Lecture Notes in Computer Science 7954

Commenced Publication in 1973
Founding and Former Series Editors:
Gerhard Goos, Juris Hartmanis, and Jan van Leeuwen

Michael Jacobson   Michael Locasto
Payman Mohassel   Reihaneh Safavi-Naini (Eds.)

Applied Cryptography and Network Security

11th International Conference, ACNS 2013
Banff, AB, Canada, June 25-28, 2013
Proceedings

 Springer

Volume Editors

Michael Jacobson
Michael Locasto
Payman Mohassel
Reihaneh Safavi-Naini

University of Calgary, Department of Computer Science
2500 University Drive NW, Calgary, AB T2N 1N4, Canada

ISSN 0302-9743   e-ISSN 1611-3349
ISBN 978-3-642-38979-5   e-ISBN 978-3-642-38980-1
DOI 10.1007/978-3-642-38980-1
Springer Heidelberg Dordrecht London New York

Library of Congress Control Number: 2013940302

CR Subject Classification (1998): K.6.5, E.3, K.4.4, D.4.6, E.4, C.2, J.1, E.1

LNCS Sublibrary: SL 4 – Security and Cryptology

Typesetting: Camera-ready by author, data conversion by Scientific Publishing Services, Chennai, India

Printed on acid-free paper

Springer is part of Springer Science+Business Media (www.springer.com)

Preface

ACNS 2013, the 11th International Conference on Applied Cryptography and Network Security, was held during June 25–28 at Banff, Alberta, Canada.

We received 150 submissions of which 33 were accepted as regular papers (22% acceptance rate), and two as short papers. These proceedings contain the revised versions of all the papers. There were three invited talks. Srdjan Capkun, Professor of Computer Science at ETH Zurich, gave a talk entitled "Selected Topics in Wireless Physical Layer Security." Bryan Parno from Microsoft Research Redmond, gave a talk on "Bootstrapping Cloud Security Speaker," and Francois Theberge, research mathematician with the Tutte Institute for Mathematics and Computing spoke about "Ensemble Clustering for Graphs-Based Data."

The Program Committee (PC) consisted of 35 members with diverse research interest and experience. Papers were reviewed double-blind, with each paper assigned to three reviewers. During the discussion phase, when necessary, extra reviews were solicited. We ensured that all papers received fair and objective evaluation by experts and also a broader group of PC members, with particular attention paid to highlighting strengths and weaknesses of papers. The final decisions were made based on the reviews and discussion. The task of paper selection was especially challenging given the high number of strong submissions. In the end, a sizable number of strong papers could not be included in the program owing to lack of space.

We would like to sincerely thank authors of all submissions– those whose papers made it into the program and those whose papers did not. We, and the PC as a whole, were impressed by the quality of submissions contributed from all around the world. Although this made the task of selecting the final list very challenging, it gave us the opportunity to have a strong and diverse program.

We would like to extend our sincere gratitude to the Program Committee. We were very fortunate that so many talented people put such an inordinate amount of time to write reviews and actively participate in discussions for nearly three weeks. They responded to our requests for extra reviews, opinions, comments, comparisons, and inputs. We were impressed by the knowledge, dedication, and integrity of our PC. We also would like to thank many external reviewers, some contacted by us directly and some through PC members, who significantly contributed to the comprehensive evaluation of papers. A list of PC members and external reviewers appears after this note.

We would like to thank Mahabir Jhanwar, the Publicity Chair, for working closely with us throughout the whole process, providing the much needed support in every step. We would also like to thank Tongjie Zhang for handling our social media presence, Coral Burns for her work on the ACNS website, Deb Angus for logistical and administrative support, Camille Sinanan for her help with the local organization and financial administration, and, finally, Hadi Ahmadi and numerous student volunteers who helped us with the successful organization of the program.

We benefited from advice and feedback from Moti Yung and Jianying Zhou, the ACNS Steering Committee. Alfred Hofmann and his colleagues at Springer provided a meticulous service for the timely production of this volume.

We would like to thank Microsoft Research, the Pacific Institute for Mathematical Sciences (PIMS), Alberta Innovates Technology Future (AITF), and the University of Calgary for their generous support. We also gratefully acknowledge our partnership with the Tutte Institute for Mathematics and Computing (TIMC), in contributing to the success of this conference.

April 2013

Michael Jacobson
Michael Locasto
Payman Mohassel
Reihaneh Safavi-Naini

ACNS 2013

11th International Conference on
Applied Cryptography and Network Security

BANFF, Alberta, Canada
June 25–28, 2013

General Chairs

Michael Jacobson   University of Calgary, Canada
Payman Mohassel   University of Calgary, Canada

Program Chairs

Michael Locasto   University of Calgary, Canada
Reihaneh Safavi-Naini   University of Calgary, Canada

Program Committee

Bill Aiello   University of British Columbia, Canada
Giuseppe Ateniese   Sapienza University of Rome, Italy
Kevin R.B. Butler   University of Oregon, USA
Srdjan Capkun   ETH Zurich, Switzerland
Alvaro A. Cárdenas   University of Texas at Dallas, USA
Chen-Mou Cheng   National Taiwan University, Taiwan
Sherman S.M. Chow   Chinese University of Hong Kong, Hong Kong
Ed Dawson   Queensland University of Technology, Australia
Roberto Di Pietro   Università Roma Tre, Italy
Sara Foresti   Università degli Studi di Milano, Italy
Guang Gong   University of Waterloo, Canada
Stefanos Gritzalis   University of the Aegean, Greece
Guofei Gu   Texas A&M University, USA
Angelos D. Keromytis   Columbia University, USA
Evangelos Kranakis   Carleton University, Canada
Ralf Küsters   Universität Trier, Germany
Xuejia Lai   Shanghai Jiao Tong University, China
Cédric Lauradoux   INRIA, France
Ninghui Li   Purdue University, USA
Yingjiu Li   Singapore Management University, Singapore
Mark Manulis   University of Surrey, UK
Kaisa Nyberg   Aalto University, Finland
Josef Pieprzyk   Macquarie University, Australia
Bart Preneel   KU Leuven, Belgium
Christian Rechberger   DTU, Denmark

Liu, Zhen
Lombardi, Flavio
Long, Yu
Ma, Di
Malisa, Luka
Mandal, Kalikinkar
Miettinen, Markus
Mohassel, Payman
More, Sara
Mouha, Nicky
Nergiz, Ahmet Erhan
Nguyen, Lan
Niederhagen, Ruben
Nikolic, Ivica
Nikova, Svetla
Nishide, Takashi
Núñez, David
Olejnik, Lukasz
Pappas, Vasilis
Peeters, Roel
Peikert, Chris
Pointcheval, David
Polychronakis, Michalis
Popper, Christina

Radomirovic, Sasa
Ranganathan, Aanjhan
Rasmussen, Kasper
  Bonne
Rial, Alfredo
Rizomiliotis, Panagiotis
Rouselakis, Yannis
Salim, Farzad
Schmitz, Guido
Schneider, Michael
Sepehrdad, Pouyan
Shahandashti, Siamak
Soleimany, Hadi
Soriente, Claudio
Su, Dong
Tan, Xiao
Tuengerthal, Max
Tzouramanis, Theodoros
Ustaoglu, Berkant
Vahlis, Yevgeniy
Van Herrewege, Anthony
Varici, Kerem
Villani, Antonio
Vo, Binh

Vogt, Andreas
Wachsmann, Christian
Wu, Jong-Shian
Wu, Teng
Xie, Xiang
Xu, Hong
Xu, Jia
Xu, Zhaoyan
Xue, Weijia
Yang, Chao
Yang, Guomin
Yang, Yanjiang
Yu, Ching-Hua
Yuen, Tsz Hon
Zhang, Cong
Zhang, Haibin
Zhang, Jialong
Zhang, Liangfeng
Zhang, Tao
Zhou, Xuhua
Zhu, Bo

Table of Contents

Cloud Cryptography

Secure Computation

Hash Function and Block Cipher

Signature

Group-Oriented Cryptography

System Attack I

Secure Implementation – Hardware

Secure Implementation – Software

System Attack II

Group-Oriented Systems

Key Exchange and Leakage Resilience

Cryptographic Proof

Cryptosystems

Transparent, Distributed, and Replicated Dynamic Provable Data Possession

Mohammad Etemad and Alptekin Küpçü

Koç University, İstanbul, Turkey
{metemad,akupcu}@ku.edu.tr

Abstract. With the growing trend toward using outsourced storage, the problem of efficiently checking and proving data integrity needs more consideration. Starting with PDP and POR schemes, many cryptography and security researchers have addressed the problem. After the first solutions for static data, dynamic versions were developed (e.g., DPDP). Researchers also considered distributed versions of such schemes. Alas, in all such distributed schemes, the client needs to be aware of the structure of the cloud, and possibly pre-process the file accordingly, even though the security guarantees in the real world are not improved.

We propose a distributed and replicated DPDP which is transparent from the client's viewpoint. It allows for real scenarios where the cloud storage provider (CSP) may hide its internal structure from the client, flexibly manage its resources, while still providing provable service to the client. The CSP decides on how many and which servers will store the data. Since the load is distributed, we observe one-to-two orders of magnitude better performance in our tests, while availability and reliability are also improved via replication. In addition, we use persistent rank-based authenticated skip lists to create centralized and distributed variants of a dynamic version control system with optimal complexity.

1 Introduction

In recent years, cloud storage systems have gained considerable attention from both academia and industry, due to the services it can provide at lower costs. As a result, IT outsourcing has grown by 79% [5]. In the case of outsourcing storage, the client wants to upload her data to a server, and wants to rest assured that her data remains intact. She may trust the server in terms of availability, but does not necessarily trust him to keep her data intact. Indeed, the server may try to hide data loss or corruption due to hardware or software failures. When the data is large, it is not acceptable to require the client to retrieve the whole file in order to validate it, since this requires high bandwidth and time complexity [2]. This will be even more problematic if the client uses resource-constrained devices, or performs this check frequently [15].

Ateniese *et al.* [2] proposed the concept of *provable data possession* (PDP), which provides probabilistic guarantees of possession of the outsourced file. Juels and Kaliski [17] developed a similar model named *proof of retrievability* (POR). The route is followed by others [20,23,19,13,4], alas, only for static files.

M. Jacobson et al. (Eds.): ACNS 2013, LNCS 7954, pp. 1–18, 2013.

Later, dynamic cloud storage protocols were developed by Erway *et al.* [15] and Ateniese *et al.* [3], and later variants followed [22]. The DPDP scheme [15] uses rank-based authenticated skip list, which supports insertion, modification, and deletion of blocks in $O(\log n)$ time, where n is the number of blocks.

All these schemes deal with integrity checks, but if the data is lost, it can only be detected, not recovered. The instant solution to this problem is to store multiple copies of the file, and use other copies if one is corrupted. Many such solutions exist for both static and dynamic scenarios [12,9,5,7,26,27] but these schemes require the client to perform pre-computation that is on the order of the number of servers/replicas (e.g., generate multiple encoded copies of the file), and the CSP architecture is not transparent from the point of view of the client.

This imposes an unnecessary burden on the client, decreasing her efficiency, while she has no way to check whether the CSP keeps storing exactly the agreed-upon number of replicas, unless the client interacts with each server one-by-one. Even in that case, presumably the inter-server communication is much faster than the client-server communication, thus a single server in the background may be storing the data and providing proofs to multiple servers interacting with the client. Moreover, if the client takes into account the internal architecture of the CSP in the pre-computation, then the CSP cannot even improve his architecture without notifying the client (which leads to re-computations). Normally, the CSP wants to change his structure and adapt it with the world technical progress (e.g., Amazon S3 is said to store three replicas for each file [24], which may be increased or decreased with technological advancements).

In this paper, we propose a *transparent*, distributed, and replicated dynamic PDP (DR-DPDP), based on the DPDP scheme [15] (or its variants following a similar structure). The CSP's architecture is completely transparent to the client, and hence the client performs in the same way as in DPDP.

Our DR-DPDP scheme *does not decrease the guarantee on detection probability*, and hence incurs no harm to the client, while helping her get rid of pre-computation imposed solely by the architecture, and later checking data integrity toward a specific architecture. We improve the client's efficiency, and achieve *better scalability, availability and reliability* at the CSP. The CSP can flexibly manage its resources, perform its own choice of load balancing and replication schemes in the background, while still providing *provable* storage for the client. This makes DR-DPDP much easier to deploy on real systems.

We also present a provable Version Control System (VCS), achieving better, indeed optimal, complexity $O(1 + \log n)$. We further combine our DR-DPDP scheme with our VCS to obtain a distributed VCS (DVCS) scheme with the same complexity.

Contributions. The main contributions of this paper are as follows:

- We propose the first *transparent*, distributed, and replicated provable dynamic cloud storage system.

  - Our system incurs no cost over the single-server case; it actually *improves the performance* due to parallelism. Indeed, for a system with 100 servers and 10 replicas, our system performs *10 times faster* updates and proofs than a single-server storage.

- Asymptotic complexity of our system does *not* depend on the number of replicas, servers, or partitions.
- The CSP's architecture is completely transparent to the client, and can be *changed on-the-fly* with the sole decision of the CSP.

– We present a (distributed) version control system with optimal complexity.

- We map VCS operations to underlying cloud storage operations in a provable manner for the first time, and show that, in many cases, the complexity of the operation is independent of the number of versions.
- We consider the multi-client scenario for provable VCS for the first time.

1.1 Related Work

Proof of Storage. A trivial way to perform integrity check is via message authentication codes or hash functions. The client hashes her file before uploading, and stores the hash value. Later, the client retrieves the whole file, recomputes its hash, and checks if it matches the stored hash value [5]. This is not efficient since each verification requires the whole file to be transmitted. The client can divide the file into blocks, hash each block separately, and challenge a random subset of blocks. Again, all challenged blocks should be transmitted for verification [2].

Ateniese *et al.* [2] proposed a PDP scheme with which these efficiency problems have been solved. In PDP, first the client divides the file F into n blocks $(F = f_1|f_2|...|f_n)$, then computes a *tag* for each block, and finally transfers the file along with the tags to the server, deleting its local copy. Later, she sends a *challenge* to the server. Upon receipt, the server constructs a *proof* using the tags and blocks stored, and sends the proof back to the client for verification.

Juels and Kaliski [17] proposed a POR scheme where the main difference was that the client uses erasure codes to encode her file before uploading. This enables resilience against data losses at the server side: the client may reconstruct her data even if the server corrupts (deletes or modifies) a portion of it.

The PDP and POR, as well as their later variants and generalizations [20,13,4] support only static files. The first dynamic schemes were proposed simultaneously by Ateniese *et al.* [3] and Erway *et al.* [15]. Ateniese *et al.* [3] proposed the Scalable PDP, where the client pre-computes responses for pre-decided challenges and stores them on the server encrypted. This means that the number of updates and challenges a client can perform is limited and fixed.

Erway *et al.* [15] proposed a Dynamic PDP (DPDP) scheme in the standard model that supports provable unlimited updates (modify, delete, and insert) with $O(\log n)$ complexity. The scheme is based on *rank-based authenticated skip list*, in which, only the relative indexes of blocks are used, so it can efficiently support dynamism. The proof for a block is computed using values in the search path from that block up to the root of the skip list.

All these schemes deal with the *integrity* of the outsourced data, but the *availability* and *reliability* are important as well. One method to support availability and reliability is to store several copies of the file, resulting in better availability and efficiency. For example, MR-PDP [12] extends PDP, and HAIL [9] distributes POR to multiple servers, trying to balance their loads.

Barsoum *et al.* [5] proposed a multi-copy PDP scheme for *static* files, where, the client generates and uploads t distinct copies of the file. Later, she separately challenges each copy to ensure that the CSP is possessing all t copies. Hence, the scheme is similar to using t different PDP schemes.

Barsoum *et al.* later proposed two multi-copy DPDP schemes, based on tree and map structures [7,6]. In the tree-based scheme, each copy of the file is put into a Merkle hash tree, and their roots are used to construct another Merkle hash tree (the *directory*) whose root is the metadata stored at client, similar to the file system proposal of DPDP [15]. Again, the challenge-response mechanism is not transparent to the client; she must know this new structure is in place.

Zhu *et al.* [26,27] proposed a Cooperative PDP where the client generates the tags of the blocks and then sends them securely to the *organizer*. The organizer is one of the servers who is responsible for communication with the client, and determines on which server each part of file will be stored. Later, when the client challenges the organizer, he gathers together responses from multiple servers and sends a single final response back to the client. Note that the tags depend on which server is storing a particular block.

In our DR-DPDP scheme, the client is exactly a DPDP client, and all servers storing data are DPDP servers. The decision about the distribution of partitions over servers, number of servers, replication, etc. are all up to the CSP. Most importantly, the whole process is transparent to the client, and she is still guaranteed that there is at least one intact copy.

It is important to note that *the CSP may store all the data on a single server, even if the scheme directs him not to do so.* The client has no way of distinguishing such a single-server case from multi-server storage. She may try to infer via timing [10], but it is not a reliable measure since the inter-server communications are much faster than the client-server communications.

Thus, instead of trying to force the CSP, we give him the flexibility. The CSP may freely employ replication for fault tolerance and availability, and distribution for load balancing and scalability, without the need to inform the client. On the other hand, the client is still ensured that at least one working copy is present, or otherwise the CSP will get caught cheating. Therefore, the CSP is incentivized to make sure he keeps the client's data intact. Our solution does not decrease detection probability, while providing improved performance as seen in Section 5.

Version Control. One of the applications of dynamic data outsourcing schemes is outsourced *version control systems* (VCS). Pervasive examples include CVS, SVN, and Git.

Erway *et al.* [15] proposed an extension of their DPDP scheme to support version control. If the average number of blocks in a file for each version is n, and there are v versions, their VCS requires $O(\log n + \log v)$ time and space for proofs, whereas our proposal requires only $O(1 + \log n)$, which is independent of the number of versions (see [15,8,18,14,11] for optimality discussion). Furthermore, we show how to combine this VCS with our DR-DPDP to obtain distributed VCS with the same complexity. We also explicitly map VCS operations to provable operations in our DR-DPDP scheme.

2   Preliminaries

A **skip list** is a randomized data structure, that has binary tree-like properties (i.e., logarithmic operation cost). An **authenticated skip list** provides membership proofs for storing items using a collision-resistant hash function.

DPDP [15] uses a modified form of the authenticated skip lists called **rank-based authenticated skip list**, where each node v also stores the number of leaf nodes reachable from v (the *rank* of v), as shown in Figure 1a. The file F is divided into n blocks $m_1|m_2|...|m_n$, then a homomorphic tag T_i is computed for each block and put in the skip list, while the blocks are stored elsewhere. Nodes also store a label computed using a collision-resistant hash function. The client stores locally the label of the skip list's root to verify the membership proofs.

An interesting property of this tree-like structure is that the insertion, deletion, or modification of a block affects only the nodes along the path from the block up to the root. The ranks of the affected nodes can be recomputed in constant time per node in a bottom-up way [15].

To make an authenticated skip list *persistent*, the *path-copying* method is applied [1]. A block update results in a new version. The new version consists of all unchanged nodes of the previous version, plus the nodes on the path from the updated block up to the root, whose values are recomputed. Figure 1b shows the process, where a new block is inserted after the second block, at level five.

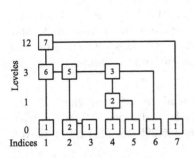
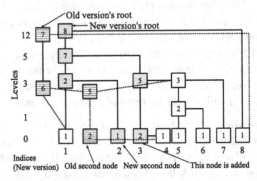

(a) Numbers inside the nodes are their ranks. The indices and levels are imaginary.

(b) Hatched nodes are specific for old version, filled in nodes are specific for new version, and white nodes are in common.

Fig. 1. A regular (a) and a persistent (b) rank-based authenticated skip list

3   DR-DPDP

DR-DPDP is a scheme that provides *transparent* distribution and replication of user data over multiple servers. There are three entities in the model as depicted in Figure 2a. The *client*, who stores data on the CSP, challenges the CSP to check the integrity of data, and updates the stored data. The *organizer*, who is one of the servers in CSP and is responsible for communication with the client and other servers (acts as a gateway or load-balancer). The *servers*, who store the user data, perform provable updates on behalf of the client, and respond to the client challenges coming via the organizer. They only communicate with the organizer and there is no inter-server communication.

It is very important to observe that even though it seems like a central entity, the organizer is not expected to perform any disk operations or expensive group operations (e.g., exponentiation). He will only perform simple hashing, and work with a very small skip list. Hence, his load will be very light, making it very easy to replicate the organizer to prevent it from becoming a bottleneck or single-point-of-failure. (Further discussion can be found in the full version [16].)

When the client wants to store a file using this scheme, she first prepares the file as in DPDP, then sends all blocks to the organizer. The organizer divides the file into partitions, each with a predefined number of blocks, and sends each partition to an agreed-upon number of servers (A partition and its rank-based authenticated skip list will be replicated on the specified number of servers.) Each server stores the blocks, builds the corresponding part of the rank-based authenticated skip list, and sends the root value back to the organizer. All servers run in parallel. Once received at least one response for each partition, the organizer builds its own part of the rank-based authenticated skip list and sends the root value as metadata to the client. All these operations are commanded by the organizer and all are transparent to the client.

The idea behind this architecture is that a big rank-based authenticated skip list is divided into multiple sub-lists; the top part is stored on the organizer, and the servers store lower parts, thereby improving scalability. Also, each sub-list will be replicated on a predefined number of servers, improving availability and reliability. Figure 2b shows the idea, where each partition is replicated on two servers. Different servers replicating the same partition are required to use the same randomness to have identical skip lists.

Remark. Note that *single-server DPDP* is a special case of ours, where $R = r_1$ in Figure 2b, and the client and server behavior is unchanged. Moreover, with small changes, 2-3/Merkle tree-based structures [25,22] can also be employed instead of rank-based authenticated skip list.

3.1   From DPDP to DR-DPDP

This section shows how to use DPDP to construct DR-DPDP. All client operations (KeyGen, PrepareUpdate, VerifyUpdate, Challenge, Verify), and server operations (PerformUpdate, Prove) are the same as DPDP. The organizer operations (PerformUpdate, Prove) are shown in Algorithms 3.1 and 3.2.

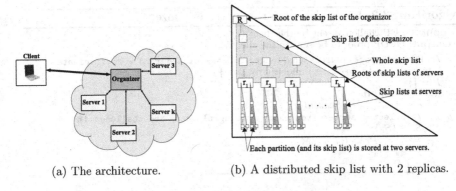

(a) The architecture. (b) A distributed skip list with 2 replicas.

Fig. 2. The DR-DPDP architecture

For an update, the client prepares the desired update command (using PrepareUpdate), and sends it to the organizer, who searches for the block indices in his skip list, figuring out which servers hold which blocks to be updated. Then, he delegates the job to the corresponding servers (All servers holding the same replicas must perform the update.) All servers perform the update in parallel and send the root value to the organizer who picks one proof and metadata per partition among replicas (possible strategies are in the full version [16]), updates his own skip list and sends the new root value to the client (Algorithm 3.1).

Algorithm 3.1. PerformUpdate run by the organizer.

Input: DPDP values sent by the client ($e(F), e(info), e(M)$).
Output: DPDP proof to be sent to the client.

1 Interpret $info$ as $\{o_1, o_2, ..., o_l\}$ // list of file block indices to be updated
2 Interpret $e(F)$ as $\{m_{o_1}, m_{o_2}, ..., m_{o_l}\}$ // list of corresponding file blocks
3 $P = \{\}$ // initialize empty proof
4 **for** $i = 1$ *to* l **do**
  // find servers storing the o_i^{th} block from the organizer's skip list
5 $loc_i, \{S_r\}_{r=0}^s \leftarrow Search(o_i)$
6 **for** $j = 1$ *to* s **do**
   // Servers perform DPDP update on own partitions, thinking of F_{i-1}
   as the current version, and M_{i-1} as the current skip list root
7   $(M_{c_j}, P_{M_{c_j}}) \leftarrow S_j.PerformUpdate\,(pk, F_{i-1}, M_{i-1}, e(m_{o_i}), e(o_i), e(M))$
  // Pick one proof P_{M_c} and one root M_c, how to pick is discussed later
8 $P = P \bigcup P_{M_c}$
  // Put new server roots to the organizer's skip list
9 $(M_c', P_{M_c}') \leftarrow PerformUpdate(pk, F_{i-1}, M_{i-1}, \{M_c\}, \{loc_i\}, e(M))$
10 $P = P \bigcup P_{M_c}'$
11 **return** M_c', P

To get an integrity proof, the client generates a challenge command as a list of blocks and random coefficients, and sends it to the organizer. Upon receipt, the organizer finds out which servers hold which blocks, decides on which servers should create the proofs (possibly based on their load), and challenges those

---

Algorithm 3.2. Prove algorithm run by the organizer.

Input: DPDP challenge sent by the client (c).
Output: DPDP proof to be sent to the client.

```
    // list of block indices challenged and associated random coefficients
1   Interpret c as {o₁, o₂, ..., oₗ} and {r₁, r₂, ..., rₗ}
2   P = {}
3   for i = 1 to l do
4       locᵢ, {Sᵣ}ˢᵣ₌₀ ← Search(oᵢ)
        // Select a server from those storing block oᵢ and challenge it
5       Sᵤ ∈ {Sᵣ}ˢᵣ₌₀
6       Pᵤ ← Sᵤ.Prove(pk, Fᵢ, Mᵢ, cᵢ)
7       P = P ∪ Pᵤ
8   return P
```

---

servers on the blocks residing in their partition. All servers generate their proofs in parallel, and send them to the organizer. Each proof consists of two parts: a skip list proof, and a combined block. The organizer sums up all combined blocks, and generates the full proof using the sub-proofs and their paths in his own skip list (from the r_is to the R in Figure 2b) as described in Algorithm 3.2.

Frequent insertions or deletions to a partition makes its size very large or small. To solve this problem, repartitioning is required. The repartitioning strategy balances the load on the servers, preserving an amortized time for challenge and update operations (further discussed in the full version [16]).

3.2   Security of DR-DPDP

Since the client-server communication is the same as in DPDP [15], we use the same security definition.

Definition 1 (Security of DR-DPDP). *A DR-DPDP scheme is secure if for any PPT adversary who can win the data possession game (from [15]) with non-negligible probability, there exists a polynomial-time extractor that can extract the challenged parts of the file by resetting and challenging the adversary.*

Theorem 1. *If DPDP scheme is secure, then our DR-DPDP scheme is secure according to Definition 1.*

Proof. All communication between the client and the organizer takes palace as in DPDP. The process is transparent to the client; she thinks as if she communicates with a DPDP server. Moreover, all servers behave as in DPDP. The only difference is how the proof is generated at the organizer, but the resulting proof will be the same as a single-server DPDP proof. Therefore, the organizer-server and inter-server communication is not a matter of security, and rather, we consider the security of client-organizer communication. If the adversary manages to create a verifying proof with non-negligible probability even though all copies of the challenged blocks are corrupted, this means that he managed to cheat either on (at least) one of the server proofs, or the organizer proof. In either case, finally, a DPDP proof is created.

If, at the end of the data possession game [15] the proof is accepted by the challenger with non-negligible probability, then the challenger can extract the requested blocks. The challenger and the extractor we use here are exactly the same as in the DPDP proof, using the 'weighted sums' as described in [15].

Therefore, under the assumption that DPDP is secure, DR-DPDP is secure. The DR-DPDP is as secure as the underlying DPDP in the sense that the client will accept the proof, as long as there is at least one intact copy of her data.

Efficiency. Assume each partition has b blocks, and we have p partitions (so $n = pb$ blocks in total). Each server holds a skip list having b leaves. The organizer has a skip list with p leaves. Since all servers run in parallel, the total time complexity of each server's PerformUpdate or Prove functions is $O(\log b)$. The organizer's skip list time is $O(\log p)$, and time for combining proofs is $O(p)$. Since $\log b + \log p = \log n$, the total complexity of DR-DPDP proofs (both computation and communication) is $O(\log n + p)$ for a file with n blocks, regardless of the number of replicas. Note that $p << n$ and mostly even $p \leq \log n$ for realistic values (e.g., $n = 100000$, $p = 10$, $\log n \sim 17$), giving total complexity of $O(\log n)$.

4   Version Control Using DPDP

In this section, we show how a persistent rank-based authenticated skip list can be used to build a Version Control System (VCS) like SVN, CVS, Git, etc. We store a file in a persistent rank-based authenticated skip list and assume that each *commit* consists of a series of updates, resulting in a new version.

To manage these versions, Erway *et al.* [15] suggests putting their roots into another rank-based authenticated skip list. But, we use a persistent rank-based authenticated skip list to store the file and its subsequent versions, and put all roots of the persistent skip list into a PDP [2] structure. (Note that a POR scheme [20,17] can also be employed here, with appropriate algorithm definitions.) Figure 3 presents an instantiation of our VCS. We assume that the client, the organizer, and the servers share a pseudorandom generator seed (or a pseudorandom function key), so that each one can perform any randomized computation independently, while obtaining the same result as the others. The main advantage of this assumption is that, when the client already has a version of the file and performs some updates on it, she can compute the persistent rank-based authenticated skip list root herself, as an honest server would do with the same randomness. She can then compute a PDP tag for that root, and send it to the organizer (or the server in single-server case). The organizer performs the update command, as the client did, and appends the PDP tag to the corresponding PDP structure.

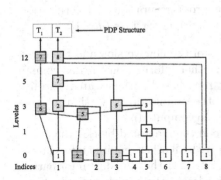

Fig. 3. Our VCS architecture

4.1   Common Utility Functions

Before describing VCS operations, we present a common utility function to be used in VCS algorithms: $GetVersion(V_i, V_j)$. This algorithm is executed by the client to request the version V_j, when she already holds V_i (which may be null).

- V_i is null or $V_i \geq V_j$: This corresponds to a checkout operation (V_i is null), or to a revert operation ($V_i \geq V_j$). In both cases, the server sends the version V_j from scratch, together with its proof.
- $V_i < V_j$: This corresponds to an update operation, where the client is trying to update to a newer version.
  - If the total number of blocks in version V_j is low compared to the number of changed blocks between V_i and V_j, then it is still better to send all these blocks to the client from scratch (together with their proof).
  - Otherwise, the server sends the differences (*delta*) and their proof separately for each version u such that $V_i < u \leq V_j$.

Normally, the server has to send all deltas starting from the client's current version, one by one, along with their PDP proofs. This requires $O(1 + ed + ed \log n)$ communication, where $d = V_j - V_i$, and e is the average size of deltas. Using the stated trick, we can reduce this complexity to $O(1 + ed)$, since sending only the deltas along with versions' PDP proofs suffices. The client can build the skip list up to the last version using his current blocks and the deltas, and verify the PDP proofs. We separate two cases for proof generation and verification, when the difference is one version ($d = 1$) or multiple versions ($d > 1$):

- **One version**: the server sends the deltas of the new version and the corresponding PDP proof (together with any other information such as commit logs). The client rebuilds the persistent rank-based authenticated skip list, and finds the root. Then, she decides on the validity of the version (by running *PDP Verify* algorithm on the root she computed).
- **Multiple versions**: the server should send the requested blocks, the aggregated PDP proof of all versions, together with all other required information. Now, if the server sends a linear combination of the versions' information, as in PDP, the client has no chance of relating them with individual versions. The client can find by herself, the *fixed-length* part of the Figure 4b, but not the *variable-length* part. If the server sends all versions' information separately, then we loose the $O(1)$ complexity of the PDP proof.

  To solve the problem, the server sends a linear combination of only variable length parts of PDP blocks of requested d versions, achieving $O(1)$ proof size. Let V_{var_k} be the variable-length portion of the PDP block associated with the kth version, V_{fix_k} be the fixed-length portion of length l_{fix}, and r_k be the random challenge sent by the client for version k.
  1. The server computes $V_{var} = \sum_{k=V_i}^{V_j} V_{var_k} * r_k$ and sends to the client.
  2. After reconstructing persistent rank-based authenticated skip lists, client computes $V_{fix} = \sum_{k=V_i}^{V_j} V_{fix_k} * r_k$ since she now knows each V_{fix_k}.

3. The client computes $V' = V_{var} * 2^{l_{fix}} + V_{fix}$ by shifting V_{var} to the left l_{fix} times and adding V_{fix}. One can easily verify that V' corresponds exactly to the combined block in a PDP proof. From this point on, the client may perform regular PDP verification using the combined tags received as part of the PDP proof.[1]

4.2   VCS Operations

Sink [21] states common functionalities of a VCS. We now show how each of these functionalities are supported by our scheme in a provable manner.

- **Create:** The first upload command issued by the client, creates the repository. One can check if the first version (and hence the repository) is stored by the server, using the common utility functions described above.
- **Update:** The client calls the $GetVersion(V_i, V_j)$ to request the last version V_j from the server and update her *local/working copy*, who is at version V_i.
- **Checkout:** Similar to update with the difference that the client does not have any local copy. She calls $GetVersion(null, V_j)$.
- **Add, edit, delete:** These operations are done locally on the working copy.
- **Diff:** To find the differences between two versions, the server (the organizer in the distributed case) sends the two versions along with their proof to client who can find the differences using a diff algorithm. Alternatively, only deltas with their proofs can be sent.
- **Commit:** After performing all updates on its working copy, the client must commit. Using our above-mentioned trick, the client computes the root of the persistent rank-based authenticated skip list after updates, and a PDP tag for that root. The client sends a DPDP update command with the updated blocks, and a PDP append command for the tag of the new version's root to the server at once. The server(s) update using the above utility functions.
- **Revert:** The client wants to drop what has been changed after some version V_i, and go back to version V_j (possibly $V_j = V_i$). She simply runs $GetVersion(V_i, V_j)$ with the server where V_i is the current version of the client's local copy.
- **Log:** With each commit, the client may provide some logging information (e.g., time and author of the change made, and a summary of changes). The client adds this log to the PDP block related to the version, and builds the PDP tag of the whole block (Figure 4b).
- **Tag:**[2] Name of a branch, can be managed in the same way as 'Log' above.
- **Branch** This operation creates another line of development, and is useful especially in development environments where different groups work on different parts of a project. A version is determined by branch number and version number within the branch. Figure 4a shows a visualization of branching.

---

[1] We use the version of PDP that does not employ the knowledge-of-exponent assumption and does not take the hash value of the block [2].

[2] Not to be confused with a PDP tag.

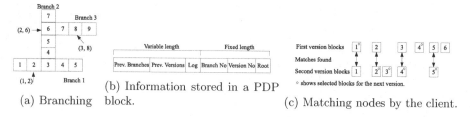

(a) Branching   (b) Information stored in a PDP block.   (c) Matching nodes by the client.

Fig. 4. (a)Branching, (b)PDP block structure, and (c)merge

We store these information about each version: the branch and version number, the root of the corresponding rank-based authenticated skip list, the previous branch that this one was generated from, version of the previous branch that this one has began, the log, and maybe the tag (see Figure 4b).

- **Merge:** This is to combine together two versions of two different/same branches and make a new version in a new/same branch. In development environments, for example, two groups of developers work on their sub-projects separately, and at the end they want to merge what they have done. This operation consists of the following steps: (1) the client requests the two versions of its interest, (2) the server sends those two versions to the client, along with their DPDP and PDP proofs as described in our utility functions, (3) the client runs an algorithm to find and match corresponding nodes of the versions (the skip lists), and then, determines the new version (e.g., Figure 4c) and computes its PDP tag. She then sends all the new version blocks and its PDP tag to the server.
- **Lock:** We believe provably locking something in a client-server setting is a hard (or possibly impossible) problem and consider it out of scope.

4.3   Extensions and Analysis

Multi-client VCS. Our discussion above assumes the same client keeps committing and also retrieving versions. In the single-client case, the client keeps information about the last version, preventing the server from cheating. But, in a multi-client system, the server may cheat and send a previous version –a *replay attack* where the server behaves as if some commit never occurred– to the client (other than the client who created the last version and knows some information about that). The scheme proposed by Erway *et al.* [15] as an extension to DPDP is also vulnerable to this attack. Therefore, some level of inter-client communication is required to prevent the server/organizer from cheating. Each client, after each commit, broadcasts information about her commit to other clients, or puts it on a trusted bulletin board. Just the last version number (and branch number) of the commit needs to be shared between the clients. Sharing of any secret information is *not* necessary (thus the bulletin board can be *public*). We assume the clients trust each other, since they modify the same repository. Now that each client knows the latest version number (of each branch), the server will be caught if he sends a different version.

Distributed VCS. When the client is composed of multiple devices, all connecting to the server to commit or update data, i.e., in software development environments, the above-mentioned central VCS does not suit well, and a distributed VCS (DVCS) is needed.

Using persistent rank-based authenticated skip list, the proposed DR-DPDP scheme can be used to build a DVCS. Each server stores a persistent rank-based authenticated skip list whose roots will be stored in another rank-based authenticated skip list at the organizer. The organizer stores the roots of his own persistent rank-based authenticated skip list (for versions) in the PDP structure. With each update, a new distributed persistent rank-based authenticated skip list will be built. The organizer sends the new version's root back to the client. Once the client verified the value of the new root, it computes a PDP tag for the root, and sends it to the organizer for storage. The organizer manages the PDP and communication with the client; hence the distributed architecture is transparent to the client.

Efficiency. A proof has two parts: a PDP proof for the version information, and a DPDP proof for the data in that version. The former requires $O(1)$, while the latter needs time and communication complexity $O(\log n)$. The client's storage is $O(1)$, and proof verification complexity is $O(1 + \log n)$ for one version.

4.4   Security of VCS

Definition 2 (Security game for VCS). *Played between the adversary who acts as a VCS server, and a challenger who plays the role of a VCS client. Full PDP and DPDP game description can be found on the original papers [2,15]. There are two kinds of VCS commands: update and retrieve. Update commands (i.e., create, commit, branch, and merge) change data on the server, while retrieve commands (i.e., update, checkout, diff, and revert) ask the server to give some parts of the stored files.*

Key Generation. *The challenger runs the $KeyGen(1^k) \rightarrow (sk, pk)$, stores public and private keys (pk, sk), and sends the public key pk to the adversary.*

Query. *The adversary specifies an update F and the related information $info$ specifying type of the update (e.g., , create, branch, merge), and sends them all to the challenger. The challenger runs Commit on them and sends the results to the adversary, who replies with the new metadata and proof, which will be verified by the challenger. The adversary will be notified about the result, and he can repeat this interaction polynomially-many times.*

Setup. *The adversary creates a new repository, using the Create command. Then, the above-mentioned interaction is performed again. The challenger updates her local metadata only for the updates whose proofs are accepted.*

Challenge. *Let F denote the final version of the file as created by the adversary using the verifying updates in the setup phase. Also, the challenger holds the latest verified metadata. The challenger creates a challenge by picking a* *random version and running the algorithm GetVersion with the adversary, who replies with a proof. The adversary wins if the received proof is accepted.*

Definition 3 (VCS security). *A VCS scheme is secure if for any PPT adversary who can win the VCS security game with non-negligible probability, there exists a polynomial-time extractor who can extract the challenged version of the file with non-negligible probability by resetting and challenging the adversary.*

Theorem 2. *Our VCS (DVCS) is secure according to Definition 3, assuming that PDP and DPDP (DR-DPDP) are secure.*

Proof. Both VCS and DVCS work in the same way except that DVCS uses DR-DPDP in the background, so here we only consider the VCS. We already proved that DR-DPDP is secure if DPDP is secure.

A VCS is not secure if the server can prepare proofs accepted by the client when the requested blocks are corrupted, or the blocks used to generate the proof belong to another version. This can be done by creating a DPDP proof, even though (some parts of) the requested challenges do not exist, or a PDP proof, using an old version of the file, to convince the client.

The VCS challenger combines a PDP and a DPDP challenger. She runs the $KeyGen(1^k) \to (sk, pk)$ which calls the $DPDP.KeyGen(1^k) \to (sk_{DPDP}, pk_{DPDP})$ and $PDP.KeyGen(1^k) \to (sk_{PDP}, pk_{PDP})$, sets $sk = (sk_{PDP}, sk_{DPDP})$ and $pk = (pk_{PDP}, pk_{DPDP})$, stores public and private keys (pk, sk), and sends only the public key pk to the adversary..

Whenever the adversary requests a commit, the challenger runs $DPDP.PrepareUpdate$ on the update request from the adversary, and performs $DPDP.PerformUpdate$ locally to find the root of the new version. She computes a PDP tag for this root using $PDP.TagBlock$, and sends the output of $DPDP.PrepareUpdate$ together with the PDP tag to the adversary.

At the challenge phase of the security game, the challenger runs $GetVersion$ on a random challenge. One may think of this as sending a random version number and a series of random blocks in that version (think of this as corresponding to deltas in $GetVersion$). The adversary's response need to include the DPDP root of challenged version, its PDP proof, the challenged blocks of the version, and the DPDP proof of the blocks. The PDP block contains only one data (the DPDP root of challenged version), therefore, can be extracted easily if the PDP proof is accepted (using $PDP.CheckProof$). The extractor simply outputs this data, and is correct since PDP is assumed to be secure. Then, the challenger runs $DPDP.Verify$ to verify the DPDP proof. If it is accepted by the challenger with non-negligible probability, the challenger can extract the requested blocks, again as described in the DPDP security proof [15] solving linear equations.

Therefore, under the assumption that PDP and DPDP (DR-DPDP) are secure, our VCS (DVCS) is secure.

Efficiency. After a file was stored on a server, for each update we store the difference from the previous version, the delta, which needs $\log n$ storage per different block. The storage complexity at the client is $O(1)$, proof generation, communication complexity, and verification are all $O(1 + \log n)$.

5   Performance

In this section, we compare performance of our DR-DPDP scheme with single-server DPDP. We obtained rank-based authenticated skip list performance numbers from a prototype implementation. All numbers are taken on a regular 2.5GHz machine with 4 cores (but the test running on a single core), with 4GB RAM and Ubuntu 11.10 operating system. The performance numbers are averages from 50 runs. We consider an example scenario with these properties:

- There are 100 servers, and no server stores more than one partition or replica.
- As we increase the number of replicas, the number of partitions will decrease.
- We assume 100000 blocks in total. If each block is 1/2KB, this gives a 50MB VCS (e.g., Tcl CVS repository), while 16KB blocks give a stored file of size 1.6GB. In both cases, it provides a realistic large number.

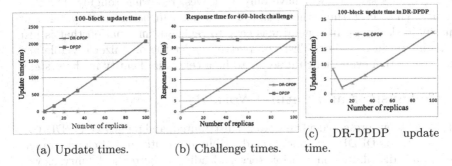

(a) Update times.   (b) Challenge times.   (c) DR-DPDP update time.

Fig. 5. Update and challenge times in DPDP and DR-DPDP

Figure 5a represents the *total* time taken for a 100-block *update* command in DPDP and DR-DPDP, assuming that the servers in DR-DPDP execute in parallel (except the organizer, who waits for servers' responses first). In single-server DPDP, as the number of replicas grows, the update time will grow linearly, since there is a single server that performs the update on all replicas sequentially. But, in DR-DPDP, the update command is executed by all servers in parallel, and there is no noticeable growth in update time, due to the load balancing property of the distributed scheme.

As the number of replicas grows in DR-DPDP, each server receives challenge commands for a larger number of blocks, therefore the response time will be increased; as shown in Figure 5b. While, in single-server DPDP, the server will select a single replica to respond to challenge commands, and hence, the response time does not depend on the number of replicas. As expected, when all servers store the whole file (100-server 100-replica case), the DR-DPDP performance is equivalent to single-server DPDP, but availability, reliability, and fault-tolerance benefits still do exist (all servers must fail simultaneously for harm to occur).

An interesting property of our proposed scheme is that when the number of replicas is small (the number of partitions is large, and each partition stores a small number of blocks), the size of organizer's rank-based authenticated skip list becomes large. In this case, the computation time in the organizer becomes greater than that of the servers, becoming a bottleneck. Therefore, the total challenge or update time will be large. As the number of replicas grows, the number of partitions falls down, leading to a decrease in the size of the organizer's rank-based authenticated skip list. Since the computation time in the organizer is reduced, the total challenge or update time will decrease. At some point, the total challenge or update time will be minimum, after which the size of each partition becomes large, and hence, the computation time of servers gets large and becomes the bottleneck. Therefore, the total challenge or update time will again increase. This is shown in Figure 5c. Based on the specifications of the underlying hardware, each CSP can determine the optimum number of replicas and partitions (about 10 replicas were the best in our test scenario).

As for the organizer, consider 10-replica case in the scenario above. This means the organizer's skip list will have only 10 leaves, requiring roughly 0.8KB of memory. Thus, everything the organizer performs can be in memory, without requiring disk access. In general it is easy to replicate information that is just 0.8KB in size in real time. These properties render the organizer a viable and attractive option even though it seems to be a centralized entity in the system.

6   Conclusions and Future Work

In this paper, we presented a transparent, distributed, and replicated DPDP. Our scheme extends DPDP to support the distributed architecture of cloud storage. User data is distributed on multiple servers, leading to better scalability, as well as availability and reliability since several servers may store the same partition. We also used persistent rank-based authenticated skip list to create a VCS with optimal complexity ($O(\log n)$), and its distributed version (DVCS).

It is interesting to note that some ideas from RAFT [10] may be employed on top of our work. One of the main ideas in RAFT is to correlate the response time of the cloud with the number of hard drives. In our DR-DPDP scheme, it will be related to the number of different servers employed, since each independent server can run in parallel. This way, the client may have an idea about fault tolerance of the system. Yet, we leave such an analysis as future work.

Acknowledgement. We would like to acknowledge the support of TÜBİTAK, the Scientific and Technological Research Council of Turkey, under project number 112E115. We also thank Ertem Esiner and Adilet Kachkeev.

References

1. Anagnostopoulos, A., Goodrich, M., Tamassia, R.: Persistent authenticated dictionaries and their applications. In: Davida, G.I., Frankel, Y. (eds.) ISC 2001. LNCS, vol. 2200, pp. 379–393. Springer, Heidelberg (2001)

2. Ateniese, G., Burns, R., Curtmola, R., Herring, J., Kissner, L., Peterson, Z., Song, D.: Provable data possession at untrusted stores. In: CCS 2007. ACM (2007)
3. Ateniese, G., Di Pietro, R., Mancini, L.V., Tsudik, G.: Scalable and efficient provable data possession. In: SecureComm 2008, pp. 9:1–9:10. ACM (2008)
4. Ateniese, G., Kamara, S., Katz, J.: Proofs of storage from homomorphic identification protocols. In: Matsui, M. (ed.) ASIACRYPT 2009. LNCS, vol. 5912, pp. 319–333. Springer, Heidelberg (2009)
5. Barsoum, A., Hasan, M.: Provable possession and replication of data over cloud servers. CACR, University of Waterloo 32 (2010)
6. Barsoum, A., Hasan, M.: Enabling data dynamic and indirect mutual trust for cloud computing storage systems (2011)
7. Barsoum, A., Hasan, M.: On verifying dynamic multiple data copies over cloud servers. Technical report, Cryptology ePrint Archive, Report 2011/447 (2011)
8. Blum, M., Evans, W., Gemmell, P., Kannan, S., Naor, M.: Checking the correctness of memories. Algorithmica 12(2), 225–244 (1994)
9. Bowers, K., Juels, A., Oprea, A.: Hail: A high-availability and integrity layer for cloud storage. In: CCS 2009, pp. 187–198. ACM (2009)
10. Bowers, K.D., van Dijk, M., Juels, A., Oprea, A., Rivest, R.L.: How to tell if your cloud files are vulnerable to drive crashes. In: CCS 2011. ACM (2011)
11. Clarke, D., Devadas, S., van Dijk, M., Gassend, B., Suh, G.E.: Incremental multiset hash functions and their application to memory integrity checking. In: Laih, C.-S. (ed.) ASIACRYPT 2003. LNCS, vol. 2894, pp. 188–207. Springer, Heidelberg (2003)
12. Curtmola, R., Khan, O., Burns, R., Ateniese, G.: Mr-pdp: Multiple-replica provable data possession. In: ICDCS 2008, pp. 411–420. IEEE (2008)
13. Dodis, Y., Vadhan, S., Wichs, D.: Proofs of retrievability via hardness amplification. In: Reingold, O. (ed.) TCC 2009. LNCS, vol. 5444, pp. 109–127. Springer, Heidelberg (2009)
14. Dwork, C., Naor, M., Rothblum, G.N., Vaikuntanathan, V.: How efficient can memory checking be? In: Reingold, O. (ed.) TCC 2009. LNCS, vol. 5444, pp. 503–520. Springer, Heidelberg (2009)
15. Erway, C., Küpçü, A., Papamanthou, C., Tamassia, R.: Dynamic provable data possession. In: CCS 2009, pp. 213–222. ACM (2009)
16. Etemad, M., Küpçü, A.: Transparent, distributed, and replicated dynamic provable data possession. Cryptology ePrint Archive, Report (2013)
17. Juels, A., Kaliski Jr., B.S.: Pors: proofs of retrievability for large files. In: CCS 2007, pp. 584–597. ACM, New York (2007)
18. Naor, M., Rotblum, G.: Complexity of online memory checking. In: FOCS (2005)
19. Sebé, F., Ferrer, J.D., Ballesté, A.M., Deswarte, Y., Quisquater, J.: Efficient remote data possession checking in critical information infrastructures. In: TKDE 2008 (2008)
20. Shacham, H., Waters, B.: Compact proofs of retrievability. In: Pieprzyk, J. (ed.) ASIACRYPT 2008. LNCS, vol. 5350, pp. 90–107. Springer, Heidelberg (2008)
21. Sink, E.: Version Control by Example, 1st edn. Pyrenean Gold Press (2011)
22. Wang, Q., Wang, C., Li, J., Ren, K., Lou, W.: Enabling public verifiability and data dynamics for storage security in cloud computing. In: Backes, M., Ning, P. (eds.) ESORICS 2009. LNCS, vol. 5789, pp. 355–370. Springer, Heidelberg (2009)
23. Zeng, K.: Publicly verifiable remote data integrity. In: Chen, L., Ryan, M.D., Wang, G. (eds.) ICICS 2008. LNCS, vol. 5308, pp. 419–434. Springer, Heidelberg (2008)

24. Zhao, L., Ren, Y., Xiang, Y., Sakurai, K.: Fault-tolerant scheduling with dynamic number of replicas in heterogeneous systems. In: HPCC 2010, pp. 434–441 (2010)
25. Zheng, Q., Xu, S.: Fair and dynamic proofs of retrievability. In: Proc. of the First ACM Conf. on Data and App. Security and Privacy, pp. 237–248. ACM (2011)
26. Zhu, Y., Hu, H., Ahn, G.-J., Yu, M.: Cooperative provable data possession for integrity verification in multi-cloud storage. IEEE TPDS 99(PrePrints) (2012)
27. Zhu, Y., Wang, H., Hu, Z., Ahn, G.-J., Hu, H., Yau, S.S.: Efficient provable data possession for hybrid clouds. In: CCS 2010, pp. 756–758. ACM, New York (2010)

Client-Controlled Cryptography-as-a-Service in the Cloud

Sören Bleikertz[1], Sven Bugiel[2], Hugo Ideler[2],
Stefan Nürnberger[2], and Ahmad-Reza Sadeghi[2]

[1] IBM Research - Zurich, Rüschlikon, Switzerland
sbl@zurich.ibm.com
[2] TU Darmstadt / CASED, Darmstadt, Germany
{sven.bugiel, hugo.ideler, stefan.nuernberger,
ahmad.sadeghi}@trust.cased.de

Abstract. Today, a serious concern about cloud computing is the protection of clients' data and computations against various attacks from outsiders as well as against the cloud provider. Moreover, cloud clients are rather limited in implementing, deploying and controlling their own security solutions in the cloud. The provider theoretically has access to stored keys in dormant images and deploying keys during run-time is infeasible because authenticating running VM instances is not possible.

In this paper, we present a security architecture that allows for establishing secure client-controlled Cryptography-as-a-Service (CaaS) in the cloud: Our *CaaS* enables clients to be in control of the provisioning and usage of their credentials and cryptographic primitives. They can securely provision keys or even implement their private virtual security module (e.g., vHSM or SmartCard). All clients' cryptographic operations run in a protected client-specific secure execution domain. This is achieved by modifying the Xen hypervisor and leveraging standard Trusted Computing technology. Moreover, our solution is legacy-compatible by installing a transparent cryptographic layer for the storage and network I/O of a VM. We reduced the privileged hypercalls necessary for administration by 79%. We evaluated the effectiveness and efficiency of our design which resulted in an acceptable performance overhead.

1 Introduction

Cloud computing offers IT resources, including storage, networking, and computing platforms, on an on-demand and pay-as-you-go basis. This promise of operational and monetary benefits has already encouraged various organizations to shift from a *"classical"* on-premise to a cloud-based service deployment of their workloads [12].

To secure those services, typically cryptographic security mechanisms are installed. Usually, these mechanisms require long-term secrets, e.g. SSL/TLS-secured web services need a secret key stored in the virtual machine (VM) for authentication purposes. Naturally, such long-term secrets are a valuable target for attackers that compromise the client's service. In the classical on-premise

M. Jacobson et al. (Eds.): ACNS 2013, LNCS 7954, pp. 19–36, 2013.

datacenters, clients had the ability to incorporate security devices like Hardware Security Modules (HSMs) or SmartCards in order to protect their cryptographic credentials and operations. While this threat still holds in a cloud-based deployment [1,13,14], the difference is that the incorporation of security hardware is virtually impossible as cloud providers strictly prohibit physical customizations or access to their facilities. Additionally, outsourced data and computations are an easy prey for insider attackers at the provider's side since the client has willingly delegated control over his resources to the provider [25]. Controlling running instances of virtual machines, e.g. starting, stopping and maintaining them, is a necessity for every virtualization solution and is done by instructing the hypervisor from a privileged management domain which by default has ultimate access to all virtual machines. Insider attackers have access to this privileged domain and hence put clients' cryptographic credentials that are stored and processed in VMs at risk. This leads to trusting the cloud provider not to eavesdrop on the data. Consequently, it is desirable to build a cloud architecture that not only provides means to protect secrets even when the VM is exploited, but to also allow the client to deploy keys securely to the cloud without insiders being able to spy on it.

Cryptography-as-a-Service. In this paper, we present a security architecture that allows for provisioning *secret-less* client VMs in clouds and separating client's cryptographic primitives and credentials into a *client-controlled* and *protected* cryptographic domain (DomC). In contrast to other work that also advocates self-managed cloud services [9,39], we specifically built a solution that not only allows the establishment of a trust anchor and provisioning of user secret keys, but which also provides the protection of legacy VMs that were not tailored for our solution. We base our solution on the well-established concepts of a) segregating and encapsulating cryptographic operations and keys from the vulnerable client VM into a separate domain (DomC); and b) a trusted hypervisor that efficiently and effectively protects the separate DomC against a compromised or malicious management domain by subjecting it to the principle of least privilege. In contrast to related work, we overcome the aforementioned problem of actually deploying keys for use in the cloud. This requires novel security extensions to the VM life cycle management to protect the DomC during storage, transit, and instantiation, and to tightly couple it to the corresponding client's workload VM.

Contribution. We present the design and implementation of Cryptography-as-a-Service (*CaaS*), a solution to a practical security problem of clouds based on well-established and widely available technology. Our contributions are as follows:

- We present a dedicated, client-specific domain DomC for the client's cryptographic primitives and credentials that can be securely deployed with secrets by the client without the possibility for insiders or external attackers to gain access to them. Based on our security extensions to the hypervisor and well-established Trusted Computing technology, DomC can be protected from malicious insiders and outsiders in a reasonable adversary model. In particular, we focus on integrating this protection in the entire VM life-cycle including deployment, instantiation, migration, and suspension.

- Clients can leverage their DomC in two different usage-modes: a) *Virtual Security Module* and b) *Secure Virtual Device*. Case a) emulates a virtual hardware security device, like an HSM/TPM, attached to the client VM while case b) interposes a transparent layer between the client VM and peripheral devices (disk or network) which encrypts all I/O data to/from those devices and hence protects *unaware* legacy OSes.
- We present the reference implementation of *CaaS* based on the Xen hypervisor and evaluate its performance for full disk encryption of attached storage and for a software-based HSM and its effectiveness with respect to different existing attack scenarios.
- Our modifications of the Xen hypervisor de-privilege the formerly privileged domain and separate former monolithic components into small, single-purpose and protected domains with a trusted computing base (TCB) that is orders of magnitudes smaller than the original version.

2 Model and Requirements

In the cloud service model hierarchy, we target the most general level *Infrastructure-as-a-Service* (IaaS) as depicted in Figure 1. In IaaS clouds, *Clients* rent virtual resources such as network and virtual machines from the provider and configure them according to their needs. Commonly, these VMs run public services such as web services offered to *End-Users* over the Internet.

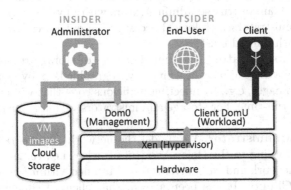

Fig. 1. Typical IaaS cloud model including our adversary and trust model

We focus on the popular Xen hypervisor [3] and consequently use the Xen terminology. The clients' VM is denoted as DomU, meaning *unprivileged* domains that are guests on the hypervisor and have no direct hardware access. While there can be many DomU executing in parallel on the Xen hypervisor, there exists only one persistent *privileged* management domain, denoted Dom0. This domain is usually not exposed to outsiders. Xen is a bare-metal hypervisor only concerned with the separation of virtual domains and their scheduling. It defers device emulation tasks to Dom0, that holds the necessary rights to access hardware resources. Thus, Dom0 is naturally the place for the cloud infrastructure management software and their *Administrators* to operate in.

Besides computation, IaaS clouds normally also provide *Cloud Storage*. This storage is not just used for workload data but also to save the *VM images*, i.e., binary representations of VM states, from which DomUs are instantiated. In newer cloud usage models like cloud app stores [8], clients are also able to publicly provide their VM image and share it with other clients.

2.1   Trust Model and Assumptions

From a client's perspective, one of the most debated issues in cloud computing security is the trust placed in the cloud provider. In order to build a reasonable and practical trust model we do not assume a fully untrusted provider, but rather consider the involved actors and possible attacker types on the provider's side. We consider the following actors in our attacker model:

Compute Administrator. On a commodity hypervisor, Dom0 and thus administrators, have read/write access to the memory of a running VM which is necessary for VM creation or, e.g., VM introspection. Hence, they are able to eavesdrop on data or even inject arbitrary code in the client's running VMs as shown by [25]. Thus, we do not trust the Dom0. We only consider attacks from administrators with *logical* access to the physical servers, e.g., by operating in the privileged management domain Dom0, and *not* attackers with physical access. This attacker model stems from practical scenarios, where datacenters are operated by a small team of trusted administrators with physical access and a large number of administrators with logical access, often outsourced and provided by third parties with limited trust.[1]

Storage Administrator. For administrators of storage resources, we consider an adversary that aims at learning cryptographic keys by inspecting or by modifying VM images, e.g., by injecting malicious code that will extract cryptographic keys at run-time. For storage administrators we allow physical access to hardware.

Network Administrator. We model the network administrators (omitted in Figure 1) according to the Dolev-Yao [16] attacker, i.e., the attacker has full control of the network and can eavesdrop and tamper with *all* network traffic.

Malicious Clients. It has been shown, that clients frequently store (and forget) security-critical information, such as cryptographic keys, in their public, shared VM images [8]. A malicious client can easily investigate those images and extract these information.

End-Users. Public (web-)services are a gateway for malicious intruders that compromise a VM, for instance, due to a vulnerability in the provided services.

---

[1] Note that purely cryptographic approaches [4,7,19] protect even against physical attacks. However, they are still impractical due to their enormous complexity overhead.

Hypervisor. We *exclude* run-time attacks on the hypervisor, as this is an open research problem and out of scope of this paper. Under this assumption, we consider a trustworthy hypervisor in the sense that the client can deploy mechanisms to verify the trustworthiness of the code a hypervisor is constituted of. This is accomplished using standardized trusted computing mechanisms such as *authenticated boot* and *remote attestation* [36] (cf. Section 3).

Denial-of-Service Attack. We *exclude* Denial-of-Service attacks from our model. This is motivated by the fact that the privileged domain Dom0, although not trusted, cannot be completely excluded from all operational and management tasks, and thus is always able to block correct operation.

2.2 Objectives and Requirements

Our main security objective is the protection of the client's cryptographic keys and operations in the cloud, similar to well-known SmartCards. We consider the following main security requirements to ensure the secure storage and usage of cryptographic credentials and operations in the client's VM:

1. Protection of long-term secrets of client VMs at runtime, i.e., an attacker who compromised the workload VM DomU or a malicious/compromised management domain Dom0 cannot extract this information from the DomU VM.
2. The same must hold for the DomU's integrity at rest, i.e., the client's dormant DomU VM image must be protected such that an attacker can neither extract credentials from it nor unnoticeably tamper with it.
3. Secure VM management operations, i.e., suspension and migration of the client DomU VM must preserve the integrity and confidentiality of DomU's state on the source and target platform as well as during transit/storage.

3 Design and Implementation

In this section, we introduce the architecture and design decisions of Cryptography-as-a-Service (*CaaS*). The vital part of this paper is the deployment of secret keys to the secure environment DomC. In the first subsection 3.1, we explain the idea of our solution, followed by our security extensions to the hypervisor.

Prerequisites. We assume the availability of a hardware trust anchor on the cloud nodes in the form of a Trusted Platform Module (TPM). The TPM is used to securely attest the node's platform state [36]. For brevity, the following descriptions involve only one cloud client, however, we stress that the presented solutions can be easily applied to multiple client scenarios as well. Moreover, we apply the term *encryption* to abstractly describe a cryptographic mechanism for both confidentiality *and* integrity protection, i.e., authenticated encryption.

3.1   General Idea

Figure 2 illustrates the *CaaS* architecture using Xen. We achieve our goals by (1) severing the client's security sensitive operations and data in DomU into a *client-controlled* secure environment denoted DomC; (2) we degrade Dom0 to an untrusted domain but retain it's purpose as administrative domain. This is achieved by extracting the domain management code (building, transferring, destroying VMs) and making this code run bare-metal in a new virtual machine. The resulting small trusted domain builder (DomT) then has exactly enough code and privileges to build new domains and makes the fully-blown management Dom0 being a part of the TCB obsolete. Instead, Dom0 now merely forwards commands to DomT. The necessary modifications in the Xen hypervisor are described in subsection 3.2.

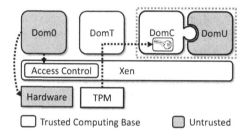

Fig. 2. Basic idea of *CaaS*: Establishment of a separate security-domain, denoted as DomC, for critical cryptographic operations

To implement DomC and DomT as separate domains running on Xen without the need for a full-fledged operating system, we leveraged *Mini-OS* [34], which is a minimal stub domain directly interfacing with the Xen hypervisor. DomC exposes cryptographic library functions to the corresponding coupled workload VM (DomU) or automatically interposes external devices used by DomU to transparently encrypt/decrypt them. The privileged operations that traditionally would be done by Dom0, like domain building, domain migration etc. are segregated to a single-purpose stub domain DomT, the Trusted Domain Builder.

Usage Modes of DomC. Xen uses a *split driver* model for device drivers. It provides a front-end and a back-end module (cf. Figure 3). The latter controls the actual physical device while the former provides a virtualized representation of that device to VMs. In *CaaS*, we leverage this split-driver mechanism to connect DomC as a Xen virtual device to DomU. Figure 3 shows the two operation modes of DomC that we describe below: *Virtual Security Module* and *Secure Device Proxy*.

Virtual Security Module. In this mode of operation, DomC resembles a security module such as an HSM. In this mode, DomU has to be aware of the DomC so that

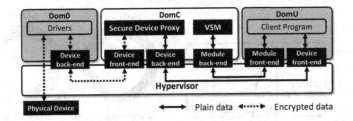

Fig. 3. Usage Modes: DomU can use DomC either as *Virtual Security Module* (VSM) or to secure its storage or network data with a transparent proxy

it can use its interface for outsourcing traditional cryptographic operations like an SSL/TLS wrapper for a web service running in the VM. In our prototypical implementation DomC emulates an HSM and provides a standardized PKCS#11-compliant interface for DomU.

Secure Device Proxy. In this mode, DomC acts as a transparent layer between DomU and external devices, such as attached storage medium or network card. We use this layer as a convenient building block for advanced applications such as booting fully encrypted VM images (cf. Section 3.3) or for legacy VMs that still want to profit from full-disk encryption. To achieve the pass-through, we chain two front-end-back-end communication channels. The first channel exists between DomC and Dom0 where DomC connects to a device offered by Dom0 (e.g., storage or network). The second channel exists between DomC and DomU, where DomC provides an identical device interface to DomU. DomC encrypts and decrypts on-the-fly all data in this stream. Although it is technically feasible that DomC writes directly to the physical device, routing encrypted I/O streams through Dom0 avoids implementing (redundantly) device drivers in each DomC.

Both modes are not mutually exclusive. A transparent encryption layer can be used while DomU is yet aware of the DomC and additionally uses it for explicit cryptographic operations.

3.2 Security Extensions to the Xen Hypervisor

While the above mentioned modes seem not to require any changes to the Xen hypervisor, default Xen does not prevent Dom0 from reading/writing another VM's memory. To prevent that, we added security extensions to the Xen hypervisor:

1. Additional Mandatory Access Control for low-level resources (e.g., memory) to isolate the client's DomC from any other domain including Dom0 (Fig. 4(a)).
2. The binary privileged/unprivileged hypercall scheme was made more fine-grained to drastically de-privilege Dom0 and to support certain hypercalls only for certain domains, namely DomT and DomC (Fig. 4(b)).

In default Xen, different mechanisms to access foreign memory of other domains exist (cf. Figure 4(a)):

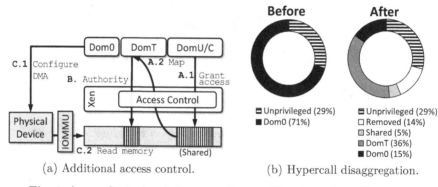

(a) Additional access control.   (b) Hypercall disaggregation.

Fig. 4. Access Control and disaggregation modifications of our Xen version

Privileged Domains. In default Xen, Dom0 is always able to map the memory pages of another domain since it needs to set up a new domain's memory before it is running. In order to remove this privilege, we separated the domain building functionality into DomT. To this extent we ported the Xen domain managment library libxl to Mini-OS to reside in DomT. Additionally, Xen's binary privileged/unprivileged hypercall scheme which allowed Dom0 to map arbitrary foreign memory needed to be refined in order to support different domains with different privileges. This new access control is enforced in the logic of the Xen hypervisor for mapping foreign memory pages into a domain's memory range by extending the Xen Security Module (XSM) accordingly. The privilege of Dom0 to access foreign memory is then disabled in the hypervisor while Dom0 needs to forward domain management requests (building, migrating, destroying) to DomT which has now memory authority (step B). The concept of disaggregating code from Dom0 was pioneered by Murray et al. [24] and enhanced in our design.

Grant tables. Grant tables are the default mechanism for establishing shared memory pages between different domains (e.g. for split drivers). The owning domain can discretely grant access to its memory pages to other domains (step A.1), which are then able to map these shared pages into their own memory space (step A.2). In *CaaS*, no additional access control on Grant Tables is required, as DomU and DomC are in control of their own pages and thus can by default deny any access from other domains.

IOMMU. A potential security risk are physical devices featuring Direct Memory Access (DMA), having access to the entire physical memory. DMA is configured by the domain that is in control of the physical hardware (by default Dom0; step C.1). We require hardware support in the form of an IOMMU (step C.2) to exclude the whole VM and Xen memory from the DMA range.

3.3   Detailed Image Setup Workflow

To ensure that the client can entrust her secrets and images to the cloud, we leverage standard Trusted Computing protocols for the Trusted Platform Module (TPM) [36]. This technology provides the means to establish a trusted end-to-end channel since the client can encrypt data such that only a platform in a certain trusted state S (i.e., running our modified version of Xen) is able to decrypt this data. Technically, this is realized using a TPM certified binding key (sk_{TPM}, pk_{TPM}) where the secret key sk_{TPM} is bound to the platform state S. The certificate *cert* proves that the key-pair was created by a genuine TPM and hence the binding property holds. To make the same key available on all cloud nodes, we use *migratable* keys, i.e., its usage is bound to one or more trustworthy platform states but not a particular platform. For brevity, we omit the setup of this TPM key from our protocol and refer to related work [10]. An *authenticated boot* [35] measures the platform state, during boot. Moreover, we make use of a TPM feature called *locality* to ensure that only the trusted hypervisor (i.e. not Dom0) is able to use the certified binding key sk_{TPM} and to further allow Dom0 to still use the TPM, however, not at the locality reserved for the hypervisor. The pseudocode in algorithm 1 depicts the setup process of the client and trust establishment in detail.

Algorithm 1. Pseudocode for Setup Steps

1: get $(cert, pk_{TPM})$ from cloud node
2: **if** VALIDATE$(cert, pk_{TPM})$ **then**
3:     $k \leftarrow$ GENERATESYMMETRICKEY()
4:     $domCimage \leftarrow$ CREATECUSTOMDOMCIMAGE()
5:     INJECTKEY$(domCimage, k)$
6:     $enc_u \leftarrow$ ENCRYPT$(domUimage, k)$
7:     $enc_c \leftarrow$ ENCRYPT$(domCimage, pk_{TPM})$
8:     $ID \leftarrow$ UPLOADANDREGISTER(enc_c, enc_u)
9: **end if**

After the client verified pk_{TPM} using the certificate *cert* (line 2), she generates at least one new secret k (line 3) and securely injects that secret into her local plaintext image of DomC (line 5). DomC is able to act as transparent cryptographic protection (e.g., encryption) of an attached block storage (*Secure Device Proxy* mode) or as a SmartCard using key k. The DomU image is encrypted under k (step 6) and the configured DomC image is encrypted under pk_{TPM} (line 7) which constitutes the trusted channel explained earlier. Both encrypted images are then uploaded and registered in the cloud under a certain *ID* (line 8). Using *ID*, the client can manage her images, e.g., launch an instance from her DomU image.

3.4   Detailed Launching Workflow

The instantiation of the uploaded encrypted DomU image can be divided in two steps as shown in Figure 5: First, and only once after booting our modified Xen, DomT is started with memory authority for the purpose of domain creation (step 1). Additionally, the locality of the TPM is set up in such a way that DomT is the

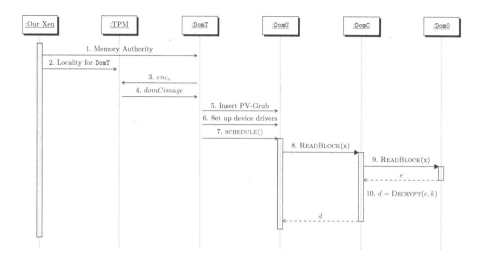

Fig. 5. Booting DomU and coupling with corresponding DomC

only one allowed to use sk_{TPM} (step 2). DomT uses this sk_{TPM} to decrypt the
DomC image *domCimage* with the aid of the TPM[2] (steps 3 & 4). DomT inserts the
Xen bootloader PV-Grub[3] into the still pristine DomU image which is necessary
for DomU to be able to boot from a device offered by DomC (step 5). Then, the
front-end devices (cf. Figure 3) are set up to be available to PV-Grub to boot
from (step 6). Once DomU is scheduled for the first time (step 7) and tries to
read a block from the attached virtual disk (step 8), it gets transparently routed
through DomC which reads the actual sectors from the traditional disk provided
by Dom0 and decrypts them for DomU (steps 9 & 10).

Suspension and Live Migration. In order to support live migration, the
standard Xen migration protocol needs to be wrapped but in essence works
unaffectedly from the perspective of the client and DomU. Since we ported the
Dom0 Xen interface (`libxl`) to DomT, the live migration request in Dom0 is simply
forwarded to DomT which has access to any DomU's memory. DomT then migrates
a running VM on-the-fly by first attesting the target host's integrity using its
certificate *cert* and by piecemeal transmission of the memory content to the
new trusted target host. Instead of migrating plaintext VM memory from one
Node to another, the memory must be encrypted, since migration requires the
involvement of Dom0 and a potentially untrusted network.

To restore the transferred state on the target platform, DomC has to be migrated as well in order to decrypt the migrated DomU state on the target plat-

---

[2] The use of asymmetric cryptography in the TPM is an abstraction. Technically, the
decryption using a TPM is more involved and requires wrapping a symmetric key
with the pk_{TPM}/sk_{TPM} pair.

[3] http://wiki.xen.org/wiki/PvGrub

form. Restoring a VM state requires platform-dependent modifications to the state, such as rebuilding the memory page-tables. DomT's domain building code performs these modifications on DomU during DomU's resumption. Afterwards the new DomC is able to decrypt and resume the DomU state on the target platform and the old DomC on the source platform can be discarded. To achieve the protection of the transferred DomC state, this state is encrypted under the TPM key pk_{TPM}. Thus, only a target node running our trustworthy hypervisor is able to decrypt and resume the DomC state. We need to make sure that the version of our trusted Xen is not run outside of a trusted datacenter, e.g. our partly trusted cloud provider. For the sake of simplicity, in our proof-of-concept implementation we only allowed to migrate to other secure hosts that are within the same class-C-network. In case of suspension, the protocol works identical, except that the "target platform" is cloud storage to which the protected DomC and DomU states are saved by DomT.

4   Security

In this section we discuss how our architecture protects the client's cryptographic keys with regard to the requirements and adversary model defined in Section 2. We also discuss the corner cases that our architecture does not handle.

Compute Administrator. Our solution protects against a malicious *Compute Administrator*. This is guaranteed by the logical isolation of domains by the trusted hypervisor and the de-privileged management domain in which the administrators operate. Extracting the domain building process to DomT combined with the TPM based protocols (cf. Section 3.2) ensures that Dom0 cannot access DomT, DomC's or DomU's memory in plaintext. We empirically verified the mitigation of known attacks to extract confidential information from VMs [25].

Any modifications Dom0 does on the encrypted images during launch will lead to integrity verification failures and abortion of the launch, and hence form a denial-of-service. The same holds for the saved, encrypted state of DomU and DomC during migration and suspension. As mentioned in our adversary model, we exclude compute administrators with physical access, since it seems there exists no practical solution against these attacks yet.

Storage Administrator. Our solutions protects against a malicious *Storage Administrator* by storing images only in encrypted and integrity protected form. Thus, this attacker cannot extract any sensitive information from the images and any modification to the images before loading them into memory results in a denial-of-service attack. Solutions against replay attacks of outdated images, which we do not consider in this paper, can also be based on the TPM [29,37].

Network Administrator. Images and VM states are protected (encrypted and integrity checked) during provision to the cloud, transfer between cloud nodes and storage during migration and suspension, respectively. Thus, a malicious *Network Administrator* cannot extract the client's keys from intercepted network data. However, dropping network traffic or tampering with it will lead to a denial-of-service attack. Freshness of network communications to protect against replay attacks or injection of non-authentic data is easily achieved by using message nonces or by establishing session keys.

End-Users. If an external attacker gains full (i.e. root) access to DomU, the attacker can misuse DomC as an oracle, e.g., to sign arbitrary messages in the client's name. This problem also applies to HSMs. A common countermeasure is an auditing mechanism within DomC that detects misuse based on heuristics (e.g., usage thresholds). The secrets however remain protected in DomC.

Malicious Clients. Since keys are neither stored nor processed within a customer VM, there is no risk of accidentally sharing them in public VM images. Thus, our solution protects against *Malicious Clients*, who inspect shared public VM images for credentials.

Adherence. Due to our isolation from the management domain, the cloud provider can no longer monitor the client's behaviour. This is a potential invitation to hide malicious/criminal activities such as providing illegal content. Other solutions [9] tackled this issue by installing a mutually trusted observer for the client VM's activities, which simultaneously preserves the client VM's privacy and checks the client's activity for conformance.

5   Performance Evaluation

We evaluated the performance overhead induced by offloading cryptographic operations to DomC for both the Secure Device Proxy and Virtual Security Module modes. Our test machine is a Dell Optiplex 980 with an Intel QuadCore i7 3.2GHz CPU, 8GB RAM, and a Western Digital WD5000AAKS - 75V0A0 hard-drive connected via SATA2.

Secure Device Proxy. This setup consists of the Xen v4.1.2 hypervisor with our extensions, an Arch Linux Dom0 (kernel 3.2.13), a Debian DomU (kernel 3.2.0) and a Mini-OS based DomC and DomT. All domains and the hypervisor execute in 64-bit mode and each guest domain has been assigned one physical core. DomU and DomT have been assigned 256 MB of RAM while each DomC runs with 32 MB. All I/O data streams from DomU to the virtual block storage are passing through DomC and are transparently encrypted using AES-128 in CBC-ESSIV mode based on code ported to Mini-OS from the disk-encryption subsystem *dm-crypt* of the Linux kernel. We measure four scenarios:

Traditional. Standard Xen setup without an interposed DomC and no encryption.

dm-crypt in DomU. This extends the *Traditional* scenario with AES-128 CBC-ESSIV mode encryption of I/O data in DomU using dm-crypt.

DomC pass-through. This scenario interposes DomC between DomU and Dom0 to merely pass-through I/O without encryption.

DomC (AES-128). This scenario extends the pass-through scenario with AES-128 CBC-ESSIV en-/decryption in DomC.

In a traditional Linux running as DomU, block device buffering is used for reads and writes, where writes occur asynchronously. In this setup, the performance overhead was negligible. To give a worst-case scenario, in this throughput benchmark we measure the induced performance overhead with all caching disabled and additionally only read/write random sectors to avoid hard disk buffer effects. The bandwidth measurements were taken using the fio tool[4] in the DomU. For each of the aforementioned four combinations measurements were taken with each read or write lasting exactly 10 minutes (see Figure 6). Performance measurements with asynchronous I/O, disk buffers left on (default Linux settings) and linear reads produced almost negligible overhead but had a high standard deviation.

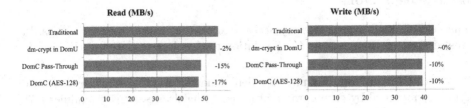

Fig. 6. Disk throughput performance

Virtual Security Module. Our setup consists of *SoftHSM*[5], a software-based implementation of a HSM that can be accessed via a PKCS#11 interface. We compare two scenarios: **a)** where *SoftHSM* is running in a Linux-based DomC, and **b)** when running inside a DomU and being accessed directly. In scenario **a**, the server resides within DomC and the client in DomU, and the communication is realized through our backend-frontend Virtual Security Module interface. In scenario **b**, both server and client reside in DomU and the network loopback device is used.

We measure the performance of RSA signing using an HSM. This is a typical scenario found in practice, e.g., CAs signing TLS certificates or signing of domain names within the DNSSEC system. In particular we are focusing on the latter scenario and leverage the benchmark software `ods-hsmspeed` from the OpenDNSSEC project[6]. As parameters for `ods-hsmspeed`, we selected 8 threads requesting signatures from the HSM, RSA1024 as the signing algorithm, and varying number of total signatures requested ranging from 1 to 10000.

Our results are illustrated in Figure 7. When requesting a low number of signatures, i.e., only 1 or 10, the costs for the connection and benchmark setup are more profound. However in practical scenarios, we expect a large number of signatures that are requested. Comparing the performance in terms of signatures per second between a *SoftHSM* residing in DomU vs. DomC, we notice a less than 3% overhead when offloading the cryptographic operations to DomC.

---

[4] FIO disk benchmark – http://freecode.com/projects/fio

[5] http://www.opendnssec.org/softhsm/

[6] http://www.opendnssec.org/

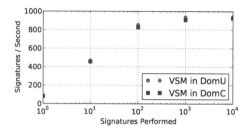

Fig. 7. Comparing the signing performance of a software-based HSM residing in DomU vs. DomC

6   Related Work

The field of cloud security is very active and touches various research areas. In this section, we compare our *CaaS* solution to the closest related work.

Trusted Computing. In physical deployments, cryptographic services are typically provided by cryptographic tokens [2], hardware-security modules [17], generic PKCS#11-compliant modules, e.g. smart cards, and the Trusted Platform Module (TPM) [36]. In our approach, we study how such cryptographic services can also be securely provided in virtualized form in cloud deployments.

To provide TPM functionality to virtual machines, virtual TPMs have been proposed [5,28] and secure migration of VM-vTPM pairs by Danev et al. [15]. Our *CaaS* is conceptually a generalized form of such as a service, since DomC could also provide a vTPM daemon. However, in contrast to [5], our solution does not rely on a security service running within a potentially malicious Dom0.

Providing a cryptographic service over a network has been considered in large-scale networks, such as peer-to-peer or grid systems, by Xu and Sandhu [40]. Berson et al. propose a *Cryptography-as-a-Network-Service* [6] for performance benefits, by using a central service equipped with cryptographic hardware accelerators. Our *CaaS* targets specifically multi-tenant cloud environments and aims at tightly but securely coupling the client and her credentials to enable advanced applications such as transparent encryption of storage.

Different cloud architectures that rely on trusted computing have been proposed that ensure protected execution of virtual machines. The Trusted Cloud Computing Platform (TCCP) [31] by Santos et al. and the architecture proposed by Schiffman et al. [33] use TCG remote attestation to prove the trustworthiness of the cloud's compute nodes. Our approach also builds on Trusted Computing technology but with the goal to protect cryptographic operations and credentials from external and internal attackers. Santos et al. extended their TCCP architecture to address the problems of binary-based attestation [32] and data sealing with an approach very similar to property-based attestation [27].

Virtualization Security. Research that advocates the benefits of virtualization technology for security purposes has a long-standing history, even decades before the advent of cloud computing [20,21,26], and has introduced concepts that establish secure (virtual) execution environments [11,18]. They implement the concept of moving the security management to the virtualization layer by providing two different execution security contexts for VMs on top of a trusted VMM. Our architecture differs from those in that we provide client-controlled cryptographic primitives for multi-tenant virtualized environments (such as clouds) and thus have to tackle the challenges of how to securely provision and use those primitives in the presence of a malicious cloud management domain.

Other related works leverage nested virtualization to advocate similar goals as *CaaS*. Williams et al. introduced the *Xen-Blanket* [39], which adds an additional virtualization layer, empowering clients to avoid cloud provider lock-in. The *CloudVisor* [41] architecture by Zhang et al. adds a small hypervisor beneath the Xen hypervisor to protect client's DomU against an untrusted or compromised VMM or Dom0 (including encrypted VM images). However, nested virtualization induces an unacceptable performance overhead and usually requires introspection. In *CaaS*, we *avoid* nested virtualization and instead apply Murray's concept of Dom0 disaggregation [24] on top of the commodity Xen hypervisor, which is assumed trustworthy. We note, that hardening hypervisors against attacks is an active, orthogonal research area [38] from which our solution benefits.

The closest related work to ours, is the *Self-Service Cloud* (SSC) framework by Butt et al. [9], which was developed independently and in parallel to our work. In SSC, clients are able to securely spawn their own meta-domain, including their own user Dom0, in which they are in control of deployed (security) services, such as DomU introspection, storage intrusion detection, or storage encryption. This meta-domain is isolated from an untrusted Dom0 using a mandatory access control framework in the Xen hypervisor (XSM [30]). In contrast to SSC, our *CaaS* takes care of client-controlled cryptographic operations and builds the basis for the actual key provisioning. We tackle the challenge of how to protect and securely use our DomC, running isolated but tightly coupled to its DomU. This requires modifications to the VM life cycle management, i.e., secure migration/suspension of DomU and instantiating fully encrypted DomU images.

Secure Execution Environment. Instead of relying on the trustworthiness of the virtualization layer, DomC would ideally run in a Secure Execution Environment (SEE) that is available as a hardware security extension on modern CPUs, e.g., *Flicker* by McCune et al. [23]. However, invocations of SEE suffer from the critical drawback that they incur a significant performance penalty. Consequently, this makes them unsuitable for streaming operations such as encryption of data of arbitrary length. McCune et al. address this issue with their *TrustVisor* [22] by leveraging hardware virtualization support of modern platforms, trusted computing technology, and a custom minimal hypervisor to establish a better performing SEE. Conceptually, TrustVisor is related to our *CaaS* from the perspective of isolating security sensitive code in an SEE. However, TrustVisor is designed to protect this code from an untrusted legacy OS while

CaaS targets the specific scenario of cloud environments and thus faces more complex challenges: First, *CaaS* has to address an additional virtualization layer to multiplex multiple clients' VMs. Second, our adversary model must consider a partially untrusted cloud provider and malicious co-located clients.

7 Conclusion and Future Work

In this paper we present the concept of secret-less virtual machines based on a client-controlled Cryptography-as-a-Service (*CaaS*) architecture for cloud infrastructures. Analogously to Hardware Security Modules in the physical world, our architecture segregates the management and storage of cloud clients' keys as well as all cryptographic operations into a secure crypto domain, denoted DomC, which is tightly coupled to the client's workloads VMs. Extensions of the trusted hypervisor enable clients to securely provision and use their keys and cryptographic primitives in the cloud. DomC can be used as virtual security module, e.g., vHSM, or as a transparent encryption layer between the client's VM and e.g. legacy storage. Furthermore, these extensions protect DomC in a reasonable adversary model from any unauthorized access that tries to extract cryptographic material from the VM – either from a privileged management domain or from outside the VM. The flexible nature of DomC allows for building more advanced architectures, such as Trusted Virtual Domains [10], on top of our CaaS. Evaluation of full disk encryption with our reference implementation showed that DomC imposes a minimal performance overhead. Future work aims at methods to mitigate run-time attacks against DomU, which enable an attacker to misuse the securely stored credentials. An avenue to mitigate this issue would be to install usage quotas heuristics in order to detect misuse. Further, secure logging in DomC would support post-misuse analysis.

Acknowledgments. This research has been supported by the European Union's Seventh Framework Programme (FP7/2007-2013) under grant agreement n°257243 (TClouds project: http://www.tclouds-project.eu).

References

1. AlertLogic. An empirical analysis of real world threats: State of cloud security report (2012),
   http://www.alertlogic.com/resources/state-of-cloud-security-report/
2. Anderson, R., Bond, M., Clulow, J., Skorobogatov, S.: Cryptographic processors – a survey. Proceedings of the IEEE 94(2), 357–369 (2006)
3. Barham, P., Dragovic, B., Fraser, K., Hand, S., Harris, T., Ho, A., Neugebauer, R., Pratt, I., Warfield, A.: Xen and the Art of Virtualization. In: 19th ACM Symposium on Operating Systems Principles (SOSP 2003). ACM (2003)
4. Ben-David, A., Nisan, N., Pinkas, B.: FairplayMP: a system for secure multi-party computation. In: 15th ACM Conference on Computer and Communications Security (CCS 2008). ACM (2008)

5. Berger, S., Cáceres, R., Goldman, K.A., Perez, R., Sailer, R., van Doorn, L.: vtpm: virtualizing the trusted platform module. In: 15th Conference on USENIX Security Symposium. USENIX (2006)

6. Berson, T., Dean, D., Franklin, M., Smetters, D., Spreitzer, M.: Cryptography as a Network Service. In: Network and Distributed Systems Security Symposium, NDSS 2001 (2001)

7. Bogdanov, D., Laur, S., Willemson, J.: Sharemind: A framework for fast privacy-preserving computations. In: Jajodia, S., Lopez, J. (eds.) ESORICS 2008. LNCS, vol. 5283, pp. 192–206. Springer, Heidelberg (2008)

8. Bugiel, S., Nürnberger, S., Pöppelmann, T., Sadeghi, A.-R., Schneider, T.: AmazonIA: When Elasticity Snaps Back. In: 18th ACM Conference on Computer and Communications Security (CCS 2011). ACM (October 2011)

9. Butt, S., Lagar-Cavilla, H.A., Srivastava, A., Ganapathy, V.: Self-service cloud computing. In: 19th ACM Conference on Computer and Communications Security (CCS 2012). ACM (October 2012)

10. Catuogno, L., et al.: Trusted Virtual Domains – Design, Implementation and Lessons Learned. In: Chen, L., Yung, M. (eds.) INTRUST 2009. LNCS, vol. 6163, pp. 156–179. Springer, Heidelberg (2010)

11. Chen, X., Garfinkel, T., Lewis, E.C., Subrahmanyam, P., Waldspurger, C.A., Boneh, D., Dwoskin, J., Ports, D.R.: Overshadow: a virtualization-based approach to retrofitting protection in commodity operating systems. ACM SIGOPS (2008)

12. Chen, Y., Sion, R.: To cloud or not to cloud?: musings on costs and viability. In: 2nd ACM Symposium on Cloud Computing (SOCC 2011). ACM (2011)

13. CVE-2007-4993. Bug in pygrub allows guests to execute commands in dom0

14. CVE-2008-1943. Buffer overflow in xensource allows to execute arbitrary code

15. Danev, B., Masti, R.J., Karame, G.O., Capkun, S.: Enabling secure VM-vTPM migration in private clouds. In: 27th Annual Computer Security Applications Conference (ACSAC 2011). ACM (2011)

16. Dolev, D., Yao, A.: On the security of public key protocols. IEEE Transactions on Information Theory 29(2), 198–208 (1983)

17. Dyer, J.G., Lindemann, M., Perez, R., Sailer, R., van Doorn, L., Smith, S.W., Weingart, S.: Building the IBM 4758 secure coprocessor. IEEE Computer (2001)

18. Garfinkel, T., Pfaff, B., Chow, J., Rosenblum, M., Boneh, D.: Terra: a virtual machine-based platform for trusted computing. In: 19th ACM Symposium on Operating Systems Principles (SOSP 2003). ACM (2003)

19. Gentry, C.: Fully homomorphic encryption using ideal lattices. In: 41st Annual ACM Symposium on Theory of Computing. ACM (2009)

20. Kelem, N., Feiertag, R.: A separation model for virtual machine monitors. In: IEEE Computer Society Symposium on Research in Security and Privacy, pp. 78–86 (May 1991)

21. Madnick, S.E., Donovan, J.J.: Application and analysis of the virtual machine approach to information system security and isolation. In: Workshop on Virtual Computer Systems. ACM (1973)

22. McCune, J., Li, Y., Qu, N., Zhou, Z., Datta, A., Gligor, V., Perrig, A.: TrustVisor: Efficient TCB reduction and attestation. In: IEEE Symposium on Security and Privacy (SP 2010). IEEE (2010)

23. McCune, J., Parno, B., Perrig, A., Reiter, M., Isozaki, H.: Flicker: An execution infrastructure for TCB minimization. In: 3rd European Conference on Computer Systems (EuroSys 2008). ACM (2008)

24. Murray, D.G., Milos, G., Hand, S.: Improving xen security through disaggregation. In: 4th Int. Conference on Virtual Execution Environments (VEE 2008). ACM (2008)
25. Rocha, F., Correia, M.: Lucy in the sky without diamonds: Stealing confidential data in the cloud. In: 41st International Conference on Dependable Systems and Networks Workshops (DSNW 2011). IEEE (2011)
26. Rushby, J.M.: Proof of separability: A verification technique for a class of a security kernels. In: Dezani-Ciancaglini, M., Montanari, U. (eds.) Programming 1982. LNCS, vol. 137, pp. 352–367. Springer, Heidelberg (1982)
27. Sadeghi, A.-R., Stüble, C.: Property-based attestation for computing platforms: caring about properties, not mechanisms. In: Workshop on New Security Paradigms (NSPW 2004). ACM (2004)
28. Sadeghi, A.-R., Stüble, C., Winandy, M.: Property-based TPM virtualization. In: Wu, T.-C., Lei, C.-L., Rijmen, V., Lee, D.-T. (eds.) ISC 2008. LNCS, vol. 5222, pp. 1–16. Springer, Heidelberg (2008)
29. Sadeghi, A.-R., Wolf, M., Stüble, C., Asokan, N., Ekberg, J.-E.: Enabling fairer digital rights management with trusted computing. In: Garay, J.A., Lenstra, A.K., Mambo, M., Peralta, R. (eds.) ISC 2007. LNCS, vol. 4779, pp. 53–70. Springer, Heidelberg (2007)
30. Sailer, R., Jaeger, T., Valdez, E., Caceres, R., Perez, R., Berger, S., Griffin, J.L., van Doorn, L.: Building a mac-based security architecture for the xen open-source hypervisor. In: 21st Annual Computer Security Applications Conference (ACSAC 2005). IEEE (2005)
31. Santos, N., Gummadi, K., Rodrigues, R.: Towards trusted cloud computing. In: Hot topics in cloud computing (HotCloud 2009). USENIX (2009)
32. Santos, N., Rodrigues, R., Gummadi, K.P., Saroiu, S.: Policy-sealed data: A new abstraction for building trusted cloud services. In: 21st USENIX Security Symposium. USENIX (2012)
33. Schiffman, J., Moyer, T., Vijayakumar, H., Jaeger, T., McDaniel, P.: Seeding clouds with trust anchors. In: ACM Workshop on Cloud Computing Security (CCSW 2010). ACM (2010)
34. Thibault, S.: Stub domains: A step towards dom0 disaggregation (2010), http://www.xen.org/files/xensummitboston08/SamThibault_XenSummit.pdf
35. Trusted Computing Group (TCG). TCG specification architecture overview, revision 1.4 (2007)
36. Trusted Computing Group (TCG). Trusted platform module specifications (2008)
37. van Dijk, M., Rhodes, J., Sarmenta, L.F.G., Devadas, S.: Offline untrusted storage with immediate detection of forking and replay attacks. In: 2007 ACM workshop on Scalable trusted computing (STC 2007). ACM (2007)
38. Wang, Z., Jiang, X.: Hypersafe: A lightweight approach to provide lifetime hypervisor control-flow integrity. In: 2010 IEEE Symposium on Security and Privacy (SP 2010). IEEE (2010)
39. Williams, D., Jamjoom, H., Weatherspoon, H.: The xen-blanket: virtualize once, run everywhere. In: 7th ACM European Conference on Computer Systems (EuroSys 2012). ACM (2012)
40. Xu, S., Sandhu, R.: A scalable and secure cryptographic service. In: Barker, S., Ahn, G.-J. (eds.) Data and Applications Security 2007. LNCS, vol. 4602, pp. 144–160. Springer, Heidelberg (2007)
41. Zhang, F., Chen, J., Chen, H., Zang, B.: Cloudvisor: retrofitting protection of virtual machines in multi-tenant cloud with nested virtualization. In: 23rd ACM Symposium on Operating Systems Principles (SOSP 2011). ACM (2011)

CloudHKA: A Cryptographic Approach for Hierarchical Access Control in Cloud Computing

Yi-Ruei Chen[1,*], Cheng-Kang Chu[2], Wen-Guey Tzeng[1], and Jianying Zhou[2]

[1] Department of Computer Science, National Chiao Tung University, Taiwan
[2] Institute for Infocomm Research, Singapore
yrchen.cs98g@nctu.edu.tw, {ckchu,jyzhou}@i2r.a-star.edu.sg,
wgtzeng@cs.nctu.edu.tw

Abstract. Cloud services are blooming recently. They provide a convenient way for data accessing, sharing, and processing. A key ingredient for successful cloud services is to control data access while considering the specific features of cloud services. The specific features include great quantity of outsourced data, large number of users, honest-but-curious cloud servers, frequently changed user set, dynamic access control policies, and data accessing for light-weight mobile devices. This paper addresses a cryptographic key assignment problem for enforcing a hierarchical access control policy over cloud data.

We propose a new hierarchical key assignment scheme *CloudHKA* that observes the Bell-LaPadula security model and efficiently deals with the user revocation issue practically. We use CloudHKA to encrypt outsourced data so that the data are secure against honest-but-curious cloud servers. CloudHKA possesses almost all advantages of the related schemes, e.g., each user only needs to store one secret key, supporting dynamic user set and access hierarchy, and provably-secure against collusive attacks. In particular, CloudHKA provides the following distinct features that make it more suitable for controlling access of cloud data. (1) A user only needs a constant computation time for each data accessing. (2) The encrypted data are securely updatable so that the user revocation can prevent a revoked user from decrypting newly and previously encrypted data. Notably, the updates can be outsourced by using public information only. (3) CloudHKA is secure against the legal access attack. The attack is launched by an authorized, but malicious, user who pre-downloads the needed information for decrypting data ciphertexts in his authorization period. The user uses the pre-downloaded information for future decryption even after he is revoked. Note that the pre-downloaded information are often a small portion of encrypted data only, e.g. the header-cipher in a hybrid encrypted data ciphertext. (4) Each user can be flexibly authorized the access rights of WRITE or READ, or both.

Keywords: Access control, hierarchical key assignment, key management, Bell-LaPadula security model, outsourced data, cloud computing, proxy re-encryption.

* The research was supported in part by projects NSC-101-2221-E-009-074-MY3 (National Science Council, Taiwan) and SecDC-112172014 (A*STAR, Singapore).

M. Jacobson et al. (Eds.): ACNS 2013, LNCS 7954, pp. 37–52, 2013.

1   Introduction

Outsourcing data to cloud server (CS) becomes popular in these years. A data provider (DP) no longer stores a large quantity of data locally. A user can access them from anywhere at any time. However, the outsourced data often contain sensitive information and CS naturally becomes a target of attacks. Even worse, CS itself could distribute DP's data for illegal profit. Therefore, DP does not want to disclose his data to CS. Furthermore, DP wants to control access to data of different sensitive levels. Only the authorized users can access the data with certain security levels. We want to enforce a designated access control policy for users over cloud data.

This work considers the hierarchical access control (HAC) policy. By the policy, data are organized into security classes SC_1, SC_2, ..., SC_n, which are partially ordered with a binary relation $\prec$. $SC_j \prec SC_i$ means that the security level of SC_i is higher than that of SC_j. If a user is authorized to read data at SC_i, he is also entitled to read data at SC_j for $SC_j \prec SC_i$. The HAC policy is widely used in various computer systems, e.g., military, government, secure database, and Pay-TV systems.

Hierarchical key assignment (HKA) is a cryptographic method for enforcing HAC policies [1]. An HKA scheme consists of a set of cryptographic keys SK_1, SK_2, ..., SK_n such that if $SK_j \prec SK_i$, SK_j can be derived by using SK_i. To enforce an HAC policy $\mathcal{P}$ for hierarchical data, a datum at SC_j is encrypted into ciphertext by using SK_j. A user who is authorized to read the data at SC_i is assigned SK_i. Thus, the user can decrypt the data at SC_j, which is lower than SC_i, by using SK_i to derive SK_j.

An important issue in designing an HKA scheme is to revoke an authorized user u from his associated class, say SC_i. DP needs to remove u's access rights for the following two kinds of data:

- *Newly encrypted data at SC_z for $SC_z \preceq SC_i$:* The encrypted data under new encryption keys after revoking u.
- *Previously encrypted data at SC_z for $SC_z \preceq SC_i$:* The encrypted data under previous encryption keys before revoking u.

To prevent u from decrypting newly encrypted data at SC_z, DP can encrypt data by new keys and distribute the new keys to the non-revoked users only. Nevertheless, since non-revoked users needs to access previously encrypted data at SC_z, they should keep all old keys. The key management cost is high if revocation occurs frequently.

To prevent u from decrypting previously encrypted data by using his old keys, DP can decrypt previously encrypted data and encrypt them with new keys, which are distributed to non-revoked users only. Thus, the revoked user u cannot use his old keys to decrypt previously encrypted data. Simultaneously, a non-revoked user needs to keep the newest key of his associated class only. However, since data are of a large quantity, DP needs substantial time in processing them. A common solution is to use the hybrid encryption technique for data encryption.

DP randomly chooses a data encryption key K for encrypting data into body-cipher and then encrypts K into header-cipher under a cryptographic key SK_i. In processing data, CS only needs to update the header-cipher and the much larger body-ciphers are no need to be changed. It saves computation time significantly. Nevertheless, the solution causes a new issue, which we call it the *legal access attack*. An authorized, but malicious, user may decrypt all decryptable header-ciphers to obtain K's. The user can use these K's to decrypt body-ciphers in the future even after he is revoked. Furthermore, in processing data, if decryption and encryption operations are done in the CS side, CS gets to know the content of data. Face to the above issues, we want a solution that updates encrypted data without disclosing the content to CS and entailing high overhead for DP and CS. Simultaneously, we hope that the solution is secure against the legal access attack.

We consider the Bell-LaPadula security model [5] for HAC policies. The model consists of two security properties: (1) The *simple security property* requires that a user cannot read the data at a higher security class. (2) The *⋆(star)-property* requires that a user cannot write data at a lower security class. To observe the security model in an HKA scheme, we separate SK_i into a write- and read-key pair ($\mathtt{WriteK}_i, \mathtt{ReadK}_i$) for encrypting and decrypting data at SC_i, respectively. A user at SC_i is authorized to obtain $\mathtt{ReadK}_i$, which is used to read (decrypt) the data at SC_z for $SC_z \preceq SC_i$. For data writing (encryption), the user is only authorized to obtain those $\mathtt{WriteK}_z$ of SC_z for $SC_i \preceq SC_z$. The separation provides flexibility in authorizing data access right of READ or WRITE, or both.

Our Contribution. We provide a practical *CloudHKA* scheme for controlling access for encrypted data in cloud computing. CloudHKA is a novel HKA scheme that observes the Bell-LaPadula security model and efficiently deals with the above issues in user revocation. The design of CloudHKA considers the specific features of cloud services. The specific features include great quantity of outsourced data, large number of users, honest-but-curious cloud servers, frequently changed user set, dynamic access control policies, and data accessing for light-weight mobile devices.

In detail, CloudHKA has the following features.

(1) *Optimal secret key size hold by each user.* Each authorized user at SC_i keeps *one* secret distribution-key $\mathtt{DistK}_i$.

(2) *Outsourceable computation in key derivation.* An authorized user can securely outsource computation for deriving a read-key to CS. He needs to do *three* decryption operations only.

(3) *Outsourceable data update in user revocation.* To revoke a user u, DP can outsource data update operations to CS. CS needs to update header-cipher and a small portion (the size is the same as header-cipher) of body-cipher only. After updating previously encrypted data, u cannot decrypt them with his old distribution-keys and the non-revoked users can decrypt them with their newest distribution-keys. In particular, only the distribution-key of u's associated class needs to be updated. It leads that the key re-distribution occurs in u's associated class only.

(4) *Secure against the legal access attack.* CloudHKA enforces that an authorized user cannot pre-download the needed information for decrypting body-cipher by only accessing a small portion of encrypted data. Therefore, the legal access attack can be prevented by denying uncommon (large traffic) data access from a user.

(5) *Flexible user access right authorization.* Each user can be authorized the access rights of WRITE or READ, or both.

(6) *Provable-security.* CloudHKA is formally shown to be message indistinguishability secure. Even if CS and a set of users collude, they cannot determine the original datum (that is not entitled to be derived by them) from an encrypted datum with non-negligible probability.

Figure 1 shows the system overview of CloudHKA. The detailed construction is illustrated in Section 3. The system consists of CS, DP, and users. CS is operated by cloud service providers. It is assumed to have bountiful storage space and computation power. DP outsources his data to CS with a self-defined HAC policy $\mathcal{P}$. DP is free to add or delete data in CS and change the access control policy. DP can execute his code over CS to manage his data. A user can be authorized to read or write data in CS. Typically, a user is assumed to have limited storage space and computing power. We assume that CS is always on-line, but DP and users are only on-line when necessary.

Related Works. Akl and Taylor [1] first addressed the problem of assigning cryptographic keys in an access hierarchy. They proposed an HKA scheme to enforce an HAC policy. After that, many researches proposed methods for improving performance, supporting dynamic access control policies, or providing distinct features [2,3,13,17,20,21,25,27,31]. Atallah et al. formalized the security requirement for HKA schemes and provided an efficient and provably-secure HKA scheme against *key recovery* attacks [3]. Recently, they proposed another scheme with security against *key-indistinguishability* attacks [2]. They also addressed the problem of reducing key derivation time for each user in a deep access hierarchy. The result is obtained by maintaining extra public system information.

Sahai and Waters [24] proposed an attribute-based encryption (ABE) scheme that provides fine-grained data access control. Most ABE schemes enforce monotone access policies over encrypted data [6,14,16,18,23,24,30]. An ABE scheme allows a user to encrypt data into ciphertexts according to a policy. Only the users with a set of attributes that satisfy the policy can decrypt the ciphertexts. Nevertheless, many ABE schemes do not address the issue of dynamic user set and dynamic access policy. Boldyreva et al. [8] addressed the issue of revoking a user with time. They periodically distribute the updated keys to non-revoked users for decrypting newly encrypted data. Yu et al. [30] proposed a revocable ABE scheme for revoking a user immediately. In contrast, Hur and Noh [18] proposed a revocable ABE scheme with immediate attribute and user revocation capability. Sahai et al. [23] proposed the revocable storage ABE scheme that deals with the issue of efficiently preventing a revoked user from decrypting previously encrypted data. In addition to the user revocation issue, decryption time of the existing ABE schemes grows with the depth of access formula. Green

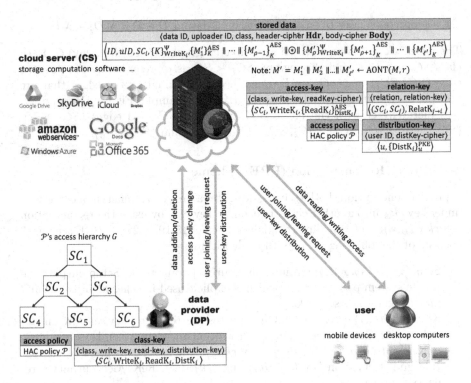

Fig. 1. A system overview of our CloudHKA

et al. [16] proposed a method of uotsoucing the overhead for users in decryption. Additionally, the size of user secret key or ciphertext in existing ABE schemes grows proportionally in the number of associated attributes. Designing an ABE scheme with a constant size of a user secret key and a ciphertext is still an open problem.

2   Preliminaries

2.1   HAC Policy with the Bell-LaPadula Security Model

An HAC policy $\mathcal{P}$ is a 5-tuple $(\mathcal{SC}, \prec, \mathcal{U}, \mathcal{D}, \lambda)$, where $\mathcal{SC} = \{SC_i : 1 \leq i \leq n\}$ is a set of security classes, $\prec$ is a binary relation over $\mathcal{SC} \times \mathcal{SC}$, $\mathcal{U}$ is a set of users, $\mathcal{D}$ is a set of data, and $\lambda : \mathcal{U} \cup \mathcal{D} \to \mathcal{SC}$ is a security function that associates each user and datum with a security class. $(\mathcal{SC}, \prec)$ forms a partial order set (poset), where $SC_j \prec SC_i$ means that the security level of class SC_i is higher than that of SC_j. To observe the Bell-LaPadula security model, $\mathcal{P}$ requires the following two properties.

1) *Simple security property*: A user $U \in \mathcal{U}$ cannot read a datum $D \in \mathcal{D}$ if $\lambda(U) \prec \lambda(D)$.

2) *-property*: A user $U \in \mathcal{U}$ cannot write a datum $D \in \mathcal{D}$ if $\lambda(D) \prec \lambda(U)$.

The poset $(\mathcal{SC}, \prec)$ is represented as a directed graph (access hierarchy) G. Each class SC_i is a node and the relation $SC_j \prec SC_i$ is represented by the directed edge (SC_i, SC_j) in G. G can be simplified by eliminating the edges that are implied by the transitive closure property. For example, Figure 1 has an access hierarchy G with the nodes SC_1, SC_2, ..., SC_6 and edges (SC_1, SC_2), (SC_1, SC_3), (SC_2, SC_4), (SC_2, SC_5), (SC_3, SC_5), and (SC_3, SC_6).

2.2   Proxy Re-Encryption (PRE) Scheme

A proxy re-encryption (PRE) scheme delegates a proxy to re-encrypt a ciphertext under key ek_A into another ciphertext under key ek_B by using the re-encryption key $rk_{A \to B}$ without revealing the plaintext [4,7,9,15,19,26,28]. A PRE scheme Ψ consists of the following six poly-time algorithms:

- Setup$(\tau) \to (sp, \mathcal{MK})$. On input a security parameter κ, Setup outputs the public system parameter sp (which is explicit used in other algorithms) and master secret key set $\mathcal{MK}$.
- KeyGen$(\mathcal{MK}, i) \to (ek_i, dk_i)$. On input the master secret key set $\mathcal{MK}$ and an index i, KeyGen outputs a pair of encryption and decryption keys (ek_i, dk_i).
- ReKeyGen$((ek_i, dk_i), (ek_j, dk_j))^1 \to rk_{i \to j}$. On input two pairs of encryption and decryption key (ek_i, dk_i) and (ek_j, dk_j), ReKeyGen outputs a re-encryption key $rk_{i \to j}$.
- Enc$(ek_i, m) \to c_i$. On input an encryption key ek_i and a plaintext m, Enc output a ciphertext c_i.
- ReEnc$(rk_{i \to j}, c_i) \to c_j$. On input a re-encryption key $rk_{i \to j}$ and ciphertext c_i, ReEnc output a ciphertext c_j under ek_j.
- Dec$(dk_i, c_i) \to m$. On input a decryption key dk_i and ciphertext c_i, Dec outputs a plaintext m.

These algorithms satisfy the following two requirements.

- For all $(ek_i, dk_i) \leftarrow$ KeyGen$(\mathcal{MK}, i)$, Dec$(dk_i,$ Enc$(ek_i, m)) = m$,
- For all $rk_{i \to j} \leftarrow$ ReKeyGen$((ek_i, dk_i),$ $(ek_j, dk_j))$, Dec$(dk_j,$ ReEnc$(rk_{i \to j},$ Enc$(ek_i, m))) = m$.

Ψ is *uni-directional* if $rk_{j \to i}$ cannot be derived from $rk_{i \to j}$. It is *multi-hop* if a ciphertext can be re-encrypted many times in a sequence.

For security, a uni-directional PRE scheme is IND-CPA secure if, for a given ciphertext, a collusive set of malicious entities cannot determine which message, m_0 or m_1, is encrypted under an uncorrupted ek_i. A malicious entity is the proxy, a non-user, or an authorized user with a partial set of decryption keys. The formal security notion is described in the full version of this paper [10].

---

[1] For the construction of a PRE scheme, it is preferable to compute $rk_{i \to j}$ in a *non-interactive* way, that is, without using the secret key dk_j. While using PRE scheme as a building block in our scheme, an interactive PRE scheme is also suitable.

2.3 All-Or-Nothing Transformation

All-or-nothing transformation (AONT) AONT is an unkeyed and randomized function with the property that it is hard to compute the whole message unless the entire function output is known [22]. AONT maps an ℓ-block message $X = X_1||X_2||\cdots||X_\ell$ and a random string r to an ℓ'-block string $Y = Y_1||Y_2||\cdots||Y_{\ell'}$. AONT satisfies the following properties:

- Given X and r, $Y \leftarrow \mathsf{AONT}(X,r)$ can be computed efficiently.
- Given Y, $X \leftarrow \mathsf{AONT}^{-1}(Y)$ can be computed efficiently.
- If any block of Y is lost, it is infeasible to recover X.

3 Our CloudHKA

3.1 Overview

The construction of CloudHKA is based on a uni-directional and multi-hop PRE scheme Ψ. Assume that the given HAC policy is $\mathcal{P}$, which is represented by a directed graph $G = (V, E)$. For each class $SC_i \in V$, DP generates a pair of write- and read-key $(\mathsf{WriteK}_i, \mathsf{ReadK}_i)$. A message that is encrypted by using WriteK_i can be decrypted by using ReadK_i. A user who obtains the write-key WriteK_i is authorized the WRITE right for SC_i. A user who obtains the read-key ReadK_i is authorized the READ right for SC_i and its lower classes. Although the pair of write- and read-key is like the pair of public- and private-key of a public-key system, neither of them can be published to a public domain in CloudHKA. A write-key WriteK_z is given to a user at SC_i (through a secure channel) when he requests to write data into SC_z for $SC_i \preceq SC_z$.

In data outsourcing, a datum M at SC_i is transformed into

$$M' = M_1'||M_2'||\cdots||M_{\ell'}' \leftarrow \mathsf{AONT}(M,r)$$

and then encrypted in the form

$$\langle \text{data ID, uploader ID, class, header-cipher, body-cipher,} \rangle$$
$$= \langle ID, uID, SC_i, \mathsf{Hdr}_{ID}^{SC_i} = \{K\}_{\mathsf{WriteK}_i}^{\Psi}, \mathsf{Body}_{ID}^{SC_i} = \{M_1'\}_K^{\mathsf{AES}}||\cdots||\{M_{\rho-1}'\}_K^{\mathsf{AES}}||$$
$$\circledast\ ||\{M_\rho'\}_{\mathsf{WriteK}_i}^{\Psi}||\{M_{\rho+1}'\}_K^{\mathsf{AES}}||\cdots||\{M_{\ell'}'\}_K^{\mathsf{AES}}\rangle, \qquad (1)$$

where

- uID is a user who stores (uploads) his data into CS,
- $\{K\}_{\mathsf{WriteK}_i}^{\Psi}$ and $\{M_\rho'\}_{\mathsf{WriteK}_i}^{\Psi}$ are respectively the ciphertexts of a randomly chosen AES encryption key K and ρ-th block of M' under WriteK_i,
- $\rho \in \{1, 2, \cdots, \ell'\}$ only known by CS and DP,
- $\circledast$ is a special symbol for marking the start position of $\mathsf{Body}_{ID}^{SC_i}[\rho]$, and
- $\{M_\omega'\}_K^{\mathsf{AES}}$ is the ciphertext of M_ω' for $\omega \in \{1, 2, \ldots, \ell'\} \setminus \{\rho\}$ under K.

Before CS storing an encrypted datum into SC_i, he should authenticate that the associated class of a data uploader is no lower than SC_i. It observes the $\star$-property.

For each relation $(SC_j, SC_i) \in E$, DP generates a (public) relation-key $\mathtt{RelatK}_{i \to j}$ that is used to re-encrypt a header-cipher and body-cipher (ρ-th block) of SC_i into that of SC_j. Assume that a user who is authorized the READ right of SC_j wants to read (decrypt) datum ID encrypted as (1). CS re-encrypts $\{K\}^{\Psi}_{\mathtt{WriteK}_i}$ and $\{M'_{\rho}\}^{\Psi}_{\mathtt{WriteK}_i}$ into $\{K\}^{\Psi}_{\mathtt{WriteK}_j}$ and $\{M'_{\rho}\}^{\Psi}_{\mathtt{WriteK}_j}$ by using the relation-key $\mathtt{RelatK}_{i \to j}$. The user then decrypts $\{K\}^{\Psi}_{\mathtt{WriteK}_j}$ and $\{M'_{\rho}\}^{\Psi}_{\mathtt{WriteK}_j}$ to obtain K and M'_{ρ} by using $\mathtt{ReadK}_j$. By using K to decrypt $\{M'_{\omega}\}^{AES}_K$ for $\omega \in \{1, 2, \ldots, \ell'\} \setminus \{\rho\}$, the user obtains M'_{ω} and combines it with M'_{ρ} to recover $M \leftarrow \mathsf{AONT}^{-1}(M')$. The concept can be easily extended for the case with $d = dst_G(SC_j, SC_i) > 1$, where $dst_G(SC_j, SC_i)$ is the distance between SC_j and SC_i in the access hierarchy G.

To revoke a user u at SC_i, DP does the following procedures.

- Removing WRITE right: DP simply removes u from his SC_i in $\mathcal{P}$. Then, u's WRITE right of SC_z for $SC_i \preceq SC_z$ is removed since he cannot pass CS's authentication in data writing.
- Removing READ right: This part can be separated into two cases.

  (1) Preventing u from decrypting newly encrypted data at SC_z for $SC_z \preceq SC_i$: DP re-generates SC_z's key pair and related relation-keys. Then, the new data at SC_z will be encrypted under the new write-key of SC_z. The new read-key of SC_z is distributed to the non-revoked users only.

  (2) Preventing u from decrypting previously encrypted data at SC_z for $SC_z \preceq SC_i$: DP sends CS a (public) transform-key $\mathtt{TranK}_z$ for transforming (re-encrypting) SC_z's header-ciphers and body-ciphers under the old write-key into the new one under the new write-key. Thus, only the non-revoked users who obtain the new read-keys can decrypt the updated header-ciphers and body-ciphers.

Remark. The data encryption form in (1) enforces a user accesses the whole body-cipher for decryption. Assume that an authorized user u at SC_i wants to access a datum ID in (1). u needs to obtain K and M'_{ρ} by using $\mathtt{ReadK}_i$ so that he can recover M. To obtain M'_{ρ}, u needs to find the start position of $\{M'_{\rho}\}^{\Psi}_{\mathtt{WriteK}_i}$. Since u does not know ρ, he needs to find ⊛ by accessing whole $\mathtt{Body}^{SC_i}_{ID}$ (or the part before meeting ⊛.) This design effectively prevents the legal access attack. In the legal access attack, u pre-downloads K and M'_{ρ} for each datum. However, u does not know the position of ⊛ until the whole body-cipher is retrieved. In CloudHKA, a authorized, but malicious, user needs to access a large portion of a data for pre-downloading the needed information for decryption. A large collection of pre-downloaded information will cause traffic in accessing. A traffic limitation mechanism (with a specified policy according to the system) can easily deny the legal access attack. For example, in a protected database, the amount of transmitted data for each user in a time period is often limited.

3.2 The Construction

Let $\Psi = (\Psi.\text{Setup}, \Psi.\text{KeyGen}, \Psi.\text{ReKeyGen}, \Psi.\text{Enc}, \Psi.\text{ReEnc}, \Psi.\text{Dec})$ be a uni-directional and multi-hop PRE scheme. Let AES be a symmetric key encryption scheme with key generation, encryption, and decryption algorithms (AES.G, AES.E, AES.D). Let PKE be an asymmetric key (or public-key) encryption scheme with key generation, encryption, and decryption algorithms (PKE.G, PKE.E, PKE.D). Let AONT be an all-or-nothing transformation function that maps an ℓ-block message and a random string to an ℓ'-block string.

To simplify the description of our scheme, we assume that two system entities of CS, DP, and users can authenticate the identity of each other. The integrity and correctness of messages or data transmitted between two system entities can be verified by each other.

System Setup. DP defines an initial HAC policy $\mathcal{P} = (\mathcal{SC}, \prec, \mathcal{U}, \mathcal{D}, \lambda)$ with n security classes $SC_1, SC_2, \ldots, SC_n$. Assume that $\mathcal{P}$ is represented as an access hierarchy $G = (V, E)$. Then, DP generates $(sp, \mathcal{MK}) \leftarrow \Psi.\text{Setup}(\kappa)$ with a given security parameter κ and associates each $SC_i \in V$ with the following keys and tokens.

- Write- and read-key pair $(\text{WriteK}_i, \text{ReadK}_i) \leftarrow \Psi.\text{KeyGen}(\mathcal{MK}, i)$.
- Distributed-key $\text{DistK}_i \leftarrow \text{AES.G}(\kappa)$.
- ReadKey-cipher $\{\text{ReadK}_i\}_{\text{DistK}_i}^{\text{AES}} \leftarrow \text{AES.E}(\text{DistK}_i, \text{ReadK}_i)$.

DP associates each relation $(SC_j, SC_i) \in E$ a relation-key

$$\text{RelatK}_{i \to j} \leftarrow \Psi.\text{ReKeyGen}((\text{WriteK}_i, \text{ReadK}_i), (\text{WriteK}_j, \text{ReadK}_j)).$$

Finally, DP uploads $\mathcal{P}$, $\langle SC_i, \text{WriteK}_i, \{\text{ReadK}_i\}_{\text{DistK}_i}^{\text{AES}} \rangle$ for $SC_i \in V$, and $\langle (SC_j, SC_i), \text{RelatK}_{i \to j} \rangle$ for $(SC_j, SC_i) \in E$ to CS. DP keeps $\mathcal{P}$ and $\langle SC_i, \text{WriteK}_i, \text{ReadK}_i, \text{DistK}_i \rangle$ for $SC_i \in V$ locally. Each user u of the system generates his public- and private-key pair (pk_u, sk_u).

Access Right Authorization. Assume that DP associates a user u with a class SC_i in $\mathcal{P}$. To authorize u the READ right of SC_z for $SC_z \prec SC_i$, DP uses u's public-key pk_u to encrypt the distribution-key DistK_i as a distKey-cipher

$$\{\text{DistK}_i\}_u^{\text{PKE}} \leftarrow \text{PKE.E}(pk_u, \text{DistK}_i)$$

and uploads $\langle u, \{\text{DistK}_i\}_u^{\text{PKE}} \rangle$ to CS. CS forwards $\{\text{DistK}_i\}_u^{\text{PKE}}$ to u and u decrypts it to obtain DistK_i. To observe the $\star$-property, CS gives the current WriteK_z to u when u requests to write data into SC_z for $SC_i \preceq SC_z$.

Data Writing. To write a datum M into SC_i, an uploader uID computes $M' \leftarrow \text{AONT}(M, r)$, where r is a random string. uID then generates a data encryption key $K \leftarrow \text{AES.G}(\kappa)$, randomly chooses an index $\rho \in \{1, 2, \ldots, \ell'\}$, and sends CS the encrypted data in the form

$$\langle \rho, SC_i, \text{C}_1, \text{C}_2 \rangle = \langle \rho, SC_i, \{K\}_{\text{WriteK}_i}^{\Psi}, \{M_1'\}_K^{\text{AES}} || \cdots || \{M_{\rho-1}'\}_K^{\text{AES}} ||$$
$$\circledast \, || \{M_\rho'\}_{\text{WriteK}_i}^{\Psi} || \{M_{\rho+1}'\}_K^{\text{AES}} || \cdots || \{M_{\ell'}'\}_K^{\text{AES}} \rangle.$$

After receiving the data, CS checks the validity of the writing request from uID. If uID is associated with SC_z for $SC_i \preceq SC_z$, CS selects a unique data identity ID and stores the data with the format

$$\langle \text{data ID, uploader ID, class, header-cipher, body-cipher} \rangle$$
$$= \langle ID, uID, SC_i, \text{Hdr}_{ID}^{SC_i} = \text{C}_1, \text{Body}_{ID}^{SC_i} = \text{C}_2 \rangle. \tag{2}$$

CS keeps ρ as a secret. The value will be used when CS needs to update body-ciphers.

Data Reading. Assume that an authorized user u at SC_j wants to read a datum encrypted as (2). If $SC_i \preceq SC_j$, CS re-encrypts the header-cipher and body-cipher as follows. Let $d = dst_G(SC_j, SC_i)$.

– Extract the relation-keys on the path from SC_i to SC_j as $\text{RelatK}_{v_1 \to v_2}$, $\text{RelatK}_{v_2 \to v_3}$, ..., $\text{RelatK}_{v_d \to v_{d+1}}$, where $v_1 = i$ and $v_{d+1} = j$.
– For each v_z from v_1 to v_d, replace $\{K\}_{\text{WriteK}_{v_z}}^{\Psi}$ and $\{M'_\rho\}_{\text{WriteK}_{v_z}}^{\Psi}$ as

$$\{K\}_{\text{WriteK}_{v_{z+1}}}^{\Psi} \leftarrow \Psi.\text{ReEnc}(\text{RelatK}_{v_z \to v_{z+1}}, \{K\}_{\text{WriteK}_{v_z}}^{\Psi}),$$

$$\{M'_\rho\}_{\text{WriteK}_{v_{z+1}}}^{\Psi} \leftarrow \Psi.\text{ReEnc}(\text{RelatK}_{v_z \to v_{z+1}}, \{M'_\rho\}_{\text{WriteK}_{v_z}}^{\Psi}).$$

CS returns $\langle \text{C}_0, \text{C}_1, \text{C}_2 \rangle = \langle \{\text{ReadK}_j\}_{\text{DistK}_j}^{\text{AES}}, \text{Hdr}_{ID}^{SC_j}, \text{Body}_{ID}^{SC_j} \rangle$ to u. After receiving the ciphertexts, u decrypts C_0 to obtain ReadK_j by using his (newest) DistK_j. u finds ⊛ to extract $\{M'_\rho\}_{\text{WriteK}_j}^{\Psi}$ from C_2. Then, u decrypts C_1 and $\{M'_\rho\}_{\text{WriteK}_j}^{\Psi}$ to obtain K and M'_ρ by using ReadK_j. u then decrypts the other blocks of C_2 to obtain M'_ω for $\omega \in \{1, 2, \ldots, \ell'\} \setminus \{\rho\}$ by using K. Finally, u combines M'_ρ and M'_ω's as M' and recovers $M \leftarrow \text{AONT}^{-1}(M')$.

Data Deletion. A datum can be deleted by its uploader only. To delete a datum ID, its uploader with identity uID sends a deletion request of ID to CS. CS deletes the datum ID and its associated information.

User Revocation with Outsourceable Data Update. Assume that DP wants to revoke a user u from SC_i.

– Removing u's WRITE right: DP simply updates his HAC policy. Hereafter, when u wants to write data into SC_z for $SC_i \preceq SC_z$, he cannot pass CS's validity check in data writing.
– Removing u's READ right:
  (1) To remove u's READ right for newly encrypted data at SC_z for $SC_z \preceq SC_i$: DP re-generates the key pair of SC_z as $(\text{WriteK}'_z, \text{ReadK}'_z)$ and affected relation-keys. DP then updates the affected readKey-ciphers as follows.
    • For $SC_z \prec SC_i$, DP updates SC_z's readKey-cipher as $\{\text{ReadK}'_z\}_{\text{DistK}_z}^{\text{AES}}$.
    • For SC_i, DP updates SC_i's distribution-key as DistK'_i and readKey-cipher as $\{\text{ReadK}'_i\}_{\text{DistK}'_i}^{\text{AES}}$.
    DP distributes the updated distribution-key DistK'_i to the non-revoked users at SC_i. For each non-revoked user $\bar{u}$, DP updates $\langle \bar{u}, \{\text{DistK}_i\}_{\bar{u}}^{\text{PKE}} \rangle$ as $\langle \bar{u}, \{\text{DistK}'_i\}_{\bar{u}}^{\text{PKE}} \rangle$.

(2) To remove u's READ right for previously encrypted data at SC_z for $SC_z \preceq SC_i$: DP sends CS a transform-key

$$\texttt{TranK}_z \leftarrow \Psi.\texttt{ReKeyGen}((\texttt{WriteK}_z, \texttt{ReadK}_z), (\texttt{WriteK}'_z, \texttt{ReadK}'_z)).$$

CS uses $\texttt{TranK}_z$ to update each SC_z's header-cipher and ρ-th block of body-cipher as

$$\{K\}^{\Psi}_{\texttt{WriteK}'_z} \leftarrow \Psi.\texttt{ReEnc}(\texttt{TranK}_z, \{K\}^{\Psi}_{\texttt{WriteK}_z}),$$

$$\{M'_\rho\}^{\Psi}_{\texttt{WriteK}'_z} \leftarrow \Psi.\texttt{ReEnc}(\texttt{TranK}_z, \{M'_\rho\}^{\Psi}_{\texttt{WriteK}_z}).$$

Updates of Access Hierarchy. The update operations include relation insertion, relation deletion, class insertion, and class deletion.

– *Relation insertion.* To insert a new relation (SC_j, SC_i), DP generates a new $\texttt{RelatK}_{i \rightarrow j} \leftarrow \Psi.\texttt{ReKeyGen}((\texttt{WriteK}_i, \texttt{ReadK}_i), (\texttt{WriteK}_j, \texttt{ReadK}_j))$ and uploads the updated HAC policy and $\langle(SC_j, SC_i), \texttt{RelatK}_{i \rightarrow j}\rangle$ to CS.

– *Relation deletion.* To delete a relation (SC_j, SC_i), DP needs to prevent the users at SC_i from re-encrypting the header-ciphers and body-cipher of SC_z into that of SC_j for $SC_z \preceq SC_i$. The procedure is like to revoke a "psuedo-user" from SC_i. The differences are that DP does not need to re-generate (1) SC_i's distribution-key and readKey-cipher and (2) (SC_j, SC_i)'s relation-key. There is no need to distribute the new distribution-key of SC_i.

– *Class insertion.* To insert a class SC_i, DP generates $(\texttt{WriteK}_i, \texttt{ReadK}_i)$, $\texttt{DistK}_i$, and $\{\texttt{ReadK}_i\}^{\texttt{AES}}_{\texttt{DistK}_i}$ and uploads the updated HAC policy and $\langle SC_i, \texttt{WriteK}_i, \{\texttt{ReadK}_i\}^{\texttt{AES}}_{\texttt{DistK}_i}\rangle$ to CS. DP then runs the relation insertion procedure to insert the incoming and outgoing relations of SC_i.

– *Class deletion.* To delete a class SC_i, DP deletes SC_i's associated parameters in CS and runs the relation deletion procedure for every SC_i's incoming and outgoing relations.

4 Analysis

4.1 Performance Analysis

This section illustrates the performance of CloudHKA. We compare CloudHKA with the first HKA scheme [1] and recent two HKA schemes [2,3] in Table 1. To our best knowledge, the schemes in [2,3] provide most features up to now and are provably-secure.

Storage Cost. In CloudHKA, each user at SC_i stores the distribution-key $\texttt{DistK}_i$. In the other three schemes, the secret key size for each user is also one.

Key Derivation Cost. In CloudHKA, when a user u at SC_j requests to read a datum at SC_i for $SC_i \preceq SC_j$, CS runs $d = dst_G(SC_j, SC_i)$ times of $\Psi.\texttt{ReEnc}$ to re-encrypt the header-cipher under $\texttt{WriteK}_i$ into the header-cipher under $\texttt{WriteK}_j$. u then runs one AES.D to obtain $\texttt{ReadK}_j$ and two $\Psi.\texttt{Dec}$ to

Table 1. A comparison of our CloudHKA with previous HKA schemes

	AT [1]	AFB [3]	ABFF [2]	CloudHKA
			Storage cost		
#(user secret key)	1	1	1	1
		Key derivation cost (for a user u at SC_j to derive a key of SC_i)			
Full computation	t_{Exp}	$d \cdot (t_H + t_{\mathrm{XOR}})$	$2d \cdot (t_H + t_{\mathrm{AES.D}}) + t_H$	$2d \cdot t_{\Psi.\mathrm{ReEnc}} + 2t_{\Psi.\mathrm{Dec}} + t_{\mathrm{AES.D}}$
Outsourceable computation	-	-	-	$2d \cdot t_{\Psi.\mathrm{ReEnc}}$
		User revocation cost (revoking a user u from SC_i)			
Rekey	-	$O(|E_i| + \sum_{SC_z \in V_i} n_z)$	$O(|V_i| + |E_i| + n_i)$	$O(|V_i| + |E_i| + n_i)$
Full data update	-	$\#c(u) \cdot (t_{\mathrm{AES.D}} + t_{\mathrm{AES.E}})$	$\#c(u) \cdot (t_{\mathrm{AES.D}} + t_{\mathrm{AES.E}})$	$|V_i| \cdot t_{\Psi.\mathrm{ReKeyGen}} + 2 \cdot \#c(u) \cdot t_{\Psi.\mathrm{ReEnc}}$
Outsourceable data update	-	-	-	$2 \cdot \#c(u) \cdot t_{\Psi.\mathrm{ReEnc}}$
		User access right authorization			
Read-Write	√	√	√	√
Read-only	-	-	-	√
Write-only	-	-	-	√
		Security			
Security game	-	Key-Recovery	Key-Indistinguishability	Message-Indistinguishability
Building block	-	PRF family	PRF family and AES	Uni-directional PRE

† Exp: A modular exponentiation over a large group.
† H: A cryptographic hash function.
† t_f: The computation time of function f.

obtain K and M'_ρ. The total key derivation cost of the other three schemes are also linear in d. Nevertheless, only CloudHKA can outsource most of the computation operations to CS so that a user only needs constant computation time in key derivation. Note that in [1], although the computation operation only contains a modular exponentiation, the size of the used group equals to the size of the multiplication of d large co-prime numbers. The computation time in key derivation is still linear to d.

User Revocation Cost. In CloudHKA, to revoke a user u at SC_i, the rekey operation for DP contains: (1) $|V_i|$ times of Ψ.KeyGen, Ψ.ReKeyGen, and AES.E, (2) one AES.G, (3) $|E_i|$ times of Ψ.ReKeyGen, (4) n_i times of PKE.E, and (5) $2 \cdot \#c(u)$ times of Ψ.ReEnc, where $V_i = \{SC_z : SC_z \preceq SC_i\}$ is the set of SC_i and its lower classes, $E_i = \{(SC_\xi, SC_z) : SC_z \in V_i\}$ is the set of relations related to the classes in V_i, n_i is the number of users (excluding u) at SC_i, and $\#c(u)$ is the number of decryptable data ciphertexts of u. The distribution-key update only occurs in the class SC_i, the distribution of the new distribution-key is needed for the non-revoked users at SC_i only. Note that the extended HKA scheme in [2] is the first HKA scheme supporting this kind of *local key re-distribution* property. To let the non-revoked users decrypt previously encrypted data, in CloudHKA, DP only needs to run $|V_i|$ times of Ψ.ReKeyGen to generate the needed transform-keys to CS. CS can update every u's decryptable header-cipher into the one under the new write-key by using Ψ.ReEnc. In other three HKA schemes, to update all u's decryptable ciphertexts, DP needs to download them, decrypt them with old data encryption keys, encrypt them with new data encryption keys, and then upload them to CS.

4.2 Bell-LaPadula Security Model Observation

Our CloudHKA observes the simple security property and ⋆-property. The uni-directional property of Ψ ensures that a relation-key RelatK$_{j \to i}$ cannot be reversed. Thus, it is not possible to compute the inverted header-cipher and body-cipher re-encryptions from class SC_i to its lower class SC_j. Therefore, CloudHKA observes the simple security property. The $\star$-property is observed in CloudHKA since CS only allows a user at SC_i to write data into SC_i and its higher classes. Note that giving all write-keys to CS does not violate the $\star$-property since CS does not have the READ right of any class in the policy.

4.3   Security Analysis

In this section, we formally show that CloudHKA ensures data confidentiality based on the security of PRE schemes. We also demonstrate that the user revocation mechanism in CloudHKA removes the access rights of a revoked user.

To simplify our security analysis, we assume that the encryption schemes AES and PKE are IND-CPA secure. For example, AES with CBC mode and ElGamal suit our need, respectively. The IND-CPA security of an encryption scheme ensures that an unauthorized user cannot distinguish an encrypted distribution-key, read-key, or datum from an encrypted random string. By the assumption, CloudHKA ensures that only an authorized user can obtain legal distribution-keys and read-keys. Then, the security of our CloudHKA only relies on the security of PRE scheme Ψ for protecting (K, M'_ρ).

User- and Read-Key Authorization. In CloudHKA, DP stores $\mathtt{DistK}_i$ as $\{\mathtt{DistK}_i\}_u^{\mathsf{PKE}}$ under user u's individual public-key pk_u for a user u at SC_i. Only u can decrypt $\{\mathtt{DistK}_i\}_u^{\mathsf{PKE}}$ to obtain $\mathtt{DistK}_i$. DP stores $\mathtt{ReadK}_i$ as $\{\mathtt{ReadK}_i\}_{\mathtt{DistK}_i}^{\mathsf{AES}}$. Only an authorized user who is assigned $\mathtt{DistK}_i$ can obtain $\mathtt{ReadK}_i$.

Data Confidentiality. Our goal is to show that even if CS and a set of malicious users collude, for a given SC_{i*}'s header-cipher and ρ-th block body-cipher pair $(\mathtt{Hdr}_{ID}^{SC_{i*}}, \mathtt{Body}_{ID}^{SC_{i*}}[\rho])$ that encrypts either $m_0 = (K_0, M'_{\rho,0})$ or $m_1 = (K_1, M'_{\rho,1})$, it is hard for the collusive entities to determine the original message of the ciphertext pair. The original messages m_0 and m_1 are chosen by the collusive entities. A malicious user can be a non-user, a revoked user, or an authorized user. They are not authorized to read the data at SC_z for $SC_{i*} \preceq SC_z$. The formal security notion for message-indistinguishable HKA and detailed proof of the following theorem is described in the full version [10].

Theorem 1. *Our CloudHKA is message-indistinguishable if the underlying PRE scheme Ψ is IND-CPA secure.*

Revocation of Access Rights. We illustrate that the user revocation mechanism in CloudHKA removes the WRITE and READ rights of a revoked user.

- *Preventing a revoked user from writing data.* To revoke a user from SC_i, DP removes u from SC_i in his HAC policy directly. Then, the request of writing operations from u will not pass CS's validity check. u is no longer allowed to write data into SC_z for $SC_i \preceq SC_z$.
- *Preventing a revoked user from reading newly encrypted data.* The rekey operation for revoking u ensures that u cannot decrypt newly encrypted data. We give an illustration with the following three parts:

- u *cannot obtain the updated* $\mathtt{ReadK}'_i$. The readkey-cipher of SC_i is updated as $\{\mathtt{ReadK}'_i\}^{\mathsf{AES}}_{\mathtt{DistK}'_i}$. Only the non-revoked users at SC_i can update the distribution-key as $\mathtt{DistK}'_i$ for decrypting $\{\mathtt{ReadK}'_i\}^{\mathsf{AES}}_{\mathtt{DistK}'_i}$ to obtain $\mathtt{ReadK}'_i$.
- u *no longer decrypts new ciphertext pair* $(\mathtt{Hdr}'^{SC_z}_{ID}, \mathtt{Body}'^{SC_z}_{ID}[\rho])$ *for* $SC_z \preceq SC_i$. Since u cannot obtain $\mathtt{ReadK}'_i$, u cannot decrypt $(\mathtt{Hdr}'^{SC_z}_{ID}, \mathtt{Body}'^{SC_z}_{ID}[\rho])$. The relation-keys $\mathtt{RelatK}_{z \to \xi}$ for $SC_z \preceq SC_i$ are re-generated by using the updated key pairs. u cannot use the new (or old) relation-keys to re-encrypt new $(\mathtt{Hdr}'^{SC_z}_{ID}, \mathtt{Body}'^{SC_z}_{ID}[\rho])$ into the old one under $\mathtt{WriteK}_z$. Thus, u cannot derive the original message in $(\mathtt{Hdr}'^{SC_z}_{ID}, \mathtt{Body}'^{SC_z}_{ID}[\rho])$.
- u *no longer decrypts new body-ciphers* $\mathtt{Body}'^{SC_z}_{ID}$ *for* $SC_z \preceq SC_i$. Since u cannot decrypt the new $(\mathtt{Hdr}'^{SC_z}_{ID}, \mathtt{Body}'^{SC_z}_{ID}[\rho])$ for $SC_z \preceq SC_i$ to obtain (K, M'_ρ), he cannot recover M by computing $\mathsf{AONT}^{-1}(M')$.

- *Preventing a revoked user from reading previously encrypted data.* In revoking a user u from SC_i, DP sends a transform-key $\mathtt{TranK}_z$ for each SC_z, $SC_z \preceq SC_i$. CS uses $\mathtt{TranK}_z$ to update (re-encrypt) each old $(\mathtt{Hdr}^{SC_z}_{ID}, \mathtt{Body}^{SC_z}_{ID}[\rho])$ as a new $(\mathtt{Hdr}'^{SC_z}_{ID}, \mathtt{Body}'^{SC_z}_{ID}[\rho])$. Hereafter, when u requests to read old datum ID, CS returns the new $\langle \{\mathtt{ReadK}'_z\}^{\mathsf{AES}}_{\mathtt{DistK}'_z}, \mathtt{Hdr}'^{SC_z}_{ID}, \mathtt{Body}'^{SC_z}_{ID} \rangle$. Since u cannot obtain $\mathtt{DistK}'_z$, he cannot obtain (K, M'_ρ) and recover M.

5   Discussion

This section introduces some existing desirable PRE schemes for CloudHKA. Then, we demonstrate that CloudHKA can be slightly extended for dealing with the following extra issues in practical system. (Please refer to the full version [10] for detailed illustrations.)

- *Issue 1.* The outsourced data stored in CS may be altered by unexpected bit flips from system errors or accidentally deleted by CS. (Solution: To apply data integrity check schemes such as hash-then-sign.)
- *Issue 2.* The re-encryption operations in key derivation and ciphertext update may cause some unexpected errors. (Solution: To apply IND-CCA secure PRE schemes [26,28])
- *Issue 3.* The rekey cost in computation and communication for distributing a new distribution-key of SC_i is linear in the number of users at SC_i. (Solution: To apply a tree-based group key management (GKM) scheme [11,12,29] to maintain distribution-key among a dynamic set of users at each class.)

6   Conclusion

In this paper we propose a practical CloudHKA for controlling data access in cloud computing. CloudHKA observes the Bell-Lapadula security model. We use ciphertext re-encryption technique to minimize the computation cost for a user in key derivation and for DP and CS in ciphertext update. CloudHKA deals with the user revocation issue practically and provides flexible authorization of data access rights. Simultaneously, CloudHKA is secure against the legal access attack. The proposed CloudHKA is formally shown to be message-indistinguishable by assuming IND-CPA security of the underlying PRE scheme.

References

1. Akl, S.G., Taylor, P.D.: Cryptographic solution to a problem of access control in a hierarchy. ACM Transactions on Computer Systems 1(3), 239–248 (1983)
2. Atallah, M.J., Blanton, M., Fazio, N., Frikken, K.B.: Dynamic and efficient key management for access hierarchies. ACM Transactions on Information and System Security 12(3) (2009)
3. Atallah, M.J., Frikken, K.B., Blanton, M.: Dynamic and efficient key management for access hierarchies. In: Proceedings of the ACM Conference on Computer and Communications Security (CCS), pp. 190–202 (2005)
4. Ateniese, G., Fu, K., Green, M., Hohenberger, S.: Improved proxy re-encryption schemes with applications to secure distributed storage. ACM Transactions on Information and System Security 9(1), 1–30 (2006)
5. Bell, D.E., Lapadula, L.J.: Secure computer systems: Unified exposition and multics interpretation. Technical Report MTR-2997, Mitre Corporation, Bedford, Massachusetts (1976)
6. Bethencourt, J., Sahai, A., Waters, B.: Ciphertext-policy attribute-based encryption. In: Proceedings of the IEEE Symposium on Security and Privacy (S&P), pp. 321–334 (2007)
7. Blaze, M., Bleumer, G., Strauss, M.: Divertible protocols and atomic proxy cryptography. In: Nyberg, K. (ed.) EUROCRYPT 1998. LNCS, vol. 1403, pp. 127–144. Springer, Heidelberg (1998)
8. Boldyreva, A., Goyal, V., Kumar, V.: Identity-based encryption with efficient revocation. In: ACM Conference on Computer and Communications Security (CCS), pp. 417–426 (2008)
9. Canetti, R., Hohenberger, S.: Chosen-ciphertext secure proxy re-encryption. In: Proceedings of ACM Conference on Computer and Communications Security (CCS), pp. 185–194 (2007)
10. Chen, Y.-R., Chu, C.-K., Tzeng, W.-G., Zhou, J.: Cloudhka: A cryptographic approach for hierarchical access control in cloud computing. Cryptology ePrint Archive, Report 2013/208 (2013), http://eprint.iacr.org/
11. Chen, Y.-R., Tygar, J.D., Tzeng, W.-G.: Secure group key management using unidirectional proxy re-encryption schemes. In: Proceedings of the IEEE International Conference on Computer Communications (INFOCOM), pp. 1952–1960 (2011)
12. Chou, K.-Y., Chen, Y.-R., Tzeng, W.-G.: An efficient and secure group key management scheme supporting frequent key updates on pay-tv systems. In: Proceedings of the IEEE Asia-Pacific Network Operations and Management Symposium (APNOMS), pp. 1–8 (2011)
13. Crampton, J., Martin, K.M., Wild, P.R.: On key assignment for hierarchical access control. In: Proceedings of the IEEE Computer Security Foundations Workshop (CSFW), pp. 98–111 (2006)
14. Goyal, V., Pandey, O., Sahai, A., Waters, B.: Attribute-based encryption for fine-grained access control of encrypted data. In: Proceedings of the ACM Conference on Computer and Communications Security (CCS), pp. 89–98 (2006)

15. Green, M., Ateniese, G.: Identity-based proxy re-encryption. In: Katz, J., Yung, M. (eds.) ACNS 2007. LNCS, vol. 4521, pp. 288–306. Springer, Heidelberg (2007)

16. Green, M., Hohenberger, S., Waters, B.: Outsourcing the decryption of abe ciphertexts. In: Proceedings of the USENIX Security Symposium (2011)

17. Harn, L., Lin, H.-Y.: A cryptographic key generation scheme for multilevel data security. Computers & Security 9(6), 539–546 (1990)

18. Hur, J., Noh, D.K.: Attribute-based access control with efficient revocation in data outsourcing systems. IEEE Transactions on Parallel and Distributed Systems 22(7), 1214–1221 (2011)

19. Luo, S., Shen, Q., Chen, Z.: Fully secure unidirectional identity-based proxy re-encryption. In: Kim, H. (ed.) ICISC 2011. LNCS, vol. 7259, pp. 109–126. Springer, Heidelberg (2012)

20. MacKinnon, S.J., Taylor, P.D., Meijer, H., Akl, S.G.: An optimal algorithm for assigning cryptographic keys to control access in a hierarchy. IEEE Transactions on Computers 34(9), 797–802 (1985)

21. Ray, I., Ray, I., Narasimhamurthi, N.: A cryptographic solution to implement access control in a hierarchy and more. In: ACM Symposium on Access Control Models and Technologies (SACMAT), pp. 65–73 (2002)

22. Rivest, R.L.: All-or-nothing encryption and the package transform. In: Biham, E. (ed.) FSE 1997. LNCS, vol. 1267, pp. 210–218. Springer, Heidelberg (1997)

23. Sahai, A., Seyalioglu, H., Waters, B.: Dynamic credentials and ciphertext delegation for attribute-based encryption. In: Safavi-Naini, R. (ed.) CRYPTO 2012. LNCS, vol. 7417, pp. 199–217. Springer, Heidelberg (2012)

24. Sahai, A., Waters, B.: Fuzzy identity-based encryption. In: Cramer, R. (ed.) EUROCRYPT 2005. LNCS, vol. 3494, pp. 457–473. Springer, Heidelberg (2005)

25. De Santis, A., Ferrara, A.L., Masucci, B.: Efficient provably-secure hierarchical key assignment schemes. Theoretical Computer Science 412(41), 5684–5699 (2011)

26. Shao, J., Liu, P., Cao, Z., Wei, G.: Multi-use unidirectional proxy re-encryption. In: Proceedings of IEEE International Conference on Communications (ICC), pp. 1–5 (2011)

27. Tzeng, W.-G.: A time-bound cryptographic key assignment scheme for access control in a hierarchy. IEEE Transactions on Knowledge and Data Engineering (TKDE) 14(1), 182–188 (2002)

28. Wang, H., Cao, Z., Wang, L.: Multi-use and unidirectional identity-based proxy re-encryption schemes. Information Sciences 180(20), 4042–4059 (2010)

29. Wong, C.K., Gouda, M.G., Lam, S.S.: Secure group communications using key graphs. IEEE/ACM Transactions on Network 8(1), 16–30 (2000)

30. Yu, S., Wang, C., Ren, K., Lou, W.: Achieving secure, scalable, and fine-grained data access control in cloud computing. In: Proceedings of the IEEE International Conference on Computer Communications (INFOCOM), pp. 534–542 (2010)

31. Zhong, S.: A practical key management scheme for access control in a user hierarchy. Computers & Security 21(8), 750–759 (2002)

Computing on Authenticated Data
for Adjustable Predicates

Björn Deiseroth, Victoria Fehr, Marc Fischlin, Manuel Maasz,
Nils Fabian Reimers, and Richard Stein

Darmstadt University of Technology, Germany

Abstract. The notion of P-homomorphic signatures, introduced by Ahn
et al. (TCC 2012), generalizes various approaches for public computations on authenticated data. For a given predicate P anyone can derive a
signature for a message m' from the signatures of a set of messages M,
as long as $P(M, m') = 1$. This definition hence comprises notions and
constructions for concrete predicates P such as homomorphic signatures
and redactable signatures.

In our work we address the question of how to combine P_i-
homomorphic schemes for different predicates $P_1, P_2, \ldots$ to create a
richer and more flexible class of supported predicates. One approach
is to statically combine schemes for predicates into new schemes for logical formulas over the predicates, such as a scheme for AND ($P_1 \wedge P_2$).
The other approach for more flexibility is to derive schemes which allow
the signer to dynamically decide which predicate to use when signing a
message, instead of supporting only a single, fixed predicate.

We present two main results. One is to show that one can indeed devise solutions for the static combination for AND, and for dynamically
adjustable solutions for choosing the predicate on the fly. Moreover, our
constructions are practical and add only a negligible overhead. The other
main result is an impossibility result for static combinations. Namely, we
prove that, in contrast to the case of AND, many other formulas like the
logical OR ($P_1 \vee P_2$) and the NOT ($\neg P$) do not admit generic combinations through so-called canonical constructions. This implies that
one cannot rely on general constructions in these cases, but must use
other methods instead, like finding new predicate-specific solutions from
scratch.

1 Introduction

The notion of P-homomorphic signatures has been put forward by Ahn et al. [1]
as a generalization of several concurrent approaches to compute on authenticated data. The predicate P takes as input a set of messages M and determines the admissible messages m' which can be derived from M, and for which
a signature can be publicly computed from the signatures for the messages
in M. Examples covered by such signatures include homomorphic signatures
[14,19,13,6,16,18,3,8,7,15,11] where m' is the sum of all messages in M, transitive signatures [20,5,23,26,25,10] where m' describes a path in a graph given by

M. Jacobson et al. (Eds.): ACNS 2013, LNCS 7954, pp. 53–68, 2013.
© Springer-Verlag Berlin Heidelberg 2013

M, and redactable signatures [19,24,21,2,17,12,22,9] where m' is a substring of the single message M.

Ahn et al. [1] proposed two general security notions for P-homomorphic signatures. The first one is unforgeability and says that one should not be able to forge signatures for fresh messages which have not been signed before, and which are not publicly derivable. The other notion is called context hiding and provides strong privacy. It says that a derived signature for an admissible message m' and freshly created signatures for m' have statistically close distributions. This guarantees for instance that the original message in case of redactable signatures remains hidden. The context hiding notion has been subsequently refined in [4].

P-Homomorphic Signatures with Adjustable Predicates. While the abstract notion of P-homomorphic signatures is very handy for arguing about the security of solutions, any construction so far, even the ones in [1,4], are for a specific fixed predicate P, such as quoting substrings of a message. What is currently unknown is how to adjust solutions for fixed predicates in the following sense:

- One desirable option may be the possibility to combine a set of given homomorphic schemes for predicates $P_1, P_2, \ldots$ into one for a new P-homomorphic signature scheme. Here, P may be a simple combination such as $P_1 \wedge P_2$ or $P_1 \vee P_2$, or describe even more complex functions. An example are two redactable schemes, one allowing for redaction only at the front of the message (P_1), and the other one enabling redaction only at the end (P_2). Then a $P_1 \vee P_2$-homomorphic scheme would be a scheme for quoting substrings, by first pruning at the front and then truncating in another step at the end. Note that the problem here is to present a general transformation which supports a rich set of combinations from, say, basic predicates $P_1, P_2, \ldots$, instead of having to build schemes for P from scratch.
- Another desirable feature, which is not offered by the previous ability to combine predicates, is that signer can decide "on the fly" for each signature which predicate P the signature should support. Here, the set of admissible predicates is only bound by the universe $\mathcal{P}$ of predicates for which such signature schemes have been devised yet. This would allow to make the set of admissible message derivates depend on the message itself, e.g., supporting selective redaction for different messages.

We call general constructions with the first property *statically adjustable* because the combined predicate P is fixed at the time of key generation. The latter schemes are called *dynamically adjustable*. Both approaches have their merits and display their full power only in combination. One can first derive (statically) adjustable schemes for a larger universe $\mathcal{P}$, and then use this universe for the dynamically adjustable scheme.

Constructing Schemes with Statically Adjustable Predicates. We first investigate simple static combinations such as $P_1 \wedge P_2$, $P_1 \vee P_2$, and $\neg P$. Having solutions for these cases would immediately allow arbitrarily complex combinations of predicates. Our first result is to confirm for the logical AND that the "componentwise" solution works: sign each message with the schemes for predicates P_1, P_2 individually, and derive signatures by applying the corresponding algorithms for each component.

Our main result is to show that the logical OR, $P_1 \vee P_2$, in general does not admit *canonical* constructions. Such canonical constructions can combine given signatures of the individual schemes into one for the $P_1 \vee P_2$ predicate, and can vice versa split any signature for the OR into parts for the individual schemes. Our AND construction is of this type. Our negative result for the OR holds for (almost) arbitrary predicates P_1, P_2, essentially only excluding trivial examples like $P_1 \vee P_1$. Note that we cannot hope to show a similar result for *non*-canonical solutions, as for some cases we know constructions from scratch for $P_1 \vee P_2$ (e.g., for quotable substrings).

We actually present a more general result, saying that one cannot find canonical constructions for any predicate combination $f(P_1, P_2, \dots)$ if one is able to efficiently find a derivable message m' under $f(P_1, P_2, \dots)$ and from a message set M, such that m' is not derivable under one of the predicates individually. This excludes the AND case, because any derivable message m' in $P_1 \wedge P_2$ must be also valid according to both in P_1 and P_2. Yet, this notion includes the OR case if m' can be derived under one predicate, and therefore the OR, but not under the other predicate. It also covers the NOT case straightforwardly, because if m' is derivable under $f(P_1) = \neg P_1$, then it is clearly not derivable under P_1. The impossibility result holds even if the canonical construction depends on f and the predicates. Put differently, it seems that the only general and non-trivial solutions for statically adjustable predicates are the ones for logical ANDs.

Constructing Schemes with Dynamically Adjustable Predicates. Does the negative result for statically adjustable parameters also rule out solutions for the dynamic case? Not necessarily, because in this case we assume that the signer adaptively chooses the predicate P from the universe $\mathcal{P}$ for which constructions are already known. Indeed we show that the "certify-then-sign" construction provides a solution in this case: use a regular signature scheme to certify a public key for the P-homomorphic scheme for the chosen predicate $P \in \mathcal{P}$ and sign the message under the secret key for P. Some care must be taken, though, because in order to preserve context hiding the key pair for the P-homomorphic scheme must remain fixed throughout the life time.

2 Preliminaries

We recall the definition and security notions of P-homomorphic signatures, as given in [1,4], and adopt them slightly for our adjustable setting.

2.1 Adjustable $\mathcal{P}$-homomorphic Signature Schemes

We assume a fixed but public universe $\mathcal{P}$ of predicates $P_1, P_2, \dots$, each predicate associated with a publicly known P_i-homomorphic signature scheme. A predicate $\mathsf{P}_i : 2^{\mathcal{M}} \times \mathcal{M} \to \{0,1\}$ indicates whether a set of messages M allows to derive another message m' from the message space $\mathcal{M}$ or not. We give the signer and the verifier the predicate P in question as additional input. In case of a single fixed predicate P, as for the statically adjustable setting, where the universe $\mathcal{P}$ is a singleton, this is an invariant for the scheme and could be ignored by both algorithms. In fact, in this case the notion basically coincides with the definition of a P-homomorphic scheme, the only difference being the predicate given to the signers and verifier as additional input. In this sense the definition of schemes with statically adjustable predicates is a rehash of the notion of P-homomorphic signatures. We stress that we do not suggest to change the terminology for P-homomorphic schemes. The reader should bear in mind, however, that schemes with statically adjustable predicates in this paper implicitly assume a *construction* from selected P-homomorphic schemes underneath. In light of this it matches the dynamic counterpart where predicates are chosen adaptively for each signature.

We simplify the notation below, and write $\mathsf{Verify}(pk, M, \Sigma, \mathsf{P})$ as shorthand for $\bigwedge_{m \in M} \mathsf{Verify}(pk, m, \sigma_m, \mathsf{P})$ with $\Sigma = \{\sigma_m\}_{m \in M}$. Similarly, we sometimes write $\Sigma \leftarrow \mathsf{Sign}(sk, M, \mathsf{P})$ for $\Sigma = \{\mathsf{Sign}(sk, m, \mathsf{P}) \mid m \in M\}$.

Definition 1 (Adjustable $\mathcal{P}$-homomorphic Signature Scheme). *A (statically or dynamically) adjustable $\mathcal{P}$-homomorphic signature scheme is a tuple of PPT algorithms (KeyGen, Sign, SignDer, Verify) such that:*

- *$(sk, pk) \leftarrow \mathsf{KeyGen}(1^\lambda)$ maps the security parameter $\lambda \in \mathbb{N}$, given in unary, to a key pair.*
- *$\sigma \leftarrow \mathsf{Sign}(sk, m, \mathsf{P})$ on input the secret key sk, a message $m \in \mathcal{M}$, and a predicate $\mathsf{P} \in \mathcal{P}$ returns a signature σ to m and P.*
- *$\sigma' \leftarrow \mathsf{SignDer}(pk, M, \Sigma, m', \mathsf{P})$ takes as input the public key pk, a set of messages $M \subseteq \mathcal{M}$ along with signatures $\Sigma = \{\sigma_m\}_{m \in M}$, a message $m' \in \mathcal{M}$, and the predicate $\mathsf{P} \in \mathcal{P}$ to be applied, and outputs a signature σ' (or a special symbol $\perp$ indicating failure).*
- *$b \leftarrow \mathsf{Verify}(pk, m, \sigma, \mathsf{P})$, given the public key pk, a signature σ, a message $m \in \mathcal{M}$, and a predicate $\mathsf{P} \in \mathcal{P}$, returns 1 if the signature is valid for the given message, and 0 if not.*

We assume the usual correctness condition, namely, that for any $\lambda \in \mathbb{N}$, any $(sk, pk) \leftarrow \mathsf{KeyGen}(1^\lambda)$, any $(m, M, m') \in \mathcal{M} \times 2^{\mathcal{M}} \times \mathcal{M}$ and any $\mathsf{P} \in \mathcal{P}$ we have:

- *if $\sigma \leftarrow \mathsf{Sign}(sk, m, \mathsf{P})$, then $\mathsf{Verify}(pk, m, \sigma, \mathsf{P}) = 1$ with probability 1; and*
- *for any $\Sigma = \{\sigma_m\}_{m \in M}$, if $\mathsf{Verify}(pk, M, \Sigma, \mathsf{P}) = 1$ and $P(M, m') = 1$, then for any $\sigma' \leftarrow \mathsf{SignDer}(pk, M, \Sigma, m', \mathsf{P})$ we have $\mathsf{Verify}(pk, m', \sigma', \mathsf{P}) = 1$ with probability 1.*

2.2   Unforgeability

For any predicate P and set M of messages it is convenient to consider the set of messages which can be derived (recursively) from M through P. Hence, similar to [1], we define $P(M) = \{m' \in \mathcal{M} \mid P(M, m') = 1\}$ for any $M \subseteq \mathcal{M}$, as well as $P^0(M) = M$ and $P^i(M) = P(P^{i-1}(M))$ for $i > 0$. Let $P^*(M) = \bigcup_{i \in \mathbb{N}_0} P^i(M)$. We sometimes switch between the set $P^*(M)$ and its predicate analogue, with $P^*(M, m') = 1$ iff $m' \in P^*(M)$. Unless mentioned differently, we assume that any predicate can be evaluated efficiently.

We also presume, without further mentioning it, that predicates are *monotone*, that is, $P(M') \subseteq P(M)$ if $M' \subseteq M$. It follows inductively that $P^*(M') \subseteq P^*(M)$ in this case as well. This is necessary to ensure that, below in the unforgeability game, the set of messages for which a signature can be trivially derived from known signatures for M, does not shrink by asking for more signatures.[1] An alternative is to consider below all subsets $M' \subseteq M$ and declare that any message which is in $P(M')$ to be a message for which a signature is trivial to derive from the signatures for messages in M'.

We again consider both the static and the dynamic case simultaneously, with the understanding that the predicate is fixed in the static case via $\mathcal{P} = \{P\}$.

Definition 2 (Unforgeability). *A (statically or dynamically) adjustable $\mathcal{P}$-homomorphic signature scheme (KeyGen, Sign, SignDer, Verify) is called* unforge-able, *if any PPT adversary $\mathcal{A}$ has a negligible advantage in the following game:*

1. *The challenger $\mathcal{C}$ generates the key pair $(sk, pk) \leftarrow$ KeyGen(1^λ) and gives pk to the adversary $\mathcal{A}$. The challenger initializes two empty sets T and Q.*
2. *$\mathcal{A}$ interleaves adaptively the following queries:*
   - *Signing queries: $\mathcal{A}$ chooses a message $m \in \mathcal{M}$ and a predicate $P \in \mathcal{P}$, upon which $\mathcal{C}$ returns a unique handle h to $\mathcal{A}$, runs $\sigma \leftarrow$ Sign(sk, m, P), and stores (h, m, σ, P) in T.*
   - *Derivation queries: $\mathcal{A}$ chooses a set of handles $\boldsymbol{h} = \{h_i\}_i$, a message $m' \in \mathcal{M}$ and a predicate P. The challenger $\mathcal{C}$ retrieves the tuples $(h_i, m_i, \sigma_i, P_i)$ from T and returns $\perp$ if one of these tuples does not exist, $P_i \neq P$ for some i, or $P(M, m') = 0$. Otherwise, the challenger returns a unique handle h' to $\mathcal{A}$, runs $\sigma' \leftarrow$ SignDer($pk, M, \{\sigma_m\}_{m \in M}, m', P$) for $M = \{m_i\}_i$ and stores (h', m', σ', P) in T.*
   - *Reveal queries: If $\mathcal{A}$ chooses a handle h then $\mathcal{C}$ returns $\perp$ if there does not exist a tuple of the form (h, m, σ, P) in T. Otherwise, it returns σ to $\mathcal{A}$ and adds (m, σ, P) to the set Q.*
3. *$\mathcal{A}$ outputs a pair (m, σ, P) and wins if the following conditions hold:*
   - *Verify(pk, m, σ, P) = 1, and*
   - *$m \notin P^*(M_P)$, where $M_P = \{m \in \mathcal{M} \mid (m, *, P) \in Q\}$, the set of messages in the query set Q for the same predicate P.*

Note that the condition on $m \notin P^*(M_P)$ can be relaxed by considering the set M of messages which have been signed under *some* predicate (and not only those which have been signed under the same predicate P as in the forgery attempt). In the static case both cases coincide, of course.

---

[1] Interestingly, this is not stipulated explicitly in previous works [1,4]. Still, the predicates for the constructions there satisfy this property. It is, nonetheless, generally required for a reasonable definition in order to avoid trivial examples of schemes which are formally unforgeable, but intuitively insecure.

2.3 Context Hiding

The original definition of Ahn et al. [1] requires a strong privacy requirement, basically saying that a derived signature (from previously signed messages M), and a fresh signature for the new message m' are statistically close. It follows that a derived signature does not leak any information about the starting messages M, and thus implies other common privacy notions for, say, redactable signature schemes [9]. Still, the notion has been strengthened in [4] to adaptive context hiding and complete context hiding, basically saying that derived signatures (for messages with any valid signatures) and fresh signatures are close. The generalization to valid signatures as input, instead of only signed messages, allows to cover previously excluded cases like rerandomizable signatures.

While the notion of adaptive context hiding is game-based, the notion of complete context hiding is defined through statistically close distributions of signatures. It is convenient for us here to present the latter definition also through a game, but considering *unbounded* adversaries (as opposed to *efficient* adversaries for adaptive context hiding). Otherwise the notions are identical. Our game-based definition of complete context hiding can be seen easily to be equivalent to the distributional approach in [4].

Definition 3 ((Complete and Adaptive) Context Hiding). *A (statically or dynamically) adjustable $\mathcal{P}$-homomorphic signature scheme ($\mathsf{KeyGen}, \mathsf{Sign}, \mathsf{SignDer}, \mathsf{Verify}$) is called* completely *(resp. adaptively)* context hiding, *if any unbounded (resp. PPT) adversary $\mathcal{A}$ has a negligible advantage in the following game:*

1. *The challenger $\mathcal{C}$ generates the key pair $(sk, pk) \leftarrow \mathsf{KeyGen}(1^\lambda)$ and gives (sk, pk) to the adversary $\mathcal{A}$.*
2. *The adversary selects a set M of messages, and set $\{\sigma_m\}_{m \in M}$ of signatures, a predicate $P \in \mathcal{P}$, and a message m' and hands it to the challenger. If $P(M, m') = 0$ or if $\mathsf{Verify}(pk, M, \{\sigma_m\}_{m \in M}, P) = 0$ then the challenger immediately returns $\perp$. Else it picks a random bit $b \leftarrow \{0, 1\}$ and computes a derived siganture $\sigma' \leftarrow \mathsf{SignDer}(pk, M, \{\sigma_m\}_{m \in M}, m', P)$ if $b = 0$, and a fresh signature $\sigma' \leftarrow \mathsf{Sign}(sk, m', P)$ in case $b = 1$. It returns σ' to the adversary.*
3. *Eventually the adversary outputs a bit $b^* \in \{0, 1\}$ and wins if $b^* = b$. The advantage of $\mathcal{A}$ is defined to be $\boldsymbol{Adv}(\mathcal{A}) = \left|\mathrm{Prob}[b^* = b] - \frac{1}{2}\right|$.*

Some remarks are in place. First note that the adversary can ask the challenger only once. A standard hybrid argument shows that this remains true for multiple (polynomially many) queries for which the challenger re-uses the same bit b. For both cases, the static and the dynamic one, the advantage grows by a factor proportional to the number of queries.

Secondly, note that in the dynamically adjustable case we do not aim to hide the predicate P which has been used to compute the signature. In a stronger requirement one could demand that the actual predicate remains hidden, either among all predicates from the universe, or among the predicates for which the public derivation algorithm would succeed. The former would require a super-polynomial set $\mathcal{P}$ (else the privacy attacker could probe the derivation algorithms for all predicates). The latter would mean a trade-off between privacy, usability, and the signer's intention for restricting the class of admissible public operations: if the signature would hide the corresponding predicate among multiple possibilities, then signatures for a different predicate than the original choice may be derivable. This would imply that the signer loses some control about the (in)ability to derive further signatures. Hence, we do not pursue such stronger requirements here.

3 Statically Adjustable Computations

In this section we investigate statically adjustable constructions for the basic operations AND, OR, and NOT. As explained in the introduction, we can give a general solution for AND, but cannot hope to give (general) transformations for the other two cases.

Below we consider combinations for arbitrary functions f over a fixed[2] number q of predicates $P_1, P_2, \ldots, P_q$. We assume that such a function $f(P_1, P_2, \ldots, P_q)$ over the predicates itself constitutes a predicate and defines a set of derivable messages from M in a straightforward way, by evaluating the predicates for (M, m') and plugging the results into the formula. If viewed as sets, our basic examples for OR, AND, and NOT can then be written as $f_\vee(P_1, P_2)(M) = P_1(M) \cup P_2(M)$, and $f_\wedge(P_1, P_2)(M) = P_1(M) \cap P_2(M)$, as well as $f_\neg(P_1)(M) = M \setminus P_1(M)$.

Note that one could more generally also define $f(P_1, P_2, \ldots, P_q)$ for divisible message sets $M = (M_1, M_2, \ldots, M_q)$ by evaluating $f(M, m')$ as a logical formula over $P_1(M_1, m'), \ldots, P_q(M_q, m')$, i.e., assigning only the i-th part M_i of M to the i-th predicate, instead of using the same set M for all predicates. This can be captured in our notion with a single M by having the predicates P_i first project M onto M_i and then evaluating the actual predicate on (M_i, m'). For sake of readability we use the simpler notion with identical M.

We also assume that the message spaces $\mathcal{M}_i$ of all schemes are identical. This can always be achieved by setting $\mathcal{M} = \bigcap_{i=1}^{q} \mathcal{M}_i$. Note that, if message spaces are not identical this in principle allows to distinguish, say, in case of OR which predicate can be used to create a signature for some message. Since this would violate the idea of privacy immediately, we restrict ourselves to the case of identical message spaces.

3.1 Statically Adjustable Computations for AND

We first confirm that the solution to sign each message component-wise under a set of public keys yields a secure solution for the AND. Instead of considering only two predicates we allow to combine any fixed number q of predicates.

---

[2] Note that, in general, the number of combined predicates is specific for the scheme and must not depend on the security parameter, i.e., the design of the scheme does not change with the security parameter. In this sense the number q of predicates is constant in the security parameter.

Construction 1 (AND-Construction). *Let* $(KeyGen_i, Sign_i, SignDer_i, Verify_i)$ *be* P_i-*homomorphic signature schemes for predicates* $P_1, \ldots, P_q$. *Then the following scheme* $(KeyGen, Sign, SignDer, Verify)$ *is a P-homomorphic signature scheme for* $P = P_1 \wedge \ldots \wedge P_q$:

- $KeyGen(1^\lambda)$ *runs* $(sk_i, pk_i) \leftarrow KeyGen_i(1^\lambda)$ *for all* $i = 1, 2, \ldots, q$, *and outputs* $sk = (sk_1, \ldots, sk_q)$ *and* $pk = (pk_1, \ldots, pk_q)$.
- $Sign(sk, m, P)$ *computes* $\sigma_i \leftarrow Sign_i(sk_i, m, P_i)$ *for all* i *and returns* $\sigma = (\sigma_1, \ldots, \sigma_q)$.
- $SignDer(pk, M, \Sigma, m', P)$ *first checks that* $P_i(M, m') = 1$ *for all* i, *and then creates* $\sigma_i' \leftarrow SignDer_i(pk_i, M, \Sigma_i, m', P_i)$ *where* Σ_i *is the set of projections on the i-th component for each signature tuple in* $\Sigma = \{\sigma_m\}_{m \in M}$. *It returns* $\sigma' = (\sigma_1', \ldots, \sigma_q')$.
- $Verify(pk, M, \Sigma, P)$ *returns* 1 *if and only if* $Verify_i(pk_i, M, \Sigma_i, P_i) = 1$ *for all* i *(where again* Σ_i *is the set of projections on the i-th component for each signature in* Σ *).*

Correctness follows easily from the correctness of the underlying P_i-homomorphic schemes.

Proposition 1. *For any constant* q *and any unforgeable and completely (resp. adaptively) context-hiding* P_i-*homomorphic schemes, Construction 1 (AND-Construction) is unforgeable and completely (resp. adaptively) context-hiding.*

For concrete parameters our proof shows that the advantage of breaking unforgeability resp. context hiding for the AND scheme is bounded by the sum of the advantages for the corresponding property over all P_i-homomorphic schemes.

Proof. We first show unforgeability, then context hiding.

Unforgeability Assume that there exists a successful adversary $\mathcal{A}$ against unforgeability (Definition 2) for the P-homomorphic signature scheme where $P = P_1 \wedge \ldots \wedge P_q$. For each $i \in \{1, 2, \ldots, q\}$, we first construct an adversary $\mathcal{A}_i$ against the unforgeability of the underlying P_i-homomorphic signature schemes:

- $\mathcal{A}_i$ initially receives pk_i from the challenger $\mathcal{C}_i$ for the game against the P_i-homomorphic signature schemes.
- $\mathcal{A}_i$ creates an initially empty table T' and runs $(sk_j, pk_j) \leftarrow KeyGen_j(1^\lambda)$ for all $j = 1, 2, \ldots, q$, $j \neq i$ to create the other keys.
- $\mathcal{A}_i$ invokes adversary $\mathcal{A}$ against the AND-scheme on $pk = (pk_1, \ldots, pk_q)$.
- For every signing query (m, P) from $\mathcal{A}$, adversary $\mathcal{A}_i$ creates a signing query for message m and the predicate P_i for its challenger and gets the handle h, then computes $\sigma_j \leftarrow Sign_j(sk_j, m, P_j)$ for all $j \neq i$, and stores (j, h, m, σ_j, P_j) in T'.
- For every derivation query $(\{h\}, m', P)$ of $\mathcal{A}$, adversary $\mathcal{A}_i$ passes a derivation query for the corresponding handles $(\{h\}, m', P_i)$ to its challenger to receive a handle h'. If $h' \neq \bot$ adversary $\mathcal{A}_i$ looks up all entries (j, h, m, σ_m, P_j) for

$j \neq i$ in T' for the queried handles in $\{h\}$ to form $M = \{m\}$, internally checks $P_j(M, m') = 1$, and computes $\sigma'_j \leftarrow \mathsf{SignDer}_j(pk_j, M, \{\sigma_m\}_{m \in M}, m', P_j)$. If no error occurs it returns h' to $\mathcal{A}$ and stores $(j, h', m', \sigma'_j, P_j)$ in T' for all $j \neq i$; else it returns $\bot$.

- For every reveal request $\mathcal{A}_i$ runs a reveal request for the corresponding handle h, combines the reply σ_i with the values σ_j from entries (j, h, m, σ_j, P_j) in T' to σ and sends it to $\mathcal{A}$; in case of an error it simply returns $\bot$.
- When $\mathcal{A}$ eventually outputs a tuple (m, σ, P), then $\mathcal{A}_i$ outputs the tuple (m, σ_i, P_i) for the i-th component σ_i in σ.

Note that for each i adversary $\mathcal{A}_i$ perfectly simulates an attack of $\mathcal{A}$ on the P-homomorphic scheme with the help of its challenger, such that $\mathcal{A}$ would output a successful forgery with the same probability in the simulation as in the original attack. By construction, we also have that the message set M_P of queries $(m, *, P)$ in $\mathcal{A}$'s queries in the simulation is identical to the set M_{P_i} for queries $(m, *, P_i)$ of $\mathcal{A}_i$ to its challenger for each i. Hence, from $m \notin P^*(M_P)$ it follows that $m \notin P_i^*(M_{P_i})$ for some $i \in \{1, 2 \ldots, q\}$. Furthermore, since verification succeeds for all components, it also holds that $\mathsf{Verify}_i(pk_i, m, \sigma, P_i) = 1$ for this i.

In other words, any successful forgery yields a successful forgery against (at least) one of the underlying schemes. It follows that the probability of breaking unforgeability for the AND scheme is bounded from above by the sum of the probabilities to break each underlying scheme.

Context Hiding. Assume next that there exists a successful adversary $\mathcal{A}$ against context hiding (Definition 3) for our P-homomorphic signature scheme with $P = P_1 \wedge \ldots \wedge P_q$. As in the case of unforgeability we construct, for each $i \in \{1, 2, \ldots, q\}$, an adversary $\mathcal{A}_i$ against context hiding of the i-th scheme. The advantage of $\mathcal{A}$ will be bounded from above by the sum over all advantages of the $\mathcal{A}_i$'s via a standard hybrid argument. Furthermore, each $\mathcal{A}_i$ will be efficient if $\mathcal{A}$ is, such that the claim remains true for adaptive context hiding.

Adversary $\mathcal{A}_i$ receives a pair (sk_i, pk_i) from its challenger and creates the other key pairs (sk_j, pk_j) for $j \neq i$ by running $\mathsf{KeyGen}_j(1^\lambda)$. It hands $sk = (sk_1, \ldots, sk_q)$ and $pk = (pk_1, \ldots, pk_q)$ to adversary $\mathcal{A}$ and waits for the adversary to create a challenge request M, Σ, m'. For each signature σ_m in Σ adversary $\mathcal{A}_i$ extracts the i-th component and thereby forms the set Σ_i. It passes M, m', and Σ_i to its own challenger to receive a signature σ'_i (or an error message). It creates the signatures σ'_j for $j < i$ by running the signing algorithm on m'; for $j > i$ it runs the signature derivation algorithm on M, m', Σ_j to create the remaining signatures σ'_j. In all cases it checks the validity of the predicates and signatures. If there is an error it returns $\bot$ to the adversary $\mathcal{A}$, and $(\sigma'_1, \ldots, \sigma'_q)$ otherwise. If $\mathcal{A}$ eventually outputs a bit b^* then $\mathcal{A}_i$, too, outputs this bit and stops.

For the analysis note that $\mathcal{A}_1$, given that its challenger uses $b = 0$, describes the case that all signatures are derived via $\mathsf{SignDer}$. It follows that the probability of $\mathcal{A}$ correctly outputting 0 for derived signatures in the attack (and thus in the perfect simulation through $\mathcal{A}_1$) is exactly the probability that $\mathcal{A}_1$ returns 0, given $b = 0$ in its challenge. Analogously, given $b = 1$ adversary $\mathcal{A}_q$ only creates fresh signatures via Sign in all components, hence given $b = 1$ the probability that $\mathcal{A}_q$ returns 0 is exactly the same that $\mathcal{A}$ outputs 0 in the case that all signatures are fresh. A standard hybrid argument now yields: $\mathbf{Adv}(\mathcal{A}) = \sum_{i=1}^{q} \mathbf{Adv}(\mathcal{A}_i)$. This proves context hiding. □

3.2 Statically Adjustable Computations for OR and NOT

Our impossibility result holds for canonical constructions which combine P_i-homomorphic schemes in a general way, ruling out specific constructions which ignore the underlying schemes and builds a new scheme from scratch. We require four algorithms, one for synthesizing public keys of the individual schemes into one for the combined scheme (PKComb), one for splitting keys (PKSplit), one for combining signatures (SigComb), and one to divide signatures for the combined scheme into signatures for the individual schemes (SigSplit). The latter is usually necessary to reduce the security to the security of the individual schemes.

For sake of readability we follow the statistical indistinguishability approach also used for (complete) context hiding, and require that the distributions of the algorithms above for combining and splitting keys and signatures have identical distributions as if running the actual algorithms of the combined scheme directly. As our proof below shows our impossibility result can be extended to cover computationally indistinguishable distributions.

Definition 4 (Canonical Construction). *Let f be a functional predicate over predicates $P_1, \ldots, P_q$ for a fixed number q of predicates. A statically adjustable $f(P_1, \ldots, P_q)$-homomorphic signature scheme* (KeyGen, Sign, SignDer, Verify) *is a canonical construction out of P_i-homomorphic signature schemes* (KeyGen$_i$, Sign$_i$, SignDer$_i$, Verify$_i$) *if there exist PPT algorithms* (PKComb, PKSplit, SigComb, SigSplit) *such that:*

Identical distribution of combined keys: *The following random variables are identically distributed:*
 - *Let $(pk, sk) \leftarrow$ KeyGen(1^λ) and output pk;*
 - *Let $(pk_i, sk_i) \leftarrow$ KeyGen$_i(1^\lambda)$ for all i, $pk \leftarrow$ PKComb$(pk_1, \ldots, pk_q)$, output pk,*

Identical distribution of split keys: *The following random variables are identically distributed:*
 - *Let $(pk, sk) \leftarrow$ KeyGen(1^λ) and output $(pk_1, \ldots, pk_q) \leftarrow$ PKSplit(pk);*
 - *Let $(pk_i, sk_i) \leftarrow$ KeyGen$_i(1^\lambda)$ for all i, output $(pk_1, \ldots, pk_q)$,*

Identical distribution of combined signatures: *For any PPT algorithm $\mathcal{F}$ the following pairs of random variables are identically distributed:*
 - *Run $M \leftarrow \mathcal{F}(1^\lambda)$. Compute $(pk, sk) \leftarrow$ KeyGen(1^λ) and output $\Sigma \leftarrow$ Sign$(sk, M, f(P_1, \ldots, P_q))$;*
 - *Run $M \leftarrow \mathcal{F}(1^\lambda)$. For all i, compute $(pk_i, sk_i) \leftarrow$ KeyGen$_i(1^\lambda)$ along with $\Sigma_i \leftarrow$ Sign$_i(sk_i, M, P_i)$. Synthesize the public key via $pk \leftarrow$ PKComb$(pk_1, \ldots, pk_q)$ and output $\Sigma \leftarrow$ SigComb$(pk, pk_1, \ldots, pk_q, \Sigma_1, \ldots, \Sigma_q, M)$.*

Splitting Signatures: *For any PPT algorithm $\mathcal{F}'$ we have that for $(pk_i, sk_i) \leftarrow \mathsf{KeyGen}_i(1^\lambda)$ for all i, $pk \leftarrow \mathsf{PKComb}(pk_1, \ldots, pk_q)$, $(M, m') \leftarrow \mathcal{F}'(1^\lambda)$ where $m' \in f(P_1, \ldots, P_q)(M)$, $\Sigma_i \leftarrow \mathsf{Sign}_i(sk_i, M, P_i)$, $\Sigma \leftarrow \mathsf{SigComb}(pk_1, \ldots, pk_q, \Sigma_1, \ldots, \Sigma_q, M)$, $\sigma' \leftarrow \mathsf{SignDer}(pk, M, \Sigma, m', f(P_1, \ldots, P_q))$, the probability that $(\sigma'_1, \ldots, \sigma'_q) \leftarrow \mathsf{SigSplit}(pk, pk_1, \ldots, pk_q, m', \sigma')$ does not contain some valid component and thus $\mathsf{Verify}_i(pk_i, m', \sigma'_i) = 0$ for all i, is negligible.*

In other words, SigSplit returns at least one valid signature for one of the underlying predicates with sufficiently high probability. Our AND-construction is canonical in the above sense: PKComb and SigComb both concatenate their inputs (and PKSplit divides the concatenated keys again), and SigSplit simply returns the signature itself. Note that the definition allows PKComb, PKSplit, SigComb, and SigSplit to depend on the given predicates P_i; the construction only follows a canonical pattern.

In what follows, we need to exclude trivial examples like $P_1 \vee P_2 = P_1 \vee P_1$. Hence, for the OR we assume below the existence of a message m' which can be derived from a set of messages M under one predicate, but not the other predicate. This clearly prevents $P_1 = P_2$. More generally, and to include for instance also the NOT case, we assume that m' can be derived under $f(P_1, P_2, \ldots)$ but not under one of the predicates; the excluded predicate P_i can be arbitrary, but the output distribution of m' does not depend on this choice. The latter is necessary to ensure that m' does not contain any information about the predicate's index i. Furthermore, we assume that such pairs (M, m') are efficiently computable. We discuss an illuminating example after the definition.

Definition 5 (Efficiently Distinguishable Predicates). *Let f be a functional predicate over predicates $P_1, \ldots, P_q$. Consider a statically adjustable $f(P_1, \ldots, P_q)$-homomorphic signature scheme (KeyGen, Sign, SignDer, Verify). Then the predicates are called* efficiently distinguishable *with respect to f, if there exists a PPT algorithm $\mathcal{F}$ such that for any $i \in \{1, 2, \ldots, q\}$ and for any $(M, m') \leftarrow \mathcal{F}(1^\lambda, i)$, we have $m' \in (f(P_1, \ldots, P_q)(M) \setminus P_i^*(M))$. Moreover, for any $i, j \in \{1, 2, \ldots, q\}$ the distribution of m' (over the coin tosses of $\mathcal{F}$) in the output of $\mathcal{F}(1^\lambda, i)$ resp. $\mathcal{F}(1^\lambda, j)$ is identical.*

Let us demonstrate the property for the introductory example of two redactable signature schemes (with message space $\mathcal{M} = \{0, 1\}^*$), one allowing to drop message bits only at the front (predicate P_1), and the other one only at the end (P_2). Consider the OR predicate $P_1 \vee P_2$ describing a scheme for quotable substrings. Then $\mathcal{F}$ can simply pick $m' = 0^\lambda$ and for $i = 1$ output $M = \{0^\lambda 1\}$, and for $i = 2$ it returns $M = \{10^\lambda\}$ instead. Clearly, for $i = 1$ one can derive m' from M via P_2 and therefore for the OR, but not via P_1, because the '1' at the end cannot be redacted through P_1. The same argument holds vice versa for $i = 2$, and the (trivial) distributions on m' are identical for both $i = 1$ and $i = 2$. Hence, this examples has efficiently distinguishable predicates.

The case of NOT is even simpler. Algorithm $\mathcal{F}$ simply needs to find some M and some m' which lies in $(\neg P(M)) \setminus P^*(M) = \mathcal{M} \setminus P^*(M)$, i.e., if m' is not derivable according to $\mathsf{P}^*(M)$. Finally note that constructions based only on AND cannot be distinguishable, since $(\mathsf{P}_1(M) \cap \mathsf{P}_2(M)) \setminus \mathsf{P}_i^*(M) = \emptyset$ for any i.

Theorem 1. *Let f be a functional predicate over predicates $\mathsf{P}_1, \ldots, \mathsf{P}_q$ for a fixed number q of predicates. Assume further that the predicates are efficiently distinguishable with respect to f. Then there is no adaptively context-hiding, statically-adjustable $f(\mathsf{P}_1, \ldots, \mathsf{P}_q)$-homomorphic signature scheme which is a canonical construction out of unforgeable P_i-homomorphic signature schemes.*

The proof idea is as follows. Essentially we show how to forge a signature for one of the underlying schemes. For this we use the distinguishability of the predicates to create a set of messages M and a message m' which is derivable by $f(\mathsf{P}_1, \ldots, \mathsf{P}_q)(M)$ but does not lie in $\mathsf{P}_i^*(M)$ for some i. Then we ask for signatures for the messages in M, and derive a signature for m' via the public operation SignDer for the combined scheme and for $f(\mathsf{P}_1, \ldots, \mathsf{P}_q)$. Splitting up the signature into its components via SigSplit we obtain (with sufficiently large probability) a valid signature for m' under the i-th scheme. But since $m' \notin \mathsf{P}_i^*(M)$ we thus create a valid forgery, contradicting the security of the underlying scheme. In the course of the proof we use the context hiding property to show that the "skewed" choice of M, m' (with $m' \notin \mathsf{P}_i^*(M)$) does not bias the success probability of SigSplit for returning a valid signature component for the i-th scheme significantly. The formal proof appears in the full version.

We stress that the impossibility result holds for the computational notion of *adaptive* context hiding (with efficient distinguishers), which even strengthens our result. As mentioned before, a slightly more involved argument allows to extend the result also to algorithms PKComb, PKSplit, SigComb whose output is only computationally indistinguishable from the one of the original algorithms (instead of being identical). This requires some additional steps to prove that gradually replacing the algorithms does not change the behavior of SigSplit in the above proof significantly.

4   Dynamically Adjustable Computations

In the dynamic case we assume a polynomial universe $\mathcal{P}$ of predicates such that there exists a P_i-homomorphic scheme for each $\mathsf{P}_i \in \mathcal{P}$. We furthermore assume that given (a description of) P_i one can efficiently recover the corresponding scheme, e.g., if the universe consists only of a fixed number of predicates. Vice versa, we assume that P_i is identifiable from the scheme's public key pk_i. This in particular implies that the public keys for predicates must be unique. For simplicity we assume an ordering on predicates in $\mathcal{P}$ and often identify the predicate P_i and the scheme with its number i according to this order. We simply call sets $\mathcal{P}$ as above *efficient*.

In the construction we need to assume that for a given predicate identifier i there is a fixed yet (pseudo)random key pair $(sk_i, pk_i) \leftarrow \mathsf{KeyGen}_i(1^\lambda)$, generated according to the key generation algorithm for the scheme for predicate P_i. This key pair remains identical for all signature requests for P_i. For a polynomial universe $\mathcal{P}$ this can be in principle implemented by generating the keys (sk_i, pk_i) when creating the scheme's keys (sk, pk), and storing them in sk. In practice this may indeed be admissible for a small number of predicates, a more applicable approach may be to generate the keys on the fly via a pseudorandom function. Namely, store a key κ of a pseudorandom function in sk, and to create the key pair for predicate P_i, recover the (pseudo)random output $\omega_i = \mathsf{PRF}(\kappa, P_i)$ and re-run $\mathsf{KeyGen}_i(1^\lambda; \omega_i)$ for ω_i to derive the same pair (sk_i, pk_i) as before. For unforgeability it can be formally shown via standard techniques that this solution is (quasi) as secure as generating fresh key pairs and maintaining a table to look up previous keys; for context hiding, however, one requires an additional assumption on the security of the underlying scheme to preserve privacy, as discussed in the full version.

Similarly, the public keys pk_i and their (fixed) certificates $cert_i$ may be published at once, or may be attached to each signature upon creation. Below we adopt the latter solution as it rather complies with our notion of (stateless) $\mathcal{P}$-homomorphic signatures. Hence, below we assume for simplicity that the efficient universe $\mathcal{P}$ stores all pairs (sk_i, pk_i) with once-created certificates $cert_i$ at the beginning in sk. For certification we use a regular signature scheme which we can subsume as a special case under P-homomorphic schemes, without considering a SignDer algorithm nor context hiding. If we define $\mathsf{P}(M) = M$ for this scheme, unforgeability for this "homomorphic" scheme corresponds to the common notion of unforgeability for regular schemes.

Construction 2 (Certify-Then-Sign Construction). *Let $\mathcal{P}$ be an efficient set of predicates $P_1, P_2, \ldots, P_q$. Let $(\mathsf{KeyGen}_0, \mathsf{Sign}_0, \mathsf{Verify}_0)$ be a regular signature scheme. Define the following dynamically adjustable $\mathcal{P}$-homomorphic signature scheme $(\mathsf{KeyGen}, \mathsf{Sign}, \mathsf{SignDer}, \mathsf{Verify})$:*

- *$\mathsf{KeyGen}(1^\lambda)$ generates $(sk_0, pk_0) \leftarrow \mathsf{KeyGen}_0(1^\lambda)$, generates key pairs $(sk_i, pk_i) \leftarrow \mathsf{KeyGen}_i(1^\lambda)$ for all predicates P_i, and certificates $cert_i \leftarrow \mathsf{Sign}_0(sk_0, pk_i)$ for all i. It returns $sk = (sk_0, \{(sk_i, pk_i, cert_i)\}_i)$ and $pk = pk_0$.*
- *$\mathsf{Sign}(sk, m, P_i)$ looks up $(sk_i, pk_i, cert_i)$ for P_i in sk and computes $\sigma_i \leftarrow \mathsf{Sign}_i(sk, m)$ and returns $\sigma = (\sigma_i, pk_i, cert_i)$.*
- *$\mathsf{SignDer}(pk, M, \Sigma, m', P')$ checks that all signatures carry the same pk_i and $cert_i$ for predicate P_i, that $P' = P_i$, that $P_i(M, m') = 1$, that $\mathsf{Verify}_i(pk_i, M, \Sigma) = 1$, and, if all checks succeed, computes $\sigma'_i \leftarrow \mathsf{SignDer}_i(pk_i, M, \Sigma, m')$ and returns $\sigma' = (\sigma'_i, pk_i, cert_i)$.*
- *$\mathsf{Verify}(pk, m, \sigma, P)$ checks that P corresponds to the public key in $(\sigma_i, pk_i, cert_i)$, that $\mathsf{Verify}_0(pk, pk_i, cert_i) = 1$, and that $\mathsf{Verify}_i(pk_i, m, \sigma_i) = 1$. Only if all checks succeed, it returns 1.*

It is straightforward to verify that the above construction is correct in the sense that genuine (fresh and derived) signatures are accepted by Verify. This follows from the correctness properties of the regular scheme and of the P_i-homomorphic ones.

Proposition 2. *Assume that the signature scheme $(\mathsf{KeyGen}_0, \mathsf{Sign}_0, \mathsf{Verify}_0)$ and all P_i-homomorphic schemes are unforgeable according to Definition 2. Then the*

Certify-then-Sign Construction 2 is also unforgeable for the efficient universe $\mathcal{P} = \{P_1, \ldots, P_q\}$ *for the fixed number q of predicates.*

In terms of concrete security, the success probability of any adversary against the construction is (for similar running time) bounded from above by the probability of forging certificates, plus q times the maximal advantage against any of the schemes from $\mathcal{P}$.

Proof. Assume that there exists a successful forger $\mathcal{A}$. Then this adversary is able to forge with non-negligible probability a signature $\sigma^* = (\sigma, pk, cert)$ for a message m such that, in particular, $\mathsf{Verify}_0(pk_0, pk, cert) = 1$. Note that if the probability that $\mathcal{A}$ succeeds and that pk does not match any of the keys pk_i created by the signer for the predicates P_i, was non-negligible, then this would straightforwardly contradict the unforgeability of the certification scheme. Namely, construct an algorithm $\mathcal{A}_0$ against the certification scheme which, on input pk_0, creates the polynomial number of key pairs $(sk_i, pk_i) \leftarrow \mathsf{KeyGen}_i(1^n)$ and asks for signatures $cert_i$ for all pk_i from the signing oracle, and then emulates the attack of $\mathcal{A}$ with the help of the secret keys. If $\mathcal{A}$ eventually outputs $\sigma^* = (\sigma, pk, cert)$, then $\mathcal{A}_0$ returns $pk, cert$ as the forgery attempt.

If the probability that $\mathcal{A}$ would succeed for a fresh pk with non-negligible probability as defined above, then our efficient algorithm $\mathcal{A}_0$, which perfectly simulates the actual attack, would then successfully forge a signature $cert$ for a new "message" pk with non-negligible probability. Since this would contradict the unforgeability of the certification scheme, we can assume that this case happens with negligible probability only. It follows that $\mathcal{A}$ must succeed with non-negligible probability for a key $pk = pk_i$ for some (unique) i, such that $\mathsf{Verify}_i(pk_i, m, \sigma, P_i) = 1$, and the message is not trivially derivable under the corresponding predicate P_i from the signing queries for P_i.

Note that the specific choice pk_i may depend on the adversary's randomness. However, there must exist at least one predicate P_i (among the q schemes) such that $\mathcal{A}$ succeeds for this key fixed pk_i with non-negligible probability. We can now derive an adversary $\mathcal{A}_i$ successfully forging signatures for this P_i-homomorphic scheme. Adversary $\mathcal{A}_i$ receives from the challenger the public key pk_i and gets access to a Sign_i-oracle. It generates (sk_0, pk_0) and all other key pairs (sk_j, pk_j) and signs all of them, including pk_i. The adversary $\mathcal{A}_i$ then runs $\mathcal{A}$ on pk_0, supplying all signatures requests for $P_j \neq P_i$ with the help of the secret keys, and using the external signing oracle for P_i. If $\mathcal{A}$ finally returns m and $(\sigma, pk, cert)$ then $\mathcal{A}_i$ returns m and σ_i.

Note that, if $\mathcal{A}$ has a non-negligible success probability for forging under the key pk_i, then $\mathcal{A}_i$ has the same success probability. This follows as the signature verifies under pk_i, and if the message m is not derivable from $\mathcal{A}$'s queries for P_i, then this is also true for $\mathcal{A}_i$. This, however, would contradict the unforgeability assumption about the P_i-homomorphic scheme. $\square$

Proposition 3. *Assume that all P_i-homomorphic schemes are completely (resp. adaptively) context-hiding according to Definition 3. Then the Certify-*

then-Sign Construction 2 is also completely (resp. adaptively) context-hiding for an efficient universe $\mathcal{P} = \{P_1, P_2, \ldots, P_q\}$ *of a fixed number q of predicates.*

The proof is similarly to the unforgeability case and omitted for space reasons.

Acknowledgments. We thank the anonymous reviewers for comments. Marc Fischlin was supported by a Heisenberg grant Fi 940/3-1 of the German Research Foundation (DFG).

References

1. Ahn, J.H., Boneh, D., Camenisch, J., Hohenberger, S., Shelat, A., Waters, B.: Computing on authenticated data. In: Cramer, R. (ed.) TCC 2012. LNCS, vol. 7194, pp. 1–20. Springer, Heidelberg (2012)
2. Ateniese, G., Chou, D.H., de Medeiros, B., Tsudik, G.: Sanitizable signatures. In: De Capitani di Vimercati, S., Syverson, P.F., Gollmann, D. (eds.) ESORICS 2005. LNCS, vol. 3679, pp. 159–177. Springer, Heidelberg (2005)
3. Attrapadung, N., Libert, B.: Homomorphic network coding signatures in the standard model. In: Catalano, D., Fazio, N., Gennaro, R., Nicolosi, A. (eds.) PKC 2011. LNCS, vol. 6571, pp. 17–34. Springer, Heidelberg (2011)
4. Attrapadung, N., Libert, B., Peters, T.: Computing on authenticated data: New privacy definitions and constructions. In: Wang, X., Sako, K. (eds.) ASIACRYPT 2012. LNCS, vol. 7658, pp. 367–385. Springer, Heidelberg (2012)
5. Bellare, M., Neven, G.: Transitive signatures based on factoring and RSA. In: Zheng, Y. (ed.) ASIACRYPT 2002. LNCS, vol. 2501, pp. 397–414. Springer, Heidelberg (2002)
6. Boneh, D., Freeman, D., Katz, J., Waters, B.: Signing a linear subspace: Signature schemes for network coding. In: Jarecki, S., Tsudik, G. (eds.) PKC 2009. LNCS, vol. 5443, pp. 68–87. Springer, Heidelberg (2009)
7. Boneh, D., Freeman, D.M.: Homomorphic signatures for polynomial functions. In: Paterson, K.G. (ed.) EUROCRYPT 2011. LNCS, vol. 6632, pp. 149–168. Springer, Heidelberg (2011)
8. Boneh, D., Freeman, D.M.: Linearly homomorphic signatures over binary fields and new tools for lattice-based signatures. In: Catalano, D., Fazio, N., Gennaro, R., Nicolosi, A. (eds.) PKC 2011. LNCS, vol. 6571, pp. 1–16. Springer, Heidelberg (2011)
9. Brzuska, C., et al.: Redactable signatures for tree-structured data: Definitions and constructions. In: Zhou, J., Yung, M. (eds.) ACNS 2010. LNCS, vol. 6123, pp. 87–104. Springer, Heidelberg (2010)
10. Camacho, P., Hevia, A.: Short transitive signatures for directed trees. In: Dunkelman, O. (ed.) CT-RSA 2012. LNCS, vol. 7178, pp. 35–50. Springer, Heidelberg (2012)
11. Catalano, D., Fiore, D., Warinschi, B.: Efficient network coding signatures in the standard model. In: Fischlin, M., Buchmann, J., Manulis, M. (eds.) PKC 2012. LNCS, vol. 7293, pp. 680–696. Springer, Heidelberg (2012)
12. Chang, E.-C., Lim, C.L., Xu, J.: Short redactable signatures using random trees. In: Fischlin, M. (ed.) CT-RSA 2009. LNCS, vol. 5473, pp. 133–147. Springer, Heidelberg (2009)

13. Charles, D., Jain, K., Lauter, K.: Signatures for network coding. Int. J. Inf. Coding Theory 1(1), 3–14 (2009)
14. Desmedt, Y.: Computer security by redefining what a computer is. In: Proceedings of the 1992-1993 Workshop on New Security Paradigms, NSPW 1992-1993, pp. 1992–1993. ACM (1993)
15. Freeman, D.M.: Improved security for linearly homomorphic signatures: A generic framework. In: Fischlin, M., Buchmann, J., Manulis, M. (eds.) PKC 2012. LNCS, vol. 7293, pp. 697–714. Springer, Heidelberg (2012)
16. Gennaro, R., Katz, J., Krawczyk, H., Rabin, T.: Secure network coding over the integers. In: Nguyen, P.Q., Pointcheval, D. (eds.) PKC 2010. LNCS, vol. 6056, pp. 142–160. Springer, Heidelberg (2010)
17. Haber, S., Hatano, Y., Honda, Y., Horne, W., Miyazaki, K., Sander, T., Tezoku, S., Yao, D.: Efficient signature schemes supporting redaction, pseudonymization, and data deidentification. In: Abe, M., Gligor, V. (eds.) ASIACCS 2008, pp. 353–362. ACM Press (March 2008)
18. Johnson, R., Walsh, L., Lamb, M.: Homomorphic signatures for digital photographs. In: Danezis, G. (ed.) FC 2011. LNCS, vol. 7035, pp. 141–157. Springer, Heidelberg (2012)
19. Johnson, R., Molnar, D., Song, D., Wagner, D.: Homomorphic signature schemes. In: Preneel, B. (ed.) CT-RSA 2002. LNCS, vol. 2271, pp. 244–262. Springer, Heidelberg (2002)
20. Micali, S., Rivest, R.L.: Transitive signature schemes. In: Preneel, B. (ed.) CT-RSA 2002. LNCS, vol. 2271, pp. 236–243. Springer, Heidelberg (2002)
21. Miyazaki, K., Susaki, S., Iwamura, M., Matsumoto, T., Sasaki, R., Yoshiura, H.: Digital documents sanitizing problem. Technical Report ISEC2003-20. IEICE (2003)
22. Nojima, R., Tamura, J., Kadobayashi, Y., Kikuchi, H.: A storage efficient redactable signature in the standard model. In: Samarati, P., Yung, M., Martinelli, F., Ardagna, C.A. (eds.) ISC 2009. LNCS, vol. 5735, pp. 326–337. Springer, Heidelberg (2009)
23. Shahandashti, S.F., Salmasizadeh, M., Mohajeri, J.: A provably secure short transitive signature scheme from bilinear group pairs. In: Blundo, C., Cimato, S. (eds.) SCN 2004. LNCS, vol. 3352, pp. 60–76. Springer, Heidelberg (2005)
24. Steinfeld, R., Bull, L., Zheng, Y.: Content extraction signatures. In: Kim, K.-c. (ed.) ICISC 2001. LNCS, vol. 2288, pp. 285–304. Springer, Heidelberg (2002)
25. Wang, L., Cao, Z., Zheng, S., Huang, X., Yang, Y.: Transitive signatures from braid groups. In: Srinathan, K., Rangan, C.P., Yung, M. (eds.) INDOCRYPT 2007. LNCS, vol. 4859, pp. 183–196. Springer, Heidelberg (2007)
26. Yi, X.: Directed transitive signature scheme. In: Abe, M. (ed.) CT-RSA 2007. LNCS, vol. 4377, pp. 129–144. Springer, Heidelberg (2006)

Towards Efficient Private Distributed Computation on Unbounded Input Streams*

(Extended Abstract)

Shlomi Dolev[1], Juan Garay[2], Niv Gilboa[3],
Vladimir Kolesnikov[4], and Yelena Yuditsky[1]

[1] Department of Computer Science, Ben Gurion University of the Negev, Israel
{dolev,yuditsky}@cs.bgu.ac.il
[2] AT&T Labs – Research, Florham Park, NJ
garay@research.att.com
[3] Deptartment of Communication Systems Engineering, Ben-Gurion University of the Negev,
Beer-Sheva, Israel
niv.gilboa@gmail.com
[4] Bell Laboratories, Murray Hill, NJ
kolesnikov@research.bell-labs.com

Abstract. In the problem of private "swarm" computing, n agents wish to securely and distributively perform a computation on common inputs, in such a way that even if the entire memory contents of some of them are exposed, no information is revealed about the state of the computation. Recently, Dolev, Garay, Gilboa and Kolesnikov [ICS 2011] considered this problem in the setting of information-theoretic security, showing how to perform such computations on input streams of *unbounded length*. The cost of their solution, however, is exponential in the size of the Finite State Automaton (FSA) computing the function.

In this work we are interested in efficient (i.e., polynomial time) computation in the above model, at the expense of *minimal* additional assumptions. Relying on the existence of one-way functions, we show how to process unbounded inputs (but of course, polynomial in the security parameter) at a cost *linear* in m, the number of FSA states. In particular, our algorithms achieve the following:

- In the case of (n, n)-reconstruction (i.e., in which all n agents participate in the reconstruction of the distributed computation) and at most $n - 1$ agents are corrupted, the agent storage, the time required to process each input symbol, and the time complexity for reconstruction are all $O(mn)$.

- In the case of $(n - t, n)$-reconstruction (where only $n - t$ agents take part in the reconstruction) and at most t agents are corrupted, the agents' storage and time required to process each input symbol are $O(m\binom{n-1}{n-t})$. The complexity of reconstruction is $O(mt)$.

* This research has been supported by the Israeli Ministry of Science and Technology (MOST), the Institute for Future Defense Technologies Research named for the Medvedi, Shwartzman and Gensler Families, the Israel Internet Association (ISOC-IL), the Lynne and William Frankel Center for Computer Science at Ben-Gurion University, Rita Altura Trust Chair in Computer Science, *Israel Science Foundation* (grant number 428/11), Cabarnit Cyber Security MAGNET Consortium, MAFAT and Deutsche Telekom Labs at BGU.

M. Jacobson et al. (Eds.): ACNS 2013, LNCS 7954, pp. 69–83, 2013.

We achieve the above through a carefully orchestrated use of pseudo-random generators and secret-sharing, and in particular a novel share re-randomization technique which might be of independent interest.

1   Introduction

Distributed computing has become an integral part of a variety of systems, including cloud computing and "swarm" computing, where n agents perform a computation on common inputs. In these emerging computing paradigms, security (i.e., privacy and correctness) of the computation is of a primary concern. Indeed, in swarm computing, often considered in military contexts (e.g., unmanned aerial vehicle (UAV) operation), security of the data and program state is of paramount importance; similarly, one persistent challenge in the field of cloud computing is ensuring the privacy of users' data, demanded by government, commercial, and even individual cloud users.

In this work, we revisit the notion of *perennial* private distributed computation, first considered by Dolev, Garay, Gilboa and Kolesnikov [8]. In such a computation, an unbounded sequence of commands (or inputs) are interpreted by several machines (agents) in a way that no information about the inputs as well as the state of the computation is revealed to an adversary who is able to "corrupt" the agents and examine their internal state, as long as up to a predetermined threshold of the machines are corrupted.

Dolev *et al.* were able to provide very strong (unconditional, or information-theoretic) security for computations performed by a finite-state machine (FSA), at the price however of the computation being efficient only for a small set of functions, as in general the complexity of the computation is exponential in the size (number of states) of the FSA computing the function.

In this work, we minimally weaken the original model by additionally assuming the existence of one-way functions (and hence consider polynomial-time adversaries—in the security parameter; more details below), and in return achieve very high efficiency in some cases as a function of the size of the FSA. We stress that we still consider computation on *a priori* unbounded number of inputs, and where the online (input-processing) phase incurs *no communication*. We now describe the model in more detail.

The setting. As in [8], we consider a distributed computation setting in which a party, whom we refer to as *the dealer*, has a finite state automaton (FSA) $\mathcal{A}$ which accepts an (*a priori* unbounded) stream of inputs $x_1, x_2, \ldots$ received from an external source. The dealer delegates the computation to agents $A_1, \ldots, A_n$, by furnishing them with an implementation of $\mathcal{A}$. The agents receive, in a synchronized manner, all the inputs for $\mathcal{A}$ during the online input-processing phase, where no communication whatsoever is allowed. Finally, given a signal from the dealer, the agents terminate the execution, submit their internal state to the dealer, who computes the state of $\mathcal{A}$ and returns it as output.

We consider an attack model where an entity, called the adversary, Adv, is able to adaptively "corrupt" agents (i.e., inspect their internal state) during the online execution phase, up to a threshold[1] $t < n$. We do not aim at maintaining the privacy of the

---

[1] We note that more general access structures may be naturally employed with our constructions.

automaton $\mathcal{A}$; however, we wish to protect the secrecy of the state of $\mathcal{A}$ and the inputs' history. We note that Adv may have external information about the computation, such as partial inputs or length of the input sequence, state information, etc. This auxiliary information, together with the knowledge of $\mathcal{A}$, may exclude the protection of certain configurations, or even fully determine $\mathcal{A}$'s state. We stress that this cannot be avoided in any implementation; thus, our goal is to prevent the leakage or derivation by Adv of any knowledge from seeing the execution traces that Adv did not already possess.

As mentioned above, our constructions relying on one-way functions dictates that the computational power of entities (adversary, agents), be polynomially bounded (in κ, the security parameter). Similarly, our protocols run on input streams of polynomial length. At the same time, we do not impose an *a priori* bound on its length; moreover, the size of the agents' state is independent of it. This allows to use agents of the same (small) complexity (storage and computational power) in all situations.

Our contributions. Our work is the first significant extension of the work of [8]. Towards the goal of making never-ending and private distributed computation practical, we introduce an additional (minimal) assumption of existence of one-way functions (and hence pseudo-random number generators [PRGs]), and propose the following constructions:

- A scheme with (n, n) reconstruction (where all n agents participate in reconstruction), where the storage and processing time per input symbol is $O(mn)$ for each agent. The reconstruction complexity is $O(mn)$.

- A scheme with $(n - t, n)$ reconstruction (where t corrupted agents do not take part in the reconstruction), where the above costs are $O(m\binom{n-1}{n-t})$.[2]

Regarding tools and techniques, the carefully orchestrated use of PRGs and secret-sharing techniques [17] allows our protocols to hide the state of the computation against an adaptive adversary by using share re-randomization. Typically, in the context of secret sharing, this is simply done by the addition of a suitable (i.e., passing through the origin) random polynomial. However, due to the no-communication requirement, share re-randomization is more challenging in our setting, particularly so in the more general case of the $(n - t, n)$-reconstruction protocol. We achieve share re-randomization by sharing PRG seeds among the players in a manner which allows players to achieve sufficient synchronization of their randomness, which is resilient to t corruptions.

Related work. Reflecting a well-known phenomenon in distributed computing, where a single point of failure needs to be avoided, a team of agents (e.g., UAVs) that collaborate in a mission is more robust than a single agent trying to complete a mission by itself (e.g., [1, 3]). Several techniques have been suggested for this purpose; another related line of work is that of automaton splitting and replication, yielding designs that can tolerate faults and as well as provide some form of privacy of the computation (see, e.g., [6–8, 10, 11]). As mentioned above, only [8] addresses the unbounded-input-stream scenario.

---

[2] For some values of t, e.g., $t = O(n)$, this quantity would be exponential in n. This however does not contradict our assumption on the computational power of the participants; rather, it simply means that, given κ, for some values of n and t this protocol cannot be executed in the allowed time.

Recall that in *secure multi-party computation* [2, 4, 13], n parties, some of which might be corrupted, are to compute an n-ary (public) function on their inputs, in such a way that no information is revealed about them beyond what is revealed by the function's output. At a high level, we similarly aim in our context to ensure the correctness and privacy of the distributed computation. However, as explained in [8], our setting is significantly different from that of MPC, and MPC definitions and solutions cannot be directly applied here. The reason is two-fold: MPC protects players *individual* inputs, whereas in our setting the inputs are common to all players. Secondly, and more importantly, MPC operates on inputs of fixed length, which would require an *a priori* estimate on the maximum input size s_{max} and agents' storage linear in s_{max}. While unbounded inputs could be processed, by for example processing them "in blocks," this would require communication during the online phase, which is not allowed in our setting. Refer to [8] for a more detailed discussion on the unbounded inputs setting *vis-à-vis* MPC's.

We note that using recently proposed fully-homomorphic encryption (FHE— [12] and follow-ups) trivially solves the problem we pose, as under FHE the agents can simply compute arbitrary functions. In fact, plain additively homomorphic encryption (e.g., [15]) can be used to encrypt the current state of the FSA and non-interactively update it as computation progresses, in a manner similar to what is described in our constructions (see the high-level intuition in Section 3). We note that, firstly, public-key encryption and, dramatically so, FHE, suffer from orders-of-magnitude computational overhead, as compared to the symmetric-key operations that we rely on. Perhaps more importantly, in this work we aim at minimizing the assumptions needed for efficient unbounded private distributed computation.

Finally, and as mentioned above, the problem of share re-randomization and conversion has been considered in the literature. Related to our setting, Cramer, Damgård and Ishai [5] for example consider the problem of locally converting a secret sharing of a value into another secret sharing of the same value.

Organization of the paper. The remainder of the paper is organized as follows. In Section 2 we present in more detail the model, definitions and building blocks that we use throughout the paper. We dedicate Section 3 to a high-level description of our constructions, while in Section 4 we present them in detail. The full privacy analysis is presented in the full version of the paper [9].

2 Model and Definitions

A *finite-state automaton* (FSA) $\mathcal{A}$ has a finite set of states ST, a finite alphabet Σ, and a transition function $\mu : ST \times \Sigma \longrightarrow ST$. In this work we do not assume an initial state or a terminal state for the automaton, i.e., it may begin its execution from any state and does not necessarily stop.

We already described in the previous section the distributed computation setting— dealer, agents, adversary, and unbounded input stream—under which the FSA is to be executed. In more detail, we assume a *global clock* to which all agents are synchronized. We will assume that no more than one input symbol arrives during any clock tick. By *input stream*, we mean a sequence of input symbols arriving at a certain schedule of clock ticks. Abusing notation, we will sometimes refer to the input without explicit reference to the schedule. (We note that the global clock requirement can in principle be removed if we allow the input schedule to be leaked to Adv.)

We also mentioned that Adv is allowed to corrupt agents as the execution of the protocol proceeds. We consider the so-called *passive* or *semi-honest* adversary model, where corrupted agents can combine their views in order to learn protected information, but are not allowed to deviate from the protocol. Furthermore, each agent can be corrupted only once during an execution. When it does, Adv can view the entire contents of a corrupted agent's memory, but does not obtain any of the global inputs.

Incidentally, we consider event processing by an agent as an *atomic operation*. That is, agents cannot be corrupted during an execution of state update. This is a natural and easily achievable assumption, which allows us to not worry about some tedious details. The computation is then considered to be secure, if any two executions (possibly on different inputs and initial states—defined more formally below) are "similarly" distributed.

This model of security for distributed computation on unbounded input streams was introduced by Dolev *et al.* [8] as the *progressive corruption* model (PCM), allowing Adv to be computationally unbounded, and in particular requiring that the distributions of the two executions (again, more formally defined below) be identical.

In this work we use a variant of PCM, applying the following two weakenings to the PCM definition:

1.   Rather than requiring that the distributions of executions be identical, we require them to be *computationally* indistinguishable. This means that we guarantee security only against polynomial-time-bounded adversaries.

2.   We require indistinguishability of executions for the *same* corruption timeline (and, of course, different input streams). This means that, for example, agent IDs are now allowed to be included in the agents' views. (We use agent IDs in one of our constructions.) We stress that this is not a significant security weakening, as essentially we only allow the adversary to differentiate among the agents' identities; the inputs and current state of the computation remain computationally hidden.

We now present our amended PCM definition. We first formalize the notion of *corruption timeline* and the view of the adversary.

Definition 1. *A corruption timeline ρ is a sequence $\rho = ((A_1, \tau_1), \ldots, (A_k, \tau_k))$, where $A_1, \ldots, A_k$ are the corrupted agents and $\tau_1, \ldots, \tau_k$ ($\tau_1 \leq \ldots \leq \tau_k$) denote the time when the corresponding corruption took place. The* length *of a corruption timeline is $|\rho| = k$.*

We denote by $\mathrm{VIEW}_\rho^\Pi(X, s)$ the probability distribution of the aggregated internal states of corrupted agents at the time of corruption, when executed on input X and initial state s.

Definition 2 (Computational Privacy in the Progressive Corruption Model). *We say that a distributed computation scheme Π is t-private in the Progressive Corruption Model (PCM) if for every two states $s_1, s_2 \in ST$, polynomial-length input streams*

X_1, X_2, and any corruption timeline ρ, $|\rho| \le t$,

$$\text{VIEW}_\rho^\Pi(X_1, s_1) \overset{c}{\approx} \text{VIEW}_\rho^\Pi(X_2, s_2).$$

Here, '$\overset{c}{\approx}$' denotes the computational indistinguishability of two distributions.

Tools and Building Blocks. A pseudo-random generator (PRG) is a function of the form $G : X \to Y$, where X and Y are typically of the form $\{0,1\}^k$ and $\{0,1\}^{k+l}$, respectively, for some positive integers k, l. Recall that PRGs are known to exist based on the existence of one-way functions, and that the security property of a PRG guarantees that it is computationally infeasible to distinguish its output on a value chosen uniformly at random from X from a value chosen uniformly at random from Y (see, e.g., [14]). In our setting, we will further assume that the old values of the PRG seeds are securely erased by the agents upon use and hence are not included in the view of the adversary.

The other basic tool that our protocols make use of is (n, t)-*secret sharing* [17], where, essentially, a secret piece of information is "split" into shares and handed out to a set of n players by a distinguished player called *the dealer*, in such a way that up to a threshold $t < n$ of the players pulling together their shares are not able to learn anything about it, while $t + 1$ are able to reconstruct the secret. We present the specific instantiations of secret sharing as needed in the corresponding sections.

3 Overview of Our Approach

Let $\mathcal{A}$ be a publicly known automaton with m states. We assume that we have some ordering of the states of $\mathcal{A}$, which are denoted by corresponding labels. Every agent stores the description of the automaton. In addition, during the computation, for every state s_j of $\mathcal{A}$, every agent A_i computes and stores its current label ℓ_j^i. As mentioned above, all agents receive a global input stream $\Gamma = \gamma_1, \gamma_2, ...\gamma_i, ...$ and perform computation in synchronized time steps.

At a high level, the main idea behind our constructions is that the state labels will be shares (à la secret sharing [17]) of a secret which identifies the currently active state of $\mathcal{A}$. More specifically, for each of the m automaton states, the n state labels (held by the n agents) will be shares of value 1 if the state is currently active, and shares of 0 otherwise. We will show how the players' local computation on their shares will ensure that this property is maintained throughout the computation on the entire input stream Γ. When the input stream Γ is fully processed (or a stop signal is issued), the agents recover the current state by reconstructing the secrets corresponding to each automaton state. At the same time, shares of the secrets (when not taken all together) reveal no information on the current state of $\mathcal{A}$.

We now present additional high-level details on two variants of the approach above. Recall that we consider the semi-honest adversary model, where corrupted players are not allowed to deviate from the protocol, but combine their views in order to learn protected information.

(n, n)-reconstruction. In this scenario, we require that all n agents participate in the reconstruction of the secret (corrupted players are considered semi-honest and hence honestly provide their computed shares).

At the onset of computation, the shares are initialized using an (n, n) additive secret-sharing scheme, such that the initial state labels are the sharing of 1, and labels of each of the other states are shares of 0. When processing a global input symbol γ, each agent computes a new label for a state s by summing the previous labels of all states s' such that $\mu(s', \gamma) = s$. It is easy to see that, due to the fact that we use additive secret sharing, the newly computed shares will maintain the desired secret-sharing property. Indeed, say that on input symbol γ, u states transition into state s. If all of them were inactive and their labels were shares of 0's, then the newly computed shares will encode a 0 (as the sum of u 0's). Similarly, if one of the u predecessor states was active and its label shared a 1, then the new active state s will also correspond to a share of 1.

A technical problem arises in the case of "empty" states, i.e., those that do not have incoming transitions for symbol γ, and hence their labels are undefined. Indeed, to hide the state of the automaton from the adversary who corrupts agent(s), we need to ensure that each label is a random share of the appropriate secret. Hence, we need to generate a random 0-share for each empty state without communication among the agents.

In the (n, n) sharing and reconstruction scenario, we will non-interactively generate these labels pseudo-randomly as follows. Each pair of agents (A_i, A_j) will be assigned a random PRG seed $seed_{ij}$ Then, at each event (e.g., processing input symbol γ), each agent A_i will pseudo-randomly generate a string r_j using each of the seeds $seed_{ij}$, and set the label of the empty state to be the sum of all strings r_j. This is done for each empty state independently. The PRG seeds are then (deterministically) "evolved" thereby erasing from the agent's view the knowledge of the labels' provenance, and making them all indistinguishable from random. As all agents are synchronized with respect to the input and the shared seeds, it is easy to see that the shares generated this way reconstruct a 0, since each string r_j will be included twice in the total sum, and hence will cancel out (we will use an appropriate [e.g., XOR-based] secret-sharing scheme such that this is ensured.).

Finally, and intuitively, we observe that PCM security will hold since the view of each corrupted agent only includes pseudo-randomly generated labels for each state and the current PRG seed value. As noted above, even when combined with the views of other corrupted players, the labels are still indistinguishable from random.

(n − t, n)-reconstruction. In this scenario, up to t corrupted agents do not take part in the reconstruction (this is motivated by the possibility of agents (UAVs) being captured or destroyed by the adversary). Agents who submit their inputs are doing so correctly. Thus, here we require $n > 2t$.

We will take our (n, n)-reconstruction solution as the basis, and adapt and expand it as follows. First, in order to enable reconstruction with $n - t (= t + 1)$ agents, we will use (n, t) additive secret-sharing (such as Shamir's [17]). Second, as before, we will use a PRG to generate labels, but now we will have a separate seed for each subset of agents of size $n - t + 1$. Then, at each event (e.g., processing of an input symbol), each agent A_i, for each of the groups he belongs to, will update its shares by generating a random (n, t)-secret sharing of a 0 using the randomness generated by applying G to the group's seed. Then, agent A_i will use the share thus generated for the i-th agent as its own, and set the label of the empty state to be the sum of all such shares.

Here we note that, since agents are excluded from some of the groups, and that in this scenario up to t agents might not return their state during reconstruction, special care must be taken in the generation of the re-randomizing polynomials so that all agents have invariantly consistent shares, *even for groups they do not belong to*, and that any set of agents of size $t + 1$ enable the reconstruction of the secrets. (See Section 4.2 for details.) The above is done for each empty state independently. As before, the PRG seeds are then (deterministically) "evolved," making them all indistinguishable from random.

Algorithm 1: Template algorithm for agent A_i, $1 \leq i \leq n$, for label and state update.

Input: An input symbol γ.
Output: New labels for every state.
1: **if** γ is initialized **then**
2:     $\ell^i_j := \sum_{k, \mu(s_k, \gamma) = s_j} \ell^i_k$ (the sum is calculated over some field $\mathbb{F}$, depending on the scheme).
3: **end if**
4: **for** every $T \in \mathcal{T}$ s.t. $A_i \in T$ **do**
5:     Compute $B^T S^T \leftarrow G(seed^T_r)$, where $B^T = b^T_1 b^T_2 ... b^T_m$, and $b^T_j \in \mathbb{F}$, $1 \leq j \leq m$.
6:     $seed^T_{r+1} := S^T$.
7:     **for** $j = 1$ to m **do**
8:         $\ell^i_j := \ell^i_j + R_j$, where R_j is a scheme-specific pseudo-random quantity.
9:     **end for**
10: **end for**

Remark 1. This approach reveals the length and schedule of the input Γ processed by the players. Indeed, the stored seeds (or more precisely, their evolution which is traceable by the adversary simply by corrupting at different times players who share a seed) do reveal to the adversary the number of times the update function has been invoked. We hide this information by requiring the agents to run updates at each clock tick.

Algorithm 1 summarizes the update operations performed by agent A_i ($1 \leq i \leq n$) during the r-th clock cycle. The key point is the generation of R_j, the label re-randomizing quantity. Notice also that in every clock cycle, there may or may not be an input symbol received by the agent; if the agent did not receive any input, we assume that the input symbol is not initialized.

4 The Constructions in Detail

4.1 The (n, n)-Reconstruction Protocol

We start our formalization of the intuition presented above with the case where all n out of the n agents participate in the state reconstruction. The protocol for this case, which we call $\Pi^{(n,n)}$, is presented below.

Protocol $\Pi^{(n,n)}$. The protocol consists of three phases:

Initialization. The dealer secret-shares among the agents a secret value for each state, such that the value for the initial state is 1 and for all the other states is 0. This is done as follows. Agent A_i ($1 \le i \le n$) is given a a random binary string $x_1^i x_2^i ... x_m^i$, with the constraints that

$$x_{init}^1 + x_{init}^2 + ... + x_{init}^n \equiv 1 \bmod 2,$$

where *init* is the index of the initial state of the computation, and for every $1 \le j \ne init \le m$,

$$x_j^1 + x_j^2 + ... + x_j^n \equiv 0 \bmod 2.$$

Each agent then proceeds to assign its state labels as $\ell_j^i \leftarrow x_j^i$.

Event Processing. Each agent runs Algorithm 1, updating its labels and computing the new seeds for the PRG. Let $\mathcal{T}$ be the set of all possible agents' pairs. For line 8 of Algorithm 1, each agent A_i now computes

$$R_j = \sum_{T \in \mathcal{T}, A_i \in T} (b_j^T)_r.$$

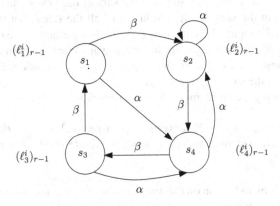

Fig. 1. *The internal state of agent A_i before a transition*

Reconstruction. All agents submit their internal states to the dealer, who reconstructs the secrets corresponding to each state, by adding (mod 2) the shares of each state, and determines and outputs the currently active state (the one whose reconstructed secret is 1).

Before proving the correctness and privacy achieved by the protocol, we illustrate the operation of the online (Event Processing) phase with the following example; refer to Figures 1 and 2. The two figures describe the execution of the protocol on an automaton with four states and two possible inputs. Figure 1 presents the internal state of agent A_i

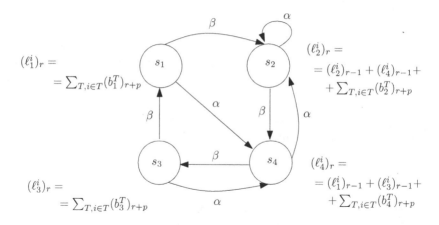

Fig. 2. *The internal state of agent A_i after an α transition*

after the $(r-1)$-th clock cycle. The agent holds the original automaton and has a label for each of the four states, $(\ell_1^i)_{r-1}$, $(\ell_2^i)_{r-1}$, $(\ell_3^i)_{r-1}$ and $(\ell_4^i)_{r-1}$.

Figure 2 shows the changes in the agent's internal state compared to Figure 1 after the r-th clock cycle. We also assume that in this clock cycle the agents receive an input symbol α. The new labels for each state are the sum of old labels and pseudo-random values. The labels in the sum are the old labels of all the states that transition to the current state given the input. Thus, the new $(\ell_2^i)_r$ includes a sum of the old $(\ell_2^i)_{r-1}$ and the old $(\ell_4^i)_{r-1}$, while the new $(\ell_3^i)_r$ doesn't include any labels in its sum because there is no state that transitions to s_3 after an α input. The pseudo-random addition to each state $j = 1, \ldots, 4$ is the sum $\sum_{T, i \in T}(b_j^T)_r$.

We start by proving the correctness of the construction.

Proposition 1. *At every Event Processing step of protocol $\Pi^{(n,n)}$, the secret corresponding to the current state in the computation is 1 and for all other states the secret is 0.*

Proof. The proof is by induction on the number of steps r that the automaton performs, i.e., the number of clock cycles.

For the base case, if we consider the state of the protocol after the initialization step and before the first clock cycle, i.e., at $r = 0$, then the statement is true by our definition of the label assignments. Let us first consider the case where at the r-th step an input symbol γ_r from Γ is received. Following the protocol, agent A_i's new label for state j becomes

$$\ell_j^i \longleftarrow \sum_{\substack{k\,:\\ \mu(s_k, \gamma_r) = s_j}} \ell_k^i + \sum_{A_i \in T}(b_j^T)_r.$$

Consider now the next state of the computation in the automaton; we wish to show that the secret corresponding to that state will be 1. Let $curr$ be the index of the current state of the automaton, and $next$ be the index corresponding to the next state; by definition,

$\mu(s_{curr}, \gamma_r) = s_{next}$. Then,

$$\ell^i_{next} \longleftarrow \sum_{\substack{k\,:\\ \mu(s_k,\gamma_r)=s_{next}}} \ell^i_k =$$

$$\ell^i_{curr} + \sum_{\substack{k \neq curr\,:\\ \mu(s_k,\gamma_r)=s_{next}}} \ell^i_k + \sum_{i \in T}(b^T_j)_r.$$

By the induction hypothesis, we know that

$$\sum_{i=0}^n \ell^i_{curr} \equiv 1 \pmod 2$$

and for $k \neq curr$,

$$\sum_{i=0}^n \ell^i_k \equiv 0 \pmod 2.$$

Thus, if we sum over all the agents:

$$\sum_{i=0}^n \left(\ell^i_{curr} + \sum_{\substack{k \neq curr\,:\\ \mu(s_k,\gamma_r)=s_{next}}} \ell^i_k + \sum_{i \in T}(b^T_j)_r \right)$$

$$= \sum_{i=0}^n \ell^i_{curr} + \sum_{\substack{k \neq curr\,:\\ \mu(s_k,\gamma_r)=s_{next}}} \sum_{i=0}^n \ell^i_k$$

$$+ \sum_{i=0}^n \sum_{i \in T}(b^T_j)_r \equiv 1 + 0 \equiv 1 \pmod 2.$$

This is because in $\sum_{i=1}^n \sum_{i \in T}(b^T_j)_r$, every $(b^T_j)_r$ appears exactly twice in this sum, once for every element in T. Using similar arguments one can see that all the other states will resolve to 0.

In the case that in the r-th step no input symbol is received, due to the fact that we just add the random strings in the same way as in the case above, we again get that the secret corresponding to the current state of the computation is 1, and for all others is 0. □

Proposition 2. *Protocol $\Pi^{(n,n)}$ is $(n-1)$-private in the PCM model according to Definition 2.*

Proof (sketch). Recall that the underlying observation is that when a corruption takes place (which cannot happen during the label-update procedure), the agent's state includes the current labels and PRG seeds which have already been evolved, and hence cannot be correlated with the label shares previously generated.

Without loss of generality, consider the case where Adv corrupts all but one agent according to an arbitrary corruption timeline, and assume, say, agent A_1 is not corrupted. We argue that the view of the adversary is indistinguishable from a view corresponding to (randomly) initialized agents $A_2, ..., A_n$ on the given automaton and any initial state. In other words, the view of the adversary is indistinguishable from the view he would obtain if he corrupted the agents simultaneously and before any input was processed. Once we prove that, the proposition follows.

The view of each corrupted agent includes $n - 1$ seeds that he shares with other agents and the FSA labels which are secret shares of 0 or a 1. We argue that, from the point of view of the adversary, these labels are *random* shares of either 0 or 1. This follows from the PRG property that an evolved seed cannot be correlated with a prior output of the PRG, and from the fact that A_1 remains uncorrupted. Indeed, the newly generated "empty" states' labels look random since the adversary cannot link them to the PRG seeds in his view. The other states' labels look random to the adversary since they are XORed with A_1's label.

Thus, the total view of the adversary consists of random shares of 0 and 1, and is hence indistinguishable from the one corresponding to the initial state.   □

We now calculate the time and storage complexity of $\Pi^{(n,n)}$. At every step of the computation, each agent pseudo-randomly generates and XORs $n - 1$ strings. Further, each agent holds a small constant-length label for each automaton state, and $n - 1$ PRG seeds, yielding an $O(m + n)$ memory requirement.

4.2   The $(n - t, n)$-Reconstruction Protocol

Recall that in this case, up to t of the agents might not take part in the reconstruction, and thus $n > 2t$.

A straightforward (albeit costly) solution to this scenario would be to execute $\Pi^{(n,n)}$ independently for every subset of agents of size $t + 1$ (assuming for simplicity $n = 2t + 1$). This would involve each agent A_i holding $\binom{n-1}{t}$ copies of the automaton $\mathcal{A}$, one copy for each such subset which includes A_i, and updating them all, as in $\Pi^{(n,n)}$, according to the same input symbol. Now, during the reconstruction, the dealer can recover the output from any subset of $t + 1$ agents. The cost of this approach would be as follows. Every agent holds $\binom{n-1}{t}$ automata (one for every $t+1$ tuple that includes this agent), and executes $\Pi^{(n,n)}$, which requires $O(m + t)$ memory, resulting in a total cost of $O\left(\binom{n-1}{t} \cdot (m+t)\right)$, with the cost of computation per input symbol being proportional to storage's. In the sequel, we will refer to this approach as $\Pi_{\text{naive}}^{(n-t,n)}$.

We now present $\Pi^{(n-t,n)}$, an improved $(n - t, n)$ reconstruction scheme, whose intuition was already presented in Section 3. The protocol uses Shamir's secret-sharing scheme [17], which we now briefly review. Let $\mathbb{F}$ be a field of size greater than n, and $s \in \mathbb{F}$ be the secret. The dealer randomly generates coefficients $c_1, c_2, ..., c_t$ from $\mathbb{F}$ and construct the following polynomial of degree t, $f(x) = s + c_1 x + c_2 x^2 + ... + c_t x^t$. The dealer gives each participant $A_i, 1 \leq i \leq n$, the value $f(i)$. It can be easily seen that one can reconstruct the secret from any subset of at least $t + 1$ points, and no information about the secret is revealed by t points (or less).

Protocol $\Pi^{(n-t,n)}$. As before, the protocol consists of three phases:

Initialization. Using Shamir's secret sharing as described above, the dealer shares a secret 1 for the initial state and 0 for all other states. In addition, the dealer generates a random seed for every set of $n - (t - 1) = n - t + 1$ agents, and gives each agent the seeds for the sets it belongs to. Let $\mathcal{T}$ be the set of all possible subsets of $n - t + 1$ agents.

Event Processing. Each agent runs Algorithm 1 updating its labels, as follows.

Let $T \in \mathcal{T}$ and j, $1 \le j \le m$, be a state of the automaton. Upon obtaining value b_j^T (refer to Algorithm 1), the agents in T (individually) construct a degree-t polynomial, P_j^T, by defining its value on the following $t + 1$ field points: 0, all the points i such that $A_i \notin T$, and k such that k is the minimal agent's index in T (the choice of which point in T is arbitrary). Now define $P_j^T(0) = 0$, $P_j^T(i) = 0 \ \forall A_i \notin T$, and $P_j^T(k) = b_j^T$.

Observe that by this definition, *every* agent $A_i \in T$ can use polynomial interpolation to compute $P_j^T(i)$, since the only required information is b_j^T (and the knowledge of set membership).

Let polynomial P_j be defined as $P_j = \sum_{T \in \mathcal{T}} P_j^T$. Each agent A_i now computes $P_j(i)$ (note that this is possible since the values corresponding to sets the agent does not belong to is set to 0), and updates the j-th label, $1 \le j \le m$, in Algorithm 1 by setting $R_j = P_j(i)$ in line 8.

Reconstruction. At least $t + 1$ agents submit their internal state to the dealer, who, for every $j = 1, \ldots, m$, views the j-th labels of $t + 1$ agents as shares in a Shamir secret-sharing scheme. The dealer reconstructs all the m secrets using the scheme's reconstruction procedure, and determines and outputs the currently active state (whose recovered secret is equal to 1).

Proposition 3. *At every Event Processing step of protocol* $\Pi^{(n-t,n)}$, *the shared secret for the current state in the computation is 1 and for all the other (inactive) states, the shared secret is 0. Furthermore, $t + 1$ agents can jointly reconstruct all secrets.*

Proof. We prove the proposition by induction on the number of clock cycles r. We show that at each clock cycle r, for every state s_j, the n labels $\ell_j^1, \ldots, \ell_j^n$ are points on a degree t polynomial Q_j whose free coefficient is 1 if j is the current state and 0 otherwise.

At initialization, the claim is true by our definition of the label assignments.

Assume that the induction hypothesis is correct after $r - 1$. We prove the hypothesis for the r-th step. Assume first that in this step the agents receive an input letter γ_r, and denote the current state by s_{curr}. By our definition, the new label of the state j of agent i is

$$\ell_j^i \longleftarrow \sum_{\substack{k \ : \\ \mu(s_k, \gamma_r) = s_j}} \ell_k^i + P_j(i),$$

or, equivalently,

$$\ell_j^i \longleftarrow \sum_{\substack{k \ : \\ \mu(s_k, \gamma_r) = s_j}} Q_k(i) + P_j(i).$$

For every $j, 1 \le j \le m$, define polynomial Q'_j as

$$Q'_j = \sum_{\substack{k:\\ \mu(s_k, \gamma_r)=s_j}} Q_k + P_j.$$

Therefore, $Q'_j(i) = \ell^i_j$ for every j and every i. In addition, since every Q_k is of degree t and so is P_j, we deduce that Q'_j is also of degree t. We finish proving the induction step by showing that $Q'_j(0) = 1$ only for the correct state.

Let $\mu(s_{curr}, \gamma_r) = s_{next}$. By induction, $Q_{curr}(0) = 1$ and $Q_j(0) = 0$ for any $j \ne curr$. Furthermore, by construction $P_j(0) = 0$, and therefore $Q'_{curr}(0) = 1$. Since $Q_j(0) = 0$ for any $j \ne curr$, we have that $Q'_j(0) = 0$ for any $j \ne next$.

If the agents do not receive any input symbol in the r-th clock cycle, then the claim follows by similar arguments as above.   □

Proposition 4. $\Pi^{(n-t,n)}$ *is t-private in the PCM model according to Definition 2.*

At a high level, the proof follows the steps of the proof of Proposition 2. The full details of the privacy analysis are presented in the full version of the paper [9].

We now calculate the costs incurred by the protocol. The space complexity of each agent is as follows. An agent holds a label for every state, i.e. $m \cdot (\lceil log|\mathbb{F}| \rceil + 1)$ bits. Additionally every agent holds $\binom{n-1}{n-t} = \binom{n-1}{t-1}$ seeds, where every seed is of size len. Thus, in total we have $\binom{n-1}{t-1} \cdot len + m \cdot (\lceil log|\mathbb{F}| \rceil + 1)$ bits. Each step of the Event Processing phase requires $O(m\binom{n-1}{t-1})$ time for seed manipulation and field operations. Reconstruction (by the dealer) is just interpolation of m polynomials of degree t.

References

1. Ben-Shahar, O., Dolev, S., Dolgin, A., Segal, M.: Direction Election in Flocking Swarms. In: Proc. of the DIALM-POMC Joint Workshop on Foundations of Mobile Computing, pp. 73–80 (2010)
2. Ben-Or, M., Goldwasser, S., Wigderson, A.: Completeness theorems for non-cryptographic fault-tolerant distributed computation. In: Proc. 20th STOC, pp. 1–10 (1988)
3. Bamberger Jr., R., Watson, D., Scheidt, D., Moore, K.: Flight Demonstrations of Unmanned Aerial Vehicle Swarming Concepts. Johns Hopkins APL Technical Digest 27(1), 41–55 (2006)
4. Chaum, D., Crépeau, C., Damgård, I.: Multiparty unconditionally secure protocols. In: Proc. 20th STOC, pp. 11–19 (1988)
5. Cramer, R., Damgård, I., Ishai, Y.: Share Conversion, Pseudorandom Secret-Sharing and Applications to Secure Computation. In: Kilian, J. (ed.) TCC 2005. LNCS, vol. 3378, pp. 342–362. Springer, Heidelberg (2005)
6. Dolev, S., Gilboa, N., Kopeetsky, M., Persiano, G., Spirakis, P.: Information Security for Sensors by Overwhelming Random Sequences and Permutations. In: Proc. of the DIALM-POMC Joint Workshop on Foundations of Mobile Computing (2010)
7. Dolev, S., Garay, J., Gilboa, N., Kolesnikov, V.: Swarming Secrets. In: 47th Annual Allerton Conference on Communication, Control, and Computing (2009)
8. Dolev, S., Garay, J., Gilboa, N., Kolesnikov, V.: Secret Sharing Krohn-Rhodes: Private and Perennial Distributed Computation. In: Innovations in Computer Science (ICS), pp. 32–44 (2011)

9. Dolev, S., Garay, J., Gilboa, N., Kolesnikov, V., Yuditsky, Y.: Towards Efficient Private Distributed Computation on Unbounded Input Streams, Cryptology ePrint Archive, Report 2013/220

10. Dolev, S., Kopeetsky, M., Shamir, A.: RFID Authentication Efficient Proactive Information Security within Computational Security. Theory Comput. Syst. 48(1), 132–149 (2011)

11. Dolev, S., Lahiani, L., Yung, M.: Secret Swarm Unit Reactive k-Secret Sharing. Ad Hoc Networks 10(7), 1291–1305 (2012)

12. Gentry, C.: Fully homomorphic encryption using ideal lattices. In: Proc. 41st STOC, pp. 169–178 (2009)

13. Goldreich, O., Micali, S., Wigderson, A.: How to play any mental game or a completeness theorem for protocols with honest majority. In: Proc. 19th STOC, pp. 218–229 (1987)

14. Goldreich, O.: Foundations of Cryptography: Basic Tools. Cambridge University Press (2000)

15. Paillier, P.: Public-Key Cryptosystems Based on Composite Degree Residuosity Classes. In: Stern, J. (ed.) EUROCRYPT 1999. LNCS, vol. 1592, pp. 223–238. Springer, Heidelberg (1999)

16. Pfitzmann, B., Waidner, M.: Composition and integrity preservation of secure reactive systems. In: Proc. of the 7th ACM conference on Computer and Communications Security (CCS), pp. 245–254 (2000)

17. Shamir, A.: How to Share a Secret. Communications of the ACM 22(11), 612–613 (1979)

From Oblivious AES to Efficient and Secure Database Join in the Multiparty Setting[*]

Sven Laur[2,3], Riivo Talviste[1,2], and Jan Willemson[1,3]

[1] Cybernetica, Ülikooli 2, Tartu, Estonia
[2] Institute of Computer Science, University of Tartu, Liivi 2, Tartu, Estonia
[3] Software Technology and Applications Competence Center, Ülikooli 2, Tartu, Estonia

Abstract. AES block cipher is an important cryptographic primitive with many applications. In this work, we describe how to efficiently implement the AES-128 block cipher in the multiparty setting where the key and the plaintext are both in a secret-shared form. In particular, we study several approaches for AES S-box substitution based on oblivious table lookup and circuit evaluation. Given this secure AES implementation, we build a universally composable database join operation for secret shared tables. The resulting protocol scales almost linearly with the database size and can join medium sized databases with 100,000 rows in few minutes, which makes many privacy-preserving data mining algorithms feasible in practice. All the practical implementations and performance measurements are done on the SHAREMIND secure multiparty computation platform.

1 Introduction

Many information systems need to store and process private data. Encryption is one of the best ways to assure confidentiality, as it is impossible to learn anything from encrypted data without knowledge of the private key. However, the number of processing steps one can carry out on encrypted data is rather limited unless we use fully homomorphic encryption. Unfortunately, such encryption schemes are far from being practical even for moderate-sized data sets [21].

Another compelling alternative is share-computing, since it assures data confidentiality and provides a way to compute on secret shared data, which is several magnitudes more efficient than fully homomorphic encryption. In this setting, data is securely shared among several parties so that individual parties learn

---

[*] This research was supported by the ERDF through EXCS and STACC; the ESF Doctoral Studies and Internationalisation Programme DoRa and by Estonian institutional research grant IUT2-1.

This research was, in part, funded by the U.S. Government. The views and conclusions contained in this document are those of the authors and should not be interpreted as representing the official policies, either expressed or implied, of the U.S. Government. Distribution Statement A (Approved for Public Release, Distribution Unlimited).

M. Jacobson et al. (Eds.): ACNS 2013, LNCS 7954, pp. 84–101, 2013.
© Springer-Verlag Berlin Heidelberg 2013

nothing about shared values during the computations and the final publication of output shares reveals only the desired output(s). For most share-computing systems, even a coalition of parties cannot learn anything about private data unless the size of a coalition is over a threshold.

Development and implementation of such multi-party computing platforms is an active research area. FairPlayMP [5], SecureSCM [2], SEPIA [13], SHARE-MIND [8], VMCrypt [31] and TASTY [24] computing platforms represent only some of the most efficient implementations and share-computing has been successfully applied to real-world settings [10,9].

Note that various database operations are particularly important in privacy-preserving data processing. Efficient and secure protocols for most key operations on secret-shared databases are already known, see [30]. The most notable operation still missing is database join based on secret-shared key columns. This operation can be used e.g. for combining customer data coming from different organisations or linking the results of statistical polls into a single dataset.

Our main theoretical contribution is an efficient multi-party protocol for database join, which combines oblivious shuffle with pseudorandom function evaluation on secret-shared data. In practice, we instantiate the pseudorandom function with the AES-128 block cipher and implement it on the SHAREMIND platform [8]. The latter is a non-trivial task, since the input and the secret key are secret-shared in this context. The resulting AES-evaluation protocol is interesting in its own right. First, AES is becoming a standard performance benchmark for share-computing platforms [18,25,34,28] and thus we can directly compare how well the implementation on the SHAREMIND platform does. Second, a secret-shared version of AES can be used to reduce security requirements put onto the key management of symmetric encryption [18]. In brief, we can emulate trusted hardware encryption in the cloud by sharing a secret key among several servers.

2 Preliminaries

AES. Advanced Encryption Standard (AES) is a symmetric block cipher approved by the National Institute of Standards and Technology [32]. AES takes a 128-bit block of plaintext and outputs 128 bits of corresponding ciphertext. AES can use cipher keys with lengths of 128, 192 or 256 bits. In our work we will only use AES-128, which denotes AES with 128-bit keys.

Sharemind Platform. SHAREMIND platform is a practical and secure share-computing framework for privacy-preserving computations [8], where the private data is shared among three parties referred to as *miners*. In its original implementation, SHAREMIND uses additive secret sharing on 32-bit integers, i.e., a secret s is split into three shares s_1, s_2, s_3 such that $s = s_1 + s_2 + s_3 \bmod 2^{32}$. In this work, we use bitwise sharing where the secret can be reconstructed by XOR-ing individual shares: $s = s_1 \oplus s_2 \oplus s_3$.

The current SHAREMIND implementation is guaranteed to be secure only if the adversary can observe the internal state of a single miner node. Thus, we report performance results only for the *semi-honest setting*. Additionally, we show how to generalise our approach to malicious setting. The latter is rather straightforward, as all protocols are based only on secure addition and multiplication protocols. Although the bitwise sharing alone is not secure against *malicious corruption*, shared message authentication codes can be used to guarantee integrity of secret sharings throughout the computations [19,33].

Security Definitions and Proofs. We use standard security definitions based on ideal versus real world paradigm. In brief, security is defined by comparing a real protocol with an ideal implementation where a trusted third party privately collects all inputs, does all computations and distributes outputs to corresponding parties. We say that a protocol is secure if any plausible attack against real protocol can be converted to an attack against ideal protocol such that both attacks have comparable resource consumption and roughly the same success rate, see standard treatments [22,14,15] for further details.

A canonical security proof uses a wrapper (*simulator*) to link a real world adversary with the ideal world execution model. More precisely, the simulator has to correctly fake missing protocol messages and communicate with the trusted party. As most protocols are modularly built from sub-protocols, security proofs can be further compacted. Namely, if all sub-protocols are *universally composable*, then we can prove the security in the hybrid model where executions of all sub-protocols are replaced with ideal implementations [15].

Since almost all share-computing platforms including SHAREMIND provide universally composable data manipulation operations, we use this composability theorem to omit unnecessary details from security proofs (see also [8]).

Efficiency Metrics in Protocol Design. Real-life efficiency of a protocol execution depends on the number of rounds and the total amount of messages sent over communication channels. The actual dependency is too complicated to analyse directly. Hence, we consider two important sub-cases. When the total communication is small compared to channel bandwidths, then the running time depends linearly on the number of rounds. If the opposite holds, then running time depends linearly on the communication complexity.

3   Share-Computing Protocol for AES Block Cipher

The overall structure of our protocol follows the standard AES algorithm specification [32]. However, there are some important differences stemming from the fact that the secret key and the message is bitwise secret shared and we have to use share-computing techniques. Fortunately, three out of four sub-operations are linear and thus can be implemented by doing local share manipulations. The efficiency of the AES protocol implementation is determined by SubWord() and SubBytes() operations that evaluate the S-box on secret-shared data. The SubWord() function used in key expansion applies the S-box independently to each byte of its input word. Similarly, the SubBytes() function uses the S-box independently on each byte of the 4-word state given as the argument.

3.1 S-Box Evaluation Protocol Based on Oblivious Selection

As the AES S-box is a non-linear one-to-one mapping of byte values, it can be implemented as 256 element lookup table. In our setting, the input of the S-box is secret shared and we need oblivious array selection to get the shares of the right table entry. The latter can be achieved by using various techniques from [30]. First, we must convert the input x into a zero-one index vector z where all entries, except one, are zeros. The non-zero vector element z_x corresponds to the entry in the S-box array that we want to pick as the output. More precisely, let $x_7x_6\ldots x_0$ be the bit-representation of the input x and $i_7i_6\ldots i_0$ be the bit-representation of an index i. Then $z_i = [x_7 = i_7] \wedge \cdots \wedge [x_0 = i_0]$ and the shares of index vector z can be computed by evaluating multinomials

$$z_i = (x_7 \oplus i_7 \oplus 1) \cdots (x_0 \oplus i_0 \oplus 1) \ . \tag{1}$$

For example, the first entry can be computed as $z_0 = (1 \oplus x_7)(1 \oplus x_6)\ldots(1 \oplus x_0)$ and the second entry as $z_1 = (1 \oplus x_7)(1 \oplus x_6)\ldots(1 \oplus x_1)x_0$.

Note that each multinomial z_i is of of degree 8 and thus 1792 secure multiplications over $\mathbb{F}_2$ are needed. To reduce the number of communication rounds, we gather terms $b_{ij} = x_j \oplus i_j \oplus 1$ into eight 256 element vectors:

$$\boldsymbol{b}_7 = (b_{0,7},\ldots,b_{255,7}),\ldots,\boldsymbol{b}_0 = (b_{0,0},\ldots,b_{255,0})$$

and use vectorised bitwise multiplications to multiply all eight terms in the same row. If we do them sequentially, then the computation of index vector requires seven multiplication rounds. With tree-style evaluation strategy we can reduce the number of multiplication rounds to three. For that, we must evaluate same level brackets in parallel for $z = ((\boldsymbol{b}_7 \cdot \boldsymbol{b}_6) \cdot (\boldsymbol{b}_5 \cdot \boldsymbol{b}_4)) \cdot ((\boldsymbol{b}_3 \cdot \boldsymbol{b}_2) \cdot (\boldsymbol{b}_1 \cdot \boldsymbol{b}_0))$. The multiplicative complexity of this step can be further decreased by utilising the underlying recursive structure of the index vector, as proposed by Launchbury et al. [28]. For comparison, we also reimplemented their solution.

As the second step, we must compute scalar product between the indicator vector z and 256-element output table y of the S-box. As elements of y are 8-bit long whereas elements of z are from $\mathbb{F}_2$, we must select output bits one by one. Let $\boldsymbol{y}_j = (y_{0,j},\ldots,y_{255,j})$ denote the vector of jth bits in the output table y. Then the jth output bit f_j of the S-box can be computed as

$$f_j = \langle \boldsymbol{z}, \boldsymbol{y}_j \rangle = \sum_{i=0}^{255} z_i \, y_{ij} \tag{2}$$

over $\mathbb{F}_2$. Since the output table y is public, all operations can be done locally and the second step does not contribute to the communication complexity.

3.2 S-Box Evaluation Protocol Based on Circuit Evaluation

The oblivious indexing as a generic approach is bound to provide a protocol with sub-optimal multiplication complexity, as the two stage evaluation of output bits f_j forces us to compute terms z_i that are dropped in the equation (2).

We can address this issue by secure computation techniques based on branching programs [26]. For that, we must convert the expression for f_j into a binary decision diagram $\mathcal{B}$ with minimal number of decision nodes. After that we must build a corresponding arithmetic circuit that evaluates $\mathcal{B}$ in bottom-up manner. As each decision node introduces two secure multiplications, the efficiency of the resulting protocol is determined by the shape of $\mathcal{B}$. Let c denote the total number of decision nodes and d denote the longest path in $\mathcal{B}$. Then the resulting protocol consists of $2c$ secure multiplication operations over $\mathbb{F}_2$, which can be arranged into d rounds of parallel multiplications.

Although this approach produces significant gains, we can use recent findings in hardware optimisation to boost efficiency further. Circuit minimisation for the AES S-box is a widely studied problem in the hardware design with many known results. In this work, we use the designs by Boyar and Peralta [11,12]. Note that their aim was to minimise the total number of gates and the overall circuit depth, while we need a circuit with minimal number of multiplication gates (AND operations) and with paths that contain as few multiplications as possible, i.e., have a low multiplicative depth. Hence, their best design with 128 gates is not the best for our purposes, as it contains 34 multiplications and its multiplicative depth is 4, while their older design [11] contains 32 multiplication and has a multiplicative circuit depth 6. Of course, the multiplicative depth plays also important role in the protocol, when the bandwidth is high, hence, the newer design might have advantages when only a few AES evaluations are performed.

As extended versions of both articles contain straight-line C-like programs for their circuits, it is straightforward to implement the corresponding secure evaluation protocol with a minor technical tweak. As byte is the smallest data unit supported by network communication libraries, entire byte is used to send elements of $\mathbb{F}_2$ over the network during a secure multiplication protocol. We can eliminate this bloat by doing eight multiplications in parallel, since eight individual values can be packed into the same byte.

It is straightforward to achieve this grouping for the SubBytes() function, as it evaluates 16 S-boxes in parallel. Consequently, if we treat original variables as 16-element bit-vectors, we can evaluate all 16 copies of the original circuit in parallel without altering the straight-line program. For the SubWord() function, additional regrouping is necessary, as it evaluates only four S-boxes in parallel. It is sufficient if we must split all multiplications into pairs that can be executed simultaneously so that we can do eight multiplications in parallel.

3.3 Security Analysis for the Entire Protocol

Note that all three versions of the AES S-box evaluation algorithms are arithmetic circuits consisting of addition and multiplication gates. Hence, it is straightforward to prove the following result.

Theorem 1. *If a share-computing framework provides universally composable protocols for bitwise addition, bitwise multiplication and bit decomposition, then all three AES S-box implementations are universally composable. Any universally composable AES S-box implementation gives a rise to a universally composable share-computing protocol for the AES block cipher.*

Proof. The proof follows directly from the universal composability theorem as we use share-computing protocols to evaluate arithmetic circuits. $\square$

Note that this result holds for any corruption model including the SHAREMIND framework, which provides security against one-out-three static passive corruption. To get security against active corruption, the underlying secret sharing scheme must support both bitwise addition and multiplication while being verifiable. There are two principal ways to achieve this.

First, we can embed elements of $\mathbb{F}_2$ into some larger finite field $\mathbb{F}_{2^t}$ with extension element α and then use standard verifiable secret sharing schemes which support secure multiplication over $\mathbb{F}_{2^t}$. On top of that it is rather straightforward to implement universally composable bit decomposition [17], which splits a secret $x \in \mathbb{F}_{2^t}$ into a vector of shared secrets $x_{t-1}, \ldots, x_0$ such that $x = x_{t-1}\alpha^{t-1} + \cdots x_1\alpha + x_0$. As a consequence, all three assumptions of Theorem 1 are satisfied and we get a secure protocol for evaluating AES. However, there is a significant slowdown in the communication due to prolonged shares.

Alternatively, we can use oblivious message authentication [19] to protect individual bits without extending shares. However, this step attaches a long secret shared authentication code to each bit. To avoid slowdown, we can authenticate long bit vectors with a singe authentication code. The latter fits nicely into the picture, as we have to evaluate 16 circuits in parallel.

3.4 Further Tweaks of the AES Evaluation Protocol

Block ciphers are often used to encrypt many messages under the same secret key. In such settings, it is advantageous to encrypt several messages in parallel in order to reduce the number of communication rounds. The latter is straightforward in the SHAREMIND platform, as it naturally supports parallel operations with vectors. The corresponding vectorised AES protocol takes in a vector of plaintext shares and a vector of shared keys and outputs a vector of cipher text shares. As another efficiency tweak note that we need to execute that key scheduling only once if the secret key is fixed during the encryption. Hence,we can run the key scheduling protocol separately and store the resulting shares of all 128-bit round keys for later use. The corresponding separation of pre-processing and online phases decreases amortised complexity by a fair margin.

3.5 Efficiency Metrics and Real-Life Performance

Having established essentially four methods with very different complexity parameters, we need to compare their real-life performance. For that we have implemented four versions of SubBytes() routines on the SHAREMIND platform

Table 1. Performance results of various S-box evaluation algorithms

Protocol	Multiplicative depth	Running time (1 evaluation)	Multiplicative complexity	Running time (4096 evaluations)
ObSel	3	32.5 ms	1792	9051 ms
Lddam	3	**31.1** ms	304	1109 ms
BCirc-1	6	69.6 ms	32	148 ms
BCirc-2	4	40.8 ms	34	**127** ms

and measured the actual performance. The tests were done on a cluster where each of the three SHAREMIND miners was deployed in a separate machine. The computers in the cluster were connected by an ethernet local area network with link speed of 1 Gbps. Each computer in the cluster had 48 GB of RAM and a 12-core 3 GHz CPU with Hyper Threading. The channels between the computers were also encrypted using 256-bit elliptic curve key agreement and the ChaCha stream cipher [7] provided by the underlying RakNet networking library [1]. While the choice of ChaCha is not standard, the best known attacks against it are still infeasible in practice [4].

We considered algorithms in two different settings. First, we measured the time needed to complete a single evaluation of SubBytes() function. Second, we measured how much time does it take to evaluate 4096 SubBytes() calls in parallel. The first setting corresponds to the case where various delays have dominant impact on the running-time, whereas the effect of communication complexity dominates in the second case. Table 1 compares theoretical indicators[1] and practical performance for all four protocols. The ObSel protocol is based on oblivious selection vector and Lddam is the same protocol with reduced number of multiplications [28]. Protocols based on Boolean circuits designed by Boyar and Peralta are denoted by BCirc-1, BCirc-2.

The results clearly show that multiplicative depth and complexity are good theoretical performance measures for optimising the structure of arithmetic circuits, as they allow us to predict the running times with $10 - 20\%$ precision. Each communication round costs $10 - 12$ ms in single operation mode and each multiplication operation adds $3.5 - 5.1$ ms to amortised running-time.

Secondly, we measured amortised cost of the AES evaluation protocol with precomputed round keys, see Figure 1. As expected, various algorithms have different saturation points where further parallelisation does not decrease the amortised cost any more. In particular, note that for few blocks the amortised costs of Lddam and circuit evaluation algorithms BCirc-1 and BCirc-2 is comparable, i.e., the advantage of circuit evaluation manifests only if we encrypt around 80 plaintexts in parallel. Also, note that the newer design BCirc-2 with smaller multiplicative depth performs better when the number of encryption calls is between $100 - 10,000$. After that the impact of communication complexity becomes more prevalent and the BCirc-1 protocols becomes more efficient.

---

[1] As all multiplications are carried over $\mathbb{F}_2$, we do not have to compensate for various input lengths and can just count the number of multiplications.

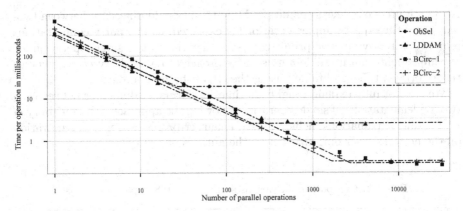

Fig. 1. Performance of AES evaluation protocols using precomputed round keys

As the final test, we measured the running time of the AES protocol with and without key scheduling. Table 2 depicts the corresponding results. As before, we give the running times for a single encryption operation and limiting cost of a single operation if many encryptions are done in parallel. Mode I denotes encryption with key expansion and mode II denotes encryption with pre-expanded secret key. Again, the results are in good correspondence. The cost of a single operation is roughly two times slower with the key expansion[2], since computing a shared round key requires one parallel invocation of S-boxes. For the amortised cost, the theoretical speedup should be 1.25 as there are 20 S-box invocation per round in the mode I and 16 invocations per round in the mode II. The difference in actual speedup factors suggest existence of some additional bottlenecks in our key-expansion algorithms.

Table 2. Performace results for various AES evaluation algorithms

	Single operation			Amortised cost		
	Mode I	Mode II	Ratio	Mode I	Mode II	Ratio
OBSEL	682 ms	343 ms	1.99	20.34 ms	18.69 ms	1.09
LDDAM	**652** ms	**323** ms	2.02	4.16 ms	2.51 ms	1.66
BCIRC-1	1329 ms	664 ms	2.00	0.48 ms	**0.29** ms	1.68
BCIRC-2	890 ms	443 ms	2.01	**0.37** ms	0.32 ms	1.17

Table 3 compares our results with the state of the art in oblivious AES-128 evaluation protocols. To make results comparable, the table contains results only for the semi-honest setting. In most cases, authors report the performance of

---

[2] The slowdown can be further reduced to 1.2 if we compute next subkey in parallel with the AES round to reduce multiplicative depth of the circuit.

AES with pre-shared keys (mode II). More than tenfold difference between two-party and three-party implementations is expected, as two-party computations require costly asymmetric primitives. Note that the cost of single operation for our implementation in Table 3 uses the approach of Launchbury et al., whereas the amortized time is obtained using the circuit-based approach.

We can not fully explain roughly 20 times performance difference between the two implementations of single operation following the approach of Launchbury et al. Possible explanations include measurement error and extreme concentration on the network layer optimization by the authors of [28].

Table 3. Comparison of various secure AES-128 implementations

Authors	Reference	Setting	Mode	Single operation	Amortised cost
Pinkas et al.	[34]	2-party	II	5000 ms	— ms
Huang et al.	[25]	2-party	II	200 ms	— ms
Damgård and Keller	[18]	3-party	I	2000 ms	— ms
Launchbury et al.	[28]	3-party	II	**14.28** ms	3.10 ms
This work		3-party	II	323 ms	**0.29** ms

4   Secure Database Join

As mentioned in the introduction, secure database join is a way to combine several data sources in privacy-preserving manner. In this work, we consider the most commonly used *equi-join*[3] operation, which merges tables according to one of few key columns using the equality comparison in the join predicate. In many cases, the key value is unique, such as social security number or name and postal code combined. The uniqueness assumption significantly simplifies our task. The need to deal with the colliding keys significantly increases the complexity of the protocols, and this case is handled in the extended version of the paper [29].

An ideal secure inner join protocol takes two or more secret-shared database tables and produces a new randomly ordered secret-shared table that contains the combined rows where the join predicate holds. The parties should learn nothing except for the number of rows in the new database. The random reordering of the output table is necessary to avoid unexpected information propagation when some entries are published either for input or for the output table.

Let m_1 and m_2 denote the number of rows and n_1 and n_2 the number of columns in the input tables. Then it is straightforward to come up with a solution that uses $\Theta(m_1 m_2)$ oblivious comparison operations by mimicking a naïve database join algorithm. We can obliviously compare all the possible key pairs, shuffle the whole database, open the comparison column and remove all the rows with the equality bit set to 0. It is straightforward to prove that this protocol is secure, since it mimics the actions of ideal implementation in verbatim. We will refer to this algorithm as NAIVEJOIN and treat it as a baseline solution.

---

[3] The authors adapt the Structured Query Language (SQL) terminology in this paper.

Database shuffling phase

1. Miners obliviously shuffle each database table T_i.
   Let T_i^* denote the resulting shuffled table with a key column $\boldsymbol{k}_i^*$.

Encryption and join phase

2. Miners choose a pseudorandom permutation π_s by generating a shared key s.
3. Miners obliviously evaluate π_s on all shared key columns $\boldsymbol{k}_i^*$.
4. Miners publish all values $\pi_s(k_{ij}^*)$ and use standard database join to merge the tables based on columns $\pi_s(\boldsymbol{k}_i^*)$. Let T^* be the resulting table.

Optional post-processing phase for colliding keys

5. If there are some non-unique keys in some key column $\pi_s(\boldsymbol{k}_i^*)$, miners should perform additional oblivious shuffle on the secret-shared table T^*

Protocol 1. Secure implementation of PRPJOIN operation

4.1 Secure Inner Join Based on Unique Key Column

As the first step towards a more efficient algorithm, consider a setting where the computing parties (miners) obliviously apply pseudorandom permutation π_s to encrypt the key column. As π_s is a pseudorandom permutation (a block cipher depending on an unknown key s) and all the values in the key column are unique, the resulting values look completely random if none of the miners knows π_s. Hence, it is secure to publish all the encryptions of key columns. Moreover, the tables can be correctly joined using the encryptions instead of key values.

However, such a join still leaks some information – miners learn which database rows in the first table correspond to the database rows in the second table. By shuffling the rows of initial tables, this linking information is destroyed. The resulting algorithm is depicted as Protocol 1. We emphasise that in each step all the tables are in secret-shared form. In particular, each miner carries out step 4 with its local shares and thus the table T^* is created in a secret-shared form. Note that we have also added step 5 to deal with the case of colliding keys. This case will be discussed in the extended version of the paper [29].

As the actual join operation is performed on public (encrypted) values, the construction works also for the *left* and *right outer joins*, where either the left or right table retains all its rows, whether a row with a matching key exists in the other table or not. These outer joins are common in data analysis. For instance, given access to supermarket purchases and demographic data, we can use outer join to add person's wealth and his/her home region to each transaction, given that both tables contain social security number. As the data about some persons might be missing from the demographic database, miners must agree on predefined constants to use instead of real shares if the encrypted key is missing. In this case, optional post-processing step is needed to hide rows with dummy values. However, the post-processing phase does not hide the number of missing data entries. We discuss this issue in the extended version of the paper [29].

Theorem 2. *Let $\mathcal{P} = (\pi_s)$ be a pseudorandom permutation family. If a share-computing framework provides universally composable protocols for database shuffle and oblivious evaluation of $\pi_s(x)$ from secret shared values of x and s, and there are no duplicate key values in any of the input tables, then the PRPJOIN protocol is universally composable in the computational model.*

Proof (Sketch). For clarity, let us analyse the security in the modified setting where $\mathcal{P}$ is the set of all permutations and Steps 1–4 are performed by trusted third party. Let m be the number of rows in the final database table and y_1 and y_2 the vectors of encrypted values published during PRPJOIN protocol. For obvious reasons, $|y_1 \cap y_2| = m$ and the set $y_1 \cup y_2$ consists of $m_1 + m_2 - m$ values, which are chosen randomly from the input domain without replacement. As Step 1 guarantees that the elements in y_1 and y_2 are in random order, it is straightforward to simulate y_1 and y_2 given only the number of rows m.

Hence, the simulation of the protocol is straightforward. First, the simulator forwards all input shares and gets back the final output shares and thus learns m. After that it generates shares for the shuffled databases by creating the correct number of valid shares of zero. As the adversarial coalition is small enough, the adversary cannot distinguish them from valid shares. Next, it generates y_1 and y_2 according to the specification given above and forwards the values to the adversary together with properly aligned output shares such that a semihonest adversary would assemble the database of output shares in the correct way.

It is easy to see that the simulation is perfect in the semihonest model. The same is true for the malicious model with honest majority, since honest parties can always carry out all the computations without the help from the adversarial coalition. In case of dishonest majority, the adversarial coalition is allowed to learn its output and then terminate the protocol. In our case, the simulator must terminate the execution when the adversarial coalition decides to stop after learning the encrypted vectors y_1 and y_2.

We can use the same simulation strategy for the original protocol where the trusted third party uses a pseudorandom permutation family. As the key s is unknown to all parties, the joint output distributions of the real and hybrid worlds are computationally indistinguishable. The latter is sufficient, as security in the hybrid model carries over to the real world through universal composability of share shuffling and oblivious function evaluation protocols. $\square$

Efficiency. By combining the secure oblivious AES evaluation and the oblivious shuffle from [30], we get an efficient instantiation of the PRPJOIN protocol. For all database sizes, the resulting protocol does $\Theta(m_1 + m_2)$ share-computing operations and $\Theta(m_1 \log m_1 + m_2 \log m_2)$ public computation operations.[4]

---

[4] The theoretical asymptotic complexity is higher, as the size of the database can be only polynomial in the security parameter and thus oblivious PRF evaluation takes $\mathsf{poly}(m)$ steps. Consequently, the protocol is asymptotically more efficient than the naive solution as long as the PRF evaluation is sub-linear in the database size.

Offline phase

  1. Generate shared random keys (k_{ij}) for the Carter-Wegman construction.

Online hashing phase

  2. Treat each key tuple as a long bit string $\boldsymbol{x} = (x_s, \ldots, x_1)$.
  3. Use secure scalar product algorithm to compute the secret shared hash code:

$$h(\boldsymbol{k}_j, \boldsymbol{x}) = x_s k_{sj} + \cdots + x_1 k_{1j} \ .$$

Protocol 2. Oblivious hashing OHASH

4.2 Secure Inner Join Based on Unique Multi-column Key Values

Let us now consider the case when database tables are joined based on several columns, such as name and birth date. We can reduce this kind of secure join to the previous case by using oblivious hashing. An ε-*almost universal hash function* is a function $h : \mathcal{K} \times \mathcal{M} \to \mathcal{T}$ that compresses message into shorter tags so that the following inequality holds:

$$\forall x \neq x' \in \mathcal{M} : \quad \Pr\left[k \leftarrow \mathcal{K} : h(k, x) = h(k, x')\right] \leq \varepsilon.$$

Such a function can be used to reduce the length of the unique key that spans over several columns. However, this function must support efficient oblivious evaluation. The Carter-Wegman construction [16]

$$h(\boldsymbol{k}, \boldsymbol{x}) = x_s k_s + \cdots + x_2 k_2 + x_1 k_1$$

is a good candidate for our application as it consist of a few simple operations and it is $2^{-\ell}$ almost universal when computations are done over the field $\mathbb{F}_{2^\ell}$. Another compelling alternative is to use several independent Carter-Wegman functions over $\mathbb{F}_2$. For ℓ independently chosen keys, the collision probability is still $2^{-\ell}$. In the semihonest model, the communication complexity of the resulting oblivious hashing protocols is the same, as the amount of communication scales linearly wrt the bit length. For the malicious models, the trade-offs depend on exact implementation details of multiplication protocol. The resulting algorithm for oblivious hashing is depicted as Protocol 2.

Theorem 3. *If a share-computing framework provides universally composable protocols for addition and multiplication over $\mathbb{F}_2$, the OHASH protocol is universally composable in the information theoretical model. For ε-almost universal hash function and m invocations of OHASH the probability that two different inputs lead to the same output is upper bounded by $\frac{1}{2} m^2 \varepsilon$.*

Proof (Sketch). The claim about security is evident as multiplication together with addition is sufficient to implement scalar product over $\mathbb{F}_2$. The collision probability follows from the union bound $\Pr\left[\text{collision}\right] \leq \binom{m}{2} \cdot \varepsilon \leq \frac{m^2 \varepsilon}{2}$. $\qquad\square$

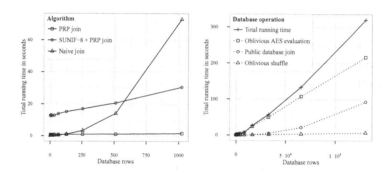

Fig. 2. Benchmarking results for the oblivious database join operation

Efficiency. A collision in the same key column invalidates the assumptions of Theorem 2, whereas a collision between keys of different tables introduces fraudulent entry in the resulting table. Hence, the size of Carter-Wegman construction must be chosen so that the probability of a collision event is negligible. By using 2^{-80} as the failure probability, we get that 128 bit Carter-Wegman construction allows us to operate up to 33.5 million table entries, which is clearly more than a secure database join protocol can handle in feasible time. To handle around million entries with the same failure probability it is sufficient to use 119-bit Carter-Wegman construction. However, note that the standard implementation of OHASH that computes each bit of the MAC separately and thus duplicates the data vector for each bit, has a larger communication complexity than oblivious AES. Experiments show that for 288 bit input and 128-bit output the complexity of a single OHASH is around 25 ms while the amortised complexity is around 5.7 ms. The corresponding numbers are 11 ms and 0.012 ms for the optimised OHASH protocol detailed in Appendix A. To put the results into context, note that unoptimised OHASH is over 10 times slower than oblivious AES, while the optimised OHASH has almost no impact to performance of the equi-join protocol as its running time is around 5%.

4.3   Benchmarking Results

We measured the performance of two secure database join protocols with the same setup as we used for timing the oblivious AES evaluation. For the experiment, we measured how much time it takes to join two database tables consisting of five 32-bit columns including the single column key. Both databases were of the same size and each key in one table had exactly one matching key in the other table. For AES, we used the BCIRC-1 version of the protocol as it has the lowest amortised cost for tables with thousands of rows.

Results depicted in Figure 2 clearly indicate that PRPJOIN protocols is much more efficient even for modest database sizes and it scales nearly linearly. More precisely, the only non-linear performance component is public database join operation, which is known to take $\Theta(m \log m)$ operations. The exact balance between oblivious AES evaluation and database shuffle depends on the number of columns. As the oblivious database shuffle scales linearly with the number of columns, the fraction of time spent on shuffling increases linearly with the number of columns. However, the slope is rather small.

For instance, consider two database tables with 10,000 rows each. Then the amount of time spent on oblivious shuffle becomes comparable with oblivious AES evaluation only if the number of columns per table exceeds 180 for our experimental setting. Hence, we can safely conclude that the oblivious database join is feasible in practical applications.

The NAIVEJOIN algorithm spends most of its time doing oblivious database shuffle. The shuffle operation itself is efficient, but the share size of the database is big. Even for two tables consisting of 1000 rows we must shuffle a database with million rows. Hence, it is affordable only for small databases.

4.4   Comparison with Related Work

Protocols for privacy-preserving database join have been proposed before. However, none of them are applicable in our model where input and output tables are secret shared. One of the first articles on privacy-preserving datamining showed how exponentiation can be used to compute equi-join in two-party case [3]. However, their protocol reveals the resulting database.

Freedman *et al.* showed how oblivious polynomial evaluation and balanced hashing can be used to implement secure set intersection [20]. The resulting two-party protocol is based on additively homomorphic encryption and has complexity $\Theta(m_1 m_2)$ without balanced hashing. The latter significantly reduces the amount of computations by splitting the elements into small distinct groups. The same idea is not directly applicable in our setting, since our data is secret shared, while their protocol assumes that key columns are local inputs.

Oblivious polynomial evaluation is not very useful in our context, as it is shorthand for the test $x \in \{b_1, \ldots, b_k\}$ which requires $\Theta(k)$ multiplications, while the PRPJOIN protocol does all such comparisons publicly.

Hazay and Lindell [23] have also proposed a similar solution that uses pseudorandom permutation to hide initial data values and performs secure set intersection on ciphertexts. However, they are working in a two-party setting where one of the parties learns the intersection.

5   Conclusion

In this paper we showed that there are several compelling ways to implement oblivious AES evaluation in a multi-party setting where the plaintext and the ciphertext are shared between the parties. As the second important contribution, we described and benchmarked efficient protocols for joining secret-shared databases.

Our benchmarking results showed that it is possible to get throughputs around 3500 blocks per second for the oblivious AES, which is the fastest three-party

MPC implementation known to the authors. In general, any block cipher based on substitution permutation networks (SPN) is a good candidate for oblivious evaluation as long as the Sbox has low multiplicative complexity and the rest of the cipher is linear over $\mathbb{F}_{2^k}$. Experimental results allow us to conclude that throughput around 350 blocks per second is achievable for any comparable SPN cipher, as the evaluation method of [28] is applicable for any Sbox.

Note that the AES key schedule is appropriate for oblivious evaluation, as all the round keys can be computed on demand. Consequently, the usage of pre-shared round keys reduces the running time for a single operation only by 25%. The only way to get more efficient oblivious evaluation protocols is to use Sbox constructions with smaller multiplicative complexity than 32. However, these Sboxes are also more likely to be weaker against linear cryptanalysis and algebraic attacks. Thus, it would be really difficult to come up with more compelling block cipher for multi-party setting – any secure block cipher designed for the oblivious evaluation, is also a good ordinary block cipher.

For the database join, we showed how to combine oblivious evaluation of almost universal hashing and pseudorandom functions to get a collision resistant pseudorandom function, which can handle arbitrary sized database keys. The resulting PRPJOIN protocol works under the assumption that all key column entries are unique. Although we can always fall back to NAIVEJOIN and preserve security without this restriction, the performance penalty is excessive. A better solution remained out of the space restrictions of this paper and is presented in the extended version [29].

From a truly theoretical viewpoint, the question whether sub-quadratic complexity for oblivious database join is achievable depends on existence of pseudorandom functions with low multiplicative complexity. The latter is an interesting open question. Another practically more important open question is to find new almost universal hash function constructions with lower multiplicative complexity or to prove that current constructions are optimal. The circuit complexity of universal hash functions has been studied in the context of energy efficiency [27], the main goal has been minimisation of total circuit complexity which is a considerably different minimisation goal.

References

1. Raknet – multiplayer game network engine, http://www.jenkinssoftware.com
2. SecureSCM. Technical report D9.1: Secure Computation Models and Frameworks (July 2008), http://www.securescm.org
3. Agrawal, R., Evfimievski, A., Srikant, R.: Information sharing across private databases. In: Proceedings of the 2003 ACM SIGMOD 2003, pp. 86–97. ACM, New York (2003)
4. Aumasson, J.-P., Fischer, S., Khazaei, S., Meier, W., Rechberger, C.: New Features of Latin Dances: Analysis of Salsa, ChaCha, and Rumba. In: Nyberg, K. (ed.) FSE 2008. LNCS, vol. 5086, pp. 470–488. Springer, Heidelberg (2008)

5. Ben-David, A., Nisan, N., Pinkas, B.: FairplayMP: a system for secure multi-party computation. In: Proceedings of ACM CCS 2008, pp. 257–266. ACM, New York (2008)

6. Chor, N.G.B., Naor, M.: Private information retrieval by keywords. Cryptology ePrint Archive, Report 1998/003 (1998), http://eprint.iacr.org/

7. Bernstein, D.J.: ChaCha, a variant of Salsa20 (2008), http://cr.yp.to/chacha.html

8. Bogdanov, D., Laur, S., Willemson, J.: Sharemind: A Framework for Fast Privacy-Preserving Computations. In: Jajodia, S., Lopez, J. (eds.) ESORICS 2008. LNCS, vol. 5283, pp. 192–206. Springer, Heidelberg (2008)

9. Bogdanov, D., Talviste, R., Willemson, J.: Deploying secure multi-party computation for financial data analysis (Short Paper). In: Keromytis, A.D. (ed.) FC 2012. LNCS, vol. 7397, pp. 57–64. Springer, Heidelberg (2012)

10. Bogetoft, P., et al.: Secure multiparty computation goes live. In: Dingledine, R., Golle, P. (eds.) FC 2009. LNCS, vol. 5628, pp. 325–343. Springer, Heidelberg (2009)

11. Boyar, J., Peralta, R.: A New Combinational Logic Minimization Technique with Applications to Cryptology. In: Festa, P. (ed.) SEA 2010. LNCS, vol. 6049, pp. 178–189. Springer, Heidelberg (2010)

12. Boyar, J., Peralta, R.: A small depth-16 circuit for the AES S-box. In: Gritzalis, D., Furnell, S., Theoharidou, M. (eds.) SEC 2012. IFIP AICT, vol. 376, pp. 287–298. Springer, Heidelberg (2012)

13. Burkhart, M., Strasser, M., Many, D., Dimitropoulos, X.: SEPIA: Privacy-preserving aggregation of multi-domain network events and statistics. In: Proceedings of the USENIX Security Symposium 2010, Washington, DC, USA, pp. 223–239 (2010)

14. Canetti, R.: Security and composition of multiparty cryptographic protocols. J. Cryptology 13(1), 143–202 (2000)

15. Canetti, R.: Universally composable security: A new paradigm for cryptographic protocols. In: Proceedings of FOCS 2001, pp. 136–145 (2001)

16. Carter, L., Wegman, M.N.: Universal classes of hash functions. J. Comput. Syst. Sci. 18(2), 143–154 (1979)

17. Damgård, I., Fitzi, M., Kiltz, E., Nielsen, J.B., Toft, T.: Unconditionally secure constant-rounds multi-party computation for equality, comparison, bits and exponentiation. In: Halevi, S., Rabin, T. (eds.) TCC 2006. LNCS, vol. 3876, pp. 285–304. Springer, Heidelberg (2006)

18. Damgård, I., Keller, M.: Secure multiparty AES. In: Sion, R. (ed.) FC 2010. LNCS, vol. 6052, pp. 367–374. Springer, Heidelberg (2010)

19. Damgård, I., Pastro, V., Smart, N.P., Zakarias, S.: Multiparty computation from somewhat homomorphic encryption. In: Safavi-Naini, R. (ed.) CRYPTO 2012. LNCS, vol. 7417, pp. 643–662. Springer, Heidelberg (2012)

20. Freedman, M.J., Nissim, K., Pinkas, B.: Efficient Private Matching and Set Intersection. In: Cachin, C., Camenisch, J.L. (eds.) EUROCRYPT 2004. LNCS, vol. 3027, pp. 1–19. Springer, Heidelberg (2004)

21. Gentry, C., Halevi, S.: Implementing Gentry's Fully-Homomorphic Encryption Scheme. In: Paterson, K.G. (ed.) EUROCRYPT 2011. LNCS, vol. 6632, pp. 129–148. Springer, Heidelberg (2011)

22. Goldreich, O.: The Foundations of Cryptography. Basic Applications, vol. 2. Cambridge University Press (2004)

23. Hazay, C., Lindell, Y.: Constructions of truly practical secure protocols using standard smartcards. In: ACM Conference on Computer and Communications Security, pp. 491–500 (2008)

24. Henecka, W., Kögl, S., Sadeghi, A.-R., Schneider, T., Wehrenberg, I.: TASTY: tool for automating secure two-party computations. In: Proceedings of ACM CCS 2010, pp. 451–462. ACM (2010)

25. Huang, Y., Evans, D., Katz, J., Malka, L.: Faster Secure Two-Party Computation Using Garbled Circuits. In: Proceedings of 20th USENIX Security Symposium, pp. 8–12 (2011)

26. Ishai, Y., Paskin, A.: Evaluating branching programs on encrypted data. In: Vadhan, S.P. (ed.) TCC 2007. LNCS, vol. 4392, pp. 575–594. Springer, Heidelberg (2007)

27. Kaps, J.-P., Yuksel, K., Sunar, B.: Energy scalable universal hashing. IEEE Trans. Comput. 54(12), 1484–1495 (2005)

28. Launchbury, J., Diatchki, I.S., DuBuisson, T., Adams-Moran, A.: Efficient lookup-table protocol in secure multiparty computation. In: Proceedings of ICFP, pp. 189–200. ACM (2012)

29. Laur, S., Talviste, R., Willemson, J.: From oblivious AES to efficient and secure database join in the multiparty setting. Cryptology ePrint Archive, Report 2013/203 (2013), http://eprint.iacr.org/

30. Laur, S., Willemson, J., Zhang, B.: Round-Efficient Oblivious Database Manipulation. In: Lai, X., Zhou, J., Li, H. (eds.) ISC 2011. LNCS, vol. 7001, pp. 262–277. Springer, Heidelberg (2011)

31. Malka, L.: Vmcrypt: modular software architecture for scalable secure computation. In: Proceedings of ACM CCS 2011, pp. 715–724. ACM, New York (2011)

32. National Institute of Standards and Technology (NIST). Advanced Encryption Standard (AES). Federal Information Processing Standards Publications, FIPS-197 (2001)

33. Nielsen, J.B., Nordholt, P.S., Orlandi, C., Burra, S.S.: A new approach to practical active-secure two-party computation. In: Safavi-Naini, R. (ed.) CRYPTO 2012. LNCS, vol. 7417, pp. 681–700. Springer, Heidelberg (2012)

34. Pinkas, B., Schneider, T., Smart, N.P., Williams, S.C.: Secure two-party computation is practical. In: Matsui, M. (ed.) ASIACRYPT 2009. LNCS, vol. 5912, pp. 250–267. Springer, Heidelberg (2009)

A   Carter-Wegman MAC Protocol Proof

As the computation of Carter-Wegman hash function is essentially a matrix-vector multiplication over the field $\mathbb{F}_2$, we can use an optimisation technique, which is applicable in many other matrix multiplication settings. The corresponding protocol is depicted as Protocol 3. We use double brackets to denote secret shared values, e.g. the secret shared version of $s = s_1 \oplus s_2 \oplus s_3$ is shown as $[\![s]\!]$, where party $\mathcal{P}_i$ holds s_i. For double indices, the second index shows which party holds the bitstring and the first shows for which output bit it will be used for. Since all values are bitwise shared, we can operate with individual bits of the shares. Operations on individual bits use superscript bit index notation.

Theorem 4. *Assume that the shares of m are correctly generated. Then Protocol 3 is correct and secure against single passively corrupted miner.*

Input-ouputput specification

Protocol input is a shared s-bit value $[\![m]\!]$ and shared s-bit keys $[\![k_1]\!], \ldots, [\![k_\ell]\!]$.
Protocol output is a shared ℓ-bit MAC value $[\![c]\!]$.

Precomputation phase

1. Each miner $\mathcal{P}_i$ generates ℓ random bits $r_i^1, \ldots, r_i^\ell \leftarrow \mathbb{Z}_2$.

Data distribution phase

3. Miner $\mathcal{P}_1$ sends s-bit shares $m_1, k_{1,1}, \ldots, k_{\ell,1}$ to $\mathcal{P}_2$.
   Miner $\mathcal{P}_2$ sends s-bit shares $m_2, k_{1,2}, \ldots, k_{\ell,2}$ to $\mathcal{P}_3$.
   Miner $\mathcal{P}_3$ sends s-bit shares $m_3, k_{1,3}, \ldots, k_{\ell,3}$ to $\mathcal{P}_1$.

Post-processing phase

5. Each miner $\mathcal{P}_i$ computes $w_{ij}^t \leftarrow m_i^t \wedge k_{j,i}^t \oplus m_{i-1}^t \wedge k_{j,i}^t \oplus m_i^t \wedge k_{j,i-1}^t$
   for each key $j \in \{1, \ldots, \ell\}$ and bit $t \in \{1, \ldots, s\}$ and sums them
   up together with re-randomisation $c_i^j \leftarrow w_{ij}^1 \oplus \cdots \oplus w_{ij}^s \oplus \oplus r_i^j \oplus r_{i-1}^j$.

Protocol 3. More efficient protocol for Carter-Wegman MAC

Proof (Sketch). For each bit c^j of MAC the correctness follows from

$$[\![c^j]\!] = \bigoplus_{i=1}^{3} \left(\bigoplus_{t=1}^{s} m_i^t \wedge k_{j,i}^t \oplus m_{i-1}^t \wedge k_{j,i}^t \oplus m_i^t \wedge k_{j,i-1}^t \right) \oplus r_i^j \oplus r_{i-1}^j$$

$$= \bigoplus_{i=1}^{3} \bigoplus_{t=1}^{s} \left(m_i^t \wedge k_{j,i}^t \oplus m_{i-1}^t \wedge k_{j,i}^t \oplus m_i^t \wedge k_{j,i-1}^t \right) = \bigoplus_{t=1}^{s} (m^t \wedge k_j^t) = h(k_j, m)$$

since the inner most sum contains all combinations of $m_a \wedge k_b$.

For the security analysis, it is sufficient to consider the corruption of $\mathcal{P}_2$ who receivers all shares owned by $\mathcal{P}_1$. Note that two shares out of three have always uniform distribution. Hence, it is trivial to simulate all messages received by $\mathcal{P}_2$. Since $\mathcal{P}_2$ is semihonest, the simulator can extract shares of the message and keys from the input of $\mathcal{P}_2$ and submit them to the trusted party who will return shares $c_2^1, \ldots, c_2^\ell$. Since the simulator knows what random values $r_2^1, \ldots, r_2^\ell$ $\mathcal{P}_2$ is going to use, it can pick $r_1^1, \ldots, r_1^\ell$ so that $\mathcal{P}_2$ will indeed output $c_2^1, \ldots, c_2^\ell$. We leave the detailed analysis of the simulation construction to the reader. $\qquad \square$

Private Database Queries Using Somewhat Homomorphic Encryption

Dan Boneh[1], Craig Gentry[2], Shai Halevi[2], Frank Wang[3], and David J. Wu[1]

[1] Stanford University
{dabo,dwu4}@cs.stanford.edu
[2] IBM Research
craigbgentry@gmail.com, shaih@alum.mit.edu
[3] MIT
frankw@mit.edu

Abstract. In a private database query system, a client issues queries to a database and obtains the results without learning anything else about the database and without the server learning the query. While previous work has yielded systems that can efficiently support disjunction queries, performing conjunction queries privately remains an open problem. In this work, we show that using a polynomial encoding of the database enables efficient implementations of conjunction queries using somewhat homomorphic encryption. We describe a three-party protocol that supports efficient evaluation of conjunction queries. Then, we present two implementations of our protocol using Paillier's additively homomorphic system as well as Brakerski's somewhat homomorphic cryptosystem. Finally, we show that the additional homomorphic properties of the Brakerski cryptosystem allow us to handle queries involving several thousand elements over a million-record database in just a few minutes, far outperforming the implementation using the additively homomorphic system.

1 Introduction

Enabling private database queries is an important research problem that arises in many real-world settings. The problem can be thought of as a generalization of symmetric private information retrieval (SPIR) [3,8] where clients can retrieve records by specifying complex queries. For example, the client may ask for the records of all people with age 25 to 29 who also live in Alaska, and the server should return these records without learning anything about the query. The client should learn nothing else about the database contents.

In this work we explore the use of somewhat homomorphic encryption (SWHE) [5] for the design of private database query protocols. In particular, we show that certain polynomial encodings of the database let us implement interesting query types using only homomorphic computations involving low-degree polynomials. There are now several encryption schemes [1,2] that efficiently support the necessary low-degree homomorphic computations on encrypted data needed for our constructions.

M. Jacobson et al. (Eds.): ACNS 2013, LNCS 7954, pp. 102–118, 2013.

Unfortunately, being a generalization of SPIR, private database queries is subject to all the same inherent inefficiency constraints as SPIR. To understand these limitations let us consider the two parties involved in the basic setup: the client and the server. The server has a database and the client has a query. We seek a protocol that gives the client only those records that match its query without the server learning any information about the query. In this setting the server must process the entire database for every query; otherwise, it would learn that the unprocessed records do not match the query. Moreover, the server has to return to the client as much data as the number of records in the database, or else the database would learn some information about the number of records that match the query. Thus, for large databases, the server is forced to do a considerable amount of work, rendering such systems impractical in most scenarios.

To overcome these severe limitations we modify the basic model a bit and consider a setting in which the database server is split into two entities called the "server" and the "proxy." Privacy holds as long as these two entities do not collude. This approach was taken by De Cristofaro et al. [4], who designed a system that supported private evaluation of a few simple query types and demonstrated performance similar to a non-private off-the-shelf MySQL system. However, the architecture of De Cristofaro et al. could not handle conjunctive queries: for instance, the client could ask for all the records with age=25 OR name='Bob', but could not ask for the records with age=25 AND name='Bob'. Another multi-party architecture for performing private database queries is proposed in [13]. In this case, the server constructs an encrypted document index which is stored on an index server (e.g., "proxy" in our setting). To submit queries, the client interacts with a query router. One of the limitations of this scheme is that for each query, the server has to perform a computation on each record in the database, which does not scale well to very large databases.

In this work, we develop protocols that can efficiently support conjunction queries over large databases using an architecture similar to [4]. We rely on somewhat homomorphic encryption schemes [1,2] that efficiently support low-degree homomorphic computations on encrypted data.

1.1 Security Model

The functionality that our protocol implements gives the client the indices of the records that match its query. The client should learn nothing about the data beyond this set and the server and proxy should learn nothing about the query beyond what is explicitly leaked.

More precisely, security for the client means that if the client issues one of two adversarially-chosen queries with the same number of attributes, the adversarial server cannot distinguish between them. Security for the server means that for any fixed query and two adversarially-chosen databases for which the query matches the same set of records, the client cannot distinguish the two databases.

In this paper, we adopt the honest-but-curious security model. Our protocols can be enhanced to handle malicious adversaries using generic tools such as [10]. It is an interesting open problem to design more efficient protocols in the malicious settings specific to the private database queries problem. Security holds as long as the server and the proxy do not collude. This is very similar to the assumptions made in [13].

1.2   Our Protocol

The protocol and tools we present in this work are aimed at revealing to the client *the indices* of the records that match its query, leaving it to a standard follow-up protocol to fetch the records themselves. The approach that underlies our protocol is to encode the database as one or more polynomials and then manipulate these polynomials using the client's query so as to obtain a new polynomial whose roots are the indices of the matching records. This representation is well suited for conjunction queries, since it allows us to use techniques similar to the Kissner-Song protocol for (multi-)set intersection [11].

In our protocol, the three parties consist of a client with a query, a proxy that has an inverted index for the database, and a server that prepared the inverted index during a pre-processing step and now keeps only the keys that were used to create this inverted index. Specifically, the server keeps some "hashing keys" and the secret key for a SWHE scheme. For every attribute-value pair (a, v) in the database, the inverted index contains a record $(\mathsf{tg}, \mathsf{Enc}(A(x)))$ where tg is a tag, computed as $\mathsf{tg} = \mathrm{Hash}(\text{``}a = v\text{''})$, and $A(x)$ is a polynomial whose roots are exactly the records indices r that contain this attribute-value pair.

An example query supported by our protocol is:

$$\texttt{SELECT} \star \texttt{FROM db WHERE } a_1 = v_1 \texttt{ AND } \cdots \texttt{ AND } a_t = v_t.$$

Given this query, the client (with oblivious help from the server) computes the tags $\mathsf{tg}_i = \mathrm{Hash}(\text{``}a_i = v_i\text{''})$ for $i = 1, \ldots, t$ and sends them to the proxy. The proxy fetches the corresponding encrypted polynomials $A_i(x)$ from the inverted index, chooses random polynomials $R_i(x)$ of "appropriate degrees" and computes the encrypted polynomial $B(x) = \sum_{i=1}^{t} R_i(x) A_i(x)$. The proxy returns the encrypted B to the client, who again uses oblivious help from the server to decrypt B, and then factors it to find its roots, which are the indices of the matching records (with high probability).

One drawback of this protocol is that the proxy can tell when two different queries share the same attribute-value pair (since the client will send the same tag in both). In Section 3.3, we show that using quadratic-homomorphic encryption, we can mitigate this drawback somewhat, providing a privacy/bandwidth tradeoff that the client can tune to its needs.

Bandwidth reduction and other optimizations. Another drawback of the protocol above is that the degree of the encrypted polynomial B returned by the proxy (which determines the size of the response) depends on the *largest* number of records that match any of the attribute-value pairs in the query. For example, if the client query was "$\texttt{SELECT} \star \texttt{FROM db WHERE gender=`male' AND zipcode=12345}$," the response size will be at least as large as the number of males in the database, even if there are only a few people with zipcode 12345.

In Section 3.2, we describe how to reduce this degree (and bandwidth) by observing that the minimum-degree polynomial that encodes the intersection is the gcd of the A_i's. We show that the somewhat homomorphic properties of the cryptosystem can be used to approximate the gcd. Our discussion here will lead to a storage/homomorphism tradeoff. We present additional optimizations in Section 3.3. In Section 3.4 we show that we can take advantage of homomorphic batching [6,14]) to further speed up the computation.

Implementation and performance results. We implemented our three-party protocol using both the additive homomorphic Paillier cryptosystem [12] and a variant of Brakerski's system [1] that supports a single multiplicative homomorphism. Our implementation, described in Section 4, shows that the use of multiplicative homomorphisms greatly improves performance and bandwidth over the strictly additive implementation using Paillier.

2 Preliminaries

2.1 Homomorphic Encryption

Fix a particular plaintext space $\mathcal{P}$ which is a ring (e.g., $\mathcal{P} = \mathbb{F}_2$). Let $\mathcal{C}$ be a class of arithmetic circuits over the plaintext space $\mathcal{P}$. A somewhat homomorphic (public-key) encryption relative to $\mathcal{C}$ is specified by the procedures KeyGen, Enc, Dec (for key generation, encryption, and decryption, respectively) and the additional procedure Eval that takes a circuit from $\mathcal{C}$ and one ciphertext per input to that circuit, and returns one ciphertext per output of that circuit.

The security requirement is the usual notion of semantic security [9]: it should be hard to distinguish between the encryption of any two adversarially-chosen messages, even if the public key is known to the adversary. The functionality requirement for homomorphic schemes [5] is that for every circuit $\pi \in \mathcal{C}$ and every set of inputs to π, if we choose at random the keys, then encrypt all the inputs, then run the Eval procedure on these ciphertexts and decrypt the result, we will get the same thing as evaluating π on this set of inputs (except perhaps with negligible probability). An important property of SWHE schemes is *circuit privacy*, which means that even the holder of the secret key cannot learn from the evaluated ciphertext anything about the circuit, beyond the output.

In this work we use "low degree" somewhat homomorphic encryption, namely homomorphic encryption schemes relative to the class of low degree polynomials. While our basic protocol requires only additive homomorphism, some of our optimizations require that the scheme support polynomials of higher degree.

2.2 Polynomial Arithmetic and Set-Intersection

We provide a brief overview of the techniques underlying the Kissner-Song set-intersection protocol [11]. Our setting is different than that considered in [11], hence also our use of these techniques is somewhat different. Roughly, Kissner and Song considered the case where each party has a set and they want to compute the intersection of all their sets. In our case we have one party holding all the sets (the server), and another party that determines which of these sets should participate in the intersection (the client).

The idea behind the Kissner-Song protocol is to fix a large field $\mathbb{F}$ and represent a set $S \subset \mathbb{F}$ by a polynomial A_S that has zeros in all the elements of S, that is $A_S(x) = \prod_{s \in S}(x - s)$. To compute the intersection of many sets S_i, we construct a polynomial B whose zeros are the intersection of these sets. Clearly, if some point $s \in \mathbb{F}$ is contained in all the sets S_i, then $A_{S_i}(s) = 0$ for all i, and therefore, if we compute B as a linear combination of the A_{S_i}'s, then also $B(s) = 0$. On the other hand, if $A_{S_i}(s) \neq 0$ for some i and B is a *random* linear combination of the A_{S_i}'s, then with high probability $B(s) \neq 0$.

The Kissner-Song approach is therefore to choose the field $\mathbb{F}$ sufficiently larger than the "universe" U of valid points (e.g., we have $S_i \subseteq U \subsetneq \mathbb{F}$), then take B to be a random linear combination of the A_{S_i}'s, and show that with high probability, the only roots of B that come from U are the ones corresponding to the intersection of the S_i's. The following lemma is easy to prove using the above arguments:

Lemma 1. *Fix a finite field $\mathbb{F}$ and a "universe" $U \subset \mathbb{F}$, let $S_1, \ldots, S_t \subseteq U$ be subsets of the universe and for each S_i, let $A_{S_i}(x) = \prod_{s \in S_i}(x - s)$.*

(i) Let $\rho_1, \ldots, \rho_{t-1}$ be random scalars in $\mathbb{F}$, let $A'(x) = A_{S_t} + \sum_{i<t} \rho_i A_{S_i}(x)$, and denote the set of roots of A' by $S_{A'}$. Then $\Pr[S_{A'} \cap U = \bigcap_i S_i] \geq 1 - |U|/|\mathbb{F}|$.

(ii) Let R_1, R_2 be random polynomials in $\mathbb{F}[x]$ of some given degrees $d_1, d_2 \geq 0$. Let $B(x) = A_1(x)R_1(x) + A_2(x)R_2(x)$, and S_B be the set of roots of B. Then $\Pr[S_B \cap U = S_1 \cap S_2] \geq 1 - |U|/|\mathbb{F}|$.

The harder part is to show that the random linear combination B does not leak information on the A_{S_i}'s beyond their intersection. For this to hold, the coefficients of the linear combination cannot be scalars in $\mathbb{F}$, they must be themselves polynomials of high-enough degree. Specifically, we use the following lemma which is a slight generalization of [11, Lemma 1]:

Lemma 2. *Fix a finite field $\mathbb{F}$ and two co-prime polynomials $A_1(x), A_2(x) \in \mathbb{F}[x]$, of degrees $d_1 = \deg(A_1)$ and $d_2 = \deg(A_2)$. Also, fix some integer $D_1 \geq d_1 - 1$, and let $D_2 = d_2 + D_1 - d_1$. Next, choose uniformly at random a degree-D_2 polynomial $R_1(x) \in \mathbb{F}[x]$ and a degree-D_1 polynomial $R_2(x) \in \mathbb{F}[x]$ and set $B(x) = A_1(x) \cdot R_1(x) + A_2(x) \cdot R_2(x)$. Then, $B(x)$ is distributed uniformly among all the polynomials of degree $d_1 + D_2 = D_1 + d_2$ over $\mathbb{F}$.*

Proof. Omitted due to space constraints. See appendix of the full version. □

Corollary 1. *Fix a finite field $\mathbb{F}$ and two polynomials $A_1(x), A_2(x) \in \mathbb{F}[x]$, with degrees d_1 and d_2, respectively. Let $G(x) = \gcd(A_1(x), A_2(x))$. Also fix some integer $D_1 \geq d_1 - 1$, and let $D_2 = d_2 + D_1 - d_1$. Then choosing uniformly at random a degree-D_2 polynomial $R_1(x) \in \mathbb{F}[x]$ and a degree-D_1 polynomial $R_2(x) \in \mathbb{F}[x]$ and setting $B(x) = A_1(x) \cdot R_1(x) + A_2(x) \cdot R_2(x)$, the polynomial*

$B(x)$ *is distributed uniformly among all the polynomials of degree* $d_1 + D_2$ *over* $\mathbb{F}$ *which are divisible by* $G(x)$.

Proof. Follows by applying Lemma 2 to the co-prime polynomials $A_1'(x) = A_1(x)/G(x)$ and $A_2'(x) = A_2(x)/G(x)$. $\qquad\qquad\qquad\qquad\qquad\qquad\qquad\square$

Intersection of two sets. If $A_{S_1}(x)$, $A_{S_2}(x)$ are polynomials that represent sets S_1, S_2, respectively, then $\gcd(A_{S_1}, A_{S_2})$ is the polynomial that represents their intersection. In this case, Corollary 1 says that setting $B = A_{S_1} R_1 + A_{S_2} R_2$ for R_1, R_2 of "appropriate degrees" yields a random multiple of $G(x)$ that leaks "no information" about A_1, A_2 beyond their intersection and the sum of their sizes.[1]

Intersection of many sets. In this setting, we are given the polynomials A_{S_i}, $i = 1, 2, \ldots, t$, with $d_i = \deg(A_{S_i})$. Without loss of generality, let d_t be the largest degree. We first choose random scalars, $\rho_i \in \mathbb{F}$ for $i = 2, \ldots, t$, and compute the degree-d_t polynomial $A'(x) = A_{S_t}(x) + \sum_{2 \le i < t} \rho_i A_{S_i}(x)$. Then we choose two random polynomials $R_1(x)$ of degree $d_t - 1$ and $R'(x)$ of degree $d_1 - 1$ and set $B(x) = A_{S_1}(x)R_1(x) + A'(x)R'(x)$.

Clearly $\gcd(A_{S_1}, A_{S_2}, \ldots, A_{S_t})$ divides $\gcd(A_{S_1}, A')$. Also Lemma 1 (applied to $U = S_1$ and $S_i' = S_i \cap S_1$) implies that with probability at least $1 - d_1/|\mathbb{F}|$ we have $\gcd(A_{S_1}, A') = \gcd(A_{S_1}, A_{S_2}, \ldots, A_{S_t})$. It follows from Corollary 1 that when the size of $\mathbb{F}$ is super-polynomially larger than d_1, the distribution of $B(x)$ is statistically close to uniform over the degree-$(d_1 + d_t - 1)$ polynomials divisible by $\gcd(A_{S_1}, A_{S_2}, \ldots, A_{S_t})$.

Reducing the degree. To reduce the degree of the resulting polynomials, instead of using $A'(x) = \sum_i \rho_i A_{S_i}(x)$, we compute the polynomial $A''(x) = A'(x) \bmod A_{S_1}(x)$ of degree $d_1 - 1$. Choosing at random $R_1(x)$ of degree $d_1 - 1$ and $R''(x)$ of degree d_1, we set $B(x) = A_1(x)R_1(x) + A''(x)R''(x)$. Correctness and secrecy follow from the observation that since $A''(x) = A'(x) \bmod A_{S_1}(x)$, $\gcd(A_{S_1}, A'') = \gcd(A_{S_1}, A')$.

3   The Three-Party Protocol

In this section, we describe the three-party setting that we adopt in this paper (which is similar to the "Isolated-Box" architecture in [4]). In this architecture, in addition to the client and server there is a third party, a proxy, that holds an "encrypted" inverted index of the database records. For each attribute-value pair in the database, the proxy holds a tag that identifies the pair, along with a set of record indices that contain the pair. Specifically, for each attribute-value pair in the database (e.g., "name=Joe"), the inverted index contains the following:

$$\langle \mathsf{PRF}_s(\text{"name=Joe"}), \quad \text{encrypted-set-of-record-indices} \rangle \qquad (1)$$

---

[1] We can pad to a pre-determined degree to hide the information about the sizes.

where the PRF key s is held by the server and the set of record indices contains all the records where the attribute "name" has value "Joe."

When the client wants to fetch the records with name=Joe, it engages in a protocol for oblivious-PRF-evaluation with the server and learns the tag $\mathrm{PRF}_s($"name=Joe"$)$. It then engages in a protocol with the proxy to learn the set of indices corresponding to this tag. To make a conjunction query, the client sends multiple tags to the proxy and at the end of the protocol, learns the records in the intersection of all the sets.

3.1   Our Basic 3-Party Protocol

The task of computing conjunctions is closely related to set intersection. Indeed, an attribute-value pair (e.g., "name=Joe") implicitly defines a set of records that contains this pair. The proxy needs to send the intersection of all these sets to the client, without learning anything about the sets themselves.

Using the technique of Kissner and Song described in Section 2.2, we represent each set as a polynomial whose roots are the elements of that set. Thus, in the row of the inverted index with tag $\mathrm{PRF}_s($"name=Joe"$)$, we do not store the set of indices S containing this attribute-value pair, but rather the polynomial $A_S(x) = \prod_{s \in S}(x - s)$, encrypted using our SWHE scheme. Note that the SWHE scheme is used to encrypt each *coefficient* of the polynomial A_S. To issue a conjunctive query (say, "name=Joe" and "age=28"), the client does the following:

1. Use oblivious-PRF-evaluation to obtain from the server the tags $\mathrm{tg}_1, \ldots, \mathrm{tg}_t$ corresponding to each of the attribute-value pairs. The client sends all the tags to the proxy.
2. The proxy collects the encrypted polynomials A_i corresponding to the tags tg_i and then computes a polynomial $B(x)$ as a "random linear combination" of the $A_i(x)$'s:
   (i) Letting $d_i = \deg(A_i)$ and assuming that the A_i's are ordered by degree ($d_1 \leq d_2 \leq \cdots \leq d_t$), the proxy first chooses random scalars $\rho_2, \ldots, \rho_{t-1}$ and computes the degree-d_t polynomial $A'(x) = A_t + \sum_{2 \leq i < t} \rho_i A_i(x)$.
   (ii) Then the proxy chooses two random polynomials $R_1(x)$ of degree $d_t - 1$ and $R'(x)$ of degree $d_1 - 1$ and sets $B(x) = A_1(x)R_1(x) + A'(x)R'(x)$. The proxy uses the additive homomorphism of the scheme to compute the encrypted coefficients of the polynomial B from the encrypted coefficients of the A_i's and the plaintext ρ_i, R_1 and R'. The proxy sends the encrypted $B(x)$ to the client.
3. The client and server engage in another protocol to decrypt $B(x)$ (encrypted under the server's key). At the conclusion of this protocol, the client knows $B(x)$ and the server knows nothing.
4. The client factors $B(x)$ and finds its roots, which are the indices of the records that the client is interested in. While $B(x)$ may have superfluous roots, we use a large-enough space so that with high probability these roots are identified as invalid and discarded.

Once the client knows the indices of the records that match its query, it can use PIR/ORAM protocols to fetch the encrypted records, then engage in another oblivious decryption protocol with the server to decrypt them.

Security. Secrecy against an honest-but-curious proxy is ensured by the fact that the tags do not leak to the proxy anything about the attribute-value pairs that were used to generate them (because the tag-generation function is pseudorandom), and the encrypted polynomials do not leak anything due to the semantic security of the SWHE cryptosystem. Note that our security model only ensures privacy for a single query. If the client issues multiple queries then the proxy may learn relations between these queries. We briefly discuss multiple queries in Section 3.3.

Secrecy against an honest-but-curious client follows from Corollary 1 and the circuit-privacy property of the SWHE scheme. Specifically, Corollary 1 implies that the polynomial B by itself does not leak anything about the A_i's beyond their intersection (and the size $d_1 + d_t$), and circuit-privacy of the cryptosystem means that the evaluated ciphertext encrypting B does not leak anything else.

3.2 Reducing Communication via Modular Reduction

The communication complexity of the basic solution above is determined by the degree of the polynomial B, which is tied to the size of the largest set in the intersection (e.g., the highest degree d_t). Using some more homomorphic operations, we can make the degree of B as low as $2d_1 - 1$, namely it can be tied to the size of the smallest set S_1 rather than the largest set S_t.

To this end, we use the optimization from Section 2.2, where instead of using $A'(x) = A_t(x) + \sum_{2 \le i < t} \rho_i A_i(x)$, the proxy uses $A''(x) = A' \bmod A_1(x)$. We note that given the encrypted coefficients of both the polynomial $A'(x)$ of degree d_t and the *monic* polynomial $A_1(x)$ of degree d_1, we can homomorphically reduce A' modulo A_1 as long as our SWHE scheme supports formulas of degree $d_t - d_1$. To see this, notice that given the encryption $\mathsf{Enc}(\alpha'_{d_t})$ of the top coefficient of A', we can reduce the degree of A' by one by setting $A'' = A' - \alpha'_{d_t} \cdot A_1(x) \cdot x^{d_t - d_1}$. Clearly the degree of A' is one less than that of A' and it satisfies $A'' \equiv A'$ $(\bmod\ A_1)$.

However, reducing modulo A_1 can be done using more limited homomorphism if the proxy is given not just the encryption of A_1 but also some other ciphertexts. For example, suppose the proxy is given the encryption $\mathsf{Enc}(x^i \bmod A_1)$ for $i = d_1 + 1, d_1 + 2, d_1 + 3, \ldots, d_t$. Then given the encryptions of all the coefficients of A', $\mathsf{Enc}(\alpha'_0), \ldots, \mathsf{Enc}(\alpha'_{d_t})$, the proxy computes the encryption of the reduced polynomial as $\mathsf{Enc}(A' \bmod A_1) = \mathsf{Enc}(\sum_{i=0}^{d_t} \alpha'_i (x^i \bmod A_1))$. Since the proxy has the encryptions of all the α'_i's and the $(x^i \bmod A_1)$'s, then it is enough if our SWHE scheme supports only quadratic formulas, such as [7,1].

The above two procedures for computing polynomial modular reduction represent two extremes on the storage/homomorphism tradeoff. Perhaps a better tradeoff can be obtained by storing only logarithmically many encrypted polynomials corresponding to A_1, and using a SWHE scheme supporting formulas of degree $O(\log d_t)$. Denoting $\Delta = d_t - d_1$, the proxy is given the encryptions $\mathsf{Enc}(x^{d_1+2^i} \bmod A_1)$ for $i = 0, 1, \ldots, \lceil \log \Delta \rceil$. Given these encryptions and the encryptions of the coefficients of A', reducing A' modulo A_1 homomorphically can be done in $\lceil \log \Delta \rceil$ steps. See appendix of full version for more details.

3.3   Other Optimizations and Variations

Returning two polynomials. The most expensive operation that the client performs in our protocol is factoring the polynomial B. Even with the bandwidth reduction trick from above, its degree is still twice as large as the degree of the smallest A_i, which can be much higher than the degree of the gcd of the A_i's.

A simple trick that can be used here is to have the proxy send to the client two encrypted polynomials. Namely, after the proxy computes the polynomial A' in Step 2(i), it repeats Step 2(ii) twice, that is, choose polynomials R_1, R' and S_1, S' and set $B(x) = A_1(x)R_1(x) + A'(x)R'(x)$ and $C(x) = A_1(x)S_1(x) + A'(x)S'(x)$. The proxy sends the encrypted B and C to the client, who engages in an oblivious decryption protocol with the server to decrypt both. Then the client computes the gcd of the two polynomials B and C, and with high probability this polynomial is the gcd of all the A_i's, which hopefully has much lower degree than B, C themselves.

Obscuring relations between different queries. One problem with the basic solution above is that the client sends to the proxy all the tags $\mathsf{tg}_i = \mathsf{PRF}_s(\mathrm{attr}_i = \mathrm{value}_i)$, so the proxy can tell when a given tg_i is used in multiple queries. This problem can be mitigated by adding spurious tags to the request, but without changing the result of the final intersection. The idea is to have the client send to the proxy pairs (tg_i, s_i) where tg_i is a tag for an attribute-value pair and s_i is an encryption of a bit $\sigma_i \in \{0, 1\}$. By using a quadratic-homomorphic encryption scheme (such as [7]), the proxy can choose its randomizers $R_i(x)$ and compute an encryption of the polynomial $B(x) = \sum_i R_i(x) \cdot (\sigma_i \cdot A_i(x))$. The client will send some spurious tags tg_i with $\sigma_i = 0$, thus obscuring the tags that it is really interested in, but without changing the result of the intersection.

3.4   Speedups via Batching

One appealing optimization that applies to the protocol in this paper is to use "batch homomorphic encryption" where a single ciphertext represents a vector of encrypted values and a single homomorphic operation on two such ciphertexts applies the homomorphic operation component-wise to the entire vector. This way, for the cost of a single homomorphic operation we get to compute on an entire vector of encrypted plaintexts. This is a cryptographic analogue of the Single Instruction Multiple Data (SIMD) architecture and is supported by recent fully homomorphic encryption systems [1,14,2,6].

We take advantage of batching in our context by splitting the database into a few small partial databases and running the same query against all parts in parallel. When using the techniques from [14,2,6] (for the ring-LWE-based homomorphic encryption) we can pack in each ciphertext ℓ different plaintext elements (where ℓ is typically in the range of 500-10,000). We can then break an r-record database into ℓ smaller databases, each with $\approx r/\ell$ records.

In the three-party setting, with each tag $\mathsf{tg}_i = \mathsf{PRF}_s(\text{“attr}_i = \mathsf{val}_i\text{”})$, we keep encryptions of ℓ different polynomials, one for each part of the database. These are placed in the ℓ "plaintext slots" of the ciphertexts, so the number of ciphertexts that needs to be kept is only as large as the degree of the largest of these ℓ polynomials. (If the records are split between the parts uniformly, then we expect this degree to be roughly a factor of ℓ smaller than it would be if we keep everything as a single database.) A client query will still be processed in the exact same way as in the previous sections, but now the client will get back from the proxy not a single encrypted polynomial $B(x)$ but ℓ different polynomials $B_j(x)$, one for each of plaintext slot. The client gets the decryption of all these B_i's from the server, factors them all, and takes the union of their roots to be the set of records that match the query.

4   Implementing the Three-Party Protocol

We implemented the basic three-party protocol from Section 3 using both the Paillier cryptosystem [12] and a variant of Brakerski's leveled homomorphic system [1]. Because the Paillier cryptosystem only supports additive homomorphism, we can only support the basic protocol, without the batching (Section 3.4) and modular reduction optimizations (Section 3.2). In contrast, Brakerski's leveled homomorphic scheme supports a bounded number of homomorphic additions and multiplications. To demonstrate the effectiveness of our optimizations we conducted a set of experiments with batching and modular reduction using Brakerski's cryptosystem. Since most of our described optimizations pertain specifically to the problem of oblivious set intersection, we focus our experimental analysis on this portion of the three-party protocol.

In this section, we show that support for batching (Section 3.4) in Brakerski's system is critical for evaluating large queries. Specifically, for large queries, the Paillier system becomes intractable, leaving the Brakerski system as the only suitable option. We also demonstrate that the modular reduction optimization (Section 3.2) yields substantial reductions in *both* computation time and network bandwidth on queries where there is a large disparity in the sizes of the record sets corresponding to the tags. In one case, we show a 4X improvement in *both* processing time and bandwidth using modular reduction.

4.1   Homomorphic Encryption Schemes

Paillier cryptosystem. Recall that the Paillier cryptosystem works over $\mathbb{Z}_{n^2}^*$ for an RSA-modulus n of unknown factorization. The scheme has plaintext space $\mathcal{P} = \mathbb{Z}_n$ and ciphertext space $\mathbb{Z}_{n^2}^*$. The scheme is additively homomorphic, with

Table 1. Parameters used to achieve 128-bit security in the Brakerski system. The false positive rate is fixed at 10^{-3}.

Experiment	Ring Modulus Φ_m	Plaintext Slots $\varphi(m)$	Plaintext Modulus p	Ciphertext Modulus q
NoMR	$m = 5939$	$\varphi(m) = 5938$	$p = 1000032577$	$\log_2 q = 181$
MR, MRNoKS	$m = 7867$	$\varphi(m) = 7866$	$p = 1000021573$	$\log_2 q = 238$

homomorphic addition implemented by multiplying the corresponding ciphertexts in $\mathbb{Z}_{n^2}^*$. Similarly, we can homomorphically multiply a ciphertext $c \in \mathbb{Z}_{n^2}^*$ by a constant $a \in \mathbb{Z}_n$ by computing $c^a \bmod n^2$.

Brakerski's leveled homomorphic cryptosystem. We also use the ring-LWE-based variant of Brakerski's scale-invariant homomorphic cryptosystem [1]. Specifically, our implementation operates over polynomial rings modulo a cyclotomic polynomial. Let $\Phi_m(x)$ denote the mth cyclotomic polynomial. Then, we work over the ring $R = \mathbb{Z}[x]/\Phi_m(x)$. Specifically, we take our plaintext space to be $\mathcal{P} = R_p = \mathbb{Z}_p[x]/\Phi_m(x)$ and our ciphertext space to be $R_q = \mathbb{Z}_q[x]/\Phi_m(x)$ for some $q > p$. In this scheme, our secret keys and ciphertexts are *vectors* of elements in R_q. Homomorphic addition is implemented by adding the corresponding ciphertexts. We can multiply a ciphertext $\mathbf{c}$ by a constant $a \in R_p$ by computing $a\mathbf{c}$. Finally, homomorphic multiplication is performed using a tensor product. Note that when we homomorphically multiply two ciphertexts, the resulting ciphertext is encrypted under a tensored secret key. Using a technique called *key-switching*, we can transform the product ciphertext into a regular ciphertext encrypted under the original secret key. We refer readers to [1] for further details.

As noted in Section 3.4, one of the main advantages of using a ring-LWE-based homomorphic scheme is the fact that we can pack multiple plaintext messages into one ciphertext using a technique called batching. To use batching we partition a database with r records into ℓ separate databases, each containing approximately r/ℓ records. Correspondingly, the the degrees of the polynomials in each database are reduced roughly by a factor of ℓ. In our implementation, $\ell \geq 5000$, so this translates to a substantial improvement in performance.

We now consider a choice for the plaintext modulus p for use in the Brakerski scheme. From Lemma 1, we have that the probability of a false positive (mistaking an element not in the intersection to be in the intersection) is given by $|U| / |\mathbb{F}_p|$. If we tolerate a false positive rate of at most $0 < \lambda < 1$, then we require that $|\mathbb{F}_p| \geq \frac{1}{\lambda} |U| = \frac{r}{\lambda}$, where r is the number of records in the database. Additionally, to maximize the number of plaintext slots, we choose p such that $p = 1 \pmod{m}$. To summarize, we choose our plaintext modulus p such that $p = 1 \pmod{m}$ and $p \geq \frac{r}{\lambda}$.

4.2   Experimental Setup

We implemented the three-party protocol using both the Paillier and Brakerski cryptosystems as the underlying homomorphic encryption scheme. Our implementation was done in C++ using the NTL library over GMP. Our code was compiled using g++ 4.6.3 on Ubuntu 12.04. We ran all timing experiments on cluster machines with multicore AMD Opteron processors running at 2.1 GHz. The machines had 512 KB of cache and 96 GB of available memory. All of our experiments were conducted in a single-threaded, single-processor environment. Memory usage during the computation generally stayed below 10 GB.

In the Paillier-based scheme, we used a 1024-bit RSA modulus for all of our experiments. For the Brakerski system, we chose parameters m, p, q to obtain 128-bit security and a false positive rate of $\lambda = 10^{-3}$. See appendix of full version for derivation of parameters. Since the Brakerski system supports both the batching and modular reduction optimizations described in Section 3.4 and Section 3.2, respectively, we considered three different experimental setups to assess the viability of these optimizations. Below, we describe each of our experiments. The parameters used in our SWHE scheme for each setup are given in Table 1.

NoMR: *Brakerski scheme without modular reduction.* In the NoMR setup, we just used the batching capabilities of the Brakerski system. Note that this setup only required homomorphic addition, and *not* homomorphic multiplication, and thus, allowed us to use smaller parameters in the Brakerski system.

MR: *Brakerski scheme with modular reduction.* In the MR setup, we considered the modular reduction optimization from Section 3.2. In the final step of the three-party protocol, the proxy computes the polynomial $B(x) = A_1(x)R_1(x) + A'(x)R'(x)$ where $\deg(A_1) \leq \deg(A')$. When we perform modular reduction, we compute $A'(x) \pmod{A_1(x)}$ followed by $B(x) \pmod{A_1(x)}$. This optimization reduces the degree of the polynomial $B(x)$ that the proxy sends to the client as well as the cost of the computation of $B(x)$. To perform this optimization, the SWHE scheme must support at least one multiplication, thus requiring larger parameters for security. Consequently, each homomorphic operation takes longer, but since we are performing fewer operations overall, the modular reduction can yield substantial gains for certain queries. Due to the cost of homomorphic multiplications, we just consider the case of doing a single multiply.

MRNoKS: *Brakerski scheme with modular reduction but without key switching.* When we homomorphically multiply two ciphertexts in the Brakerski system, we obtain a tensored ciphertext (e.g., a higher-dimensional ciphertext) encrypted under a tensored secret key. Normally, we perform a key-switching operation that transforms the tensored ciphertext into a new ciphertext encrypted under the normal secret key. If left unchecked, the length of the ciphertexts grows exponentially with the number of successive multiplications. Thus, the key-switching procedure is important for constraining the length of the ciphertexts. In our application, we perform a single multiplication, and so the key-switching procedure may be unnecessary. Since the key-switching operation has non-negligible cost, we can achieve improved performance at the expense of slightly longer ciphertexts (and thus, increased bandwidth) by not performing the key switch.

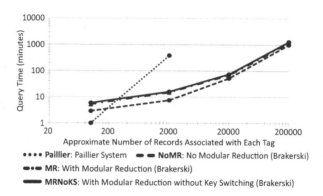

Fig. 1. Timing tests on *balanced* queries using the Paillier cryptosystem and the three setups of the Brakerski cryptosystem described in Section 4.2. All queries were conducted over a database consisting of 10^6 records. Each query consisted of five tags; the approximate number of records associated with each tag is indicated on the plot above. Note that the running time with Paillier became too large when the database had more than 2,000 records per tag and as a result the Paillier line stops at 2,000.

Query type. In each of our experiments, we operated over a database with 10^6 records and performed queries consisting of five tags. Let $d_1 \leq d_2 \leq \cdots \leq d_5$ denote the number of elements associated with each tag $\mathsf{tg}_1, \ldots, \mathsf{tg}_5$. We profiled our system on two different sets of queries: *balanced* queries and *unbalanced* queries. In a balanced query, the number of elements associated with each tag was approximately the same: $d_1 \approx d_2 \approx \cdots \approx d_5$.

In an unbalanced query, the number of elements associated with each tag varies significantly. Specifically, d_1 is at most 5% of d_5. As discussed in Section 1, queries like these where we compute an intersection of a large set with a much smaller set are very common and so, it is important that we can perform such queries efficiently. For each query, we measured the computation time as well as the total network bandwidth required by each of our setups. Note that due to the poor scalability of the Paillier system, we were not able to perform the full set of experiments using the Paillier cryptosystem.

4.3   Experimental Results

Balanced queries. In the first set of experiments, we considered the run-time and bandwidth requirements for performing balanced queries. In particular, we constructed a database with 10^6 records and where each tag in the database was associated with approximately d records (for d ranging from 100 to 200,000). We executed these queries on the four different setups described above (Paillier, NoMR, MR, and MRNoKS). Our timing and bandwidth measurements are summarized in Fig. 1 and Fig. 2. Because the query execution time dominated the cost of the computation, we just present the cost of performing the query.

We compare the computational cost and network bandwidth required by each of our setups described in Section 4.2 for evaluating balanced queries. From

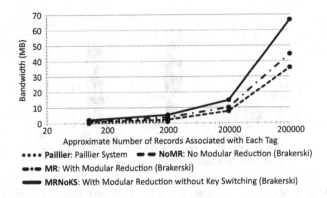

Fig. 2. Bandwidth measurements on *balanced* queries using the Paillier cryptosystem and the three different setups of the Brakerski cryptosystem. Same setup as in Fig. 1.

Fig. 1, we see that the Paillier system is faster for small queries involving sets of several hundred records. This is due to the simplicity and low computational overhead of the Paillier cryptosystem compared to Brakerski's leveled homomorphic cryptosystem. However, the run time scales quadratically with the size of the underlying sets, so for queries with over 2,000 elements, the Paillier system becomes completely impractical. While the performance using Brakerski's system also scales quadratically with the number of records, batching allows us to split the main database $\mathcal{D}$ into ℓ slices, each with approximately $\frac{|\mathcal{D}|}{\ell}$ records. Thus, we were able to reduce the degree of the polynomials we needed to multiply by a factor of approximately $\ell > 5000$. In turn, batching allows for approximately a factor of ℓ increase in the number of records the system could handle. Using Brakerski's system, we are able to handle queries for tags consisting of 200,000 records. These results also indicate that in terms of both bandwidth and computation time, the modular reduction optimization from Section 3.2 is ineffective when we have *balanced* queries. This is because the modular reduction optimization is designed for cases where there is a large disparity between the sizes of the smallest and largest sets. When the size of each set is approximately equal, the larger parameters needed to support the modular reduction optimization coupled with the computational cost of performing the optimization resulted in worse performance overall. Thus, for balanced queries, it is advantageous to just use the Brakerski system without additional optimizations.

Unbalanced queries. We also considered the case where the underlying sets are unbalanced, that is, cases where the smallest set contains at most 5% of the number of records in the largest set. Due to the poor scalability of the Paillier system, we only performed the queries using our three Brakerski setups. Our results are summarized in Fig. 3 and Fig. 4.

When working with unbalanced queries, the modular reduction optimization (with or without key switching) reduces the necessary bandwidth. Despite the fact that each individual ciphertext is larger when we perform modular reduction

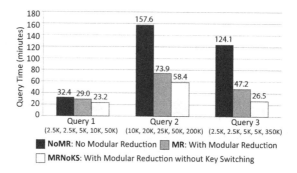

Fig. 3. Timing tests on *unbalanced* queries using the three different setups of the Brakerski system (described in Section 4.2). All queries were conducted over a database consisting of 10^6 records. Each query consisted of five tags; the number of records associated with each tag is shown in parenthesis in the corresponding graphs.

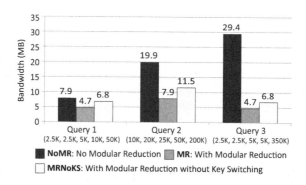

Fig. 4. Bandwidth measurements on *unbalanced* queries using the three different setups of the Brakerski system. Same setup as in Fig. 3.

(due to the larger parameters in the Brakerski system), the polynomials also have much lower degree (degree given by $2d_1 - 1$ rather than $d_1 + d_5 - 1$). The larger the difference between d_1 and d_5, the more substantial the bandwidth reduction. Furthermore, performing modular reduction also translated to faster query processing. Recall that in the last step of the proxy computation, the proxy multiplies a polynomial of degree $d_5 - 1$ with one of degree $d_1 - 1$. If we use modular reduction, the multiplication is instead performed on two polynomials of degree d_1 and $d_1 - 1$. From our experiments, we see that when $d_1 = 10,000$ and $d_5 = 200,000$ (Query 2), the MRNoKS setup is about 2.7 times faster. When this gap is even larger with $d_1 = 2,500$ and $d_5 = 350,000$ (Query 3), we observe that the MRNoKS setup is almost 4.7 times faster than the NoMR system. Even with key switching in this case (Query 3), modular reduction still reduces the run time by a factor of 2.6. In both MR and MRNoKS, the bandwidth on this very unbalanced query is reduced by more than a factor of 4 compared to the baseline without the modular reduction optimization.

To summarize, performing the modular reduction optimization is greatly beneficial, both in terms of computation time as well as in terms of network bandwidth, when there is a large difference between the sizes of the underlying sets. As we have demonstrated, it is possible to achieve over a 4X improvement in *both* computation time and network bandwidth on certain queries, making modular reduction a very viable optimization in practice.

5   Conclusion

This paper presents new protocols and tools that can be used to construct a private database query system supporting a rich set of queries. We showed how a polynomial representation of the database allows for efficient evaluation of private conjunction queries. The basic schemes only require an additively homomorphic system like Paillier, but we showed that significant performance improvements can be obtained using a stronger homomorphic system that supports both homomorphic additions and a few homomorphic multiplications. Our experiments quantify this improvement showing a real-world example where lattice-based homomorphic systems can outperform their factoring-based counterparts.

Acknowledgements. This work is supported by IARPA via DoI/NBC contract number D11PC20202. The U.S. Government is authorized to reproduce and distribute reprints for Governmental purposes notwithstanding any copyright annotation thereon. Disclaimer: The views and conclusions contained herein are those of the authors and should not be interpreted as necessarily representing the official policies or endorsements, either expressed or implied, of IARPA, DoI/NBC, or the U.S. Government.

References

1. Brakerski, Z.: Fully homomorphic encryption without modulus switching from classical GapSVP. In: Safavi-Naini, R. (ed.) CRYPTO 2012. LNCS, vol. 7417, pp. 868–886. Springer, Heidelberg (2012)
2. Brakerski, Z., Gentry, C., Vaikuntanathan, V.: Fully homomorphic encryption without bootstrapping. In: Innovations in ITCS 2012 (2012)
3. Chor, B., Kushilevitz, E., Goldreich, O., Sudan, M.: Private information retrieval. J. ACM 45(6), 965–981 (1998)
4. De Cristofaro, E., Lu, Y., Tsudik, G.: Efficient techniques for privacy-preserving sharing of sensitive information. In: McCune, J.M., Balacheff, B., Perrig, A., Sadeghi, A.-R., Sasse, A., Beres, Y. (eds.) Trust 2011. LNCS, vol. 6740, pp. 239–253. Springer, Heidelberg (2011)
5. Gentry, C.: A fully homomorphic encryption scheme. Ph.D. thesis, Stanford University (2009), http://crypto.stanford.edu/craig
6. Gentry, C., Halevi, S., Smart, N.P.: Fully homomorphic encryption with polylog overhead. In: Pointcheval, D., Johansson, T. (eds.) EUROCRYPT 2012. LNCS, vol. 7237, pp. 465–482. Springer, Heidelberg (2012)

7. Gentry, C., Halevi, S., Vaikuntanathan, V.: A simple BGN-type cryptosystem from LWE. In: Gilbert, H. (ed.) EUROCRYPT 2010. LNCS, vol. 6110, pp. 506–522. Springer, Heidelberg (2010)
8. Gertner, Y., Ishai, Y., Kushilevitz, E., Malkin, T.: Protecting data privacy in private information retrieval schemes. In: STOC 1998, pp. 151–160 (1998)
9. Goldwasser, S., Micali, S.: Probabilistic encryption. Journal of Computer and System Sciences 28(2), 270–299 (1984)
10. Ishai, Y., Prabhakaran, M., Sahai, A.: Founding cryptography on oblivious transfer – efficiently. In: Wagner, D. (ed.) CRYPTO 2008. LNCS, vol. 5157, pp. 572–591. Springer, Heidelberg (2008)
11. Kissner, L., Song, D.: Privacy-preserving set operations. In: Shoup, V. (ed.) CRYPTO 2005. LNCS, vol. 3621, pp. 241–257. Springer, Heidelberg (2005)
12. Paillier, P.: Public-key cryptosystems based on composite degree residuosity classes. In: Stern, J. (ed.) EUROCRYPT 1999. LNCS, vol. 1592, pp. 223–238. Springer, Heidelberg (1999)
13. Raykova, M., Cui, A., Vo, B., Liu, B., Malkin, T., Bellovin, S.M., Stolfo, S.J.: Usable, Secure, Private Search. IEEE Security and Privacy, 53–60 (October 2012)
14. Smart, N.P., Vercauteren, F.: Fully homomorphic SIMD operations (2011), Manuscript at http://eprint.iacr.org/2011/133

BLAKE2: Simpler, Smaller, Fast as MD5

Jean-Philippe Aumasson[1], Samuel Neves[2], Zooko Wilcox-O'Hearn[3],
and Christian Winnerlein[4]

[1] Kudelski Security, Switzerland
jeanphilippe.aumasson@gmail.com
[2] University of Coimbra, Portugal
sneves@dei.uc.pt
[3] Least Authority Enterprises, USA
zooko@zooko.com
[4] Ludwig Maximilian University of Munich, Germany
codesinchaos@gmail.com

Abstract. We present the hash function BLAKE2, an improved version
of the SHA-3 finalist BLAKE optimized for speed in software. Target
applications include cloud storage, intrusion detection, or version control
systems. BLAKE2 comes in two main flavors: BLAKE2b is optimized
for 64-bit platforms, and BLAKE2s for smaller architectures. On 64-
bit platforms, BLAKE2 is often faster than MD5, yet provides security
similar to that of SHA-3: up to 256-bit collision resistance, immunity
to length extension, indifferentiability from a random oracle, etc. We
specify parallel versions BLAKE2bp and BLAKE2sp that are up to 4
and 8 times faster, by taking advantage of SIMD and/or multiple cores.
BLAKE2 reduces the RAM requirements of BLAKE down to 168 bytes,
making it smaller than any of the five SHA-3 finalists, and 32% smaller
than BLAKE. Finally, BLAKE2 provides a comprehensive support for
tree-hashing as well as keyed hashing (be it in sequential or tree mode).

1   Introduction

The SHA-3 Competition succeeded in selecting a hash function that comple-
ments SHA-2 and is much faster than SHA-2 in hardware [1]. There is nevertheless a demand for fast software hashing for applications such as integrity
checking and deduplication in filesystems and cloud storage, host-based intrusion
detection, version control systems, or secure boot schemes. These applications
sometimes hash a few large messages, but more often a lot of short ones, and
the performance of the hash directly affects the user experience.

Many systems use faster algorithms like MD5, SHA-1, or a custom function
to meet their speed requirements, even though those functions may be insecure.
MD5 is famously vulnerable to collision and length-extension attacks [2,3], but
it is 2.53 times as fast as SHA-256 on an Intel Ivy Bridge and 2.98 times as fast
as SHA-256 on a Qualcomm Krait CPU.

Despite MD5's significant security flaws, it continues to be among the most
widely-used algorithms for file identification and data integrity. To choose just
a handful of examples, the OpenStack cloud storage system [4], the popular

M. Jacobson et al. (Eds.): ACNS 2013, LNCS 7954, pp. 119–135, 2013.

version control system Perforce, and the recent object storage system used internally in AOL [5] all rely on MD5 for data integrity. The venerable md5sum unix tool remains one of the most widely-used tools for data integrity checking. The Sun/Oracle ZFS filesystem includes the option of using SHA-256 for data integrity, but the default configuration is to instead use a non-cryptographic 256-bit checksum, for performance reasons. The Tahoe-LAFS distributed storage system uses SHA-256 for data integrity, but is investigating a faster hash function [6].

Some SHA-3 finalists outperform SHA-2 in software: for example, on Ivy Bridge BLAKE-512 is 1.41 times as fast as SHA-512, and BLAKE-256 is 1.70 times as fast as SHA-256. BLAKE-512 reaches 5.76 cycles per byte, or approximately 579 mebibytes per second, against 411 for SHA-512, on a CPU clocked at 3.5GHz. Some other SHA-3 submissions are competitive in speed with BLAKE and Skein, but these have been less analyzed and generally inspire less confidence (e.g., due to distinguishers on the compression function).

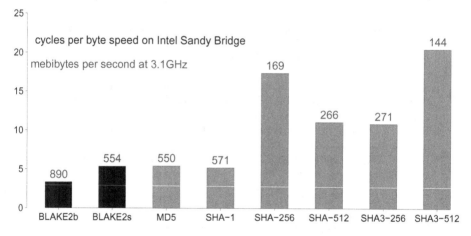

Fig. 1. Speed comparison of various popular hash functions, taken from eBACS's "hydra7" measurements. SHA-3 and BLAKE2 have no known security issues. SHA-1, MD5, SHA-256, and SHA-512 are susceptible to length-extension. SHA-1 and MD5 are vulnerable to collisions. MD5 is vulnerable to cheap chosen-prefix collisions.

BLAKE thus appears to be a good candidate for fast software hashing. Its security was evaluated by NIST in the SHA-3 process as having a "very large security margin", and the cryptanalysis published on BLAKE was noted as having "a great deal of depth" (see §4).

But as observed by Preneel [7], its design "reflects the state of the art in October 2008"; since then, and after extensive cryptanalysis, we have a better understanding of BLAKE's security and efficiency properties. We therefore introduce BLAKE2, an improved BLAKE with the following properties:

- **Faster than MD5** on 64-bit Intel platforms
- **32% less RAM** required than BLAKE
- Direct support, with no overhead, of
  - **Parallelism** for many-times faster hashing on multicore or SIMD CPUs
  - **Tree hashing** for incremental update or verification of large files
  - **Prefix-MAC** for authentication that is simpler and faster than HMAC
  - **Personalization** for defining a unique hash function for each application
- **Minimal padding**, faster and simpler to implement

Fig. 1 presents our results on the Sandy Bridge, and compares them against other common hash functions, and the SHA-3 winner Keccak.

The rest of this paper is structured as follows: §2 describes how BLAKE2 differs from BLAKE, §3 discusses its efficiency on various platforms and reports preliminary benchmarks, and §4 discusses its security.

2 Description of BLAKE2

The BLAKE2 family consists of two main algorithms:

- **BLAKE2b** is optimized for *64-bit platforms* — including NEON-enabled ARMs — and produces digests of any size between 1 and 64 bytes.
- **BLAKE2s** is optimized for *8- to 32-bit platforms*, and produces digests of any size between 1 and 32 bytes.

Both are designed to offer security similar to that of an ideal function producing digests of same length. Each one is portable to any CPU, but can be up to twice as fast when used on the CPU size for which it is optimized; for example, on a Tegra 2 (32-bit ARMv7-based SoC) BLAKE2s is expected to be about twice as fast as BLAKE2b, whereas on an AMD A10-5800K (64-bit, Piledriver microarchitecture), BLAKE2b is expected to be more than 1.5 times as fast as BLAKE2s.

Since BLAKE2 is very similar to BLAKE, we first describe the changes introduced with BLAKE2. We refer to https://blake2.net for the full version of the BLAKE2 paper, or https://131002.net/blake for a complete specification of BLAKE.

2.1 Fewer Rounds

BLAKE2b does *12 rounds* and BLAKE2s does *10 rounds*, against 16 and 14 respectively for BLAKE. Based on the security analysis performed so far, and on reasonable assumptions on future progress, it is unlikely that 16 and 14 rounds are meaningfully more secure than 12 and 10 rounds (as discussed in §4). Recall that the initial BLAKE submission [8] had 14 and 10 rounds, respectively, and that the later increase [9] was motivated by the high speed of BLAKE (i.e., it could afford a few extra rounds for the sake of conservativeness), rather than by cryptanalysis results.

This change gives a direct speed-up of about 25% and 29%, respectively, on long inputs. Speed on short inputs also significantly improves, though by a lower ratio, due to the overhead of initialization and finalization.

2.2 Rotations Optimized for Speed

BLAKE is a so-called ARX algorithm, that is, it is based on a sequence of xors, modular additions, and word rotations.

The core function (G) of BLAKE-512 performs four 64-bit word rotations of respectively 32, 25, 16, and 11 bits. BLAKE2b replaces 25 with 24, and 11 with 63:

- Using a 24-bit rotation allows SSSE3-capable CPUs to perform two rotations in parallel with a single SIMD instruction (namely, pshufb), whereas two shifts plus a logical OR are required for a rotation of 25 bits. This reduces the arithmetic cost of the G function, in recent Intel CPUs, from 18 single cycle instructions to 16 instructions, a 12% decrease.
- A 63-bit rotation can be implemented as an addition (doubling) and a shift followed by a logical OR. This provides a slight speed-up on platforms where addition and shift can be realized in parallel but not two shifts (i.e., some recent Intel CPUs). Additionally, since a rotation right by 63 is equal to a rotation left by 1, this may be slightly faster in some architectures where 1 is treated as a special case.

No platform suffers from these changes. For an in-depth analysis of optimized implementations of rotations, we refer to a previous work by two co-designers of BLAKE2 [10].

Past experiments by the BLAKE designers as well as third parties suggest that known differential attacks are unlikely to get significantly better (cf. §4).

2.3 Minimal Padding and Finalization Flags

BLAKE2 pads the last data block *if and only if necessary, with null bytes*. If the data length is a multiple of the block length, no padding byte is added. This implies that if the message length is a multiple of the block length, no padding byte is added. The padding thus does not include the message length, as in BLAKE, MD5, or SHA-2.

To avoid weaknesses, e.g. exploiting fixed points, BLAKE2 introduces *finalization flags* f_0 and f_1, as auxiliary inputs to the compression function:

- The security functionality of the padding is transferred to a finalization flag f_0, a word set to ff...ff if the block processed is the last, and to 00...00 otherwise. The flag f_0 is 64-bit for BLAKE2b, and 32-bit for BLAKE2s.
- A second finalization flag f_1 is used to signal the last node of a layer in tree-hashing modes (see §§2.10). When processing the last block—that is, when f_0 is ff...ff—the flag f_1 is also set to ff...ff if the node considered is the last, and to 00...00 otherwise.

The finalization flags are processed by the compression function as described in §2.4.

BLAKE2s thus supports hashing of data of at most $2^{64} - 1$ bytes, that is, almost 16 exbibytes (the amount of memory addressable by 64-bit processors). BLAKE2b's upper bound of $2^{128} - 1$ bytes ought to be enough for anybody.

2.4   Fewer Constants

Whereas BLAKE used 8 word constants as IV plus 16 word constants for use in the compression function, BLAKE2 uses a total of *8 word constants, instead of 24*. This saves 128 ROM bytes and 128 RAM bytes in BLAKE2b implementations, and 64 ROM bytes and 64 RAM bytes in BLAKE2s implementations.

The compression function initialization phase is modified to:

$$\begin{pmatrix} v_0 & v_1 & v_2 & v_3 \\ v_4 & v_5 & v_6 & v_7 \\ v_8 & v_9 & v_{10} & v_{11} \\ v_{12} & v_{13} & v_{14} & v_{15} \end{pmatrix} \leftarrow \begin{pmatrix} h_0 & h_1 & h_2 & h_3 \\ h_4 & h_5 & h_6 & h_7 \\ IV_0 & IV_1 & IV_2 & IV_3 \\ t_0 \oplus IV_4 & t_1 \oplus IV_5 & f_0 \oplus IV_6 & f_1 \oplus IV_7 \end{pmatrix}$$

Note the introduction of finalization flags f_0 and f_1, in place of BLAKE's redundant counter.

The G functions of BLAKE2b (left) and BLAKE2s (right) are defined as:

$$a \leftarrow a + b + m_{\sigma_r(2i)} \qquad\qquad a \leftarrow a + b + m_{\sigma_r(2i)}$$
$$d \leftarrow (d \oplus a) \ggg 32 \qquad\qquad d \leftarrow (d \oplus a) \ggg 16$$
$$c \leftarrow c + d \qquad\qquad c \leftarrow c + d$$
$$b \leftarrow (b \oplus c) \ggg 24 \qquad\qquad b \leftarrow (b \oplus c) \ggg 12$$
$$a \leftarrow a + b + m_{\sigma_r(2i+1)} \qquad\qquad a \leftarrow a + b + m_{\sigma_r(2i+1)}$$
$$d \leftarrow (d \oplus a) \ggg 16 \qquad\qquad d \leftarrow (d \oplus a) \ggg 8$$
$$c \leftarrow c + d \qquad\qquad c \leftarrow c + d$$
$$b \leftarrow (b \oplus c) \ggg 63 \qquad\qquad b \leftarrow (b \oplus c) \ggg 7$$

Note the aforementioned change of rotation counts.

Omitting the constants in G gives an algorithm similar to the (unattacked) BLAZE toy version[1]. Constants in G initially aimed to guarantee early propagation of carries, but it turned out that the benefits (if any) are not worth the performance penalty, as observed by a number of cryptanalysts. This change saves two xors and two loads per G, that is, 16% of the total arithmetic (addition and xor) instructions.

2.5   Little-Endian

BLAKE, like SHA-1 and SHA-2, parses data blocks in the big-endian byte order. Like MD5, *BLAKE2 is little-endian*, because the large majority of target platforms is little-endian (AMD and Intel desktop processors, most mainstream ARM systems). Switching to little-endian may provide a slight speed-up, and often simplifies implementations.

Note that in BLAKE, the counter t is composed of two words t_0 and t_1, where t_0 holds the least significant bits of the integer encoded. This little-endian convention is preserved in BLAKE2.

---

[1] See https://131002.net/blake/toyblake.pdf

2.6   Counter in Bytes

The counter t counts *bytes rather than bits*. This simplifies implementations and reduces the risk of error, since target applications measure data volumes in bytes rather than bits.

Note that BLAKE supported messages of arbitrary bit size for the sole purpose of conforming to NIST's requirements. However, as discussed on the SHA-3 mailing list, there is no evidence of an actual need to support this. As observed during the first months of the competition, the support of arbitrary bit sizes was the origin of several bugs in reference implementations (including that of BLAKE).

2.7   Salt Processing

BLAKE's predecessor LAKE [11] introduced the built-in support for a salt, to simplify the use of randomized hashing within digital signature schemes (although the RMX transform [12] can be used with arbitrary hash functions).

In BLAKE2 the salt is processed as a one-time input to the hash function, through the IV, rather than as an input to each compression function. This simplifies the compression function, and saves a few instructions as well as a few bytes in RAM, since the salt does not have to be stored anymore. Using salt-independent compression functions has only negligible practical impact on security, as discussed in §4.

2.8   Parameter Block

The parameter block of BLAKE2 is *xored with the IV* prior to the processing of the first data block. It encodes parameters for secure tree hashing, as well as key length (in keyed mode) and digest length.

The parameters are described below, and the block structure is shown in Tables 1 and 2:

- General parameters:
    - **Digest byte length** (1 byte): an integer in $[1, 64]$ for BLAKE2b, in $[1, 32]$ for BLAKE2s
    - **Key byte length** (1 byte): an integer in $[0, 64]$ for BLAKE2b, in $[0, 32]$ for BLAKE2s (set to 0 if no key is used)
    - **Salt** (16 or 8 bytes): an arbitrary string of 16 bytes for BLAKE2b, and 8 bytes for BLAKE2s (set to all-NULL by default)
    - **Personalization** (16 or 8 bytes): an arbitrary string of 16 bytes for BLAKE2b, and 8 bytes for BLAKE2s (set to all-NULL by default)
- Tree hashing parameters:
    - **Fanout** (1 byte): an integer in $[0, 255]$ (set to 0 if unlimited, and to 1 only in sequential mode)
    - **Maximal depth** (1 byte): an integer in $[1, 255]$ (set to 255 if unlimited, and to 1 only in sequential mode)

Table 1. BLAKE2b parameter block structure (offsets in bytes)

Offset	0	1	2	3
0	Digest length	Key length	Fanout	Depth
4	Leaf length			
8 12	Node offset			
16	Node depth	Inner length	RFU	
20 24 28	RFU			
32 ... 44	Salt			
48 ... 60	Personalization			

- **Leaf maximal byte length** (4 bytes): an integer in $[0, 2^{32} - 1]$, that is, up to 4 GiB (set to 0 if unlimited, or in sequential mode)
- **Node offset** (8 or 6 bytes): an integer in $[0, 2^{64} - 1]$ for BLAKE2b, and in $[0, 2^{48} - 1]$ for BLAKE2s (set to 0 for the first, leftmost, leaf, or in sequential mode)
- **Node depth** (1 byte): an integer in $[0, 255]$ (set to 0 for the leaves, or in sequential mode)
- **Inner hash byte length** (1 byte): an integer in $[0, 64]$ for BLAKE2b, and in $[0, 32]$ for BLAKE2s (set to 0 in sequential mode)

This is 50 bytes in total for BLAKE2b, and 32 bytes for BLAKE2s. Any bytes left are reserved for future and/or application-specific use, and are NULL. Values spanning more than one byte are written in *little-endian*. Note that tree hashing may be keyed, in which case leaf instances hash the key followed by a number of bytes equal to (at most) the maximal leaf length.

Table 2. BLAKE2s parameter block structure (offsets in bytes)

Offset	0	1	2	3
0	Digest length	Key length	Fanout	Depth
4	Leaf length			
8	Node offset			
12	Node offset (cont.)		Node depth	Inner length
16 20	Salt			
24 28	Personalization			

2.9   Keyed Hashing (MAC and PRF)

When keyed (that is, when the field key length is non-zero), BLAKE2 sets the first data block to the key padded with zeros, the second data block to the first block of the message, the third block to the second block of the message, etc. Note that the padded key is treated as arbitrary data, therefore:

- The counter t includes the 64 (or 128) bytes of the key block, regardless of the key length.
- When hashing the empty message with a key, BLAKE2b and BLAKE2s make only one call to the compression function.

The main application of keyed BLAKE2 is as a message authentication code (MAC): BLAKE2 can be used securely in prefix-MAC mode, thanks to the indifferentiability property inherited from BLAKE [13]. Prefix-MAC is faster than HMAC, as it saves at least one call to the compression function. Keyed BLAKE2 can also be used to instantiate PRFs, for example within the PBKDF2 password hashing scheme.

2.10   Tree Hashing

The parameter block supports arbitrary tree hashing modes, be it binary or ternary trees, arbitrary-depth updatable tree hashing or fixed-depth parallel hashing, etc. Note that, unlike other functions, BLAKE2 does not restrict the leaf length and the fanout to be powers of 2.

Basic mechanism. Informally, tree hashing processes chunks of data of "leaf length" bytes independently of each other, then combines the respective hashes using a tree structure wherein each node takes as input the concatenation of "fanout" hashes. The "node offset" and "node depth" parameters ensure that each invocation to the hash function (leaf of internal node) uses a different hash function. The finalization flag f_1 signals when a hash invocation is the last one at a given depth (where "last" is with respect to the node offset counter, for both leaves and intermediate nodes). The flag f_1 can only be non-zero for the last block compressed within a hash invocation, and the root node always has f_1 set to ff...ff.

The tree hashing mechanism is illustrated on Figures 2 and 3, which show layout of trees given different parameters and different input lengths. On those figures, octagons represent leaves (i.e., instances of the hash function processing input data), double-lined nodes (including leaves) are the last nodes of a layer, and thus have the flag f_1 set). Labels "$i{:}j$" indicate a node's depth i and offset j.

We refer to [14] for a comprehensive overview of secure tree hashing constructions.

Message parsing. Unless specified otherwise, we recommend that data be parsed as contiguous blocks: for example, if leaf length is 1024 bytes, then the first 1024-byte data block is processed by the leaf with offset 0, the subsequent 1024-byte data block is processed by the leaf with offset 1, etc.

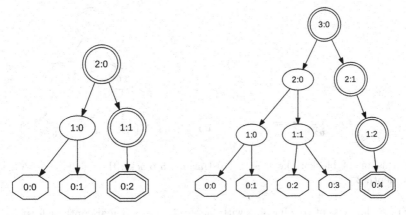

(a) Hashing 3 blocks: the tree has depth 3.

(b) Hashing 5 blocks: the tree has depth 4.

Fig. 2. Layouts of tree hashing with fanout 2, and maximal depth at least 4

Special cases. We highlight some special cases of tree hashing:

- **Unlimited fanout**: When the fanout is unlimited (parameter set to 0), then the root node hashes the concatenation of as many leaves are required to process the message. That is, the depth of the tree is always 2, regardless of the maximal depth parameter. Nevertheless, changing the maximal depth parameter changes the final hash value returned. We thus recommend to set the depth parameter to 2.
- **Dealing with saturated trees**: If a tree hashing instance has fanout $f \geq 2$, maximal depth $d \geq 2$, and leaf maximal length $\ell \geq 1$ bytes, then up to $f^{d-1} \cdot \ell$ can be processed within a single tree. If more bytes have to be hashed, the fanout of the root node is extended to hash as many digests as necessary to respect the depth limit. This mechanism is illustrated on Figure 4. Note that if the maximal depth is 2, then the value does not affect the layout of the tree, which is identical to that of a tree hash with unlimited fanout.

Generic tree parameters. Tree parameters supported by the parameter block allow for a wide range of implementation trade-offs, for example to efficiently support updatable hashing, which is typically an advantage when hashing many (small) chunks of data.

Although optimal performance will be reached by choosing the parameters specific to one's application, we specify the following parameters for a *generic tree mode*: binary tree (i.e., fanout 2), unlimited depth, and leaves of 4 KiB (the typical size of a memory page).

Updatable hashing example. Assume one has to provide a digest of a 1-tebibyte filesystem disk image that is updated every day. Instead of recomputing the

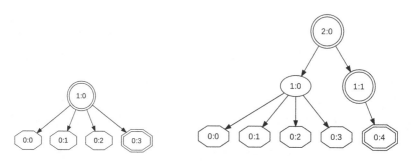

(a) Hashing 4 blocks: the tree has depth 2.

(b) Hashing 5 blocks: the tree has depth 3.

Fig. 3. Layouts of tree hashing with fanout 4, and maximal depth at least 3

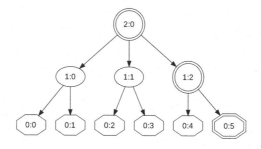

Fig. 4. Tree hashing with maximal depth 3, fanout 2, but a root with larger fanout due to the reach of the maximal depth

digest by reading all the 2^{40} bytes, one can use our generic tree mode to implement an updatable hashing scheme:

1. Apply the generic tree mode, and store the $2^{40}/4096 = 2^{28}$ hashes from the leaves as well as the $2^{28} - 2$ intermediate hashes
2. When a leaf is changed, update the final digest by recomputing the 28 intermediate hashes

If BLAKE2b is used with intermediate hashes of 32 bytes, and that it hashes at a rate of 500 mebibytes per second, then step 1 takes approximately 35 minutes and generates about 16 gibibytes of intermediate data, whereas step 2 is instantaneous.

Note however that much less data may be stored: For many applications it is preferable to only store the intermediate hashes for larger pieces of data (without increasing the leaf size), which reduces memory requirement by only storing "higher" intermediate values. For example, storing intermediate values for 4 MiB chunks instead of all 4 KiB leaves reduces the storage to only 16 MiB.

Indeed, using 4 KiB leaves allows applications with different piece sizes (as long as they are powers-of-two of at least 4 KiB) to produce the same root hash, while allowing them to make different granularity vs. storage trade-offs.

2.11   Parallel Hashing: BLAKE2sp and BLAKE2bp

We specify 2 parallel hash functions (that is, with depth 2 and unlimited leaf length):

- BLAKE2bp runs *4 instances* of BLAKE2b in parallel
- BLAKE2sp runs *8 instances* of BLAKE2s in parallel

These functions use a different *parsing rule* than the default one in §§2.10: The first instance (node offset 0) hashes the message composed of the concatenation of all message blocks of index zero modulo 4; the second instance (node offset 1) hashes blocks of index 1 modulo 4, etc. Note that when the leaf length is unlimited, parsing the input as contiguous blocks would require the knowledge of the input length before any parallel operation, which is undesirable (e.g. when hashing a stream of data of undefined length, or a file received over a network).

When hashing one single large file, and when incrementability is not required, such parallel modes with unlimited leaf length seem the most appropriate, since

- They *minimize the computation overhead* by doing only one non-leaf call to the sequential hash function
- They *maximize the usage of the CPU* by keeping multiple cores and instruction pipelines busy simultaneously
- They require *realistic bandwidth and memory*

Within a parallel hash, the same parameter block, except for the node offset, is used for all 4 or 8 instances of the sequential hash.

3   Performance

BLAKE2 is much faster than BLAKE, mainly due to its reduced number of rounds. On long messages, the BLAKE2b and BLAKE2s versions are expected to be approximately 25% and 29% faster, ignoring any savings from the absence of constants, optimized rotations, or little-endian conversion. The parallel versions BLAKE2bp and BLAKE2sp are expected to be 4 and 8 times faster than BLAKE2b and BLAKE2s on long messages, when implemented with multiple threads on a CPU with 4 or more cores (as most desktop and server processors: AMD FX-8150, Intel Core i5-2400S, etc.). Parallel hashing also benefits from advanced CPU technologies, as previously observed [10, §5.2].

Public domain C and C# code of BLAKE2 is available on https://blake2.net. We are developing a tool b2sum similar to, and aiming to replace, md5sum.

3.1 Why BLAKE2 Is Fast in Software

BLAKE2, along with its parallel variant, can take advantage of the following architectural features, or combinations thereof:

Instruction-level parallelism. Most modern processors are superscalar, that is, able to run several instructions per cycle through pipelining, out-of-order execution, and other related techniques. BLAKE2 has a natural instruction parallelism of 4 instructions within the G function; processors that are able to handle more instruction-level parallelism can do so in BLAKE2bp, by interleaving independent compression function calls. Examples of processors with notorious amount of instruction parallelism are Intel's Core 2, i7, and Itanium or AMD's K10, Bulldozer, and Piledriver.

SIMD instructions. Many modern processors contain *vector units*, which enable SIMD processing of data. Again, BLAKE2 can take advantage of vector units not only in its G function, but also in tree modes (such as the mode proposed in §§2.11), by running several compression instances within vector registers. Microarchitectures with SIMD capabilities are found in recent Intel and AMD CPUs, NEON-extended ARM-based SoC, PowerPC and Cell CPUs.

Multiple cores. Limits in both semiconductor manufacturing processes, as well as instruction-level parallelism have driven CPU manufacturers towards yet another kind of coarse-grained parallelism, where multiple independent CPUs are placed inside the same die, and enable the programmer to get thread-level parallelism. While sequential BLAKE2 does not take advantage of this, the parallel mode described in §§2.11, and other tree modes, can run each intermediate hashing in its own thread. Candidate processors for this approach are recent Intel and AMD chips, the IBM Cell, and recent ARM, UltraSPARC and Loongson models.

3.2 64-Bit CPUs

We have submitted optimized BLAKE2 implementations to eBACS [15], that take advantage of the AVX and XOP instruction sets. Table 3 reports the timings obtained in two key architectures: Intel's Sandy Bridge (hydra7) and AMD's Bulldozer (hydra6). The full set of results is available at http://bench.cr.yp.to/results-hash.html.

Table 3. Speed, in cycles per byte, of BLAKE2 in sequential mode

Microarchitecture	BLAKE2b			BLAKE2s		
	Long	1536	64	Long	1536	64
Sandy Bridge	3.32	3.81	9.00	5.34	5.35	5.50
Bulldozer	5.29	5.30	11.95	8.20	8.21	7.91

Compared to the best known timings for BLAKE [10],

- On Sandy Bridge, BLAKE2b is 71.99% faster than BLAKE-512, and BLAKE2s is 40.26% faster than BLAKE-256,
- On Bulldozer, BLAKE2b is 30.25% faster than BLAKE-512, and BLAKE2s is 43.78% faster than BLAKE-256.

Due to the lack of native rotation instructions on SIMD registers, the speedup of BLAKE2b is greater on the Intel processors, which benefit not only from the round reduction, but also from the easier-to-implement rotations.

On short messages, the speed advantage of the improved padding on BLAKE2 is quite noticeable. On Sandy Bridge, no other cryptographic hash function measured in eBACS[2] (including MD5 and MD4) is faster than BLAKE2s on 64-byte messages, while BLAKE2b is roughly as fast as MD4.

Like BLAKE, BLAKE2 will benefit from the AVX2 instruction set, which will appear in the upcoming Haswell microarchitecture by Intel. The analysis performed in [10, §4] for BLAKE applies to BLAKE2 as well, except for the constants, which reduce the number of instructions per compression function: techniques such as parallelized message loading or message caching can thus be applied to BLAKE2b and BLAKE2s. Adapting the estimates in [10, §§4.4], one obtains a lower bound of 2.62 cycles per byte for BLAKE2b on AVX2-enabled CPUs. Another bound can be defined for implementations on Haswell *not using* SIMD, but rather exploiting the additional integer execution port: this enables 4 parallel arithmetic operations and 3 parallel rotations per cycle, leading to a lower bound of $(10/4 + 4/3) \times 4 \times 2 \times 12/128 = 2.87$ cycles per byte. It remains unclear whether SIMD implementations will be faster than non-SIMD ones, on Haswell.

Compared to Keccak's SHA-3 final submission, BLAKE2 does quite well on 64-bit hardware. On Sandy Bridge, the 512-bit Keccak$[r = 576, c = 1024]$ hashes at 20.46 cycles per byte, while the 256-bit Keccak$[r = 1088, c = 512]$ hashes at 10.87 cycles per byte.

Keccak is, however, a very versatile design. By lowering the capacity from $4n$ to $2n$, where n is the output bit length, one achieves $n/2$-bit security for both collisions and second preimages [16], but also higher speed. We estimate that a 512-bit Keccak$[r = 1088, c = 512]$ would hash at about 10 cycles per byte on high-end Intel and AMD CPUs, and a 256-bit Keccak$[r = 1344, c = 256]$ would hash at roughly 8 cycles per byte. This parametrization would put Keccak at a performance level superior to SHA-2, but at a substantial cost in second-preimage resistance. BLAKE2 does not require such tradeoffs, and still offers much higher speed.

3.3 Low-End Platforms

A typical implementation of BLAKE-256 in *embedded software* stores in RAM at least the chaining value (32 bytes), the message (64 bytes), the constants

---

[2] http://bench.cr.yp.to/results-hash.html#amd64-hydra7

(64 bytes), the permutation internal state (64 bytes), the counter (8 bytes), and the salt, if used (16 bytes); that is, 232 bytes, and 248 with a salt. BLAKE2s reduces these figures to *168 bytes*—recall that the salt doesn't have to be stored anymore—that is, a gain of respectively 28% and 32%. Similarly, BLAKE2b only requires 336 bytes of RAM, against 464 or 496 for BLAKE-512.

3.4   Hardware

Hardware directly benefit from the 29% and 25% speed-up in sequential mode, due to the round reduction, for any message length. Parallelism is straightforward to implement by replicating the architecture of the sequential hash. BLAKE2 enjoys the same degrees of freedom as BLAKE to implement various space-time tradeoffs (horizontal and vertical folding, pipelining, etc.). In addition, parallel hashing provides *another dimension for trade-offs* in hardware architectures: depending on the system properties (e.g. how many input bits can be read per cycle), one may choose between, for example, BLAKE2sp based on 8 high-latency compact cores, or BLAKE2s based on a single low-latency unrolled core.

4   Security

BLAKE2 builds on the high confidence built by BLAKE in the SHA-3 competition. Although BLAKE2 performs fewer rounds than BLAKE, this does not imply lower security (it does imply a lower *security margin*), as explained below.

4.1   BLAKE Legacy

The security of BLAKE2 is closely related to that of BLAKE, since they rely on a similar core permutation originally used in Bernstein's ChaCha stream cipher [17] (itself a variant of Salsa20 [18], co-winner in the eSTREAM project[3]).

Since 2009, at least 14 research papers have described cryptanalysis results on reduced versions of BLAKE. The most advanced attacks on the BLAKE as hash function—as opposed to its building blocks—are *preimage attacks on 2.5 rounds* by Ji and Liangyu, with respective complexities 2^{241} and 2^{481} for BLAKE-256 and BLAKE-512 [19]. Most research actually considered reduced versions of the compression function or core permutation of BLAKE, regardless of the constraints imposed by the IV. The most recent results of this type are the following

- A distinguisher on 6 rounds of the permutation of BLAKE-256, with complexity 2^{456}, by Dunkelman and Khovratovich [20];
- A boomerang distinguisher on 8 rounds of the core permutation of BLAKE-512, with complexity 2^{242}, by Biryukov, Nikolic, and Roy [21] (recent work questions the correctness of this result [22]).

---

[3] See http://www.ecrypt.eu.org/stream/

The exact attacks as described in research papers may not directly apply to BLAKE2, due to the changes of rotation counts (typically, differential characteristics for BLAKE do not apply to BLAKE2). Nevertheless, we expect attacks on reduced BLAKE with n rounds to adapt to BLAKE2 with n rounds, though with slightly different complexities.

4.2   Implications of BLAKE2 Tweaks

We have argued that the reduced number of rounds and the optimized rotations are unlikely to meaningfully reduce the security of BLAKE2, compared to that of BLAKE. We summarize the security implications of other tweaks:

Salt-independent compressions. BLAKE2 salts the hash function in the IV, rather than each compression. This preserves the uniqueness of the hash function for any distinct salt, but facilitates multicollision attacks relying on offline precomputations (see [23,24]). However, this leaves fewer "controlled" bits in the initial state of the compression function, which complicates the finding of fixed points.

Many valid IVs. Due to the high number of valid parameter blocks, BLAKE2 admits many valid initial chaining values. For example, if an attacker has an oracle that returns collisions for random chaining values and messages, she is more likely to succeed in attacking the hash function because she has many valid targets, rather than a valid one. However, such a scenario assumes that (free-start) collisions can be found efficiently, that is, that the hash function is already broken. Note that the best collision-like results on BLAKE are near-collisions for the compression function with 4 *reordered* rounds [25,26].

Simplified padding. The new padding does not include the message length of the message, unlike BLAKE. However, it is easy to see that the length is indirectly encoded through the counter, and that the padding preserves the unambiguous encoding of the initial padding. That is, the padding simplification does not affect the security of the hash function. Nevertheless, it may be desirable to have a formal proof.

References

1. Chang, S., Perlner, R., Burr, W.E., Turan, M.S., Kelsey, J.M., Paul, S., Bassham, L.E.: Third-Round Report of the SHA-3 Cryptographic Hash Algorithm Competition. NISTIR 7896, National Institute for Standards and Technology (November 2012)
2. Stevens, M., Sotirov, A., Appelbaum, J., Lenstra, A., Molnar, D., Osvik, D.A., de Weger, B.: Short chosen-prefix collisions for MD5 and the creation of a rogue CA certificate. In: Halevi, S. (ed.) CRYPTO 2009. LNCS, vol. 5677, pp. 55–69. Springer, Heidelberg (2009)

3. Duong, T., Rizzo, J.: Flickr's API Signature Forgery Vulnerability (September 2009),
   http://netifera.com/research/
4. Slipetskyy, R.: Security issues in OpenStack. Master's thesis, Norwegian University of Science and Technology (2011)
5. Pollack, D.: HSS: A simple file storage system for web applications. In: 26th Large Installation System Administration Conference, LISA 2012 (2012)
6. Haver, E., Ruud, P.: Experimenting with SHA-3 candidates in Tahoe-LAFS. Technical report, Norwegian University of Science and Technology (2010)
7. Preneel, B.: The First 30 Years of Cryptographic Hash Functions and the NIST SHA-3 Competition. In: Pieprzyk, J. (ed.) CT-RSA 2010. LNCS, vol. 5985, pp. 1–14. Springer, Heidelberg (2010)
8. Aumasson, J.P., Henzen, L., Meier, W., Phan, R.C.W.: SHA-3 proposal BLAKE. Submission to NIST (Round 1/2) (2008)
9. Aumasson, J.P., Henzen, L., Meier, W., Phan, R.C.W.: SHA-3 proposal BLAKE. Submission to NIST (Round 3) (2010)
10. Neves, S., Aumasson, J.P.: Implementing BLAKE with AVX, AVX2, and XOP. Cryptology ePrint Archive, Report 2012/275 (2012),
    http://eprint.iacr.org/2012/275
11. Aumasson, J.-P., Meier, W., Phan, R.C.-W.: The hash function family LAKE. In: Nyberg, K. (ed.) FSE 2008. LNCS, vol. 5086, pp. 36–53. Springer, Heidelberg (2008)
12. Halevi, S., Krawczyk, H.: Strengthening digital signatures via randomized hashing. In: Dwork, C. (ed.) CRYPTO 2006. LNCS, vol. 4117, pp. 41–59. Springer, Heidelberg (2006)
13. Chang, D., Nandi, M., Yung, M.: Indifferentiability of the Hash Algorithm BLAKE. Cryptology ePrint Archive, Report 2011/623 (2011),
    http://eprint.iacr.org/2011/623
14. Bertoni, G., Daemen, J., Peeters, M., Assche, G.V.: Sufficient conditions for sound tree and sequential hashing modes. Cryptology ePrint Archive, Report 2009/210 (2009),
    http://eprint.iacr.org/2009/210
15. Bernstein, D.J., Lange, T. (eds.): eBACS: ECRYPT Benchmarking of Cryptographic Systems (accessed November 1, 2012)
16. Bertoni, G., Daemen, J., Peeters, M., Van Assche, G.: On the indifferentiability of the sponge construction. In: Smart, N.P. (ed.) EUROCRYPT 2008. LNCS, vol. 4965, pp. 181–197. Springer, Heidelberg (2008)
17. Bernstein, D.J.: ChaCha, a variant of Salsa20, http://cr.yp.to/chacha.html
18. Bernstein, D.J.: Snuffle 2005: the Salsa20 encryption function,
    http://cr.yp.to/snuffle.html
19. Ji, L., Liangyu, X.: Attacks on round-reduced BLAKE. Cryptology ePrint Archive, Report 2009/238 (2009), http://eprint.iacr.org/2009/238
20. Dunkelman, O., Khovratovich, D.: Iterative differentials, symmetries, and message modification in BLAKE-256. In: ECRYPT2 Hash Workshop (2011)
21. Biryukov, A., Nikolić, I., Roy, A.: Boomerang attacks on BLAKE-32. In: Joux, A. (ed.) FSE 2011. LNCS, vol. 6733, pp. 218–237. Springer, Heidelberg (2011)
22. Leurent, G.: ARXtools: A toolkit for ARX analysis. In: The Third SHA-3 Candidate Conference (March 2012)

23. Biham, E., Dunkelman, O.: A framework for iterative hash functions - HAIFA. Cryptology ePrint Archive, Report 2007/278 (2007), http://eprint.iacr.org/2007/278
24. Joux, A.: Multicollisions in iterated hash functions. Application to cascaded constructions. In: Franklin, M. (ed.) CRYPTO 2004. LNCS, vol. 3152, pp. 306–316. Springer, Heidelberg (2004)
25. Guo, J., Matusiewicz, K.: Round-reduced near-collisions of blake-32. Accepted for presentation at WEWoRC 2009 (2009)
26. Su, B., Wu, W., Wu, S., Dong, L.: Near-collisions on the reduced-round compression functions of Skein and BLAKE. In: Heng, S.-H., Wright, R.N., Goi, B.-M. (eds.) CANS 2010. LNCS, vol. 6467, pp. 124–139. Springer, Heidelberg (2010)

Cryptophia's Short Combiner
for Collision-Resistant Hash Functions

Arno Mittelbach

Darmstadt University of Technology, Germany
www.cryptoplexity.de,
arno.mittelbach@cased.de

Abstract. A combiner for collision-resistant hash functions takes two functions as input and implements a hash function with the guarantee that it is collision-resistant if one of the functions is. It has been shown that such a combiner cannot have short output (Pietrzak, Crypto 2008); that is, its output length is lower bounded by roughly $2n$ if the ingoing functions output n-bit hash values. In this paper, we present two novel definitions for hash function combiners that allow to bypass the lower bound: the first is an extended semi-black-box definition. The second is a new game-based, fully black-box definition which allows to better analyze combiners in idealized settings such as the random-oracle model or indifferentiability framework (Maurer, Renner, and Holenstein, TCC 2004). We then present a new combiner which is robust for pseudorandom functions (in the traditional sense), which does not increase the output length of its underlying functions and which is collision-resistant in the indifferentiability setting. Our combiner is particularly relevant in practical scenarios, where security proofs are often given in idealized models, and our combiner, in the same idealized model, yields strong security guarantees while remaining *short*.

Keywords: hash functions, combiners, collision resistance, multi-property combiner.

1 Introduction

A Story. Once upon a time little Cryptess was walking through her favorite forest. As usual she was thinking about a hard problem and thus did not pay much attention on where she was going. It thus came that she suddenly found herself on a beautiful glade that she had never seen before. In its center she could make out what seemed to be a fairy flapping her wings in a welcoming pattern. Little Cryptess slowly approached the fairy and politely asked "Hello little one, who are you?" The fairy responded "I am the fairy Cryptophia and since you have found my magical glade, I grant you one wish." Little Cryptess did not take long to come up with a wish: "Can you build me a hash-function combiner that while being robust for collision resistance does not increase the output length of the hash functions?" "Of course I can", said the fairy. "Here it is. But beware,

M. Jacobson et al. (Eds.): ACNS 2013, LNCS 7954, pp. 136–153, 2013.
© Springer-Verlag Berlin Heidelberg 2013

it is a magical combiner. Given access to two hash functions H_1 and H_2 and a message M it returns $H_1(M)$ if and only if H_1 is 'more' collision-resistant than H_2. Else it returns $H_2(M)$". Cryptess thought for a moment and then replied "I am sorry Cryptohia, but your combiner is utterly useless. It is not robust for collision resistance after all. Assume I give it access to two uniformly random functions $\mathcal{R}_1$ and $\mathcal{R}_2$ and I am given an oracle that computes collisions for the combiner. As the oracle will only provide collisions for $\mathcal{R}_1$ no efficient reduction can compute collisions for $\mathcal{R}_2$. This, as you should know, violates the definition of robustness and thus your combiner is useless to me." With this she turned around and went home.

Hash-Function Combiners. Hash functions are an important cryptographic primitive but, as with many primitives, efficient constructions used in practice are based on heuristics [40,34,8]. As history has shown, with time, it is not unlikely that cryptanalysts find plausible attacks [45,43,42,44,19,3,14] and it is thus a natural question to ask whether we can hedge against the failure of an implemented hash function.

A hash-function combiner is a construction which, given access to two or more hash functions, itself implements a hash function that, however, comes with certain guarantees. A combiner is called *robust* for some property π if it guarantees to satisfy property π provided that sufficiently many input functions do. The simplest version (and the one usually used in practice) is a combiner which takes two hash functions as input and hedges against the failure of one of them, i.e., it obeys π if either of the input functions does. This will also be the variant that we examine more closely in this paper. A practical example of the application of hash-function combiners are the original versions of the TLS and SSL protocols [24,20].

Assume C^{H_1,H_2} is a hash-function combiner given access to two hash functions H_1 and H_2, then robustness for property π is usually defined via a reductionist approach. That is, the combiner is called robust for π if there exists a reduction $\mathcal{P}$ such that if $\mathcal{P}$ is given access to any (breaking-)oracle $\mathcal{B}$ that breaks π on the combiner with non-negligible probability, then $\mathcal{P}^{\mathcal{B},H_1,H_2}$ must in turn break π on both input hash functions (H_1 **and** H_2) with non-negligible probability.

There are two folklore combiners for hash functions. The *concatenation combiner* $C_\|^{H_1,H_2}(M) := H_1(M)\|H_2(M)$ is, amongst others, robust for collision resistance (it should be difficult to find two distinct messages that hash to the same value). It is easy to see that a collision on the combiner directly yields collisions for both input functions. In other words, for a message pair (M, M') with $M \neq M'$ it holds that $C^{H_1,H_2}(M) = C^{H_1,H_2}(M')$ if and only if $H_1(M) = H_1(M')$ and $H_2(M) = H_2(M')$. The concatenation combiner is, however, not robust for pseudorandomness (no efficient distinguisher that is only given black-box access should be able to distinguish between the hash function and a randomly chosen function with the same domain and codomain). On the other hand, the *exclusive-or combiner* $C_\oplus^{H_1,H_2}(M) := H_1(M) \oplus H_2(M)$ which computes the bitwise exclusive-or on the outputs of the two hash functions is robust for pseudorandomness if instantiated with two independent hash functions.

However, it is not robust for collision resistance, nor even collision-resistant preserving. Hash-function combiners that are robust for multiple properties, in particular for collision resistance and pseudorandomness together, have been studied by Fischlin et al. [21,22].

Short Combiners. If we assume that H_1 and H_2 take on values in $\{0,1\}^n$ then the concatenation combiner doubles the output length, whereas the exclusive-or combiner does not. Furthermore, it is a common property that all combiners robust for collision resistance share: their output length is in the order of the sum of the output lengths of the input hash functions.

This observation lead to the question whether *short* hash-function combiners (combiners with an output length significantly shorter than that of the concatenation combiner) that are robust for collision resistance exist [12]. It has been shown that this is not the case, i.e., there exists a lower bound on the output length for combiners that are robust for collision resistance as well as for related properties [12,13,36,37,30] where the lower bound is roughly the output length achieved by the concatenation combiner.[1]

Cryptophia's Magical Combiner. Cryptess rejected Cryptophia's magical combiner on the grounds that it is not *robust* for collision resistance. Indeed, she was right, as the combiner only evaluates one of the two functions a collision on the combiner cannot possibly yield information about collisions for the other function. On the other hand, the robustness definition is usually only given for black-box combiners, i.e., combiners that only get black-box access to the hash functions; Cryptophia's magical combiner is, however, clearly not black-box. Nevertheless, what this shows is that the robustness definition requires the combiner, in some sense, to be stronger than both input hash functions which in turn leads to the lower bound on the output-length of combiners for collision resistance. This, however, goes against the intuition of what a combiner should capture: it should be at least as strong as the stronger of the two functions, but not necessarily stronger.

Contributions and Outline. In this paper we examine the current definition of robust combiners and the reason why it is necessary for combiners that are robust for collision resistance to satisfy a lower bound on their output-length (Section 3). In Section 3.2, we extend the definition (in a semi black-box way) in order to better capture the intuition: a combiner does only need to be as strong as the strongest input function and not necessarily stronger. We then present a new game-based definition for combiners (Section 3.3) which also allows to bypass the lower bounds while still being fully black-box. This second notion

---

[1] A recent framework by Baecher et al. [4] allows to precisely characterize reductions (and thus separation results) in terms of the level of black-boxness used by the construction and the reduction. In terms of the impossibility result for short combiners it can be shown that the ruled-out reductions are of the type NNN meaning that it holds even if the construction or the accompanying security reduction were using non-black-box techniques. See the full-version of this work [31] for further details.

is tailored to analyze combiners in idealized models such as the random oracle model (ROM; [7]) or the indifferentiability framework introduced by Maurer, Renner and Holenstein [28,17] giving guarantees of the form: *the combiner has property π if one of the input functions is* ideal *even if the other function is completely under the control of the adversary and possibly even based on the first function.* We go on to present a new construction for a combiner which we analyze in this new model (Section 4). The combiner does not increase the output length of its ingoing functions while guaranteeing collision resistance (and related properties) provided that one of the two input functions is indifferentiable from a random oracle (assuming ideal compression functions). Finally, we show that our combiner is robust for pseudorandomness under the "traditional" definition of robustness without needing to assume independence (as is the case for the "standard" xor-combiner). This yields the first multi-property combiner with short output length, which is robust for pseudorandomness and which gives additional guarantees about collision resistance and related properties such as pre-image resistance or target collision resistance.

2   Preliminaries

Lower-case letters, such as $n \in \mathbb{N}$, usually represent natural numbers and by 1^n we denote the unary representation of n. Upper-case letters in standard typeface, like M, stand for bit-strings which we usually call messages. By $\{0,1\}^n$ we denote the set of all bit-strings M of length $|M| = n$, while $\{0,1\}^*$ denotes the set of all bit-strings. For bit-strings $X, Y \in \{0,1\}^*$ we denote with $X\|Y$ their concatenation and with $X \oplus Y$ the bit-wise exclusive-or (XOR) operation. If $\mathcal{X}$ is a set then by $M \leftarrow \mathcal{X}$ we mean that M is chosen uniformly from $\mathcal{X}$. If $\mathcal{X}$ is a distribution then $M \leftarrow \mathcal{X}$ denotes that M is chosen according to the distribution.

If $\mathcal{A}$ is an algorithm (often also called adversary) that has black-box access to one or more oracles $\mathcal{O}_1, ..., \mathcal{O}_z$ we denote this by adding them in superscript, i.e., $\mathcal{A}^{\mathcal{O}_1,...,\mathcal{O}_z}$. By $X \leftarrow \mathcal{A}(M)$ we denote that algorithm $\mathcal{A}$ on input M outputs value X. Throughout this paper we assume 1^n to be a security parameter and we call an algorithm efficient if it runs in polynomial time in the security parameter.

If X is a random variable, $\Pr[X = x]$ denotes the probability that X takes on value x. By $\mathrm{H}_\infty(X)$ we denote the min-entropy of variable X, defined as

$$\mathrm{H}_\infty(X) := \min_{x \in \mathrm{Supp}(X)} \log(1/\Pr[X = x])$$

where the probability is over X. The (average) conditional min-entropy of random variable X conditioned on variable Z is defined (in the style of [1]) as

$$\tilde{\mathrm{H}}_\infty(X|Z) := \min_{\mathcal{A}} \log(1/\Pr[X = \mathcal{A}(Z)])$$

where the probability is over X and Z and the random coins of $\mathcal{A}$ (which has no efficiency bounds).

2.1   Hash Functions and their Properties

Formally, a hash function $\mathcal{H}$ is defined as a family of functions together with a key generation algorithm **HKGen** that picks one of the functions to be used. That is, a *hash function (family)* is a pair of efficient algorithms $\mathcal{H} = (\mathbf{HKGen}, H)$ where $\mathbf{HKGen}(1^n)$ is a probabilistic algorithm that takes as input the security parameter 1^n and outputs a key k, while deterministic algorithm $H_k(M) :=$ $H(k, M)$ takes a key k and message $M \in \{0,1\}^*$ as input and outputs a hash value $H_k(M) \in \{0,1\}^n$. Note that we will drop the subscript and simply write $H(M)$ whenever the key is clear from context.

Collision Resistance and Related Properties. A hash function $\mathcal{H}$ is called *collision-resistant* (cr) if no efficient adversary can find two distinct messages (M, M') such that $H_k(M) = H_k(M')$. More formally, a hash function is called collision-resistant, if for any efficient adversary $\mathcal{A}$ there exists a negligible function negl such that:

$$\mathbf{Adv}^{\mathrm{cr}}_{\mathcal{H}}(\mathcal{A}) := \Pr\left[\begin{array}{cc} k \leftarrow \mathbf{HKGen}(1^n); & M \neq M' \;\wedge \\ (M, M') \leftarrow \mathcal{A}(k) & H_k(M) = H_k(M') \end{array} \right] \leq \mathtt{negl}(n)$$

where the probability is over the choice of key and $\mathcal{A}$'s internal coin tosses.

Two closely related properties are *second pre-image resistance* (spr) and *target collision resistance* (tcr) (see [41] for an overview of several variants of these notions). Here the adversary's task is not to find an arbitrary collision but a specific one, in case of second pre-image resistance the target message is sampled according to a distribution $\mathcal{M}$ whereas for target collision resistance the target message is specified by a first-round adversary.[2]

Finally, we consider another variant of second pre-image resistance called *pre-image resistance* (also often referred to as *one-wayness*). In the pre-image resistance experiment a message M is again chosen according to some distribution $\mathcal{M}$. Given only the resulting hash value $H_k(M)$ (and not message M) and key k, the adversary's task is to find a corresponding pre-image M', i.e., a message M' such that $H_k(M) = H_k(M')$.

Pseudorandomness and Message Authentication Codes. Besides collision resistance and its variants, hash functions are often assumed to be *pseudorandom* (or a pseudorandom function; prf) or *secure message authentication codes*. Here the adversary is not given access to the hash function's key but only to a black-box implementing the hash function, i.e., the key is kept private at all times. A hash function $\mathcal{H}$ is called *pseudorandom* if no efficient adversary can tell whether it is given black-box access to the hash function $\mathcal{H}$ or to a random

---

[2] Note that target collision resistant hash functions are also known as universal one-way hash functions [33].

function f with the same domain and range. More formally, for any efficient adversary $\mathcal{A}$ there exists a negligible function $\texttt{negl}$ such that:

$$\mathbf{Adv}_{\mathcal{A}}^{\mathrm{prf}}(\mathcal{A}) := \left| \mathrm{Pr}_k\left[\mathcal{A}^{H_k}(1^n) = 1 \right] - \mathrm{Pr}_f\left[\mathcal{A}^f(1^n) = 1 \right] \right| \leq \texttt{negl}(n)$$

The probability is over the adversary's random coins and the choice of key in the first part and the choice of function in the second, respectively.

A hash function is called a *secure message authentication code* (mac) if no adversary given only black-box access to a hash oracle can find a message and corresponding hash value (without querying the oracle on the corresponding message) with noticeable probability. The probability is over the choice of key k and the adversary's internal coin tosses.

Random Oracles and Indifferentiability. Many security proofs are given in the random oracle model (ROM; [7]) where hash functions are modeled as ideal, i.e., as truly random functions (e.g., [16,5,6,11]). While random oracles have no structure at all hash functions, on the other hand, are usually built from a fixed-length compression function and some iteration scheme defining how arbitrarily long messages are hashed [29,18,40,27,8].

The *indifferentiability* notion introduced by Maurer, Renner and Holenstein in [28] can be seen as a generalization of indistinguishability that allows to better analyze constructions—such as hash functions—where internal state is publicly available. Coron et al. [17] applied the notion to hash functions and proved several hash constructions to be indifferentiable from a random oracle. The composition theorem for indifferentiability allows to reduce the security of a scheme in the random oracle model to the security of the compression function, in case the random oracle is implemented by a hash construction that is indifferentiable from a random oracle. As a compression function is a much more graspable object than a random oracle, indifferentiability has become an accepted design criterion for hash functions; indeed, many candidates to the SHA-3 competition [35], including the winner Keccak [8] enjoy proofs of indifferentiability [15,2,32,9,10].

3   A Novel Definition of Combiners for Hash Functions

3.1   Black-Box Combiners for Hash Functions

Combiners for hash functions are traditionally defined in the following fashion (see, for example, [12,37] for a version of this definition for collision resistance): a hash-function combiner robust for property π (e.g., collision resistance) is a construction that given black-box access to two hash functions $\mathcal{H}_1$ and $\mathcal{H}_2$ implements a hash function which obeys property π as long as $\mathcal{H}_1$ or $\mathcal{H}_2$ obeys property π. Formally, a hash-function combiner $\mathcal{C} := (\mathbf{CKGen}, C, \mathcal{P})$, robust for property π, is a triple of efficient algorithms, where $\mathbf{CKGen}(1^n, \mathbf{HKGen}_1, \mathbf{HKGen}_2)$ generates keys for hash functions $\mathcal{H}_1$ and $\mathcal{H}_2$ and possibly some additional key k_C for the combiner. Algorithm C is an efficient deterministic algorithm that on input keys k_{H_1}, k_{H_2}, k_C and $M \in \{0,1\}^*$ returns a hash value $C_{k_{H_1}, k_{H_2}, k_C}(M)$

in target domain $\{0,1\}^n$. We will usually simply write $C^{H_1,H_2}(M)$. Algorithm $\mathcal{P}$ is a security reduction, i.e., $\mathcal{P}$ is a probabilistic polynomial-time oracle Turing machine that given access to a (breaking-)oracle $\mathcal{B}$ that breaks property π on the combiner (for example, samples collisions) breaks property π on both hash functions $\mathcal{H}_1$ and $\mathcal{H}_2$. Note that $\mathcal{B}$ may be inefficient.

The classical combiner for collision resistance (and related properties) is the *concatenation combiner* defined as

$$C_{\|}^{H_1,H_2}(M) := H_1(M)\|H_2(M) \ .$$

Obviously, any collision on the combiner $C_{\|}$ directly yields collisions for hash functions H_1 and H_2. The same applies for second pre-image resistance, target collision resistance and pre-image resistance. This combiner is, however, trivially not robust for pseudorandomness. The traditional combiner for pseudorandomness is the *exclusive-or combiner*

$$C_{\oplus}^{H_1,H_2}(M) := H_1(M) \oplus H_2(M)$$

although one has to make the additional assumption that the two functions are independent. Under this assumption the combiner is robust for pseudorandomness, message authentication codes and indifferentiability [23,26]. Without this additional assumption it is, however, not even pseudorandomness preserving. Take two (keyed) random oracles $H_1, H_2 : \{0,1\}^* \to \{0,1\}^n$ where H_2 is defined as $H_2 := H_1 \oplus 1^n$. Individually, these two functions are information-theoretically indistinguishable from random functions. The XOR-combiner would, however, implement the constant 1^n-function. The exclusive-or combiner is also not robust for collision resistance, even assuming independent functions, as a collision on the combiner does not require collisions under both input functions.

Short Combiners for Collision Resistance. A crucial difference between the two classical combiners (apart from being robust for different properties) is that the concatenation combiner doubles the output length, i.e., if the two input hash functions have range $\{0,1\}^n$, then the concatenation combiner outputs hash values in $\{0,1\}^{2n}$ while the exclusive-or combiner only outputs bit-strings of length n. A natural question to ask is: can we do better? That is, *does a secure combiner for collision resistance, which has a significantly shorter output length than the concatenation combiner, exist?* This question was first posed by Boneh and Boyen in [12] and has since been answered negatively [12,13,36,37]: combiners, robust for collision resistance, with significantly shorter output length than the concatenation combiner do not exist. Recently, a similar result was proved for second pre-image resistance, target collision resistance and pre-image resistance [30].

Let us quickly sketch the proof idea for collision-resistance. Assume we have a combiner for two hash functions with range $\{0,1\}^n$. If the combiner compresses its output to below $2n$ bits, then by the pigeonhole principle, there must exist collisions that result from compression rather than from collisions on the original hash functions. This allows to show the existence of an adversary which only samples such collisions that result from compression (note that the breaking oracle does *not* need to be efficient and can, thus, search for such a collision). Naturally, these collisions do not help any security reduction $\mathcal{P}$ in finding collisions on the input hash functions. For example, assume the input hash functions are random oracles: then, a collision on the combiner which solely results from compression does not provide any help in finding a collision for one of the random oracles. This allows to show that no security reduction can exist if the combiner compresses. Hence, combiners with short output-length do not exist.

3.2 Extending the Traditional Definition

In the introduction we saw that Cryptophia's magical combiner is not robust for collision resistance under the traditional definition of robustness. In the following we extend the traditional definition of combiners for collision-resistant hash functions such that it also captures the "magical" combiner. To this end, we need to relax the requirements on the security reduction $\mathcal{P}$ while ensuring that, in doing so, we won't label any insecure combiners "secure". The idea is to call a combiner robust for some property π if the advantage of any efficient adversary against the combiner is upper-bounded by the maximal advantage of *any* efficient adversary against any of the two input hash functions. That is, the combiner needs to be at least as *strong* as the better of the two functions, but not necessarily stronger.

To formalize the idea, we need a notion of the maximum advantage of any adversary against some property π.

Definition 1. *Let $t \in \mathbb{N}$ be a natural number and n be a security parameter. The maximum t-advantage $\mathbf{AdvMax}_\pi^t$ against property π on hash function $\mathcal{H}$ is defined as the maximum advantage of any adversary running in time t against property π on hash function $\mathcal{H}$:*

$$\mathbf{AdvMax}_\pi^t(\mathcal{H}, 1^n) := \max_{\mathcal{A}} \mathbf{Adv}_{\mathcal{A}}^\pi(\mathcal{H}, 1^n) \quad s.t. \ \mathcal{A} \ runs \ in \ time \ t$$

We now present an extension to the current black-box definition of robust combiners for hash functions. We extend the original definition such that all robust combiners remain robust under the new definition but we relax the requirements on the security reduction such that the combiner does not need to be stronger than any of the input functions.

Definition 2 (extension). *Let n be a security parameter. Let $\mathcal{C} := (\mathbf{CKGen}, C)$ be a combiner for hash functions $\mathcal{H}_1$ and $\mathcal{H}_2$ as defined earlier. Let π be a property on hash functions. We say $\mathcal{C}$ is a robust combiner for property π if $\mathcal{C}$ is robust under the original definition, or if for all $t \in \mathbb{N}$:*

$$\mathbf{AdvMax}_\pi^t(\mathcal{C}, 1^n) \leq \min\left(\mathbf{AdvMax}_\pi^t(\mathcal{H}_1, 1^n), \mathbf{AdvMax}_\pi^t(\mathcal{H}_2, 1^n)\right)$$

Note that any combiner that is robust for some property π under the traditional definition is also robust under our new definition. The introduced loophole, however, allows a combiner to be robust even if no security reduction $\mathcal{P}$ exists. In this case, the combiner must guarantee that the advantage for any adversary running in time t against property π on either $\mathcal{H}_1$ or $\mathcal{H}_2$ denotes an upper-bound on the advantage of any adversary running in time t against the combiner.

Discussion. The extended definition captures the security of the "magical" (non black-box) combiner. However, being a semi-black-box notion, it seems difficult to design an actual (non-magical) combiner exploiting the loophole offered by this notion. In the following section we build upon the ideas developed so far and present a fully black-box model which also allows to circumvent the lower bound on the output length. For this, we strengthen the assumption on the "input functions" requesting that one of the functions is ideal. Knowing that one of the functions is ideal then allows us to model that the combiner should be as strong as the ideal function, while it can "ignore" the second function.

3.3 Secure Combiners in Idealized Models

In this section we use a different and more practical approach to bypass the lower bound. We present a novel game-based security notion for black-box combiners that is tailored to be used in the idealized random oracle setting. Being black-box makes it easy to design combiners for this new notion and assuming, to a certain extend, idealized functions allows us to bypass the lower bound. In short, a combiner proven secure in our new notion provides the guarantee that it has a certain property as long as one of the two functions is ideal even in case the other function is highly dependent upon the first; this is modeled by giving the adversary full control over the second function.

We say that a combiner C is *ideally secure* for some property π if no adversary can win the *ideally secure combiner game* (see Figure 1). For this we consider a two-stage adversary $\mathcal{A} = (\mathcal{A}_1, \mathcal{A}_2)$, where $\mathcal{A}_1$ outputs some state st and a description of an efficient function that can contain special oracle

Ideally Secure Combiner$_{\mathcal{A}}^{C}$
$H_{\mathcal{A}}^{\mathcal{R}}, st \longleftarrow \mathcal{A}_1(1^n)$
$\mathcal{R}, k \longleftarrow$ sample RO and keys[3]
return $\mathcal{A}_2^{\mathcal{R}, H_{\mathcal{A}}^{\mathcal{R}}}(st, k)$ breaks π for combiner $C^{\mathcal{R}, H_{\mathcal{A}}^{\mathcal{R}}}$ or $C^{H_{\mathcal{A}}^{\mathcal{R}}, \mathcal{R}}$

Fig. 1. Security of Combiners in Idealized Settings

gates to call a random oracle. Then a random oracle $\mathcal{R}$ and a key k for the combiner are sampled. We say the adversary wins the game if $\mathcal{A}_2$ breaks property π on combiner C initialized with the random oracle and the function output by $\mathcal{A}_1$: that is, $\mathcal{A}_2$ breaks property π on either combiner $C^{\mathcal{R}, H_{\mathcal{A}}^{\mathcal{R}}}$ or on combiner $C^{H_{\mathcal{A}}^{\mathcal{R}}, \mathcal{R}}$ (note the different order of oracles).

---

[3] In the *Ideally Secure Combiner* game (and in following security games) the random oracle is sampled such that its domain and range matches allowed hash functions and the keys are sampled using the key generation algorithm of combiner C.

Definition 3. *A combiner C is called* ideally secure *for property π if no efficient adversary $\mathcal{A} = (\mathcal{A}_1, \mathcal{A}_2)$ can win the* Ideally Secure Combiner *game (Figure 1) with non-negligible advantage.*

The security guarantees given in this model are that the combiner has property π as long as one of the two functions is a random oracle. Furthermore, security may be reduced to the security of compression functions, when analyzing the security in the indifferentiability model [28]. We find this notion particularly useful from a practical point of view as many security proofs are only given in the random oracle model (to name a few [16,5,6,11]) and a combiner proven secure under our new notion allows us to hedge against the failure of the instantiation of the random oracle in the corresponding scheme. Furthermore, while our new notion makes stronger assumptions about the ingoing hash functions it allows to bypass the restrictions given by the traditional definition. As these stronger assumptions are, however, frequently needed in security proofs for practical constructions, we do not loose anything by also applying the very same assumptions in the examinations of combiners to be used in these schemes. On the other hand, there is lots to gain.

Further note that our new notion is far from trivial to fulfill although we know that one of the two functions is ideal to begin with. Take the exclusive-or combiner (compare Section 3.1) as an example. If one of the functions can depend on the other, most, if not all properties are easily breakable. Let, for example, adversary $\mathcal{A}_1$ output function $H_{\mathcal{A}}^{\mathcal{R}}(M) := \mathcal{R}(M)$. In this setting the exclusive-or combiner would implement the constant zero function $C_\oplus(M) = \mathcal{R}(M) \oplus \mathcal{R}(M)$ which is, of course, not collision-resistant or pseudorandom.

Remark 1. Recently, Ristenpart et al. [39] gave the somewhat surprising result that the indifferentiability composition theorem does not hold in general but only in what they call *single-stage settings*. A game is called single-stage if we can assume a single global adversary. Note that this applies to all but one of the security games considered in this paper (see Figures 1 and 2), as we usually allow adversaries to pass on their current state without any restrictions. For the exception, Lemma 2, it can be shown that it falls into the class of *secure-1-pass-games* in the terminology of [25]. The authors in [25] study multi-stage games for which indifferentiability (with certain additions) suffices to allow composition. For games falling into their class of *secure-1-pass-games* no additions are needed and thus plain indifferentiability is sufficient to allow composition. The idea, why access to the underlying compression function does not yield any advantage is that all "interesting" random oracle evaluations (notably, $\mathcal{R}(m \oplus k_3)$, cf. Figure 3) have a block-length of exactly 1. Thus, length extension attacks via the computation of inner compression function evaluations do not yield any advantage over directly computing the full hash value.

4 A Short Multi-property Combiner for Hash Functions

In this section we present a new black-box combiner for two hash functions that does not increase the output length. The combiner is robust for pseudorandomness (under the traditional definition of robust combiners) without needing to assume independence of the input functions (cf. Section 3.1). Further, it is *ideally secure* (cf. Definition 3) for collision resistance, second pre-image resistance, target collision resistance and pre-image resistance, that is, it holds these properties if one of the hash functions is instantiated with a random oracle or if one of the functions is indifferentiable from a random oracle (assuming an ideal compression function, also see remark at end of last the section).

Our construction is based on the exclusive-or combiner where each message block is preprocessed. To ease on notation, we will not explicitly model the key generation stage for hash functions but implicitly assume that the functions are chosen from a family of functions (i.e., the key is implicit in the hash function).

Construction 1. *Let* $H_1, H_2 : \{0,1\}^* \rightarrow \{0,1\}^n$ *be two hash functions and* $m_1 \| \ldots \| m_\ell := M \| pad(M)$ *be a message from the joint domain of both hash functions padded to a multiple of the block length n. The combiner is given by*

$$C^{H_1,H_2}(M) := G_1^{H_1,H_2}(M) \oplus G_2^{H_1,H_2}(M)$$

where G_1 and G_2 are stateless and deterministic constructions given by

$$G_1^{H_1,H_2}(M) := H_1 \left(\tilde{m}_1^1 \| \ldots \| \tilde{m}_\ell^1 \right) \qquad G_2^{H_1,H_2}(M) := H_2 \left(\tilde{m}_1^2 \| \ldots \| \tilde{m}_\ell^2 \right)$$

with preprocessed blocks

$$\tilde{m}_j^1 := H_2(1 \| m_j \oplus k_1) \oplus m_j \oplus k_2 \oplus H_1(1 \| m_j \oplus k_3)$$
$$\tilde{m}_j^2 := H_1(0 \| m_j \oplus k_4) \oplus m_j \oplus k_5 \oplus H_2(0 \| m_j \oplus k_6)$$

for $j := 1, \ldots, \ell$ and for independently chosen keys $k_i \in \{0,1\}^n$ for $i = 1, ..., 6$.

Let us examine the combiner more closely before proving its security. First notice that the combiner is symmetric, that is, it makes no difference if functions H_1 and H_2 are interchanged. Function $G_1(M)$ can be thought of as simply calling hash function H_1 on some preprocessed input. If the original input $m_1 \| \ldots \| m_\ell := M \| pad(M)$ consisted of ℓ blocks, then the preprocessed input also consists of ℓ blocks. Each block m_i is preprocessed independently and becomes

$$H_2(1 \| m_i \oplus k_1) \oplus m_i \oplus k_2 \oplus H_1(1 \| m_i \oplus k_3) \ .$$

The idea behind this construction is that the outer most hash function in G_1 (i.e., $H_1(\cdot)$) cannot, given its input, guess (or rather compute) the input that is going into the outer most hash function in G_2, i.e., $H_2(\cdot)$. This will become more evident when we prove security for various properties. Furthermore, note that we achieve domain separation between the calls to functions within G_1 and G_2 (i.e., calls to H_1 and H_2 are prefixed by 1 for G_1 and by 0 for G_2).

Finally, we want to note that the combiner can be efficiently implemented. If we take as measure the number of hash block evaluations then the combiner increases the number of evaluations by a factor of 3. However, in contrast to other multi-property combiners [21,22] it is completely parallelizable as each block is preprocessed independently of others.

$FindPreImage_{\mathcal{A}}$	$FindCollision_{\mathcal{A}}$
$\mathcal{R}, k_1, \ldots k_6 \longleftarrow$ sample RO and keys	$\mathcal{R}, k_1, \ldots k_6 \longleftarrow$ sample RO and keys
$H_{\mathcal{A}}^{\mathcal{R}}, st, \mathcal{X} \longleftarrow \mathcal{A}_1(1^n)$	$H_{\mathcal{A}}^{\mathcal{R}}, st \longleftarrow \mathcal{A}_1(1^n)$
$\tau \longleftarrow \mathcal{X}$	$(M, M') \longleftarrow \mathcal{A}_2^{\mathcal{R}, H_{\mathcal{A}}^{\mathcal{R}}}(st, k_1, \ldots, k_6)$
$M \longleftarrow \mathcal{A}_2^{\mathcal{R}, H_{\mathcal{A}}^{\mathcal{R}}}(st, C^{\mathcal{R}, H_{\mathcal{A}}^{\mathcal{R}}}(\tau), k_1, \ldots, k_6)$	return $(C^{\mathcal{R}, H_{\mathcal{A}}^{\mathcal{R}}}(M) = C^{\mathcal{R}, H_{\mathcal{A}}^{\mathcal{R}}}(M'))$
return $(C^{\mathcal{R}, H_{\mathcal{A}}^{\mathcal{R}}}(M) = C^{\mathcal{R}, H_{\mathcal{A}}^{\mathcal{R}}}(\tau))$	

Fig. 2. Security Games

4.1   Security Analysis

We will first show that the combiner is pre-image resistant if one of its input functions is a random oracle. Remember that the basic XOR-combiner is not necessarily pre-image resistant even if instantiated with two random oracles (see Sections 3.1 and 3.3). We give the security experiments necessary for the following proofs in Figure 2.

Proposition 1. *Construction 1 is ideally secure for pre-image resistance (ow). That is, for any efficient adversary $\mathcal{A}$ which outputs efficiently sampleable distributions $\mathcal{X}$ with super-logarithmic min-entropy $(\mathrm{H}_\infty(\mathcal{X}) \in \omega(n))$ it holds that its advantage in the* FindPreImage *game is bound by*

$$Adv_{\mathcal{A}}^{\text{FindPreImage}}(1^n) \leq q_{\mathcal{A}} \cdot 2^{-\,\mathrm{H}_\infty(\mathcal{X})}$$

where $q_{\mathcal{A}}$ denotes an upper-bound on the number of combiner evaluations.

We prove Proposition 1 via an intermediate result about the preprocessed message blocks $\tilde{m}_j^b$ (cf. Construction 1). These we regard as "preprocessing functions" of the form $\{0,1\}^n \to \{0,1\}^n$ with oracle access to hash functions H_1 and H_2, parameterized by keys k_1, k_2, k_3, taking message blocks $m \in \{0,1\}^n$ as input and outputting a preprocessed message block; we write $\tilde{m}_{k_1, k_2, k_3}^{H_1, H_2}(m)$. We show that these pre-processed message blocks are, in fact, random variables with min-entropy n bits over the choice of random oracle and keys k_1, k_2, k_3. By applying the union bound, we can then argue that if an efficient adversary with access to the random oracle and keys $k_1, \ldots, k_3$ can choose message m it can at most reduce the entropy to $n - \mathcal{O}(\log n)$ bits, where the logarithmic reduction is bound by the number of random oracle evaluations.

Lemma 1. *The preprocessed blocks $\tilde{m}_{k_1, k_2, k_3}^{H_1, H_2}(\cdot)$ in Construction 1 are random variables with min-entropy n; that is, if $H_b := \mathcal{R}$ for $b \in \{1, 2\}$ is a random oracle, then it holds for all message blocks $m \in \{0,1\}^n$ and functions H_{2-b+1} with restrictions as in Construction 1 that*

$$\tilde{\mathrm{H}}_\infty\left(\tilde{m}_{k_1, k_2, k_3}^{H_1, H_2}(m) | m, k_1, k_2, k_3\right) = n \qquad (1)$$

where the probability is over the choice of random oracle $\mathcal{R}$ and keys $k_1, \ldots, k_3$.

To prove Lemma 1 we consider the following distribution (see Figure 3). The distribution is parameterized by an (efficient) algorithm $\mathcal{A}$, a random oracle from the function space $\{0,1\}^* \to \{0,1\}^n$ and uniformly and

$$\underline{\mathbf{Dist}_{\mathcal{A}}^{\mathcal{R},k_1,k_2,k_3}(m)}$$

$$m' \longleftarrow \mathcal{A}^{\mathcal{R}}(1^n, m \oplus k_3)$$

$$\mathbf{return}\ \mathcal{R}(m \oplus k_1) \oplus m \oplus k_2 \oplus m'$$

Fig. 3. Adv. Controlled Distribution

independently chosen keys k_1, k_2, k_3 from $\{0,1\}^n$. To compute the mapping for message m, adversary $\mathcal{A}$ receives value $m \oplus k_3$ and outputs a message m'. Value $\mathcal{R}(m \oplus k_1) \oplus m \oplus k_2 \oplus m'$ is returned as sample.

Proof (of Lemma 1). In the adversarial distribution (Figure 3), the adversary can be regarded as the adversarially created function $H_{\mathcal{A}}^{\mathcal{R}}(\cdot)$ in Construction 1. Thus, we have that the min-entropy of the adversarial distribution (instantiated with any efficient adversary $\mathcal{A}$) is an upper bound for the min-entropy of $\tilde{m}_{k_1,k_2,k_3}^{H_1,H_2}$:

$$\tilde{\mathrm{H}}_\infty\left(\tilde{m}_{k_1,k_2,k_3}^{H_1,H_2}(m)|m,k_1,k_2,k_3\right) \geq \tilde{\mathrm{H}}_\infty\left(\mathrm{Dist}_{\mathcal{A}}^{\mathcal{R},k_1,k_2k_3}(m)|m,k_1,k_2,k_3\right)$$

As the keys are chosen uniformly at random from $\{0,1\}^n$ and in particular independently of the random oracle, we know that for every message m value $\mathcal{R}(m \oplus k_1)$ is uniformly distributed and thus:

$$\tilde{\mathrm{H}}_\infty\left(\mathcal{R}(m \oplus k_1) \oplus m \oplus k_2|m,k_1,k_2,k_3\right) = n$$

To estimate the min-entropy of distribution $\mathrm{Dist}_{\mathcal{A}}^{\mathcal{R},k_1,k_2k_3}(\cdot)$ we thus need to analyze the effect of value m' as output by adversary $\mathcal{A}$ on input $m \oplus k_3$. In order to output m' such that the min-entropy of

$$\tilde{\mathrm{H}}_\infty\left(\mathcal{R}(m \oplus k_1) \oplus m \oplus k_2 \oplus m'|m,k_1,k_2,k_3\right) \tag{2}$$

is less than n bits, adversary $\mathcal{A}$ itself must have sufficient information on $\mathcal{R}(m \oplus k_1) \oplus m \oplus k_2$ given its sole input $m \oplus k_3$. To model, that $\mathcal{A}$ has access to the random oracle, we add its list of queries to the conditions. Let $\mathtt{qry}(\mathcal{A}^{\mathcal{R}}(m \oplus k_3))$ denote the query-answer pairs of $\mathcal{A}$ to the random oracle on input $m \oplus k_3$. Note that this is a random variable over the coins of $\mathcal{A}$ and the random oracle $\mathcal{R}$. Then, we can formalize the uncertainty of $\mathcal{A}$ about value $\mathcal{R}(m \oplus k_1) \oplus m \oplus k_2$ by

$$\tilde{\mathrm{H}}_\infty\left(\mathcal{R}(m \oplus k_1) \oplus m \oplus k_2|m \oplus k_3, \mathtt{qry}(\mathcal{A}^{\mathcal{R}}(m \oplus k_3))\right) \tag{3}$$

It is easily seen that this denotes an upper bound for

$$\tilde{\mathrm{H}}_\infty\left(\mathcal{R}(m \oplus k_1) \oplus k_2|m, \mathtt{qry}(\mathcal{A}^{\mathcal{R}}(m))\right) \tag{4}$$

where we removed the distortion of m by k_3 on the conditions, which in turn allows us to remove message m from the conditioned side. Note that values k_2 and $\mathcal{R}(m \oplus k_1)$ are uniformly distributed and independent (k_2 is chosen independently of $\mathcal{R}$ and similarly m and k_1 are chosen independently of $\mathcal{R}$). Thus we can analyze the two terms going into the exclusive-or operation individually; that is,

$$\tilde{\mathrm{H}}_\infty\left(k_2 \oplus \mathcal{R}(m \oplus k_1)|m, \mathtt{qry}(\mathcal{A}^{\mathcal{R}}(m))\right) \geq$$
$$\max\left(\tilde{\mathrm{H}}_\infty\left(k_2|m, \mathtt{qry}(\mathcal{A}^{\mathcal{R}}(m))\right), \tilde{\mathrm{H}}_\infty\left(\mathcal{R}(m \oplus k_1)|m, \mathtt{qry}(\mathcal{A}^{\mathcal{R}}(m))\right)\right) \tag{5}$$

As m is independent of keys k_1 and k_2 we have that both terms in the max-operation have n bits of entropy and thus

$$\tilde{H}_\infty \left(k_2 \oplus \mathcal{R}(m \oplus k_1) | m, \texttt{qry}(\mathcal{A}^{\mathcal{R}}(m)) \right) = n. \tag{6}$$

Thus, adversary $\mathcal{A}$ cannot output m' such that the entropy in (2) is reduced. $\square$

By an application of the union bound it follows that for any message m that is generated by an efficient adversary $\mathcal{A}^{H_1,H_2}(k_1, k_2, k_3)$ which is given the keys and that has oracle access to the hash functions, the min-entropy of $\tilde{m}_{k_1,k_2,k_3}^{H_1,H_2}(m)$ is at most reduced by logarithmically (in n) many bits (see full version [31] for details).

Lemma 2. *Let the setup be as in Lemma 1. Then, for all efficient adversaries $\mathcal{A}$ it holds that*

$$\tilde{H}_\infty \left(\tilde{m}_{k_1,k_2,k_3}^{H_1,H_2}(m) | m \leftarrow \mathcal{A}^{H_1,H_2}(1^n, k_1, k_2, k_3), k_1, k_2, k_3 \right) \geq n - \mathcal{O}(\log q) \tag{7}$$

where q is an upper bound on random oracle evaluations by H_{2-b+1} and adversary $\mathcal{A}$. The probability is over the choice of keys k_1, k_2, k_3, random oracle $\mathcal{R}$ and $\mathcal{A}$'s internal coin tosses.

Remark 2. We have examined Lemma 1 in the random oracle model using the information theoretic min-entropy notion. We can also analyze it in the privately keyed standard model assuming a pseudorandom function instead of a random oracle. For this we need to switch to a computational version of entropy such as HILL entropy (see [38] for an introduction). The proof works analogously.

We now prove Proposition 1 by showing that the advantage of any adversary in winning the *FindPreImage* game is bounded by $q_\mathcal{A} \cdot 2^{-\text{H}_\infty(\mathcal{X})}$ where $q_\mathcal{A}$ is the number of combiner evaluations. Let us first examine the *FindPreImage* game. In a first step, a random oracle $\mathcal{R}$ is sampled from the space of all functions of the form $\{0,1\}^* \rightarrow \{0,1\}^n$ together with keys $k_1, \ldots, k_6$. Adversary $\mathcal{A}_1$ is then given the security parameter and it outputs a target distribution $\mathcal{X}$, some state st, and a description of a hash function $H_\mathcal{A}^\mathcal{R}$ which can contain special gates to evaluate random oracle $\mathcal{R}$ (note that $\mathcal{A}_1$ does not get access to $\mathcal{R}$ while constructing $H_\mathcal{A}^\mathcal{R}$ and that distribution $\mathcal{X}$ must have super-logarithmic min-entropy given state st). In a next step a target message τ is sampled from distribution $\mathcal{X}$. Then, adversary $\mathcal{A}_2$ is given keys $k_1, \ldots, k_6$ and and hash value $C^{\mathcal{R},H_\mathcal{A}^\mathcal{R}}(\tau)$ and is given oracle access to $\mathcal{R}$ and $H_\mathcal{A}^\mathcal{R}$. It wins if it outputs a message M which, under the combiner, yields value $C^{\mathcal{R},H_\mathcal{A}^\mathcal{R}}(\tau)$, i.e.: $C^{\mathcal{R},H_\mathcal{A}^\mathcal{R}}(M) = C^{\mathcal{R},H_\mathcal{A}^\mathcal{R}}(\tau)$.

Proof (Proposition 1). Let us examine the preprocessed message blocks going into $G_2^{\mathcal{R},H_\mathcal{A}^\mathcal{R}}$ (cf. Construction 1) for some message $m_1, \ldots, m_\ell := M \| PAD(M)$. Each block is of the form

$$\mathcal{R}(0 \parallel m_i \oplus k_4) \oplus m_i \oplus k_5 \oplus H_\mathcal{A}^\mathcal{R}(0 \parallel m_i \oplus k_6) \tag{8}$$

By Lemma 2 we can assume each of these blocks to be a random variable with min-entropy n bits (note that the factor $\log(q)$ of Lemma 2 is implicit in the number of random oracle queries by the adversary) and thus the combined blocks (via concatenation) to be a random variable of also at least n bits. The same necessarily holds for for the blocks going into $G_1^{\mathcal{R},H_{\mathcal{A}}^{\mathcal{R}}}$. Furthermore, by achieving domain separation for the random oracle calls (prefixing the input with 0 and 1, respectively) within $G_1^{\mathcal{R},H_{\mathcal{A}}^{\mathcal{R}}}(\cdot)$ and $G_2^{\mathcal{R},H_{\mathcal{A}}^{\mathcal{R}}}(\cdot)$, we can assume the random variables for blocks of G_1 to be independent of those for blocks of G_2.

If U_n and U_n' are independent random variables from the message space to $\{0,1\}^n$ with min-entropy n bits, then we can write the combiner $C^{\mathcal{R},H_{\mathcal{A}}^{\mathcal{R}}}$ as

$$C^{\mathcal{R},H_{\mathcal{A}}^{\mathcal{R}}}(M) := \mathcal{R}(U_n(M)) \oplus H_{\mathcal{A}}^{\mathcal{R}}(U_n'(M))$$

Hence, the probability for any message M to be mapped to $C^{\mathcal{R},H_{\mathcal{A}}^{\mathcal{R}}}(\tau)$ under the combiner is 2^{-n}. As one possible pre-image (namely τ) is contained in the support of distribution $\mathcal{X}$, the best strategy for an adversary is to sample messages from $\mathcal{X}$, which allows us to upper bound the advantage of an adversary winning in the *FindPreImage* game by

$$\mathbf{Adv}_{\mathcal{A}}^{FindPreImage}(1^n) \leq q_{\mathcal{A}} \cdot 2^{-\mathrm{H}_\infty(\mathcal{X})}$$

where $q_{\mathcal{A}}$ denotes the number of combiner queries by adversary $\mathcal{A}_2$. □

For second pre-image and target collision resistance it suffices to slightly change the *FindPreImage* game to adapt it to the specifics in the examined property.

Collision resistance is examined using the *FindCollision* game (see Figure 2). We show that the advantage of any efficient adversary is bound by $q_{\mathcal{A}}^2 \cdot 2^{-(n+1)}$ where $q_{\mathcal{A}}$ denotes the number of combiner evaluations. In short we show that as the inputs to the outer hash functions in G_1 and G_2 have entropy at least $n - \mathcal{O}(\log q)$ bits, the problem of finding collisions can be rewritten as finding collisions for

$$\mathcal{R}(U_n(M)) \oplus \mathcal{R}(U_n(M')) = H_{\mathcal{A}}^{\mathcal{R}}(U_n'(M)) \oplus H_{\mathcal{A}}^{\mathcal{R}}(U_n'(M))$$

where U_n and U_n' are again independent random variables mapping from $\{0,1\}^*$ to $\{0,1\}^n$ and having n bits of min-entropy (again the logarithmic factor is hidden in the number of U_n evaluations by the adversary). We refer to the full version [31] for details.

4.2   Pseudorandomness

Finally, we show that our combiner is robust for pseudorandomness and ideally secure for message authentication codes. For pseudorandomness we can directly show robustness in the standard model (that is, without assuming a random oracle). We want to stress that, in contrast to the exclusive-or combiner, we do not need to assume that the two ingoing functions H_1 and H_2 are independent (cf. Section 3.1).

Proposition 2. *The combiner given in construction 1 is robust for pseudorandomness.*

Proof (sketch). We have already argued that we can analyze Lemma 1 and Lemma 2 also in the standard model, using computational analogues of entropy (see remark following Lemma 2). Thus, assuming that H_1 is pseudorandom, Lemma 2 yields that the input to $G_1^{H_1,H_2}(M) := H_1(\tilde{M})$ has sufficiently high computational min-entropy and hence G_1 is pseudorandom. Due to the symmetric design of the combiner, this also yields that $G_2^{H_1,H_2}$ is pseudorandom if H_2 is pseudorandom. Note, that due to the domain separation, the inputs to the outer hash evaluations in G_1 and G_2 are independent and thus the further analysis can be reduced to the analysis of the exclusive-or combiner which we know to be robust for pseudorandom functions assuming independent inputs.   □

Acknowledgments. I thank the anonymous reviewers for their valuable comments. This work was supported by CASED (www.cased.de).

References

1. Alwen, J., Dodis, Y., Wichs, D.: Leakage-resilient public-key cryptography in the bounded-retrieval model. In: Halevi, S. (ed.) CRYPTO 2009. LNCS, vol. 5677, pp. 36–54. Springer, Heidelberg (2009)
2. Andreeva, E., Mennink, B., Preneel, B.: On the indifferentiability of the Grøstl hash function. In: Garay, J.A., De Prisco, R. (eds.) SCN 2010. LNCS, vol. 6280, pp. 88–105. Springer, Heidelberg (2010)
3. Aoki, K., Sasaki, Y.: Meet-in-the-middle preimage attacks against reduced SHA-0 and SHA-1. In: Halevi, S. (ed.) CRYPTO 2009. LNCS, vol. 5677, pp. 70–89. Springer, Heidelberg (2009)
4. Baecher, P., Brzuska, C., Fischlin, M.: Notions of black-box reductions, revisited. Cryptology ePrint Archive, Report 2013/101 (2013), http://eprint.iacr.org/
5. Bellare, M., Boldyreva, A., O'Neill, A.: Deterministic and efficiently searchable encryption. In: Menezes, A. (ed.) CRYPTO 2007. LNCS, vol. 4622, pp. 535–552. Springer, Heidelberg (2007)
6. Bellare, M., Brakerski, Z., Naor, M., Ristenpart, T., Segev, G., Shacham, H., Yilek, S.: Hedged public-key encryption: How to protect against bad randomness. In: Matsui, M. (ed.) ASIACRYPT 2009. LNCS, vol. 5912, pp. 232–249. Springer, Heidelberg (2009)
7. Bellare, M., Rogaway, P.: Random oracles are practical: A paradigm for designing efficient protocols. In: Ashby, V. (ed.) ACM CCS 1993, pp. 62–73. ACM Press (November 1993)
8. Bertoni, G., Daemen, J., Peeters, M., Assche, G.V.: The keccak SHA-3 submission. Submission to NIST (Round 3) (2011), http://keccak.noekeon.org/Keccak-submission-3.pdf
9. Bertoni, G., Daemen, J., Peeters, M., Van Assche, G.: On the indifferentiability of the sponge construction. In: Smart, N.P. (ed.) EUROCRYPT 2008. LNCS, vol. 4965, pp. 181–197. Springer, Heidelberg (2008)

10. Bhattacharyya, R., Mandal, A., Nandi, M.: Indifferentiability characterization of hash functions and optimal bounds of popular domain extensions. In: Roy, B., Sendrier, N. (eds.) INDOCRYPT 2009. LNCS, vol. 5922, pp. 199–218. Springer, Heidelberg (2009)
11. Boldyreva, A., Cash, D., Fischlin, M., Warinschi, B.: Foundations of non-malleable hash and one-way functions. In: Matsui, M. (ed.) ASIACRYPT 2009. LNCS, vol. 5912, pp. 524–541. Springer, Heidelberg (2009)
12. Boneh, D., Boyen, X.: On the impossibility of efficiently combining collision resistant hash functions. In: Dwork, C. (ed.) CRYPTO 2006. LNCS, vol. 4117, pp. 570–583. Springer, Heidelberg (2006)
13. Canetti, R., Rivest, R., Sudan, M., Trevisan, L., Vadhan, S.P., Wee, H.M.: Amplifying collision resistance: A complexity-theoretic treatment. In: Menezes, A. (ed.) CRYPTO 2007. LNCS, vol. 4622, pp. 264–283. Springer, Heidelberg (2007)
14. De Cannière, C., Rechberger, C.: Preimages for reduced SHA-0 and SHA-1. In: Wagner, D. (ed.) CRYPTO 2008. LNCS, vol. 5157, pp. 179–202. Springer, Heidelberg (2008)
15. Chang, D., Nandi, M., Yung, M.: Indifferentiability of the hash algorithm BLAKE. Cryptology ePrint Archive, Report 2011/623 (2011), http://eprint.iacr.org/
16. Chevallier-Mames, B., Phan, D.H., Pointcheval, D.: Optimal asymmetric encryption and signature paddings. In: Ioannidis, J., Keromytis, A.D., Yung, M. (eds.) ACNS 2005. LNCS, vol. 3531, pp. 254–268. Springer, Heidelberg (2005)
17. Coron, J.-S., Dodis, Y., Malinaud, C., Puniya, P.: Merkle-damgård revisited: How to construct a hash function. In: Shoup, V. (ed.) CRYPTO 2005. LNCS, vol. 3621, pp. 430–448. Springer, Heidelberg (2005)
18. Damgård, I.: A design principle for hash functions. In: Brassard, G. (ed.) CRYPTO 1989. LNCS, vol. 435, pp. 416–427. Springer, Heidelberg (1990)
19. De Cannière, C., Rechberger, C.: Finding SHA-1 characteristics: General results and applications. In: Lai, X., Chen, K. (eds.) ASIACRYPT 2006. LNCS, vol. 4284, pp. 1–20. Springer, Heidelberg (2006)
20. Dierks, T., Rescorla, E.: The Transport Layer Security (TLS) Protocol Version 1.2. RFC 5246 (Proposed Standard) (August 2008), http://www.ietf.org/rfc/rfc5246.txt, updated by RFCs 5746, 5878, 6176
21. Fischlin, M., Lehmann, A.: Multi-property preserving combiners for hash functions. In: Canetti, R. (ed.) TCC 2008. LNCS, vol. 4948, pp. 375–392. Springer, Heidelberg (2008)
22. Fischlin, M., Lehmann, A., Pietrzak, K.: Robust multi-property combiners for hash functions revisited. In: Aceto, L., Damgård, I., Goldberg, L.A., Halldórsson, M.M., Ingólfsdóttir, A., Walukiewicz, I. (eds.) ICALP 2008, Part II. LNCS, vol. 5126, pp. 655–666. Springer, Heidelberg (2008)
23. Fischlin, M., Lehmann, A., Wagner, D.: Hash function combiners in TLS and SSL. In: Pieprzyk, J. (ed.) CT-RSA 2010. LNCS, vol. 5985, pp. 268–283. Springer, Heidelberg (2010)
24. Freier, A., Karlton, P., Kocher, P.: The Secure Sockets Layer (SSL) Protocol Version 3.0. RFC 6101 (Historic) (August 2011), http://www.ietf.org/rfc/rfc6101.txt
25. In Submission: Salvaging indifferentiability in a multi-stage setting (2013)
26. Lehmann, A.: On the Security of Hash Function Combiners. Ph.D. thesis, TU Darmstadt (März 2010), http://tuprints.ulb.tu-darmstadt.de/2094/
27. Liskov, M.: Constructing an ideal hash function from weak ideal compression functions. In: Biham, E., Youssef, A.M. (eds.) SAC 2006. LNCS, vol. 4356, pp. 358–375. Springer, Heidelberg (2007)

28. Maurer, U., Renner, R., Holenstein, C.: Indifferentiability, impossibility results on reductions, and applications to the random oracle methodology. In: Naor, M. (ed.) TCC 2004. LNCS, vol. 2951, pp. 21–39. Springer, Heidelberg (2004)
29. Merkle, R.C.: One way hash functions and DES. In: Brassard, G. (ed.) CRYPTO 1989. LNCS, vol. 435, pp. 428–446. Springer, Heidelberg (1990)
30. Mittelbach, A.: Hash combiners for second pre-image resistance, target collision resistance and pre-image resistance have long output. In: Visconti, I., De Prisco, R. (eds.) SCN 2012. LNCS, vol. 7485, pp. 522–539. Springer, Heidelberg (2012)
31. Mittelbach, A.: Cryptophia's short combiner for collision-resistant hash functions. Cryptology ePrint Archive, Report 2013/210 (2013), http://eprint.iacr.org/
32. Moody, D., Paul, S., Smith-Tone, D.: Improved indifferentiability security bound for the JH mode. Cryptology ePrint Archive, Report 2012/278 (2012), http://eprint.iacr.org/
33. Naor, M., Yung, M.: Universal one-way hash functions and their cryptographic applications. In: 21st ACM STOC, pp. 33–43. ACM Press (May 1989)
34. National Institute of Standards and Technology: FIPS 180-3, Secure Hash Standard, Federal Information Processing Standard (FIPS), Publication 180-3. Tech. rep., Department of Commerce (August 2008)
35. NIST: NIST SHA-3 Competition, http://csrc.nist.gov/groups/ST/hash/sha-3/index.html
36. Pietrzak, K.: Non-trivial black-box combiners for collision-resistant hash-functions don't exist. In: Naor, M. (ed.) EUROCRYPT 2007. LNCS, vol. 4515, pp. 23–33. Springer, Heidelberg (2007)
37. Pietrzak, K.: Compression from collisions, or why CRHF combiners have a long output. In: Wagner, D. (ed.) CRYPTO 2008. LNCS, vol. 5157, pp. 413–432. Springer, Heidelberg (2008)
38. Reyzin, L.: Some notions of entropy for cryptography (2011), http://www.cs.bu.edu/~reyzin/papers/entropy-survey.pdf
39. Ristenpart, T., Shacham, H., Shrimpton, T.: Careful with composition: Limitations of the indifferentiability framework. In: Paterson, K.G. (ed.) EUROCRYPT 2011. LNCS, vol. 6632, pp. 487–506. Springer, Heidelberg (2011)
40. Rivest, R.: The MD5 Message-Digest Algorithm. RFC 1321 (Informational) (April 1992), http://www.ietf.org/rfc/rfc1321.txt, updated by RFC 6151
41. Rogaway, P., Shrimpton, T.: Cryptographic hash-function basics: Definitions, implications, and separations for preimage resistance, second-preimage resistance, and collision resistance. In: Roy, B., Meier, W. (eds.) FSE 2004. LNCS, vol. 3017, pp. 371–388. Springer, Heidelberg (2004)
42. Sasaki, Y., Aoki, K.: Finding preimages in full MD5 faster than exhaustive search. In: Joux, A. (ed.) EUROCRYPT 2009. LNCS, vol. 5479, pp. 134–152. Springer, Heidelberg (2009)
43. Stevens, M., Sotirov, A., Appelbaum, J., Lenstra, A., Molnar, D., Osvik, D.A., de Weger, B.: Short chosen-prefix collisions for MD5 and the creation of a rogue CA certificate. In: Halevi, S. (ed.) CRYPTO 2009. LNCS, vol. 5677, pp. 55–69. Springer, Heidelberg (2009)
44. Wang, X., Yin, Y.L., Yu, H.: Finding collisions in the full SHA-1. In: Shoup, V. (ed.) CRYPTO 2005. LNCS, vol. 3621, pp. 17–36. Springer, Heidelberg (2005)
45. Wang, X., Yu, H.: How to break MD5 and other hash functions. In: Cramer, R. (ed.) EUROCRYPT 2005. LNCS, vol. 3494, pp. 19–35. Springer, Heidelberg (2005)

Generic Attacks for the Xor of k Random Permutations

Jacques Patarin

Université de Versailles
45 avenue des Etats-Unis
78035 Versailles Cedex - France

Abstract. Xoring the output of k permutations, $k \geq 2$ is a very simple way to construct pseudo-random functions (PRF) from pseudo-random permutations (PRP). Moreover such construction has many applications in cryptography (see [2,3,4,5] for example). Therefore it is interesting both from a theoretical and from a practical point of view, to get precise security results for this construction. In this paper, we will describe the best attacks that we have found on the Xor of k random n-bit to n-bit permutations. When $k = 2$, we will get an attack of computational complexity $O(2^n)$. This result was already stated in [2]. On the contrary, for $k \geq 3$, our analysis is new. We will see that the best known attacks require much more than 2^n computations when not all of the 2^n outputs are given, or when the function is changed on a few points. We obtain like this a new and very simple design that can be very useful when a security larger than 2^n is wanted, for example when n is very small.

Keywords: Pseudorandom functions, pseudorandom permutations, Luby-Rackoff backwards, generic attacks.

1 Introduction

The problem of converting pseudorandom permutations (PRP) into pseudorandom functions (PRF) named "Luby-Rackoff backwards" was first considered in [3]. This problem is obvious if we are interested in an assymptotical security model (since a PRP is then a PRF), but not if we are interested in achieving more optimal and concrete security bounds. More precisely, the loss of security when regarding a PRP as a PRF comes from the "birthday attack" which can distinguish a random permutation from a random function of n bits to n bits, in $2^{\frac{n}{2}}$ operations and $2^{\frac{n}{2}}$ queries. In [5] (Theorem 2 p.474), it has been proved that the Xor of k PRP gives a PRF with security at least in $O(2^{\frac{k}{k+1}n})$. (For $k = 2$ this gives $O(2^{\frac{2}{3}n})$). Moreover in [2], it has been proved that the Xor of two PRP gives a PRF with security at least in $O(2^n/n^{\frac{2}{3}})$ and at most in $O(2^n)$, which is much better than the birthday bound in $O(2^{\frac{n}{2}})$. Similarly in [8], it has been proved that in fact the security is at least in (and therefore exactly in) $O(2^n)$ for this problem to distinguish the Xor of two PRP from a PRF. An interesting question is "Can we hope to get even better bound than $O(2^n)$ with

M. Jacobson et al. (Eds.): ACNS 2013, LNCS 7954, pp. 154–169, 2013.
© Springer-Verlag Berlin Heidelberg 2013

more than two Xor, particularly if not all the 2^n inputs/outputs are given to the cryptanalysis ?" In this paper, we will study this question. Let F_k denote the Xor of k random permutations. Let G_k denote the function F_k except on a few secret (or public) points x_i where $G(x_i)$ is random (for example it can be only the point 0). We will distinguish 4 kinds of attack scenarios:

1. The adversary has access to the full codebook of F_k, i.e. exactly all the 2^n pairs of function input and function output.
2. The adversary has access to almost, but not all, the entire codebook of F_k, i.e. to m pairs with $m \simeq 2^n$ and $m < 2^n$.
3. The adversary wants to attack G_k (instead of F_k) and he has access to the full codebook of G_k.
   Moreover, in these scenarios 2 and 3 we will also assume that the adversary has access to a generator of such functions F_k (or G_k), i.e. has access to μ such functions and he wants to distinguish these μ functions from μ random independent functions.
4. Finally, in scenario 4, we will be as in scenario 2 except that:
   a. The adversary has access to only one function F_k (not a generator).
   b. We look in this scenario 4 for the best Advantage that the adversary can get even if this mathematical value is $\ll 1$ (and therefore cannot be used to distinguish).

To analyze these scenarios, we will introduce what we call "stable" attacks and "unstable" attacks. An attack will be called "stable" if the attack is still valid with a similar complexity when a few points of the functions are changed to truly random values. We will present the best "stable" and "unstable" attacks that we have found on the Xor of k functions, $k \geq 2$ when we study a generator of such functions (not only one such function). We will see that in Scenario 1, the best security bound is indeed in $O(2^n)$, but in Scenario 2 and 3, the best attacks have an even greater complexity. So it gives candidate schemes to build PRF from PRP in a still very simple way and with potentially even better security. Since building PRF from PRP has many applications (see [2,3,4]), we think that these results are really interesting both from theoretical and from practical point of view.

The paper is organised as follows. We will analyse Scenario 1 in section 2, Scenario 2 in section 3 and 4, Scenario 3 in section 5 and Scenario 4 in sections 6 and 7. Then we will analyse the case where the k Xor are done on only one permutation (instead of k independant permutations) in section 8. Some other variants and open problems are presented in section 9. Finally, the results obtained are summarized in section 10. We have decided to present in Appendices the computation of all the mean values and standard deviations needed.

2   Scenario 1 on $f_1 \oplus f_2 \oplus \ldots \oplus f_k$ with $O(2^n)$ Computations

Notations: In all this paper we will denote $I_n = \{0,1\}^n$. F_n will be the set of all applications from I_n to I_n, and B_n the set of all permutations from I_n to

I_n. So $|I_n| = 2^n$, $|F_n| = 2^{n \cdot 2^n}$, and $|B_n| = (2^n)!$. $x \in_R A$ will mean that x is randomly chosen in A, with a uniform distribution.

Aim: In this section we want to distinguish $f \oplus g$, with $f, g \in_R B_n$ from $h \in_R F_n$.

Attack. We analyze a function G, we want to know if $G = f \oplus g$, $f, g \in_R B_n$, or if $G = h$, $h \in_R F_n$. If we have access to all the 2^n values $G(x)$, then we can compute $T = \oplus_{i=1}^{2^n} G(i)$. If $G = f \oplus g$, then with probability 1, we have $T = 0$. (Proof: If f is a permutation we have $\oplus_{i=1}^{2^n} f(i) = \oplus_{i=1}^{2^n} i = 0$ and similarly $\oplus_{i=1}^{2^n} g(i) = 0$, so $\oplus_{i=1}^{2^n} f(i) \oplus g(i) = 0$). If $G = h$, $h \in_R F_n$, then we have $T = 0$ with probability $\frac{1}{2^n}$. Therefore, by computing T, we can distinguish $f \oplus g$ from h with a very good probability. This attack is in $O(2^n)$ computations, with $O(2^n)$ input/output values.

Aim with $k \geq 3$: We want to distinguish $f_1 \oplus f_2 \oplus \ldots \oplus f_k$, with $f_1, f_2, \ldots, f_k \in_R B_n$ from $h \in_R F_n$.

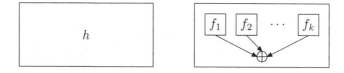

Fig. 1. Our attack distinguish between a function and the xor of k permutations

Attack. We use exactly the same attack: by computing T, we can distinguish $f_1 \oplus f_2 \oplus \ldots \oplus f_k$ from h with a very good probability. This attack is in $O(2^n)$ computations, with $O(2^n)$ input/output values.

Therefore, it seems that 2^n is the best security result that we can get with k Xor of permutations, for all k. However we can notice that if instead of having $f_1 \oplus f_2 \oplus \ldots \oplus f_k$, we use a function G such that $G = f_1 \oplus f_2 \oplus \ldots \oplus f_k$ except on a few points (or even except only on 0), and on these few points the output of G is truly random, then the above attack fails. We will say that this attack is "unstable". More precisely, we will define "stable" attacks as follows:

Definition. We want to distinguish a function G of F_n (generated by a function generator) from truly random functions $f \in_R F_n$ with an attack A. Let $P(n)$ be a polynomial in n and $x_1, \ldots x_\phi$ be ϕ points randomly chosen in I_n with $\phi \leq P(n)$. Let $\Phi = \{x_1, \ldots x_\phi\}$. Let $G' = G$ on all the points of $F_n - \Phi$ and $G'(x_i)$ be truly random on all $x_i \in \Phi$. Then if for each such sets Φ the attack A is polynomial (in n) against G', we will say that this attack is stable on G.

Remark: It is possible to store a few random points with $O(n)$ random bits, i.e. polynomial in n, but to store a random function of F_n, we need $n \cdot 2^n$ random bits, i.e. not polynomial in n. To avoid an "unstable" attack on G, we have to change the design of G only on a few points. However to avoid a "stable" attack on G, the design of G must be deeply changed.

3   Scenario 2 on $f \oplus g$ with $O(2^{2n})$ Computations

Aim: we want to distinguish a generator A of functions $f \oplus g$, with $f, g \in_R B_n$, from a generator B of functions h, with $h \in_R F_n$; i.e. we can have access to more than one test function G, these G functions are generated from A or from B and we have to distinguish these two cases with a non negligible probability. Moreover for each G function, we have access to all the inputs/outputs, except a few points. (Or alternatively, from generator A, $G = f \oplus g$ except on a few points).

Attack. We will count the number N of collisions on the functions G. Therefore if we have access to m inputs/outputs for G, $G(x_i) = y_i$ for $1 \leq i \leq m$, N is the number of (i, j), $1 \leq i < j \leq m$ such that $G(x_i) = G(x_j)$. (In our attack we will generally choose $m \simeq 2^n$ but we will not need $m = 2^n$.)

Case of Random Functions. We know that for a random function of F_n, we have $E(N) = \frac{m(m-1)}{2 \cdot 2^n}$ and $\sigma(N) = O(\frac{m}{\sqrt{2^n}})$ where $E(N)$ denotes the mean value of N, and $\sigma(N)$ denotes the standard deviation of N. (See Appendix A for the proof of these results). Therefore, for a generator with μ such functions,

$$E(N) = \frac{\mu \cdot m(m-1)}{2 \cdot 2^n} \quad \text{and} \quad \sigma(N) = O(\frac{\sqrt{\mu} \cdot m}{\sqrt{2^n}})$$

(Since if $X_1, \ldots, X_n$ are n independent events with $E(X_i) = E$ and $\sigma(X_i) = \sigma$, we have $E(X_1 + \ldots + X_n) = nE$ and $\sigma(X_1 + \ldots X_n) = \sqrt{n}\sigma$. Here the generator generates independent functions $h_1, \ldots h_n$).

Case of $f \oplus g$. We know that if $G = f \oplus g$, with $f, g \in_R B_n$, we have

$$E(N) = \frac{m(m-1)}{2} \cdot \frac{1}{2^n - 1} \quad \text{and} \quad \sigma(N) = O(\frac{m}{\sqrt{2^n}}),$$ (see Appendix B for the proof of these results). Therefore, for a generator with μ such functions,

$$E(N) = \frac{\mu \cdot m(m-1)}{2} \cdot \frac{1}{2^n - 1}$$

(This shows that we have in average slightly more collisions with $f \oplus g$ than with h), and

$$\sigma(N) = O(\frac{\sqrt{\mu}m}{\sqrt{2^n}})$$

From Bienayme-Tchebichev theorem we know that we will be able to distinguish h from $f \oplus g$ with a good probability when

$$\sigma(N)_h << |E(N)_h - E(N)_{f \oplus g}|$$

and

$$\sigma(N)_{f \oplus g} << |E(N)_h - E(N)_{f \oplus g}|$$

(This is a sufficient condition to distinguish h from $f \oplus g$.)
Here these conditions give:

$$\frac{\sqrt{\mu}m}{\sqrt{2^n}} << \frac{\mu \cdot m(m-1)}{2 \cdot 2^{2n}}$$

For $m \simeq 2^n$, this gives: $\mu \geq 2^n$ and the complexity of this attack is in $O(\mu \cdot m)$ computations, i.e. in $O(2^{2n})$.

Conclusion: This is a "stable attack" on $f \oplus g$ with $O(2^{2n})$ computations (see section 5 to see why this attack is "stable").

Remark: This is the best "stable" generic attack on $f \oplus g$ that we have found.

4   Scenario 2 on $f_1 \oplus f_2 \oplus \ldots \oplus f_k$ with $O(2^{(2k-2)n})$ Computations

Aim: we want to distinguish a generator A of functions $f_1 \oplus f_2 \oplus \ldots \oplus f_k$, with $f_1, \ldots f_k \in_R B_n$ from a generator B of functions $h \in_R F_n$. We assume that we have access to m inputs/outputs values for each function G, with $m \neq 2^n$ (but $m \simeq 2^n$ if we want), i.e. we look for a stable attack (the attack will still be valid if a few inputs/outputs of G are changed).

Remark: Section 3 was a special case of section 4 with $k = 2$.

Attack. We will count the number N of collisions on all the functions G. Therefore, if we have access to m inputs/outputs for each function G, N is the number of (i, j), $i < j$, such that: $G(x_i) = G(x_j)$.

Case of Random Functions. We have seen in Section 3 (and in Appendix B) that for a random function of F_n, we have:

$$E(N) = \frac{m(m-1)}{2 \cdot 2^n} \quad \text{and} \quad \sigma(N) = O(\frac{m}{\sqrt{2^n}})$$

Therefore, for a generator with μ such functions,

$$E(N) = \frac{\mu \cdot m(m-1)}{2 \cdot 2^n} \quad \text{and} \quad \sigma(N) = O(\frac{\sqrt{\mu} \cdot m}{\sqrt{2^n}})$$

Case of $f_1 \oplus f_2 \oplus \ldots \oplus f_k$. We know that if $G = f_1 \oplus f_2 \oplus \ldots \oplus f_k$, with $f_1, f_2, \ldots f_k \in_R B_n$, we have

$$E(N) = \frac{m(m-1)}{2} \cdot \frac{1}{2^n} \Big[1 + \frac{(-1)^k}{(2^n - 1)^{k-1}} \Big]$$

and $\sigma(N) = O(\frac{m}{\sqrt{2^n}})$, (Proof: see Appendix C). Therefore, for a generator with μ such functions,

$$E(N) = \frac{\mu \cdot m(m-1)}{2} \cdot \frac{1}{2^n} \Big[1 + \frac{(-1)^k}{(2^n - 1)^{k-1}} \Big] \quad \text{and} \quad \sigma(N) = O(\frac{\sqrt{\mu} m}{\sqrt{2^n}})$$

From Bienayme-Tchebichev theorem we know that we will be able to distinguish h from $f_1 \oplus f_2 \oplus \ldots \oplus f_k$ with a good probability when

$$\sigma(N)_h << |E(N)_h - E(N)_{f_1 \oplus \ldots \oplus f_k}|$$

and

$$\sigma(N)_{f_1 \oplus \ldots \oplus f_k} << |E(N)_h - E(N)_{f_1 \oplus \ldots \oplus f_k}|$$

(This is a sufficient condition to distinguish h from $f_1 \oplus \ldots \oplus f_k$).

Here these conditions give:

$$\frac{\sqrt{\mu m}}{\sqrt{2^n}} << \frac{\mu \cdot m^2}{2^{kn}}$$

For $m \simeq 2^n$, this gives: $\mu \geq 2^{(2k-3)n}$ and therefore the complexity of this attack is in $O(\mu \cdot m)$ computations, i.e. in $O(2^{(2k-2)n})$.

5 Analysis of Scenario 3

Let G^* be perfectly random on φ points, and $G^*(x) = f_1(x) \oplus f_2(x) \oplus \ldots \oplus f_k(x)$, with $f_1, \ldots, f_k \in_R B_n$, on the $2^n - \varphi$ other points. Let ϕ be the set of the φ special points. Let assume that we know G^* on m points x_i, such that φ' of these point are in Φ and $m - \varphi'$ are not in Φ, $\varphi' \leq \varphi$. Let N be the number of collisions $G^*(x_i) = G^*(x_j)$, with $i < j$. We have: $N = N_1 + N_2 + N_3$ with

N_1 = number of collisions with $x_i \notin \phi$ and $x_j \notin \phi$, $i < j$.

N_2 = number of collisions with $x_i \notin \phi$ and $x_j \in \phi$, $i < j$.

N_3 = number of collisions with $x_i \in \phi$ and $x_j \in \phi$, $i < j$.

We have $E(N) = E(N_1) + E(N_2) + E(N_3)$. From Theorem 1 of Appendix C, we have:

$$E(N_1) = \frac{(m - \varphi')(m - \varphi' - 1)}{2} \cdot \frac{1}{2^n}[1 + \frac{(-1)^k}{(2^n - 2)^{k-1}}]$$

Moreover, $E(N_2) = \frac{\varphi'(m-\varphi')}{2^n}$ and $E(N_3) = \frac{\varphi'(\varphi'-1)}{2 \cdot 2^n}$. Therefore

$$E(N) = \frac{m(m-1)}{2} \cdot \frac{1}{2^n} + \frac{(m - \varphi')(m - \varphi' - 1)}{2} \cdot \frac{1}{2^n} \frac{(-1)^k}{(2^n - 1)^{k-1}}$$

So if $m \simeq 2^n$ and $\varphi << 2^n$, we have $\varphi' << 2^n$ and

$$|E(N)_{G^*} - E(N)_{f \in_R F_n}| \simeq \frac{1}{2 \cdot (2^n - 1)^{k-2}}$$

Therefore this attack by counting N for G^* will work with the same complexity as the attack by counting N on $f_1(x) \oplus f_2(x) \oplus \ldots \oplus f_k(x)$ as long as $\varphi << 2^n$, so we say that this attack is "stable". (This also means that "scenario 3" and "scenario 2" have the same conplexity).

6 Scenario 4: Best Known Advantage on a Single $f \oplus g$ with $m < 2^n$

Let h be the single function of F_n that we want to study. h can be $h \in_R F_n$, or h can be $h = f \oplus g$ with $f, g \in_R B_n$. We assume that we know h on m points x_i: $h(x_i) = y_i$, $\forall i$, $1 \leq i \leq m$. Let N be the number of collisions on these m points, i.e. N is the number of (i,j), $1 \le i < j \le m$ such that: $y_i = y_j$.

First case: $m \ll \sqrt{2^n}$. Let ϕ be this attack:

- if $N = 0$ then ϕ outputs 0.
- if $N \ne 0$ (i.e. $N \ge 1$) then ϕ outputs 1.

Let $p_1 = Pr_{h \in_R F_n}(\phi(h) = 1)$, and $p_1^* = Pr_{f,g \in_R B_n}(\phi(f \oplus g) = 1)$. If $m \ll \sqrt{2^n}$, $p_1 \simeq \frac{m(m-1)}{2.2^n}$, and $p_1^* \simeq \frac{m(m-1)}{2.2^n}(1+\frac{1}{2^n})$ (cf Appendix B). Therefore, if $m \ll \sqrt{2^n}$, $Adv(\phi) = |p_1 - p_1^*| \simeq \frac{m(m-1)}{2.2^{2n}}$. This shows that if $m \ll \sqrt{2^n}$, the Advantage, Adv_m to distinguish $h \in_R F_n$ from $f \oplus g$, $f, g \in_R B_n$ is at least in $O(\frac{m(m-1)}{2^{2n}})$. (This value is $\ll 1$ and therefore too small to distinguish).

Remark. When $m = 1$, $m = 2$ and $m = 3$, the exact values for Adv_m are given in [9]. More precisely in [9], it is shown that $Adv_1 = 0$, $Adv_2 = \frac{1}{2^n(2^n-1)} \simeq \frac{1}{2^{2n}}$, $Adv_3 = \frac{1}{2^{2n}}\left(\frac{3.2^{2n}-12.2^n+4}{(2^n-1)(2^n-2)}\right) \simeq \frac{3}{2^{2n}}$.

Second case: $\sqrt{2^n} \ll m \ll 2^n$. Let Ψ be this attack:

- if $N \ge \frac{m(m-1)}{2.2^n}$, then Ψ outputs 1.
- if $N < \frac{m(m-1)}{2.2^n}$, then Ψ outputs 0.

(Ψ is a "2-point" attack). If $(f,g) \in_R B_n$ we have $E(N) = \frac{m(m-1)}{2.(2^n-1)} \simeq \frac{m(m-1)}{2.2^n}(1+\frac{1}{2^n})$ and $\sigma(N) \simeq \frac{m}{\sqrt{2}\sqrt{2^n}}$ (cf Appendix B). If $\sqrt{2^n} \ll m \ll 2^n$, then the distribution of N is similar to the Gaussian distribution of density $\frac{1}{\sqrt{2\pi}\sigma}e^{-\frac{(x-E(N))^2}{2\sigma^2}}$. Therefore we have: $Adv(\Psi) = O(\frac{\Delta E(N)}{\sigma})$, $Adv(\Psi) = O(\frac{m}{2^{\frac{3n}{2}}})$. This shows that if $\sqrt{2^n} \ll m \ll 2^n$, the Advantage to distinguish $h \in_R F_n$ from $f \oplus g$, $f, g \in_R B_n$ is at least $O(\frac{m}{2^{\frac{3n}{2}}})$. (This value is $\ll 1$, this is why in scenarios 2 and 3 we used a generator of functions).

7   Scenario 4: Best Known Advantage on $f_1 \oplus f_2 \oplus \ldots \oplus f_k$ with $m < 2^n$

First case: $m \ll \sqrt{2^n}$. Let ϕ be the attack ϕ seen in section 6. Let $p_1 = Pr_{h \in_R F_n}(\phi(h) = 1)$ as in section 6. let $p_1^*(k) = Pr_{f_1,\ldots,f_k \in_R B_n}(\phi(f_1 \oplus f_2 \oplus \ldots f_k) = 1)$. If $m \ll \sqrt{2^n}$, $p_1 \simeq \frac{m(m-1)}{2.2^n}$ and $p_1^*(k) \simeq \frac{m(m-1)}{2.2^n}(1 + \frac{(-1)^k}{(2^n-1)^{k-1}})$ (cf Appendix C). Therefore if $m \ll \sqrt{2^n}$, $Adv(\phi) = |p_1 - p_1^*(k)| \simeq \frac{m(m-1)}{2.2^{kn}}$. This shows that if $m \ll \sqrt{2^n}$, the Advantage, Adv_m to distinguish $h \in_R F_n$ from $f_1 \oplus f_2 \oplus \ldots \oplus f_k$, $f_1,\ldots,f_k \in_R B_n$, is at least $O(\frac{m(m-1)}{2^{kn}})$.

Second case: $\sqrt{2^n} \ll m \ll 2^n$. Let Ψ be the attack Ψ seen in section 6. If $h \in_R F_n$ we have $E(N) = \frac{m(m-1)}{2.2^n}$. If $f_1,\ldots,f_k \in_R B_n$ we have $E(N) = \frac{m(m-1)}{2.2^n}(1 + \frac{(-1)^k}{(2^n-1)^{k-1}})$ and $\sigma(N) \simeq \frac{m}{\sqrt{2}\sqrt{2^n}}$ (cf Appendix C). If $\sqrt{2^n} \ll m \ll 2^n$, then the distribution of N is similar to the Gaussian distribution of density $\frac{1}{\sqrt{2\pi}\sigma}e^{-\frac{(x-E(N))^2}{2\sigma^2}}$. Therefore we have: $Adv(\Psi) = O(\frac{\Delta E(N)}{\sigma})$, $Adv(\Psi) = O(\frac{m}{2^{(k-\frac{1}{2})n}})$. This shows that if $\sqrt{2^n} \ll m \ll 2^n$, the Advantage to distinguish $h \in_R F_n$ from $f \oplus \ldots \oplus f_k$,

$f, \ldots, f_k \in_R B_n$ is at least $O(\frac{m}{2^{(k-\frac{1}{2})n}})$. (This value is $\ll 1$, this is why in scenarios 2 and 3 we used a generator of functions).

8 A Simple Variant of the Schemes with Only One Permutation

Variant with 2 Xor
Instead of $G = f_1 \oplus f_2$, $f_1, f_2 \in_R B_n$, we can study $G'(x) = f(x\|0) \oplus f(x\|1)$, with $f \in_R B_n$ and $x \in I_{n-1}$. This variant was already introduced in [2]. There are many common results between G and G' but also a few differences. It is possible to prove that our attacks (stable and unstable) on G are also valid on G' with similar properties. The (unstable) attack of Section 2 in $O(2^n)$ is also valid for G', since $\oplus_{x=1}^{2^n} G'(x) = \oplus_{i=1}^{2^n} i = 0$, and the number of collisions for the (stable) attacks of Section 3 will be similar for G and G'.

   A Specific Attack on G'
There is however a specific attack on G' that do not exist on G since $\forall x \in I_n, G'(x) \neq 0$. Therefore, if we know m outputs y_i of G, we can test if $\forall i, 1 \leq i \leq m, y_i \neq 0$ (#). The probability of this event is 1 on G' and $(1 - \frac{1}{2^n})^m \simeq e^{-\frac{m}{2^n}}$ on $f \in_R F_n$. Therefore if $\frac{m}{2^n}$ is not close to 0, we can distinguish $f \in_R F_n$ from G' with a good probability. We will call $\mathcal{A}$ this attack. Like the attack on $\oplus_{i=1}^{2^n} G(i)$, this attack $\mathcal{A}$ requires $O(2^n)$ queries and $O(2^n)$ computations. (This attack was already described in [2].) However unlike the attack on $\oplus_{i=1}^{2^n} G(i)$, this attack $\mathcal{A}$ does not requires $m = 2^n$, but only to have $\frac{m}{2^n}$ not close to 0.

   Stability of the Attack
Let G'_ϕ be the function G', except on ϕ randomly and secretly chosen points x_i, and on these points G'_ϕ is perfectly random. The probability of (#) is 1 on G', is $(1 - \frac{1}{2^n})^\phi \simeq e^{\frac{\phi}{2^n}} \simeq 1 - \frac{\phi}{2^n}$ on G'_ϕ and is $\simeq e^{-\frac{m}{2^n}}$ on $f \in_R F_n$. Therefore, if ϕ is $\leq P(n)$ and if $m \simeq 2^n$, with $p(n)$ a polynomial in n, the probability of (#) is about 1 on G'_ϕ, and is about $\frac{1}{e}$ on $f \in_R F_n$, so this attack $\mathcal{A}$ is still able to distinguish G'_ϕ from $f \in_R F_n$. Therefore $\mathcal{A}$ is "stable" with our definition of "stable".

   Variant with ≥ 3 Xor
With 3 Xor, instead of $G(x) = (f_1 \oplus f_2 \oplus f_3)(x)$, if $x \neq 0$, with $f_1, f_2, f_3 \in_R B_n$, and $G(0)$ random, we can study $G'(x) = f(x\|00) \oplus f(x\|01) \oplus f(x\|10)$, if $x \neq 0$, with $f \in_R B_n$ and $x \in I_{n-2}$, $G'(0)$ random. Now $G'(x)$ can have the value 0, and as with $f \oplus g \oplus h$, $f, g, h \in B_n$ with this design the best known attacks have complexity greater than $O(2^n)$. More generally, with k Xor, instead of using k random permutations of B_n, we can use only one. From a theoretical point of view the analysis, attacks and results will be similar if the number of Xor is ≥ 3 (cf Appendices D and E), but from a practical point of view these variants may be sometime a bit better since they use only one random permutation of B_n.

9   Other Variants and Open Problems

Let assume, for example, that we want to build a pseudo-random function of F_n from two random permutations of B_n. We have

$$|B_n|^2 = \left((2^n)!\right)^2 \simeq \left((2^n)^{2^n} \cdot e^{-2^n} \sqrt{2\pi \cdot 2^n}\right)^2 \simeq 2^{2n \cdot 2^n} e^{-2 \cdot 2^n} (2\pi \cdot 2^n)$$

Here we use Stirling formula and $|F_n| = (2^n)^{2^n} = 2^{n \cdot 2^n}$. So $|B_n|^2 \geq |F_n|$ and therefore, from an information theoretic point of view, we may imagine to transform a random element of B_n^2 in a pseudo-random element of F_n with a security bound much better than $O(2^n)$. In fact, if we have a very small probability that the transformation fails, i.e. gives no element of F_n, then we may even hope to get a perfectly random element of F_n when the construction works.

Remark. A similar problem arise when we want to transform for example a perfectly random integer x of $[1, 11]$ into a perfectly random integer y of $[1, 2]$. We can decide that if $x \in \{1, 2, 3, 4, 5\}$ then $y = 1$, and if $x \in \{6, 7, 8, 9, 10\}$ then $y = 2$, and if $x = 11$, then no output y is given. Then when an output y is given, y is perfectly random in $[1, 2]$.

It may be interesting to design a similar transformation from B_n^2 to F_n, i.e. with a high probability the construction will give an output, and when it gives an output, this output will be a perfectly random element of F_n. However, we want to perform only $O(n)$ operations (or polynomial in n) to get the output (as $(f_1 \oplus g_2)(x)$ where only 2 operations are needed), not $O(2^n)$. Therefore, this problem may have no solution. However, it may exist some designs with better security results than our constructions with the same number of operations. In any case, it is an interesting and open question to evaluate the best possible designs when only $O(n)$ (or a polynomial in n) operations are possible to evaluate $G(x)$. Of course another open question is: Are our generic attacks the best possible attacks on our constructions (with k Xor and a few random points)?

10   Summary of the Results

- k denotes the number of Xor: $f_1 \oplus f_2 \oplus \ldots \oplus f_k$.
- In "scenario 1" we present the number of computations required in a CPA-2 (Adaptive chosen plaintext attack) to distinguish $f_1 \oplus f_2 \oplus \ldots \oplus f_k$ (with $f_1, \ldots, f_k \in_R B_n$) from a truly random function $h \in_R F_n$ when the adversary has access to the **full** codebook. This number is proved to be at

Table 1. Best known attacks for the Xor of k permutations

k	Scenario 1	Scenario 2 and 3	Scenario 4, $m \ll \sqrt{2^n}$	Scenario 4, $\sqrt{2^n} \ll m \ll 2^n$
2	2^n	$\leq 2^{2n}$	$Adv \geq O(\frac{m(m-1)}{2^{2n}})$	$Adv \geq O(\frac{m}{2^{\frac{3}{2}}})$
3	2^n	$\leq 2^{4n}$	$Adv \geq O(\frac{m(m-1)}{2^{3n}})$	$Adv \geq O(\frac{m}{2^{\frac{5}{2}}})$
4	2^n	$\leq 2^{6n}$	$Adv \geq O(\frac{m(m-1)}{2^{4n}})$	$Adv \geq O(\frac{m}{2^{\frac{7}{2}}})$
k	2^n	$\leq 2^{(2k-2)n}$	$Adv \geq O(\frac{m(m-1)}{2^{kn}})$	$Adv \geq O(\frac{m}{2^{(k-\frac{1}{2})n}})$

least in $O(2^n/n^{\frac{2}{3}})$ (security results of [2]) at least in $O(2^n)$ (security results of [8]), and at most in $O(2^n)$ ("unstable" attack of Section 2) when all the 2^n inputs/outputs are given), and therefore exactly in $O(2^n)$.

- "Scenario 2" is like "scenario 1" except that we have access to m input/output pairs, with $m \simeq 2^n$ but $m < 2^n$, and that we use a generator of such functions.

- In "scenario 3" we present the number of computations required in a CPA-2 (Adaptive chosen plaintext attack) to distinguish G from a truly random function $h \in_R F_n$ where G is equal to $f_1 \oplus f_2 \oplus \ldots \oplus f_k$ (with $f_1, \ldots, f_k \in_R B_n$) on all the points except on a few points x_i where $G(x_i)$ is random. (For example it can be only on the point 0). Moreover, we use a generator of such functions G.

"$\leq$" denotes the fact that we give here the best known attack. We see that in scenarios 2 and 3 the number of computations can be much larger than in scenario 1. Therefore the design of G can be very efficient in some applications.

- In Scenario 4 we present the best Advantage that we have found when we try to attack in CPA-2 a **single** $f_1 \oplus f_2 \oplus \ldots \oplus f_k$ with m queries, (not a generator), with $\sqrt{2^n} \ll m \ll 2^n$. (These values for Adv are always $\ll 1$, this is why in Scenarios 2 and 3 we needed more than one function to distinguish). "$\geq$" denotes the fact that we give here the best known advantage, but better Advantage may exist.

With the variant of section 8 (i.e. with only one permutation), the results obtained are the same as for $f_1 \oplus f_2 \oplus \ldots \oplus f_k$ except for $k = 2$.

Table 2. Best known attacks for the variant of section 8 (i.e. k Xor on only one permutation)

k	Scenario 1	Scenario 2 and 3	Scenario 4, $m \ll \sqrt{2^n}$	Scenario 4, $\sqrt{2^n} \ll m \ll 2^n$
2	2^n	2^n	$Adv \geq O(\frac{m}{2^n})$	$Adv \geq O(\frac{m}{2^n})$
3	2^n	$\leq 2^{4n}$	$Adv \geq O(\frac{m(m-1)}{2^{3n}})$	$Adv \geq O(\frac{m}{2^{\frac{5n}{2}}})$
4	2^n	$\leq 2^{6n}$	$Adv \geq O(\frac{m(m-1)}{2^{4n}})$	$Adv \geq O(\frac{m}{2^{\frac{7n}{2}}})$
k	2^n	$\leq 2^{(2k-2)n}$	$Adv \geq O(\frac{m(m-1)}{2^{kn}})$	$Adv \geq O(\frac{m}{2^{(k-\frac{1}{2})n}})$

11   Conclusion

In this paper, we have designed new schemes to build PRF from PRP. On these schemes we use k Xor instead of two, on all the points except a few, and on these few points, we have a truly random output. On these new schemes, we have shown that the best known generic attacks have a complexity much larger than $O(2^n)$. Therefore these schemes might be very useful when we want to generate random functions from random permutations with a small value of n and a high security (security in 2^{80} for example and $n < 80$).

References

1. Aiello, W., Venkatesan, R.: Foiling Birthday Attacks in Length-Doubling Transformations - Benes: A Non-Reversible Alternative to Feistel. In: Maurer, U.M. (ed.) EUROCRYPT 1996. LNCS, vol. 1070, pp. 307–320. Springer, Heidelberg (1996)
2. Bellare, M., Impagliazzo, R.: A Tool for Obtaining Tighter Security Analyses of Pseudorandom Function Based Constructions, with Applications to PRP to PRF Conversion. ePrint Archive 1999/024: Listing for 1999 (1999)
3. Bellare, M., Krovetz, T., Rogaway, P.: Luby-Rackoff Backwards: Increasing Security by Making Block Ciphers Non-invertible. In: Nyberg, K. (ed.) EUROCRYPT 1998. LNCS, vol. 1403, pp. 266–280. Springer, Heidelberg (1998)
4. Hall, C., Wagner, D., Kelsey, J., Schneier, B.: Building PRFs from PRPs. In: Krawczyk, H. (ed.) CRYPTO 1998. LNCS, vol. 1462, pp. 370–389. Springer, Heidelberg (1998)
5. Lucks, S.: The Sum of PRPs Is a Secure PRF. In: Preneel, B. (ed.) EUROCRYPT 2000. LNCS, vol. 1807, pp. 470–487. Springer, Heidelberg (2000)
6. Mandal, A., Patarin, J., Nachef, V.: Indifferentiability beyond the Birthday Bound for the Xor of Two Public Random Permutations. In: Gong, G., Gupta, K.C. (eds.) INDOCRYPT 2010. LNCS, vol. 6498, pp. 69–81. Springer, Heidelberg (2010)
7. Maurer, U., Pietrzak, K.: The Security of Many-Round Luby-Rackoff Pseudo-Random Permutations. In: Biham, E. (ed.) EUROCRYPT 2003. LNCS, vol. 2656, pp. 544–561. Springer, Heidelberg (2003)
8. Patarin, J.: A Proof of Security in $O(2^n)$ for the Xor of Two Random Permutations. In: Safavi-Naini, R. (ed.) ICITS 2008. LNCS, vol. 5155, pp. 232–248. Springer, Heidelberg (2008)
9. Patarin, J.: Security in $O(2^n)$ for the Xor of Two Random Permutations — Proof with the standard H technique. This paper is available from the author

Appendices

A   Mean Value and Standard Deviation of Collisions on Random Functions

Aim. Let f be a random function from I_n to I_n. We assume that we know f on m distinct points x_i: $\forall i$, $1 \le i \le m$, $f(x_i) = y_i$. Let N be the number of collisions on these values y_i. We want to evaluate $E(N)$ (the mean value of N when $f \in_R F_n$) and $\sigma(N)$ (the standard deviation of N when $f \in_R F_n$).

Computation of $E(N)$. Let $\delta_{ij} = 1 \Leftrightarrow f(x_i) = f(x_j)$ and $\delta_{ij} = 0 \Leftrightarrow \delta_{ij} \ne 1$. We have $N = \sum_{i<j} \delta_{ij}$. Therefore, $E(N) = \sum_{i<j} E(\delta_{ij})$. Moreover

$$E(\delta_{ij}) = Pr_{\substack{i \ne j \\ f \in_R B_n}} \left(f(x_i) = f(x_j) \right) = \frac{1}{2^n}$$

Therefore $E(N) = \frac{m(m-1)}{2 \cdot 2^n}$.

Computation of $\sigma(N)$.

$$V(N) = V\left(\sum_{i<j} \delta_{ij} \right) = \sum_{i<j} V(\delta_{ij}) + \sum_{\substack{i<j,\ k<l, \\ (i,j) \ne (k,l)}} Cov(\delta_{ij}, \delta_{kl})$$

where $Cov(\delta_{ij}, \delta_{kl})$ denotes the covariance of $(\delta_{ij}, \delta_{kl})$:

$$Cov(\delta_{ij}, \delta_{kl}) = E(\delta_{ij} \cdot \delta_{kl}) - E(\delta_{ij})E(\delta_{kl})$$

We have:

$$V(\delta_{ij}) = E(\delta_{ij}^2) - E(\delta_{ij})^2 = \frac{1}{2^n} - \frac{1}{2^{2n}}$$

We now have to evaluate $E(\delta_{ij} \cdot \delta_{kl})$.

Case 1: i, j, k, l are pairwise distinct. Then

$$E(\delta_{ij} \cdot \delta_{kl}) = Pr_{f \in_R B_n}\big(f(x_i) = f(x_j) \text{ and } f(x_k) = f(x_l)\big) = \frac{1}{2^{2n}}$$

Case 2: In i, j, k, l, we have exactly 3 distinct values. For example $i = k$. Then

$$E(\delta_{ij} \cdot \delta_{kl}) = Pr_{f \in_R B_n}\big(f(x_i) = f(x_j) = f(x_l)\big) = \frac{1}{2^{2n}}$$

Therefore all the covariance are 0 and we have:

$$V(N) = \frac{m(m-1)}{2}\Big(\frac{1}{2^n} - \frac{1}{2^{2n}}\Big) \quad \text{and} \quad \sigma(N) = \sqrt{V(N)} = O\Big(\frac{m}{\sqrt{2^n}}\Big)$$

B   Mean Value and Standard Deviation of Collisions on $f \oplus g$, $f, g \in_R B_n$

Aim. Let $G = f \oplus g$, with $f, g \in_R B_n$. We assume that we know G on m distinct points x_i: $\forall i, 1 \le i \le m$, $G(x_i) = y_i$. Let N be the number of collisions on these m values y_i. We want to evaluate $E(N)$ (the mean value of N when $f, g \in_R B_n$) and $\sigma(N)$ (the standard deviation of N when $f, g \in_R B_n$).

Computation of $E(N)$. Let $\delta_{ij} = 1 \Leftrightarrow G(x_i) = G(x_j)$ and $\delta_{ij} = 0 \Leftrightarrow \delta_{ij} \ne 1$. We have $N = \sum_{i<j} \delta_{ij}$. Therefore, $E(N) = \sum_{i<j} E(\delta_{ij})$. Moreover

$$E(\delta_{ij}) = Pr_{\substack{i \ne j, \\ f, g \in_R B_n}} \big(g(x_i) \oplus g(x_j) = f(x_i) \oplus f(x_j)\big)$$

When f is fixed, $f \in B_n$, $f(x_i) \oplus f(x_j)$ is a value different from 0. Therefore the probability when $g \in_R B_n$ that $g(x_i) \oplus g(x_j) = f(x_i) \oplus f(x_j)$ is exactly $\frac{1}{2^n - 1}$. So

$$E(\delta_{ij}) = \frac{1}{2^n - 1} \quad \text{and} \quad E(N) = \frac{m(m-1)}{2} \cdot \frac{1}{2^n - 1}$$

Computation of $\sigma(N)$.

$$V(N) = V\Big(\sum_{i<j} \delta_{ij}\Big) = \sum_{i<j} V(\delta_{ij}) + \sum_{\substack{i<j, \, k<l \\ (i,j) \ne (k,l)}} Cov(\delta_{ij}, \delta_{kl}) \quad (*)$$

where $Cov(\delta_{ij}, \delta_{kl})$ denotes the covariance of $(\delta_{ij}, \delta_{kl})$:

$$Cov(\delta_{ij}, \delta_{kl}) = E(\delta_{ij} \cdot \delta_{kl}) - E(\delta_{ij})E(\delta_{kl})$$

We have:
$$V(\delta_{ij}) = E(\delta_{ij}^2) - E(\delta_{ij})^2 = \frac{1}{2^n - 1} - \frac{1}{(2^n - 1)^2}$$

We now have to evaluate $E(\delta_{ij} \cdot \delta_{kl})$

Case 1: i, j, k, l are pairwise distinct. Then

$$E(\delta_{ij} \cdot \delta_{kl}) = Pr_{f,g \in_R B_n} \begin{pmatrix} g(x_i) \oplus g(x_j) = f(x_i) \oplus f(x_j) \\ g(x_k) \oplus g(x_l) = f(x_k) \oplus f(x_l) \end{pmatrix}$$

When $f(x_i)$, $f(x_j)$, $f(x_k)$, $f(x_l)$, $g(x_j)$, $g(x_l)$ are fixed, $g(x_i)$ and $g(x_k)$ are fixed with

$$g(x_i) = g(x_j) \oplus f(x_i) \oplus f(x_j) \quad \text{and} \quad g(x_k) = g(x_l) \oplus f(x_k) \oplus f(x_l)$$

(and these conditions may be compatible or not with g being a permutation). If we did not have these two equalities, for $g(x_i)$ we would have $(2^n - 2)$ possibilities ($g(x_i) \notin \{g(x_j), g(x_l)\}$), and for $g(x_k)$ we would have $(2^n - 3)$ possibilities ($g(x_k) \notin \{g(x_i), g(x_j), g(x_l)\}$). So,

$$E(\delta_{ij} \cdot \delta_{kl}) \leq \frac{1}{(2^n - 2)(2^n - 3)}$$

Therefore

$$E(\delta_{ij} \cdot \delta_{kl}) - E(\delta_{ij})E(\delta_{kl}) \leq \frac{1}{(2^n - 2)(2^n - 3)} - \frac{1}{(2^n - 1)^2}$$

$$\leq \frac{3 \cdot 2^n}{(2^n - 1)^2(2^n - 2)(2^n - 3)} \leq O(\frac{1}{2^{3n}})$$

Case 2: in i, j, k, l, we have exactly 3 distinct values. For example $i = k$. Then

$$E(\delta_{ij} \cdot \delta_{kl}) = Pr_{f,g \in B_n} (f(x_i) \oplus g(x_i) = f(x_j) \oplus g(x_j) = f(x_l) \oplus g(x_l))$$

When $f(x_i)$, $f(x_j)$, $f(x_l)$, $g(x_i)$ are fixed, $g(x_j)$ and $g(x_l)$ are fixed with

$$\begin{cases} g(x_j) = f(x_i) \oplus g(x_i) \oplus f(x_j) \\ g(x_l) = f(x_i) \oplus g(x_i) \oplus f(x_l) \end{cases}$$

(and these conditions may be compatible or not with g being a permutation). If we did not have these two equalities, for $g(x_j)$ we would have $(2^n - 1)$ possibilities ($g(x_j) \neq g(x_i)$) and for $g(x_l)$, we would have $(2^n - 2)$ possibilities ($g(x_l) \notin \{g(x_i), g(x_j)\}$). So

$$E(\delta_{ij} \cdot \delta_{kl}) \leq \frac{1}{(2^n - 1)(2^n - 2)}$$

Therefore

$$E(\delta_{ij} \cdot \delta_{kl}) - E(\delta_{ij})E(\delta_{kl}) \leq \frac{1}{(2^n - 1)(2^n - 2)} - \frac{1}{(2^n - 1)^2}$$

$$\leq \frac{1}{(2^n - 1)^2 (2^n - 2)} \leq O(\frac{1}{2^{3n}})$$

So from $(*)$ we get

$$V(N) \leq \frac{m(m-1)}{2} (\frac{1}{2^n - 1} - \frac{1}{(2^n - 1)^2}) + O(\frac{m^4}{2^{3n}})$$

So

$$V(N) \leq O(\frac{m^2}{2^n}) + O(\frac{m^4}{2^{3n}})$$

Since $m \leq 2^n$, $V(N) \leq O(\frac{m^2}{2^n})$ and therefore $\sigma(N) \leq O(\frac{m}{\sqrt{2^n}})$.

C   Mean Value and Standard Deviation of Collisions on $f_1 \oplus f_2 \oplus \ldots \oplus f_k$

Theorem 1 *Let $G = f_1 \oplus f_2 \oplus \ldots \oplus f_k$, $f, g \in_R B_n$, with $f_1, f_2, \ldots, , f_k \in_R B_n$. Let assume that we know G on m distinct points x_i: $\forall i$, $1 \leq i \leq m$, $G(x_i) = y_i$. Let N_k be the number of collisions on these m points: $N_k = $ the number of (i, j), $1 \leq i < j \leq m$ such that $y_i = y_j$. Then*

$$E(N_k) = \frac{m(m-1)}{2} \cdot \frac{1}{2^n} [1 + \frac{(-1)^k}{(2^n - 1)^{k-1}}]$$

where $E(N_k)$ denotes the mean value of N_k when $f_1, f_2, \ldots, f_k$ are randomly chosen in B_n.

To prove this theorem we will first need a lemma.

Lemma 1. *If $x_i \neq x_j$, we have*

$$\text{if } \varphi \neq 0, \quad Pr_{f \in B_n}\big(f(x_i) \oplus f(x_j) = \varphi\big) = \frac{1}{2^n - 1}$$

$$\text{and if } \varphi = 0, \quad Pr_{f \in B_n}\big(f(x_i) \oplus f(x_j) = \varphi\big) = 0$$

Proof of Lemma 1
If $\varphi = 0$, $f(x_i) \neq f(x_j)$ since f is a permutation. If $\varphi \neq 0$, when $f(x_i)$ is fixed, $f(x_j)$ is fixed to the value of $\varphi \oplus f(x_i)$, so instead of having $2^n - 1$ possible values for $f(x_j)$ we have one when $f(x_i)$ is fixed.

Proof of Theorem 1
Let $\delta_{ij} = 1 \Leftrightarrow G(x_i) = G(x_j)$ and $\delta_{ij} = 0 \Leftrightarrow \delta_{ij} \neq 1$. We have $N_k = \sum_{i<j} \delta_{ij}^k$, so $E(N_k) = \sum_{i<j} E(\delta_{ij}^k)$. We will compute $E(\delta_{ij}^k)$ by induction on k.

$$E(\delta_{ij}^k) = Pr_{f_1, \ldots, f_k \in_R B_n} [f_1(x_i) \oplus \ldots \oplus f_k(x_i) = f_1(x_j) \oplus \ldots \oplus f_k(x_j)]$$

So from Lemma 1 above,

$$E(\delta_{ij}^k) = \frac{1}{2^n - 1} Pr_{f_1,\dots,f_{k-1} \in_R B_n} \left[f_1(x_i) \oplus \dots \oplus f_{k-1}(x_i) \neq f_1(x_j) \oplus \dots \oplus f_{k-1}(x_j) \right]$$

$$E(\delta_{ij}^k) = \frac{1}{2^n - 1} \left[1 - E(\delta_{ij}^{k-1}) \right] \quad (*)$$

If $k = 1$ we have $E(\delta_{ij}^1) = Pr_{f_1 \in B_n}(f_1(x_i) = f_1(x_j)) = 0$ $(**)$ (since f_1 is a permutation and $x_i \neq x_j$). Now from $(*)$ and $(**)$ we get immediately by induction on k that

$$E(\delta_{ij}^k) = \frac{1}{2^n} \left[1 + \frac{(-1)^k}{(2^n - 1)^{k-1}} \right]$$

and therefore,

$$E(N_k) = \frac{m(m-1)}{2} E(\delta_{ij}^k) = \frac{m(m-1)}{2} \cdot \frac{1}{2^n} \left[1 + \frac{(-1)^k}{(2^n - 1)^{k-1}} \right]$$

as claimed. Moreover the standard deviation can be computed exactly as in Appendix B, or alternatively by using the fact that $G = f_1 \oplus f_2 \oplus \psi$ where ψ is a function independant of $f_1 \oplus f_2$. We get the same result: $\sigma(N_k) \leq O(\frac{m}{\sqrt{2^n}})$.

Remark. This result is not surprising: by Xoring k permutations, $k \geq 3$ instead of 2, we expect to obtain a better or at least as good pseudorandom permutation. Since we have seen that $\sigma(N)$ for $k = 2$ and $\sigma(N)$ for a random function are less than or equal to $O(\frac{m}{\sqrt{2^n}})$, it is natural that for $k \geq 3$ we also have the same result $\sigma(N) \leq O(\frac{m}{\sqrt{2^n}})$.

D   Mean Value of Collisions on $f(x\|\alpha) \oplus f(x\|\beta)$, $f \in_R B_n$

Let $G'(x) = f(x\|\alpha) \oplus f(x\|\beta)$, $f \in_R B_n$, with $\alpha \neq \beta$. We assume that we know G' on m distinct points x_i: $\forall i, 1 \leq i \leq m$, $G'(x_i) = y_i$. Let N be the number of collisions on these m values y_i. We want to evaluate $E(N)$, the mean value of N when $f \in_R B_n$. Let $\delta_{ij} = 1 \Leftrightarrow G'(x_i) = G'(x_j)$ and $\delta_{ij} = 0 \Leftrightarrow \delta_{ij} \neq 1$. We have $N = \sum_{i<j} \delta_{ij}$. Therefore $E(N) = \sum_{i<j} E(\delta_{ij})$. Moreover $E(\delta_{ij}) = Pr_{f \in_R B_n}(f(x_i\|\alpha) \oplus f(x_i\|\beta) \oplus f(x_j\|\alpha) = f(x_j\|\beta))$. So $E(\delta_{ij}) = Pr_{f \in_R B_n}(f(a) \oplus f(b) \oplus f(c) = f(d))$ where a, b, c, d are pairwise distinct. When $f(a)$, $f(b)$ and $f(b)$ are fixed, then $f(d)$ can have any value $\notin \{f(a), f(b), f(c)\}$ with probability exactly $\frac{1}{2^n-3}$ (and $f(d) \in \{f(a), f(b), f(c)\}$ with probability 0). Moreover $f(a) \oplus f(b) \oplus f(c) \in \{f(a), f(b), f(c)\}$ is not possible since f is a permutation. Therefore $E(\delta_{ij}) = \frac{1}{2^n-3}$ and $E(N) = \frac{m(m-1)}{2.(2^n-3)} \simeq \frac{m(m-1)}{2.2^n}(1 + \frac{3}{2^n})$.

E   Mean Value of Collisions on $f(x\|\alpha_1) \oplus \dots \oplus f(x\|\alpha_k)$, $f \in_R B_n$

Let $G'_k(x) = f(x\|\alpha_1) \oplus \dots \oplus f(x\|\alpha_k)$, $f \in_R B_n$, with $\alpha_1, \alpha_2, \dots \alpha_k$ pairwise distinct. We assume that we know G'_k on m distinct points x_i: $\forall i, 1 \leq i \leq$

m, $G'_k(x_i) = y_i$. Let N_k be the number of collisions on these m values y_i. We want to evaluate $E(N_k)$, the mean value of N when $f \in_R B_n$. Let $\delta_{ij} = 1 \Leftrightarrow G'_k(x_i) = G'_k(x_j)$ and $\delta_{ij} = 0 \Leftrightarrow \delta_{ij} \neq 1$. We have $N_k = \sum_{i<j} \delta_{ij}$. Therefore $E(N_k) = \sum_{i<j} E(\delta_{ij})$. Let $p_k = E(\delta_{ij}) = Pr_{f \in_R B_n}(f(x_i\|\alpha_1) \oplus \ldots \oplus f(x_i\|\alpha_k) = f(x_j\|\alpha_1) \oplus \ldots \oplus f(x_j\|\alpha_k)) = Pr_{f \in_R B_n}(f(a_1) \oplus f(a_2) \oplus \ldots \oplus f(a_{2k-1}) = f(a_{2k}))$ where $a_1, a_2, \ldots, a_{2k}$ are pairwise distinct. When $f(a_1), \ldots f(a_{2k-1})$ are fixed, then $f(a_{2k})$ can have any value $\notin \{f(a_1), \ldots, f(a_{2k-1})\}$ with probability exactly $\frac{1}{2^n - (2k-1)}$ (and $f(a_{2k}) \in \{f(a_1), \ldots, f(a_{2k-1})\}$ with probability 0). Therefore we have: $p_k = (1 - (2k-1)p_{k-1}) \cdot \frac{1}{2^n - (2k-1)}$ (∗) (since $\forall i, 1 \leq i \leq 2k-1$ we have the probability exactly $1 - p_{k-1}$ that $f(a_1) \oplus f(a_2) \oplus \ldots f(a_{2k-1}) = f(a_i)$). For example, from $p_1 = 0$ (since f is a bijection), we get from (∗): $p_2 = \frac{1}{2^n-3}$ (as already found in Appendix D), and then $p_3 = (1 - 5p_2) \cdot \frac{1}{2^n-5} = \frac{1}{2^n}(1 - \frac{15}{2^{2n} - 8 \cdot 2^n + 15})$. More generally, from (∗) and $p_2 = \frac{1}{2^n-3}$, we get easily by induction that:
$$p_k = \frac{1}{2^n}\left[1 + \frac{(-1)^k \cdot 3.5.7\ldots(2k-1)}{2^{(k-1)n}(1-\frac{3}{2^n})(1-\frac{5}{2^n})\ldots(1-\frac{2k-1}{2^n})}\right]. \text{ Therefore } E(N_k) = \frac{m(m-1)}{2}p_k =$$
$$\frac{m(m-1)}{2.2^n}\left[1 + O(\frac{1}{2^{(k-1)n}})\right], \text{ with } O(\frac{1}{2^{(k-1)n}}) = \frac{(-1)^k \cdot 3.5.7\ldots(2k-1)}{2^{(k-1)n}(1-\frac{3}{2^n})(1-\frac{5}{2^n})\ldots(1-\frac{2k-1}{2^n})}.$$

Preimage Attacks on Feistel-SP Functions: Impact of Omitting the Last Network Twist

Yu Sasaki

NTT Secure Platform Laboratories
3-9-11 Midori-cho, Musashino-shi, Tokyo 180-8585 Japan
sasaki.yu@lab.ntt.co.jp

Abstract. In this paper, generic attacks are presented against hash functions that are constructed by a hashing mode instantiating a Feistel or generalized Feistel networks with an SP-round function. It is observed that the omission of the network twist in the last round can be a weakness against preimage attacks. The first target is a standard Feistel network with an SP round function. Up to 11 rounds can be attacked in generic if a condition on a key schedule function is satisfied. The second target is a 4-branch type-2 generalized Feistel network with an SP round function. Up to 15 rounds can be attacked in generic. These generic attacks are then applied to hashing modes of ISO standard ciphers Camellia-128 without FL and whitening layers and CLEFIA-128.

Keywords: Feistel, generalized Feistel, SP round function, hashing modes, meet-in-the-middle attack, preimage attack, Camellia, CLEFIA.

1 Introduction

Designing secure and efficient symmetric-key primitives is a long-term challenge in the cryptographic community. One of the most successful designs is AES [7,28]. Since then, many designs use an AES-based transformation as a core of their algorithms. An unique design philosophy of AES is the omission of the diffusion called MixColumns in the last round. The purpose of this design is making the encryption and decryption algorithms symmetric, while it does not lower the provable security bound against differential and linear cryptanalysis. However, the omission impacts to the security for other cryptanalytic approaches. Dunkelman and Keller discussed its impact in [8]. Sasaki also showed that the omission could be exploited by an attacker in several hashing modes [21].

Another widely used design approach is the Feistel network, which was firstly used in DES [5], and the generalized Feistel network (GFN) [29]. The computation structures of Feistel network and 4-branch type-2 GFN are shown in Fig. 1. In the Feistel network, the data is separated into the left and right halves $L\|R$, and then R is updated by $R \oplus F(k, L)$, where F is called a round function and k represents a subkey. Finally, the left and right halves are exchanged, $i.e.$, $R \oplus F(k, L)\|L$. The ciphertext is computed by iterating this transformation several times. As shown in Fig. 1, several designs omit the network twist in the last

M. Jacobson et al. (Eds.): ACNS 2013, LNCS 7954, pp. 170–185, 2013.

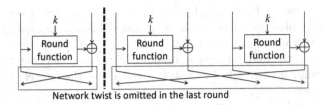

Network twist is omitted in the last round

Fig. 1. Left: sketch of Feistel network, Right: sketch of 4-branch type-2 GFN

round, for example, DES [5] and ISO standard ciphers Camellia [2,12], CLEFIA [27,13], and HIGHT [10,12]. The omission of the last network twist makes the encryption and decryption algorithms symmetric.

Here, we raise a simple question; *What is the impact of omitting the last network twist in the Feistel network and GFN with respect to the security?* This paper answers this question by showing an attack against Feistel based hash functions that works more efficiently when the last network twist is omitted.

One may say that analyzing hash functions constructed by a Feistel cipher, especially for dedicated algorithms such as Camellia and CLEFIA, is meaningless unless someone develops a system that actually implements their hashing modes. However, we believe such analysis is important from the following reason.

> Non-cryptographic experts do not always tell cryptographers which hash function algorithm they implemented. Such information is sometimes never opened. Thus, it is important for cryptographers to prepare for the potential use by non-experts. Hashing modes based on an n-bit block-cipher, *e.g.* the Matyas-Meyer-Oseas (MMO) mode [16, Algorithm 9.41], is internationally standardized by ISO [11]. Camellia and CLEFIA are also internationally standardized by ISO [12,13]. MMO-Camellia and MMO-CLEFIA are important candidates for the potential use by non-experts because giving a guideline of good technology to non-experts is one of the purposes of the standardization.

So far, several researchers have studied the security of Feistel functions. Knudsen and Rijmen showed a collision attack for 7 rounds in the MMO mode [15]. Sasaki and Yasuda analyzed the Feistel network with an Substitution-Permutation (SP) round function. They showed a collision attack for a half of the state for 11 rounds in the MMO mode [24]. The attack was later improved and implemented on reduced-round Camellia [23]. Moon *et al.* presented preimage attacks on Feistel network, GFN, and Misty network with an SP round function [17]. They attacked 6 rounds of a Feistel-SP function and 9 rounds of a 4-branch type-2 GFN-SP function.

Our Contributions. In this paper, we present meet-in-the-middle (MitM) preimage attacks against hash functions that are constructed by the MMO or other Preneel-Govaerts-Vandewalle (PGV) modes [20] instantiating a Feistel or 4-branch Type-2 GFN ciphers with an SP-round function. Regarding the Feistel network, 11 rounds can be attacked when an attacker can control several bits of the last round subkey by choosing the first round subkey. Regarding 4-branch type-2 GFN, 15 rounds can be attacked when the relation between the first-round and the last-round subkeys is random. If the last network twist is not omitted. the number of attacked rounds is 6 and 10 for the Feistel and 4-branch type-2 GFN, respectively,

The MitM attack separates the target algorithm into two parts called *forward chunk* and *backward chunk* so that each chunk includes several bits which are independent of the other chunk. Such bits are called *free bits*. So far, there are two types of the MitM attacks. One is setting the free bits in the key and the other is setting the free bits in the internal state. In this paper, we take the second approach.[1] Note that, during the computation of one chunk, all previous work treat the free bits for the other chunk as unknown.

Our attacks are based on the following two ideas. Note that these ideas are not specific for SP-round functions.

1. The omission of the last network twist can be exploited by the splice-and-cut technique [3]. When the last and then first rounds are computed in this order, the input value to the round function do not change. Therefore, if the subkey values are identical, the impact of these two rounds cancel each other. The same situation also occurs between the second last and the second rounds. In the hash function, the key value can be chosen by the attacker and thus the round-shrink can be caused deliberately. Note that the cancellation of the round function was exploited by Gauravaram *et al.* [9]. Our discovery is that the cancellation gives more impacts when the last network twist is omitted.

2. During the computation of one chunk, free bits for the other chunk do not have to be completely independent as long as they linearly relate to the computation. Therefore, for the computation of each chunk, we trace how the free bits for the other chunk relate rather than treat them as unknown immediately. Our attack on 4-branch type-2 GFN traces the linearity over 10 rounds, and thus the idea works efficiently.

We apply these techniques to block-ciphers Camellia-128 without the FL and whitening layers and CLEFIA-128 in hashing modes. Camellia is a Feistel-SP cipher but its P-layer does not satisfy the maximum branch number. Thus, the attack can be extended compared to the generic case. We show an attack up to 13 rounds of Camellia-128 hashing modes. CLEFIA adopts 4-branch Type-2 GFN but uses two different diffusion matrices for the diffusion switching mechanism [25,26]. This increases the security and thus the attack becomes worse than the generic case. We show an attack up to 12 rounds of CLEFIA-128 hashing modes.

---

[1] Setting free bits in the key is impossible without defining a key schedule algorithm.

2   Preliminaries

2.1   Specification of Camellia

Camellia was jointly designed by NTT and Mitsubishi Electric Corporation. It is widely standardized or recommended, *e.g.*, ISO [12], NESSIE [19], and CRYP-TREC [6]. This paper attacks Camellia-128, where both of the key and block sizes are 128 bits. We attack a weak variant of Camellia-128 where computations called FL and whitening layers are omitted.

Let M and K be a 128-bit plaintext and a secret key, respectively. Eighteen 64-bit round keys $k_0, \ldots, k_{17}$ are generated from K. Let X_r^L and X_r^R ($0 \leq r \leq 18$) be left and right 64-bits of the internal state in each round. The plaintext is loaded into $X_0^L \| X_0^R$. Then, $X_r^L = X_{r-1}^R \oplus F(X_{r-1}^L, k_{r-1})$ and $X_r^R = X_{r-1}^L$ for $1 \leq r \leq 17$ is computed up to the second last round. In the last round, The ciphertext $X_{18}^L \| X_{18}^R$ is computed by $X_{18}^L = X_{17}^L$ and $X_{18}^R = X_{17}^R \oplus F(X_{17}^L, k_{17})$, namely, the last network twist is omitted.

The key schedule takes a 128-bit key K as input and firstly produces another 128-bit value K_A. We later analyze subkey values k_0, k_1, k_{11}, and k_{12}. These subkeys are defined as $k_0 \| k_1 = K_A$, k_{11} is the right half of ($K_A \lll 60$), and k_{12} is the left half of ($K \lll 94$).

The round function consists of a 64-bit subkey addition, S-box transformation, and a diffusion called P-layer. The size of each S-box is 8 bits, and thus 8 S-boxes are applied. Let $(z_0 \| z_1 \| \cdots \| z_7)$ be 64-bit values input to the P-layer. The output $(z_0' \| z_1' \| \cdots \| z_7')$ is computed as follows. Here, $z[s, t, u, \cdots]$ means $z_s \oplus z_t \oplus z_u \oplus \cdots$. The branch number of P is only 5. This is different from the case of an MDS matrix multiplication.

$$z_0' = z[0,2,3,5,6,7], \quad z_2' = z[0,1,2,4,5,7], \quad z_4' = z[0,1,5,6,7], \quad z_6' = z[2,3,4,5,7],$$
$$z_1' = z[0,1,3,4,6,7], \quad z_3' = z[1,2,3,4,5,6], \quad z_5' = z[1,2,4,6,7], \quad z_7' = z[0,3,4,5,6].$$

2.2   Specification of CLEFIA

CLEFIA is a block-cipher proposed at FSE 2007 by Shirai *et al.* [27]. It is standardized by ISO [13] as a lightweight cipher. In this paper, we attack CLEFIA-128, where both of the block size and the key size are 128 bits. It adopts the type-2 generalized Feistel structure with 4 branches and consists of 18 rounds. Two round functions F^L and F^R consist of a 32-bit subkey addition, an S-box transformation, and a multiplication by an MDS matrix. The size of each S-box is 8 bits, and thus 4 S-boxes are applied in each of the left and right functions. MDS matrices for the left and right functions are different.

Let M and K be a 128-bit plaintext and a secret key, respectively. Thirty-six 32-bit subkeys $k_0, \ldots, k_{35}$ and four 32-bit whitening keys wk_0, wk_1, wk_2, wk_3 are generated from K. Let $X_r^0 \| X_r^1 \| X_r^2 \| X_r^3$ ($0 \leq r \leq 18$) be an input internal state in each round. The plaintext is loaded into $X_0^0 \| X_0^1 \| X_0^2 \| X_0^3$. Then, the second and fourth words are updated by the pre-whitening operation, *i.e.*, $X_0^1 \leftarrow$

$X_0^1 \oplus wk_0$ and $X_0^3 \leftarrow X_0^3 \oplus wk_1$. Then, internal state is updated by the following computation up to the second last round (for $1 \le r \le 17$);

$$X_r^0 = X_{r-1}^3 \oplus F^R(X_{r-1}^2, k_{2r-1}), \quad X_r^1 = X_{r-1}^0,$$
$$X_r^2 = X_{r-1}^1 \oplus F^L(X_{r-1}^0, k_{2r-2}), \quad X_r^3 = X_{r-1}^2.$$

In the last round, $X_{18}^0 \| X_{18}^1 \| X_{18}^2 \| X_{18}^3$ is computed by $X_{18}^0 = X_{17}^0, X_{18}^1 = X_{17}^1 \oplus F^L(X_{17}^0, k_{34}), X_{18}^2 = X_{17}^2, X_{18}^3 = X_{17}^3 \oplus F^R(X_{17}^2, k_{35})$, namely, the last network twist is omitted. Finally, the second and fourth words are updated by the post-whitening operation, $i.e.$, $X_{18}^1 \leftarrow X_{18}^1 \oplus wk_2$ and $X_{18}^3 \leftarrow X_{18}^3 \oplus wk_3$, and $X_{18}^0 \| X_{18}^1 \| X_{18}^2 \| X_{18}^3$ is output as the ciphertext.

2.3   Feistel and 4-Branch Type-2 GFN with an SP Round Function

In this paper, we firstly analyze generic Feistel and 4-Branch Type-2 GFN structures with an SP round function. Analyzing such generic structure can be seen many papers [4,14,17,23,24,26]. These structures are generally represented by several parameters $i.e.$, the block size N, the S-box size c, and the number of S-boxes in each round b. The attack strategy and efficiency depends on these parameters. In this paper, to make a comparison of attacks against Camellia and CLEFIA clear, we fix the parameters to $(N, c, b) = (128, 8, 8)$ for the standard Feistel and $(N, c, b) = (128, 8, 4)$ for 4-branch type-2 GFN.

An SP round function consists of three operations: subkey addition, S-layer, and P-layer. In the subkey addition, a subkey is XORed to the state. In the S-layer, b S-boxes with the size of c bits are applied. In the P-layer, a linear computation whose branch number is $b+1$ is performed. An MDS multiplication is an example of the operation. We assume that all round functions are identical. We also assume that whitening operations are not performed.

Hereafter we use the notations S_i and P_i for the standard Feistel to represent the state immediately after the S-layer and P-layer in round i, respectively. For 4-branch type-2 GFN, we use the notations S_i^L, S_i^R, P_i^L, and P_i^R to further distinguish the left and right round functions.

2.4   Domain Extension and Hashing Modes

Main targets of this paper are compression functions which are constructed by PGV modes with a Feistel-SP or GFN-SP cipher. For simplicity, we explain the attack on the compression function constructed by the Davies-Meyer mode [16, Algorithm 9.42] or MMO mode, in which the compression function output is computed by an XOR of plaintext and ciphertext.

Suppose that the compression function is constructed by the Davies-Meyer mode and the hash function is constructed by the narrow-pipe Merkle-Damgård domain extension. It is well known that a pseudo-preimage attack on the compression function with a complexity of 2^x can be converted to a preimage attack on the hash function with a complexity of $2^{((x+N)/2)+1}$ [16, Fact 9.99]. If the MMO mode is adopted, the attack is converted to a second preimage attack on the hash function with the same complexity.

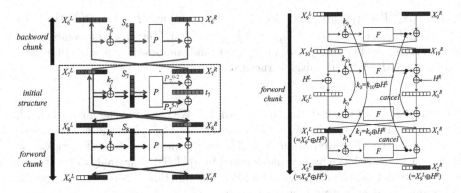

Fig. 2. 3 rounds including the 1-round initial structure   **Fig. 3.** 4-round shrink for generic Feistel

3   Preimage Attacks on Feistel-SP and GFN-SP Functions

3.1   Attacks on 11-round Feistel-SP Compression Function

The attack is a MitM attack with the splice-and-cut [3], initial structure [22], and indirect-partial matching [1]. This attack only can work if a condition on the key schedule function is satisfied. (Later we show the condition can be satisfied for 13-round Camellia-128.) The attacked rounds are from round 0 to round 10.

The attacker firstly searches for a key value satisfying the condition. Then, for the fixed key value, the MitM attack is performed. During the MitM attack, 4 rounds will be shrunken when we analyze the last and first rounds sequentially with the splice-and-cut technique. The valid pair can be identified by efficiently matching the results from two chunks with skipping several rounds.

1-round Initial Structure Plus 2 Rounds (Rounds 6 to 8). The attack starts from round 7 by constructing the initial structure. The detailed construction is given in Fig. 2. Throughout this paper, free bytes for the forward chunk and values depending of them are shown in blue, while free bytes for the backward chunk and values depending of them are shown in red. Grey bytes are fixed during the MitM attack. In the computation for each chunk, free bytes of the other chunk are regarded as unknown value which are shown with blank squares. Although one of the technical contributions of this paper is tracing linear relations of free bytes for the other chunk, this technique does not lead to any advantage for the case of a generic Feistel-SP. Hence, in this attack, to make the attack simple, we do not trace linear relations.

The computation for each chunk starts from choosing the value of the free bytes. The free bytes for the forward chunk and backward chunk are the last three bytes of X_7^L and the first three bytes of X_7^L, respectively. Because P is a linear operation, the impact from the free bytes for each chunk, denoted by P_7^{0-2} and P_7^{5-7} can be computed independently, *i.e.*, $P_7^{0-2} = P\big(S(X_7^L[0] \oplus$

$k_7[0]) \| S(X_7^L[1] \oplus k_7[1]) \| S(X_7^L[2] \oplus k_7[2]) \| 0 \| 0 \| 0 \| 0 \| 0)$ and $P_7^{5-7} = P(0 \| 0 \| 0 \| 0 \| 0 \| 0 \|$ $S(X_7^L[5] \oplus k_7[5]) \| S(X_7^L[6] \oplus k_7[6]) \| S(X_7^L[7] \oplus k_7[7]))$. Therefore, two chunks can be computed independently. In Fig. 2, one round computation is added for both chunks after the 1-round initial structure.

4-round Shrink (Rounds 9, 10, 0, and 1). We continue the forward chunk after Fig. 2. The next 4 rounds are given in Fig. 3. The splice-and-cut technique is used, namely, after we obtain $X_{11}^L \| X_{11}^R$ we obtain the values of $X_0^L \| X_0^R$ by taking an XOR with the hash value denoted by $H^L \| H^R$. The analysis for these 4 rounds does not use the property of an SP-round function. Therefore, we describe the round function in a more generic form.

With a straight-forward method, the forward chunk cannot continue even two rounds because the unknown three bytes at X_9^L makes all bytes of X_{10}^L unknown and all bytes of X_{11}^R unknown. However, we observe that, with the help of the omission of the network twist after round 10, we can cancel the round function output in round 10, $F(X_{10}^L \oplus k_{10})$, by the one in round 0, $F(X_0^L \oplus k_0)$, with setting $k_0 = k_{10} \oplus H^L$. This is because $F(X_0^L \oplus k_0) = F((X_{10}^L \oplus H^L) \oplus (k_{10} \oplus H^L)) = F(X_{10}^L \oplus k_{10})$. Then, we can preserve the known bytes of X_9^L in X_1^L. Moreover, because X_1^L and X_9^L have the relation H^R, we can cancel the impact of round 9 with the one in round 1 by setting $k_1 = k_9 \oplus H^R$.

In the end, after 4 rounds, X_2^L and X_2^R become $X_9^R \oplus H^L$ and $X_9^L \oplus H^R$, respectively. This is stronger than just skipping 4 rounds because the unknown bytes (X_9^L) are moved to the right half of the state (X_2^R) which is not used to update the next round.

We set two $N/2$-bit conditions on the key. If the output of the key schedule function is uniformly distributed, satisfying this condition will take the same cost as the brute-force preimage attack. However, satisfying this condition is often possible because the key schedule function is usually light. For example, if some bits of the secret key are used as subkeys *e.g.* DES [5] and XTEA [18], satisfying the condition is trivial. Moreover, in some ciphers, the last-round subkey can be directly generated from the secret key for achieving on-the-fly key generation for decryption, *e.g.* HIGHT [10]. In such a case, the condition is easily satisfied.

4-round Match (Rounds 2 to 5). The remaining 4 rounds are shown in Fig. 4. If we compute 2 rounds in backwards, all bytes become unknown due to the three unknown bytes of X_6^R. Hence, the direct match cannot be applied.

We observe that the computation over three rounds denoted by bold lines in Fig. 4 is linear. The equation is $S_5 \leftarrow P^{-1}(P(S_3) \oplus X_3^R \oplus X_6^L)$. By applying a linear transformation, this part can be converted into a partial match. A simplified description of these computations is given in Fig. 5. The transformed equation is $S_5 \leftarrow S_3 \oplus P^{-1}(X_3^R) \oplus P^{-1}(X_6^L)$. Note that the attacker knows all values of X_3^R and X_6^L. Hence, $P^{-1}(X_3^R)$ and $P^{-1}(X_6^L)$ can be computed in each chunk independently of the other chunk. In more details, in the forward chunk, we compute $S_3 \oplus P^{-1}(X_3^R)$ and store them in a table. In the backward chunk,

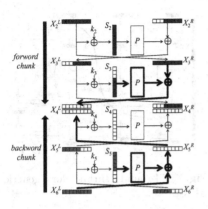

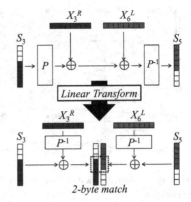

Fig. 4. The match over 4 rounds   **Fig. 5.** Detailed matching procedure

we compute $S_5 \oplus P^{-1}(X_6^L)$ and check the match. Because 2 bytes are overlapped between these values, 2-byte match can be performed.

Attack Procedure. The attack procedure for a target $H^L \| H^R$ is as follows.

1. Find a key value K such that $k_0 = k_{10} \oplus H^L$ and $k_1 = k_9 \oplus H^R$ are satisfied.
2. For all choices of the ten fixed-byte values, $X_7^L[3,4]$ and t_7, do as follows.
3. Choose three free bytes for the forward chunk, $X_7^L[5,6,7]$, and compute the value of $S_3 \oplus P^{-1}(X_3^R)$. Store the results in a table.
4. Choose three free bytes for the backward chunk, $X_7^L[0,1,2]$, compute the value of $S_5 \oplus P^{-1}(X_6^L)$, and check if the same value exists in the table with respect to the 3rd and 4th bytes.
5. If the match is found, check the match of all bits with the corresponding free bytes for both chunks. If all bits match, output it as a pseudo-preimage.

The complexity for Step 1 depends on the key schedule function. Let T_{key} be the complexity of Step 1. Step 2 iterates the following steps 2^{80} times. For each value of Step 2, Step 3 is iterated 2^{24} times, and requires 2^{24} amount of memory. Step 4 is also iterated 2^{24} times. The sum of the complexities for Steps 3 and 4 is about 2^{24} 11-round compression function computations. Strictly speaking, the attacker does not have to compute the shrunken 4 rounds. Here, we ignore its impact. After Step 4, $2^{24+24-16} = 2^{32}$ values will remain. These values are examined in Step 5 that requires 2^{32} 11-round compression function computations. Finally, this 2^{32} computations are iterated by 2^{80} times due to Step 2, which results in 2^{112} 11-round compression function computations. Note that, for a fixed key, all output values of the compression function cannot be produced. Hence, the success probability of the attack is $1 - 1/e \approx 0.63$. Note that the attack can be iterated as long as several key values satisfying the conditions are available.

In summary, the total computational complexity is $T_{key} + 2^{112}$ computations and the memory requirement is 2^{24} internal-state values. Suppose that T_{key} is

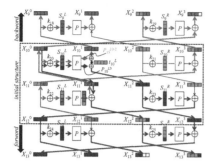
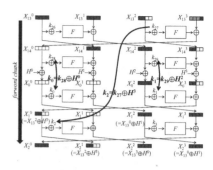

Fig. 6. 4 rounds with 2-round initial structure

Fig. 7. 4-round shrink for generic GFN-SP

much smaller than 2^{112} 11-round computations. Then, the attack is converted to the preimage attack or the second preimage attack on the hash function with a complexity of $2^{((112+128)/2)+1} = 2^{121}$ computations.

Let us discuss the comparison with the case where the last network twist is not omitted. In this case, the cancellation property cannot be exploited in the MitM attack. We focus on the identical pattern of the known byte positions between (X_9^L, X_9^R) and (X_3^L, X_3^R). This indicates that if we remove rounds 9, 10, 0, 1, and 2, in total 5 rounds, the MitM attack can work. Hence, the number of attacked rounds is 6, which is significantly smaller than the case without the last network twist.

3.2   Attacks on 15-round Type-2 GFN-SP Compression Function

2-round Initial Structure Plus 2 Rounds (Rounds 9 to 12). The attack starts from round 10 by constructing a 2-round initial structure. The detailed construction is given in Fig. 6. Hereafter, yellow bytes represent the ones that are linearly dependent of free bytes for the other chunk.

Inside the 2-round initial structure, we need to ensure that the impact from two chunks do not mix. Here, we explain the computation of each chunk.

Forward Chunk: The free byte for the forward chunk (blue) is $X_{10}^0[3]$. In round 10, Because P is linear, the impact from $X_{10}^0[3]$ denoted by P_{10}^{L3} is independently computed from the backward chunk *i.e.*, $P_{10}^{L3} = P(0\|0\|0\| S(X_{10}^0[3] \oplus k_{20}[3]))$. In round 11, suppose that the value of P_{11}^{L3} is independent of the backward chunk. Then, the output of round 11 is computed by simply computing the round function.

Backward Chunk: The free bytes for the forward chunk (red) are $X_{12}^1[2]$ and $X_{12}^1[3]$. We only choose 1-byte (256) possibilities for these two bytes so that P_{11}^{L3} in round 11 can be a fixed value. In details, we first choose the value of $S_{11}^L[2]$ and then choose the corresponding $S_{11}^L[3]$ that makes P_{11}^{L3} be a predetermined fixed value. The value of $S_{11}^L[3]$ depends on the specification of P. In general, we can have unique candidate of $S_{11}^L[3]$ due to the linearity of P. After we choose $S_{11}^L[2], S_{11}^L[3]$, we compute $X_{12}^1[2], X_{12}^1[3]$ by XORing $k_{22}[2], k_{22}[3]$. In round 10, P_{10}^{L0-2} can be computed independently of the forward chunk as explained before. In the end, X_{10}^1 can be computed independently of the forward chunk.

In Fig. 6, one round computation is added for both chunks after the 2-round initial structure. Note that $X_{13}^2[2,3]$ is linearly affected by the free bytes for the backward chunk, $X_{12}^1[2,3]$. Similarly, $X_9^3[3]$ is linearly affected by the free byte for the forward chunk, $X_{10}^0[3]$.

4-round Shrink (Rounds 13, 14, 0 to 2). 4 rounds after Fig. 6 is shown in Fig. 7. After we obtain $X_{15}^0 \| \cdots \| X_{15}^3$, we obtain $X_0^0 \| \cdots \| X_0^3$ by taking an XOR with the hash value $H^0 \| \cdots \| H^3$. The analysis does not use the property of an SP-round function, thus the round function is described in a more generic form.

We observe that, with the help of the omission of the network twist after round 14, we can cancel the round function output in round 14, $F(X_{14}^0 \oplus k_{28})$ and $F(X_{14}^2 \oplus k_{29})$, by the ones in round 0, $F(X_0^0 \oplus k_0)$ and $F(X_0^2 \oplus k_1)$, with setting $k_0 = k_{28} \oplus H^0$ and $k_1 = k_{29} \oplus H^2$. Then, we can preserve the known bytes. Moreover, because X_1^0 and X_{13}^2 have the relation H^3, we can cancel the impact of $F(X_{13}^2 \oplus k_{27})$ in round 13 by setting $k_2 = k_{27} \oplus H^3$.

Similar to the attack on the Feistel network in Sect. 3.1, byte positions affected by the other chunk moved from the input side to the output side of the round function. This helps the attacker in subsequent rounds. Note that $X_2^1[2,3]$ is still only linearly affected by the free bytes for the backward chunk.

Different from the attack on a Feistel network, we only set three $N/4$-bit conditions on the subkeys. These $3N/4$-bit relations can be satisfied by the brute force search with a complexity of $2^{3N/4}$ key schedule function.

7-round Match (Rounds 3 to 9). The remaining 7 rounds are shown in Fig. 8. If we compute 3 rounds in backwards and 4 rounds in forwards, the direct match cannot be applied. We then use the linear computation over three rounds denoted by bold lines in Fig. 8. The equation is $S_8^R \leftarrow p^{-1}(P(S_6^L) \oplus X_6^1 \oplus X_9^0)$. A simplified description is given in the top of Fig. 9. By applying a linear transformation, this part can be converted into a partial match. The transformed equation is $S_8^R \leftarrow S_6^L \oplus P^{-1}(X_6^1) \oplus P^{-1}(X_9^0)$. X_6^1 consists of the values dependent of the forward chunk and the free bytes for the backward chunk, X_{12}^1. This is shown in the middle of Fig. 9. Then, we further apply a transformation as the bottom of Fig. 9, and perform the 3-byte match. In more details, in the forward chunk, we compute $P^{-1}(X_6^1)$ and store them in a table. In the backward chunk, we compute $S_8^R \oplus P^{-1}(S_9^0) \oplus S_6^L \oplus P^{-1}(X_{12}^1)$ and check the match. Because 3 bytes are overlapped, 3-byte match can be performed.

Attack Summary. Due to the limited space, if omit the detailed attack procedure. In summary, the total computational complexity is 2^{120} 15-round computations and 2^{96} key-schedule computations. The memory requirement is

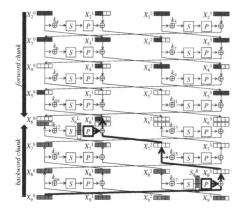
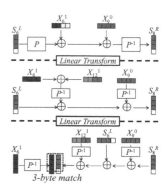

Fig. 8. 7 rounds including the matching procedure

Fig. 9. Details of the matching procedure

2^8 internal state. The attack is converted to the preimage or the second preimage attack on the hash function with a complexity of $2^{((120+128)/2)+1} = 2^{125}$ computations. Similarly to Sect. 3.1, the success probability is 0.63. The attack can be iterated as long as several key values are available.

Let us discuss the comparison with the case where the last network twist is not omitted. Known byte positions between $(X_{14}^0, \ldots, X_{14}^3)$ and $(X_4^0, \ldots, X_4^3)$ are identical. Therefore if we remove rounds 14, 0, 1, 2, and 3, in total 5 rounds, the MitM attack can work. Hence, the number of attacked rounds is 10, which is significantly smaller than the case without the last network twist.

4   Application to 13-round Weakened Camellia-128

We analyze hashing modes of Camellia-128 without the FL and whitening layers. Because the P-layer of Camellia does not satisfy the maximum branch number, the attack is extended by 2 rounds compared to the generic case.

2-round Initial Structure. 2-round initial structure can be constructed by exploiting a small branch number of the Camellia's P-layer. 4 rounds, from round 7 to 10, are shown in Fig. 10. The initial structure is located in round 8 and 9.

The forward chunk starts from a single free byte of $X_8^L[7]$. During round 8, it affects the single byte of $S_8[7]$. For the output value of P in rounds 8 and 9, the impact from the first 7 bytes denoted by P_8^{0-6}, P_9^{0-6} can be independently computed of the impact from the 7th bytes denoted by P_8^7, P_9^7. $S_8[7]$ gives influence to 6 bytes of $X_8^L[0, 1, 2, 4, 5, 6]$. The important point here is that $X_9^L[7]$, which is later used as a free variable for the backward chunk, is not affected by $X_8^L[7]$. $X_8^L[7]$ also affects to a single byte of $X_9^R[7]$. We later show that this byte is not

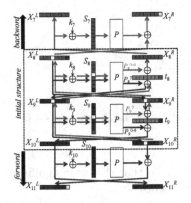 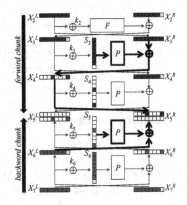

Fig. 10. Initial structure for Camellia   **Fig. 11.**   Matching   procedure   for
Camellia

affected by the free byte of the backward chunk. Computations during round 9 and round 10 are straight-forward.

The backward chunk starts from a single free byte of $X_{10}^R[7]$. During round 9, it affects the single byte of $S_9[7]$. Then, $S_9[7]$ gives influence to 6 bytes of $X_9^R[0,1,2,4,5,6]$. It surely does not affect to $X_9^R[7]$, which is the free byte for the forward chunk. $X_{10}^R[7]$ also affects to $X_9^L[7]$. As mentioned in the previous paragraph, $X_9^L[7]$ is not affected by the forward chunk. Thus, no contradiction occurs. Computations during round 8 and round 7 are straight-forward.

Matching Procedure. The 4-round shrink (round 11 to round 12 and round 0 to round 1) exploiting the omission of the last network twist is exactly the same as the attack on a generic case in Sect. 3.1. After 4 rounds, X_2^L and X_2^R become $X_{11}^R \oplus H^L$ and $X_{11}^L \oplus H^R$, respectively.

We match the results of two chunks in the remaining 5 rounds (round 2 to round 6). These rounds are described in Fig. 11. The form of the match is the same as Fig. 4, hence we omit the details. The equation for the match is written as $S_5 = S_3 \oplus P^{-1}(X_3^R) \oplus P^{-1}(X_6^L \oplus X_8^L[7])$, thus $S_5 \oplus P^{-1}(X_6^L) = S_3 \oplus P^{-1}(X_3^R \oplus X_8^L[7])$. 2 bytes of the left-hand-side and 7 bytes of the right-hand-side can be independently computed, and we can match 1 byte of them.

Analysis of the Key Schedule. For the 4-round shrink, we need to satisfy two conditions of subkeys; $k_0 = k_{12} \oplus H^L$ and $k_1 = k_{11} \oplus H^R$. According to the specification, $k_0 \| k_1 = K_A$, k_{11} is the right half of $(K_A \lll 60)$, and k_{12} is the left half of $(K \lll 94)$. Our strategy is choosing K_A so that the condition $k_1 = k_{11} \oplus H^R$ is deterministically satisfied, and satisfy $k_0 = k_{12} \oplus H^L$ with probability 2^{-64}. The details of the analysis is as follows. See its illustration in Fig. 12. The goal is finding 2^{64} 128-bit values K_A that satisfy $k_1 = k_{11} \oplus H^R$, where k_1 is the right half of K_A, and k_{11} is the right half of $(K_A \lll 60)$. For simplicity, we assume $H^R = 0$ in below. This is trivially extended for any H^R.

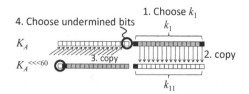

Fig. 12. Analysis of Camellia key schedule function. Each cell represents 4 bits.

1. Choose a 64-bit value of the right half of K_A so that the most significant 4 bits and the the least significant 4 bits are identical.
2. Copy the remaining 60 bits of k_1 to the corresponding bits of k_{11}. These also fix 60 bits of K_A.
3. The remaining 4 bits of K_A can be any value. In other words, we obtain 2^4 key values K_A that satisfy $k_1 = k_{11}$.
4. Finally, we have 60-bit choices for the value of the right half of K_A fixed at Step 1. Thus, we can find $2^4 \cdot 2^{60} = 2^{64}$ values of K_A that satisfy $k_1 = k_{11}$.

From 2^{64} values of K_A with $k_1 = k_{11} \oplus H^R$, we will find one that also satisfies $k_0 = k_{12} \oplus H^L$. Note that the success probability of the key search is 0.63, and we cannot expect more than 1 key.

Summary. We first search for a key value satisfying two conditions for the 4-round shrink. This is done with a complexity of 2^{64} key schedule function. We then start the MitM attack. Both of the forward and backward chunks include 1 free byte, and we match 1 byte of the results from two chunks. Hence, the pseudo-preimage is found faster than the brute force attack by a factor of 2^8, which is 2^{120} computations. The success probability is about $0.63^2 \approx 0.40$ due to the key search phase and the MitM phase. If it succeeds, the pseudo-preimage is converted to the preimage or the second preimage attack on a hash function with a complexity of 2^{125}.

5   Application to 12-round CLEFIA-128

Because F functions are different between the left half and the right half in CLEFIA, the number of attacked rounds is reduced by 3 compared to a generic case. Instead, conditions for subkeys is reduced from $3N/4$ to $N/4$ bits. Interestingly, the whitening operations do not impact to the attack very much.

2-round Initial Structure. The construction of the initial structure is basically the same as the one in Fig. 6. However, because the number of attacked rounds changes, we change the starting position of the backward chunk from the left half to the right half. We also increase the number of free bytes from 1 to 2. The detailed construction for 4 rounds, from round 6 to round 9, is shown in Fig. 13. Due to the similarity to Fig. 6, we omit the detailed explanation.

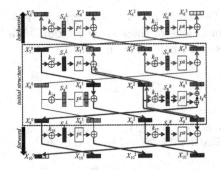
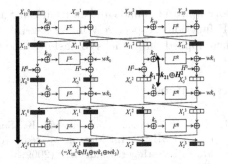

Fig. 13. 2-round initial structure for CLEFIA-128

Fig. 14. 4-round shrink that requires an $n/4$-bit condition. The shrink only occurs in the same function.

4-round Shrink. The cancellation only occurs if the F function in consecutive two rounds are identical. Hence, we only make the cancellation between F^R in round 11 and F_R in round 0 by setting an $N/4$-bit condition $k_1 = k_{21} \oplus H^2$. This makes 32 bits of X_2^0 unknown, and the number of attacked rounds is reduced compared to a generic 4-branch type-2 GFN.

Matching Procedure. Again, the different F functions in the left half and the right half prevent the efficient matching over 2 P-layers. Hence, we use the indirect-partial matching technique [1], which enables us to match 4 bytes of the state. Due to the limited space, we omit the figure, but it can be derived in the same way as other attacks.

Summary. We first search for a key value satisfying $N/4$-bit condition for the 4-round shrink. This is done with a complexity of 2^{32} key schedule function. Note that several keys satisfying the condition can be generated by iterating the procedure. We then start the MitM attack. Both of the forward and backward chunks include 2 free bytes, and we match 4 bytes of the results from two chunks. Hence, the pseudo-preimage is found faster than the brute force attack by a factor of 2^{16}, which is 2^{112} computations. Because several keys are available, the success probability can become close to 1. Finally, the pseudo-preimage is converted to the preimage or the second preimage attack on a hash function with a complexity of 2^{121}.

6   Concluding Remarks

In this paper, we analyzed hash functions constructed by a generic Feistel and 4-branch type-2 GFN with an SP function. We showed that the omission of the last network twist can be utilized in the MitM preimage attack. Our attacks can work up to 11 rounds and 15 rounds for a Feistel-SP and 4-branch type-2 GFN-SP functions respectively under several conditions of the subkey relations. We then applied our attacks to hashing modes of Camellia-128 and CLEFIA-128.

References

1. Aoki, K., Guo, J., Matusiewicz, K., Sasaki, Y., Wang, L.: Preimages for step-reduced SHA-2. In: Matsui, M. (ed.) ASIACRYPT 2009. LNCS, vol. 5912, pp. 578–597. Springer, Heidelberg (2009)
2. Aoki, K., Ichikawa, T., Kanda, M., Matsui, M., Moriai, S., Nakajima, J., Tokita, T.: Camellia: A 128-Bit Block Cipher Suitable for Multiple Platforms - Design and Analysis. In: Stinson, D.R., Tavares, S. (eds.) SAC 2000. LNCS, vol. 2012, pp. 39–56. Springer, Heidelberg (2001)
3. Aoki, K., Sasaki, Y.: Preimage Attacks on One-Block MD4, 63-Step MD5 and More. In: Avanzi, R.M., Keliher, L., Sica, F. (eds.) SAC 2008. LNCS, vol. 5381, pp. 103–119. Springer, Heidelberg (2009)
4. Bogdanov, A., Shibutani, K.: Double SP-Functions: Enhanced Generalized Feistel Networks. In: Parampalli, U., Hawkes, P. (eds.) ACISP 2011. LNCS, vol. 6812, pp. 106–119. Springer, Heidelberg (2011)
5. Coppersmith, D.: The data encryption standard (DES) and its strength against attacks. IBM Journal of Research and Development 38(3), 243–250 (1994)
6. Cryptography Research and Evaluation Committees (CRYPTREC). e-Government recommended ciphers list (2003)
7. Daemen, J., Rijmen, V.: The design of Rijndeal: AES – the Advanced Encryption Standard (AES). Springer (2002)
8. Dunkelman, O., Keller, N.: The effects of the omission of last round's MixColumns on AES. Inf. Process. Lett. 110(8-9), 304–308 (2010)
9. Gauravaram, P., Leurent, G., Mendel, F., Naya-Plasencia, M., Peyrin, T., Rechberger, C., Schläffer, M.: Cryptanalysis of the 10-Round Hash and Full Compression Function of SHAvite-3-512. In: Bernstein, D.J., Lange, T. (eds.) AFRICACRYPT 2010. LNCS, vol. 6055, pp. 419–436. Springer, Heidelberg (2010)
10. Hong, D., Sung, J., Hong, S.H., Lim, J.-I., Lee, S.-J., Koo, B.-S., Lee, C.-H., Chang, D., Lee, J., Jeong, K., Kim, H., Kim, J.-S., Chee, S.: HIGHT: A New Block Cipher Suitable for Low-Resource Device. In: Goubin, L., Matsui, M. (eds.) CHES 2006. LNCS, vol. 4249, pp. 46–59. Springer, Heidelberg (2006)
11. International Organization for Standardization. ISO/IEC 10118-2:1994, Information technology – Security techniques – Hash-functions – Part 2: Hash-functions using an n-bit block cipher algorithm (2010)
12. ISO/IEC 18033-3:2010. Information technology–Security techniques–Encryption Algorithms–Part 3: Block ciphers (2010)
13. ISO/IEC 29192-2:2011. Information technology–Security techniques–Lightweight cryptography–Part 2: Block ciphers (2011)
14. Kang, H., Hong, D., Moon, D., Kwon, D., Sung, J., Hong, S.: Known-key attacks on generalized Feistel schemes with SP round function. IEICE Transactions 95-A(9), 1550–1560 (2012)
15. Knudsen, L.R., Rijmen, V.: Known-Key Distinguishers for Some Block Ciphers. In: Kurosawa, K. (ed.) ASIACRYPT 2007. LNCS, vol. 4833, pp. 315–324. Springer, Heidelberg (2007)

16. Menezes, A.J., van Oorschot, P.C., Vanstone, S.A.: Handbook of Applied Cryptography. CRC Press (1997)
17. Moon, D., Hong, D., Kwon, D., Hong, S.: Meet-in-the-Middle preimage attacks on hash modes of generalized Feistel and Misty schemes with SP round function. IEICE Transactions 95-A(8), 1379–1389 (2012)
18. Needham, R.M., Wheeler, D.J.: TEA extensions. Technical report, Computer Laboratory, University of Cambridge (October 1997)
19. New European Schemes for Signatures, Integrity, and Encryption(NESSIE). NESSIE PROJECT ANNOUNCES FINAL SELECTION OF CRYPTO ALGORITHMS (2003)
20. Preneel, B., Govaerts, R., Vandewalle, J.: Hash functions based on block ciphers: A synthetic approach. In: Stinson, D.R. (ed.) CRYPTO 1993. LNCS, vol. 773, pp. 368–378. Springer, Heidelberg (1994)
21. Sasaki, Y.: Meet-in-the-middle preimage attack on AES hashing modes and an application to Whirlpool. In: Joux, A. (ed.) FSE 2011. LNCS, vol. 6733, pp. 378–396. Springer, Heidelberg (2011)
22. Sasaki, Y., Aoki, K.: Finding preimages in full MD5 faster than exhaustive search. In: Joux, A. (ed.) EUROCRYPT 2009. LNCS, vol. 5479, pp. 134–152. Springer, Heidelberg (2009)
23. Sasaki, Y., Emami, S., Hong, D., Kumar, A.: Improved known-key distinguishers on Feistel-SP ciphers and application to Camellia. In: Susilo, W., Mu, Y., Seberry, J. (eds.) ACISP 2012. LNCS, vol. 7372, pp. 87–100. Springer, Heidelberg (2012)
24. Sasaki, Y., Yasuda, K.: Known-key distinguishers on 11-round Feistel and collision attacks on its hashing modes. In: Joux, A. (ed.) FSE 2011. LNCS, vol. 6733, pp. 397–415. Springer, Heidelberg (2011)
25. Shirai, T., Preneel, B.: On Feistel ciphers using optimal diffusion mappings across multiple rounds. In: Lee, P.J. (ed.) ASIACRYPT 2004. LNCS, vol. 3329, pp. 1–15. Springer, Heidelberg (2004)
26. Shirai, T., Shibutani, K.: Improving immunity of Feistel ciphers against differential cryptanalysis by using multiple MDS matrices. In: Roy, B., Meier, W. (eds.) FSE 2004. LNCS, vol. 3017, pp. 260–278. Springer, Heidelberg (2004)
27. Shirai, T., Shibutani, K., Akishita, T., Moriai, S., Iwata, T.: The 128-bit block-cipher CLEFIA (extended abstract). In: Biryukov, A. (ed.) FSE 2007. LNCS, vol. 4593, pp. 181–195. Springer, Heidelberg (2007)
28. U.S. Department of Commerce, National Institute of Standards and Technology. Specification for the ADVANCED ENCRYPTION STANDARD (AES) (Federal Information Processing Standards Publication 197) (2001)
29. Zheng, Y., Matsumoto, T., Imai, H.: On the construction of block ciphers provably secure and not relying on any unproved hypotheses. In: Brassard, G. (ed.) CRYPTO 1989. LNCS, vol. 435, pp. 461–480. Springer, Heidelberg (1990)

Constructing Practical Signcryption KEM from Standard Assumptions without Random Oracles

Xiangxue Li[1,2], Haifeng Qian[1,*], Yu Yu[3], Yuan Zhou[4], and Jian Weng[5]

[1] Department of Computer Science and Technology, East China Normal University
hfqian@cs.ecnu.edu.cn
[2] State Key Laboratory of Integrated Services Networks, Xidian University
[3] Institute for Interdisciplinary Information Sciences, Tsinghua University
[4] Network Emergency Response Technical Team/Coordination Center, China
[5] Department of Computer Science, Jinan University

Abstract. We present a direct construction for signcryption Key Encapsulation Mechanism (KEM) without random oracles under standard complexity assumptions. Chosen-ciphertext security is proven in the standard model under the DBDH assumption, and unforgeability is proven in the standard model under the CDH assumption. The proof technique allows us to achieve strong unforgeability from the weakly unforgeable Waters signature. The validity of the ciphertext of our signcryption KEM can be verified publicly, without knowledge of the decryption key.

Keywords: Signcryption, KEM, Standard Model, Standard Assumption.

1 Introduction

Signcryption [25] provides confidentiality and non-repudiation simultaneously for the messages sent over an insecure channel, at lower costs of computation and communication than those required in both signature-then-encryption ($\mathcal{StE}$) and encryption-then-signature ($\mathcal{EtS}$) approaches. Thus, protocols based on signcryption are considerably more efficient than those traditional approaches that combine both encryption and signature. One may apply signcryption to obtain a performance-enhanced protocol which contributes to the practical and engineering side of real-world applications [20,21,12,22,11].

For long messages, it is quite inefficient in the real-life applications to apply signcryption directly. Inspired by traditional hybrid encryption techniques, Dent [9] generalized the KEM paradigm to the signcryption setting by proposing new security criteria and a construction for the signcryption KEM (SC-KEM) to provide in KEM the authentication service. Such a construction combines the convenience of a signcryption with the efficiency of a symmetric-key system [8]. By using such a construction, a random session key is first encapsulated by a signcryption KEM, then the data (plaintext) is encrypted by the session key, and finally two ciphertexts are both sent over an insecure channel.

---

* Corresponding author.

M. Jacobson et al. (Eds.): ACNS 2013, LNCS 7954, pp. 186–201, 2013.

1.1   The State of the Art

Dent [9,10] introduced the concept of signcryption KEM which includes an authentication in KEM by constructing two signcryption KEM schemes with insider security and outsider security, respectively. A signcryption scheme is outsider secure if it is secure against attacks made by any third party, i.e., attacks made by an entity who is neither the sender nor the receiver. This is a weaker notion of security than has been traditionally dealt with by signcryption schemes, a notion known as insider security. Actually, the work [10] improved the model in [9] (which only covers outsider security) by providing a signcryption KEM with insider security such that the resultant scheme is secure against attacks against the confidentiality of the message made by any third party and from forgery attacks made by any person except the sender.

However, insider security proposed by Dent [10] is only considered for authenticity. In other words, the model in [10] allows an attacker to recover the symmetric key generated by signcryption KEM during the attacks. Comparatively, the stronger notion named full insider security [2,23] protects the sender's authenticity even against the receiver, and the receiver's privacy even against the sender, at the same time.

Recently, Tan proposed in [23] a signcryption KEM with full insider security. Much different from those schemes [9,10], Tan's SC-KEM is proven secure in the standard model whose security does not rely on random oracles. Another signcryption KEM in the standard model was presented in [18] which is shown more efficient than Tan's scheme in terms of computational cost and communication overhead.

1.2   Motivation

Concrete constructions for signcryption KEM are evaluated according to the following perspectives: (1) the complexity assumptions on which security of the construction is based; (2) the expansion of a single ciphertext; (3) the operational assumption of setting up the construction practically; and other interesting features (e.g., public verifiability of the ciphertext).

All existing constructions of SC-KEM need the recipient's private keys to verify the validity of the ciphertexts. Hence these schemes can not be used in applications where a ciphertext need to be validated by any third party that knows the public key of the sender as in usual signature scheme. As a technically higher standard, public verifiability of ciphertexts enables any member of the public to independently fully verify the accuracy of a ciphertext [1,14]. Additionally, the constructions in [9] and [10] are proven secure in the random oracle model that serves as a heuristic. Although those in [18] and [23] are without random oracles, yet they utilize standard signatures as building blocks, thus we can't reduce the computation and the size of a single ciphertext fewer than the underlying signature, and the readers may refer to section 4 for more details on the sizes of standard model based signatures; on the other hand, the construction in [18] is based on non-standard GHDH assumption [16]. For all, the question of constructing a signcryption KEM that is secure under the standard assumptions without random oracles (and achieving public verifiability) remains open.

1.3 Our Contributions

In this paper we provide an elegant construction for SC-KEM to give a positive answer to the question. Our signcryption KEM achieves the following desirable features simultaneously, compared with the previous constructions.

1. *Full Insider Security* (FIS): Our SC-KEM is proven secure in the standard model with respect to insider adversaries.
2. *Standard Complexity Assumptions*: Security of our SC-KEM relies on the well-established DBDH and the CDH assumptions. Prior to our work, the SC-KEM scheme [18] requires non-standard assumption (i.e., the Gap Hashed Diffie-Hellman assumption [16]) to prove security in the standard model.
3. *Small Ciphertext Expansion*: The ciphertext of our SC-KEM consists of three elements of $\mathbb{G}$. It outperforms all known standard model-based constructions (that use strongly unforgeable signatures as building block) because according to the state of the art [19] a strongly unforgeable signature contains at least 3 group elements since each Waters signature, the only known signature secure under CDH assumption without random oracles, has two group elements. Our construction is also comparable to, though not quite as efficient as, the Dent signcryption KEM schemes [9,10] in the random oracle model.
4. *Additional Interesting Features*: On one hand, our construction enjoys *simple setup operation* since it only needs one key generation algorithm to generate the keys of both the sender and the receiver. Whereas, two different key generation algorithms are required in [18] and [23] respectively to generate the key pairs of the sender and the receiver. Thus, the setup process of these SC-KEM schemes is more complicate than that of ours. On the other hand, in the standard model based SC-KEM schemes in [18,23] only the receiver has the capability of verifying the correctness of a ciphertext as the private key of the receiver is required in verifying operation; whereas in our SC-KEM scheme, a given ciphertext can get checked for validity solely based on the knowledge of the public keys of the parties.

2 Preliminaries

2.1 Bilinear Group

Consider the following setting: Let $\mathbb{G}$ and $\mathbb{G}_T$ be two multiplicative cyclic groups of prime order p; the group action on $\mathbb{G}$, $\mathbb{G}_T$ can be computed efficiently; g is a generator of $\mathbb{G}$; $e : \mathbb{G} \times \mathbb{G} \to \mathbb{G}_T$ is an efficiently computable map with the following properties [3,4,24]: Bilinear: for all $u, v \in \mathbb{G}$ and $a, b \in \mathbb{Z}_p$, $e(u^a, v^b) = e(u, v)^{ab}$; Efficiently computable: $e(u, v)$ is efficiently computable for any input pair $(u, v) \in \mathbb{G} \times \mathbb{G}$; Non-degenerate: $e(g, g) \neq 1$. We say that $\mathbb{G}$ is a bilinear group if it satisfies these requirements.

2.2 Complexity Assumptions

Definition 1 (DBDH). *Let a, b, c and z be random from $\mathbb{Z}_p$, g the generator of $\mathbb{G}$ of prime order p. The (t, ε)-DBDH assumption says that there is no algorithm $\mathcal{A}$ that can distinguish the tuple $(g^a, g^b, g^c, e(g, g)^{abc})$ from the tuple $(g^a, g^b, g^c, e(g, g)^z)$ in time t with advantage ε, where the advantage of $\mathcal{A}$ is defined as the probability*

$$\text{Adv}_{\mathcal{A}}^{\text{DBDH}} = \left| \Pr[\mathcal{A}(g^a, g^b, g^c, e(g, g)^{abc}) = 1] - \Pr[\mathcal{A}(g^a, g^b, g^c, e(g, g)^z) = 1] \right|.$$

Definition 2 (CDH). *In a bilinear group $\mathbb{G}$, the computational Diffie-Hellman problem is: given $(g, g^a, g^b) \in \mathbb{G}^3$ for some (randomly chosen) $a, b \in_R \mathbb{Z}_p$, to find $g^{ab} \in \mathbb{G}$. The success probability of an algorithm $\mathcal{A}$ in solving the CDH problem on $\mathbb{G}$ is defined as*

$$\text{Adv}_{\mathcal{A}}^{\text{CDH}} \stackrel{\text{def}}{=} \Pr\left[\mathcal{A}(g, g^a, g^b) = g^{ab} : a, b \stackrel{R}{\longleftarrow} \mathbb{Z}_p \right].$$

The probability is over the random choice of g from $\mathbb{G}$, of a, b from $\mathbb{Z}_p$, and the coin tosses of $\mathcal{A}$. $\mathcal{A}$ (t, ε)-breaks the CDH problem on $\mathbb{G}$ if $\mathcal{A}$ runs in time at most t, and $\text{Adv}_{\mathcal{A}}^{\text{cdh}}$ is at least ε.

2.3 Collision Resistant Hash Function

Definition 3 (CRHF). *Let $\mathcal{H} = \{H_k\}$ be a hash family of functions $H_k : \{0, 1\}^* \to \{0, 1\}^n$ indexed by k. We say that algorithm $\mathcal{A}$ (t, ε_{cr})-breaks the collision-resistance of $\mathcal{H}$ if*

$$\Pr[\mathcal{A}(k) = (x, x') : H_k(x) = H_k(x'), x \neq x'] \geq \varepsilon_{cr},$$

where the probability is over the random choice of k and the random bits of $\mathcal{A}$. $\mathcal{H}$ is (t, ε_{cr})-collision-resistant if no t-time adversary has advantage at least ε_{cr} in breaking the collision-resistance of $\mathcal{H}$.

2.4 Definition of Signcryption KEM

Definition 4 (SC-KEM). *A signcryption KEM consists of three algorithms:*

KeyGen(1^λ): *key generation algorithm, on input a security parameter λ, outputs the sender's public/private key pair (pk_s, sk_s) and the receiver's public/private key pair (pk_r, sk_r). We write $(pk, sk) = $ KeyGen(1^λ).*

KeyEnc(sk_s, pk_r): *key encapsulation algorithm, on input the sender's private key sk_s and the receiver's public key pk_r, outputs a symmetric key K which may be used in the subsequent data encapsulation mechanism, and a ciphertext C which is an encapsulation of the key K. We write $(K, C) = $ KeyEnc(sk_s, pk_r).*

KeyDec(pk_s, sk_r, C): *key decapsulation algorithm, on input the sender's public key pk_s, the receiver's private key sk_r and the encapsulation C of some symmetric key K, outputs either the symmetric key K or the error symbol $\perp$ in case the ciphertext is not valid. We write $K = $ KeyDec(pk_s, sk_r, C).*

Correctness requires that for all public/private key pair $(pk_s, sk_s), (pk_r, sk_r)$ it follows $K = $ KeyDec(pk_s, sk_r, C) for all $(K, C) = $ KeyEnc(sk_s, pk_r).

2.5   Security Model of SC-KEM

We borrow the following models which are commonly used in the literature [9,10,18,23]. The paper focuses on the direct construction for SC-KEM without random oracles under standard complexity assumptions, in the security models.

Confidentiality. The attack model [18,23] of confidentiality for a signcryption KEM is defined in the following game, termed the IND-CCA2 game, played between a hypothetical challenger $\mathcal{C}$ and a two-phase attacker $\mathcal{A}$.

- **Setup**: On input a given security parameter λ, the challenger $\mathcal{C}$ runs the key generation algorithm KeyGen(1^λ) to produce the sender's key pair $(pk_s^\star, sk_s^\star)$ and the receiver's key pair $(pk_r^\star, sk_r^\star)$, and sends $(pk_s^\star, sk_s^\star)$ and $pk_r^\star$ to the attacker $\mathcal{A}$, while keeping $sk_r^\star$ secret.
- **Phase 1**: During this phase, $\mathcal{A}$ may make the polynomially bounded queries of key decapsulation. In a key decapsulation query, $\mathcal{A}$ submits to the challenger $\mathcal{C}$ a ciphertext C associated with the sender's public key pk_s for key decapsulation. Herein, the public key pk_s may be generated by $\mathcal{A}$ as it wishes. The challenger $\mathcal{C}$ performs key decapsulation operation for $\mathcal{A}$ in the algorithm KeyDec by using the private key $sk_r^\star$ and then sends the result $K = \mathsf{KeyDec}(pk_s, sk_r^\star, C)$ or $\perp$ (if C is not valid) to $\mathcal{A}$.
- **Challenge**: At the end of Phase 1, $\mathcal{C}$ performs the algorithm KeyEnc by using the private key $sk_s^\star$ and the public key $pk_r^\star$, and obtains the result $(K_0^\star, C^\star) = \mathsf{KeyEnc}(sk_s^\star, pk_r^\star)$. $\mathcal{C}$ also chooses a random bit $b \in \{0,1\}$ and a random symmetric key $K_1^\star$ with the requirement that $K_1^\star$ and $K_0^\star$ are of the same length. Lastly, $\mathcal{C}$ gives $\mathcal{A}$ the tuple $(K_b^\star, C^\star)$ as the challenge.
- **Phase 2**: During this phase, $\mathcal{A}$ may make the queries as in **Phase 1**, while differently we do not allow $\mathcal{A}$ to query the key decapsulation for the ciphertext $C^\star$ under the the sender's public key $pk_s^\star$.
- **Guess**: Eventually, $\mathcal{A}$ outputs a bit b', and it wins the game if $b = b'$.

The advantage of the adversary $\mathcal{A}$ is defined as the probability $\mathsf{Adv}_{\mathcal{A}}^{\mathsf{IND}} = |2\Pr[b = b'] -$

Definition 5 (Confidentiality). *We say $\mathcal{A}$ (t, q_d, ε)-breaks the IND-CCA2 security of the signcryption KEM, if $\mathcal{A}$ wins the IND-CCA2 game with the advantage ε in time t after making q_d key decapsulation queries. A signcryption KEM is said to achieve the IND-CCA2 security if no polynomially bounded adversary has a non-negligible advantage in winning the IND-CCA2 game.*

Unforgeability. The notion of strongly existential unforgeability for a signcryption KEM [18,23] is defined by the SUF game, played between a hypothetical challenger $\mathcal{C}$ and an attacker $\mathcal{F}$ below. For a given security parameter λ:

- **Setup:** The challenger $\mathcal{C}$ runs the key generation algorithm KeyGen(1^λ) (defined in definition 4) to produce the sender's key pair $(pk_s^\star, sk_s^\star)$ and the receiver's key pair $(pk_r^\star, sk_r^\star)$, and sends $pk_s^\star$ and $(pk_r^\star, sk_r^\star)$ to the attacker $\mathcal{F}$, while keeping $sk_s^\star$ secret.

- **Attack:** During this phase, $\mathcal{F}$ may make the polynomially bounded queries of key encapsulation. In a key encapsulation query, the challenger $\mathcal{C}$ performs key encapsulation operation for $\mathcal{F}$ in the algorithm KeyEnc by using the private key $sk_s^\star$ and the public key $pk_r^\star$, obtains the result $(K, C) =$ KeyEnc$(sk_s^\star, pk_r^\star)$, and sends C to $\mathcal{F}$.
- **Forgery:** Eventually, the attacker $\mathcal{F}$ outputs a ciphertext $C^\star$ with the requirement that $C^\star$ is not one of the outputs of the key encapsulation queries. $\mathcal{F}$ wins the game if $C^\star$ is valid, i.e., KeyDec$(pk_s^\star, sk_r^\star, C^\star) \neq \perp$.

The advantage of $\mathcal{F}$ is defined as the probability of success in winning the game: $\mathrm{Adv}_{\mathcal{F}}^{\mathsf{SUF}} = \Pr[\mathsf{Win}]$.

Definition 6 (Unforgeability). *We say the signcryption KEM is (t, q_e, ε)-forgeable if $\mathcal{F}$ wins the SUF game with the advantage ε in time t after making q_e key encapsulation queries. A signcryption KEM achieves strongly existential unforgeability if no polynomially-bounded adversary can win the SUF game with non-negligible advantage.*

Definition 7 (Public Verifiability). *We say the signcryption KEM has public verifiability of ciphertexts if any member of the public can independently fully verify the accuracy of a ciphertext without relying on any secret information.*

3 The Proposed Signcryption KEM

Let $\mathbb{G}$ be a group of prime order p, for which there exists an efficiently computable bilinear map into $\mathbb{G}$. The size of the group is determined by the security parameter. Additionally, let $e : \mathbb{G} \times \mathbb{G} \to \mathbb{G}_T$ denote the bilinear map and g be the corresponding generator, along with $u', u_1, u_2, \ldots, u_n, f, h, v, w \in \mathbb{G}$. Let $G : \{0,1\}^* \to \{0,1\}^n$, $H : \{0,1\}^* \to \mathbb{Z}_p$ be two collision resistant hash functions. Our construction is described as follows.

KeyGen(1^λ): A probabilistic polynomial-time sender/receiver key generation algorithm, chooses $x_s, x_r \in_R \mathbb{Z}_p$, sets $sk_s = x_s$, $pk_s = g^{x_s}$, $sk_r = x_r$, $pk_r = g^{x_r}$, and outputs the public/private key pair (pk_s, sk_s) for the sender and the public/private key pair (pk_r, sk_r) for the receiver.

keyEnc(sk_s, pk_r):
1. Randomly choose $k, \ell \in_R \mathbb{Z}_p$.
2. Compute $K = e(h, pk_r)^k$, $\sigma_1 = g^k$, $\sigma_2 = g^\ell$, $t_1 = G(\sigma_1, pk_s, pk_r)$,
3. Let $\mathcal{T} \subset \{1, 2, \ldots, n\}$ be the set of indices such that $t_1[i] = 1$ where $t_1[i]$ is the i-th bit of t_1.
4. Compute $t_2 = H(\sigma_1, \sigma_2, pk_s, pk_r)$, $\sigma_3 = f^{x_s} \cdot \left(u' \prod_{i \in \mathcal{T}} u_i \right)^\ell (v^{t_2} w)^k$.
5. Let $C = (\sigma_1, \sigma_2, \sigma_3)$ and return (K, C).

Different from the constructions in [18,23], a ciphertext C of our SC-KEM scheme is only composed of three elements in $\mathbb{G}$.

KeyDec(pk_s, sk_r, C):

1. Compute $t_1 = G(\sigma_1, pk_s, pk_r)$, $t_2 = H(\sigma_1, \sigma_2, pk_s, pk_r)$.
2. If

$$e(g, \sigma_3) = e(f, pk_s) \cdot e\left(\sigma_2, u' \prod_{i \in \mathcal{T}} u_i\right) \cdot e\left(\sigma_1, v^{t_2} w\right),$$

return

$$K = e(\sigma_1, h^{x_r});$$

otherwise return $\perp$.

It can be verified easily that the construction satisfies the correctness. Note that unlike previous SC-KEM constructions, the validity of the ciphertext of ours can get checked by anyone who only knows the public keys.

4   Comparisons

Prior to proving the security of our construction, we compare in this section our SC-KEM with the SC-KEM schemes in the literature [9,10,23,18]. Table 1 shows the comparisons.

The schemes in [18] and [23] need strongly unforgeable signatures as building block. Without random oracles, several signature schemes can be shown to be strongly unforgeable under relatively strong or standard assumptions.

Gennaro, Halevi, and Rabin [13], and Cramer and Shoup [7] constructed strongly unforgeable signatures based on the Strong-RSA assumption, and the signatures are composed of one element in $\mathbb{Z}_n$ (n is the RSA modulus) [13], and one element in $\mathbb{Z}_n$ and two elements in a group $\mathbb{G}$ (n is the RSA modulus, $|\mathbb{G}| \geq 160$) [7], respectively; Boneh and Boyen [3] constructed a strongly unforgeable signature based on the Strong-Diffie-Hellman assumption, and the signature consists of an element in $\mathbb{G}$ and an element in $\mathbb{Z}_p$; Boneh, Shen, and Waters [5] constructed a strongly unforgeable signature based on the standard computational Diffie-Hellman assumption, and the signature contains two elements in $\mathbb{G}$ and an element in $\mathbb{Z}_p$; Kang et al. [15] constructed a short signature scheme based on the computational Diffie-Hellman assumption, and the signature is composed of an element in $\mathbb{G}$ and an element in $\mathbb{Z}_p$.

We also notice that there are several generic transformations proposed to convert weak unforgeability into strong unforgeability. According to the shortest generic transformation [19] so far, in terms of signature size expansion, the transformation increases the resulting signature by one group element. For example, when we use the transformation to convert the Waters signature, the only known signature secure under standard CDH assumption without random oracles, into a strongly unforgeable one, the resultant signature contains three elements in $\mathbb{G}$.

The idea behind our SC-KEM construction is to combine the technique in the Waters signatures [24] with that in transforming identity-based encryption to CCA-secure public key encryption [6,17]. Different from the previous SC-KEM methods, we present a direct construction which does not rely on the use of any strongly unforgeable signature scheme. All known constructions for

Table 1. Comparisons of SC-KEM Schemes

	S/R KG	Size	ROM/Standard model	SA	PV	FIS
Dent[9]	1A	$1|\mathbb{G}|$	ROM	CDH	NO	NO
Dent[10]	1A	$2|\mathbb{Z}_q|$	ROM	GDH	NO	NO
Tan[23]	2A	$3|\mathbb{G}| + |\mathsf{sig}|$	Standard	DDH+SUF	NO	YES
Li[18]	2A	$2|\mathbb{G}| + |\mathsf{sig}|$	Standard	GHDH +SUF	NO	YES
Ours	1A	$3|\mathbb{G}|$	Standard	DBDH+CDH	YES	YES

S/R KG: Sender/Receiver Key Generation Algorithms; Size: Ciphertext Expansion Size; 1A: the key generation algorithm generates the public/private key pairs for both the sender and the receiver; 2A: two separate key generation algorithms are required, one for the sender, another for the receiver; $|\mathbb{G}|$, $|\mathsf{sig}|$: the bit lengths of the representation for elements in the underlying group $\mathbb{G}$, and for the signature generated by the underlying signature scheme, respectively (and $|\mathsf{sig}| \geq |\mathbb{G}| + |\mathbb{Z}_p|$ according to the state of the art on standard model based signatures); SA: Security Assumption; PV: Public Verifiability; FIS: Full Insider Security; GDH: Gap Diffie-Hellman; SUF: Strong Unforgeability of the underlying signature scheme; GHDH: Gap Hashed Diffie-Hellman.

SC-KEM schemes in the standard model are 'generic': they involve running a standard strongly unforgeable signature scheme and are thus not very efficient in ciphertext expansion as well as the computational performance.

5 Proving The Security

5.1 Confidentiality

Theorem 1. *If there exists an adversary $\mathcal{A}$ that can (t, q_d, ε)-break the IND-CCA2 security of our SC-KEM (q_d is the total number of the key decapsulation queries), then one can construct an algorithm $\mathcal{B}$ that (t', ε')-breaks the DBDH problem assuming that H is (t, ε_{cr})-collision resistant, where T_e, T_p are the running-time of the exponentiation in $\mathbb{G}$ and the pairing respectively, and*

$$\varepsilon' \geq \frac{\varepsilon}{2} - \varepsilon_{cr} - \frac{q_d}{p}, t' \leq t + \mathcal{O}(6 \cdot q_d + n + 12)T_e + \mathcal{O}(6 \cdot q_d)T_p, \qquad (1)$$

Proof. Our idea of the proof is to utilize the adversary $\mathcal{A}$ that (t, q_d, ε)-breaks the IND-CCA2 security of our signcryption KEM, to construct an algorithm $\mathcal{B}$ that first simulates the environment of the IND-CCA2 game, and then uses the output of $\mathcal{A}$ to solve the DBDH problem.

Assume that algorithm $\mathcal{B}$ is given as input a random 5 tuple (g, g^a, g^b, g^c, Z) where $Z = e(g, g)^{abc}$ or $e(g, g)^z$ for a, b, c, z randomly chosen from $\mathbb{Z}_p$. Algorithm $\mathcal{B}$'s goal is to output 1 if $Z = e(g, g)^{abc}$ and 0 otherwise. $\mathcal{B}$ does the following to achieve the goal.

Setup. $\mathcal{B}$ randomly chooses $\alpha_0, \alpha_1, \alpha_2, \ldots, \alpha_n, \alpha_v, \alpha_w, \beta_v, s, \gamma$ and x_s from $\mathbb{Z}_p$, then sets

$$\sigma_2^\star = g^s, u' = g^{\alpha_0}, u_1 = g^{\alpha_1}, u_2 = g^{\alpha_2}, \ldots, u_n = g^{\alpha_n}, h = g^b, f = g^\gamma, v = g^{\alpha_v} h^{\beta_v},$$

$$t_2^\star = H(g^c, g^s, pk_s^\star, pk_r^\star), \ w = g^{\alpha_w} h^{-\beta_v t_2^\star}, \ pk_s^\star = g^{x_s}, \ sk_s^\star = x_s, \ pk_r^\star = g^a.$$

Finally $\mathcal{B}$ gives $\mathcal{A}$ the parameters u', u_1, u_2, ..., u_n, f, h, v, w and keys $pk_s^\star$, $sk_s^\star$, $pk_r^\star$.

All the parameters and keys we give here have the same distribution as those used in our construction. Thus, $\mathcal{B}$ provides a perfect simulation in this phase.

Phase 1. When $\mathcal{A}$ submits a query $(pk_s, C = (\sigma_1, \sigma_2, \sigma_3))$ for key decapsulation, $\mathcal{B}$ responds as follows:

1. Compute $t_1 = G(\sigma_1, pk_s, pk_r^\star)$, $t_2 = H(\sigma_1, \sigma_2, pk_s, pk_r^\star)$.
2. Check

$$e(g, \sigma_3) \stackrel{?}{=} e(f, pk_s) \cdot e\left(\sigma_2, u' \prod_{i \in \mathcal{T}} u_i\right) \cdot e(\sigma_1, v^{t_2} w), \tag{2}$$

   if not, return $\bot$.
3. If $t_2 = t_2^\star$, abort (this event is denoted as CRFail); otherwise randomly choose r from $\mathbb{Z}_p$ and compute

$$
\begin{aligned}
D_1 &= (g^a)^{-\frac{\alpha_v \cdot t_2 + \alpha_w}{\beta_v(t_2 - t_2^\star)}} \cdot (v^{t_2} w)^r = h^a \cdot (h^a)^{-\frac{\beta_v(t_2 - t_2^\star)}{\beta_v(t_2 - t_2^\star)}} \cdot (g^a)^{-\frac{\alpha_v \cdot t_2 + \alpha_w}{\beta_v(t_2 - t_2^\star)}} \cdot (v^{t_2} w)^r \\
&= h^a \cdot \left(g^{\alpha_v \cdot t_2 + \alpha_w} h^{\beta_v(t_2 - t_2^\star)}\right)^{-\frac{a}{\beta_v(t_2 - t_2^\star)}} \cdot (v^{t_2} w)^r \\
&= h^a \cdot (v^{t_2} w)^{-\frac{a}{\beta_v(t_2 - t_2^\star)}} \cdot (v^{t_2} w)^r = h^a \cdot (v^{t_2} w)^{r - \frac{a}{\beta_v(t_2 - t_2^\star)}}, \\
D_2 &= g^r \cdot (g^a)^{-\frac{1}{\beta_v(t_2 - t_2^\star)}} = g^{r - \frac{a}{\beta_v(t_2 - t_2^\star)}}.
\end{aligned}
$$

   Let $\eta = r - \frac{a}{\beta_v(t_2 - t_2^\star)}$, we have $D_1 = h^a \cdot (v^{t_2} w)^\eta$, $D_2 = g^\eta$.
4. Compute

$$\Delta = \sigma_3 \cdot (pk_s)^{-\gamma} \cdot (\sigma_2)^{-\alpha_0 - \sum\limits_{i \in \mathcal{T}} \alpha_i}. \tag{3}$$

   Since $C = (\sigma_1, \sigma_2, \sigma_3)$ can pass the verification equation (2), we have

$$pk_s = g^x, \ \sigma_1 = g^k, \ \sigma_2 = g^\ell, \ \sigma_3 = f^x \cdot \left(u' \prod_{i \in \mathcal{T}} u_i\right)^\ell (v^{t_2} w)^k,$$

   for some $x, k, \ell \in \mathbb{Z}_p$. Thus, we know that

$$
\begin{aligned}
\Delta &= \sigma_3 \cdot (pk_s)^{-\gamma} \cdot (\sigma_2)^{-\alpha_0 - \sum\limits_{i \in \mathcal{T}} \alpha_i} = \sigma_3 \cdot (g^x)^{-\gamma} \cdot (g^\ell)^{-\alpha_0 - \sum\limits_{i \in \mathcal{T}} \alpha_i} \\
&= \sigma_3 \cdot (g^\gamma)^{-x} \cdot \left(u' \prod_{i \in \mathcal{T}} u_i\right)^{-\ell} \\
&= f^x \cdot \left(u' \prod_{i \in \mathcal{T}} u_i\right)^\ell (v^{t_2} w)^k \cdot (f)^{-x} \cdot \left(u' \prod_{i \in \mathcal{T}} u_i\right)^{-\ell} = (v^{t_2} w)^k.
\end{aligned}
$$

5. Return

$$K = \frac{e(\sigma_1, D_1)}{e(D_2, \Delta)}.$$

   Note that K is correct because

$$
\begin{aligned}
e(\sigma_1, D_1) &= e\left(\sigma_1, h^a \cdot (v^{t_2} w)^\eta\right) = e(\sigma_1, h^a) \cdot e\left(g^k, (v^{t_2} w)^\eta\right) \\
&= K \cdot e\left(g^\eta, (v^{t_2} w)^k\right) = K \cdot e(D_2, \Delta).
\end{aligned} \tag{4}
$$

Challenge. In this phase, $\mathcal{B}$ generates the challenge ciphertext for the adversary $\mathcal{A}$ as follows.

1. Set $\sigma_1^\star = g^c$ and compute $t_1^\star = G(\sigma_1^\star, pk_s^\star, pk_r^\star)$;
2. Compute $\sigma_3^\star = (g^\gamma)^{x_s} \cdot \left(u' \prod_{i \in \mathcal{T}^\star} u_i \right) \cdot (g^c)^{\alpha_v \cdot t_2^\star + \alpha_w}$;
3. Set $K_0^\star = Z$, $C^\star = (\sigma_1^\star, \sigma_2^\star, \sigma_3^\star)$;
4. Choose a random bit $\theta \in \{0,1\}$ and a random key $K_1^\star \in \mathbb{G}_T$;
5. Return $(K_\theta^\star, C^\star)$ as the challenge.

The ciphertext $C^\star$ is valid and can pass the Equation (2) since

$$
\sigma_3^\star = (g^\gamma)^{x_s} \cdot \left(u' \prod_{i \in \mathcal{T}^\star} u_i \right)^s \cdot (g^c)^{\alpha_v \cdot t_2^\star + \alpha_w} = f^{x_s} \cdot \left(u' \prod_{i \in \mathcal{T}^\star} u_i \right)^s \cdot (g^{\alpha_v \cdot t_2^\star + \alpha_w})^c
$$

$$
= f^{x_s} \cdot \left(u' \prod_{i \in \mathcal{T}^\star} u_i \right)^s \cdot \left((g^{\alpha_v} \cdot h^{\beta_v})^{t_2^\star} \cdot (g^{\alpha_w} \cdot h^{-\beta_v t_2^\star}) \right)^c
$$

$$
= f^{x_s} \cdot \left(u' \prod_{i \in \mathcal{T}^\star} u_i \right)^s \cdot \left(v^{t_2^\star} w \right)^c.
$$

Phase 2. $\mathcal{B}$ responds to the queries of $\mathcal{A}$ as it does in Phase 1, except denying to answer the query of the challenge ciphertext $C^\star$ w.r.t. $pk_s^\star$.

Guess. Eventually $\mathcal{A}$ outputs a bit θ' as its guess for θ.

Algorithm $\mathcal{B}$ outputs 1 if $\theta' = \theta$ (denoted by ASuc), and 0 if $\theta' \neq \theta$.

Analysis. In the following, we analyze $\mathcal{B}$'s probability of success in solving the Decisional Bilinear Diffie-Hellman problem. We first present the following claim.

Claim. $\Pr[\mathsf{CRFail}] \leq \varepsilon_{cr} + \frac{q_d}{p}$, where q_d is the number of the key decapsulation queries made by $\mathcal{A}$.

Proof. For any valid ciphertext $C = (\sigma_1, \sigma_2, \sigma_3)$, event CRFail happens only when one of the following two events takes place:

1. Event CR, $(\sigma_1, \sigma_2, pk_s, pk_r^\star) \neq (\sigma_1^\star, \sigma_2^\star, pk_s^\star, pk_r^\star) \wedge t_2 = t_2^\star$;
2. Event Fail, $(\sigma_1, \sigma_2, pk_s, pk_r^\star) = (\sigma_1^\star, \sigma_2^\star, pk_s^\star, pk_r^\star)$.

Actually, event Fail can't happen in **Phase 2** because if $(\sigma_1, \sigma_2, pk_s, pk_r^\star) = (\sigma_1^\star, \sigma_2^\star, pk_s^\star, pk_r^\star)$ and $C = (\sigma_1, \sigma_2, \sigma_3)$ is valid (which can be verified by Equation (2)), then $\sigma_3 = \sigma_3^\star$ must hold. However, the challenge ciphertext $(\sigma_1^\star, \sigma_2^\star, \sigma_3^\star)$ with respect to $(pk_s^\star, pk_r^\star)$ is not allowed to be queried. Thus we know $(pk_s, C = (\sigma_1, \sigma_2, \sigma_3))$ can't be queried as well in **Phase 2**. Therefore, event Fail may happen in **Phase 1**, but must not happen in **Phase 2**.

The adversary cannot know the challenge ciphertext in Phase 1 because it is information-theoretically hidden in Phase 1. Then, the event $\mathcal{A}$ submits a ciphertext identical to the challenge one with the same sender's public key happens with probability at most $\frac{1}{p}$. And event Fail happens with probability at most $\frac{q_d}{p}$ for the q_d queries in **Phase 1**, i.e., $\Pr[\mathsf{Fail}] \leq \frac{q_d}{p}$.

Event CR, $(\sigma_1, \sigma_2, pk_s, pk_r^\star) \neq (\sigma_1^\star, \sigma_2^\star, pk_s^\star, pk_r^\star) \wedge t_2 = t_2^\star$, implies $\mathcal{B}$ finds a collision for H by utilizing $\mathcal{A}$. Therefore, $\Pr[\mathsf{CR}] \leq \varepsilon_{cr}$.

Thus, we know $\mathcal{B}$'s abortion probability is bounded by $\Pr[\mathsf{CRFail}] = \Pr[\mathsf{CR}] + \Pr[\mathsf{Fail}] \leq \varepsilon_{cr} + \frac{q_d}{p}$. $\qquad\square$

Now we can compute the probability that $\mathcal{B}$ in the above game outputs 1 given Z with either $Z = e(g,g)^{abc}$ or $Z = e(g,g)^z$ where a,b,c,z are randomly chosen from $\mathbb{Z}_p$. Let ASuc be the event that the adversary $\mathcal{A}$ succeeds in guessing θ (i.e., $\theta' = \theta$).

Due to the simulation, it follows that if $Z = e(g,g)^{abc}$ then the challenge ciphertext $C^\star = (\sigma_1^\star, \sigma_2^\star, \sigma_3^\star)$ is a valid key encapsulation of $K_0^\star = Z$ under $(sk_s^\star, pk_r^\star)$. Therefore, $\mathcal{B}$ provides a perfect simulation unless event CRFail happens. Namely, $\mathcal{A}$'s view is identical to that in the real attack game unless event CRFail happens. So we have the following result.

$$\Pr\left[\mathcal{B}(g^a, g^b, g^c, Z = e(g,g)^{abc}) = 1\right] = \Pr\left[(\text{ASuc}|Z = e(g,g)^{abc}) \bigwedge (\neg\text{CRFail})\right]$$
$$\geq \Pr\left[\text{ASuc}|Z = e(g,g)^{abc}\right] - \Pr\left[\text{CRFail}\right] \geq \Pr\left[\theta = \theta'|Z = e(g,g)^{abc}\right] - \varepsilon_{cr} - \frac{q_d}{p}$$
$$= \frac{\text{Adv}_{\mathcal{A}}^{\text{IND}}+1}{2} - \varepsilon_{cr} - \frac{q_d}{p} = \frac{\varepsilon+1}{2} - \varepsilon_{cr} - \frac{q_d}{p}.$$
$$\tag{5}$$

If $Z = e(g,g)^z$, then the challenge ciphertext $C^\star = (\sigma_1^\star, \sigma_2^\star, \sigma_3^\star)$ is an invalid key encapsulation of $K_0^\star = Z$ under $(sk_s^\star, pk_r^\star)$. In this case, both $K_0^\star = Z$ and $K_1^\star$ are random. Therefore, $\mathcal{A}$ succeeds in guessing θ with probability at most $\frac{1}{2}$. Thus, we have

$$\Pr\left[\mathcal{B}(g^a, g^b, g^c, Z = e(g,g)^z) = 1\right] = \Pr\left[(\text{ASuc}|Z = e(g,g)^z) \bigwedge (\neg\text{CRFail})\right]$$
$$\leq \Pr\left[\text{ASuc}|Z = e(g,g)^z\right] = \Pr\left[\theta = \theta'|Z = e(g,g)^z\right] = \frac{1}{2}. \tag{6}$$

Combining Equation (5) and Equation (6), we conclude that

$$\varepsilon' = \text{Adv}_{\mathcal{B}}^{\text{DBDH}} = \left|\Pr[\mathcal{A}(g^a, g^b, g^c, e(g,g)^{abc}) = 1] - \Pr[\mathcal{A}(g^a, g^b, g^c, e(g,g)^z) = 1]\right|$$
$$\geq \frac{\varepsilon+1}{2} - \varepsilon_{cr} - \frac{q_d}{p} - \frac{1}{2} = \frac{\varepsilon}{2} - \varepsilon_{cr} - \frac{q_d}{p}.$$

Finally, for the running-time of $\mathcal{B}$, we mainly take into account the running-time t of $\mathcal{A}$, the exponentiations and the pairings in the key decapsulation queries, and the exponentiation of generating the parameters. This takes time at most $t + \mathcal{O}(6 \cdot q_d + n + 12)T_e + \mathcal{O}(6 \cdot q_d)T_p$, where T_e is the running-time of the exponentiation in $\mathbb{G}$, T_p is the running-time of the pairing, and q_d is the number of key decapsulation queries.

5.2   Unforgeability

Our signcryption KEM satisfies strong unforgeability as defined in definition 6. The following theorem formally proves its unforgeability. Note that we can conclude that the proposed construction is asymptotically unforgeable under the CDH assumption if the underlying hash function is collision resistant, as the Waters signature [24] itself can be reduced to the CDH assumption.

Theorem 2 (Unforgeability). *Our signcryption KEM is (t, q_s, ε)-strongly un-forgeable assuming the Waters signature is $(t + \mathcal{O}(q_s), q_s, \varepsilon/2)$-existentially un-forgeable, the CDH assumption $(t + \mathcal{O}(q_s), (\varepsilon - \varepsilon_{cr})/2q_s)$-holds in $\mathbb{G}$, and H is (t, ε_{cr})-collision resistant.*

Proof. The SUF game defines the strong unforgeability for signcryption KEM, and is played by an adversary and the challenger. Suppose there is an adversary $\mathcal{A}$ which can win the SUF game in time t with probability ε. $\mathcal{A}$ is first equipped with the public parameters and the keys $pk_s^\star, pk_r^\star, sk_r^\star$. $\mathcal{A}$ can make q_s key encapsulation queries and will be given $\Sigma = \{C_i = (\sigma_{i1}, \sigma_{i2}, \sigma_{i3}) | i = 1, 2, \ldots, q_s\}$ on these queries. Let $\Sigma_1 = \{\sigma_{i1} | i = 1, 2, \ldots, q_s\}$, and let $C^* = (\sigma_1^*, \sigma_2^*, \sigma_3^*)$ be the forgery $\mathcal{A}$ eventually produces. As $C^* \notin \Sigma$, we can then distinguish between two types of forgeries:

Type I. A forgery where $\sigma_1^* \notin \Sigma_1$. In this case we denote the adversary as type I forger $\mathcal{A}_I$.

Type II. A forgery where $\sigma_1^* = \sigma_{l1}$ and $\sigma_2^* \neq \sigma_{l2}$ for some $l \in \{1, 2, \ldots, q_s\}$. In this case we denote the adversary as type II forger $\mathcal{A}_{II}$.

Note that if $\sigma_1^* = \sigma_{l1}$ and $\sigma_2^* = \sigma_{l2}$, then $\sigma_3^* = \sigma_{l3}$ because given $(pk_s^\star, pk_r^\star)$, σ_1^* and σ_2^* (resp., σ_{l1} and σ_{l2}) uniquely determines σ_3^* (resp., σ_{l3}) that implies $C^* (= C_l)$ is not a valid forgery.

A successful adversary $\mathcal{A}$ must output a forgery of either Type I or Type II. We will show that a Type I forger $\mathcal{A}_I$ can be used to break the existential unforgeability of the Waters signature, and a Type II forger $\mathcal{A}_{II}$ can be used to solve the CDH problem if H is collision resistant. The simulator can flip a coin at the beginning of the simulation to guess which type of forgery the adversary will produce and set up the simulation appropriately. In both cases the simulation is perfect. We start by describing how to use a Type II forgery which is the more interesting case.

Type II Forgery. Suppose $\mathcal{A}_{II}$ is a Type II adversary which (t, q_s, ε)-breaks strong unforgeability of our signcryption KEM, producing a Type II forgery. We construct an adversary $\mathcal{B}_{II}$ that can $(t, \frac{1}{q_s}(\varepsilon - \varepsilon_{cr}))$-break the Computational Diffie-Hellman problem if the hash function is (t, ε_{cr})-collision resistant.

Suppose $\mathcal{B}_{II}$ is given (g, g^a, g^b) associated with the bilinear group parameters $\mathsf{pp} = (\mathbb{G}, \mathbb{G}_T, e, g)$ and its goal is to output g^{ab}. To utilize the forger $\mathcal{A}_{II}$, the simulator $\mathcal{B}_{II}$ simulates the environment of the SUF game.

Setup. $\mathcal{B}_{II}$ generates the parameters, the public key of the sender, and the private/public key pair of the receiver.

1. Randomly choose $\alpha_0, \alpha_1, \ldots, \alpha_n, \alpha_v, \alpha_w, x_s, s, \gamma$ and x_r from $\mathbb{Z}_p$.

2. Set

$$u' = g^{\alpha_0}, u_1 = g^{\alpha_1}, u_2 = g^{\alpha_2}, \ldots, u_n = g^{\alpha_n}, f = g^b, h = g^\gamma, v = g^{\alpha_v} f,$$

$$pk_r^\star = g^{x_r}, sk_r^\star = x_r, pk_s^\star = g^{x_s}, t_2^\star = H(g^a, g^s, pk_s^\star, pk_r^\star), w = g^{\alpha_w} f^{-t_2^\star}.$$

3. Give $\mathcal{A}_{II}$ the parameters $u', u_1, u_2, \ldots, u_n, f, h, v, w$ and the keys $pk_s^\star, sk_r^\star, pk_r^\star$.

Encapsulation Queries. Suppose $\mathcal{A}_{II}$ issues q_s key encapsulation queries. $\mathcal{B}_{II}$ first picks up $j^* \in \{1, 2, \ldots, q_s\}$ randomly, then responds to the i-th query as follows ($i = 1, 2, \ldots, q_s$):

1. If $i \neq j^\star$, select k, η randomly from $\mathbb{Z}_p$, and return $C_i = (\sigma_{i1}, \sigma_{i2}, \sigma_{i3})$ where $\sigma_{i1} = g^k$, $\sigma_{i2} = g^\eta$, $t_1 = G(g^k, pk_s^\star, pk_r^\star)$, $t_2 = H(g^k, g^\eta, pk_s^\star, pk_r^\star)$ and

$$\sigma_{i3} = (g^b)^{x_s} \cdot \left(u' \prod_{i \in \mathcal{T}} u_i \right)^\eta \cdot (v^{t_2} \cdot w)^k;$$

2. If $i = j^\star$, return $C_i = (\sigma_{j^\star 1}, \sigma_{j^\star 2}, \sigma_{j^\star 3})$ where $\sigma_{j^\star 1} = g^a$, $\sigma_{j^\star 2} = g^s$, $t_1^\star = G(g^a, pk_s^\star, pk_r^\star)$,

$$\sigma_{j^\star 3} = (g^b)^{x_s} \cdot \left(u' \prod_{i \in \mathcal{T}^\star} u_i \right)^s \cdot (g^a)^{\alpha_v t_2^\star + \alpha_w}.$$

3. Update $\Sigma = \Sigma \bigcup \{C_i\}$ (where we let Σ be initially empty).
Indeed, the ciphertext $C_{j^\star} = (\sigma_{j^\star 1}, \sigma_{j^\star 2}, \sigma_{j^\star 3})$ is valid because $\sigma_{j^\star 1} = g^a$, $\sigma_{j^\star 2} = g^s$,

$$\begin{aligned}
\sigma_{j^\star 3} &= (g^b)^{x_s} \cdot \left(u' \prod_{i \in \mathcal{T}^\star} u_i \right)^s \cdot (g^a)^{\alpha_v t_2^\star + \alpha_w} \\
&= (g^b)^{x_s} \cdot \left(u' \prod_{i \in \mathcal{T}^\star} u_i \right)^s \cdot \left((g^{\alpha_v} f)^{t_2^\star} \cdot (g^{\alpha_w} f^{-t_2^\star}) \right)^a \quad (7) \\
&= (g^b)^{x_s} \cdot \left(u' \prod_{i \in \mathcal{T}^\star} u_i \right)^s \cdot \left(v^{t_2^\star} \cdot w \right)^a .
\end{aligned}$$

Output. In this phase, $\mathcal{A}_{\mathrm{II}}$ eventually outputs its forgery $C^* = (\sigma_1^*, \sigma_2^*, \sigma_3^*)$ of Type II (implying $\sigma_1^* \in \Sigma_1$), $\mathcal{B}_{\mathrm{II}}$ does the following to extract g^{ab} for solving the CDH problem.

1. If ($\sigma_1^* = \sigma_{j^\star 1}$ and $\sigma_2^* \neq \sigma_{j^\star 2}$), compute $t_1^\star = G(\sigma_1^*, pk_s^\star, pk_r^\star)$, $t_2 = H(\sigma_1^*, \sigma_2^*, pk_s^\star, pk_r^\star)$.
2. If $t_2 = t_2^\star$, abort (we denote this as event ColF); otherwise compute

$$\Delta = \frac{\sigma_3^*}{(g^b)^{x_s} \cdot (\sigma_2^*)^{\alpha_0 + \sum\limits_{i \in \mathcal{T}^\star} \alpha_i} \cdot (\sigma_1^*)^{\alpha_w + t_2 \alpha_v}}. \quad (8)$$

3. Return $(\Delta)^{\frac{1}{t_2 - t_2^\star}}$.
As $C^* = (\sigma_1^*, \sigma_2^*, \sigma_3^*)$ is a valid forgery, we have, for some $\ell \in \mathbb{Z}_p$:

$$\sigma_1^* = g^a, \quad \sigma_2^* = g^\ell, \quad \sigma_3^* = (g^b)^{x_s} \cdot \left(u' \prod_{i \in \mathcal{T}^\star} u_i \right)^\ell \cdot (v^{t_2} w)^a,$$

$$\begin{aligned}
\Delta &= \frac{\sigma_3^*}{(g^b)^{x_s} \cdot (\sigma_2^*)^{\alpha_0 + \sum\limits_{i \in \mathcal{T}^\star} \alpha_i} \cdot (\sigma_1^*)^{\alpha_w + t_2 \alpha_v}} \\
&= \frac{(g^b)^{x_s} \cdot \left(u' \prod\limits_{i \in \mathcal{T}^\star} u_i \right)^\ell \cdot (v^{t_2} w)^a}{(g^b)^{x_s} \cdot (\sigma_2^*)^{\alpha_0 + \sum\limits_{i \in \mathcal{T}^\star} \alpha_i} \cdot (\sigma_1^*)^{\alpha_w + t_2 \alpha_v}} \\
&= \frac{(g^b)^{x_s} \cdot \left(g^{\alpha_0 + \sum\limits_{i \in \mathcal{T}^\star} \alpha_i} \right)^\ell \cdot \left((g^{\alpha_v} \cdot f)^{t_2} \cdot (g^{\alpha_w} f^{-t_2^\star}) \right)^a}{(g^b)^{x_s} \cdot (\sigma_2^*)^{\alpha_0 + \sum\limits_{i \in \mathcal{T}^\star} \alpha_i} \cdot (\sigma_1^*)^{\alpha_w + t_2 \alpha_v}} \\
&= \frac{(g^{\alpha_v t_2 + \alpha_w} f^{t_2 - t_2^\star})^a}{(\sigma_1^*)^{\alpha_w + t_2 \alpha_v}} = \frac{(\sigma_1^*)^{\alpha_w + t_2 \alpha_v} \cdot (f^a)^{t_2 - t_2^\star}}{(\sigma_1^*)^{\alpha_w + t_2 \alpha_v}} = (g^{ab})^{t_2 - t_2^\star}.
\end{aligned}$$

Thus, $\Delta^{\frac{1}{t_2 - t_2^*}} = g^{ab}$. Namely, when $\mathcal{A}_{II}$ outputs a valid forgery C^* of Type II (denoted as event ASuc), $\mathcal{B}_{II}$ can successfully solve the CDH problem if $\sigma_1^* = \sigma_{j^*1}$ and event ColF doesn't happen.

Since j^* is information theoretically hidden from $\mathcal{A}_{II}$, both event ASuc and event ColF are independent from event $\sigma_1^* = \sigma_{j^*1}$. Then we have $\Pr[\sigma_1^* = \sigma_{j^*1}] \geq \frac{1}{q_s}$, and

$$
\begin{aligned}
\Pr[g^{ab} \leftarrow \mathcal{B}(g, g^a, g^b)] &= \Pr[\text{ASuc} \wedge \neg\text{ColF} \wedge \sigma_1^* = \sigma_{j^*1}] \\
&= \Pr[\text{ASuc} \wedge \neg\text{ColF}] \cdot \Pr[\sigma_1^* = \sigma_{j^*1}] \\
&\geq \frac{\Pr[\text{ASuc} \wedge \neg\text{ColF}]}{q_s} \\
&\geq \frac{\Pr[\text{ASuc}] - \Pr[\text{ColF}]}{q_s} \\
&= \frac{\varepsilon - \Pr[\text{ColF}]}{q_s}
\end{aligned}
$$

If event ColF happens, we get a collision of H. Thus $\Pr[\text{ColF}] \leq \varepsilon_{cr}$. From Equation (5.2), we have

$$
\Pr[g^{ab} \leftarrow \mathcal{B}(g, g^a, g^b)] \geq \frac{\varepsilon - \varepsilon_{cr}}{q_s}.
$$

The running time of $\mathcal{B}_{II}$ is close to that of $\mathcal{A}_{II}$ except $(4q_s + 12) \cdot T_e$ in simulation where T_e is the running time of the exponentiation in $\mathbb{G}$.

Type I Forgery. Suppose $\mathcal{A}_I$ is a Type I forger which (t, q_s, ε)-breaks the strong unforgeability of our signcryption KEM, producing a Type I forgery. We can construct an adversary $\mathcal{B}_I$ that (t, ε)-breaks (existential unforgeability of) the Waters signature of the form $\left(g^r, g_2^\alpha \left(u' \prod_{i \in \mathcal{M}} u_i \right)^r \right)$. Refer to [24] for more details on the Waters signatures.

Suppose $\mathcal{B}_I$ is given a public key $g_1 = g^a$ along with the parameters $\text{pp} = (\mathbb{G}, \mathbb{G}_T, e, g, u', u_1, u_2, \ldots, u_n, g_2, G)$ and a signing oracle $\mathcal{O}_w$ that returns the Waters signatures on requested messages. Its goal is to output a Waters signature on some fresh message which is not among $\mathcal{B}_I$'s chosen messages. To utilize $\mathcal{A}_I$, the adversary $\mathcal{B}_I$ simulates the environment of the SUF game.

Setup. In this phase, $\mathcal{B}_I$ generates the remaining parameters and the public key of the sender and the private/public key pair of the receiver.

1. Randomly choose α_v, α_w, γ and x_r from $\mathbb{Z}_p$.
2. Set $f = g_2, h = g^\gamma, v = g^{\alpha_v}, w = g^{\alpha_w}, pk_r^\star = g^{x_r}, sk_r^\star = x_r, pk_s^\star = g_1$.
3. Give $\mathcal{A}_I$ the parameters $u', u_1, u_2, \ldots, u_n, f, h, v, w$ and the keys $pk_s^\star, sk_r^\star, pk_r^\star$.

Encapsulation Queries. When $\mathcal{A}_I$ makes key encapsulation queries, $\mathcal{B}_I$ simulates the encapsulation oracle as follows:

1. Select k randomly from $\mathbb{Z}_p$, and compute $\sigma_1 = g^k$.
2. Submit $M = (g^k, pk_s^\star, pk_r^\star)$ to the oracle $\mathcal{O}_w$ and obtain the signature $(\sigma_{w1}, \sigma_{w2})$ on M.
3. Set $t_2 = H(g^k, \sigma_{w1}, pk_s^\star, pk_r^\star)$, $\sigma_1 = g^k$, $\sigma_2 = \sigma_{w1}$.
4. Return $C = (\sigma_1, \sigma_2, \sigma_3)$ where $\sigma_3 = \sigma_{w2} \cdot (\sigma_1)^{\alpha_v t_2 + \alpha_w} = \sigma_{w2} \cdot (v^{t_2} w)^k$.
5. Update $\mathbb{M} = \mathbb{M} \bigcup \{M\}$ (where we let $\mathbb{M}$ be initially empty).

Output. Eventually $\mathcal{A}_I$ outputs its forgery $C^* = (\sigma_1^*, \sigma_2^*, \sigma_3^*)$ of Type I (namely, σ_1^* is not included in any $(\sigma_1, \sigma_2, \sigma_3)$ returned by the encapsulation oracle), $\mathcal{B}_I$ does the following to obtain a new forgery for the Waters signature:

1. Set $M^* = (\sigma_1^*, pk_s^\star, pk_r^\star)$ and $t_2^* = H(\sigma_1^*, \sigma_2^*, pk_s^\star, pk_r^\star)$;
2. Compute $\sigma_{w2}^\star = \sigma_3^* \cdot (\sigma_1^*)^{-\alpha_v t_2^* - \alpha_w}$, and return $(M^*, (\sigma_{w1}^\star = \sigma_2^*, \sigma_{w2}^\star))$.

Note that $M^* \notin \mathbb{M}$ as σ_1^* is not included in any $(\sigma_1, \sigma_2, \sigma_3)$ returned by the encapsulation oracle. Meanwhile, $(\sigma_{w1}^\star = \sigma_2^*, \sigma_{w2}^\star)$ is a valid forgery of the Waters signature because, for $k = \log_g \sigma_1^*$ and $\ell = \log_g \sigma_2^*$, we have

$$\sigma_{w2}^\star = \sigma_3^* \cdot (\sigma_1^*)^{-\alpha_v t_2^* - \alpha_w} = \sigma_3^* \cdot (v^{t_2^*} w)^{-k} = g_2^a \cdot (u' \prod_{i \in \mathcal{T}^\star} u_i)^\ell,$$

where $\mathcal{T}^\star \subset \{1, 2, \ldots, n\}$ is the set of indices such that $G(M^\star)[i] = 1$, and $G(M^\star)[i]$ is the i-th bit of $G(M^\star)$.

The probability of $\mathcal{B}_I$'s success in forging a Waters signature is the same as that of $\mathcal{A}_I$'s success in outputting a forgery of Type I. The running times of $\mathcal{A}_I$ and $\mathcal{B}_I$ are almost the same except for $2q_s$ exponentiation computations in simulation. $\qquad\square$

Acknowledgement. This work has been supported by the National Natural Science Foundation of China (Grant Nos. 61272536, 61172085, 61103221, 61021004, 61070249, U1135004, 61170080, 11061130539 and 60703031).

References

1. El Aimani, L.: Generic constructions for verifiable signcryption. In: Kim, H. (ed.) ICISC 2011. LNCS, vol. 7259, pp. 204–218. Springer, Heidelberg (2012)
2. An, J.H., Dodis, Y., Rabin, T.: On the security of joint signature and encryption. In: Knudsen, L.R. (ed.) EUROCRYPT 2002. LNCS, vol. 2332, pp. 83–107. Springer, Heidelberg (2002)
3. Boneh, D., Boyen, X.: Short signatures without random oracles. In: Cachin, C., Camenisch, J.L. (eds.) EUROCRYPT 2004. LNCS, vol. 3027, pp. 56–73. Springer, Heidelberg (2004)
4. Boneh, D., Franklin, M.: Identity-based encryption from the Weil pairing. SIAM Journal on Computing 32(3), 586–615 (2003)
5. Boneh, D., Shen, E., Waters, B.: Strongly unforgeable signatures based on computational diffie-hellman. In: Yung, M., Dodis, Y., Kiayias, A., Malkin, T. (eds.) PKC 2006. LNCS, vol. 3958, pp. 229–240. Springer, Heidelberg (2006)
6. Boyen, X., Mei, Q., Waters, B.: Direct chosen ciphertext security from identity-based techniques. In: Proceedings of ACM CCS 2005, pp. 320–329 (2005)
7. Cramer, R., Shoup, V.: Signature schemes based on the strong RSA assumption. ACM TISSEC 3(3), 161–185 (2000)
8. Cramer, R., Shoup, V.: Design and analysis of practical public-key encryption schemes secure against adaptive chosen ciphertext attack. SIAM Journal on Computing 33(1), 167–226 (2004)

9. Dent, A.W.: Hybrid signcryption schemes with outsider security. In: Zhou, J., López, J., Deng, R.H., Bao, F. (eds.) ISC 2005. LNCS, vol. 3650, pp. 203–217. Springer, Heidelberg (2005a)

10. Dent, A.W.: Hybrid signcryption schemes with insider security. In: Boyd, C., González Nieto, J.M. (eds.) ACISP 2005. LNCS, vol. 3574, pp. 253–266. Springer, Heidelberg (2005b)

11. Dent, A., Zheng, Y.: Practical signcryption. In: Information Security and Cryptography. Springer (2010)

12. Gamage, C., Leiwo, J., Zheng, Y.: Encrypted message authentication by firewalls. In: Imai, H., Zheng, Y. (eds.) PKC 1999. LNCS, vol. 1560, pp. 69–81. Springer, Heidelberg (1999)

13. Gennaro, R., Halevi, S., Rabin, T.: Secure hash-and-sign signatures without the random oracle. In: Stern, J. (ed.) EUROCRYPT 1999. LNCS, vol. 1592, pp. 123–139. Springer, Heidelberg (1999)

14. Ji, P., Yang, M.: Verifiable short signcryption without random oracle. In: Wireless Communications, Networking and Mobile Computing, pp. 2270–2273 (2007)

15. Kang, L., Tang, X., Lu, X., Fan, J.: A short signature scheme in the standard model. IACR Eprint archive (2007), http://eprint.iacr.org/2007/398

16. Kiltz, E.: Chosen-ciphertext secure key-encapsulation based on gap hashed Diffie-Hellman. In: Okamoto, T., Wang, X. (eds.) PKC 2007. LNCS, vol. 4450, pp. 282–297. Springer, Heidelberg (2007)

17. Kiltz, E., Galindo, D.: Direct chosen-ciphertext secure identity-based key encapsulation without random oracles. In: Batten, L.M., Safavi-Naini, R. (eds.) ACISP 2006. LNCS, vol. 4058, pp. 336–347. Springer, Heidelberg (2006)

18. Li, F., Shirase, M., Takagi, T.: Efficient signcryption key encapsulation without random oracles. In: Yung, M., Liu, P., Lin, D. (eds.) Inscrypt 2008. LNCS, vol. 5487, pp. 47–59. Springer, Heidelberg (2009)

19. Liu, J.K., Au, M.H., Susilo, W., Zhou, J.: Short generic transformation to strongly unforgeable signature in the standard model. In: Gritzalis, D., Preneel, B., Theoharidou, M. (eds.) ESORICS 2010. LNCS, vol. 6345, pp. 168–181. Springer, Heidelberg (2010)

20. Matsuura, K., Zheng, Y., Imai, H.: Compact and flexible resolution of CBT multicast key-distribution. In: Masunaga, Y., Tsukamoto, M. (eds.) WWCA 1998. LNCS, vol. 1368, pp. 190–205. Springer, Heidelberg (1998)

21. Park, B., Lee, W.: ISMANET: a secure routing protocol using identity-based signcryption scheme for mobile ad-hoc networks. IEICE Transactions on Communications E88-B(6), 2548–2556 (2005)

22. Park, N., Moon, K., Chung, K.-I., Won, D.H., Zheng, Y.: A security acceleration using XML signcryption scheme in mobile grid web services. In: Lowe, D.G., Gaedke, M. (eds.) ICWE 2005. LNCS, vol. 3579, pp. 191–196. Springer, Heidelberg (2005)

23. Tan, C.: Insider-secure signcryption KEM/tag-KEM schemes without random oracles. In: Proceedings of International Conference on Availability, Reliability and Security - ARES 2008, pp. 1275–1281 (2008)

24. Waters, B.: Efficient identity-based encryption without random oracles. In: Cramer, R. (ed.) EUROCRYPT 2005. LNCS, vol. 3494, pp. 114–127. Springer, Heidelberg (2005)

25. Zheng, Y.: Digital signcryption or how to achieve cost(signature & encryption) ≪ cost (signature)+ cost(encryption). In: Kaliski Jr., B.S. (ed.) CRYPTO 1997. LNCS, vol. 1294, pp. 165–179. Springer, Heidelberg (1997)

Sequential Aggregate Signatures Made Shorter

Kwangsu Lee[1,*], Dong Hoon Lee[1,**], and Moti Yung[2,3]

[1] Korea University, Korea
{guspin,donghlee}@korea.ac.kr
[2] Columbia University, USA
moti@cs.columbia.edu
[3] Google Inc., USA

Abstract. Sequential aggregate signature (SAS) is a special type of public-key signature that allows a signer to add his signature into a previous aggregate signature in sequential order. In this case, since many public keys are used and many signatures are employed and compressed, it is important to reduce the sizes of signatures and public keys. Recently, Lee et al. proposed an efficient SAS scheme with short public keys and proved its security without random oracles under static assumptions. In this paper, we propose an improved SAS scheme that has a shorter signature size compared with that of Lee et al.'s SAS scheme. Our SAS scheme is also secure without random oracles under static assumptions. To achieve the improvement, we devise a new public-key signature scheme that supports multi-users and public re-randomization. Compared with the SAS scheme of Lee et al., our SAS scheme employs new techniques which allow us to reduce the size of signatures by increasing the size of the public keys (obviously, since signature compression is at the heart of aggregate signature this is a further step in understanding the aggregation capability of such schemes).

1 Introduction

Aggregate signature is a relatively new type of public-key signature (PKS) that allows a signer to aggregate different signatures generated by different signers on different messages into a short aggregate signature [6]. Aggregate signature has many applications like signing certificate chains, proxy signing, secure routing protocols, and more. After the introduction of aggregate signature by Boneh, Gentry, Lynn, and Shacham [6], many aggregate signature schemes were proposed by using bilinear groups [1,2,4,6,10,11,13,15,17,21] and trapdoor permutations [7,18,20]. However, the security of many aggregate signature schemes was proven in the random oracle model. The random oracle model was very

* Supported by the MKE (The Ministry of Knowledge Economy), Korea, under the ITRC (Information Technology Research Center) support program (NIPA-2012-H0301-12-3007) supervised by the NIPA (National IT Industry Promotion Agency).
** Supported by the National Research Foundation of Korea (NRF) grant funded by the Korea government (MEST) (No. 2010-0029121).

M. Jacobson et al. (Eds.): ACNS 2013, LNCS 7954, pp. 202–217, 2013.
© Springer-Verlag Berlin Heidelberg 2013

successful to prove the security of practical schemes, but the security proof in the random oracle model is not entirely sound [8] and schemes in the standard model are needed. Standard model solutions for the cases of sequential aggregate signature (introduced in [18]) [13,15,17,21] (where signatures are aggregated in a sequence, as in applications like certification chains), and synchronized aggregate signature (where all signers share a synchronized same value, as introduced by [10]) [1] were given.

A sequential aggregate signature (SAS) scheme without random oracle assumption is what we concentrate on here, such a scheme was first proposed by Lu et al. [17], but the public-key size of this scheme is too large since the scheme is based on the PKS scheme of Waters [22]. In public-key based aggregate signature, reducing the size of public keys is very important since a verifier should retrieve all the public keys of signers to check the validity of the aggregate signature, and needless to say the size of the aggregated signature is important as well. The importance of constructing a SAS scheme with short public keys was addressed by Lu et al. [17], but they left it as an interesting open problem. Schröder proposed the first SAS scheme with short public keys based on the Camenisch-Lysyanskaya (CL) signature scheme [21], but it is only secure under the interactive LRSW assumption. Recently, Lee et al. [15] proposed another SAS scheme with short public keys based on the identity-based encryption (IBE) scheme of Lewko and Waters [16] and proved its security without random oracles under static assumptions.

1.1 Our Contributions

In this paper, we revisit the SAS scheme of Lee et al. [15] and propose an improved SAS scheme with shorter signature size. The proposed SAS scheme trades off signature for public-key size since the signature size of our SAS scheme is shorter than that of Lee et al.'s SAS scheme by two group elements but the public-key size of our SAS scheme is longer by two group elements. To construct the SAS scheme with shorter signature size that supports sequential aggregation, we first propose a new PKS scheme and prove its security without random oracles under static assumptions. Additionally, we propose a multi-signature (MS) scheme with shorter signature size and shorter public parameters and prove its security without random oracles under static assumptions.

We suggest new ideas, and technically speaking, we construct a PKS scheme that supports multi-users and public re-randomization for a SAS scheme with shorter signature size. We start the construction from the PKS scheme derived from the IBE scheme of Lewko and Waters [16] (as was done earlier). However, this directly converted PKS scheme does not support multi-users and public re-randomization as pointed out by Lee et al. [15] since the elements $g, u, h \in \mathbb{G}$ cannot be published in the public key. Lee et al. solved this problem by modifying the verification algorithm of the PKS scheme, but the size of signatures increased by two group elements. In this paper, we solve this obstacle in a different way and publish $gw_1^{c_g}, uw_1^{c_u}, hw_1^{c_h} \in \mathbb{G}$ in the public key instead of publishing $g, u, h \in \mathbb{G}$ to maintain the same size of signatures (loosely speaking, we lift the verification parameters to the exponent). However, note that this method increases the size of public keys by two group elements compared with that of Lee et al.'s scheme since additional group elements should be published in the public key to make public $gw_1^{c_g}, uw_1^{c_u}, hw_1^{c_h}$.

1.2 Related Work

Aggregate Signature. The concept of aggregate signatures was introduced by Boneh et al. [6], and they proposed the first aggregate signature scheme in bilinear groups. Their aggregate signature scheme is the only unique one that supports full aggregation, but the security is proven in the random oracle model and the verification algorithm requires l number of pairing where l is the number of signers in the aggregate signature. To remedy this situation, other types of aggregate signatures were introduced.

Lysyanskaya et al. [18] introduced the concept of sequential aggregate signature (SAS) and proposed a SAS scheme in trapdoor permutations. Lu et al. [17] proposed the first SAS scheme without random oracles, but the size of public keys is very large. To reduce the size of public keys, SAS schemes with short public key was proposed [13, 15, 21]. Recently, SAS schemes that do not require a verifier to check the validity of the previous signature were proposed [7, 9]. Boldyreva et al. [4] proposed an identity-based sequential aggregate signature scheme in bilinear groups and proved its security under an interactive assumption. Recently Gerbush et al. [11] proposed a modified identity-based sequential aggregate signature scheme in composite order bilinear groups and proved its security in the random oracle model under static assumptions.

Gentry and Ramzan [10] introduced the concept of synchronized aggregate signature and proposed an identity-based synchronized aggregate signature scheme in the random oracle model. Ahn et al. [1] proposed an synchronized aggregate signature scheme and proved its security without random oracles. Recently, Lee et al. [13] proposed a synchronized aggregate signature scheme with shorter aggregate signatures based on the CL signature and proved its security in the random oracle model.

Multi-signature. The concept of multi-signature (MS) was introduced by Itakura and Nakamura [12]. MS is a special type of aggregate signatures where all signers generate signatures for the same message. Micali et al. [19] defined the first formal security model of MS and proposed a MS scheme based on the Schnorr signature. Boldyreva defined a general security model for multi-signatures and proposed a MS scheme in bilinear groups that is secure in the random oracle model [3]. Lu et al. [17] proposed the first MS scheme that is secure without random oracles by modifying their SAS scheme. Recently, Lee et al. [15] proposed a MS scheme with short public parameters and proved its security without random oracles.

2   Preliminaries

In this section, we define asymmetric bilinear groups and introduce complexity assumptions in this bilinear groups.

2.1   Asymmetric Bilinear Groups

Let $\mathbb{G}, \hat{\mathbb{G}}$ and $\mathbb{G}_T$ be multiplicative cyclic groups of prime order p. Let $g, \hat{g}$ be generators of $\mathbb{G}, \hat{\mathbb{G}}$. The bilinear map $e : \mathbb{G} \times \hat{\mathbb{G}} \to \mathbb{G}_T$ has the following properties:

1. Bilinearity: $\forall u \in \mathbb{G}, \forall \hat{v} \in \hat{\mathbb{G}}$ and $\forall a, b \in \mathbb{Z}_p$, $e(u^a, \hat{v}^b) = e(u, \hat{v})^{ab}$.
2. Non-degeneracy: $\exists g, \hat{g}$ such that $e(g, \hat{g})$ has order p, that is, $e(g, \hat{g})$ is a generator of $\mathbb{G}_T$.

We say that $\mathbb{G}, \hat{\mathbb{G}}, \mathbb{G}_T$ are bilinear groups with no efficiently computable isomorphisms if the group operations in $\mathbb{G}, \hat{\mathbb{G}}$, and $\mathbb{G}_T$ as well as the bilinear map e are all efficiently computable, but there are no efficiently computable isomorphisms between $\mathbb{G}$ and $\hat{\mathbb{G}}$.

2.2   Complexity Assumptions

We employ three static assumptions in prime order (asymmetric) bilinear groups. Assumptions 1 and 2 were introduced by Lewko and Waters [16], while Assumption 3 has been used extensively.

Assumption 1 (LW1). Let $(p, \mathbb{G}, \hat{\mathbb{G}}, \mathbb{G}_T, e)$ be a description of the asymmetric bilinear group of prime order p with the security parameter λ. Let $g, \hat{g}$ be generators of $\mathbb{G}, \hat{\mathbb{G}}$ respectively. The assumption is that if the challenge values

$$D = ((p, \mathbb{G}, \hat{\mathbb{G}}, \mathbb{G}_T, e), g, g^b, \hat{g}, \hat{g}^a, \hat{g}^b, \hat{g}^{ab^2}, \hat{g}^{b^2}, \hat{g}^{b^3}, \hat{g}^c, \hat{g}^{ac}, \hat{g}^{bc}, \hat{g}^{b^2 c}, \hat{g}^{b^3 c}) \text{ and } T$$

are given, no PPT algorithm $\mathcal{B}$ can distinguish $T = T_0 = \hat{g}^{ab^2 c}$ from $T = T_1 = \hat{g}^d$ with more than a negligible advantage. The advantage of $\mathcal{B}$ is defined as $\mathbf{Adv}_{\mathcal{B}}^{A1}(\lambda) = \big| \Pr[\mathcal{B}(D, T_0) = 0] - \Pr[\mathcal{B}(D, T_1) = 0] \big|$ where the probability is taken over the random choice of $a, b, c, d \in \mathbb{Z}_p$.

Assumption 2 (LW2). Let $(p, \mathbb{G}, \hat{\mathbb{G}}, \mathbb{G}_T, e)$ be a description of the asymmetric bilinear group of prime order p. Let $g, \hat{g}$ be generators of $\mathbb{G}, \hat{\mathbb{G}}$ respectively. The assumption is that if the challenge values

$$D = ((p, \mathbb{G}, \hat{\mathbb{G}}, \mathbb{G}_T, e), g, g^a, g^b, g^c, \hat{g}, \hat{g}^a, \hat{g}^{a^2}, \hat{g}^{bx}, \hat{g}^{abx}, \hat{g}^{a^2 x}) \text{ and } T$$

are given, no PPT algorithm $\mathcal{B}$ can distinguish $T = T_0 = g^{bc}$ from $T = T_1 = g^d$ with more than a negligible advantage. The advantage of $\mathcal{B}$ is defined as $\mathbf{Adv}_{\mathcal{B}}^{A2}(\lambda) = \big| \Pr[\mathcal{B}(D, T_0) = 0] - \Pr[\mathcal{B}(D, T_1) = 0] \big|$ where the probability is taken over the random choice of $a, b, c, x, d \in \mathbb{Z}_p$.

Assumption 3 (Decisional Bilinear Diffie-Hellman). Let $(p, \mathbb{G}, \hat{\mathbb{G}}, \mathbb{G}_T, e)$ be a description of the asymmetric bilinear group of prime order p. Let $g, \hat{g}$ be generators of $\mathbb{G}, \hat{\mathbb{G}}$ respectively. The assumption is that if the challenge values

$$D = ((p, \mathbb{G}, \hat{\mathbb{G}}, \mathbb{G}_T, e), g, g^a, g^b, g^c, \hat{g}, \hat{g}^a, \hat{g}^b, \hat{g}^c) \text{ and } T$$

are given, no PPT algorithm $\mathcal{B}$ can distinguish $T = T_0 = e(g, \hat{g})^{abc}$ from $T = T_1 = e(g, \hat{g})^d$ with more than a negligible advantage. The advantage of $\mathcal{B}$ is defined as $\mathbf{Adv}_{\mathcal{B}}^{A3}(\lambda) = \big| \Pr[\mathcal{B}(D, T_0) = 0] - \Pr[\mathcal{B}(D, T_1) = 0] \big|$ where the probability is taken over the random choice of $a, b, c, d \in \mathbb{Z}_p$.

3 Public-Key Signature

In this section, we propose an efficient public-key signature (PKS) scheme with short public keys that supports multi-users and public re-randomization, and prove its security without random oracles under static assumption.

3.1 Construction

To construct a PKS scheme with short public keys that supports multi-users and public re-randomization, we can derive a PKS scheme with short public keys from the IBE scheme in prime order groups of Lewko and Waters [16] by applying the transformation of Naor [5] and representing the signature in $\mathbb{G}$ to reduce the size of signatures. However, this PKS scheme does not support multi-users and public re-randomization since the elements $g, u, h \in \mathbb{G}$ cannot be published in the public key. Lee et al. [15] solved this problem by re-randomizing the verification elements of the signature verification algorithm, but the number of signatures increased by two group elements, and our main issue here is further compression of the signature size.

To this end, we present another solution for the above problem that allows the elements g, u, h to be safely published in the public key. In the PKS scheme of Lewko and Waters [16], if $g, u, h \in \mathbb{G}$ are published in the public key, then the simulator of the security proof can easily distinguish normal verification components from semi-functional verification components of the signature verification algorithm for a forged signature without the help of an adversary. Thus the simulator of Lewko and Waters sets the CDH value into the elements g, u, h to prevent the simulator from creating these elements. Our idea for solving this problem is to lift the published values into the exponent and publish $gw_1^{c_g}, uw_1^{c_u}, hw_1^{c_h}$ that are additionally multiplied with random elements instead of directly publishing g, u, h. In this case, the simulator can create these elements since the random exponents c_g, c_u, c_h can be used to cancel out the CDH value embedded in the elements g, u, h. Additionally, the simulator cannot distinguish the changes of verification components for the forged signature because of the added elements $w_1^{c_g}, w_1^{c_u}, w_1^{c_h}$. This solution does not increase the number of group elements in the signatures, rather it increases the number of public keys since additional elements $w_2^{c_g}, w^{c_g}, w_2^{c_u}, w^{c_u}, w_2^{c_h}, w^{c_h}$ should be published.

Our PKS scheme in prime order bilinear groups is described as follows:

PKS.KeyGen(1^λ): This algorithm first generates the asymmetric bilinear groups $\mathbb{G}, \hat{\mathbb{G}}$ of prime order p of bit size $\Theta(\lambda)$. It chooses random elements $g, w \in \mathbb{G}$ and $\hat{g} \in \hat{\mathbb{G}}$. Next, it selects random exponents $\nu, \phi_1, \phi_2 \in \mathbb{Z}_p$ and sets $\tau = \phi_1 + \nu\phi_2$. It also selects random exponents $\alpha, x, y \in \mathbb{Z}_p$ and sets $u = g^x, h = g^y, \hat{u} = \hat{g}^x, \hat{h} = \hat{g}^y, w_1 = w^{\phi_1}, w_2 = w^{\phi_2}$. It outputs a private key $SK = (\alpha, x, y)$ and a public key by selecting random values $c_g, c_u, c_h \in \mathbb{Z}_p$ as

$$PK = \big(\ gw_1^{c_g}, w_2^{c_g}, w^{c_g},\ uw_1^{c_u}, w_2^{c_u}, w^{c_u},\ hw_1^{c_h}, w_2^{c_h}, w^{c_h},\ w_1, w_2, w,$$
$$\hat{g}, \hat{g}^\nu, \hat{g}^{-\tau},\ \hat{u}, \hat{u}^\nu, \hat{u}^{-\tau},\ \hat{h}, \hat{h}^\nu, \hat{h}^{-\tau},\ \Lambda = e(g, \hat{g}),\ \Omega = e(g, \hat{g})^\alpha\ \big).$$

PKS.Sign(M, SK): This algorithm takes as input a message $M \in \mathbb{Z}_p$ and a private key $SK = (\alpha, x, y)$. It selects random exponents $r, c_1, c_2 \in \mathbb{Z}_p$ and outputs a signature as

$$\sigma = \big(\ W_{1,1} = (gw_1^{c_g})^\alpha((uw_1^{c_u})^M(hw_1^{c_h}))^r w_1^{c_1},$$
$$W_{1,2} = (w_2^{c_g})^\alpha((w_2^{c_u})^M w_2^{c_h})^r w_2^{c_1},\ W_{1,3} = (w^{c_g})^\alpha((w^{c_u})^M w^{c_h})^r w^{c_1},$$
$$W_{2,1} = (gw_1^{c_g})^r w_1^{c_2},\ W_{2,2} = (w_2^{c_g})^r w_2^{c_2},\ W_{2,3} = (w^{c_g})^r w^{c_2}\ \big).$$

PKS.Verify(σ, M, PK): This algorithm takes as input a signature σ on a message $M \in \mathbb{Z}_p$ under a public key PK. It chooses a random exponent $t \in \mathbb{Z}_p$ and computes verification components as

$$V_{1,1} = \hat{g}^t,\ V_{1,2} = (\hat{g}^\nu)^t,\ V_{1,3} = (\hat{g}^{-\tau})^t,$$
$$V_{2,1} = (\hat{u}^M \hat{h})^t,\ V_{2,2} = ((\hat{u}^\nu)^M \hat{h}^\nu)^t,\ V_{2,3} = ((\hat{u}^{-\tau})^M \hat{h}^{-\tau})^t.$$

Next, it verifies that $\prod_{i=1}^3 e(W_{1,i}, V_{1,i}) \cdot \prod_{i=1}^3 e(W_{2,i}, V_{2,i})^{-1} \overset{?}{=} \Omega^t$. If this equation holds, then it outputs 1. Otherwise, it outputs 0.

If we implicitly sets $\tilde{c}_1 = c_g\alpha + (c_u M + c_h)r + c_1$, $\tilde{c}_2 = c_g r + c_2$, then the signature is restated as the following form

$$W_{1,1} = g^\alpha(u^M h)^r w_1^{\tilde{c}_1},\ W_{1,2} = w_2^{\tilde{c}_1},\ W_{1,3} = w^{\tilde{c}_1},$$
$$W_{2,1} = g^r w_1^{\tilde{c}_2},\ W_{2,2} = w_2^{\tilde{c}_2},\ W_{2,3} = w^{\tilde{c}_2}.$$

3.2 Security Analysis

We prove the security of our PKS scheme without random oracles under static assumptions. To prove the security, we use the dual system encryption technique of Lewko and Waters [16]. The dual system encryption technique was originally developed to prove the full-model security of IBE and its extensions, but it also can be used to prove the security of PKS by using the transformation of Naor [5]. Recently Lee et al. [15] proved the security of their PKS scheme by using the dual system encryption technique, and Gerbush et al. [11] developed the dual form signature technique that is a variation of the dual system encryption technique to prove the security of theirs PKS schemes.

Theorem 1. *The above PKS scheme is existentially unforgeable under a chosen message attack if Assumptions 1, 2, and 3 hold.*

Proof. Before proving the security, we first define two additional algorithms for semi-functional types. For the semi-functionality, we set $f = g^{y_f}, \hat{f} = \hat{g}^{y_f}$ where y_f is a random exponent in $\mathbb{Z}_p$.

PKS.SignSF. The semi-functional signing algorithm first creates a normal signature using the private key. Let $(W'_{1,1}, \ldots, W'_{2,3})$ be the normal signature of a message M with random exponents $r, c_1, c_2 \in \mathbb{Z}_p$. It selects random exponents $s_k, z_k \in \mathbb{Z}_p$ and outputs a semi-functional signature as

$$\sigma = \big(\ W_{1,1} = W'_{1,1} \cdot (f^{-\nu})^{s_k z_k}, \ W_{1,2} = W'_{1,2} \cdot f^{s_k z_k}, \ W_{1,3} = W'_{1,3},$$
$$W_{2,1} = W'_{2,1} \cdot (f^{-\nu})^{s_k}, \ W_{2,2} = W'_{2,2} \cdot f^{s_k}, \ W_{2,3} = W'_{2,3} \ \big).$$

PKS.VerifySF. The semi-functional verification algorithm first creates a normal verification components using the public key. Let $(V'_{1,1}, \ldots, V'_{2,3})$ be the normal verification components with a random exponent $t \in \mathbb{Z}_p$. It chooses random exponents $s_c, z_c \in \mathbb{Z}_p$ and computes semi-functional verification components as

$$V_{1,1} = V'_{1,1}, \ V_{1,2} = V'_{1,2} \cdot \hat{f}^{s_c}, \ V_{1,3} = V'_{1,3} \cdot (\hat{f}^{-\phi_2})^{s_c},$$
$$V_{2,1} = V'_{2,1}, \ V_{2,2} = V'_{2,2} \cdot \hat{f}^{s_c z_c}, \ V_{2,3} = V'_{2,3} \cdot (\hat{f}^{-\phi_2})^{s_c z_c}.$$

Next, it verifies that $\prod_{i=1}^{3} e(W_{1,i}, V_{1,i}) \cdot \prod_{i=1}^{3} e(W_{2,i}, V_{2,i})^{-1} \stackrel{?}{=} \Omega^t$. If this equation holds, then it outputs 1. Otherwise, it outputs 0.

If the semi-functional verification algorithm is used to verify a semi-functional signature, then an additional random element $e(f, \hat{f})^{s_k s_c (z_k - z_c)}$ is left in the left part of the above verification equation. If $z_k = z_c$, then the semi-functional verification algorithm succeeds. In this case, we say that the signature is *nominally* semi-functional.

The security proof uses a sequence of games $\mathbf{G}_0, \mathbf{G}_1, \mathbf{G}_2, \mathbf{G}_3$: The first game $\mathbf{G}_0$ will be the original security game and the last game $\mathbf{G}_3$ will be a game such that an adversary $\mathcal{A}$ has no advantage. Formally, the hybrid games are defined as follows:

Game $\mathbf{G}_0$. This game is the original security game. In this game, the signatures that are given to $\mathcal{A}$ are normal and the challenger use the normal verification algorithm **PKS.Verify** to check the validity of the forged signature of $\mathcal{A}$. Note that $\mathcal{A}$ can forge a normal signature or a semi-functional signature to win this game since normal or semi-functional signatures are always verified in the normal verification algorithm.

Game $\mathbf{G}_1$. This game is almost identical to $\mathbf{G}_0$ except that the challenger use the semi-functional verification algorithm **PKS.VerifySF** to check the validity of the forged signature of $\mathcal{A}$. Note that $\mathcal{A}$ should forge a normal signature to win this game since semi-functional signatures cannot be verified in the semi-functional verification algorithm.

Game $\mathbf{G}_2$. This game is the same as the $\mathbf{G}_1$ except that the signatures that are given to $\mathcal{A}$ will be semi-functional. At this moment, the signatures are semi-functional and the challenger use the semi-functional verification algorithm **PKS.VerifySF** to check the validity of the forged signature. Suppose that $\mathcal{A}$ makes at most q signature queries. For the security proof, we define a sequence of hybrid games $\mathbf{G}_{1,0}, \ldots, \mathbf{G}_{1,k}, \ldots, \mathbf{G}_{1,q}$ where $\mathbf{G}_{1,0} = \mathbf{G}_1$. In $\mathbf{G}_{1,k}$, a normal signature is given to $\mathcal{A}$ for all j-th signature queries such that $j > k$ and a semi-functional signature is given to $\mathcal{A}$ for all j-th signature queries such that $j \leq k$. It is obvious that $\mathbf{G}_{1,q}$ is equal to $\mathbf{G}_2$.

Game $\mathbf{G}_3$. This final game differs from $\mathbf{G}_2$ in that the challenger always rejects the forged signature of $\mathcal{A}$ by replacing the element Ω in the verification equation to a random element. Therefore, the advantage of this game is zero since $\mathcal{A}$ cannot win this game.

To prove the security using the dual system encryption technique, we should show that it is hard for $\mathcal{A}$ to forge a normal signature and a semi-functional signature. At first, from the indistinguishability between $\mathbf{G}_0$ and $\mathbf{G}_1$, we obtain that $\mathcal{A}$ can forge a normal signature with a non-negligible probability while he cannot forge a semi-functional signature when only normal signatures are given to $\mathcal{A}$. To finish the proof, we additionally should show that it is hard for $\mathcal{A}$ to forge a normal signature. From the indistinguishability between $\mathbf{G}_1$ and $\mathbf{G}_2$, we obtain that the probability of $\mathcal{A}$ to forge a normal signature does not change when the signatures given to $\mathcal{A}$ are changed from a normal type to a semi-functional type. Finally, from the indistinguishability between $\mathbf{G}_2$ and $\mathbf{G}_3$, we obtain that it is hard for $\mathcal{A}$ to forge a normal signature when only semi-functional signatures are given to the adversary. Therefore, we have the unforgeability of the adversary through the indistinguishability of hybrid games. □

Lemma 1. *If Assumption 1 holds, then no polynomial-time adversary can distinguish between G_0 and G_1 with non-negligible advantage.*

Lemma 2. *If Assumption 2 holds, then no polynomial-time adversary can distinguish between G_1 and G_2 with non-negligible advantage.*

Lemma 3. *If Assumption 3 holds, then no polynomial-time adversary can distinguish between G_2 and G_3 with non-negligible advantage.*

The proof of Lemma 1 is given in Appendix A and the proofs of other lemmas are given in the full version of this paper [14].

4 Sequential Aggregate Signature

In this section, we propose an efficient sequential aggregate signature (SAS) scheme with short public keys and prove its security without random oracles.

4.1 Definitions

The concept of SAS was introduced by Lysyanskaya et al. [18]. In SAS, all signers first generate public keys and private keys, and then publishes their public keys.

To generate a sequential aggregate signature, a signer may receive an aggregate-so-far from a previous signer, and creates a new aggregate signature by adding his signature to the aggregate-so-far in sequential order. After that, the signer may send the aggregate signature to a next signer. A verifier can check the validity of the aggregate signature by using the pubic keys of all signers in the aggregate signature. A SAS scheme is formally defined as follows:

Definition 1 (Sequential Aggregate Signature). *A sequential aggregate signature (SAS) scheme consists of four PPT algorithms* **Setup, KeyGen, AggSign,** *and* **AggVerify,** *which are defined as follows:*

Setup(1^λ). *The setup algorithm takes as input a security parameter* 1^λ *and outputs public parameters* PP.

KeyGen(PP). *The key generation algorithm takes as input the public parameters* PP, *and outputs a public key* PK *and a private key* SK.

AggSign$(AS', \mathbf{M}, \mathbf{PK}, M, SK)$. *The aggregate signing algorithm takes as input an aggregate-so-far* AS' *on messages* $\mathbf{M} = (M_1, \ldots, M_l)$ *under public keys* $\mathbf{PK} = (PK_1, \ldots, PK_l)$, *a message* M, *and a private key* SK, *and outputs a new aggregate signature* AS.

AggVerify$(AS, \mathbf{M}, \mathbf{PK})$. *The aggregate verification algorithm takes as input an aggregate signature* AS *on messages* $\mathbf{M} = (M_1, \ldots, M_l)$ *under public keys* $\mathbf{PK} = (PK_1, \ldots, PK_l)$, *and outputs either 1 or 0 depending on the validity of the sequential aggregate signature.*

The correctness requirement is that for each PP *output by* **Setup,** *for all* (PK, SK) *output by* **KeyGen,** *any* M, *we have that* **AggVerify**(**AggSign**$(AS', \mathbf{M}', \mathbf{PK}', M, SK), \mathbf{M}' \| M, \mathbf{PK}' \| PK) = 1$ *where* AS' *is a valid aggregate-so-far signature on messages* $\mathbf{M}'$ *under public keys* $\mathbf{PK}'$.

The security model of SAS was defined by Lysyanskaya et al. [18], but we use the security model of Lu et al. [17] that requires for an adversary to register key-pair of other signers except the target signer. The security model of SAS is formally defined as follows:

Definition 2 (Security). *The security notion of existential unforgeability under a chosen message attack is defined in terms of the following experiment between a challenger* $\mathcal{C}$ *and a PPT adversary* $\mathcal{A}$:

1. **Setup:** $\mathcal{C}$ *first initializes a certification list* CL *as empty. Next, it runs* **Setup** *to obtain public parameters* PP *and* **KeyGen** *to obtain a key pair* (PK, SK), *and gives* PK *to* $\mathcal{A}$.
2. **Certification Query:** $\mathcal{A}$ *adaptively requests the certification of a public key by providing a key pair* (PK, SK). *Then* $\mathcal{C}$ *adds the key pair* (PK, SK) *to* CL *if the key pair is a valid one.*
3. **Signature Query:** $\mathcal{A}$ *adaptively requests a sequential aggregate signature (by providing an aggregate-so-far* AS' *on messages* $\mathbf{M}'$ *under public keys* $\mathbf{PK}'$), *on a message* M *to sign under the challenge public key* PK, *and receives a sequential aggregate signature* AS.

4. **Output:** *Finally (after a sequence of the above queries), $\mathcal{A}$ outputs a forged sequential aggregate signature AS^* on messages $\mathbf{M}^*$ under public keys $\mathbf{PK}^*$. $\mathcal{C}$ outputs 1 if the forged signature satisfies the following three conditions, or outputs 0 otherwise: 1) $\mathbf{AggVerify}(AS^*, \mathbf{M}^*, \mathbf{PK}^*) = 1$, 2) The challenge public key PK must exists in $\mathbf{PK}^*$ and each public key in $\mathbf{PK}^*$ except the challenge public key must be in CL, and 3) The corresponding message M in $\mathbf{M}^*$ of the challenge public key PK must not have been queried by $\mathcal{A}$ to the sequential aggregate signing oracle.*

The advantage of $\mathcal{A}$ is defined as $\mathbf{Adv}_{\mathcal{A}}^{SAS} = \Pr[\mathcal{C} = 1]$ where the probability is taken over all the randomness of the experiment. A SAS scheme is existentially unforgeable under a chosen message attack if all PPT adversaries have at most a negligible advantage in the above experiment.

4.2 Construction

To construct a SAS scheme from a PKS scheme, the PKS scheme should support multi-users by sharing some elements among all signers and the randomness of signatures should be sequentially aggregated to a single value. We can employ the randomness reuse method of Lu et al. [17] to aggregate the randomness of signatures. To apply the randomness reuse method, we should re-randomize the aggregate signature to prevent a forgery attack. Thus we build on the PKS scheme of the previous section that supports multi-users and public re-randomization to construct a SAS scheme.

The SAS scheme in prime order bilinear groups is described as follows:

SAS.Setup(1^λ): This algorithm first generates the asymmetric bilinear groups $\mathbb{G}, \hat{\mathbb{G}}$ of prime order p of bit size $\Theta(\lambda)$. It chooses random elements $g, w \in \mathbb{G}$ and $\hat{g} \in \hat{\mathbb{G}}$. Next, it selects random exponents $\nu, \phi_1, \phi_2 \in \mathbb{Z}_p$ and sets $\tau = \phi_1 + \nu\phi_2$, $w_1 = w^{\phi_1}, w_2 = w^{\phi_2}$. It publishes public parameters by selecting a random value $c_g \in \mathbb{Z}_p$ as

$$PP = \left(gw_1^{c_g}, w_2^{c_g}, w^{c_g}, w_1, w_2, w, \hat{g}, \hat{g}^\nu, \hat{g}^{-\tau}, \Lambda = e(g, \hat{g}) \right).$$

SAS.KeyGen(PP): This algorithm takes as input the public parameters PP. It selects random exponents $\alpha, x, y \in \mathbb{Z}_p$ and sets $\hat{u} = \hat{g}^x, \hat{h} = \hat{g}^y$. It outputs a private key $SK = (\alpha, x, y)$ and a public key by selecting random values $c'_u, c'_h \in \mathbb{Z}_p$ as

$$PK = \left(uw_1^{c_u} = (gw_1^{c_g})^x w_1^{c'_u}, w_2^{c_u} = (w_2^{c_g})^x w_2^{c'_u}, w^{c_u} = (w^{c_g})^x w_2^{c'_u}, \right.$$
$$hw_1^{c_h} = (gw_1^{c_g})^y w_1^{c'_u}, w_2^{c_h} = (w_2^{c_g})^y w_2^{c'_u}, w^{c_h} = (w^{c_g})^y w_2^{c'_u},$$
$$\left. \hat{u}, \hat{u}^\nu = (\hat{g}^\nu)^x, \hat{u}^{-\tau} = (\hat{g}^{-\tau})^x, \hat{h}, \hat{h}^\nu = (\hat{g}^\nu)^y, \hat{h}^{-\tau} = (\hat{g}^{-\tau})^y, \Omega = \Lambda^\alpha \right).$$

SAS.AggSign($AS', \mathbf{M}', \mathbf{PK}', M, SK$): This algorithm takes as input an aggregate-so-far $AS' = (S'_{1,1}, \ldots, S'_{2,3})$ on messages $\mathbf{M}' = (M_1, \ldots, M_{l-1})$ under public keys $\mathbf{PK}' = (PK_1, \ldots, PK_{l-1})$ where $PK_i = (u_i w_1^{c_{u,i}}, \ldots, \Omega_i)$, a message

$M \in \mathbb{Z}_p$, a private key $SK = (\alpha, x, y)$ with $PK = (uw_1^{c_u}, \ldots, \Omega)$ and PP. It first checks the validity of AS' by calling **SAS.AggVerify**$(AS', \mathbf{M}', \mathbf{PK}')$. If AS' is not valid, then it halts. If the public key PK of SK does already exist in $\mathbf{PK}'$, then it halts. Next, it selects random exponents $r, c_1, c_2 \in \mathbb{Z}_p$ and outputs an aggregate signature as

$$AS = (\ S_{1,1} = S_{1,1}'(gw_1^{c_g})^\alpha (S_{2,1}')^{xM+y} \cdot \prod_{i=1}^{l-1}((u_i w_1^{c_{u,i}})^{M_i}(h_i w_1^{c_{h,i}}))^r ((uw_1^{c_u})^M (hw_1^{c_h}))^r w_1^{c_1},$$

$$S_{1,2} = S_{1,2}'(w_2^{c_g})^\alpha (S_{2,2}')^{xM+y} \cdot \prod_{i=1}^{l-1}((w_2^{c_{u,i}})^{M_i}(w_2^{c_{h,i}}))^r ((w_2^{c_u})^M w_2^{c_h})^r w_2^{c_1},$$

$$S_{1,3} = S_{1,3}'(w^{c_g})^\alpha (S_{2,3}')^{xM+y} \cdot \prod_{i=1}^{l-1}((w^{c_{u,i}})^{M_i}(w^{c_{h,i}}))^r ((w^{c_u})^M w^{c_h})^r w^{c_1},$$

$$S_{2,1} = S_{2,1}' \cdot (gw_1^{c_g})^r w_1^{c_2}, \ S_{2,2} = S_{2,2}' \cdot (w_2^{c_g})^r w_2^{c_2}, \ S_{2,3} = S_{2,3}' \cdot (w^{c_g})^r w^{c_2} \ ).$$

SAS.AggVerify$(AS, \mathbf{M}, \mathbf{PK})$: This algorithm takes as input a sequential aggregate signature AS on messages $\mathbf{M} = (M_1, \ldots, M_l)$ under public keys $\mathbf{PK} = (PK_1, \ldots, PK_l)$ where $PK_i = (u_i w_1^{c_{u,i}}, \ldots, \Omega_i)$. It first checks that any public key does not appear twice in $\mathbf{PK}$ and that any public key in $\mathbf{PK}$ has been certified. If these checks fail, then it outputs 0. If $l = 0$, then it outputs 1 if $S_1 = S_2 = 1$, 0 otherwise. It chooses a random exponent $t \in \mathbb{Z}_p$ and computes verification components as

$$C_{1,1} = \hat{g}^t, \ C_{1,2} = (\hat{g}^\nu)^t, \ C_{1,3} = (\hat{g}^{-\tau})^t,$$

$$C_{2,1} = \prod_{i=1}^{l}(\hat{u}_i^{M_i}\hat{h}_i)^t, \ C_{2,2} = \prod_{i=1}^{l}((\hat{u}_i^\nu)^{M_i}\hat{h}_i^\nu)^t, \ C_{2,3} = \prod_{i=1}^{l}((\hat{u}_i^{-\tau})^{M_i}\hat{h}_i^{-\tau})^t.$$

Next, it verifies that $\prod_{i=1}^{3} e(S_{1,i}, C_{1,i}) \cdot \prod_{i=1}^{3} e(S_{2,i}, C_{2,i})^{-1} \overset{?}{=} \prod_{i=1}^{l} \Omega_i^t$. If this equation holds, then it outputs 1. Otherwise, it outputs 0.

4.3   Security Analysis

Theorem 2. *The above SAS scheme is existentially unforgeable under a chosen message attack if the PKS scheme is existentially unforgeable under a chosen message attack.*

Proof. Suppose there exists an adversary $\mathcal{A}$ that forges the above SAS scheme with non-negligible advantage ϵ. A simulator $\mathcal{B}$ that forges the PKS scheme is first given: a challenge public key $PK_{PKS} = (gw_1^{c_g}, w_2^{c_g}, w^{c_g}, uw_1^{c_u}, \ldots, w^{c_h}, w_1, w_2, w, \hat{g}, \hat{g}^\nu, \hat{g}^{-\tau}, \hat{u}, \ldots, \hat{h}^{-\tau}, \Lambda, \Omega)$. Then $\mathcal{B}$ that interacts with $\mathcal{A}$ is described as follows:

Setup: $\mathcal{B}$ first constructs $PP = (gw_1^{c_g}, w_2^{c_g}, w^{c_g}, w_1, w_2, w, \hat{g}, \hat{g}^\nu, \hat{g}^{-\tau}, \Lambda)$ and $PK^* = (uw_1^{c_u}, \ldots, w^{c_h}, \hat{u}, \ldots, \hat{h}^{-\tau}, \Omega)$ from PK_{PKS}. Next, it initializes a certification list CL as an empty one and gives PP and PK^* to $\mathcal{A}$.

Queries: $\mathcal{A}$ may adaptively requests certification queries or sequential aggregate signature queries. If $\mathcal{A}$ requests the certification of a public key by providing a public key $PK_i = (u_i w_1^{c_{u,i}}, \ldots, \Omega_i)$ and its private key $SK_i = (\alpha_i, x_i, y_i)$, then $\mathcal{B}$ checks the private key and adds the key pair (PK_i, SK_i) to CL. If $\mathcal{A}$ requests a sequential aggregate signature by providing an aggregate-so-far AS' on messages $\mathbf{M}' = (M_1, \ldots, M_{l-1})$ under public keys $\mathbf{PK}' = (PK_1, \ldots, PK_{l-1})$, and a message M to sign under the challenge private key of PK^*, then $\mathcal{B}$ proceeds the aggregate signature query as follows:

1. It first checks that the signature AS' is valid and that each public key in $\mathbf{PK}'$ exits in CL.
2. It queries its signing oracle that simulates **PKS.Sign** on the message M for the challenge public key PK^* and obtains a signature σ.
3. For each $1 \le i \le l - 1$, it constructs an aggregate signature on message M_i using **SAS.AggSign** since it knows the private key that corresponds to PK_i. The result signature is an aggregate signature for messages $\mathbf{M}' \| M$ under public keys $\mathbf{PK}' \| PK^*$ since this scheme does not check the order of aggregation. It gives the result signature AS to $\mathcal{A}$.

Output: Finally, $\mathcal{A}$ outputs a forged aggregate signature $AS^* = (S_{1,1}^*, \ldots, S_{2,3}^*)$ on messages $\mathbf{M}^* = (M_1, \ldots, M_l)$ under public keys $\mathbf{PK}^* = (PK_1, \ldots, PK_l)$ for some l. Without loss of generality, we assume that $PK_1 = PK^*$. $\mathcal{B}$ proceeds as follows:

1. $\mathcal{B}$ first checks the validity of AS^* by using **SAS.AggVerify**. Additionally, the forged signature should not be trivial: the challenge public key PK^* must be in $\mathbf{PK}^*$, and the message M_1 must not be queried by $\mathcal{A}$ to the signature query oracle.
2. For each $2 \le i \le l$, it parses $PK_i = (u_i w_1^{c_{u,i}}, \ldots, \Omega_i)$ from $\mathbf{PK}^*$, and it retrieves the private key $SK_i = (\alpha_i, x_i, y_i)$ of PK_i from CL. It then computes

$$W_{1,1} = S_{1,1}^* \prod_{i=2}^{l} \left(g^{\alpha_j} (S_{2,1}^*)^{x_i M_i + y_i} \right)^{-1}, \quad W_{1,2} = S_{1,2}^* \prod_{i=2}^{l} \left((S_{2,2}^*)^{x_i M_i + y_i} \right)^{-1},$$

$$W_{1,3} = S_{1,3}^* \prod_{i=2}^{l} \left((S_{2,3}^*)^{x_i M_i + y_i} \right)^{-1}, \quad W_{2,1} = S_{2,1}^*, \quad W_{2,2} = S_{2,2}^*, \quad W_{2,3} = S_{2,3}^*.$$

3. It outputs $\sigma = (W_{1,1}, \ldots, W_{2,3})$ as a non-trivial forgery of the PKS scheme since it did not make a signing query on M_1.

The public parameters and the public key are correctly distributed, and the sequential aggregate signatures are also correctly distributed since this scheme does not check the order of aggregation. The result signature $\sigma = (W_{1,1}, \ldots, W_{2,3})$ of the simulator is a valid PKS signature on the message M_1 under the public key PK^* since it satisfies the following equation:

$$\prod_{i=1}^{3} e(W_{1,i}, V_{1,i}) \cdot \prod_{i=1}^{3} e(W_{2,i}, V_{2,i})^{-1}$$

$$= e(S_{1,1}^*, \hat{g}^t) \cdot e(S_{1,2}^*, \hat{g}^{\nu t}) \cdot e(S_{1,4}^*, \hat{g}^{-\tau t}) \cdot e(\prod_{i=2}^{l} g^{\alpha_i}, \hat{g}^t)^{-1}.$$

$$e(S_{2,1}^*, \prod_{i=2}^{l}(\hat{u}_i^{M_i}\hat{h}_i)^t)^{-1} \cdot e(S_{2,2}^*, \prod_{i=2}^{l}(\hat{u}_i^{M_i}\hat{h}_i)^{\nu t})^{-1} \cdot e(S_{2,3}^*, \prod_{i=2}^{l}(\hat{u}_i^{M_i}\hat{h}_i)^{-\tau t})^{-1}.$$

$$e(S_{2,1}^*, (\hat{u}^{M_1}\hat{h})^t)^{-1} \cdot e(S_{2,2}^*, (\hat{u}^{M_1}\hat{h})^{\nu t})^{-1} \cdot e(S_{2,3}^*, (\hat{u}^{M_1}\hat{h})^{-\tau t})^{-1}$$

$$= e(S_{1,1}^*, C_{1,1}) \cdot e(S_{1,2}^*, C_{1,2}) \cdot e(S_{1,3}^*, C_{1,3}) \cdot e(\prod_{i=2}^{l} g^{\alpha_i}, \hat{g}^t)^{-1}.$$

$$e(S_{2,1}^*, \prod_{i=1}^{l}(\hat{u}_i^{M_i}\hat{h}_i)^t)^{-1} \cdot e(S_{2,2}^*, \prod_{i=1}^{l}(\hat{u}_i^{M_i}\hat{h}_i)^{\nu t})^{-1} \cdot e(S_{2,3}^*, \prod_{i=1}^{l}(\hat{u}_i^{M_i}\hat{h}_i)^{-\tau t})^{-1}.$$

$$= \prod_{i=1}^{3} e(S_{1,i}^*, C_{1,i}) \cdot \prod_{i=1}^{3} e(S_{2,i}^*, C_{2,i})^{-1} \cdot e(\prod_{i=2}^{l} g^{\alpha_i}, \hat{g}^t)^{-1} = \prod_{i=1}^{l} \Omega_i^t \cdot \prod_{i=2}^{l} \Omega_i^{-t} = \Omega_1^t$$

where $\delta_i = x_i M_i + y_i$ and $\tilde{s}_2 = \sum_{i=2}^{l}(x_i M_i + y_i)s_1 + s_2$. This completes our proof.

4.4 Discussions

Multi-signature. A MS scheme can be easily constructed from our SAS scheme by moving some group elements in the public key to the public parameters. This scheme is also secure without random oracles under static assumptions and the signature size of this scheme is shorter than that of Lee et al.'s MS scheme [15].

5 Conclusion

In this paper, we improved the SAS scheme of Lee et al. [15] by reducing the size of aggregate signatures and similarly proved its security without random oracles under static assumptions. To reduce the size of signatures, we first devised a PKS scheme that supports multi-users and public re-randomization and proved its security using the dual system encryption technique. The proposed SAS scheme of this paper trades off signature size against public-key size compared with the scheme of Lee et al. since the signature size of our scheme decreases by two group elements but the public-key size increases by two group elements (but signatures are many and a public key is published once). Our techniques include lifting and randomization of verification parameters used in the previous scheme.

References

1. Ahn, J.H., Green, M., Hohenberger, S.: Synchronized aggregate signatures: new definitions, constructions and applications. In: ACM Conference on Computer and Communications Security, pp. 473–484 (2010)
2. Bellare, M., Namprempre, C., Neven, G.: Unrestricted aggregate signatures. In: Arge, L., Cachin, C., Jurdziński, T., Tarlecki, A. (eds.) ICALP 2007. LNCS, vol. 4596, pp. 411–422. Springer, Heidelberg (2007)

3. Boldyreva, A.: Threshold signatures, multisignatures and blind signatures based on the gap-diffie-hellman-group signature scheme. In: Desmedt, Y.G. (ed.) PKC 2003. LNCS, vol. 2567, pp. 31–46. Springer, Heidelberg (2002)
4. Boldyreva, A., Gentry, C., O'Neill, A., Yum, D.H.: Ordered multisignatures and identity-based sequential aggregate signatures, with applications to secure routing. Cryptology ePrint Archive, Report 2007/438 (2010), http://eprint.iacr.org/2007/438
5. Boneh, D., Franklin, M.: Identity-based encryption from the weil pairing. In: Kilian, J. (ed.) CRYPTO 2001. LNCS, vol. 2139, pp. 213–229. Springer, Heidelberg (2001)
6. Boneh, D., Gentry, C., Lynn, B., Shacham, H.: Aggregate and verifiably encrypted signatures from bilinear maps. In: Biham, E. (ed.) EUROCRYPT 2003. LNCS, vol. 2656, pp. 416–432. Springer, Heidelberg (2003)
7. Brogle, K., Goldberg, S., Reyzin, L.: Sequential aggregate signatures with lazy verification from trapdoor permutations. In: Wang, X., Sako, K. (eds.) ASIACRYPT 2012. LNCS, vol. 7658, pp. 644–662. Springer, Heidelberg (2012)
8. Canetti, R., Goldreich, O., Halevi, S.: The random oracle methodology, revisited. J. ACM 51(4), 557–594 (2004)
9. Fischlin, M., Lehmann, A., Schröder, D.: History-free sequential aggregate signatures. In: Visconti, I., De Prisco, R. (eds.) SCN 2012. LNCS, vol. 7485, pp. 113–130. Springer, Heidelberg (2012)
10. Gentry, C., Ramzan, Z.: Identity-based aggregate signatures. In: Yung, M., Dodis, Y., Kiayias, A., Malkin, T. (eds.) PKC 2006. LNCS, vol. 3958, pp. 257–273. Springer, Heidelberg (2006)
11. Gerbush, M., Lewko, A., O'Neill, A., Waters, B.: Dual form signatures: An approach for proving security from static assumptions. In: Wang, X., Sako, K. (eds.) ASIACRYPT 2012. LNCS, vol. 7658, pp. 25–42. Springer, Heidelberg (2012)
12. Itakura, K., Nakamura, K.: A public-key cryptosystem suitable for digital multisignatures. NEC Research & Development (71), 1–8 (1983)
13. Lee, K., Lee, D.H., Yung, M.: Aggregating cl-signatures revisited: Extended functionality and better efficiency. Cryptology ePrint Archive, Report 2012/562 (2012), http://eprint.iacr.org/2012/562
14. Lee, K., Lee, D.H., Yung, M.: Sequential aggregate signatures made shorter. Cryptology ePrint Archive (2013), http://eprint.iacr.org/
15. Lee, K., Lee, D.H., Yung, M.: Sequential aggregate signatures with short public keys: Design, analysis and implementation studies. In: Kurosawa, K., Hanaoka, G. (eds.) PKC 2013. LNCS, vol. 7778, pp. 423–442. Springer, Heidelberg (2013)
16. Lewko, A., Waters, B.: New techniques for dual system encryption and fully secure HIBE with short ciphertexts. In: Micciancio, D. (ed.) TCC 2010. LNCS, vol. 5978, pp. 455–479. Springer, Heidelberg (2010)
17. Lu, S., Ostrovsky, R., Sahai, A., Shacham, H., Waters, B.: Sequential aggregate signatures and multisignatures without random oracles. In: Vaudenay, S. (ed.) EUROCRYPT 2006. LNCS, vol. 4004, pp. 465–485. Springer, Heidelberg (2006)
18. Lysyanskaya, A., Micali, S., Reyzin, L., Shacham, H.: Sequential aggregate signatures from trapdoor permutations. In: Cachin, C., Camenisch, J.L. (eds.) EUROCRYPT 2004. LNCS, vol. 3027, pp. 74–90. Springer, Heidelberg (2004)
19. Micali, S., Ohta, K., Reyzin, L.: Accountable-subgroup multisignatures: extended abstract. In: Reiter, M.K., Samarati, P. (eds.) ACM Conference on Computer and Communications Security, pp. 245–254. ACM (2001)

20. Neven, G.: Efficient sequential aggregate signed data. In: Smart, N.P. (ed.) EUROCRYPT 2008. LNCS, vol. 4965, pp. 52–69. Springer, Heidelberg (2008)
21. Schröder, D.: How to aggregate the cl signature scheme. In: Atluri, V., Diaz, C. (eds.) ESORICS 2011. LNCS, vol. 6879, pp. 298–314. Springer, Heidelberg (2011)
22. Waters, B.: Efficient identity-based encryption without random oracles. In: Cramer, R. (ed.) EUROCRYPT 2005. LNCS, vol. 3494, pp. 114–127. Springer, Heidelberg (2005)

A   Security Proofs of Lemmas

A.1   The Proof of Lemma 1

The proof of this lemma is almost similar to the proof of Lemma 1 in [16] except that the public key is generated differently and the proof is employed in the PKS setting. Suppose there exists an adversary $\mathcal{A}$ that distinguishes between $\mathbf{G}_0$ and $\mathbf{G}_1$ with non-negligible advantage. A simulator $\mathcal{B}_1$ that solves Assumption 1 using $\mathcal{A}$ is given: a challenge tuple $D = ((p, \mathbb{G}, \hat{\mathbb{G}}, \mathbb{G}_T, e),$ $k, k^b, \hat{k}, \hat{k}^a, \hat{k}^b, \hat{k}^{ab^2}, \hat{k}^{b^2}, \hat{k}^{b^3}, \hat{k}^c, \hat{k}^{ac}, \hat{k}^{bc}, \hat{k}^{b^2c}, \hat{k}^{b^3}c)$ and T where $T = T_0 = \hat{k}^{ab^2c}$ or $T = T_1 = \hat{k}^{ab^2c+d}$. Then $\mathcal{B}_1$ that interacts with $\mathcal{A}$ is described as follows: $\mathcal{B}_1$ first chooses random exponents $\phi_2, A, B, \alpha \in \mathbb{Z}_p$, random values $y_g, y_u, y_h, y_w \in \mathbb{Z}_p$. It computes $w_1 = w^{\phi_1} = (k^b)^{y_w}, w_2 = w^{\phi_2} = k^{y_w\phi_2}, w = k^{y_w}$ by implicitly setting $\phi_1 = b$. It implicitly sets $c_g = -b/y_w + c'_g, c_u = -bA/y_w + c'_u, c_h = -bB/y_w + c'_h, \nu = a, \tau = b + a\phi_2$ and publishes a public key by selecting random values $c'_g, c'_u, c'_h \in \mathbb{Z}_p$ as

$$gw_1^{c_g} = k^{y_g}w_1^{c'_g}, \ w_2^{c_g} = (k^b)^{-b_2}w_2^{c'_g}, \ w^{c_g} = (k^b)^{-1}w^{c'_g},$$

$$uw_1^{c_u} = k^{y_u}w_1^{c'_u}, \ w_2^{c_u} = (k^b)^{-b_2A}w_2^{c'_u}, \ w^{c_u} = (k^b)^{-A}w^{c'_u},$$

$$hw_1^{c_h} = k^{y_h}w_1^{c'_h}, \ w_2^{c_h} = (k^b)^{-b_2B}w_2^{c'_h}, \ w^{c_h} = (k^b)^{-B}w^{c'_h}, \ w_1, \ w_2, \ w,$$

$$\hat{g} = \hat{k}^{b^2}\hat{k}^{y_g}, \ \hat{g}^{\nu} = \hat{k}^{ab^2}(\hat{k}^a)^{y_g}, \ \hat{g}^{-\tau} = (\hat{k}^{b^3}(\hat{k}^b)^{y_g}(\hat{k}^{ab^2})^{b_2}(\hat{k}^a)^{y_gb_2})^{-1},$$

$$\hat{u} = (\hat{k}^{b^2})^A\hat{k}^{y_u}, \ \hat{u}^{\nu} = (\hat{k}^{ab^2})^A(\hat{k}^a)^{y_u}, \ \hat{u}^{-\tau} = ((\hat{k}^{b^3})^A(\hat{k}^b)^{y_u}(\hat{k}^{ab^2})^{Ab_2}(\hat{k}^a)^{y_ub_2})^{-1},$$

$$\hat{h} = (\hat{k}^{b^2})^B\hat{k}^{y_h}, \ \hat{h}^{\nu} = (\hat{k}^{ab^2})^B(\hat{k}^a)^{y_h}, \ \hat{h}^{-\tau} = ((\hat{k}^{b^3})^B(\hat{k}^b)^{y_h}(\hat{k}^{ab^2})^{Bb_2}(\hat{k}^a)^{y_hb_2})^{-1},$$

$$\Lambda = e(k^{b^3}, \hat{k}^b) \cdot e(k^{b^2}, \hat{k})^{2y_g} \cdot e(k, \hat{k})^{y_g^2}, \ \Omega = \Lambda^{\alpha}.$$

It implicitly sets $g = k^{b^2}k^{y_g}, u = (k^{b^2})^A k^{y_u}, h = (k^{b^2})^B k^{y_h}$, but it cannot create these elements since k^{b^2} is not given. Additionally, it sets $f = k, \hat{f} = \hat{k}$ for the semi-functional signature and verification. $\mathcal{A}$ adaptively requests a signature for a message M. To response this sign query, $\mathcal{B}_1$ first selects random exponents $r, c'_1, c'_2 \in \mathbb{Z}_p$. It implicitly sets $c_1 = -b(\alpha + (AM + B)r)/y_w + c'_1, c_2 = -br_1/y_w + c'_2$ and creates a normal signature as

$$W_{1,1} = k^{y_g\alpha + (y_uM + y_h)r}(w_1)^{c'_1}, \ W_{1,2} = (W_{1,3})^{\phi_2}, \ W_{1,3} = (k^b)^{-(\alpha + (AM + B)r)}w^{c'_1},$$

$$W_{2,1} = k^{y_gr}(w_1)^{c'_2}, \ W_{2,2} = (W_{2,3})^{\phi_2}, \ W_{2,3} = (k^b)^{-r}w^{c'_2}.$$

Finally, $\mathcal{A}$ outputs a forged signature $\sigma^* = (W_{1,1}^*, \ldots, W_{2,3}^*)$ on a message M^* from $\mathcal{A}$. To verify the forged signature, $\mathcal{B}_1$ first chooses a random exponent $t \in \mathbb{Z}_p$ and computes verification components by implicitly setting $t = c$ as

$$V_{1,1} = \hat{k}^{b^2 c}(\hat{k}^c)^{y_g}, \quad V_{1,2} = T(\hat{k}^{ac})^{y_g}, \quad V_{1,3} = ((\hat{k}^{b^3 c})(\hat{k}^{bc})^{y_g}(T)^{\phi_2}(\hat{k}^{ac})^{y_g \phi_2})^{-1},$$

$$V_{2,1} = (\hat{k}^{b^2 c})^{AM^*+B}(\hat{k}^c)^{y_u M^* + y_h}, \quad V_{2,2} = (T)^{AM^*+B}(\hat{k}^{ac})^{y_u M^* + y_h},$$

$$V_{2,3} = ((\hat{k}^{b^3 c})^{AM^*+B}(\hat{k}^{bc})^{y_u M^* + y_h}(T)^{\phi_2(AM^*+B)}(\hat{k}^{ac})^{\phi_2(y_u M^* + y_h)})^{-1}.$$

Next, it verifies that $\prod_{i=1}^{3} e(W_{1,i}^*, V_{1,i}) \cdot \prod_{i=1}^{3} e(W_{2,i}^*, V_{2,i})^{-1} \overset{?}{=} \Omega^t$. If this equation holds, then it outputs 0. Otherwise, it outputs 1.

To finish this proof, we show that the distribution of the simulation is correct. We first show that the distribution using $D, T_0 = \hat{k}^{ab^2 c}$ is the same as $\mathbf{G}_0$. The public key is correctly distributed as

$$gw_1^{c_g} = (k^{b^2} k^{y_g})(k^{by_w})^{-b/y_w + c_g'} = k^{y_g} w_1^{c_g'},$$

$$uw_1^{c_u} = (k^{b^2 A} k^{y_u})(k^{by_w})^{-bA/y_w + c_u'} = k^{y_u} w_1^{c_u'},$$

$$hw_1^{c_h} = (k^{b^2 B} k^{y_h})(k^{by_w})^{-bB/y_w + c_h'} = k^{y_h} w_1^{c_h'}.$$

The simulator cannot create g, u, h since k^{b^2} is not given in the assumption, but it can create $gw_1^{c_g}, uw_1^{c_u}, hw_1^{c_h}$ since c_g, c_u, c_h can be used to cancel out k^{b^2}. The signature and the verification components are also correctly distributed since these are similar to the simulation in [16]. We next show that the distribution of the simulation using $D, T_1 = \hat{k}^{ab^2 c + d}$ is the same as $\mathbf{G}_1$. We only consider the distribution of the verification components since T is only used in the verification components. The difference between T_0 and T_1 is that T_1 additionally has $\hat{k}^d$. Thus $V_{1,2}, V_{1,3}, V_{2,2}, V_{2,3}$ that have T in the simulation additionally have $\hat{k}^d, (\hat{k}^d)^{\phi_2}, (\hat{k}^d)^{AM^*+B}, (\hat{k}^d)^{\phi_2(AM^*+B)}$ respectively. If we implicitly set $s_c = d, z_c = AM^* + B$, then the verification components of the forged signature are semi-functional since A and B are information-theoretically hidden to the adversary.

How to Share a Lattice Trapdoor: Threshold Protocols for Signatures and (H)IBE

Rikke Bendlin[1,*], Sara Krehbiel[2], and Chris Peikert[2,**]

[1] Department of Computer Science, Aarhus University
[2] School of Computer Science, Georgia Institute of Technology

Abstract. We develop secure *threshold* protocols for two important operations in lattice cryptography, namely, generating a hard lattice Λ together with a "strong" trapdoor, and sampling from a discrete Gaussian distribution over a desired coset of Λ using the trapdoor. These are the central operations of many cryptographic schemes: for example, they are exactly the key-generation and signing operations (respectively) for the GPV signature scheme, and they are the public parameter generation and private key extraction operations (respectively) for the GPV IBE. We also provide a protocol for trapdoor delegation, which is used in lattice-based hierarchical IBE schemes. Our work therefore directly transfers all these systems to the threshold setting.

Our protocols provide information-theoretic (i.e., statistical) security against adaptive corruptions in the UC framework, and they are robust against up to $\ell/2$ semi-honest or $\ell/3$ malicious parties (out of ℓ total). Our Gaussian sampling protocol is both noninteractive and efficient, assuming either a trusted setup phase (e.g., performed as part of key generation) or a sufficient amount of interactive but offline precomputation, which can be performed before the inputs to the sampling phase are known.

1 Introduction

A *threshold* cryptographic scheme [18] is one that allows any quorum of h out of ℓ trustees to jointly perform some privileged operation(s), but remains correct and secure even if up to some $t < h$ of the parties behave adversarially. For example, in a threshold signature scheme any h trustees can sign an agreed-upon message, and no t malicious players (who may even pool their knowledge and coordinate their actions) can prevent the signature from being produced, nor forge a valid signature on a new message. Similarly, a threshold encryption scheme requires at least h trustees to decrypt a ciphertext.

* Supported by the Danish National Research Foundation and The National Science Foundation of China (under the grant 61061130540) for the Sino-Danish Center for the Theory of Interactive Computation, within which part of this work was performed; and also from the CFEM research center (supported by the Danish Strategic Research Council). Part of this work was performed while visiting the Georgia Institute of Technology.
** Supported by the Alfred P. Sloan Foundation and the National Science Foundation under CAREER Award CCF-1054495. Any opinions, findings, and conclusions or recommendations expressed in this material are those of the author(s) and do not necessarily reflect the views of the National Science Foundation.

M. Jacobson et al. (Eds.): ACNS 2013, LNCS 7954, pp. 218–236, 2013.
© Springer-Verlag Berlin Heidelberg 2013

Threshold cryptography is very useful for both distributing trust and increasing robustness in systems that perform high-value operations, such as certificate authorities (CAs) or private-key generators in identity-based encryption (IBE) systems.

Desirable efficiency properties in a threshold system include: (1) efficient local computation by the trustees; (2) a minimal amount of interaction—i.e., one broadcast message from each party—when performing the privileged operations; and (3) key sizes and public operations that are independent of the number of trustees. For example, while it might require several parties to *sign* a message, it is best if the signature can be *verified* without even being aware that it was produced in a distributed manner.

Over the years many elegant and rather efficient threshold systems have been developed. To name just a few representative works, there are simple variants of the El-Gamal cryptosystem, Canetti and Goldwasser's [13] version of the CCA-secure Cramer-Shoup cryptosystem [17], and Shoup's [35] version of the RSA signature scheme. These systems, along with almost all others in the literature, are based on number-theoretic problems related to either integer factorization or the discrete logarithm problem in cyclic groups. As is now well-known, Shor's algorithm [34] would unfortunately render all these schemes insecure in a "post-quantum" world with large-scale quantum computers.

Lattice-based cryptography. Recently, *lattices* have been recognized as a viable foundation for quantum-resistant cryptography, and the past few years have seen the rapid growth of many rich lattice-based systems. A fruitful line of research, starting from the work of Gentry, Peikert and Vaikuntanathan (GPV) [22], has resulted in secure lattice-based hash-and-sign signatures and (hierarchical) identity-based encryption schemes [15,1], along with many more applications (e.g., [23,10,9,2]). All these schemes rely at heart on two nontrivial algorithms: the key-generation algorithm produces a lattice Λ together with a certain kind of "strong" trapdoor (e.g., a short basis of Λ) [3,6], while the signing/key-extraction algorithms use the trapdoor to randomly sample a short vector from a *discrete Gaussian distribution* over a certain coset $\Lambda + \mathbf{c}$, which is determined by the message or identity [22]. Initially, both tasks were rather complicated algorithmically, and in particular the Gaussian sampling algorithm involved several adaptive iterations, so it was unclear whether either task could be efficiently and securely distributed among several parties. Recently, however, both key generation and Gaussian sampling have been simplified and made more efficient and parallel [30,25]. This is the starting point for our work.

Our results. We give threshold protocols for the main nontrivial operations in lattice-based signature and (H)IBE schemes, namely: (1) generating a lattice Λ together with a strong trapdoor of the kind recently proposed in [25], (2) sampling from a discrete Gaussian distribution over a desired coset of Λ, and (3) delegating a trapdoor for a higher-dimensional extension of Λ. Since these are the only secret-key operations used in the signature and (H)IBE schemes of [22,15,1,25] and several other related works, our protocols can be plugged directly into all those schemes to distribute the signing algorithms and the (H)IBE private-key generators. In the full version of this paper we show how this is (straightforwardly) done for the simplest of these applications, namely, the GPV signature and IBE schemes [22]; other applications work similarly.

Our protocols have several desirable properties:

- They provide *information-theoretic* (i.e., statistical) security for *adaptive* corruptions. By information-theoretic security, we mean that the security of the key-generation and sampling protocols *themselves* relies on no computational assumption—instead, the application alone determines the assumption (usually, the Short Integer Solution assumption [4,26] for digital signatures, and Learning With Errors [32] for identity-based encryption). We work in a version of the universal composability (UC) framework [12], specialized to the threshold setting, and as a result also get strong security guarantees for protocols under arbitrary composition.
- They work for an optimal threshold of $h = t + 1$ for semi-honest adversaries, and $h = 2t + 1$ for active (malicious) adversaries. (Recall that h is the number of honest parties needed to successfully execute the protocol, and the robustness threshold t is an upper bound on the number of dishonest parties.)
- The public key and trapdoor "quality" (i.e., the width of the discrete Gaussian that can be sampled using the trapdoor; smaller width means higher quality) are essentially the same as in the standalone setting. In particular, their sizes are independent of the number of trustees; the individual shares of the trapdoor are the same size as the trapdoor itself; and the protocols work for the same lattice parameters as in the standalone setting, up to small constant factors.
- They have *noninteractive* and very efficient *online* phases (corresponding to the signing or key-extraction operations), assuming either (1) a setup phase in which certain shares are distributed by a trusted party (e.g., as part of key generation), or (2) the parties themselves perform a sufficient amount of interactive precomputation in an offline phase (without relying on any trusted party).

Regarding the final item, the trusted setup model is the one used by Canetti and Goldwasser [13] for constructing threshold chosen ciphertext-secure threshold cryptosystems: as part of the key-generation process, a trusted party also distributes shares of some appropriately distributed secrets to the parties, which they can later use to perform an *a priori* bounded number of noninteractive threshold operations. Or, in lieu of a trusted party, the players can perform some interactive precomputation (offline, before the desired coset is known) to generate the needed randomness. The downside is that this precomputation is somewhat expensive, since the only solution we have for one important step (namely, sampling shares of a Gaussian-distributed value over $\mathbb{Z}$) is to use somewhat generic information-theoretic multiparty computation tools. On the plus side, the circuit for this sampling task is rather shallow, with depth just slightly super-constant $\omega(1)$, so the round complexity of the precomputation is not very high. We emphasize that the expensive precomputation is executed offline, before the applications decides which lattice cosets will be sampled from, and that the online protocols remain efficient and non-interactive.

Our protocols rely on the very simple form of the new type of strong trapdoor recently proposed in [25], and the parallel and offline nature of recent standalone Gaussian sampling algorithms [30,25].[1] A key technical challenge is that the security of the

---

[1] In particular, it appears very difficult to implement, in a noninteractive threshold fashion, iterative sampling algorithms like those from [24,22] which use the classical trapdoor notion of a short basis.

sampling algorithms from [30,25] crucially relies on the secrecy of some intermediate random variables known as "perturbations." However, in order to obtain a noninteractive protocol we need the parties to publicly reveal certain information about these perturbations. Fortunately, we can show that the leaked information is indeed simulatable, and so security is unharmed. See Section 3 and in particular Lemma 1 for further details.

Open problems. In addition to simple, non-interactive protocols for discrete Gaussian sampling with trusted setup, the full version of this paper provides protocols that avoid both trusted setup and online interaction. These protocols are designed as follows: first, we give efficient protocols that use (offline) access to a functionality $\mathcal{F}_{\mathsf{SampZ}}$, which produces shares of Gaussian-distributed values over the integers $\mathbb{Z}$ (see Section 4 and the full version for details). Then, we show how to instantiate $\mathcal{F}_{\mathsf{SampZ}}$ using a (somewhat inefficient) interactive protocol using generic MPC techniques. It remains an interesting open problem to design protocols without trusted setup whose *offline precomputation* is efficient and/or non-interactive as well. An efficient realization of $\mathcal{F}_{\mathsf{SampZ}}$ would yield such a solution, but there may be other routes as well.

Another intriguing problem is to give a simple and noninteractive threshold protocol for inverting the LWE function $g_\mathbf{A}(\mathbf{s}, \mathbf{e}) = \mathbf{s}^t \mathbf{A} + \mathbf{e}^t \bmod q$ (for short error vector $\mathbf{e}$) using a shared trapdoor. We find it surprising that, while in the standalone setting this inversion task is conceptually and algorithmically much simpler than Gaussian sampling, we have not yet been able to find a simple threshold protocol for it.[2] Such a protocol could, for example, be useful for obtaining threshold analogues of the chosen ciphertext-secure cryptosystems from [29,25], without going through a generic IBE-to-CCA transformation [8].

Related work in threshold lattice cryptography. A few works have considered lattice cryptography in the threshold setting. For encryption schemes, Bendlin and Damgård [7] gave a threshold version of Regev's CPA-secure encryption scheme based on the learning with errors (LWE) problem [32]. Related work by Myers *et al.* [27] described threshold decryption for fully homomorphic cryptosystems. Xie *et al.* [36] gave a threshold CCA-secure encryption scheme from any lossy trapdoor function (and hence from lattices/LWE [31]), though its public key and encryption runtime grow at least linearly with the number of trustees. For signatures, Feng *et al.* [21] gave a threshold signature scheme where signing proceeds sequentially through each trustee, making the scheme highly interactive; also, the scheme is based on NTRUSign, which has been broken [28]. Cayrel *et al.* [16] gave a lattice-based threshold *ring* signature scheme, in which at least t trustees are needed to create an *anonymous* signature. In that system, each trustee has its own public key, and verification time grows linearly with the number of trustees. In summary, lattice-based threshold schemes to date have either been concerned with distributing the *decryption* operation in public-key cryptosystems, and/or have lacked key efficiency properties typically asked of threshold systems (which our protocols do

---

[2] We note that it is possible to give a threshold protocol using a combination of Gaussian sampling and trapdoor delegation [15,25], but it is obviously no simpler than Gaussian sampling alone.

enjoy). Also, other important applications such as (H)IBE have yet to be realized in a threshold manner.

Organization. The remainder of the paper is organized as follows. In Section 2 we recall the relevant background on lattices, secret sharing, and the UC framework. In Section 3 we review the standalone key-generation and discrete Gaussian sampling algorithms of [25], present our functionalities for these algorithms in the threshold setting, and show how these functionalities can be implemented efficiently and noninteractively using trusted setup. We additionally provide a functionality and protocol for trapdoor delegation. In Section 4 we remove the trusted setup assumption and show how to implement the key generation functionality. Due to space restrictions, we refer to the full version for implementations of the Gaussian sampling functionalities using offline interaction instead of trusted setup. The full version also details a simple example application of our protocols, namely, a threshold version of the GPV signature scheme [22] realizing the threshold signature functionality of [5].

2   Preliminaries

We denote the reals by $\mathbb{R}$ and the integers by $\mathbb{Z}$. For a positive integer ℓ, we let $[\ell] = \{1, \ldots, \ell\}$. A symmetric real matrix Σ is *positive definite*, written $\Sigma > 0$, if $\mathbf{z}^t \Sigma \mathbf{z} > 0$ for all nonzero $\mathbf{z}$. Positive definiteness defines a partial ordering on real matrices: we say that $\mathbf{X} > \mathbf{Y}$ if $\mathbf{X} - \mathbf{Y} > 0$. We say that $\mathbf{X}$ is a *square root* of a positive definite matrix Σ, written $\mathbf{X} = \sqrt{\Sigma}$, if $\mathbf{X}\mathbf{X}^t = \Sigma$. The largest singular value (also called spectral norm or operator norm) of a real matrix $\mathbf{X}$ is defined as $s_1(\mathbf{X}) = \max_{\mathbf{u} \neq \mathbf{0}} \|\mathbf{X}\mathbf{u}\| / \|\mathbf{u}\|$. For convenience, we sometime write a scalar s to mean the scaled identity matrix $s\mathbf{I}$, whose dimension will be clear from context.

2.1   Lattices and Gaussians

A *lattice* Λ is a discrete additive subgroup of $\mathbb{R}^m$ for some $m \geq 0$. In this work we are only concerned with full-rank integer lattices, which are subgroups of $\mathbb{Z}^m$ with finite index. Most recent cryptographic applications use a particular family of so-called *q-ary* integer lattices, which contain $q\mathbb{Z}^m$ as a sublattice for some integer q, which in this work will always be bounded by $\text{poly}(n)$. For positive integers n and q, let $\mathbf{A} \in \mathbb{Z}_q^{n \times m}$ be arbitrary, and define the full-rank m-dimensional q-ary lattice

$$\Lambda^\perp(\mathbf{A}) = \{\mathbf{z} \in \mathbb{Z}^m : \mathbf{A}\mathbf{z} = \mathbf{0} \bmod q\}.$$

For any $\mathbf{u} \in \mathbb{Z}_q^n$ admitting an integral solution $\mathbf{x} \in \mathbb{Z}^m$ to $\mathbf{A}\mathbf{x} = \mathbf{u} \bmod q$, define the coset (or shifted lattice)

$$\Lambda_\mathbf{u}^\perp(\mathbf{A}) = \Lambda^\perp(\mathbf{A}) + \mathbf{x} = \{\mathbf{z} \in \mathbb{Z}^m : \mathbf{A}\mathbf{z} = \mathbf{u} \bmod q\}.$$

We define the Gaussian function $\rho \colon \mathbb{R}^m \to (0, 1]$ as $\rho(\mathbf{x}) = \exp(-\pi\langle \mathbf{x}, \mathbf{x}\rangle) = \exp(-\pi\|\mathbf{x}\|^2)$. Generalizing to any nonsingular $\mathbf{B} \in \mathbb{R}^{m \times m}$, we define the Gaussian function with parameter $\mathbf{B}$ as

$$\rho_\mathbf{B}(\mathbf{x}) := \rho(\mathbf{B}^{-1}\mathbf{x}) = \exp\left(-\pi \cdot \mathbf{x}^t \Sigma^{-1} \mathbf{x}\right),$$

where $\Sigma = \mathbf{B}\mathbf{B}^t > 0$. Because $\rho_\mathbf{B}$ is distinguished only up to Σ, we usually refer to it as $\rho_{\sqrt{\Sigma}}$, and refer to Σ as its *covariance matrix*. For a lattice coset $\Lambda + \mathbf{c}$ and covariance matrix $\Sigma > 0$, the *discrete Gaussian distribution* $D_{\Lambda+\mathbf{c},\sqrt{\Sigma}}$ is defined to assign probability proportional to $\rho_{\sqrt{\Sigma}}(\mathbf{x})$ to each $\mathbf{x} \in \Lambda + \mathbf{c}$, and zero elsewhere. That is, $D_{\Lambda+\mathbf{c},\sqrt{\Sigma}}(\mathbf{x}) := \rho_{\sqrt{\Sigma}}(\mathbf{x})/\rho_{\sqrt{\Sigma}}(\Lambda + \mathbf{c})$. A discrete Gaussian is said to be *spherical* with parameter $s > 0$ if its covariance matrix is $s^2\mathbf{I}$.

In some of our proofs we use the notion of the *smoothing parameter* $\eta_\epsilon(\Lambda)$ of a lattice Λ [26], generalized to arbitrary covariances. For reasons associated with the smoothing parameter, throughout the paper we often attach a factor $\omega_n = \omega_n(n) = \omega(\sqrt{\log n})$ to Gaussian parameters $\sqrt{\Sigma}$ (or ω_n^2 to covariance matrices Σ), which represents an arbitrary fixed function that grows asymptotically faster than $\sqrt{\log n}$. In exposition we usually omit reference to these factors, but we always retain them where needed in formal expressions. The full version gives further background on lattices and Gaussians.

2.2 The GPV Schemes

As mentioned in the introduction, the two non-trivial algorithmic steps of many lattice-based cryptographic schemes are generating a lattice $\Lambda = \Lambda^\perp(\mathbf{A})$ together with a strong trapdoor $\mathbf{R}$, and sampling from discrete Gaussian distributions over a given coset of Λ. In Section 3, we give functionalities and protocols for these tasks in the threshold setting.

Here we briefly recall the well-known GPV signature scheme from [22], which uses these operations (GenTrap and SampleD), and serves as an immediate application of the present work. The scheme is parametrized by a security parameter n, modulus q, and message space $\mathcal{M}$, and it uses a hash function $H : \mathcal{M} \to \mathbb{Z}_q^n$ which is modeled as a random oracle. At a high level, $\mathsf{GenTrap}(n, q, m)$ (for sufficiently large m) generates a matrix $\mathbf{A} \in \mathbb{Z}_q^{n \times m}$ with distribution statistically close to uniform, together with a trapdoor $\mathbf{R}$. Using these, $\mathsf{SampleD}(\mathbf{A}, \mathbf{R}, \mathbf{u}, s)$ generates a Gaussian sample (for any sufficiently large parameter s) over the lattice coset $\Lambda_\mathbf{u}^\perp(\mathbf{A})$. The signature scheme consists of the following three algorithms:

- $\mathsf{KeyGen}(1^n)$: Let $(\mathbf{A}, \mathbf{R}) \leftarrow \mathsf{GenTrap}(n, q, m)$ and output verification key $vk = \mathbf{A}$ and signing key $sk = \mathbf{R}$.
- $\mathsf{Sign}(sk, \mu \in \mathcal{M})$: If (μ, σ) is already in local storage, output signature σ. Otherwise, let $\mathbf{x} \leftarrow \mathsf{SampleD}(\mathbf{A}, \mathbf{R}, H(\mu), s)$, store (μ, σ), and output signature $\sigma = \mathbf{x}$.
- $\mathsf{Verify}(vk, \mu, \sigma = \mathbf{x})$: If $\mathbf{A}\mathbf{x} = H(\mathbf{m})$ and $\mathbf{x}$ is sufficiently short, then accept; otherwise, reject.

See [22] for the proof of (strong) unforgeability under worst-case lattice assumptions. Another immediate application of the present work is the identity-based encryption (IBE) scheme of [22], where vk and sk above are the master public and secret keys, respectively, and signatures on identities are the secret keys for individual identities.

2.3 Secret Sharing

In this work we need to distribute secret lattice vectors among ℓ players so that any sufficiently large number of players can reconstruct the secret, but no group of $t < \ell$ or fewer players collectively get any information about the secret. Because a lattice Λ is an *infinite* additive group (and in particular is not a field), it is not immediately amenable to standard secret-sharing techniques like those of [33]. There is a rich theory of secret sharing for arbitrary additive groups and modules, e.g., [19,20]. We refer to the full version of this paper for secret sharing details, and simply note here that a variant of the Shamir secret sharing scheme has the desired properties.

Our notation is as follows: Let G be any finite abelian (additive) group. We denote player i's share of some value $v \in G$ by $[\![v]\!]^i$, and the tuple of all such shares by $[\![v]\!]$.

2.4 UC Framework

We frame our results in the Universal Composability (UC) framework [12,11]. In the UC framework, security is defined by considering a probabilistic polynomial-time (PPT) machine $\mathcal{Z}$, called the environment. In coordination with an adversary that may corrupt some of the players, $\mathcal{Z}$ chooses inputs and observes the outputs of a protocol executed in one of two worlds: a "real" world in which the parties interact with each other in some specified protocol π while a dummy adversary $\mathcal{A}$ (controlled by $\mathcal{Z}$) corrupts players and controls their interactions with honest players, and an "ideal" world in which the players interact directly with a *functionality* $\mathcal{F}$, while a simulator $\mathcal{S}$ (communicating with $\mathcal{Z}$) corrupts players and controls their interactions with $\mathcal{F}$. The views of the environment in these executions are respectively denoted $\mathsf{REAL}_{\pi,\mathcal{A},\mathcal{Z}}$ and $\mathsf{IDEAL}_{\mathcal{F},\mathcal{S},\mathcal{Z}}$, and the protocol is said to realize the functionality if these two views are indistinguishable. In this work we are concerned solely with statistical indistinguishability (which is stronger than the computational analogue), denoted by the relation $\overset{s}{\approx}$.

Definition 1. *We say that a protocol π statistically realizes a functionality $\mathcal{F}$ (or alternatively, is a UC-secure implementation of $\mathcal{F}$) if for any probabilistic polynomial-time (PPT) adversary $\mathcal{A}$, there exists a PPT simulator $\mathcal{S}$ such that for all PPT environments $\mathcal{Z}$, we have $\mathsf{IDEAL}_{\mathcal{F},\mathcal{S},\mathcal{Z}} \overset{s}{\approx} \mathsf{REAL}_{\pi,\mathcal{A},\mathcal{Z}}$.*

What makes this definition so strong and useful is the general *composition theorem* [12], which (informally) states that any UC-secure protocol remains secure under concurrent general composition. This allows for the modular design of functionalities and protocols which can be composed to produce secure higher-level protocols.

UC framework for threshold protocols. We consider a specialized case of the UC framework that is appropriate for modeling threshold protocols. All of our functionalities are called with a session ID of the form $sid = (\mathcal{P}, sid')$, where $\mathcal{P}$ is a set of ℓ parties representing the individual trustees in the threshold protocol. We prove security against t-limited adversaries, which may adaptively corrupt a bounded number t of the parties over the entire lifetime of a protocol. Corruptions can occur before or after any invoked protocol/functionality command, but not during its execution. At the time of corruption, the entire view of the player to that point (and beyond) is revealed to the adversary; in particular, we do not assume secure erasures. For robustness, we additionally require that when the environment issues a command to a functionality/protocol, it always does so for at least h honest parties in the same round.

In the case of semi-honest corruptions, namely when corrupted parties reveal their protocol traffic to the adversary but always execute the protocol faithfully, we prove security for $t < |\mathcal{P}|/2$ and $h = t + 1$. In the case of malicious corruptions, namely when corrupted parties send messages on behalf of the adversary that are not necessarily consistent with the protocol, we prove security for $t < |\mathcal{P}|/3$ and $h = 2t + 1$. These parameters come directly from the secrecy and robustness guarantees of the secret sharing scheme described in Section 2.3.

Many of our protocols require the parties to maintain and use consistent local states, corresponding to certain shared random variables that are consumed by the protocols. We note that synchronizing their local states may be nontrivial, if not every party is involved with executing every command. For this reason we assume some mechanism for coordinating local state, such as those like hashing suggested in [13], which deals with similar synchronization issues.

3   Threshold KeyGen, Gaussian Sampling, and Delegation

In this section, we present UC functionalities and protocols for generating a lattice with a shared trapdoor, for sampling from a coset of that lattice, and for securely delegating a trapdoor of a higher-dimensional extension of the lattice. As an example application of these functionalities, we describe threshold variants of the GPV signature and IBE schemes [22] in the full version. Other signature and (H)IBE schemes (e.g., [15,1,25]) can be adapted similarly (where delegation is needed for HIBE).

In Section 3.1 we recall the recent standalone (non-threshold) key generation and discrete Gaussian sampling algorithms of [25], which form the basis of our protocols. In Section 3.2 we present the two main functionalities $\mathcal{F}_{\text{KG}}$ (key generation) and $\mathcal{F}_{\text{GS}}$ (Gaussian sampling) corresponding to the standalone algorithms. We also define two lower-level "helper" functionalities $\mathcal{F}_{\text{Perturb}}$ and $\mathcal{F}_{\text{Correct}}$, and show how they can be realized noninteractively using either trusted setup or offline precomputation. In Section 3.3 we give an efficient noninteractive protocol that realizes $\mathcal{F}_{\text{GS}}$ using access to $\mathcal{F}_{\text{Perturb}}$ and $\mathcal{F}_{\text{Correct}}$. In Section 3.4 we give a functionality and protocol for trapdoor delegation.

Since key generation tends to be rare in applications, $\mathcal{F}_{\text{KG}}$ can be realized using trusted setup; alternatively, later in Section 4 we realize $\mathcal{F}_{\text{KG}}$ without trusted setup using some lower-level functionalities described there. We additionally realize $\mathcal{F}_{\text{Perturb}}$ and $\mathcal{F}_{\text{Correct}}$ with these and other lower-level functionalities in the full version of the paper.

3.1   Trapdoors and Standalone Algorithms

We recall the notion of a (strong) lattice trapdoor and associated algorithms recently introduced by Micciancio and Peikert [25]; see that paper for full details and proofs. Let n and q be positive integers and $k = \lceil \lg q \rceil$. Define the "gadget" vector $\mathbf{g} = (1, 2, 4, \dots, 2^{k-1}) \in \mathbb{Z}_q^k$ and matrix $\mathbf{G} := \mathbf{I}_n \otimes \mathbf{g}^t \in \mathbb{Z}_q^{n \times nk}$, the direct sum of n copies of $\mathbf{g}^t$. The k-dimensional lattice $\Lambda^\perp(\mathbf{g}^t) \subset \mathbb{Z}^k$, and hence also the nk-dimensional lattice $\Lambda^\perp(\mathbf{G})$, has smoothing parameter bounded by $s_{\mathbf{g}} \cdot \omega_n$, where $s_{\mathbf{g}} \leq \sqrt{5}$ is a known constant. There are efficient algorithms that, given any desired syndrome $u \in \mathbb{Z}_q$, sample from a discrete Gaussian distribution over the coset $\Lambda_u^\perp(\mathbf{g}^t)$ for any given parameter

$s \geq s_{\mathbf{g}} \cdot \omega_n$. Since $\Lambda^\perp(\mathbf{G}) \subset \mathbb{Z}^{nk}$ is the direct sum of n copies of $\Lambda^\perp(\mathbf{g}^t)$, discrete Gaussian sampling over a desired coset $\Lambda_{\mathbf{u}}^\perp(\mathbf{G})$ (with parameter $s \geq s_{\mathbf{g}} \cdot \omega_n$) can be done by concatenating n independent samples over appropriate cosets of $\Lambda^\perp(\mathbf{g}^t)$.

Definition 2 ([25]). *Let $m \geq nk$ be an integer and define $\bar{m} = m - nk$. For $\mathbf{A} \in \mathbb{Z}_q^{n \times m}$, we say that $\mathbf{R} \in \mathbb{Z}_q^{\bar{m} \times nk}$ is a trapdoor for $\mathbf{A}$ with tag $\mathbf{H}^* \in \mathbb{Z}_q^{n \times n}$ if $\mathbf{A} [\begin{smallmatrix} \mathbf{R} \\ \mathbf{I} \end{smallmatrix}] = \mathbf{H}^* \cdot \mathbf{G}$. The quality of the trapdoor is defined to be the spectral norm $s_1(\mathbf{R})$.*

Note that $\mathbf{H}^*$ is uniquely determined and efficiently computable from $\mathbf{R}$, because $\mathbf{G}$ contains the n-by-n identity as a submatrix. Note also that if $\mathbf{R}$ is a trapdoor for $\mathbf{A}$ with tag $\mathbf{H}^*$, then it is also a trapdoor for $\mathbf{A_H} := \mathbf{A} - [\mathbf{0} \mid \mathbf{HG}]$ with tag $\mathbf{H}^* - \mathbf{H} \in \mathbb{Z}_q^{n \times n}$.

The key-generation algorithm of [25] produces a parity-check matrix $\mathbf{A} \in \mathbb{Z}_q^{n \times m}$ together with a trapdoor $\mathbf{R}$ having desired tag $\mathbf{H}^*$. It does so by choosing (or being given) a uniformly random $\bar{\mathbf{A}} \in \mathbb{Z}_q^{n \times \bar{m}}$ and a random $\mathbf{R} \in \mathbb{Z}^{\bar{m} \times nk}$ having small $s_1(\mathbf{R})$, and outputs $\mathbf{A} = [\bar{\mathbf{A}} \mid \mathbf{H}^* \cdot \mathbf{G} - \bar{\mathbf{A}}\mathbf{R}]$. For sufficiently large $m \geq Cn \lg q$ (where C is a universal constant) and appropriate distribution of $\mathbf{R}$, the output matrix $\mathbf{A}$ is uniformly random, up to $\mathrm{negl}(n)$ statistical distance.

The discrete Gaussian sampling algorithm of [25] is an instance of the "convolution" approach from [30]. It works in two phases:

1. In the *offline* "perturbation" phase, it takes as input a parity-check matrix $\mathbf{A}$, a trapdoor $\mathbf{R}$ for $\mathbf{A}$ with some tag $\mathbf{H}^* \in \mathbb{Z}_q^{n \times n}$, and a Gaussian parameter $s \geq Cs_1(\mathbf{R})$ (where C is some universal constant). It chooses Gaussian perturbation vectors $\mathbf{p} \in \mathbb{Z}^m$ (one for each future call to the online sampling step) having non-spherical covariance $\Sigma_{\mathbf{p}}$ that depends only on s and the trapdoor $\mathbf{R}$.

2. In the *online* "syndrome correction" phase, it is given a syndrome $\mathbf{u} \in \mathbb{Z}_q^n$ and a tag $\mathbf{H} \in \mathbb{Z}_q^{n \times n}$. As long as $\mathbf{H}^* - \mathbf{H} \in \mathbb{Z}_q^{n \times n}$ is invertible, it chooses $\mathbf{z} \in \mathbb{Z}^{nk}$ having Gaussian distribution with parameter $s_{\mathbf{g}} \cdot \omega_n$ over an appropriate coset of $\Lambda^\perp(\mathbf{G})$, and outputs $\mathbf{x} = \mathbf{p} + [\begin{smallmatrix} \mathbf{R} \\ \mathbf{I} \end{smallmatrix}]\mathbf{z} \in \Lambda_{\mathbf{u}}^\perp(\mathbf{A_H})$, where $\mathbf{p}$ is a fresh perturbation from the offline step.

Informally, the perturbation covariance $\Sigma_{\mathbf{p}}$ of $\mathbf{p}$ is carefully designed to cancel out the trapdoor-revealing covariance of $\mathbf{y} = [\begin{smallmatrix} \mathbf{R} \\ \mathbf{I} \end{smallmatrix}]\mathbf{z}$, so that their sum has a (public) spherical Gaussian distribution. More formally, the output $\mathbf{x}$ has distribution within $\mathrm{negl}(n)$ statistical distance of $D_{\Lambda_{\mathbf{u}}^\perp(\mathbf{A_H}), s \cdot \omega_n}$, and in particular does not reveal any information about the trapdoor $\mathbf{R}$ (aside from an upper bound s on $s_1(\mathbf{R})$, which is public).

We emphasize that for security, it is essential that none of the intermediate values $\mathbf{p}, \mathbf{z}$ or $\mathbf{y} = [\begin{smallmatrix} \mathbf{R} \\ \mathbf{I} \end{smallmatrix}]\mathbf{z}$ be revealed, otherwise they could be correlated with $\mathbf{x}$ to leak information about the trapdoor $\mathbf{R}$ that could lead to an attack like the one given in [28].

3.2   Functionalities for Threshold Sampling

Ideal functionalities for threshold key generation and discrete Gaussian sampling are specified in Figure 1 and Figure 2, respectively; they internally execute the standalone algorithms described above.

Functionality $\mathcal{F}_{\mathrm{KG}}$

Generate: Upon receiving $(\mathrm{gen}, sid, \bar{\mathbf{A}} \in \mathbb{Z}_q^{n \times \bar{m}}, \mathbf{H}^* \in \mathbb{Z}_q^{n \times n}, z)$ from at least h honest parties in $\mathcal{P}$:
- Choose $\mathbf{R} \leftarrow D_{\mathbb{Z}, z \cdot \omega_n}^{\bar{m} \times nk}$, and compute a sharing $[\![\mathbf{R}]\!]$ over $\mathbb{Z}_q$. Let $\mathbf{A} = [\bar{\mathbf{A}} \mid \mathbf{H}^* \cdot \mathbf{G} - \bar{\mathbf{A}}\mathbf{R}]$.
- Send $(\mathrm{gen}, sid, \mathbf{A}, [\![\mathbf{R}]\!]^i)$ to each party i in $\mathcal{P}$, and $(\mathrm{gen}, sid, \mathbf{A}, \mathbf{H}^*, z)$ to the adversary.

Fig. 1. Key generation functionality

To realize $\mathcal{F}_{\mathrm{KG}}$ in the trusted setup model (as used in [13]) we can simply let the trusted party play the role of $\mathcal{F}_{\mathrm{KG}}$, because key generation is a one-time setup. Without trusted setup, we give in Section 4 a simple and efficient protocol that realizes $\mathcal{F}_{\mathrm{KG}}$ using a simple integer-sampling functionality $\mathcal{F}_{\mathrm{SampZ}}$. This in turn can be realized using general-purpose multiparty computation tools.

Functionality $\mathcal{F}_{\mathrm{GS}}$

Initialize: Upon receiving $(\mathrm{init}, sid, \mathbf{A}, [\![\mathbf{R}]\!]^i, \mathbf{H}^*, s, B)$ from at least h honest parties i in $\mathcal{P}$:
- Reconstruct $\mathbf{R}$ and store $sid, \mathbf{A}, \mathbf{R}, \mathbf{H}^*, s$, and B.
- Send (init, sid) to each party in $\mathcal{P}$, and $(\mathrm{init}, sid, \mathbf{A}, \mathbf{H}^*, s, B)$ to the adversary.

Sample: Upon receiving $(\mathrm{sample}, sid, \mathbf{H} \in \mathbb{Z}_q^{n \times n}, \mathbf{u} \in \mathbb{Z}_q^n)$ from at least h honest parties in $\mathcal{P}$, if $\mathbf{H}^* - \mathbf{H} \in \mathbb{Z}_q^{n \times n}$ is invertible and fewer than B calls to sample have already been made:
- Sample $\mathbf{x} \leftarrow D_{\Lambda_{\mathbf{u}}^{\perp}(\mathbf{A}_{\mathbf{H}}), s \cdot \omega_n}$ using the algorithm from [25] with trapdoor $\mathbf{R}$.
- Send $(\mathrm{sample}, sid, \mathbf{x})$ to all parties in $\mathcal{P}$, and $(\mathrm{sample}, sid, \mathbf{H}, \mathbf{u}, \mathbf{x})$ to the adversary.

Fig. 2. Gaussian sampling functionality

We realize $\mathcal{F}_{\mathrm{GS}}$ in Section 3.3. For modularity, the following subsections first define two lower-level functionalities $\mathcal{F}_{\mathrm{Perturb}}$ and $\mathcal{F}_{\mathrm{Correct}}$ (Figures 3 and 4), which respectively generate the perturbation and syndrome-correction components of the standalone sampling algorithm. We describe how these helper functionalities can be realized efficiently and noninteractively using trusted setup, and the full version of this paper realizes them without trusted setup. The $\mathcal{F}_{\mathrm{GS}}$, $\mathcal{F}_{\mathrm{Perturb}}$, and $\mathcal{F}_{\mathrm{Correct}}$ functionalities are all initialized with a bound B on the number of Gaussian samples that they will produce in their lifetimes. This is so that the trusted setup/offline precomputation phases of our protocols can prepare sufficient randomness to support noninteractive online phases. (If the bound B is reached, then the parties can just initialize new copies of $\mathcal{F}_{\mathrm{GS}}$, $\mathcal{F}_{\mathrm{Perturb}}$, $\mathcal{F}_{\mathrm{Correct}}$.)

Perturbation. Our perturbation functionality $\mathcal{F}_{\mathrm{Perturb}}$ (Figure 3) corresponds to the offline perturbation phase of the standalone sampling algorithm. The perturb command does not take any inputs, so it (and any realization) can be invoked offline, before the result is needed. With trusted setup, the functionality can be realized trivially by just precomputing and distributing (shares of) B samples in the initialization phase, which the parties then draw from in the online phase. Without trusted setup $\mathcal{F}_{\text{Perturb}}$ can be realized relatively efficiently using $\mathcal{F}_{\text{Samp}\mathbb{Z}}$ and some standard low-level MPC functionalities (for multiplication and blinding).

Note that $\mathcal{F}_{\text{Perturb}}$ distributes shares $[\![\mathbf{p}]\!]^i$ of a perturbation $\mathbf{p}$ to the players, which themselves do not reveal any information about $\mathbf{p}$ to the adversary, just as in the standalone Gaussian sampling algorithm. However, in order for the perturbation to be useful in the later online syndrome-correction phase, the parties will need to know (and so $\mathcal{F}_{\text{Perturb}}$ reveals) some partial information about $\mathbf{p}$, namely, the syndromes $\bar{\mathbf{w}} = [\bar{\mathbf{A}} \mid -\bar{\mathbf{A}}\mathbf{R}] \cdot \mathbf{p} \in \mathbb{Z}_q^n$ and $\mathbf{w} = [\mathbf{0} \mid \mathbf{G}] \cdot \mathbf{p} \in \mathbb{Z}_q^n$. This is the main significant difference with the standalone setting, in which these same syndromes are calculated internally but never revealed. Informally, Lemma 1 below shows that the syndromes are uniformly random (up to negligible error), and hence can be simulated without knowing $\mathbf{p}$. Furthermore, $\mathbf{p}$ will still be a usable perturbation even after $\bar{\mathbf{w}}, \mathbf{w}$ are revealed, because it has an appropriate (non-spherical) Gaussian parameter which sufficiently exceeds the smoothing parameter of the lattice coset to which it belongs. (This fact will be used later in the proof of security for our $\mathcal{F}_{\text{GS}}$ realization.)

Functionality $\mathcal{F}_{\text{Perturb}}$

Initialize: Upon receiving (init, $sid, \mathbf{A}_{-\mathbf{H}^*} = [\bar{\mathbf{A}} \mid -\bar{\mathbf{A}}\mathbf{R}], [\![\mathbf{R}]\!]^i, s, B$) from at least h honest parties i in $\mathcal{P}$:

- Reconstruct $\mathbf{R}$ to compute covariance matrix $\Sigma_{\mathbf{p}} = s^2 - s_{\mathbf{g}}^2 \begin{bmatrix} \mathbf{R} \\ \mathbf{I} \end{bmatrix} [\, \mathbf{R}^t \; \mathbf{I} \,]$ and store sid, $\mathbf{A}_{-\mathbf{H}^*}$, and $\Sigma_{\mathbf{p}}$.
- Send (init, sid) to all parties in $\mathcal{P}$, and (init, $sid, \mathbf{A}_{-\mathbf{H}^*}, s, B$) to the adversary.

Perturb: Upon receiving (perturb, sid) from at least h honest parties in $\mathcal{P}$, if fewer than B calls to perturb have already been made:

- Choose $\mathbf{p} \leftarrow D_{\mathbb{Z}^m, \sqrt{\Sigma_{\mathbf{p}}} \cdot \omega_n}$.
- Compute $\bar{\mathbf{w}} = \mathbf{A}_{-\mathbf{H}^*} \cdot \mathbf{p} \in \mathbb{Z}_q^n$ and $\mathbf{w} = [\mathbf{0} \mid \mathbf{G}] \cdot \mathbf{p} \in \mathbb{Z}_q^n$.
- Send (perturb, $sid, \bar{\mathbf{w}}, \mathbf{w}$) to the adversary, and receive back shares $[\![\mathbf{p}]\!]^i \in \mathbb{Z}_q^m$ for each currently corrupted party i in $\mathcal{P}$.
- Generate a uniformly random sharing $[\![\mathbf{p}]\!]$ consistent with the received shares.
- Send (perturb, $sid, [\![\mathbf{p}]\!]^i, \bar{\mathbf{w}}, \mathbf{w}$) to each party i in $\mathcal{P}$.

Fig. 3. Perturbation functionality

Lemma 1. *Let $\bar{\mathbf{A}} \in \mathbb{Z}_q^{n \times \bar{m}}$ be uniformly random for $\bar{m} = m - nk \geq n \lg q + \omega(\log n)$, and let*

$$\mathbf{B} = \begin{bmatrix} \bar{\mathbf{A}} & -\bar{\mathbf{A}}\mathbf{R} \\ & \mathbf{G} \end{bmatrix} = (\bar{\mathbf{A}} \oplus \mathbf{G}) \begin{bmatrix} \mathbf{I} & -\mathbf{R} \\ & \mathbf{I} \end{bmatrix} \in \mathbb{Z}_q^{2n \times (\bar{m} + nk)}$$

(where $\oplus$ denotes the direct sum). Then with all but $\text{negl}(n)$ probability over the choice of $\bar{\mathbf{A}}$, we have $\eta_\epsilon(\Lambda^\perp(\mathbf{B})) \leq \sqrt{5}(s_1(\mathbf{R}) + 1) \cdot \omega_n$ for some $\epsilon = \text{negl}(n)$.

In particular, for $\mathbf{p} \leftarrow D_{\mathbb{Z}^m, \sqrt{\Sigma_{\mathbf{p}}}}$ *where* $\sqrt{\Sigma_{\mathbf{p}}} \geq 6(s_1(\mathbf{R}) + 1) \cdot \omega_n \geq 2\eta_\epsilon(\Lambda^\perp(\mathbf{B}))$, *the syndrome* $\mathbf{u} = \begin{bmatrix} \bar{\mathbf{w}} \\ \mathbf{w} \end{bmatrix} = \mathbf{B}\mathbf{p} \in \mathbb{Z}_q^{2n}$ *is* $\mathrm{negl}(n)$-*far from uniform, and the conditional distribution of* $\mathbf{p}$ *given* $\mathbf{u}$ *is* $D_{\Lambda_{\mathbf{u}}^\perp(\mathbf{B}), \sqrt{\Sigma_{\mathbf{p}}}}$.

Proof. By [25, Lemma 2.4], we have $\eta_{\epsilon'}(\Lambda^\perp(\bar{\mathbf{A}})) \leq 2 \cdot \omega_n$ (with overwhelming probability) for some $\epsilon' = \mathrm{negl}(n)$. Also as shown in [25], we have $\eta_{\epsilon'}(\Lambda^\perp(\mathbf{G})) \leq \sqrt{5} \cdot \omega_n$. This implies that

$$\eta_\epsilon(\Lambda^\perp(\bar{\mathbf{A}} \oplus \mathbf{G})) \leq \sqrt{5} \cdot \omega_n$$

where $(1 + \epsilon) = (1 + \epsilon')^2$, and in particular $\epsilon = \mathrm{negl}(n)$.

Since $\mathbf{T} = \begin{bmatrix} \mathbf{I} & -\mathbf{R} \\ & \mathbf{I} \end{bmatrix}$ is unimodular with inverse $\mathbf{T}^{-1} = \begin{bmatrix} \mathbf{I} & \mathbf{R} \\ & \mathbf{I} \end{bmatrix}$, it is easy to verify that $\Lambda^\perp(\mathbf{B}) = \mathbf{T}^{-1} \cdot \Lambda^\perp(\bar{\mathbf{A}} \oplus \mathbf{G})$, and hence

$$\eta_\epsilon(\Lambda^\perp(\mathbf{B})) \leq s_1(\mathbf{T}^{-1}) \cdot \eta_\epsilon(\Lambda^\perp(\bar{\mathbf{A}} \oplus \mathbf{G})) \leq \sqrt{5}(s_1(\mathbf{R}) + 1) \cdot \omega_n.$$

Syndrome Correction. Our syndrome correction functionality $\mathcal{F}_{\text{Correct}}$ (Figure 4) corresponds to the syndrome-correction step of the standalone sampling algorithm. Because its output $\mathbf{y}$ must lie in a certain coset $\Lambda_{\mathbf{v}}^\perp(\mathbf{A})$, where $\mathbf{v}$ depends on the desired syndrome $\mathbf{u}$, the functionality must be invoked online. As indicated in the overview, the standalone algorithm samples $\mathbf{z} \leftarrow \Lambda_{\mathbf{v}}^\perp(\mathbf{G})$ and defines $\mathbf{y} = \begin{bmatrix} \mathbf{R} \\ \mathbf{I} \end{bmatrix} \mathbf{z}$. The functionality does the same, but outputs only shares of $\mathbf{y}$ to their respective owners. This ensures that no information about $\mathbf{y}$ is revealed to the adversary. (Note that the input $\mathbf{v}$ itself is not revealed in the standalone algorithm, but in our setting $\mathbf{v}$ is determined solely by public information like the tags $\mathbf{H}^*, \mathbf{H}$ and the syndromes $\bar{\mathbf{w}}, \mathbf{w}$ of the perturbation $\mathbf{p}$.)

Functionality $\mathcal{F}_{\text{Correct}}$

Initialize: Upon receiving $(\text{init}, sid, [\![\mathbf{R}]\!]^i, B)$ from at least h honest parties i in $\mathcal{P}$:
- Reconstruct $\mathbf{R}$ and store sid, $\mathbf{R}$, and B.
- Send (init, sid) to all parties in $\mathcal{P}$, and (init, sid, B) to the adversary.

Correct: Upon receiving $(\text{correct}, sid, \mathbf{v})$ from at least h honest parties in $\mathcal{P}$, if fewer than B calls to correct have already been made:
- Sample $\mathbf{z} \leftarrow D_{\Lambda_{\mathbf{v}}^\perp(\mathbf{G}), s_{\mathbf{g}} \cdot \omega_n}$ and compute $\mathbf{y} = \begin{bmatrix} \mathbf{R} \\ \mathbf{I} \end{bmatrix} \mathbf{z}$.
- Send $(\text{correct}, sid, \mathbf{v})$ to the adversary, receive shares $[\![\mathbf{y}]\!]^i \in \mathbb{Z}_q^m$ for each corrupted party i, and generate a uniformly random sharing $[\![\mathbf{y}]\!]$ consistent with these shares.
- Send $(\text{correct}, sid, [\![\mathbf{y}]\!]^i)$ to each party i in $\mathcal{P}$.

Fig. 4. Syndrome correction functionality

Realizing $\mathcal{F}_{\text{Correct}}$ with a noninteractive protocol relies crucially on the *parallel* and *offline* nature of the corresponding step of sampling a coset of $\Lambda^\perp(\mathbf{G})$ in the algorithm of [25]. In particular, we use the fact that without knowing $\mathbf{v}$ in advance, that algorithm can precompute *partial* samples for each of the $q = \mathrm{poly}(n)$ scalar values $v \in \mathbb{Z}_q$, and then linearly combine n such partial samples to answer a query for a full syndrome $\mathbf{v} \in \mathbb{Z}_q^n$.

In the trusted setup model, the protocol realizing $\mathcal{F}_{\text{Correct}}$ is as follows.

1. In the offline phase, a trusted party uses the trapdoor $\mathbf{R}$ (with tag $\mathbf{H}^*$) to distribute shares as follows. For each $j \in [n]$ and $v \in \mathbb{Z}_q$, the party initializes queues $Q^i_{j,v}$ for each party i, does the following B times, and then gives each of the resulting queues $Q^i_{j,v}$ to party i.
   - Sample $\mathbf{z}_{j,v} \leftarrow D_{\Lambda^\perp_v(\mathbf{g}^t), s_{\mathbf{g}} \cdot \omega_n}$.
   - Compute $\mathbf{y}_{j,v} = [\begin{smallmatrix} \mathbf{R} \\ \mathbf{I} \end{smallmatrix}] (\mathbf{e}_j \otimes \mathbf{z}_{j,v})$, where $\mathbf{e}_j \in \mathbb{Z}^n$ denotes the jth standard basis vector. Note that

   $$\mathbf{A}_{\mathbf{H}} \cdot \mathbf{y}_{j,v} = (\mathbf{H}^* - \mathbf{H})\mathbf{G} \cdot (\mathbf{e}_j \otimes \mathbf{z}_{j,v}) = (\mathbf{H}^* - \mathbf{H})(v \cdot \mathbf{e}_j),$$

   where as always, $\mathbf{A}_{\mathbf{H}} = \mathbf{A} - [\mathbf{0} \mid \mathbf{HG}]$ for any $\mathbf{H} \in \mathbb{Z}_q^{n \times n}$.
   - Generate a sharing for $\mathbf{y}_{j,v}$, and add $[\![\mathbf{y}_{j,v}]\!]^i$ to queue $Q^i_{j,v}$ for each party $i \in \mathcal{P}$.
2. In the online phase, upon receiving $(\text{correct}, \textit{sid}, \mathbf{v})$, each party i dequeues an entry $[\![\mathbf{y}_{j,v_j}]\!]^i$ from Q_{j,v_j} for each $j \in [n]$, and locally outputs $[\![\mathbf{y}]\!]^i = \sum_{j \in [n]} [\![\mathbf{y}_{j,v_j}]\!]^i$. Note that by linearity and the secret-sharing homomorphism, the shares $[\![\mathbf{y}]\!]^i$ recombine to some $\mathbf{y} = [\begin{smallmatrix} \mathbf{R} \\ \mathbf{I} \end{smallmatrix}] \mathbf{z} \in \mathbb{Z}^m$ for some Gaussian-distributed $\mathbf{z}$ of parameter $s_{\mathbf{g}} \cdot \omega_n$, such that $\mathbf{A}_{\mathbf{H}} \cdot \mathbf{y} = (\mathbf{H}^* - \mathbf{H}) \cdot \mathbf{v} \in \mathbb{Z}_q^n$.

The full version gives an efficient protocol for $\mathcal{F}_{\text{Correct}}$, without trusted setup. It populates the local queues $Q^i_{j,v}$ in the offline phase in a distributed manner, using the shares of $\mathbf{R}$ together with access to $\mathcal{F}_{\text{SampZ}}$ and standard share-blinding $\mathcal{F}_{\text{Blind}}$ and multiplication $\mathcal{F}_{\text{Mult}}$ functionalities. In short, it samples (shares of) the values $\mathbf{z}_{j,v}$ from the coset $\Lambda^\perp_v(\mathbf{g}^t)$ using $\mathcal{F}_{\text{SampZ}}$, the homomorphic properties of secret sharing, and $\mathcal{F}_{\text{Blind}}$. Then using $\mathcal{F}_{\text{Mult}}$ it computes (shares of) $\mathbf{y}_{j,v} = [\begin{smallmatrix} \mathbf{R} \\ \mathbf{I} \end{smallmatrix}] (\mathbf{e}_j \otimes \mathbf{z}_{j,v})$.

Legal Uses of the Functionalities. Putting the key-generation and Gaussian sampling operations into separate functionalities $\mathcal{F}_{\text{KG}}$ and $\mathcal{F}_{\text{GS}}$, and realizing $\mathcal{F}_{\text{GS}}$ using these helper functionalities, aids modularity and simplifies the analysis of our protocols. However, as a side effect it also raises a technical issue in the UC framework, since environments can in general provide functionalities with arbitrary inputs, even on behalf of honest users. The issue is that $\mathcal{F}_{\text{GS}}$, $\mathcal{F}_{\text{Perturb}}$, and $\mathcal{F}_{\text{Correct}}$ are all designed to be initialized with some common, *valid* state—namely, shares of a trapdoor $\mathbf{R}$ for a matrix $\mathbf{A}$ as produced by $\mathcal{F}_{\text{KG}}$ on valid inputs—but it might be expensive or impossible for the corresponding protocols to check the consistency and validity of those shares. Moreover, such checks would be unnecessary in the usual case where an application protocol, such as a threshold signature scheme, initializes the functionalities as intended.[3]

Therefore, we prove UC security for a restricted class of environments $\mathscr{Z}$ that always initialize our functionalities with valid arguments. In particular, environments in $\mathscr{Z}$ can instruct parties to instantiate $\mathcal{F}_{\text{KG}}$ only with arguments $\bar{\mathbf{A}}, z$ corresponding to a statistically secure instantiation of the trapdoor generator from [25]. Similarly, $\mathcal{F}_{\text{GS}}$ (and

---

[3] This issue is not limited to our setting, and can arise anytime the key-generation and secret-key operations of a threshold scheme are put into separate functionalities. We note that using "joint state" [14] does not appear to resolve the issue, because it only allows multiple instances of the *same* protocol to securely share some joint state.

$\mathcal{F}_{\text{DelTrap}}$) can be initialized only with a matrix $\mathbf{A}$, tag $\mathbf{H}^*$, and shares of a trapdoor $\mathbf{R}$ matching those of a prior call to the gen command of $\mathcal{F}_{\text{KG}}$, and with a sufficiently large Gaussian parameter $s \geq Cs_1 \cdot \omega_n$, where s_1 is a high-probability upper bound on $s_1(\mathbf{R})$ for the trapdoor $\mathbf{R}$ generated by $\mathcal{F}_{\text{KG}}$. (The functionalities $\mathcal{F}_{\text{Perturb}}$ and $\mathcal{F}_{\text{Correct}}$ are not intended for direct use by applications, but for proving the security of their realizations we also require that they be initialized using a prior output of $\mathcal{F}_{\text{KG}}$.) These restrictions are all described more formally in the full version of the paper.

We emphasize that these restrictions on the environment are not actually limiting in any meaningful way, since our functionalities are only intended to serve as subroutines in higher-level applications. As long as an application protocol obeys the above conditions in its use of $\mathcal{F}_{\text{KG}}$ and $\mathcal{F}_{\text{GS}}$ (and $\mathcal{F}_{\text{DelTrap}}$), the UC framework's composition theorem will still hold for the application itself, *without* any restriction on the environment.

3.3 Gaussian Sampling Protocol

Figure 5 defines a protocol π_{GS} that realizes the Gaussian sampling functionality $\mathcal{F}_{\text{GS}}$ in the $(\mathcal{F}_{\text{Perturb}}, \mathcal{F}_{\text{Correct}})$-hybrid model. Its sample command simply makes one call to each of the main commands of $\mathcal{F}_{\text{Perturb}}$ and $\mathcal{F}_{\text{Correct}}$, adjusting the requested syndrome as necessary to ensure that the syndrome of the final output is the desired one. (This is done exactly as in the standalone algorithm.) The shares of the perturbation $\mathbf{p}$ and syndrome-correction term $\mathbf{y}$ are then added locally and announced, allowing the players to reconstruct the final output $\mathbf{x} = \mathbf{p} + \mathbf{y}$. The security of π_{GS} is formalized in Theorem 1, and proved via the simulator $\mathcal{S}_{\text{GS}}$ in Figure 6.

An essential point is that given the helper functionalities, the protocol π_{GS} is completely *noninteractive*, i.e., no messages are exchanged among the parties, except when broadcasting their shares of the final output. Similarly, recall that our realizations of $\mathcal{F}_{\text{Perturb}}$ and $\mathcal{F}_{\text{Correct}}$ are also noninteractive, either when using trusted setup or offline pre-computation. In other words, in the fully realized sampling protocol, where the helper functionalities are replaced by their respective realizations, the parties can sample from any desired coset using only local computation, plus one broadcast of the final output shares. We emphasize that this kind of noninteractivity is nontrivial, because the number of possible cosets is exponentially large.

Theorem 1. *Protocol π_{GS} statistically realizes $\mathcal{F}_{\text{GS}}$ in the $(\mathcal{F}_{\text{Perturb}}, \mathcal{F}_{\text{Correct}})$-hybrid model for t-limited environments in $\mathscr{Z}$.*

Proof (sketch). Essentially, the simulator $\mathcal{S}_{\text{GS}}$ in Figure 6 just maintains consistent sharings of $\mathbf{p} = 0$ and $\mathbf{y} = \mathbf{x}$ for each call to sample, and releases player i's shares of these values (on behalf of $\mathcal{F}_{\text{Perturb}}$ and $\mathcal{F}_{\text{Correct}}$) upon corruption of player i. The fact that $\mathbf{p}$ and $\mathbf{y}$ in $\mathcal{S}_{\text{GS}}$ are from incorrect distributions is not detectable (even statistically) by the environment $\mathcal{Z}$, because it sees at most t shares of each, and the shares are consistent with announced shares of $\mathbf{x} = \mathbf{p} + \mathbf{y}$.

The only other significant issues relate to (1) the syndromes $\bar{\mathbf{w}}, \mathbf{w}$ output publicly by $\mathcal{F}_{\text{Perturb}}$ in the $(\mathcal{F}_{\text{Perturb}}, \mathcal{F}_{\text{Correct}})$-hybrid world, versus the simulator's choices of those values (on behalf of $\mathcal{F}_{\text{Perturb}}$) in the ideal world; and (2) the distribution (conditioned

---

Protocol π_{GS} in the $(\mathcal{F}_{Perturb}, \mathcal{F}_{Correct})$-hybrid model

Initialize: On input $(\text{init}, sid, \mathbf{A}, [\![\mathbf{R}]\!]^i, \mathbf{H}^*, s, B)$, party i stores $\mathbf{H}^*$, calls $\mathcal{F}_{Perturb}(\text{init}, sid, \mathbf{A}_{-\mathbf{H}^*}, [\![\mathbf{R}]\!]^i, s, B)$ and $\mathcal{F}_{Correct}(\text{init}, sid, [\![\mathbf{R}]\!]^i, B)$, and outputs (init, sid).

Sample: On input $(\text{sample}, sid, \mathbf{H}, \mathbf{u})$, if $\mathbf{H}^* - \mathbf{H} \in \mathbb{Z}_q^{n \times n}$ is invertible, and if fewer than B calls to sample have already been made, then party i does:

- Call $\mathcal{F}_{Perturb}(\text{perturb}, sid)$ and receive $(\text{perturb}, sid, [\![\mathbf{p}]\!]^i, \bar{\mathbf{w}}, \mathbf{w})$.
- Compute $\mathbf{v} = (\mathbf{H}^* - \mathbf{H})^{-1}(\mathbf{u} - \bar{\mathbf{w}}) - \mathbf{w} \in \mathbb{Z}_q^n$.
- Call $\mathcal{F}_{Correct}(\text{correct}, sid, \mathbf{v})$ and receive $(\text{correct}, sid, [\![\mathbf{y}]\!]^i)$.
- Broadcast $[\![\mathbf{x}]\!]^i = [\![\mathbf{p}]\!]^i + [\![\mathbf{y}]\!]^i$ and reconstruct $\mathbf{x} = \mathbf{p} + \mathbf{y}$.
- Output $(\text{sample}, sid, \mathbf{x})$.

Fig. 5. Gaussian sampling protocol

Simulator $\mathcal{S}_{GS}$

Initialize: Upon receiving $(\text{init}, sid, \mathbf{A}, \mathbf{H}^*, s, B)$ from $\mathcal{F}_{GS}$, reveal to $\mathcal{Z}$ (init, sid) as outputs of both $\mathcal{F}_{Perturb}$ and $\mathcal{F}_{Correct}$ to each currently corrupted party and any party that is corrupted in the future.

Sample: Upon receiving $(\text{sample}, sid, \mathbf{H}, \mathbf{u}, \mathbf{x})$ from $\mathcal{F}_{GS}$:

- Choose uniform and independent $\bar{\mathbf{w}}, \mathbf{w} \in \mathbb{Z}_q^n$ and compute $\mathbf{v} = (\mathbf{H}^* - \mathbf{H})^{-1}(\mathbf{u} - \bar{\mathbf{w}}) - \mathbf{w} \in \mathbb{Z}_q^n$.
- On behalf of $\mathcal{F}_{Perturb}$, send $(\text{perturb}, sid, \bar{\mathbf{w}}, \mathbf{w})$ to $\mathcal{Z}$ and receive back shares $[\![\mathbf{p}]\!]^i$ for each currently corrupted party i in $\mathcal{P}$. Generate a uniformly random sharing $[\![\mathbf{p}]\!]$ of $\mathbf{p} = \mathbf{0}$ consistent with these shares. Send $(\text{perturb}, sid, [\![\mathbf{p}]\!]^i, \bar{\mathbf{w}}, \mathbf{w})$ to each corrupted party i in $\mathcal{P}$ on behalf of $\mathcal{F}_{Perturb}$.
- On behalf of $\mathcal{F}_{Correct}$, send $(\text{correct}, sid, \mathbf{v})$ to $\mathcal{Z}$ and receive back shares $[\![\mathbf{y}]\!]^i$ for each currently corrupted party i in $\mathcal{P}$. Generate a uniformly random sharing $[\![\mathbf{y}]\!]$ of $\mathbf{y} = \mathbf{x}$ consistent with these shares. Send $(\text{correct}, sid, [\![\mathbf{y}]\!]^i)$ to each corrupted party i in $\mathcal{P}$ on behalf of $\mathcal{F}_{Correct}$.
- Broadcast $[\![\mathbf{x}]\!]^i = [\![\mathbf{p}]\!]^i + [\![\mathbf{y}]\!]^i$ on behalf of each honest party i.

Corruption: When $\mathcal{Z}$ requests to corrupt party i, for each previous call to sample, reveal the corresponding messages $(\text{perturb}, sid, [\![\mathbf{p}]\!]^i, \bar{\mathbf{w}}, \mathbf{w})$ and $(\text{correct}, sid, [\![\mathbf{y}]\!]^i)$ to party i on behalf of $\mathcal{F}_{Perturb}$ and $\mathcal{F}_{Correct}$, respectively.

Fig. 6. Simulator for π_{GS}

---

on any fixed $\bar{\mathbf{w}}, \mathbf{w})$ of the final output $\mathbf{x}$ in both worlds. For item (1), as proved in Lemma 1, in the hybrid world the syndromes $\bar{\mathbf{w}}, \mathbf{w}$ are jointly uniform and independent (up to negligible statistical distance) over the choice of $\mathbf{p}$ by $\mathcal{F}_{Perturb}$, just as they are when produced by the simulator. Moreover, conditioned on any fixed values of $\bar{\mathbf{w}}, \mathbf{w}$, the distribution of $\mathbf{p}$ in the hybrid world is a discrete Gaussian with covariance $\Sigma_{\mathbf{p}}$ over a certain lattice coset $\Lambda_{\mathbf{u}}^{\perp}(\mathbf{B})$, and the actual value of $\mathbf{p}$ from this distribution is perfectly hidden by the secret-sharing scheme.

For item (2), the above facts imply that in the hybrid world, $\mathbf{x} = \mathbf{p} + \mathbf{y}$ has spherical discrete Gaussian distribution $D_{\Lambda_{\mathbf{u}}^{\perp}(\mathbf{A_H}), s}$, just as the output $\mathbf{x}$ of $\mathcal{F}_{GS}$ does in the ideal world (up to negligible statistical error in both cases). The proof is almost word-for-word identical to that of the "convolution lemma" from [25], which guarantees the correctness of the standalone sampling algorithm (as run by $\mathcal{F}_{GS}$ in the ideal world). The only slight difference is that in the hybrid world, $\mathbf{p}$'s distribution (conditioned on any fixed values of $\bar{\mathbf{w}}, \mathbf{w}$) is a discrete Gaussian with parameter $\sqrt{\Sigma_{\mathbf{p}}}$ over a fixed coset of $\Lambda^{\perp}(\mathbf{B})$, instead of over $\mathbb{Z}^m$ as in the standalone algorithm. Fortunately, Lemma 1 says that $\sqrt{\Sigma_{\mathbf{p}}} \geq 2\eta_{\epsilon}(\Lambda^{\perp}(\mathbf{B}))$, and this is enough to adapt the proof from [25] to the different distribution of $\mathbf{p}$.

Finally, by the homomorphic properties of secret sharing, the shares $[\![\mathbf{p}]\!]^i + [\![\mathbf{y}]\!]^i$ announced by the honest parties are jointly distributed exactly as a fresh sharing of $\mathbf{x}$ as produced by the simulator. We conclude that the hybrid and real views are statistically indistinguishable, as desired.

3.4 Trapdoor Delegation

Here we sketch a straightforward use of the above protocols to do distributed trapdoor delegation, which is used in hierarchical IBE schemes. Due to space restrictions, we leave the formal definition of a trapdoor delegation functionality, protocol, and proof of security to the full version of the paper.

The functionality $\mathcal{F}_{\text{DelTrap}}$ corresponds to the algorithm DelTrap in [25] for delegating a lattice trapdoor. That algorithm works as follows: given a trapdoor $\mathbf{R}$ for some $\mathbf{A} \in \mathbb{Z}_q^{n \times m}$, and an extension $\mathbf{A}' = [\mathbf{A_H} | \mathbf{A_1}] \in \mathbb{Z}_q^{n \times (m+nk)}$ (where $\mathbf{A_H} = \mathbf{A} - [\mathbf{0} \mid \mathbf{HG}]$ as always) and tag $\mathbf{H}' \in \mathbb{Z}_q^{n \times n}$, it outputs a trapdoor $\mathbf{R}'$ for $\mathbf{A}'$ with tag $\mathbf{H}'$, where the distribution of $\mathbf{R}'$ is Gaussian (and in particular is independent of $\mathbf{R}$). It does this simply by sampling Gaussian columns of $\mathbf{R}'$ to satisfy the relation $\mathbf{A_H} \cdot \mathbf{R}' = \mathbf{H}' \cdot \mathbf{G} - \mathbf{A_1}$. In the threshold setting, where the parties have a sharing of the trapdoor $\mathbf{R}$, a distributed protocol for this process is trivial in the $\mathcal{F}_{GS}$-hybrid model: the parties simply use $\mathcal{F}_{GS}$ to sample the columns of $\mathbf{R}'$, using the public columns of $\mathbf{H}' \cdot \mathbf{G} - \mathbf{A_1}$ as the desired syndromes.

4   Key Generation without Trusted Setup

Here we show how to implement the key-generation functionality $\mathcal{F}_{KG}$ without any trusted setup, instead using access to two low-level functionalities $\mathcal{F}_{\text{Blind}}$ and $\mathcal{F}_{\text{SampZ}}$. Informally, $\mathcal{F}_{\text{Blind}}$ takes shares of some value and returns to each party a fresh sharing of the same value, and $\mathcal{F}_{\text{SampZ}}$ distributes shares of a discrete Gaussian-distributed value over the integer lattice $\mathbb{Z}$ (or equivalently, $\mathbb{Z}^{h \times w}$ for some $h, w \geq 1$). The full definitions of these functionalities, which we use for realizing other functionalities without trusted setup, are given in the full version of the paper along with descriptions of interactive protocols realizing them offline. A simplified version of $\mathcal{F}_{\text{SampZ}}$ that is sufficient for realizing $\mathcal{F}_{KG}$ is given in Figure 7.

The protocol π_{KG} realizing $\mathcal{F}_{KG}$ in the $(\mathcal{F}_{\text{SampZ}}, \mathcal{F}_{\text{Blind}})$-hybrid model is straightforward given the homomorphic properties of the secret-sharing scheme and the simple operation of the standalone trapdoor generator, which just multiplies a public uniform matrix $\bar{\mathbf{A}}$ with a secret Gaussian-distributed matrix $\mathbf{R}$. The parties get shares

---

Functionality $\mathcal{F}_{\mathrm{Samp\mathbb{Z}}}$

Sample: Upon receiving (sample, $sid, h \times w, z, d$) from at least h honest parties in $\mathcal{P}$:
- Sample $\mathbf{X} \leftarrow D_{\mathbb{Z}, z \cdot \omega_n}^{h \times w}$ and generate a fresh sharing $[\![\mathbf{X}]\!]$ over $\mathbb{Z}_{q^d}$.
- Send (sample, $sid, [\![\mathbf{X}]\!]^i$) to each party i in $\mathcal{P}$ and (sample, $sid, h \times w, z, d$) to the adversary.

Fig. 7. Integer sampling functionality

of a Gaussian-distributed trapdoor $\mathbf{R}$ using $\mathcal{F}_{\mathrm{Samp\mathbb{Z}}}$, then announce *blinded* shares of $\mathbf{A}_1 = -\bar{\mathbf{A}}\mathbf{R} \bmod q$ and reconstruct $\mathbf{A}_1$ to determine the public key $\mathbf{A} = [\bar{\mathbf{A}} \mid \mathbf{A}_1]$. The blinding is needed so that the announced shares reveal only $\mathbf{A}_1$, and not anything more about the honest parties' shares $[\![\mathbf{R}]\!]^i$ themselves. The formal protocol π_{KG} is given in Figure 8.

Protocol π_{KG} in the $(\mathcal{F}_{\mathrm{Samp\mathbb{Z}}}, \mathcal{F}_{\mathrm{Blind}})$-hybrid model

Generate: On input (gen, $sid, \bar{\mathbf{A}} \in \mathbb{Z}_q^{n \times \bar{m}}, \mathbf{H}^* \in \mathbb{Z}_q^{n \times n}, z$), party i does:
- Call $\mathcal{F}_{\mathrm{Samp\mathbb{Z}}}$(sample, $sid, \bar{m} \times nk, z, 1$) and receive (sample, $sid, [\![\mathbf{R}]\!]^i$).
- Call $\mathcal{F}_{\mathrm{Blind}}$(blind, $sid, -\bar{\mathbf{A}}[\![\mathbf{R}]\!]^i$) and receive (blind, $sid, [\![\mathbf{A}_1]\!]^i$).
- Broadcast $[\![\mathbf{A}_1]\!]^i$ and reconstruct $\mathbf{A}_1 = -\bar{\mathbf{A}}\mathbf{R}$ from the announced shares.
- Output (gen, $sid, \mathbf{A} = [\bar{\mathbf{A}} \mid \mathbf{H}^* \cdot \mathbf{G} + \mathbf{A}_1], [\![\mathbf{R}]\!]^i$).

Fig. 8. Key generation protocol

The announced (blinded) shares $-\bar{\mathbf{A}}[\![\mathbf{R}]\!]^i$ form a uniformly random (and independent of the honest parties' outputs $[\![\mathbf{R}]\!]^i$) sharing of $\mathbf{A}_1 = -\bar{\mathbf{A}}\mathbf{R}$. This is the heart of the security analysis; a simulator for demonstrating security is given in the full version.

Theorem 2. *Protocol π_{KG} statistically realizes $\mathcal{F}_{KG}$ in the $(\mathcal{F}_{Samp\mathbb{Z}}, \mathcal{F}_{Blind})$-hybrid model for t-limited environments in $\mathscr{L}$.*

References

1. Agrawal, S., Boneh, D., Boyen, X.: Efficient lattice (H)IBE in the standard model. In: Gilbert, H. (ed.) EUROCRYPT 2010. LNCS, vol. EUROCRYPT, pp. 553–572. Springer, Heidelberg (2010)
2. Agrawal, S., Freeman, D.M., Vaikuntanathan, V.: Functional encryption for inner product predicates from learning with errors. In: Lee, D.H., Wang, X. (eds.) ASIACRYPT 2011. LNCS, vol. 7073, pp. 21–40. Springer, Heidelberg (2011)
3. Ajtai, M.: Generating hard instances of the short basis problem. In: Wiedermann, J., Van Emde Boas, P., Nielsen, M. (eds.) ICALP 1999. LNCS, vol. 1644, pp. 1–9. Springer, Heidelberg (1999)
4. Ajtai, M.: Generating hard instances of lattice problems. Quaderni di Matematica 13, 1–32 (2004); Preliminary version in STOC 1996

5. Almansa, J.F., Damgård, I.B., Nielsen, J.B.: Simplified threshold RSA with adaptive and proactive security. In: Vaudenay, S. (ed.) EUROCRYPT 2006. LNCS, vol. 4004, pp. 593–611. Springer, Heidelberg (2006)

6. Alwen, J., Peikert, C.: Generating shorter bases for hard random lattices. Theory of Computing Systems 48(3), 535–553 (2011); Preliminary version in STACS 2009

7. Bendlin, R., Damgård, I.: Threshold decryption and zero-knowledge proofs for lattice-based cryptosystems. In: Micciancio, D. (ed.) TCC 2010. LNCS, vol. 5978, pp. 201–218. Springer, Heidelberg (2010)

8. Boneh, D., Canetti, R., Halevi, S., Katz, J.: Chosen-ciphertext security from identity-based encryption. SIAM J. Comput. 36(5), 1301–1328 (2007)

9. Boneh, D., Freeman, D.M.: Homomorphic signatures for polynomial functions. In: Paterson, K.G. (ed.) EUROCRYPT 2011. LNCS, vol. 6632, pp. 149–168. Springer, Heidelberg (2011)

10. Boneh, D., Freeman, D.M.: Linearly homomorphic signatures over binary fields and new tools for lattice-based signatures. In: Public Key Cryptography, pp. 1–16 (2011)

11. Canetti, R.: Universally composable security: A new paradigm for cryptographic protocols. Cryptology ePrint Archive, Report 2000/067 (2000), http://eprint.iacr.org/

12. Canetti, R.: Universally composable security: A new paradigm for cryptographic protocols. In: FOCS, pp. 136–145 (2001)

13. Canetti, R., Goldwasser, S.: An efficient *threshold* public key cryptosystem secure against adaptive chosen ciphertext attack. In: Stern, J. (ed.) EUROCRYPT 1999. LNCS, vol. 1592, pp. 90–106. Springer, Heidelberg (1999)

14. Canetti, R., Rabin, T.: Universal composition with joint state. In: Boneh, D. (ed.) CRYPTO 2003. LNCS, vol. 2729, pp. 265–281. Springer, Heidelberg (2003)

15. Cash, D., Hofheinz, D., Kiltz, E., Peikert, C.: Bonsai trees, or how to delegate a lattice basis. In: Gilbert, H. (ed.) EUROCRYPT 2010. LNCS, vol. 6110, pp. 523–552. Springer, Heidelberg (2010)

16. Cayrel, P.-L., Lindner, R., Rückert, M., Silva, R.: A lattice-based threshold ring signature scheme. In: Abdalla, M., Barreto, P.S.L.M. (eds.) LATINCRYPT 2010. LNCS, vol. LATIN-CRYPT, pp. 255–272. Springer, Heidelberg (2010)

17. Cramer, R., Shoup, V.: A practical public key cryptosystem provably secure against adaptive chosen ciphertext attack. In: Krawczyk, H. (ed.) CRYPTO 1998. LNCS, vol. 1462, pp. 13–25. Springer, Heidelberg (1998)

18. Desmedt, Y.G., Frankel, Y.: Threshold cryptosystems. In: Brassard, G. (ed.) CRYPTO 1989. LNCS, vol. 435, pp. 307–315. Springer, Heidelberg (1990)

19. Desmedt, Y., Frankel, Y.: Perfect homomorphic zero-knowledge threshold schemes over any finite abelian group. SIAM J. Discrete Math. 7(4), 667–679 (1994)

20. Fehr, S.: Span programs over rings and how to share a secret from a module. Master's thesis, ETH Zurich, Institute for Theoretical Computer Science (1998)

21. Feng, T., Gao, Y., Ma, J.: Changeable threshold signature scheme based on lattice theory. In: International Conference on E-Business and E-Government, pp. 1311–1315 (2010)

22. Gentry, C., Peikert, C., Vaikuntanathan, V.: Trapdoors for hard lattices and new cryptographic constructions. In: STOC, pp. 197–206 (2008)

23. Dov Gordon, S., Katz, J., Vaikuntanathan, V.: A group signature scheme from lattice assumptions. In: Abe, M. (ed.) ASIACRYPT 2010. LNCS, vol. 6477, pp. 395–412. Springer, Heidelberg (2010)

24. Klein, P.N.: Finding the closest lattice vector when it's unusually close. In: SODA, pp. 937–941 (2000)

25. Micciancio, D., Peikert, C.: Trapdoors for lattices: Simpler, tighter, faster, smaller. In: Pointcheval, D., Johansson, T. (eds.) EUROCRYPT 2012. LNCS, vol. 7237, pp. 700–718. Springer, Heidelberg (2012)

26. Micciancio, D., Regev, O.: Worst-case to average-case reductions based on Gaussian measures. SIAM J. Comput. 37(1), 267–302 (2007); Preliminary version in FOCS 2004
27. Myers, S., Sergi, M., Shelat, A.: Threshold fully homomorphic encryption and secure computation. Cryptology ePrint Archive, Report 2011/454 (2011), http://eprint.iacr.org/
28. Nguyen, P.Q., Regev, O.: Learning a parallelepiped: Cryptanalysis of GGH and NTRU signatures. J. Cryptology 22(2), 139–160 (2009); Preliminary version in Eurocrypt 2006
29. Peikert, C.: Public-key cryptosystems from the worst-case shortest vector problem. In: STOC, pp. 333–342 (2009)
30. Peikert, C.: An efficient and parallel gaussian sampler for lattices. In: Rabin, T. (ed.) CRYPTO 2010. LNCS, vol. 6223, pp. 80–97. Springer, Heidelberg (2010)
31. Peikert, C., Waters, B.: Lossy trapdoor functions and their applications. In: STOC, pp. 187–196 (2008)
32. Regev, O.: On lattices, learning with errors, random linear codes, and cryptography. J. ACM 56(6), 1–40 (2009); Preliminary version in STOC 2005
33. Shamir, A.: How to share a secret. Commun. ACM 22(11), 612–613 (1979)
34. Shor, P.W.: Polynomial-time algorithms for prime factorization and discrete logarithms on a quantum computer. SIAM J. Comput. 26(5), 1484–1509 (1997)
35. Shoup, V.: Practical threshold signatures. In: Preneel, B. (ed.) EUROCRYPT 2000. LNCS, vol. 1807, pp. 207–220. Springer, Heidelberg (2000)
36. Xie, X., Xue, R., Zhang, R.: Efficient threshold encryption from lossy trapdoor functions. In: Yang, B.-Y. (ed.) PQCrypto 2011. LNCS, vol. 7071, pp. 163–178. Springer, Heidelberg (2011)

Toward Practical Group Encryption*

Laila El Aimani[1,**] and Marc Joye[2]

[1] Gemalto, 6 rue de la verrerie, 92197 Meudon Cedex, France
[2] Technicolor, 975 avenue des Champs Blancs, 35576 Cesson-Sévigné Cedex, France

Abstract. A group encryption scheme allows anyone to form a ciphertext for a given group member while keeping the receiver's identity private. At the same time, the encryptor is capable of proving that some (anonymous) group member is able to decrypt the ciphertext and, optionally, that the corresponding plaintext satisfies some *a priori* relation (to prevent sending bogus messages). Finally, in case of a dispute, the identity of the intended receiver can be recovered by a designated authority. In this paper, we abstract a generic approach to construct group encryption schemes. We also introduce several new implementation tricks. As a result, we obtain group encryption schemes that significantly improve the state of the art. Both interactive and non-interactive constructions are considered.

Keywords: Group encryption, Canetti-Halevi-Katz paradigm, homomorphic encryption, structure-preserving signatures, (non)-interactive zero-knowledge.

1 Introduction

Basically, group signature schemes [7] allow a registered group member to conceal her identity when issuing digital signatures. However, any group signature can be opened by a designated group authority to reveal the signature's originator. In a dual way, group encryption schemes [12] provide revocable anonymity to the ciphertext's receiver. More specifically, a group encryption scheme is a public-key encryption scheme augmented with special properties: (1) the receiver's identity is hidden among the set of group members, (2) an opening authority is able to uncover the receiver's identity if need be, and (3) the ciphertext's originator is able to convince a verifier that (3-a) the ciphertext can be decrypted by a group member, (3-b) the opening authority can open the ciphertext and revoke the anonymity, and (3-c) the corresponding plaintext satisfies some *a priori* relation.

The additional features enjoyed by group encryption schemes make them suitable for a number of privacy-aware applications. One of them resides in secure oblivious retriever storage where anonymous credentials may move between computing elements (computer, mobile unit, etc...). Asynchronous transfer, which does not require the presence of all devices (subject to the transfer) at the same time, may resort to an untrusted server for storing temporarily the encrypted credentials. Group encryption can be employed in implementing such a storage server where it is guaranteed that (1) the server

---

* The full version [2] is available at the Cryptology ePrint Archive.
** This work was done while the first author was working at Technicolor.

M. Jacobson et al. (Eds.): ACNS 2013, LNCS 7954, pp. 237–252, 2013.

stores well formed encrypted credentials; (2) the credentials have a legitimate anonymous retriever (3) if necessary, an authority is able to pin down the identity of the retriever. Further scenarios where group encryption can be utilized are described in [12,6].

Related Work. The concept of group encryption was first formalized by Kiayias, Tsiounis, and Yung [12]. They also provide a modular design to build such schemes along with a concrete instantiation. Their realization achieves a ciphertext size of 2.4 kB and a well-formedness proof of approximately 70 kB for an 80-bit security level and a 2^{-50} soundness error. The main criticism to the proposal lies in entailing interaction with the verifier in order to prove the validity of the ciphertext. In fact, interaction can be cumbersome in situations where the encryptor needs to run the proof several times with different verifiers, as this would require remembering all the random coins used to form the ciphertext.

This shortcoming was addressed in subsequent works. First, Qin *et al.* [15] suggested a closely related primitive with non-interactive proofs of well-formedness of the ciphertext using the random oracle idealization. Then, Cathalo, Libert, and Yung [6] provided the first non-interactive realization of group encryption in the standard model. Their ciphertext and proof are also significantly shorter than those of [12] (the ciphertext size is 1.25 kB and the proof size is 16.125 kB for a 128-bit security level). However, the dark side of this non-interactive proposal resides in the expensive cost of the proof verification (several thousands of pairings) due to the recourse to Groth-Sahai [11]'s system.

To summarize the state of the art in group encryption, there is on the one hand an interactive proposal with a rather consequent size of the ciphertext and its proof of well-formedness, but which has the merit of having an efficient verification of this proof, and on the other hand, there is a non-interactive realization which significantly reduces the size of the ciphertext and its validity proof, but which is characterized by its computationally demanding proof verification.

It would be nice to combine the best of the two works and come up with a scheme with short ciphertexts and proofs, and where both the interactive and non-interactive setting are efficiently supported. This is the main contribution of this paper.

Contributions and Underlying Ideas. We propose a new design strategy for group encryption which significantly improves the performance. Two main ideas underlay our constructions.

First, instead of assembling highly secure components, we start with weaker — and so more efficient — primitives to get a group encryption scheme secure in a weak sense. The so-obtained scheme is next converted with a generic transform into a fully-secure group encryption scheme. In addition to efficiency, starting with weaker components also brings diversity and permits to develop further schemes, under various security assumptions. As a by-product, we show that the transform used to upgrade the security in group encryption applies to tag-based encryption and allows also to uplift the security in this primitive while preserving the verifiability properties.

Second, we encrypt only an alias of the receiver's public key in order to realize the opening functionality, leading consequently to important extra savings in both size and computation. In fact, the prior works [12,6] include in the ciphertext an encryption (using the opening authority's public key) of the receiver's public key in order to implement the opening function. Since a public key often consists of a vector of group elements, [12,6] use a chosen ciphertext secure encryption to encrypt each component of the key. We remark that such an operation is unnecessary as the public keys are all maintained in a public database. Therefore, encrypting only an alias of the key (which will be recorded along with the key in the database) is enough for this functionality. The opening authority needs then to execute the extra step of looking up the database for the key corresponding to the alias, however we note that resorting to the opening function is only done in case of disputes and occurs thus rarely.

Our new generic construction accepts many practical instantiations which support both interactive and non-interactive validity proofs. For instance, we get for a 128-bit security level, a concrete realization in the standard model with a ciphertext size of 0.4 kB, an interactive proof of 1 kB, a non-interactive proof of 2 kB which requires 325 pairing evaluations (vs. 3895 in [6]) for the verification.

Finally, we note that due to space constraints, all technical details, proofs, and analyzes of our results, are deferred to the long version [2].

2   Group Encryption: Syntax and Security Model

In this section, we review the formal definition of group encryption, as introduced in [12]. We also present the corresponding security notions.

It is useful to introduce some notation. For a two-party protocol between A and B, we represent its execution as $\langle output_A \mid output_B \rangle \leftarrow \langle A(input_A), B(input_B) \rangle$-$(common\text{-}input)$. The security properties are described through experiments where the adversary is given access to oracles. We write $\mathcal{A}^{\texttt{oracle}(\cdot)}$ to denote that adversary $\mathcal{A}$ has access to oracle $\texttt{oracle}(\cdot)$. When a query is not allowed, we use the symbol $\neg$: $\mathcal{A}^{\texttt{oracle}^{\neg(\text{some query})}}(\cdot)$.

2.1   Syntax

A *group encryption scheme* consists of the following algorithms/protocols:

$\texttt{setup}(1^\kappa)$. On input a security parameter κ, this probabilistic algorithm generates the public parameters *param* of the scheme. Although not always explicitly mentioned, *param* will serve as an input to all the algorithms/protocols that follow.

$(\mathcal{G}_r, \mathcal{R}, \texttt{sample}_\mathcal{R})$. This tuple of algorithms is part of the setup procedure and is needed for verifiability; *i.e.*, proving that the decryption of a certain ciphertext satisfies a given relation. In this sense, $\mathcal{G}_r$ generates the key pair $(pk_\mathcal{R}, sk_\mathcal{R})$ of the relation $\mathcal{R}$ from a security parameter. Similarly to [12,6], $sk_\mathcal{R}$ can be empty if the relation $\mathcal{R}$ is publicly sampleable (*e.g.*, the Diffie-Hellman relation in bilinear groups). On input the key pair of the relation $\mathcal{R}$, algorithm $\texttt{sample}_\mathcal{R}$ produces a pair (x, w) consisting of an instance x and a witness w for the relation $\mathcal{R}$. The polynomial-time testing procedure $\mathcal{R}(x, w)$ returns 1 iff (x, w) belongs to the relation based on the public parameter $pk_\mathcal{R}$.

keygen$_\mathsf{E}(param)$. This probabilistic algorithm outputs the key pair $(pk_\mathsf{E}, sk_\mathsf{E})$ of the entity E in the system; E can either be the group manager GM who manages the set of receivers (group members), or the opening authority OA that recovers the receiver's identity from a given ciphertext, or a group member User who receives ciphertexts.

join $= \langle \mathsf{J}_{\mathsf{User}}(param), \mathsf{GM}(sk_\mathsf{GM}) \rangle (pk_\mathsf{GM})$. This is an interactive protocol between GM and the potential joining group member $\mathsf{J}_{\mathsf{User}}$. The latter sends her public key pk to GM and prospectively proves the correctness of her key, whereas GM issues (at the end) a certificate $cert_{pk}$ that marks the effectiveness of the user's membership. GM stores additionally the pair $(pk, cert_{pk})$ in a public directory $database$.

encrypt$(pk_\mathsf{GM}, pk_\mathsf{OA}, pk, w, L)$. On input the respective public keys pk_GM and pk_OA of GM and OA, the (certified) public key pk of the receiver, this algorithm encrypts the witness w to produce a ciphertext ψ for a certain label L (which specifies the "context" of the encryption).

prove $= \langle \mathcal{P}(w, coins_\psi), \mathcal{V}(param) \rangle (pk_\mathsf{GM}, pk_\mathsf{OA}, pk_\mathcal{R}, x, \psi, L)$. This is an interactive protocol between a sender $\mathcal{P}$ (acting as the prover) who has generated the ciphertext ψ and any verifier $\mathcal{V}$; in this protocol, the sender uses the random coins used to produce ψ in order to prove that there is a group member whose key is registered in $database$ and who is capable of decrypting ψ, under label L, and recovering a witness w such that $(x, w) \in \mathcal{R}$. At the end of the protocol, the verifier outputs 1 if the proof is accepted, and 0 otherwise.

decrypt(sk, ψ, L). On input the private key sk of the group user, this algorithm decrypts the ciphertext ψ, under label L, and outputs the witness w (or a failure symbol $\perp$).

open$(sk_\mathsf{OA}, \psi, L)$. On input the private key sk_OA of OA and a ciphertext ψ with corresponding label L, this algorithm outputs the public key pk under which ψ was created.

Remark 1. The verifiability of encryption is optional; if it is not desired, the relation $\mathcal{R}$ can be set to the trivial relation that includes any string of fixed size as a witness.

2.2   Security Model

In addition to correctness, we require the following properties in a group encryption scheme.

Soundness. In a soundness attack, the adversary creates adaptively the intended group of receivers communicating with the genuine group manager. The adversary is successful if it can produce a ciphertext ψ and a corresponding proof of validity w.r.t. a relation $\mathcal{R}$ with a chosen $pk_\mathcal{R}$ such that (1) ψ is invalid, or (2) opening ψ results in an invalid public key or a value which is not equal to the public key of any group member. We adhere to the same formal definition of [12,6]. This definition involves an oracle reg$(sk_\mathsf{GM}, \cdot)$ that simulates the group manager GM and maintains a repository $database$ that comprises the registered public keys along with their certificates. The space of valid ciphertexts is denoted by $\mathcal{L}_{ciphertext}^{x, L, pk_\mathcal{R}, pk_\mathsf{GM}, pk_\mathsf{OA}, pk}$ and is given by

$$\left\{ \mathrm{encrypt}(pk_\mathsf{GM}, pk_\mathsf{OA}, pk, w, L) \colon (x, w) \in \mathcal{R} \text{ and } pk \in database \right\}$$

The space of valid public keys is denoted by $\mathcal{L}_{PK}^{param}$. A group encryption scheme satisfies soundness if for any polynomial-time adversary $\mathcal{A}$, the experiment below returns 1 with negligible probability.

Experiment $\mathbf{Exp}_{\mathcal{A}}^{\text{soundness}}(\kappa)$

1. $param \leftarrow \text{setup}(1^{\kappa})$;
2. $(pk_{\text{GM}}, sk_{\text{GM}}) \leftarrow \text{keygen}_{\text{GM}}(1^{\kappa}, param)$; $(pk_{\text{OA}}, sk_{\text{OA}}) \leftarrow \text{keygen}_{\text{OA}}(1^{\kappa}, param)$;
3. $(aux, pk_{\mathcal{R}}, x, \psi, L) \leftarrow \mathcal{A}^{\text{reg}(sk_{\text{GM}}, \cdot)}(param, pk_{\text{GM}}, pk_{\text{OA}}, sk_{\text{OA}})$;
4. $\langle done \mid out \rangle \leftarrow \langle \mathcal{A}(aux), \mathcal{V}(param) \rangle (pk_{\text{GM}}, pk_{\text{OA}}, pk_{\mathcal{R}}, x, \psi, L)$;
5. If $(out = 0)$ return 0;
6. $pk \leftarrow \text{open}(sk_{\text{OA}}, \psi, L)$;
7. If $(pk \notin database)$ or $(pk \notin \mathcal{L}_{PK}^{param})$ or $(\psi \notin \mathcal{L}_{ciphertext}^{x, L, pk_{\mathcal{R}}, pk_{\text{GM}}, pk_{\text{OA}}, pk})$ return 1 else return 0.

Message Security. The message security captures the property that an adversary cannot learn any information whatsoever on a message from an encryption of it. Strong security guarantees require that this holds true even when the adversary has adaptive access to a decryption oracle. For group encryption, it is also assumed that the adversary may control the group manager and the opening authority, and that he has access to the prove oracle in the challenge phase. We let IND-CCA denote the corresponding security notion. There is a weaker notion, denoted IND-sl-wCCA, where the adversary commits to the target label beforehand (selective-label attacks) and is not allowed to issue decryption queries involving the target label (weak chosen-ciphertext attacks).

Formally, a group encryption scheme meets the IND-sl-wCCA notion if the success probability of any polynomial-time adversary $\mathcal{A}$ to distinguish among encryptions of a chosen message and of a random message is at most negligibly better (in security parameter κ) than $1/2$ in the experiment that follows. In this experiment we use the following notation (similar to that in [12,6].

- $\text{decrypt}^{\neg(\cdot, L)}(sk, \cdot)$: is a stateless decryption oracle which is restricted not to decrypt ciphertexts w.r.t. the label L.
- $\text{CH}_{\text{ror}}^{b}(1^{\kappa}, pk, w, L)$: is a real-or random challenge oracle that is only queried once. It returns $\psi, coins_{\psi}$ such that $\psi \leftarrow \text{encrypt}(pk_{\text{GM}}, pk_{\text{OA}}, pk, cert_{pk}, w, L)$ if $b = 1$, and $\psi \leftarrow \text{encrypt}(pk_{\text{GM}}, pk_{\text{OA}}, pk, cert_{pk}, w', L)$ otherwise, where w' is a random plaintext chosen uniformly in the space of messages of length 1^{κ}. In both cases $coins_{\psi}$ denote the random coins used to produce ψ.
- $\text{prove}_{\mathcal{P}, \mathcal{P}'}^{b}(pk_{\text{GM}}, pk_{\text{OA}}, pk_{\mathcal{R}}, x, L, \psi)$: this a stateful oracle that the adversary can query on multiple occasions. If $b = 1$, it runs the real prover $\mathcal{P}$ (of the prove procedure) using the private inputs $w, coins_{\psi}, pk, cert_{pk}$ to produce a real proof (the common input being $pk_{\text{GM}}, pk_{\text{OA}}, pk_{\mathcal{R}}, x, L, \psi$). If $b = 0$, the oracle runs a simulator $\mathcal{P}'$ on the same common input $pk_{\text{GM}}, pk_{\text{OA}}, pk_{\mathcal{R}}, x, L, \psi$, but which is deprived from the private input $w, coins_{\psi}$ ($\mathcal{P}'$ may have access to $pk, cert_{pk}$), to generate a simulated proof. As pointed in [12,6], designing an efficient simulator $\mathcal{P}'$ is part of proving the security.

Experiment $\mathbf{Exp}_{\mathcal{A}}^{\text{IND-sl-wCCA}}(\kappa)$

1. $param \leftarrow \texttt{setup}(1^\kappa)$;
2. $(aux, pk_{\text{GM}}, pk_{\text{OA}}, L) \leftarrow \mathcal{A}(param)$;
3. $\langle pk, sk, cert_{pk} \mid aux, pk, cert_{pk} \rangle \leftarrow \langle \mathsf{J}_{\text{User}}(param), \mathcal{A}(aux) \rangle (pk_{\text{GM}})$;
4. $(aux, x, w, pk_{\mathcal{R}}) \leftarrow \mathcal{A}^{\texttt{decrypt}^{\neg(\cdot, L)}(sk, \cdot)}(aux)$; ▷ Find stage
5. If $(x, w) \notin \mathcal{R}$ then abort;
6. $b \xleftarrow{R} \{0, 1\}$; $(\psi, coins_\psi) \leftarrow \mathsf{CH}_{\text{ror}}^b(1^\kappa, pk, w, L)$;
7. $b^\star \leftarrow \mathcal{A}^{\texttt{prove}_{\mathcal{P}, \mathcal{P}'}^b(pk_{\text{GM}}, pk_{\text{OA}}, pk_{\mathcal{R}}, x, L, \psi), \texttt{decrypt}^{\neg(\cdot, L)}(sk, \cdot)}(aux, \psi)$; ▷ Guess stage
8. If $(b = b^\star)$ return 1 else return 0.

To get the full IND-CCA security level, the above experiment is modified in a way such that:

(i) the adversary is required to select the target label L only at the end of its find stage, and

(ii) the adversary is no longer restricted in its decryption queries (with the sole exception of the pair (ψ, L) in its guess stage) — in particular, the adversary is allowed to issue decryption queries including the target label L.

Anonymity. The notion of anonymity is described in an analogous way and comes with similar variations. The goal of the adversary is now to distinguish among two possible receivers given the encryption of a same witness under two different public keys. Of course, the adversary does not control the opening authority (and so is given the public opening key pk_{OA}).

The formal definition of selective-label anonymity against weak chosen-ciphertext attacks (in short, ANO-sl-wCCA) follows. The notion of ANO-sl-wCCA is met if the success probability of any polynomial-time adversary $\mathcal{A}$ is at most negligibly better than $1/2$. The formal definition of ANO-CCA (anonymity against chosen-ciphertext attacks) is obtained by modifying the experiment as for the IND-CCA notion (see above). Similarly to [12,6], we introduce the following notations:

- $\texttt{open}^{\neg(\cdot, L)}(sk_{\text{OA}}, \cdot)$: is a stateless opening oracle, for the key pk_{OA}, which is restricted not to open ciphertexts w.r.t. the label L.
- $\mathsf{CH}_{\text{anon}}^b(pk_{\text{GM}}, pk_{\text{OA}}, pk_0, pk_1, w, L)$: is a challenge oracle that is queried once. It returns $\psi, coins_\psi$ such that $\psi \leftarrow \texttt{encrypt}(pk_{\text{GM}}, pk_{\text{OA}}, pk_b, cert_b, w, L)$ and $coins_\psi$ denote the coins used to produce ψ.
- $\texttt{User}(pk_{\text{GM}})$: is a stateful oracle that simulates two executions of J_{User} to introduce two honest users in the group. It uses a string keys where the outputs of the two executions are written.

Experiment $\mathbf{Exp}_{\mathcal{A}}^{\text{ANO-sl-wCCA}}(\kappa)$

1. $param \leftarrow \texttt{setup}(1^\kappa)$; $(pk_{\text{OA}}, sk_{\text{OA}}) \leftarrow \texttt{keygen}_{\text{OA}}(1^\kappa, param)$;

2. $(aux, pk_{\mathsf{GM}}, L) \leftarrow \mathcal{A}(param); aux \leftarrow \mathcal{A}^{\mathsf{User}(pk_{\mathsf{GM}}),\mathsf{open}^{\neg(\cdot,L)}(sk_{\mathsf{OA}},\cdot)}(aux, pk_{\mathsf{OA}});$
   If keys $\neq (pk_0, sk_0, cert_{pk_0}, pk_1, sk_1, cert_{pk_1})$ return 0;

3. $(aux, x, w, pk_{\mathcal{R}}) \leftarrow \mathcal{A}^{\mathsf{open}^{\neg(\cdot,L)}(sk_{\mathsf{OA}},\cdot),\ \mathsf{decrypt}^{\neg(\cdot,L)}(sk_0,\cdot),\ \mathsf{decrypt}^{\neg(\cdot,L)}(sk_1,\cdot)}(aux);$

4. If $(x, w) \notin \mathcal{R}$ return 0;

5. $b \xleftarrow{R} \{0,1\}; (\psi, coins_\psi) \leftarrow \mathsf{CH}^b_{\mathsf{anon}}(pk_{\mathsf{GM}}, pk_{\mathsf{OA}}, pk_0, pk_1, w, L);$

6. $b^\star \leftarrow \mathcal{A}^{\mathsf{prove}_{\mathcal{P}},\mathsf{open}^{\neg(\cdot,L)}(sk_{\mathsf{OA}},\cdot),\ \mathsf{decrypt}^{\neg(\cdot,L)}(sk_0,\cdot),\ \mathsf{decrypt}^{\neg(\cdot,L)}(sk_1,\cdot)}(aux, \psi);$

7. If $(b = b^\star)$ return 1 else return 0.

3 Building Group Encryption Schemes

In this section we present our new strategy to build efficient group encryption schemes. We start by providing a construction which achieves "weak" security properties from "weakly secure" components. Next, we use a technique evocative of the Canetti-Halevi-Katz transformation to upgrade the security of the resulting construction into full-fledged CCA security.

In the rest of this paper, and in order to avoid confusion, we use a dot notation to refer the different components; for instance, $\varGamma.\mathtt{encrypt}()$ refers to the encryption algorithm of public-key scheme $\varGamma$, $\varSigma.pk$ to the public key of signature scheme $\varSigma$, etc.

3.1 A Generic Construction

Our construction for group encryption departs from the specific constructions in [12,6] in encrypting only an *alias* to the public key (computed using a function H) instead of encrypting the entire public key. As will become apparent, such a change drastically reduces the cost and size of the resulting encryption. Moreover, and similarly to [6], it does not include the commitment on the public key (and potentially on its certificate) in the ciphertext.

Let $\varGamma^{\mathsf{User}} = (\mathtt{keygen}, \mathtt{encrypt}, \mathtt{decrypt})$ and $\varGamma^{\mathsf{OA}} = (\mathtt{keygen}, \mathtt{encrypt}, \mathtt{decrypt})$ be two public-key encryption schemes with labels. Let further $\varSigma = (\mathtt{keygen}, \mathtt{sign}, \mathtt{verify})$ be a signature scheme. We assume that the message space of $\varSigma$ includes the public-key space of $\varGamma^{\mathsf{User}}$. Finally, let H denote a collision-resistant function from the public key space of $\varGamma^{\mathsf{User}}$ to the message space of $\varGamma^{\mathsf{OA}}$.

The properties required for H to guarantee an efficient $\mathtt{prove}$ algorithm/protocol are described in the next section. Actually, even the collision-resistance property can be weakened as we will see later since GM has some control over the public keys she certifies, and therefore may proceed to simple measures in case a collision occurs.

$\mathtt{setup}(1^\kappa)$. This algorithm invokes the setup algorithms for the building blocks (namely, $\varGamma^{\mathsf{User}}$, $\varGamma^{\mathsf{OA}}$, and $\varSigma$), and outputs $param$. The public parameters $param$ are input to all the subsequent algorithms/protocols and further include the description of a relation $\mathcal{R}$ along with a key pair $(pk_{\mathcal{R}}, sk_R)$ necessary for sampling pairs (x, w) where $(x, w) \in \mathcal{R}$ and w belongs to the message space of $\varGamma^{\mathsf{User}}$. Finally, $\mathtt{setup}$ outputs also a description of a collision-resistant function H which maps elements from the public key space of $\varGamma^{\mathsf{User}}$ into elements in the message space of $\varGamma^{\mathsf{OA}}$.

$\texttt{keygen}_{\textsf{GM}}(1^\kappa)$. This algorithm invokes $\Sigma.\texttt{keygen}(1^\kappa)$ and outputs $(pk_{\textsf{GM}}, sk_{\textsf{GM}}) = (\Sigma.pk, \Sigma.sk)$.

$\texttt{keygen}_{\textsf{OA}}(1^\kappa)$. This algorithm invokes $\Gamma^{\textsf{OA}}.\texttt{keygen}(1^\kappa)$ and outputs $(pk_{\textsf{OA}}, sk_{\textsf{OA}}) = (\Gamma^{\textsf{OA}}.pk, \Gamma^{\textsf{OA}}.sk)$.

$\texttt{keygen}_{\textsf{User}}(1^\kappa)$. This algorithm invokes $\Gamma^{\textsf{User}}.\texttt{keygen}(1^\kappa)$ and outputs $(pk_{\textsf{User}}, sk_{\textsf{User}}) = (\Gamma^{\textsf{User}}.pk, \Gamma^{\textsf{User}}.sk)$ as a key pair for the group member User.

$\texttt{join} = \langle J_{\textsf{User}}, \textsf{GM}(sk_{\textsf{GM}})\rangle(pk_{\textsf{GM}})$. The potential joining group member $J_{\textsf{User}}$ wishing to join the group sends her public key $pk_{\textsf{User}}$ (obtained after calling $\texttt{keygen}_{\textsf{User}}$) to GM, and the latter replies with the certificate $cert_{pk_{\textsf{User}}} = \Sigma.\texttt{sign}_{\Sigma.sk}(pk_{\textsf{User}})$. GM then stores $(pk_{\textsf{User}}, H(pk_{\textsf{User}}), cert_{pk_{\textsf{User}}})$ in a public directory $database$. (We stress that for any two different $pk_{\textsf{User}}$ and $pk'_{\textsf{User}}$, the values of $H(pk_{\textsf{User}})$ and $H(pk'_{\textsf{User}})$ will be different.)

$\texttt{encrypt}(pk_{\textsf{GM}}, pk_{\textsf{OA}}, pk_{\textsf{User}}, w, L)$. This algorithm first produces an encryption ψ_1 using $\Gamma^{\textsf{User}}$ on w with the public key $pk_{\textsf{User}}$ under label L, and then encrypts $H(pk_{\textsf{User}})$ in ψ_2 using $\Gamma^{\textsf{OA}}$ under label L with public key $pk_{\textsf{OA}}$. The ciphertext consists of the pair (ψ_1, ψ_2).

$\texttt{prove} = \langle \mathcal{P}(w, coins_\Psi), \mathcal{V}(param)\rangle(pk_{\textsf{GM}}, pk_{\textsf{OA}}, pk_{\mathcal{R}}, x, \psi, L)$. $\mathcal{P}$ who created the ciphertext $\psi = (\psi_1, \psi_2)$ uses the coins used to produce ψ in order to prove to $\mathcal{V}$:
- knowledge of the message underlying ψ_1 and that it forms a witness for the instance x w.r.t. the relation $\mathcal{R}$;
- knowledge of the decryption of ψ_2 and that it corresponds to the value of the function H on the public key under which ψ_1 is created;
- knowledge of a certificate on the public key used to create ψ_1.

These proofs are detailed in Section 4.

$\texttt{decrypt}(sk_{\textsf{User}}, \psi, L)$. This algorithm parses ψ as (ψ_1, ψ_2), invokes $\Gamma^{\textsf{User}}.\texttt{decrypt}$ on (ψ_1, L), and outputs the result of this decryption, say w, if $(x, w) \in \mathcal{R}$, and $\perp$ otherwise.

$\texttt{open}(sk_{\textsf{OA}}, \psi, L)$. This algorithm parses ψ as (ψ_1, ψ_2), invokes $\Gamma^{\textsf{OA}}.\texttt{decrypt}$ on (ψ_2, L), then looks up $database$ for the preimage w.r.t. H of such a decryption, and outputs the result of this search.

Theorem 1. *The construction of § 3.1 yields a group encryption scheme with*

1. IND-sl-wCCA *message security if* $\Gamma^{\textsf{User}}$ *is a tag-based encryption scheme having indistinguishability of encryptions under selective-tag weak chosen-ciphertext attacks, and* $\texttt{prove}$ *is zero knowledge.*
2. ANO-sl-wCCA *anonymity if* $\Gamma^{\textsf{User}}$ *is a tag-based encryption scheme having indistinguishability of keys under selective-tag weak chosen-ciphertext attacks,* $\Gamma^{\textsf{OA}}$ *is a tag-based encryption scheme having indistinguishability of encryptions under selective-tag weak chosen-ciphertext attacks, and* $\texttt{prove}$ *is zero knowledge.*
3. *soundness if the proof underlying* $\texttt{prove}$ *is sound and the used certification scheme is* EUF-CMA *secure.*   □

3.2   A Canetti-Halevi-Katz Like Paradigm for Group Encryption

Canetti, Halevi, and Katz [4] provide a method that transforms any selective-identity chosen-plaintext secure identity-based scheme into one with full-fledged chosen-ciphertext security. The transformation, referred to as the *CHK transform*, consists in signing the ciphertext, result of encryption with the weakly secure identity-based encryption scheme, using a one-time signature scheme, wherein the "identity" is given by the verification key. Concurrently, MacKenzie, Reiter, and Yang [14] present a method for converting a weakly chosen-ciphertext secure tag-based encryption scheme to a fully secure public-key encryption scheme. Finally, Kiltz [13] combines the ideas of [4,14,3] in order to derive chosen-ciphertext secure public-key encryption schemes from selective-tag weakly chosen-ciphertext secure tag-based encryption schemes using one-time signatures.

Interestingly and analogously to [13], we can now turn a weakly secure group encryption scheme as per Theorem 1 into a group encryption scheme with full message security (*i.e.*, IND-CCA) and full anonymity (*i.e.*, ANO-CCA). Let $\mathcal{GE}^*$ be a group encryption satisfying the notions of IND-sl-wCCA and ANO-sl-wCCA. Given $\mathcal{GE}^*$, we construct a group encryption scheme $\mathcal{GE}$ meeting the strong notions of IND-CCA and ANO-CCA as depicted in Fig. 1. The conversion uses a one-time signature scheme $\mathfrak{S} = (\mathtt{keygen}, \mathtt{sign}, \mathtt{verify})$.

Theorem 2. *The group encryption scheme $\mathcal{GE}$ obtained from the conversion in Fig. 1 has* IND-CCA *message-security and* ANO-CCA *anonymity if $\mathcal{GE}^*$ is* IND-sl-wCCA *and* ANO-sl-wCCA, *and $\mathfrak{S}$ is a strongly secure one-time signature scheme.*   □

$\boxed{\mathcal{GE}.\mathtt{encrypt}(pk_{\mathsf{GM}}, pk_{\mathsf{OA}}, pk_{\mathsf{User}}, w, L)}$

1. $(\mathfrak{S}.pk, \mathfrak{S}.sk) \leftarrow \mathfrak{S}.\mathtt{keygen}(1^\kappa)$;
2. $\psi^* \leftarrow \mathcal{GE}^*.\mathtt{encrypt}(pk_{\mathsf{GM}}, pk_{\mathsf{OA}}, pk_{\mathsf{User}}, w, \mathfrak{S}.pk)$;
3. $\sigma \leftarrow \mathfrak{S}.\mathtt{sign}(\mathfrak{S}.sk, \psi^* \| L)$;
4. Return $\psi \leftarrow (\psi^*, \mathfrak{S}.pk, \sigma)$.

$\boxed{\mathcal{GE}.\mathtt{decrypt}(sk_{\mathsf{User}}, \psi, L)}$

1. Parse ψ as $(\psi^*, \mathfrak{S}.pk, \sigma)$;
2. If $\mathfrak{S}.\mathtt{verify}(\mathfrak{S}.pk, \psi^* \| L) = \perp$ then return $\perp$;
3. Else return $\mathcal{GE}^*.\mathtt{decrypt}(sk_{\mathsf{User}}, \psi^*, \mathfrak{S}.pk)$.

Fig. 1. Conversion

Remark 2. This transformation can be also used to upgrade the security in TBE (from sl-wCCA to full CCA indistinguishability and anonymity). In [13], Kiltz suggests to achieve this task via a CCA secure public key encryption (PKE): first derive a CCA secure PKE from an sl-wCCA secure TBE, then identify the pair "(message,tag)" in the TBE by the message "message∥tag" in the PKE.
Our transform has the merit of preserving the algebraic structure of the message to be encrypted. This impacts positively the verifiability of the encryption; *i.e.*, proving knowledge of the message underlying the CCA encryption is as efficient as proving knowledge of the message underlying its sl-wCCA encryption.

4   Efficient Instantiations

The sender of the message, in the construction provided in the previous section, is compelled to provide the following proof in the `prove` procedure:

$$
\begin{aligned}
\mathsf{PoK} = \{(pk, cert_{pk}, w) \; : \; & cert_{pk} = \Sigma.\mathtt{sign}_{\Sigma.sk}(pk) \; \wedge \\
& \psi_1 = \Gamma^{\mathsf{User}}.\mathtt{encrypt}_{pk}(w) \; \wedge \\
& \psi_2 = \Gamma^{\mathsf{OA}}.\mathtt{encrypt}_{pk_{\mathsf{OA}}}(H(pk)) \; \wedge \\
& (x, w) \in \mathcal{R} \\
& \} \; (\psi_1, \psi_2, \Sigma.pk, pk_{\mathsf{OA}}, x)
\end{aligned}
$$

where the private input of the prover are the coins used to form ψ_1, ψ_2 in addition to pk, $cert_{pk}$, and m.

According to whether we want to provide an interactive or a non-interactive `prove` procedure, the components underlying the construction have to satisfy different conditions:

Non-interactive Setting. We can provide a non-interactive zero knowledge (NIZK) `prove` if the language defined by this procedure is compatible with the Groth-Sahai proof system [11]. In fact, [11] provides efficient NIZK or NIWI proofs for a number of languages that cover pairing-product equations, multi-scalar multiplication, and quadratic equations.

In this case, the common reference string (CRS) needs to be part of the `setup` algorithm. Besides, the private input of the prover has to consist of only group elements. Moreover, the building blocks, namely Σ, Γ^{User}, Γ^{OA}, H, and $\mathcal{R}$ need to perform only group or pairing (if bilinear groups are involved) operations on this private input. For example, we can consider structure-preserving signatures [9,8,1] for the certification scheme Σ, Kiltz'[13] or Cash *et al.*'s [5] (described in Fig. 3) encryption schemes for both Γ^{User} or Γ^{OA}, the discrete logarithm or the Diffie-Hellman relation for $\mathcal{R}$, and any function H performing group or pairing operations on the input. Note however that the statements underlying `prove` that consist of pairing-product equations need to be of special form in order to accept zero knowledge proofs (otherwise `prove` will be only witness-indistinguishable).

Interactive Setting. While having a number of useful properties, non-interactive proofs built from Groth-Sahai's proof system suffer the high verification cost due to the pairing evaluations in the verification. Therefore, it would be judicious to support the construction in the previous section with an interactive variant of `prove`. This will decree different conditions on the building blocks. The essence of these conditions consists in manipulating the private input, which has to comprise only group elements, through homomorphic maps.

The rest of this section is organized as follows. Subsection 1 will introduce formally the classes of the different components Σ, Γ^{User}, Γ^{OA}, H, and $\mathcal{R}$ that will lead to an efficient *interactive* `prove`. Subsection 2 describes explicitly the *interactive* `prove` protocol in case the building blocks are instantiated from the previously presented classes.

Finally, we provide a concrete realization of group encryption in Subsection 3 and compare the resulting performances with those of the prior proposals [12,6].

4.1 Building Blocks

Definition 1 (The class $\mathbb{S}$ of certification schemes). $\mathbb{S}$ *is the set of all digital signatures* Σ *for which there exists a pair of efficient algorithms,* convert *and* retrieve, *where* convert *inputs a verification key vk, a key pk (to be certified), and a valid signature* $cert_{pk}$ *(w.r.t. vk) on pk, and outputs a tuple* (S, R) *such that:*

1. *R is information theoretically independent from $cert_{pk}$ and pk. I.e. There exists an algorithm* simulate *that inputs a verification key vk from the verification key space and outputs a string statistically indistinguishable from R.*
2. *There exists an algorithm* compute *that on the input vk and R, computes a description of a map $F : (\mathbb{G}_S, *_S) \times (\mathbb{G}_{pk}, *_{pk}) \to (\mathbb{G}_F, \circ_F)$:*
   - *where $(\mathbb{G}_S, *_S)$ and $(\mathbb{G}_{pk}, *_{pk})$ are groups and $\mathbb{G}_F$ is a set equipped with the binary operation $\circ_F$,*
   - *$\forall (S, pk), (S', pk') \in (\mathbb{G}_S, *_S) \times (\mathbb{G}_{pk}, *_{pk}): F(S *_S S', pk *_{pk} pk') = F(S, pk) \circ_F F(S', pk').$*
   and an I such that $F(S, pk) = I$.
3. *The* retrieve *algorithm inputs a candidate tuple (S, R, pk) (satisfying the above conditions) and vk, and outputs a key $\widetilde{pk}$ and a valid certificate $\widetilde{cert_{\widetilde{pk}}}$ on it w.r.t. vk.*

Informally, this class includes signature schemes where the signature on a given message can be converted into a "simulatable" part (denoted by R in the definition) that does not reveal any information about the signature or the message to be signed (denoted by pk), and a "vital" part (denoted by S) such that S and pk form a preimage, by a homomorphic map F, of some quantity I computed only from R and the public parameters. The last condition dictated by the retrieve algorithm guarantees the non-triviality of the map F; given (S, R, pk) satisfying $F(S, pk) = I$ (I computed as prescribed by the definition), one can come up with a pair of a message and a valid signature on it w.r.t. the same verification key.

Definition 2 (The class $\mathbb{R}$ of relations). $\mathbb{R}$ *is the set of relations $\mathcal{R}$ such that there exists an algorithm which inputs an instance x from the set of instances $\mathbb{G}_x$ (in addition to the public parameters) and outputs a description of a map $F_{\mathcal{R}} : (\mathbb{G}_w, *_w) \to (\mathbb{G}_{\mathcal{R}}, \circ_{\mathcal{R}})$ where:*

- *$\mathbb{G}_w$ is the set of witnesses that is a group for $*_w$, and $\mathbb{G}_{\mathcal{R}}$ is a set equipped with the binary operation $\circ_{\mathcal{R}}$,*
- *$\forall w, w' \in \mathbb{G}_w, : F_{\mathcal{R}}(w *_w w') = F_{\mathcal{R}}(w) \circ_{\mathcal{R}} F_{\mathcal{R}}(w').$*

and an $I_{\mathcal{R}}$ such that $F_R(w) = I_{\mathcal{R}} \Leftrightarrow (x, w) \in \mathcal{R}$.

Examples of such functions include the discrete logarithm or the Diffie-Hellman (in bilinear groups) functions. Likewise, one can prove knowledge of a witness corresponding to a given instance thanks to the homomorphic property of $F_{\mathcal{R}}$.

Definition 3 (The class $\mathbb{E}_1$ of encryption schemes). $\mathbb{E}_1$ *is the set of tag-based encryption (TBE) schemes Γ that have the following properties:*

1. *The message space $\mathbb{G}_w$ and the public key space $\mathbb{G}_{pk}$ are groups with respect to $*_w$ and $*_{pk}$ respectively.*
2. *Let $w \in \mathbb{G}_w$ be a message and e its encryption with respect to a tag t under a public key pk. On the common input pk, w, e, and t, there exists an efficient zero knowledge proof of w being the decryption of e with respect to the key pk and the tag t. The private input of the prover is the randomness used to produce the encryption e.*
3. *Given an encryption e of some message under some public key w.r.t. a given tag t, there exists an efficient algorithm* compute *which inputs e and outputs a public key $pk' \in \mathbb{G}_{pk}$, a message w', and its encryption $e' = \Gamma.\text{encrypt}_{pk'}(w', t)$, under the key pk' w.r.t. the same tag t, such that:*
   - *The probability distributions of the random variables $pk' \in \mathbb{G}_{pk}$ and $w' \in \mathbb{G}_w$ are indistinguishable from uniform, where the probability is taken over the ciphertext e, the tag t, and the random coins of* compute*.*
   - *One can define a group operation $\circ_e$ on the set*

$$\mathcal{E} = \{e' : (pk', w', e') \leftarrow \Gamma.\text{compute}(e, t)\}$$

   such that $\Gamma.\text{encrypt}_{pk' *_{pk} pk}(w' *_w w, t) = e' \circ_e e$, where w and pk are the message and public key underlying the encryption e respectively. Moreover, given the randomnesses used to produce e and e', one can deduce (using only the public parameters) the randomness used to produce $e' \circ_e e$ on $w' *_w w$ under the key $pk' *_{pk} pk$.

The class $\mathbb{E}_1$ informally comprises encryption schemes that possess efficient proofs of correctness of decryption (i.e. proofs that a given ciphertext correctly decrypts to a given message) in addition to being homomorphic w.r.t. both the message and the public key. This might seem restrictive at a first glance, however, it turns out that the ElGamal-based family of encryption schemes satisfy nicely the properties required in the above definition. We note as an illustration the tag-based variant of the modified Cramer-Shoup scheme [5] described in Fig. 3.

Definition 4 (The class $\mathbb{H}$ of functions). $\mathbb{H}$ *is the set of functions $H : \mathbb{G}_{pk} \to \mathbb{G}_H$ such that:*

   - $\mathbb{G}_{pk}$ *is a group w.r.t. some binary operation $*_{pk}$, and $\mathbb{G}_H$ is a set equipped with a binary operation $*_H$.*
   - $\forall pk, pk' \in \mathbb{G}_H : H(pk *_{pk} pk') = H(pk) *_H H(pk')$.

It is natural to require that $H(pk)$ for some public key pk in *database* identifies pk uniquely; i.e. there are no different pk and pk' in *database* that map to the same value by the function H. In this sense, requiring H to be collision-resistant seems natural, however we remark that in our application of group encryption, GM has some control over the public keys she certifies, and therefore may proceed to simple measures (see [2, Appendix E.3]) in case a collision occurs.

Definition 5 (The class $\mathbb{E}_2$ of encryption schemes). $\mathbb{E}_2$ *is the set of tag-based encryption schemes Γ that have the following properties:*

1. *The message space is a group $\mathbb{G}_H$ w.r.t. some binary operation $*_H$ and the ciphertext space $\mathcal{C}$ is a set equipped with some binary operation $\circ_c$.*
2. *Let $h \in \mathbb{G}_H$ be a message and e its encryption with respect to a given key pk and a given tag t. On the common input pk, t, h, and e, there exists an efficient zero knowledge proof of h being the decryption of e with respect to t under the key pk. The private input of the prover is the randomness used to produce the encryption e.*
3. *$\forall h, h' \in \mathbb{G}_H, \forall pk, \forall t$: $\Gamma.\text{encrypt}_{pk}(h *_H h', t) = \Gamma.\text{encrypt}_{pk}(h, t) \circ_c \Gamma.\text{encrypt}_{pk}(h', t)$. Moreover, given the randomness used to encrypt h in $\Gamma.\text{encrypt}_{pk}(h, t)$ and h' in $\Gamma.\text{encrypt}_{pk}(h', t)$, one can deduce (using only the public parameters) the randomness used to produce $\Gamma.\text{encrypt}_{pk}(h, t) \circ_c \Gamma.\text{encrypt}_{pk}(h', t)$ on $h *_H h'$.*

Examples of encryption schemes in the above class include Kiltz' [13] and Cash et al.'s [5] (described in Fig. 3) tag-based encryption schemes.

4.2 The prove Protocol

In this paragraph, we instantiate the construction in Section 3 with the following constituents:

1. A signature scheme Σ from Class $\mathbb{S}$ with key pair (sk_{GM}, pk_{GM}), and corresponding function
   $$F : (\mathbb{G}_S, *_S) \times (\mathbb{G}_{pk}, *_{pk}) \to (F(\mathbb{G}_S \times \mathbb{G}_{pk}), \circ_F).$$
2. An encryption scheme Γ_1 from Class $\mathbb{E}_1$ with public key space $(\mathbb{G}_{pk}, *_{pk})$, message space $(\mathbb{G}_w, *_w)$, and with ciphertext subset $(\mathcal{E}, \circ_e)$ (as defined in Definition 3).
3. A relation $\mathcal{R}$ from Class $\mathbb{R}$ with instance space $\mathbb{G}_x$ and witness space $(\mathbb{G}_w, *_w)$.
4. A function H from Class $\mathbb{H}$ with domain $(\mathbb{G}_{pk}, *_{pk})$ and codomain $(\mathbb{G}_H, *_H)$.
5. An encryption scheme Γ_2 from Class $\mathbb{E}_2$ with key pair (sk_{OA}, pk_{OA}), message space $(\mathbb{G}_H, *_H)$, and ciphertext space $(\mathcal{C}, \circ_c)$.

Theorem 3. *The prove protocol depicted in Fig. 2 is an efficient zero knowledge proof of knowledge with the special soundness property.* □

Theorem 4. *The construction in Section 3 is sound if the prove protocol satisfies the special soundness property, and the used certification scheme is EUF-CMA secure.* □

4.3 A Concrete Realization

In this subsection, we consider bilinear groups with $e\colon \mathbb{G}_1 \times \mathbb{G}_2 \to \mathbb{G}_T$. Moreover, we instantiate this system with the Λ_{sxdh} setting which refers to the case of asymmetric pairings for which the DDH assumption holds in both $\mathbb{G}_1$ and $\mathbb{G}_2$.

We instantiate the construction in Section 3 with the following bricks:

1. The signature scheme from [1]. The scheme signs messages in $\mathbb{G}_2^4$.

Prover P	Verifier V

Compute $I_\mathcal{R}$ as in Def 2

$(S, R) \leftarrow \text{convert}(pk_\text{GM}, pk, cert_{pk})$

$(pk', w', e_1') \leftarrow \Gamma_1.\text{compute}(e_1)$

$S' \xleftarrow{R} \mathbb{G}_S$

$f' = F(S', pk')$

$f'_\mathcal{R} = F_\mathcal{R}(w')$

$h' = H(pk')$

$e_2' = \Gamma_2.\text{encrypt}_{pk_\text{OA}}(h')$

$$\xrightarrow{\quad R, f', e_1', f'_\mathcal{R}, e_2' \quad}$$

Compute I as in Def 1

$$\xleftarrow{\quad b \quad} \qquad b \xleftarrow{R} \{0,1\}^\ell$$

$$\xrightarrow{\quad z_S = S' *_S S^b, z_{pk} = pk' *_{pk} pk^b \quad}$$

$$\xrightarrow{\quad z_w = w' *_w w^b, z_h = h' *_H h^b \quad}$$

$$\xleftrightarrow{\quad \text{PoK}_1\{e_1' \circ_e e_1^b = \Gamma.\text{encrypt}_{z_{pk}}(z_w, t)\} \quad}$$

$$\xleftrightarrow{\quad \text{PoK}_2\{e_2' \circ_c e_2^b = \Gamma.\text{encrypt}_{pk_\text{OA}}(z_h, t)\} \quad}$$

Accept if:

$F(z_S, z_{pk}) = f' \circ_F I^b$,

$F_\mathcal{R}(z_w) = f'_\mathcal{R} \circ_\mathcal{R} I_\mathcal{R}^b$,

$H(z_{pk}) = z_h$,

PoK_1 and PoK_2 are valid.

Fig. 2. Proof system for membership to the language $\{(w, pk, cert_{pk}): e_1 = \Gamma_1.\text{encrypt}_{pk}(w, t) \quad \wedge \quad e_2 = \Gamma_2.\text{encrypt}_{pk_\text{OA}}(H(pk), t) \quad \wedge \quad cert_{pk} = \Sigma.\text{sign}_{sk_\text{GM}}(pk) \quad \wedge \quad (x, w) \in \mathcal{R}\}$ Common input: $(e_1, e_2, t, x, pk_\text{OA}, pk_\text{GM})$ and Private input: $(w, pk, cert_{pk})$ and randomness used to produce e_1 and e_2.

2. The encryption scheme described in Fig. 3 to instantiate both Γ^User and Γ^OA. The message space of both Γ^User and Γ^OA is the group $\mathbb{G}_2$.

3. The relation $\mathcal{R}: (x = [X, Y], w) \in \mathcal{R} \Leftrightarrow e(X, Y) = e(g, w)$, where g is a known generator of $\mathbb{G}_1$.

4. The function H mapping an element $(X_1, \ldots, X_4) \in \mathbb{G}_2^4$ to $\prod_{i=1}^4 X_i^{a_i}$, where $a_1, \ldots, a_4$ are public elements in $\mathbb{Z}_d$ (d is order of $\mathbb{G}_2$). The collision-resistance of H is analyzed in the full version of the paper.

5. The one-time signature from [10].

We summarize in this chart the performances of our realization compared to those of [12] and [6]. (IP stands for interactive proof, whereas NIP stands for non-interactive proof).

[Setup]	Choose a group $(\mathbb{G}, \cdot)$ generated by g with prime order d.
[Keygen]	Choose $x_1, \widetilde{x}_1, x_2, \widetilde{x}_2 \xleftarrow{R} \mathbb{Z}_d$ then compute
	$X_i \leftarrow g^{x_i}$ and $\widetilde{X}_i \leftarrow g^{\widetilde{x}_i}$ for $i = 1, 2$
	set $pk \leftarrow \{X_i, \widetilde{X}_i\}_{i=1,2}$ and $sk \leftarrow \{x_i, \widetilde{x}_i\}_{i=1,2}$.
[Encrypt]	For a message $m \in \mathbb{G}$ and a tag $t \in \mathbb{Z}_d$:
	choose $r \xleftarrow{R} \mathbb{Z}_d$,
	compute $c_1 \leftarrow g^r$, $c_2 \leftarrow (X_1^t \widetilde{X}_1)^r$, $c_3 \leftarrow (X_2^t \widetilde{X}_2)^r$, and $c_4 = m X_1^r$,
	set the ciphertext to (c_1, c_2, c_3, c_4).
[Decrypt]	Given a ciphertext $c = (c_1, c_2, c_3, c_4)$ and a tag t:
	check that $c_2 = c_1^{t x_1 + \widetilde{x}_1}$ and that $c_3 = c_1^{t x_2 + \widetilde{x}_2}$
	if it is not the case, return $\perp$, otherwise:
	compute the plaintext as $m \leftarrow c_4 c_1^{-x_1}$.

Fig. 3. TBE variant of the Modified Cramer-Shoup [5]

	[12]	[6]	Our scheme
Ciphertext (kB)	2.5	1.25	0.4
IP size (kB)	70	–	1
# of pairings in IP	0	–	14
NIP size (kB)	–	16.125	2
# of pairings in NIP	–	3895	325

Fig. 4. Comparison

References

1. Abe, M., Fuchsbauer, G., Groth, J., Haralambiev, K., Ohkubo, M.: Structure-preserving signatures and commitments to group elements. In: Rabin, T. (ed.) CRYPTO 2010. LNCS, vol. 6223, pp. 209–236. Springer, Heidelberg (2010)
2. El Aimani, L., Joye, M.: Toward practical group encryption. IACR Cryptology ePrint Archive, Report 2012/155 (2012), http://eprint.iacr.org/
3. Boneh, D., Katz, J.: Improved efficiency for CCA-secure cryptosystems built using identity-based encryption. In: Menezes, A. (ed.) CT-RSA 2005. LNCS, vol. 3376, pp. 87–103. Springer, Heidelberg (2005)
4. Canetti, R., Halevi, S., Katz, J.: Chosen-ciphertext security from identity-based encryption. In: Cachin, C., Camenisch, J.L. (eds.) EUROCRYPT 2004. LNCS, vol. 3027, pp. 207–222. Springer, Heidelberg (2004)
5. Cash, D.M., Kiltz, E., Shoup, V.: The twin diffie-hellman problem and applications. In: Smart, N.P. (ed.) EUROCRYPT 2008. LNCS, vol. 4965, pp. 127–145. Springer, Heidelberg (2008)
6. Cathalo, J., Libert, B., Yung, M.: Group encryption: Non-interactive realization in the standard model. In: Matsui, M. (ed.) ASIACRYPT 2009. LNCS, vol. 5912, pp. 179–196. Springer, Heidelberg (2009)
7. Chaum, D., van Heyst, E.: Group signatures. In: Davies, D.W. (ed.) EUROCRYPT 1991. LNCS, vol. 547, pp. 257–265. Springer, Heidelberg (1991)
8. Fuchsbauer, G.: Automorphic Signatures in Bilinear Groups and an Application to Round-Optimal Blind Signatures. Cryptology ePrint Archive, Report 2009/320 (2009), http://eprint.iacr.org/

9. Groth, J.: Homomorphic Trapdoor Commitments to Group Elements. IACR Cryptology ePrint Archive 2009, 7 (2009)
10. Groth, J.: Simulation-sound NIZK proofs for a practical language and constant size group signatures. In: Lai, X., Chen, K. (eds.) ASIACRYPT 2006. LNCS, vol. 4284, pp. 444–459. Springer, Heidelberg (2006)
11. Groth, J., Sahai, A.: Efficient non-interactive proof systems for bilinear groups. In: Smart, N.P. (ed.) EUROCRYPT 2008. LNCS, vol. 4965, pp. 415–432. Springer, Heidelberg (2008)
12. Kiayias, A., Tsiounis, Y., Yung, M.: Group encryption. In: Kurosawa, K. (ed.) ASIACRYPT 2007. LNCS, vol. 4833, pp. 181–199. Springer, Heidelberg (2007)
13. Kiltz, E.: Chosen-ciphertext security from tag-based encryption. In: Halevi, S., Rabin, T. (eds.) TCC 2006. LNCS, vol. 3876, pp. 581–600. Springer, Heidelberg (2006)
14. MacKenzie, P.D., Reiter, M.K., Yang, K.: Alternatives to non-malleability: Definitions, constructions, and applications. In: Naor, M. (ed.) TCC 2004. LNCS, vol. 2951, pp. 171–190. Springer, Heidelberg (2004)
15. Qin, B., Wu, Q., Susilo, W., Mu, Y.: Publicly verifiable privacy-preserving group decryption. In: Yung, M., Liu, P., Lin, D. (eds.) Inscrypt 2008. LNCS, vol. 5487, pp. 72–83. Springer, Heidelberg (2009)

Experimental Analysis of Attacks on Next Generation Air Traffic Communication

Matthias Schäfer[1], Vincent Lenders[2], and Ivan Martinovic[3]

[1] TU Kaiserslautern, Germany
schaefer@cs.uni-kl.de
[2] Armasuisse, Switzerland
vincent.lenders@armasuisse.ch
[3] University of Oxford, UK
ivan.martinovic@cs.ox.ac.uk

Abstract. This work studies the security of next generation air traffic surveillance technology based on Automatic Dependent Surveillance – Broadcast (ADS-B). ADS-B is already supported by a majority of international aircraft and will become mandatory in 2020 for most airspaces worldwide. While it is known that ADS-B might be susceptible to different spoofing attacks, the complexity and impact of launching these attacks has been debated controversially by the air traffic control community. Yet, the literature remains unclear on the requirements of launching ADS-B attacks in real-world environments, and on the constraints which affect their feasibility. In this paper, we take a scientific approach to systematically evaluate realistic ADS-B attacks. Our objective is to shed light on the practicability of different threats and to quantify the main factors that impact the success of such attacks. Our results reveal some bad news: attacks on ADS-B can be inexpensive and highly successful. Using a controlled experimental design, we offer insights from a real-world feasibility analysis that leads to the conclusion that any safety-critical air traffic decision process should not rely exclusively on the ADS-B system.

Keywords: NextGen, ADS-B, Attacks, Security, Threats, Air Safety.

1 Introduction

Air traffic control (ATC) systems face large challenges in modern civil aviation. Controllers have to separate an increasing number of aircraft in their airspace. The European Organisation for the Safety of Air Navigation (EUROCONTROL) predicts almost a doubling of instrument flight rules (IFR) movements between 2009 and 2030 [1], which means higher air traffic density and therefore higher separation complexity. At the same time, civil aviation faces an increasing risk of terrorist or other attacks, necessitating protection.

To reliably meet separation minima, i.e. to manage the distances of aircraft to each other, controllers need accurate information about position, velocity and heading of all aircraft in their airspace. This information is retrieved from

M. Jacobson et al. (Eds.): ACNS 2013, LNCS 7954, pp. 253–271, 2013.

different sources such as flight progress strips, direct radio communications with the pilot and – most importantly – radar systems [2]. Conventional radar systems can be classified in primary surveillance radars (PSR) or secondary surveillance radars (SSR). PSRs are independent and do not require cooperation of aircraft. They transmit high-frequency signals that are reflected by the target. By receiving and evaluating the resulting echoes, the range, angular direction, velocity and even the size and shape of a target can be determined [3]. To meet higher demands in accuracy, SSR relies on transponders in aircraft, which respond to interrogations by ground stations. The responses contain the precise altitude and other information such as identification codes or information about technical problems. While SSR is still independent, it requires cooperation from the aircraft to function properly.

Driven by the ever growing air traffic volume and the shortcomings of PSR and SSR (mainly accuracy and cost), several efforts are underway to develop a new air traffic surveillance system that relies on satellite based navigation systems (NextGen in the US and SESAR in Europe [4,5]). The automatic dependent surveillance broadcast system (ADS-B) represents the most prominent system that has been mandated by EUROCONTROL in Europe and the FAA in America. In ADS-B, aircraft continuously determine their own position based on on-board navigational systems (e.g. GPS) and periodically broadcast it to surrounding ground sensors and aircraft. In contrast to PSR and SSR, the ADS-B system is not independent and requires full cooperation of the aircraft.

ADS-B support will be mandatory by 2020 in most airspaces in the world. Countries such as Australia and Canada have already started deploying ADS-B ground sensors at a nation-wide scale. By now, most airlines have reacted to this mandate and updated their aircraft with ADS-B capabilities. However, most aircraft manufacturers target a complete equipage by 2020.

ADS-B has evolved out of technologies whose development dates back to World War II. Back then, the designers did not have a modern adversarial model in mind. This deficiency led to a lack of modern security mechanisms and makes the air-ground data link vulnerable to multiple attacks. Even though the security threats and vulnerabilities of ADS-B have been identified and discussed by air navigation safety organizations [6,7] and open literature [8,9] for years, the common belief is still that existing vulnerabilities are difficult to exploit because doing so requires high-end equipment and precise positioning of the attacker. Recent research on security of ADS-B considers the difficulty to launch message injection and deletion attacks to be medium to hard [10,11] because the attacker must craft and transmit valid ADS-B messages.

In 2010, the FAA released the findings of its security certification and accreditation procedures [6]. This report includes comments from various entities, including the U.S. Department of Defense, expressing concerns that parties could monitor transmissions, that broadcasts could be used to target and harm aircraft, and that timing signals could be subject to interruption. However, the FAA concludes that "*using ADS-B data does not subject an aircraft to any increased risk compared to the risk that is experienced today*".

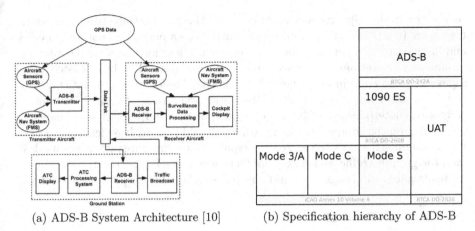

(a) ADS-B System Architecture [10]   (b) Specification hierarchy of ADS-B

Fig. 1. ADS-B Overview

These statements, however, mostly rely on qualitative and subjective assessments of the authors or of interviewed people. Considering the technical progress made in the past decades, such as the availability of low-cost software-defined radios, the above statement might underestimate the capabilities of a realistic wireless adversary.

Only recent publications at the computer security events Black Hat 2012 [12] and DEF CON 2012 [13] took practical feasibility of attacks with modern equipment into account. While these publications brought the ADS-B security issues to a wider attention, they did not offer much insights in the threat model.

Hence, the goal of this paper is to take a scientific approach to systematically evaluate the sophisticated ADS-B attacks, in particular those that result in malicious manipulation of radar screens based on injecting ghost aircraft, modifying an aircrafts position, or deleting the presence of an existing aircraft. To provide basic means for the development of countermeasures based on a realistic wireless adversary, we identify constraints an attacker faces under the special conditions of ADS-B. Instead of considering the limits for individual attacks, we break the attacks down into a few basic attack primitives and theoretically derive limits on placement and timing given by the large distances, message formats, and signal propagation characteristics.

Since ADS-B will only be globally deployed and adopted in 2020, the impact of the analyzed attacks on real-world air traffic safety can only be speculated today. Nevertheless, we hope that the insights of this paper will serve responsible authorities to better asses the security risks related to attacks on ADS-B and to be considered in the ongoing deployment and wide-scale adoption of ADS-B.

2   Background on ADS-B

The automatic dependent surveillance broadcast system (ADS-B) is a new paradigm to monitor the airspace and the FAA refers to ADS-B as the satellite-based successor of radar [4]. An overview of the ADS-B system architecture is shown in Figure 1a. In ADS-B, every aircraft computes its own position via on-board GPS and broadcasts it in periodic position messages. These messages are recorded by ground sensor stations and other aircraft in proximity. The broadcasted messages may also contain other fields like velocity, identification, intent, urgency code, and uncertainty level. Each ADS-B equipped aircraft or vehicle automatically starts determining and broadcasting its position and velocity when moving. Depending on the equipment class, the aircraft additionally broadcasts intent information once it enters the en route airspace. Receiving subsystems are used to monitor ground traffic and detect conflicts when moving on the runway. In en route airspaces, aircraft and ground sensors use ADS-B for situational awareness.

2.1 1090 ES Data Link

The ADS-B specification mainly describes the function of broadcasting information. Two standards are proposed as data link. The first alternative is the Universal Access Transceiver (UAT). UAT is specifically designed for ADS-B and other aviation services (e.g. traffic information broadcasting service) to overcome constraints of legacy systems. It establishes a channel with a data rate of 1 Mbps and operates at 978 MHz. Because UAT requires aircraft to be equipped with new hardware (transceivers), the FAA decided to use UAT only in general aviation[1] which is also practice in Europe [6].

For scheduled air transportation, ADS-B uses a mechanism of SSR Mode S, so called extended squitter, to broadcast the aircraft's state vector on the 1090 MHz channel. This combination of ADS-B and Mode S Extended Squitter is also referred to as 1090ES ADS-B (see Figure 1b). Typically, the ADS-B function is directly included into Mode S transponders. As 1090ES ADS-B is the major data link for scheduled air transportation, we focus our security investigations in this work on this standard and do not consider UAT any further.

3   Attacks on 1090ES ADS-B

As there are no cryptographic mechanisms implemented in the ADS-B protocol, messages can be trivially injected, modified or deleted by an attacker who has full control over the wireless channel in a Dolev-Yao [14] manner. However, as shown later, there are several hurdles to overcome for real-world attackers.

3.1 Passive Attacks

An inherent characteristic of wireless networks is the broadcast nature of RF communication. Since ADS-B messages are not encrypted, they can be recorded by an adversary and misused to obtain unique identifiers of aircraft as well as accurate position trajectories. Besides commercially available ADS-B receivers[2],

---

[1] General aviation refers to all civil flights not belonging to scheduled air transports.
[2] http://www.kinetic-avionics.co.uk/

Table 3. Example information about an aircraft provided by ADS-B and publicly available sources

Call sign	XYZ
ICAO ID	XYZ
Country	XYZ
Position	XYZ
Altitude	37700,ft
Heading	144°
Speed	395 kn
Climbing rate	896 ft/m

(a) ADS-B

Flight No.	XYZ
Owner	XYZ
Start	XYZ
Destination	XYZ
Scheduled arrival	19:25
Aircraft Model	Airbus A320-214
Seats	126-168
Engine	CFM56-5B4/P

(b) Publicly available sources

there are even services available on the Internet[3] which provide digitized live ADS-B data to the public. For more sophisticated traffic analyses, there is e.g. a Mode S and ADS-B capable open-source GNU Radio module[4] available. We extended this receiver to eavesdrop and analyze ADS-B traffic and signals.

The FAA argues in [6] that using ADS-B data does not subject an aircraft to any increased risk compared to the risk that is experienced today without ADS-B. Yet, privacy concerns are addressed partially by an identifier-based mechanism that provides pseudonymity for ADS-B communication. Furthermore, particular active attacks rely on the knowledge derived by passive eavesdropping of ADS-B messages, i.e. eavesdropping is often the first step involved in active attacks. By combining ADS-B provided data with other publicly available data sources (e.g. official databases provided by aviation authorities), attackers can retrieve enough information to launch targeted attacks. Table 3 shows information on a random aircraft retrieved from ADS-B and publicly available sources.

To get an idea of how much information an attacker could retrieve from eavesdropping ADS-B traffic, we conducted a one week measurement. The receiver was placed on top of a four-storied office building in an urban environment with an airport nearby.

In this week, we have seen 18545 flights of 3041 different aircraft from different countries. Some of these aircraft crossed our reception range in up to 10 flights in one day on their flights back and forth between national airports. On average, each aircraft was visible for roughly 10 minutes. We observed nearly every kind of aircraft ranging from light (< 7031 kg) to heavy aircraft (> 136078 kg), high vortex, high performance (> 5 g acceleration) and high speed (> 400 kn) aircraft, gliders and rotorcraft. By doing long-term measurements over large areas, attackers can derive statistics about persons, airlines or companies. For instance, detailed statistics about destinations, delays or fleet can be used to maintain useful datasets about competitors and their business activities. In addition, we were able to create the Received Signal Strength (RSS) map shown in Figure 2a

---

[3] http://www.flightradar24.com/
[4] https://www.cgran.org/wiki/gr-air-modes

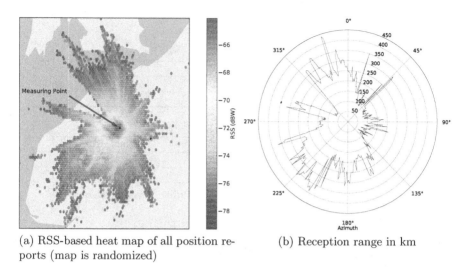

(a) RSS-based heat map of all position re-   (b) Reception range in km
ports (map is randomized)

Fig. 2. Signal strength and range of our measurements

with our dataset. RSS profiling-based localization techniques (see e.g. [15] for details) or multilateration can be used to locate aircraft, even if they conceal their position as in case of military aircraft.

Our measurements conclude that the reception quality and range with low cost equipment is remarkable. By positioning our receiver on the roof of a seven-floor building in another experiment on a day with optimal clear weather, we were able to receive messages over distances of up to a maximum of 450 km (compare Figure 2b). This shows that it is easily feasible to monitor the ADS-B traffic of hundreds of aircraft at the same time with a single low-cost receiver.

3.2   Active Attacks

While passive attacks are mainly affecting privacy and might not result in severe risks for air-traffic safety, this section focuses on our main threat model, which is an active attacker. In the following we describe active attacks that may result in severe threats to air traffic safety including attacks on air traffic monitors and automated assisting systems like collision avoidance (TCAS) and pilots.

It is important to keep in mind that we consider ADS-B only, i.e. not in combination with other surveillance technologies. More complex attack scenarios which include combined attacks on several technologies simultaneously are imaginable but beyond the scope of this paper. Furthermore they would require detailed knowledge of the actual implementations of surveillance systems, which are apparently kept under tight wraps by the respective authorities.

Attacker Model: The following active attacks are based on three basic attack primitives: message injection, message deletion and message modification. For now, we assume that the attacker has full control over the wireless communication channel and is able to *inject, delete and modify* any ADS-B message. Functional and timing requirements will be derived in Section 5.

Ghost Aircraft Injection: Based on fake message injection, ADS-B messages of a non-existing (ghost) aircraft are broadcasted on the ADS-B communication channel. This attack was presented conceptually in [9,10,11]. Target of this attack could be any legitimate ADS-B receiver. The ghost aircraft should have realistic properties (position, velocity, ID) in order to be indistinguishable from real aircraft without additional information sources. On the ground, air traffic controllers could be confused or distracted by ghost aircraft. Ghost aircraft could appear as both, taxiing and flying aircraft and combined with poor visibility, this could force controllers to deny landings or instruct aircraft to change their altitude and/or course unnecessarily. In the air, on-board ADS-B-based collision avoidance systems offer attackers a simple way to distract pilots. Again, with poor visibility, pilots primarily make decisions based on their instruments what makes them vulnerable to malicious interference. Deep knowledge about the behavior of collision avoidance systems and a systematic injection of ghost aircraft enable attackers to force collision avoidance systems to instruct pilots to change their course, velocity and/or altitude almost arbitrarily. The injection of ghost aircraft would not directly result in a crash since pilots still make their own decisions. But due to the increased situational complexity, this attack could result in life threatening decisions made by confused pilots and controllers.

Ghost Aircraft Flooding: Based on the same techniques as the previous attack, i.e. message injection, ghost aircraft flooding is the injection of multiple aircraft simultaneously [10]. This attack aims primarily at a denial of service of the controller's surveillance system. Contrary to single ghost aircraft injections, this attack is obvious. By using realistic ghost aircraft, the presence of ghost and real aircraft are hard to distinguish for controllers. The impact of flooding an airborne aircraft with ghost aircraft is unclear, since no tests with collision avoidance systems are reported so far and the detailed implementation of ADS-B-based collision avoidance systems is not publicly available. On the ground, both, airport and airspace surveillance systems can be a target. By covering the airport or airspace with ghost aircraft, management of runways or airborne aircraft is impossible without the support of other surveillance technologies.

Virtual Trajectory Modification: This new attack aims at modifying the trajectory of an *existing* aircraft, which broadcasts correct ADS-B position reports. The attack can be implemented in two ways: by combining message deletion and injection or directly via message modification technique. The former variant deletes all position reports of the target aircraft and replays them slightly modified. The latter variant modifies the position reports in the air. This attack benefits from inaccuracies of other surveillance technologies like primary surveillance radar (PSR), since a tolerant data fusion with e.g. ADS-B and PSR provided data might not reveal these slight inconsistencies. With a smooth takeover, this attack might remain undetected and could lead to wrong instructions by air traffic controllers or delayed reactions of collision avoidance systems.

False Alarm Attack: Similar to the virtual trajectory modification, the attacker deletes and re-injects or modifies messages of a real aircraft in order to indicate a fake alarm. Like Mode S, ADS-B provides mechanisms to indicate emergencies or unlawful interferences such as aircraft hijacking. Such an attack results in confusion and focuses the attention of responsible persons on the target aircraft. Furthermore it may initiate other processes such as the denial of the permission to land or penalty charges for airlines. The detection of this deception on higher levels than the physical layer is hard, since e.g. voice radio must be considered to be untrustworthy in case of a hijacked aircraft.

Ground Station Flooding: Continuous jamming attacks on a ground sensor or aircraft result in high losses and deletion of messages. ADS-B-based ATC cannot provide service any more due to failure of communications. The threat of this attack is well-known [9,11,10] and considered to be of low difficulty. This attack would force ATC to switch to other, less efficient or less accurate surveillance and control methods. Especially in high density areas (e.g. around major international airports), a sudden failure of the surveillance or collision avoidance systems is described as *devastating* by controllers and could result in confusion and human failure with fatal consequences. ATC would have to redirect aircraft blindly into other airspaces via voice radio – assuming that voice radio is not attacked as well. If the attacker is strong enough to also jam the communication between aircraft, collision avoidance systems would fail. As history has shown, without the support of collision avoidance systems, collisions are likely to happen. Especially in climbing or descending phases since pilots might miss nearby aircraft due to their limited perspective.

Aircraft Disappearance: Failure of collision avoidance systems and confusion at ground sensors when correlating several data sources can be caused by deleting all messages of a target aircraft with message deletion techniques. By doing so, the attacker prevents aircraft from being detected by ADS-B ground stations or other aircraft. This attack is similar to ground station flooding but more subtle, since the absence of a single aircraft is – if detected – more likely due to failure of avionics than of ground station hardware. If detected, this attack could force the target aircraft to land for safety checks. In case of the attack remaining undetected, the aircraft is not protected by ADS-B-based systems such as collision avoidance, what could have fatal consequences.

Aircraft Spoofing: In order to spoof and outflank surveillance facilities, the ICAO 24 bit address may be spoofed. This can be achieved through combining message deletion and message injection. In addition, the ICAO address in transponders can be reprogrammed by any person who is able to access the cockpit. Masquerading as a friendly aircraft reduces causes for alarm when an unexpected aircraft is detected by other surveillance technologies like PSR.

4   Implementation, Demonstration and Results

This section demonstrates the ghost aircraft injection, ghost aircraft flooding, ground station flooding and virtual trajectory modification attacks with COTS

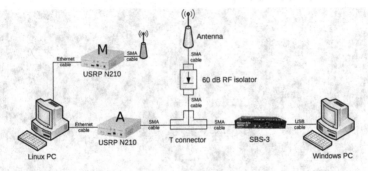

Fig. 3. Experimental setup with additional safety precautions. The attacker's target is an SBS-3 ADS-B receiver which is connected to an isolated antenna and the attacker's signal output. Just in case of a signal leakage, the attacker uses an additional receiver to detect the leakage and terminate the attack immediately.

hardware. Within a controlled environment, we were able to launch these attacks in a realistic manner.

4.1 Safety Precautions and Hardware Setup

Due to the criticality of this topic and the legal requirements concerning usage of wireless channels, a safe and yet realistic practical evaluation of the above attacks poses special challenges. At first and most important, all experiments *must not* affect real systems in any way. It must be ensured that none of the attacker's signals can be perceived by a real system. At the same time, a realistic evaluation requires that the attacker's signal underlies realistic channel characteristics including noise and ADS-B traffic from other aircraft.

To fulfill both requirements, we used in consultation with the respective regulatory authority the experimental setup depicted in Figure 3. The target of our attacks was an SBS-3 ADS-B receiver which receives real ADS-B messages via an antenna and forwards them to a PC running a special radar-style visualization software (Kinetic Avionic's BaseStation). The attacker consists out of an off-the-shelf Linux-based PC and an Ettus' USRP N210 SDR (A). To ensure that the attacker's signals do not interfere with real communications, we connected a 60 dB RF isolator ahead of the antenna which attenuates signals unidirectionally in the direction of the antenna. By additionally reducing the transmission power of the attacker's USRP to the least possible value, the signal emitted by the antenna should be imperceptible by any other receivers than our SBS-3 receiver.

As an additional safety precaution, the attacker's PC is connected to a second USRP N210 (M) which runs a GNU Radio-based ADS-B receiver. For the case of an unexpected leakage of the attacker's messages, this receiver is programmed such that it terminates all attacks immediately on reception of a message sent by the attacker. In order to enhance the sensitivity of this *safety monitor*, we disabled the check for valid CRC checksums.

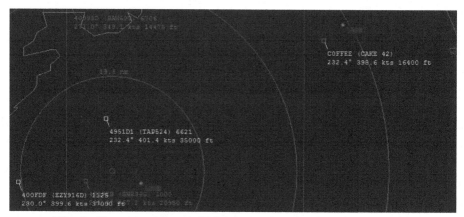

Fig. 4. Ghost aircraft with ICAO 24-bit ID 0xC0FFEE (north east)

4.2 Implementation

We used the SDR USRP N210 to inject and receive ADS-B messages and to generate jamming signals. The USRP is connected to a host computer that generates samples and sends the digitalized signal data to the USRP via Ethernet. Then, the USRP shifts the software-generated signal from the baseband to the desired frequency using digital up converters, converts the digital to an analog signal and emits it. Together with the open-source software development toolkit for software radios, GNU Radio, the USRP provides a suitable foundation for our implementations at low-cost ($1800-$2500).

For our attacks, we implemented a signal generator block which enables us to generate arbitrary pulse position modulated messages including the preamble according to [16]. A script written in Python generates arbitrary messages and passes them to the signal generator. It generates IQ-samples that are transported to the USRP via Ethernet. A jammer for message deletion attacks is realized with a Gaussian noise waveform generator that covers the full downlink channel of Mode S. For eavesdropping on messages, we extended the open-source GNU Radio Mode S receiver module[5] such that it stores the decoded ADS-B messages plus signal properties (RSSI, SNR, ...) to a database. To inject realistic ADS-B messages, we implemented a library that simulates arbitrary flights. It calculates the trajectory and all required ADS-B messages at the requested rates.

So as not to decrease the implementation complexity for attacks, we skip further implementation details and will not disclose any part of our source code.

4.3 Results

Ghost Aircraft Injection: Our implementation simulates a flight of an aircraft with a fake identity from a starting coordinate to a target coordinate at

---
[5] https://www.cgran.org/wiki/gr-air-modes

a given velocity and altitude. The aircraft disappears after arrival. During the ghost flight, the software generates the respective ADS-B position and velocity reports, each with a rate of 2 Hz, and identification reports at 0.2 Hz, i.e. once in 5 seconds. As Figure 4 illustrates, the radar software of SBS-3 shows our injected ghost aircraft flying inconspicuously from the airport in north east to the airport in south-west at an altitude of ~16400 ft and a velocity of ~400 kn. Except in its obviously fake identifier, the ghost aircraft does not differ from real aircraft.

Ghost Aircraft Flooding: The ghost aircraft flooding implementation generates a given number of ghost aircraft using the ghost aircraft injection implementation but with random (yet realistic) parameters. The starting and target coordinates of each ghost aircraft are set to random coordinates within a target area. The altitude and ground speed are selected randomly from a range between 16400 and 32800 ft and 200 and 600 kts respectively. When starting the attack, all generated ghost aircraft perform simulated random flights back and forth between their start and destination coordinates while sending out the same messages with the same rates as in the ghost aircraft injection above. As Figure 5b shows, this attack results in a complete loss of situational awareness. Due to the random distribution, it is difficult and time-consuming to determine whether an aircraft is real or not. One notable effect of this attack was the freezing of the BaseStation-Software for several minutes due to the heavy workload caused by the high number injected aircraft. Some SSR implementations detect the sudden appearance of targets as a failure of the system and initiate a reboot-procedure, what equals a failure of the system for several minutes. It would be easy for an attacker to cause such a failure if ADS-B receivers are implemented similarly.

Ground Station Flooding: In this experiment, the attacker emits a continuous white noise jamming waveform. This waveform interferences at the SBS-3 resulting in complete deletion of all messages. By executing the attack, the noise level is significantly increased. As Figure 5a shows, a successful reception and demodulation of messages on the 1090 MHz channel is not possible any more, resulting in a complete denial of service.

Virtual Trajectory Modification: We implemented the virtual trajectory modification attack with the combination of the message deletion and message injection attack techniques. First, the attacker deletes all messages at the ground sensor by generating constant interference as in the previous ground station flooding attack. At the same time, the attacker uses an additional ADS-B receiver to capture and forward all but the target aircraft's messages. The forwarded messages are transmitted at a higher power than the interference. Except for the injected position updates of the modified aircraft trajectory, all aircraft position updates reflect the correct position. The result of this attack was an authentic radar screen (similar to Figure 4) while the trajectory of the target aircraft was modified from the start of our attack. Without any other sources of information, it is hardly possible to recognize this modification since we implemented a smooth takeover.

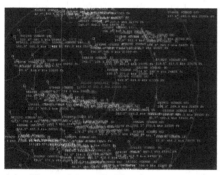 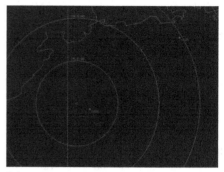

(a) Ghost Aircraft Flooding: 100 randomly distribution ghost aircraft appear
in the specified area and fly back and forth
between two random coordinates.

(b) Ground Station Flooding: By emitting
white noise, all ADS-B messages sent by
aircraft in range are destroyed what results in an empty radar screen.

Fig. 5. Snapshots of Kinetic Avionic's BaseStation under Ghost Aircraft Flooding and
Ground Station Flooding attacks.

5   Feasibility and Requirements Analysis

This section provides a better understanding of the actual threat of the eavesdropping, injection, deletion, and modification attack primitives by analyzing
their actual requirements under a *realistic* attacker model. In particular, we analyze the timing, positioning and signal power constraints for the attacker and
derive practical bounds for these parameters.

5.1   Passive Attacks

The attacker's reception range must include the position of all target aircraft to
perform passive attacks. The range depends on the received signal-to-noise ratio
(SNR) at the attacker and must satisfy $P_{PA}/N_A > \delta$, where P_{PA} is the received
signal power of the aircraft's signal at the attacker, N_A the noise floor of the
attacker's receiver, and δ the minimum SNR to correctly decode a message. High
gain antennas and a sensitive receiver which is capable of decoding messages with
very low SNR can increase the reception range. Another important factor is the
position of the receiver. Our experiments showed that obstacles and geographic
conditions can reduce the range significantly. Figure 2b illustrates the strong
dependency of the range from environmental conditions. A high building at an
azimuth of 305° resulted in a massive reduction of the reception range in this
direction.

5.2   Active Attacks

All active attacks presented in Section 3 use either message injection, message deletion, message modification, or combinations of these as basic attack mechanisms. This section analyzes the limits of these attack primitives. Especially the signal power, timing and positioning constraints are considered.

Message Injection: Since no authentication is required at message level in ADS-B, injecting false messages requires an attacker to implement a transmitter that generates correctly modulated signals in the right message format. Hence, the requirement for a successful message injection attack at ground sensor node G is $P_{AG}/N_G > \delta$, where P_{AG} represents the received power at the ground sensor G emitted by the attacker A, N_G the noise floor at the ground sensor and δ the required minimal SNR to correctly demodulate the signal. For ADS-B receivers that use omni-directional antennas, false messages may be injected from any location as the receiver is not able to discriminate false position messages based on the incoming angle of arrival. However, even when rotating directional antennas are used (e.g. SSR antennas), injecting false messages from a different angle is possible because directional antennas usually have significant side-lobes and will receive the signal even when it does not arrive at the main lobe [17]. The same holds for message deletion and modification attacks.

For attacks that require numerous message injections, the number of messages to be injected is limited by the bandwidth of the channel. The number of injected ghost aircraft is limited by the bandwidth as follows. For 1090 ES ADS-B, each message transmission lasts $120\,\mu s$. Assuming each of the n ghost aircraft sends on average m messages per second, n is limited by $n \leq 1\,s/(m \cdot 120\,\mu s)$. If each aircraft broadcasts its position and velocity with a rate of $2\,Hz$ each and identification once in $5\,s$, n has an upper bound of 1984. We successfully tested the ghost aircraft flooding attack with this configuration and it turned out that the bottleneck of this attack is indeed the bandwidth of the ADS-B channel.

Message Deletion: This attack can be realized in two ways: by means of destructive or constructive interference. With destructive interference, the attacker attempts to annihilate the signal at the sensor by transmitting the inverse of the signal from the legitimate node. As the received signal by the sensor is the superposition of both signals, the resulting signal is erased or at least highly attenuated. This type of interference requires very precise timing and synchronization with the carrier phase and frequency in order to achieve the desired annihilation [18]. This synchronization is hardly achievable with moving aircraft and we will not consider it in this work.

Constructive interference is much easier to achieve as the synchronization requirements are less strict. With constructive interference, the aircraft's signal will experience a higher level of bit errors. The checksum parity field of the extended squitter allows the correction of at most 5 bit errors in a message. Messages with more than 5 bit errors are not correctable anymore and have to be discarded by ground sensors. The requirement for constructive interference at a ground sensor G is

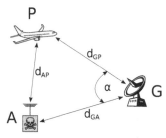

Fig. 6. Attacker Scenario

Table 4. Time offsets for deletion decision in message deletion attacks

Deletion decision field	Time offset t_D
ICAO address	40 μs
identification	96 μs
position	96 μs
emergency code	51 μs
positioning integrity (NIC_p)	48 μs
positioning accuracy (NAC_p)	83 μs

$$\frac{P_{PG}}{P_{AG} + N_G} < \beta, \tag{1}$$

where P_{PG} is the received signal power of the aircraft P's legitimate message and β the threshold for the minimal required SNR to decode messages correctly. The factor β is highly dependent on the signal waveform used by the attacker and how well the receiver is able to suppress this kind of interference with appropriate filters. For a waveform with a white Gaussian distribution with zero mean, the interference can be viewed as noise and β is equal to δ.

To delete all messages on the channel, requirement (1) is sufficient. However, if the attacker aims at deleting messages selectively, additional timing requirements are given. To delete selected messages, the attacker must continuously listen to the medium, interpret incoming messages, and interfere only with the desired messages before they are completely received at the ground sensor. This form of reactive jamming requires stringent timing in order to hit the message at the receiver. In the following, we derive the timing and placement requirements for this type of selective message deletion.

Let d_{GP} denote the distance between ground sensor (G) and aircraft (P), d_{GA} the distance between ground sensor and attacker (A), d_{AP} the distance between attacker and aircraft, and α the angle between the attacker A and the aircraft P as seen from the ground station G (see Figure 6). Signal propagation speed is assumed to be the speed of light c. The respective signal propagation times t_{GP}, t_{GA} and t_{AP} are then given by

$$t_{GP} = \frac{d_{GP}}{c} \qquad t_{GA} = \frac{d_{GA}}{c} \qquad t_{AP} = \frac{d_{AP}}{c}$$

Let further t_D denote the time offset of the message portion, which is used by the reactive jammer to decide whether it should jam or not, to the first pulse of the preamble. For instance, when an attacker relies on the ICAO 24 bit address of an extended squitter, t_D is 40 μs[6]. A list of different values of t_D for possible deletion decision fields is given in Table 4. Finally, t_R denotes the reaction time of the attacker, i.e. the hardware switching time between the moment when the decision to delete the message is made until the actual interference is emitted by the attacker. Selective message deletion attacks are then feasible if and only

---

[6] 8 μs preamble + 5 μs downlink format + 3 μs capability field + 24 μs ICAO address.

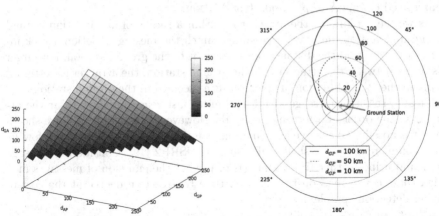

(a) Depending on d_{GP} and d_{AP}. Constant parameters are $t_{msg} = 120\,\mu s$, $t_D = 40\,\mu s$ and $t_R = 0\,\mu s$ (worst case)

(b) Depending on the angle α between attacker and aircraft at the ground station. Messages are selected by the attacker based on their ICAO 24 bit ID ($\Rightarrow$ $d_R = 20.09$ km)

Fig. 7. Upper bound of the distance d_{GA} (in km) between ground station and attacker for message deletion attacks

if $t_R < t_{msg} - t_D + t_{GP} - t_{AP} - t_{GA} - 5\,\mu s$ holds, where t_{msg} is the message transmission time (120 μs in this case) and the 5 μs subtracted on the right-hand side results from the minimum of 5 wrong bits required to destroy the messages successfully (due to the CRC). Otherwise, the injected interference would arrive too late at the ground sensor and the intended deletion of the message would fail. Due to this, the attacker's position is contrained by $d_{GA} < d_{GP} - d_{AP} + (t_{msg} - t_D - t_R - 5\mu s) \cdot c$. The graph shown in Figure 7a shows an upper bound for d_{GA} when deleting messages based on the aircraft address ($t_D = 40\mu s$) and for a reaction time of zero (worst case). This result shows that this attack always benefits from far distances between ground station and aircraft and short distances between attacker and ground station.

However, the attacker has a clear advantage because he can adjust his position such that the angle α is optimal to him. Assume for example an attacker that is positioned close to an airport. Since all aircraft will land and start along the same direction, he may optimize his attack range without the need to reduce its distance to the ground station. For the attacker's reaction and distance requirements in relation to the angle α, we use the law of cosines and get

$$d_{GA} < \frac{d_R \cdot d_{GP} + \frac{d_R^2}{2}}{d_R + d_{GP} \cdot (1 - \cos\alpha)} \qquad (2)$$

where $d_R = (t_{msg} - t_D - t_R - 5\mu s) \cdot c$. Figure 7b shows an upper bound for d_{GA} when deleting messages based on the aircraft address and with zero reaction delay ($t_R = 0$). The curves represent an upper bound on d_{GA} for different angles α and fixed distances $d_{GP} = 100, 50$ and $10\,\mathrm{km}$.

As we see, as long as the attacker is within a radius of about $10\,\mathrm{km}$ around the ground station, he may successfully launch the message deletion attack independent of α and the distance of the aircraft to the ground station. For larger distances between the attacker and the ground station, the attacker is better off being in the same direction of the aircraft as seen from the ground station.

Clearly, selective message deletion requires fast reaction times t_R at the attacker in the order of a few microseconds. However, Wilhelm et al. have shown that it is possible to achieve fast jamming reaction times in the order of a few μs with commercial off-the-shelf SDRs such as USRP2 [19]. Considering message rates and using further traffic analysis to predict the emission of messages may relax these constraints on the reaction time to a certain degree at the cost of higher detection complexity.

Message Modification: The goal of message modification attacks is to modify a message while it is being transmitted over the air. There are two possible techniques to manipulate messages during transmission — overshadowing and bit-flipping. When overshadowing, the attacker's signal is of such high power relative to the legitimate transmission that the original message (or parts of it) appears as noise. With bit-flipping, the attacker superimposes the radio signal such that one or several bits are converted from one to zero or vice versa. Bit flipping requires precise synchronization to the carrier phase and frequency and is hence extremely difficult to achieve for moving targets like aircraft and is therefore not considered in this work [18].

To overshadow the signal of a legitimate aircraft transmitter, $P_{AG}/P_{PG} > \gamma$ must hold, where γ is a fixed threshold value defining the minimum signal-to-interference ratio (SIR) at which the attacker's signal is decoded without error.

The timing and distance requirements are slightly more strict than for the message deletion attack. Let t_M denote the offset of the message portion to be modified to the last bit of the field that is used by the attacker to decide whether it should modify the actual message or not. For instance, when an attacker wants to modify the sixteenth bit of the message data (ME) field based on the ICAO 24 bit address in the aircraft address (AA) field, t_M is $16\,\mu s$ since the ME field is directly after the AA field. On-the-fly modification attacks are then feasible if and only if the following constraint on the attacker's reaction time is satisfied:

$$t_R < t_M + \frac{d_{GA} + d_{GP} - \sqrt{d_{GA}^2 + d_{GP}^2 - 2\,d_{GA}\,d_{GP}\cos\alpha}}{c} \tag{3}$$

Otherwise, the injected modification signal arrives too late at the aircraft and the intended modification of the message fails. Due to this, we can formulate the following constraint on the attacker's position:

$$d_{GA} < \frac{d_{GP} + \frac{c}{2} \cdot (t_M - t_R)}{1 + \frac{d_{GP} \cdot (1 - \cos\alpha)}{c \cdot (t_M - t_R)}}. \tag{4}$$

Since a CRC checksum is used to detect transmission errors, the CRC must be further modified by the attacker in any case to preserve the validity of the message. This does not pose a challenge since all transmitted bits are known to the attacker and he is therefore able to calculate the new CRC of the modified message and modify the CRC as well.

An additional timing challenge lies in the estimation of the signal propagation delays t_{GP}, t_{AP}, and t_{AG}. The attacker needs to precisely estimate these delays such that its overshadowing signal arrives at the correct time of the bits to be modified. An overall estimation precision below 1 μs is necessary to inject its modified bit sequence at the correct message position at the ground sensor. This synchronization is however easy to achieve since the exact positions of the aircraft are known to the attacker from the received ADS-B messages.

To summarize this section, the following statements can be concluded from this section. While message eavesdropping and message injection are only constrained by signal power, the message deletion and message modification attacks have additional constraints with regard to timing and position. Nevertheless, we have shown that these constraints are not major hurdles. An attacker can launch these attacks with low-cost software radio equipment at distances of up to ten km to the ground station independent on the aircraft constellation in the sky. By carefully positioning itself with the correct angle, an attacker may even increase its attack range beyond 100 km from the ground station.

6   Related Work on ADS-B Security

While the aviation community already expressed reservations about the lack of security mechanisms[7], research on ADS-B security as found in the open literature has focused on the identification of vulnerabilities and subjective risk analysis. This section provides a summary of open literature on ADS-B security.

Korzel and Andrisani already identified potential threats resulting from unverified ADS-B reports in 2004 [8]. They proposed verification and validation techniques to verify the reported state of an aircraft, signal conformance in terms of the reported position vs. true physical position and intent conformance. They use a suite of Kalman filters to estimate the state of an aircraft and multilateration to compare signal properties with the reported position. The focus of their work is however not on security aspects and no concrete adversarial model is considered by the authors. In addition, they do not investigate particular threats resulting from the lack of security mechanisms.

In 2007, Valovage discusses several enhancements to ADS-B including security services such as authentication and confidentiality with cryptographic methods [20]. They propose an authentication scheme in terms of pre-shared keys and cryptographic hash sums.

In 2009, Wood interviewed six professionals affiliated with the aviation community [21]. Based on their subjective assessments, they conducted a security risk analysis. The work is focused on three central aspects: comparing the ADS-B network design to government and commercial industry network security standards, identifying several similarities and differences between the introduced

---

[7] http://www.airsport-corp.com/adsb2.htm

ADS-B network and industry standard computer networks. They also analyzed the behavior of ADS-B when faced with common computer network threats such as denial of service, session hijacking, and network eavesdropping attacks. They offer a brief analysis of threats and vulnerabilities concerning confidentiality, integrity and availability of ADS-B. In contrast to our work, the assessments of threats are based on the subjective experience of the interviewed people. Hence, there is no systematic evaluation and feasibility analysis of these threats from a technical perspective.

Sampigethaya et al. identified several attacks in 2010 and proposed solutions based on cooperative groups of aircraft to mitigate threats to airborne surveillance [9,22]. Furthermore, they designed a security simulation concept and simulation tool which allows users to model and quantify the impact of ADS-B exploits. However, they do not provide any statements about the feasibility of attacks on the ADS-B data link. The overall objective of attackers in their model is to degrade accuracy and performance, while more sophisticated attacks are not at the focus of their analysis. In 2010, Purton et al. performed an analysis of the threats, opportunities, weaknesses and strengths (TOWS analysis) of the ADS-B system [11]. They identified several threats to different communication links (GPS, propagation path, ground infrastructure), rated their likelihood and severity, and derived strategic actions. They only provide qualitative judgments about likelihood and severity based on the high-level assessments of the authors. Again, no detailed technical investigations are made to provide realistic statements on feasibility of specific attacks. The primary objective of McCallie et al. in their work in 2011 was to establish a taxonomy to classify attacks on ground stations and aircraft based on ADS-B message injection, jamming and interception [10]. Additionally, they provided valuable security recommendations, which request more transparency of security certifications and accreditation procedures, and a complete security analysis of the whole NextGen system design. They motivate the integration of security as an additional objective in SSR development and an adequate education on security aspects to the aviation community. Attacks are considered to be of low difficulty only if specialized hardware and software are readily available. Compared to their work, we see our contribution as an important step forward in understanding the severity of the threats.

7   Conclusion

ADS-B is an air-traffic surveillance technology that will become mandatory for regulating airspace in 2020. One of the main objectives of this technology is to increase the safety of the worldwide air traffic by increasing the aircraft positioning accuracy. The main objective of this work was to investigate practical attacks against ADS-B and to offer insights from a real-world evaluation. We believe that by providing these insights, this work will help ATC and regulation authorities to realistically assess the risks that this technology will pose when fully operational. We conclude that without appropriate countermeasures, critical air traffic management decision processes should not rely on ADS-B derived data. Finally, we hope that the rule makers and regulators involved in the

ADS-B standardization process will recognize the criticality of the described threats and include security as one of its key requirements in future releases.

References

1. Statistics and Forecast Service: Long-Term Forecast: IFR Flight Movements 2010 – 2030. EEC Technical Report CND/STATFOR Doc415, EUROCONTROL (2010)
2. Carswell, C.M. (ed.) Reviews of Human Factors and Ergonomics, vol. 4, pp. 195–244. Human Factors and Ergonomics Society (2008)
3. Skolnik, M.I.: Radar handbook, 3rd edn. McGraw-Hill Professional (2007)
4. Federal Aviation Administration: NextGen Implementation Plan (March 2011)
5. SESAR Consortium: The ATM Target Concept. Technical report (2007)
6. Federal Aviation Administration: Automatic Dependent Surveillance—Broadcast (ADS-B) Out Performance Requirements To Support Air Traffic Control (ATC) Service; Final Rule. Federal Register 75(103), 14 CFR Part 91 (May 2010)
7. ICAO: Safeguarding International Civil Aviation Against Acts of Unlawful Interference, 9th edn., Annex 17: Security (2011)
8. Krozel, J., Andrisani, D., Ayoubi, M.A., Hoshizaki, T., Schwalm, C.: Aircraft ADS-B Data Integrity Check. In: AIAA Aviation, Technology, Integration, and Operations Conference Proceedings (September 2004)
9. Sampigethaya, K., Poovendran, R.: Visualization & assessment of ADS-B security for green ATM. In: 2010 IEEE/AIAA 29th Digital Avionics Systems Conference (DASC), pp. 3.A.3-1–3.A.3-16 (October 2010)
10. McCallie, D., Butts, J., Mills, R.: Security analysis of the ADS-B implementation in the next generation air transportation system. International Journal of Critical Infrastructure Protection 4, 78–87 (2011)
11. Purton, L., Abbass, H., Alam, S.: Identification of ADS-B System Vulnerabilities and Threats. In: Australian Transport Research Forum (October 2010)
12. Costin, A.: Ghost is in the air(traffic). Black Hat USA (July 2012)
13. Haines, B.: Hacker + Airplanes = No Good Can Come of This. In: DEF CON®20 Hacking Conference (July 2012)
14. Dolev, D., Yao, A.: On the security of public key protocols. IEEE Transactions on Information Theory 29(2), 198–208 (1983)
15. Mao, G., Fidan, B., Anderson, B.D.: Wireless sensor network localization techniques. Computer Networks 51(10), 2529–2553 (2007)
16. ICAO: Annex 10: Aeronautical Telecommunications, 4th edn., vol. IV. Surveillance and Collision Avoidance Systems (2007)
17. Stevens, M.: Secondary surveillance radar. Artech House (1988)
18. Pöpper, C., Tippenhauer, N.O., Danev, B., Capkun, S.: Investigation of Signal and Message Manipulations on the Wireless Channel. In: Atluri, V., Diaz, C. (eds.) ESORICS 2011. LNCS, vol. 6879, pp. 40–59. Springer, Heidelberg (2011)
19. Wilhelm, M., Martinovic, I., Schmitt, J.B., Lenders, V.: Reactive jamming in wireless networks: how realistic is the threat? In: Proceedings of the Fourth ACM Conference on Wireless Network Security, WiSec 2011, pp. 47–52 (2011)
20. Valovage, E.: Enhanced ADS-B Research. IEEE Aerospace and Electronic Systems Magazine 22(5), 35–38 (2007)
21. Wood, R.G.: A security risk analysis of the data communications network proposed in the nextgen air traffic control system. PhD thesis, Stillwater, OK, USA (2009)
22. Sampigethaya, K., Poovendran, R., Bushnell, L.: Assessment and mitigation of cyber exploits in future aircraft surveillance. In: IEEE Aerospace Conference (March 2010)

Launching Generic Attacks on iOS
with Approved Third-Party Applications

Jin Han[1], Su Mon Kywe[2], Qiang Yan[2], Feng Bao[1], Robert Deng[2],
Debin Gao[2], Yingjiu Li[2], and Jianying Zhou[1]

[1] Institute for Infocomm Research
[2] Singapore Management University

Abstract. iOS is Apple's mobile operating system, which is used on
iPhone, iPad and iPod touch. Any third-party applications developed for
iOS devices are required to go through Apple's application vetting process and appear on the official iTunes App Store upon approval. When an
application is downloaded from the store and installed on an iOS device,
it is given a limited set of privileges, which are enforced by iOS application sandbox. Although details of the vetting process and the sandbox
are kept as black box by Apple, it was generally believed that these iOS
security mechanisms are effective in defending against malwares.

In this paper, we propose a generic attack vector that enables third-
party applications to launch attacks on non-jailbroken iOS devices. Following this generic attack mechanism, we are able to construct multiple
proof-of-concept attacks, such as cracking device PIN and taking snapshots without user's awareness. Our applications embedded with the attack codes have passed Apple's vetting process and work as intended
on non-jailbroken devices. Our proof-of-concept attacks have shown that
Apple's vetting process and iOS sandbox have weaknesses which can be
exploited by third-party applications. We further provide corresponding
mitigation strategies for both vetting and sandbox mechanisms, in order
to defend against the proposed attack vector.

1   Introduction

Digital mobile devices, such as smartphones and tablets, have been increasingly
used for personal and business purposes in recent years. iOS from Apple is one
of the most popular mobile operating systems in terms of the number of users.
By Jan 2013, 500 millions of iOS devices had been sold worldwide and Apple's
iTunes App Store contained over 800,000 iOS third-party applications, which
had been downloaded for more than 40 billion times [1].

Third-party applications are pervasively installed on iOS devices as they provide various functions that significantly extend the usability of the mobile devices. On the other hand, these third-party applications pose potential threats
to personal and business data stored on the devices. Thus, Apple adopts various
security measures on its iOS platform to protect the device from malicious third-
party applications. Among these security measures, Apple's application vetting

M. Jacobson et al. (Eds.): ACNS 2013, LNCS 7954, pp. 272–289, 2013.

process and the iOS application sandbox are considered as the fundamental mechanisms that protect users from security and privacy exploits.

Each iOS third-party application is required to go through a vetting process before it is published on the official iTunes App Store, which is the only source of obtaining applications without jailbreaking an iOS device. Although details of the vetting process are kept secret, it is generally regarded as highly effective since no harmful malware on non-jailbroken devices has been reported on iTunes App Store [2,3]. Only graywares, which stealthily collect sensitive user data, were found on iTunes Store. These graywares were immediately removed from the store upon discovery [4].

When an application is downloaded and installed on an iOS device, it is given a limited set of privileges [5], which are enforced by the application sandbox. With the sandbox restrictions, an application cannot access files and folders of other applications. In order to access the required user data or control system hardware (e.g. Bluetooth or WiFi), applications need to call respective iOS APIs which are hooked by the sandbox so that validations of these API invocations are performed dynamically. The sandbox mechanism serves as the last line of defense which restricts malicious applications from accessing privileged system services, abusing user data or exploiting resources of other applications.

Due to the closed-source nature of iOS platform, the implementation details of security mechanisms used by iOS (including vetting process and application sandbox) are not officially documented. As a result, to our best knowledge, there is no systematic security analysis conducted for iOS platform, which has been generally believed as one of the most secure commodity operating systems [6].

In this paper, we make the first attempt in constructing generic attacks on iOS platform. Existing ad hoc attacks usually require root privilege [7,8,9] and thus work only on jailbroken iOS devices. In contrast, our attacks are intended to work on non-jailbroken iOS devices, which are protected by both vetting process and application sandbox. Thus, we propose an attack vector which include two attack stages: 1) In the first stage, malicious applications which are embedded with attack codes need to pass Apple's vetting process in order to appear in the official iTunes App Store; 2) In the second stage, after users have downloaded these applications onto their iOS devices, the attack codes need to bypass the restriction of the iOS sandbox in order to perform malicious functionalities. We realize both attack stages by exploiting the weaknesses of the vetting process and the iOS sandbox. With the proposed generic attack vector, we implement seven proof-of-concept attacks, such as cracking device PIN and taking screenshots without user's awareness, which impose serious threats to the security and privacy of iOS users. Most of our attacks implemented work on both iOS 5 and iOS 6. We implement multiple iOS applications and embed our attack codes into these applications, which are then submitted to the iTunes App Store. These applications with attack codes have passed the vetting process and all our attacks work effectively on non-jailbroken iOS devices[1]. Our proof-of-concept attacks and

---

[1] Due to privacy concerns, we embedded secret triggers in our applications so that public users will not be affected by the attack codes in these applications.

further validation experiments indicate that the current vetting process and iOS sandbox have vulnerabilities that can be exploited by malicious third-party applications to escalate their privileges and launch serious attacks on non-jailbroken iOS devices.

In order to defend against the proposed attacks, we further discuss several mitigation methods which could enhance both vetting process and iOS application sandbox. Some of these methods utilize existing iOS security features, thus can be conveniently implemented and deployed on the current iOS platform. We have notified Apple all of our findings and shared all our attack codes with Apple's product security team. By the time this paper was accepted, Apple is still in the progress of addressing the security issues we have discovered.

In summary, this paper makes the following contributions:

- We provide a generic attack vector which exploits the weaknesses of both vetting process and iOS application sandbox. The attack vector consists of two attack stages and can be used to construct serious attacks that work on non-jailbroken iOS devices.
- We implement seven proof-of-concept attacks with the attack vector proposed. We embed these attack codes into multiple applications we implemented and all the applications are able to pass the vetting process and appear on official iTunes Store.
- We suggest several mitigation methods to defend against our attacks. These methods include improvements on both the vetting process and the application sandbox, which can be deployed on the iOS platform conveniently.

2   Background and Threat Model

2.1   iOS Platform Overview

iOS platform follows a closed-source model, where source code of the underlying architecture and implementation details of its security mechanisms are not available to the public. Though it is debatable whether such obscurity provides better security, iOS has been generally believed as one of the most secure commodity operating systems [6]. Unlike other mobile platforms, third-party applications on iOS are given a more restricted set of privileges [5]. In addition, any third-party application developed for iOS must go through Apple's application vetting process before it is published on the official iTunes App Store. While some users and developers favor to have such restrictions for better security, others prefer to have more controls over the device for additional functionalities, such as allowing to install pirated software and allowing applications to change the themes of the device. To attain such extended privileges, an iOS device needs to be jailbroken. Jailbreaking is a process of installing modified kernel patches which allow a user to have root access of the device so that any unsigned third-party applications can run on it. Although jailbreaking is legal [10], it violates Apple's End User License Agreement and voids the warranties of the purchased devices. Jailbreaking is also known to expose to potential security attacks [7,8].

Application Vetting Process. Without jailbreaking a device, the only way of installing a third-party application on iOS is via the official iTunes App Store. Any application that is submitted to iTunes Store needs to be reviewed by Apple before it is published on the store. This review process is known as *Apple's application vetting process*. The vetting covers several aspects, including detection of malware, detection of copyright violations, and quality inspection of submitted applications. Although the vetting process is kept secret by Apple, it is generally regarded as highly effective as no harmful malware has been reported on iTunes Store [3,2]. Only grayware (which stealthily collects user data) had been reported and was removed from the store upon reporting [4,3].

Application Sandbox. iOS utilizes another security measure – application sandbox – to restrict privileges of third-party applications running on a device. The sandbox is implemented as a set of fine-grained access controls, enforced at the kernel level. Under the sandbox restrictions, an application cannot access files and folders of other applications. In order to access user data or control system hardware, applications also need to call respective Application Programming Interfaces (APIs) provided on iOS. These APIs are hooked by the sandbox so that validations of API invocations can be performed dynamically. The sandbox serves as the last line of security defense which limits malicious applications from accessing system services or exploiting resources of other applications.

iOS Frameworks and APIs. To facilitate development of third-party applications, a collection of *frameworks* are provided in Cocoa Touch [11], which include both public frameworks and private frameworks. Public frameworks are application libraries officially provided to third-party developers while private frameworks are intended only for Apple's internal developers. Each framework provides a set of APIs with which applications can access required system resources and services. Similar to frameworks, APIs can also be categorized into public APIs and private APIs.

Public APIs allow third-party applications to access a limited set of user information and control hardware of iOS devices, such as camera, Bluetooth and WiFi. In contrast, private APIs are the APIs that are meant to be used by Apple's internal developers. Private APIs may exist in both public and private frameworks. Though not officially documented, private APIs include various functions which could be used by a third-party application to escalate its restricted privileges. Thus, Apple explicitly forbids third-party developers from using private APIs and rejects applications once the use of private APIs is detected. On the other hand, private APIs can still be used by applications that are designed to run on jailbroken devices. Such applications are available through Cydia [12], which is an unofficial application market built for jailbroken iOS devices.

2.2 Threat Model

In this paper, we are interested in finding out the possible attacks which can be performed by third-party applications on non-jailbroken iOS devices, as illustrated in Figure 1. The success of such attacks depends on two major factors: 1) whether the corresponding malicious applications can pass Apple's vetting process and appear in the official iTunes App Store; and 2) whether malicious function calls can bypass the restriction of the iOS sandbox. We embed all our proof-of-concept attack codes in the applications we develop, which have passed Apple's vetting process and have been digitally signed by Apple. Thus, our attacks embedded in these applications are able to work on both jailbroken and non-jailbroken iOS devices.

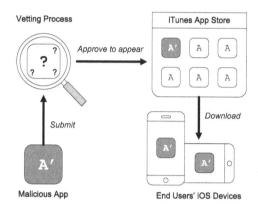

Fig. 1. Threat model

3   Generic Attack Vector

As introduced in Section 2, iOS private APIs exist in both private frameworks and part of public frameworks. When used by third-party applications, private APIs may provide additional privileges to the applications and thus are explicitly forbidden by the vetting process. We choose to utilize private APIs to construct our attacks which perform various malicious functionalities. In this section, we first present two ways of dynamically invoking private APIs which enable the malicious applications to pass the vetting process without being detected. Such dynamic loading mechanisms guarantee the success of the first stage in the proposed attack vector. For the second attack stage, in order to identify useful private APIs that are not restricted by iOS application sandbox, we manually analyze and test each iOS framework. Utilizing the useful private APIs we identified, we manage to implement multiple serious attacks that cover a wide range of privileged functionalities. These attacks can be embedded in any third-party applications, and they work effectively on non-jailbroken iOS devices.

Although our attack vector includes two stages, these two stages are not isolated – what private API needs to be utilized decides the way of its dynamic invocation. Thus, in the following, we first use SMS-sending and PIN-cracking attacks as two examples to explain the underlying mechanisms of the entire attack vector. We then introduce other attacks we implemented utilizing the same attack vector and discuss the implications of these attacks.

3.1 Attacks via Dynamically Loaded Frameworks

When implementing a third-party iOS application that uses private APIs, the normal process is to link the corresponding framework statically (in the application's Xcode [13] project), and import the framework headers in the application's source code. For example, if a developer wants to send SMS programmatically in his application, CoreTelephony.framework needs to be linked, and CTMessage-Center.h needs to be imported in the application code. After preparing those preconditions, the SMS-sending private API can then be called as follows:

```
[[CTMessageCenter sharedMessageCenter]
    sendSMSWithText:@"A testing SMS"
    serviceCenter:nil
    toAddress:@"+19876543210"];
```

In the above code, the static method sharedMessageCenter returns an instance of CTMessageCenter class, and then invokes the private API call "sendSMSWithText: serviceCenter:toAddress:", which performs the SMS-sending functionality on iOS 5. Third-party application can utilize this method to send premium-rate SMS, and the sent SMS will not even appear in the SMS outbox (more precisely, it does not appear in the default iOS Message application[2]). Thus, a user would be totally unaware of such malicious behavior until the user receives his next phone bill.

However, this standard way of invoking private APIs can be easily detected by the vetting process, even though only the executable binary of the compiled application is submitted for vetting. One way of detecting this API call is to simply use string matching (e.g., "grep") on the binary, as the name of the function call appears in the binary's objc_methname segment (and also other segments). Moreover, the framework name and class name also appear in the binary as imported symbols. In this example SMS-sending code, although CoreTelephony is a public framework, CTMessageCenter.h is a private header (i.e., CTMessageCenter is a private class); thus, importing it in the source code can be detected by performing static analysis on the application's binary file. In order to pass Apple's vetting process, the application cannot link the framework statically.

To avoid being detected, the framework has to be loaded dynamically and the required classes and methods need to be located dynamically. In our attacks, we utilize Objective-C runtime classes and methods to achieve this goal. The example SMS attack code that illustrates the dynamic loading mechanism is given as follows:

---

[2] Another way of sending SMS programmatically on iOS 5 is to utilize MFMessageComposeViewController. However, this method is easy to be noticed as the SMS sent would appear in the default Message application.

```
1: NSBundle *b = [NSBundle bundlewithPath:@"/System/Library
   /Frameworks/CoreTelephony.framework"];
2: [b load];
3: Class c = NSClassFromString(@"CTMessageCenter");
4: id mc = [c performSelector:NSSelectorFromString(@"sharedMessage
   Center")];
5: // call "sendSMSWithText:serviceCenter:toAddress:" dynamically
   by utilizing NSInvocation
. . .
```

In the above code, the first two lines are used to load the CoreTelephony framework dynamically, without linking this framework in the application's source code. The path of this library is fixed on every iOS device, which is under the /System/Library/Frameworks/ folder. Note that not only public frameworks can be loaded dynamically, private frameworks (which is under /System/Library/Private-Frameworks/) can also be loaded dynamically using the same method. According to our experiments, Apple's sandbox does not check the parameter of [NSBundle load] to forbid accessing these frameworks under /System/Library folder.

NSClassFromString at the third line is a function which can locate the corresponding class in memory by passing it the class name, which is similar to the "Class.forName()" method in Java reflection. At the fourth line, the sharedMessage-Center method is called via "performSelector:". At last, in order to call a method with more than 2 parameters (which is "sendSMSWithText:serviceCenter:toAddress:" in this case), the NSInvocation class is utilized.

Although the above code dynamically invokes the private API call, it may need certain obfuscation in order to avoid the detection from static analysis during the vetting process[3]. The last step of generating the actual attack code is to obfuscate all the strings appearing in the above example code. There are various ways of obfuscating strings in the source code. One simple technique is to create a constant string which includes all 52 letters (both upper and lower cases), 10 digits and common symbols. Then all the strings appeared in the above code can be generated dynamically at runtime by selecting corresponding positions from this constant string. Some of our applications utilize this method to obfuscate strings in the attack codes, and some others adopt a complex obfuscation mechanism, which involves bitwise operations and certain memory stack operations that are more difficult to be detected.

3.2 Attacks via Private C Functions

Information about private Objective-C classes and methods in the Cocoa Touch frameworks can be obtained from the iOS runtime headers [14], which are generated using runtime introspection tool such as RuntimeBrowser [15]. An example

---

[3] Actually according to our experiments, obfuscation may not be necessary, as the vetting process does not seem to check all text segments in the binary. In our experiments, we have tried to embed this SMS-sending code in one application which does not utilize obfuscation, and the application passed the vetting process.

of directly utilizing these Objective-C private APIs has been introduced in the previous subsection. However, Objective-C private classes and methods are not the only private APIs we are able to use in third-party applications.

When we reverse engineer the binary files of each framework, we find that there are a number of C functions in these frameworks that can be invoked by our application, which do not appear in the iOS runtime headers [14] and cannot be found with RuntimeBrowser [15]. In order to invoke these C functions, we need to dynamically load the framework binary and locate the function at runtime. The following code segment is part of our PIN-cracking code, which illustrates how we realize the dynamic invocation for private C functions.

```
void *b = dlopen("/System/Library/PrivateFrameworks
    /MobileKeyBag.framework/MobileKeyBag", 1);
int (*f)(id, id, id) = dlsym(b, "MKBKeyBagChangeSystemSecret");
...
int r = f(oldpwd, newpwd, pubdict);
...
```

In the above code segment, we use dlopen() to load the binary file of the private framework MobileKeyBag, which returns an opaque handle for this dynamic library. Utilizing this handle and dlsym(), we are then able to locate the address where the given symbol MKBKeyBagChangeSystemSecret is loaded into memory. This address is then casted into a function pointer so that it can be directly invoked later on in our attack code.

Although the above code segment may look simple, it is actually not easy to identify which C functions we should invoke to serve for our attack purpose, especially when only framework binary is given. Even after the C functions are identified and located, it takes further tedious work to figure out the correct parameter types and values to pass to the C functions. And in many cases, even all parameters are correct, these functions may be restricted by iOS sandbox and thus will not function correctly within third-party applications. To speed up the manual reverse engineering process when analyzing the given framework binaries, we build our own static analysis tool (which is based on IDA Pro.[16]) to disassemble the framework binary and obtain assembly instructions that are relatively easy to read.

By manually analyzing the private framework ManagedConfiguration, we find out that the changePasscodeFrom:to:outError: method of MCPasscodeManager is used to reset the password of the iOS device. However, we are not able to directly invoke this Objective-C method because the device needs to be "unlocked" first with current device password (possibly due to sandbox restrictions). Thus, we need to find a way of bypassing such restriction. Digging into the assembly code of the changePasscodeFrom:to:outError: method, we find out that it eventually invokes the MKBKeyBagChangeSystemSecret C function in MobileKeyBag to reset the password, which is allowed to be directly invoked under the sandbox restrictions. Further analysis and experiments are then conducted to figure out the correct parameters used to invoke MKBKeyBagChangeSystemSecret.

Our analysis reveals that the MKBKeyBagChangeSystemSecret function accepts three parameters, all of which have the type of (NSData*). The first parameter is the data of the old password, which can be converted from password string. The second parameter is the data of the new password. The third parameter, however, is an NSDictionary containing the "keyboard type" of the current password, which must be converted into NSData with [NSPropertyListSerialization dataFromPropertyList:format:errorDescription:]. One simple way of obtaining this NS-Dictionary data is to utilize the private framework ManagedConfiguration. However, in our attack code, to minimize the number of frameworks loaded, we utilize another private C function MKBKeyBagCopySytemSecretBlob[4] in MobileKeyBag to obtain this NSDictionary, which is then passed to MKBKeyBagChangeSystemSecret as the third parameter.

After this MKBKeyBagChangeSystemSecret function is successfully invoked, the rest of the attack code is straight forward – we simply use brute force to crack the password. 4-digit PIN has been widely used to lock iOS devices and has a password space of 10^4. When using our application to crack a device PIN on iPhone 5, it takes 18.2 minutes on the average (of 16 trials on two iPhone 5 devices) to check the whole PIN space (10^4). This gives an average speed of 9.2 PINs per second. To further speed up the cracking, we build a PIN dictionary so that common PINs are checked first. If the given PIN is in birthday format (mmdd/ddmm), it takes about 40 seconds to crack the PIN on average. Note that since our PIN-cracking attack uses the low level C functions, it will not trigger the "wrong password" event on the iOS device which is implemented at higher level (Objective-C functions) in the framework code. Thus, there is no limit on the number of attempts for our brute force attacks when cracking the device PIN. It is the same procedure to crack 4-digit PIN and complex password using our method, but the latter will take much longer time than PIN due to its large password space.

3.3 Other Implemented Attacks and Implications

The *SMS-sending* attack and the *PIN-cracking* attack introduced above explain how the entire attack vector is constructed. The former uses private Objective-C functions (Section 3.1), while the latter uses private C functions (Section 3.2). With the same dynamic invocation mechanisms which are able to bypass the vetting process, other attacks can also be implemented, as long as we can identify sensitive private APIs that are overlooked by the iOS sandbox.

We manually analyze the 180+ public and private iOS frameworks and manage to identify seven sets of sensitive APIs that are not restricted by iOS sandbox. Utilizing these APIs and the dynamic invocation mechanisms, we implement seven attacks, which are listed in Table 1. The corresponding frameworks and

---

[4] Note that it is not a spelling error in this MKBKeyBagCopySytemSecretBlob function. The key word "System" in this function name is spelled as "Sytem" by Apple's programmers. This detail further shows that in this attack, we utilize a function which Apple programmers may not expect to be used by third-party applications.

Table 1. The seven attacks implemented and their applicability

#	Attack Name	Description	iOS 5	iOS 6	iPhone	iPad[*]
1	PIN-cracking	Crack and retrieve the PIN of the device.	✓	✓	✓	✓
2	Call-blocking	Block all incoming calls or the calls from specified numbers.	✓	✓	✓	–
3	Snapshot-taking	Continuously take snapshots for current screen (even the app is at background).	✓	✓	–	✓
4	Secret-filming[**]	Open camera secretly and take photos or videos without the user's awareness.	✓	✓	✓	✓
5	Tweet-posting	Post tweets on Twitter without user's interaction.	✓	✓	✓	✓
6	SMS-sending	Send SMS to specified numbers without the user's awareness.	✓	–	✓	–
7	Email-sending	Send emails using user's system email accounts without the user's awareness.	✓	–	✓	✓

[*] The call-blocking and SMS-sending attacks do not work on iPad, simply because iPad does not have corresponding functionalities since it is not a phone device.
[**] This secret-filming attack can be implemented purely with iOS public APIs.

key APIs utilized are listed in Table 2 in the appendix. We embed our attack codes in multiple applications we develop, and all those applications have passed Apple's vetting process and appeared in the official iTunes App Store.

Most of the attacks in Table 1 work on both iOS 5 and iOS 6 (which is the default iOS version on iPhone 5). The last two attacks (*SMS-sending* and *email-sending*) currently only work on iOS 5, but not iOS 6. The APIs of sending SMS and emails on iOS 6 have been substantially changed to prevent such attacks (which will be further analyzed in Section 4).

The severity of most of our attacks would be significantly increased when the attack code is embedded in an application that can keep running at the background. Take the snapshot attack as an example. By calling the private API [UIWindow createScreenIOSurface], an application can capture the current screen content of the device. When continuously running at the background, this application can take snapshots of the device periodically, and send these snapshots back to the developer's server for further analysis[5]. Such *snapshot-taking* attack may reveal user's email content, photos and even bank account information, thus it should be avoided on any mobile devices.

Similar to the *snapshot-taking* attack, the *call-blocking* and *PIN-cracking* attacks also become more serious when they are used in an application that can continuously run at the background, which have been verified in our experi-

---

[5] The snapshot attack code is embedded into one of our applications which can keep running at background utilizing audio playing feature. This application also passed Apple's vetting process and it sends out snapshots every 5 seconds once triggered.

ments. However, the *secret-filming* attack does not work when in background. The current implementation of the iOS camera service requires that an application utilizing this service be not in the background status. Nevertheless, even if the *secret-filming* attack works only when the application is in the foreground, it is still a serious threat to user privacy. Considering that when a user is playing a game on the iOS device, and the game secretly opens the cameras and takes photos periodically without the user's notice. In our experiments, we have verified that both front and back cameras can be used, and the sound can be muted when taking videos or photos programmatically in our applications.

We emphasize that all these attacks are implemented with secret triggers in the applications that are submitted to iTunes Store. The attacks are only launched on our testing devices after certain sequences of secret buttons have been pressed in the applications. However, note that in the application codes, such triggers are just "if-else" statements. Thus, if the trigger conditions were replaced with an "if-true" condition, these attacks could be launched on any user device with such applications. Therefore, the secret triggers used in our proof-of-concept applications do not affect the conclusions drawn from our experiments.

Besides the seven attacks we have implemented, our attack vector can be used to construct other attacks as long as there are security sensitive functions on iOS that are not restricted by iOS sandbox. As each iOS version will include new functionalities to the platform, each iOS update may introduce new attacks from malicious third-party applications based on our attack vector.

4   Attack Mitigation

Our proof-of-concept attacks have shown that Apple's current vetting and sandbox mechanisms have weaknesses which can be exploited by third-party applications to escalate their privileges and perform serious attacks on iOS users. In this section, we first suggest improvements on the vetting process to mitigate the security threats caused by dynamic invocations. We then propose enhancements on the iOS sandbox to further defend against our attacks utilizing private APIs.

4.1   Improving Application Vetting Process

Static analysis can be used to determine all the API calls which are not invoked with reflection (i.e., dynamic invocations), and it can provide the list of frameworks that are statically linked in the application. Thus, an automated static analysis is able to detect the standard way of invoking private APIs, as what is probably being used by Apple in its current vetting process. In addition, we suggest to improve the existing static analysis to detect suspicious applications based on certain code signatures. For example, one suspicious code signature could be applications containing any dlopen() or [NSBundle load] invocations whose parameters are not constant strings (which match the cases of our attacks). However, as the static analysis alone is not sufficient to determine whether a suspicious application is indeed a malware or not, manual examination and dynamic analysis should be utilized to examine such suspicious applications.

In many cases, manual examination may not be able to find malicious behaviors of the examined applications, because the malicious functions may not be preformed for every execution. Instead, they can be designed in the way that such functions are only triggered when certain conditions have been satisfied. Examples of such conditions include time triggers or button triggers (as what have been used in our applications). When a malicious application uses such trigger strategy, the manual inspection may not find any suspicious behaviors during the vetting process. Such malicious applications can only be detected by utilizing fuzz testing [16] (or in the extreme case, using symbolic execution [17]), where different inputs are used to satisfy every condition of the application code. Furthermore, in order to determine whether sensitive user data are transferred out of the device, dynamic taint analysis [18] is an effective approach to serve this purpose. However, since it is expensive to apply fuzz testing and dynamic taint analysis on every application, the vetting process may choose to run such examinations only on selected suspicious applications.

4.2   Enhancement on iOS Sandbox

Dynamic Parameter Inspection. From the perspective of iOS sandbox, a straightforward defense to our attacks that utilize the dynamic loading functions (such as [NSBundle load] and dlopen()) is to forbid third-party applications to invoke these functions. However, it is not practical to completely forbid the invocation of dynamic loading functions, since frameworks, libraries and many other resources need to be dynamically loaded for benign purposes at runtime. Even Apple's official code, including both framework code and application code (which is automatically generated by Xcode), utilizes dynamic loading functions extensively to load resources at runtime. On the other hand, since sensitive APIs can be hooked by utilizing the application sandbox, the parameters of these APIs can be checked at runtime. Thus, it is useful if Apple's sandbox is modified in the way that the parameter values passed to dynamic loading functions are examined, and accessing files under a specific folder is forbidden.

One way of implementing this approach is to forbid the third-party applications to dynamically load any frameworks under "/System/Library/" folder. However, a sophisticated attacker may be able to completely reverse engineer a given framework binary, locate all the code regions in the binary that are needed for launching his attack, and then copy only the needed code regions from the binary and insert into his application code. In this way, he does not need to dynamically load framework binaries in his malicious applications. Therefore, this parameter-inspection approach is not able to completely defend against the proposed attacks, though it can increase the complexity for the adversary to construct these attacks.

Privileged IPC Verification. Another technique of enhancing the sandbox is to dynamically check the privilege of the identity which makes sensitive API calls. For example, a third-party application should not have the privilege to invoke

MKBKeyBagChangeSystemSecret API, which is used in our PIN-cracking attack. Such private APIs should only be invoked by processes or services with the system privilege. However, directly restricting the access to private APIs may not effectively prevent the attacks. By analyzing the implementation of several private APIs (in assembly code), we find that the private APIs eventually use interprocess communication (IPC) methods, which communicate with the system service process, to complete the functionalities of the private APIs. For example, MKBKeyBagChangeSystemSecret API uses perform_command() method to communicate with the system service (with service_bundle_id = "com.apple.mobile.keybagd"). This means that instead of invoking private APIs, an application can also use such IPC method to directly send command to the system service process to perform the same functionality.

In order to defend against such attacks, for each privileged system service, the recipient of the command (which is the service process itself) needs to check the sender of the command to verify whether the sender has the valid privilege to make such IPC. To enable this IPC verification, the system service process needs to maintain a list of privileged IPC commands which are checked dynamically when an IPC is received. Compared to the parameter-inspection approach, privileged IPC verification provides better defense against the *PIN-cracking, call-blocking* and *snapshot-taking* attacks as the corresponding privileged functionalities should not be used by any third-party applications. However, this approach alone is not sufficient to mitigate the other four attacks listed in Table 1. For these four attacks, the corresponding functionalities should be provided to applications due to usability reasons, but at the same time, it needs to be ensured that user interactions are involved when these functionalities are performed.

Service Delegation Enhancement. On iOS 6, Apple starts using the XPC Service, which allows processes to communicate with each other asynchronously so that it can be used for privilege separation. Originally on iOS 5, the SMS and email APIs are implemented as "View Controller" classes that are created and used within a third-party application process. Therefore, applications can manipulate these view controller classes to send out SMSes and emails programmatically without users' interaction. However, on iOS 6, the SMS and email functionalities are now delegated to another system process utilizing XPC Service, which is completely out of the process space of third-party applications. Thus, a third-party application on iOS 6 is no longer able to send SMSes or emails programmatically without user's interaction.

Although currently iOS 6 has not implemented the service delegation mechanism for the Twitter service, the *tweet-posting* attack can be prevented using this mechanism, as it follows exactly the same service model as SMS and email. The *secret-filming* attack, however, cannot be easily mitigated using such service delegation. Instead of using a unified user interface, iOS enables third-party applications to create their own customized user interfaces for taking photos or videos. If the same service delegation mechanism is applied, then the camera interface will be identical across different applications as it is provided by system service. Thus, more precisely, service delegation is able to defend against camera device abuse, but its implementation may greatly impact user experience.

System Notifiers for Sensitive Functionalities. In order to mitigate the threat of secret filming, while preserving the functionality and flexibility of using camera in third-party applications on iOS, one possible solution is to add a half-transparent system notifier on the screen (e.g., at the upper-right corner), whenever the camera device is being used. This notifier can be shown using the XPC mechanism so that the notifier is handled by a system daemon process, which is outside of the control of third-party applications. In this way, whenever the camera is being used (either taking photos or taking videos), the system notifier is shown on the screen to alert the user.

By enhancing the current iOS platform with the 1) privileged IPC verification, 2) comprehensive service delegation, and 3) extended system notifiers, it will be able to defend against all the seven attacks we construct. Note that since iOS is a close-source platform, it is extremely difficult (if not impossible) for us to implement these mitigation methods we proposed, and thus it is one of the limitations in our work. However, we have shared all our mitigation suggestions with Apple so that Apple's product security team may choose some of these methods to fix the sandbox. From the partial knowledge that is revealed by our attacks and the mitigation analysis, it may be inferred that the current iOS sandbox implementation is quite complex and its privilege check is not complete. Due to its complexity and also its trade-off nature against usability, it may not be easy to completely fix the iOS sandbox to prevent future attacks.

5   Discussions

On the current iOS platform, when an application plays an audio file (e.g., .mp3), normally a music-playing notifier (i.e., the ▶ symbol) is shown in the status bar on top of the screen. However, this only happens when the application is implemented following the standard programming rules, which require the application code to call [[UIApplication sharedApplication] beginReceivingRemote-ControlEvents]. This API call registers the application in the system service so as to receive remote events, such as when a user presses the control buttons on earphone. In the background running application we implement, however, this API is not invoked and our application simply calls the basic audio playing APIs to play a silent music in an infinite loop. As a result, *no notifier is shown on the status bar when our application is running at the background*, thus the iOS user may be totally unaware of the existence of this security threat. In addition to playing audio, there are other means of enabling background running, such as VOIP and tracking locations. Thus, besides the system notifier for the camera functionality (Section 4.2), we suggest to add another system notifier specifically designed to indicate that an application is running at the background. Upon seeing this notifier, a user can force close any background applications that are not being used. This will not only enhance security but also save device battery.

The PIN-cracking attack code introduced in Section 3.2 not only can be used to steal device PIN and send it to an external server, but can also be used to reset the current PIN to another value so that the legitimate user is not able to unlock the device. In iOS settings, there is an option to "erase all data on this device after 10 failed passcode attempts". If this option is enabled on a device and our PIN-cracking code resets the PIN, it could make a user panic if he is unable to unlock the device after several trials of inputting his original password. Again note that our PIN-cracking attack itself will not trigger the "wrong password" event on the iOS device and thus, there is no limit on the number of brute forcing trials for our attack code when cracking the device PIN.

With the attack codes we shared with Apple's product security team, the PIN-cracking vulnerability has been fixed in the newly released iOS 6.1 (January 2013). However, other security issues we discovered are still in the process of being addressed. Note that the conclusions about the vetting process and sandbox given in this paper are inferences based on observations from our experiments, as the details of the vetting process and sandbox are kept as black box by Apple. The ground truth may become available to the public when Apple decides to turn major components of iOS into open source in the future, as what has been done for Mac OS X [19].

6   Related Work

Spyphone [20] is a prototype application, developed for iOS 3.1.2, which illustrates that a wide list of user data can be accessed on iOS by third-party applications. However, Spyphone does not use any private APIs – it only invokes public APIs and reads public files to access user data in order to enable itself to appear in iTunes Store [20], which is completely different from our malicious applications implemented. In addition, the security enforcement of iOS has been significantly improved since then so that a large portion of user data that can be accessed by Spyphone on iOS 3 is forbidden to access since iOS 5.

Malwares, such as iKee [7] and Dutch 5 ransom [8] worms, have been found on iOS. However, these worms only work on jailbroken iOS devices where an SSH server is installed with the default root password unchanged. Other iOS malwares known to the public, such as iSAM created by Damopoulos et al. [9] (which focuses more on malware propagation methods), also exploit vulnerabilities exist only on jailbroken iOS devices, which are different from our work.

Felt et al. [3] conduct a survey on the modern mobile malware in the wild, which encompasses all known iOS, Symbian, and Android malwares that spread between January 2009 and June 2011. They find that (i) all the 4 iOS malwares they identified work only on jailbroken iOS devices, and none were listed in the iTunes App Store; and (ii) only graywares are found on iTunes App Store which are then removed by Apple. These findings are confirmed by Egele et al. [21], in which they develop a static analysis tool, PiOS, to detect privacy leakages in iOS applications. They perform static analysis on more than one thousand third-party iOS applications and find out that only a few applications are graywares which stealthily access user data without user's awareness.

Extensive researches have been conducted on the other popular mobile platform – Android. Privilege escalation attacks on Android are proposed by [22], and the defense mechanisms for such attacks are introduced by Bugiel et al. [23]. Enck et al. [24] performs static analysis of Android applications using the decompiler they developed. Dynamic taint analysis on third-party Android applications is performed by TaintDroid [25]. Comprehensive surveys on mobile security are provided by Becher et al. [26] and Egners et al. [27].

The closest work to our research is the work by Miller [28]. By exploiting the security flaw he found, he managed to get iOS devices to run unsigned codes which are dynamically downloaded by his proof-of-concept malicious application. Miller's attack mechanism provides an alternative for the first stage of our proposed attack vector. However, Apple has removed his application from the iTunes App Store and released a fix for the security flaw. Thus, our dynamic invocation used in the first stage, to our best knowledge, is the only way of bypassing the vetting process. Although our mechanism is not complex, it is a very effective way of allowing malicious applications appear in the official application store. Furthermore, by performing sophisticated analysis on all existing iOS frameworks, we identify seven sets of sensitive APIs which are not restricted by iOS sandbox and thus can be utilized by any malicious applications.

7 Conclusion

The original goal of this work is to answer a simple (but not easy) research question: is there a generic attack vector which enables third-party applications to launch attacks on non-jailbroken iOS devices? Two pre-conditions need to be satisfied in answering this question: (i) the third-party application has to pass the vetting process and appear on the official application store; and (ii) the corresponding attack codes must break through the restrictions of iOS sandbox in order to work on non-jailbroken iOS devices.

In this paper, we constructed effective mechanisms which allow any third-party application to invoke private APIs without being detected by the vetting process. By utilizing such mechanisms and exploiting the vulnerabilities in the application sandbox, we implemented seven proof-of-concept attacks which can cause serious damages to iOS users. Finally, we suggested mitigation mechanisms to enhance the current vetting process and iOS sandbox. Our paper fills the gap in the current mobile security literature where most research efforts are conducted on Android platform. We have shared all our findings with Apple's product security team. In January 2013, Apple released iOS 6.1 and fixed the PIN-cracking vulnerability we discovered in iOS 6.0, while other security issues presented in this paper still remain unsolved.

Acknowledgments. This work was partially supported by project SecSG-EPD090005RFP(D) funded by Energy Market Authority, Singapore. We also thank the anonymous reviewers for their valuable insights and comments.

References

1. Apple Press Info: App Store Tops 40 Billion Downloads with Almost Half in 2012 (January 2013), http://www.apple.com/pr/library/2013/01/07App-Store-Tops-40-Billion-Downloads-with-Almost-Half-in-2012.html
2. Safe and Savvy: How secure is your iPhone (June 2012), http://safeandsavvy.f-secure.com/2012/06/29/how-secure-is-your-iphone/
3. Felt, A.P., Finifter, M., Chin, E., Hanna, S., Wagner, D.: A survey of mobile malware in the wild. In: Proceedings of the ACM Workshop on Security and Privacy in Smartphones and Mobile Devices, pp. 3–14 (2011)
4. TrendLabs: Malware for iOS? Not Really (June 2012), http://blog.trendmicro.com/trendlabs-security-intelligence/malware-for-ios-not-really/
5. Han, J., Yan, Q., Gao, D., Zhou, J., Deng, R.H.: Comparing Mobile Privacy Protection through Cross-Platform Applications. In: Proceedings of the Network and Distributed System Security Symposium (February 2013)
6. macgasm.net: IT Professionals Rank iOS As Most Secure Mobile OS (August 2012), http://www.macgasm.net/2012/08/17/it-professionals-rank-ios-as-most-secure-mobile-os/
7. NakedSecurity: First iphone worm discovered - ikee changes wallpaper to rick astley photo (November 2009), http://nakedsecurity.sophos.com/2009/11/08/iphone-worm-discovered-wallpaper-rick-astley-photo/
8. NakedSecurity: Hacked iphones held hostage for 5 euros, http://nakedsecurity.sophos.com/2009/11/03/hacked-iphones-held-hostage-5-euros/
9. Damopoulos, D., Kambourakis, G., Gritzalis, S.: iSAM: An iPhone Stealth Airborne Malware. In: Camenisch, J., Fischer-Hübner, S., Murayama, Y., Portmann, A., Rieder, C. (eds.) SEC 2011. IFIP AICT, vol. 354, pp. 17–28. Springer, Heidelberg (2011)
10. Kravets, D.: ABCNews: Jailbreaking iPhone Legal, U.S. Government Says, http://abcnews.go.com/Technology/story?id=11254253
11. iOS Technology Overview: Cocoa Touch, https://developer.apple.com/technologies/ios/cocoa-touch.html
12. Freeman, J.: Cydia, an alternative to Apple's App Store for jailbroken iOS devices, http://cydia.saurik.com/
13. Apple Developer: Xcode, Apple's integrated development environment for creating apps for Mac and iOS, https://developer.apple.com/xcode/
14. Seriot, N.: iOS 6 runtime headers, https://github.com/nst/iOS-Runtime-Headers
15. Seriot, N.: Objective-C Runtime Browser, for Mac OS X and iOS, https://github.com/nst/RuntimeBrowser/
16. Godefroid, P., Levin, M.Y., Molnar, D.A.: Automated Whitebox Fuzz Testing. In: Proceedings of the Network and Distributed System Security Symposium (2008)
17. Person, S., Yang, G., Rungta, N., Khurshid, S.: Directed incremental symbolic execution. In: Proceedings of the 32nd ACM SIGPLAN Conference on Programming Language Design and Implementation, pp. 504–515 (2011)
18. Kang, M.G., McCamant, S., Poosankam, P., Song, D.: DTA++: Dynamic Taint Analysis with Targeted Control-Flow Propagation. In: Proceedings of the Network and Distributed System Security Symposium (2011)
19. apple.com: Apple Open Source Projects, http://www.apple.com/opensource/
20. Seriot, N.: iPhone Privacy. In: Black Hat DC (2010)

21. Egele, M., Kruegel, C., Kirda, E., Vigna, G.: PiOS: Detecting Privacy Leaks in iOS Applications. In: Proceedings of the Network and Distributed System Security Symposium (2011)
22. Felt, A.P., Wang, H.J., Moshchuk, A., Hanna, S., Chin, E.: Permission re-delegation: attacks and defenses. In: Proceedings of the 20th USENIX Security Symposium (2011)
23. Bugiel, S., Davi, L., Dmitrienko, A., Fischer, T., Sadeghi, A.R., Shastry, B.: Towards taming privilege-escalation attacks on android. In: Annual Network & Distributed System Security Symposium (February 2012)
24. Enck, W., Octeau, D., McDaniel, P., Chaudhuri, S.: A study of android application security. In: USENIX Security Symposium (2011)
25. Enck, W., Gilbert, P., Chun, B.G., Cox, L.P., Jung, J., McDaniel, P., Sheth, A.N.: Taintdroid: an information-flow tracking system for realtime privacy monitoring on smartphones. In: OSDI (2010)
26. Becher, M., Freiling, F.C., Hoffmann, J., Holz, T., Uellenbeck, S., Wolf, C.: Mobile Security Catching Up? Revealing the Nuts and Bolts of the Security of Mobile Devices. In: Proceedings of the IEEE Symposium on Security and Privacy (2011)
27. Egners, A., Marschollek, B., Meyer, U.: Hackers in Your Pocket: A Survey of Smartphone Security Across Platforms, Technical Report (2012)
28. Miller, C.: Apple lets malware into App Store (2011), http://nakedsecurity.sophos.com/2011/11/08/apples-app-store-security-compromised/

A   Details in Attack Implementations

The frameworks and key APIs utilized in our attacks are given in Table 2.

Table 2. The frameworks and key APIs utilized for the seven attacks implemented

#	Attack	Frameworks	Classes*	Functions
1	PIN-cracking	MobileKeyBag	—	MKBKeyBagChangeSystemSecret MKBKeyBagCopySytemSecretBlob
2	Call-blocking	CoreTelephony	—	CTTelephonyCenterGetDefault CTTelephonyCenterAddObserver CTCallCopyAddress CTCallDisconnect
3	Snapshot-taking	UIKit	UIWindow UIImage	createScreenIOSurface initWithIOSurface:
4	Secret-filming	AVFoundation CoreMedia CoreVideo	AVCaptureDevice AVCaptureDeviceInput AVCaptureVideoDataOutput AVCaptureSession	devices deviceInputWithDevice:error: setSampleBufferDelegate:queue: startRunning
5	Tweet-posting	Twitter	TWTweetComposeViewController	setCompletionHandler: setInitialText: send:
6	SMS-sending	CoreTelephony	CTMessageCenter	sharedMessageCenter sendSMSWithText:serviceCenter:-toAddress:
7	Email-sending	Message AppSupport	MailAccount CPDistributedMessagingCenter	defaultMailAccountForDelivery uniqueId centerNamed: sendMessageAndReceiveReplyName-e:userInfo:error:

* The symbol of "—" in the Class field indicates that the corresponding attack does not utilize any Objective-C classes, but only utilizes private C functions.

Hardware Architectures for MSP430-Based Wireless Sensor Nodes Performing Elliptic Curve Cryptography

Erich Wenger

Graz University of Technology
Institute for Applied Information Processing and Communications
Inffeldgasse 16a, 8010 Graz, Austria
erich.wenger@iaik.tugraz.at

Abstract. Maximizing the battery lifetime of wireless sensor nodes and equipping them with elliptic curve cryptography is a challenge that requires new energy-saving architectures. In this paper, we present an architecture that drops a hardware accelerator between CPU and RAM. Thus neither the CPU nor the data memory need to be modified. In a detailed comparison with a software-only and a dedicated hardware architecture, we show that the drop-in concept is smaller than the dedicated hardware module, while achieving similarly fast runtimes. Most interesting for micro-chip manufacturers is that only 4 kGE of chip area need to be committed for the dedicated drop-in accelerator.

Keywords: MSP430, ASIC, Hardware, Software, Elliptic Curve Cryptography, Wireless Sensor Nodes.

1 Introduction

Privacy, authenticity, and confidentiality pose three of the most challenging current demands on wireless sensor networks. To solve those requirements the use of cryptography is essential. Unfortunately, it is hardly possible to solve this challenge using only symmetric cyphers. The most promising solutions are based on asymmetric cryptography, in particular Elliptic Curve Cryptography (ECC).

Efficiently implementing ECC is a complex task, especially when a designer also needs to be aware of the capabilities of the entities of a sensor network: A sensor node usually comes with a microprocessor, a sensor (e.g., for humidity), a wireless communication interface (e.g., IEEE 802.15.4 [16], ZigBee [31]), and a battery, which should keep the sensor-node alive for a lifetime (some years) within a hostile environment. This means that a solution to the initial requirements should be light-weight and efficient. For maximizing the battery live and keeping the price of a sensor node at a minimum, ECC has to be implemented with care. To realize the scope of the difficulty, be aware that within the time required for a single elliptic-curve point multiplication, several hundreds of symmetric encryptions and decryptions can be preformed. Thus ECC has a major impact on both communication latency and energy consumption.

M. Jacobson et al. (Eds.): ACNS 2013, LNCS 7954, pp. 290–306, 2013.
© Springer-Verlag Berlin Heidelberg 2013

A lot of research has been focused on efficiently and securely implementing ECC. The research is performed based on three different approaches: one is based on efficiently implementing ECC in software, one is based on adding dedicated hardware, and one is a combination of the two preceding approaches. Several papers discuss the use of assembly optimizations [12], instruction-set extensions [6,10], and dedicated ECC hardware designs [19,20]. The drawback of those techniques are the relatively low performance, the requirement to change the microprocessor, and the potential waste of precious chip area, respectively. As CPU vendors usually do not give away the source code of microprocessors, but obfuscated code instead, adding new instructions is a troublesome task. Dedicated hardware modules provide locally optimized solutions, but ignore the existence of already available hardware modules. Our paper fills this gap.

Our contribution. In this paper, we perform a fair comparison (common algorithms, technologies, tools) of three different hardware architectures, all capable of performing ECC. Using an openMSP430 at the core, we present (i) an area and speed-optimized software solution, (ii) a dedicated hardware module, and most importantly (iii) a novel ECC 'drop-in' architecture. For the drop-in architecture, a lightweight ECC accelerator is placed right between the CPU and its data memory. It requires less chip area than a dedicated hardware module, while being similarly fast. Compared to the optimized software solution, the energy consumption is reduced by a factor of 28, which certainly will make a major impact on the lifetime of a wireless sensor node. The drop-in concept is also most interesting for micro-chip manufacturers as only 4 kGE of dedicated chip area need to be committed for the drop-in accelerator.

The paper is structured as follows. Section 2 gives a short introduction on how to securely implement ECC and Section 3 discusses different architectures for ECC. The most promising architectures are then implemented within Sections 4–6 and compared within Section 7. Conclusions are drawn within Section 8.

2   A Short Introduction to ECC

Elliptic curves, used for cryptography, are built on top of finite fields. As finite field, one can either choose a prime field or a binary extension field. Prime fields are fast in software as they are based on integers and integer multipliers are available in nearly all (embedded) microprocessors. Binary-extension fields on the other hand are built on polynomials, which when implemented in hardware do not have the drawback of carry propagation. However, in software a multiplication of two polynomials has to be realized using branches, which are vulnerable to side-channel attacks.

The for us most interesting standardized elliptic curves [1,2,23] are all based on the Weierstrass equation: $y^2 + a_1xy + a_3y = x^3 + a_2x^2 + a_4x + a_6$. Depending on whether prime or binary-extension fields are used, this equation is simplified to $y^2 = x^3 + ax + b$ or $y^2 + xy = x^3 + ax^2 + b$, respectively. Also the formulas used to perform point additions and doublings depend on the used finite field. For further information, the reader is referred to standard literature on elliptic curves [3,13].

Table 1. ECC formulas used within this paper

| | | | Finite-field operations per key bit | | |
Formula	Field	Registers	Add/Subtract	Square	Multiply
Hutter et al. [15]	$\mathbb{F}_p$	$7 + 3 = 10$	17	4	12
López and Dahab [22]	$\mathbb{F}_{2^m}$	$5 + 3 = 8$	3	5	6

For the following comparison, it is important that all implementations are based on a common methodology. For the constant-runtime software implementations, the integer and polynomial arithmetic has been separated from the reduction operation. The reduction is performed using only simple shift and addition operations. Thereby advantage was taken of the used prime and irreducible polynomial. To perform an inversion in constant time, an exponentiation, based on Fermat's little theorem ($a^{q-2} \equiv a^{-1} \bmod (q)$) is used. For binary-extension fields an optimized inversion algorithm based on Itoh and Tsujii [17] is used.

More important than the used finite field is that ECC implementations are vulnerable to side-channel attacks [7]. Attackers can use runtime information, power consumption profiles, or induce faults to recover the secret key. This is a significant problem for the easily accessible wireless sensor nodes that usually are deployed within unsafe environments. Thus, a methodology must be utilized that minimizes the potential threats.

In this paper we take advantage of differential addition formulas optimized for Montgomery ladders. Table 1 gives a short summary of the used formulas. By using a Montgomery ladder, the underlying finite-field operations are independently performed from the used private scalar. Thus a key-independent constant runtime is achievable under the assumption that all finite-field operations are performed in constant time (which they are). The formulas are also lightweight. Only 7/5 registers are required during the point double-and-add operations. For the recovery of the y-coordinate another two registers are needed which store the original base point. Another register that stores the private scalar is also included in all comparisons within this paper.

To further increase the resistance against power-analysis attacks one would use Randomized Projective Coordinates [5] and to resist fault attacks, perform point verifications before and after each point multiplication. In practice the resistance against those attacks is verified by performing real-world evaluations. As those evaluations would go beyond the scope of this paper, they have not (yet) been done. However, the algorithms and methodologies used for our implementations are applicable to build real-world secure hardware.

3   Architectures

The decision regarding the best architecture is most important for a final design as it greatly influences area, runtime, power, and energy characteristics. Only by considering all requirements and the system as a whole, a *global optimum*

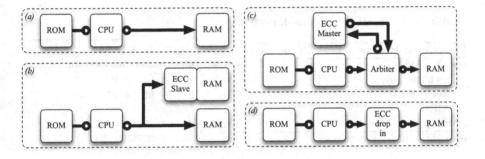

Fig. 1. Microprocessor-based architectures

can be found. By optimizing a single (e.g., ECC) component it is probable to reach a *local optimum* only. Figure 1 shows four different architectures which are based on microprocessors, as microprocessors are the central component in all currently available sensor nodes. The ECC-independent components, such as the wireless interface and the actual sensor, are considered to be constants and therefore independent from the used architecture.

(a) The most straight-forward solution is to perform and optimize ECC in software[1]. The hardware designer only has to make sure that the data memory is sufficiently large and the assembly-optimized ECC code is placed within the program memory. The microprocessor (CPU) is then used to execute the code. In Figure 1, the program memory is simplified as ROM and the data memory as RAM. As ECC is very resource demanding and a software-only solution is in most cases insufficiently slow, one could add a memory-mapped ECC co-processor.

(b) Co-processors have already been extensively studied and optimized in related work [19,20]. However, comparing area and power results of designs that use different technologies and tools is inaccurate. Therefore, Section 5 presents an ECC co-processor on-par with related work.

The drawback of so-called ECC slaves is that they waste chip area by having their own memory. A solution in which the global RAM is reused is preferable. Even when area-efficient RAM macros are used, practical evaluations show that one RAM macro with more entries is smaller than two RAM macros with fewer entries (c.f. 128 × 8-bit: 2,073 GE vs. 256 × 8-bit: 2,897 GE). An ECC accelerator without RAM, which only performs finite-field operations would be a solution. Unfortunately, for this solution the CPU has to manually move operands from the RAM to the ECC slave and vice versa, thus wasting potential performance.

(c) An ECC circuit which, like the CPU, is capable of accessing the global data memory by itself solves that problem: an ECC bus master. This assumes that the used microprocessor must support a multi-master scenario, which embedded

---

[1] Section 4 discusses this solution.

Table 2. HW synthesis of openMSP430 [24]

Functional Blocks	Chip-Area [GE]
openMSP430	7,801
Execution unit	5,536
Register file	2,709
ALU	693
Multiplier	1,826
openMSP430 w/o Multiplier	5,958

Algorithm 1. Accessing the 16-bit memory-mapped multiplier

```
1: MOV R4, &MPY
2: MOV R5, &OP2
3: NOP
4: MOV @RESLO, R6
5: MOV @RESHI, R7
```

light-weight microprocessors usually do not. Also, the required arbiter can have a significant impact on the total chip area.

(d) A more sophisticated concept is to unite the ECC master with the arbiter. This within the context of ECC novel concept "drops" an ECC accelerator right between the CPU and the data memory. From the viewpoint of the CPU it behaves as simple ECC slave and does not hinder any access to the data memory. From the viewpoint of the drop-in module, direct access to the data memory is possible. Advantageous is also that neither the CPU (compared to instruction-set extensions) nor the data-memory need to be modified. Section 6 discusses this solution in more detail.

Tools. For this paper we use the 130 nm low-leakage ASIC technology by UMC with the Faraday design libraries in combination with area-efficient single-port register-based RAM macros. For hardware synthesis Cadence RTL Compiler v08.10, for place-and-route and power simulation Cadence First Encounter v08.10, and for simulation Cadence NCSim v08.20 are used. In this technology, one gate equivalent is equal to $5.12\,\mu m^2$. All evaluations are performed at 1 MHz and can easily be synthesized to exceed an operating frequency of 50–100 MHz.

4   ECC on openMSP430

At the core of all previously discussed hardware designs is a microprocessor. The selection of an appropriate microprocessor crucially influences the final run-time, chip area, power, and energy results. The MSP430 [27] developed by Texas Instruments, is considered to be a role model when it comes to low-cost and low-power applications. It is currently already used for the sensor-node platforms BEAN, COOKIES, EPIC mode, PowWow, Shimmer, TelosB, T-Mote Sky, and XM1000, just to name a few. The MSP430 is a 16-bit RISC processor with a Von Neumann architecture. This is important for saving data memory, as constants do not have to be loaded to the expensive RAM before they are used. The MSP430 comes with 16 16-bit registers, where R0 is the program counter, R1 is the stack pointer, R2 is the status register, and R3 is the constant-generator register. So only 12 registers (R4–R15) are useable as general-purpose registers. The

---

Algorithm 2. $ACC \leftarrow ACC + (A[0] \times B[2]) + (A[1] \times B[1]) + (A[2] \times B[0])$.

```
1: ADD   #4    , OPB         9: MOV  @OPA   , &MAC
2: MOV   @OPA+, &MPY        10: MOV  @OPB   , &OP2
3: MOV   @OPB , &OP2        11: SUB  #4     , OPA
4: DECD  OPB               12: ADD  @RESLO , ACCO
5: MOV   @OPA+, &MAC        13: ADDC @RESHI , ACC1
6: MOV   @OPB , &OP2        14: ADDC @SUMEXT, ACC2
7: DECD  OPB               15: MOV  ACCO   , 4(DEST)
8: ADD   @SUMEXT, ACC2      16: CLR  ACCO
```

MSP430 comes with only 27 instructions, from which none is a multiplication instruction. To perform a 16-bit integer multiplication, the MSP430 optionally has a memory-mapped multiplier. This will be discussed in detail later.

4.1 openMSP430

As our desired goal is a microprocessor-based hardware design, we need a hardware model of the MSP430. Olivier Girard programmed a synthesizable Verilog clone of the MSP430, called openMSP430 [24]. This clone fully supports the instruction set of the original MSP430 (with nearly identical timings), interrupts, and power-saving modes. It optionally comes with a 16×16-bit hardware multiplier, watchdog, timer, and GPIOs. A first evaluation of this core is depicted in Table 2. An openMSP430 without data or program memory (which will be chosen appropriately) requires 7,801 GE. Most of this chip area is spent on the execution unit (71 %), and the hardware multiplier (23 %). Without the multiplier, which is not necessary for binary-field based ECC, the openMSP430 only requires 5,958 GE.

4.2 Integer Arithmetic

In order to perform a 16-bit integer multiplication, four memory accesses are necessary. Algorithm 1 shows the assembly code necessary to multiply R4 with R5 and to store the product in R6 and R7. The code shown in Algorithm 1 needs $4 + 4 + 1 + 2 + 2 = 13$ cycles to complete.

As multiple words are needed to represent integers within the used finite field, the multi-precision product-scanning multiplication technique of Comba [4] is used. Algorithm 2 sketches the used methodology. Three registers are used to hold pointers to the operands (OPA and OPB) and the result (DEST), three registers for the accumulator (ACC0-2) and three registers to hold addresses of the memory-mapped multiplier (RESLO, RESHI, and SUMEXT). In order to avoid loading the product after each multiplication, multiply-accumulate operations are performed directly within the memory-mapped multiplier. The overflowing bit stored within the SUMEXT register needs to be loaded within line 8. After line 14, the accumulated product resides within the registers ACC0-2. This technique has already been presented by Gouvêa and López [8].

Table 3. Comparison with related work

Algorithm 3. 64 × 1-bit polynomial multiplication

```
1: RLA B0        8: XOR #0, C0
2: JNC +10       9: XOR #0, C1
3: XOR A0, C0   10: XOR #0, C2
4: XOR A1, C1   11: XOR #0, C3
5: XOR A2, C2   12: NOP
6: XOR A3, C3   13: NOP
7: JMP +12
```

Curve	Type	ROM [Bytes]	RAM [Bytes]	Runtime [kCycles]
Gouvêa et al. [9] and Szczechowiak et al. [26]				
secp160r1 [9]	$\mathbb{F}_p$	23,300	2,800	2,528
sect163k1 [9]	$\mathbb{F}_{2^m}$	27,800	3,600	2,032
Custom [26]	$\mathbb{F}_p$	31,300	2,900	5,898
sect163k1 [26]	$\mathbb{F}_{2^m}$	32,100	2,800	8,519
ours on MSP430				
secp160r1	$\mathbb{F}_p$	4,230	282	5,721
sect163r2	$\mathbb{F}_{2^m}$	4,126	294	7,447

4.3 Polynomial Arithmetic

As the MSP430 lacks a carry-less multiplier, a polynomial multiplication has been implemented using branch operations. Algorithm 3 shows a 64 × 1-bit polynomial multiplication which was used to build a 64 × 32-bit multiplication. The 64 × 32-bit multiplication can be performed without the use of a single, costly memory load or store operation. Using the methodology of Karatsuba and Ofman a three-way split of a single 192-bit multiplication to 6 64-bit multiplications has been performed. On the MSP430 a 64 × 32-bit polynomial multiplication takes 383 cycles and a 192-bit polynomial multiplication takes 6,089 cycles. For constant runtime, lines 8-13 in Algorithm 3 perform dummy operations. Without the dummy operations, a speedup of 23 % is possible on average. For comparison, a 192-bit integer multiplication takes 2,254 cycles and therefore is 2.7 times faster. Gouvêa et al. [9] report an assembly optimized implementation for sect163k1 which only needs 3,907 cycles, but their implementation is not safe from timing attacks.

4.4 Software Results

Four standardized elliptic curves providing security-levels of 80–96 bits have been implemented. secp192r1 and sect163r2 are chosen because they are the smallest elliptic curves within the NIST standard [2,23], still providing a sufficient level of security. secp160r1 has been chosen because it is popularly used within related work. As c2tnb191v1 [1] provides a similar security level as secp192r1 (95 vs 96 bits) it can be used for comparison.

Note that Table 3 shows the runtimes of our software implementation, simulated on a cycle-accurate model of the MSP430, while Table 4 shows the slightly better runtimes for an openMSP430. In Appendix A a detailed comparison of all software implementations is depicted.

In literature many speed-optimized ECC implementations for the MSP430 have been reported [9,21,26,28] (cf. Table 3). Because of the extentsively performed assembler optimization, our software implementation outperforms the related work of Szczechowiak et al. [26] that also requires larger memories. The

Table 4. Synthesized software implementations of ECC on the openMSP430

Curve	Type	Security [Bits]	ROM [Bytes]	RAM [Bytes]	ROM [GE]	RAM [GE]	Area [GE]	Runtime [kCycles]	Power [µW]	Energy [µJ]
secp160r1	$\mathbb{F}_p$	80	4,230	282	5,907	3,175	16,638	5,445	55.9	304.3
secp192r1	$\mathbb{F}_p$	96	4,846	322	6,173	3,400	17,128	8,650	53.9	466.7
sect163r2	$\mathbb{F}_{2^m}$	81	4,126	294	5,737	3,275	14,167	7,217	49.1	354.3
c2tnb191v1	$\mathbb{F}_{2^m}$	95	3,994	310	5,735	3,375	14,014	8,376	55.4	463.8

fastest (ECDSA) implementation was done by Gouvêa et al. [9] in 2012. Compared to our implementations, they report twofold faster runtimes at the expense of 7 times larger program and 12 times larger data memories. As we synthesize the program memory and choose appropriately large RAM macros, their implementation would result in a significantly larger hardware design, compared to ours.

Table 4 shows the measured chip area, runtime, power, and energy results for the four implemented elliptic curves. The biggest impact of up to 60 % on the total chip area is due to the size of the program memory and data memory. For the elliptic curves over $\mathbb{F}_{2^m}$ the integer multiplier has been removed. The binary-field-based ECC implementations are about 16 % smaller and similarly fast, compared to the prime-field-based ECC implementations. For sect163r2 the used 176-bit polynomial multiplier which is based on the 192-bit multiplication algorithm discussed before, renders the runtime results inferior compared to secp160r1.

The elliptic curve requiring the least amount of energy is secp160r1 (303.3 µJ). However, the biggest potential for hardware optimizations (cf. [29]) lies within binary-field based elliptic curves (354.3 µJ). Therefore sect163r2 alias NIST B-163 has been selected for the following hardware implementations.

5   Stand-Alone ECC Hardware

The dedicated hardware design used for this paper (cf. Figure 2) is strongly related to the works of Kumar and Paar [19] and Lee et al. [20], but uses a different memory architecture. As register-based memory is most expensive, it is replaced by latches, which are 27 % smaller in the used 130 nm technology. As latches are not synchronous, the depicted circuit only works because a common Work register is placed before the latches. At the positive clock level, activated via the clock gate (CG), the latch inherits the contents stored within the Work register. A single multiplexer is used to select the content of a latch which is then used as operand OpA for the datapath. The datapath consists of an MSB-first digit-serial multiplier, an adder, and optionally a squaring unit. For the multiplication, an operand is split into W-bit sized parts which are stored in OpB. d of the W bits are then concurrently handled within the multiplication circuit. Dependent on the desired speed grade, it is possible to increase the size of d, or to use a dedicated squaring circuit. For interfacing the module with an external W-bit wide bus, the existing multiplexers are reused. For memory

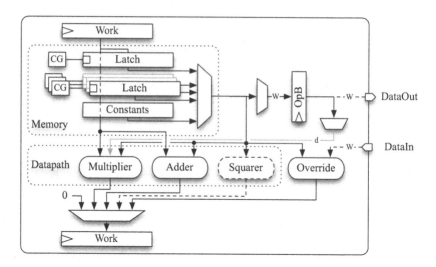

Fig. 2. Dedicated ECC hardware

storing operations, W of the N-bit wide bus are overridden by the externally driven bus signal.

5.1   Stand-Alone ECC Hardware Results

A complete ECC coprocessor including datapath, controlpath, memory, private scalar, modifiable base point, and resulting point with recovered y-coordinate needs at least 11,778 GE and up to 341,835 cycles. Table 5 summarizes our results for different d parameters. Adding a dedicated 1-cycle squaring unit only costs 884 GE (7.5 %) of additional hardware, but improves the runtime by a factor of approximately two. The most energy-efficient circuit is using $d = 2$. The circuit with the best scaled area-runtime product (SARP) is using $d = 4$.

Compared to related work [14,19,20,25,30], our designs are smaller or faster and therefore provide a better area-time product. In terms of power and energy, which are highly dependent on the used technology, our results are similar to related work.

The chip area shown in Table 5 does not include the area needed by the MSP430 (5,958 GE), its data memory (8 × 16-bit RAM – 1,443 GE), and its program memory (354 bytes – 801 GE). So all our dedicated ECC hardware designs need additional 8,202 GE of hardware in order to provide the full functionality of an MSP430.

The major drawback of the ECC hardware module is the inefficient data memory. Unfortunately, there are no efficient RAM macros with a 163-bit interface. Even though latches are used, the memory requires 6,924 GE, or 59 % of the total hardware area. A comparable register-based RAM macro with 8 × 163 = 1, 467 bits requires only 2,600 GE. That is 62 % less. For the drop-in concept discussed in the next section, such an area-efficient RAM macro is used.

Table 5. Synthesis results of the dedicated ECC hardware design without MSP430

Design	Technology [nm]	Area [GE]	Runtime [kCycles]	Power [µW]	Energy [µJ]	SARP
$d = 1$ w/o squ.	130	11,778	341,835	63.3	21.6	5.2
$d = 1$ w/ squ.	130	12,662	174,025	71.5	12.4	2.8
$d = 2$ w/ squ.	130	13,307	93,997	78.4	7.4	1.6
$d = 4$ w/ squ.	130	14,552	53,489	140.1	7.5	1.0
Kumar and Paar [19] $d = 1$	350	15,094	376,864	788.0	297.0	7.3
Hein et al. [14]	180	11,904	296,299	101.9	30.2	4.5
Lee et al. [20] $d = 1$	130	12,506	302,457	32.4	9.8	4.9
Lee et al. [20] $d = 5$	130	20,316	83,375	48.9	4.1	2.2

6 Drop-in Concept

The drop-in concept has some similarities with instruction-set extensions. The drawback of ISE is that the HW designer needs to be able to modify both the controlpath and the datapath of the used processor, as well as the corresponding software toolchain. A different solution, based on a memory mapped carry-less multiply-accumulate unit has similarly large access times as the already existing integer multiply-accumulate unit of the MSP430. Therefore, it would only make a minor impact on the ECC runtime.

The drop-in concept provides full advantage even when the hardware designer is not able to modify the used microprocessor. Performance similar to dedicated ECC hardware is achievable and the verification and validation process regarding the used microprocessor does not have to be redone. The drop-in concept is also flexible: A hardware designer can shift control logic between the program memory and the dedicated hardware module. In this paper the drop-in module is designed to efficiently perform finite-field arithmetic (addition, squaring, and multiplication) only. The finite-field inverse as well as the point-multiplication algorithm are implemented in software.

As interface, the drop-in module provides three address, a command, and a status register. Before each operation, the address registers are written with two source and a destination memory address, and the operation is started by writing the command register. The status register is then polled to check whether the operation has been finished. Actually, experiments showed that waiting at the beginning of the finite-field operations for the previous operations to finish is more performant. In this way the CPU and the drop-in module can partly work in parallel.

6.1 Drop-in Architecture

Figure 3 shows the architecture of the drop-in module. The data-bus is depicted in red and orange, the address bus in blue. The drop-in module consists of a lightweight arbiter, controlpath, and datapath. If both the CPU and the drop-in module want to access the data memory, the currently pending operation within

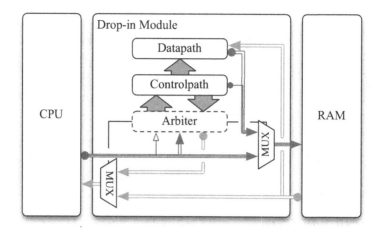

Fig. 3. Drop-in module for Elliptic Curve Cryptography

the drop-in module is put on hold and the CPU is given access to the data memory. Therefore the drop-in module needs to be specially prepared for the case in which it is put on hold. For our ECC design, only 7 1-bit registers are necessary to provide this functionality. As a side note, the openMSP430 does not support to have delayed memory access.

The datapath within the drop-in module is very similar to the datapath of the dedicated ECC hardware module. Figure 4 shows that only two N-bit registers and a W-bit register are necessary for an MSB-first digit-serial multiplier. In each cycle, the N bits of OpA are multiplied with d bits of OpB, which are added to a d-bit shifted intermediate product, stored within the N-bit Work register. The $(N+d)$-bit sum is then reduced and used to update the Work register. At the beginning of the algorithm, Work is initialized with zero and OpA is initialized with the value stored within the data memory. The W-bit chunks of OpB are loaded on-demand, as it is shown within Figure 5 (d). When the multiplication is finished, the result within Work is stored back to the data memory.

Optionally, a dedicated squaring unit can be used. In our implementation (Figure 5 (a)), OpA is loaded from the data memory, the squaring is performed within a single cycle, and the result is stored back to the data memory. The datapath of the addition is not shown in Figure 4 as it only is a simple XOR-gate. For the finite-field addition (Figure 5 (b)) three times $\lceil N/W \rceil$ memory operations are necessary.

If at any moment, the CPU needs to do some (real-time) interrupt handling and needs access to the data memory, the operation in progress within the drop-in module is simply halted and continued when the data memory bus is free to use (Figure 5 (c)).

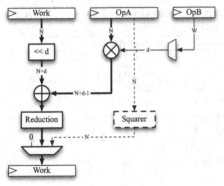

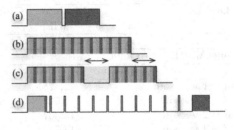

Fig. 5. Bus access during squaring (a), addition (b), addition with stall (c), and multiplication (d) operations. Memory operations regarding OpA, OpB, and Dest are colored in blue, green, and red, respectively

Fig. 4. Datapath of the ECC drop-in

6.2 Drop-in Concept Hardware Results

Similar to before, the drop-in module was evaluated for different configurations (cf. Table 6). Independent of the size of the digit-serial multiplier and the availability of a squaring unit, the size of the CPU (5,715 GE), the program memory (1,426 bytes – 2,635 GE), and the data memory (222 bytes – 2,875 GE) are constant. The drop-in module only needs between 4,114 GE and 6,760 GE in chip area.

This is the most interesting number for microchip manufacturers. As not every customer actually needs ECC, they want to leave out unnecessary components, as they produce unnecessary costs. On the other hand, customers that require performant ECC can take advantage of the drop-in ECC module. Compared to a dedicated ECC hardware module, which requires 12–15 kGE, the drop-in module requires only a fraction of it: 35 %.

6.3 Related Work

In 2009, Guo and Schaumont [11] identified the data bus as potential bottleneck for ECC designs. Cause of that, they add the necessary data memory to the dedicated ECC accelerator to keep the number of necessary bus accesses at a minimum. Thus their ECC accelerator becomes more like a dedicated hardware module. As it is an FPGA design, a comparison with our work is impracticable.

Most comparable to our drop-in concept is the work of Koschuch et al. [18]. They implemented a memory-less ECC accelerator and used a DMA controller for efficiently accessing the data memory. Their architecture is best comparable with the previously discussed architecture *(c)*. Their DMA controller is 1,029 GE large, their ECC accelerator is 11,618 GE large, and their total design for $\mathbb{F}_{2^{191}}$ requires 29,491 GE. For a scalar multiplication, they require 1,416 kCycles. Thus their design is slower and larger than our drop-in designs.

Table 6. Synthesis results of all ECC hardware architectures at 1 MHz for `sect163r2`

Design	Module [GE]	Chiparea [GE]	Runtime [Cycles]	Power [μW]	Energy [μJ]
Architecture *(a)* – Software-only implementation					
openMSP430 w/o mult.	-	14,167	7,216,905	49.1	354.3
Architecture *(b)* – Dedicated ECC Hardware Accelerator					
$d = 1$ w/o squ.	11,778	19,980	342,724	93.8	32.1
$d = 1$ w/ squ.	12,662	20,864	174,910	112.9	19.7
$d = 2$ w/ squ.	13,307	21,509	94,882	152.4	14.5
$d = 4$ w/ squ.	14,552	22,754	54,376	181.7	9.9
Architecture *(d)* – Drop-in Module Based					
$d = 1$ w/o squ.	4,114	15,282	467,370	66.1	30.9
$d = 1$ w/ squ.	4,895	16,121	303,202	77.6	23.5
$d = 2$ w/ squ.	5,512	16,738	224,222	73.6	16.5
$d = 4$ w/ squ.	6,760	17,986	182,130	70.0	12.8

7 Comparison of Implemented Architectures

In the previous sections, architectures *(a)* - a plain software implementation, *(b)* - a dedicated ECC hardware module, and *(d)* - a drop-in module - have been presented and discussed in connection with the appropriate related work. Thereby all implementations are on-par with related work or outperform related work. Most important however is the comparison of the three implemented architectures *(a,b,d)* with each other.

Table 6 shows the area, runtime, power, and energy values of all architectures. The column 'Module' gives the area for the dedicated ECC hardware blocks, while 'Chiparea' accumulates the program memory, the data memory, the microprocessor, and the special hardware module. The runtimes of architecture *(b)* now include the calling overhead needed to trigger and poll the dedicated hardware module. In comparison to Table 5, the area and power values now also include the RAM, ROM, and CPU.

The smallest of all implementations is the plain software implementation *(a)* needing only 14,167 GE. Both the drop-in solution *(d)* (15,282 GE) and the dedicated hardware solution *(b)* (19,980 GE) are larger. However, those solutions are up to 132 times faster and up to 36 times more energy efficient. Thus architecture *(a)* can be considered as fall-back solution, but is practically to slow for most relevant applications. The runtime is nearly one second at a common sensors-node frequency of 8 Mhz.

Thus the question is whether architecture *(b)* or *(d)* is better. The drop-in concept *(d)* is 22 % smaller and requires 50 % less power. On the other hand, architecture *(b)* is faster. The comparison is visualized in Figure 6, which prints the chiparea values versus the runtimes. The dashed lines indicate constant area-runtime products. After investigating the results in detail, our conclusion is that both architectures *(b)* and *(d)* have the very right of existence. However, if the application requires that a point multiplication is finished within, e.g., 30 ms

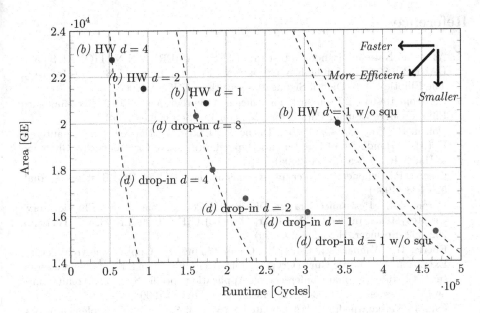

Fig. 6. Area-runtime-characteristics of the various ECC architectures

(@ 8 MHz), architecture *(d)* based on the drop-in concept with $d = 2$ is the smallest and therefore best solution.

8   Conclusion

This work proofs that the drop-in concept is a viable alternative to previously existing plain software and dedicated hardware solutions. Both the presented software-only and the presented dedicated hardware solution enable a fair comparison using a common side-channel aware methodology and identical tools. The software implementation is (supposed to be) side-channel secure and needs 7–12 times less memory compared to latest related work. The hardware implementation is more area-efficient compared to related work, because a specially designed data memory is used. However, a plain hardware implementation is not aware of the versatile MSP430, which is usually available in wireless sensor nodes. Hereby the drop-in concept provides a novel solution which actually is smaller than the hardware module based architecture, while being similarly fast, and requiring 36 times less energy than the dedicated software solution. This makes the newly presented drop-in concept a great solution for microchip and sensor-node manufacturers.

Acknowledgments. The research described in this paper has been supported, in part, by the European Commission through the ICT Program under contract ICT-SEC-2009-5-258754 TAMPRES.

References

1. American National Standards Institute (ANSI). AMERICAN NATIONAL STANDARD X9.62-2005. Public Key Cryptography for the Financial Services Industry, The Elliptic Curve Digital Signature Algorithm, ECDSA (2005)
2. Certicom Research. Standards for Efficient Cryptography, SEC 2: Recommended Elliptic Curve Domain Parameters, Version 1.0 (September 2000)
3. Cohen, H., Frey, G., Avanzi, R., Doche, C., Lange, T., Nguyen, K., Vercauteren, F. (eds.): Handbook of Elliptic and Hyperelliptic Curve Cryptography. Chapman & Hall/CRC, Boca Raton (2006)
4. Comba, P.: Exponentiation cryptosystems on the IBM PC. IBM Systems Journal, 526–538 (1990)
5. Coron, J.-S.: Resistance against Differential Power Analysis for Elliptic Curve Cryptosystems. In: Koç, Ç.K., Paar, C. (eds.) CHES 1999. LNCS, vol. 1717, pp. 292–302. Springer, Heidelberg (1999)
6. Eberle, H., Wander, A., Gura, N., Chang-Shantz, S., Gupta, V.: Architectural Extensions for Elliptic Curve Cryptography over $GF(2^m)$ on 8-bit Microprocessors. In: IEEE International Conference on Application-specific Systems, Architectures and Processors, pp. 343–349. IEEE Computer Society (2005)
7. Fan, J., Verbauwhede, I.: An Updated Survey on Secure ECC Implementations: Attacks, Countermeasures and Cost. In: Naccache, D. (ed.) Quisquater Festschrift. LNCS, vol. 6805, pp. 265–282. Springer, Heidelberg (2012)
8. Gouvêa, C.P.L., López, J.: Software Implementation of Pairing-Based Cryptography on Sensor Networks Using the MSP430 Microcontroller. In: Roy, B., Sendrier, N. (eds.) INDOCRYPT 2009. LNCS, vol. 5922, pp. 248–262. Springer, Heidelberg (2009)
9. Gouvêa, C.P.L., Oliveira, L., López, J.: Efficient Software Implementation of Public-Key Cryptography on Sensor Networks Using the MSP430X Microcontroller. Journal of Cryptographic Engineering 2, 19–29 (2012)
10. Großschädl, J., Savaş, E.: Instruction Set Extensions for Fast Arithmetic in Finite Fields $GF(p)$ and $GF(2^m)$. In: CHES, pp. 133–147 (2004)
11. Guo, X., Schaumont, P.: Optimizing the HW/SW boundary of an ECC SoC design using control hierarchy and distributed storage. In: DATE, pp. 454–459 (2009)
12. Gura, N., Patel, A., Wander, A., Eberle, H., Shantz, S.C.: Comparing Elliptic Curve Cryptography and RSA on 8-Bit CPUs. In: CHES, pp. 119–132 (2004)
13. Hankerson, D., Menezes, A.J., Vanstone, S.: Guide to Elliptic Curve Cryptography. Springer (2004)
14. Hein, D., Wolkerstorfer, J., Felber, N.: ECC Is Ready for RFID – A Proof in Silicon. In: Avanzi, R.M., Keliher, L., Sica, F. (eds.) SAC 2008. LNCS, vol. 5381, pp. 401–413. Springer, Heidelberg (2009)
15. Hutter, M., Joye, M., Sierra, Y.: Memory-Constrained Implementations of Elliptic Curve Cryptography in Co-Z Coordinate Representation. In: Nitaj, A., Pointcheval, D. (eds.) AFRICACRYPT 2011. LNCS, vol. 6737, pp. 170–187. Springer, Heidelberg (2011)
16. IEEE. IEEE Standard 802.15.4-2003: Wireless Medium Access Control (MAC) and Physical Layer (PHY) Specifications for Low-Rate Wireless Personal Area Networks (LR-WPANs) (May 2003)
17. Itoh, T., Tsujii, S.: Effective recursive algorithm for computing multiplicative inverses in $GF(2^m)$. Electronic Letters, 334–335 (1988)

18. Koschuch, M., Großschädl, J., Page, D., Grabher, P., Hudler, M., Krüger, M.: Hardware/Software Co-Design of Public-Key Cryptography for SSL Protocol Execution in Embedded Systems. In: Workshop on Embedded Systems Security, pp. 63–79 (2009)

19. Kumar, S.S., Pàar, C.: Are standards compliant Elliptic Curve Cryptosystems feasible on RFID? In: Workshop on RFID Security – RFIDSec 2006 (2006)

20. Lee, Y.K., Sakiyama, K., Batina, L., Verbauwhede, I.: Elliptic-Curve-Based Security Processor for RFID. IEEE Transactions on Computers 57(11), 1514–1527 (2008)

21. Liu, A., Ning, P.: TinyECC: A Configurable Library for Elliptic Curve Cryptography in Wireless Sensor Networks. In: International Conference on Information Processing in Sensor Networks, pp. 245–256 (2008)

22. López, J., Dahab, R.: Fast Multiplication on Elliptic Curves over $GF(2_m)$ without Precomputation. In: Koç, Ç.K., Paar, C. (eds.) CHES 1999. LNCS, vol. 1717, pp. 316–327. Springer, Heidelberg (1999)

23. National Institute of Standards and Technology (NIST). FIPS-186-3: Digital Signature Standard, DSS (2009)

24. Olivier Girard. openMSP430 (2013), http://opencores.org/project,openmsp430

25. Öztürk, E., Sunar, B., Savaş, E.: Low-Power Elliptic Curve Cryptography Using Scaled Modular Arithmetic. In: Joye, M., Quisquater, J.-J. (eds.) CHES 2004. LNCS, vol. 3156, pp. 92–106. Springer, Heidelberg (2004)

26. Szczechowiak, P., Oliveira, L.B., Scott, M., Collier, M., Dahab, R.: NanoECC: Testing the Limits of Elliptic Curve Cryptography in Sensor Networks. In: Verdone, R. (ed.) EWSN 2008. LNCS, vol. 4913, pp. 305–320. Springer, Heidelberg (2008)

27. Texas Instruments. MSP430C11x1 - Mixed Signal Microcontroller (2008), http://focus.ti.com

28. Wang, H., Sheng, B., Li, Q.: Elliptic Curve Cryptography-based Access Control in Sensor Networks. International Journal of Security and Networks, 127–137 (2006)

29. Wenger, E., Hutter, M.: Exploring the design space of prime field vs. binary field ECC-hardware implementations. In: Laud, P. (ed.) NordSec 2011. LNCS, vol. 7161, pp. 256–271. Springer, Heidelberg (2012)

30. Wolkerstorfer, J.: Is Elliptic-Curve Cryptography Suitable for Small Devices? In: Workshop on RFID and Lightweight Crypto, pp. 78–91 (2005)

31. ZigBee Alliance. The ZigBee Alliance Website, http://www.zigbee.org/

A   Implementation Runtimes

Table 7 lists the constant key-independent runtimes of all implementations done for this paper. Architectures *(b)* and *(d)* implemented the elliptic curve sect163r2.
We distinguish between runtimes for the original MSP430 and the open-MSP430. The runtimes of the openMSP430 are better, because several instructions of the openMSP430 perform the same operation in less cycles than the original MSP430. In average, the openMSP430 is 5 % faster for the prime field based elliptic curves (secp160r1, secp192r1) and 3 % faster for the binary field based elliptic curves (sect163r2, c2tnb191v1).

Table 7. Runtimes for finite-field addition/subtraction (ADD), squaring (SQU), multiplication (MUL), inversion (INV), and point-multiplication (P-MUL) operations

Implementation	ADD [Cycles]	SQU [Cycles]	MUL [Cycles]	INV [Cycles]	P-MUL [Cycles]
(a) MSP430 secp160r1	163	1,905	1,905	327,366	5,721,420
(a) MSP430 secp192r1	191	2,559	2,559	526568	9,100,128
(a) MSP430 sect163r2	109	852	6,604	199,815	7,446,677
(a) MSP430 c2tnb191v1	118	778	6,566	229,297	8,610,906
(a) openMSP430 secp160r1	161	1,808	1,808	310,812	5,445,010
(a) openMSP430 secp192r1	189	2,426	2,426	499,331	8,650,455
(a) openMSP430 sect163r2	107	781	6,446	186,653	7,216,905
(a) openMSP430 c2tnb191v1	116	725	6,420	217,209	8,376,138
(b) HW $d = 1$ w/o squ	2	174	174	29,754	341,835
(b) HW $d = 1$	2	1	174	1,728	174,025
(b) HW $d = 2$	2	1	93	999	93,997
(b) HW $d = 4$	2	1	52	630	53,489
(d) drop-in $d = 1$ w/o squ	40	208	208	36,419	467,370
(d) drop-in $d = 1$	40	38	208	9,963	303,202
(d) drop-in $d = 2$	40	38	128	9,227	224,222
(d) drop-in $d = 4$	40	38	80	8,843	182,130

Beyond Full Disk Encryption: Protection on Security-Enhanced Commodity Processors[*]

Michael Henson and Stephen Taylor

Thayer School of Engineering, Dartmouth College

Abstract. Modern computer systems exhibit a major weakness in that code and data are stored in the clear, unencrypted, within random access memory. As a result, numerous vulnerabilities exist at every level of the software stack. These vulnerabilities have been exploited to gather confidential information (e.g. encryption keys) and inject malicious code to overcome access controls and other protections. Full memory encryption (FME) would mitigate the vulnerabilities but the CPU-memory bottleneck presents a significant challenge to designing a usable system with acceptable overheads. Recently, security hardware, including encryption engines, has been integrated on-chip within commodity processors such as the Intel i7, AMD bulldozer, and multiple ARM variants. This paper describes on-going work to develop and measure a clean-slate operating system – Bear – that leverages on-chip encryption to provide confidentiality of code and data. While Bear operates on multiple platforms, memory encryption work is focused on the Freescale i.MX535 (ARM Cortex A8) using its integrated encryption engine.

Keywords: Memory encryption, data in use, security-enhanced commodity processors, secure microkernel, mobile platform security.

1 Background and Threat Model

Current operating system designs have sought to utilize a *static* base of trust and extend trust into software through deliberate layering [Arbaugh et al. 1997]. Modern computer systems, even those protected by full disk encryption (FDE) [Brink 2009], exhibit a major weakness in that code and data are stored in the clear, unencrypted, within *memory*. These sensitive details are not only available to applications; they are known to persist in multiple unexpected locations (kernel and application), for longer than traditionally thought, even after an application exits [Chow et al. 2004], [Dunn et al. 2012], [Tang et al. 2012]. Unfortunately, this invalidates basic security assumptions rendering it possible to gather confidential information, including encryption keys, passwords, and other sensitive information that can be used to undermine trust [Halderman et al. 2008], [Boileau 2006], [Steil 2005], [Henson and Taylor, 2012]. To exacerbate the problem, memory vulnerabilities extend to *every level of the software*

---

[*] This material is based on research sponsored by the Defense Advanced Research Projects Agency (DARPA) under agreement number FA8750-09-1-0213.

M. Jacobson et al. (Eds.): ACNS 2013, LNCS 7954, pp. 307–321, 2013.

stack and the opportunities for exploitation extend well beyond physical attack to include remote attacks over the Internet: techniques have evolved that allow malicious code to be injected into device drivers, operating system kernels, and user processes.

To exploit memory vulnerabilities, numerous attack vectors have been developed. In a cold boot attack, for example, memory is frozen using a refrigerant and then removed from the computer. It is then quickly placed into a specially designed system that reads out its content, targeting encryption keys and other sensitive information. This particular attack has recently been shown to be applicable to smart phone devices as well as traditional desktops via the forensic recovery of scrambled telephones (FROST) operating system [Muller et al. 2012]. Besides capturing the encryption key, FROST was used to capture other code and data to include photos, websites visited, e-mails, contact lists, networking credentials and complete ELF binaries. Another particularly effective attack, bus-snooping/injecting, allows information to be captured or inserted via the bus lines between system components [Boileau 2006].

The threat model for this work involves an adversary gaining physical access to a computer system with sufficient resources and motivation (e.g. criminal and point of sale systems or government sponsored attacker and mobile military systems) to pursue the vulnerabilities mentioned above. For example, the smart phone of a diplomat may be confiscated for a period of time while transiting through airport security. Methods of physical access may be used to capture memory and/or disk contents for offline analysis with the sole purpose of the attack being data exfiltration. In another example, an unmanned aerial system (UAS) might be captured and control programs reverse engineered to enable the attack of other similar systems.

In contrast to research on intrusion detection, our research group is focused on exploring methods to *increase attacker workload*, undermining surveillance, forensics and persistence while *reducing the attack surface*. This paper focuses on one such method -- *memory encryption* – explored within the context of a modern microkernel.

2   Related Work

In effect, the increasing adoption of full disk encryption (FDE) has pushed the vulnerabilities associated with persistent data on disk down into the next level of the memory hierarchy, which has proven equally vulnerable. The key concept by which vulnerabilities were mitigated on disk was encryption: encrypting the disk provided confidentiality preventing access to sensitive information. By migrating the same solution down into RAM, it may be possible to circumvent similar attacks at this lower level of the memory hierarchy. This constrains the *boundary* available to an attack to lie at the *processor itself*, presenting a barrier that, in most cases, cannot be defeated without mechanical or electrical destruction of the processor chip. Attacks on the device are possible, for example, by etching away the chip walls with acid to reveal internal bus lines, or electromagnetic and differential power analyses [Pope 2008], [Kocher et al. 1999]. These approaches clearly increase the attacker workload by at least an order of magnitude, require expert knowledge, and cannot be exploited remotely over a network [Suh et al. 2007]. Moreover, while tamper resistant mechanisms are already available that significantly increase the barrier to entry [Chari et al. 1999], protecting circuits from invasive and side-channel attacks is an open research area.

Although the concept of *memory encryption* has been actively researched for over three decades, it has yet to be used at the core of operating system designs to provide confidentiality of code and data [Henson and Taylor 2012]. The literature on memory encryption is largely concerned with three core approaches based on hardware enhancements [Lie et al. 2000], [Rogers et al. 2005], [Su et al. 2009], operating system enhancements [Chhabra et al. 2011], [Chen et al. 2008], [Peterson 2010], and specialized industrial applications [Dallas 1997], [Arnold and Doorn 2004], [Steil and Domke 2008]. Unfortunately, almost all of the hardware and operating system enhancements have only been implemented through simulation or emulation, and as a result, the claims have yet to be validated and quantified on practical systems. The few processors that implement memory encryption are characterized by low speeds and small addressable memory (<=16 bits) at use in low throughput (e.g. point-of-sale, set top TV access, etc.) applications or specialized gaming systems.

Recently, security hardware, including encryption engines, has been integrated within commodity processors such as the Intel i7, AMD bulldozer, and multiple ARM variants; however, systems developers have yet to embrace these specialized, often vendor-specific, features [Vasudevan et al. 2011]. Little practical experimentation has been conducted and the improvements in security and performance have yet to be quantified [Henson and Taylor 2012]. While this new hardware has not been used to protect an entire system, there are examples of its use to protect particular applications. Several papers have highlighted approaches to mitigate attacks on FDE. For example, Tresor [Muller et al. 2011], aims to protect the FDE key by storing it only inside the CPU and performing encryption/decryption within that boundary. Unfortunately, this technique is inadequate since it is possible to recover the key via a DMA injection attack on unprotected memory [Blass and Robertson 2012]. In another example, memory vulnerabilities were used to undermine the memory encryption protections of the Xbox 360. In the original Xbox, the key was stored in plaintext and transmitted across the southbridge bus. The key was captured in a bus-snooping attack, which led to compromise of the gaming system and to the subsequent growth of the Xbox mod-chip industry [Steil 2005]. In the updated Xbox 360, memory encryption is used to protect against such attacks; however, it appears that the process stack is not encrypted and this has led to another successful compromise [Steil and Domke 2008].

Unfortunately, little work has been performed to explore the trade space of using security enhanced commodity processors to implement *full memory encryption* (FME): encrypting all components of a process – stack, heap, code and data. Although more recent processors make memory encryption less costly, it remains unclear if FME is viable for everyday use or is limited to constrained tactical applications. In past ME work, overhead has been measured at the coarse granularity of an entire process without regard to process sub-components. The relationship between the overhead costs and security gains for encrypting particular process components needs to be understood (e.g. is there a particular component that can be protected with low overhead yet holds high value code/data). This work is the first to implement ME on a commodity processor, thereby allowing investigation of the low-level implementation details and the cost/security tradeoffs at sub-process component granularity.

Memory vulnerabilities are common in systems ranging from servers and standard desktops to mobile computing devices (e.g. smart phones, tablets, laptops, etc.). However, usage patterns toward the mobile end of the spectrum may exacerbate the situation since many users of smart phones rarely reboot these systems maintaining them in an "always on" fashion [Karlson et al. 2009]. In fact, in a study of the Android operating system, 6 out of 14 applications permanently maintained their passwords in RAM. Additionally, mobile devices are more likely to be lost or stolen providing physical access to possible adversaries. In NYC, for example, 49% of the population has experienced mobile phone theft and/or loss [Tang et al. 2012]. Mobile devices, such as Android based smart phones, are beginning to be used in forward deployed military areas. These phones are loaded with information such as local maps, objectives, and blue force tracker (friendly unit) locations. Unfortunately, these phones (and other devices such as remotely piloted airframes with similar embedded processors) could easily fall into enemy hands. In fact, a recent U.S. Air Force document entitled Air Force Cyber Vision 2025 highlights the need for trust-based techniques to protect captured mobile devices in adversarial territory against reverse engineering efforts [United 2012]. While ME should be considered for both standard desktop and mobile devices, the work described here targets the ARM Cortex A8 which is common to many smart phones and tablets, including Apple's iPhone 3GS and 4, iPad first generation, iPod touch 3rd and 4th generations, and Samsung Galaxy Tablet to name a few.

3   Approach

The approach described in this paper is to implement memory encryption within a clean-slate microkernel design – *Bear* – leveraging security-enhanced commodity processors to ensure that code and data *never appear in the clear outside the processor chip boundary* as shown in Figure 1. The motivation for a "from scratch" kernel rests on the desire to conduct experiments in the context of a minimalist, secure microkernel. The design separates core functions into protected layers typical of modern microkernel designs such as MINIX [Tannenbaum and Woodhull 2006]. Monolithic operating systems, such as Linux and Windows, contain millions of lines of code and have a large runtime footprint providing ample opportunity for exploitation. In addition, they rarely enforce protections and allow device drivers direct access to kernel-space. In contrast, the Bear system used in this research involves approximately 3000 lines of code, with a runtime footprint of less than 50Kbytes on the ARM A8, making it an ideal platform to explore the tradeoffs involved in memory encryption in the presence of a small attack surface. All potentially compromised device drivers are executed in user-space, where they are non-deterministically regenerated to refresh trust and undermine persistence. Versions of the system operate on 64-bit Intel X86-based multi-core blade servers and ARM M3, A8, and A9 processors. On 64-bit systems MULTICs style protections are strictly enforced through paging structures to increase attacker workload; these added protection techniques are not used in the experiments described here in order to quantify the baseline overheads independently.

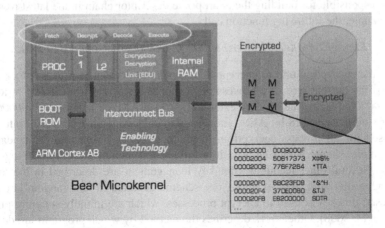

Fig. 1. General Approach for Memory Encryption

Hardware. ARM licenses the design of the basic processor (e.g. the A8) while various vendors build them with additional functionality. The exploration of memory encryption described here is focused on Freescale's i.MX535 applications processor. Critical components of the processor for this research include the internal RAM (iRAM-128 KB + 16 KB "secure"), symmetric asymmetric hashing and random accelerator (SAHARA), L1/L2 cache (32KB Harvard L1, 256KB L2), and the NEON single instruction multiple data (SIMD) coprocessor. These components are common to other ARM processors that include security hardware. Most of the techniques in the memory encryption literature targeting hardware involve modifying the fetch-decode-execute (FDE) engine to include decryption (fetch-decrypt-decode-execute) while adding encryption acceleration and internal storage space. Without specialized FDDE hardware, data can not be decrypted and placed directly into caches and execution pipelines. This results in a requirement for significant internal space in which to store and operate on sensitive, plaintext information.

SAHARA implements AES, DES and 3DES encryption, MD5, SHA-1, SHA-224, and SHA-256 hashing and hardware based (ring oscillator) random number generation. It also provides its own DMA controller with an AHB bus interface to reduce the interaction/burden on the primary CPU. For AES encryption, SAHARA includes electronic codebook (ECB), cipher-block chaining (CBC), counter (CTR) and counter with CBC-MAC (CCM) modes of operation. Descriptors are used to notify SAHARA of blocks of memory (internal or external) for encryption/decryption. Internal (secure) registers are cleared after a descriptor chain has completed processing to provide for usage by multiple, mutually distrusting processes. Completion of encryption/decryption is signaled via an interrupt. The encryption-decryption unit (EDU), is controlled via a *descriptor chain*, consisting of six 32-bit words. Each bit or group of bits (generally 2-3) are selected to enable the hardware module (e.g., encryption, authentication, random number generation), algorithm (e.g. RSA, DES), mode of operation (e.g. electronic codebook, cipher block chaining) and other details. A security API was developed to hide proprietary Freescale encryption details and is responsible for building the appropriate descriptor chain in the latest prototype. For example, the following function call:

$$EDU('E', 0x000001A0, 0xF8000000, 0x70000000, 0xF801FFFD);$$

causes the encryption unit to encrypt (E=encrypt, D=decrypt) a process block of 416 bytes -- the current size of a process descriptor and stack -- from iRAM at location $0xF8000000$, placing the result in external RAM (eRAM) at location $0x70000000$. For simplicity, a 128-bit AES symmetric key is downloaded via JTAG into iRAM and used for all process encryption. In practice an out-of-channel or standard key distribution scheme would be used in a full system implementation [Mel and Baker 2001]. Several other techniques for key management are described in the memory encryption literature. For example, one scheme generates a new random key at system reset; this key is used to encrypt processes, which are initially stored in plaintext [Chen et al. 2008]. Other work describes the method by which programs are delivered encrypted. Programs developed externally are encrypted using a public key. The private key, stored inside the processor, is used to decrypt the program in iRAM. The program is then re-encrypted with a randomly generated symmetric key to improve encryption performance. Regardless of the key generation and escrow techniques used, the keys are *never* available in eRAM. In the work described in this paper, there is space for storage of many keys whereas several of the approaches to protecting FDE schemes rely on internal registers (e.g. SSE, debug, etc.) limiting storage to a small number of keys [Muller et al. 2011], [Muller et al. 2012].

Static Encrypted Processes. The initial memory encryption proof-of-concept was implemented on the ARM A8 processor, using the Freescale SAHARA encryption engine, with the MMU and cache disabled. In this method, only the code is encrypted, using 128-bit AES symmetric-key encryption, and stored on disk as part of the executable binary. Other process components (data, stack, heap) are never encrypted as they remain within the protected iRAM. A small bootloader stored in internal ROM is responsible for initializing the hardware and loading the microkernel over the JTAG interface directly into iRAM. Next, a shell is bootstrapped using the on-board USART connection to allow programs to be executed. User processes are added to the scheduling queue and executed from iRAM. The microkernel then begins execution by decrypting the user process code and storing it into iRAM. This technique, referred to as *static encrypted processes,* only performs decryption once at code loading and is relevant to embedded systems where processes fit entirely within iRAM [Henson and Taylor 2013]. Measurements detailed in Section 4 quantify the overhead of this approach. Other than the one-time initial decryption cost (dependent upon the size of the process code), there is little evidence of overhead using this method. Since embedded processors are continually increasing on-chip memory, this technique represents an increasingly practical, low-overhead approach to memory encryption.

Dynamic Encrypted Processes. A more general case, *dynamic encrypted processes*, occurs where there is sufficient memory pressure (i.e. processes + data are larger than available iRAM) to force processes back to eRAM during execution. Process components include code, data (global/static), stack and heap, and iRAM buffers are created for each. The prototype allows swapping of encrypted processes to eRAM. Process segments are stored in eRAM in encrypted form and brought into iRAM, decrypted, and executed on-demand. Segments are re-encrypted before being sent back to eRAM with the exception of code, which does not change. In the absence of an enabled MMU, this movement of code and data required some virtual memory management (e.g. updating of stack pointers, addresses, program counters, jump addresses, etc.) where all segments of a given type correspond to a single internal buffer. This management was taken care of via modifications to the process creation, context switching and heap allocation routines. Figure 2 illustrates how the prototype encrypts the process control block (PCB) and stack (as one chunk); dynamically allocated memory and code are encrypted separately. The process context switch provides a natural point at which to perform decryption of these segments. Since the prototype does not utilize a paging mechanism, there is no similar point at which to intercede in accesses to global/static data, which are solely controlled by the compiler. Therefore, global/static data currently remains in iRAM.

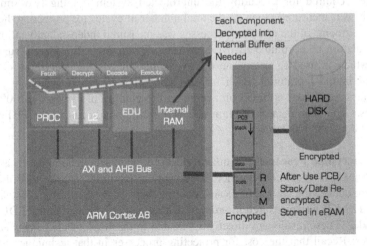

Fig. 2. Dynamic Encrypted Processes – Cache Disabled

The PCB-stack and code segments are of predetermined sizes while the size of the heap segments are not known a-priori. Depending on the size of the allocated segment, two alternative approaches are available. If it is small enough to fit within iRAM (after taking into consideration the space occupied by the kernel and other segments) then the whole segment is decrypted and placed within the internal data buffer in a similar fashion to the code and PCB-stack. However, if the segment is too large, then decryption of data on-demand at the size appropriate to the application (or smallest size possible) is used.

For a strenuous test of worst-case heap performance, a radix-2, in-place fast Fourier transform (FFT) based on the Tukey-Cooley algorithm was used to gauge the overhead [Press et al. 1992]. The smallest size for decryption in AES is a block of 16 Bytes. Since the data in each component of the FFT (real and imaginary part) take up one word each (4 Bytes), additional overhead is introduced in order to align the smaller data with the algorithm requirements. Whereas the unprotected version implements a simple swap of two of the real and imaginary components, the protected version must determine the appropriate 16 Byte aligned address to decrypt into the internal buffers for each component. Then the proper half of the 16 Bytes must be identified after which the swap is performed in iRAM, data re-encrypted and stored back to eRAM.

4   Measurement

Since the performance degradation of memory encryption results in less likelihood of its use, it is an extremely important factor in the comparison of different schemes. First, the cost of decryption was quantified in terms of total number of cycles for generic data blocks, using the Cortex A8 performance monitors. Next, the total number of cycles required for executing the unprotected system running two simple user processes was measured. Finally, the total number of cycles for protecting the various process segments of the two user processes was measured independently, allowing for the calculation of accumulated overhead (i.e. slowdown). The system runs at 800 MHz, which is used to determine the cycles-per-bit cost of decryption commonly provided in the literature. Each measurement of the context switching segments (PCB-stack and code) is based on averaging the number of cycles for 1000 context switches. The heap data encryption is tested with a single run of the FFT program using a large (128 KB) array.

Static Encrypted Processes. To quantify decryption speed, generic data was used as the data itself is of no consequence to decryption overhead. The average number of cycles for decrypting chunks of eRAM ranging from 16 Bytes (the smallest size possible) to 128 KB was measured in order to determine performance of the EDU in AES 128 mode. These results are directly applicable to the implemented *static encrypted processes*: Recall that the cost for protecting processes in that technique is the one-time cost of decryption of code. The results of the decryption tests are shown in Table 1 below. The overhead associated with initializing the EDU (key expansion, etc.) is approximately 8096 cycles (as shown in the first row of the table). For the other rows, the cycles per bit cost of decryption is calculated by dividing the approximate cycles by the number of bits decrypted. For example, decrypting a chunk at the smallest possible size of 16 Bytes results in a cost of approximately 71.5 cycles per bit (9152 cycles/16*8). As the decryption chunk increases the overhead remains constant so that the measure of cycles per bit decreases (better performance). This trend is shown graphically in Figure 3 below. After 4KB, the improvement in cycles per bit is reduced dramatically. The ARM Cortex A8 architecture supports page sizes of 4 KB,

64 KB, 1 MB, and 16 MB. These measurements suggest that decryption overhead may be about the same whether 4 KB or larger page sizes are selected in future implementations. They also suggest that any granularity less than 4KB (e.g. a cache line of 64 Bytes) is sub-optimal.

Table 1. Overhead for Decryption of Various Sizes (Chunks) of Memory

Data Size in Bytes	Average Cycles	Std Dev	Cycles per bit
Overhead	8096	40	N/A
16	9152	65	71.5
32	9664	60.9	37.7
64 (Cache line)	10496	384.5	20.5
128	11712	55.4	11.4
256	14208	590.7	6.9
512	19776	376.3	4.8
1024	30080	577.2	3.7
2048	50688	578.2	3.1
4096 (Page size)	91776	578.7	2.8
8192	181632	401.8	2.77
16384	355584	716.8	2.71
32768	702720	566.2	2.68
65536	1397184	560.3	2.66
131072	2785792	658.7	2.66

ARM processors are targeted for operations in constrained space and power environments. It is likely because of this that the performance of the EDU on the Cortex A8 is slow relative to figures presented in the memory encryption literature (which tends to target X86 processors). In AEGIS [Suh et al. 2007], a single AES unit is estimated at 86,655 gates. Yet, AEGIS is demonstrated with an OR1200 soft core in FPGA with a total size of approximately 60,000 gates (meaning the AES unit is 144% of the original core size). Recall that encryption hardware has been added to other processors such as Intel's i5 and i7 and AMD bulldozer chipsets. Intel's advanced encryption standard-new instructions (AES-NI) provide a significant speedup over both software and ARM hardware-enhanced encryption. The authors of this paper ran an implementation of TrueCrypt's encryption algorithm benchmark test on a Mac-Book Pro with an Intel i7 dual-core, 2.66 GHz CPU. Using a 5 MB buffer in RAM, the throughput averages 202 MB/s without AES-NI support, and 1 GB/s with it – approximately 119 cycles for 64 Bytes. This represents an improvement of 88 times over the 10,496 cycles measured on the i.MX535 (as shown above). While x86 based processors do not tend to include user accessible iRAM, the combination of improved decryption performance and large caches in those systems might enable some form of memory encryption protection. Intel has recently filed a patent for processors incorporating memory encryption, perhaps indicating a move toward support in commodity processors [Gueron et al. 2013].

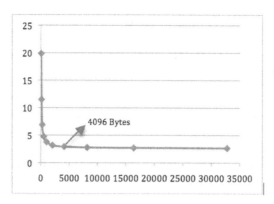

Fig. 3. Graph of Cycles/bit Vs. Number of Bytes Decrypted (64 B through 32 KB)

Dynamic Encrypted Processes. The measurements for protecting the PCB-stack and code are shown below in Table 2. The system schedules two simple processes in a round-robin fashion and for these measurements the scheduling quantum was set to 200 milliseconds, resulting in approximately 300 context switches per minute. The process behavior has nothing to do with the costs of protection since the costs are incurred during the context switch, not process execution. As in previous experiments, all measurements are averaged over 1000 context switches. The unprotected context switch routine averages approximately 20 microseconds as shown in the first row of the table. The overhead for protecting the segments is fairly large: a factor of approximately 2.9 to protect the PCB-stack and 3.4 times for both the PCB-stack and code when compared to the unprotected context. However, this cost is only incurred on average 300 times per minute. Thus the total overhead per minute is about 14,700 microseconds (.0147 seconds) giving ~1.5 seconds of overhead after 100 minutes of execution. This indicates that context and code protection are viable even without the benefit of the MMU and cache. While the size of the context and code were fixed for these experiments (416 and 672 Bytes respectively) the results from Table 1 suggest that larger component sizes (e.g. 4 KB page size) would more effectively hide the cost of the EDU initialization overhead.

Table 2. Overhead for PCB-Stack and Code Protection

Component within Context Switch	Average Cycles	Std Dev	Execution Time @ 800 MHz	Overhead
Unprotected	16064	70	20 us	N/A
PCB-Stack	47296	682	59 us	2.9
Code	23800	400	30 us	1.5
PCB-Stack & Code	54976	856	69 us	3.4

Table 3 shows the overhead of decryption of data in the FFT problem with 128 KB arrays holding the real and imaginary data components. Since 128 KB was too large to fit into iRAM, on-demand decryption was implemented at the size that most closely approximates data accesses (16 Bytes). The cycles per bit cost of decryption is large at the 16 Byte size (~71.5). In summary, about 17.2 billion cycles were required to execute the unprotected FFT. Providing encryption protection during the bit reversal (first half of the FFT) only requires an additional 3.2 billion cycles (20.4 billion cycles total). Encrypting all data for the entire FFT operation requires approximately 20 billion additional cycles (37.2 billion cycles total): resulting in a slow down of approximately 2.2 times over the unprotected execution. Memory accesses in the FFT problem are pathological, providing a thorough (worst-case) evaluation of our memory encryption approach.

Table 3. Overhead for Data Protection in FFT Function

FFT Data Structure @ 128 KB	Average Cycles	Std Dev	Execution Time @ 800 MHz	Overhead
Unprotected	17269347514	70	21.6 s	N/A
Bit Reversal Only	20438649003	682	25.5 s	1.2
Fully Protected	37197691328	400	46.5 s	2.2

In reality, most mobile processor packages include SIMD cores, such as the NEON processor to optimize algorithms like the FFT. Mobile system use tends to be characterized by applications such as chat, e-mail, and those displaying spatial/temporal locality (e.g. photo viewing). It is reasonable to believe that the performance on these more typical workloads will be considerably improved even without optimization of the on-demand decryption techniques used in this work.

It is important to understand the performance characteristics of the worst-case (on-demand decryption) scenario where decryption overhead is added directly to memory access time. It was anticipated that performing memory encryption without the benefit of the MMU and cache (including prefetching etc.) would yield excessively large overheads. While this was the case for the FFT data-structure access, PCB-stack and code protection were surprisingly efficient. Further, the slowdown for the FFT (2.2x) is considerably less than that reported in the simulation results of a similar technique that took advantage of caching mechanisms but lacked encryption hardware. In that work, slowdowns of 2.53x and 8.5x were measured when utilizing a 4 KB page with a 256 KB and 64 KB L2 cache respectively [Chen et al. 2008].

While the use of MMU/cache will make the system more closely approximate those of smart-phones, there are many examples where the techniques already developed in this work could be applicable. For example, many devices at the lower end of the embedded spectrum, including the large number of *smart electric meters* recently deployed, tend not to include MMU's [McLaughlin et al. 2010].

5   Future Work

A valuable next step is to take advantage of the ARM Cortex A8's MMU and cache. However, effectively modifying the fetch-decode-execute cycle requires a way to decrypt pages brought on-chip before they are loaded into the cache. The A8 architecture includes a built-in preload engine (PLE) that can be used to move data to and from the L2 cache under software control [ARM]. This engine will be used to load the cache with decrypted data and instructions, with iRAM continuing to act as a workspace and extension to L1/L2 cache. Additionally, the NEON SIMD coprocessor is tightly coupled with the L2 cache, which may provide another method for update. Enabling the cache (and other optimization mechanisms such as prefetching) should provide significant improvement over the current decrypt-on-demand prototype.

While there are many current requirements for a from-scratch microkernel (especially in the military), this work can be expanded to incorporate currently popular operating systems. A Bear *microvisor*, quite similar to the microkernel, has already been developed. Efforts are currently under way to enable the NetBSD (5.0.1) operating system to boot on top of the microvisor, protecting it with Bear's security mechanisms. After experimenting with MMU-enabled memory encryption, the techniques will be added to the microvisor's capabilities. The microvisor can then be used on future ARM hardware (supporting virtualization) to boot mobile operating systems (e.g. Android).

6   Conclusions

This paper describes a clean-slate operating system design that leverages security-enhanced commodity processors to ensure that code and data *never appear in the clear outside the processor chip boundary*. By utilizing the SAHARA security hardware of the Freescale i.MX535 processor, the system provides memory encryption with various granularities of a process. The current work utilizes on-demand decryption whereby the overhead for decrypting code and data is added directly to the fetch-decode cost. In this way, an upper bound on the overhead associated with memory encryption is established. The experimental overhead associated with the protection of process PCB-stack and code is surprisingly small.

Few operating system developers have taken advantage of the new security hardware available in many commodity processors. There are various projects that utilize some aspects of this hardware, for example, to protect the key in FDE. Since sensitive data is left in memory for relatively long periods of time, it is logical to conclude that the protections afforded "data at rest" on disk should also apply to memory. By forcing an attacker to rely on brute-force attacks against encrypted memory (or other relatively difficult attacks on the chip itself) we seek to *increase attacker workload* enough to dissuade or delay the attack, allowing for mission completion (or protection of user information). The overhead displayed in the work described here suggests this protection is feasible today with security-enhanced commodity processors. While the concept of memory encryption has existed for over three decades, there are still no general-purpose, commercial-off-the-shelf solutions integrated with secure operating systems. Unfortunately, while full disk encryption seems to be the state-of-the art, it is insufficient for the protection of systems holding sensitive information.

Notice. The U.S. Government is authorized to reproduce and distribute reprints for Governmental purposes notwithstanding any copyright notation thereon. The views and conclusions contained herein are those of the authors and should not be interpreted as necessarily representing the official policies or endorsements, either expressed or implied, of the Defense Advanced Research Projects Agency (DARPA) or the U.S. Government.

References

Arbaugh, A., Farber, D., Smith, J.: A secure and reliable bootstrap architecture. In: Proceedings of the 1997 IEEE Symposium on Security and Privacy (SP 1997). IEEE Computer Society, Washington, DC (1997)

Arnold, T., Doorn, L.: The IBM PCIXCC: a new cryptographic coprocessor for the IBM eserver. The IBM Journal of Research and Development, 120–126 (2004)

Blass, E., Robertson, W.: TRESOR-HUNT: Attacking CPU-Bound Encryption. In: Proceedings of the 28th Annual Computer Security Applications Conference (December 2012)

Blunden, B.: The Rootkit Arsenal: Escape and Evasion in the Dark Corners of the System. Jones and Bartlett Publishers, Inc., USA (2009)

Anderson, R., Kuhn, M.: Tamper resistance – a cautionary note. In: Proceedings of the Second USENIX Workshop on Electronic Commerce, vol. 2, pp. 1–11 (1996)

Barrantes, E., Ackley, D., Forrest, S., Palmer, T., Sefanovic, D., Zovi, D.: Randomized Instruction Set Emulation to Disrupt Binary Code Injection Attacks. In: Proceedings of the 10th ACM Conference on Computer and Communications Security (CCS 2003), pp. 281–289 (October 2003)

Boileau, A.: Hit by a Bus: Physical Access Attacks with Firewire. Presented at Ruxcon (2006)

Brink, D.: Full-disk encryption on the rise. Aberdeen Research Group Report (September 2009)

Casey, E., Fellows, G., Geiger, M., Stellatos, G.: The growing impact of full disk encryption on digital forensics. Digital Investigation 8, 129–134 (2011)

Chari, S., Jutla, C.S., Rao, J.R., Rohatgi, P.: Towards sound approaches to counteract power-analysis attacks. In: Wiener, M. (ed.) CRYPTO 1999. LNCS, vol. 1666, pp. 398–412. Springer, Heidelberg (1999)

Chhabra, S., Rogers, B., Solihin, Y., Prvulovic, M.: SecureMe: a hardware-software approach to full system security. In: Proceedings of the International Conference on Supercomputing (ICS) (May 2011)

Chhabra, S., Solihin, Y.: i-NVMM: a secure non-volatile main memory system with incremental encryption. In: Proceedings of the International Symposium on Computer Architecture (ISCA) (June 2011)

Chen, X., Dick, R., Choudary, A.: Operating system controlled processor-memory bus encryption. In: Proceedings of DATE (2008)

Chow, J., Pfaff, B., Garfinkel, T., Christopher, K., Rosenblum, M.: Understanding data lifetime via whole system simulation. In: Proceedings of the USENIX Security Symposium (August 2004)

Cortex-A Series Programmer's Guide, Version: 2.0, http://infocenter.arm.com/help/index.jsp?topic=/ com.arm.doc.den0013b/index.html

Dallas Semiconductor. Secure microcontroller data book. Dallas (1997)

Duc, G., Keryell, R.: CryptoPage: an efficient secure architecture with memory encryption, integrity and information leakage protection. In: Proceedings of the Annual Computer Security Applications Conference, ACSAC (2006)

Gueron, S., Savagaonkar, U., McKeen, F., Rozas, C., Durham, D., Doweck, J., Mulla, O., Anati, I., Greenfield, Z., Maor, M.: Method and apparatus for memory encryption with integrity check and protection against replay attacks. WO patent number 2013002789 (January 3, 2013)

Halderman, J., Schoen, S., Heninger, N., Clarkson, W., Paul, W., Calandrino, J., Feldman, A., Appelbaum, J., Felten, E.: Lest we remember: cold boot attacks on encryption keys. In: Proceedings of the USENIX Security Symposium (February 2008)

Hennessy, J., Patterson, D.: Computer Architecture, 4th edn. A Quantitative Approach. Morgan Kaufmann Publishers Inc., San Francisco (2006)

Henson, M., Taylor, S.: Memory Encryption: A Survey of Existing Techniques. Submitted to ACM Computing Surveys (July 2012), Available as Thayer Technical Report TR13-001 at http://thayer.dartmouth.edu/tr/reports

Henson, M., Taylor, S.: Attack Mitigation through Memory Encryption of Security Enhanced Commodity Processors. In: Hart, D. (ed.) The Proceedings of the 8th International Conference on Information Warfare and Security (ICIW 2013), pp. 265–268 (March 2013)

i.MX53 Multimedia Applications Processor Reference Manual, http://www.freescale.com/webapp/sps/site/prod_summary.jsp?cod e=IMX53QSB&fpsp=1&tab=Documentation_Tab

Karlson, A.K., Meyers, B.R., Jacobs, A., Johns, P., Kane, S.K.: Working overtime: Patterns of smartphone and PC usage in the day of an information worker. In: Tokuda, H., Beigl, M., Friday, A., Brush, A.J.B., Tobe, Y. (eds.) Pervasive 2009. LNCS, vol. 5538, pp. 398–405. Springer, Heidelberg (2009)

Kocher, P., Jaffe, J., Jun, B.: Differential power analysis. In: Wiener, M. (ed.) CRYPTO 1999. LNCS, vol. 1666, pp. 388–397. Springer, Heidelberg (1999)

Kgil, T., Falk, L., Mudge, T.: ChipLock: support for secure microarchitectures. ACM Sigarch 33(1) (March 2005)

Kuhn, M.: Cipher instruction search attack on the bus-encryption security microcon-troller DS5002FP. IEEE Transactions on Computing 47, 1153–2257 (1998)

Lee, M., Ahn, M., Kim, E.: I2SEMS: interconnects-independent security enhances shared memory multiprocessor systems. In: Proceedings of the International Conference on Parallel Architectures and Compilation Techniques, PACT (2007)

Lie, D., Thekkath, C., Mitchell, M., Lincoln, P., Boneh, D., Mitchell, J., Horowitz, M.: Architectural support for copy and tamper resistant software. In: Proceedings of the 9th Conference on Architectural Support for Programming Languages and Operating Systems (ASPLOS), pp. 168–177 (2000)

McLaughlin, S., Podkuiko, D., Delozier, A., Miadzverzhanka, S., McDaniel, P.: Embedded firmware diversity for smart electric meters. In: Proceedings of the 5th USENIX Workshop on Hot Topics in Security, HotSec 2010, Wshington, DC, USA, August 1-8 (2010)

Mel, H., Baker, D.: Cryptography Decrypted. Addison-Wesley, Upper Saddle River (2001)

Muller, T., Freiling, F., Dewald, A.: TRESOR runs encryption securely outside RAM. In: Proceedings of the 20th USENIX Conference on Security (2011)

Müller, T., Taubmann, B., Freiling, F.C.: TreVisor: OSIndependent Software-Based Full Disk Encryption Secure Against Main Memory Attacks. In: Bao, F., Samarati, P., Zhou, J. (eds.) ACNS 2012. LNCS, vol. 7341, pp. 66–83. Springer, Heidelberg (2012)

Nagarajan, V., Gupta, R., Krishnaswamy, A.: Compiler-assisted memory encryption for embedded processors. In: HiPPEAC, pp. 7–22 (2007)

Peterson, P.: Cryptkeeper: improving security with encrypted RAM. In: Proceedings of the IEEE International Conference on Technologies for Homeland Security (HST), pp. 120–126 (November 2010)

Press, W., Teukolsky, S., Vetterling, W., Flannery, B.: Numerical Recipes in C, 2nd edn. Cambridge University Press, Cambridge (1992)

Rogers, B., Solihin, Y., Prvulovic, M.: Memory predecryption: hiding the latency overhead of memory encryption. ACM SIGARCH Computer Architecture News 33(1), 27–33 (2005)

Rogers, B., Prvulovic, M., Solihin, Y.: Efficient data protection for distributed shared memory multiprocessors. In: Proceedings of the 15th International Conference on Parallel Architectures and Compilation Techniques (PACT) (September 2006)

Shi, W., Lee, H., Ghosh, M., Lu, C.: Architectural support for high speed protection of memory integrity and confidentiality in multiprocessor systems. In: Proceedings of the 13th International Conference on Parallel Architecture and Compilation Techniques, PACT (2004)

Steil, M.: 17 mistakes Microsoft made in the Xbox security system. In: Proceedings of the 22nd Chaos Communication Congress (2005)

Steil, M., Domke, F.: The Xbox 360 Security System and its Weaknesses (August. 2008), Google TechTalk available at
http://www.youtube.com/watch?v=uxjpmc8ZIxM

Su, L., Martinez, A., Guillemin, P., Cerdan, S., Pacalet, R.: Hardware mechanism and performance evaluation of hierarchical page-based memory bus protection. In: Proceedings of the Conference on Design, Automation and Test in Europe, DATE (2009)

Suh, G., O'Donell, C., Devadas, S.: Aegis: a single-chip secure processor. IEEE Design and Test of Computers 24(6), 570–580 (2007)

Suh, G., Clarke, D., Gassend, B., Dijk, M., Devadas, S.: Efficient memory integrity verification and encryption for secure processors. In: Proceedings of the 36th International Symposium on Microarchitecture (2005)

Tanenbaum, Woodhull: Operating Systems: Design and Implementation. Prentice-Hall (2006)

Tang, Y., Ames, P., Bhamidipati, S., Bijlani, A., Geambasu, R., Sarda, N.: CleanOS: Limiting mobile data exposure with idle eviction. In: OSDI (2012)

United States Air Force Cyberspace Science and Technology Vision. AF/ST TR 12-01 (December 2012),
http://www.globalsecurity.org/security/library/policy/usaf/cybervision2025_afd-130327-306.pdf

Vasudevan, A., Owusu, E., Zhou, Z., Newsome, J., McCune, J.: Trustworthy execution on mobile devices: what security properties can my mobile platform give me? Carnegie Mellon University CyLab Technical Report 11-023 (November 2011)

Yan, C., Rogers, B., Englender, D., Solihin, Y., Prvulovic, M.: Improving cost performance and security of memory encryption and authentication. In: Proceedings of the 33rd International Symposium on Computer Architecture (June 2006)

NEON Implementation of an Attribute-Based Encryption Scheme

Ana Helena Sánchez and Francisco Rodríguez-Henríquez*

Computer Science Department, CINVESTAV-IPN
asanchez@computacion.cs.cinvestav.mx, francisco@cs.cinvestav.mx

Abstract. In 2011, Waters presented a ciphertext-policy attribute-based encryption protocol that uses bilinear pairings to provide control access mechanisms, where the set of user's attributes is specified by means of a linear secret sharing scheme. Some of the applications foreseen for this protocol lie in the context of mobile devices such a smartphones and tablets, which in a majority of instances are powered by an ARM processor supporting the NEON vector set of instructions. In this paper we present the design of a software cryptographic library that implements a 127-bit security level attribute-based encryption scheme over mobile devices equipped with a 1.4GHz Exynos 4 Cortex-A9 processor and a developing board that hosts a 1.7 GHz Exynos 5 Cortex-A15 processor. For the latter platform and taking advantage of the inherent parallelism of the NEON vector instructions, our library computes a single optimal pairing over a Barreto-Naehrig curve approximately 2 times faster than the best timings previously reported on ARM platforms at this level of security. Further, using a 6-attribute access formula our library is able to encrypt/decrypt a text/ciphertext in less than 7.5mS and 15.67mS, respectively.

Keywords: Atribute based-encryption, pairing-based protocols, Barreto-Naehrig curves, elliptic curve scalar multiplication, ARM processor.

1 Introduction

It was long assumed that the task of computing a single bilinear pairing was rather expensive, so much so that when assessing the complexity of a given protocol, a designer could safely ignore the computational cost of all the other cryptographic components included in it. Nevertheless, in the last few years we have witnessed a dramatic reduction in the timing required to calculate a single pairing, which has had the side effect that the computation of the other ancillary functions associated to pairing-based protocols have acquired a renewed importance. Some examples of these auxiliary blocks include, fixed/variable point

---

* A portion of this work was performed while the author was visiting University of Waterloo.

M. Jacobson et al. (Eds.): ACNS 2013, LNCS 7954, pp. 322–338, 2013.
© Springer-Verlag Berlin Heidelberg 2013

scalar multiplication for elliptic curves defined over finite fields and their extensions, the projection of arbitrary strings to a random point in those elliptic curves, exponentiation in field extensions, *etc.* Furthermore, as pointed out in [15], several pairing-based protocols admit further optimizations, such as the computation of fixed-argument pairings and products of pairings.

Unfortunately as of today, very few works have analyzed in detail the complexity and overall computational weight of non-pairing cryptographic operations in a given protocol. This lack of research in the implementation of pairing-based protocols is especially acute for mobile platforms such as the ones using ARM processors.

An important number of major IT players such as Apple, Samsung, Sony, to name just a few, have adopted the ARM Cortex family of processors for powering their tablets, smartphones and other mobile devices. A majority of those devices support the vector set of instructions NEON. In spite of their ever increasing popularity, it is only until recently that some research works have studied the implementation of cryptographic primitives over ARM processor platforms.

Among the research papers reporting pairing implementations in the ARM Cortex family of processors are [1] and [10]. In [1], authors propose the idea that affine coordinates could be more attractive than the projective ones when implementing pairings in constrained devices, whereas the software library of [10] reports the current record in the computation of a single asymmetric pairing at the 128, 224 and 320-bit security levels. As for the implementation of pairing-based protocols on mobile devices, the only work that we are aware of is [2], where the authors described the design of an attribute-based encryption scheme able to preserve the confidentiality of the medical electronic records generated within a hospital environment.

In this work we present the design of a software library that implements Waters' attribute-based encryption scheme [16], over a set of mobile device platforms equipped with the latest models of the ARM Cortex family of processors and the vectorized set of instructions NEON. Our library was specifically tailored for computing optimal pairings over Barreto-Naehrig curves at the 127-bit security level. When executed on a developing board that hosts a 1.7 GHz Exynos 5 Cortex-A15 processor, our software computes a single optimal pairing in approximately 5.84M clock cycles, which is about two times less than the estimated cycling count reported in [10] for a single pairing computation over a TI 1.2GHz OMAP 4460 Cortex-A9 processor.

Our library also implements single/multi-pairing computations with fixed/variable input points, as well as other auxiliary functions associated with most pairing-based protocols such as scalar multiplication and the projection of arbitrary strings to elliptic curve points defined over extension finite fields, among others. In particular, when executed on the Cortex-A15 processor mentioned above and when using an access formula composed of six attributes, our library computes the encryption/decryption primitives of Waters' attributed-based encryption protocol in less than 12.75M clock cycles and 26.64M clock cycles, roughly equivalent to 7.5mS and 15.67mS, respectively.[1]

2 Mathematical Background

Let p be a prime, and let E be an elliptic curve defined over the finite field $\mathbb{F}_p$. Let r be a prime with $r \mid \#E(\mathbb{F}_p)$ and $\gcd(r, p) = 1$. The embedding degree k is defined as the smallest positive integer such that $r \mid (p^k - 1)$. In this paper, only the Barreto-Naehrig (BN) pairing-friendly family of elliptic curves [4] was considered for pairing implementation. All BN curves have embedding degree $k = 12$ and they are defined by the equation $E : y^2 = x^3 + b, b \in \mathbb{F}_p^*$, where the characteristic p of the prime field, the group order r, an the trace of Frobenius t are parametrized as,

$$p(z) = 36z^4 + 36z^3 + 24z^2 + 6z + 1; \tag{1}$$
$$r(z) = 36z^4 + 36z^3 + 18z^2 + 6z + 1;$$
$$t(z) = 6z^2 + 1,$$

where $z \in \mathbb{Z}$, is an arbitrary integer known as the BN parameter, such that $p(z)$ and $r(z)$ are prime numbers. BN curves admit a sextic degree twist curve, defined as $\tilde{E}(\mathbb{F}_{p^2}) : Y^2 = X^3 + b/\xi$, where $\xi \in \mathbb{F}_{p^2}$ is neither a square nor a cube in $\mathbb{F}_{p^2}$.

Let $\pi : (x, y) \mapsto (x^p, y^p)$ be the p-th power Frobenius endomorphism. The trace of the Frobenius is defined as $t = p + 1 - \#E(\mathbb{F}_p)$. Let $\mathbb{G}_1 = \{P \in E[r] : \pi(P) = P\} = E(\mathbb{F}_p)[r]$, where $\mathbb{G}_1$ is the 1-eigenspace of π acting on $E[r]$. Let $\Psi : \tilde{E} \to E$ be the associated twisting isomorphism. Let $\tilde{Q} \in \tilde{E}(\mathbb{F}_{p^2})$ be a point of order r; then $Q = \Psi(\tilde{Q}) \notin E(\mathbb{F}_p)$. The group $\mathbb{G}_2 = \langle Q \rangle$ is the p-eigenspace of π acting on $E[r]$. Let $\mathbb{G}_T$ denote the order-r subgroup of $\mathbb{F}_{p^{12}}^*$. The bilinear pairing studied in this paper is defined as the non-degenerate map $\hat{a}_{opt} : \mathbb{G}_2 \times \mathbb{G}_1 \to \mathbb{G}_T$, corresponding to the optimal ate pairing given as:

$$\hat{a}_{opt} : \mathbb{G}_2 \times \mathbb{G}_1 \to \mathbb{G}_T \tag{2}$$
$$(Q, P) \mapsto [f_{s,Q}(P) \cdot \ell_{(s)Q, \pi(Q)}(P) \cdot$$
$$\ell_{(s)Q + \pi(Q), \pi^2(Q)}(P)]^{(p^{12} - 1)/r}$$

where $f_{s,Q}$ is a Miller function of length $s = 6z + 2$, which is a rational function in $\bar{\mathbb{F}}_p(E)$ with divisor $\mathrm{div}(f_{s,R}) = s[R] - [sR] - (s - 1)[\mathcal{O}]$, while ℓ_{Q_1, Q_2} is the line equation given by the point addition of $Q_1 \in \mathbb{G}_2$ and $Q_2 \in \mathbb{G}_2$. Algorithm 1 computes the optimal pairing as defined in Eq. (2).

---

[1] An open source code of our software library is available at http://sandia.cs.cinvestav.mx/index.php?n=Site.NEONabe

---

Algorithm 1. Optimal ate pairing

Require: $P \in \mathbb{G}_1$, $Q \in \mathbb{G}_2$
Ensure: $g = \hat{a}_{opt}(Q, P)$
1: Write $s = 6z+2$ as $s = \sum_{i=0}^{l-1}$, $s_i \in \{-1, 0, 1\}$

2: $T \leftarrow Q$, $f \leftarrow 1$
3: **for** $i = l - 2 \rightarrow 0$ **do**
4:   $f \leftarrow f^2 \cdot \ell_{T,T}(P)$, $T \leftarrow 2T$
5:   **if** $s_i = 1$ **then**
6:     $f \leftarrow f \cdot \ell_{T,Q}(P)$, $T \leftarrow T + Q$

7:   **else if** $s_i = -1$ **then**
8:     $f \leftarrow f \cdot \ell_{T,-Q}(P)$, $T \leftarrow T - Q$
9:   **end if**
10: **end for**
11: $Q_1 \leftarrow \pi(Q)$, $Q_2 \leftarrow \pi^2(Q)$
12: $f \leftarrow f \cdot \ell_{T,Q_1}(P)$, $T \leftarrow T + Q_1$, $f \leftarrow f \cdot \ell_{T,-Q_2}(P)$, $T \leftarrow T - Q_2$
13: $g \leftarrow f^{(p^{12}-1)/r}$
14: **return** g

---

3 Tower Extension Field Arithmetic

Efficient arithmetic over extension finite fields is a necessary requirement in the development of high-performance pairing-based schemes. In this work, we represent $\mathbb{F}_{p^{12}}$ using the same tower extension employed in [3], namely, we first construct a quadratic extension, which is followed by a quadratic and cubic extensions of it and finally by a quadratic one, using the following irreducible binomials,

- $\mathbb{F}_{p^2} = \mathbb{F}_p[u]/(u^2 - \beta)$, where $\beta = -1$
- $\mathbb{F}_{p^4} = \mathbb{F}_{p^2}[V]/(V^2 - \xi)$, where $\xi = u + 1$
- $\mathbb{F}_{p^6} = \mathbb{F}_{p^2}[V]/(V^3 - \xi)$, where $\xi = u + 1$
- $\mathbb{F}_{p^{12}} = \mathbb{F}_{p^6}[W]/(W^2 - V)$ or $\mathbb{F}_{p^4}[T]/(T^3 - V)$

Furthermore, as in [3] we selected $z = -(2^{62} + 2^{55} + 1)$, which using Eq. 1 yields a prime $p \equiv 3 \bmod 4$. This allows for a faster arithmetic over $\mathbb{F}_{p^2}$, since the multiplication by the constant β reduces to a simple subtraction. For the computation of the pairing final exponentiation, cyclotomic subgroup arithmetic $\mathbb{G}_{\Phi_6}(\mathbb{F}_{p^2})$ [9] was extensively used.

Algorithm 2. Montgomery product

Require: prime p, p', $r = 2^k$ and $\tilde{a}, \tilde{b} \in \mathbb{F}_p$
Ensure: $\tilde{c} = \text{MontPr}(\tilde{a}, \tilde{b})$
1: $t \leftarrow \tilde{a} \cdot \tilde{b}$
2: $u \leftarrow (t + (t \cdot p' \bmod r) \cdot p)/r$
3: **if** $u > p$ **then**
4:   **return** $u - p$
5: **else**
6:   **return** u
7: **end if**

3.1 Field Multiplication Over $\mathbb{F}_p$

The single most important base field arithmetic operation is modular multiplication, which is defined as $c = a \cdot b \bmod p$, with $a, b, c \in \mathbb{F}_p$. Since in general BN primes are not suitable for fast reductions, this operation was performed via the Montgomery multiplication algorithm. The Montgomery product is defined as, $\tilde{c} = \tilde{a} \cdot \tilde{b} \cdot r^{-1} \bmod p$, where $\tilde{a}, \tilde{b} \in \mathbb{F}_p$ are given as, $\tilde{a} = a \cdot r \bmod p$ and $\tilde{b} = b \cdot r \bmod p$, respectively. This formulation allows trading the costly division by p with divisions by r, where $r = 2^k$ with $k - 1 < |p| < k$. If required, the modular product c, can be easily recovered using $c = \tilde{c} \cdot r^{-1} \bmod p$. Algorithm 2 shows the classical version of the Montgomery product, which expects as input parameter an integer p' that can be precomputed before hand using Bezout's identity for two co-prime integers, namely, $r \cdot r^{-1} - p \cdot p' = 1$.

In our library both, the Separated Operand Scanning (SOS) and the Coarsely Integrated Operand Scanning (CIOS) multi-precision Montgomery product variants as described in [13] were implemented. The SOS method computes first the integer product $t = a \cdot b$, followed by the Montgomery reduction step that calculates u such that $u = (t + m \cdot p)/r$, where $m = t \cdot p' \pmod{r}$. In this case $r = 2^{wn}$, where w is the wordsize of the processor and $n = \lfloor (\lfloor \log_2 p \rfloor + 1)/w \rfloor$. The CIOS method interleaves the calculations corresponding to the integer product with the ones required for getting u. Since in both methods, the reduction is implemented word by word, then the operation $m = t \cdot p' \bmod r$ can be performed replacing p' by $p'_0 = p' \bmod 2^w$, which redounds in a more efficient computation. According to [13], the CIOS variant is more efficient than the SOS one. Nevertheless, the later method allows lazy reduction, which was the reason why we implemented both variants.

3.2   Extension Field Arithmetic Computational Cost

Let us denote by (a, m, s, i) and $(\tilde{a}, \tilde{m}, \tilde{s}, \tilde{i})$ the computational cost of the addition, multiplication, squaring and inversion operations over $\mathbb{F}_p$ and $\mathbb{F}_{p^2}$, respectively. The field arithmetic procedures used in this work extensively exploits lazy reduction, which closely resembles the approaches adopted in [3,10]. Let $\tilde{m}_E$, $\tilde{s}_E$ and $\tilde{r}_E$ denote integer multiplication, integer squaring and reduction over $\mathbb{F}_{p^2}$, respectively, where $\tilde{m} = \tilde{m}_E + \tilde{r}_E$ and $\tilde{s} = \tilde{s}_E + \tilde{r}_E$. The rationale behind the costs given in Table 1, can be summarized as follows.

The cost of reductions over $\mathbb{F}_{p^2}$ is twice the cost of reduction over $\mathbb{F}_p$, i.e., $\tilde{r}_E = 2r_E$. At a field extension $\mathbb{F}_{p^d}$, $d = 2^i 3^j$, $i, j \in \mathbb{Z}^+$; the product $c = a \cdot b$, $a, b, c \in \mathbb{F}_{p^d}$ can be computed with $3^i 6^j$ integer multiplications and $2^i 3^j$ reductions modulo p (Theorem 1 of [3]). Field inversion was based on the procedure described in [10]. In the case of the quadratic and twelfth field extensions $\mathbb{F}_{p^2}$ and $\mathbb{F}_{p^{12}}$, field squaring was computed using the complex method at a cost of 2 multiplications. The inversion of an element $A = a_0 + a_1 u \in \mathbb{F}_{p^2}$ was obtained through the identity $(a_0 + a_1 u)^{-1} = (a_0 - a_1 u)/(a_0^2 - \beta a_1^2)$. In $\mathbb{F}_{p^4}$ the squaring was implemented at a cost of $3\tilde{s}$. This operation is required for computing squarings in the cyclotomic group $\mathbb{G}_{\Phi_6}(\mathbb{F}_{p^2})$, having a cost of 3 squarings over $\mathbb{F}_{p^4}$. The asymmetric squaring formula for cubic extensions of [5] was used in the field $\mathbb{F}_{p^6}$ at a cost of $2\tilde{m} + 3\tilde{s}$. Inversion in $\mathbb{F}_{p^6}$ has a computational complexity of $9\tilde{m} + 3\tilde{s} + i$ [11]. Notice that m_ξ stands for a multiplication by the constant ξ.

Table 1. Computational cost of the tower extension field arithmetic

Field	Addition	Multiplication	Squaring	Inversion
$\mathbb{F}_{p^2}$	$\tilde{a}=2a$	$\tilde{m} = 3m_E + 2r_E + 8a + m_\beta$	$\tilde{s} = 2m_E + 2r_E + 3a$	$\tilde{i} = 2m_E + r_E + 2m + 2a + i$
$\mathbb{F}_{p^4}$	$2\tilde{a}$		$3\tilde{s} + m_\xi + 4\tilde{a}$	
$\mathbb{F}_{p^6}$	$3\tilde{a}$	$6\tilde{m}_E + 3\tilde{r}_E + 2m_\xi + 24\tilde{a}$	$2\tilde{m}+3\tilde{s}+2m_\xi+9\tilde{a}$	$9\tilde{m}_E + 3\tilde{s}_E + 7\tilde{r}_E + 4m_\xi + 10\tilde{a} + \tilde{i}$
$\mathbb{F}_{p^{12}}$	$6\tilde{a}$	$18\tilde{m}_E + 6\tilde{r}_E + 7m_\xi + 96\tilde{a}$	$12\tilde{m}_E + 6\tilde{r}_E + 6m_\xi + 63\tilde{a}$	$25\tilde{m}_E+9\tilde{s}_E+16\tilde{r}_E+13m_\xi +79\tilde{a} + \tilde{i}$
$\mathbb{G}_{\Phi_6}(\mathbb{F}_{p^2})$			$9\tilde{s} + 4m_\xi + 30\tilde{a}$	$3\tilde{a}$

3.3 Field Arithmetic Implementation Using NEON

The performance of a field arithmetic library is strongly influenced by the processor micro-architecture features, the size of the operands and the algorithms and programming techniques associated to them. In our case, the size of the operands is of 254 bits, which conveniently allows the usage of lazy reduction. The word size in the ARM processors is of 32 bits and the processors considered in this work include the NEON vector set of instructions.

Algorithm 3. Computing double integer product with NEON

Require: $a = (a_0, a_1)$, $b = (b_0, b_1)$, $c = (c_0, c_1)$ and $d = (d_0, d_1)$
Ensure: $F = a \cdot b$, $G = c \cdot d$
1: $F \leftarrow 0$, $G \leftarrow 0$
2: **for** $i = 0 \to 1$ **do**
3:     $C_1 \leftarrow 0$, $C_2 \leftarrow 0$
4:     **for** $j = 0 \to 1$ **do**
5:         $(C_1, S_1) \leftarrow F_{i+j} + a_j \cdot b_i + C_1$, $(C_2, S_2) \leftarrow G_{i+j} + c_j \cdot d_i + C_2$,
6:         $F_{i+j} = S_1$, $G_{i+j} = S_2$
7:     **end for**
8:     $F_{i+n} = C_1$, $G_{i+n} = C_2$
9: **end for**
10: **return** F, G

NEON is a 128-bit Single Instruction Multiple Data (SIMD) architecture extension for the ARM Cortex family of processors. NEON architecture has 32 registers of 64 bits (*doubleword*), which can be viewed as 16 registers of 128 bits (*quadword*). Our library mostly made use of two intrinsic instructions:

uint64x2_t vmull_u32 (uint32x2_t, uint32x2_t);
uint64x2_t vmlal_u32 (uint64x2_t, uint32x2_t, uint32x2_t).

The first one performs two 32-bit integer multiplications storing the corresponding result into two 64-bit registers. The second one performs a multiplication that is accumulated with the addition of a 64-bit scalar. Algorithm 3 illustrates the usage of NEON for computing the double integer product $F = a \cdot b$, $G = c \cdot d$. This is the core operation for the SOS Montgomery multiplication variant. Each field element a, b, c, d is represented with two 32-bit words. Figure 1 depicts the NEON dataflow of this algorithm.

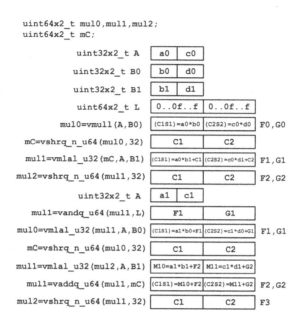

```
uint64x2_t mul0,mul1,mul2;
uint64x2_t mC;
```

uint32x2_t A	a0	c0	
uint32x2_t B0	b0	d0	
uint32x2_t B1	b1	d1	
uint64x2_t L	0..0f..f	0..0f..f	
mul0=vmull(A,B0)	(C1S1)=a0*b0	(C2S2)=c0*d0	F0,G0
mC=vshrq_n_u64(mul0,32)	C1	C2	
mul1=vmlal_u32(mC,A,B1)	(C1S1)=a0*b1+C1	(C2S2)=c0*d1+C2	F1,G1
mul2=vshrq_n_u64(mul1,32)	C1	C2	F2,G2
uint32x2_t A	a1	c1	
mul1=vandq_u64(mul1,L)	F1	G1	
mul0=vmlal_u32(mul1,A,B0)	(C1S1)=a1*b0+F1	(C2S2)=c1*d0+G1	F1,G1
mC=vshrq_n_u64(mul0,32)	C1	C2	
mul1=vmlal_u32(mul2,A,B1)	M10=a1*b1+F2	M11=c1*d1+G2	
mul1=vaddq_u64(mul1,mC)	(C1S1)=M10+F2	(C2S2)=M11+G2	F2,G2
mul2=vshrq_n_u64(mul1,32)	C1	C2	F3

Fig. 1. NEON Implementation of Algorithm 3

Algorithm 4. NEON multiplication over $\mathbb{F}_{p^2}$

Require: $A = a_0 + a_1 u$, $B = b_0 + b_1 u \in \mathbb{F}_{p^2}$
Ensure: $C = A \cdot B \in \mathbb{F}_{p^2}$
1: $s \leftarrow a_0 + a_1$
2: $t \leftarrow b_0 + b_1$
3: $(d_0, d_1) \leftarrow mule_{NEON}(s, t, a_0, b_0)$
4: $d_2 \leftarrow mul256(a_1, b_1)$
5: $d_0 \leftarrow d_0 - d_1 - d_2$
6: $d_1 \leftarrow d_1 - d_2$
7: $(c_1, c_0) \leftarrow red_{NEON}(d_0, d_1)$
8: **return** $C = c_0 + c_1 u$

Because of their ability to perform two multiplications at once, NEON instructions are very useful for accelerating arithmetic computations. However, data loading and storing is in general costly since the NEON registers have to be fed by storing data into consecutive 32-bit ARM registers. Hence, in order to take a real advantage of NEON, load/store instructions should be avoided as much as possible, which is easier to accomplish if the arithmetic algorithms are specified with little data dependency among the multiplier operands. In the case of $\mathbb{F}_{p^2}$ arithmetic, two independent multiplications over $\mathbb{F}_p$ were implemented using NEON as follows. Let us consider $|p| = 254$ bits and define the following three functions: mul_{NEON}, $mule_{NEON}$ and red_{NEON}. The first one performs two independent multiplications in $\mathbb{F}_p$ using the CIOS method, *i.e.* given $a, b, c, d, f, g \in \mathbb{F}_p$, define mul_{NEON} as $(f, g) \leftarrow mul_{NEON}(a, b, c, d)$ where $f = a \cdot b \bmod p$ and $g = c \cdot d \bmod p$. The second function $mule_{NEON}$ performs two integer multiplications: $(F, G) \leftarrow mule_{NEON}(a, b, c, d)$, with $a, b, c, d \in \mathbb{F}_p$, $F = a \cdot b$ and $G = c \cdot d$,

---

Algorithm 5. NEON Squaring over $\mathbb{F}_{p^2}$

Require: $A = a_0 + a_1 u \in \mathbb{F}_{p^2}$
Ensure: $C = A^2 \in \mathbb{F}_{p^2}$
1: $c_0 \leftarrow a_0 - a_1$
2: $c_2 \leftarrow a_0 + a_1$
3: $(c_1, c_0) \leftarrow mul_{NEON}(a_0, a_1, c_0, c_2)$
4: $c_1 \leftarrow 2c_1$
5: **return** $C = c_0 + c_1 u$

---

where $|G| = |F| = 508$ bits. Finally, the third function red_{NEON} implements the Montgomery reduction defined as $(f, g) \leftarrow red_{NEON}(F, G)$, where $f, g \in \mathbb{F}_p$ and $|G| = |F| = 512$ bits. Making use of the aforementioned functions, Algorithms 4 and 5 compute a multiplication and a squaring in $\mathbb{F}_{p^2}$, respectively. Notice that In step 4 of Alg. 4 the function $mul256$ stands for a single integer multiplication.

4 Elliptic Curve Arithmetic

Elliptic curve points were represented using projective Jacobian coordinates, where a BN elliptic curve E is given as $Y^2 = X^3 + BZ^6$. A point $(X_1 : Y_1 : Z_1)$ in E corresponds to the affine point $(X_1/Z_1^2, Y_1/Z_1^3)$, with $Z_1 \neq 0$. The point at infinity $\mathcal{O}$ is represented as $(1, 1, 0)$, whereas the additive inverse of $(X_1 : Y_1 : Z_1)$ is $(X_1 : -Y_1 : Z_1)$.

Algorithm 6. Point doubling with Jacobian coordinates

Require: $P = (X_1 : Y_1 : Z_1) \in \mathbb{G}_1$
Ensure: $2P = (X_3 : Y_3 : Z_3) \in \mathbb{G}_1$
1: $(t_1, t_4) \leftarrow mul_{NEON}(Y_1, Y_1, 3X_1, X_1)$
2: $(t_2, t_3) \leftarrow mul_{NEON}(4X_1, t_1, 4t_1, 2t_1)$
3: $(X_3, Z_3) \leftarrow mul_{NEON}(t_4, t_4, 2Y_1, Z_1)$
4: $X_3 \leftarrow X_3 - 2t_2$
5: $Y_3 \leftarrow t_4 \cdot (t_2 - X_3) - t_3$
6: **return** $(X_3 : Y_3 : Z_3)$

Algorithm 7. Mixed point addition

Require: $P = (X_1 : Y_1 : Z_1)$ and $Q = (X_2 : Y_2 : 1) \in \mathbb{G}_1$
Ensure: $R = P + Q = (X_3 : Y_3 : Z_3) \in \mathbb{G}_1$
1: $t_1 \leftarrow Z_1^2$
2: $(t_2, t_3) \leftarrow mul_{NEON}(Z_1, t_1, X_2, t_1)$
3: $t_5 \leftarrow t_3 - X_1$
4: $(t_4, t_7) \leftarrow mul_{NEON}(Y_2, t_2, t_5, t_5)$
5: $(t_8, t_9) \leftarrow mul_{NEON}(t_7, t_5, t_7, X_1)$
6: $t_6 \leftarrow t_4 - Y_1$
7: $(X_3, Z_3) \leftarrow mul_{NEON}(t_6, t_6, Z_1, t_5)$
8: $X_3 \leftarrow X_3 - (t_8 + 2t_9)$
9: $(Y_3, t_0) \leftarrow mul_{NEON}(t_6, t_9 - X_3, Y_1, t_8)$
10: $Y_3 \leftarrow Y_3 - t_0$
11: **return** $(X_3 : Y_3 : Z_3)$

Point Doubling. Given $P = (X_1 : Y_1 : Z_1)$, the point $2P = (X_3 : Y_3 : Z_3)$ can be calculated with 4 squarings and 3 multiplications according to the next sequence of operations,

$$t_1 \leftarrow Y_1^2,\, t_2 \leftarrow 4X_1 \cdot t_1,\, t_3 \leftarrow 8t_1^2,\, t_4 \leftarrow 3X_1^2,$$
$$X_3 \leftarrow t_4^2 - 2t_2,\, Y_3 \leftarrow t_4 \cdot (t_2 - X_3) - t_3,\, Z_3 \leftarrow 2Y_1 \cdot Z_1$$

Mixed Point Addition. Let $P = (X_1 : Y_1 : Z_1)$ with $Z_1 \neq 0$ and $Q = (X_2 : Y_2 : 1)$, for $P \neq \pm Q$, the addition $R = P + Q = (X_3 : Y_3 : Z_3)$ can be obtained at a cost of 3 squarings and 8 multiplications according to the next sequence,

$$t_1 \leftarrow Z_1^2,\, t_2 \leftarrow Z_1 \cdot t_1,\, t_3 \leftarrow X_2 \cdot t_1,\, t_4 \leftarrow Y_2 \cdot t_2,\, t_5 \leftarrow t_3 - X_1,$$
$$t_6 \leftarrow t_4 - Y_1,\, t_7 \leftarrow t_5^2,\, t_8 \leftarrow t_7 \cdot t_5,\, t_9 \leftarrow X_1 \cdot t_7,$$
$$X_3 \leftarrow t_6^2 - (t_8 + 2t_9),\, Y_3 \leftarrow t_6 \cdot (t_9 - X_3) - Y_1 \cdot t_8,\, Z_3 \leftarrow Z_1 \cdot t_5$$

Taking advantage of the inherent parallelism of the above sequences, a NEON implementation of the point addition and point doubling operations is shown in Algorithms 6 and 7, respectively.

4.1   Efficient Techniques for Computing Scalar Multiplication

The elliptic curve scalar multiplication operation computes the multiple $R = [\ell]P$, with $\ell \in \mathbb{Z}_r$, $P, R \in E(\mathbb{F}_p)$, which corresponds to the point resulting of adding P to itself ℓ times. The average cost of computing $[\ell]P$ by a random $n-$bit scalar ℓ using the customary double-and-add method is of about, $nD + \frac{n}{2}A$, where A is the cost of a point addition, and D is the cost of a point doubling.

The customary method to speed up this operation reduces the Hamming weight of the scalar ℓ by representing it in its non-adjacent form (NAF). The technique can be easily extended to the w-NAF representation, namely, $\ell = \sum_{i=0}^{n-1} \ell_i 2^i$, $|\ell_i| \leq 2^{w-1}$, and at most one of any w consecutive digits is non-zero, with $\ell_{n-1} \neq 0$, where the length n is at most one bit larger than the bitsize of the scalar n and the resulting Hamming weight is approximately $1/(w+1)$. The estimated cost of the scalar multiplication reduces to, $nD + \frac{n}{w+1}A$, plus the cost of the precomputation of the multiples $P_i = [i]P$, for $i \in [1, 3, \ldots, 2^{w-1} - 1]$. Due to this exponential penalty, in most applications a rather conservative value of $w \in [3, 5]$ is selected.

When the point P is fixed, some form of the comb method is usually preferred. Given an w-window size and a known-point P, one can pre-compute for all of the possible bit strings $(a_{w-1}, \ldots, a_0)$ the following 2^w multiples of P: $[a_{w-1}, \ldots, a_2, a_1, a0]P = a_{w-1}2^{(w-1)d}P + \ldots + a_2 2^{2d}P + a_1 2^d P + a_0 P$. Then, the scalar ℓ is scanned column-wise by recoding it into d blocks each one with a bit length of w bits, where $d = |r|/w$. The computational and storage costs of the comb method is of $d(A + D)$, and a look-up table of 2^w points, respectively. Notice that the storage cost can be reduced to a half by using a signed representation of the scalar ℓ. A further speedup in the computation of the scalar multiplication can be achieved if there exists an efficient-computable endomorphism ψ over $E/\mathbb{F}_p$ such that $\psi(P) = \lambda P$ [8]. In the case of BN curves, given a cube root of unity $\beta \in \mathbb{F}_p$, one has that the mapping $\psi : E_1 \to E_1$ defined as, $(x, y) \to (\beta x, y)$ and $\mathcal{O} \to \mathcal{O}$, is an endomorphism over $\mathbb{F}_p$ with a characteristic polynomial given as $\lambda^2 + \lambda \equiv -1 \mod r$, $\lambda = 36z^4 - 1$. The scalar ℓ can be rewritten as $\ell \equiv \ell_0 + \ell_1\lambda \bmod r$, where $|\ell_i| < |\sqrt{r}|$, which allows to compute the scalar multiplication as, $[\ell]P = [\ell_0]P + [\ell_1]\psi(P)$, at an approximate cost of $[D + (2^{w-2} - 1)A] + \left[\frac{n}{w+1}A + \frac{n}{2}D\right]$.

In the case that the scalar multiplication in $\mathbb{G}_2$, *i.e.* the computation of the multiple $S = [\ell]Q$, with $\ell \in \mathbb{Z}_r$, $Q, S \in E(\mathbb{F}_{p^2})$, is of interest, one can take advantage of the Frobenius endomorphism to extend the two-dimensional GLV method to a four dimension version using the GS approach [7]. Let E be a BN elliptic curve over $\mathbb{F}_p$ with embedding degree $k = 12$ and let $\tilde{E}(\mathbb{F}_{p^2})$ be the sixth degree twist of E. Let π_p be the Frobenius operator in E, then $\psi = \phi^{-1}\pi_p\phi$ is an endomorphism on $\tilde{E}$ such that $\psi : \tilde{E}(\mathbb{F}_{p^2}) \to \tilde{E}(\mathbb{F}_{p^2})$. Then for $Q \in \tilde{E}(\mathbb{F}_{p^2})$, it holds that $\psi^k(Q) = Q$, $\psi(Q) = pQ$, and ψ satisfies $\psi^4 - \psi^2 + 1 = 0$. Since $p \equiv t - 1 \bmod r$, the scalar ℓ can be decomposed as $\ell = \ell_0 + \ell_1\lambda + \ell_2\lambda^2 + \ell_3\lambda^3$ with $\lambda = t - 1$ and $|\ell_i| \approx |r|/4$, which allows to compute the scalar multiplication in $\mathbb{G}_2$, as, $[\ell]Q = [\ell_0]Q + [\ell_1]\psi(Q) + [\ell_2]\psi^2(Q) + [\ell_3]\psi^3(Q)$, at an approximate cost of $[D + (2^{w-2} - 1)A] + \left[\frac{n}{w+1}A + \frac{n}{4}D\right]$.

Likewise, in the case of the exponentiation in $\mathbb{G}_T$, the operation f^e with $f \in \mathbb{G}_T, e \in \mathbb{Z}_r$ can then be accomplished by rewriting the exponent e in base p as, $e = e_0 + e_1 \cdot p + e_2 \cdot p^2 + e_3 \cdot p^3$, with $|e_i| \approx |r|/4$, followed by the computation, $f^e = f^{e_0} \cdot f^{e_1^p} \cdot f^{e_2^{p^2}} \cdot f^{e_3^{p^3}}$. Notice that the Frobenius mapping e^{p^i} for $i = 0, \ldots, 3$, has a negligible computational cost. Notice also that the identity $f^p = f^\lambda = f^{6x^2}$, holds.

5 Bilinear Pairing Arithmetic

In this section we briefly describe the Miller's loop and final exponentiation computations as well as the algorithm utilized to perform multi-pairing computations.

Miller Loop. The main operations of Algorithm 1 are the evaluation of the tangent line $\ell_{T,T}$ and the doubling of the point T; as well as the secant line evaluation and the computation of the point addition $T + P$. The most efficient way to perform above operations is through the usage of standard projective coordinates, where the projective point $(X_1 : Y_1 : Z_1)$ in the elliptic curve E corresponds to the affine point $(X_1/Z_1, Y_1/Z_1)$. Given the curve $\tilde{E}/\mathbb{F}_{p^2}$ defined as $\tilde{E} : y^2 = x^3 + b'$ whose projective form is $Y^2Z = X^3 + bZ^3$, one can calculate $2T = (X_3 : Y_3 : Z_3) \in E'(\mathbb{F}_{p^2})$ using the formulas [3]:

$$X_3 = \frac{X_1Y_1}{2}(Y_1^2 - 9b'Z_1^2)$$
$$Y_3 = \left[\frac{1}{2}(Y_1^2 + 9b'Z_1^2)\right]^2 - 27b'^2Z_1^4$$
$$Z_3 = 2Y_1^3Z_1$$

whereas the line $\ell_{T,T}$ evaluated on $P = (x_P, y_P) \in E(\mathbb{F}_p)$ is given as,

$$\ell_{T,T}(P) = -2Y_1Z_1y_P + 3X_1^2x_Pw + (3b'Z_1^2 - Y_1^2)w^3 \in \mathbb{F}_{p^{12}}$$

In the same way, given the points $T = (X_1, Y_1, Z_1), Q = (X_2, Y_2, 1) \in E'(\mathbb{F}_{p^2})$ and $P = (x_P, y_P) \in E(\mathbb{F}_p)$ one can calculate the point addition $R = T + Q = (X_3, Y_3, Z_3)$ and $\ell_{T,Q}(P)$ as [3]:

$$\ell_{T,Q}(P) = \lambda y_P - \theta x_P w + (\theta X_2 - \lambda Y_2) w^3,$$

$$X_3 = \lambda(\lambda^3 + Z_1 \theta^2 - 2X_1 \lambda^2)$$
$$Y_3 = \theta(3X_1 \lambda^2 - \lambda^3 - Z_1 \theta^2) - Y_1 \lambda^3$$
$$Z_3 = Z_1 \lambda^3$$

where $\theta = Y_1 - Y_2 Z_1$ and $\lambda = X_1 - X_2 Z_1$.

Another important aspect of the Miller's algorithm is the multiplication of the Miller variable f by the line (either tangent or secant) evaluation. However, the evaluation of the lines $\ell_{Q,Q}$ and $\ell_{T,Q}$ produce a sparse element in the group $\mathbb{F}_{p^{12}}^*$ with half of its coefficients having a zero value, which motivates the idea that any product of $f \in \mathbb{F}_{p^{12}}$ with $\ell_{Q,Q}$ or $\ell_{T,Q}$ should be performed using a procedure specially tailored for computing sparse multiplications.

Final Exponentiation. The exponent $e = (p^k - 1)/r$ in the BN final exponentiation can be broken into two parts as,

$$(p^{12} - 1)/r = [(p^{12} - 1)/\Phi_{12}(p)] \cdot [\Phi_{12}(p)/r],$$

where $\Phi_{12}(p) = p^4 - p^2 + 1$ denotes the twelfth cyclotomic polynomial evaluated in p. Computing the map $f \mapsto f^{(p^{12}-1)/\Phi_{12}(p)}$ is relatively inexpensive, costing only a few multiplications, inversions, and inexpensive p-th exponentiations in $\mathbb{F}_{p^{12}}$. Raising to the power $d = \Phi_{12}(p)/r = (p^4 - p^2 + 1)/r$ is considered more difficult. This part was computed using a multiple d' of d where $r \nmid d$ as discussed in [6], which allowed a lower number of operations. Using the BN parameter z, the exponentiation of $g^{d'(z)}$ requires the calculation of the following addition chain,

$$f^z \mapsto f^{2z} \mapsto f^{4z} \mapsto f^{6z} \mapsto f^{6z^2} \mapsto f^{12z^2} \mapsto f^{12z^3},$$

which requires 3 exponentiations by z, 3 squarings an one multiplication over $\mathbb{F}_{p^{12}}$. Finally, given the variables $a = g^{12z^3} \cdot g^{6z^2} \cdot g^{6z}$ and $b = a \cdot (g^{2z})^{-1}$, the exponentiation of $g^{d'(z)}$ is calculated as follows:

$$g^{d'(z)} = \left[a \cdot g^{6z^2} \cdot g \right] \cdot [b]^p \cdot [a]^{p^2} \cdot [b \cdot g^{-1}]^{p^3} \in \mathbb{F}_{p^{12}}^{\times}$$

Since $g \in \mathbb{G}_{\Phi_6}(\mathbb{F}_{p^2})$, the cost of $g^{d'(z)}$ is 3 Frobenius operators, 3 exponentiations by z, 10 multiplications in $\mathbb{F}_{p^{12}}$ and 3 squarings in $\mathbb{G}_{\Phi_6}(\mathbb{F}_{p^2})$. It should be noted that we use the Karabina compressed squaring formulas [12] for performing the exponentiation-by-z step.

Multipairing. Products of pairings are computations required in Waters' attribute-based protocol. For this operation, one can make use of the pairing bilinear property to group pairings sharing one of the input parameters. If all the pairings share a common input point, then one can exchange n pairing products by $n - 1$ point additions and a single pairing using the identity,

$$\prod_{i=0}^{n-1} e(Q, P_i) = e(Q, \sum_{i=0}^{n-1} P_i),$$

If a product of pairings is still needed, and the previous method was already exploited, there is still room for obtaining significant speedups. For instance, one can compute this product by performing a multi-pairing (or simultaneous product of pairings), by exploiting the well-known techniques employed in the multi-exponentiation setting. In essence, in a multipairing computation not only the costly final exponentiation step can be shared, but also, one can share both the Miller variable f, and the squaring computations performed in the step 4 of Algorithm 1. A further performance improvement can be achieved if the point Q in $\mathbb{G}_2$ is known in advance, since in this case one can pre-compute some of the operations involved in the line evaluations. In particular, the cost of computing the line evaluated at the point $P \in \mathbb{G}_1$ given as, $\ell_{.,.}(P) = l_0 y_P + l_1 x_P w + l_2 w^3$, reduces to two scalar multiplications since l_0, l_1, l_2, can be precomputed offline.

6   Attribute Based-Encryption

Attribute-Based Encryption (ABE) is a relatively new encryption scheme where an identity is seen as a set of attributes. In this scheme a user can access to some resources only if she had a set of privileges (called attributes) satisfying a control access policy previously defined. The policy is described through a boolean formula, which can be represented by an access structure and can be implemented using a linear secret-sharing scheme (LSSS) [14, 16]. The LSSS structure is described by the pair (M, ρ), where $M \in \mathbb{F}_r$ is an $u \times t$ matrix, where u, t are the number of required attributes and the access policy threshold, respectively; whereas ρ is a label function that according to the policy links each row of the matrix M to an attribute. For the sake of efficiency and as Scott did in [15], we reformulate the protocol from its original symmetric setting to an asymmetric one where some scheme parameters are conveniently defined in $\mathbb{G}_1$ whereas others are in $\mathbb{G}_2$. The ABE scheme is made up of four algorithms [16]: Setup, Encrypt, Key Generation and Decrypt, as described next.

Setup. This algorithm takes as input the security parameter λ and the set of U attributes. The security parameter becomes the main criterion to select the groups $\mathbb{G}_1$ and $\mathbb{G}_2$ of order r and the generators $P \in \mathbb{G}_1$ and $Q \in \mathbb{G}_2$. The points $H_1, \ldots, H_U \in \mathbb{G}_1$ are generated from the attribute universe and two random integers $a, \alpha \in \mathbb{F}_r$, are chosen at random. The public key is published as, $\mathrm{PK} = \{P, Q, e(Q, P)^\alpha, [a]P, H_1, \ldots, H_U\}$. Additionally, the authority establishes $\mathrm{MSK} = [\alpha]P$ as her master secret key. This algorithm has a cost of one pairing, two scalar multiplications and U MapToPoint functions. Notice that it is assumed that the elements P, Q, $[a]P$ and $e(Q, P)^\alpha$ are all known in advance. On the contrary, the points $H_1, \ldots H_U$ were not considered as fixed points since the attribute universe has a variable length, a fact that is also reflected in the storage cost.

Encrypt. The algorithm for encryption takes as input the public key PK, the message $\mathcal{M}$ to be encrypted, and the LSSS access structure (M, ρ), where $M \in \mathbb{F}_r$ is an $u \times t$ matrix as described above. The algorithm starts by randomly selecting a column vector $v = (s, y_2, \ldots, y_t)^T \in \mathbb{F}_r^n$ that will be used to securely share the secret exponent s. For $i = 1$ to u, it calculates $\lambda_i = M_i \cdot v$ where M_i is the $1 \times t$ vector corresponding to the i-th row of M. The scalars $r_1, \ldots, r_u \in \mathbb{F}_r$ are also randomly chosen. Then, the cipher CT is published as follows:

$$
CT = \begin{cases}
C = \mathcal{M}e(Q, P)^{\alpha s}, C' = [s]Q, \\
(C_1 = [\lambda_1]([a]P) - [r_1]H_{\rho(1)}, D_1 = [r_1]Q), \\
\vdots \\
(C_u = [\lambda_u]([a]P) - [r_u]H_{\rho(u)}, D_u = [r_u]Q),
\end{cases}
$$

which is sent along with the LSSS access structure (M, ρ).

The comb method was applied to compute scalar multiplications involving the fixed points Q, P and $[a]P$. In the same way, one can apply a variation of this method to obtain the powering of $e(Q, P)^\alpha$ by the exponent s. The GLV method was used to compute scalar multiplications with the points $H_i \in \mathbb{G}_1$. Hence the cost of encryption is one multiplication and one fixed exponentiation in $\mathbb{G}_T$, u fixed point multiplications in $\mathbb{G}_1$, $u + 1$ fixed point multiplications in $\mathbb{G}_2$ and u point multiplication in $\mathbb{G}_1$.

Key Generation. This algorithm takes as input the master secret key MSK = αP and a set of attributes S. First the algorithm selects a random number $t \in \mathbb{F}_r$, then it generates the attribute-based private key as follows,

$$
SK = \{ K = [\alpha]P + [t]([a]P), L = [t]Q, \forall x \in S \ K_x = [t]H_x \}
$$

Let N be the number of attributes on S, since the points aP and Q are known, the cost of this algorithm is one fixed point multiplication in $\mathbb{G}_1$, one fixed point in $\mathbb{G}_2$ and N point multiplications in $\mathbb{G}_1$. For the first two scalar multiplications the *comb* method was used, and the GLV method for the rest.

Decrypt. This algorithm takes as inputs the cipher CT with the access structure (M, ρ) and the private key SK for a set S. Suppose S satisfies the access structure and define $I \subset \{1, 2, \ldots, u\}$ as $I = \{i : \rho(i) \in S\}$. Let $\{\omega_i \in \mathbb{Z}\}_{i \in I}$ be the set of constants such that if λ_i is a valid share of a secret s according to M, then $\sum_{i \in I} \omega_i \lambda_i = \Delta s$ with $\Delta \in \mathbb{F}_r$. The decryption algorithm first computes:

$$
\left(e(L, \sum_{i \in I} [\omega_i] C_i) \prod_{i \in I} e(D_i, [\omega_i] K_{\rho(i)}) \right)^{\frac{1}{\Delta}} / e(C', K) = e(P, Q)^{-\alpha s}, \tag{3}
$$

Followed by the multiplication of this value by C as defined in Eq. (3). If S satisfies the access structure this should recover the message $\mathcal{M}$.

The variable Δ guarantees low size constants ω_i, i.e., $|\omega_i| < 64$ bits, which allows us to perform the scalar multiplications involving these constants using a w-NAF method. We called this operation *short scalar multiplication*. Let $N < u$ be the number of elements of I, then the computational cost of Eq. (3) is of $2N$ short multiplications in $\mathbb{G}_1$, an $N + 2$ multipairing computation, N point additions in $\mathbb{G}_1$ and one exponentiation in $\mathbb{G}_T$ which can be computed using the GS method. Also, since $L \in \mathbb{G}_2$ is a known point, its lines evaluations were precomputed.

Table 2. Clock cycle comparison for Single pairing computations

Work	Processor	10^3 clock cycles for 254 bits						
		$\tilde{a}$	$\tilde{m}$	$\tilde{s}$	i	ML	FE	Pairing
[1]	Tegra 2^a	1.42	8.18	5.20	26.61	$26,320$	$24,690$	$51,010$
[10]	Apple A5^b	0.25	3.48	2.88	19.19	$8,338$	$5,483$	$13,821$
	TI OMAP^c	0.16	3.37	2.53	16.86	$8,231$	$5,258$	$13,489$
	(ASM)	0.12	2.95	2.48	16.60	$7,376$	$4,510$	$11,886$
This Work	Tegra 2^a	0.17	3.41	2.41	39.25	$8,313$	$5,269$	$13,582$
	Exynos^d	0.17	3.42	2.41	39.21	$8,348$	$4,607$	$13,618$
	(NEON)	0.16	2.29	2.00	60.37	$5,758$	$3,794$	$9,477$
	Exynos^e	0.14	1.36	0.86	29.01	$3,388$	$2,353$	$5,838$

a. NVidia Tegra 2 (ARM v7) Cortex-A9 a 1.0 GHz (C)

b. iPad 2 (ARM v7) Apple A5 Cortex-A9 a 1.0 GHz (C)

c. Galaxy Nexus (ARM v7) TI OMAP 4460 Cortex-A9 a 1.2 GHz (Two versions: C and ASM)

d. Galaxy Note (ARM v7) Exynos 4 Cortex-A9 a 1.4 GHz (Two versions: C and NEON)

e. Arndaleboard (ARM v7) Exynos 5 Cortex-A15 a 1.7 GHz (NEON)

7 Implementation Results

This section presents the main implementation results classified into three subsections: bilinear pairings, scalar multiplication and the ABE scheme timings.

7.1 Pairing Timings

Let us recall that $(\tilde{a}, \tilde{m}, \tilde{s}, \tilde{i})$ denote the computational cost of the addition, multiplication, squaring and inversion operations over $\mathbb{F}_{p^2}$. These field arithmetic operations are used to perform a single pairing computation, a task that as it was described in section 5, can be split into two main parts: the Miller Loop (ML) and the Final Exponentiation (FE).

Using above definitions, Table 2 presents a comparison against the works [1] and [10] In [1] a pairing library that employs affine coordinates was presented, whereas [10] reports an assembler optimized pairing library using standard projective coordinates.

7.2   Costs of the Scalar Multiplication and Field Exponentiation

Table 3 shows the timings obtained for the computation of scalar multiplication in the groups $\mathbb{G}_1$ and $\mathbb{G}_2$, and the field exponentiation in the group $\mathbb{G}_T$. The computation of the scalar multiplication using the w-NAF approach was only utilized for small 64-bit scalars, with $w = 3$. The comb method was the choice for computing fixed point scalar multiplication with a window size of $w = 8$. We stress that the w-NAF was used in combination with both the GLV and GS methods.[2]

Table 3. Scalar mult. and exponentiation timings (in 10^3 clock cycles)

Processor	$\mathbb{G}_1$ Mult.			$\mathbb{G}_2$ Mult.			$\mathbb{G}_T$ Exp.		
	w-NAF	GLV	Comb	w-NAF	GS	Comb	w-NAF	GS	Comb
Tegra 2	779	1977	626	2059	4190	1745	2643	5998	2727
Exynos 4	785	1973	627	2096	4189	1742	2633	4777	2155
(NEON)	676	1698	556	1493	2933	1214	1827	4102	1863
Exynos 5	337	822	251	797	1571	636	1125	2522	1121

Table 4. ABE scheme with 6 attributes (Timings in 10^3 clock cycles)

Processor	Key Generation	Encryption	Decryption ($\Delta = 1$)	Decryption ($\Delta > 1$)
Tegra 2	18,340	31,830	63,870	74,140
Exynos 4	18,270	29,480	63,810	73,930
Exynos 4 (NEON)	15,333	24,167	43,980	50,808
Exynos 5	7,617	12,748	26,638	31,161

7.3   Attribute-Based Encryption Costs

We could not compare our ABE scheme timings against [2], because this work only implements the decryption algorithm and it does not present the exact timings. Table 4 reports the timings obtained when a 6-attribute policy is employed in the three main primitives of the ABE protocol, namely, key generation, encryption and decryption that were discussed in section 6. Note that for the decryption algorithm we present the cases when $\Delta = 1$ and $\Delta > 1$ (see Eq. 3).

8   Conclusion

We presented a cryptographic library that implements Waters' attribute encryption scheme in mobile devices operated with ARM processors. The main primitives developed were bilinear pairings and scalar multiplications in different flavors. Our library uses four different scalar multiplications according to the

---

[2] A description of the w-NAF GLS and GS methods for computing scalar multiplications was given in subsection 4.1.

group, scalar size and the type of the point (either fixed or variable), providing a 127 bits security level and achieving record timings for the computation of a single bilinear pairing at this level of security when implemented on the Exynos-5 Cortex-A15 processor.

A key factor that helps us to achieve faster timings than previously reported works was the usage of the NEON technology that allows a better exploitation of the inherent parallelism present in several field and elliptic curve arithmetic operations. It is illustrative to analyze the Exynos-4 scalar multiplication timings shown in Table 3. where NEON produces savings of about 14%, 30% and 15% in the computations over the $\mathbb{G}_1, \mathbb{G}_2$ and $\mathbb{G}_T$ groups, respectively. Notice that the significant better performance of NEON in the computations over $\mathbb{G}_2$ are a consequence of the rich parallelism extracted for the field squaring and multiplication over $\mathbb{F}_{p^2}$ as it was explained in Section 4.

Another interesting aspect to remark is the performance comparison of our work against [1] for the single pairing computation at the 127 bit security level. As shown in Table 2, *without using* NEON, the two libraries perform essentially the same when implemented in the Tegra 2 and Apple A5 processors, respectively. However, taking advantage of NEON, our library outperforms the library in [1] by approximately 20% when implemented in the Exynos 4 and TI OMAP processors, respectively. Moreover, when implemented in the Exynos 5 processor, our library is a bit more than two times faster than the software in [1]. We conclude that the Cortex A-15 micro-architecture and its improved NEON unit, provide a significantly better performance for cryptographic application implementations.

Acknowledgments. We wish to thank Peter Schwabe for explaining us how to perform accurate clock cycle counts on ARM processors and for giving us feedback on the first draft of the paper and Armando Faz-Hernández for benchmarking our software in the Exynos 5 Cortex-A15 processor. We also thank Alfred Menezes for commenting on the earlier draft. The second author acknowledges partial support from CONACyT project 132073

References

1. Acar, T., Lauter, K., Naehrig, M., Shumow, D.: Affine pairings on ARM. In: Abdalla, M., Lange, T. (eds.) Pairing 2012. LNCS, vol. 7708, pp. 203–209. Springer, Heidelberg (2013)
2. Akinyele, J.A., Lehmann, C., Green, M., Pagano, M., Peterson, Z., Rubin, A.: Self-Protecting Electronic Medical Records Using Attribute-Based Encryption. In: Bhattacharya, A., Dasgupta, P., Enck, W. (eds.) The 1st ACM Workshop on Security and Privacy in Smartphones and Mobile Devices SPSM 2011, pp. 75–86. ACM (2010)
3. Aranha, D.F., Karabina, K., Longa, P., Gebotys, C.H., López, J.: Faster Explicit Formulas for Computing Pairings over Ordinary Curves. In: Paterson, K.G. (ed.) EUROCRYPT 2011. LNCS, vol. 6632, pp. 48–68. Springer, Heidelberg (2011)

4. Barreto, P.S.L.M., Naehrig, M.: Pairing-friendly elliptic curves of prime order. In: Preneel, B., Tavares, S. (eds.) SAC 2005. LNCS, vol. 3897, pp. 319–331. Springer, Heidelberg (2006)
5. Chung, J., Hasan, M.A.: Asymmetric Squaring Formulas. In: Kornerup, P., Muller, J.-M. (eds.) Proceedings of the 18th IEEE Symposium on Computer Arithmetic, pp. 113–122. IEEE Computer Society (2007)
6. Fuentes-Castañeda, L., Knapp, E., Rodríguez-Henríquez, F.: Faster hashing to $\mathbb{G}_2$. In: Miri, A., Vaudenay, S. (eds.) SAC 2011. LNCS, vol. 7118, pp. 412–430. Springer, Heidelberg (2012)
7. Galbraith, S.D., Scott, M.: Exponentiation in Pairing-Friendly Groups Using Homomorphisms. In: Galbraith, S.D., Paterson, K.G. (eds.) Pairing 2008. LNCS, vol. 5209, pp. 211–224. Springer, Heidelberg (2008)
8. Gallant, R.P., Lambert, R.J., Vanstone, S.A.: Faster Point Multiplication on Elliptic Curves with Efficient Endomorphisms. In: Kilian, J. (ed.) CRYPTO 2001. LNCS, vol. 2139, pp. 190–200. Springer, Heidelberg (2001)
9. Granger, R., Scott, M.: Faster squaring in the cyclotomic subgroup of sixth degree extensions. In: Nguyen, P.Q., Pointcheval, D. (eds.) PKC 2010. LNCS, vol. 6056, pp. 209–223. Springer, Heidelberg (2010)
10. Grewal, G., Azarderakhsh, R., Longa, P., Hu, S., Jao, D.: Efficient implementation of bilinear pairings on ARM processors. In: Knudsen, L.R., Wu, H. (eds.) SAC 2012. LNCS, vol. 7707, pp. 149–165. Springer, Heidelberg (2013)
11. Hankerson, D., Menezes, A., Scott, M.: Software implementation of pairings (Chapter 12). In: Joye, M., Neven, G. (eds.) Identity-based Cryptography. Cryptology and Information Security, vol. 2, pp. 188–206. IOS Press (2009)
12. Karabina, K.: Squaring in cyclotomic subgroups. Math. Comput. 82(281) (2013)
13. Koc, C.K., Acar, T., Kaliski Jr., B.S.: Analyzing and Comparing Montgomery Multiplication Algorithms. IEEE Micro 16(3), 26–33 (1996)
14. Liu, Z., Cao, Z.: On efficiently transferring the linear secret-sharing scheme matrix in ciphertext-policy attribute-based encryption. IACR Cryptology ePrint Archive, 2010:374 (2010)
15. Scott, M.: On the Efficient Implementation of Pairing-Based Protocols. In: Chen, L. (ed.) IMACC 2011. LNCS, vol. 7089, pp. 296–308. Springer, Heidelberg (2011)
16. Waters, B.: Ciphertext-policy attribute-based encryption: An expressive, efficient, and provably secure realization. In: Catalano, D., Fazio, N., Gennaro, R., Nicolosi, A. (eds.) PKC 2011. LNCS, vol. 6571, pp. 53–70. Springer, Heidelberg (2011)

Fast and Maliciously Secure
Two-Party Computation Using the GPU

Tore Kasper Frederiksen and Jesper Buus Nielsen*

Department of Computer Science, Aarhus University
{jot2re,jbn}@cs.au.dk

Abstract. We describe, and implement, a maliciously secure protocol for two-party computation in a parallel computational model. Our protocol is based on Yao's garbled circuit and an efficient OT extension. The implementation is done using CUDA and yields fast results for maliciously secure two-party computation in a financially feasible and practical setting by using a consumer grade CPU and GPU. Our protocol further uses some novel constructions in order to combine garbled circuits and an OT extension in a parallel and maliciously secure setting.

1 Introduction

Secure two-party computation (2PC) is the area of cryptography concerned with two mutually distrusting parties who wish to securely compute an arbitrary function on their joint and private input without leaking any information. The area was introduced in 1982 by Yao [25], specifically for the *semi honest* case where both parties are assumed to follow the prescribed protocol. Yao showed how to construct such a protocol using a technique referred to as the *garbled circuit approach*. Later, a solution in the *malicious* setting, where one of the parties might deviate from the prescribed protocol in an arbitrary manner, was given in [4]. Another approach for malicious security, called the *cut-and-choose approach*, involves running several instances of garbled circuits in parallel, with some random instances being completely revealed to verify that the other party has behaved honestly. Efficient 2PC and secure multi-party computation (MPC) have many practical applications. The first case of this is described in [2], where MPC was used for deciding the price of a national sugar beet auction in Denmark. Other applications for 2PC and MPC include voting, anonymous identification, privacy preserving database queries etc.

Recently a lot of research has gone into making 2PC efficient enough to be practical, cf. [7,13,15,18,19,21]. Most previous approaches have focused on doing this in a sequential model [13,15,18]. However, the recent evolution of processors seems to indicate a convergence of speed, whereas the amount of cores in processors seem to increase. Thus, constructing algorithms and cryptographic protocols

---

* Partially supported by the Danish Council for Independent Research via DFF Starting Grant 10-081612. Partially supported by the European Research Commission Starting Grant 279447.

M. Jacobson et al. (Eds.): ACNS 2013, LNCS 7954, pp. 339–356, 2013.

that work well in a parallel model will be paramount for hardware based efficiency increases in the future, which is why we take the parallel approach to increase the speed of 2PC.

Previous work in "parallel cryptography" started with [22], where a cluster of either CPUs or GPUs was used to execute 3072 semi honest protocols for 1-out-of-2 oblivious transfer (OT) followed by gate garbling/degarbling in parallel.[1] In [12] 512 cores of a cluster was used to do OT along with circuit garbling in parallel to achieve malicious security using the cut-and-choose approach. In this manner they managed to use the inherit parallelism of the cut-and-choose approach to achieve very fast and maliciously secure 2PC. Any other work taking a parallel approach to cryptography that we know of focuses either on attacks e.g. [24] or simultaneous applications of more primitive cryptographic computations e.g. [20].

Contributions. Our main contribution is a careful implementation, along with a general protocol, for maliciously secure 2PC using a *Same Instruction, Multiple Data (SIMD)*, or *Parallel Random Access Model (PRAM)* computation device. Our protocol is UC secure in the *Random Oracle Model (ROM)*, *OT-hybrid model* and based on Yao's garbled circuit approach [25] along with the *OT extension* (See Section 2) of [18] and a few novel ideas. Computationally our protocol relies solely on symmetric primitives, except for a few seed OTs used in the OT extension which only need to be done once for each pair of parties. Furthermore, our protocol is of constant round complexity and, assuming access to enough cores, computationally bounded only by the number of layers in the circuit to be computed and the block size of a hash function. Using a NVIDIA GPU as our SIMD device, we make several experiments and show that our approach is orders of magnitude more efficient on current *consumer hardware* than any other protocol based on garbled circuits. Finally, we show that this approach is the fastest yet documented assuming a "practical", yet malicious, setting.[2]

Notation. We let $\|$ denote string concatenation and let $r[i]$ be the i'th element of a string r. We let ℓ be the statistical security parameter and κ be the computational security parameter. In particular we let $H(\cdot)$ denote a hash function with a digest of κ bits (in our implementation this will be 160 bits). We assume that Alice is the circuit *constructor* and Bob is the circuit *evaluator* and we will use their names and roles interchangeably.

Overview. Section 2 introduces the idea of parallel implementations and the overall structure of our computation device of choice; the GPU. In Section 3 we go through the overall structure of our protocol. Later, in Section 4 we go

---

[1] 1-out-of-2 OT is the protocol where the first party, Alice, gives as input two bitstrings (x_0, x_1), and the second party, Bob, inputs a bit b. Bob learns x_b but gets no information on x_{1-b} and Alice gets no information on b.

[2] We refer to "practical" as either financially feasible for a consumer and/or having a liberal statistical security parameter.

through the ideas used to make our protocol suitable in the SIMD model. Then, in Section 5 we discuss the implementation details and finally in Section 6 we review our results.

2 Background

Parallel Approach. In our approach we assume access to a massive parallel computation device which is capable of executing the same instruction on each processor in parallel, but on different pieces of data. Our protocol does not make any assumption on whether such a device has access to shared memory between the processors, or only access to local memory. This applies completely for write privileges, but also for read privileges with only a constant memory usage penalty.

We decided to implement our protocol using the GPU, the motivation being that GPUs are part of practically all mid- to high-end consumer computers. Furthermore, using the GPU eliminates the security problems from outsourcing the computation to a non-local cluster. Also, assuming access to a local cluster seems to be an unrealistic assumption for general practical applications. Using gaming consoles or multi-cores CPUs might also be an option. However, even the latest and best of these have orders of magnitude processors less than the latest GPUs.

Our implementation is done using the CUDA framework which is an extension to C and C++ that allows using NVIDIA GPUs for general computational tasks. This is done by making CUDA programs. Such a program does not purely run on the GPU. It consists of both general C classes, which run on the CPU, and CUDA classes which run on the GPU since the GPU can not communicate directly with the Operating System (OS).

In order to motivate our specific implementation choices it is necessary to describe a general CUDA enabled GPU: Each GPU consists of several (up to 192) *streaming multiprocessors* (SM), each of these again contains between 8 and 192 *streaming processors* (SP), depending on the architecture of the GPU. Each of the SPs within a given SM always performs the same operations at a given point in time, but on different pieces of data. Furthermore, each of these SMs contains 64 KB of *shared memory* along with a few kilobytes of constant cache, which all of the SPs within the given SM must share. For storage of variables each SM contains 64K 32-bit registers which is shared amongst all the SPs. Thus all the threads being executed by a given SM must share all these resources.

We now introduce some notation and concepts which are used in the general purpose GPU community and which we will also use in this paper; a GPU is called a *device* and the non-GPU parts of a computer is called the *host*. This means that the CPU, RAM, hard drive, etc., are part of the host. The code written for the host will be used to interact with the OS, that is, it will do all the IO operations needed by the CUDA program. The host code is also responsible for copying the data to and from the device, along with launching code on the device. Each procedure running on a device without interaction with the host is called a *kernel*. Before launching a kernel the host code should complete all needed IO and copy all the data needed by the kernel to the device's RAM. The RAM of the device is referred to as *global memory*. After a kernel has terminated the host can copy the results from the global memory of the device to its own memory, before it launches another kernel.

A kernel is more than just a procedure of code, it also contains specifications of how many times in parallel the code should be executed and any type of synchronization needed between the parallel executions. A kernel consists of code which is executed in a *grid*. A grid is a 2-dimensional matrix of *blocks*. Each block is a 3-dimensional matrix of threads. Each thread is executed once and takes up one SP during its execution. When all the threads, of all the blocks in the grid, have been executed the kernel terminates. The threads in each block are executed in *warps*, which is a sequence of 32 threads. Thus, the threads must be partitioned into blocks in multiples of the warp size, and contain no branching. The threads can then be executed completely independently and in arbitrary order.

Furthermore, to achieve the fastest execution time one should *coalescence* the data in global memory. That is, to "sort" the data such that the word thread 1 needs is located next to the word thread 2 needs and so on. This makes it possible to load these 32 words for the warp in one go, thus limiting the usage of bandwidth, and in turn significantly increasing the speed of the program. This advice on memory organisation is also relevant for the data in the shared memory. Finally, it is a well known fact [3] that the bottleneck for most applications of the massive parallelism offered by CUDA is the memory bandwidth, thus it should always be a goal to limit the frequency of which a program access data in the global memory.

Maliciously Secure Garbled Circuits. For completeness we now sketch how a generic garbled circuit is constructed. We are given a Boolean circuit description, C, of the Boolean function we wish to compute, f, from which we construct a garbled circuit, GC. For simplicity we assume that each gate consists of two input wires and one output wire. However, we allow the output wire to split into two or more if the output of a given gate is needed as input to more than one other gate. Each wire in C has a unique label, and we give the corresponding wire in GC the same label. Each wire w has two keys associated, k_w^0 and k_w^1, which are independent uniformly random bitstrings. Here k_w^0 represents the bit 0 and k_w^1 represents the bit 1. If the bit on wire w in C is 0, then the value on wire w in GC will be k_w^0, otherwise it will be k_w^1. Each gate in GC consists of a *garbled computation table*. This table is used to find the correct value of the output wire given the correct keys for the input wires. For a gate of C call the left input wire l, the right input wire r and the output wire o. Assume the functionality of the gate is given by $G(\sigma, v) = \rho$ where $\sigma, v, \rho \in \{0, 1\}$, then the garbled computation table is a random permutation of the four ciphertexts $C_{\sigma,v} = E_{k_l^\sigma}\left(E_{k_r^v}\left(k_o^\rho\right)\right) = E_{k_l^\sigma}\left(E_{k_r^v}\left(k_o^{G(\sigma,v)}\right)\right)$ for all four possible input pairs, (σ, v), using some symmetric encryption function, $E_{key}(\cdot)$. I.e., the entries in the garbled computation table consists of "double encryptions" of the output wire's values, where the keys for each double encryption corresponds to exactly one combination of the input wires' values. The encryption algorithm is constructed such that given k_l^σ and k_r^υ it is possible to recognize and correctly decrypt $C_{\sigma,\upsilon}$, but it is not possible to learn any information about the remaining three encryptions.

Optimized Garbled Circuits. To determine which entry in the garbled computation table is the correct one to decrypt we use permutation bits [21]. The idea is to associate a *permutation bit*, $\pi_i \in \{0,1\}$, with each wire, i, in GC. The value on i is then defined as $k_i^b \parallel c_i$ where $c_i = \pi_i \oplus b$ with b being the bit wire i should represent. We call c_i the *external value*. The garbled computation table is then

$$\left[c_l, \ c_r \ : \ \mathrm{E}_{k_l^{b_l}, k_r^{b_r}}^{Gid \parallel c_l \parallel c_r} \left(k_o^{G(b_l, b_r)} \parallel c_o \right) \right]_{l=0, r=0}^{1,1},$$

where $c_l = \pi_l \oplus b_l$, $c_r = \pi_r \oplus b_r$, and $c_o = \pi_o \oplus G(b_l, b_r)$, *sorted* on $c_l \parallel c_r$. This means that given the keys of the input wires the evaluator can decide which entry he needs to decrypt, without learning anything about the bits the wires represent. The encryption function for the keys in the garbled computation table is defined as follows:

$$\mathrm{E}_{k_l, k_r}^s(k_o) = k_o \oplus \mathrm{KDF}^{|k_o|}(k_l, k_r, s),$$

where $\mathrm{KDF}^{|k_o|}(k_l, k_r, s)$ is a *key derivation function* with an output of $|k_o|$ bits, independent of the two input keys, k_l and k_r in isolation, and which depends on the value of some salt, s. As we assume the ROM, we are able to specify the KDF as follows:

$$\mathrm{KDF}^{|k_o|}(k_l, k_r, s) = \mathrm{H}(k_l \parallel k_r \parallel s) .$$

This means that the encryption function essentially can be reduced to a single invocation of a robust hash function with output length κ (assuming $\kappa \geq |k_o|$).

We further include the optimization from [11] which will make it possible to evaluate all the XOR gates in the circuit for "free". Free here means that no garbled computation table needs to be constructed or transmitted. The trick is to have a *global key* Δ, which is a uniformly random bitstring of the same length as the wire keys, and then let $k_i^1 = k_i^0 \oplus \Delta$ for all wires i. Regarding the external values, this implies that $\pi_i \oplus 1 = \pi_i \oplus 0 \oplus 1$. So, in order to compute an XOR gate simply compute XOR of the keys of the two input wires of the gate, that is $k_o \parallel c_o = k_l \oplus k_r \parallel c_l \oplus c_r$. Finally, we also eliminate a row of the garbled computation table using the approach of [17]. The trick is to let one of the output keys be the result of the KDF on one input key pair. This key pair is the one where the external values are 0, i.e., $c_l = 0$ and $c_r = 0$. I.e.:

$$k_o^{G(\pi_l \oplus 0, \pi_r \oplus 0)} \parallel c_o = \mathrm{KDF}^{\kappa+1}\left(k_l^{\pi_l \oplus 0}, \ k_r^{\pi_r \oplus 0}, \ Gid \parallel 0 \parallel 0 \right) .$$

Depending on the type of gate, this again uniquely specifies the permutation bit of the output wire as $c_o = \pi_o \oplus G(\pi_l \oplus 0, \pi_r \oplus 0)$. The other output key is given using Δ. The three remaining entries in the garbled computation table are then the appropriate encryptions of these two output keys.

Optimized Approaches to Cut-and-Choose Malicious Security. In general OT is an expensive primitive, and if the evaluator has a large input to the circuit this can contribute significantly to the execution time of the whole protocol. However, the amount of "actual" OTs we need to complete can be significantly reduced by using an *OT extension*: Beaver showed in [1] that given a number of OTs it is possible to "extend" these to give a polynomial number of random OTs which can easily be changed to specific OTs. Thus, making it possible to do a few OTs once, and extend these almost indefinitely. The idea of an OT extension has been optimized even further in [8] and [18] to yield significant practical advantages. Our protocol uses a slightly modified version of the OT extension presented in [18].

The cut-and-choose approach in itself is unfortunately not enough to make a semi honestly secure protocol maliciously secure. In fact, several problems arise from using cut-and-choose to get security against a malicious adversary, these problems can be categorized as follows:

1. "Consistency of input bits"; both parties need to use the same input in all the cut-and-choose instances to ensure that the majority of the garbled circuit evaluations are consistent and that a corrupt evaluator does not learn the output of the function on different inputs.
2. "Selective failure attack"; we must make sure that both the keys the constructor inputs in the OT phase are correct, to avoid giving away a particular bit values of the evaluator's input, depending on failure or not of the evaluation.

Letting $|x|$ be the size of the constructor's input and ℓ the statistical security parameter then the first problem can be solved using $O(|x| \cdot \ell^2)$ commitments to verify consistency in all possible cut-and-choose cases [13]. A more efficient approach is to construct a Diffie-Hellman pseudo random synthesizer, which limits the complexity to $O(|x| \cdot \ell)$ symmetric and asymmetric operations and also solves the selective failure attack [15]. Yet another solution is based on claw-free functions [23].

The selective failure problem can also be solved using different techniques. In [13] it is shown how to do this using a circuit extension which increases the amount of input bits of the evaluator by a factor ℓ. In [23] the problem is solved using a special version OT, known as *comitting OT*.

Our solution is different; we solve the problem of the consistency in the constructor's input bits by using a circuit extension and the consistency of the evaluator by extending each OT by a factor ℓ using the random oracle. The selective failure attack is handled by a novel combination of the OT extension and the use of the free-XOR approach in the garbled circuit. We use these constructions to achieve parallel scalability.

3 High Level Description

We now describe the overall structure of our protocol. For simplicity we assume that only the evaluator is supposed to receive output from the computation. If we wish to compute a circuit where the constructor should also receive output then the circuit extension approach of [13], or the signed output approach of [23], will work directly in our protocol and be scalable in parallel.

Abstractly our protocol can be described as follows:

1. Given a statistical security parameter, ℓ, such that the probability of a total breakdown is at most $2^{-\ell}$, along with a Boolean circuit C, the constructor extends the circuit to get a new circuit, C', that includes a consistency check. Using the description C', the constructor constructs $\ell' = 3.22 \cdot \ell$ GCs in parallel.[3]

2. The constructor then hashes each of the ℓ' GCs along with the keys for the evaluator's output, and sends the digests to the evaluator. These digests makes it possible to avoid sending half of the garbled computation tables as mentioned in [5]. This ends the *garbling phase*.

3. The constructor then sends both of the keys of the evaluator's output wires to the evaluator.

4. The constructor and evaluator engage in OT in order for the evaluator to learn the keys corresponding to his input for all ℓ' circuits. We call this the *OT phase*.

   (a) The constructor and evaluator complete a modified OT extension which is a 1-out-of-2 OTs of random bitstrings.

   (b) For each of these OTs the constructor extends the two random outputs to a $\ell' \cdot \kappa$ "random" bitstring. The first representing the 0-keys of the ℓ' garbled circuits and the other the 1-keys.

   (c) Similarly the evaluator extends his output of each OT to a $\ell' \cdot \kappa$ "random" bitstring, representing either the 0 or 1 keys of the ℓ' garbled circuits depending on his choice in the OT.

   (d) From the circuit generation the constructor will have a 0 and 1 key for each wire in each GC. The constructor then XORs each of the "random" bitstrings she learned from the modified OT extension with the appropriate keys from the circuit generation and sends all these differences to the evaluator.

   (e) The evaluator uses these bitstrings to find the correct input keys for the GCs by a simple XOR operation.

5. The parties then select $\ell'/2$ circuits for verification (using a coin-tossing protocol) and the constructor sends the random seeds used to generate these circuits to the evaluator. We call this and the following three steps for the *cut-and-choose phase*.

6. Using the seeds the evaluator regenerates the circuits' garbled computation tables along with the keys of the output wires and verifies that they are

---

[3] The constant increase in the amount of GCs stems from the fact that cut-and-choose of ℓ circuits only corresponds to statistical security of $2^{-0.311\ell}$ [15].

correct by hashing them and checking equality with the digests he has already received in Step 2. He also uses the seeds to generate the input keys for the GCs. He uses these keys, the differences he received in the OT phase, along with his outputs from the OT phase, to reconstructs both the 0 and 1 keys and uses these values to verify that the constructor sent the correct differences in the OT phase.

7. After these checks the constructor sends the input keys in correspondence with her input, along with the garbled computation tables of the $\ell'/2$ circuits for which the evaluator was *not* given the seeds.

8. The evaluator then hashes the garbled computation tables of these circuits and verifies them against the hash digests he received in Step 2. He then degarbles the circuits to achieve the output keys along with their respective external values. In the end he then checks consistency of these outputs. We call this the *evaluation phase*.

9. If all checks pass, then the evaluator maps the output keys to their corresponding bits and take the majority of the decrypted outputs of the $\ell'/2$ circuits to be the overall output of the protocol.

4   Specific Details

The Garbled Circuit. First of all, we modify the circuit of the function we wish to compute in order to embed a consistency check for the constructor's input. Assume the function we wish to compute is defined by f as $f(x, y) = (f_1(x, y), f_2(x, y))$ with $|x| = \tau_a$, $|y| = \tau_b$ and $f_1(x, y)$ being the (possibly empty) output the constructor is supposed to learn and $f_2(x, y)$ being the output the evaluator is supposed to learn. We now define a new function f' as $f'((x, s), (y, r)) = (f_1(x, y), (f_2(x, y), t))$ where $s \in_R \{0, 1\}^\ell$, $r \in_R \{0, 1\}^{\tau_a + \ell}$ and $t \in \{0, 1\}^\ell$. To compute t define a matrix $\mathbf{M} \in \{0, 1\}^{\ell \times \tau_a}$ where the i'th row is the first τ_a bits of $r << i$ where $<<$ denotes the bitwise left shift, i.e. $\mathbf{M}_{i,j} = r[i+j]$. Using this matrix the computation of t is defined as $t = (\mathbf{M} \cdot x) \oplus s$, assuming all binary vectors are in column form.

With this modification the new function computes the same as the original, but requires ℓ extra random bits of input from the constructor and $\tau_a + \ell$ extra random bits from the evaluator. However, the new function returns ℓ extra bits to the evaluator. These ℓ extra bits will work as digest bits and can be used to check that the constructor is consistent with her inputs to the GCs by verifying that they are the same in all the garbled circuits which are evaluated.

This augmentation works since the new function computes, besides the original functionality, a family of universal hash functions where the auxiliary input from both parties defines a particular hash function from this family. The auxiliary output of the augmented function is then the digest of the constructor's input in this universal hash function. The proof that the augmentation is indeed a family of universal hash functions was shown in [16]. Thus this gives statistical security $2^{-\ell}$ when augmenting the function with an ℓ bit digest.

We turn this new function, f', into a circuit description which we then parse. The parsing consists of finding all the gates which can be computed using only the input wires, calling this set of gates for layer 0. We then find all the gates, not in layer 0, that can be computed using only the input wires and the output wires of the gates in layer 0, calling this layer for layer 1. We continue in this manner until all gates have been assigned a unique layer. The interesting thing to notice here is that we now have a partition of the gates in such a manner that all gates in a single layer can be constructed or evaluated in parallel, in an arbitrary order, only requiring that gates at lower levels have been constructed or evaluated beforehand. Thus, given the keys of the input wires we can construct the garbled computation tables of the gates in layer 0 in an arbitrary order. Moreover, the heavy part of these computations, encryption, can be done in a SIMD manner. The only part of the construction that varies, depending on the type of gate, is which entries in the garbled computation table that should represent a 0-key and which that should represent a 1-key. Notice, however, since we implement the free XOR approach this problem is eliminated, as we can simply multiply the global key with the output of the given gate and always XOR this into the garbled computation table entry which is already representing a 0-key. Still, using the free XOR approach gives another problem, that is the need to further partition each layer into sets of XOR gates and non-XOR gates, in order to achieve complete SIMD *or* to keep the amount of layers and instead execute each layer like it *only* consists of XOR gates *and* execute it like *only* consists of non-XOR gates and only use the relevant result of each of the gates.

Finally, it should be noted that the global key we choose needs to be the same for all the gates in one GC, but different for each of the GCs we make to allow opening in cut-and-choose. Keeping these changes, and this way to parallelize in mind, the protocol for construction is the same as the optimized protocol for generic GC generation previously described, repeated ℓ' times.

The evaluation proceeds in almost the same manner as in the generic garbled circuit evaluation. However, we still use the same paradigm for parallelization as in the construction phase; we degarble each gate in a given layer, in all the $\ell'/2$ circuits, in parallel. Finally, having degarbled all gates, and thus found the keys on the output wires. The evaluator uses the output keys previously received by the constructor to find the bits of his output. The evaluator then checks for a selective failure attack by verifying that each of the ℓ digest bits, on all of the $\ell'/2$ circuits, has the same values. If that is not the case then the evaluator outputs failure. Finally, the evaluator takes the majority of the outputs to be his outputs.

The Modified OT Extension. We use the approach from [18] for the core of our modified OT extension. However, we make a few changes to reduce as many operations as possible to parallel computable hashes of short bitstrings.

Assuming the existence of random oracles and a secure implementation of a κ-bit 1-out-of-2 OT as an ideal resource, the protocol is UC secure against a malicious adversary. For the rest of this section we let τ be the amount of bits in the evaluator's input for the augmented circuit, i.e. $\tau = \tau_b + \tau_a + \ell$.

Define the evaluator's (Bob's) input to the augmented circuit as a bitstring of $y' = y \parallel r$ of τ bits, where y is his original input. Define $H(\cdot)$ to be a hash function with κ bits output. The modified OT extension goes as follows:

1. Bob chooses $\lceil \frac{8}{3}\kappa \rceil$ pairs of seeds, each consisting of κ random bits. That is, for each $i = 1, \ldots \lceil \frac{8}{3}\kappa \rceil$ let $(l_i^0, l_i^1) \in_R \{0,1\}^\kappa \times \{0,1\}^\kappa$ be the i'th seed pair.
2. Alice now samples $\lceil \frac{8}{3}\kappa \rceil$ random bits, $x_1, \ldots, x_{\lceil \frac{8}{3}\kappa \rceil} \in_R \{0,1\}$.
3. Alice and Bob then run $\lceil \frac{8}{3}\kappa \rceil$ OTs where, for $i = 1, \ldots, \lceil \frac{8}{3}\kappa \rceil$, Bob offers (l_i^0, l_i^1) and Alice selects x_i, and receives $l_i^{x_i}$.
4. Now, for each of the $i = 1, \ldots, \lceil \frac{8}{3}\kappa \rceil$ pairs of random bits Bob computes the following two vectors of τ bits, using $id_{i,j}$ as a unique ID:

$$L_i^0 = H\left(id_{i,0}\|l_i^0\right)\|H\left(id_{i,1}\|l_i^0\right)\|\ldots\|H\left(id_{i,\tau/\kappa}\|l_i^0\right),$$
$$L_i^1 = H\left(id_{i,0}\|l_i^1\right)\|H\left(id_{i,1}\|l_i^1\right)\|\ldots\|H\left(id_{i,\tau/\kappa}\|l_i^1\right).$$

5. Now, in the same manner Alice extends each of her outputs of the OT from their original length of κ bits, into strings of τ bits. Thus, Alice computes $L_i^{x_i} = H\left(id_{i,0}\|l_i^{x_i}\right)\|H\left(id_{i,1}\|l_i^{x_i}\right)\|\ldots\|H\left(id_{i,\tau/\kappa}\|l_i^{x_i}\right)$.
6. Now, for each $i = 1, \ldots, \lceil \frac{8}{3}\kappa \rceil$ Bob computes a bitstring, $\lambda_i = L_i^0 \oplus L_i^1 \oplus y'$, and sends these to Alice.
7. For each $i = 1, \ldots, \lceil \frac{8}{3}\kappa \rceil$ Alice computes a bitstring as follows

$$L'^{x_i}_i = L_i^{x_i} \oplus (x_i \cdot \lambda_i) = L_i^0 \oplus (x_i \cdot y').$$

8. Alice then picks a uniformly random permutation $\pi : \left\{1, \ldots, \lceil \frac{8}{3}\kappa \rceil \right\} \to \left\{1, \ldots, \lceil \frac{8}{3}\kappa \rceil \right\}$ where, for all i, $\pi(\pi(i)) = i$, and sends these to Bob. Furthermore, define $S(\pi) = \{i | i \leq \pi(i)\}$, that is, for each pair, the smallest index is in $S(\pi)$.
9. Now, for all the $\lfloor \frac{4}{3}\kappa \rfloor$ indexes $i \in S(\pi)$ do the following:
   (a) Alice computes $d_i = x_i \oplus x_{\pi(i)}$ and sends these to Bob.
   (b) Alice and Bob both compute $Z_i = \left(L'^{x_i}_i \oplus L'^{x_{\pi(i)}}_{\pi(i)}\right)$. This is possible for Bob since d_i uniquely determines the way to compute Z_i, i.e. if he should XOR L_i^0 with y'.
10. For all $i \in S(\pi)$, Alice and Bob concatenate Z_i and evaluate equality using the protocol for equality of [18], modified for parallel computation (see the full version of this article), and abort if they are not equal.
11. For each $i = 1, \ldots, \lfloor \frac{4}{3}\kappa \rfloor$ and for each $j = 1, \ldots, \tau$ Alice defines K_j to be the string consisting of the j'th bits from all the strings $L'^{x_i}_i$, i.e. $K_j = L'^{x_1}_1[j]\|L'^{x_2}_2[j]\|\ldots\|L'^{x_{\lfloor \frac{4}{3}\kappa \rfloor}}_{\lfloor \frac{4}{3}\kappa \rfloor}[j]$. This means that she gets τ keys consisting of $\lfloor \frac{4}{3}\kappa \rfloor$ bits.
12. Now, for each $i = 1, \ldots, \lfloor \frac{4}{3}\kappa \rfloor$ and for each $j = 1, \ldots, \tau$ Bob sets M_j to be the string consisting of the j'th bits from all the strings L_i^0, i.e. $M_j = L_2^0[j]\|L_2^0[j]\|\ldots\|L^0_{\lfloor \frac{4}{3}\kappa \rfloor}[j]$.

13. Alice lets Γ_A be the string consisting of all the bits x_i for $i \in S(\pi)$, i.e. $\Gamma_A = x_1 \| x_2 \| \dots \| x_{\lfloor \frac{4}{3}\kappa \rfloor}$.

14. Bob now computes $Y_j = H(M_j)$ and achieves $(Y_0, \dots, Y_\tau)$. He then extends each of these to ℓ' random values. That is, for each $i = 1, \dots, \ell'$ he computes $Y_j^i = H(id_{i,j} \| Y_j)$.

15. Alice computes $X_j^0 = H(K_j)$ and $X_j^1 = H(K_j \oplus \Gamma_A)$ and achieves $((X_1^0, X_1^1), \dots, (X_\tau^0, X_\tau^1))$. She then extends each of these pairs to pairs of ℓ' random values. Specifically for each $i = 1, \dots, \ell'$ she computes the following:

$$\left(X_j^{0,i}, X_j^{1,i} \right) = \left(H\left(id_{i,j} \| X_j^0 \right), H\left(id_{i,j} \| X_j^1 \right) \right).$$

If the parties have been honest it should be the case, that for each $i = 1, \dots, \ell'$ and $j = 1, \dots, \tau$ we have $Y_j^{y'[j],i} = X_j^{y'[j],i}$.

Fitting It Together. After completing the modified OT extension Bob has $\tau \cdot \ell'$ keys of length κ. However, these keys are not consistent with the random keys used for the ℓ' circuits. So, for each of the $\tau \cdot \ell'$ pairs of keys Alice has, she computes the difference between the keys she achieved as a result of the modified OT extension and the actual keys to the given GCs. That, is for each $i = 1, \dots, \ell'$ and each $j = 1, \dots, \tau$ she computes $\delta_j^{0,i} = X_j^{0,i} \oplus k_j^{0,i}$ and $\delta_j^{1,i} = X_j^{1,i} \oplus k_j^{1,i}$ where $k_j^{0,i}$ is the 0-key and $k_j^{1,i}$ is the 1-key for the particular wire, j, in the particular GC, i. Alice then sends all the pairs of δs to Bob. For each pair, Bob can only know one X value, that is, either $X_j^{0,i}$ or $X_j^{1,i}$, because of the hiding property of the OT. This means that Bob can compute exactly his choice of key, but not the other. This follows from the security of the free-XOR approach, along with the power of the random oracle for constructing $X_j^{0,i}$ and $X_j^{1,i}$, i.e. they work as one-time-pads for the keys. Thus, we get a linking between the modified OT extension and the GCs.

Finally, Alice also computes a digest of each of her outputs from the OT phase and sends these to Bob. That is, for each $i = 1, \dots, \ell'$ and each $j = 1, \dots, \tau$ she computes and sends $\chi_j^{0,i} = H(X_j^{0,i})$ along with $\chi_j^{1,i} = H(X_j^{1,i})$ to Bob.

After the cut-and-choose phase Bob will know the following bitstrings for each of his input wires in $\ell'/2$ of the GCs:

- Both the keys for the current input wire, i.e. k^0, $k^1 = k^0 \oplus \Delta$.
- Exactly one output of the OT phase, X^b, for his input bit, b, on the current wire.
- Both the difference bitstrings for the current input wire, i.e. δ^0 and δ^1.
- A digest for both the possible outcomes of the OT phase, i.e. $\chi^0 = H(X^0)$, $\chi^1 = H(X^1)$.

To verify that δ^0 and δ^1 are correct he computes

$$\delta'^b = k^b \oplus X^b, \quad X'^{\neg b} = \delta^b \oplus \delta^{\neg b} \oplus \Delta, \quad \chi^{\neg b} = H(X'^{\neg b}).$$

He accepts if and only if $\delta'^b = \delta^b$ and $\chi'^{\neg b} = \chi^{\neg b}$. The intuition of why the check on $\chi'^{\neg b}$ is sufficient for the key $k^{\neg b}$ is as follows: If $\delta^{\neg b}$ is incorrect then $X'^{\neg b} \neq X^{\neg b}$, in which case, with overwhelming probability, $H(X'^{\neg b}) \neq H(X^{\neg b})$. Now, since Alice does not know which $\ell'/2$ GCs Bob will pick as check circuits, she cannot guess in which of the δ bitstrings she can cheat without being detected. Furthermore, as Bob can check both δ^0 and δ^1, she does not learn anything about his input choices either. In conclusion this little trick prevents a selective failure attack from the constructor.

Parallel Complexity. First see that many of the computationally heavy calculations in the protocol are hashes. Next, notice that these hashes are of "small" bitstrings, bounded by $O(\kappa)$. Now by our approach to parallelization of the garbling and degarbling process we notice that the complexity becomes bounded by the length of the input to the KDF and the depth of the circuit to securely compute. Thus, assuming access to enough parallel processors the garbling and degarbling time will be bounded by $O(\kappa \cdot d)$ where d is the depth of the circuit to garble.

Regarding the modified OT extension notice that all the hashes to be computed in a given step of the modified OT extension can be done independently of each other, and thus in parallel. Looking at these steps from each party's point of view, we see that Step 4 is the step requiring the most computations for Bob. Assume w.l.o.g. that $\tau > \kappa$ then if Bob has access to $p \leq \left\lceil \frac{8}{3}\kappa \right\rceil \cdot \tau$ processors the amount of bits he needs to hash sequentially in the SIMD parallel model is $O(\tau \cdot \kappa^2/p)$. If he has access to more processors then the amount of bits to hash sequentially is only $O(\kappa)$. For Alice the greatest amount of hashes are computed in Step 15. If she has access to $p \leq \tau$ processors then the amount of bits she needs to hash sequentially in said model is $O(\tau \cdot \kappa/p)$. If she has access to more processors, then the amount of bits to hash is only $O(\kappa)$. In conclusion, the overall parallel computational complexity of the protocol is $O(\kappa \cdot d)$, not including the seed OTs.

Finally, note that the communication complexity needed for this protocol is asymptotically the same as for the OT extension described in [18], that is $O(\kappa \cdot (\kappa + \tau)) = O(\kappa \cdot (\kappa + \ell \cdot \tau))$ bits, both for Alice, Bob and in total.

5   Implementation

We now describe how we constructed our implementation in CUDA in order to achieve high efficiency, based on the knowledge of the device hardware and scheduling. It should be noted that we use SHA-1 with 160 bits digest and 512 bits blocks as our hash function.

Garbling. First, notice that we will have a case of SIMD for every circuit in ℓ'. Thus, it is obvious to have each thread in a warp processing a distinct circuit and thus having the blocks be 1-dimensional, consisting of a constant amount of warps. This structure will give us both high block occupancy, and no more than ℓ' threads in each block. We chose to have blocks consist of 32 threads since preliminary tests showed this to be a good choice.

Next we notice that all gates within a single layer can be computed in arbitrary order, thus it is obvious to have one grid dimension be the amount of gates in each layer. Furthermore, as we cannot know which order the blocks will be computed in, we will need to have an iteration of kernel launches, one launch for each layer in the circuit, in order to have the output keys of the previous layer computed and ready for computing the next layer.

Regarding memory management, we first copy the seeds onto the device, and then compute the global keys for all the circuits and the 0 keys for all the input wires in all the circuits, using a unique seed for each circuit. This is done by hashing the seed along with a unique ID in order to get a "random" key (remember we assume the ROM). Afterwards, using the generated keys, we initiate a loop of kernel launches in order to compute each layer of keys and garbled computation table entries in each circuit. Between all these launches, all the currently computed keys, along with the global keys, remain in the global memory of the device so they can be used by the next kernels. Furthermore, we keep all the currently computed garbled computation tables on the device so that all the results can be copied to the host as a batch after all the kernels have finished. In order to save memory we only store the 0-key for each wire, since the 1-key can be efficient computed by simply XORing it with the appropriate global key for a given circuit.

Finally notice that the structure of the kernel for degarbling is the same as for garbling. The only difference is that before the initial launch the garbled computation table for the whole circuit is copied from the host into the global memory along with the initial input keys, one key for each of the 2τ input wires, and a description of the circuit.

Memory Coalescing. We memory coalesced all the data we used, both in the global memory and in the shared memory. As both keys and garbled computation table entries consists of 160 bits (the digest size of SHA-1), i.e. five 32-bit words, we stored all data in *segments* of $32 \cdot 5 = 160$ words. The first entry is the first word of thread 1, the second entry is the first word of thread 2, and so on up to entry 33, which then contains the second word of thread 1, entry 34 contains the second word of thread 2 and so on. Thus, all data access is coalesced in a multiple of the warp size.

The Modified OT Extension. Unlike the generation and evaluation of the GCs, the modified OT extension involves many phases, several of which are depended on the previous phases and results from interacting with the other party. This means that we cannot have a single kernel, or even a single kernel function, in order to complete all the steps of the protocol for each party.

Like we did for the GCs we have coalesced all memory in blocks of 32 words. We also make segments, which consists of $5 \cdot 32 = 160$ words, such that each segment hold a coalesced hash values or a small κ bit data array, for 32 threads. For this reason we again construct kernels to use blocks of 32 threads.

Using this choice, no coalescence conversion needs to be done to use the data from the modified OT extension with our implementation of GCs. Furthermore, this choice will still keep an efficient and scalable organisation of the memory. Also, as all the data we use for computations here is completely independent, we get the possibility of only launching a single kernel for each step of the protocol in order to avoid kernel launch overhead, resulting from the iterative launching of kernels.

The kernels needed in Step 4 and 5, and Step 14 and 15, are almost the same so we only include a description of Step 4 and 5.

Step 4 and 5. Step 4, involves hashing $2 \cdot \lceil \frac{8}{3} \kappa \rceil$ seeds τ/κ times. In order to avoid redundant data copying of L_i^0 and L_i^1 to the device when we need to construct λ_i, we compute parts of all the three vectors, L_i^0, L_i^1 and λ_i, in each thread. That is, we include Step 6 in the kernel. To save memory usage and bandwidth we let all the 32 threads of a single block use the same pair of seeds, thus we make each thread in a block compute 160 bits of each of the three vectors L_i^0, L_i^1 and λ_i for the same i. Next, one dimension of the grid is responsible for computing all τ bits of the three vectors, L_i^0, L_i^1 and λ_i, and thus contains $\lceil \frac{\tau}{32 \cdot \kappa} \rceil$ threads. The other dimension of the grid is responsible for doing this for each of the $\lceil \frac{8}{3} \kappa \rceil$ vectors that need to be computed. Step 5 proceeds in the same manner, except each block only uses a single seed and each thread only computes a single digest.

6   Experimental Results and Conclusions

For benchmarking our implementation we used the circuit for oblivious 128-bit AES encryption. This circuit is used as benchmark in many previous works including [6,7,15,18]. What makes this circuit a good benchmark is its relatively random structure, its relatively large size, along with its interesting usage for oblivious encryption.

To get the most diverse results we ran our experiments with several different statistical security parameters from 2^{-9} to 2^{-119}. We ran the experiments on two consumer grade desktop computers connected directly by a cross-over cable. At the time of writing each of these machines had a purchase price of less than \$1600.

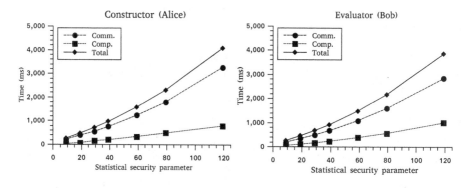

Fig. 1. Timings in milliseconds for both Alice and Bob under different statistical security parameters when computing oblivious 128 bit AES

Table 1. Timing comparison of secure two party computation protocols evaluating oblivious 128 bit AES. d is the depth of the circuit to be computed.

	Security	ℓ	Model	Rounds	Time (s)	Equipment
[7]	Semi honest	-	ROM	$O(1)$	0.20	Desktop
This work	Malicious	2^{-9}	ROM	$O(1)$	0.30	Desktop w. GPU
This work	Malicious	2^{-29}	ROM	$O(1)$	0.83	Desktop w. GPU
[12]	Malicious	2^{-80}	SM	$O(1)$	1.4	Cluster, 512 nodes
[18]	Malicious	2^{-58}	ROM	$O(d)$	1.6	Desktop
This work	Malicious	2^{-59}	ROM	$O(1)$	1.8	Desktop w. GPU
This work	Malicious	2^{-79}	ROM	$O(1)$	2.7	Desktop w. GPU
[12]	Malicious	2^{-80}	SM	$O(1)$	115	Cluster, 1 node

Both machines had similar specifications: an Intel Ivy Bridge i7 3.5 GHz quad-core processor, 8 GB DDR3 RAM, an Intel series-520 180 GB SSD drive, an MSI Z77 motherboard with gigabit LAN and an MSI GPU with an NVIDIA GTX 670 chip and 2 GB GDDR5 RAM. The machines ran the latest version (at the time) of Linux Mint with all updates installed. The experiments were repeated 30 times each and no front end applications were running on either of the machines. These results are summarized in Table. 2 and visualized in Fig. 1. These timings include every aspect of the protocol including loading circuit description and randomness along with communication between the host and device and communication between the parties. However, in the same manner as done in [18] the timing of seed OTs have not been included as this is a computation that practically only is needed once between two parties and thus will get amortized out in a practical context. From these timings we see that the bottleneck of the protocol is the communication complexity. This becomes increasingly obvious the higher the statistical security parameter is.

We believe that our protocol approach along with the implementation yield the best practical results for maliciously secure two-party computation. This is so since the faster timings of [12] is achieved using a large grid with an estimated purchase price of at least \$129,168 per party[4] which might not be feasible in the majority of use cases. It should further be noted that their only timings are for statistical security 2^{-80} and that we do not expect a lower security parameter to yield a significant increase in speed due to their approach in parallelization which uses one core per garbled circuit. I.e. they would not be able to utilize more than 28 or 94 cores per player if using statistical security 2^{-9} respectively 2^{-29}. Thus using a less conservative statistical security parameter it seems highly plausible that our protocol implementation will match the pricey grid computer implementation of [12].

Next notice that the approach of [18] achieves a slightly faster result for a conservative statistical security parameter. However, their round complexity is asymptotically greater than ours which could yield performance issues if the protocol were to be executed on the Internet since several packet transmission

---

[4] Price estimate of a Sun Blade X3-2B with 256 nodes.

Table 2. Timing in milliseconds when computing oblivious 128 bit AES under different statistical security parameters. Communication is on LAN using a cross-over cable.

ℓ	9		19		59	
	Alice	Bob	Alice	Bob	Alice	Bob
IO	4.29 ±	4.83 ±	4.56 ±	5.10 ±	5.75 ±	6.35 ±
	0.0370	0.357	0.0290	0.477	0.00432	0.573
OT (total)	37.1 ±	24.4 ±	39.0 ±	24.6 ±	42.9 ±	24.2 ±
	8.48	5.86	9.33	6.01	9.27	5.61
OT (comm.)	31.5 ±	17.3 ±	32.6 ±	17.4 ±	32.8 ±	15.9 ±
	8.47	5.92	9.32	5.92	9.29	5.66
OT (comp.)	5.55 ±	7.05 ±	6.40 ±	7.18 ±	10.1 ±	8.35 ±
	0.154	0.408	0.0468	0.383	0.371	0.317
GC (total.)	230 ±	235 ±	441 ±	434 ±	1543 ±	1466 ±
	0.844	6.10	1.44	6.14	5.81	7.36
GC (comm.)	194 ±	182 ±	366 ±	327 ±	1207 ±	1080 ±
	0.704	6.06	2.52	6.06	3.25	6.76
GC (comp.)	35.7 ±	53.2 ±	75.1 ±	107 ±	336 ±	386 ±
	0.376	0.626	2.36	0.732	3.45	3.32
Total	271 ±	265 ±	484 ±	464 ±	1591 ±	1497 ±
	8.38	8.27	9.55	9.62	10.9	9.81
(execution)	300		539		1833	

must be initialized several times during the execution. Furthermore, their timings are based on amortization of 54 instances (or 27 if one is happy with statistical security 2^{-55}). Finally, by an artifact of their approach choosing a lower security parameter will not give significant performance improvements. In particular, a factor 2 in execution time seems to be the absolute maximal time improvement possible by an arbitrary reduction of the statistical security.

In conclusion, we have showed that the construction of a parallel protocol for 2PC in the SIMD parallel model with implementation on the GPU can yield very positive results.

Acknowledgment. The authors would like to thank Benny Pinkas, Thomas Schneider, Nigel P. Smart and Stephen C. Williams for supplying the base circuit which we augmented for our implementation and Roberto Trifiletti for supplying the code we used for circuit parsing.

References

1. Beaver, D.: Correlated pseudorandomness and the complexity of private computations. In: STOC 1996, pp. 479–488. ACM (1996)
2. Bogetoft, P., et al.: Secure multiparty computation goes live. In: Dingledine, R., Golle, P. (eds.) FC 2009. LNCS, vol. 5628, pp. 325–343. Springer, Heidelberg (2009)
3. Nvidia Corporation. NVIDIA CUDA C Programming Best Practices Guide. Technical report (2012)

4. Goldreich, O., Micali, S., Wigderson, A.: How to play any mental game or a completeness theorem for protocols with honest majority. In: STOC 1987, pp. 218–229. ACM (1987)
5. Goyal, V., Mohassel, P., Smith, A.: Efficient two party and multi party computation against covert adversaries. In: Smart, N.P. (ed.) EUROCRYPT 2008. LNCS, vol. 4965, pp. 289–306. Springer, Heidelberg (2008)
6. Henecka, W., Kögl, S., Sadeghi, A.-R., Schneider, T., Wehrenberg, I.: Tasty: tool for automating secure two-party computations. In: ACM Conference on Computer and Communications Security, pp. 451–462. ACM (2010)
7. Huang, Y., Evans, D., Katz, J., Malka, L.: Faster secure two-party computation using garbled circuits. In: USENIX Security Symposium (2011)
8. Ishai, Y., Kilian, J., Nissim, K., Petrank, E.: Extending oblivious transfers efficiently. In: Boneh, D. (ed.) CRYPTO 2003. LNCS, vol. 2729, pp. 145–161. Springer, Heidelberg (2003)
9. Ishai, Y., Prabhakaran, M., Sahai, A.: Founding cryptography on oblivious transfer – efficiently. In: Wagner, D. (ed.) CRYPTO 2008. LNCS, vol. 5157, pp. 572–591. Springer, Heidelberg (2008)
10. Kolesnikov, V., Sadeghi, A.-R., Schneider, T.: From dust to dawn: Practically efficient two-party secure function evaluation protocols and their modular design. Cryptology ePrint Archive, Report 2010/079 (2010), http://eprint.iacr.org/
11. Kolesnikov, V., Schneider, T.: Improved garbled circuit: Free XOR gates and applications. In: Aceto, L., Damgård, I., Goldberg, L.A., Halldórsson, M.M., Ingólfsdóttir, A., Walukiewicz, I. (eds.) ICALP 2008, Part II. LNCS, vol. 5126, pp. 486–498. Springer, Heidelberg (2008)
12. Kreuter, B., Shelat, A., Shen, C.-H.: Billion-gate secure computation with malicious adversaries. In: 21th USENIX Conference on Security Symposium, p. 14. USENIX (2012)
13. Lindell, Y., Pinkas, B.: An efficient protocol for secure two-party computation in the presence of malicious adversaries. In: Naor, M. (ed.) EUROCRYPT 2007. LNCS, vol. 4515, pp. 52–78. Springer, Heidelberg (2007)
14. Lindell, Y., Pinkas, B.: A proof of security of yao's protocol for two-party computation. J. Cryptology 22(2), 161–188 (2009)
15. Lindell, Y., Pinkas, B.: Secure two-party computation via cut-and-choose oblivious transfer. In: Ishai, Y. (ed.) TCC 2011. LNCS, vol. 6597, pp. 329–346. Springer, Heidelberg (2011)
16. Mansour, Y., Nisan, N., Tiwari, P.: The computational complexity of universal hashing. In: Structure in Complexity Theory Conference, p. 90. IEEE (1990)
17. Naor, M., Pinkas, B., Sumner, R.: Privacy preserving auctions and mechanism design. In: ACM Conference on Electronic Commerce, pp. 129–139. ACM (1999)
18. Nielsen, J.B., Nordholt, P.S., Orlandi, C., Burra, S.S.: A new approach to practical active-secure two-party computation. In: Safavi-Naini, R. (ed.) CRYPTO 2012. LNCS, vol. 7417, pp. 681–700. Springer, Heidelberg (2012)
19. Nielsen, J.B., Orlandi, C.: LEGO for two-party secure computation. In: Reingold, O. (ed.) TCC 2009. LNCS, vol. 5444, pp. 368–386. Springer, Heidelberg (2009)
20. Nishikawa, N., Iwai, K., Kurokawa, T.: High-performance symmetric block ciphers on multicore CPU and GPUs. International Journal of Networking and Computing 2(2) (2012)
21. Pinkas, B., Schneider, T., Smart, N.P., Williams, S.C.: Secure two-party computation is practical. In: Matsui, M. (ed.) ASIACRYPT 2009. LNCS, vol. 5912, pp. 250–267. Springer, Heidelberg (2009)

22. Pu, S., Duan, P., Liu, J.-C.: Fastplay-a parallelization model and implementation of SMC on cuda based GPU cluster architecture. IACR Cryptology ePrint Archive, 2011:97 (2011)
23. Shelat, A., Shen, C.-H.: Two-Output Secure Computation with Malicious Adversaries. In: Paterson, K.G. (ed.) EUROCRYPT 2011. LNCS, vol. 6632, pp. 386–405. Springer, Heidelberg (2011)
24. Xu, L., Lin, D., Zou, J.: ECDLP on GPU. IACR Cryptology ePrint Archive, 2011:146 (2011)
25. Yao, A.C.: Protocols for secure computations. In: FOCS 1982, pp. 160–164. IEEE (1982)

Comparing the Pairing Efficiency over Composite-Order and Prime-Order Elliptic Curves [*]

Aurore Guillevic[1,2]

[1] Laboratoire Chiffre – Thales Communications and Security
4 avenue des Louvresses – 92622 Gennevilliers Cedex – France
[2] Crypto Team – DI – École Normale Supérieure
45 rue d'Ulm – 75230 Paris Cedex 05 – France
aurore.guillevic@ens.fr

Abstract. We provide software implementation timings for pairings over composite-order and prime-order elliptic curves. Composite orders must be large enough to be infeasible to factor. In the literature, protocols use orders which are product of 2 up to 5 large prime numbers. Our contribution is three-fold. First, we extend the results of Lenstra concerning the RSA modulus sizes to multi-prime modulus, for various security levels. We then implement a Tate pairing over a composite order supersingular curve and an optimal ate pairing over a prime-order Barreto-Naehrig curve, both at the 128-bit security level. Thirdly we use our implementation timings to deduce the total cost of the homomorphic encryption scheme of Boneh, Goh and Nissim and its translation by Freeman in the prime-order setting. We also compare the efficiency of the unbounded Hierarchical Identity Based Encryption protocol of Lewko and Waters and its translation by Lewko in the prime order setting. Our results strengthen the previously observed inefficiency of composite-order bilinear groups and advocate the use of prime-order group whenever possible in protocol design.

Keywords: Tate pairing, optimal ate pairing, software implementation, composite-order group, supersingular elliptic curve, Barreto-Naehrig curve.

1 Introduction

Bilinear structures of composite-order groups provide new possibilities for cryptosystems. In 2005, Boneh, Goh and Nissim [7] introduced the first public-key homomorphic encryption scheme using composite-order groups equipped with a pairing. The scheme permits several homomorphic additions and one multiplication on few bits. The security relies on the subgroup decision assumption. They applied this tool to on-line voting and universally verifiable computation. Decryption time grows exponentially w. r. t. the input size so this approach

---

[*] Full version is available on ePrint, report 2013/218.

M. Jacobson et al. (Eds.): ACNS 2013, LNCS 7954, pp. 357–372, 2013.

for homomorphic encryption is not yet very practical for large data but the idea was developed for other interests. In the last seven years, many cryptographic schemes were built using composite-order groups. In 2005, a Hierarchical Identity Based Encryption (HIBE) was proposed by Boneh, Boyen and Goh [6]. It relies on the ℓ-bilinear Diffie-Hellman exponent assumption. In 2009, Waters introduced the Dual System Encryption method [25], resulting in very interesting properties for security proofs. In 2011, Lewko and Waters published a HIBE relying on the subgroup decision assumption. HIBE has become very practical in the sense that the maximal hierarchy depth is not static i.e. can be augmented without resetting all the system parameters.

The subgroup decision assumption is that given a group G of composite order $p_1 p_2 = N$ (e.g. an RSA modulus), it is hard do decide whether a given element $g \in G$ is in the subgroup of order p_1 without knowing p_1 and p_2. N must be infeasible to factor to achieve this hardness. This results in very large parameter sizes, e.g. $\log_2 N = 3072$ or 3248 for a 128-bit security level, according to NIST or ECRYPT II recommendations. Moreover, the pairing computation is much slower in this setting but exact performances were not given yet. To reduce the parameter sizes, Freeman [11] proposed to use a copy of the (e.g. 256-bit) same prime-order group instead of a group whose order (of e.g. 3072 bits) has two or more distinct primes. His paper provides conversions of protocols and in particular of the BGN scheme, from the composite-order to the prime-order setting. Then Lewko at Eurocrypt 2012 [19] provided a generic conversion. These conversions achieve much smaller parameter sizes but have a drawback: they need not only one but several pairings. More precisely, Lewko's conversion for the HIBE scheme needs at least $2n$ pairings over a prime order group (of e.g. 256-bit) instead of one pairing over a n-prime composite order group (of e.g. 3072-bit).

The translated protocols remain interesting because it is commonly assumed that a pairing is much slower over a composite-order than over a prime-order elliptic curve. An overhead factor around 50 (at an estimate attributed to Scott) was given in [11, §1] for a 80-bit security level. A detailed and precise comparison would be interesting and useful to protocol designers and application developers.

The Number Field Sieve (NFS) algorithm is the fastest method to factor a two-prime modulus. Lenstra studied carefully its complexity and made recommendations. Lenstra stated that at a 128-bit security level, an RSA modulus can have no more than 3 prime factors of the same size, 4 factors at a 192-bit level and 5 at a 256-bit level [17, §4]. We complete his work to obtain the modulus sizes with more than two prime factors, at these three security levels. We then find supersingular elliptic curves of such orders and benchmark a Tate paring over these curves. We also implemented an optimal ate pairing over a prime-order Barreto-Naehrig curve, considered as the fastest pairing (at least in software). With these timings, we are able to estimate the total cost of the protocols in composite-order and prime-order settings. We then compare the BGN protocol [7] in the two settings and do the same for the unbounded HIBE protocol of Lewko and Waters [20] and its translation [19, §B].

Organization of the Paper. Section 2 presents our results on the modulus sizes with more than two prime factors, at the 128, 192 and 256-bit security level. In Sec. 3, we present the possibilities to construct pairing-friendly elliptic curves of composite order and our choice for the implementation. We develop a theoretical estimation of each pairing in Sec. 4. Our implementation results are presented in Sec. 5.

2   Parameter Sizes

In this section, we extend Lenstra's estimates [17] to RSA modulus sizes with up to 8 prime factors. We present in Tab. 1 the usual key length recommendations from http://www.keylength.com. The NIST recommendations are the less conservative ones. A modulus of length 3072 is recommended to achieve a security level equivalent to a 128 bit symmetric key. The ECRYPT II recommendations are comparable: 3248 bit modulus are suggested.

Table 1. Cryptographic key length recommendations, January 2013. All key sizes are provided in bits. These are the minimal sizes for security.

Method	Date	Symmetric	Asymmetric	Discrete Log Key	Group	Elliptic curve	Hash function
Lenstra / Verheul	2076	129	6790–5888	230	6790	245	257
Lenstra Updated	2090	128	4440–6974	256	4440	256	256
ECRYPT II (EU)	2031–2040	128	3248	256	3248	256	256
NIST (US)	> 2030	128	3072	256	3072	256	256
FNISA (France)	> 2020	128	4096	200	4096	256	256
NSA (US)	–	128	–	–	–	256	256
RFC3766	–	128	3253	256	3253	242	–

We consider the Number Field Sieve attack (NFS, see e.g. [18] for an overview) whose complexity is given by [17, §3.1]:

$$L[N] = \exp(1.923(\log N)^{1/3}(\log \log N)^{2/3}) \text{ (NFS)} \tag{1}$$

and the Elliptic Curve Method (ECM) that depends on the modulus size and on the size of the smallest prime p_i in the modulus. This attack is less efficient for a modulus of only two prime factors but become competitive for more prime factors. We consider that all the prime factors p_i have the same size. The ECM complexity is [17, §4]

$$E[N, p_i] = (\log_2 N)^2 \exp(\sqrt{2}(\log p_i)^{1/2}(\log \log p_i)^{1/2}) \text{ (ECM)}. \tag{2}$$

It is assumed in [17, §3.1] that a k-bit RSA modulus offers the same *computational security* as a symmetric cryptosystem of d-bit security and speed comparable to singe DES if $L[2^k] = 50 \cdot 2^{d-56} \cdot L[2^{512}]$. The author argues that speed-up in symmetric implementation affects slightly the complexity thus is not taken into account. We used this formula to compute Tab. 2. These assumptions may be considered controversial, anyone can consider more conservative ones thus obtain slightly different results.

The first line in Tab. 2 appears in [17, Tab. 1]. The threshold between NFS and ECM is represented through bold font. We do not consider security levels under 128 bits. For a 128-bit security level, a modulus of 3224 bits with two prime factors (of 1612 bits) is enough to prevent the NFS attack and the attack with ECM is much slower. This attack becomes significantly more efficient than the NFS one against a modulus with 5 prime factors (each of the same size). A modulus of 4040 bits instead of 3224 bits must be considered. For 8 primes in the modulus, the size is almost doubled: 6344 bits instead of 3224 bits and each prime factor is 793-bit long. Table 2 could be used by protocol designers to set the size of the security parameter λ. Our Tab. 2 can also be used when setting the parameter sizes for protocols (or security proofs) relying on the Φ-hiding assumption. In 2010 at Crypto, Kiltz, O'Neill and Smith [15] used this assumption to obtain a nice result about RSA-OAEP. Then at Africacrypt in 2011, Herrmann [13] explained new results about the security of this assumption. We emphasize that setting the security parameter λ in protocols is not completely straightforward if the modulus contains more than 3 prime factors.

Table 2. RSA-Multi-Prime modulus size from 2 (see [17, Tab. 1]) up to 8 prime factors

Equiv.	AES-128				AES-192				AES-256			
Nb of	min		max		min		max		min		max	
primes	$\log p_i$	$\log N$	$\log p_i$	$\log N$	$\log p_i$	$\log N$	$\log p_i$	$\log N$	$\log p_i$	$\log N$	$\log p_i$	$\log N$
2	1322	2644	1612	3224	3449	6898	3959	7918	6920	13840	7694	15388
3	882	2646	1075	3225	2299	6897	2640	7920	4614	13842	5129	15387
4	694	**2776**	815	**3260**	1725	6900	1980	7920	3460	13840	3847	15388
5	687	**3435**	808	**4040**	1484	**7420**	1654	**8270**	2768	13840	3078	15390
6	682	**4092**	802	**4812**	1476	**8856**	1646	**9876**	2544	**15264**	2760	**16560**
7	677	**4739**	797	**5579**	1470	**10290**	1639	**11473**	2535	**17745**	2752	**19264**
8	673	**5384**	793	**6344**	1464	**11712**	1633	**13064**	2528	**20224**	2744	**21952**

3   Composite-Order Elliptic Curves

For a detailed introduction to pairings, see e.g. [14, Ch. IX]. Let E be an elliptic curve defined over a prime field $\mathbb{F}_p$. A pairing is a bilinear, non-degenerate and efficient map $e : G_1 \times G_2 \to G_T$. From an algebraic point of view, G_1 and G_2 are two *necessarily distinct* subgroups of $E(\overline{\mathbb{F}_p})$, of same order n. If $n \mid \#E(\mathbb{F}_p)$ then $G_1 \subset E(\mathbb{F}_p)$, this is the common setup. Let k be the smallest integer such that $n \mid p^k - 1$, k is the *embedding degree*. Then $G_2 \subset E(\mathbb{F}_{p^k})$ and $G_T \subset \mathbb{F}_{p^k}^*$. For supersingular or some of the $k = 1$ curves, an efficient isomorphism is available from G_1 into G_2. This gives a symmetric pairing and we can use the notation $G_1 = G_2$ to implicitly denote the use of the isomorphism in the pairing computation. In the remaining of this section, we will use the algebraic interpretation of G_1 and G_2. In other words, we will assume that they are two distinct subgroups of E, of same order n. The target group G_T is the order-n (multiplicative) subgroup of $\mathbb{F}_{p^k}^*$. G_1 and G_2 have to be strong enough against a generic attack to a discrete logarithm problem. The third group G_T is more vulnerable because computing a discrete logarithm in a finite field is easier with the index calculus attack. Its size has to be enlarged.

Finding optimal pairing-friendly elliptic curves is an active field of research (see the survey [10]). At a 128-bit security level, the optimal choice would be to construct an elliptic curve whose order is a prime of 256 bits and over a prime finite field of the same size. For an embedding degree $k = 12$, an element in the third group is 3072 bit long in order to match the NIST recommendations. Such optimal pairing-friendly curves exist [3] (Barreto-Naehrig (BN) curves), but have a special form: the parameters p (defining the finite field), n (elliptic curve order) and t (trace) are given by degree 4 polynomials. We have $p(x) = 36x^4 + 36x^3 + 24x^2 + 6x + 1$, $n(x) = 36x^4 + 36x^3 + 18x^2 + 6x + 1$ and $t(x) = 6x^2 + 1$.

3.1   Issues in Composite-Order Elliptic Curve Generation

For our particular purpose, the pairing-friendly elliptic curve order has to contain a composite-order modulus N. Hence the order is chosen *before* the other curve parameters and no special form can be imposed to N. For example, finding such an elliptic curve over a non-prime field (e.g. in characteristic 2 or 3) is completely infeasible at the moment. As for BN curves, all the complete pairing-friendly elliptic curve families in the survey [10], defined by polynomials, are not convenient.

Secondly, the parameter sizes of composite-order elliptic curves are not optimal. The curve order should be hN with h a cofactor as small as possible. Due to the Hasse bound, the size of p (defining $\mathbb{F}_p$) is the same as the size of hN. This means that the prime field $\mathbb{F}_p$ already achieves the recommended size (say, 3072) to avoid an index calculus attack. Consequently, an embedding degree $k = 1$ is enough. As G_1 and G_2 are distinct, an embedding degree of 1 means that both G_1 and G_2 are subgroups of $E(\mathbb{F}_p)$, then $N^2 \mid E(\mathbb{F}_p)$ and $\log_2 p \geqslant 2\log_2 N$. This mean that for a 3072 bit modulus N, p will have more than 6144 bits. Such curves exist, for example see [16, §6] or more recently [8]. The elliptic curve point coordinates are more than 6144 bit long.

Tate pairing computation is described in Alg. 2. It consists in a Miller loop over the considered elliptic curve group order. A final exponentiation in $\mathbb{F}_{p^k}^*$ at the end is performed to obtain a unique pairing value. Optimal ate pairing computation on a BN curve is detailed in Alg. 1. Convenient supersingular curves do not benefit from pairing optimization such as η_T pairing, as the trace is zero (in large characteristic), or decomposition of the Miller loop length, as there is no efficiently computable endomorphism over $\mathbb{F}_p$ on such curves, except the scalar multiplication. For ordinary curves with $6 \mid k$ and $D = 3$ (BN curves) or $4 \mid k$ and $D = 1$, the complex multiplication induces an easy computable endomorphism thus permits to reduce the Miller loop length up to a factor 4.

Pairing computation over curves of embedding degree 2 needs multiplications over $\mathbb{F}_p$ and $\mathbb{F}_{p^2}$ with $\log_2 p = 1536$. Pairing computation over curves of embedding degree 1 needs multiplications over $\mathbb{F}_p$ with $\log_2 p = 3072$. Recently in [26] it was shown that self-pairings on these particular curves may be speed-up thanks to the distortion map. Zhao et. al. gave efficient formulas of Weil pairing with denominator elimination thanks to the distortion map, although $k = 1$ instead of $k = 2$. Such ordinary $k = 1$ curves with efficient endomorphisms are rare. Few constructions are proposed in [8]. More work is needed to determine in which cases pairings on these curves are competitive with $k = 2$ curves.

As mentioned in recent works, some properties (cancelling, projecting) are achieved with only composite-order elliptic curves or only asymmetric pairings. More precisely, at Asiacrypt 2012, Seo [23] presented results on the impossibility of projecting pairings in certain cases. An ordinary composite-order elliptic curve is the only choice in this case. Such constructions are possible, see e.g. Boneh, Rubin and Silverberg paper [8] but this seems to be the worst case in terms of parameter sizes and efficiency.

3.2   Our Choices

If we want to reduce the size of p (hence of G_1), we can choose a supersingular elliptic curve of embedding degree $k = 2$. This means that $G_1 \subset E(\mathbb{F}_p)$, $G_2 \not\subset E(\mathbb{F}_p)$ and both G_1 and G_2 are subgroups of $E(\mathbb{F}_{p^2})$.

$$G_1 \text{ and } G_2 \subset E(\mathbb{F}_{p^2}) \Big| N^2 \mid \#E(\mathbb{F}_{p^2})$$
$$\Big|$$
$$G_1 \subset E(\mathbb{F}_p) \Big| N \mid \#E(\mathbb{F}_p),\ N^2 \nmid \#E(\mathbb{F}_p)$$

A supersingular elliptic curve of given subgroup order and embedding degree 2 is easy to construct:

1. Let N be a composite-order modulus.
2. Find the smallest integer h, $4 \mid h$, such that $hN - 1$ is prime.
3. Let $p = hN - 1$. The elliptic curve $E(\mathbb{F}_p) : y^2 = x^3 - x$ is supersingular, of order $hN = p + 1$ and embedding degree 2.

As $p = 3 \mod 4$, -1 is not a square in $\mathbb{F}_p$. If $\mathbb{F}_{p^2} = \mathbb{F}_p[Z]/(Z^2 + 1)$, a distortion map is available: $\phi : E(\mathbb{F}_{p^2}) \to E(\mathbb{F}_{p^2})$, $(x, y) \mapsto (-x, Zy)$. In particular, $\phi(G_1) = G_2$ and the pairing is symmetric. As mentioned above, the improved pairing variant denoted η_T is not possible as this supersingular curve has trace 0 ($\#E(\mathbb{F}_p) = p + 1$). We implemented a Tate pairing on this curve. The parameter sizes for a security level equivalent to AES-128 are summarized in Tab. 3. We assume that the points on the elliptic curves are in compressed representation.

4   Theoretical Estimation

In this section we will estimate the number of multiplications over the base field for each pairing in Tab. 3.

Table 3. Parameter sizes for prime order and composite order pairing-friendly elliptic curves, minimum and maximum in theory, according to Tab. 2

Elliptic curve, order		size of G_1 order $\log_2 N$ min – max	size of elts in G_1 $\log_2 p$ min – max	emb. deg. k	size of elts in G_2	size of elts in G_T $k\log_2 p$ min – max
BN, prime order		256	256 – 269	12	512 – 538	3072 – 3224
supersingular curve / Composite order	Prime order	256	1322 – 1612	2	As for elts in G_1	2644 – 3224
	2 primes	2644 – 3224	$\geqslant 2646$ – $\geqslant 3226$			$\geqslant 5292$ – $\geqslant 6452$
	3 primes	2646 – 3225	$\geqslant 2648$ – $\geqslant 3227$			$\geqslant 5296$ – $\geqslant 6454$
	4 primes	2776 – 3260	$\geqslant 2778$ – $\geqslant 3262$			$\geqslant 5556$ – $\geqslant 6524$
	5 primes	3435 – 4040	$\geqslant 3437$ – $\geqslant 4042$			$\geqslant 6874$ – $\geqslant 8084$
	6 primes	4092 – 4812	$\geqslant 4094$ – $\geqslant 4814$			$\geqslant 8188$ – $\geqslant 9628$
	7 primes	4739 – 5579	$\geqslant 4741$ – $\geqslant 5581$			$\geqslant 9482$ – $\geqslant 11162$
	8 primes	5384 – 6344	$\geqslant 5386$ – $\geqslant 6346$			$\geqslant 10772$ – $\geqslant 12692$

4.1 Prime Order BN Curve

We aim to implement a state of the art optimal ate pairing on a BN curve. We use various techniques described e.g. in [21,5]. A careful operation count is detailed in Alg. 1 since it may be of independent interest. We use the finite field arithmetic described in [9] and [12] for speeding up the pairing final exponentiation and exponentiations in G_T. Operation counts in Tab. 4 describe our choices according to recommendations made in [9]. The arithmetic operations in $\mathbb{F}_p$ are denoted M_p for a multiplication, S_p for a square, I_p for an inversion and HW denotes the Hamming weight. We build the extensions as $\mathbb{F}_{p^2} = \mathbb{F}_p[X]/(X^2 - \alpha)$, $\mathbb{F}_{p^6} = \mathbb{F}_{p^2}[Y]/(Y^3 - \beta)$, $\mathbb{F}_{p^{12}} = \mathbb{F}_{p^6}[Z]/(Z^2 - \gamma)$. M_α, M_β and M_γ denote resp. a multiplication by α, β and γ, performed with few additions if α, β and γ are well chosen. For exponentiation in $\mathbb{F}_{p^k}$, $S_{\Phi_6(p^2)}$ denotes the improved squaring formula from [12]. Details are provided in Alg. 1 which computes $e_{\text{OptAte}}(P, \psi_6(Q)) = f^{\frac{p^{12}-1}{r}}$ with $f = f_{6x+2,\psi_6(Q)}(P) \cdot \ell_{[6x+2]\psi_6(Q),\pi_p(\psi_6(Q))}(P) \cdot \ell_{[6x+2]\psi_6(Q)+\pi_p(\psi_6(Q)),-\pi_p^2(\psi_6(Q))}(P)$ with ψ_6 the sextic twist map, π_p the p-power Frobenius and π_{p^2} the p^2-power Frobenius.

Table 4. Approximation of arithmetic operations in finite field extensions

$M_{p^{12}} = 3M_{p^6} + 5A_{p^6} + 1M_\gamma$	$\to 54M_p$	$S_{p^{12}} = 2M_{p^6} + 4A_{p^6} + 2M_\gamma$	$\to 36M_p$
$M_{p^6} = 6M_{p^2} + 13A_{p^2} + 2M_\beta$	$\to 18M_p$	$S_{p^6} = 2M_{p^2} + 3S_{p^2} + 10A_{p^2} + 2M_\beta$	$\to 12M_p$
$M_{p^2} = 3M_p + 5A_p + 1M_\alpha$	$\to 3M_p$	$S_{p^2} = 2M_p + 4A_p + 2M_\alpha$	$\to 2M_p$

4.2 Supersingular Curve

A Tate pairing may not benefit from the previous optimizations. We can still simplify the Miller loop thanks to the even embedding degree ($k = 2$). The denominators cancel in the final exponentiation thus we can remove them in the

---

Algorithm 1. Optimal ate pairing $e_{\text{OptAte}}(P, \psi_6(Q))^{\frac{p^{12}-1}{n}}$ on a BN curve

Input: $E(\mathbb{F}_p)$, $P(x_P, y_P) \in E(\mathbb{F}_p)[n]$, $Q(x_Q, y_Q) \in E'(\mathbb{F}_{p^2})[n]$, t, x
Output: $e_{\text{OptAte}}(P, \psi_6(Q)) \in \boldsymbol{\mu}_n \subset \mathbb{F}_{p^{12}}^*$

1   $R(X_R : Y_R : Z_R) \leftarrow (x_Q : y_Q : 1)$; $f \leftarrow 1$; $s \leftarrow 6x + 2$
2   **for** $m \leftarrow \lfloor \log_2(s) \rfloor - 1, \ldots, 0$ **do**
3      $(R, \ell) \leftarrow g(R, P)$ $6M_{p^2} + 5S_{p^2} + 4M_p = 32M_p$
4      $f \leftarrow f^2 \cdot \ell$ $S_{p^{12}} + 13M_{p^2} = 36 + 39 = 75M_p$
5   **if** $s_m = 1$ **then**
6          $(R, \ell) \leftarrow h(R, Q, P)$ $10M_{p^2} + 3S_{p^2} + 4M_p = 40M_p$
7          $f \leftarrow f \cdot \ell$ $13M_{p^2} = 39M_p$

8   $Q_1 \leftarrow \pi_p(Q)$ $M_{p^2} = 3M_p$
9   $Q_2 \leftarrow \pi_{p^2}(Q)$ $2M_p$
10 $(R, \ell) \leftarrow h(R, Q_1, P)$ $6M_{p^2} + 5S_{p^2} + 4M_p = 32M_p$
11 $f \leftarrow f \cdot \ell$ $13M_{p^2} = 39M_p$
12 $(R, \ell) \leftarrow h(R, Q_2, P)$ $6M_{p^2} + 5S_{p^2} + 4M_p = 32M_p$
13 $f \leftarrow f \cdot \ell$ $13M_{p^2} = 39M_p$
                                1. 8 to 1. 13: $147M_p$
       Miller Loop: $147M_p + \log_2(6x + 2) \cdot 107M_p + \text{HW}(6x + 2) \cdot 79M_p$

14 $f \leftarrow f^{p^6-1}$ $3M_{p^6} + 2S_{p^6} + 10M_{p^2} + 3S_{p^2} + 2M_p + 2S_p + I_p = 118M_p + I_p$
15 $f \leftarrow f^{p^2+1}$ $10M_p + M_{p^{12}} = 64M_p$
16 **if** $x < 0$ **then**
17   $a \leftarrow f^{6|x|-5}$ $\log_2(6x + 5)S_{\Phi_6(p^2)} + \text{HW}(6x + 5)M_{p^{12}}$
18 **else** $(f^{p^6} = f^{-1})$
19   $a \leftarrow (f^{p^6})^{6x+5}$
20 $b \leftarrow a^p$ $5M_{p^2} = 15M_p$
21 $b \leftarrow ab$ $M_{p^{12}} = 54M_p$
22 Compute f^p, f^{p^2} and f^{p^3} $5M_{p^2} + 10M_p + 5M_{p^2} = 40M_p$
23 $c \leftarrow b \cdot (f^p)^2 \cdot f^{p^2}$ $S_{\Phi_6(p^2)} + 2M_{p^{12}} = 126M_p$
24 $c \leftarrow c^{6x^2+1}$ $\log_2(6x^2 + 1)S_{\Phi_6(p^2)} + \text{HW}(6x^2 + 1)M_{p^{12}}$
25 $f \leftarrow f^{p^3} \cdot c \cdot b \cdot (f^p \cdot f)^9 \cdot a \cdot f^4$ $7M_{p^{12}} + 5S_{\Phi_6(p^2)} = 468M_p$
           Exponentiation $f \leftarrow f^{(p^6-1)(p^2+1)(p^4-p^2+1)/n}$:
  $(885 + 18\log_2(6x + 5) + 54\text{HW}(6x + 5) + 18\log_2(6x^2 + 1) + 54\text{HW}(6x^2 + 1))M_p + I_p$
26 **return** f

---

computations. Details are provided in Alg. 2 with ψ_2 the distortion map from G_1 into G_2.

The algorithm for a supersingular elliptic curve of composite order is the same as Alg. 2. In addition, we take $n = N$ the modulus, hence $\log_2 n = 3072$ for example. By construction, the cofactor h will be as small as possible, resulting in very cheap final exponentiation, e.g. $\log_2 h = 12$. We detail in Tab. 5 the different estimations for a pairing computation.

Algorithm 2. Tate pairing $e_{\text{Tate}}(P, \psi_2(Q))^{\frac{p^2-1}{n}}$ on a supersingular curve

---

Input: $E(\mathbb{F}_p) : y^2 = x^3 + ax$, $P(x_P, y_P), Q(x_Q, y_Q) \in E(\mathbb{F}_p)[n]$, n
Output: $e_{Tate}(P, \psi_2(Q)) \in \mu_n \subset \mathbb{F}_{p^2}^*$

1 $R(X_R : Y_R : Z_R) \leftarrow (x_P : y_P : 1)$; $f \leftarrow 1$; for $m \leftarrow \lfloor \log_2(n) \rfloor - 1, \ldots, 0$ do
2    $(R, \ell) \leftarrow g(R, Q)$ $8M_p + 6S_p$
3    $f \leftarrow f^2 \cdot \ell$ $S_{p^2} + M_{p^2} = 5M_p$
4   if $n_m = 1$ then
5      $(R, \ell) \leftarrow h(R, P, Q)$ $11M_p + 3S_p$
6      $f \leftarrow f \cdot \ell$ $M_{p^2} = 3M_p$

          Miller loop: $\log_2 n \cdot (13M_p + 6S_p) + \text{HW}(n) \cdot (14M_p + 3S_p)$
7 $f \leftarrow f^{p-1}$ $2M_p + I_p$
8 $f \leftarrow f^{(p+1)/n} = f^h$ $\log_2 h\ S_{p^2} + \text{HW}(h)M_{p^2}$
9 **return** f Final exp.: $\log_2 h\ S_{p^2} + \text{HW}(h)M_{p^2} + 2M_p + I_p$

Table 5. Estimations for pairings on prime-order and composite-order elliptic curves, assuming that for a composite-order supersingular curve, $\log_2 N$ is as in Tab. 2, $\text{HW}(N) = \log_2 N/2$, $\log_2 h = 12$ and $\text{HW}(h) = 5$, and for a BN curve, $\log_2 n = \log_2 p = 256$, $\text{HW}(x) = 4, \text{HW}(6x + 5) = 10, \text{HW}(6x^2 + 1) = 33$.

Curve	Pairing	nb primes	Miller loop min – max	Final exp. ($+ I_p$) min – max
BN	opt. ate	1	$7204\ M_p$	$6669\ M_p$
supersingular (SsC)	Tate	1	$4224M_p + 1728S_p$	$3730M_p - 4745M_p$
		2	$52880M_p + 19830S_p - 64480M_p + 24180S_p$	
		3	$52920M_p + 19845S_p - 64500M_p + 24187S_p$	
		4	$55520M_p + 20820S_p - 65200M_p + 24450S_p$	
		5	$68700M_p + 25762S_p - 80800M_p + 30300S_p$	$41M_p + I_p$
		6	$81840M_p + 30690S_p - 96240M_p + 36090S_p$	
		7	$94780M_p + 35542S_p - 111580M_p + 41842S_p$	
		8	$107680M_p + 40380S_p - 126880M_p + 47580S_p$	

5   Implementation Results

We implemented in C the above pairings (Tab. 3), we compiled with gcc 4.4.3 and ran the software implementation on a 2.6 GHz Intel Celeron 64 bits PC with 1 GB RAM and Ubuntu 10.04.4 LTS OS. The developed code is part of a proprietary library, the LibCryptoLCH developed at Thales Communications & Security (France). The finite field arithmetic uses the Montgomery representation and the modular multiplication is written in x86-64 assembly language. Our timings are competitive compared to others proprietary generic libraries such as the one used at Microsoft Research [1]. The Authors in [1] develop a C library then add different optimized assembly part of code for x86 or ARMv7 processors. They run their library on a x86-64, Intel Core2 E6600 @ 2.4 GHz, Windows 7 (64-bit) and on a ARM, dual-core Cortex A9 @ 1GHz, Windows device. They obtain a pairing on average at 55.19 ms (ARM) and 6.31 ms (x86-64) in projective coordinates and 51.01 ms (ARM) and 5.92 ms (x86-64) in affine coordinates, over a BN curve of 254 bit prime order group. Our timings are slightly slower than other state-of-the-art ones can be ([21,2]) because our software is not optimized for a particular sparse prime number which might result in very specific and optimized modular reduction.

Results are presented in Fig. 1. We did not plot our timings on a BN curve as the spots would be on the x axis because of the scale. We present in Tab. 6 our results for a BN curve, a prime-order and a composite two-prime order supersingular curve. The first line shows our results of an implementation of an optimal ate pairing on a Barreto-Naehrig curve, see for example [24,5,21] on how to implement it efficiently. We choose a quite sparse but still random parameter $x = $ 0x580000000000100d resulting in quite sparse prime order and prime field. Our modular reduction is not optimized for this value. Our extension field is optimized for towers built with binomials with small coefficients. For instance the first extension is built as $\mathbb{F}_{p^2} \simeq \mathbb{F}_p[X]/(X^2+1)$ as $p \equiv 3 \mod 4$ which allows a fast reduction $\mod X^2+1$ in the Karatsuba multiplication. The second extension is built as $\mathbb{F}_{p^{12}} \simeq \mathbb{F}_{p^2}[Y]/(Y^6-2)$ resulting in fast polynomial reduction too. Our implementation perform a pairing in 5.05 ms in average which is comparable to the 5.73 ms over an x86-64 Intel Core2 E6600 of the Microsoft Research Team [1, Tab.2].

Table 6. Timings for exponentiation in milliseconds (ms), Ate and Tate pairings on prime order n and composite order $n = n_1 \cdots n_i$ elliptic curves for different security levels

Pairing	$\log_2 n$	$\log_2 n_i$	$\log_2 p$	$\frac{k\cdot}{\log_2 p}$	Miller Loop	F. Exp.	Pairing	Exp. G_1	g^{P_i} G_1	Exp. G_2	Exp. G_T	g^{P_i} G_T
BN,o.ate	256	–	256	3072	2.35	2.70	5.05	0.55	–	1.91	5.16	–
	269	–	269	3228	3.22	3.80	7.29	0.77	–	2.56	5.98	–
(1), Tate	256	–	1536	3072	19.70	20.50	40.20	8.30	–	–	2.20	–
(2), Tate	1024	512	1036	3072	56.88	0.10	56.98	24.38	13.12	–	7.81	3.9
(2), Tate	2048	1024	2059	4118	392.50	0.40	392.90	172.5	86.25	–	50.63	25.8
(2), Tate	3072	1536	3083	6166	1295.6	0.7	1296.3	586.2	301.8	–	166.10	81.9
(3), Tate	3072	1024	3083	6166	1275.6	0.7	1276.3	556.9	222.5	–	174.88	60.1

For this 128-bit security level, a pairing on an elliptic curve of composite order with two primes is 254 times slower than over a prime-order elliptic curve (1.27 s compared to 5.05 ms). The Miller loop is very expensive, indeed it runs over N without any possible significant optimization as explained in Sec. 3.1. The final exponentiation is very cheap because it consists in $f^{(p-1)h} = (f^p \cdot f^{-1})^h$ computed with one inversion, one multiplication, one Frobenius map and one very small exponentiation (h is only a dozen bits) in $\mathbb{F}_{p^2}$.

5.1 Application to BGN Cryptosystem

In 2005, Boneh, Goh and Nissim published in [7] a somewhat homomorphic encryption scheme which can add several times different ciphertexts, perform one

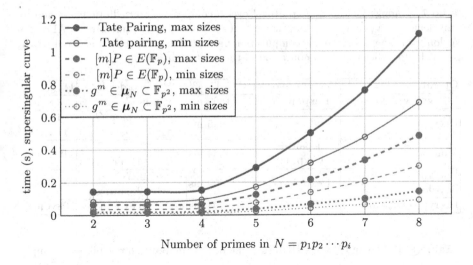

Fig. 1. Execution time (s) on average for a scalar multiplication on $E(\mathbb{F}_p)$, an exponentiation in $\boldsymbol{\mu}_N \subset F_{p^2}$ and a Tate pairing over a composite-order supersingular curve

multiplication then continue to add ciphertexts. Freeman proposed a conversion to a prime-order setting in [11]. We compare the two settings. Our results show that the whole protocol is much slower on a composite-order elliptic curve, as presented in Tab. 7. Due to lack of space, we briefly present our results, a detailed version of the protocol in the two settings is available in the online full version[1]. We assumed that to compute several pairings on the same curve, we compute each Miller loop, then multiply the outputs and apply a single final exponentiation. There are four distinct products of two or three pairings in the second protocol.

The arithmetic on the composite-order elliptic curve $E(\mathbb{F}_p)$ is more than 3 times slower than in $G_T \subset \mathbb{F}_{p^2}$, this means that the encryptions and exponentiations for decryption in G_T are more efficient. The converse is observed over a prime-order elliptic curve. This protocol over an optimal prime-order elliptic curve is dramatically faster than over a composite-order elliptic curve. More precisely, the exponentiation in the decryption step is 161 times faster in G_1, 57 times faster in G_2 and 2 times faster in G_T over a prime-order elliptic curve than over a composite-order one.

5.2 Application to Hierarchical Identity Based Encryption

In this section, we detail and implement the Hierarchical Identity Based Encryption (HIBE in the following) of Lewko and Waters published at Eurocrypt 2011 [20] and compare it with its translation in the prime-order setting due to Lewko [19]. Due to lack of space, we don't recall the protocol here. For a

---

[1] http://eprint.iacr.org/2013/218.

Table 7. Timings for the BGN protocol over a composite order elliptic curve and its equivalent over a prime order elliptic curve for a security level equivalent to AES-128. We don't consider a discrete log computation because this is not the scope of our paper, see e.g. [4] for efficient DL computation in this particular setting.

Operation	Composite-order E.C. [7, §3]		Prime-order E.C. [11, §5]	
Encrypt or Add	1 exp. in G_1	1300 ms	1 exp. in G_1 and G_2	3.8 ms
Decrypt	$C^{p_1} \in G_1$	645 ms	π_1: 4 exp. in G_1	4.0 ms
			π_2: 4 exp. in G_2	11.2 ms
Multiply	1 pairing + 1 exp. in G_T	3364 ms	1 exp. in G_1 and G_2 + 4×(3 pairings)	119.8 ms
Encrypt or Add	1 exp. in G_T	409 ms	1 exp. in G_1 and G_2 + 4×(2 pairings)	87.8 ms
Decrypt (without DL)	$C^{p_1} \in G_T$	204 ms	$\pi_t(C)$ 16 exp. in G_T	108.8 ms

Table 8. Lewko and Waters HIBE scheme over a composite order bilinear group

Operation	Randomness complexity	Computation	Timing $j = 3$ Tab. 6
Setup	$N = p_1p_2p_3$, 5 elts $\in G_{1(p_1)}$, 1 elt $\in \mathbb{Z}_N$	1 pairing	1.27 s
KeyGen	$3j - 1$ elts in $\mathbb{Z}_N$	$7j$ exp. in G_1	11.55 s
Encrypt	$j + 1$ elts $\in Z_N$	$4 + 4j$ exp. in G_1, 1 exp. in G_T	8.96 s
Delegate $j \to j + 1$	$3j + 2$ elts in $\mathbb{Z}_N$	$7(j + 1)$ exp. in G_1	15.40 s
Decryption	–	$4j$ pairings	5.08 s

brief description on the scheme, see our full online version and for the complete description, see [20]. We present our implementation results in Tab. 8.

We also studied the Lewko HIBE translation in prime order bilinear group. We only consider in Tab. 9 the Setup, Encrypt, KeyGen, Delegate and Decrypt steps written only from practical point of view, with $m = 6$. For a complete description of the scheme with $m = 10$ for the security proof, see [19, §B.3] and [19, §2.2] for notations. Moreover the scheme in [19] is described with a symmetric pairing. We apply the protocol to an asymmetric pairing to improve its practical efficiency. There are two possible approaches. We can set the secret keys in G_1 and the ciphertexts in G_2 to optimise the needs in secured memory which can be quite expensive in constrained devices. Or we can set in G_2 the secrets keys (with double secured memory) and set in G_1 the ciphertexts to improve the bandwidth. We will choose this second option.

Vectors of group elements are considered and denoted $v = (v_1, \ldots, v_m) \in \mathbb{F}_r^m$ (with r the subgroup prime order of an elliptic curve), and for $g_1 \in G_1$ (recall that this is an elliptic curve and not a finite field despite the multiplicative notation), $g_1^v = (g_1^{v_1}, g_1^{v_2}, \ldots, g_1^{v_m}) \in G_1^m$. Moreover, for any $a \in \mathbb{F}_r$ and $v, w \in \mathbb{F}_r^m$, we have: $g_1^{av} = (g_1^{av_1}, g_1^{av_2}, \ldots, g_1^{av_m})$, $g_1^{v+w} = (g_1^{v_1+w_1}, g_1^{v_2+w_2}, \ldots, g_1^{v_m+w_m})$. The corresponding pairing is defined as follows, with e a *one dimensional* bilinear pairing: $e_m(g_1^v, g_2^w) = \prod_{i=1}^m e(g_1^{v_i}, g_2^{w_i}) = e(g_1, g_2)^{v \cdot w} \in G_T \subset \mathbb{F}_{p^k}^*$. The pairing e_m costs m pairings e. More precisely, as e_m is a product of m pairings, it costs m Miller loops then one final exponentiation if we set e to be a (variant of a) Tate pairing.

Setup$(\lambda \to$ PP, MSK). The setup algorithm takes in the security parameter λ and chooses a bilinear group G_1 of sufficiently large prime order r and a generator g_1; G_2 of same prime order r with a generator g_2 and finally G_T of same order r. Let $g_T = e(g_1, g_2)$ be a generator of G_T. Let $e : G_1 \times G_2 \to G_T$ denote the bilinear map. We set $m = 6$. Hence

$$e_m = e_6 : G_1^6 \times G_2^6 \to G_T$$
$$(g_1^v, g_2^w) \mapsto \prod_{i=1}^6 e(g_1^{v_i}, g_2^{w_i})$$

The algorithm samples random dual orthonormal bases, $(\mathbb{D}, \mathbb{D}^*) \leftarrow \text{Dual}(\mathbb{F}_r^m)$. Let $d_1, \ldots, d_6$ denote the elements of $\mathbb{D}$ and $d_1^*, \ldots, d_6^*$ denote the elements of $\mathbb{D}^*$. They satisfy the property $d_i \cdot d_i^* = \psi \in \mathbb{F}_r^*$ $\forall i$ and $d_i \cdot d_j^* = 0$ (mod r) for $i \neq j$. It also chooses random exponents $\alpha_1, \alpha_2, \theta, \sigma, \gamma, \xi \in \mathbb{F}_r$. The public parameters are

$$\text{PP} = \left\{ G_1, G_2, G_T, r, e(g_1, g_2)^{\alpha_1 d_1 \cdot d_1^*}, e(g_1, g_2)^{\alpha_2 d_2 \cdot d_2^*}, g_1^{d_1}, \ldots, g_1^{d_6} \right\}, \quad (3)$$

and the master secret key is

$$\text{MSK} = \left\{ \alpha_1, \alpha_2, g_2^{d_1^*}, g_2^{d_2^*}, g_2^{\gamma d_1^*}, g_2^{\xi d_2^*}, g_2^{\theta d_3^*}, g_2^{\theta d_4^*}, g_2^{\sigma d_5^*}, g_2^{\sigma d_6^*} \right\} . \quad (4)$$

KeyGen$((\mathcal{I}_1, \ldots, \mathcal{I}_j), \text{MSK}, \text{PP}) \to \text{SK}_\mathcal{I}$. The key generation algorithm chooses uniformly at random values $r_1^i, r_2^i \in \mathbb{F}_r$ for $1 \leqslant i \leqslant j$. It also chooses random values $y_1, \ldots, y_j \in \mathbb{F}_r$ and $w_1, \ldots, w_j \in \mathbb{F}_r$ s. t. $y_1 + y_2 + \ldots + y_j = \alpha_1$ and $w_1 + w_2 + \ldots + w_j = \alpha_2$. For each $1 \leqslant i \leqslant j$ it computes $K_i := g_2^{y_i d_1^* + w_i d_2^* + r_1^i \mathcal{I}_i \theta d_3^* - r_1^i \theta d_4^* + r_2^i \mathcal{I}_i \sigma d_5^* - r_2^i \sigma d_6^*} \in G_2$. The secret key is:

$$\text{SK}_\mathcal{I} := \left\{ g_2^{\gamma d_1^*}, g_2^{\xi d_2^*}, g_2^{\theta d_3^*}, g_2^{\theta d_4^*}, g_2^{\sigma d_5^*}, g_2^{\sigma d_6^*}, K_1, \ldots, K_j \in G_2 \right\}. \quad (5)$$

Encrypt$(\text{M}, (\mathcal{I}_1, \ldots, \mathcal{I}_j), \text{PP}), \to \text{CT}$. The encryption algorithm chooses s_1, s_2 and t_1^i, t_2^i for $1 \leqslant i \leqslant j$ uniformly randomly from $\mathbb{F}_r$. It computes

$$C_0 := M e(g_1, g_2)^{\alpha_1 s_1 d_1 \cdot d_1^*} e(g_1, g_2)^{\alpha_2 s_2 d_2 \cdot d_2^*} \in G_T \quad (6)$$

(note that $e(g_1, g_2)^{\alpha_1 d_1 \cdot d_1^*}$ and $e(g_1, g_2)^{\alpha_2 d_2 \cdot d_2^*}$ are in PP). It computes also

$$C_i := g_1^{s_1 d_1 + s_2 d_2 + t_1^i d_3 + \mathcal{I}_i t_1^i d_4 + t_2^i d_5 + \mathcal{I} t_2^i d_6} \quad (7)$$

for $1 \leqslant i \leqslant j$. The ciphertext is $\text{CT} := \{C_0 \in G_T, C_1, \ldots, C_j \in G_1\}$.

Delegate(PP, $SK_{\mathcal{I}}$, $\mathcal{I}_{j+1}$) $\to$ $SK_{\mathcal{I}|\mathcal{I}_{j+1}}$. The delegation algorithm chooses random values $\omega_1^i, \omega_2^i \in \mathbb{F}_r$ for $1 \leqslant i \leqslant j + 1$. It also chooses random values $y_1', \ldots, y_j' \in \mathbb{F}_r$ and $w_1', \ldots, w_j' \in \mathbb{F}_r$ s.t. $y_1' + y_2' + \ldots + y_{j+1}' = 0$ and $w_1' + w_2' + \ldots + w_{j+1}' = 0$. It takes in a secret key $SK_{\mathcal{I}}$ with elements denoted as above. It computes $K_i' := K_i \cdot g_2^{y_i' \gamma d_1^* + w_i' \xi d_2^* + \omega_1^i \mathcal{I}_i \theta d_3^* - \omega_1^i \theta d_4^* + \omega_2^i \mathcal{I}_i \sigma d_5^* - \omega_2^i \sigma d_6^*} \in G_2$ for $1 \leqslant i \leqslant j$ and $K_{j+1} := g_2^{y_{j+1}' \gamma d_1^* + w_{j+1}' \xi d_2^* + \omega_1^{j+1} \mathcal{I}_{j+1} \theta d_3^* - \omega_1^{j+1} \theta d_4^* + \omega_2^{j+1} \mathcal{I}_{j+1} \sigma d_5^* - \omega_2^{j+1} \sigma d_6^*} \in G_2$. $SK_{\mathcal{I}|\mathcal{I}_{j+1}}$ is formed as

$$\left\{ g_2^{\gamma d_1^*}, g_2^{\xi d_2^*}, g_2^{\theta d_3^*}, g_2^{\theta d_4^*}, g_2^{\sigma d_5^*}, g_2^{\sigma d_6^*} (\text{ from } SK_{\mathcal{I}}), K_1', \ldots, K_j', K_{j+1} \in G_2 \right\} . \quad (8)$$

Decryption(CT, $SK_{\mathcal{I}}$) $\to$ M. Assuming $(\mathcal{I}_1, \ldots, \mathcal{I}_j)$ is a prefix of $(\mathcal{I}_1, \ldots, \mathcal{I}_\ell)$, the decryption algorithm computes $B := \prod_{i=1}^{j} e_m(C_0, K_i)$. The message is then computed as $M = C_0/B$.

Table 9. Lewko HIBE scheme translation over prime order bilinear group

Operation	Randomness complexity	Computation	Timing Tab. 6 $j = 3, m = 6$
Setup	r, $2m^2$ elts in $\mathbb{F}_r$ for $(\mathbb{D}, \mathbb{D}^*)$, 6 elts $\in \mathbb{F}_r$	1 pairing e, 2 exp. in G_T, m^2 exp. in G_1, $m(m+2)$ exp. in G_2	127 ms
KeyGen	$2j + 2(j-1)$ elts $\in \mathbb{F}_r$	$j \cdot m^2$ exp. in G_2, some mult. in $\mathbb{F}_p$ and G_2	206 ms
Encrypt	$2 + 2j$ elts in $\mathbb{F}_r$	$j \cdot m^2$ exp. in G_1, 2 exp. in G_T, some mult. in $\mathbb{F}_p$	70 ms
Delegate $j \to j+1$	$2(j+1) + 2j$ elts in $\mathbb{F}_r$	$(j+1)m^2$ exp. in G_2	80 ms
Decryption	–	$j \cdot m$ pairings e	45.0 ms

Each step is summarized in Tab. 9. We chose a hierarchy depth of $j = 3$. We can say that this instantiation (Tab. 9) is 10 times more efficient than with a composite-order elliptic curve (Tab 8) for Setup, 56 times for KeyGen, 128 times for Encrypt, 192 times for Delegate and 112 times for Decryption. In other words, the important operations of delegation, encryption and decryption are more than hundred times faster over a prime-order bilinear curve with an asymmetric pairing compared to a composite-order supersingular curve with a symmetric pairing.

6   Conclusion

We studied well-known protocols based on composite-order or prime-order elliptic curves. We justified the sizes of the composite orders when more than two primes are present in the modulus. We analyzed the Number Field Sieve complexity and the Elliptic Curve Method to find the size bounds. We then compared the cost of the homomorphic encryption scheme of Boneh, Goh and Nissim over a composite-order and the corresponding scheme over a prime-order pairing-friendly elliptic curve given by Freeman. In the former case, a pairing took 3 s, compared to 13 ms in the latter case. Even with 12 pairings instead of one in the Multiply step of the protocol, the prime-order translation remained 28 times faster. We also compared the unbounded HIBE protocol of Waters and Lewko and its translation given by Lewko. The prime-order setting is between 10 times to 192 times faster than the composite-order setting. Despite useful properties of bilinear composite-order structures to design new protocols, the resulting schemes are not very competitive compared to protocols relying on other assumptions which in particular, need prime-order bilinear structures with asymmetric pairings. Some special protocols need extra properties such as cancelling and projecting pairings. Only composite-order groups or supersingular curves achieve these properties.

We recommend to avoid composite-order groups whenever possible. Moreover, we did not investigate multi-exponentiation techniques to compute simultaneously several pairings on the same elliptic curve, neither did we use the Frobenius map to decompose exponents when performing exponentiation in $\mathbb{F}_{p^{12}}$. Hence some speed-ups are still available for protocols in the prime-order setting.

Acknowledgements. We thank the reviewers of the ACNS conference for their detailed and useful comments. Thanks to Damien Vergnaud and the cryptology engineers of Thales for their help and support. This work was supported in part by the French ANR-09-VERS-016 BEST Project.

References

1. Acar, T., Lauter, K., Naehrig, M., Shumow, D.: Affine pairings on ARM. In: Abdalla, M., Lange, T. (eds.) Pairing 2012. LNCS, vol. 7708, pp. 203–209. Springer, Heidelberg (2013)
2. Aranha, D.F., Karabina, K., Longa, P., Gebotys, C.H., López, J.: Faster explicit formulas for computing pairings over ordinary curves. In: Paterson (ed.) [22], pp. 48–68
3. Barreto, P.S.L.M., Naehrig, M.: Pairing-friendly elliptic curves of prime order. In: Preneel, B., Tavares, S. (eds.) SAC 2005. LNCS, vol. 3897, pp. 319–331. Springer, Heidelberg (2006)
4. Bernstein, D.J., Lange, T.: Computing small discrete logarithms faster. In: Galbraith, S., Nandi, M. (eds.) INDOCRYPT 2012. LNCS, vol. 7668, pp. 317–338. Springer, Heidelberg (2012)
5. Beuchat, J.-L., González-Díaz, J.E., Mitsunari, S., Okamoto, E., Rodríguez-Henríquez, F., Teruya, T.: High-speed software implementation of the optimal ate pairing over Barreto-Naehrig curves. In: Joye, M., Miyaji, A., Otsuka, A. (eds.) Pairing 2010. LNCS, vol. 6487, pp. 21–39. Springer, Heidelberg (2010)
6. Boneh, D., Boyen, X., Goh, E.-J.: Hierarchical identity based encryption with constant size ciphertext. In: Cramer, R. (ed.) EUROCRYPT 2005. LNCS, vol. 3494, pp. 440–456. Springer, Heidelberg (2005)

7. Boneh, D., Goh, E.-J., Nissim, K.: Evaluating 2-DNF formulas on ciphertexts. In: Kilian, J. (ed.) TCC 2005. LNCS, vol. 3378, pp. 325–341. Springer, Heidelberg (2005)

8. Boneh, D., Rubin, K., Silverberg, A.: Finding composite order ordinary elliptic curves using the Cocks-Pinch method. Journal of Number Theory 131(5), 832–841 (2011)

9. Devegili, A.J., Héigeartaigh, C.O., Scott, M., Dahab, R.: Multiplication and squaring on pairing-friendly fields. Cryptology ePrint Archive, Report 2006/471 (2006)

10. Freeman, D., Scott, M., Teske, E.: A taxonomy of pairing-friendly elliptic curves. J. Cryptology 23(2), 224–280 (2010)

11. Freeman, D.M.: Converting pairing-based cryptosystems from composite-order groups to prime-order groups. In: Gilbert, H. (ed.) EUROCRYPT 2010. LNCS, vol. 6110, pp. 44–61. Springer, Heidelberg (2010)

12. Granger, R., Scott, M.: Faster squaring in the cyclotomic subgroup of sixth degree extensions. In: Nguyen, P.Q., Pointcheval, D. (eds.) PKC 2010. LNCS, vol. 6056, pp. 209–223. Springer, Heidelberg (2010)

13. Herrmann, M.: Improved cryptanalysis of the multi-prime ϕ - hiding assumption. In: Nitaj, A., Pointcheval, D. (eds.) AFRICACRYPT 2011. LNCS, vol. 6737, pp. 92–99. Springer, Heidelberg (2011)

14. Blake, I.F., Seroussi, G., Smart, N.P.: Advances in Elliptic Curve Cryptography. Cambridge University Press (2005)

15. Kiltz, E., O'Neill, A., Smith, A.: Instantiability of RSA-OAEP under chosen-plaintext attack. In: Rabin, T. (ed.) CRYPTO 2010. LNCS, vol. 6223, pp. 295–313. Springer, Heidelberg (2010)

16. Koblitz, N., Menezes, A.: Pairing-based cryptography at high security levels. In: Smart, N.P. (ed.) Cryptography and Coding 2005. LNCS, vol. 3796, pp. 13–36. Springer, Heidelberg (2005)

17. Lenstra, A.K.: Unbelievable security: Matching AES security using public key systems. In: Boyd, C. (ed.) ASIACRYPT 2001. LNCS, vol. 2248, pp. 67–86. Springer, Heidelberg (2001)

18. Lenstra, A.K., Lenstra, H.W.J. (eds.): The development of the number field sieve. Lecture Notes in Mathematics, vol. 1554. Springer, Heidelberg (1993)

19. Lewko, A.: Tools for simulating features of composite order bilinear groups in the prime order setting. In: Pointcheval, D., Johansson, T. (eds.) EUROCRYPT 2012. LNCS, vol. 7237, pp. 318–335. Springer, Heidelberg (2012)

20. Lewko, A.B., Waters, B.: Unbounded HIBE and attribute-based encryption. In: Paterson (ed.) [22], pp. 547–567

21. Naehrig, M., Niederhagen, R., Schwabe, P.: New software speed records for cryptographic pairings. In: Abdalla, M., Barreto, P.S.L.M. (eds.) LATINCRYPT 2010. LNCS, vol. 6212, pp. 109–123. Springer, Heidelberg (2010)

22. Paterson, K.G. (ed.): EUROCRYPT 2011. LNCS, vol. 6632. Springer, Heidelberg (2011)

23. Seo, J.H.: On the (im)possibility of projecting property in prime-order setting. In: Wang, X., Sako, K. (eds.) ASIACRYPT 2012. LNCS, vol. 7658, pp. 61–79. Springer, Heidelberg (2012)

24. Vercauteren, F.: Optimal pairings. IEEE Transactions on Information Theory 56(1), 455–461 (2010)

25. Waters, B.: Dual system encryption: Realizing fully secure IBE and HIBE under simple assumptions. In: Halevi, S. (ed.) CRYPTO 2009. LNCS, vol. 5677, pp. 619–636. Springer, Heidelberg (2009)

26. Zhao, C., Zhang, F., Xie, D.: Faster computation of self-pairings. IEEE Transactions on Information Theory 58(5), 3266–3272 (2012)

FROST
Forensic Recovery of Scrambled Telephones

Tilo Müller and Michael Spreitzenbarth

Department of Computer Science
Friedrich-Alexander University of Erlangen-Nuremberg
{tilo.mueller,michael.spreitzenbarth}@cs.fau.de

Abstract. At the end of 2011, Google released version 4.0 of its Android operating system for smartphones. For the first time, Android smartphone owners were supplied with a disk encryption feature that transparently encrypts user partitions. On the downside, encrypted smartphones are a nightmare for IT forensics and law enforcement, because brute force appears to be the only option to recover encrypted data by technical means. However, RAM contents are necessarily left unencrypted and, as we show, they can be acquired from live systems with physical access only. To this end, we present the data recovery tool FROST (*Forensic Recovery of Scrambled Telephones*). Using Galaxy Nexus devices from Samsung as an example, we show that it is possible to perform cold boot attacks against Android smartphones and to retrieve valuable information from RAM. This information includes personal messages, photos, passwords and the encryption key. Since smartphones get switched off only seldom, and since the tools that we provide must not be installed before the attack, our method can be applied in real cases.

1 Introduction

In 2011, 83 percent of the American adults had a cell phone from which 42 percent had a phone that can be classified as a *smartphone* [1]. Android is today the most common smartphone platform, followed by iOS, Blackberry OS, and Windows Phone. Since most consumers use their smartphones for both business and personal applications, missing devices often contain personal and corporate data. For example, the survey *The Lost Smartphone Problem* [2] on 439 U.S. organizations objectively determined that in a 12-month period 142,708 out of 3,297,569 employee smartphones were lost or stolen, i.e., 4.3 percent per year. 5,034 of these smartphones were known to be subject to theft, while the others were "missing". Only 9,298 smartphones were recovered within the time of the study. Results like those make clear that people must take precautions to secure their smartphones against physical loss. The most popular method to protect data against physical loss is encrypting it with AES. Android, for example, enables users to encrypt their user partition with AES since version 4.0, which was released in October 2011. However, encryption technologies are ambivalent as they also enable criminals to hide digital evidence, so that encrypted smartphones have a serious impact on digital forensics.

M. Jacobson et al. (Eds.): ACNS 2013, LNCS 7954, pp. 373–388, 2013.

Contributions. In this paper, we aim at recovering valuable information from encrypted smartphones. Roughly speaking, we analyze the characteristics of the *remanence effect* [3] on smartphones, prove that Android's boot sequence enable us to perform *cold boot attacks* [4], and show that valuable information can be retrieved from RAM. To this end, we present our recovery tool FROST (*Forensic Recovery of Scrambled Telephones*). FROST can be loaded to a smartphone *after* we got physical access to it, and *without* the need to have user privileges before. We carried out our experiments exemplarily for Galaxy Nexus devices. In detail, our contributions are:

1. *Evaluation of the Remanence Effect*: We analyze the characteristics of the remanence effect on smartphones for the first time. According to previous results on PCs, the decay of bits in RAM correlates with both the operating temperature of a device and its time without power. However, contradictory to previous results, we show that the remanence interval on smartphones is shorter. 50% of all bits are decayed after 2-4s, depending on the device temperature.

2. *Cold Boot Attacks*: The bootloader of Galaxy Nexus devices (and many other Android-driven smartphones) can be unlocked with physical access only. Unlocking the bootloader does *not* destroy RAM contents, but it requires us to reboot the smartphone. According to our results about the remanence effect, we can reboot a smartphone quickly while preserving a significant amount of RAM. After rebooting a Galaxy Nexus device, unlocking its bootloader, and booting up our recovery tool, we were still able to recover much sensitive information. Among others, we recovered emails, photos, contacts, calendar entries, WiFi credentials, and even the disk encryption key.

3. *Breaking Disk Encryption*: If a bootloader is already unlocked *before* we gain access to a device, we can break disk encryption. The keys that we recover from RAM then allow us to decrypt the user partition. However, if a bootloader is locked, we need to unlock it first in order to boot FROST, and the unlocking procedure wipes the user partition (but preserves RAM contents). Since bootloaders of Galaxy Nexus devices are locked by default, and since we conjecture that most people do not unlock them, disk encryption can mostly not be broken in real cases. In addition we integrated a brute force option that breaks disk encryption for short PINs.

The fact that user partitions are wiped out when unlocking the bootloader is a serious limitation of our method. Forensic experts from law enforcement might not be allowed to delete a user partition in order to retrieve digital evidence from RAM. Any data on disk would irretrievably be lost. However, this depends on the actual case and the respective legislation of the country. In any event, criminals do not care about this fact and it is therefore important to discuss the attack vector "RAM" irrespectively of its forensic application. With FROST, we are always able to acquire memory dumps from switched-on Galaxy Nexus devices, and we conjecture that our attack can be extended to a wider range of devices with the tools that we provide. A tutorial, a photo series, source codes, and precompiled binaries of our project are available at www1.cs.fau.de/frost/.

2   Background Information

We now provide necessary background information about the encryption support in Android 4.0 and subsequent versions (Sect. 2.1). We then give information about the remanence effect, and about cold boot attacks on PCs (Sect. 2.2). Finally, we give details about our device under test, namely the Samsung Galaxy Nexus (Sect. 2.3).

2.1   Disk Encryption Since Android 4.0

With Android 4.0, support for AES-based disk encryption was introduced. While third party apps that extend the functionality of Android smartphones are primarily written in Java, disk encryption resides entirely in system space and is written in C. Android's encryption feature builds upon *dm-crypt*, which has been available in Linux kernels for years. Dm-crypt relies on the *device-mapper* infrastructure and the *Crypto API* of the Linux kernel. It provides a flexible way to encrypt block devices by creating a virtual encryption layer on top of all kinds of abstract block devices, including real devices, logical partitions, loop devices, and swap partitions. Writing to a mapped device gets encrypted and reading from it gets decrypted. Although dm-crypt is suitable for *full disk encryption* (FDE), Android does not encrypt full disks but only user partitions.

Dm-crypt is kept modular and supports different ciphers and modes of operation, including AES, Twofish and Serpent, as well as CBC and XTS. Android 4.0 makes use of the cipher mode `aes-cbc-essiv:sha256` with 128-bit keys [5]. The AES-128 *data encryption key* (DEK) is encrypted with an AES-128 *key encryption key* (KEK), which is in turn derived from the user PIN through the *password-based key derivation function 2* (PBKDF2) [6]. Using two different keys, namely the DEK and the KEK, renders cumbersome reencryption in the case of PIN changes unnecessary. The encrypted DEK as well as the *initialization vector* (IV) for PBKDF2 are random numbers taken from `/dev/urandom`. These values are stored inside a *crypto footer* of the disk. The crypto footer can either be an own partition or it can be placed at the last 16 kilobytes of an encrypted partition. The crypto footer becomes important for our implementation because it holds necessary information to decrypt encrypted partitions.

Unlike iOS, which automatically activates disk encryption when a PIN is set, Android's encryption is disabled by default. Activating it manually takes up to an hour for the initial process and cannot be undone. Furthermore, it can only be activated if PIN-locks or passwords are in use. In Android, PINs consist of 4 to 16 numeric characters, and passwords consists of 4 to 16 alphanumeric characters with at least one letter. New screen locking mechanisms like pattern-locks and face recognition are less secure, and so Google forbids them in combination with disk encryption. Pattern-locks, for example, can be broken by *Smudge Attacks* [7], and face recognition can simply be tricked by showing a photo of the smartphone owner [8].

2.2 Remanence Effect and Cold Boot Attacks

Adversaries with physical access to their target can perform *cold boot attacks* against encrypted PCs. Cold boot attacks have become publicly known in 2008, when Halderman et al. [4] proved that the *remanence effect* can be exploited to recover disk encryption keys from RAM. The remanence effect, however, has already been known since decades and is neither specific to encryption keys nor to memory chips of PCs [3,9]. The remanence effect says that contents of volatile memory fade away gradually over time, rather than disappearing immediately after power is cut. It also says that low temperatures slow down the fading process. Anderson and Kuhn first outlined attacks exploiting the remanence effect of cooled down memory chips [10]. In applied cryptography, the remanence effect is also used as a timing source [11], and as an entropy source [12].

On PCs, secret keys can be traced in RAM after a reboot from malicious USB drives, due to the remanence effect. Above that, cooled down RAM chips can physically be replugged into another PC. The replug variant is more generic than the reboot variant, because it works irrespectively of BIOS and boot sequence settings. With a recovered secret key, adversaries can decrypt the hard disk and eventually access all data. Cold boot attacks are generic and constitute a threat to all disk encryption solutions. However, it has not been reported yet if, and *how*, cold boot attacks are applicable against ARM-based devices such as smartphones and tablets. According to Halderman et al., by cooling down RAM chips the *remanence interval* is extended from 30 seconds up to ten minutes. According to our results, the remanence interval on smartphones is much shorter (see Sect. 3.2). An interesting question at the beginning was if we can obtain a physical RAM dump from smartphones at all? Unlike x86 PCs, Android devices have soldered RAM chips that we cannot unplug, and no bootable USB ports. Hence, we had to find another way to boot system code. The popular trend towards open bootloaders in recent Android devices opened more avenues for attack. Galaxy Nexus devices (and many other Android-driven smartphones) have now bootloaders that can be manipulated with physical access only.

2.3 Samsung Galaxy Nexus

For our purpose, we have chosen the Galaxy Nexus from Samsung because it was the first device with Android 4.0 and consequently, it was the first Android-based smartphone with encryption support. Moreover, it is an official Google phone, meaning that it comes with an official Android version from Google which is not modified by the phone manufacturer. Official Google releases are most amenable for an in-depth security analysis, and flaws can be generalized best to a wider class of devices.

The Galaxy Nexus family comes with an OMAP4 chip from Texas Instruments (4460) which has a Cortex-A9 CPU implementing ARMv7. The partition layout of an encrypted Galaxy Nexus device is given in Fig. 1. Most of the thirteen partitions can be ignored for our purpose, except userdata, metadata and recovery. The userdata partition contains the encrypted filesystem, the metadata partition is the crypto footer that holds necessary information for decryption, and

block device	partition name	description
/dev/block/mmcblk0p1	xloader	bootloader code
/dev/block/mmcblk0p2	sbl	bootloader code
/dev/block/mmcblk0p3	efs	static information like IMEI
/dev/block/mmcblk0p4	param	boot parameters
/dev/block/mmcblk0p5	misc	system settings like carrier ID
/dev/block/mmcblk0p6	dgs	unknown *(zero filled on all devices)*
/dev/block/mmcblk0p7	boot	boot code
/dev/block/mmcblk0p8	**recovery**	recovery image
/dev/block/mmcblk0p9	radio	radio firmware (GSM)
/dev/block/mmcblk0p10	system	Android operating system
/dev/block/mmcblk0p11	cache	cache (e.g., for user apps)
/dev/block/mmcblk0p12	**userdata**	user data (encrypted)
/dev/block/mmcblk0p13	**metadata**	crypto footer

Fig. 1. Partition layout of an encrypted Samsung Galaxy Nexus device

the recovery partition is a partition that holds a *second* bootable Linux. The recovery partition is different from the main Android system (which is stored on the system partition). It can be compared best with a rescue system of ordinary PCs and allows basic operations on the hard disk without booting into full Android. The recovery partition plays a vital role in our cold boot attack, because we make use of it to boot our own system code.

3   Cold Boot Attacks on Galaxy Nexus Smartphones

We now give an evaluation about the remanence effect on Galaxy Nexus devices and probe the effectiveness of cold boot attacks. To this end, we rely on our recovery tool FROST; we describe the technical details of FROST in Sect. 4. We now describe how FROST can be booted (Sect. 3.1). Based on FROST, we then examine how the operating temperature of a Galaxy Nexus device correlates with the decay of bits (Sect. 3.2). Afterwards, we have a look at personal data that we can gain from RAM when the phone is encrypted (Sect. 3.3). Finally, we have a look to the special case when bootloaders are already unlocked before accessing the phone (Sect. 3.4). If so, we can break Android's encryption feature entirely and decrypt all data on the phone.

3.1   Booting the FROST Recovery Image

The question we answer in this section is, how do we reboot a smartphone and run FROST if physical access to it has just been gained? An important point at the beginning is to ensure that the device has sufficient power for a live analysis. Otherwise, it must be charged, because once an encrypted device loses power, all possibilities other than brute force are lost to gain data from it. After charging, the device must be *cooled down* in order to increase the remanence interval (see

Sect. 3.2). As a rule of thumb, we experienced good results when putting the device into a $-15°C$ freezer for 60 minutes. Before that, it should be packed up in a freezer bag in order to protect it against water condensation.

After the phone has been charged and cooled down, we can reboot it. Since the Galaxy Nexus device has no reset button (like most other smartphones), we have to reboot it by unplugging the battery briefly. Shutting the device down from the lock screen is too slow and valuable information in RAM would get lost. In order to boot up the device quickly after reinserting the battery, the power button must already been held *before* removing the battery. The entire process has to happen so quickly that the phone is without power only for a few hundred milliseconds. Once a smartphone is up again, the risk of losing RAM contents is defeated, because neither unlocking the bootloader nor booting into FROST destroys any important memory lines according to our tests.

Additionally, the buttons *volume up* and *volume down* must be held during boot to enter the *fastboot* mode. Once the phone is in fastboot mode, it can be connected to a PC via USB. First, we assume the bootloader is locked. If so, we have to run `fastboot oem unlock` first. This command requires us to confirm the following warning on the phone: "To prevent unauthorized access to your personal data, unlocking the bootloader will also delete all personal data from your phone". Once we confirm this warning, the encrypted user partition gets wiped. However, "all personal data" is not deleted from the phone – RAM contents are preserved.

Next, FROST must be booted. This can be done in two different ways. Either we run `fastboot flash recovery frost.img` to install it persistently on the recovery partition, or we run `fastboot boot <kernel> [ramdisk]` to start FROST temporarily. The latter is interesting for forensic investigations in the case that the bootloader was already unlocked, because it then prevents the forensic examiner from modifying the state of the phone (which might be illegal depending on the case and/or country). However, if the bootloader must get unlocked first, the state of the phone must be modified anyway. In that case, either the first or the second command can be used interchangeable. Again, criminals most likely do not care about changing the phone state, and thus it is important to discuss both attack vectors, irrespectively of their forensic applicability.

After installing FROST to the recovery partition of a phone, the *recovery mode* option must be selected from the phone's boot menu in order to launch FROST. With the help of FROST, personal data and even encryption keys can now be recovered (see Sect. 3.3 and Sect. 3.4). We strongly recommend to practice the entire procedure several times before carrying it out in real cases. The time of battery removal is critical and the entire procedure must happen quickly (see Sect. 3.2).

3.2   The Remanence Effect

We now analyze the remanence effect of RAM on Galaxy Nexus devices. That is, we analyze the number of decayed bits in RAM after power is cut, in dependence of the operating temperature of a phone and the time of battery removal. Earlier

	ε	$0.5 - 1s$	$1 - 2s$	$3 - 4s$	$5 - 6s$
5 – 10 °C	0 (0%)	2 (0%)	1911 (5%)	8327 (25%)	24181 (73%)
10 – 15 °C	0 (0%)	976 (2%)	2792 (8%)	18083 (55%)	25041 (76%)
15 – 20 °C	0 (0%)	497 (1%)	4575 (13%)	20095 (61%)	25433 (77%)
20 – 25 °C	0 (0%)	421 (1%)	16461 (50%)	23983 (73%)	27845 (84%)
25 – 30 °C	1 (0%)	2204 (6%)	16177 (49%)	27454 (83%)	28661 (87%)

Fig. 2. Number of bit flipping errors per physical page (in total and percentage) in dependence of the phone temperature and the time of battery removal

in our investigations, we recognized that the chance to recover personal data with FROST increases considerably if the phone is cold. We then experimented with putting the phone into a fridge and into a freezer, and we got even better success rates. In the following we give exact benchmarks for this effect.

Fig. 2 lists the bit error rate of memory pages as a function of the device temperature and the time without power before reboot. To determine the device temperature we utilized an infrared thermometer and pointed it to the exactly same position on the phone's motherboard each test run. To cool down the phone, we put it into a -15 °C freezer. 25–30 °C is the normal operating temperature of a Galaxy Nexus, 20–25 °C is reached after 10 minutes, 15–20 °C after 20 minutes, 10–15 °C after 40 minutes, and 5–10 °C after 60 minutes inside the freezer. In several test cases, we never observed damage to the phone when putting it into the freezer for 60 minutes or less (longer periods have not been tested).

To determine the bit error rate, we used FROST to fill memory pages at fixed physical addresses entirely with 0xff. The page size in Android is 4,096 and so we filled each page with $4,096 \cdot 8 = 32,768$ bits. After booting into FROST, as described in Sect. 3.1, we reconsidered the pages that we recently filled and counted the bits that were now zero. By this means, we got the total number of decayed bits and we were able to estimate the overall bit error rate, as listed in Fig. 2. Note that the highest possible bit error rate is 87.5%, and not 100%, because the passive state of 50% of RAM lines is 0xc0, and not 0x00. We reproduced our test for different physical addresses, and all pages exhibited the same behavior.

The most inaccurate measures in our test set-up are the times that a device is without power. According to Sect. 3.1, for rebooting a Galaxy Nexus quickly the battery must be removed manually. Milliseconds are crucial for the number of decayed bits, but the mechanic task of battery removal cannot be handled exactly. Therefore, with ε we define the quickest unplugging/replugging procedure that we "were able to perform"; we claim this was consistently below 500 ms. Moreover, we define four intervals up to six seconds, and say that we replugged the battery "somewhen" within these intervals. We explain inconsistencies of our results given in Fig. 2 and 3 mostly with inaccurate timings.

In Fig. 3, we visualized the data set from Fig. 2. It becomes clear that the bit error rate of RAM increases with both the temperature and the time without power. For example, at a temperature of approximately 25 °C we have a bit error rate of 50% after two seconds, whereas the corresponding bit error rate at

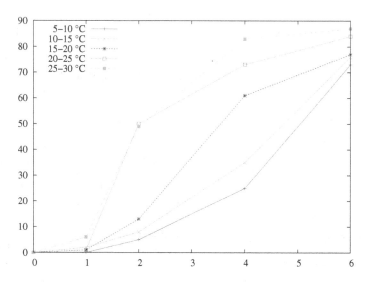

Fig. 3. Bit error ratio (y-axis) in dependence of time (x-axis) and temperatures. The bit error rate decreases with both lower temperatures and shorter times without power.

Fig. 4. A Droid-bitmap in RAM of a Galaxy Nexus device after 0, ε, 0.5s, 1s, 2s, 4s, and 6s without power. The cold boot attacks have been deployed at room temperature.

temperatures around 10 °C is only 5%. Hence, besides replugging the battery quickly, putting a device into a freezer increases the chance to recover personal data from RAM notably.

In Fig. 4, we visualized the remanence effect on Galaxy Nexus devices by visualizing decayed bits as a series of Droid bitmaps. For this series, we used 4096-byte bitmaps that exactly fit into one physical page. We used bitmaps rather than JPEGs to visualize bit errors, because using JPEGs entire blocks get destroyed rather than single pixels. We then increased the interval that the phone was without power during boot successively from ε to 6 seconds. Whenever the bitmap header got destroyed, we fixed it manually in order to display the image. Fig. 4 graphically shows the remanence effect and the distribution of bit errors. It also shows that the passive state of the first half of a physical RAM page is 0x00, while the passive state of the second half is 0xc0.

In contrast to Halderman et al., who considered the remanence effect on PCs, we cannot cool down RAM chips below 0°C without risking serious damage to the phone's hardware. Particularly the display and the battery are likely to suffer damage from temperatures below 0°C. Nevertheless, for temperatures above 0°C our experiments reveal shorter remanence intervals than those identified by Halderman et al. [4]. But, as we see in the next section, the shorter remanence intervals still enable us to perform cold boot attacks against smartphones.

3.3   Recovery of Personal Data

We now investigate which data we can forensically recover from encrypted smartphones through cold boot attacks. Specifically, we are after personal data and digital evidence such as address book contacts, documents, messages, photos, and calendar entries. For our main case, we set up a Galaxy Nexus as personal phone and used it for everyday communications over a week. We then took a photo and did a phone call immediately before the attack. Our goal was to recover as much personal data from the entire week as possible, and the time before the attack in particular. To this end, we attacked the phone by means of FROST and took a memory dump. The memory dump of our test case was near optimal, i.e., we cooled down the phone below 10°C and replugged the battery so quickly that we had a bit error ratio of about 0% according to Fig. 2. Hence, we conjecture we recovered nearly everything that was available in RAM.

We then examined the memory dump with known system utilities like *strings* and *hexdump*, and made use of data recovery programs like *PhotoRec*. Besides photos, PhotoRec can recover websites, text files, databases, sound files, source codes, and binary programs from raw memory images. From the memory dump, we were able to recover 68 JPEG and 199 PNG pictures, 36 OGG tracks, 295 HTML and 386 XML files, 215 SQlite databases, 28 ZIP and 105 JAR archives, 1214 ELF binaries, 485 JAVA source codes, and 6, 331 text files.

We then analyzed all recovered data sets thoroughly. While most PNG images that we recovered were system images and logos (and hence, of no interest for us) many JPEG files were *personal photos*. We were able to recover both the picture that was recently taken and older pictures. We were surprised when we even recovered pictures that were taken with another smartphone weeks before the attack. The reason was that these pictures got synchronized in the background via Dropbox (a common filehoster). For the photo we took immediately before the attack, we could recover two variants, a small thumbnail and a high-resolution variant. For the other photos, we could only retrieve the small thumbnail.

As stated above, most PNG images that we recovered were system files, but also the Wikipedia and Wikimedia logos were available. Indeed, we surfed to *wikipedia.org* in the week before the attack, and it was one of the webpages we accessed last, but we did not access it immediately before the attack. Even though, we could also trace its HTML source in RAM. Moreover, we found residues of other webpages in RAM, too. Besides that, we found personal text files and recent emails in RAM. And we found the *entire chat-history* of WhatsApp (a popular messenger). We also explicitly searched for names of our contact list, and we found each name to be present in RAM several times. Near the memory locations where we identified a name, we found respective phone numbers,

Personal information	fully recovered	partly recovered	not recovered
Address book contacts	✓		
Calendar entries		✓	
Emails and messaging		✓	
GPS coordinates			✓
High resolution pictures		✓	
Recent phone calls			✓
Thumbnail pictures	✓		
Web browsing history		✓	
WhatsApp history	✓		
WiFi credentials	✓		

Fig. 5. Set of personal information that we exemplarily searched for. Most of the data we search for could at least partly be recovered.

email addresses, and other contact details. We also found the remaining entries of our contact list that we did not explicitly search for, indicating that the entire address book is in RAM. Additionally, we recovered dates like birthdays from Jorte Calendar, indicating that also the calendar is in RAM. Interestingly, we even found plaintext passwords. Actually, we did search for the SSID of our department WiFi and we could easily locate the according username and password in plaintext. We did not enter the password right before the attack but days before; the password is probably loaded into RAM each time before connecting to the WiFi.

Overall, we recovered dozens of personal information from RAM with known recovery tools and common system utilities. However, we could not locate all information that we were looking for. We tried to find the call history, i.e., we wanted to find out which number has been dialed last, but we were not successful. Likely, this information is in RAM but we failed to identify the respective memory structure. We also failed to recover GPS coordinates when we wanted to construct a movement profile. However, we are confident that more information can be retrieved from RAM with more efforts in the future. Fig. 5 summarizes our results.

3.4   Recovery of the Disk Encryption Key

Apart from personal data, we were also able to recover the disk encryption keys (given that no or only a few bits were decayed). However, on devices where the bootloader is locked, the bootloader must get unlocked first (see Sect. 3.1). On current Galaxy Nexus devices, the unlocking process deletes the userdata and cache partition. We verified that Google actually *wipes* the userdata and cache partition, meaning that these partitions get zero-filled. As a consequence, it becomes pointless to retrieve encryption keys from RAM, although this is still possible.

Since the wiping process is induced by the telephone software rather than the PC, it cannot easily be bypassed. And since the bootloader of a new Galaxy Nexus is locked by default, we conjecture that most Galaxy Nexus devices have *locked* bootloaders. However, it is generally a device-dependent property whether a bootloader is locked or unlocked by default, and whether partitions get wiped during unlocking or not. The first series of Galaxy Nexus devices, did *not* delete user partitions when unlocking the bootloader [13]. Later versions of the Galaxy Nexus apparently delete userdata partitions but do not wipe them if the phone is not encrypted [14]. Other devices, like the Samsung Galaxy SII, are shipped with unlocked bootloaders even by default [15], such that unlocking is never necessary.

If we find a bootloader to be unlocked, then FROST can even be applied to break disk encryption, i.e., to decrypt the entire user partition. In that case, it is pointless to discuss which personal data apart from the key can be recovered from RAM (see Sect. 3.3), because we have access to the entire disk. We built necessary key recovery and decryption tools into FROST. In short, we go over all physical memory pages in order to trace AES key schedules. For details, see Sect. 4.

To conclude, for all Android-based smartphones with an unlocked bootloader, or those that can get unlocked without wiping the user partition, we can perform cold boot attacks on the disk encryption key. For all other devices, we can "only" perform cold boot attacks to retrieve valuable information from RAM.

4   Implementation of the FROST Recovery Image

We now present details on the implementation of the FROST recovery image. Technically, FROST is a set of recovery tools that we developed and compounded together into an easy-to-use GUI. Notably, FROST displays a GUI that allows forensic examiners to acquire full memory dumps, to recover encryption keys directly on the phone, to unlock the encrypted user partition with recently recovered keys, and to crack weak PINs with brute force. We come back to these points in the subsequent sections.

4.1   Linux Kernel Module and GUI

The centerpiece of FROST are its loadable Linux kernel modules (LKMs). Accessing physical memory requires system level privileges, and to gain system level privileges we load LKMs. As a basis for our recovery image, we chose the recovery image from *ClockworkMod*, which is a known provider for custom Android ROMs. We integrated our FROST LKM, as well as user mode utilities and third party tools, into the ClockwordMod recovery image and modified it's GUI such that forensic data recovery can be operated comfortably. Users can choose between one of the following options in the FROST GUI:

- *Telephone encryption state*: To check the encryption state of the phone, we try to mount the userdata partition and check whether that succeeds.
- *Key recovery*: This option searches for AES keys (see Sect. 4.2). On success, the recovered key is displayed to the user and saved internally for later use.

- *RAM dump via USB*: This option saves a full memory dump of the smart-phone to the PC for offline analysis.
- *Crack 4-digit PINs*: Performs brute force attacks against weak PINs (see Sect. 4.3). Recovered PINs and keys are displayed and the key is saved for later use.
- *Decrypt and mount data*: Decrypts the user partition with recently recovered keys.

The key recovery mode optimized for Galaxy Nexus devices finishes in about $9s$. To create a full memory dump of 700 MB (which is the RAM size of a Galaxy Nexus) takes $3m\ 9s$. To load memory dumps to the PC, we make use of the LiME module [16]. LiME parses a kernel structure to learn physical memory addresses and each physical page is then transferred over TCP to the computer. Alternatively, LiME allows to save physical memory dumps to user partitions, but this is not an option in FROST because we assume user partitions are encrypted. To decrypt the userdata partition, we integrated a statically linked ARM binary of the *dmsetup* utility [17]. This option becomes available only if one of the key recovery methods or the brute force approach were successful, i.e., if the decryption key is known.

A precompiled version of the FROST recovery image for Galaxy Nexus devices is on our website (`http://www1.cs.fau.de/frost`). Above that, we provide the code of the FROST LKM and our user mode utilities as open source, such that similar images can easily be built for a wider class of devices. You may use these components independently of the recovery image.

4.2   AES Key Recovery

Our key recovery algorithm in FROST is based on the known utility *aeskeyfind* [4]. Aeskeyfind searches for AES keys in a given memory image from x86 PCs by identifying AES key schedule patterns in RAM. Contrary to aeskeyfind, FROST is implemented for ARM and searches for AES keys *on-the-fly*, i.e., directly on the phone. In comparison to x86, the endianness of key bytes in ARM is reversed, for example, such that exisiting algorithms had to be adapted. Our optimized code recovers AES keys in less than 10 seconds directly on the phone (whereas aeskeyfind requires always about 10 minutes). An exemplary FROST output is given in Fig. 6.

Our key recovery LKM basically supports two search modes: *quick search* and *full search*. Quick search is highly optimized for Galaxy Nexus devices and looks for AES keys at certain RAM addresses. In detail, we have chosen the address space 0xc5000000 to 0xd0000000 because all our tests revealed that AES key schedules are placed in this range. In quick search mode, the recovery process finishes within seconds. This mode, however, might fail on other devices because the search space might be too specific. Therefore, we implemented the full search mode that considers the entire physical RAM. The full search mode uses a sliding window mechanism that looks at each physical RAM page twice. In quick search mode, AES key schedules which are spread over multiple pages, are missed. In

```
adb> insmod frost.ko fullsearch=0 ; dmesg

key-32: 4ee35476397b76905828a89f3d9b872f
      : ccb6671af6eebffe94ea1bc87c0948e4
key-32: 4ee35476397b76905828a89f3d9b872f
      : ccb6671af6eebffe94ea1bc87c0948e4
key-16: bcdbc55cf809cb5989e58a40ecbb7164
key-16: bcdbc55cf809cb5989e58a40ecbb7164

Summarizing 4 keys found.
```

Fig. 6. Keys recovered with the FROST LKM

```
adb> ./crackpin

    magic: D0B5B1C4
   encdek: 3c4ac402c6095ed46cf4f1e2281a1f3e
     salt: 19043211840adfde95110c7f99263d6c

>>  KEK: 2165534cc66099714a8226753d70b576
>>  IV:  05cb47cf3a98d77e563bb4cfcde791aa
>>  DEK: bcdbc55cf809cb5989e58a40ecbb7164
>>  PIN: [2323]
```

Fig. 7. Key and PIN recovered with brute fore

practice, however, this is unlikely; in 50 test cases, we never observed an AES key schedule that was spread over two pages (the page size in Android is 4096 bytes).

If neither the quick search mode nor the full search mode succeeds, the memory image is too noisy, meaning that too many bits decayed during cold booting (see Sect. 3.2). As stated above, our key recovery algorithm is based on the utility aeskindfind. Aeskeyfind discards key candidates as soon as a given threshold of bits is reached that are not in line with a typical key schedule structure. If this threshold is too high, pseudo keys are identified from irrelevant memory regions. But if the threshold is too low, the recovery algorithm becomes prone to decayed bits from cold booting. As a tradeoff value that is based on results of our experiments, we have chosen 64 as default threshold in FROST. That means, 64 out of 1280 bits can be disturbed per key schedule at maximum. In other words, the bit error ratio is not allowed to exceed 5% to be able to identify key schedules in FROST.

To overcome the situation that no key bits can be recovered due to noisy images, we implemented a third search mode. During our RAM analysis, we recognized that AES keys are typically present in memory *five times*: once in the context of an AES forward schedule, once in the context of an AES backward schedule, and three times as a stand-alone bit sequence. Stand-alone bit sequences are commonly hard to identify as keys, because keys themselves have no structure. Only their corresponding key schedules have a structure. To exploit these occurrences, we implemented a search mode that is less generic but offers good results in practice: Rather than searching for key schedule patterns, we look after "magic strings" that appear near the desired key. From several test runs we know fixed offsets from magic strings to key locations. Given these offsets are correct, we can recover key bits independently of key schedules. However, this procedure is optimized for Galaxy Nexus devices and specific Android versions; offsets may change in upcoming releases.

The key recovery code of FROST was developed and tested on Galaxy Nexus devices, but it works for other Android-based smartphones, too. It is a part of our project which is *platform-independent*, meaning that it even runs on non-

Android systems. For example, we have successfully tested parts of our module on a PandaBoard with Ubuntu. In general, FROST's key recovery code can be used on all ARM devices where you have a Linux shell with root access.

4.3   PIN Cracking through Brute Force

PINs are still the most frequent screen lock in use today. But long PINs are too inconvenient for most people that work on their phones on a daily basis, because they must be entered for each interaction with the device, e.g., for giving a call, for writing a message, and for taking a photo. Consequently, people commonly use short PINs of only 4-8 digits. That is a concern, because in Android the screen lock PIN necessarily equals the PIN that is used to derive the disk encryption key. Consequently, besides cold boot attacks, short PINs are another weak point of Android's encryption feature. (Note that we find the restriction that encryption passwords must equal screen lock PINs in Android unnecessary and dangerous. In practice, it is more time consuming to crack a visual PIN prompt than to perform automated brute force attacks against encrypted filesystems.)

In 2012, Cannon and Bradford [18] presented details about Android's encryption system and gave instructions on how to break it with brute force attacks against the PIN. They published their findings in form of a Python script that breaks Android encryption offline, meaning that it runs on an x86 PC after the userdata and metadata partition have been retrieved "somehow". Basically, we reimplemented their Python script in C and cross-compiled it for the ARM architecture, so that we can perform efficient attacks directly on the phone, without the need to download the user partition. To this end, we cross-compiled the *PolarSSL* library for Android, an open source library similar to OpenSSL which is more light-weight and easier to use and integrate. We then statically linked our PIN cracking program with the PolarSSL library, because Android does not support dynamic linking. Both the source code and the statically linked binary are available on our webpage; an exemplary output of it is given in Fig. 7.

PINs with four digits are cracked within $2m$ $58s$ at maximum, i.e., in one and a half minute on average. Although we only implemented the important 4-digit case yet, we can estimate that 5-digit PINs are cracked in about $15m$, 6-digit PINs in $2h$ $30m$, and 7-digit PINs in about $25h$.

5   Future Work and Conclusions

To defeat physical access attacks, disk encryption has become an essential security mechanism for mobile devices. Virtually all PC operating systems support disk encryption since years, and smartphones now provide encryption, too. However, when losing an Android-based smartphone, chances are to lose valuable information even though encryption was used. The remanence effect shows up on smartphones, and as we have proven, it can be exploited with cold boot attacks to retrieve personal data. We believe that our study about Android's encryption is important for two reasons: First, it reveals a significant security gap that users should be aware of. Since smartphones are switched off only seldom, the severity of this gap is more concerning than on PCs. Second, we provide the recovery utility FROST which allows law enforcement to recover data from encrypted smartphones comfortably.

We have several plans for future improvements of FROST. First, we want to make our recovery image available for more Android devices than just the Galaxy Nexus. We already provide device independent system utilities like the FROST LKM and the PIN cracking program on our webpage, so that forensic examiners can compose recovery images for other devices also on their own. We provide appropriate howtos and source codes of our project for that. From an academic point of view, it is more important to analyze Android's memory structures in-depth in future. For example, we were not able to recover GPS coordinates and the list of recent phone calls yet, but we believe that this information is present in RAM.

To conclude, we have proven that smartphones can be attacked by cold boot attacks. To this end, we have shown that on Galaxy Nexus devices low temperatures raise the success rate of cold boot attacks (remanence effect). We also presented FROST, a tool that recovers personal data from encrypted smartphones. The biggest limitation of FROST to date, however, is that it requires an unlocked bootloader for breaking encryption entirely. Recovering the disk encryption key is always possible, but searching for it becomes pointless when the bootloader was locked (because the user partition gets wiped during unlocking). Nevertheless, personal data can *always* be recovered from RAM.

Countermeasures against cold boot attacks are difficult. On x86 PCs, solutions like TRESOR and TreVisor [19,20] perform encryption on CPU registers only, thereby thwarting attempts to reveal sensitive key material from RAM. However, such solutions are limited to encryption keys and cannot protect RAM contents in general. Protecting all information in RAM is assumed to be infeasible, which in turn proves the severity of tools like FROST.

Acknowledgments. We would like to thank Felix Freiling, Johannes Götzfried, Andreas Kurtz, Sven Schmitt, Johannes Stüttgen, and Stefan Vömel for helpful comments on the topic of our study.

References

1. Smith, A.: 35% of American adults own a smartphone. Pew Internet and American Life Project. Pew Research Center (July 2011)
2. Ponemon Institute LLC. The Lost Smartphone Problem: Benchmark study of U.S. organizations. In: Ponemon Institute Research Report. sponsored by McAfee (October 2011)
3. Gutmann, P.: Data Remanence in Semiconductor Devices. In: Proceedings of the 10th USENIX Security Symposium, Washington, D.C. USENIX Association (August 2001)

4. Halderman, J.A., Schoen, S.D., Heninger, N., Clarkson, W., Paul, W., Calandrino, J.A., Feldman, A.J., Appelbaum, J., Felten, E.W.: Lest We Remember: Cold Boot Attacks on Encryptions Keys. In: Proceedings of the 17th USENIX Security Symposium, San Jose, CA, August 2008, pp. 45–60. Princeton University, USENIX Association (August 2008)

5. Android Open Source Project (AOSP). Notes on the implementation of encryption in Android 3.0, source.android.com/tech/encryption/

6. Turan, M., Barker, E., Burr, W., Chen, L.: Special Publication 800-132: Recommendation for Password-Based Key Derivation. Technical report, NIST, Computer Security Division, Information Technology Laboratory (December 2010)

7. Aviv, A.J., Gibson, K., Mossop, E., Blaze, M., Smith, J.M.: Smudge Attacks on Smartphone Touch Screens. In: WOOT 2010, 4th USENIX Workshop on Offensive Technologies. Department of Computer and Information Science, University of Pennsylvania (August 2010)

8. Kumar, M.: Android facial recognition based unlocking can be fooled with photo. The Hacker News (November 2011), http://thehackernews.com/

9. Skorobogatov, S.: Data Remanence in Flash Memory Devices. In: Rao, J.R., Sunar, B. (eds.) CHES 2005. LNCS, vol. 3659, pp. 339–353. Springer, Heidelberg (2005)

10. Anderson, R., Kuhn, M.: Tamper Resistance – a Cautionary Note. In: The Second USENIX Workshop on Electronic Commerce Proceedings, Oakland, California, pp. 1–11. USENIX Association (November 1996)

11. Rahmati, A., Salajegheh, M., Holcomb, D., Sorber, J., Burleson, W., Fu, K.: TARDIS: Time and Remanence Decay in SRAM to Implement Secure Protocols on Embedded Devices withou Clocks. In: 21st USENIX Security Symposium, Bellevue, WA, UMass Amherst, USENIX Association (August 2012)

12. Saxena, N., Voris, J.: We Can Remember It for You Wholesale: Implications of Data Remanence on the Use of RAM for True Random Number Generation on RFID Tags. In: 5th Workshop on RFID Security (RFIDSec), Leuven, Belgium, Polytechnic Institute of New York University (July 2009)

13. xdadevelopers. Google Play Nexus not wiping after Bootloader Unlock. Thread 1650830 (April 2012), http://forum.xda-developers.com

14. xdadevelopers. Internal Memory Data Recovery - Yes We Can! Thread 1994705 (November 2012), http://forum.xda-developers.com

15. xdadevelopers. GT-i9100 Galaxy SII FAQ. Thread 1046748 (April 2011), http://forum.xda-developers.com

16. Sylve, J.: LiME - Linux Memory Extractor. In: ShmooCon 2012, Washingtion, D.C. Digital Forensics Solutions, LLC (January 2012)

17. Zugelder, M.: androidcrypt.py (April 2012), https://github.com/michael42/androidcrypt.py/

18. Cannon, T., Bradford, S.: Into the Droid: Gaining Access to Android User Data. In: DefCon 2012. VIA Forensics (July 2012)

19. Müller, T., Freiling, F., Dewald, A.: TRESOR Runs Encryption Securely Outside RAM. In: 20th USENIX Security Symposium, San Francisco, California. University of Erlangen-Nuremberg, USENIX Association (August 2011)

20. Müller, T., Taubmann, B., Freiling, F.C.: TreVisor: OS-Independent Software-Based Full Disk Encryption Secure Against Main Memory Attacks. In: Bao, F., Samarati, P., Zhou, J. (eds.) ACNS 2012. LNCS, vol. 7341, pp. 66–83. Springer, Heidelberg (2012)

Attacking Atmel's CryptoMemory EEPROM with Special-Purpose Hardware

Alexander Wild, Tim Güneysu, and Amir Moradi

Horst Görtz Institute for IT Security, Ruhr University Bochum, Germany
{alexander.wild,tim.gueneysu,amir.moradi}@rub.de

Abstract. Atmel's CryptoMemory devices are non-volatile memories with cryptographically secured access control. Recently, the authentication mechanism of these devices have been shown to be severely vulnerable. More precisely, to recover the secret key the published attack requires only two to six days of computation on a cluster involving 200 CPU cores. In this work, we identified and applied theoretical improvements to this attack and mapped it to a reconfigurable computing cluster, known as RIVYERA. Our solution provides significantly higher performance exceeding the previous implementation by a factor of 7.27, revealing the secret key obtained from the internal state in 0.55 days on average using only 30 authentication frames.

1 Introduction

In 2002 Atmel introduced a secure memory device with authentication called CryptoMemory [2,13] which is basically an Electrically Erasable Programmable Read-Only Memory (EEPROM) augmented with a secure access control unit.

Due to the low cost and simplicity of deployment the device is employed in a wide range of commercial products, e.g., as key storage of the HDCP system in NVIDIA's graphic cards [16], Labgear's digital satellite receivers [15], Microsoft's Zune Player [7] and SanDisk's Sansa Connect [9] using the CryptoMemory as part of their DRM system implementation. Further examples of CryptoMemory deployment are printer and printer cartridge manufacturers like Dell, Ricoh, Xerox, and Samsung [14]. Furthermore, Atmel's CryptoMemory is placed in authentication tokens from Digitrade [6] and Datakey Electronics [1].

The specification of the Atmel cipher was kept secret till ACM CCS 2010 where Garcia et al. presented their findings obtained from reverse engineering [8]. They also showed significant weaknesses by analyzing the authentication protocol. One year later Biryukov et al. published a more efficient method which – with a probability of 50% – is capable of extracting the secret key from 30 authentication recordings [4]. This attack runs on a computing cluster with 200 Central Processing Unit (CPU) cores and needs two to six days to recover the secret. Another attack based on power side-channels has also been reported in [3]. This attack lasting a few minutes, however, needs physical access to the device and a special side-channel measurement setup to extract the secret key from about 100 power traces.

M. Jacobson et al. (Eds.): ACNS 2013, LNCS 7954, pp. 389–404, 2013.

Our contribution: In this work, we improve and map the best known cryptanalytic attack on CryptoMemory devices published in [4] to special-purpose hardware, namely the RIVYERA S3-5000 reconfigurable computing cluster [17]. Our improvement of the cryptanalytic setup in addition to our hardware-based implementation leads to a speedup factor of 7.27 compared to the previously reported results. In short, our implementation is able to extract the internal state of the cipher from 30 authentication frames within 0.55 days on average which impressively demonstrates that none of the products mentioned above can be considered as secure. Given a cluster such as RIVYERA, our attack configuration is also a power-efficient solution. For a run with 30 frames, the hardware cluster consumes 8.6KWh instead of 245.76KWh the CPU cluster per attacked device.

Outline: In Section 2 we provide preliminary information on CryptoMemory, previously published attacks and RIVYERA. Improvements of the attack are presented in Section 3. Section 4 and 5 deals with our implementation architectures before we compare our results in Section 6 with those of a CPU-based implementation. Finally, our conclusions are given by Section 7.

2   Background

In this section we briefly restate the required background of our work. The section includes specification of the targeted cipher, the underlying protocol, the attack of [4], and our computing cluster.

2.1   CryptoMemory Stream Cipher

The cipher state consists of four shift registers - the left, middle, right and feedback register.

Definition 1. *The state* $S = (l, m, r, f)$ *is an element of* $\mathbb{F}_2^{117}$ *and consists of:*

$$
\begin{aligned}
\textit{Left Register:} \quad & l = (l_0, l_1 \ldots, l_6) \in (\mathbb{F}_2^5)^7 \\
\textit{Middle Register:} \quad & m = (m_0, m_1 \ldots, m_6) \in (\mathbb{F}_2^7)^7 \\
\textit{Right Register:} \quad & r = (r_0, r_1 \ldots, r_4) \in (\mathbb{F}_2^5)^5 \\
\textit{Feedback Register:} \quad & f = (f_0, f_1) \in (\mathbb{F}_2^4)^2
\end{aligned}
$$

For every cipher tick, the input $a \in \mathbb{F}_2^8$ is processed during the transition of S to the successor state S'. The state transition is executed in three steps. First, the input values a and f are merged and XORed to several bits in the l, m, and r registers. Second, the left, middle, and right registers are shifted to the right and their feedback value is calculated with the help of a bitwise left rotation and modular addition. Third, the f register is shifted to the left and the new calculated cipher output nibble becomes the new first element of f. Figure 1 provides an overview of the cipher operation. The core operations of the cipher are given by the following definitions:

Definition 2. *The bitwise left rotation operator* $L : \mathbb{F}_2^n \to \mathbb{F}_2^n$ *is defined by:*

$$L(x_0 x_1 \ldots x_{n-1}) = (x_1 \ldots x_{n-1} x_0)$$

Definition 3. *Let* $\oplus$ *be a bitwise XOR operator* $\mathbb{F}_2^n \times \mathbb{F}_2^n \to \mathbb{F}_2^n$.

Definition 4. *The modular addition operator* $\boxplus : \mathbb{F}_2^n \times \mathbb{F}_2^n \to \mathbb{F}_2^n$ *is defined as:*

$$x \boxplus y = \begin{cases} x + y(\mod 2^n - 1) & \text{if } x = y = 0 \text{ or } x + y \neq 0 (\mod 2^n - 1) \\ 2^n - 1 & \text{otherwise} \end{cases}$$

Definition 5. *Let* a *and* b *be defined as:* $a \in \mathbb{F}_2^8$ *and* $b = a \oplus f_0 f_1$. *Further, the successor state* $S' = (l', m', r', f')$ *is defined as follows:*

$$l_0' := l_3 \boxplus L(l_6), \qquad l_3' := l_2 \oplus b_3 b_4 b_5 b_6 b_7, \qquad l_{i+1}' := l_i \quad i \in \{0,1,3,4,5\}$$
$$m_0' := m_5 \boxplus L(m_6), \qquad m_5' := m_4 \oplus b_4 b_5 b_6 b_7 b_0 b_1 b_2, \qquad m_{j+1}' := m_j \quad j \in \{0,1,2,3,5\}$$
$$r_0' := r_2 \boxplus r_4, \qquad r_2' := r_1 \oplus b_0 b_1 b_2 b_3 b_4, \qquad r_{k+1}' := r_k \quad k \in \{0,2,3\}$$
$$f_0' := f_1, \qquad f_1' := output(S')$$

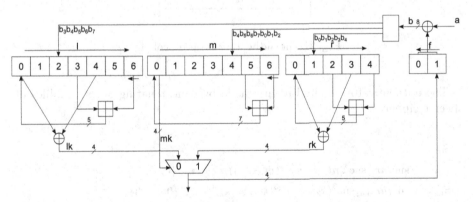

Fig. 1. The CryptoMemory keystream generator [4]

Definition 6. *The cipher output function is defined as follows while* i *is a bit-selector:*

$$output(S')_i = \begin{cases} lk_i = (l_0' \oplus l_4')_{i+1}, & \text{if } m_{0,i+3}' = 0 \\ rk_i = (r_0' \oplus r_3')_{i+1}, & \text{if } m_{0,i+3}' = 1 \end{cases} \quad i \in \{0,\ldots,3\}$$

Definition 7. *Let suc be the state transition function with input a, S and output S′ = suc(a, S). Further, sucⁿ(a, S) is defined as multiple application of suc transforming S into its n-th successor state.*

$$suc^1(a, S) := suc(a, S)$$
$$suc^n(a, S) := suc^{n-1}(a, suc(a, S)) \; for \; n > 1$$

2.2 Mutual Authentication Protocol

Apart from the authentication between reader and memory, the authentication protocol is used to initialize the CryptoMemory device and requires the exchange of three messages. The first one contains a nonce $nt \in (\mathbb{F}_2^8)^8$ sent from the memory to the reader. The second message consists of another nonce $nr \in (\mathbb{F}_2^8)^8$ and a calculated authenticator $ar \in (\mathbb{F}_2^4)^{16}$ sent from reader to the memory device. As the last message, the memory device calculates its authenticator $at \in (\mathbb{F}_2^4)^{16}$ and sends it to the reader. Figure 2 depicts the protocol from which the resulting tuple $(nr, nt, ar, \text{and } at)$ is defined as an authentication frame.

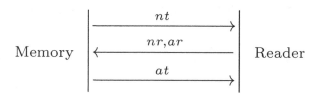

Fig. 2. The authentication protocol [4]

The authenticators ar and at are made by concatenating output nibbles of specific cipher states.

$S_0 := 0$

$S_{i+1} := \text{suc}(nr_i, \text{suc}^3(nt_{2i+1}, \text{suc}^3(nt_{2i}, S_i)))$ $\quad i \in \{0, \ldots, 3\}$

$S_{i+5} := \text{suc}(nr_{i+4}, \text{suc}^3(k_{2i+1}, \text{suc}^3(k_{2i}, S_{i+4})))$ $\quad i \in \{0, \ldots, 3\}$

$S_9 := \text{suc}^5(0, S_8), \quad S_{10} := \text{suc}(0, S_9), \quad S_i := \text{suc}^6(0, S_{i-1}) \quad i \in \{11, 13, \ldots, 23\}$

$S_i := \text{suc}(0, S_{i-1}) \quad i \in \{12, 14, \ldots, 24\}, \quad S_i := \text{suc}(0, S_{i-1}) \quad i \in \{25, 26, \ldots, 38\}$

$ar_i := \text{output}(S_{i+9}) \quad i \in \{0, 1, \ldots, 15\}$

$at_0 := 15, \quad at_1 := 15, \quad at_i := \text{output}(S_{i+23}) \quad i \in \{2, 3, \ldots, 15\}$

2.3   A Probabilistic Attack on CryptoMemory

This section introduces the published attack by Biryukov et al. [4] which requires knowledge of some eavesdropped authentication frames to reconstruct the cipher state S_8 and S_4. Then a meet-in-the-middle attack is applied to extract the secret key k from the cipher states. The reconstruction of S_8 is the most computationally intensive part and is based on three phases. We start with the generation of state candidates for the right register r. Based on these given candidates we similarly obtain state hypotheses for the left register l. As the third step, we finally compute candidates matching the middle register m for each given left-right register tuple.

Right Register. The attack is based on an exhaustive search for all possible S_{24} states of the right register r and uses a correlation test to filter invalid guesses. This is performed by guessing r, calculating the register output for 16 consecutive ticks and counting the equivalent bits to ar_{14}, ar_{15}, at_i for $i = 2, \ldots 15$. If the sum of coincident bits is below a certain threshold T_r, the candidate is discarded. These steps are repeated until all candidates for r are checked.

Left Register. The next step is to recover the left register and is repeated for each remaining candidate of r. First, lk_i is defined as the intermediate output of l and $l_{S_0} = \{l_0, l_1, l_2, l_3, l_4, l_5, l_6\}$ as the starting point for the calculation. In fact, some bits of lk are known - in particular the cipher output bits that cannot be created by the right register.

Combining the state update function and the state output function, this results in the following equations for the first six output nibbles of the left register:

$$lk_1 = (l_3 \boxplus L(l_6)) \oplus l_3, \quad lk_2 = (l_2 \boxplus L(l_5)) \oplus l_2, \quad lk_3 = (l_1 \boxplus L(l_4)) \oplus l_1,$$
$$lk_4 = (l_0 \boxplus L(l_3)) \oplus l_0, \quad lk_5 = (l_7 \boxplus L(l_2)) \oplus l_7, \quad lk_6 = (l_8 \boxplus L(l_1)) \oplus l_8.$$

The equations above show that lk_i depends only on two variables. Based on these equations the following sets are defined which hold tuples of l_i and l_j.

$$H_0 = \{l_3, l_6\}, \quad H_1 = \{l_2, l_5\}, \quad H_2 = \{l_1, l_4\}, \quad H_3 = \{l_0, l_3\},$$
$$H_4 = \{l_7, l_2\}, \quad H_5 = \{l_8, l_1\}, \quad H_6 = \{l_9, l_0\}.$$

With the known parts of lk_i, H_i can be reduced to only those that match the aforementioned equations. The cardinality of each set strongly depends on the number of known bits in lk_i. Let $N_H(lk_i)$ be the number of known bits in lk_i. Note that register cells are used in more than one set. For example, l_3 is part of H_0 and H_3.

$$H_{0,3} = H_0 \cap H_3 = \{l_3\}, \quad H_{1,4} = H_1 \cap H_4 = \{l_2\},$$
$$H_{2,5} = H_2 \cap H_5 = \{l_1\}, \quad H_{3,6} = H_3 \cap H_6 = \{l_0\}$$

H_i and H_{i+3} can be further reduced by keeping only tuples that consist in l_{3-i} and create the intersection set $H_{i,i+3}$. Additionally, H_0, H_3, and H_6 are combined to $H_{0,3,6} = \{l_0, l_3, l_6\}$ to do a similar reduction by keeping only possible intersection values.

A yet unresolved problem is to choose a good starting point S_0 to maximize the reduction effect. A solution to this problem $\Psi(i)$ can be obtained from

$$\Psi(i) = \sum_{j \in \{1,3,4,8\}} N_H(lk_{i+j}) \quad \text{for } 1 \leq i \leq 7.$$

This function considers the reduction effect on $A = \{l_0, l_1, l_3, l_4, l_6\}$ of a chosen starting state S_0. Let $J = \arg\max_{1 \leq i \leq 7} \Psi(i)$; then, the optimal starting point is S_{24+J} to have the maximum reduction effect on A.

Theorem 1. *If A is defined as $A = \{l_0, l_1, l_3, l_4, l_6\}$ then $\{lk_0, lk_1, lk_3, lk_4, lk_7, lk_8, lk_{11}, lk_{15}\}$ depend only on A, $\{lk_{-1}\}$ on $\{l_5\}$ and A, and $\{lk_5, lk_{12}\}$ on A and l_2 for any chosen starting point l_{S_0}.*

Theorem 1 points out that some register cells exist with more impact on the output stream than others. Hence, the best starting point is the one with the most known bits in A. The proof of Theorem 1 can be found in [5]. Note that $\Psi(i)$ is defined over $1 \leq i \leq 7$ and if $J = 7$, only lk_i up to $i = 8$ can be used for the reduction. Due to the fact that J can be at minimum 1, the (lk_{-1}, lk_5) tuple can be combined with H_1 similar to the intersection set $H_{0,3,6}$ for further reduction.

After the reduction steps, the remaining set H_1 and A are combined to reconstruct all possible internal states S_{24+J} of the left register. In order to cover all lk_i the created candidates are clocked forward and finally backward from l_{S_0} to the original state S_{24}. Keep in mind for this step that l_0 and l_1 has to be XORed with their corresponding feedback byte to get the original values. For further reduction all restored candidates are filtered with the same correlation test as that of the right register but using T_l as the chosen threshold.

Middle Register. The most time-consuming part is the recovery of the middle register that we mapped to hardware as explained in Section 5. Assume that possible candidate pairs for the left and the right register have been generated according to the two steps expressed before. These candidates represent the state S_{24}. The following steps are then performed for each candidate pair.

Let mk_i be the output bits of the middle register. Some bits of mk_i can be restored with the help of rk_i and lk_i. Note that mk_i are the four right most bits of m_j. Due to that, information about m_0, m_7, m_8, ..., m_{21} is extracted. In order to use all gathered information about the middle register cells the attack starts from the state S_{30}.

Depending on the output and update function the following equations are extracted:

$$mk_7 = m_7 \boxplus L(m_0), \quad mk_i = m_i \boxplus L(m_{i-1}) \quad i \in \{8, \ldots, 15\}.$$

Similar to the reconstruction of the left register, all possible tuples for the middle register cells of state S_{30} are grouped together to form the sets Q_i. For example, Q_0 holds all tuples of m_7 and m_0 that are able to create mk_7. In comparison to the reconstruction of the left register, there are some known bits of m_i that do not depend on other register cells. The cardinality of Q_i also correlates with the number of known bits in mk_{i+7}, m_{i+7}, and m_{i+6}.

$$Q_0 = \{m_7, m_0\}, \quad Q_1 = \{m_8, m_7\}, \quad Q_2 = \{m_9, m_8\}, \quad Q_3 = \{m_{10}, m_9\},$$
$$Q_4 = \{m_{11}, m_{10}\}, \quad Q_5 = \{m_{12}, m_{11}\}, \quad Q_6 = \{m_{13}, m_{12}\}, \quad Q_7 = \{m_{14}, m_{13}\},$$
$$Q_8 = \{m_{15}, m_{14}\}$$

Figure 3 shows which information is used by each Q_i. It is shown that all gained information is used in the sets and which relations they have. In the following it is explained how these relations are used to minimize the number of possible S_{30} candidates.

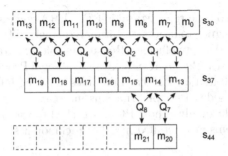

Fig. 3. This diagram shows in which data set which information is processed, structured by the candidate state of the middle register

Q_i and Q_{i+1} can be shrunk by keeping only tuples that exist in the intersection set $Q_{i,i+1}$ with the same pattern value m_j. To maximize the reduction effect a good starting point needs to be chosen again. Let $I = \arg\min_{0 \leq i \leq 8} |Q_i|$ where $|Q_i|$ is the cardinality of Q_i. Then, the reduction process is started from $Q_I = \{m_j, m_k\}$ with $k = 0$ or $k = j - 1$. In other words, each Q_i is compared with Q_{i+1} for $I \leq i \leq 7$. Q_i is also compared with Q_{i-1} for $1 \leq i \leq I$.

$$Q_{0,1} = Q_0 \cap Q_1 = \{m_7\}, \quad Q_{1,2} = Q_1 \cap Q_2 = \{m_8\}, \quad Q_{2,3} = Q_2 \cap Q_3 = \{m_9\},$$
$$Q_{3,4} = Q_3 \cap Q_4 = \{m_{10}\}, \quad Q_{4,5} = Q_4 \cap Q_5 = \{m_{11}\}, \quad Q_{5,6} = Q_5 \cap Q_6 = \{m_{12}\},$$
$$Q_{6,7} = Q_6 \cap Q_7 = \{m_{13}\}, \quad Q_{7,8} = Q_7 \cap Q_8 = \{m_{14}\}$$

Now, the reduced Q_i sets are combined to fill the middle register cells six downto three of state S_{30}. This partially filled register is checked immediately by

$$mk_{14} = (m_{14} \oplus b_{S_{36}}) \boxplus L(m_{13} \oplus b_{S_{35}}) = (m_8 \boxplus L(m_7)) \boxplus L(m_7 \boxplus L(m_0)),$$
$$mk_{15} = (m_{15} \oplus b_{S_{37}}) \boxplus L(m_{14} \oplus b_{S_{36}}) = (m_9 \boxplus L(m_8)) \boxplus L(m_8 \boxplus L(m_7)).$$

This verification is performed by calculating m_{13}, m_{14} and m_{15} from m_0, m_7, m_8, and m_9. Then the new calculated values are XORed with their feedback byte and it is checked if the tuple (m_{14}, m_{13}) is included in Q_7 and if the tuple (m_{15}, m_{14}) is a part of Q_8. If this is not the case, the partial candidate is discarded and register cells 3 to 6 are filled with the next combination. Otherwise, cell 2 to 0 are filled from Q_3, Q_4, and Q_5 in the same way like cell 3 and 4 to complete the register candidate of state S_{30}. In order to get full cipher candidates of the same state the middle register is clocked backwards to state S_{24}.

As the final step of the state recovering process, the complete internal state $S_{24} = (l, m, r, f)$ is clocked backwards to state S_8 and the corresponding output is compared with ar_{13} to ar_0. This final step usually filters all invalid candidates. A correct state S_8 of a frame only persists if it was previously not discarded by the correlation tests performed on the right and left register candidates.

2.4 RIVYERA Special-Purpose Hardware Cluster

In this work we employ the reconfigurable RIVYERA computing cluster system which is specially designed to process cryptanalytic tasks. The Redesign of the Incredibly Versatile Yet Energy-efficient, Reconfigurable Architecture (RIVYERA) cluster is populated with 128 Spartan-3 XC3S5000 Field Programmable Gate Arrays (FPGAs) distributed over 16 card modules. The modules are plugged into a backplane that provides a systolic ring bus interconnect for high-performance communication. Additionally, a host PC is attached to the ring bus via PCI Express and both systems are installed in a 19" rackmount system [10,11,18,19].

3   Advanced Candidate Filtering

The attack described previously creates candidates for each register sequentially. The candidates for the left register are chosen from the output stream of a right register candidate, and the middle register candidates are based on the output stream of a left and a right register candidate. The output function of the left and the right register is a simple XOR. The XOR operation of the binary complement $\bar{x}_0$ and $\bar{x}_1$ of an arbitrary x_0 and x_1 results in the same output y.

The update function of both register acts as following:

$$l_3 \boxplus L(l_6) = l_0 \qquad\qquad r_2 \boxplus r_4 = r_0 \qquad\qquad (1)$$

$$\bar{l}_3 \boxplus L(\bar{l}_6) = \bar{l}_0 \text{ when } l_3 \neq L(\bar{l}_6) \qquad \bar{r}_2 \boxplus \bar{r}_4 = \bar{r}_0 \text{ when } r_2 \neq \bar{r}_4 \qquad (2)$$

The probability that the condition in Equation (2) is not given for a register is $\frac{1}{32}$. To create the output stream the right register candidate is clocked 16 times. So the probability that the condition is not met during this time is $(1 - \frac{1}{32})^{16} = 0.6017$. Summarizing the previous facts leads to a 60% chance that r as well as $\bar{r}$ produce the same output stream. In case r passes the correlation test, $\bar{r}$ passes the correlation test as well. This behavior also occurs for left register candidates. Due to the fact that the left register candidates are only based on the cipher output stream and the right register output stream, r and $\bar{r}$ produce the same left register candidate list. The middle register candidates are also based only on the output streams lk and rk which means that the tuples (l,r), $(\bar{l},r)$, $(l,\bar{r})$ and $(\bar{l},\bar{r})$ produces the same middle register candidate list, when the conditions in Equation (2) are satisfied during register output generation.

The attack performs inverted cipher ticks for a register candidate triple (l,m,r) and checks whether it matches to the known ar_i nibbles. For an inverted cipher tick a modular subtraction is necessary which is defined as follows:

Definition 8. *The modular subtraction operator* $\boxminus : \mathbb{F}_2^n \times \mathbb{F}_2^n \to \mathbb{F}_2^n$ *is defined as:*

$$x \boxminus y = \begin{cases} x - y(\mod 2^n - 1) & \text{if } x \neq y \\ 2^n - 1 \text{ or } 0 & \text{otherwise} \end{cases}$$

Note that the modular subtraction is non-injective. In case of $x = y$, the result of the modular subtraction can be 0 or $2^n - 1$. The attack, should consider both cases; in the later steps the wrong guess will be filtered out when not matching with ar_i.

For the modulo subtraction we observe a similar behavior as for the modulo addition. The condition in Equation (3) is due to the non-injectivity of the operator.

$$l_0 \boxminus l_4 = L(l_6) \qquad\qquad r_0 \boxminus r_3 = r_4$$
$$\bar{l}_0 \boxminus \bar{l}_4 = L(\bar{l}_6) \text{ when } l_0 \neq l_4 \qquad \bar{r}_0 \boxminus \bar{r}_3 = \bar{r}_4 \text{ when } r_0 \neq r_3 \qquad (3)$$

Summarizing all these facts leads to the following conclusion. The attack performs inverse cipher ticks for the triple (r,m,l) to check its consistency with the known ar_i nibbles. If r, $\bar{r}$ and l, $\bar{l}$ exist in the list of candidates, we validate the triples $(l,m,\bar{r})$, $(\bar{l},m,r)$, $(\bar{l},m,\bar{r})$ at the same time. Also, if (l,m,r) is not the correct internal state, $(l,m,\bar{r})$, $(\bar{l},m,r)$, and $(\bar{l},m,\bar{r})$ will not be the correct one either. Therefore, we can remove $\bar{l}$ and $\bar{r}$ from the list of candidates which generate the same output stream as l and r. For a remaining candidate S_8 the complementary left and right register candidates have to be checked separately if they are feasible as well. Our experiments have shown that with this additional filtering the number of right and left register candidates are reduced to 68%. In total we only process – on average – 46.24% of the original left and right candidate list.

4   Mapping Components to Hardware

Most parts of the attack will be executed in software and only the most time-consuming parts are mapped to hardware. In this context, the interfaces between software and hardware are of major importance to allow a smooth transition of data in both directions. As a first step we implement the calculations of the middle register reconstruction process in hardware. The transition from software to hardware at this point requires only a very limited number of data transfers.

Moreover, this is indeed the most time-consuming part (about 98.8 % of the attack time).

Attacking m begins with the reconstruction of Q_i and searches for the smallest set. The subsequent reduction on this step compares possible register cell candidates. In our hardware implementation we should merge these two steps so that the generation and reduction of the register cell candidates are performed at once. In order to check whether m_i is part of Q_j and Q_{j+1} it is necessary to check if (a) m_i contains the known bits from the fragmentary middle register output stream and (b) there must be at least one m_{i+1} and one m_{i-1} each of which contains the fragmentary known bits and is not removed. Each of them also must be able to create in conjunction with m_i an arbitrary m_{k+1} and m_k, respectively, that each contains the corresponding known bits. If both conditions are fulfilled, m_i is a valid register cell candidate.

Due to our merging technique we do not know which set is the smallest one. So we always start the generation with Q_8 and continue the calculation iteratively until we have created Q_0. With Q_0 we perform the generation and reduction steps again for all sets from Q_0 to Q_8. During the creation of the sets, either register cell candidates from previously generated sets are used or the candidates are generated with the help of the known mk_i bits as described in Section 5.1.

After generation the valid tuples need to be stored in memory. One problem is that we do not know in advance how many valid tuples we will receive but we have to allocate a fixed amount of memory in hardware. So we assume the worst case memory complexity for the Q_i sets: $2^7 \cdot 2^7 \cdot 14 \cdot 9$ bits. This translates to 126 Block Random-Access Memory (BRAM) blocks with 18kB each, but a Spartan-3 5000 only provides 108 BRAMs. Due to the sequential nature of the reduction, an on-the-fly calculation of the candidates will result in an enormous increase of time. An alternative method is to store the information of valid tuples in relation matrices. In a relation matrix the information of the register cell values is encoded in the position of a special flag which indicates if the register cell combination is valid or not. The usage of relation matrices reduces the memory complexity to: $2^7 \cdot 2^7 \cdot 9$ bits, which needs in total only 9 BRAM blocks to hold the necessary information. This storage method directly leads to the next challenge: the efficient reconstruction of register cell values. Obviously, due to the cell candidate dependencies a bitwise search for each candidate is ineffective.

Finally, the hardware instantiation of an Inverse Cipher Tick (ICT) is not trivial as well. Each modular subtraction for an ICT is non-injective so for some values the result is ambiguous and incorrect values need to be sorted out a few ICTs later. This backtracking behavior complicates a straightforward hardware implementation using parallelism or pipelining techniques so that we decided to implement multiple iterative ICT modules instead for maximum performance.

5   Implementation

In this section we give an overview of the hardware implementation of the attack including advanced candidate filtering. Each of the 128 FPGAs is configured with the same configuration. The design contains two independent attack cores to which a controller forwards data depending on which module is waiting for a new dataset. Each attack component contains a module to generate Q_i tables that iteratively creates register cell candidates and stores them in the BRAMs. Then, a module reconstructs complete middle register candidates from the previously generated relation matrices (Buffered Pipeline) and distributes the candidates to a free ICT module. The ICT module performs inverse cipher ticks and validates the candidate by examining its compliance with ar_i. Figure 4 depicts the top-level design of our implementation.

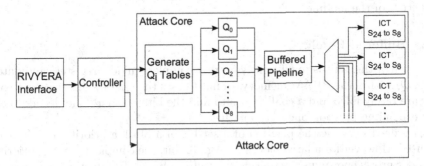

Fig. 4. The top-level design of our hardware implementation

5.1   Generating Q_i Tables

The Q_i generating module iteratively fills Q_i with valid register cell tuples and starts with Q_8. First, the design uses just a counter and the partial reconstructed

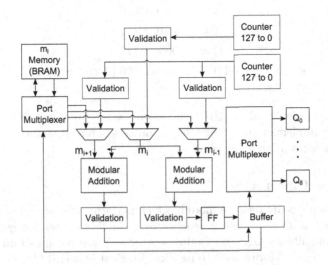

Fig. 5. Design of the Q_i generation module

output stream to reduce the amount of possible candidates for m_{15}, m_{14} and m_{13}. The possible register cell candidates are then fed into a modular adder that calculates m_{21} and m_{20} which are directly verified by the known bits. Based on the results, a BRAM block for Q_8 is filled with a stream of bits that represents valid tuples for m_{15} and m_{14}. After the calculation of Q_8 is completed, the module continues with the calculation of Q_7. At this point possible previously defined candidates for m_{14} are present in memory and the module repeats these steps until Q_0 is generated. Next it performs the same procedure again in the reverse direction, i.e., from Q_1 to Q_8 to achieve a maximum effect reducing the number of possible register cell candidates. Figure 5 shows an overview of the structure of the module.

5.2   Buffered Pipeline

The goal of this unit is to efficiently extract complete middle register candidates from Q_i within the BRAM memory. In most cases the relation matrices in memory are rarely filled and a challenge is to find the bits set in Q_i and decode their corresponding position one after another.

In order to decode the position of a set bit in a block a priority decoder can be used. However for a large blocksize, e.g., 32-bit, the complexity of the priority decoder grows enormously requiring a lot of resources. To save the resources we filter one set bit out of the block and use a simple decoder to extract the position of this single set bit. The filtering is realized with the following approach:

Let α be a binary block. Instead of using a priority decoder one can calculate $\alpha \wedge (\alpha \oplus (\alpha - 1))$ which contains at most a single one bit and passes this to a binary decoder. This process can be iteratively repeated by replacing α by $\alpha \oplus (\alpha \wedge (\alpha \oplus (\alpha - 1)))$. For clarification an example is given in the following:

$$\alpha = \ldots 101001000$$
$$\alpha - 1 = \ldots 101000111$$
$$\alpha \oplus (\alpha - 1) = \ldots 000001111$$
$$\alpha \wedge (\alpha \oplus (\alpha - 1)) = \ldots 000001000 \text{ (decoder input)}$$

This technique always filters the right most set bit from an arbitrary binary block. In our implementation this filtering process is repeated until each one bit in a block is appropriately decoded.

5.3   Inverse Cipher Tick

The ICT module is an iterative module which performs inverse cipher ticks until S_8 of a cipher state candidate is reached or a candidate does not generate the known output nibbles ar_i. The module starts with the receipt of an incoming candidate of S_{24} and forwards it to its First In, First Out (FIFO) unit. A candidate coming out of the FIFO is fed into the modular subtractor which calculates the right most cells of the three main state registers. Due to the non-injective property of modular subtraction, the output of the modular subtractor is selected by a special flag (0 by default). A decision unit calculates these flags and ensures that – in case of multiple ambiguous results – all possible combinations are considered. Two final modules update the feedback register and validate with ar_i. In case of a positive result, the newly generated state is fed into the FIFO for the next ICT– until either finally S_8 is reached or validation fails in a later step. Figure 6 depicts a block diagram of the ICT module.

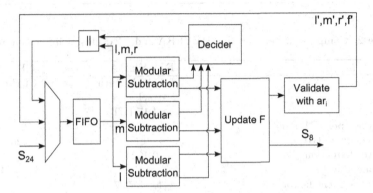

Fig. 6. The internal structure of an ICT module

6   Results

In this section we present the results of our hardware implementation obtained using Xilinx ISE Foundation 14.3 for synthesis and place and route. The design with two attack cores of which each contains 17 ICT modules is synthesized and runs at the frequency of 100MHz. The utilized resources on each Spartan-3 5000 are shown in Table 1.

Essentially, the attack speed strongly depends on the frequency of operation and the number of attack components and ICT modules per core. The integrated FIFO component of each module has a data width of 125 bits which results in the utilization of 4 BRAM primitives on a Spartan-3. The complete hardware design is limited by BRAM blocks, i.e., a generic design configuration with two attack cores based on BRAM can only instantiate 7 ICT modules per core. For a better resource utilization a dedicated LUT-based version of the ICT modules was generated to instantiate the internal FIFO. This alternative implementation allows us to instantiate 10 additional ICT modules per core. Table 1 shows the resource consumptions of both ICT versions on a Spartan-3 5000.

Next we compare the throughput of the CPU-based cluster implementation in [4] with our hardware implementation on RIVYERA. Note that exact cycle counts are not available for the implementation given in [4]. Therefore we restrict our comparison to the data as shown in Table 2.

Table 1. Resource consumption of a dedicated RAM-based ICT BRAM-based ICT and for the complete design (two attack components and 17 ICT) on a Spartan-3 5000 FPGA

Resource	DRAM ICT	BRAM ICT	Complete	Available
Slices	808	482	28.298	33.280
Lookup Tables (LUTs)	1058	469	45.600	66.560
Slice Registers	460	317	28.199	66.560
BRAM	0	4	103	104

Table 2. Comparison between the RIVYERA and CPU cluster implementation

Aspect	RIVYERA	CPU
Parallelization	128 FPGAs with 2 attack cores and 17 ICT	200 CPU cores
Clock Cycles per ICT step	5	2^7
Clock Frequency [GHz]	0.1	2.26
Candidate Reduction (1/r)	0.4624	1
Total Time [days]	0.55	$\frac{2+6}{2} = 4$
Total improvement factor	$\frac{4}{0.55} = 7.27$	1
Performance equivalency	1 FPGA $\equiv$	11.36 CPUs
Power Consumption per Device [KW]	0.65	2.56
Power Consumption per Attack [KWh]	$0.65 \cdot 13.23 = 8.6$	$2.56 \cdot 96 = 245.76$
Cost Reduction	28.58	1

In order to determine the attack speed of our solution, we measure the validation time for a left and right register pair. 300 randomly generated frames are chosen to compute the average time needed for register pair validation. On average one attack unit is able to check one left/right register candidate tuple in 0.8 seconds. To have a 50% chance for a successful attack we need 30 frames similarly as stated in [4]. On average 23 right and $2^{19.527}$ left register candidates are generated out of 30 frames what leads to a total running time of the attack to reconstruct the internal state in about 13 hours (0.55 days).

Apart from performance, the cost for running an attack is of utmost importance. The CPU-based attack was run on a rented Amazon Elastic Compute Cloud (EC2) cluster but unfortunately, RIVYERA is not for rent. For a fair comparison, we therefore compare the running costs of the attack by estimating the power consumption for both attack implementations. The RIVYERA S-3 5000 takes on average $650W$ while two Intel Xeon L5640 CPUs including peripherals approximately demand $(60W \cdot 2) + 40W = 160W$ [12] for the complete system. To run the attack in the given time as stated in [4], at least 16 such computing systems are required. The power consumption in Table 2 shows again the advantage of special-purpose hardware over CPU-based attack clusters.

Despite the performance improvement with the Spartan-3 5000, we can achieve even higher performance with later FPGA devices. In particular, the RIVYERA S6-LX150 which can be equipped with 256 Spartan-6 LX150 offers by far more logic and performance but was not available in the course of this work. However, to provide at least estimates, we adapted our design for the Spartan-6 LX150 on which we can instantiate the double amount of attack cores with 17 ICT modules each. Additionally, we can run the design at double clock frequency due to the newer FPGA technology (200MHz) which results in an additional performance speed-up by factor of four.

7   Conclusion

The hardware implementation presented in this work improves the attack on CryptoMemory devices by Biryukov et al. [4] by introducing an additional candidate filtering step reducing the computation complexity to a half. By mapping the most time consuming parts to FPGA hardware, our solution runs in total 7.27 times faster than the previously reported results using 30 authentication frames. This enables the complete recovery of the secret internal state of the CryptoMemory cipher on average in less than 0.55 days. Finally, our hardware attack is 28.58 times cheaper considering power consumption compared to [4] using a CPU-based cluster.

Acknowledgements. The authors would like to thank Alex Biryukov, Ilya Kizhvatov and Bin Zhang for useful discussions and for their kindness providing parts of their attack script.

References

1. Atmel Corporation. CryptoMemory for Removable Storage Devices and Reprogrammable Keys, http://www.cryptomemorykey.com/pdfs/ AtmelCryptoMemoryFlier.pdf (retrieved April 15, 2013)
2. Atmel Corporation. CryptoMemory specification (2007), http://www.atmel.com/ Images/doc5211.pdf (retrieved April 15, 2013)
3. Balasch, J., Gierlichs, B., Verdult, R., Batina, L., Verbauwhede, I.: Power Analysis of Atmel CryptoMemory – Recovering Keys from Secure EEPROMs. In: Dunkelman, O. (ed.) CT-RSA 2012. LNCS, vol. 7178, pp. 19–34. Springer, Heidelberg (2012)
4. Biryukov, A., Kizhvatov, I., Zhang, B.: Cryptanalysis of the Atmel Cipher in SecureMemory, CryptoMemory and CryptoRF. In: Lopez, J., Tsudik, G. (eds.) ACNS 2011. LNCS, vol. 6715, pp. 91–109. Springer, Heidelberg (2011)
5. Biryukov, A., Kizhvatov, I., Zhang, B.: Cryptanalysis of the Atmel Cipher in SecureMemory, CryptoMemory and CryptoRF. IACR Cryptology ePrint Archive, p. 22 (2011)
6. Digitrade   GmbH,   http://www.digittrade.de/shop/index.php/cat/c66_ HS256S-High-Security.html (April 15, 2013)
7. Dipert, B.: The Zune HD: more than an iPod touch wanna-be? In: EDN (2009)

8. Garcia, F., van Rossum, P., Verdult, R., Wichers Schreur, R.: Dismantling Secure-Memory, CryptoMemory and CryptoRF. In: CCS 2010, pp. 250–259. ACM (2010)
9. Giacomelli, M.: SanDisk Sansa Connect, http://www.rockbox.org/wiki/SansaConnect
10. Güneysu, T., Kasper, T., Novotný, M., Paar, C., Rupp, A.: Cryptanalysis with COPACOBANA. IEEE Transactions on Computers 57(11), 1498–1513 (2008)
11. Güneysu, T., Pfeiffer, G., Paar, C., Schimmler, M.: Three Years of Evolution: Cryptanalysis with COPACOBANA. In: SHARCS 2009, pp. 9–10 (2009)
12. Intel. Intel Xeon Processor 5600 Series: Product Brief, http://www.intel.com/content/dam/www/public/us/en/documents/product-briefs/xeon-5600-brief.pdf (April 15, 2013)
13. Jarboe, M.: Introduction to CryptoMemory. Atmel Applications Journal 3, 28 (2004)
14. József, S.: AT88SC0204 ChipResetter, http://chipreset.atw.hu/6/index61.html (April 15, 2013)
15. Labgear. Labgear HDSR300 High Definition Satellite Receiver. User Guide, http://www.free-instruction-manuals.com/pdf/p4789564.pdf (April 15, 2013)
16. NVIDIA Corporation. Checklist for Building a PC that Plays HD DVD or Blue-ray Movies, ftp://download.nvidia.com/downloads/pvzone/Checklist_for_Building_a_HDPC.pdf (retrieved April 15, 2013)
17. SciEngines GmbH, http://www.sciengines.com
18. Xilinx. Spartan-3 FPGA Family: Complete Data Sheet. Product Documentation (November 2005)
19. Xilinx. Spartan-3 Generation FPGA User Guide. Product Documentation (June 2011)

Keystroke Timing Analysis of on-the-fly Web Apps

Chee Meng Tey[1], Payas Gupta[1], Debin Gao[1], and Yan Zhang[2]

[1] Singapore Management University
{cmtey.2008,payas.gupta.2008,dbgao}@smu.edu.sg
[2] State Key Laboratory Of Information Security, Institute of Information
Engineering, Chinese Academy of Sciences
zhangyan@iie.ac.cn

Abstract. The Google Suggestions service used in Google Search is one example of an interactivity rich Javascript application. In this paper, we analyse the timing side channel of Google Suggestions by reverse engineering the communication model from obfuscated Javascript code. We consider an attacker who attempts to infer the typing pattern of a victim. From our experiments involving 11 participants, we found that for each keypair with at least 20 samples, the mean of the inter-keystroke timing can be determined with an error of less than 20%.

1 Introduction

Fig. 1. Suggestions for 'secure'

Rich and complex Javascript (JS) applications provide sophisticated GUI updates and fast client-server communications that approaches the capabilities of traditional desktop applications. For example, Google Instant [1] and Google Suggestion(GS) [2] allow users to view results and suggestions on–the–fly while typing search queries. The front-end JS communicates using HTTP(s) with the back-end server in response to various events such as keypress. Figure 1 and Table 1 shows respectively the GS interface and HTTP requests when a user types in the search term 'secure'. In this paper we explore whether the improved GUI creates a timing side channel. We hope a detailed study of one application yields insights on the threats that may apply to the entire class of such applications.

Related work. Similar side channels attack had been demonstrated by Chen et al. [3] (inferring encrypted JS traffic from packet size) and Song et al [4] (reducing search space of SSH passwords from packet timing). This paper differs from prior work in the following ways. It is the first to analyse JS timing side channels and use it to derive typing patterns, which raise a privacy concern as prior research showed that typing patterns are unique and allows user identification [5,6,7,8]. Moreover, personalized typing patterns improves the SSH attacks

M. Jacobson et al. (Eds.): ACNS 2013, LNCS 7954, pp. 405–413, 2013.

Table 1. Query scenarios: (a) Slow typing. (b) Typing correction. (c) Typing s, e, c, then choosing *secure* from the suggestions. (d) Fast typing (not handled in this paper)

(a)	(b)	(c)	(d)

(a)	(b)	(c)	(d)
`GET /s?...&q=s&`	`GET /s?...&q=s&`	`GET /s?...&q=s&`	`GET /s?...&q=sec&`
`GET /s?...&q=se&`	`GET /s?...&q=se&`	`GET /s?...&q=se&`	`GET /s?...&q=secur&`
`GET /s?...&q=sec&`	`GET /s?...&q=sev&`	`GET /s?...&q=sec&`	`GET /s?...&q=secure&`
`GET /s?...&q=secu&`	`GET /s?...&q=se&`	`long pause`	
`GET /s?...&q=secur&`	`GET /s?...&q=sec&`	`GET /s?...&q=secure&`	
`GET /s?...&q=secure&`	`GET /s?...&q=secu&`		
	`GET /s?...&q=secur&`		
	`GET /s?...&q=secure&`		

by Song et al. [4] and allows imitation attacks [9] on keystroke biometrics systems [10,7,5,11,12]. JS timing side channels are challenging to analyse because keystroke and network traffic timing are only loosely correlated. This is because JS applications (a) are far slower as compared to native binary applications and (b) typically run in a single threaded co-operative multitasking execution model.

Key results. In the following sections, we study GS's communication model and derive a set of techniques to construct a keypair timing model (probability distribution of keypair intervals) for each pair of keystroke from unencrypted GS traffic. We conducted a user study on 11 participants to collect their keystrokes and timings. Results show that if at least 20 samples of each keypair are available, the recovered mean timing differs from the actual mean by at most 20%. However, the recovered standard deviation is less accurate: with at least 40 samples, the maximum difference is 46%. The accuracy improves with the increase in the pool of samples indicating the effectiveness of long term attacks.

2   Communication Model

Our approach to study the GS communication model is based on both black-box testing and white-box analysis. We used the setup of Figure 2. The client under testing connects to the Google servers in the back-end through a proxy server. For blackbox testing, we captured Google query packets using a packet sniffer [13] installed on the client. For whitebox testing, we hosted a copy[1] of the Google HTML and JS files on another

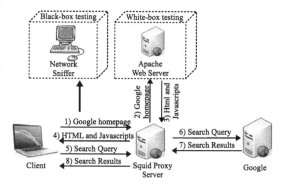

Fig. 2. Setup for black-box and white-box testing

web server and selectively redirect the proxy server [14] to fetch our copy rather than from the actual Google server. This allows us to make arbitrary changes to the scripts for our testing.

---

[1] Retrieved Apr 2012.

2.1 Approach

Black-box analysis allowed the quick identification of traffic patterns and content. For example, we quickly found that different network traffic patterns are possible even for the same query (see Table 1). On the other hand, when we analysed the timings of the keypress and the packets, we encountered significant difficulty correlating them. For example, after the user pressed a key, the corresponding HTTP request can be observed on the network from between approximately 3 ms to over 100 ms later with 2 distinctive frequency peaks at around 7 ms and 45 ms. Whitebox analysis is therefore necessary.

Our approach is to first manipulate the obfuscated source code using the tool JSBeautifier [15]. The decision to host a separate copy of the script files in Figure 2 allowed us to make arbitrary changes to the JS source code independently of the Google servers. Next, we use the console logging feature of Firebug to pinpoint the code that initiated the HTTP requests. This formed the starting point for subsequent investigations, where we incrementally assign meaningful symbols to the variables and functions through (a) monitored calls to standard functions, and (b) selectively breaking execution and examining the call stack and variables. Please note that our investigation focuses specifically on the timing aspects. Hence we did not deobfuscate all the script code involved in GS. The rest of this section documents our findings.

2.2 Communication Model Obtained

JS uses an event driven execution model [16]. For GS, there are 3 classes of event handlers of interest. H_{poll} is a handler for polling events. The polling is setup and removed when the query input box receives and loses focus respectively. Although the specified polling interval is 10 ms, the actual firing interval fluctuates. The reason is likely to be due to other events firing and executing, thereby delaying the execution of this handler. H_{ui} handles UI events, e.g., keydown, keypress, keyup, etc. The same handler code fires for different events but with different closure scope. The handler function for the keydown event, named H_{ui}^{kd}, is installed during GS code initialization. The GS code includes a mechanism to defer execution of a function. H_{defer} handles the events which are deferred. The 2 key parts to this are the postMessage JS function and an array of deferred functions (Arr_{defer}). At load time, GS setups a message event handler. This handler fires when a message is posted to it using postMessage. When fired, it removes the first function from Arr_{defer} and executes it. If Arr_{defer} is not empty, it posts a message to itself and exits. Any JS code deferring execution calls a wrapper function defer which first pushes the function to defer onto the bottom of Arr_{defer} and then post a message to H_{defer}.

When a user presses and releases a key, JS fires four events in this order: keydown, keypress, input, keyup. Under normal circumstances, H_{ui}^{kd} uses the deferred execution mechanism to invokes a function named H_x to send out the network traffic. However, it is also possible for H_{poll} to run before H_{ui}^{kd}. In such a case, H_{poll} invokes H_x directly (without deferring execution) to send out the query.

Regardless of the path taken, H_x is executed at most once for each keystroke. The end result is a race (to execute H_x) between the synchronous mechanism of H_{poll} and the asynchronous mechanism of H_{ui}^{kd}, resulting in the introduction of a variable delay. The race is won mostly by H_{ui}^{kd}. Another factor affecting the execution delay is the number of task on each execution path. For example, the first keypress for GS also updates the UI in preparation for not just the suggestions of GS, but also the results of Google Instant. This additional code increases the execution delay by approximately 6 times ($\sim$45 ms).

Listing 1.

```
trace Hx
  if xhrtimer not pending then
    xhrm enter
      ...
    exit
  end if
end trace

trace TimerEvent
  Call xhrm
end trace

procedure xhrm
  if unsent_query then
    xhri enter
      ...
    send query to Google
      ...
    exit
    timeout ← compute_timeout
    create TimerEvent
  end if
end procedure
```

A third factor affecting the delay is submission throttling [17]. Most search engines used this technology to limit the amount of search traffic to their website while the user is typing the query. In the case of GS, regardless of whether H_{poll} or H_{ui}^{kd} won the race, H_x is always invoked. The role of H_x is to send queries and receive results from the Google servers. Listing 1 shows how submission throttling is implemented in GS when H_x is invoked. The sending mechanism of GS uses a timer named xhr_{timer}. This timer is initially cleared. When H_x is invoked it checks this timer. If xhr_{timer} is cleared, H_x calls a sub function xhr_m to send out the query immediately. Otherwise, it exits without sending any HTTP traffic. When xhr_m runs, it sets up the timer xhr_{timer} to call itself (xhr_m) again after a timeout value. The detailed computation of the timeout is out of the scope of this paper, but on a fast network, this value is 100 ms. After this timer is set, xhr_m will not run again until the timer expires. Any keystrokes typed during this time accumulate and are sent together in the same HTTP request when the timer expires. If xhr_m runs but does not find any unsent query (that is, between the previous and current invocation of xhr_m, the user did not press any key), it does not set any new timer. xhr_{timer} therefore becomes cleared again. If a new key is now pressed, xhr_m will again send it out without delay. The described process then repeats itself. The implication is that correlation between keystroke and packet timing is poor whenever xhr_m is in timer mode.

3   Recovery of Keypair Timing Model

Section 2 identifies the timeout mechanism and atypical execution path as major noise contributors. Packet timings thus affected are considered unreliable. Figure 3 shows that if we discard the unreliable timing, the delay between pressing of keystroke and sending of packet becomes significantly more consistent. (t_{ks} and t_{pkt} refer to the keystroke and packet timing respectively.) This allows the recovery of the derived keypair timing model.

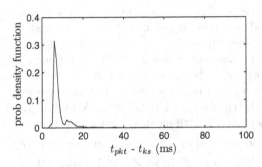

Fig. 3. Noise model

For each keypair, the recovery process involves (a) identifying the corresponding packet-pairs, (b) determining if each packet timing is reliable, (c) choosing packet-pairs where the earlier timing is reliable, (d) further dividing the chosen packet-pairs into a set where the latter packet timing is reliable and another set where it is not, (e) computing the mean and variance of the packet-pair timing model and finally (f) applying a correction to the variance to obtain the derived keypair timing model. This process requires an assumption of normally distributed timing models which are independent. Prior work [4] investigating keypair timing model found the normal distribution to be a reasonable approximation. In step (d), the size of the first set (reliable latter packet timing) is denoted by N_o. The size of the complementary set is denoted by N_u.

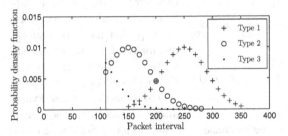

Fig. 4. Different scenarios for the building of DTM$_\text{key}$ from TM$_\text{pkt}$

In step (e), depending on the values of N_o and N_u, there can be 4 different scenarios, 3 of which are shown in figure 4. TM$_\text{key}$ denotes the keypair timing model, TM$_\text{pkt}$ denotes the packet-pair timing model, and DTM$_\text{key}$ denotes the derived keypair timing model, which is an approximation of TM$_\text{key}$ obtained by applying a variance correction to TM$_\text{pkt}$.

In type 1 scenarios, $N_u = 0$. The mean and variance are calculated directly from the observed intervals.

For type 2, $N_u < N_o$. The timeout translates to a cutoff time beyond which certain intervals are not observed. The peak though is still visible. We first estimate the median from N_u and the observable parts of the distribution. We next obtain the mean which is equal to the median. We estimated the missing part of the distribution by reflecting the observable part about the mean. From the reconstructed distribution, we can calculate the variance.

For type 3, $N_u \geq N_o$. The peak is not visible. Our aim is to fit a normal distribution (with unknown mean $\bar{x}$ and std. deviation s) based on the interval observations on the right tail. Let l denote the cutoff time (timeout + a small allowance). $\bar{x}$, s, l, α are related by $l = \bar{x} + \alpha s$, where α is a multiplier s.t. for a standard normal distributed random variable X, $\Pr(X > \alpha) = N_o/(N_o + N_u)$. The curve fitting iterates over a possible list of values for $\bar{x}$, and computes the corresponding s. The values providing the best fit (least squares) is chosen.

In type 4 scenarios, $N_o = 0$. The mean of the keypair timing is far less than the timeout, resulting in no interval observations. Hence it is not plotted in Figure 4. To recover the timing for a keypair such as $c_1 - c_2$ where c_i denotes a key pressed, we need to have the parameters of another 2 distributions: the keypair $c_2 - c_3$ and the triplet $c_1 - c_2 - c_3$. The latter 2 distributions would be observable if there exists c_3 such that $c_2 - c_3$ is much longer than the timeout.

Given two independent normally distributed random variables X and Y, the random variable $Z = X + Y$ is also normal [18] with mean $\bar{z} = \bar{x} + \bar{y}$ and standard deviation $s_z = \sqrt{s_x^2 + s_y^2}$. The relation between $c_1 - c_2$, $c_2 - c_3$ and $c_1 - c_2 - c_3$ is analogous to that of X, Y and Z. Therefore, if we let Z and Y represent the distribution for $c_1 - c_2 - c_3$ and $c_2 - c_3$ respectively, we can obtain the mean and standard deviation of the unobservable $c_1 - c_2$ from X.

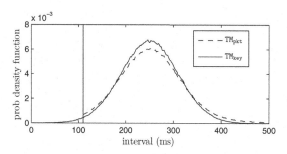

In step (f) we need to apply a correction to the variance but not the mean. This is because there is residual noise even after accounting for the timeout and atypical execution path. This noise affects both timing observations of a packet-pair. It cancels out for the interval mean, but adds to the variance. Figure 5 shows this effect for a keypair. To compute the required variance correction, we use a simple heuristic. A Monte Carlo simulation based on the model of Section 2 computes the observed variance for a set of variances. The differences are stored in a table and looked up whenever a correction is needed.

Fig. 5. Difference in the $p.d.f.$ of $\mathrm{TM_{key}}$ compared to the corresponding $p.d.f.$ of $\mathrm{TM_{pkt}}$

4   User Study

To verify the theory of Section 3, we conducted a user study. 11 participants are asked to install a plugin on their browser which captures the keystroke timings of GS queries. The duration of the study ranges from 32 to 49 days. Users are allowed to inspect and delete any sensitive entries in the capture log before submission. Towards the end of the study, users with too few queries were given a chance to go through a Q&A worksheet using Google to find the answers. This is so that they get more opportunities in using Google search. The collected keystrokes are anonymised and post processed to retain only English alphabets and the SPACE char. Queries with BACKSPACE are broken up. The resulting logs are consolidated on a single machine running Ubuntu 11.10 (AMD Athlon(tm) 64 X2 Dual Core Processor 4000+ 2110 MHz with 3 GB RAM). The keystrokes in each query are injected programmatically using the `uinput` [19] interface and the corresponding query packets are collected.

Table 2. Statistics of user study. Q: total number of queries by user. KS: total keystrokes typed. KP: total keypairs typed. TP: total char sequence. KP_{obs}: sum of N_o for all keypairs. TP_{obs}: sum of N_o for all triplets. N_{sig}: total number of keypair/triplets for which $N_o \geq 10$. This is also the number of recovered $p.d.f.$

S/N	Q	KS	KP	TP	KP_{obs}	TP_{obs}	N_{sig}
1	502	3114	2612	2110	642	487	6
2	421	2666	2245	1824	682	506	7
3	1206	6607	5401	4195	2447	1715	93
4	688	4243	3555	2867	601	403	6
5	593	3604	3011	2418	1368	993	34
6	774	4592	3818	3044	1752	1284	58
7	405	2517	2112	1707	733	561	8
8	696	4610	3914	3218	1181	893	29
9	327	2163	1836	1509	270	185	1
10	1041	6042	5001	3960	2359	1697	96
11	700	3964	3264	2564	1233	853	29

The outcome of the user study is shown in Table 2. There is a positive correlation between the number of queries submitted and the number of $p.d.f.$ (last column) recovered in DTM_{key} for each participant. This suggests that long term collection of queries would recover far more $p.d.f.$ than our user study. The outcome of the methods for type 1 to type 2 are shown in Figure 6. Relatively fewer samples were collected for type 3 and type 4 due to the low probability of finding observations at the tail and finding both triplet and keypair accounts. The outcome for these methods are omitted due to brevity of space. Generally, the mean can be recovered accurately although larger observations tend to result in more accuracy. The variance, on the other hand, is less accurate, particularly for fewer observations. Like the mean, however, the accuracy improves as the observations increases.

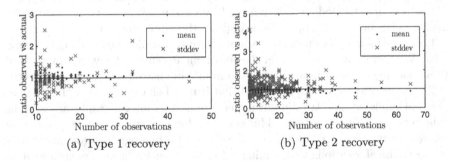

(a) Type 1 recovery   (b) Type 2 recovery

Fig. 6. Recovery of $p.d.f.$ from various types of packet observations

4.1 The Optimal Timeout

Given that the current timeout value of 100ms allows the derivation of DTM_{key} (from TM_{pkt}), we also investigated the possible countermeasures. These countermeasures are equally applicable to any JS application with rich interactivity that wishes to deny potential adversary the opportunity for UI events harvesting. We conducted a Monte Carlo simulation using the set of keystroke data collected from the user study. We varied the GS timeout and computed the simulated packet timing based on the noise model and the findings of Section 2.

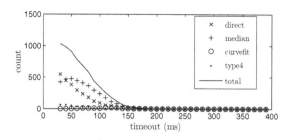

Figure 7 shows the variation of the count of recovered keypairs and triplets vs the timeout. Choosing a timeout figure of 200-250 ms eliminates most observations, but the responsiveness is more than halved. Given that in Listing 1, xhr_m exits timeout

Fig. 7. Variation of the total recovered keypair or triplets for all users given a particular timeout setting

mode whenever there is no keystroke activity in the previous timeout cycle, an alternative is to increase the number of timeout cycles to 3 while keeping the timeout unchanged at 100 ms. This eliminates all observable intervals without affecting the responsiveness.

5 Limitations

In our study, the keypair timing model is based on keydown-keydown intervals. Many biometric authentication techniques use such intervals [10,11,5]. Our work therefore affects such systems. However, biometric authentication is not limited to just keydown-keydown metrics. Keydown-keyup, keyup-keydown and even keypress pressure are examples of alternatives. For the first 2, active attacks injecting malicious Javascript code can capture both keydown and keyup, but this is not investigated in this paper. Keypress pressure however, cannot be measured by Javascript applications and are therefore unaffected.

The keystroke injection part of the user study was done on a dedicated machine. We therefore did not model the additional execution delay that may result if the machine is also running multiple compute intensive processes concurrently.

The description of GS [2] indicated that it may behave differently in different geographical locations. We did not manage to isolate any geographically specific code during our investigations. This is either due to our limitations or different source code was delivered to different locations. Our findings therefore apply only to geographical locations with similar settings as our evaluation environment.

6 Conclusions

In this paper, we investigated the recovery of personalized keystroke timing information using GS. We found that it is possible to construct a user's typing pattern from the timing of the queries sent over the network. This is of concern because the availability of typing pattern is a prerequisite for (a) achieving the best outcome in timing side channel attacks and (b) imitation attacks on keystroke biometrics. It can also be used to identify users. This suggests that logs recording network traffic of interactive Javascript applications should be considered confidential and handled accordingly. Otherwise, the operators of search engines as well as proxy server administrators can mine the typing pattern of their users from the traffic logs. We suggest that designers consider alternative options such as multiple timeout cycles to shut down the leak effectively.

References

1. Google Instant, http://goo.gl/WI9Zu
2. Autocomplete, http://goo.gl/jv3fQ
3. Chen, S., Wang, R., Wang, X., Zhang, K.: Side-channel leaks in web applications: A reality today, a challenge tomorrow. In: Proceedings of the 2010 IEEE Symposium on Security and Privacy, SP 2010, pp. 191–206. IEEE Computer Society, Washington, DC (2010)
4. Song, D.X., Wagner, D., Tian, X.: Timing analysis of keystrokes and timing attacks on ssh. In: Proceedings of the 10th conference on USENIX Security Symposium, SSYM 2001, vol. 10, p. 25. USENIX Association, Berkeley (2001)
5. Araujo, L., Sucupira, J. L., Lizarraga, M., Ling, L., Yabu-Uti, J.: User authentication through typing biometrics features. Trans. Sig. Proc. 53(2), 851–855 (2005)
6. Killourhy, K.S.: A Scientific Understanding of Keystroke Dynamics. Dissertation, Carnegie Mellon University (2012)
7. Peacock, A., Ke, X., Wilkerson, M.: Typing patterns: A key to user identification. IEEE Security and Privacy 2(5), 40–47 (2004)
8. Monrose, F., Rubin, A.D.: Keystroke dynamics as a biometric for authentication. Future Gener. Comput. Syst. 16(4), 351–359 (2000)
9. Tey, C.M., Gupta, P., Gao, D.: I can be You: Questioning the use of Keystroke Dynamics as Biometrics. In: Proceedings of the Network and Distributed System Security Symposium (NDSS), San Diego, CA (February 2013)
10. Joyce, R., Gupta, G.: Identity authentication based on keystroke latencies. Commun. ACM 33(2), 168–176 (1990)
11. Haider, S., Abbas, A., Zaidi, A.: A multi-technique approach for user identification through keystroke dynamics. In: IEEE International Conference on Systems, Man and Cybernetics, SMC 2000, pp. 1336–1341 (2000)
12. Killourhy, K., Maxion, R.: Why did my detector do that?!: predicting keystroke-dynamics error rates. In: Jha, S., Sommer, R., Kreibich, C. (eds.) RAID 2010. LNCS, vol. 6307, pp. 256–276. Springer, Heidelberg (2010)
13. Tcpdump, http://www.tcpdump.org
14. Squid, http://www.squid-cache.org/Intro/
15. JSBeautifier, http://jsbeautifier.org/
16. DOM Events, http://en.wikipedia.org/wiki/DOM_events
17. Mahemoff, M.: Ajax Design Patterns. O'Reilly Media, Inc. (2006)
18. Normal Sum Distribution, http://goo.gl/wfaMz
19. Uinput, http://thiemonge.org/getting-started-with-uinput

Terrorism in Distance Bounding: Modeling Terrorist-Fraud Resistance

Marc Fischlin and Cristina Onete

CASED & Technische Universität Darmstadt
www.cryptoplexity.de

Abstract. In distance-bounding protocols, verifiers use a clock to measure the time elapsed in challenge-response rounds, thus upper-bounding their distance to the prover. This should prevent man-in-the-middle (MITM) relay attacks. Distance-bounding protocols may aim to prevent several attacks, amongst which terrorist fraud, where a dishonest prover helps the adversary to authenticate, but without passing data that allows the adversary to later authenticate on its own. Two definitions of terrorist-fraud resistance exist: a very strong notion due to Dürholz et al. [6] (which we call SimTF security), and a weaker, fuzzier notion due to Avoine et al. [1]. Recent work [7] indicates that the classical countermeasures to terrorist fraud, though intuitively sound, do *not* grant SimTF security. Two questions are posed in [7]: (1) Is SimTF security achievable? and (2) Can we find a definition of terrorist-fraud resistance which both captures the intuition behind it *and* enables efficient constructions?

We answer both questions affirmatively. For (1) we show the first provably SimTF secure distance-bounding scheme in the literature, though superior terrorist-fraud resistance comes here at the cost of security. For (2) we provide a game-based definition for terrorist-fraud resistance (called GameTF security) that captures the intuition suggested in [1], is formalized in the style of [6], and is strong enough for practical applications. We also prove that the SimTF-insecure [7] Swiss-Knife protocol *is* GameTF-secure. We argue that high-risk scenarios require a stronger security level, closer to SimTF security. Our SimTF secure scheme is also strSimTF secure.

1 Introduction

Authentication protocols, run between a *prover* and a *verifier*, allow the verifier to either accept the prover as legitimate or reject it if it is illegitimate. Authentication is used in e.g. public transport, Passive Keyless and Start (PKES) systems, and personal identification. Secure authentication schemes must prevent impersonation attacks, i.e. the verifier must always reject illegitimate provers. However, security models in authentication do not usually capture man-in-the-middle (MITM) relay attacks, where an adversary authenticates by just forwarding data between the prover and verifier. Such attacks, called mafia fraud [4], have been implemented in various application scenarios like Bluetooth [15,9], smart- and RFID cards [5,10,13], e-Passports [12], e-voting [16], and PKES [8].

M. Jacobson et al. (Eds.): ACNS 2013, LNCS 7954, pp. 414–431, 2013.

Introduced in [3], distance bounding detects mafia fraud, or rather, the delay caused by relays in the MITM adversary. Here the verifier uses a clock to upper-bound its (communication) distance to the prover, by measuring the time elapsed between sending a challenge and receiving the response. If the roundtrip time is at most equal to a threshold t_{max}, the response is *in time*, presumably sent by a prover in the verifier's *proximity*. Thus, t_{max} denotes a maximum trusted distance to the verifier, which can be a few millimeters, some centimeters, or more. Time measurements are usually round-based; most protocols consist of rounds (or phases [6]), which are either *lazy* (slow) —if the clock is *not* used— or *time-critical* (fast) —if the clock measures time-of-flight. The digital-analog system in [17] ensures that distance-bounding protocols can be implemented in practice, detecting pure relays for up to 41 cm. Many distance-bounding protocols are designed for resource-constrained devices, e.g. RFID tags.

In this paper we focus on one of the four main goals of distance-bounding protocols, namely *terrorist fraud* resistance. Terrorist fraud is an attack where the MITM adversary is helped by a dishonest prover to authenticate (but this help should *not* allow the adversary to authenticate later). For example, simply passing the secret key is prohibited, but revealing some secret information which can be used in a single execution is admissible. Two previous frameworks [1,6] define this attack differently. This controversy is unfortunately not unique in the area of distance bounding, where, though the intuition behind the security model has been known for decades, the formalization of it is still debatable. No previous definition of terrorist-fraud resistance seems quite "right", being either too weak or too strong, depending on the (limitations of the) adversary's power. Essentially, there are two main model features which limit the adversary's power: its interaction with the prover (should it be just in slow, or also in fast phases?), and the restriction on the prover do to help. Both existing frameworks [1,6] allow the prover and adversary to interact only in lazy phases (however, we argue that restriction is unnecessary and artificial). Furthermore, while [1] greatly restrict the prover and dismiss most attacks (provers may only forward data that leaves the secret key statistically hidden [2]), the model of [6] allows the prover to forward almost any data, thus excluding very few attacks (the prover can even send bits of the key if the adversary can use them more in the session where the prover helps than in later sessions). We argue that, while the former model allows very efficient constructions, it is too weak in the sense that it might not prevent real attacks. Yet, the latter notion is too strong in the sense that it is not attained by schemes employing classical (and intuitively effective) countermeasures to terrorist fraud.[1]

---

[1] Concretely, the attack in [7] is aimed at the protocols of Reid et al. [18] and the Swiss-Knife protocol [14]. In fact, slightly modified versions of these protocols are used, since the circular dependency between the secret key and the time-critical responses in the original schemes makes it hard to prove mafia and impersonation resistance. In [7] a single instance of the secret key sk is replaced in each protocol by another key sk^*. Yet, the terrorist attack in [7] works against the original, as well as the modified schemes.

Contributions. In this paper we answer the following questions, posed by [7]:

1. Can the definition of Dürholz et al. actually be achieved?
2. Can we "rightly" define terrorist-fraud resistance, such that we capture the intuition *and* enable efficient constructions?

We mainly focus on (2), but we also answer question (1) affirmatively. We prove that the challenging notion of [6] (which we call SimTF security, because it uses a simulation-based definition) is achievable. Yet, in order to attain SimTF security, our protocol (the first SimTF secure scheme in the literature) becomes more vulnerable to other attacks. This may indicate that SimTF security cannot be achieved *efficiently*. Our scheme modifies the Swiss-Knife protocol [14], introducing a "back door" for the simulator, which can authenticate either by learning the long-term secret (from the adversary's state) or by luck (the verifier accepts an incorrect authentication string with some probability). Our scheme inherits the mafia and distance-fraud resistance of the Swiss-Knife protocol, which many protocols lack [7], but due to the "back door" for proving SimTF with decreased security levels.

In answer to (2) we propose a sufficiently strong, game-based notion of terrorist-fraud resistance, called GameTF-security. We start from the intuition of [1], but formalize it as in [6], striving towards a unified security framework. A protocol is GameTF-secure if any adversary authenticating with the prover's help can authenticate unaided with better-than-mafia-fraud probability. This notion also captures the intuition of terrorist-fraud resistance: it requires that the information gained from the prover during the terrorist attack (which constitutes the terrorist adversary's state) will not lead, once the prover stops helping, to an authentication probability higher than for a mafia adversary. Note that the mafia-fraud success probability is a natural lower bound for the unaided adversary, since, once the prover stops helping, the adversary finds itself exactly in the MITM mafia scenario, with only its state to give it any advantage. This notion captures the exact intuition behind terrorist fraud and indeed, we can prove that the SimTF insecure, modified Swiss-Knife protocol [7], *is* GameTF secure (as intuition indicates it should be).

Our GameTF notion is strong enough for, e.g., public transport ticketing mechanisms. Yet, terrorist fraud affects high-security applications like e-Passports and e-voting much more (see discussion in Section 5); thus stronger definitions are needed. We propose a natural extension of SimTF-security, where adversaries also access the prover online, during the authentication attempt (excepting relay scheduling, of course). Our *strong simulation-based terrorist-fraud model* (strSimTF) is stronger than SimTF security, but also achievable: in fact, our SimTF-secure scheme is also strSimTF-secure.

For completeness, we also give a full security diagram featuring our notions and SimTF security. Interestingly, our strSimTF and GameTF models are independent of each other; however, a scheme that is strSimTF-secure *and* mafia-fraud resistant is also GameTF-secure. We also show that, though our GameTF definition resembles the notion in [1], it does *not* imply mafia-fraud resistance (as [1] argues). The full diagram appears in Fig. 3.

2   Preliminaries

We first review the terminology of [6], particularly terrorist fraud (SimTF) resistance. The setting we consider is that of a single prover $\mathcal{T}$ and a single verifier $\mathcal{R}$, sharing a secret key sk generated by an algorithm Kg.[2] In the RFID setting, the provers are RFID *tags* and the verifier is a *reader*; this is the terminology used in [6]. The reader has a clock and stores sk in an internal database. The interaction between $\mathcal{T}$ and $\mathcal{R}$, i.e. the protocol, is run in phases, which are either *time-critical* (if $\mathcal{R}$ measures roundtrip times, matching them against a threshold $t_{\max}$), or *lazy* (if the clock is not used). The following *timing parameters* are considered: the number N_c of time-critical phases; the threshold roundtrip time $t_{\max}$; the number $T_{\max}$ of time-critical phases that may exceed $t_{\max}$; and the number $E_{\max}$ of time-critical phases with erroneous responses[3].

In [6], $\mathcal{T}$ and $\mathcal{R}$ interact in *sessions*, indexed by session id's sid and associated with transcripts containing all the exchanged messages in sid. For mafia and terrorist fraud, sessions are run between 2 out of these 3 parties: the tag $\mathcal{T}$, the reader $\mathcal{R}$, and a MITM adversary $\mathcal{A}$. In *reader-tag* sessions, $\mathcal{A}$ observes honest prover-verifier interaction. In *adversary-tag sessions*, $\mathcal{A}$ interacts with the honest $\mathcal{T}$, impersonating a reader. In *reader-adversary* sessions, $\mathcal{A}$ impersonates the prover to $\mathcal{R}$. In reader-tag sessions, $\mathcal{A}$ may not interfere with the protocol run; to run a MITM attack, $\mathcal{A}$ opens parallel reader-adversary and adversary-tag sessions. We quantify the adversary in terms of its runtime t and the number of sessions it runs, i.e. q_{OBS} reader-tag, $q_{\mathcal{R}}$ reader-adversary, and $q_{\mathcal{T}}$ adversary-tag sessions. The advantage ϵ of $\mathcal{A}$ is its success probability (see below).

As in [6], we denote messages i to j exchanged in session sid by $\Pi_{\text{sid}}[i\ldots j]$, while $\Pi_{\text{sid}}[1\ldots]$ denotes *all* the messages exchanged in sid. An abstract, *universal* clock variable clock (distinct from the reader's *local* clock) keeps track of the order in which messages are sent. The integer clock(sid, k) is assigned to the k-th protocol message, which is delivered in session sid to an honest party. This party's reply is associated with clock(sid, $k+1$) = clock(sid, k) + 1 (i.e. clock is augmented by 1). If the adversary opens two parallel sessions, then clock(sid, k) < clock(sid*, k) if $\mathcal{A}$ sends the k-th message in session sid* after the k-th message in session sid.

Mafia fraud. In [6], each attack is defined by restricting the adversary's interactions to a number of allowed *tainted* phases. In mafia fraud, a phase is *tainted* if pure relaying takes place (in reality this is detected by the clock). The adversary can taint at most $T_{\max}$ rounds, thus accounting for expected transmission delays; in practice, $T_{\max}$ should be very low. More formally [6]:

---

[2] Though distance bounding is usually run in a symmetric setting, our results extend to public-key settings too.

[3] The values $T_{\max}$ and $E_{\max}$ are not classical parameters in distance bounding, but were introduced in [6] to account for unreliable time-critical transmissions. Also note that Dürholz et al. use a misnomer (also often found in the literature) in talking about *identification* rather than *authentication* schemes: indeed, the protocols output an accept/reject bit, not an identity.

Definition 1 (Tainted Time-Critical Phase, [6]). *A time-critical phase* $\Pi_{\mathsf{sid}}[k \ldots k + 2\ell - 1] = (m_k, \ldots, m_{k+2\ell-1})$ *for* $k, \ell \geq 1$ *of a reader-adversary session* sid, *with the* k-*th message being received by the adversary, is* tainted *by the phase* $\Pi_{\mathsf{sid}^*}[k \ldots k + 2\ell - 1] = (m_k^*, \ldots, m_{k+2\ell-1}^*)$ *of an adversary-tag session* sid^* *if for all* $i = 0, 1, \ldots, \ell - 1$ *we have:*

$$(m_k, \ldots, m_{k+2\ell-1}) = (m_k^*, \ldots, m_{k+2\ell-1}^*),$$
$$clock(\mathsf{sid}, k + 2i) < clock(\mathsf{sid}^*, k + 2i),$$
$$and \quad clock(\mathsf{sid}, k + 2i + 1) > clock(\mathsf{sid}^*, k + 2i + 1).$$

Insight: pure relay. The definition excludes *only* pure relay: exact messages sent in the same order between sessions; thus an adversary who receives from $\mathcal{R}$ some input challenge bit b is allowed to flip this bit and relay it to the prover, then relaying the response. In practice, this method can be used against protocols where the computation for one input bit (say $b = 1$) is easier than for the other; in this case, $\mathcal{A}$ can fool the clock by using the faster computation. Since communication is usually very fast in distance bounding, computation delays are very significant. Dürholz et al. restrict mafia adversaries only *minimally*: they assume that the reader's clock only detects same-message relays between parties.

Definition 2 (Mafia Fraud Resistance). *For a distance-bounding authentication scheme* $\mathcal{ID}$ *with parameters* $(t_{\max}, T_{\max}, E_{\max}, N_c)$, *a* $(t, q_{\mathcal{R}}, q_{\mathcal{T}}, q_{\mathrm{OBS}})$-*mafia-fraud adversary* $\mathcal{A}$ *wins against* $\mathcal{ID}$ *if the verifier accepts in a reader-adversary session* sid *such that any adversary-tag session* sid^* *taints at most* $T_{\max}$ *time-critical phases of* sid. *Let* $\mathbf{Adv}_{\mathcal{ID}}^{mafia}(\mathcal{A})$ *denote the probability that* $\mathcal{A}$ *wins.*

We say $\mathcal{ID}$ is *mafia-fraud resistant* if any efficient mafia-fraud adversary has at most a negligible advantage to win.

The SimTF notion. In the terrorist fraud resistance notion in [6] (here called SimTF-security), the adversary may not interact with the prover during time-critical phases *at all*. This is reflected in the definition below, which states that if $\mathcal{A}$ and the malicious $\mathcal{T}'$ interact, the phase is tainted.

Definition 3 (Tainted Time-Critical Phase (SimTF)). *A time-critical phase* $\Pi_{\mathsf{sid}}[k \ldots k + 2\ell - 1] = (m_k, \ldots, m_{k+2\ell-1})$ *for* $k, \ell \geq 1$ *of a reader-adversary session* sid, *with the* k-*th message being received by* $\mathcal{A}$, *is* tainted *if there exists a session* sid' *between* $\mathcal{A}$ *and* $\mathcal{T}'$ *such that, for some* i,

$$clock(\mathsf{sid}, k) < clock(\mathsf{sid}', i) < clock(\mathsf{sid}, k + 2\ell - 1).$$

SimTF security is defined in terms of a simulator: once an adversary $\mathcal{A}$ authenticates in a reader-adversary session, its transcripts and randomness (i.e. the view $\mathsf{view}_{\mathcal{A}}$ of $\mathcal{A}$) are passed to a simulator $\mathcal{S}$ which must authenticate, by only using $\mathsf{view}_{\mathcal{A}}$, with at least as much probability. Thus, if the adversary requests (a part of) the secret key, this information is passed on to the simulator.

Definition 4 (SimTF security, [6]). *Let $\mathcal{ID}$ be an authentication scheme for parameters $(t_{\max}, T_{\max}, E_{\max}, N_c)$. Let $\mathcal{A}$ be a $(t, q_{\mathcal{R}}, q'_T)$-SimTF adversary, $\mathcal{S}$ be an algorithm with runtime $t_{\mathcal{S}}$, and $\mathcal{T}'$ be an algorithm with runtime t'. Let*

$$Adv_{\mathcal{ID}}^{terror}(\mathcal{A}, \mathcal{S}, \mathcal{T}') = p_{\mathcal{A}} - p_{\mathcal{S}}$$

where $p_{\mathcal{A}}$ is the probability that $\mathcal{R}$ accepts in one of the $q_{\mathcal{R}}$ reader-adversary sessions sid *such that at most $T_{\max}$ time-critical phases of* sid *are tainted, and $p_{\mathcal{S}}$ is the probability that, given* view$_{\mathcal{A}}$*, $\mathcal{S}$ authenticates to $\mathcal{R}$ in one of $q_{\mathcal{R}}$ subsequent executions.*

Insight: SimTF. In [1], the active adversary succeeds if: it authenticates with the prover's aid; and it authenticates (at all) without it. In fact, the prover's secret must be information-theoretically hidden. This model excludes nearly *any* information-exchange with the adversary, even if the data does not directly help authentication. As most attacks are ruled out, this definition is rather weak.

By contrast, SimTF security focuses on exactly how much the prover's information helps the simulator. Excluded are only attacks where prover data, contained in $\mathcal{A}$'s state, is directly used by $\mathcal{S}$. Thus, even if the simulator's authentication probability is significant, but not as large as the adversary's, the attack is valid. This definition is very broad, enabling syntactic attacks like the one in [7] against the scheme of Reid et al.

3   Flavors of Terrorist Fraud

In this section, we introduce two possible definitions of terrorist-fraud resistance. The first (called GameTF security, see Section 3.1) is a game-based definition capturing the intuition behind a basic terrorist-fraud attack in a manner compatible with the model of Dürholz et al. [6]. This notion is sufficient for many practical applications, e.g. logistics or ticketing in public transport. Our second notion (strSimTF security, see Section 3.2) extends, in a natural way, the simulation-based SimTF definition in [6]; this definition is extremely strong, and should be used only in high-risk applications like e-Passports or e-voting. In what follows we briefly explain our motivations for introducing the two notions, referring to previous models of terrorist-fraud resistance, and sketching our own approach towards defining terrorist-fraud attacks.

We discuss mainly two modeling aspects in defining terrorist fraud: (1) the adversary-prover interaction; and (2) the restriction on how much a prover can help. Both terrorist-fraud models in the literature [1,6] seem to agree on how to handle (1), but fundamentally disagree on how to define (2). We first discuss point (2). In this matter, Avoine et al. [1] demand that the prover's aid gives the adversary "no further advantage" to authenticate, requiring statistically-hiding properties for the prover's secret key. As discussed in Section 1 this restricts the prover very much, and thus attacks where partial key-related information is given are ruled out. By contrast, SimTF security [6] only rules out attacks where the information received from the prover can be used as effectively during the prover-aided session *and* later. We agree with the intuition of Avoine et al. that the adversary should have no "further advantage", but note that the behavior of the adversary after the prover has stopped helping it is that of a mafia fraud attacker who also retains some state information, i.e. what the prover has forwarded it before. Thus, our GameTF notion considers a pair of adversaries: a first, terrorist adversary (aided by the prover); and a second, mafia-fraud adversary sharing state with the first adversary.

We also re-consider the traditional adversary-prover interaction restriction to lazy phases (point (1) above), which seems to assume that time-critical interactions would be detected by the verifier's clock. We disagree: the clock can *only* detect queries to the prover if the messages have a *relay scheduling*, i.e. a MITM adversary receives input from the reader, then sends input to the tag; upon receiving output from the tag, it sends some output (the same, or different) to the reader. This is not the same as *pure relay* as defined for mafia fraud, see Definition 1, since in pure relay, the input and output messages must be the same. Thus, we *may* allow such adversary-prover interactions. We discuss also why we *should* allow them; and why we cannot allow the adversary *even more* freedom, e.g. by using Definition 1.

Why we should allow it. Consider a distance-bounding protocol where the dishonest $\mathcal{T}'$ and $\mathcal{R}$ share, at the end of the lazy phases, pseudo-random strings T^0, T^1, such that $T^0 \oplus T^1 = sk^*$, where sk^* is a secret key (a part of sk or an independent key). This is how terrorist fraud resistance is usually achieved.

Now assume that $\mathcal{R}$ generates challenges as follows: it first draws a random c_1 for the first round, then runs a PRF (with key sk) on input c_1 to generate a string s with $|s| \geq N_c$. Then $\mathcal{R}$ sets challenges $c_2, \dots c_{N_c}$ for the other rounds bitwise to the bits of s. That is, c_2 is set to the most significant bit of s, c_3, to the following bit, etc. Such a protocol does not exist in the literature; nevertheless, our model *should* rule out such dependency of challenges.

In each time-critical phase of the protocol, $\mathcal{R}$ sends a challenge bit c_i and expects a bit from T^{c_i} (i.e. either T^0 or T^1). At the end of the lazy phases, $\mathcal{T}'$ has computed responses T^0 and T^1. When the terrorist adversary $\mathcal{A}$ receives challenge c_1 from $\mathcal{R}$, it sends a random bit r to $\mathcal{R}$, then forwards c_1 to $\mathcal{T}'$. Now $\mathcal{T}'$ computes $c_2, \dots c_{N_c}$ and sends the appropriate responses to $\mathcal{A}$ (without revealing any information about sk^*). The adversary wins with probability $\frac{1}{2}$ (the probability that $r = T^{c_1}$).

Why this is all we can do. Mafia fraud adversaries may use relay scheduling if at least one relayed message is not the exact one $\mathcal{A}$ received from the honest party. We cannot allow this for terrorist fraud, since the dishonest prover may adapt its response in order to bypass our definition. For instance, instead of sending the correct response r for each round, it just sends $1 \oplus r$, that is, the flipped bit. Then $\mathcal{A}$ just flips the bit back and sends it to the verifier.

Consequently, we redefine tainted phases as follows:

Definition 5 (Tainted Time-Critical Phase (strSimTF)). *A time-critical phase* $\Pi_{\mathsf{sid}}[k \ldots k+2\ell-1] = (m_k, \ldots, m_{k+2\ell-1})$ *for* $k, \ell \geq 1$ *of a reader-adversary session* sid, *with the* k-*th message being received by the adversary, is* tainted *if there exists an adversary-tag session* sid* *and messages* $(m_k^*, \ldots, m_{k+2\ell-1}^*)$ *such that for all* $i = 0, 1, \ldots, \ell - 1$ *we have:*

$$clock(\mathsf{sid}, k + 2i) < clock(\mathsf{sid}^*, k + 2i),$$

$$and \quad clock(\mathsf{sid}, k + 2i + 1) > clock(\mathsf{sid}^*, k + 2i + 1).$$

3.1 GameTF Security

Our game-based terrorist fraud resistance GameTF follows the intuition of [1]. The key difference between this and SimTF security is that GameTF security rules out attacks if the attacker gains *any* advantage to authenticate later (even if this advantage is *smaller* than the adversary's success probability). Thus, we match the unaided adversary's success against a MITM attack (mafia fraud).

We consider a simulator-free two-step game, with two adversaries $\mathcal{A}$ and $\mathcal{A}^*$ sharing view view$_\mathcal{A}$, as defined in the SimTF security model.[4] Now $\mathcal{A}$ can interact with the dishonest $\mathcal{T}'$ during lazy and time-critical phases as described above (we use the notion of tainted phases in Definition 5). The second adversary $\mathcal{A}^*$ (sharing state, or view, with $\mathcal{A}$) runs a mafia fraud interaction with $\mathcal{R}$ in the presence of the prover (who is this time honest). Thus, $\mathcal{A}^*$ models the adversary *after* the prover stops helping: $\mathcal{A}^*$ must authenticate in a MITM attack, using view$_\mathcal{A}$. In SimTF security, the simulator is passive and just uses view$_\mathcal{A}$ to authenticate; however, in GameTF, $\mathcal{A}^*$ runs an active mafia-fraud interaction *and* uses view$_\mathcal{A}$. We say that $\mathcal{A}$ *is helpful* to $\mathcal{A}^*$ if $\mathcal{A}^*$ authenticates with better than mafia-fraud success probability (i.e. view$_\mathcal{A}$ shouldn't help $\mathcal{A}^*$ at all).

We sketch the differences between SimTF and GameTF security in Fig. 1. Also note that in SimTF security, $\mathcal{A}$ queries $\mathcal{T}'$ in at most $T_{\max}$ time-critical phases (tainting them). However, the GameTF adversary $\mathcal{A}$ may query $\mathcal{T}'$ in *each* time-critical phase, tainting it only if it uses relay scheduling.

Of $\mathcal{A}$ and $\mathcal{A}^*$, the former is the terrorist adversary. Its attack is *invalid* if there exists $\mathcal{A}^*$ such that $\mathcal{A}$ is helpful to $\mathcal{A}^*$, i.e. we rule out attacks where $\mathcal{A}$ learns information useful for later authentication. Schemes are GameTF secure if every terrorist adversary $\mathcal{A}$ either (i) wins with negligible probability; or (ii) there exists an adversary $\mathcal{A}^*$ to which $\mathcal{A}$ is helpful. Let $\mathcal{A}$ run in time t, using q_{OBS} reader-tag, $q_{\mathcal{R}}$ resp. reader-adversary, and $q_{\mathcal{T}'}$ adversary-tag sessions —the latter subject to Definition 5; its success probability is denoted ϵ.

When $\mathcal{A}$ stops, it forwards view$_\mathcal{A}$ to $\mathcal{A}^*$. Then $\mathcal{A}^*$ runs a mafia-fraud interaction with $\mathcal{T}$ (we omit the apostrophe as $\mathcal{T}$ is now honest). W.l.o.g., let $\mathcal{A}^*$ run in time $t^* \leq 3t$ ($\mathcal{A}^*$ runs $\mathcal{A}$ at most twice internally, with the same queries as $\mathcal{A}$), and let $\mathcal{A}^*$ run at most q_{OBS} reader-tag, $q_{\mathcal{R}}$ reader-adversary, and $q_{\mathcal{R}}$ adversary-tag sessions (since $\mathcal{A}$'s queries to $\mathcal{T}'$ deviate from protocol, we give $\mathcal{A}^*$ one adversary-tag session for each reader-adversary session). Let $\mathcal{A}^*$ win w.p. ϵ^*. We now define *helpful* terrorist adversaries and GameTF security.

---

[4] Note that any other state information is computable from view$_\mathcal{A}$, for higher runtimes.

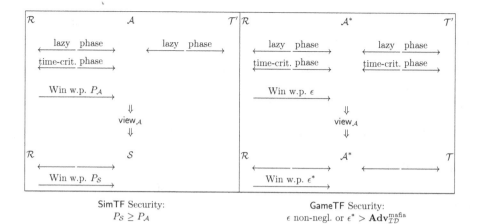

Fig. 1. Simulation and game-based security models

Definition 6. *For an authentication scheme $\mathcal{ID}$ with parameters $(t_{max}, T_{max}, E_{max}, N_c)$, let $\mathcal{A}$ be a $(t, q_{OBS}, q_{\mathcal{R}}, q_{\mathcal{T'}})$ adversary running a strSimTF interaction with $\mathcal{R}$ and $\mathcal{T'}$, and let $st = view_{\mathcal{A}}$ denote its state. We say that $\mathcal{A}$ is* helpful *to an adversary $\mathcal{A}^*$ with input st, runtime at most 3t, running at most $q_{OBS}, q_{\mathcal{R}}$, and $q_{\mathcal{T}} = q_{\mathcal{R}}$ sessions in a mafia-fraud interaction with $\mathcal{R}$ and $\mathcal{T}$, and winning with probability ϵ^* (taken over $view_{\mathcal{A}}$ and the coins of $\mathcal{A}^*$) if:*

$$\epsilon^* > Adv_{\mathcal{ID}}^{mafia},$$

where $Adv_{\mathcal{ID}}^{mafia}$ denotes the mafia fraud resistance of $\mathcal{ID}$ for a $(t, q_{OBS}, q_{\mathcal{R}}, q_{\mathcal{T}})$-mafia adversary.

Definition 7 (GameTF Security). *A distance-bounding authentication scheme $\mathcal{ID}$ with parameters $(t_{max}, T_{max}, E_{max}, N_c)$ is $(t, q_{OBS}, q_{\mathcal{R}}, q_{\mathcal{T'}}, \epsilon)$-GameTF secure if for all $(t, q_{OBS}, q_{\mathcal{R}}, q_{\mathcal{T'}})$ adversaries $\mathcal{A}$ running a strSimTF interaction, one of the following statements hold:*

- *The probability that $\mathcal{A}$ wins is upper bounded by ϵ;*
- *There exists an adversary $\mathcal{A}^*$ such that $\mathcal{A}$ is helpful to $\mathcal{A}^*$ as defined above.*

A scheme $\mathcal{ID}$ is GameTF secure if it is $(t, q_{OBS}, q_{\mathcal{R}}, q_{\mathcal{T'}}, \epsilon)$-GameTF secure for negligible ϵ.

The Swiss-Knife protocol. This section concerns the Swiss-Knife protocol of [14], modified as in [7], which we depict in Fig. 2. We use the modified version since it is mafia-fraud resistant, noting that both the original and the modified versions are SimTF-insecure [7]. Despite the attack of [6], however, the scheme prevents known terrorist attacks. In fact, we can prove its GameTF-security, confirming intuition; in particular, the syntactic attack in [7] is ruled out because the prover's help gives the adversary a significant advantage. For our GameTF proof, we use the scheme's mafia fraud resistance. In the protocol, PRF denotes a pseudorandom function, $\mathcal{ID}_\mathcal{R}$ and $\mathcal{ID}_\mathcal{T}$ are reader and tag identifiers, and const is a publicly known constant. The difference to the original scheme is the use of an independent key sk^* instead of re-using sk.

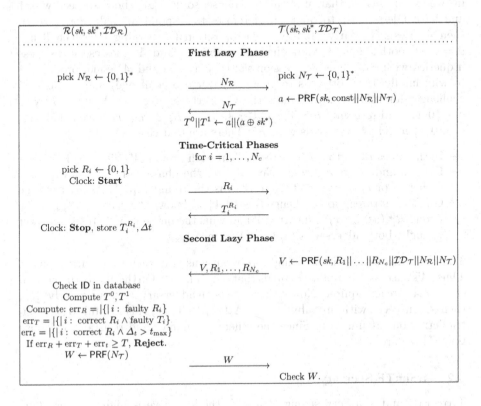

Fig. 2. The Modified Swiss-Knife protocol of [7]

Proposition 1 (GameTF Security).

Let $\mathcal{ID}$ be the protocol in Fig. 2 with parameters (t_{max}, N_c). This scheme is $(t, q_{\text{OBS}}, q_\mathcal{R}, q_{\mathcal{T}'}, \epsilon)$-GameTF secure, for $\epsilon \geq \mathbf{Adv}_{\mathcal{ID}}^{mafia}$.

Proof. Assume towards contradiction that the scheme is *not* $(t, q_{\text{OBS}}, q_\mathcal{R}, q_{\mathcal{T}'}, \epsilon)$-GameTF resistant. Then there exists a $(t, q_{\text{OBS}}, q_\mathcal{R}, q_{\mathcal{T}'})$ adversary $\mathcal{A}$ such that: (i) $\mathcal{A}$ wins with probability $\epsilon > \mathbf{Adv}_{\mathcal{ID}}^{mafia}$; *and* (ii) for all $(3t, q_{\text{OBS}}, q_\mathcal{R}, q_\mathcal{R})$-adversaries $\mathcal{A}^*$, initialized with view$_\mathcal{A}$, running a mafia fraud interaction with $\mathcal{R}$ and $\mathcal{T}$, the success probability ϵ^* of $\mathcal{A}^*$ is such that $\epsilon^* \geq \mathbf{Adv}_{\mathcal{ID}}^{mafia}$.

We construct, for each $\mathcal{A}$ as in (i) and (ii), an $\mathcal{A}^*$ with input view$_\mathcal{A}$, winning in the attack above with probability $\epsilon^* \geq \epsilon$. Thus, if $\mathcal{A}$ wins w.p. $\epsilon > \mathbf{Adv}_{\mathcal{ID}}^{mafia}$ (as in (i)), our $\mathcal{A}^*$ follows the specifications of Definition 6 and wins w.p. $\epsilon^* = \epsilon > \mathbf{Adv}_{\mathcal{ID}}^{mafia}$ (contradicting point (ii)). Thus, an adversary $\mathcal{A}$ for which points (i) and (ii) both hold does not exist.

We describe $\mathcal{A}^*$. For each session $\mathcal{A}$ runs with $\mathcal{R}$, $\mathcal{A}^*$ runs parallel sessions with $\mathcal{R}$ and resp. $\mathcal{T}$, relaying the lazy phase and running time-critical phases as follows. In the verifier-adversary session sid, $\mathcal{A}^*$ runs $\mathcal{A}$ internally, branching out in two executions, so that: if $\mathcal{A}$ taints a phase, so does $\mathcal{A}^*$ (both succeed w.p. 1 and have 1 less phase to taint); if $\mathcal{A}$ refuses to respond to challenge $\alpha_i =: \alpha$, then $\mathcal{A}^*$ uses a Go-Early strategy (see Proposition 3), querying $\mathcal{T}$ with challenge $\bar{\alpha} = \alpha \oplus 1$ (both $\mathcal{A}$ and $\mathcal{A}^*$ know the same response), and $\mathcal{A}^*$ guesses the response if queried with challenge α in session sid: this gives $\mathcal{A}$ and $\mathcal{A}^*$ equal probability to win; finally, if $\mathcal{A}$ forwards responses r_0 (for a 0 challenge) and r_1 (for a 1 challenge) for this round, $\mathcal{A}^*$ uses the Go-Early strategy, challenging $\mathcal{T}$ with $\alpha \in \{0,1\}$, and receiving R_i^α. Then $\mathcal{A}^*$ sets $R_i^{\bar{\alpha}} = R_i^\alpha \oplus r_0 \oplus r_1$; given challenge $c \in \{0,1\}$ in sid, $\mathcal{A}^*$ responds with R_i^c. There are four cases:

- Both values r_0 and r_1 are correct. Then both $\mathcal{A}$ and $\mathcal{A}^*$ win w.p. 1.
- Both r_0 and r_1 are incorrect. Now $\mathcal{A}$ loses the phase and $\mathcal{A}^*$ wins w.p. 1.
- Either r_0 or r_1 is incorrect. Now $\mathcal{A}$ wins the round w.p. $\frac{1}{2}$. As $\mathcal{A}^*$ runs the Go-Early strategy for challenge $\alpha \in \{0,1\}$, it knows the correct R_i^α, but the wrong $R_i^{\bar{\alpha}}$ (as $r_0 \oplus r_1$ is incorrect), and wins the phase w.p. $\frac{1}{2}$. If they answer wrongly, both adversaries subtract 1 from $E_{\max}$.

Thus, $\mathcal{A}^*$ wins with at least as high probability as $\mathcal{A}$ in each time-critical phase. Thus, $\mathcal{A}$'s success probability ϵ equals that of $\mathcal{A}^*$, i.e. ϵ^*. Furthermore, the parameters of $\mathcal{A}^*$ are as required. Now if there exists an adversary $\mathcal{A}$ with $\epsilon > \mathbf{Adv}_{\mathcal{ID}}^{\mathrm{mafia}}$, then $\mathcal{A}^*$ succeeds with probability $\epsilon^* > \mathbf{Adv}_{\mathcal{ID}}^{\mathrm{mafia}}$. Thus, $\mathcal{A}$ is helpful to $\mathcal{A}^*$, contradicting our assumption. Since the scheme is mafia fraud resistant, it is also GameTF secure. □

3.2 strSimTF Security

Terrorist fraud is a very strong attack. If the incentive is high (e.g. breaking e-Passport security), then dishonest provers may be willing to forward *some* secret information to ensure the adversary's success. However, SimTF security (while strong) restricts the adversary unnecessarily by not allowing it to query the prover in time-critical rounds.

We obtain our strSimTF notion by simply switching the tainted-phase definition from Definition 3 to Definition 5, and then use Definition 4. The strSimTF adversary is stronger: we show in Theorem 1 that there exist SimTF-secure schemes that are strSimTF-insecure. We also show in Section 4 that strSimTF security is achievable; this is a non-trivial statement, since the recent results of [7] cast a doubt whether *any* existing protocol is provably SimTF-secure (they are thus also strSimTF-insecure). Our construction relies on the Swiss-Knife protocol, but we introduce a back door for the simulator to authenticate.

3.3 Relating the Notions

Our full security diagram in Fig. 3 fully relates the notions. Due to space reasons, we only sketch the proofs in the Appendix.

Theorem 1 (Relations between notions). SimTF, strSimTF, GameTF *security, and mafia-fraud resistance are related as in Fig. 3. Arrows between notions indicate that security against one notion implies security against the other.*

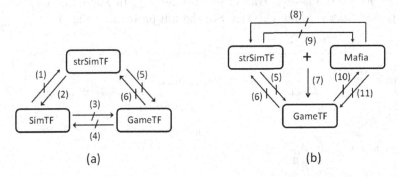

Fig. 3. Full security diagram. The "+" sign beside (7) indicates property composition.

4 Terrorist Fraud Resistant Construction

4.1 The Protocol

Our SimTF- and strSimTF-secure protocol relies on the (modified) Swiss-Knife protocol in Fig. 2, which thwarts MITM attacks by a second authentication phase. We make the following changes: (1) we add a bit to the authentication string, now denoted $0||I$ in Fig. 4 (an honest prover always sends $0||I$, but by sending $1||I$, a dishonest prover or an adversary may switch the flag a for $\mathcal{R}$, see the following point); (2) we add a flag a for $\mathcal{R}$ denoting whether the protocol runs normally (more or less as in the Swiss-Knife protocol) or exceptionally, such that during the time-critical phases, the verifier just expects $\mathcal{T}$ to echo the challenges (also see below). In our proof the simulator will try to make $\mathcal{R}$ run the protocol exceptionally, thus bypassing authentication.

Now, if the prover's first protocol response is a string of the form $1||I, N_{\mathcal{T}}, \mathcal{R}$ accepts $1||I$ as valid lazy authentication (continuing the protocol) with probability $\min\{1, 2^{-\#_1(I \oplus sk') + T_{\max} + E_{\max}}\}$; in this case the flag a is set to 1. We denote by $\#_1(I \oplus sk')$ the Hamming distance between I and sk'; thus, if the first bit is a 1, the rest of the string I should be close to sk' (an adversary can't just receive an honest $0||I$ and flip the first bit). The probability is tailored to fit the SimTF definition, where the simulator recovers some bits of sk' from a successful adversary; the bound also accounts for $\mathcal{A}$'s tainted and erroneous-response rounds (see the SimTF proof). The flag a and our second authentication method (using $1||I$ responses, with I close to sk') are artifices enabling us to prove SimTF and resp. strSimTF security. Once the flag is flipped, *any* party in $\mathcal{R}$'s proximity can authenticate, since the reader expects $\mathcal{T}$ to just echo the time-critical challenges. However, mafia fraud attackers cannot make use of this, as honest provers never send $1||sk'$ (but rather a string $0||I$, where I is output by PRF) —for mafia and impersonation security we only lose a term $q_{\mathcal{R}} \cdot 2^{-(2-\log_2 3)N_c+T_{\max}+E_{\max}}$, accounting for the probability of guessing a close-enough authentication string.

For the second lazy authentication phase, $\mathcal{T}$ runs a different PRF than before (namely, F) on the session transcript, denoted τ_{ID}. In Simulator mode (i.e. if $a = 1$), the string P is not checked. See the full protocol in Fig. 4.

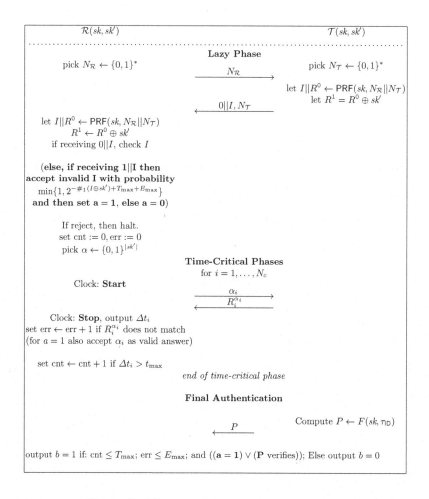

Fig. 4. SimTF secure distance-bounding protocol

4.2 Security

Here we prove our scheme SimTF- and strSimTF-secure, under the assumption that reader-adversary sessions are executed sequentially. Note that not *every* SimTF-secure scheme is also strSimTF-secure, see also Section 3.3. We also state the scheme's full distance-bounding properties, but omit the proofs for space reasons.

Theorem 2 (SimTF Security). *Let* ID *be the distance-bounding authentication scheme in Fig. 4 with parameters* $(t_{\max}, T_{\max}, E_{\max}, N_c)$. *For any* $(t, q_{\mathcal{R}}, q_{\mathcal{T}'})$- SimTF *adversary* $\mathcal{A}$ *against the scheme, mounting a sequential attack, there exists a* $t_{\mathcal{S}}$-*simulator* $\mathcal{S}$ *with* $t_{\mathcal{S}} = 2t + O(nq_{\mathcal{R}})$ *such that we have*

$$Adv_{\mathsf{ID}}^{\mathsf{SimTF}}(\mathcal{A}, \mathcal{S}, \mathcal{T}) \leq 0.$$

Proof. We describe the simulator $\mathcal{S}$. Given view$_{\mathcal{A}}$, including $\mathcal{A}$'s randomness, $\mathcal{S}$ internally runs $\mathcal{A}$ stepwise with view$_{\mathcal{A}}$, repeating the same strategy for each of its $q_{\mathcal{R}}$ sessions sid (as many sessions as $\mathcal{A}$). Namely, $\mathcal{S}$ checks if $\mathcal{A}$ sends $1||I$ and succeeds; if so, $\mathcal{S}$ sets $sk'' = I$ for sid. Else, if $\mathcal{A}$ uses $0||I$, the simulator constructs sk'' as follows: each time $\mathcal{A}$ expects α_i in the next time-critical phase, $\mathcal{S}$ branches into two executions, once sending $\alpha_i^0 = 0$ and the other time $\alpha_i^1 = 1$ to $\mathcal{A}$. It waits for $\mathcal{A}$ to answer in both branches, or query $\mathcal{T}'$ (tainting a branch). As we consider sequential executions only, there are no other options. If $\mathcal{A}$ taints or refuses one query, $\mathcal{S}$ picks sk_i'' at random; else it sets $sk_i'' = R_i^0 \oplus R_i^1$. The simulator returns to its main execution and resumes the simulation with the correct α_i. When $\mathcal{A}$ stops, $\mathcal{S}$ has predictions sk_i'' for each bit of sk_i'. If $\mathcal{A}$ succeeds in some sid with $0||C$, then there are four cases for each guessed bit sk_i'':

- The adversary taints the phase or refuses to answer both challenges. Then $\mathcal{S}$'s guessing strategy is good: by comparing the term $\#_1(I \oplus sk') - T_{\max} - E_{\max}$ (i.e. the number of bits $\mathcal{S}$ needs to predict) to the number of phases $\mathcal{A}$ needs to pass, we see that $\mathcal{S}$ gets a "wild card" for each of the at most $T_{\max}$ tainted phases. If $\mathcal{A}$ taints the phase in both branches, it succeeds for one round; however $\mathcal{S}$ then "gains" 1.5 bits by deducting one wild card off $T_{\max}$ and guessing a bit of sk' with probability $\frac{1}{2}$. Thus $\mathcal{S}$ has an advantage over $\mathcal{A}$. If, however, $\mathcal{A}$ taints exactly one branch *and* always responds correctly in the other (it always wins the round), then $\mathcal{S}$ gets half a bit from sk_i' correctly (for the untainted branch, which occurs w.p. $\frac{1}{2}$), and another half a bit from the tainted branch ($\mathcal{A}$ cannot taint another round later). On average $\mathcal{S}$ gets thus as many bits as is $\mathcal{A}$'s success probability.
- If $\mathcal{A}$ returns correct R_i^0, R_i^1, then $sk_i'' = sk_i'$, $\mathcal{A}$ wins the round, and $\mathcal{S}$ gains a bit.
- Analogously, $sk_i'' = sk_i'$ if both replies are incorrect ($\mathcal{A}$ fails here).
- If exactly one of R_i^0 and R_i^1 is correct, then sk_i'' is certainly incorrect. But then $\mathcal{A}$ too fails the phase with probability $\frac{1}{2}$. The reasoning from the first case for $T_{\max}$ applies to $E_{\max}$.

Accounting for at most $T_{\max} + E_{\max}$ tainted and erroneous phases, $\mathcal{A}$ authenticates with probability at most $2^{-\#_1(sk'' \oplus sk') + T_{\max} + E_{\max}}$. By using sk'', $\mathcal{S}$ also authenticates with the same probability. Also, if $\mathcal{S}$ reuses $sk'' = I$ for adversary executions with $1||I$, it succeeds with the same probability as $\mathcal{A}$. □

Proposition 2. *Let* ID *be the protocol in Fig. 4 with parameters* $(t_{\max}, T_{\max}, E_{\max}, N_c)$. *For any* $(t, q_{\mathcal{R}}, q_{\mathcal{T}'})$-strSimTF *adversary* $\mathcal{A}$ *against* ID, *mounting a* *sequential attack, there exists a t_S-simulator S with $t_S = 2t + O(nq_R)$ such that for any T' running in time $t_{T'}$*

$$Adv_{ID}^{terror}(A, S, T) \leq 0.$$

Proof. We extend our SimTF proof to account for time-critical queries to T', also for sequential executions. We change S as follows: if A does *not* interact with T' during time-critical phases, the simulator is the same. If A *does* query T', for each time-critical phase where A interacts with T', the simulator branches the execution for both challenges. If A refuses to forward one response or taints the phase (with relay scheduling), S guesses the bit in sk'' as before.

The old proof still stands; indeed, if the phase is *not* tainted by relaying, then either A queries T' *before* challenge α_i is sent, or T' responds *after* A has replied to R in this phase. In the former case, T' does *not* know the true challenge, as in the SimTF scenario. In the latter case, the prover's response does not help A, as the responses are pseudorandom and independent of each other, though it may help the simulator instead (since view_A contains the correct response). □

Proposition 3 (Mafia Fraud Resistance). *Let* ID *be the scheme in Figure 4 with parameters* $(t_{max}, T_{max}, E_{max}, N_c)$. *For any* (t, q_R, q_T, q_{OBS})*-mafia-fraud adversary* A *against the scheme there exist: a* (t', q')*-distinguisher* A' *against* PRF, *a* (t'', q'')*-distinguisher* A'' *against* F, *and a* (t''', q''')*-distinguisher* A''' *(where* $t', t'', t''' = t + O(n)$ *and* $q', q'', q''' = q_R + q_T + q_{OBS}$*) such that:*

$$Adv_{ID}^{mafia}(A) \leq q_R \left(\frac{1}{2}\right)^{N_c - (T_{max} + E_{max})} + \binom{q_R + q_{OBS}}{2} \cdot 2^{-(|N_R| + \lceil \frac{N_c}{2} \rceil - T_{max} - E_{max})}$$

$$+ \binom{q_T + q_{OBS}}{2} \cdot 2^{-(|N_T| + \lceil \frac{N_c}{2} \rceil - T_{max} - E_{max})} + Adv_{PRF}^{d}(A')$$

$$+ Adv_F^{d}(A'') + 2Adv_{Kg}^{d(D,U)}(A''') + q_R \cdot 2^{-(2 - \log_2 3)N_c + T_{max} + E_{max}}.$$

Proposition 4 (Distance Fraud Resistance). *Let* ID *be the scheme in Figure 4 with parameters* $(t_{max}, T_{max}, E_{max}, N_c)$. *Assume also that* Kg *is run by either the reader or a trusted third party (not the tag), such that it generates keys* sk, sk' *by drawing them uniformly at random from a distribution* D *computationally indistinguishable from the uniform random distribution. For any* (t, q_R, q_T, q_{OBS})*-distance-fraud adversary* A *against* ID *it holds that,*

$$Adv_{ID}^{dist}(A) \leq q_R \cdot \left(\frac{3}{4}\right)^{N_c - T_{max} - E_{max}} + Adv_{Kg}^{d(D,U)}(A').$$

Proposition 5 (Impersonation Security). *Let* ID *be the scheme in Figure 4 with parameters* $(t_{max}, T_{max}, E_{max}, N_c)$. *For any* (t, q_R, q_T, q_{OBS})*-impersonation adversary* A *against* ID *there exist a* (t', q')*-distinguisher* A', *resp. a* (t'', q'')*-distinguisher* A'' *against* PRF *and resp.* F *(with* $t', t'' = t + O(n)$ *and* $q', q'' = q_R + q_T + q_{OBS}$*) such that*

$$Adv_{ID(A)}^{imp} \leq q_R \cdot 2^{-|I|} + q_R \cdot 2^{-(2 - \log_2 3)N_c + T_{max} + E_{max}} + q_R \cdot Adv_{PRF}^{d}(A') +$$

$$q_R \cdot Adv_F^{d}(A') + \left(\binom{q_R + q_{OBS}}{2} \cdot 2^{-|N_R|} + \binom{q_T}{2} \cdot 2^{-|N_T|}\right) \cdot 2^{-N_c}.$$

5   Which Model to Use

The abundance of terrorist-fraud resistance definitions in the literature proves that, though this topic is crucial to distance-bounding authentication, no clear solution has been found for it. Even our present work does not give one, but rather two definitions of terrorist-fraud resistance, and proves that, though many existent schemes in the literature fail to achieve one notion (strSimTF security), they do attain the other. Which definition is better? That is a question which cannot be answered in an unequivocal way.

Simulation-based models, like SimTF and strSimTF security, formalize terrorist-fraud resistance in a very strong way, allowing the prover to help the adversary as long as the gained help cannot be used by a simulator given the adversary's view only. This is the case for the SimTF notion of [6], which we extend to better capture the attack. These strong notions *should* be used in high-risk applications, like e-voting or e-Passports, where the strongest possible security is desirable. Indeed both SimTF and strSimTF security *can* be achieved, e.g. by our scheme.

However, simulation-based security is too strong for resource-constrained devices, as it does *not* enable efficient protocols. In such scenarios, our game-based GameTF model is more appropriate, capturing the intuition of terrorist fraud resistance, but enabling more efficient schemes e.g. [14].

References

1. Avoine, G., Bingol, M.A., Karda, S., Lauradoux, C., Martin, B.: A formal framework for analyzing RFID distance bounding protocols. Journal of Computer Security - Special Issue on RFID System Security (2010)
2. Avoine, G., Lauradoux, C., Martin, B.: How secret-sharing can defeat terrorist fraud. In: Proceedings of the Fourth ACM Conference on Wireless Network Security, WISEC 2011, pp. 145–156. ACM Press (2011)
3. Brands, S., Chaum, D.: Distance-bounding protocols. In: Helleseth, T. (ed.) EUROCRYPT 1993. LNCS, vol. 765, pp. 344–359. Springer, Heidelberg (1994)
4. Desmedt, Y.: Major security problems with the 'unforgeable' (feige)-fiat-shamir proofs of identity and how to overcome them. In: SecuriCom, pp. 15–17. SEDEP Paris, France (1988)
5. Drimer, S., Murdoch, S.J.: Keep your enemies close: distance bounding against smartcard relay attacks. In: Proc. of the 16th USENIX Security Symposium on USENIX Security Symposium, article no. 7. ACM Press (2007)
6. Dürholz, U., Fischlin, M., Kasper, M., Onete, C.: A formal approach to distance-bounding RFID protocols. In: Lai, X., Zhou, J., Li, H. (eds.) ISC 2011. LNCS, vol. 7001, pp. 47–62. Springer, Heidelberg (2011)
7. Fischlin, M., Onete, C.: Provably secure distance-bounding: an analysis of prominent protocols. Accepted at the 6th Conference on Security and Privacy in Wireless and Mobile Networks ACM WISec 2013, Proceedings will follow (2013), http://eprint.iacr.org/2012/128.pdf
8. Francillon, A., Danev, B., Čapkun, S.: Relay Attacks on Passive Keyless Entry and Start Systems in Modern Cars (2010), http://eprint.iacr.org/2010/332

9. Haataja, K., Toivanen, P.: Two practical man-in-the-middle attacks on bluetooth secure simple pairing and countermeasures. Transactions on Wireless Communications 9(1), 384–392 (2010)

10. Hancke, G.P.: A practical relay attack on ISO 14443 proximity cards (2005), http://www.cl.cam.ac.uk/gh275/relay.pdf

11. Hancke, G.P., Kuhn, M.G.: An RFID distance bounding protocol. In: SECURECOMM, pp. 67–73. ACM Press (2005)

12. Hlaváč, M., Tomáč, R.: A Note on the Relay Attacks on e-Passports (2007), http://eprint.iacr.org/2007/244.pdf

13. Kfir, Z., Wool, A.: Picking virtual pockets using relay attacks on contactless smart-card systems. In: Conference on Security and Privacy for Emergency Areas in Communication Networks – SecureComm 2005, pp. 47–58. IEEE (2005)

14. Kim, C.H., Avoine, G., Koeune, F., Standaert, F.-X., Pereira, O.: The Swiss-Knife RFID distance bounding protocol. In: Lee, P.J., Cheon, J.H. (eds.) ICISC 2008. LNCS, vol. 5461, pp. 98–115. Springer, Heidelberg (2009)

15. Levi, A., Çetintaş, E., Aydos, M., Koç, Ç.K., Çağlayan, M.U.: Relay attacks on bluetooth authentication and solutions. In: Aykanat, C., Dayar, T., Körpeoğlu, İ. (eds.) ISCIS 2004. LNCS, vol. 3280, pp. 278–288. Springer, Heidelberg (2004)

16. Oren, Y., Wool, A.: Relay attacks on RFID-based electronic voting systems. Cryptology ePrint Archive, Report 2009/442 (2009), http://eprint.iacr.org/2009/422.pdf

17. Ranganathan, A., Tippenhauer, N.O., Škorić, B., Singelée, D., Čapkun, S.: Design and Implementation of a Terrorist Fraud Resilient Distance Bounding System. In: Foresti, S., Yung, M., Martinelli, F. (eds.) ESORICS 2012. LNCS, vol. 7459, pp. 415–432. Springer, Heidelberg (2012)

18. Reid, J., Nieto, J.M.G., Tang, T., Senadji, B.: Detecting relay attacks with timing-based protocols. In: ASIACCS, pp. 204–213. ACM Press (2007)

A   Full Proofs of Security Diagram

Proof (sketch). For the proofs of (8) and (9) we use the strategy in [6], reusing their counterexample to prove (8). The counterexample for (9) is the scheme in (10). Finally (1) follows trivially from the strSimTF definition. The proofs are out of order, as we group similar proofs together.

Our separation for (2) relies on our scheme in Fig. 4, modified to run $2N_c$ time-critical rounds such that $\mathcal{R}$ reveals the even-indexed challenges in advance, sending them masked with pseudorandom bits during odd-indexed rounds. However, in odd-indexed rounds, the prover must just echo the challenge.The modified scheme preserves the properties of the original one. Though distance fraud adversaries can predict even-indexed challenges, they must guess the odd-indexed ones. Mafia fraud adversaries trivially echo odd-indexed responses, but learn nothing about the encrypted even-indexed challenges. Finally, the SimTF security proof still stands since the odd-indexed rounds are trivial for both $\mathcal{A}$ and $\mathcal{S}$. However, a strSimTF adversary echoes odd-indexed challenges, using its time-critical interactions to forward the encrypted challenges in advance (thus receiving also the even-indexed challenges). Since no key information is leaked, the simulator cannot authenticate.

We prove (7) similarly to Proposition 1: let $\mathcal{ID}$ be a mafia-fraud and strSimTF-secure scheme, and assume it is *not* GameTF resistant. Assume that there exists a $(t, q_{\text{OBS}}, q_{\mathcal{R}}, q_{\mathcal{T}'})$-adversary $\mathcal{A}$ interacting in a strSimTF way such that: (i) $\mathcal{A}$ wins with non-negligible probability ϵ; (ii) all $(3t, q_{\text{OBS}}, q_{\mathcal{R}}, q_{\mathcal{R}})$ adversaries $\mathcal{A}^*$ using view$_{\mathcal{A}}$ in a mafia fraud interaction wins w.p. at most $\mathbf{Adv}_{\mathcal{ID}}^{\text{mafia}}$. By strSimTF security, for adversary $\mathcal{A}$ there exists a simulator $\mathcal{S}$, which, given view$_{\mathcal{A}}$, wins with probability $p_{\mathcal{S}} \geq \epsilon$. Now $\mathcal{A}^*$ run $\mathcal{S}$ as a black box on view$_{\mathcal{A}}$, and wins w.p. $p_{\mathcal{S}} \geq \epsilon$. Following point (ii), $\mathcal{A}^*$ must win w.p. at most $\mathbf{Adv}_{\mathcal{ID}}^{\text{mafia}}$; thus $\epsilon \leq p_{\mathcal{S}} \leq \mathbf{Adv}_{\mathcal{ID}}^{\text{mafia}}$. Then $\mathbf{Adv}_{\mathcal{ID}}^{\text{mafia}}$ is non-negligible, contradicting the assumption that $\mathcal{ID}$ is mafia-fraud resistant.

For (8) we use the Hancke-Kuhn protocol [11] except that R^0, R^1 are computed as: $R^0 \| R^1 \leftarrow \mathsf{PRF}(sk, N_{\mathcal{R}} \| N_{\mathcal{T}})$. The mafia fraud resistance of this scheme can be found in [7]; however, a GameTF adversary can query $\mathcal{T}'$ for $R^0 \| R^1$ in some session sid, giving no help for future authentication. Similarly, Mafia $\nrightarrow$ strSimTF.

For (11) we use a trick from [6], changing the protocol in Fig. 2 to allow an adversary to change a flag that makes $\mathcal{R}$ run in a special mode, expecting the conjugated response values, rather than the originals. Now a mafia adversary passes the challenges to $\mathcal{T}$, but flips the responses. However, a GameTF-adversary cannot use this trick, as relay scheduling taints the phase (even if the bits are flipped). We use the same trick for (5). In strSimTF security, $\mathcal{S}$ must win with the same probability as $\mathcal{A}$. The helpfulness of GameTF adversaries depends though on mafia fraud resistance. If mafia fraud adversaries authenticate easily, any adversary is unhelpful, even one for which there exists a simulator as in strSimTF security. We modify the scheme in Figure 4 as in (11), thus making $\mathbf{Adv}_i^{\text{mafia}} d = 1$, for the (still) strSimTF-secure scheme. However, the protocol is GameTF insecure: an adversary $\mathcal{A}$ receiving sk' from $\mathcal{T}'$: (i) wins with probability 1; (ii) all adversaries $\mathcal{A}^*$ with input view$_{\mathcal{A}}$, win w.p. at most $1 = \mathbf{Adv}_{\mathcal{ID}}^{\text{mafia}}$. The same strategy proves (3), by replacing strSimTF with SimTF security, and (4) follows from (6) and (2).

For (6), we change the scheme in Fig. 2 to allow a dishonest prover to generate and send the adversary a particular cheating lazy-phase response, making $\mathcal{R}$ run a special mode, where the challenges are predictable, but only by a prover. This breaks strSimTF security, enabling the prover to help the adversary and then forward the correct challenges; however, a simulator is unable to learn the responses, even if it knows the challenges. By contrast, if a GameTF adversary uses the cheat, it is helpful to an adversary who can then use the Go-Early strategy to learn the correct responses. $\square$

Crowdshare: Secure Mobile Resource Sharing

N. Asokan[1], Alexandra Dmitrienko[2], Marcin Nagy[5], Elena Reshetova[4],
Ahmad-Reza Sadeghi[2,3], Thomas Schneider[3], and Stanislaus Stelle[3]

[1] University of Helsinki, Finland
asokan@acm.org
[2] Fraunhofer-Institut SIT Darmstadt, Germany
{alexandra.dmitrienko,ahmad-reza.sadeghi}@sit.fraunhofer.de
[3] Technische Universität Darmstadt, Germany
{thomas.schneider,stanislaus.stelle}@cased.de
[4] Intel Open Labs, Finland
elena.reshetova@gmail.com
[5] Aalto University, Finland
marcin.nagy@gmail.com

Abstract. Mobile smart devices and services have become an integral
part of our daily life. In this context there are many compelling scenarios
for mobile device users to share resources. A popular example is tethering. However, sharing resources also raises privacy and security issues.

In this paper, we present Crowdshare, a complete framework and
its (Android) implementation for secure and private resource sharing
among nearby devices. Crowdshare provides pseudonymity for users, accountability of resource usage, and the possibility of specifying access
control in terms of social network relationships. Further, Crowdshare preserves secure connectivity between nearby devices even in the absence of
the mobile infrastructure. We have implemented Crowdshare on Android
devices and report good performance results.

1   Introduction

The popularity of inexpensive communication services like Skype, Gtalk, and
WhatsApp is increasing rapidly. They allow people to communicate with almost
the same ease as with phone calls and Short Message Service (SMS) messages,
but at a significantly lower cost to the users. However, the pre-requisite to all
such services is Internet access, which can be quite difficult to obtain in certain
situations. First, Internet access can be expensive while traveling abroad. As a
result, *tethering*, the process of sharing Internet connectivity from one device
by turning it into a wireless access point that other devices can connect to, has
gained popularity. Some devices provide tethering as part of their base functionality, while other third party applications like JoikuSpot [9] and OpenGarden [1]
can enable tethering. Second, in some situations Internet connectivity may be
impossible like in the aftermath of a disaster or while visiting rural areas with
little network coverage or when organizing demonstrations against totalitarian
regimes. In such situations, ad-hoc mesh networks among mobile devices can

M. Jacobson et al. (Eds.): ACNS 2013, LNCS 7954, pp. 432–440, 2013.

provide similar communication or data exchange services. For example, the Serval [2] project aims to preserve connectivity between mobile devices by providing MeshSMS and Call services even in the absence of the mobile support infrastructure; Nokia Instant Community [11] allows mobile devices to form an ad-hoc network to exchange messages or share content.

Naturally any such service that allows the resources of some users (providers) to be used by other users (consumers) has to identify potential security and privacy threats and provide solutions to address them. In particular, providers need to have convenient means to specify suitable *access control*. Access control may be specified in terms of membership in a service (as is done by the community-based WiFi sharing service Fon). Another natural basis to specify access control is to share internet connectivity to "friends of friends", e.g., for visitors of an organization or guests at a party. Consumers need some level of privacy which has to be balanced against the providers' need for accountability so that providers would have evidence of resource usage by consumers.

Our Goal and Contribution. In this paper we present CrowdShare: a service design and its (Android) implementation that allows users to *share connectivity*. CrowdShare distinguishes itself from other tethering and mesh networking applications through incorporating a security architecture with privacy-preserving access control based on social relationships, pseudonymity for users, and accountability of usage. Although CrowdShare focuses on connectivity sharing, the architecture is generic and can be applied to resource sharing in general.

In summary our contribution is *design and integrated implementation* of a complete generic framework for secure resource sharing among nearby devices by incorporating a *security architecture* into existing technologies for mesh networking, tethering, and social network interfaces.

2   System Model and Requirement Analysis

System Model. The system model of the CrowdShare system is depicted in Fig. 1. It consists of a trusted CrowdShare server S, a social network server N, and a set of users $\mathcal{U}$. S admits the users to join the CrowdShare service, while N provides information about friend relationships among users. Each user $U_i \in \mathcal{U}$ possesses a mobile platform which runs the CrowdShare application and enables communication of different users via the mesh network. A user U_i can play one of the following roles: (i) resource provider P, (ii) resource consumer C, or (iii) forwarding node F. P has access to (a set of) resources $\mathcal{R}$ and shares access to them with other users (e.g., Internet bandwidth, media files, or location information). P can restrict the access to his resources either to any U_i, or to a subset of users $\mathcal{F} \subset \mathcal{U}$, who are in a social relation with P in the social network (e.g., friends or friends of friends). C does not have direct access to $\mathcal{R}$ or $\mathcal{R}$ might be available but expensive, hence it consumes resources provided by P via the mesh network. Forwarding nodes F forward messages in the mesh network such that P and C can be connected over multiple hops.

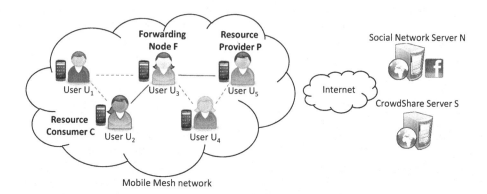

Fig. 1. CrowdShare system model

Threat Model and Security Requirements. CrowdShare and its infrastructure could be subject to several attacks. Our threat model does not cover any attacks against the operating system of the mobile device or any outside component, e.g., a remote server. Instead we concentrate on the attacks that users perform against the service itself. We focus on protecting against semi-honest adversaries that modify the CrowdShare service in order to learn sensitive information or get unauthorized access to services. We identify the following threats for CrowdShare which motivate the need for the respective security requirements.

1. **Man-in-the-middle Attacks ⇒ Channel Protection.** Devices in the ad-hoc mesh network should not be able to act as man-in-the middle that eavesdrops on or modifies messages that are routed through them. This motivates channel protection.
2. **Framing Attacks ⇒ Accountability.** C could use P's resources for illegal purposes. For instance, in the case of Internet sharing C could download a pirated song, leading the copyright owner of the song to accuse P of unauthorized use. In case of such violations, P needs the ability to give evidence that the resource was requested by a particular C. This motivates accountability.
3. **User Identification ⇒ Pseudonymity.** It should not be possible for a user to learn personally identifiable information such as the phone number or the email address of another user. This motivates pseudonymity.
4. **Unauthorized Usage ⇒ Access Control.** C should not be able to use P's resources without its consent. This motivates access control, i.e., P can attach a policy to the shared resource that needs to be fulfilled by C.

3   CrowdShare Protocols and Services

3.1   CrowdShare Protocols

Registration. The purpose of registration is to figure out a real user identity and to issue pseudonymous certificates which will be used by the CrowdShare community members for subsequent communication.

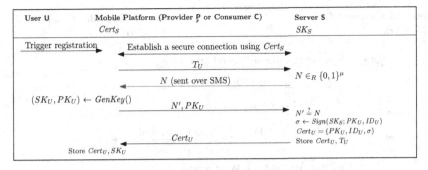

Fig. 2. Registration protocol

The registration protocol is depicted in Fig. 2. Fist, the user $U \in \mathcal{U}$ establishes a secure channel to the server S using the certificate $Cert_S$ of S that is provided together with the CrowdShare application. Next, U sends the user's phone number T_U to S, who generates a one time password (OTP) N and sends it over the short message service (SMS) back to U. In turn, U generates an asymmetric key pair (SK_U, PK_U), and sends PK_U to S together with $N' = N$. Next, S verifies if the received N' matches N sent over SMS, generates a user certificate $Cert_U$ for this user, stores $Cert_U$ together with T_U and returns $Cert_U$ to U. The received $Cert_U$ is stored together with SK_U for future use.

The user's identity is verified, because S has the assurance that the submitted phone number belongs to the user, as he was able to receive the OTP N. S keeps the mapping between certificates and phone numbers secret and reveals it only to authorized entities, e.g., in case of a subpoena.

Provider Discovery. The goal of the provider discovery protocol is to discover a resource provider P which can share its resources with resource consumer C. The corresponding protocol is shown in Fig. 3. It is initiated when the resource request cannot be served locally (e.g., the request of the web-browser for the network connectivity cannot be served due to unavailable network connection).

First, $C \in \mathcal{U}$ connects to a potential resource provider $P \in \mathcal{U}$ (using mesh networking services) and establishes a secure (i.e., authentic and confidential) channel to it based on $Cert_C$ and $Cert_P$ (i.e., certificates obtained during registration). Next, C sends the resource request over the established channel along with the description of the resource R. If R is available, P responds with *policy* which specifies conditions for resource sharing. Particularly, *policy* may allow resource sharing with friends (or friends of friends) only, or require execution of the accountability protocol in order to protect P from framing attacks. If required by *policy*, P and C additionally use *Friend-of-Friend Finder* service (cf. §3.2) to identify friend relationships and execute the *accountability protocol*. If all conditions are met, P is added to a set of suitable provider candidates $\mathcal{P}$.

The protocol repeats n times to populate $\mathcal{P}$ with n candidates, where n is a configurable system parameter. The best candidate $P^* \in \mathcal{P}$ is selected for

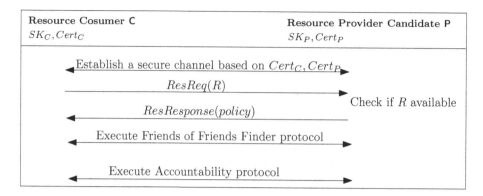

Fig. 3. Provider discovery protocol

resource sharing, while others are kept as back-ups. The availability of every P ∈ 𝒫 is monitored through listening to heart beat messages transmitted on a regular base. If any of them disappear, a new round of the provider discovery protocol is triggered to find a new candidate.

Accountability. Accountability is achieved by having C sign a resource quota request RQR that contains PK_C, the type of the resource R, and the resource leasing time τ. The resulting signature σ_{RQR} is sent to P*, verified, and stored as an evidence.

Data Channel. A data channel is used for the delivery of the resource R from P* to C. To provide confidentiality and authenticity to the data channel, we use standard techniques for setting up virtual private network (VPN) connections. Depending on the type of the shared resource, the VPN connection is either between C and P* or S (e.g., between C and S for Internet connectivity sharing).

3.2 Friends-of-Friends Finder (FoF Finder) Service

The following server-aided approach allows to determine if two users P and C, are mutual friends or friends of friends in an existing social network.

During registration, each user authorizes S to access his friend list from the social network server N and to map the social network identifiers of the user's friends (and friends of friends) to their CrowdShare membership certificates. This mapping is sent to the registering device. During provider discovery, P checks if the certificate of C belongs to one of his friends or friends of friends by comparing the certificate identifier of C with identifiers in the friends database.

The server-aided solution requires each user to learn about entities in his social graph at hop lengths > 1, e.g., the number of friends of friends he has or their certificates which serve as pseudonyms. Depending on how users have set the visibility of their friend relations in the social network, this may be information that was otherwise not available to users.

As an alternative, we also allow P and C to determine common friends by running a private set intersection (PSI) protocol directly between them. The input to PSI is a set of "capabilities" that serve as proof of the friend relationship in the social network. We use a social network application as a generic secret distribution channel to exchange capabilities among friends. Due to space limitations we do not describe this approach in detail. The interested reader is referred to our technical report [4].

4   Security Considerations

In the following we provide an informal security analysis that demonstrates that the security requirements of §2 are fulfilled.

Channel Protection. For channel protection, all protocols are executed over a secure (i.e., confidential and mutually authenticated) channel. Particularly, the registration protocol runs over a channel where the server S is authenticated based on the server certificate $Cert_S$, while the user is authenticated by verifying user's phone number. The provider discovery and accountability protocols run over the secure channel established based on mutually exchanged certificates between P and C. The resource delivery is protected by a data channel established between C and P or C and S. The former is used in use cases which are not sensitive to eavesdropping by P, e.g., in case of file sharing (a file originating from P is already known to P). The latter is applied in case if P is a subject for confidentiality requirement, e.g., when sharing Internet connectivity (to ensure P cannot eavesdrop or manipulate traffic downloaded by C).

Pseudonymity. Pseudonymity is fulfilled by deploying pseudonymous user certificates which do not include any user specific information. The only entity which can map certificates to user identities is the server S, which is trusted to keep this information confidential.

Accountability. Accountability is satisfied by deploying an accountability service which protects P from framing attacks. The signed resource quota request submitted during the accountability protocol can be used by P as evidence toward possible misuse by C. Further, the signature can be mapped to a user identity with the help of the server S, which keeps the mapping between pseudonymous user certificates and user phone numbers. Hence, the real user identity can be traced back in case of illegal usage (e.g., accessing illegal content).

Access Control. We use two access control mechanisms: (i) membership-based access control which allows users to deny non-members access to resources of members, and (ii) social-relationship-based access control which allows users to grant access to friends or friends of friends.

5   Implementation

In this section we describe the implementation of the trusted server S and the mobile device which integrates functionality of the resource consumer C, resource provider P, and a relay device F in one.

Server. The server S provides the following main functionalities: (i) registration of new CrowdShare community members and (ii) a database that includes persistent information from other services (e.g., mapping from user identities to certificates). The functionality of S is implemented in Java 1.5 and stores objects in MySQL using the Hibernate framework. The implementation has 5 188 lines of Java code (LoC).

Mobile Platform. Our implementation targets Android-based devices. We used Google's Nexus One and the HTC Desire smartphones with Cyanogenmod 7.0 images for our development. The code is written in Java (for the API level 10) and makes use of a Bouncy Castle crypto library v. 147 (written in Java). For the implementation of cryptographic primitives, we used RSA 1024 and AES 128. We used standard SSL for the establishment of the secure channel used in provider discovery and OpenVPN (from the Cyanogenmod image) for the protection of the data channel. Our Android app has a modular design. Particularly, MeshNetwork is implemented as a separate component with well-defined interfaces which can be replaced when necessary or re-used in other applications. The overall implementation excluding the MeshNetwork component has 9 441 LoC.

We adapted the implementation of the Serval open source project [6] for the instantiation of the MeshNetwork component. Serval allows mobile devices to establish mesh networking on top of ad-hoc WiFi connections. It integrates BATMAN [10], a proactive distance vector routing protocol for wireless mesh networks. Further, it supports voice calls and text messages between mesh modes (hence, this functionality is also inherited by our implementation), but it does *not* provide Internet connectivity sharing and does *not* address possible security threats, which are our main focus.

Generally, stock Android devices cannot be configured to operate in WiFi ad-hoc mode without root access. Root access is required for loading a WiFi driver, configuring it to operate in ad-hoc mode and for configuring IP settings. However, root access is not required for the usage of our FoF Finder service. To support this claim, we implemented a simple (one-hop) tethering app which uses FoF Finder service for access control. The app uses Bluetooth to run FoF Finder protocols and WiFi for tethering and does not require root privileges.

6   Performance Evaluation

For our performance tests we used a HTC Desire device as a resource provider P and Nexus One devices for the resource consumer C and the relaying node F.

Multihop Re-transmissions. Fig. 4 illustrates the performance with and without multihop re-transmissions. To perform this test, we sent a ping packet to a remote server (*www.google.de*) and estimated the delay of the received response. The test was done for the direct Internet connection (i.e., no mesh retransmissions are required), as well as for 1 hop and 2 hop indirect connections[1]. We sent 200 ping packets for each case. The delay increases with rising hop counts in the multi hop connection, which is reasonable, as each additional hop imposes additional packet delay due to re-transmissions. Further, the context switch between 3G and WiFi transmissions also adds overhead. The several peaks for the 2 hop tethering are imposed by packet loss and subsequent re-transmissions required to perform packet delivery successfully. To summarize, a hop count of 2 introduces a little delay in the range of milliseconds, which is acceptable.

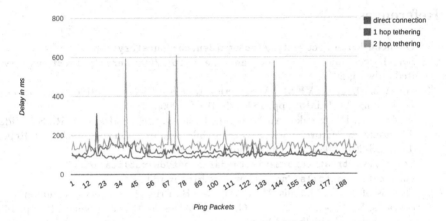

Fig. 4. Performance with and without multihop re-transmissions

7 Related work

VENETA [3] is a mobile social networking platform that, among other features, allows decentralized SMS-messaging via Bluetooth (up to 3 hops) and privacy-preserving matching of common entries in the users' address books using private set intersection. The combination of privacy-preserving profile matching and establishment of a secure channel was considered recently in [13]. Their solution allows a user to establish a shared key with another user only if their profiles match in a pre-determined set of attributes. Privacy-preserving discovery of common social contacts was considered in [5], where friends issue mutual certificates for their friendship relation. Our setting is different to all these works as we want to perform access control based on relationships in an existing social network.

---

[1] Our tests were limited by the number of available devices.

A number of projects developed ad hoc communication and resource sharing on top of mesh networks like Serval [6] and OpenGarden [1]. SCAMPI [12] provides generic discovery and a routing framework for opportunistic networks for developing versatile applications and services on top of it. Ad hoc communication has also found use cases in extreme situations where normal infrastructures are inaccessible, e.g., mines [7] and disaster-recovery scenarios [8]. In addition, we focus on privacy and security.

Acknowledgements. This work was supported in part by the German Federal Ministry of Education and Research (BMBF) within EC SPRIDE, and by the Hessian LOEWE excellence initiative within CASED.

References

[1] OpenGarden project, http://opengarden.com/ourstory.php
[2] Serval - comunicate anywhere, anytime, http://www.servalproject.org/ (visited July 26, 2012)
[3] von Arb, M., et al.: VENETA: Serverless friend-of-friend detection in mobile social networking. In: WiMob, pp. 184–189. IEEE (2008)
[4] Asokan, N., Dmitrienko, A., Nagy, M., Reshetova, E., Sadeghi, A.-R., Schneider, T., Stelle, S.: Crowdshare: Secure mobile resource sharing. Technical Report TUD-CS-2013-0084, TU Darmstadt (April 2013), http://www.trust.informatik.tu-darmstadt.de/publications/publication-details/?no_cache=1&tx_bibtex_pi1
[5] De Cristofaro, E., Manulis, M., Poettering, B.: Private discovery of common social contacts. In: Lopez, J., Tsudik, G. (eds.) ACNS 2011. LNCS, vol. 6715, pp. 147–165. Springer, Heidelberg (2011)
[6] Gardner-Stephen, P.: The serval project: Practical wireless ad-hoc mobile telecommunications (2011)
[7] Ginzboorg, P., et al.: DTN communication in a mine. In: ExtremeCom (2010)
[8] Hossmann, T., et al.: Twitter in disaster mode: Security architecture. In: CoNEXT. ACM (2011)
[9] JoikuSpot (2007), http://joikusoft.com/
[10] Neumann, A., et al.: B.A.T.M.A.N.: Better approach to mobile ad-hoc networking. IEFT Draft (2008)
[11] Nokia. Nokia Instant Community. Article in Nokia Conversations Blog (May 2010), http://conversations.nokia.com/2010/05/25/nokia-instant-community-gets-you-social/
[12] Pitkänen, M., et al.: SCAMPI: Service platform for social aware mobile and pervasive computing. Computer Communication Review 42(4) (2012)
[13] Zhang, L., et al.: Message in a sealed bottle: Privacy preserving friending in social networks. CoRR, abs/1207.7199 (2012)

Remotegrity: Design and Use of an End-to-End Verifiable Remote Voting System[*]

Filip Zagórski[1], Richard T. Carback[2], David Chaum[3],
Jeremy Clark[4], Aleksander Essex[5], and Poorvi L. Vora[6]

[1] Wrocław University of Technology
[2] Draper Laboratory
[3] Voting System Institute
[4] Carleton University
[5] Western University
[6] The George Washington University

Abstract. We propose and implement a cryptographically end-to-end verifiable (E2E) remote voting system for absentee voters and report on its deployment in a binding municipal election in Takoma Park, Maryland. Remotegrity is a hybrid mail/internet extension to the Scantegrity in-person voting system, enabling secure, electronic return of vote-by-mail ballots. It provides voters with the ability to detect unauthorized modifications to their cast ballots made by either malicious client software, or a corrupt election authority—two threats not previously studied in combination. Not only can the voter detect such changes, they can prove it to a third party without giving up ballot secrecy.

1 Introductory Remarks

In 2009, the city of Takoma Park in Maryland, United States, became the first election authority (EA) to use a cryptographically end-to-end verifiable (E2E) voting system in a public election [4]. This system, Scantegrity II [7], allows voters to verify their votes were counted correctly, while maintaining ballot secrecy. Scantegrity also provides a *dispute resolution* mechanism: in the event either the voter or the EA behaves maliciously, parties that follow the protocol should be able to prove their honesty to a third party (such as a democracy watch group). These integrity and dispute resolution protections afforded by the in-person nature of Scantegrity II, however, do not immediately extend to absentee voters submitting ballots by mail or online.

Shifting from in-person to remote voting introduces new threats, including the possibility of malicious software on the voter's computer making unauthorized (and potentially undetected) modifications to ballot selections. Although

---

[*] Full version available: http://eprint.iacr.org/2013/214. Zagórski was funded in part by NSF Awards 0937267 and 1137973 and by the Polish National Science Center (NCN) scientific project 2010-2013 with grant number N N206 369839. Clark and Essex acknowledge funding through NSERC PDF awards.

M. Jacobson et al. (Eds.): ACNS 2013, LNCS 7954, pp. 441–457, 2013.

this threat has been well studied in isolation, a major complication arises when simultaneously considering the problem of dispute resolution: a malicious EA caught cheating could spuriously blame the voters' clients for the malfeasance.

In this paper we tackle the problem of protecting against malicious software on the voter's computer while simultaneously offering a dispute resolution procedure. To that end we present Remotegrity, a remote voting extension for Scantegrity designed to extend similar protections to absentee voters as those of voters attending the polling place. We propose the Remotegrity protocol and describe an implementation which was fielded in Takoma Park's municipal election in November 2011.

Contributions. The main contributions of this paper include:

1. The Remotegrity protocol, a remote voting system providing voters with the ability to detect and prove unauthorized changes made to their ballots by malicious client software or a corrupt election authority,
2. An implementation and case study of Remotegrity in a municipal election,
3. Lessons learned from the real-world deployment of voting systems research.

2   Background

Absentee Voting. A reality of elections is that a certain portion of the electorate will be unable to physically attend a polling place during the election period, *e.g.*, due to illness, travel, or residing out of the district. Four common methods for enfranchising absentees exist. *Early voting* is most appropriate for travellers but does not assist the ill or non-resident. *Vote-by-proxy* breaches ballot secrecy and is not generally used in public-sector elections. Hosting a *polling place abroad* is suitable when a large contingency of absentees are local to the area, such as a military base or embassy in a large foreign city. It is less suitable for small-scale, *e.g.*, municipal-level, elections.

Most EAs use both early voting and a fourth method: *remote voting*. Remote voting could be either (i) available only to voters demonstrating a need, (ii) available to any voter, or (iii) mandatory for all voters. In the United States, there are respectively 27, 21, and 2 states/capital districts in these categories at the time of writing.[1] In addition 33 offer early voting.

The primary method for delivering and receiving ballots from remote voters in the United States is the postal system. Vote-by-mail enables threats not present in polling place voting: ballots could be mailed to the wrong address or lost before being received by voters; voters can demonstrate how they vote for payment or be coerced into voting a certain way; there may not be a strong mechanism to authenticate that a ballot was filled out by the intended voter (or distinguish a real ballot from impersonated fake ballots); ballots could be lost, delayed, or tampered with during their return to EA; and there are only weak guarantees of ballot secrecy from the election officials receiving the ballots.

---

[1] Absentee and Early Voting. *National Conference of State Legislators*, 4 Sept 2012.

Online Voting. Of the issues with vote-by-mail, the most significant is arguably that ballots are not always received in time—19% of mail-in ballots cast in the 2008 US election were not received in time to be counted. In response, election officials are interested in enabling electronic channels, such as email, fax, or the internet for voters to receive and return ballots. In addition to subsuming most of the issues with postal ballots, online voting introduces several of its own. Malware on a voter's computer may undetectably alter the voter's choices. Email and fax do not provide secure transport for ballots, and while websites can, this requires the assumption that voters can correctly authenticate the server (e.g., voters do not fall prey to phishing, SSL-stripping, or man-in-the-middle attacks with illegitimately obtained certificates [10]). The EA servers may be made inaccessible through a denial-of-service attack. Most importantly, a compromise of the server could allow all cast ballots to be undetectably modified.

Hybrid Internet/Mail Voting. The delay introduced by the postal system can be partially addressed by utilizing an electronic channel only for ballot receipt, or ballot return. In many U.S. counties and states, blank ballots can be downloaded and submitted by mail.[2] Conversely, ballots are received by mail and submitted online in Remotegrity. Given that the date a voter receives a blank ballot is a soft deadline, whereas the date the EA must receive the returned ballot is a hard deadline, it is arguably preferable to use the electronic channel for ballot return. Further, this enables voters to experience the full campaign before voting, and better addresses the human tendency toward procrastination. The primary concern with electronic return is security; something most commercial systems do not fully address. Remotegrity is an electronic-return voting system designed to provide secure and reliable transport, even in the presence of client-side malware, server compromise, or a corrupt EA.

End-to-End Verifiability. The use of cryptographic techniques to provide a verifiable tally while maintaining strong voter privacy has developed substantially since first proposed by Chaum in 1981 [5]. E2E polling place systems like Prêt à Voter [9] and Scantegrity [7] have been refined and are suitable for governmental elections [4,3]. E2E internet voting systems like Helios [1] and SCV [23] have been tested in binding student and organizational elections [2]. Helios is not designed to provide strong integrity when a voter's computer is malicious, and proof-of-concept vote-stealing malware has been proposed [14].

　　Client-side vulnerabilities can be addressed through a technique called *code-voting*, proposed by Chaum in 2001 [6]. With code-voting, voter choices are denoted with a set of random codes distributed to the voter out-of-band. Without knowledge of the codes, malicious devices cannot sensibly modify voter choices. Many proposals have refined this approach [16,18,17,24,19,26,15,25]. While these systems protect the voter from client-side vulnerabilities, they do not protect against a malicious EA (which knows all the codes), nor do they provide dispute resolution (see below). Remotegrity extends the code voting approach to satisfy these additional security properties.

---

[2] http://www.fvap.gov/resources/media/evswfactsheet.pdf

The literature also addresses the tangential problem of coercion-resistance in the unsupervised, remote voting setting. This line of research originated with Juels *et al.* [20]. Recent improvements include more efficient tallying [27] and the use of panic passwords [12]. These systems all assume the voter votes on a trusted machine. By contrast, code voting does not address coercion. Addressing both threats simultaneously is an open problem.

Dispute Resolution. One less obvious property an E2E voting system should provide is *dispute-freeness* [21] (or accountability [22]). If the verification of some aspect of the election fails, implying an error or fraud, the voter should be able to demonstrate that it failed and which entity is responsible. With online voting, the EA cannot assume accountability for the state of voters' computers. If vote verification fails, the EA must ensure that it is not incorrectly blamed for compromised voter machines. Likewise, voters want assurance that a malicious EA cannot modify ballots and blame the voters' computers if the modification is detected. It is also important that voters or political parties cannot easily fabricate false evidence that an election has been compromised, casting doubt on the final tally.

3   Remotegrity

Overview. Remotegrity is not a full voting system. Rather, it is a component that is combined with a traditional E2E paper ballot system like Scantegrity or Prêt à Voter to provide integrity to the process of ballot delivery. Even when ballots are submitted from an untrusted computer over an untrusted network to an untrusted EA, voters can have the same assurance that their vote will be counted correctly as they would if they cast their ballot in-person.

It utilizes two primary security mechanisms. The first is code voting which prevents malicious devices from sensibly modifying voter selections. However this is not sufficient as a fully corrupt EA could determine the set of codes and modify voter selections reliably. The second mechanism we use is that of providing each voter with a *lock-in* code placed under a scratch-off surface. The lock-in code is posted on the election website by the voter to indicate that his or her vote is correctly recorded. The scratch-off surface operates as a tamper-evident seal. If a malicious EA locks in a ballot entry that does not reflect the voter's selections, the scratch-off surface still covers the code providing physical evidence of EA malfeasance.

3.1   Cryptographic Preliminaries

Remotegrity utilizes a distributed key generation protocol DKG to generate threshold shares of a secret seed s amongst a set of trustees (*e.g.*, party officials or election observers); a pseudo-random generator, $PRG(s)$, to expand the seed into psuedo-randomness; and a cryptographic commitment function, $Comm(m, r)$, that is hiding and binding for message m and randomness r (for brevity, we denote a randomized commitment to m as $[\![m]\!]$).

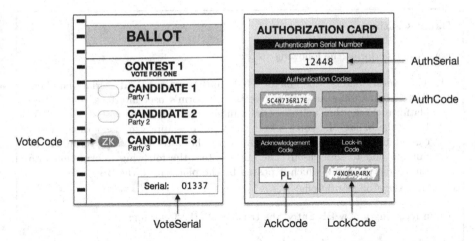

Fig. 1. Remotegrity ballot package. **Left:** marked Scantegrity II ballot showing a vote for candidate 3. **Right:** Remotegrity authorization card showing the AuthSerial and AckCode as well as an AuthCode and the LockCode as scratched off by the voter during the ballot casting protocol.

As in Scantegrity, we assume trustees can use a semi-trusted 'blackbox' computation to generate election values. This computation is not assumed to be correct, but it is assumed to keep all inputs and intermediate values private. No private state is ever stored; trustees always regenerate the state from their shares. The trade-off between the practicality offered by this model and the strong cryptographic guarantees of using a multiparty computation have been discussed elsewhere [13]. Finally we assume the existence of an append-only broadcast channel, called a bulletin board (BB).

3.2   Protocol

Voters receive a ballot package by mail which contains two parts, as shown in Figure 1. The first is a paper ballot, similar or identical to the ones used for polling place voting. In this section, we will consider composing Remotegrity with Scantegrity II ballots. Scantegrity II ballots consist of a serial number, VoteSerial, and a set of short confirmation codes, $\langle \mathsf{VoteCode}_1, \mathsf{VoteCode}_2, \ldots \rangle$. There is one code per candidate and the codes are randomly assigned to candidates and ballots. Two voters will, with high probability, receive different codes, invariant to whether they voted for the same candidate or different candidates. The codes are printed with invisible ink and revealed when the voter marks a particular candidate with a special pen (we describe how we modified the system to avoid having to mail pens to each voter in Section 4). For simplicity, we assume a single contest ballot in our description; extension to multi-contest ballots is trivial.

Ballot Casting

Each voter performs the following steps:

1. The voter enters the ballot and authorization card serial numbers $\langle$VoteSerial, AuthSerial$\rangle$ into the voting platform's user interface. The voting platform checks that neither serial number was previously posted to the BB.
2. Using the ballot, the voter selects the VoteCode appearing next their chosen candidate. Using the authorization card, the voter selects an AuthCode at random and to scratch-off. The voter enters the following information into the voting platform, which is posted by the platform to the BB:
   $\langle$VoteCode, AuthCode$\rangle$.

Upon receiving a new BB Entry, the trustees do the following:

3. The trustees check AuthCode. If it has not been used in a previously signed BB Entry and it contains valid codes, the trustees append AckCode and sign the tuple. The BB entry now reads:
   $\langle$VoteSerial, VoteCode, AuthSerial, AuthCode, AckCode, Sig(%)$\rangle$,
   where Sig(%) denotes a digital signature on all preceding elements in the tuple. If it does not contain valid codes, it marks it as invalid and signs it.

Upon receiving acknowledgement from the trustees, the voter does the following:

4. The voter checks that no modifications have been made to the BB Entry. The voter verifies AckCode and the signature. If correct, the voter submits LockCode. The BB Entry is now finalized as:
   $\langle$VoteSerial, VoteCode, AuthSerial, AuthCode, AckCode, Sig(%), LockCode$\rangle$.

After the election closes, the trustees do the following:

5. For the tuples containing a correct LockCode, the trustees input $\langle$VoteSerial, VoteCode$\rangle$ to the vote tallying system (*e.g.*, Scantegrity's BB).

Protocol 1. The vote casting procedure in Remotegrity

The second part of the ballot package is the Remotegrity authorization card. The card consists of a serial number, a set of authentication codes under scratch-off (denoted with a grey box), a short acknowledgement code, and a lock-in code under scratch-off. With *e.g.*, four authentication codes, the authorization card is denoted as:

$$\Big\langle \text{AuthSerial},\ \boxed{\text{AuthCode}_1}\ ,\ \boxed{\text{AuthCode}_2}\ ,\ \boxed{\text{AuthCode}_3}\ ,\ \boxed{\text{AuthCode}_4}\ ,\ \text{AckCode},\ \boxed{\text{LockCode}}\ \Big\rangle$$

Election Set-up

Prior to the election, all trustees do the following with a blackbox computation:

1. The trustees use DKG to derive threshold shares of a master secret.
2. The trustees use PRG to expand the master secret into a sufficient number of random codes for two authorization cards per voter.
3. For each authorization card, the trustees publish on the BB the serial number and a commitment (again using PRG for the randomness) to each code on the card:

$$\langle \mathsf{AuthSerial}, [\![\mathsf{AuthCode}_1]\!], [\![\mathsf{AuthCode}_2]\!], \ldots, [\![\mathsf{AckCode}]\!], [\![\mathsf{LockCode}]\!] \rangle$$

After the pre-election commitments are published, the EA does:

4. The EA prints the authorization cards, potentially printing more than needed and allowing a random print audit of a fraction of the cards.
5. Each eligible absentee voter is assigned and mailed a Scantegrity ballot and an authorization card. The EA retains the binding between the voter ID, VoteSerial, and AuthSerial. For each ballot, it at least publishes: $\langle \mathsf{VoteSerial}, \mathsf{AuthSerial} \rangle$. The EA can also publish which voter received which VoteSerial without compromising ballot secrecy. In either case, the number of these tuples should match the number of absentee voters.

After the election closes, an authorized set of trustees open all the commitments to authorization card codes.

Protocol 2. The trustee and EA procedures in Remotegrity

Serials are assigned sequentially and all codes are assigned random; the length of the codes should provide resistance from repeated guessing (while "short" codes only resist a single guess). The purpose of each code is not likely apparent from inspection but each code and scratch-off surface plays an integral part in preventing certain attacks; thus we will explain the protocol concurrently to a security analysis. The vote casting process is described in Protocol 1, and how the codes are derived by the EA is described in Protocol 2.

Remotegrity protocol serves a single function: to allow voters to verify that their Scantegrity ballot, $\langle \mathsf{VoteSerial}, \mathsf{VoteCode} \rangle$, is correctly posted to Scantegrity's BB. If voters could post $\langle \mathsf{VoteSerial}, \mathsf{VoteCode} \rangle$ without interference from a client-side malware or a malicious EA, Remotegrity would not be required. The codes and features of the Remotegrity authorization card and vote casting protocol can be split into two sets. The first set contains the mechanisms for addressing a malicious voting platform: a single AuthCode and AckCode. The second set contains mechanisms for detecting malicious EA actions: multiple AuthCode's, LockCode, scratch-off surfaces, and the trustees signature.

Validating Ballot Codes. The protocol assumes that the EA can determine if a VoteCode for a given VoteSerial is valid: one of the VoteCode's appearing on the ballot. To provide certain assurances, Remotegrity uses the fact that a guessed VoteCode will, with high probability, be invalid. Scantegrity has its own dispute resolution process, which can determine precisely this. Assuming the systems are governed by the same set of trustees, they can work in an online fashion to validate the VoteCode in Remotegrity ballots as they are submitted. An alternative approach is append a short message authentication code to each VoteCode, which will be stripped off when the accepted and locked-in Remotegrity ballots are posted to Scantegrity's BB. This allows validation of the codes without requiring that all the confirmation codes be online and accessible to the trustees.

Initial BB Check. In the first step of Protocol 1, the voter checks if her VoteSerial has already been voted. If the VoteSerial appears but has been rejected by the EA for having an invalid AuthCode, the voter can ignore the entry and proceed to vote with an actual AuthCode. If the VoteSerial has been voted and accepted by the EA (*i.e.*, with a published AckCode and signature), it must have been posted by an insider with knowledge of the correct authorization code or the EA signed off on something invalid. In either case, the voter can demonstrate that no authorization codes have been scratched off on her card, which is publicly linked to the serial number of the ballot, and thus the EA is accountable for the wrongfully accepted ballot.

Malicious Voting Client. Provided the VoteSerial is not on the BB, we first consider the case where the EA is honest but the voter uses a malicious voting client. Since only the voter and the EA know the values of the codes on the ballot and authorization card, the voting client cannot cast a ballot without the voter's involvement or repeatedly guessing VoteCode and AuthCode pairs. Since VoteCode is short (*e.g.*, 2 characters), AuthCode should be of a length sufficient for protection from repeated guessing (*e.g.*, 12 characters).

When the voter enters VoteCode and AuthCode, the computer could keep AuthCode and modify VoteCode. It could further simulate the voter's view of the BB to make it appear that the BB Entry was not modified. To provide detection, the voter can rely on receiving back AckCode. Since the voting client does not know the VoteCode on the ballot corresponding to its preferred candidate, at best it can chose a VoteCode randomly. With moderately high (since the code is short) probability, the EA will reject the BB Entry and not post AckCode. The voting client will then have to guess AckCode which will also fail with moderate probability. Since receiving a wrong AckCode code suggests the computer is malicious, the client has only one chance to guess and thus AckCode can be short. Diligent voters can check the BB from a secondary device to detect modifications, even in the unlikely case that the computer issues a correct guess. If such detection occurs, the voter will not lock-in the ballot. Like AuthCode, LockCode should be of a length sufficient for protection from repeated guessing.

Malicious EA. We now consider a malicious EA. First, a point of clarification: a malicious EA could be comprised of colluding trustees who reconstruct the codes, the officials who print the authorization cards, or the officials who mail them. Since the EA is ultimately accountable for all of these officials, the Remotegrity protocol protects against all of them without distinguishing which exact official is responsible.

A malicious EA knows all of the codes on the voter's authorization card, however it cannot undetectably use a code unless it is assured the voter has scratched it off. Assume an EA generated/modified BB Entry is locked-in on the BB. If the voter did not try and lock something in, LockCode is still sealed and the voter can hold the EA accountable. If the voter has scratched-off LockCode, it must be the case that the voter's correct BB Entry did appear at some point on the BB and was accepted and signed by the EA. The EA cannot apply LockCode to any BB Entry other than the one intended by the voter without signing a new BB Entry. However, signing a new BB Entry requires the entry to have an unused AuthCode. Therefore, if the EA waits for the voter to submit LockCode and immediately fabricates a new BB Entry to which it applies LockCode, it would have to use a previously unused AuthCode and any unused AuthCode would still be sealed on the voter's authentication card.

Print Audit. Voters can resolve disputes by demonstrating that codes are still sealed on the physical ballots and authorization cards they have received. However, if the EA is forced to correctly commit to the contents of the cards, many disputes can be resolved without the physical records. In order to check this consistency, a random selection of authorization cards should be audited using a publicly verifiable challenge to determine the selection [11]. For full voter-verifiability, voters could be mailed two authorization cards: one to use and the one to audit.

3.3   Other Security Properties

Dispute Resolution. We say the EA *accepts* a BB Entry if it provides an AckCode and signs the BB Entry. If the EA accepts the BB Entry as cast by the voter, we call it a *true accept*. If it accepts a BB Entry that is modified from the voter's intent, or a BB Entry it manufactured without the voter's knowledge or consent, we call it a *false-accept*. If the EA rejects a BB Entry with correct values (*e.g.*, as a denial-of-service), we call it a *false reject*. Finally, if the EA correctly rejects a BB Entry containing incorrect codes (*e.g.*, one modified by a malicious computer, as above), we call it a *true reject*.

We iterate through all the various issues with each code and how it is resolved in Table 1. The EA can always force a denial-of-service, which is unsurprising as it can accomplish this without resorting to manipulating codes. What Remotegrity does not allow is the EA to fully accept (*i.e.*, accept and lock) any ballot the voter did not cast without the voter being able to dispute it.

If the voter enters values and does not see them on the BB, he or she tries again from another computer. All true rejects occur because the EA received

Table 1. Overview of the dispute resolution process in Remotegrity

Code	Issue	Blame	Resolution
VoteSerial	Missing	Device	Voter votes from a different device.
	False Accept	N/A	BB Entry belongs to another voter.
	False Reject	EA	Voter retains authentication card and ballot as evidence.
	True Reject	Device	Voter votes from a different device.
VoteCode	False Accept	EA	Voter attempts to change vote using another AuthCode.
	False Reject	EA	Voter retains ballot as evidence.
	True Reject	Device	Voter votes from a different device.
AuthSerial	False Accept	EA	Publicly apparent since link between VoteSerial and AuthSerial is public.
	False Reject	EA	Publicly apparent since link between VoteSerial and AuthSerial is public.
	True Reject	Device	Voter votes from a different device.
AuthCode	False Accept	EA	Voter retains unscratched AuthCode codes as evidence.
	False Reject	EA	Link between AuthCode and AuthSerial is decommitted after election.
	True Reject	Device	Voter votes from a different device.
AckCode	Invalid	Device	Voter accesses ABB from a different device.
Sig(%)	Invalid	EA	Publicly apparent. Voter can request new signature.
LockCode	False Accept	EA	Voter keeps unscratched LockCode as evidence.
	False Reject	EA	Voter retains authentication card as evidence.
	True Reject	Device	Voter locks-in from a different device.

false values. This happens because of a malicious voting computer or an erring human. If a voter sees false code(s) displayed on the BB and rejected by the EA, and knows it was not erroneously entered, he or she can attempt to enter the code(s) again from another computer. If, in spite of repeated attempts, the voter always experiences a similar reject, he or she is experiencing a distributed denial of service attack from voting computers.

A false reject occurs because an EA rejects a correct code claiming that it is incorrect; that is, the voter sees the correct code on the BB but the EA rejects it. The correspondence between AuthSerial and VoteSerial is public. Additionally, commitments to valid codes—all information on an authentication card; the correspondences between VoteCode and VoteSerial (though not between VoteCode and candidates)— are opened at the end of the election. Because the EA knows the correct correspondences, the EA is shown to be cheating. A voter may also experience a reject because of a previous use (not by the voter) of AuthSerial, VoteSerial, AuthCode, or LockCode or all—this would correspond to a previous false accept by the EA.

All false accepts are accepts of either (a) invalid codes or (b) valid codes (in either case, the accept is false because the code was not entered by the voter, but can be seen on the BB). Case (a) is immediately apparent when the commitments for valid codes are opened, in a case converse to that described in false-rejects above. Because the EA knows an invalid code, its acceptance indicates a cheating EA and this is proven when the commitments are opened. For Case (b), if the false acceptance is of the VoteCode, the voter can try to re-enter the VoteCode from another computer. Because it is a short code, the computer might have guessed it correctly and used the correct VoteSerial, AuthSerial and AuthCode entered by the voter. For all other false-accepts—false accepts of LockCode or AuthCode—as well as repeated false accepts of the VoteCode, the voter should retain the unscratched-off authorization card and ballot to prove that the EA is cheating. (Here it is possible that a network of colluding dishonest voting computers would have guessed a VoteCode correctly and would repeatedly thwart the voter's attempt to change an incorrect VoteCode, but the probability is considered negligible). Note that incorrect correspondences between VoteSerial and AuthSerial are easily detected as being Case (a).

If the voter does not receive the correct AckCode, he or she attempts to vote again from another computer. Repeated failure implies an EA attempting a denial-of-service, assuming that the voter has access to at least one honest computer. This is proven when all the commitments are opened. If the voter receives an invalid signature, the entry is checked from a different computer. An invalid signature is apparent to anyone examining the BB.

Ballot Secrecy. No part of Remotegrity is dependent on the voter's selection. Secrecy of the voter's selection is fully subsumed by the Scantegrity system (or whatever E2E voting system Remotegrity is composed with). In particular, Scantegrity assumes that the printer can be trusted with knowledge of confirmation numbers, and that confirmation numbers printed in invisible ink are not visible unless exposed.

Physical Attacks on Scratch-Off Surfaces. Remotegrity does assume the integrity of scratch-off surfaces. If voters can retrieve codes without scratching-off the surface or can reapply an indistinguishable surface, they could falsely incriminate an entity for election tampering. The use of invisible ink and scratch-off is interchangeable. We present the ballots with invisible ink as per the original Scantegrity proposal, but use scratch-offs with Remotegrity as that is what was used in the election. Other physical technologies for providing tamper-resistant sealing of printed codes may be used with Remotegrity.

3.4   Optimizations

We avoid doubling-up the functionality of any of the codes to provide the clearest mapping between each code and the security functionality it serves. However to reduce the number of codes a voter must enter, codes can be combined. The serial numbers of the ballot and authorization card can be harmonized to the same value. If VoteCode and AuthCode are unique across all ballots/cards, serial numbers can be eliminated entirely. Finally, a unique AuthCode-length code could be assigned to each candidate, eliminating the need for Votecode at all. Note that this results in a fully-modified ballot style. Remotegrity is designed to interface with an existing type of ballot style, so that vote tallying can be conducted across all ballots: in-person and absentee together.

4   Deployment

Takoma Park is a municipality, sharing a city line with Washington D.C., with about 17,000 residents and 11,000 registered voters. The choice of voting system is formally made by the City Council, on recommendation by a Board of Elections (BOE) with 7 members. Ballots for municipal elections are provided in English and Spanish. Any voter can request to vote with an absentee ballot.

4.1   Preparations

We began discussion with the BOE in the early part of 2011 toward using Remotegrity in the November 2011 election. We attended their monthly board meetings and made many changes to the protocol based on their feedback.

System Test. The proposed system was tested on June 8, 2011 in the Takoma Park Community Center. The City announced the test in the city newspaper and in the senior newsletter. The test was open to anyone, and not restricted to Takoma Park voters or residents. We provided voters with a survey to fill out after they had tried the voting system. About 20 individuals participated in the test—including some BOE members—and about 17 responded to the survey on Remotegrity. From our perspective, the purpose of the test was to receive feedback on usability. It also served as an opportunity to educate potential voters on the system; as a result, we interacted significantly with voters using the system. We did not use the results as an indication of usability, due to the test's informality and small sample size, but the subjective feedback was very useful in making changes to the user interface and instructions. As one example, we modified the system so that voters did not need to enter both AuthSerial and VoteSerial; just AuthSerial.

The test was reported in the media and we presented the results to the BOE in the June meeting. The BOE outlined a number of concerns, centred around usability and security (because of the protocol's use of the internet, and the problems Washington DC had had with an internet voting trial [28]). In the July meeting, the Board members communicated to us that they had confidence in the technology, but they were concerned about the procedures, which appeared *ad hoc*, about potential security mishaps, and that the system had not been peer-reviewed. In this meeting, they communicated that they were leaning towards not using Remotegrity, but would go ahead with a mail-in Scantegrity ballot.

System Adaptations. In the August Board meeting, we proposed (to which they agreed) that the city provide voters with the option to use Remotegrity in addition to mailing back marked ballots. Only marked ballots would be counted, but voters using Remotegrity could test/"audit" the system, and, if they chose to lock-in their vote, could communicate that the system was accurately recording their vote. Instructions for "voting" and "auditing" would be sent in separate envelopes in the same package, with appropriate marking, so as not to overwhelm voters not interested in the audit.

Thus the system we finally used had some major differences with the protocol described in Section 3.2. Voters were not required to lock-in (this means that, in practice, an EA changing the vote using another AuthCode belonging to the voter could not be distinguished from the voter by a third party). Second, the Remotegrity system included ballots with visible codes (these ballots correspond to the original version of Scantegrity [8]). This avoids the requirement of mailing invisible ink development pens, however dispute resolution in the specific case of a wrong VoteCode is not possible. Third, voters needed to submit marked paper ballots by mail for votes to be counted; this eliminated any dependence on the internet, but made it possible for the EA to ignore a mailed-in ballot. However, the Scantegrity codes of the votes were posted on the election website and voters could check if their votes made it in the count.

4.2   Implementation and Server Infrastructure

Backend. The backend of the Remotegrity system contains a module, written in Java, that has similar functionality to the Scantegrity backend. Before the election, it is responsible for generating the Remotegrity data, commitments, and PDFs for printing the authorization cards. After the election, it is used to open the commitments.

Printing the Cards. The BOE anticipated that about 120 absentee voters would register. Because of the small-scale, around 200 authorization cards were printed by the Remotegrity team on a regular inkjet printer on card stock, and scratch-off stickers were applied manually. The back of each card had a printed overlay of "noise" to obfuscate the possibility of the reading of codes through the scratch-off surface using a very bright source of light.

Web-interface. The web interface was implemented with PHP and the Smarty template engine. During the election, the system was hosted in Amazon Elastic Cloud (EC2). It consisted of a load balancer that served the page over HTTPS[3], two instances of Apache servers (monitored in realtime, with auto-scale option), and one instance of an Amazon RDS (MySQL). Each server instance was only granted the right to INSERT data into the database. If needed, additional webservers could be started from the same image.

---

[3] http://takoma.remotegrity.org

Bulletin Board. Another EC2 instance ran a signing daemon written in Java. As data received from voters was inserted into the table by the webservers, the daemon would fetch and digitally sign it in realtime, inserting the signed data to a different table. This happened independently of the EA deciding to accept a ballot. Auditors had direct access to the second table.

An offline signing server (OSS) checked the validity of the submitted codes and was granted access to the AckCode codes corresponding to each possible AuthCode code. If the ballot submission was well-formed, it would sign it. As input, the OSS took an XML file containing data signed by the signing daemon, and output in XML an AckCode and signature on the entries it accepted. Both input and output files were transported to/from the OSS on a flash drive manually every 4 hours.

Testing. Both, the web interface and the backend of the system that was used during the pilot were tested by two independent researchers: Marco Ramilli and Marco Prandini. They found several security issues related to the web-interface, *e.g.*, visible system path and session control issues. These issues were fixed.

4.3 The Election

Voters were required to return their absentee ballots by mail, which still provides voters with the ability to verify correct receipt of their ballot (but limits their ability to respond and correct the ballot if it is not correct). In addition, they could opt-in to submitting their ballots electronically.

Procedure. Takoma Park election officials mailed two types of paper cards—a Scantegrity ballot and a Remotegrity authorization card—to each voter. Both cards were sent to the voter by regular mail in a single package. The ballots and authorization cards were paired at random and commitments to ⟨VoteCode, AuthCode⟩ were published. The EA assigned at random a package to a voter. They put the package into an outer envelope, stuck the voter's address on this envelope and wrote down the serial number of the authorization card next to a voter's name on a roster (this could help to remove a vote from the tally if it was intercepted by an unauthorized person and detected by a voter). Unused packages were later audited.

Result. The Remotegrity BB contains 123 entries which correspond to 119 voters. Only 5 ballots were submitted online, and two of these were not counted as the corresponding paper ballots were not mailed in. While the number of voters who used the online system was small, full preparation and a complete implementation were required to deploy the system.

Post-election. Remotegrity ballots were included in the same tally as Scantegrity ballots that were cast during election day. Both aspects of the election were audited by independent voting system experts selected by Takoma Park (on recommendation of the Remotegrity/Scantegrity teams). Neal McBurnett and Roberto Araujo conducted the audit, which included verifying the Remotegrity commitments during the pre- and post-election audit procedures. Neal McBurnett additionally audited all the unsent absentee packages.

5 Lessons Learned and Concluding Remarks

The design of secure internet voting systems is non-trivial. One of the most important lessons learned concerns the importance of a good working relationship between the system designers and the election officials. We benefitted from Takoma Park's feedback on the user interface. We believe that they, in turn, came to appreciate some of the more subtle security properties we were attempting to provide, and that their involvement helped to promote an increased sense of pride and ownership of the outcome. The other important lesson pertains to adapting voting research systems for real-world use. For example, most E2E schemes presuppose the existence of a public append-only bulletin board. Implementing this, however, proved to be a major technical challenge, which invariably leads to a relaxation of security properties. Designers of such systems must be able to adapt accordingly.

In future work, while considering scalability of the system for larger elections, we do not foresee problems and observe that it is as scalable as vote-by-mail. Also interesting from the perspective of future work is the problem of rigorous definitions and property proofs for the protocol, in a model that takes into account the properties of paper and scratch-off surfaces. Another important open problem is that of a coercion-resistant version of Remotegrity.

Finally, it was exciting to work with an election jurisdiction that sees merit in cryptographic election verification. But this was not just a case of early adoption—Takoma Park had run an E2E election before, and for the first time, we caught an exciting glimpse into the future of electronic voting in which E2E verification is the new normal.

Acknowledgements. The authors acknowledge the contributions of the voters of Takoma Park, the City Clerk, the Assistant City Clerk, and all Board of Elections members. We would like to thank Ron Rivest for his valuable remarks. The authors thank Zbigniew Golebiewski for implementing OSS and moving data between online and offline instances, sometimes in the middle of the night.

References

1. Adida, B.: Helios: web-based open-audit voting. In: USENIX Security (2008)
2. Adida, B., de Marneffe, O., Pereira, O., Quisquater, J.J.: Electing a university president using open-audit voting: Analysis of real-world use of Helios. In: EVT/WOTE (2009)
3. Burton, C., Culnane, C., Heather, J., Peacock, T., Ryan, P.Y.A., Schneider, S., Srinivasan, S., Teague, V., Wen, R., Xia, Z.: Using Pret a Voter in Victoria State elections. In: EVT/WOTE (2012)

4. Carback, R.T., Chaum, D., Clark, J., Conway, J., Essex, A., Hernson, P.S., Mayberry, T., Popoveniuc, S., Rivest, R.L., Shen, E., Sherman, A.T., Vora, P.L.: Scantegrity II election at Takoma Park. In: USENIX Security (2010)
5. Chaum, D.: Untraceable electronic mail, return addresses, and digital pseudonyms. Communications of the ACM 24(2), 84–90 (1981)
6. Chaum, D.: Surevote: Technical overview. In: WOTE (2001)
7. Chaum, D., Carback, R., Clark, J., Essex, A., Popoveniuc, S., Rivest, R.L., Ryan, P.Y.A., Shen, E., Sherman, A.T.: Scantegrity II: end-to-end verifiability for optical scan election systems using invisible ink confirmation codes. In: EVT (2008)
8. Chaum, D., Essex, A., Carback, R., Clark, J., Popoveniuc, S., Sherman, A.T., Vora, P.: Scantegrity: End-to-end voter verifiable optical-scan voting. IEEE Security and Privacy 6(3), 40–46 (2008)
9. Chaum, D., Ryan, P.Y.A., Schneider, S.: A practical voter-verifiable election scheme. In: di Vimercati, S.d.C., Syverson, P.F., Gollmann, D. (eds.) ESORICS 2005. LNCS, vol. 3679, pp. 118–139. Springer, Heidelberg (2005)
10. Clark, J., van Oorschot, P.: SSL and HTTPS: Revisiting past challenges and evaluating certificate trust model enhancements. In: IEEE Symp. Security & Privacy (2013)
11. Clark, J., Hengartner, U.: On the use of financial data as a random beacon. In: EVT/WOTE (2010)
12. Clark, J., Hengartner, U.: Selections: Internet voting with over-the-shoulder coercion-resistance. In: Danezis, G. (ed.) FC 2011. LNCS, vol. 7035, pp. 47–61. Springer, Heidelberg (2012)
13. Essex, A., Clark, J., Hengartner, U., Adams, C.: Eperio: Mitigating technical complexity in cryptographic election verification. In: EVT/WOTE (2010)
14. Estehghari, S., Desmedt, Y.: Exploiting the client vulnerabilities in internet e-voting systems: Hacking Helios 2.0 as an example. In: EVT/WOTE (2010)
15. Heiberg, S., Lipmaa, H., van Laenen, F.: On E-vote integrity in the case of malicious voter computers. In: Gritzalis, D., Preneel, B., Theoharidou, M. (eds.) ESORICS 2010. LNCS, vol. 6345, pp. 373–388. Springer, Heidelberg (2010)
16. Helbach, J., Schwenk, J.: Secure internet voting with code sheets. In: Alkassar, A., Volkamer, M. (eds.) VOTE-ID 2007. LNCS, vol. 4896, pp. 166–177. Springer, Heidelberg (2007)
17. Helbach, J., Schwenk, J., Schage, S.: Code voting with linkable group signatures. In: EVOTE (2008)
18. Joaquim, R., Ribeiro, C.: CodeVoting protection against automatic vote manipulation in an uncontrolled environment. In: Alkassar, A., Volkamer, M. (eds.) VOTE-ID 2007. LNCS, vol. 4896, pp. 178–188. Springer, Heidelberg (2007)
19. Joaquim, R., Ribeiro, C., Ferreira, P.: VeryVote: A voter verifiable code voting system. In: Ryan, P.Y.A., Schoenmakers, B. (eds.) VOTE-ID 2009. LNCS, vol. 5767, pp. 106–121. Springer, Heidelberg (2009)
20. Juels, A., Catalano, D., Jacobsson, M.: Coercion-resistant electronic elections. In: WPES (2005)
21. Kiayias, A., Yung, M.: Self-tallying elections and perfect ballot secrecy. In: Naccache, D., Paillier, P. (eds.) PKC 2002. LNCS, vol. 2274, pp. 141–158. Springer, Heidelberg (2002)
22. Kusters, R., Truderung, T., Vogt, A.: Accountability: Definition and relationship to verifiability. In: CCS (2010)

23. Kutyłowski, M., Zagórski, F.: Scratch, Click & Vote: E2E voting over the internet. In: Chaum, D., Jakobsson, M., Rivest, R.L., Ryan, P.Y.A., Benaloh, J., Kutylowski, M., Adida, B. (eds.) Towards Trustworthy Elections. LNCS, vol. 6000, pp. 343–356. Springer, Heidelberg (2010)
24. Oppliger, R., Schwenk, J., Lohr, C.: Captcha-based code voting. In: EVOTE (2008)
25. Popoveniuc, S.: Speakup: remote unsupervised voting. In: ACNS (2010)
26. Ryan, P.Y.A., Teague, V.: Pretty good democracy. In: Christianson, B., Malcolm, J.A., Matyáš, V., Roe, M. (eds.) Security Protocols 2009. LNCS, vol. 7028, pp. 111–130. Springer, Heidelberg (2013)
27. Spycher, O., Koenig, R., Haenni, R., Schläpfer, M.: A new approach towards coercion-resistant remote e-voting in linear time. In: Danezis, G. (ed.) FC 2011. LNCS, vol. 7035, pp. 182–189. Springer, Heidelberg (2012)
28. Wolchok, S., Wustrow, E., Isabel, D., Halderman, J.A.: Attacking the washington, D.C. Internet voting system. In: Keromytis, A.D. (ed.) FC 2012. LNCS, vol. 7397, pp. 114–128. Springer, Heidelberg (2012)

Exposure-Resilient One-Round Tripartite Key Exchange without Random Oracles

Koutarou Suzuki and Kazuki Yoneyama

NTT Secure Platform Laboratories
3-9-11 Midori-cho Musashino-shi Tokyo 180-8585, Japan
yoneyama.kazuki@lab.ntt.co.jp

Abstract. This paper studies Tripartite Key Exchange (3KE) which is a special case of Group Key Exchange. Though general one-round GKE satisfying advanced security properties such as forward secrecy and maximal-exposure-resilience (MEX-resilience) is not known, it can be efficiently constructed with the help of pairings in the 3KE case. In this paper, we introduce the first one-round 3KE which is MEX-resilient in the standard model, though existing one-round 3KE schemes are proved in the random oracle model (ROM), or not MEX-resilient. Each party broadcasts 4 group elements, and executes 14 pairing operations. Complexity is only three or four times larger in computation and communication than the existing most efficient MEX-resilient 3KE scheme in the ROM; thus, our protocol is adequately practical.

Keywords: authenticated key exchange, tripartite key exchange, standard model, dual-receiver encryption.

1 Introduction

Authenticated Key Exchange (AKE) is a cryptographic primitive to share a common *session key* among multiple parties through unauthenticated networks such as the Internet. This work considers the PKI-based setting that each party locally keeps his own *static secret key* (SSK) and publish a *static public key* (SPK) corresponding to the SSK. Validity of SPKs is guaranteed by a certificate authority. In a key exchange session, each party generates an *ephemeral secret key* (ESK) and sends an *ephemeral public key* (EPK) corresponding to the ESK. A session key is derived from these keys with a *key derivation function*.

In the two-party AKE (2KE) setting, many practical and provably secure AKE protocols have been introduced since [1]. For example, MQV [2] and its variants [3,4,5,6,7,8,9] achieve one-round schemes from the Diffie-Hellman (DH) assumptions. One-round protocols mean that parties send their messages independently and simultaneously only once. On the other hand, in the general group AKE (GKE) setting, to achieve one-round protocols is not so easy. A known approach [10,11] is that each party broadcasts multiple ciphertexts encrypting a common nonce to all parties, and aggregates nonces with a key derivation function. These schemes do not satisfy some important security properties such as forward secrecy. The other approach is using a multilinear map from ideal

M. Jacobson et al. (Eds.): ACNS 2013, LNCS 7954, pp. 458–474, 2013.

lattices [12]. This multilinear map is still a candidate, and the resultant GKE is impractical. Thus, to construct secure and practical one-round GKE is a challenging problem in the research area of AKE.

Interestingly, in the three-party AKE (3KE) setting (i.e., a special case of GKE), secure one-round protocols can be achieved practically thanks to pairings. Joux [13] firstly proposed one-round (unauthenticated) 3KE by extending the ordinary DH protocol to 3KE with pairings. After that, several one-round authenticated 3KE schemes are studied such as [14,15,16]. The security model for GKE in [15,16] (called the MSU model) captures a very strong security property; that is, even though an adversary can reveal any non-trivial[1] combination of ephemeral secret keys and static secret keys, any information of the session key is not exposed. We call such a property *maximal-exposure-resilience* (MEX-resilience). MEX-resilience implies various important security properties for GKE such as forward secrecy and key compromise impersonation resilience. Unfortunately, the known MEX-resilient one-round 3KE schemes [15,16] are proved in the random oracle model (ROM).

1.1 Our Contribution

We achieve the first MEX-resilient one-round 3KE scheme in the standard model (StdM). Our key idea is to utilize *dual-receiver encryption* (DRE) [17,18]. DRE allows a ciphertext to be decrypted into the same plaintext by two independent receivers. The situation of DRE is very similar to 3KE; a party tries to share common secret information with other two parties. Thus, our basic strategy is that each party broadcasts a ciphertext of DRE and aggregates three plaintexts by a pseudo-random function. However, we must carefully consider several special situations of 3KE, which do not occur in encryption; e.g., the simulator must manage decryption of the challenge ciphertext. We modify the original DRE to be able to simulate such situations correctly.

Also, we reformulate the MSU model [15,16] for GKE (called the G-CK⁺ model) by combining with one of the 'strongest' models for 2KE, CK⁺ model [3,19]. The G-CK⁺ model allows adversaries to reveal intermediate computation results of sessions in addition to the MSU model. Such a reveal capability is also considered in several security models for 2KE [20,3,8,19]. We prove that our scheme is secure in the G-CK⁺ model in the StdM under the decisional bilinear DH (DBDH) assumption.

2 Preliminaries

In this section, we recall definitions of building blocks.

Throughout this paper we use the following notations. If M is a set, then by $m \in_R M$ we denote that m is sampled uniformly from M. If $\mathcal{R}$ is an algorithm, then by $y \leftarrow \mathcal{R}(x; r)$ we denote that y is output by $\mathcal{R}$ on input x and randomness r (if $\mathcal{R}$ is deterministic, r is empty).

---

[1] If both the static key and the ephemeral key of a party in the target session are revealed, the adversary trivially obtains the session key for any protocol.

2.1 Bilinear Group

Let G and G_T be cyclic groups of prime order p where g is a generator of G. We say that $e : G \times G \to G_T$ is a bilinear map if for all $X, Y \in G$ and $a, b \in \mathbb{Z}_p$, $e(X^a, Y^b) = e(X, Y)^{ab}$, and $e(g, g) \neq 1$. We say that G is a bilinear group if e, and group operations in G and G_T can be computed efficiently.

2.2 Decisional Bilinear Diffie-Hellman Assumption

Let κ be the security parameter and p be a κ-bit prime. Let G be a bilinear group of a prime order p with a generator g, and G_T be a cyclic group of the prime order p. Let $e : G \times G \to G_T$ be a bilinear map.

The DBDH assumption is defined by two experiments, $\mathsf{Exp}^{\text{dbdh-real}}(\mathcal{D})$ and $\mathsf{Exp}^{\text{dbdh-rand}}(\mathcal{D})$. For a distinguisher $\mathcal{D}$, inputs $(g, \alpha = g^a, \beta = g^b, \gamma = g^c, \delta)$ are provided, where $(a, b, c) \in_R (\mathbb{Z}_p)^3$. $\delta = g_T^{abc}$ in $\mathsf{Exp}^{\text{dbdh-real}}(\mathcal{D})$ and $\delta \in_R G$ in $\mathsf{Exp}^{\text{dbdh-rand}}(\mathcal{D})$ where $g_T = e(g, g)$. We define advantage

$$\mathbf{Adv}^{\text{dbdh}}(\mathcal{D}) = |\Pr[\mathsf{Exp}^{\text{dbdh-real}}_{g,p}(\mathcal{D}) = 1] - \Pr[\mathsf{Exp}^{\text{dbdh-rand}}_{g,p}(\mathcal{D}) = 1]|,$$

where the probability is taken over the choices of a, b, c, δ and the random tape of $\mathcal{D}$.

Definition 1 (DBDH Assumption). *We say that the DBDH assumption in (G, G_T) holds if for all probabilistic polynomial-time (PPT) distinguisher $\mathcal{D}$ the advantage $\mathbf{Adv}^{\text{dbdh}}(\mathcal{D})$ is negligible in security parameter κ.*

2.3 Pseudo-random Function

Let κ be a security parameter and $\mathsf{F} = \{F_\kappa : Dom_\kappa \times Kspace_\kappa \to Rng_\kappa\}_\kappa$ be a function family with a family of domains $\{Dom_\kappa\}_\kappa$, a family of key spaces $\{Kspace_\kappa\}_\kappa$ and a family of ranges $\{Rng_\kappa\}_\kappa$.

Definition 2 (Pseudo-Random Function). *We say that function family $\mathsf{F} = \{F_\kappa\}_\kappa$ is the PRF family, if for any PPT distinguisher $\mathcal{D}$, $\mathbf{Adv}^{\text{prf}} = |\Pr[\mathcal{D}^{F_\kappa(\cdot)} \to 1] - \Pr[\mathcal{D}^{RF_\kappa(\cdot)} \to 1]| \leq negl$, where $RF_\kappa : Dom_\kappa \to Rng_\kappa$ is a truly random function.*

2.4 Target-Collision Resistant Hash Function

We say a function $TCR : Dom \to Rng$ is a target-collision resistant hash function if the following condition holds for a security parameter κ: For any PPT adversary $\mathcal{A}$, $\Pr[x \in_R Dom; x' \gets \mathcal{A}(x) \text{ s.t. } x \neq x' \wedge TCR(x) = TCR(x')] \leq negl$.

3   G-CK⁺ Model

In this section, we introduce a new security model, G-CK⁺ model, for GKE by combining the CK⁺ model [19] for two-party AKE and the MSU model [15,16] for GKE.

Note that we show a model specified to one-round protocols for simplicity. It can be trivially extended to any round protocol.

3.1 Protocol Participants and Initialization

Let $\mathcal{U} := \{U_1, \ldots, U_N\}$ be a set of potential protocol participants. Each party U_i is modeled as a PPT Turing machine w.r.t. security parameter κ. For party U_i, we denote static secret (public) key by SSK_i (SPK_i) and ephemeral secret (public) key by ESK_i (EPK_i). Party U_i generates its own keys, SSK_i and SPK_i, and the static public key SPK_i is linked with U_i's identity in some systems like PKI.

3.2 Session

An invocation of a protocol is called a *session*. We suppose that a session contains n parties $\{U_{j_1}, \ldots, U_{j_n}\}$, where $2 \le n \le N$. A session is managed by a tuple $(\Pi, \text{role}_i, U_{j_\ell}, \{U_{j_1}, \ldots, U_{j_n}\})$, where Π is a protocol identifier, role_i is a role identifier, and U_{j_ℓ} is a party identifier. Hereafter, for simplicity, we can suppose that $U_{j_\ell} = U_\ell$ without loss of generality. If U_j is activated with $(\Pi, \text{role}_i, U_j, \{U_1, \ldots, U_n\}, Init)$, then U_j is called the *i-th player*. The role of a party in a session is decided by the lexicographic order of party identities, and $\text{role}_i \ne \text{role}_{i'}$ for any i and i' in a session. U_j outputs EPK_j, receives $EPK_{j'}$ from $U_{j'}$ for $j' = 1, \ldots, j-1, j+1, \ldots, n$, and computes the session key SK.

If U_j is the i-th player of a session, the session is identified by $\text{sid} = (\Pi, \text{role}_i, U_j, \{U_1, \ldots, U_n\}, EPK_j)$ or $\text{sid} = (\Pi, \text{role}_i, U_j, \{U_1, \ldots, U_n\}, \{EPK_1, \ldots, EPK_n\})$. We say that U_j is the *owner* of session sid, if the third coordinate of sid is U_j. We say that U_j is a *peer* of session sid, if the third coordinate of sid is not U_j. We say that a session is *completed* if its owner computes the session key. We say $(\Pi, \text{role}_{i'}, U_{j'}, \{U_1, \ldots, U_n\}, \{EPK_1, \ldots, EPK_n\})$ is *matching session* of $(\Pi, \text{role}_i, U_j, \{U_1, \ldots, U_n\}, \{EPK_1, \ldots, EPK_n\})$, where $i' \ne i$ and $j' \ne j$.

3.3 Adversary

The adversary $\mathcal{A}$, which is modeled as a PPT Turing machine, controls all communications between parties including session activation and registrations of parties by performing the following adversary queries.

- Send(U_j, message): U_j is the receiver. The message has the following form: $(\Pi, \text{role}_i, U_j, \{U_1, \ldots, U_n\}, Init)$ for session activation, or $(\Pi, \text{role}_{i'}, U_{j'}, \{U_1, \ldots, U_n\}, EPK_{j'})$. $\mathcal{A}$ obtains the response from U_j.
- Establish(U_j, SPK_j): This query allows $\mathcal{A}$ to introduce new parties. In response, if $U_j \notin \mathcal{U}$ (due to the uniqueness of identities) then U_j with the static public key SPK_j is added to $\mathcal{U}$. Note that $\mathcal{A}$ is not required to prove the possession of the corresponding secret key SSK_j. If a party is registered by a Establish query issued by $\mathcal{A}$, then we call the party *dishonest*. If not, we call the party *honest*.

To capture exposure of secret information, the adversary $\mathcal{A}$ is allowed to issue the following queries.

- SessionReveal(sid): The adversary $\mathcal{A}$ obtains the session key SK for the session sid if the session is completed.
- StateReveal(sid): The adversary $\mathcal{A}$ obtains the session state of the owner of session sid if the session is not completed (the session key is not established yet). The session state includes all ephemeral secret keys and intermediate computation results except for immediately erased information but does not include the static secret key. Note that the protocol specifies what the session state contains.
- StaticReveal(U_j): This query allows the adversary $\mathcal{A}$ to obtain all static secret keys of the party U_j.
- EphemeralReveal(sid): This query allows the adversary $\mathcal{A}$ to obtain all ephemeral secret keys of the owner of the session sid if the session is not completed (the session key is not established yet). It is necessary to represent a MEX situation that an adversary can reveal ESKs but is prevented to obtain other session state such that the adversary trivially wins.

3.4 Freshness

For the security definition, we need the notion of freshness.

Definition 3 (Freshness). *Let* sid* = (Π, role$_i$, U_j, $\{U_1, \ldots, U_n\}$, $\{EPK_1, \ldots, EPK_n\}$) *be a completed session between honest parties* $\{U_1, \ldots, U_n\}$, *which is owned by* U_j. *If a matching session exists, then let* $\overline{\text{sid}^*}$ *be a matching session of* sid*. *We say session* sid* *is* fresh *if none of the following conditions hold:*

1. *The adversary* $\mathcal{A}$ *issues* SessionReveal(sid*), *or* SessionReveal($\overline{\text{sid}^*}$) *for any* $\overline{\text{sid}^*}$ *if* $\overline{\text{sid}^*}$ *exists,*
2. $\overline{\text{sid}^*}$ *exists, and adversary* $\mathcal{A}$ *makes either of* StateReveal(sid*) *or* StateReveal($\overline{\text{sid}^*}$),
3. $\overline{\text{sid}^*}$ *does not exist, and adversary* $\mathcal{A}$ *makes* StateReveal(sid*),
4. *adversary* $\mathcal{A}$ *makes both of* StaticReveal(U_j) *and* EphemeralReveal(sid*),
5. $\overline{\text{sid}^*}$ *exists (the owner of* $\overline{\text{sid}^*}$ *is* $U_{j'}$), *and adversary* $\mathcal{A}$ *makes both of* StaticReveal($U_{j'}$) *and* EphemeralReveal($\overline{\text{sid}^*}$),
6. $\overline{\text{sid}^*}$ *does not exist, and adversary* $\mathcal{A}$ *makes* StaticReveal($U_{j'}$) *for any intended peer* $U_{j'}$ *of* U_j *in* sid*.

3.5 Security Experiment

For the security definition, we consider the following security experiment. Initially, the adversary $\mathcal{A}$ is given a set of honest users and makes any sequence of the queries described above. During the experiment, the adversary $\mathcal{A}$ makes the following query.

- Test(sid*): Here, sid* must be a fresh session. Select random bit $b \in_R \{0, 1\}$, and return the session key held by sid* if $b = 0$, and return a random key if $b = 1$.

The experiment continues until the adversary $\mathcal{A}$ makes a guess b'. The adversary $\mathcal{A}$ *wins* the game if the test session sid* is still fresh and if the guess of the adversary $\mathcal{A}$

is correct, i.e., $b' = b$. The advantage of the adversary $\mathcal{A}$ is defined as $\mathbf{Adv}_{\Pi}^{gke}(\mathcal{A}) =$ $\Pr[\mathcal{A} \text{ wins}] - \frac{1}{2}$. We define the security as follows.

Definition 4 (G-CK$^+$ Security). *We say that a GKE protocol Π is secure in the G-CK$^+$ model if the following conditions hold:*

1. *If two honest parties complete matching sessions, then, except with negligible probability, they both compute the same session key.*
2. *For any PPT adversary $\mathcal{A}$, $\mathrm{Adv}_{\Pi}^{gke}(\mathcal{A})$ is negligible in security parameter κ for the test session* sid*.

4 Maximal-Exposure-Resilient One-Round Tripartite Key Exchange without ROs

In this section, we introduce a new one-round 3KE protocol. We use the technique of DRE with some modification. Our protocol is G-CK$^+$ secure in the StdM under the DBDH assumption.

4.1 What Is Barrier to Remove ROs?

All of known 3KE protocols in the ROM use an RO as the key derivation function. For example, in the simplest variant of the FMSU framework [16] a session key is the output of an RO as follows: Let κ be a security parameter. Let G and G_T be bilinear groups with pairing $e : G \times G \to G_T$ of order κ-bit prime p with generators g and $g_T = e(g, g)$, respectively. Party U_A, U_B and U_C own $a, b, c \in_R \mathbb{Z}_p$ as SSKs and $A = g^a, B = g^b, C = g^c \in G$ as SPKs, and $x, y, z \in_R \mathbb{Z}_p$ as ESKs and $X = g^x, Y = g^y, Z = g^z \in G$ as EPKs, respectively. Then, parties share 8 combinations of their SSKs and ESKs with pairings (i.e., $g_T^{abc}, g_T^{xbc}, g_T^{ayc}, g_T^{abz}, g_T^{xyc}, g_T^{xbz}, g_T^{ayz}$ and g_T^{xyz}). The session key SK is the output of RO inputting these shared information.

This structure helps the simulation to keep consistency between SessionReveal and Send queries in the security proof. The simulator must answer correct session keys for the SessionReveal query according to EPKs for the Send query. In the ROM, the simulator can arbitrarily chooses the output of the key derivation function without computing shared information. Thus, if the simulator cannot know the ESK corresponding to the EPK received from the Send query, he can make the session key consistent by the simulation of the RO.

Conversely, in the StdM, the simulator must compute all shared information in order to answer the session key to the SessionReveal query correctly. However, MEX includes exposure of all non-trivial combinations of SSKs and ESKs, and the simulator must embed an instance of a hard problem into unexposed keys to solve the problem. For example, we consider the case that the key derivation function in the above FMSU variant is not RO. If a, y and z are revealed, then the simulator must embed DBDH tuple $(\alpha, \beta, \gamma, \delta)$ into $X = \alpha$, $B = \beta$, $C = \gamma$, and $g_T^{xbc} = \delta$. Then, the simulator must return the correct session key for the SessionReveal and Send query though x, b and c are not known. Such a situation is hard to simulate as it is.

4.2 Modifying Dual-Receiver Encryption

A promising approach is to use techniques to simulate decryption queries in chosen ciphertext (CCA) secure encryption. Especially, for the 3KE setting, we need DRE rather than ordinary public key encryption. We use the KEM version of a CCA secure DRE [18] (CFZ DRE) to construct our basic protocol; that is, each party encapsulates a random nonce with DRE and broadcasts it to other parties. The protocol of the CFZ DRE is as follows:

Public Parameters. Let κ be a security parameter. Let G and G_T be bilinear groups with pairing $e : G \times G \to G_T$ of order κ-bit prime p with generators g and $g_T = e(g, g)$, respectively. Let $TCR : G \to \mathbb{Z}_p$ be a target collision resistance hash function.

Secret and Public Keys. The secret key of receiver U_i is $sk_i := (x_i, y_i) \in_R \mathbb{Z}_p^2$. The public key of receiver U_i is $pk_i := (X_i = g^{x_i}, Y_i = g^{y_i})$.

Encapsulation. Given pk_1 and pk_2, the sender chooses $r \in_R \mathbb{Z}_p$, and computes $R = g^r$, $\mathsf{tag} = TCR(R)$, $\pi_1 = (X_1^{\mathsf{tag}}Y_1)^r$, and $\pi_2 = (X_2^{\mathsf{tag}}Y_2)^r$. The KEM session key is $K = e(X_1, X_2)^r$, and the ciphertext is $CT = (R, \pi_1, \pi_2)$.

Decapsulation. Given pk_1, pk_2, sk_1, and CT, the receiver computes $\mathsf{tag} = TCR(R)$, and checks $e(g, \pi_1) = e(R, x_1^{\mathsf{tag}}y_1)$ and $e(g, \pi_2) = e(R, x_2^{\mathsf{tag}}y_2)$. If not, return $\perp$. Otherwise, return the KEM session key $K = e(R, X_2)^{x_1}$.

In the security proof, the simulator can handle decryption queries by utilizing the fact that tag^* corresponding to the challenge ciphertext CT^* is different from tags corresponding to ciphertexts of decryption queries. Specifically, the simulator embeds a DBDH tuple $(g, \alpha, \beta, \gamma, \delta)$ into $R^* = \alpha$, $\pi_1^* = \alpha^{d_1}$, $\pi_2^* = \alpha^{d_2}$, $X_1^* = \beta$, $Y_1^* = \beta^{-\mathsf{tag}^*} g^{d_1}$, $X_2^* = \gamma$, $Y_2^* = \gamma^{-\mathsf{tag}^*} g^{d_2}$ and $K^* = \delta$, where $d_1, d_2 \in_R \mathbb{Z}_p$ and $\mathsf{tag}^* = TCR(R^*)$. When a ciphertext $CT = (R, \pi_1, \pi_2)$ is posed, the simulator can return $K = e((\pi_1 R^{-d_1})^{(\mathsf{tag} - \mathsf{tag}^*)^{-1}}, X_2^*)$ or $K = e((\pi_2 R^{-d_2})^{(\mathsf{tag} - \mathsf{tag}^*)^{-1}}, X_1^*)$, where $\mathsf{tag} = TCR(R)$. Owing to this simulation, we can simulate the SessionReveal and Send query without knowing secret keys. It is likely that 3KE could be constructed by setting the ciphertext of the CFZ DRE as the EPK. However, a simple application of DRE does not correctly work in the 3KE setting.

First, though the adversary is prevented to pose the challenge ciphertext to the decryption oracle in the CCA game of DRE, an adversary can be forward the message, corresponding to the challenge ciphertext, in the test session for other sessions by Send query in the G-CK$^+$ model. For example, an adversary specifies U_A as the owner of the test session, and reveals the SSK of U_A. Then, the simulator embeds an element in the DBDH tuple into R^* of a part of the EPK of U_A as the simulation of the CFZ DRE. The adversary can reuse R^* as a part of the EPK of U_B in another session. In this case, the simulator must manage the decryption of it, but the original decryption simulation technique of DRE does not help him because $\mathsf{tag} = \mathsf{tag}^* = TCR(R^*)$. Thus, our first modification is that the way to generate tags is changed to be different in distinct two sessions even if the challenge ciphertext is reused. Specifically, we make tags dependent on identities of the sender and receivers. That is, if the sender is U_A, and receivers are U_B and U_C, then $\mathsf{tag} = TCR(R, U_A, U_B, U_C)$. Even if the same R is reused, the tag is different from tag because the sender is not U_A. Note that when R is reused in another session such that the sender is U_A, and receivers are U_B and U_C, the decryption simulation is not necessary because we can return δ in the DBDH tuple.

Next, we must consider the other problem. To resist exposure of all SSKs, parties must share a secret state only with their ESKs to be independent with SSKs as g_T^{xyz} in the simplest variant of the FMSU framework. If each party knows own ESK, such a secret state can be computed. Unfortunately, in the case that the simulator must embed an element in the DBDH tuple into R^* of a part of the EPK of U_A in the test session, the secret state cannot be simulated. If the test session has no matching session, and an adversary reuses R^* as EPKs of U_B and U_C, the simulator must computes the secret state from R^*. However, the simulator cannot generate it because no ESK is known. On the other hand, to resist exposure or adversarial generation of all ESKs, parties must share a secret state only with their SSKs to be independent with ESKs as g_T^{abc} in the simplest variant of the FMSU framework. A similar case as above occurs; that is, the simulator cannot generate such a secret state because no SSK is known when an element in the DBDH tuple is embedded into the SPK of a party and other parties are established by the adversary. To resolve this problem, our second modification is that each party generates an additional group element as a part of SPK, and broadcasts an additional group element as a part of EPK. Secret states corresponding to g_T^{abc} and g_T^{xyz} are generated with them. This modification allows the simulator to know ESKs and SSKs to generate secret states even if the simulator embeds an element in the DBDH tuple into EPK or SPK. In our construction (Section 4.3), EPKs R'_A, R'_B, R'_C and SPKs Z_A, Z_B, Z_C correspond to the modification.

4.3 Our Construction

Public Parameters. Let κ be a security parameter. Let G and G_T be bilinear groups with pairing $e : G \times G \to G_T$ of order κ-bit prime p with generators g and $g_T = e(g, g)$, respectively. Let $F : \{0, 1\}^* \times G_T \to \{0, 1\}^\kappa$ be a pseudo-random function where the key space for F is G_T. Let $TCR : G \to \mathbb{Z}_p$ be a target collision resistance hash function.

Secret and Public Keys. Party U_I chooses $x_I, y_I, z_I \in_R \mathbb{Z}_p$ as the static secret key. Then, U_I computes $X_I = g^{x_I}$, $Y_I = g^{y_I}$ and $Z_I = g^{z_I}$ as the static public key.

Key Exchange. We suppose a session executed by U_A, U_B and U_C.

1. U_A chooses $r_A, r'_A \in_R \mathbb{Z}_p$ as the ephemeral secret key, and computes $R_A = g^{r_A}$, $R'_A = g^{r'_A}$, $\pi_{AB} = (X_B^{\mathsf{tag}_A} Y_B)^{r_A}$, and $\pi_{AC} = (X_C^{\mathsf{tag}_A} Y_C)^{r_A}$ as the ephemeral public key, where $\mathsf{tag}_A = TCR(R_A, R'_A, U_A, U_B, U_C)$. Then, U_A broadcasts $(\Pi, \mathsf{role}_1, U_A, \{U_A, U_B, U_C\}, (R_A, R'_A, \pi_{AB}, \pi_{AC}))$ to U_B and U_C.

2. U_B chooses $r_B, r'_B \in_R \mathbb{Z}_p$ as the ephemeral secret key, and computes $R_B = g^{r_B}$, $R'_B = g^{r'_B}$, $\pi_{BA} = (X_A^{\mathsf{tag}_B} Y_A)^{r_B}$, and $\pi_{BC} = (X_C^{\mathsf{tag}_B} Y_C)^{r_B}$ as the ephemeral public key, where $\mathsf{tag}_B = TCR(R_B, R'_B, U_B, U_C, U_A)$. Then, U_A broadcasts $(\Pi, \mathsf{role}_2, U_B, \{U_A, U_B, U_C\}, (R_B, R'_B, \pi_{BA}, \pi_{BC}))$ to U_A and U_C.

3. U_C chooses $r_C, r'_C \in_R \mathbb{Z}_p$ as the ephemeral secret key, and computes $R_C = g^{r_C}$, $R'_C = g^{r'_C}$, $\pi_{CA} = (X_A^{\mathsf{tag}_C} Y_A)^{r_C}$, and $\pi_{CB} = (X_B^{\mathsf{tag}_C} Y_B)^{r_C}$ as the ephemeral public key, where $\mathsf{tag}_C = TCR(R_C, R'_C, U_C, U_A, U_B)$. Then, U_C broadcasts $(\Pi, \mathsf{role}_3, U_C, \{U_A, U_B, U_C\}, (R_C, R'_C, \pi_{CA}, \pi_{CB}))$ to U_A and U_B.

4. On receiving $(\Pi, \mathsf{role}_2, U_B, \{U_A, U_B, U_C\}, (R_B, R'_B, \pi_{BA}, \pi_{BC}))$ and $(\Pi, \mathsf{role}_3, U_C, \{U_A, U_B, U_C\}, (R_C, R'_C, \pi_{CA}, \pi_{CB}))$, U_A computes $\mathsf{tag}_B = TCR(R_B, R'_B, U_B, U_C, U_A)$ and $\mathsf{tag}_C = TCR(R_C, R'_C, U_C, U_A, U_B)$, and verify the following equations.

$$e(g, \pi_{BA}) = e(R_B, X_A^{\mathsf{tag}_B} Y_A); e(g, \pi_{BC}) = e(R_B, X_C^{\mathsf{tag}_B} Y_C);$$

$$e(g, \pi_{CA}) = e(R_C, X_A^{\mathsf{tag}_C} Y_A); e(g, \pi_{CB}) = e(R_C, X_B^{\mathsf{tag}_C} Y_B)$$

If the verification does not hold, U_A aborts. Otherwise, U_A computes the following shared information.

$$\sigma_1 = e(Z_B, Z_C)^{z_A}; \ \sigma_2 = e(X_B, X_C)^{r_A}; \sigma_3 = e(R_B, X_C)^{x_A}; \ \sigma_4 = e(X_B, R_C)^{x_A};$$

$$\sigma_5 = e(R_B, X_C)^{r_A}; \ \sigma_6 = e(X_B, R_C)^{r_A}; \sigma_7 = e(R_B, R_C)^{x_A}; \ \sigma_8 = e(R'_B, R'_C)^{r_A}$$

Then, U_A sets the session transcript $\mathsf{ST} = (U_A, (R_A, R'_A, \pi_{AB}, \pi_{AC}), U_B, (R_B, R'_B, \pi_{BA}, \pi_{BC}), U_C, (R_C, R'_C, \pi_{CA}, \pi_{CB}))$. Finally, U_A generates the session key $SK = F_{\sigma_1}(\mathsf{ST}) \oplus \cdots \oplus F_{\sigma_8}(\mathsf{ST})$, and completes the session.

5. On receiving $(\Pi, \mathsf{role}_1, U_A, \{U_A, U_B, U_C\}, (R_A, R'_A, \pi_{AB}, \pi_{AC}))$ and $(\Pi, \mathsf{role}_3, U_C, \{U_A, U_B, U_C\}, (R_C, R'_C, \pi_{CA}, \pi_{CB}))$, U_B computes $\mathsf{tag}_A = TCR(R_A, R'_A, U_A, U_B, U_C)$ and $\mathsf{tag}_C = TCR(R_C, R'_C, U_C, U_A, U_B)$, and verify the following equations.

$$e(g, \pi_{AB}) = e(R_A, X_B^{\mathsf{tag}_A} Y_B); e(g, \pi_{AC}) = e(R_A, X_C^{\mathsf{tag}_A} Y_C);$$

$$e(g, \pi_{CA}) = e(R_C, X_A^{\mathsf{tag}_C} Y_A); e(g, \pi_{CB}) = e(R_C, X_B^{\mathsf{tag}_C} Y_B)$$

If the verification does not hold, U_B aborts. Otherwise, U_B computes the following shared information.

$$\sigma_1 = e(Z_A, Z_C)^{z_B}; \ \sigma_2 = e(R_A, X_C)^{x_B}; \sigma_3 = e(X_A, X_C)^{r_B}; \ \sigma_4 = e(X_A, R_C)^{x_B};$$

$$\sigma_5 = e(R_A, X_C)^{r_B}; \ \sigma_6 = e(R_A, R_C)^{x_B}; \sigma_7 = e(X_A, R_C)^{r_B}; \ \sigma_8 = e(R'_A, R'_C)^{r_B}$$

Then, U_B sets the session transcript $\mathsf{ST} = (U_A, (R_A, R'_A, \pi_{AB}, \pi_{AC}), U_B, (R_B, R'_B, \pi_{BA}, \pi_{BC}), U_C, (R_C, R'_C, \pi_{CA}, \pi_{CB}))$. Finally, U_B generates the session key $SK = F_{\sigma_1}(\mathsf{ST}) \oplus \cdots \oplus F_{\sigma_8}(\mathsf{ST})$, and completes the session.

6. On receiving $(\Pi, \mathsf{role}_1, U_A, \{U_A, U_B, U_C\}, (R_A, R'_A, \pi_{AB}, \pi_{AC}))$ and $(\Pi, \mathsf{role}_2, U_B, \{U_A, U_B, U_C\}, (R_B, R'_B, \pi_{BA}, \pi_{BC}))$, U_C computes $\mathsf{tag}_A = TCR(R_A, R'_A, U_A, U_B, U_C)$ and $\mathsf{tag}_B = TCR(R_B, R'_B, U_B, U_C, U_A)$, and verify the following equations.

$$e(g, \pi_{AB}) = e(R_A, X_B^{\mathsf{tag}_A} Y_B); e(g, \pi_{AC}) = e(R_A, X_C^{\mathsf{tag}_A} Y_C);$$

$$e(g, \pi_{BA}) = e(R_B, X_A^{\mathsf{tag}_B} Y_A); e(g, \pi_{BC}) = e(R_B, X_C^{\mathsf{tag}_B} Y_C)$$

If the verification does not hold, U_C aborts. Otherwise, U_C computes the following shared information.

$$\sigma_1 = e(Z_A, Z_B)^{z_C}; \ \sigma_2 = e(R_A, X_B)^{x_C}; \sigma_3 = e(X_A, R_B)^{x_C}; \ \sigma_4 = e(X_A, X_B)^{r_C};$$

$$\sigma_5 = e(R_A, R_B)^{x_C}; \ \sigma_6 = e(X_A, R_B)^{r_C}; \sigma_7 = e(X_A, R_B)^{r_C}; \ \sigma_8 = e(R'_A, R'_B)^{r_C}$$

Table 1. Comparison of previous one-round 3KE schemes and our scheme

	MEX-resilient?	Resource	Assumption	Computation (#parings+ #[multi,regular]-exp)	Communication complexity
[10]	no	ROM	DDH	$0 + [0,7]^\dagger$ or $0 + [2,1]$	$20\kappa^\dagger$ or 2κ (2560 or 256)
[11]	no	StdM	DDH	$0 + [3,7]$	16κ (2048)
[14]	no	ROM	BDH	$1 + [0,3]$	4κ (512)
[15,16]	yes	ROM	GBDH	$4 + [0,7]$	4κ (512)
Ours	yes	StdM	DBDH	$14 + [2,15]$	16κ (2048)

† Since the protocol is asymmetric, the cost for a party is higher than the others.

DDH means the Decisional Diffie-Hellman assumption. BDH means the Bilinear Diffie-Hellman assumption. DBDH means the Decisional Bilinear Diffie-Hellman assumption. GBDH means the gap Bilinear Diffie-Hellman assumption. For concreteness the expected communication complexity for a 128-bit security implementation is also given. Note that computational costs are estimated without any pre-computation technique.

Then, U_C sets the session transcript $\text{ST} = (U_A, (R_A, R'_A, \pi_{AB}, \pi_{AC}), U_B, (R_B, R'_B, \pi_{BA}, \pi_{BC}), U_C, (R_C, R'_C, \pi_{CA}, \pi_{CB}))$. Finally, U_C generates the session key $SK = F_{\sigma_1}(\text{ST}) \oplus \cdots \oplus F_{\sigma_8}(\text{ST})$, and completes the session.

The session state of a session owned by U_I contains ephemeral secret keys (r_I, r'_I), shared information $(\sigma_1, \ldots, \sigma_8)$, and outputs of PRFs $(F_{\sigma_1}(\text{ST}), \ldots, F_{\sigma_8}(\text{ST}))$.

4.4 Efficiency

Our construction needs 2 regular exponentiations and 2 multi exponentiations to generate a message, 4 regular exponentiations and 8 pairings to verify received messages, and 8 regular exponentiations and 6 pairings to compute shared information for each party. The total computational cost for each party is 2 multi exponentiations, 15 regular exponentiations, and 14 pairings. A message contains 4 group elements in G, and each party broadcasts the message to two other parties. The total communication complexity (the message size sent by a party) is 16κ with an elliptic curve.

Table 1 summarizes the efficiency comparison of previous one-round 3KE schemes and our scheme. Schemes in [10] and [11] are designed for GKE, and we describe 3KE versions of them. The instantiation of [10] in Table 1 is with the ElGamal KEM as semantically secure public key encryption and the Chevallier-Mames signature [21] as existentially unforgeable signature. The instantiation of [11] in Table 1 is with the multiple Cramer-Shoup encryption [22] as CCA secure multiple KEM according to the generic construction [23].

This table hints that communication complexity grows to achieve security in the standard model, and computational cost grows to achieve MEX-resilient. Hence, our scheme is less efficient than existing schemes but still practical because complexity is only three or four times larger both in computation and communication than [15,16].

Table 2. Classification of events, when A, B and C are distinct

	SSK_A	ESK_A	SSK_B	ESK_B	SSK_C	ESK_C
E_1	r	ok	ok	r/n	ok	r/n
E_2	ok	r	ok	r/n	ok	r/n
E_3	r	ok	r	ok	r	ok
E_4	ok	r	r	ok	r	ok
E_5	r	ok	ok	r/n	r	ok
E_6	ok	r	ok	r/n	r	ok
E_7	r	ok	r	ok	ok	r/n
E_8	ok	r	r	ok	ok	r/n

"ok" means the static secret key is not revealed, or a partnered instance exists and its ephemeral secret key is not revealed. "r" means the static or ephemeral secret key may be revealed. "r/n" means the ephemeral secret key may be revealed if the corresponding partnered instance exists, or no corresponding partnered instance exists.

5   Security

We show the following theorem.

Theorem 1. *If the DBDH assumption holds, and F is a PRF, then our 3KE protocol is G-CK$^+$-secure.*

Proof. In the experiment of G-CK$^+$ security, we suppose that sid* is the session identity for the test session, and that there are N parties and at most ℓ sessions are activated per a party. Let κ be the security parameter, and let $\mathcal{A}$ be a PPT (in κ) adversary. Suc denotes the event that $\mathcal{A}$ wins. We consider eight events in Table 2, that cover all cases of the behavior of $\mathcal{A}$.

To finish the proof, we investigate events $E_i \wedge Suc$ ($i = 1, \ldots, 8$) that cover all cases of event Suc. Due to the space limitation, we only show the full proof of $E_1 \wedge Suc$ which is the most difficult event. Other events can be proved in a similar way.

5.1   Event $E_1 \wedge Suc$

We change the interface of oracle queries and the computation of the session key. These instances are gradually changed over hybrid experiments, depending on specific sub-cases. In the last hybrid experiment, the session key in the test session does not contain information of the bit b. Thus, the adversary clearly only output a random guess. We denote these hybrid experiments by $\mathbf{H}_0, \ldots, \mathbf{H}_4$, and the advantage of the adversary $\mathcal{A}$ when participating in experiment $\mathbf{H}_i$ by $\mathbf{Adv}(\mathcal{A}, \mathbf{H}_i)$.

Hybrid Experiment $\mathbf{H}_0$. This experiment denotes the real experiment for G-CK$^+$ security and in this experiment the environment for $\mathcal{A}$ is as defined in the protocol. Thus, $\mathbf{Adv}(\mathcal{A}, \mathbf{H}_0)$ is the same as the advantage of the real experiment.

Hybrid Experiment H_1. In this experiment, if session identities in two sessions are identical, the experiment halts.

When randomness in generating EPKs are identical, session identities in two sessions are also identical. However, such an event occurs with negligible probability. Thus, $|\mathbf{Adv}(\mathcal{A}, H_1) - \mathbf{Adv}(\mathcal{A}, H_0)| \leq negl$.

Hybrid Experiment H_2. In this experiment, the experiment selects parties U_A, U_B and U_C, and integer $k \in [1, \ell]$ randomly in advance. If $\mathcal{A}$ poses Test query to a session except k-th session of U_A whose the intended peers U_B and U_C, the experiment halts.

Since guess of the test session matches with $\mathcal{A}$'s choice with probability $1/N^3\ell$, $\mathbf{Adv}(\mathcal{A}, H_2) \geq (1/N^3\ell) \cdot \mathbf{Adv}(\mathcal{A}, H_1)$. After this experiment, without loss of generality, we can suppose that the intended peers of the k-th session of U_A are U_B and U_C.

Hybrid Experiment H_3. In this experiment, the computation of σ_2 in the test session is changed. Instead of computing $\sigma_2 = g_T^{r_A x_B x_C}$, it is changed as choosing $\sigma_2 \leftarrow G_T$ randomly, where we suppose that U_B and U_C are intended peers of U_A in the test session.

We construct a DBDH distinguisher $\mathcal{D}$ from $\mathcal{A}$ in H_2 or H_3. $\mathcal{D}$ performs the following steps.

Init. $\mathcal{D}$ receives a DBDH tuple $(g, \alpha, \beta, \gamma, \delta)$ as a challenge.

Setup. $\mathcal{D}$ chooses pseudo-random function $F : \{0, 1\}^* \times G_T \rightarrow \{0, 1\}^\kappa$, and provides it as a part of the public parameters.

First, $\mathcal{D}$ sets the ephemeral public key $(R_A^*, R_A'^*, \pi_{AB}^*, \pi_{AC}^*)$ of k-th session of U_A. $\mathcal{D}$ randomly chooses r_A', d_1 and d_2, and sets $R_A^* := \alpha$, $R_A'^* := g^{r_A'}$, $\pi_{AB}^* := \alpha^{d_1}$ and $\pi_{AC}^* := \alpha^{d_2}$.

Next, $\mathcal{D}$ implicitly sets all N parties' static secret and public keys. Keys of parties except U_B and U_C are generated as the protocol. If $\mathcal{A}$ poses Establish query with a party identifier and a SPK, then $\mathcal{D}$ replaces the preset SPK of the party with the given SPK. Static public keys of U_B and U_C $((X_B^*, Y_B^*, Z_B^*)$ and $(X_C^*, Y_C^*, Z_C^*))$ are set as $X_B^* := \beta$, $Y_B^* := \beta^{-tag_A^*}g^{d_1}$, $Z_B^* := g^{z_B^*}$, $X_C^* := \gamma$, $Y_C^* := \gamma^{-tag_A^*}g^{d_2}$, and $Z_C^* := g^{z_C^*}$, where $tag_A^* = TCR(R_A^*, R_A'^*, U_A, U_B, U_C)$ and $z_B^*, z_C^* \in_R \mathbb{Z}_p$.

Simulation. $\mathcal{D}$ maintains the list $\mathcal{L}_{SK}$ that contains queries and answers of SessionReveal. $\mathcal{D}$ simulates oracle queries by $\mathcal{A}$ as follows.

1. Send($U_{j_1}, \Pi, role_i, U_{j_1}, \{U_{j_1}, U_{j_2}, U_{j_3}\}, Init$):
   (a) If $j_1 = A$, $j_2 = B$, $j_3 = C$, $i = 1$, the session is k-th session of U_A, then $\mathcal{D}$ returns $(\Pi, role_1, U_A, \{U_A, U_B, U_C\}, (R_A^*, R_A'^*, \pi_{AB}^*, \pi_{AC}^*))$ and records it.
   (b) Otherwise, $\mathcal{D}$ computes the ephemeral public key as the protocol, returns it and records $(\Pi, role_i, U_{j_1}, \{U_{j_1}, U_{j_2}, U_{j_3}\}, (R_{j_1}, R_{j_1}', \pi_{j_1 j_2}, \pi_{j_1 j_3}))$.

2. Send($U_{j_2}, \Pi, role_i, U_{j_1}, \{U_{j_1}, U_{j_2}, U_{j_3}\}, EPK_{j_1}$) or Send($U_{j_3}, \Pi, role_i, U_{j_1}, \{U_{j_1}, U_{j_2}, U_{j_3}\}, EPK_{j_1}$):
   (a) If both $(\Pi, role_{i'}, U_{j_2}, \{U_{j_1}, U_{j_2}, U_{j_3}\}, EPK_{j_2})$ and $(\Pi, role_{i''}, U_{j_3}, \{U_{j_1}, U_{j_2}, U_{j_3}\}, EPK_{j_3})$ are not recorded, $\mathcal{D}$ only records $(\Pi, role_i, U_{j_1}, \{U_{j_1}, U_{j_2}, U_{j_3}\}, EPK_{j_1})$.

(b) Else if $\mathcal{D}$ checks EPK_{j_1} with pairing equations as the protocol, and the verification is not valid, then $\mathcal{D}$ rejects the session.

(c) Else if $(j_2 = A, j_1 = C)$ or $(j_3 = A, j_1 = B)$, and the session is the k-th session of U_A, then $\mathcal{D}$ sets all σ_i as follows: σ_2 is set as δ. Since $\mathcal{D}$ knows x_A, z_A, z_B^*, z_C^* and r'^*_A, σ_1, σ_3, σ_4, σ_7 and σ_8 are computed with these values. $\sigma_5 = e((\pi_{BC} R_B^{-d_2})^{(\mathsf{tag}_B - \mathsf{tag}_{A^*})^{-1}}, R_A^*)$ where $\mathsf{tag}_B = TCR(R_B, R'_B, U_B, U_C, U_A)^2$. $\sigma_6 = e((\pi_{CB} R_C^{-d_1})^{(\mathsf{tag}_C - \mathsf{tag}_{A^*})^{-1}}, R_A^*)$ where $\mathsf{tag}_C = TCR(R_C, R'_C, U_C, U_A, U_B)^3$. $\mathcal{D}$ computes the session key SK^* as the protocol, and records $(\Pi, \mathsf{role}_1, U_A, \{U_A, U_B, U_C\}, \{EPK_A, EPK_B, EPK_C\})$, $(\Pi, \mathsf{role}_2, U_B, \{U_A, U_B, U_C\}, \{EPK_A, EPK_B, EPK_C\})$ and $(\Pi, \mathsf{role}_3, U_C, \{U_A, U_B, U_C\}, \{EPK_A, EPK_B, EPK_C\})$ as the completed session and SK^* in the list $\mathcal{L}_{SK}$.

(d) Else if $j_1 = A, j_2 = B, j_3 = C$, the first content of EPK_{j_1} is R_A^*, then $\mathcal{D}$ sets all σ_i as follows: σ_2 is set as δ. Since $\mathcal{D}$ knows x_A, z_A, z_B^*, z_C^* and r'^*_A, σ_1, σ_3, σ_4, σ_7 and σ_8 are computed with these values. $\sigma_5 = e((\pi_{j_2 j_3} R_{j_2}^{-d_2})^{(\mathsf{tag}_{j_2} - \mathsf{tag}_{A^*})^{-1}}, R_A^*)$ where $\mathsf{tag}_{j_2} = TCR(R_{j_2}, R'_{j_2}, U_B, U_C, U_A)^4$. $\sigma_6 = e((\pi_{j_3 j_2} R_{j_3}^{-d_1})^{(\mathsf{tag}_{j_3} - \mathsf{tag}_{A^*})^{-1}}, R_A^*)$ where $\mathsf{tag}_{j_3} = TCR(R_{j_3}, R'_{j_3}, U_C, U_A, U_B)^5$. $\mathcal{D}$ computes the session key SK as the protocol, and records $(\Pi, \mathsf{role}_1, U_A, \{U_A, U_B, U_C\}, \{EPK_A, EPK_B, EPK_C\})$, $(\Pi, \mathsf{role}_2, U_B, \{U_A, U_B, U_C\}, \{EPK_A, EPK_B, EPK_C\})$ and $(\Pi, \mathsf{role}_3, U_C, \{U_A, U_B, U_C\}, \{EPK_A, EPK_B, EPK_C\})$ as the completed session and SK in the list $\mathcal{L}_{SK}$.

(e) Else if $j_2 = B$ (resp. $j_3 = B$), then $\mathcal{D}$ parses EPK_{j_1} into $(R_{j_1}, R'_{j_1}, \pi_{j_1 j_2}, \pi_{j_1 j_3})$, and sets σ_i as follows: Since $\mathcal{D}$ knows z_B^*, r_B and r'_B, σ_1, σ_3, σ_4, σ_7 and σ_8 are computed with these values. $\sigma_2 = e((\pi_{j_1 j_2} R_{j_1}^{-d_1})^{(\mathsf{tag}_{j_1} - \mathsf{tag}_{A^*})^{-1}}, X_{j_3})$ (resp. $\sigma_2 = e((\pi_{j_1 j_3} R_{j_1}^{-d_1})^{(\mathsf{tag}_{j_1} - \mathsf{tag}_{A^*})^{-1}}, X_{j_2})$) where $\mathsf{tag}_{j_1} = TCR(R_{j_1}, R'_{j_1}, U_{j_1}, U_B, U_{j_3})$ (resp. $\mathsf{tag}_{j_1} = TCR(R_{j_1}, R'_{j_1}, U_{j_1}, U_{j_3}, U_B)$). $\sigma_5 = e(R_{j_1}, X_{j_3})^{r_B}$ (resp. $\sigma_5 = e((\pi_{j_1 j_3} \cdot R_{j_1}^{-d_1})^{(\mathsf{tag}_{j_1} - \mathsf{tag}_{A^*})^{-1}}, R_{j_3}))$ where $\mathsf{tag}_{j_1} = TCR(R_{j_1}, R'_{j_1}, U_{j_1}, U_{j_3}, U_B)$. $\sigma_6 = e((\pi_{j_1 j_2} \cdot R_{j_1}^{-d_1})^{(\mathsf{tag}_{j_1} - \mathsf{tag}_{A^*})^{-1}}, R_{j_3})$ (resp. $\sigma_6 = e(R_{j_1}, X_{j_3})^{r_B})$ where $\mathsf{tag}_{j_1} = TCR(R_{j_1}, R'_{j_1}, U_{j_1}, U_B, U_{j_3})$. $\mathcal{D}$ computes the session key SK as the protocol, and records $(\Pi, \mathsf{role}_i, U_{j_1}, \{U_{j_1}, U_B, U_{j_3}\}, \{EPK_{j_1}, EPK_B, EPK_{j_3}\})$, $(\Pi, \mathsf{role}_{i'}, U_B, \{U_{j_1}, U_B, U_{j_3}\}, \{EPK_{j_1}, EPK_B, EPK_{j_3}\})$ and $(\Pi, \mathsf{role}_{i''}, U_{j_3}, \{U_{j_1}, U_B, U_{j_3}\}, \{EPK_{j_1}, EPK_B, EPK_{j_3}\})$ (resp. $(\Pi, \mathsf{role}_i, U_{j_1}, \{U_{j_1}, U_{j_2}, U_B\}, \{EPK_{j_1}, EPK_{j_2}, EPK_B\})$, $(\Pi, \mathsf{role}_{i'}, U_{j_2}, \{U_{j_1}, U_{j_2}, U_B\}, \{EPK_{j_1}, EPK_{j_2}, EPK_B\})$ and $(\Pi, \mathsf{role}_{i''}, U_B, \{U_{j_1}, U_{j_2}, U_B\}, \{EPK_{j_1}, EPK_{j_2}, EPK_B\}))$ as the completed session and SK in the list $\mathcal{L}_{SK}$

(f) Else if $j_2 = C$ (resp. $j_3 = C$), then $\mathcal{D}$ parses EPK_{j_1} into $(R_{j_1}, R'_{j_1}, \pi_{j_1 j_2}, \pi_{j_1 j_3})$, and sets σ_i as follows: Since $\mathcal{D}$ knows z_C^*, r_C and r'_C, σ_1, σ_3, σ_4, σ_7 and σ_8 are computed with these values. $\sigma_2 = e((\pi_{j_1 j_2} R_{j_1}^{-d_2})^{(\mathsf{tag}_{j_1} - \mathsf{tag}_{A^*})^{-1}}, X_{j_3})$ (resp. $\sigma_2 = e((\pi_{j_1 j_3} R_{j_1}^{-d_2})^{(\mathsf{tag}_{j_1} - \mathsf{tag}_{A^*})^{-1}}, X_{j_2})$) where $\mathsf{tag}_{j_1} = TCR(R_{j_1}, R'_{j_1}, U_{j_1}, U_C, U_{j_3})$ (resp. $\mathsf{tag}_{j_1} = TCR(R_{j_1}, R'_{j_1}, U_{j_1}, U_{j_3}, U_C)$). $\sigma_5 =$

---

[2] Even if $R_B = R_A^*$, the simulation validly works because $\mathsf{tag}_B \neq \mathsf{tag}_{A^*}$ always holds.
[3] Even if $R_C = R_A^*$, the simulation validly works because $\mathsf{tag}_C \neq \mathsf{tag}_{A^*}$ always holds.
[4] Even if $R_{j_2} = R_A^*$, the simulation validly works because $\mathsf{tag}_{j_2} \neq \mathsf{tag}_{A^*}$ always holds.
[5] Even if $R_{j_3} = R_A^*$, the simulation validly works because $\mathsf{tag}_{j_3} \neq \mathsf{tag}_{A^*}$ always holds.

$e(R_{j_1}, X_{j_3})^{rc}$ (resp. $\sigma_5 = e((\pi_{j_1 j_3} \cdot R_{j_1}^{-d_2})^{(\text{tag}_{j_1} - \text{tag}_{A^*})^{-1}}, R_{j_3})$) where tag_{j_1}
$= TCR(R_{j_1}, R'_{j_1}, U_{j_1}, U_{j_3}, U_C)$. $\sigma_6 = e((\pi_{j_1 j_2} \cdot R_{j_1}^{-d_2})^{(\text{tag}_{j_1} - \text{tag}_{A^*})^{-1}}, R_{j_3})$ (resp.
$\sigma_6 = e(R_{j_1}, X_{j_3})^{rc}$) where $\text{tag}_{j_1} = TCR(R_{j_1}, R'_{j_1}, U_{j_1}, U_C, U_{j_3})$. $\mathcal{D}$ com-
putes the session key SK as the protocol, and records $(\Pi, \text{role}_i, U_{j_1}, \{U_{j_1}, U_C, U_{j_3}\}, \{EPK_{j_1}, EPK_C, EPK_{j_3}\})$, $(\Pi, \text{role}_{i'}, U_C, \{U_{j_1}, U_C, U_{j_3}\}, \{EPK_{j_1}, EPK_C, EPK_{j_3}\})$ and $(\Pi, \text{role}_{i''}, U_{j_3}, \{U_{j_1}, U_C, U_{j_3}\}, \{EPK_{j_1}, EPK_C, EPK_{j_3}\})$ (resp.
$(\Pi, \text{role}_i, U_{j_1}, \{U_{j_1}, U_{j_2}, U_C\}, \{EPK_{j_1}, EPK_{j_2}, EPK_C\})$, $(\Pi, \text{role}_{i'}, U_{j_2}, \{U_{j_1}, U_{j_2}, U_C\}, \{EPK_{j_1}, EPK_{j_2}, EPK_C\})$ and $(\Pi, \text{role}_{i''}, U_C, \{U_{j_1}, U_{j_2}, U_C\}, \{EPK_{j_1}, EPK_{j_2}, EPK_C\})$)) as the completed session and SK in the list $\mathcal{L}_{SK}$

   (g) Otherwise, $\mathcal{D}$ computes the session key SK as the protocol, and records $(\Pi, \text{role}_i, U_{j_1}, \{U_{j_1}, U_{j_2}, U_{j_3}\}, \{EPK_{j_1}, EPK_{j_2}, EPK_{j_3}\})$ as the completed session and SK in the list $\mathcal{L}_{SK}$.

3. Establish(U_j, SPK_j): $\mathcal{D}$ sets U_j as a new party and SPK_j as the SPK of U_j as the definition. Note that U_A, U_B and U_C are not posed due to the freshness definition.

4. SessionReveal(sid):

   (a) If the session sid is not completed, $\mathcal{D}$ returns an error message.

   (b) Otherwise, $\mathcal{D}$ returns the recorded value SK.

5. StateReveal(sid): $\mathcal{D}$ answers the ephemeral secret key and intermediate computation results of sid as the definition. Note that the StateReveal query is not posed to sid* from the freshness definition. Thus, $\mathcal{D}$ can avoid to return the ephemeral secret key corresponding to α.

6. StaticReveal(U_j): $\mathcal{D}$ answers the static secret key of U_j as the definition. Note that the StaticReveal query is not posed to U_B and U_C in the event E_1. Thus, $\mathcal{D}$ can avoid to return static secret key corresponding to β and γ.

7. EphemeralReveal(sid): $\mathcal{D}$ answers the ephemeral secret key of sid as the definition. Note that the EphemeralReveal query is not posed to sid* in the event E_1. Thus, $\mathcal{D}$ can avoid to return the ephemeral secret key corresponding to α.

8. Test(sid): $\mathcal{D}$ responds to the query as the definition.

9. If $\mathcal{A}$ outputs a guess b', $\mathcal{D}$ outputs b'.

Analysis. The simulation is perfect except that the following event occurs: In Send query, $\text{tag}_{j_2} = \text{tag}_A^*$ or $\text{tag}_{j_3} = \text{tag}_A^*$ in case 2.(c), and $\text{tag}_{j_1} = \text{tag}_A^*$ in case 2.(d) and 2.(e). If these events occur, since $\text{tag}_{j_1} - \text{tag}_{A^*} = 0$, $\text{tag}_{j_2} - \text{tag}_{A^*} = 0$ or $\text{tag}_{j_3} - \text{tag}_{A^*} = 0$, σ_2, σ_5 or σ_6 cannot be computed correctly. This event means that $\mathcal{A}$ finds a collision in TCR. Thus, the probability that the event occurs is negligible.

It is easy to see that static public keys of U_B and U_C are distributed as in $\mathbf{H}_2$. Also, the ephemeral public key of sid* is distributed as in $\mathbf{H}_2$.

For $\mathcal{A}$, the simulation is same as the experiment $\mathbf{H}_2$ if the challenge δ is g_T^{abc}. Otherwise, the simulation is same as the experiment $\mathbf{H}_3$. Thus, if the advantage of $\mathcal{D}$ is negligible, then $|\mathbf{Adv}(\mathcal{A}, \mathbf{H}_3) - \mathbf{Adv}(\mathcal{A}, \mathbf{H}_2)| \leq negl$.

Hybrid Experiment $\mathbf{H}_4$. In this experiment, the computation of SK in the test session is changed. Instead of computing $SK = F_{\sigma_1}(\text{ST}) \oplus \cdots \oplus F_{\sigma_8}(\text{ST})$, it is changed as $SK = F_{\sigma_1}(\text{ST}) \oplus K \oplus F_{\sigma_3}(\text{ST}) \cdots \oplus F_{\sigma_8}(\text{ST})$ where $K \in_R \{0, 1\}^k$.

We construct a distinguisher $\mathcal{D}'$ between PRF $F^* : \{0, 1\}^* \times G_T \to \{0, 1\}^k$ and a random function RF from $\mathcal{A}$ in $\mathbf{H}_3$ or $\mathbf{H}_4$. $\mathcal{D}'$ performs the following steps.

Setup. $\mathcal{D}'$ sets PRF $F = F^*$, and provides it as a part of the public parameters. Also, $\mathcal{D}'$ sets all N parties' static secret and public keys.

Simulation. $\mathcal{D}'$ maintains the list $\mathcal{L}_{SK}$ that contains queries and answers of SessionReveal. $\mathcal{D}'$ simulates oracle queries by $\mathcal{A}$ as follows.

1. Send($U_{j_1}, \Pi, \text{role}_i, U_{j_1}, \{U_{j_1}, U_{j_2}, U_{j_3}\}, Init$): $\mathcal{D}'$ computes the ephemeral public key as the protocol, returns it and records $(\Pi, \text{role}_i, U_{j_1}, \{U_{j_1}, U_{j_2}, U_{j_3}\}, (R_{j_1}, R'_{j_1}, \pi_{j_1 j_2}, \pi_{j_1 j_3}))$.

2. Send($U_{j_2}, \Pi, \text{role}_i, U_{j_1}, \{U_{j_1}, U_{j_2}, U_{j_3}\}, EPK_{j_1}$) or Send($U_{j_3}, \Pi, \text{role}_i, U_{j_1}, \{U_{j_1}, U_{j_2}, U_{j_3}\}, EPK_{j_1}$):

   (a) If both $(\Pi, \text{role}_{i'}, U_{j_2}, \{U_{j_1}, U_{j_2}, U_{j_3}\}, EPK_{j_2})$ and $(\Pi, \text{role}_{i''}, U_{j_3}, \{U_{j_1}, U_{j_2}, U_{j_3}\}, EPK_{j_3})$ are not recorded, $\mathcal{D}'$ only records $(\Pi, \text{role}_i, U_{j_1}, \{U_{j_1}, U_{j_2}, U_{j_3}\}, EPK_{j_1})$.

   (b) Else if $\mathcal{D}'$ checks EPK_{j_1} with pairing equations as the protocol, and the verification is not valid, then $\mathcal{D}'$ rejects the session.

   (c) Else if $(j_2 = A, j_1 = C)$ or $(j_3 = A, j_1 = B)$, and the session is the k-th session of U_A, then $\mathcal{D}$ computes all σ_i as the protocol. $\mathcal{D}'$ poses ST to his oracle (i.e., F^* or a random function RF), obtains $K \in \{0, 1\}^\kappa$, computes the session key $SK^* = F_{\sigma_1}(\text{ST}) \oplus K \oplus F_{\sigma_3}(\text{ST}) \cdots \oplus F_{\sigma_8}(\text{ST})$, and records $(\Pi, \text{role}_1, U_A, \{U_A, U_B, U_C\}, \{EPK_A, EPK_B, EPK_C\})$, $(\Pi, \text{role}_2, U_B, \{U_A, U_B, U_C\}, \{EPK_A, EPK_B, EPK_C\})$ and $(\Pi, \text{role}_3, U_C, \{U_A, U_B, U_C\} \{EPK_A, EPK_B, EPK_C\})$ as the completed session and SK^* in the list $\mathcal{L}_{SK}$.

   (d) Otherwise, $\mathcal{D}'$ computes the session key SK as the protocol, and records $(\Pi, \text{role}_i, U_{j_1}, \{U_{j_1}, U_{j_2}, U_{j_3}\}, \{EPK_{j_1}, EPK_{j_2}, EPK_{j_3}\})$ as the completed session and SK in the list $\mathcal{L}_{SK}$.

3. Establish(U_j, SPK_j): $\mathcal{D}$ sets U_j as a new party and SPK_j as the SPK of U_j as the definition. Note that U_A, U_B and U_C are not posed due to the freshness definition.

4. SessionReveal(sid):

   (a) If the session sid is not completed, $\mathcal{D}'$ returns an error message.

   (b) Otherwise, $\mathcal{D}'$ returns the recorded value SK.

5. StateReveal(sid): $\mathcal{D}'$ answers the ephemeral secret key and intermediate computation results of sid as the definition.

6. StaticReveal(U_j): $\mathcal{D}'$ answers the static secret key of U_j as the definition.

7. EphemeralReveal(sid): $\mathcal{D}'$ answers the ephemeral secret key of sid as the definition.

8. Test(sid): $\mathcal{D}'$ responds to the query as the definition.

9. If $\mathcal{A}$ outputs a guess $b' = 0$, $\mathcal{D}'$ outputs that the oracle is the PRF F^*. Otherwise, $\mathcal{D}'$ outputs that the oracle is a random function RF.

Analysis. For $\mathcal{A}$, the simulation by $\mathcal{D}'$ is same as the experiment $\mathbf{H}_3$ if the oracle is the PRF F^*. Otherwise, the simulation by $\mathcal{D}'$ is same as the experiment $\mathbf{H}_4$. Thus, if the advantage of $\mathcal{D}'$ is negligible, then $|\mathbf{Adv}(\mathcal{A}, \mathbf{H}_4) - \mathbf{Adv}(\mathcal{A}, \mathbf{H}_3)| \le negl$.

In $\mathbf{H}_4$, the session key in the test session is perfectly randomized. Thus, $\mathcal{A}$ cannot obtain any advantage from Test query.

Therefore, $\mathbf{Adv}(\mathcal{A}, \mathbf{H}_4) = 0$, and $\Pr[E_1 \wedge Suc]$ is negligible.

References

1. Bellare, M., Rogaway, P.: Entity Authentication and Key Distribution. In: Stinson, D.R. (ed.) CRYPTO 1993. LNCS, vol. 773, pp. 232–249. Springer, Heidelberg (1994)
2. Law, L., Menezes, A., Qu, M., Solinas, J.A., Vanstone, S.A.: An Efficient Protocol for Authenticated Key Agreement. Des. Codes Cryptography 28(2), 119–134 (2003)
3. Krawczyk, H.: HMQV: A High-Performance Secure Diffie-Hellman Protocol. In: Shoup, V. (ed.) CRYPTO 2005. LNCS, vol. 3621, pp. 546–566. Springer, Heidelberg (2005)
4. LaMacchia, B.A., Lauter, K., Mityagin, A.: Stronger Security of Authenticated Key Exchange. In: Susilo, W., Liu, J.K., Mu, Y. (eds.) ProvSec 2007. LNCS, vol. 4784, pp. 1–16. Springer, Heidelberg (2007)
5. Ustaoglu, B.: Obtaining a secure and efficient key agreement protocol from (H)MQV and NAXOS. Des. Codes Cryptography 46(3), 329–342 (2008)
6. Ustaoglu, B.: Comparing *SessionStateReveal* and *EphemeralKeyReveal* for Diffie-Hellman Protocols. In: Pieprzyk, J., Zhang, F. (eds.) ProvSec 2009. LNCS, vol. 5848, pp. 183–197. Springer, Heidelberg (2009)
7. Sarr, A.P., Elbaz-Vincent, P., Bajard, J.-C.: A Secure and Efficient Authenticated Diffie–Hellman Protocol. In: Martinelli, F., Preneel, B. (eds.) EuroPKI 2009. LNCS, vol. 6391, pp. 83–98. Springer, Heidelberg (2010)
8. Sarr, A.P., Elbaz-Vincent, P., Bajard, J.-C.: A New Security Model for Authenticated Key Agreement. In: Garay, J.A., De Prisco, R. (eds.) SCN 2010. LNCS, vol. 6280, pp. 219–234. Springer, Heidelberg (2010)
9. Fujioka, A., Suzuki, K.: Designing Efficient Authenticated Key Exchange Resilient to Leakage of Ephemeral Secret Keys. In: Kiayias, A. (ed.) CT-RSA 2011. LNCS, vol. 6558, pp. 121–141. Springer, Heidelberg (2011)
10. Boyd, C., González Nieto, J.M.: Round-Optimal Contributory Conference Key Agreement. In: Desmedt, Y.G. (ed.) PKC 2003. LNCS, vol. 2567, pp. 161–174. Springer, Heidelberg (2002)
11. Gorantla, M.C., Boyd, C., González Nieto, J.M., Manulis, M.: Generic One Round Group Key Exchange in the Standard Model. In: Lee, D., Hong, S. (eds.) ICISC 2009. LNCS, vol. 5984, pp. 1–15. Springer, Heidelberg (2010)
12. Garg, S., Gentry, C., Halevi, S.: Candidate Multilinear Maps from Ideal Lattices. In: Johansson, T. (ed.) EUROCRYPT 2013. LNCS, vol. 7881, pp. 1–17. Springer, Heidelberg (2013), http://eprint.iacr.org/2012/610
13. Joux, A.: A One Round Protocol for Tripartite Diffie-Hellman. In: Bosma, W. (ed.) ANTS-IV. LNCS, vol. 1838, pp. 385–393. Springer, Heidelberg (2000)
14. Al-Riyami, S.S., Paterson, K.G.: Tripartite authenticated key agreement protocols from pairings. In: Paterson, K.G. (ed.) Cryptography and Coding 2003. LNCS, vol. 2898, pp. 332–359. Springer, Heidelberg (2003)
15. Manulis, M., Suzuki, K., Ustaoglu, B.: Modeling Leakage of Ephemeral Secrets in Tripartite/Group Key Exchange. In: Lee, D., Hong, S. (eds.) ICISC 2009. LNCS, vol. 5984, pp. 16–33. Springer, Heidelberg (2010)
16. Fujioka, A., Manulis, M., Suzuki, K., Ustaoğlu, B.: Sufficient Condition for Ephemeral Key-Leakage Resilient Tripartite Key Exchange. In: Susilo, W., Mu, Y., Seberry, J. (eds.) ACISP 2012. LNCS, vol. 7372, pp. 15–28. Springer, Heidelberg (2012)
17. Diament, T., Lee, H.K., Keromytis, A.D., Yung, M.: The dual receiver cryptosystem and its applications. In: ACM CCS 2004, pp. 330–343 (2004)
18. Chow, S.S.M., Franklin, M., Zhang, H.: Practical Dual-Receiver Encryption: Soundness, Complete Non-Malleability, and Applications. Technical Report, UC Davis (2012), http://csiflabs.cs.ucdavis.edu/~hbzhang/dual.pdf

19. Fujioka, A., Suzuki, K., Xagawa, K., Yoneyama, K.: Strongly Secure Authenticated Key Exchange from Factoring, Codes, and Lattices. In: Fischlin, M., Buchmann, J., Manulis, M. (eds.) PKC 2012. LNCS, vol. 7293, pp. 467–484. Springer, Heidelberg (2012)

20. Canetti, R., Krawczyk, H.: Analysis of Key-Exchange Protocols and Their Use for Building Secure Channels. In: Pfitzmann, B. (ed.) EUROCRYPT 2001. LNCS, vol. 2045, pp. 453–474. Springer, Heidelberg (2001)

21. Chevallier-Mames, B.: An Efficient CDH-Based Signature Scheme with a Tight Security Reduction. In: Shoup, V. (ed.) CRYPTO 2005. LNCS, vol. 3621, pp. 511–526. Springer, Heidelberg (2005)

22. Cramer, R., Shoup, V.: Design and Analysis of Practical Public-Key Encryption Schemes Secure against Adaptive Chosen Ciphertext Attack. SIAM Journal on Computing 33, 167–226 (2004)

23. Smart, N.P.: Efficient Key Encapsulation to Multiple Parties. In: Blundo, C., Cimato, S. (eds.) SCN 2004. LNCS, vol. 3352, pp. 208–219. Springer, Heidelberg (2005)

Public Key Exchange Using Semidirect Product of (Semi)Groups

Maggie Habeeb[1,*], Delaram Kahrobaei[2,**], Charalambos Koupparis[3], and Vladimir Shpilrain[4,***]

[1] California University of Pennsylvania
habeeb@calu.edu
[2] CUNY Graduate Center and City Tech, City University of New York
dkahrobaei@gc.cuny.edu
[3] CUNY Graduate Center, City University of New York
ckoupparis@gc.cuny.edu
[4] The City College of New York and CUNY Graduate Center
shpil@groups.sci.ccny.cuny.edu

Abstract. In this paper, we describe a brand new key exchange protocol based on a semidirect product of (semi)groups (more specifically, on extension of a (semi)group by automorphisms), and then focus on practical instances of this general idea. Our protocol can be based on any group, in particular on any non-commutative group. One of its special cases is the standard Diffie-Hellman protocol, which is based on a cyclic group. However, when our protocol is used with a non-commutative (semi)group, it acquires several useful features that make it compare favorably to the Diffie-Hellman protocol. Here we also suggest a particular non-commutative semigroup (of matrices) as the platform and show that security of the relevant protocol is based on a quite different assumption compared to that of the standard Diffie-Hellman protocol.

1 Introduction

It is rare that the beginning of a whole new area of science can be traced back to one particular paper. This is the case with public key cryptography; it started with the seminal paper [2].

The simplest, and original, implementation of the protocol uses the multiplicative group of integers modulo p, where p is prime and g is primitive mod p. A more general description of the protocol uses an arbitrary finite cyclic group.

* Research of Maggie Habeeb was partially supported by the NSF-LSAMP fellowship.
** Research of Delaram Kahrobaei was partially supported by a PSC-CUNY grant from the CUNY research foundation, as well as the City Tech foundation. Research of Delaram Kahrobaei and Vladimir Shpilrain was also supported by the ONR (Office of Naval Research) grant N000141210758.
*** Research of Vladimir Shpilrain was partially supported by the NSF grants DMS-0914778 and CNS-1117675.

M. Jacobson et al. (Eds.): ACNS 2013, LNCS 7954, pp. 475–486, 2013.
© Springer-Verlag Berlin Heidelberg 2013

1. Alice and Bob agree on a finite cyclic group G and a generating element g in G. We will write the group G multiplicatively.
2. Alice picks a random natural number a and sends g^a to Bob.
3. Bob picks a random natural number b and sends g^b to Alice.
4. Alice computes $K_A = (g^b)^a = g^{ba}$.
5. Bob computes $K_B = (g^a)^b = g^{ab}$.

Since $ab = ba$, both Alice and Bob are now in possession of the same group element $K = K_A = K_B$ which can serve as the shared secret key.

The protocol is considered secure against eavesdroppers if G and g are chosen properly. The eavesdropper must solve the *Diffie-Hellman problem* (recover g^{ab} from g, g^a and g^b) to obtain the shared secret key. This is currently considered difficult for a "good" choice of parameters (see e.g. [5] for details).

There is an ongoing search for other platforms where the Diffie-Hellman or similar key exchange could be carried out more efficiently, in particular with public/private keys of smaller size. This search already gave rise to several interesting directions, including a whole area of elliptic curve cryptography. We also refer the reader to [6] for a survey of proposed cryptographic primitives based on non-abelian (= non-commutative) groups. A survey of these efforts is outside of the scope of the present paper; our goal here is to suggest a new key exchange protocol based on extension of a (semi)group by automorphisms. Our protocol can be based on any group, in particular on any non-commutative group. It has some superficial resemblance to the classical Diffie-Hellman protocol, but there are several distinctive features that, we believe, give our protocol important advantages. In particular, even though the parties do compute a large power of a public element (as in the classical Diffie-Hellman protocol), they do not transmit the whole result, but rather just part of it.

We also describe in this paper some particular instances of our general protocol. In particular, we suggest a non-commutative semigroup (of matrices) as the platform and show that security of the relevant protocol is based on a quite different assumption compared to that of the standard Diffie-Hellman protocol.

We mention another, rather different, proposal [8] of a cryptosystem based on the semidirect product of two groups and yet another, more complex, proposal of a key agreement based on the semidirect product of two monoids [1]. Both these proposals are very different from ours. Also, the extended abstract [3], despite the similarity of the title, has very little overlap with the present paper. In particular, the key exchange protocol in Section 3 of the present paper is brand new.

Finally, we note that the basic construction (semidirect product) we use in this paper can be adopted, with some simple modifications, in other algebraic systems, e.g. associative rings or Lie rings, and key exchange protocols similar to ours can be built on those.

2   Semidirect Products and Extensions by Automorphisms

We include this section to make the exposition more comprehensive. The reader who is uncomfortable with group-theoretic constructions can skip to subsection 2.1.

We now recall the definition of a semidirect product:

Definition 1. *Let G, H be two groups, let $Aut(G)$ be the group of automorphisms of G, and let $\rho : H \to Aut(G)$ be a homomorphism. Then the semidirect product of G and H is the set*

$$\Gamma = G \rtimes_\rho H = \{(g, h) : g \in G, \ h \in H\}$$

with the group operation given by
$$(g, h)(g', h') = (g^{\rho(h')} \cdot g', \ h \cdot h').$$
Here $g^{\rho(h')}$ denotes the image of g under the automorphism $\rho(h')$, and when we write a product $h \cdot h'$ of two morphisms, this means that h is applied first.

In this paper, we focus on a special case of this construction, where the group H is just a subgroup of the group $Aut(G)$. If $H = Aut(G)$, then the corresponding semidirect product is called the *holomorph* of the group G. We give some more details about the holomorph in our Section 2.1, and in Section 3 we describe a key exchange protocol that uses (as the platform) an extension of a group G by a *cyclic* group of automorphisms.

2.1   Extensions by Automorphisms

A particularly simple special case of the semidirect product construction is where the group H is just a subgroup of the group $Aut(G)$. If $H = Aut(G)$, then the corresponding semidirect product is called the *holomorph* of the group G. Thus, the holomorph of G, usually denoted by $Hol(G)$, is the set of all pairs (g, ϕ), where $g \in G$, $\phi \in Aut(G)$, with the group operation given by $(g, \phi) \cdot (g', \phi') = (\phi'(g) \cdot g', \phi \cdot \phi')$.

It is often more practical to use a subgroup of $Aut(G)$ in this construction, and this is exactly what we do in Section 3, where we describe a key exchange protocol that uses (as the platform) an extension of a group G by a cyclic group of automorphisms.

Remark 1. One can also use this construction if G is not necessarily a group, but just a semigroup, and/or consider endomorphisms of G, not necessarily automorphisms. Then the result will be a semigroup; this is what we use in our Section 6.

3   Key Exchange Protocol

In the simplest implementation of the construction described in our Section 2.1, one can use just a cyclic subgroup (or a cyclic subsemigroup) of the group $Aut(G)$

(respectively, of the semigroup $End(G)$ of endomorphisms) instead of the whole group of automorphisms of G.

Thus, let G be a (semi)group. An element $g \in G$ is chosen and made public as well as an arbitrary automorphism $\phi \in Aut(G)$ (or an arbitrary endomorphism $\phi \in End(G)$). Bob chooses a private $n \in \mathbb{N}$, while Alice chooses a private $m \in \mathbb{N}$. Both Alice and Bob are going to work with elements of the form (g, ϕ^r), where $g \in G$, $r \in \mathbb{N}$. Note that two elements of this form are multiplied as follows: $(g, \phi^r) \cdot (h, \phi^s) = (\phi^s(g) \cdot h, \ \phi^{r+s})$.

1. Alice computes $(g, \phi)^m = (\phi^{m-1}(g) \cdots \phi^2(g) \cdot \phi(g) \cdot g, \ \phi^m)$ and sends **only the first component** of this pair to Bob. Thus, she sends to Bob **only** the element $a = \phi^{m-1}(g) \cdots \phi^2(g) \cdot \phi(g) \cdot g$ of the (semi)group G.

2. Bob computes $(g, \phi)^n = (\phi^{n-1}(g) \cdots \phi^2(g) \cdot \phi(g) \cdot g, \ \phi^n)$ and sends **only the first component** of this pair to Alice. Thus, he sends to Alice **only** the element $b = \phi^{n-1}(g) \cdots \phi^2(g) \cdot \phi(g) \cdot g$ of the (semi)group G.

3. Alice computes $(b, x) \cdot (a, \ \phi^m) = (\phi^m(b) \cdot a, \ x \cdot \phi^m)$. Her key is now $K_A = \phi^m(b) \cdot a$. Note that she does not actually "compute" $x \cdot \phi^m$ because she does not know the automorphism $x = \phi^n$; recall that it was not transmitted to her. But she does not need it to compute K_A.

4. Bob computes $(a, y) \cdot (b, \ \phi^n) = (\phi^n(a) \cdot b, \ y \cdot \phi^n)$. His key is now $K_B = \phi^n(a) \cdot b$. Again, Bob does not actually "compute" $y \cdot \phi^n$ because he does not know the automorphism $y = \phi^m$.

5. Since $(b, x) \cdot (a, \ \phi^m) = (a, \ y) \cdot (b, \ \phi^n) = (g, \ \phi)^{m+n}$, we should have $K_A = K_B = K$, the shared secret key.

Remark 2. Note that, in contrast with the "standard" Diffie-Hellman key exchange, correctness here is based on the equality $h^m \cdot h^n = h^n \cdot h^m = h^{m+n}$ rather than on the equality $(h^m)^n = (h^n)^m = h^{mn}$. In the "standard" Diffie-Hellman set up, our trick would not work because, if the shared key K was just the product of two openly transmitted elements, then anybody, including the eavesdropper, could compute K.

4   Computational Cost

From the look of transmitted elements in our protocol in Section 3, it may seem that the parties have to compute a product of m (respectively, n) elements of the (semi)group G. However, since the parties actually compute powers of an element of G, they can use the "square-and-multiply" method, as in the standard Diffie-Hellman protocol. Then there is a cost of applying an automorphism ϕ to an element of G, and also of computing powers of ϕ. These costs depend, of course, on a specific platform (semi)group that is used with our protocol. In our first, "toy" example (Section 5 below), both applying an automorphism ϕ and computing its powers amount to exponentiation of elements of G, which can be done again by the "square-and-multiply" method. In our main example, in Section 6, ϕ is a conjugation, so applying ϕ amounts to just two multiplications of elements in G, while computing powers of ϕ amounts to exponentiation of two elements of G (namely, of the conjugating element and of its inverse).

Thus, in either instantiation of our protocol considered in this paper, the cost of computing $(g, \phi)^n$ is $O(\log n)$, just as in the standard Diffie-Hellman protocol.

5   "Toy Example": Multiplicative $\mathbb{Z}_p^*$

As one of the simplest instantiations of our protocol, we use here the multiplicative group $\mathbb{Z}_p^*$ as the platform group G to illustrate what is going on. In selecting a prime p, as well as private exponents m, n, one can follow the same guidelines as in the "standard" Diffie-Hellman.

Selecting the (public) endomorphism ϕ of the group $\mathbb{Z}_p^*$ amounts to selecting yet another integer k, so that for every $h \in \mathbb{Z}_p^*$, one has $\phi(h) = h^k$. If k is relatively prime to $p-1$, then ϕ is actually an automorphism. Below we assume that $k > 1$.

Then, for an element $g \in \mathbb{Z}_p^*$, we have:

$$(g, \phi)^m = (\phi^{m-1}(g) \cdots \phi(g) \cdot \phi^2(g) \cdot g, \ \phi^m).$$

We focus on the first component of the element on the right; easy computation shows that it is equal to $g^{k^{m-1}+\ldots+k+1} = g^{\frac{k^m-1}{k-1}}$. Thus, if the adversary chooses a "direct" attack, by trying to recover the private exponent m, he will have to solve the discrete log problem twice: first to recover $\frac{k^m-1}{k-1}$ from $g^{\frac{k^m-1}{k-1}}$, and then to recover m from k^m. (Note that k is public since ϕ is public.)

On the other hand, the analog of what is called "the Diffie-Hellman problem" would be to recover the shared key $K = g^{\frac{k^{m+n}-1}{k-1}}$ from the triple $(g, \ g^{\frac{k^m-1}{k-1}}, \ g^{\frac{k^n-1}{k-1}})$. Since g and k are public, this is equivalent to recovering $g^{k^{m+n}}$ from the triple $(g, \ g^{k^m}, \ g^{k^n})$, i.e., this is exactly the standard Diffie-Hellman problem.

Thus, the bottom line of this example is that the instantiation of our protocol where the group G is $\mathbb{Z}_p^*$, is not really different from the standard Diffie-Hellman protocol. In the next section, we describe a more interesting instantiation, where the (semi)group G is non-commutative.

6   Matrices Over Group Rings and Extensions by Inner Automorphisms

To begin with, we note that our general protocol in Section 3 can be used with any non-commutative group G if ϕ is selected to be a non-trivial inner automorphism, i.e., conjugation by an element which is not in the center of G. Furthermore, it can be used with any non-commutative semigroup G as well, as long as G has some invertible elements; these can be used to produce inner automorphisms. A typical example of such a semigroup would be a semigroup of matrices over some ring.

In the paper [4], the authors have employed matrices over group rings of a (small) symmetric group as platforms for the (standard) Diffie-Hellman-like key exchange. In this section, we use these matrix semigroups again and consider an extension of such a semigroup by an inner automorphism to get a platform semigroup for our protocol.

Recall that a (semi)group ring $R[S]$ of a (semi)group S over a commutative ring R is the set of all formal sums

$$\sum_{g_i \in S} r_i g_i$$

where $r_i \in R$, and all but a finite number of r_i are zero.

The sum of two elements in $R[G]$ is defined by

$$\left(\sum_{g_i \in S} a_i g_i \right) + \left(\sum_{g_i \in S} b_i g_i \right) = \sum_{g_i \in S} (a_i + b_i) g_i.$$

The multiplication of two elements in $R[G]$ is defined by using distributivity.

As we have already pointed out, if a (semi)group G is non-commutative and has non-central invertible elements, then it always has a non-identical inner automorphism, i.e., conjugation by an element $g \in G$ such that $g^{-1}hg \neq h$ for at least some $h \in G$.

Now let G be the semigroup of 3×3 matrices over the group ring $\mathbb{Z}_7[A_5]$, where A_5 is the alternating group on 5 elements. Here we use an extension of the semigroup G by an inner automorphism φ_H, which is conjugation by a matrix $H \in GL_3(\mathbb{Z}_7[A_5])$. Thus, for any matrix $M \in G$ and for any integer $k \geq 1$, we have

$$\varphi_H(M) = H^{-1}MH; \ \varphi_H^k(M) = H^{-k}MH^k.$$

Now our general protocol from Section 3 is specialized in this case as follows.

1. Alice and Bob agree on public matrices $M \in G$ and $H \in GL_3(\mathbb{Z}_7[A_5])$. Alice selects a private positive integer m, and Bob selects a private positive integer n.

2. Alice computes $(M, \varphi_H)^m = (H^{-m+1}MH^{m-1} \cdots H^{-2}MH^2 \cdot H^{-1}MH \cdot M, \varphi_H^m)$ and sends **only the first component** of this pair to Bob. Thus, she sends to Bob **only** the matrix

$$A = H^{-m+1}MH^{m-1} \cdots H^{-2}MH^2 \cdot H^{-1}MH \cdot M = H^{-m}(HM)^m.$$

3. Bob computes $(M, \varphi_H)^n = (H^{-n+1}MH^{n-1} \cdots H^{-2}MH^2 \cdot H^{-1}MH \cdot M, \varphi_H^n)$ and sends **only the first component** of this pair to Alice. Thus, he sends to Alice **only** the matrix

$$B = H^{-n+1}MH^{n-1} \cdots H^{-2}MH^2 \cdot H^{-1}MH \cdot M = H^{-n}(HM)^n.$$

4. Alice computes $(B, x) \cdot (A, \varphi_H^m) = (\varphi_H^m(B) \cdot A, \ x \cdot \varphi_H^m)$. Her key is now $K_{Alice} = \varphi_H^m(B) \cdot A = H^{-(m+n)}(HM)^{m+n}$. Note that she does not actually "compute" $x \cdot \varphi_H^m$ because she does not know the automorphism $x = \varphi_H^n$; recall that it was not transmitted to her. But she does not need it to compute K_{Alice}.

5. Bob computes $(A, y) \cdot (B, \varphi_H^n) = (\varphi_H^n(A) \cdot B, \ y \cdot \varphi_H^n)$. His key is now $K_{Bob} = \varphi_H^n(A) \cdot B$. Again, Bob does not actually "compute" $y \cdot \varphi_H^n$ because he does not know the automorphism $y = \varphi_H^m$.

6. Since $(B, x) \cdot (A, \varphi_H^m) = (A, y) \cdot (B, \varphi_H^n) = (M, \varphi_H)^{m+n}$, we should have $K_{Alice} = K_{Bob} = K$, the shared secret key.

7 Security Assumptions and Analysis

In this section, we address the question of security of the particular instantiation of our protocol described in Section 6.

Recall that the shared secret key in the protocol of Section 6 is

$$K = \varphi_H^m(B) \cdot A = \varphi_H^n(A) \cdot B = H^{-(m+n)}(HM)^{m+n}.$$

Therefore, our security assumption here is that it is computationally hard to retrieve the key $K = H^{-(m+n)}(HM)^{m+n}$ from the quadruple $(H, M, H^{-m}(HM)^m, H^{-n}(HM)^n)$.

In particular, we have to take care that the matrices H and HM do not commute because otherwise, K is just a product of $H^{-m}(HM)^m$ and $H^{-n}(HM)^n$.

A weaker security assumption arises if an eavesdropper tries to recover a private exponent from a transmission, i.e., to recover, say, m from $H^{-m}(HM)^m$. A special case of this problem, where $H = I$, is the "discrete log" problem for matrices over $\mathbb{Z}_7[A_5]$, namely: recover m from M and M^m. Even this problem appears to be hard; it was addressed in [4] in more detail. In particular, statistical experiments show that for a random matrix M, matrices M^m are indistinguishable from random.

In order to verify the robustness and security of our protocol, we have experimentally addressed two questions. The first question is whether or not any information about the private exponent n is leaked from transmission. That is, for a random exponent n, how different is the matrix $(M, \varphi_H)^n$ from N, where N is random? The second point that needs verification is to determine how different the final shared key is from a random matrix. More specifically, if Alice and Bob choose secret integers m and n respectively, how different is the matrix $(M, \varphi_H)^{n+m}$ from $(M, \varphi_H)^q$, where q is of the same bit size are $n + m$.

To perform the first experimental validation we worked over $M_3(\mathbb{Z}_7[A_5])$ and used random choices of $n \in [10^{44}, 10^{55}]$. We then looked at the two distributions generated by the first component of $(M, \varphi_H)^n$ and N, where M and N are random matrices. We need to verify that the two generated distributions are in fact indistinguishable. To this end we looked at the components of each matrix and counted the frequency of occurrence of each element of A_5. We repeated this process 500 times and generated a frequency distribution table for the two distributions.

From the table, we produced $Q - Q$ (quantile) plots of the entries of the two matrices: the first component of $(M, \varphi_H)^n$ and a random matrix N. Quantile plots are a quick graphical tool for comparing two distributions. These plots essentially compare the cumulative distribution functions of two distributions. If the distributions are identical, the resulting graph will be a straight line.

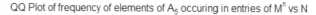

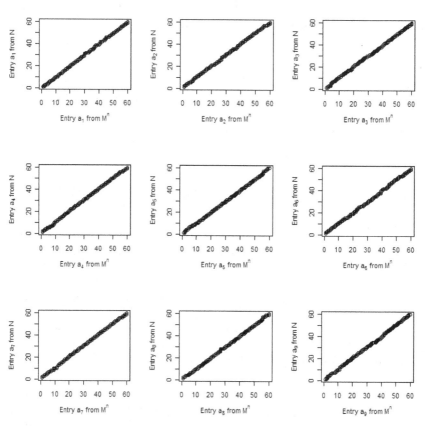

Fig. 1. Results for M^n vs. N

Figure 1 shows the resulting plots for this experiment. These graphs show that the two distributions are in fact identical, therefore suggesting that no information about a private exponent n is revealed by transmissions between Alice and Bob.

The second experiment we carried out was similar to the first one, except in this case we were comparing the first components of $(M, \varphi_H)^n$ and $(M, \varphi_H)^{a+b}$, where n, a and b are random and all of roughly the same bit size, i.e. all are integers from $[10^{44}, 10^{55}]$. This experiment helps address the DDH (decisional Diffie-Hellman) assumption by comparing the shared secret key to a random key and ensuring that no information about the former is leaked. See Figure 2 for the resulting $Q - Q$ plots. These 9 graphs suggest that the two distributions generated by these keys are in fact indistinguishable.

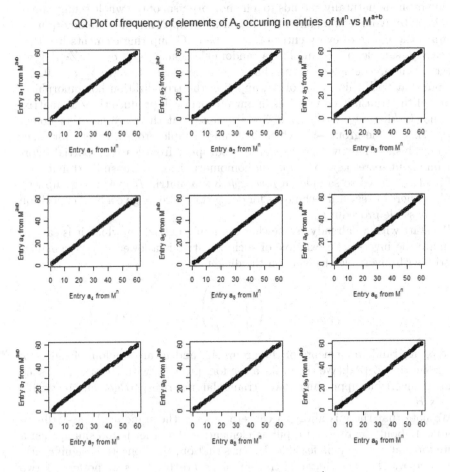

Fig. 2. Results for M^n vs. M^{a+b}

8   Parameters and Key Generation

Private exponents m and n should be of the magnitude of 2^t, where t is the security parameter, to make brute force search infeasible. Thus, m and n are roughly t bits long.

Public matrix M is selected as a random 3×3 matrix over the group ring $\mathbb{Z}_7[A_5]$, which means that each entry of M is a random element of $\mathbb{Z}_7[A_5]$. The latter means that each entry is a sum $\sum_{g_i \in A_5} c_i g_i$ of elements of the group A_5 with coefficients c_i selected uniformly randomly from $\mathbb{Z}_7$. Thus, although the bit complexity of the matrix M is fairly high ($9 \cdot 3 \cdot 60 = 1620$ bits), the procedure for sampling M is quite efficient. We want to impose one restriction on the matrix M though. There is a trivialization (sometimes called *augmentation*) homomorphism of the group ring that sends every group element to 1. This homomorphism naturally extends to a homomorphism of the whole semigroup of matrices. To avoid leaking any information upon applying this homomorphism, we want the image of every entry of M to be 0. Group ring elements like that are easy to sample: after sampling a random element $\sum_{g_i \in A_5} c_i g_i$ of $\mathbb{Z}_7[A_5]$, we select a random coefficient c_i and change it, if necessary, to have $\sum_i c_i = 0$.

Note that with this choice of M, applying the trivialization homomorphism to any of the transmitted matrices in our protocol will produce the zero matrix, thus not leaking any information. We also note that there are no other homomorphisms of the group A_5 (which is a finite simple group), except for inner automorphisms. This will prevent an eavesdropper from learning partial information about secret keys by applying homomorphisms to transmitted matrices.

Finally, we need to sample an *invertible* 3×3 matrix H over the group ring $\mathbb{Z}_7[A_5]$. There are several techniques for doing this; here we give a brief exposition of one possible procedure.

We start with an already "somewhat random" matrix, for which it is easy to compute the inverse. An example of such a matrix is a lower/upper triangular matrix, with invertible elements on the diagonal:

$$U = \begin{pmatrix} g_1 & u_1 & u_2 \\ 0 & g_2 & u_3 \\ 0 & 0 & g_3 \end{pmatrix}.$$

Here g_i are random elements of the group A_5, and u_i are random elements of the group ring $\mathbb{Z}_7[A_5]$. We then take a random product, with 20 factors, of such random invertible upper and lower triangular matrices, to get our invertible matrix H.

We note that there is always a concern (also in the standard Diffie-Hellman protocol) about the order of a public element: if the order is too small, then a brute force attack may be feasible. In our situation, this concern is significantly alleviated by the fact that our transmissions are products of powers of two different matrices rather than powers of a single matrix. Therefore, even if the order of one of the matrices happens to be small by accident, this does not mean that the product $H^{-m}(HM)^m$ will go into loop of a small size. Furthermore, since our matrix M is non-invertible, it does not have an "order", but rather a loop: $M^r = M^s$ for some positive $r \neq s$. The matrices HM and $H^{-m}(HM)^m$ are non-invertible, too, so they do not have an order either, but rather a loop. Detecting a loop is, in general, computationally much harder than computing the order of an invertible element.

9   Conclusions

We have presented a brand new key exchange protocol based on extension of a (semi)group by automorphisms and described some practical instances of this general idea. Our protocol can be based on any group, in particular on any non-commutative group. It has some superficial resemblance to the classical Diffie-Hellman protocol, but there are several distinctive features that, we believe, give our protocol important advantages:

• Even though the parties do compute a large power of a public element (as in the classical Diffie-Hellman protocol), they do not transmit the whole result, but rather just part of it.

• Since the classical Diffie-Hellman protocol is a special case of our protocol, breaking our protocol even for any cyclic group would imply breaking the Diffie-Hellman protocol.

• If the platform (semi)group is not commutative, then we get a new security assumption. In the simplest case, where the automorphism used for extension is inner, attacking a private exponent amounts to recovering an integer n from a product $g^{-n}h^n$, where g, h are public elements of the platform (semi)group. In the special case where $g = 1$ this boils down to recovering n from h^n, with public h ("discrete log" problem).

On the other hand, in the particular instantiation of our protocol, which is based on a non-commutative semigroup extended by an inner automorphism, recovering the shared secret key from public information is based on a different security assumption than the classical Diffie-Hellman protocol is. Namely, the assumption is that it is computationally hard to retrieve the shared secret key $K = h^{-(m+n)}g^{m+n}$ from the triple of elements $(h, \ h^{-m}g^m, \ h^{-n}g^n)$, assuming that g and h do not commute.

References

1. Anshel, I., Anshel, M., Goldfeld, D., Lemieux, S.: Key agreement, the Algebraic Eraser, and lightweight cryptography. Algebraic Methods in Cryptography, Contemp. Math. Amer. Math. Soc. 418, 1–34 (2006)
2. Diffie, W., Hellman, M.E.: New Directions in Cryptography. IEEE Transactions on Information Theory IT-22, 644–654 (1976)
3. Habeeb, M., Kahrobaei, D., Shpilrain, V.: A public key exchange using semidirect products of groups (extended abstract). In: Proceedings of the International Conference in Symbolic Computations and Cryptography, SCC 2010, Royal Holloway, University of London, Egham, United Kingdom (June 2010)

4. Kahrobaei, D., Koupparis, C., Shpilrain, V.: Public key exchange using matrices over group rings, Groups, Complexity, and Cryptology (to appear), http://arxiv.org/abs/1302.1625
5. Menezes, A., van Oorschot, P., Vanstone, S.: Handbook of Applied Cryptography. CRC-Press (1996)
6. Myasnikov, A.G., Shpilrain, V., Ushakov, A.: Group-based cryptography. Birkhäuser (2008)
7. Myasnikov, A.G., Shpilrain, V., Ushakov, A.: Non-commutative cryptography and complexity of group-theoretic problems. Amer. Math. Soc. Surveys and Monographs (2011)
8. Paeng, S.-H., Ha, K.-C., Kim, J.H., Chee, S., Park, C.S.: New public key cryptosystem using finite non abelian groups. In: Kilian, J. (ed.) CRYPTO 2001. LNCS, vol. 2139, pp. 470–485. Springer, Heidelberg (2001)

Leakage Resilient IBE and IPE under the DLIN Assumption

Kaoru Kurosawa[1] and Le Trieu Phong[2]

[1] Ibaraki University, Japan
kurosawa@mx.ibaraki.ac.jp
[2] NICT, Japan
phong@nict.go.jp

Abstract. In this paper, we show identity-based encryption (IBE) and inner product encryption (IPE) schemes which achieve the maximum-possible leakage rate $1-o(1)$. These schemes are secure under the decision linear (DLIN) assumption in the standard model. Specifically, even if $1-o(1)$ fraction of each private key is arbitrarily leaked, the IBE scheme is fully secure and the IPE scheme is selectively secure.

Mentioned results are in the bounded memory leakage model (Akavia et al., TCC '09). We show that they naturally extends to the continual memory leakage model (Brakerski et al., Dodis et al., FOCS '10). In this stronger model, the leakage rate becomes $1/2 - o(1)$.

Keywords: IBE, IPE, leakage resilience, DLIN assumption.

1 Introduction

1.1 Background

Leakage-resilient cryptography tries to deal with the question: "Can we do cryptography with *no perfect* secrets?". The question is natural, since generating and handling secrets is uneasy in practice, and furthermore they can be leaked by side-channel attacks. Following the research trend, in this paper we will focus on leakage resilient IBE, and IPE schemes. We will work in the following models of leakage: (1) the bounded memory leakage model of Akavia-Goldwasser-Vaikuntanathan [3], which allows arbitrary leakage on the private key for once. This is a basic model of leakage; and (2) the continual memory leakage model [12, 15], which allows leakage on the private key in many period of time. The holder of the key can update his/her key if suspecting any danger on it.

Recall that in identity-based encryption, first asked by Shamir [26], one can use arbitrary strings as public keys. The research on IBE is an active and stimulating field of cryptography, and so far IBE schemes have been constructed under several assumptions: pairing-related assumptions, quadratic residue-related assumptions and lattice-related assumptions. Akavia et al. [3] and Alwen et al. [4,5] showed that some variants of them are secure against private key leakage attacks.

M. Jacobson et al. (Eds.): ACNS 2013, LNCS 7954, pp. 487–501, 2013.

The security of these schemes is either analyzed in the random oracle model or is based on "non-static" assumption in the standard model. In the standard model, Chow et al. [14] presented a leakage resilient IBE with the leakage rate 1/3 under the DBDH assumption. Here, the leakage rate is defined as

$$\frac{\text{size of leakage permitted}}{\text{size of private key}}.$$

Also recall that inner product encryption [18] goes beyond IBE by allowing encryption under attribute vectors, while private keys are associated with predicate vectors. Let u be an encryption attribute vector, and id a predicate vector, then decryption works correctly if the inner product $\langle id, u \rangle = 0$. IPE implies IBE, since to test $id_{\text{IBE}} = id'_{\text{IBE}}$ for some identities id_{IBE} and id'_{IBE}, just check whether the inner product between vectors $id = (1, id_{\text{IBE}})$ and $u = (id'_{\text{IBE}}, -1)$ equals 0. IPE also serves as an important tool for designing encryption scheme supporting queries on encrypted data [11], and disjunctions, polynomial evaluation [18]. IPE is a class of functional encryption, which is a very active research field thanks to their potentially-wide applications.

Recently IPE (and hence IBE) have been realized under the DLIN assumption. This assumption, first formalized in [9], is very appealing and has been used in various works. In particular, Okamoto and Takashima [23] showed a general functional encryption scheme under DLIN. These schemes include IBE and IPE. Some other IBE schemes under DLIN are in [6, 8, 19]. All of these schemes are not in any leakage model. Thus in the literature, under the DLIN assumption,

- **On IBE:** No fully-secure, efficient, leakage-resilient IBE is known to achieve the maximum-possible leakage rate $1 - o(1)$.
- **On IPE:** While IPE is considerably examined recently, e.g. via [2, 18, 20, 23, 24], the case of *leakage resilient* IPE is still poorly understood. To our knowledge, no leakage resilient IPE scheme is proposed so far.

1.2   Our Contributions

Results on IBE. In this paper, we show the first leakage resilient IBE which achieves the maximum-possible leakage rate $1 - o(1)$ in the standard model under a static assumption. That is, it is fully secure under under the DLIN assumption even if $1 - o(1)$ fraction of each private key is arbitrarily leaked. Precise values are in Table 1.

Setting minimal $\ell = 3$ in Table 1, we obtain an instantiation with leakage rate $1/2 - o(1)$. The ciphertext overhead is only 6 group elements, and the private key also consists of only 6 group elements. When ℓ grows, the leakage rate increases, while ciphertexts and private keys get longer.

Note also in Table 1, the IBE in Lewko et al. [21], while tolerating master key leakage, has private key leakage rate $\frac{1}{1+c}(1 - o(1))$ for $c > 0$. This rate cannot reach $1 - o(1)$ simply because c cannot be 0 (see the caption of Table 1).

Technically, from the viewpoint of leakage resilience, our IBE scheme is based on the leakage resilient public key encryption scheme of Naor and Segev [22].

Table 1. Leakage resilient IBE in the standard model under static assumptions

IBE Schemes	Assumption	Ctxt. overhead (group elements)	Priv. key	Memory leakg. rate
Chow et al. [14]	DBDH	$|seed| + 3$	3	$1/3$
Lewko et al. [21]	$1, 2, 3$	L	L	$\frac{1}{1+c_1+c_3}(1 - O(1/L))$
Ours (Sect.4)	DLIN	2ℓ	2ℓ	$1 - \frac{3}{2\ell} - o(1)$
		6	6	$1/2 - o(1)$

Above, $c_1 = |p_1|/|p_2|, c_3 = |p_3|/|p_2|$ for some primes p_1, p_2, p_3, and $L \geq 4, \ell \geq 3$. The elements may belong to different groups, but we ignore that for simplicity. Assumptions $1, 2, 3$ are some new assumptions in composite bilinear groups (see [21] for details).

From the viewpoint of utilizing trapdoor in security reduction, it is motivated from the lattice based IBE of Agrawal, Boneh, and Boyen [1]. Perhaps surprisingly, a big difference from [1] is that we achieve the maximum possible leakage rate $1 - o(1)$, while the counterparts in [1] are not known to be leakage resilient. In fact, it seems hard to prove them leakage resilient; see Remark 1 below the proof of Theorem 2, but intuitively, the simulator in DLIN setting has more freedom than that in lattice.

Results on IPE. Going further, we propose the *first* leakage resilient IPE scheme in the literature. The scheme is selectively-secure, under the DLIN assumption, with private key leakage rate $1 - \frac{3}{2\ell} - o(1)$. Each private key consists of 2ℓ group elements, while the ciphertext overhead is of $(n+1)\ell$ group elements where n is the length of attributes. Taking $\ell = 3$ yields an instantiation with constant private key size of only 6 group elements, ciphertext overhead of $3n + 3$ group elements, with leakage rate $1/2 - o(1)$.

The design of our IPE scheme is partially inspired by the work of Agrawal et al. [2] in the lattice setting. Similarly to the above, the lattice-based scheme is not known to be leakage resilient.

Extensions to the Continual Memory Leakage Model. Above are works in which the private keys are leaked, while arbitrarily, but once. Brakerski et al. [12] and Dodis et al. [15] considered the continual memory leakage (CML) model , and particularly [12] presented a selectively secure IBE scheme. Yuen et al. [29] in turn examined the (even more stronger) continual auxiliary input model, and proposed an IBE scheme fully secure under three static assumptions in composite order pairing groups (as in [21]).

We show that our above schemes, with slight modifications, can be proved secure in the CML model of [12]. In particular, in the CML model, we present a fully secure IBE scheme, and a selectively secure IPE scheme. (Note that the IBE scheme in [12] is selectively secure, while ours is fully secure.) While selectively secure, our IPE scheme is apparently the first one in the CML model.

Recently, Yuen et al. [29] considered the continual auxiliary leakage model, where, roughly speaking, the adversary is given leakage $f(sk)$ where function f

Table 2. IBE schemes in the CML model

Schemes in CML model	Security	Memory leakage rate
Brakerski et al. [12]	selective	$\frac{1}{2} - o(1)$
Our IBE (Sect.6)	full	$\frac{1}{2} - o(1)$

is computationally uninvertible. (The schemes are in the composite-order pairing groups.) Hence their setting is different from ours.

Relation of DLIN and Lattice-Based Schemes. The CML-IBE scheme of Brakerski et al. [12] (under DLIN) can be seen as basing on Cash et al.'s IBE [13] (using lattices, not proven leakage resilient). The latter IBE is improved to obtain adaptive security in [1] in lattice setting (not proven leakage resilient). Our IBE schemes can be seen as [1]'s counterparts in DLIN setting.

Roadmap. Section 4 is for IBE, while Section 5 is for IPE. Section 6 is for IBE and IPE in the CML model. To illustrate the main ideas, we start with a simple IBE scheme, which is selectively-secure and leakage-resilient, in Sect.4.1.

2   Preliminaries

Notations. Denote $a \xleftarrow{\$} A$ as the process of taking a randomly from a set A. Let $|a|$ be the bit length of the element a, while $|A|$ be the order of the set. Let q be a prime. We call $\mathbb{PG} = (\mathbb{G}, \mathbb{G}_T, g, \hat{e} : \mathbb{G} \times \mathbb{G} \to \mathbb{G}_T)$ a pairing group if $\mathbb{G}$ and $\mathbb{G}_T$ are cyclic groups of order q. The element g is a generator of $\mathbb{G}$, and the mapping $\hat{e}$ satisfies the following properties: $\hat{e}(g, g) \neq 1$, and $\hat{e}(g^a, g^b) = \hat{e}(g, g)^{ab}$. Vectors and matrices will be in boldface. Let $\mathbb{Z}_q^{m \times n}$ be the matrices of size $m \times n$ over $\mathbb{Z}_q$. For an integer $r > 0$, the set $\mathrm{Rk}_r(\mathbb{Z}_q^{m \times n})$ contains matrices of rank r in $\mathbb{Z}_q^{m \times n}$. For a matrix $\mathbf{A}$ over $\mathbb{Z}_q$, let $g^{\mathbf{A}} = (g^{\mathbf{A}[i,j]})$, which is a matrix over $\mathbb{G}$. Also for the matrix $\mathbf{A} \in \mathbb{Z}_q^{m \times n}$, $\mathrm{span}(\mathbf{A}) = \{\mathbf{z}\mathbf{A} : \mathbf{z} \in \mathbb{Z}_q^{1 \times m}\}$, while $\ker(\mathbf{A}) = \{\mathbf{x} \in \mathbb{Z}_q^{n \times 1} : \mathbf{A} \cdot \mathbf{x} = \mathbf{0}\}$.

DLIN Assumption. The decision linear assumption, originated in [9], essentially says that given g_1^x and g_2^y, it's hard to distinguish g^{x+y} from random, where $x, y \xleftarrow{\$} \mathbb{Z}_q$, and $g_1, g_2, g \xleftarrow{\$} \mathbb{G}$. For our purpose, we will consider the matrix $g^{\mathbf{A}}$ where $\mathbf{A} \in \mathbb{Z}_q^{3 \times \ell}$ for $\ell \geq 3$ of rank either 2 or 3. If the DLIN assumption holds, then given $g^{\mathbf{A}}$, it is hard to tell the rank of $\mathbf{A}$. (See [22, full version] for a more general result.) More precisely, for any poly-time distinguisher $\mathcal{D}$, the advantage

$$\left| \Pr\left[b' = b : \begin{array}{l} \mathbf{A}_0 \xleftarrow{\$} \mathrm{Rk}_2(\mathbb{Z}_q^{3 \times \ell}), \mathbf{A}_1 \xleftarrow{\$} \mathrm{Rk}_3(\mathbb{Z}_q^{3 \times \ell}), \\ b \xleftarrow{\$} \{0,1\}, b' \leftarrow \mathcal{D}(g, g^{\mathbf{A}_b}) \end{array} \right] - \frac{1}{2} \right|$$

is negligible under the DLIN assumption.

Generalized Leftover Hash Lemma. A family of hash function $\mathcal{H} = \{h : X \to Y\}$ is called universal if $\Pr_{h \xleftarrow{\$} \mathcal{H}}[h(x) = h(x')] = 1/|Y|$ for all $x \neq x' \in X$.

Let U_Y be the uniform distribution on Y. We will make use of the following lemma.

Lemma 1 (cf. [1]). *Let $\mathcal{H} = \{h : X \to Y\}$ be a universal hash family. Let $f : X \to Z$ be some function. Then for any random variable T taking values in X, the statistical distance*

$$\Delta\Big((h, h(T), f(T)); (h, U_Y, f(T))\Big) \leq \frac{1}{2}\sqrt{\gamma(T) \cdot |Y| \cdot |Z|},$$

where $\gamma(T) = \max_t \Pr[T = t]$. In other words, if the right-hand side is negligible, $h(T)$ is almost random even given h and the side information $f(T)$.

3 Definitions for IBE and IPE in the Bounded Leakage Model

IBE and its Security Definitions. The scheme consists of algorithms (Setup, Extract, Enc, Dec). Setup generates the public parameters and master key (pp, msk). The public pp is the input to all other algorithms. Extract, on input msk and an identity id, returns the private key sk_{id}. Enc, on input id and a message m, returns a ciphertext c, which will be decrypted by an identity holding sk_{id}, yielding m.

We now recap both the leakage-resilient IND-sID-CPA security. Below, $0 < \rho_M < 1$ stands for the memory leakage rate. Maximum rate means $\rho_M = 1 - o(1)$, at which we aim.

Definition 1 (Leakage resilient IND-sID-CPA security). *An IBE scheme is IND-sID-CPA secure with leakage rate ρ_M if any poly-time adversary succeeds in the following game with probability negligibly close to $1/2$. In **identity selection**, the adversary decides and sends the target identity id^* to the challenger. Then the challenger runs Setup to generate (msk, pp), and sends pp to the adversary. In **private key generation**, the challenger runs $sk_{id^*} \leftarrow$ Extract(msk, id^*). In **query set 1**, the adversary makes queries of the following types:*

- *Extract queries $id \neq id^*$: the challenger returns $sk_{id} =$ Extract(msk, id) to the adversary.*
- *Leakage queries (leak_i, id) where id can be id^*, and leak_i is some function: the challenger returns $\text{leak}_i(sk_{id})$ to the adversary. These queries can be adaptive, and it is required that the sum of all lengths $|\text{leak}_i(sk_{id})|$ $(i \geq 1)$ is less than $\rho_M |sk_{id}|$.*
- *Reveal queries id: if $id \neq id^*$ was in a leakage query, namely sk_{id} was partially leaked, the adversary can even ask for the whole sk_{id}.*

*In **challenge** phase, the adversary gives equal-length m_0, m_1 to the challenger, who computes and sends back $c^* \leftarrow$ Enc(id^*, m_b) for $b \xleftarrow{\$} \{0, 1\}$. In **query set 2**, the adversary issues additional extract queries id with $id \neq id^*$ to which the challenger answers in the same manner as above. Finally, the adversary outputs a guess $b' \in \{0, 1\}$. It succeeds if $b' = b$.*

Definition 2 (Leakage resilient IND-ID-CPA security). *An IBE scheme is IND-ID-CPA secure with leakage rate ρ_M if any poly-time adversary succeeds in the following game with probability negligibly close to $1/2$. (1) The challenger runs* Setup *to generate (msk, pp), and sends pp to the adversary. (2) In* **query set 1,** *the adversary makes queries of the following types:*

- *Extract queries id. The challenger returns the private key $sk_{id} =$ Extract (msk, id) to the adversary.*
- *Leakage queries (leak_i, id) where leak_i is a function. The challenger returns $\mathsf{leak}_i(sk_{id})$ to the adversary.*
- *Reveal queries id: if id was in a leakage query, namely sk_{id} was partially leaked, the adversary can even ask for the whole sk_{id}.*

In **identity selection,** *the adversary decides and send the target identity id^* to the challenger. It is possible that id^* was appeared at leakage queries above, but not at reveal or extract queries.* **Query set 2** *is the same as query set 1 above, except there is no extract or reveal query on id^*. It is required that the sum of all lengths $|\mathsf{leak}_i(sk_{id})|$ $(i \geq 1)$ is less than $\rho_M|sk_{id}|$. In* **challenge** *phase, the adversary gives equal-length m_0, m_1 to the challenger, who computes and sends back $c^* \leftarrow \mathsf{Enc}(id^*, m_b)$ for $b \xleftarrow{\$} \{0,1\}$. In* **query set 3,** *the adversary can ask more of extract queries $id \neq id^*$. Finally the adversary outputs a guess $b' \in \{0,1\}$. It succeeds if $b' = b$.*

Inner Product Encryption. Consider algorithms (Setup, Extract, Enc, Dec) as in the IBE case. Here $\mathsf{Extract}(msk, id)$ produces a key sk_{id}, while $\mathsf{Enc}(u, m)$ with attribute u returns a ciphertext c of the message m. Decryption $\mathsf{Dec}(id, sk_{id}, c)$ works correctly if the inner product, defined over some group, between id and u is 0, namely $\langle id, u \rangle = 0$. Define $\mathsf{Pred}_{id}(u) = \mathtt{true}$ (resp. $\mathtt{false}$) iff $\langle id, u \rangle = 0$ (resp. $\neq 0$).

4   Proposed IBE Schemes under DLIN

4.1   Basic Scheme: Selectively Secure IBE

- Setup: Fix $\ell \geq 3$. The public parameters are $pp = (g^{\mathbf{A}_0}, g^{\mathbf{A}_1}, \mathbf{B}, g^{\mathbf{D}})$, where the matrices $\mathbf{A}_0, \mathbf{A}_1, \mathbf{B} \xleftarrow{\$} \mathbb{Z}_q^{2 \times \ell}$ and $\mathbf{D} \xleftarrow{\$} \mathbb{Z}_q^{2 \times 1}$. The master secret key is $msk = (\mathbf{A}_0, \mathbf{A}_1)$. For an identity $id \in \{0,1\}^*$, let $\mathbf{F}(id) = [\mathbf{A}_0 | \mathbf{A}_1 + H(id) \cdot \mathbf{B}] \in \mathbb{Z}_q^{2 \times 2\ell}$, where $H : \{0,1\}^* \to \mathbb{Z}_q$ is a collision-resistant hash function.
- Extract: on input id, return $sk_{id} = g^{\mathbf{v}}$ where $\mathbf{v} \in \mathbb{Z}_q^{2\ell \times 1}$ is a random vector such that

$$\mathbf{F}(id) \cdot \mathbf{v} = \mathbf{D}. \tag{1}$$

It is easy to generate such $g^{\mathbf{v}}$ from msk using linear algebra. See Appendix A for details.

- Enc: on input id and $M \in \mathbb{G}_T$, take $\mathbf{z} \xleftarrow{\$} \mathbb{Z}_q^{1\times 2}$ and compute $C = g^{\mathbf{z}\cdot\mathbf{F}(id)}$, $E = \hat{e}(g,g)^{\mathbf{z}\cdot\mathbf{D}} \cdot M$. Return (C, E) as the ciphertext.
- Dec: On input $sk_{id} = g^{\mathbf{v}}$ and $C = g^{\mathbf{c}}$, compute $K = \hat{e}(g,g)^{\mathbf{c}\cdot\mathbf{v}}$ and $M = EK^{-1}$, using the bi-linearity of $\hat{e}$, and return M. Note that if $\mathbf{c} = \mathbf{z}\mathbf{F}(id)$ then $\mathbf{c}\mathbf{v} = \mathbf{z}(\mathbf{F}(id)\mathbf{v}) = \mathbf{z}\mathbf{D}$, and the completeness follows.

Trapdoor. Instead of generating $\mathbf{A}_1$ as above, suppose that

$$\mathbf{A}_1 = \mathbf{A}_0\mathbf{R}^* - H(id^*)\mathbf{B}$$

for $\mathbf{R}^* \xleftarrow{\$} \mathbb{Z}_q^{\ell\times\ell}$ and the target identity id^*. Since $\mathbf{R}^*$ is freshly random, $\mathbf{A}_1$ is correctly distributed. The matrix $\mathbf{R}^*$ will be the trapdoor utilized in security proofs. Then from pp and $\mathbf{R}^*$, we can compute $sk_{id} = g^{\mathbf{v}}$ for any identity id ($\neq id^*$) as follows: First randomly choose $\mathbf{w} \in \mathbb{Z}_q^{\ell\times 1}$. Next consider a random $\mathbf{x} \in \mathbb{Z}_q^{\ell\times 1}$ such that

$$(H(id) - H(id^*))\mathbf{B}\mathbf{x} = -\mathbf{A}_0\mathbf{w} + \mathbf{D}. \tag{2}$$

It is easy to compute $g^{\mathbf{x}}$ from $\mathbf{B}, g^{\mathbf{A}_0}, g^{\mathbf{D}}$ given in pp. Let $\mathbf{v} = \begin{bmatrix} \mathbf{w} - \mathbf{R}^*\mathbf{x} \\ \mathbf{x} \end{bmatrix}$. We can compute $g^{\mathbf{v}}$ by using $g^{\mathbf{x}}$. This $\mathbf{v}$ satisfies eq.(1) because

$$\mathbf{F}(id)\mathbf{v} = [\mathbf{A}_0 | \mathbf{A}_0\mathbf{R}^* + (H(id) - H(id^*))\mathbf{B}] \cdot \begin{bmatrix} \mathbf{w} - \mathbf{R}^*\mathbf{x} \\ \mathbf{x} \end{bmatrix}$$
$$= \mathbf{A}_0(\mathbf{w} - \mathbf{R}^*\mathbf{x}) + (\mathbf{A}_0\mathbf{R}^* + (H(id) - H(id^*))\mathbf{B})\mathbf{x}$$
$$= \mathbf{A}_0\mathbf{w} + (H(id) - H(id^*))\mathbf{B}\mathbf{x} = \mathbf{D}$$

We show that the above $\mathbf{v}$ is correctly distributed. The solution space of eq.(1) has dimension $2\ell - 2$. On the other hand, $\mathbf{w}$ is chosen from a space of dimension ℓ, and the solution of eq.(2) has freedom $\ell - 2$ since $\mathbf{B} \in \mathbb{Z}_q^{2\times\ell}$. Hence the set of the above $\mathbf{v}$ is equal to the solution space of eq.(1), since $\ell + (\ell - 2) = 2\ell - 2$. The use of trapdoor is similar to [1] in lattice setting.

Theorem 2. *Under the DLIN assumption, the IBE scheme is IND-sID-CPA-secure, leakage resilient with rate $1 - \frac{3}{2\ell} - \frac{\eta}{\ell|q|}$ for η-bit security. The private key and ciphertext overhead are of 2ℓ group elements.*

When $\ell = 3$, the private key and ciphertext overhead are of 6 group elements, with leakage rate $1/2 - o(1)$.

Proof. Let **Game$_0$** be the real attack game against the IBE scheme (recalled in Appendix 3), and **Game$_1$** be the same as **Game$_0$** except that C^* in the challenge ciphertext is randomly chosen. We first show that the two games are indistinguishable under the DLIN assumption, whose formulation using matrices is in Sect.2. We will temporarily ignore leakage queries. Given an adversary $\mathcal{A}$

against the IBE scheme, we build $\mathcal{B}$ with input $g^{\mathbf{A}}$ telling whether random $\mathbf{A} \in \mathbb{Z}_q^{3 \times \ell}$ is of rank 2 or 3. After $\mathcal{A}$ announces the target id^*, $\mathcal{B}$ sets up the public parameter $pp = (g^{\mathbf{A}_0}, g^{\mathbf{A}_1}, \mathbf{B}, g^{\mathbf{D}})$ as follows: $g^{\mathbf{A}_0}$ is the first two rows of $g^{\mathbf{A}}$. Namely, $\mathbf{A}_0 \in \mathbb{Z}_q^{2 \times \ell}$ consists of the two rows of $\mathbf{A}$. $\mathcal{B}$ chooses $\mathbf{B} \xleftarrow{\$} \mathbb{Z}_q^{2 \times \ell}$ and $\mathbf{R}^* \xleftarrow{\$} \mathbb{Z}_q^{\ell \times \ell}$, and sets $\mathbf{A}_1 = \mathbf{A}_0 \mathbf{R}^* - H(id^*)\mathbf{B}$. Certainly $\mathcal{B}$ can compute $g^{\mathbf{A}_1}$ from $g^{\mathbf{A}_0}$. Note that by the above,

$$\mathbf{F}(id) = [\mathbf{A}_0 | \mathbf{A}_1 + H(id)\mathbf{B}] = [\mathbf{A}_0 | \mathbf{A}_0 \mathbf{R}^* + (H(id) - H(id^*))\mathbf{B}]$$

so particularly $\mathbf{F}(id^*) = [\mathbf{A}_0 | \mathbf{A}_0 \mathbf{R}^*]$. $\mathcal{B}$ chooses $\mathbf{v}^* \xleftarrow{\$} \mathbb{Z}_q^{2\ell \times 1}$ and sets $\mathbf{D} = \mathbf{F}(id^*) \cdot \mathbf{v}^* = [\mathbf{A}_0 | \mathbf{A}_0 \mathbf{R}^*] \cdot \mathbf{v}^*$ so that $\mathbf{D} \in \mathbb{Z}_q^{2 \times 1}$ is uniformly distributed, and $\mathcal{B}$ can compute $g^{\mathbf{D}}$ from $g^{\mathbf{A}_0}$. $\mathcal{B}$ then simulates $\mathcal{A}$ as follows. On extract query $id \neq id^*$, $\mathcal{B}$ computes and returns $g^{\mathbf{v}}$ as shown in the trapdoor above. On challenge query (M_0, M_1), denote $\mathbf{y}$ the third row of $\mathbf{A}$, let $b \xleftarrow{\$} \{0, 1\}$, and return

$$(C^*, E^*) = \left(g^{[\mathbf{y}|\mathbf{yR}^*]}, \hat{e}(g, g)^{[\mathbf{y}|\mathbf{yR}^*]\mathbf{v}^*} M_b \right).$$

Finally, $\mathcal{A}$ outputs b'. If $b' = b$, $\mathcal{B}$ bets that $\mathbf{A}$ is of rank 2. Otherwise, it guesses $\mathbf{A}$ is of rank 3. We will show that (C^*, E^*) is the ciphertext in $\mathbf{Game}_0$ if $\mathsf{rank}(\mathbf{A}) = 2$; while it is in $\mathbf{Game}_1$ if $\mathsf{rank}(\mathbf{A}) = 3$. First suppose that $\mathsf{rank}(\mathbf{A}) = 2$. Then $\mathbf{y}$ is a linear combination of the first two rows of $\mathbf{A}_0$, namely $\mathbf{y} = \mathbf{z}^* \mathbf{A}_0$ for some $\mathbf{z}^* \in \mathbb{Z}_q^{1 \times 2}$. Therefore

$$[\mathbf{y}|\mathbf{yR}^*] = [\mathbf{z}^*\mathbf{A}_0|\mathbf{z}^*\mathbf{A}_0\mathbf{R}^*] = \mathbf{z}^*[\mathbf{A}_0|\mathbf{A}_0\mathbf{R}^*] = \mathbf{z}^* \cdot \mathbf{F}(id^*),$$

showing that (C^*, E^*) is the ciphertext in $\mathbf{Game}_0$. Now suppose that $\mathsf{rank}(\mathbf{A}) = 3$. Then $\mathbf{y}$ is random in $\mathbb{Z}_q^{1 \times \ell}$. It suffices to prove that $\mathbf{d} = \mathbf{yR}^*$ is also random in $\mathbb{Z}_q^{1 \times \ell}$ even given $\mathbf{A}_0$, $\mathbf{U} = \mathbf{A}_0\mathbf{R}^*$, $\mathbf{y}$. It is easy to see that

$$\mathbf{A} \cdot \mathbf{R}^* = \begin{bmatrix} \mathbf{U} \\ \mathbf{d} \end{bmatrix}.$$

Therefore, for any $\mathbf{d}$, there exists a unique $\mathbf{R}^*$ such that the above equation holds because $\mathbf{A}$ is of full rank (with all but negligible probability). This means that $\mathbf{d}$ is random since $\mathbf{R}^*$ is random and hence C^* is random as expected. Thus $\mathbf{Game}_0$ and $\mathbf{Game}_1$ are indistinguishable under the DLIN assumption. Let p_i be the success probability $\Pr[b' = b]$ of the adversary $\mathcal{A}$ in $\mathbf{Game}_i$ for $i = 0, 1$, so that $|p_0 - p_1|$ is computationally negligible. We will show that $p_1 = 1/2$ to finish the proof. First C^* is now written as $C^* = g^{\mathbf{c}^*}$ for some $\mathbf{c}^* \in \mathbb{Z}_q^{1 \times 2\ell}$. Then $E^* = \hat{e}(g, g)^{\mathbf{c}^* \cdot \mathbf{v}^*} M_b$. Let $\alpha = \mathbf{c}^* \cdot \mathbf{v}^*$, and remember that $\mathbf{D} = \mathbf{F}(id^*) \cdot \mathbf{v}^*$, we obtain

$$\begin{bmatrix} \alpha \\ \mathbf{D} \end{bmatrix} = \begin{bmatrix} \mathbf{c}^* \\ \mathbf{F}(id^*) \end{bmatrix} \mathbf{v}^*.$$

In **Game**$_1$, $\mathbf{c}^*$ is random because C^* is random. Hence $\mathbf{c}^*$ is linearly independent of the two rows of $\mathbf{F}(id^*)$ with overwhelming probability. This means that α is random even given $\mathbf{c}^*, \mathbf{D}, \mathbf{F}(id^*)$ because $\mathbf{v}^*$ is random. Thus $E^* = \hat{e}(g,g)^\alpha M_b$ is random, and hence $p_1 = 1/2$ as claimed. Therefore the advantage of $\mathcal{A}$ against the IBE scheme $\left|p_0 - \frac{1}{2}\right| = |p_0 - p_1|$ is negligible under the DLIN assumption.

Let us now consider leakage resilience. Consider the leakage function f : $\mathbb{Z}_q^{2\ell} \to Z$ encoding of all leakage queries f_i, for some set Z (whose order is decided below). We want to prove that the distributions $(\mathbf{c}^*, \mathbf{c}^*\mathbf{v}^*, f(\mathbf{v}^*))$ and $(\mathbf{c}^*, \mathsf{U}_{\mathbb{Z}_q}, f(\mathbf{v}^*))$ are statistically indistinguishable, which means $\alpha = \mathbf{c}^*\mathbf{v}^*$ is randomly distributed conditioned on $\mathbf{c}^* = \log_g C^*$ and the leakage $f(\mathbf{v}^*)$.

Now re-consider the games, now with leakage queries. Since the simulator $\mathcal{B}$ for the DLIN assumption can generate $\mathbf{v}^*$, **Game**$_0$ and **Game**$_1$ are still indistinguishable even given $f(\mathbf{v}^*)$. Furthermore, in **Game**$_1$, $\mathbf{c}^*$ is random over $\mathbb{Z}_q^{1\times 2\ell}$. Let $h_{\mathbf{c}^*}(\mathbf{r}) = \mathbf{c}^*\mathbf{r}$ maps $\mathbf{r} \in \mathbb{Z}_q^{2\ell\times 1}$ to $\mathbb{Z}_q$. Since $\Pr_{\mathbf{c}^*}[h_{\mathbf{c}^*}(\mathbf{r}) = h_{\mathbf{c}^*}(\mathbf{r}')] = 1/q$ for $\mathbf{r} \neq \mathbf{r}'$, the function $h_{\mathbf{c}^*}$ is universal. Applying Lemma 1, the statistical distance of the above distributions is at most $\frac{1}{2}\sqrt{\gamma(\mathbf{v}^*) \cdot q \cdot |Z|}$ in which $\gamma(\mathbf{v}^*) = \max_{\mathbf{u}\in\mathbb{Z}_q^{2\ell}} \Pr[\mathbf{v}^* = \mathbf{u}]$.

Now that $\mathbf{v}^*$ is random satisfying $\mathbf{F}(id^*)\mathbf{v}^* = \mathbf{D}$, its freedom is $2\ell - 2$. Therefore $\gamma(\mathbf{v}^*) = q^{2-2\ell}$ so that we can choose $|Z| = q^{2\ell-3}2^{-2\eta}$ for η-bit security, namely the leakage on $\mathbf{v}^*$ can be of $(2\ell - 3)|q| - 2\eta$ bits. Therefore the leakage rate is $\frac{(2\ell-3)|q|-2\eta}{2\ell|q|} = 1 - \frac{3}{2\ell} - \frac{\eta}{\ell|q|} = 1 - o(1)$ as claimed. $\qquad\square$

Remark 1. In the above proof, the algorithm $\mathcal{B}$ against DLIN on input $g^{\mathbf{A}_0}$ chooses $\mathbf{v}^* \xleftarrow{\$} \mathbb{Z}_q^{2\ell\times 1}$ and sets $\mathbf{D} = \mathbf{F}(id^*) \cdot \mathbf{v}^* = [\mathbf{A}_0|\mathbf{A}_0\mathbf{R}^*] \cdot \mathbf{v}^*$, so that $\mathbf{v}^*$ is known to $\mathcal{B}$. In contrast, in the lattice based scheme of [1], the counterpart $\mathcal{B}$ against LWE has input $(\mathbf{A}_0, \mathbf{D})$, so it cannot choose $\mathbf{D}$, and hence cannot choose (short vector) $\mathbf{v}^*$ satisfying $\mathbf{D} = \mathbf{F}(id^*) \cdot \mathbf{v}^*(\bmod\ q)$. Therefore, it seems hard to prove the lattice-based scheme leakage resilient.

Remark 2. Above we neglect a technical point in estimating the leakage rate. Let G be an elliptic curve over $\mathbb{Z}_p$ for some prime p, so each element in G can be represented in about $|p|$ bits. Thus private key size is $|g^{\mathbf{v}^*}| \approx 2\ell|p|$ bits. Now, the rate is more precisely $\frac{|\mathrm{leak}(g^{\mathbf{v}^*})|}{|g^{\mathbf{v}^*}|} \approx \frac{(2\ell-3)|q|-2\eta}{2\ell|p|}$ so that to claim the rate $1 - o(1)$, we need $|q|/|p| \approx 1$. This requirement is satisfied by practical choices of q and p (e.g., [10, Table 1]). This remark applies as well for estimating the leakage rate in following sections.

4.2 Fully Secure Scheme under DLIN

For an identity id expressed as a bit sequence $id = id[1]||\cdots||id[m]$, consider the KEM in the previous section, yet employing the matrix

$$\mathbf{F}(id) = \left[\mathbf{A}_0 \middle| \mathbf{A}_0' + \sum_{i=1}^{m} id[i]\mathbf{A}_i\right] \in \mathbb{Z}_q^{2\times 2\ell},$$

where $\mathbf{A}_0, \mathbf{A}_1, \ldots, \mathbf{A}_m, \mathbf{A}_0' \in \mathbb{Z}_q^{2 \times \ell}$ are random matrices employed as the master secret key. In the public parameters, the matrices are given in the exponents.

Theorem 3. *Employing the above $\mathbf{F}(id)$, the IBE scheme in Section 4.1 is IND-ID-CPA-secure under the DLIN assumption, and leakage resilient with rate $1 - \frac{3}{2\ell} - \frac{\eta}{\ell|q|}$ for η-bit security. The private key and ciphertext overhead are of 2ℓ group elements.*

When $\ell = 3$, the private key and ciphertext overhead are of 6 group elements, with leakage rate $1/2 - o(1)$.

In the security reduction, we use the artificial abort technique of Waters [28]. (Note that one may also use the technique in [7] to improve the concrete security. Then the artificial abort technique is not needed either.) We construct a simulator $\mathcal{B}$ as follows. $\mathcal{B}$ first sets $J = 4Q$, where Q is the total number of (extract, leakage, reveal) queries of the adversary. $\mathcal{B}$ chooses $k \xleftarrow{\$} \{0, \ldots, m\}$ and $h_i \xleftarrow{\$} \mathbb{Z}_J$ for $i = 0, 1, \ldots, m$. $\mathcal{B}$ then constructs the matrices $\mathbf{A}_0'$ and each $\mathbf{A}_i$ (excluding $\mathbf{A}_0$) as $\mathbf{A}_0' = \mathbf{A}_0 \mathbf{R}_0 + (q - kJ + h_0)\mathbf{C}$, $\mathbf{A}_i = \mathbf{A}_0 \mathbf{R}_i + h_i \mathbf{C}$ where $\mathbf{C} \leftarrow \mathbb{Z}_q^{2 \times \ell}$, and $\mathbf{R}_i \leftarrow \mathbb{Z}_q^{\ell \times \ell}$. Then

$$\mathbf{F}(id) = \left[\mathbf{A}_0 \middle| \mathbf{A}_0 \left(\mathbf{R}_0 + \sum_{i=1}^m id[i] \mathbf{R}_i \right) + \left(q - kJ + h_0 + \sum_{i=1}^m id[i] h_i \right) \mathbf{C} \right]$$

Let $\alpha(id) = q - kJ + h_0 + \sum_{i=1}^m id[i] h_i$, $\mathcal{B}$ can succeed if $\alpha(id^*) = 0 \bmod q$, and for all extract query $id \neq id^*$, $\alpha(id) \neq 0 \bmod q$. This probability λ is lower bounded by $\lambda \geq \frac{1}{(m+1)J}\left(1 - 2\frac{Q}{J}\right)$ similarly to [28, Sect.5.2, eq.(1k)]. With probability λ,

$$\mathbf{F}(id^*) = \left[\mathbf{A}_0 \middle| \mathbf{A}_0 \left(\mathbf{R}_0 + \sum_{i=1}^m id^*[i] \mathbf{R}_i \right) \right],$$

so that the proof proceeds identically with that of Theorem 2 just by letting $\mathbf{R}^* = \mathbf{R}_0 + \sum_{i=1}^m id^*[i] \mathbf{R}_i$, except for that we use the artificial abort, and the following. $\mathcal{A}$ does not announce the target id^* at the beginning of the attack game in the model of full security. Hence $\mathcal{B}$ cannot compute $\mathbf{v}^*$ nor $g^\mathbf{D}$ as in the proof of Theorem 2.

1. Therefore $\mathcal{B}$ first chooses $\mathbf{E} \in \mathbb{Z}_q^{\ell \times 1}$ randomly and consider $\mathbf{D} \in \mathbb{Z}_q^{2 \times 1}$ such that $\mathbf{D} = \mathbf{A}_0 \mathbf{E}$. $\mathcal{B}$ computes $g^\mathbf{D}$ from $g^{\mathbf{A}_0}$ and $\mathbf{E}$. Moreover, given $\mathbf{D}$ and for $\mathbf{E} = (\mathbf{E}[1], \ldots, \mathbf{E}[\ell])^T$, we can let the components $\mathbf{E}[3], \ldots, \mathbf{E}[\ell]$ free in $\mathbb{Z}_q$ since $\mathbf{A}_0 \in \mathbb{Z}_q^{2 \times \ell}$ is of rank 2.
2. The simulation of queries depends on $\alpha(id)$: There are two cases for each query id. Firstly, if $\alpha(id) \neq 0$, the corresponding $\mathbf{v}$ is set to

$$\mathbf{v} = \left[\begin{array}{c} \mathbf{w} - (\mathbf{R}_0 + \sum_{i=1}^m id[i] \mathbf{R}_i) \mathbf{x} \\ \mathbf{x} \end{array} \right]$$

in which $\mathbf{w}$ is random and $\mathbf{x}$ satisfies $\alpha(id)\mathbf{Cx} = \mathbf{D} - \mathbf{A}_0\mathbf{w}$. Thus $sk_{id} = g^{\mathbf{v}}$ can be computed, and hence extraction, leakage, and reveal queries can be simulated. In the second case of target identity $id = id^*$, namely $\alpha(id^*) = 0$, $\mathcal{B}$ can again compute private key $sk_{id^*} = g^{\mathbf{v}^*}$ by solving $\mathbf{v}^* = (\mathbf{v}^*[1], \ldots, \mathbf{v}^*[2\ell])^T$ satisfying $[\mathbf{I}_\ell \mid \mathbf{R}^*] \cdot \mathbf{v}^* = \mathbf{E}$ where $\mathbf{I}_\ell \in \mathbb{Z}_q^{\ell \times \ell}$ is the identity matrix. It is easy to see that $g^{\mathbf{v}^*}$ is the private key for id^* by multiplying $\mathbf{A}_0$ from the left to both hand sides of the above equation. From that equation, we now have

$$\begin{bmatrix} \mathbf{v}^*[1] \\ \vdots \\ \mathbf{v}^*[\ell] \end{bmatrix} = \begin{bmatrix} \mathbf{E}[1] \\ \vdots \\ \mathbf{E}[\ell] \end{bmatrix} - \mathbf{R}^* \begin{bmatrix} \mathbf{v}^*[\ell+1] \\ \vdots \\ \mathbf{v}^*[2\ell] \end{bmatrix}.$$

Since $\mathbf{E}[3], \ldots, \mathbf{E}[\ell], \mathbf{v}^*[\ell+1], \ldots, \mathbf{v}^*[2\ell]$ can be independently random in $\mathbb{Z}_q$, there are $q^{(\ell-2)+\ell}$ choices for $\mathbf{v}^*$, so that it is from a space of dimension $2\ell - 2$ as expected. The leakage rate for η-bit security $1 - \frac{3}{2\ell} - \frac{\eta}{\ell|q|}$ is computed exactly as in the selective case.

5   Proposed IPE under DLIN

In this section we design the first leakage resilient IPE scheme under the DLIN assumption with leakage rate $1 - o(1)$. Several techniques in previous sections are re-utilized here. Below $id = (id_1, \ldots, id_n) \in \mathbb{Z}_q^n$. For $u = (u_1, \ldots, u_n) \in \mathbb{Z}_q^n$, decryption will work correctly if $\langle id, u \rangle = \sum_{i=1}^n id_i u_i = 0 \in \mathbb{Z}_q$. The scheme is as follows.

- Setup: Take $\mathbf{A}_i, \mathbf{S} \xleftarrow{\$} \mathbb{Z}_q^{2 \times \ell}$ and $\mathbf{D} \xleftarrow{\$} \mathbb{Z}_q^{2 \times 1}$, let $msk = (\mathbf{A}_0, \ldots, \mathbf{A}_n)$, and $mpk = (g^{\mathbf{A}_0}, \ldots, g^{\mathbf{A}_n}, g^{\mathbf{D}}, \mathbf{S})$.
- Extract$_{msk}(id)$: Return $g^{\mathbf{v}} \in \mathbb{G}^{2\ell \times 1}$ where $\mathbf{F}(id) \cdot \mathbf{v} = \mathbf{D}$ for $\mathbf{F}(id) = [\mathbf{A}_0 \mid \sum_{i=1}^n id_i \mathbf{A}_i]$.
- Enc$(u, M \in \mathbb{G}_T)$: Take $\mathbf{z} \xleftarrow{\$} \mathbb{Z}_q^{1 \times 2}$, return $C = g^{\mathbf{z}[\mathbf{A}_0 | \mathbf{A}_1 + u_1 \mathbf{S} | \cdots | \mathbf{A}_n + u_n \mathbf{S}]}$ and $E = e(g, g)^{\mathbf{z} \cdot \mathbf{D}} M$.
- Dec$_{g^{\mathbf{v}}}(id, C, E)$: From $C = g^{[\mathbf{y} | \mathbf{y}_1 | \cdots | \mathbf{y}_n]}$, compute

$$\prod_{i=1}^n (g^{\mathbf{y}_i})^{id_i} = g^{\sum_{i=1}^n id_i \mathbf{y}_i},$$

and hence obtain $g^{[\mathbf{y} | \sum_{i=1}^n id_i \mathbf{y}_i]}$. Pair that with the private key $g^{\mathbf{v}}$, obtaining $F = e(g, g)^{[\mathbf{y} | \sum_{i=1}^n id_i \mathbf{y}_i] \cdot \mathbf{v}} \in \mathbb{G}_T$ and finally compute the message $m = E \cdot F^{-1}$.

Correctness. Following directly from below equations: $[\mathbf{y} | \sum_{i=1}^n id_i \mathbf{y}_i] = [\mathbf{z}\mathbf{A}_0 | \mathbf{z} \sum_{i=1}^n id_i \mathbf{A}_i + \langle id, u \rangle \mathbf{z}\mathbf{S}] = [\mathbf{z}\mathbf{A}_0 | \mathbf{z} \sum_{i=1}^n id_i \mathbf{A}_i] = \mathbf{z}\mathbf{F}(id)$.

Theorem 4. *The above IPE scheme is leakage resilient under the DLIN assumption with leakage rate $1 - \frac{3}{2\ell} - \frac{\eta}{\ell|q|}$ for η-bit security.*

The proof will be given in the full version due to the lack of space.

6   Extensions to Continual Leakage

Identity-Based Encryption. To work in the CML model, following [12], we need to specify the algorithm $\mathsf{Update}_{\mathrm{user}}$ re-newing the private key of users. To do so, we choose $\mathbf{D} = \mathbf{0}$ working on $\ker(\mathbf{F}(id))$. The private key for identity $id \in \{0,1\}^m$ is $g^{[\mathbf{v}_1|\mathbf{v}_2]}$ for $\mathbf{v}_i \xleftarrow{\$} \ker(\mathbf{F}(id))$. To renew the key, the user takes $\mathbf{S} \xleftarrow{\$} \mathbb{Z}_q^{2\times2}$ and returns $g^{[\mathbf{v}_1|\mathbf{v}_2]\mathbf{S}}$. The nice effect of $\mathbf{D} = \mathbf{0}$ is that $[\mathbf{v}_1|\mathbf{v}_2]\mathbf{S}$ is also in the kernel space $\ker(\mathbf{F}(id)) \times \ker(\mathbf{F}(id))$ as required since

$$\mathbf{F}(id)[\mathbf{v}_1|\mathbf{v}_2]\mathbf{S} = [\mathbf{F}(id)\mathbf{v}_1|\mathbf{F}(id)\mathbf{v}_2]\mathbf{S} = \mathbf{0}.$$

However, due to $\mathbf{D} = \mathbf{0}$, we now have to consider an IBE scheme encrypting one bit. The scheme is described below, in which the parameter $\ell \geq 7$ (e.g., $\ell = 12$ for concreteness) affects the leakage rates. Below, security proofs are postponed to the full version due to space limit.

The IBE scheme is as follows. In Setup, the public params are $pp = (g^{\mathbf{A}_0}, \ldots, g^{\mathbf{A}_m}, g^{\mathbf{B}})$ for $\mathbf{A}_0 \xleftarrow{\$} \mathbb{Z}_q^{2\times3}$, and $\mathbf{A}_1, \ldots, \mathbf{A}_m, \mathbf{A}_0' \xleftarrow{\$} \mathbb{Z}_q^{2\times(\ell-3)}$. The master secret key is set to $msk = (\mathbf{A}_0, \ldots, \mathbf{A}_m, \mathbf{A}_0')$. Extract, for input $id \in \{0,1\}^m$, returns $sk_{id} = g^{\mathbf{v}}$ where $\mathbf{v} = [\mathbf{v}_1|\mathbf{v}_2]$ in which $\mathbf{v}_1, \mathbf{v}_2 \in \mathbb{Z}_q^{\ell\times1}$ satisfies $\mathbf{F}(id) \cdot \mathbf{v}_1 = \mathbf{F}(id) \cdot \mathbf{v}_2 = \mathbf{0}$ for

$$\mathbf{F}(id) = \left[\mathbf{A}_0 \middle| \mathbf{A}_0' + \sum_{i=1}^m id[i]\mathbf{A}_i\right] \in \mathbb{Z}_q^{2\times\ell}.$$

$\mathsf{Update}_{\mathrm{user}}$ chooses $\mathbf{S} \xleftarrow{\$} \mathbb{Z}_q^{2\times2}$ and returns $sk_{id}' = g^{[\mathbf{v}_1|\mathbf{v}_2]\cdot\mathbf{S}}$. Enc, encrypting $\mu \in \{0,1\}$, takes $\mathbf{c} \xleftarrow{\$} \mathrm{span}(\mathbf{F}(id)) = \{\mathbf{z}\mathbf{F}(id) : \mathbf{z} \in \mathbb{Z}_q^{1\times2}\}$ if $\mu = 0$; otherwise $\mathbf{c} \xleftarrow{\$} \mathbb{Z}_q^{1\times\ell}$, and returns the ciphertext $g^{\mathbf{c}}$. Dec, decrypting $g^{\mathbf{c}}$, computes $\hat{e}(g,g)^{\mathbf{c}\cdot\mathbf{v}}$ and if the result is $\hat{e}(g,g)^{\mathbf{0}}$, then returns $\mu = 0$, else returns $\mu = 1$.

Theorem 5. *The above IBE scheme is IND-ID-CPA-secure in the CML model under the DLIN assumption, with memory leakage rate $1/2 - o(1)$.*

Inner Product Encryption. The scheme is as follows. Setup takes $\mathbf{A}_{1\leq i\leq n}$, $\mathbf{S} \xleftarrow{\$} \mathbb{Z}_q^{2\times(\ell-3)}$, $\mathbf{A}_0 \xleftarrow{\$} \mathbb{Z}_q^{2\times3}$, and lets $msk = (\mathbf{A}_0, \ldots, \mathbf{A}_n)$, $mpk = (g^{\mathbf{A}_0}, \ldots, g^{\mathbf{A}_n}, \mathbf{S})$. $\mathsf{Extract}_{msk}(id)$ returns $g^{\mathbf{v}} = g^{[\mathbf{v}_1|\mathbf{v}_2]} \in \mathbb{G}^{\ell\times2}$ where with $j = 1, 2$,

$$\mathbf{F}(id) \cdot \mathbf{v}_j = \left[\mathbf{A}_0 \middle| \sum_{i=1}^n id_i\mathbf{A}_i\right] \cdot \mathbf{v}_j = \mathbf{0}.$$

$\mathsf{Update}_{\mathrm{user}}$ chooses $\mathbf{T} \xleftarrow{\$} \mathbb{Z}_q^{2\times2}$ and returns $sk_{id}' = g^{[\mathbf{v}_1|\mathbf{v}_2]\cdot\mathbf{T}}$. Algorithm $\mathsf{Enc}(u, M \in \{0,1\})$ takes $\mathbf{z} \xleftarrow{\$} \mathbb{Z}_q^{1\times2}$, and returns

$$C = g^{z[\mathbf{A}_0|\mathbf{A}_1 + u_1\mathbf{S}|\cdots|\mathbf{A}_n + u_n\mathbf{S}]}$$

if $M = 0$; otherwise choose $C \xleftarrow{\$} \mathbb{G}^{(\ell-3)n+3}$. $\mathsf{Dec}_{g^\mathbf{v}}(id, C = g^{[\mathbf{y}|\mathbf{y}_1|\cdots|\mathbf{y}_n]})$ computes $\prod_{i=1}^{n}(g^{\mathbf{y}_i})^{id_i} = g^{\sum_{i=1}^{n} id_i\mathbf{y}_i}$, and hence obtain $g^{[\mathbf{y}|\sum_{i=1}^{n} id_i\mathbf{y}_i]}$. Pair that with the private key $g^\mathbf{v}$, obtaining $F = e(g,g)^{[\mathbf{y}|\sum_{i=1}^{n} id_i\mathbf{y}_i]\cdot\mathbf{v}} \in \mathbb{G}_T$ and output $M = 0$ if $F = e(g,g)^\mathbf{0}$. Otherwise output $M = 1$.

Theorem 6. *The above IPE scheme is IND-sID-CPA-secure in the CML model under the DLIN assumption, with memory leakage rate* $1/2 - o(1)$.

References

1. Agrawal, S., Boneh, D., Boyen, X.: Efficient lattice (H)IBE in the standard model. In: Gilbert [16], pp. 553–572
2. Agrawal, S., Freeman, D.M., Vaikuntanathan, V.: Functional encryption for inner product predicates from learning with errors. Cryptology ePrint Archive, Report 2011/410 (2011), http://eprint.iacr.org/ (accepted to Asiacrypt 2011)
3. Akavia, A., Goldwasser, S., Vaikuntanathan, V.: Simultaneous hardcore bits and cryptography against memory attacks. In: Reingold, O. (ed.) TCC 2009. LNCS, vol. 5444, pp. 474–495. Springer, Heidelberg (2009)
4. Alwen, J., Dodis, Y., Naor, M., Segev, G., Walfish, S., Wichs, D.: Public-key encryption in the bounded-retrieval model. In: Gilbert [16] pp. 113–134
5. Alwen, J., Dodis, Y., Wichs, D.: Survey: Leakage resilience and the bounded retrieval model. In: Kurosawa, K. (ed.) ICITS 2009. LNCS, vol. 5973, pp. 1–18. Springer, Heidelberg (2010)
6. Bellare, M., Kiltz, E., Peikert, C., Waters, B.: Identity-based (lossy) trapdoor functions and applications. In: Pointcheval, Johansson [25], pp. 228–245
7. Bellare, M., Ristenpart, T.: Simulation without the artificial abort: Simplified proof and improved concrete security for Waters' IBE scheme. In: Joux, A. (ed.) EUROCRYPT 2009. LNCS, vol. 5479, pp. 407–424. Springer, Heidelberg (2009)
8. Bellare, M., Waters, B., Yilek, S.: Identity-based encryption secure against selective opening attack. In: Ishai [17], pp. 235–252
9. Boneh, D., Boyen, X., Shacham, H.: Short group signatures. In: Franklin, M. (ed.) CRYPTO 2004. LNCS, vol. 3152, pp. 41–55. Springer, Heidelberg (2004)
10. Boneh, D., Lynn, B., Shacham, H.: Short signatures from the Weil pairing. J. Cryptology 17(4), 297–319 (2004)
11. Boneh, D., Waters, B.: Conjunctive, subset, and range queries on encrypted data. In: Vadhan, S.P. (ed.) TCC 2007. LNCS, vol. 4392, pp. 535–554. Springer, Heidelberg (2007)
12. Brakerski, Z., Kalai, Y.T., Katz, J., Vaikuntanathan, V.: Overcoming the hole in the bucket: Public-key cryptography resilient to continual memory leakage. In: Trevisan [27], pp. 501–510, Full version available at http://eprint.iacr.org/2010/278.pdf
13. Cash, D., Hofheinz, D., Kiltz, E., Peikert, C.: Bonsai trees, or how to delegate a lattice basis. In: Gilbert [16], pp. 523–552
14. Chow, S.S.M., Dodis, Y., Rouselakis, Y., Waters, B.: Practical leakage-resilient identity-based encryption from simple assumptions. In: Al-Shaer, E., Keromytis, A.D., Shmatikov, V. (eds.) ACM Conference on Computer and Communications Security, pp. 152–161. ACM (2010)

15. Dodis, Y., Haralambiev, K., López-Alt, A., Wichs, D.: Cryptography against continuous memory attacks. In: Trevisan [27], pp. 511–520
16. Gilbert, H. (ed.): EUROCRYPT 2010. LNCS, vol. 6110. Springer, Heidelberg (2010)
17. Ishai, Y. (ed.): TCC 2011. LNCS, vol. 6597. Springer, Heidelberg (2011)
18. Katz, J., Sahai, A., Waters, B.: Predicate encryption supporting disjunctions, polynomial equations, and inner products. In: Smart, N.P. (ed.) EUROCRYPT 2008. LNCS, vol. 4965, pp. 146–162. Springer, Heidelberg (2008)
19. Lewko, A.B.: Tools for simulating features of composite order bilinear groups in the prime order setting. In: Pointcheval, Johansson [25], pp. 318–335
20. Lewko, A.B., Okamoto, T., Sahai, A., Takashima, K., Waters, B.: Fully secure functional encryption: Attribute-based encryption and (hierarchical) inner product encryption. In: Gilbert [16], pp. 62–91
21. Lewko, A.B., Rouselakis, Y., Waters, B.: Achieving leakage resilience through dual system encryption. In: Ishai [17], pp. 70–88
22. Naor, M., Segev, G.: Public-key cryptosystems resilient to key leakage. In: Halevi, S. (ed.) CRYPTO 2009. LNCS, vol. 5677, pp. 18–35. Springer, Heidelberg (2009), Full version available at
http://research.microsoft.com/en-us/um/people/gilse/
papers/KeyLeakage.pdf
23. Okamoto, T., Takashima, K.: Fully secure functional encryption with general relations from the decisional linear assumption. In: Rabin, T. (ed.) CRYPTO 2010. LNCS, vol. 6223, pp. 191–208. Springer, Heidelberg (2010)
24. Okamoto, T., Takashima, K.: Adaptively attribute-hiding (hierarchical) inner product encryption. In: Pointcheval, Johansson [25], pp. 591–608
25. Pointcheval, D., Johansson, T. (eds.): EUROCRYPT 2012. LNCS, vol. 7237, pp. 2012–2031. Springer, Heidelberg (2012)
26. Shamir, A.: Identity-based cryptosystems and signature schemes. In: Blakely, G.R., Chaum, D. (eds.) CRYPTO 1984. LNCS, vol. 196, pp. 47–53. Springer, Heidelberg (1985)
27. Trevisan, L. (ed.): 51th Annual IEEE Symposium on Foundations of Computer Science, FOCS 2010, Las Vegas, Nevada, USA, October 23-26, 2010. IEEE Computer Society (2010)
28. Waters, B.: Efficient identity-based encryption without random oracles. In: Cramer, R. (ed.) EUROCRYPT 2005. LNCS, vol. 3494, pp. 114–127. Springer, Heidelberg (2005)
29. Yuen, T.H., Chow, S.S.M., Zhang, Y., Yiu, S.M.: Identity-based encryption resilient to continual auxiliary leakage. In: Pointcheval, Johansson [25], pp. 117–134

A   Computing $g^{\mathbf{v}}$

We are given $\mathbf{F} \in \mathbb{Z}_q^{2 \times 2\ell}$, $g^{\mathbf{D}} \in \mathbb{G}^{2 \times 1}$ and want to compute $g^{\mathbf{v}} \in \mathbb{G}^{2\ell \times 1}$ where $\mathbf{Fv} = \mathbf{D}$. With all but negligible probability, we can assume that $\mathbf{F}$ as generated in our scheme is of rank 2. Solving the linear equation $\mathbf{Fv} = \mathbf{D}$ gives us $\left[\mathbf{I}_2 | \mathbf{F}_1 \right] \mathbf{v} = \mathbf{F}_2 \mathbf{D}$ where $\mathbf{I}_2$ is the 2×2 identity matrix, and $\mathbf{F}_1 \in \mathbb{Z}^{2 \times (2\ell-2)}$, $\mathbf{F}_2 \in \mathbb{Z}_q^{2 \times 2}$ depends on $\mathbf{F}$. Now let $\mathbf{w} = (\mathbf{v}[1], \mathbf{v}[2])^T$ and $\mathbf{w}' = (\mathbf{v}[3], \ldots, \mathbf{v}[2\ell])^T$ we have $\mathbf{w} + \mathbf{F}_1 \mathbf{w}' = \mathbf{F}_2 \mathbf{D}$, so that $\mathbf{w}'$ can be free, and $\mathbf{w} = \mathbf{F}_2 \mathbf{D} - \mathbf{F}_1 \mathbf{w}'$. Since $g^{\mathbf{D}}$ is given, we can compute $g^{\mathbf{w}}$, and hence $g^{\mathbf{v}}$ as well.

Batch Proofs of Partial Knowledge*

Ryan Henry and Ian Goldberg

Cheriton School of Computer Science
University of Waterloo
Waterloo, ON, Canada N2L 3G1
{rhenry,iang}@cs.uwaterloo.ca

Abstract. This paper examines "batch zero-knowledge" protocols for communication- and computation-efficient proofs of propositions composed of many simple predicates. We focus specifically on batch protocols that use Cramer, Damgård, and Schoenmakers' *proofs of partial knowledge* framework (Crypto 1994) to prove propositions that may be true even when some of their input predicates are false. Our main result is a novel system for batch zero-knowledge arguments of knowledge and equality of k-out-of-n discrete logarithms. Along the way, we propose the first general definition for batch zero-knowledge proofs and we revisit Peng and Bao's batch zero-knowledge proofs of knowledge and equality of one-out-of-n discrete logarithms (Inscrypt 2008). Our analysis of the latter protocol uncovers a critical flaw in the security proof, and we present a practical lattice-based attack to exploit it.

Keywords: Batch proof and verification, zero-knowledge, cryptanalysis, lattice-based attacks, efficiency.

1 Introduction

An interactive zero-knowledge proof is a conversation between two mutually distrusting parties—a *prover* and a *verifier*—in which the prover tries to convince the verifier that some proposition is true. The prover holds evidence (e.g., an NP witness) but is unwilling to reveal it to the verifier; the verifier, conversely, is skeptical of the prover and needs convincing. What makes a zero-knowledge proof special, therefore, is how much extra information the verifier learns: in a zero-knowledge proof, the verifier learns *nothing* beyond the veracity of the prover's claim. Zero-knowledge proofs have had profound implications for cryptography since Goldwasser, Micali, and Rackoff introduced them back in 1985 [20]; indeed, they are integral to many cryptographic protocols in the literature ranging from end-to-end verifiable voting schemes [11,25], through to anonymous blacklisting and reputation systems [2,3,33], protocols for priced symmetric private information retrieval [24], threshold ring signatures [34], verifiable mix networks [21,31], and cryptographic auctions [9], among others.

---

* An extended version of this paper is available [23].

M. Jacobson et al. (Eds.): ACNS 2013, LNCS 7954, pp. 502–517, 2013.

Alas, zero-knowledge does not come free. Each application above gives rise to at least one proposition whose "fan-in" scales with a critical system parameter (e.g., the global user count [11, 25, 34] or the size of a database [2, 3, 24, 33]). Take for example a prover and a verifier that share generators g, h and a set of n pairs of group elements $\{(g_i, h_i) = (g^{x_i}, h^{y_i}) \mid i \in [1, n]\}$ from some suitably chosen group $\mathbb{G}$. The prover wishes to prove a proposition about this entire *batch* of predicates, such as "For each $i \in [1, n]$, I know $x_i \in \mathbb{Z}_{|G|}$ such that $\log_g g_i = \log_h h_i = x_i$" or "For some $i \in [1, n]$, I know $x_i \in \mathbb{Z}_{|G|}$ such that $\log_g g_i = \log_h h_i = x_i$". The first ("AND") proposition naturally arises, e.g., in universally verifiable shuffling protocols for mix networks [31, §2.3], while the second ("OR") proposition arises, e.g., in coercion-resistant Internet voting when each voter must prove that she appears on the election roster [11, §3.5]. In both cases, the standard zero-knowledge protocols scale linearly with the number of inputs n: the prover and verifier each compute $\Theta(n)$ full-length exponentiations in $\mathbb{G}$, the verifier sends $\Theta(1)$ group elements to the prover, and the prover sends $\Theta(n)$ group elements to the verifier. In 1998, Bellare, Garay, and Rabin [4, 5] suggested *batch verification* techniques to reduce verification costs. Their "small exponents" batch verification test [5, §3.3] reduces the verifier's computation cost to just $\Theta(1)$ full-length exponentiations and $\Theta(\lambda n)$ multiplications in $\mathbb{G}$. The quantity λ is a *soundness parameter*; perhaps $\lambda = 40$ or 60 in practice.

Inspired by Bellare et al.'s small-exponent batch test, Peng, Boyd, and Dawson [30, §4.1] proposed a four-round *batch proof* of (complete) knowledge for the above "AND" proposition. The prover and verifier each compute just $\Theta(1)$ full-length exponentiations and $\Theta(\lambda n)$ multiplications in $\mathbb{G}$, the prover sends $\Theta(1)$ group elements to the verifier, and the verifier sends $\Theta(1)$ group elements and $\Theta(\lambda n)$ additional bits to the prover. More recently, Peng and Bao [28, §5.1] proposed a four-round batch proof of *partial knowledge* for the above "OR" proposition, which blends small-exponent batch testing with a special case of Cramer, Damgård, and Schoenmakers' proofs of partial knowledge [12]. The prover and verifier each compute just $\Theta(1)$ full-length exponentiations and $\Theta(\lambda n)$ multiplications in $\mathbb{G}$, and they each send and receive just $\Theta(1)$ group elements and $\Theta(\lambda n)$ additional bits. A handful of other papers [8, 15, 21, 24, 29, 31] propose similar "batch proofs" with similar "sublinear" costs.

Our contributions.

1. We propose a novel system for batch zero-knowledge arguments of knowledge and equality of k-out-of-n discrete logarithms for fixed $k \in [1, n]$. As special cases, we obtain batch "AND" proofs (n-out-of-n) and batch "OR" proofs (one-out-of-n). Our protocol has similar costs to the protocols of Peng et al. [30, §4.1] and of Peng and Bao [28, §5.1].

2. We present a practical, lattice-based attack on the soundness of Peng and Bao's protocol for batch zero-knowledge proofs of knowledge and equality of one-out-of-n pairs of discrete logatarithms. We provide a fix that uses *all-but-k mercurial commitments* [22], a variant of mercurial vector commitments [10] with a strengthened binding property.

3. We propose formal definitions for *batch zero-knowledge* proofs and proofs of knowledge. Prior treatments of batch proofs have been informal and ad hoc. Our new definitions address this with a *conciseness* property describing the asymptotic performance of a "batch" protocol relative to one formed by sequential composition of corresponding single-instance protocols.

Outline. We examine Peng and Bao's [28, §5.1] batch "OR" protocol in §2 and describe a practical attack on its soundness (the full details of which are in the extended version of this paper [23, Appendix A]). In §3, we discuss using *all-but-k mercurial commitments* [22] to repair Peng and Bao's protocol. In §4, we propose our formal definitions for batch zero-knowledge proofs and batch zero-knowledge proofs of knowledge. Our new batch protocol follows in §5. We list some potential applications in §6 and conclude in §7.

2   Peng and Bao's Batch Proof Protocol

The following protocol is due to Peng and Bao [28, §5.1]; they call it "batch ZK proof and verification of 1-out-of-n equality of logarithms". The protocol incorporates Bellare et al.'s small-exponent batch testing [5, §3.3] into both the proof and verification phases of an otherwise standard sigma protocol for proving knowledge and equality of one-out-of-n pairs of discrete logarithms. Both the prover P and verifier V know the same two generators g, h of an order-p group $\mathbb{G}$ and a set of n pairs of group elements $\{(g_i, h_i) \mid i \in [1, n]\}$, but only P knows an index $j \in [1, n]$ and exponent $x_j \in \mathbb{Z}_p^*$ such that $\log_g g_j = \log_h h_j = x_j$. The goal of the protocol is for P to convince V that she knows such a (j, x_j) pair without revealing any additional information. For ease of notation below, we define $H = [1, n] \setminus \{j\}$ for the (j, x_j) pair that honest P is proving knowledge of. We also introduce a *soundness parameter* $\lambda \in \mathbb{N}$, which tunes the cost versus soundness trade off in small-exponent batch testing.

Protocol 1. (Peng & Bao's Batch Proof of Partial Knowledge [28, §5.1]).

V1: Choose $t_i \in_R [0, 2^\lambda - 1]$ for each $i \in [1, n]$. Send $(t_1, \ldots, t_n)$ to P.

P2: Receive $(t_1, \ldots, t_n)$ from V. Choose $r \in_R \mathbb{Z}_p^*$ and $c_i \in_R [0, 2^\lambda - 1]$ for each $i \in H$. Compute $a = g^r \prod_{i \in H} g_i^{c_i t_i}$ and $b = h^r \prod_{i \in H} h_i^{c_i t_i}$. Send (a, b) to V.

V3: Receive (a, b) from P. Choose $c \in_R [0, 2^\lambda - 1]$ and send it to P.

P4: Receive c from V. Compute $c_j = c - \sum_{i \in H} c_i \bmod 2^\lambda$ and $v = r - t_j c_j x_j \bmod p$. Send $(c_1, \ldots, c_n, v)$ to V.

V5: Receive $(c_1, \ldots, c_n, v)$ from P. Output "true" if and only if $a \overset{?}{=} g^v \prod_{i=1}^n g_i^{c_i t_i}$, $b \overset{?}{=} h^v \prod_{i=1}^n h_i^{c_i t_i}$, and $c \overset{?}{\equiv} \sum_{i=1}^n c_i \pmod{2^\lambda}$, otherwise output "false".

Some remarks about Protocol 1 are in order. Perhaps surprisingly, we observe that V speaks before P does. What V sends to P in Step V1 is a list of short exponents for small-exponent batch testing. Step P2 ostensibly forces P to commit to an index j (such that $H = [1, n] \setminus \{j\}$) and to $\{c_i \mid i \in H\}$; if so, then V choosing

$c \in_R \left[0, 2^\lambda - 1\right]$ in Step V3 is equivalent to V choosing the missing $c_j \in_R \left[0, 2^\lambda - 1\right]$ for P in Step P4, which is exactly what we want for good soundness. It is trivial to verify that the protocol is *complete*; i.e., that honest P always convinces honest V. Theorem 1 in Peng and Bao's paper [28] states that "Soundness in [the above protocol] only fails with an overwhelmingly small probability [in the soundness parameter λ]." Their soundness proof works by computing an upper bound of $1/2^\lambda$ on the probability that the verification equations hold if $\log_g g_j \neq \log_h h_j$, given the following two implicit assumptions: 1) P committed to $H = [1, n] \setminus \{j\}$ and to $\{c_i \mid i \in H\}$ in Step P2, and 2) V chose c and (hence, c_j) uniformly at random from $\left[0, 2^\lambda - 1\right]$ in Step V3. *However, it is easy to see that the pair (a, b) of "commitments" that P computes and sends to V in Step P2 does not bind her to using $H = [1, n] \setminus \{j\}$; hence, the first implicit assumption in Peng and Bao's soundness proof is not guaranteed to hold when P is dishonest.* Dishonest P can exploit this observation to pass the verification equations even when the claimed equality of logarithms is false.

We give a high-level description of the attack below; interested readers can find further details in the extended version of this paper [23, Appendix A].

Overview of the attack. Suppose that P knows several (x_j, y_j) pairs such that $(g_j, h_j) = (g^{x_j}, h^{y_j})$ but $x_j \not\equiv y_j \pmod{p}$ for any of the known pairs. Partition the interval $[1, n]$ into two sets H and S, where S is a subset of indices for which P knows the above pair of discrete logarithms and H is a superset of indices for which she does not. (Note that in some reasonable settings P may know *every* such pair.) In Step P2, P computes (a, b) using this new H so that when V sends c to P in Step V3, P has $|S| - 1$ extra degrees of freedom to compute her response in Step P4. In particular, to find the missing $\{c_j \mid j \in S\}$ she solves the following system of two linear equations in $k = |S|$ unknowns:

$$0 \equiv \sum_{j \in S} c_j t_j \left(x_j - y_j\right) \pmod{p}, \text{ and} \tag{1}$$

$$c' \equiv \sum_{j \in S} c_j \pmod{2^\lambda}, \tag{2}$$

where $c' = c - \sum_{i \in H} c_i \bmod 2^\lambda$. Equation (1) implies $\sum_{j \in S} c_j t_j x_j \equiv \sum_{j \in S} c_j t_j y_j \pmod{p}$; hence, if P sets $v = r - \sum_{j \in S} c_j t_j x_j \bmod p$ in Step P4, then $(c_1, \ldots, c_n, v)$ will satisfy each verification equation in Step V5. Of course, if P just naively solves the above system of equations and obtains a solution $\{c_j \mid j \in S\}$ containing $c_{j'} \geq 2^\lambda$ for some $j' \in S$, then V may notice that P is cheating. Therefore, what P really wants to do is find a solution to the above system subject to the additional restriction that $0 \leq c_j < 2^\lambda$ for all $j \in S$.

A counting argument suggests that such "suitably small" solutions are plentiful whenever $k \cdot \lambda$ is "sufficiently large" compared to $\lg p$.[1] If **X** is an instance

---

[1] Recall that $k = |S|$ is a lower bound on the number of exponent pairs that P knows and that λ is the soundness parameter. Larger values of λ are *supposed* to result in better soundness; however, what we find is just the opposite: larger values of λ only make suitably small solutions more numerous and easier for P to find.

of the above system induced by some real interaction between P and honest V, then we heuristically expect the distribution of solutions of $\mathbf{X}$ to be uniform among all possible $\langle c_{j_1}, \ldots, c_{j_k} \rangle \in (\mathbb{Z}_p)^k$; in particular, we expect the proportion of solutions that are suitably small to be about $(2^\lambda/p)^k$. Now, only p^{k-1} of the $\langle c_{j_1}, \ldots, c_{j_k} \rangle \in (\mathbb{Z}_p)^k$ can satisfy Equation (1), and of these only about $p^{k-1}/2^\lambda$ can simultaneously satisfy Equation (2). This leads us to conclude that $\mathbf{X}$ has around $(p^{k-1}/2^\lambda)(2^\lambda/p)^k = (2^\lambda)^{k-1}/p$ suitably small solutions. In the extended version of this paper [23, Appendix A], we discuss how P can find one of these solutions by solving a short vector search problem in a particular lattice of dimension $k+3$. When k is reasonably small, P can use a standard basis reduction algorithm, such as Lenstra-Lenstra-Lovász (LLL) [27], to find a suitably small solution quickly. For example, setting $\lambda = 40$ and letting $\lg p \approx 160$, P only needs to know about $k = 5$ exponent pairs to find a suitably small solution, on average.

3   All-but-k Mercurial Commitments

Our attack on Protocol 1 is possible because P can wait until *after* she sees the challenge c in Step P4 to choose $k > 1$ of the c_i. If the "commitment" in Step P2 actually bound P to using $H = [1, n] \setminus \{j\}$ and $\{c_i \mid i \in H\}$, then Peng and Bao's upper bound of $1/2^\lambda$ on the protocol's soundness error would hold. For a direct fix, we therefore desire a special commitment that will (i) force P to commit to all but one component of $\langle c_1, \ldots, c_n \rangle$ in Step P2 and (ii) let P specify an arbitrary value for the missing component—*without betraying its position*—when she opens the commitment in Step P4. This, informally, is the binding and hiding guarantees that all-but-k mercurial commitments [22] provide when $k = 1$. More generally, an all-but-k mercurial commitment allows P to commit to an *arbitrary subset* of $n - k$ components from a length-n vector so that she is bound to these $n - k$ components but is still free to choose the k unspecified components prior to opening. V does not learn which components P chose before committing and which she chose after committing; V does, however, learn the total number 'k' of non-committed components in the opening.

We refer the reader to Henry and Goldberg's paper [22] for a more comprehensive exposition of all-but-k mercurial commitments, including formal statements of the security properties. For our own purposes, we use an abridged notation that abstracts away certain technical details.

Informal definition. An *all-but-k mercurial commitment scheme* is a 4-tuple of probabilistic polynomial-time (PPT) algorithms (ABK-Init, ABK-Commit, ABK-Open, ABK-Verify) that work as follows:

- ABK-Init outputs a common reference string PK for use in the other protocols.
- ABK-Commit_PK outputs commitments to vectors in which some subset of components is as-of-yet unspecified.

- ABK-OpenPK opens such commitments to fully specified vectors, explicitly revealing the number of components k not bound by the commitment.
- ABK-VerifyPK verifies the output of ABK-OpenPK, including the validity of k.

Repairing Peng and Bao's protocol. Given secure all-but-k mercurial commitments, it is straightforward to protect Protocol 1 from attacks like the one in §2. In Step P2, P commits to $\langle c_i \mid i \in H \rangle$ for $H = [1, n] \setminus \{j\}$. After V sends c to P in Step V3, P computes the missing c_j as usual, then opens the above commitment to $\langle c_1, \ldots, c_n \rangle$ as part of Step P4, proving as she does so that she chose only one of the c_j after committing in Step P2. Constructing a simulator and extractor for this augmented protocol is simple (and we give explicit simulator and extractor constructions for the generalized version in the extended version of this paper [23, Appendix B]); furthermore, the augmented protocol is still intuitively a "batch" protocol provided the all-but-k scheme satisfies certain efficiency requirements. In §5, we let the parameter k vary and thereby generalize the repaired Peng-Bao protocol to a system for batch zero-knowledge arguments of knowledge and equality of k-out-of-n discrete logarithms for any $k \in [1, n]$. Our protocol (including the special case just outlined) appears to be the first such batch protocol for $k \neq n$.

4   Defining Batch Zero-Knowledge Proofs

Several papers (many of which we listed in the introduction [8, 15, 21, 24, 29, 31]) propose protocols that implement what their respective authors refer to as "batch zero-knowledge proofs (of knowledge)". Regrettably, the community has no agreed upon definition of what constitutes a "batch" zero-knowledge proof. Prior works, consequently, justify the terminology using ad hoc arguments that contrast the communication cost (counted in terms of group elements transfers) and computation cost (counted in terms of full-length exponentiations) of their protocols with those of the most "obvious" protocols to implement proofs of the same propositions. (Peng et al. did suggest one definition for batch zero-knowledge proofs [30, Definition 1]; however, their definition fails to address asymptotic communication and computation costs, which we believe to be the key property differentiating the abovementioned "batch" proofs from their "non-batch" counterparts.) We therefore offer our own, very general definition for batch zero-knowledge proofs (of knowledge). We model our new definition after the standard zero-knowledge definitions (specifically, [18, Definition 3] and [6, Definition 3.1]), but add a new parameterized *conciseness* criterion that places asymptotic restrictions on how the communication and the computation costs of the interaction scale with respect to the size of the proposition under consideration. In particular, our conciseness criterion characterizes the asymptotic relationship between the number of predicates under consideration, the *soundness (or knowledge) error* of the proof, and the communication and computation cost of the resulting interaction.

Formal model. We model our prover P and verifier V as a pair of interactive functions and consider the interaction $\big(P_x(y), V_x(z)\big)$ that occurs when both functions take $x = \langle x_1, \ldots, x_n \rangle$ as common input, P takes $y = \langle y_1, \ldots, y_n \rangle$ as private input, and V takes string z as private auxiliary input. In general, some (possibly trivial) subset of (x_i, y_i) pairs satisfy a given witness relation R and z encodes arbitrary prior knowledge of V, such as a set of transcripts from earlier interactions with P. (The *transcript* of an interaction $\big(P_x(\cdot), V_x(z)\big)$, which is denoted by $\mathrm{tr}_{P,V}(x, z)$, is the string-valued random variable that records V's inputs and all correspondence with P up to the end of an interaction.)

We let φ_R be the function that maps pairs of n-tuples (x, y) as above to n-bit strings in which the ith bit is 1 if and only if $(x_i, y_i) \in R$. Intuitively, we are interested in interactions $\big(P_x(y), V_x(z)\big)$ that implement zero-knowledge proofs of the proposition $p(x, y)$ induced by R and a given language L in the following sense: $p(x, y)$ is true if and only if $\varphi_R(x, y) \in L$. Note that the pair (L, R) uniquely determines the proposition p, and vice versa. For ease of notation below, we define the language of n-tuples induced by (L, R) as $L_R = \big\{ x \mid \exists y \text{ for which } \varphi_R(x, y) \in L \big\}$. We parameterize the lengths of the x_i and y_i in a given interaction by τ; in particular, we assume throughout that the x_i are all τ bits long and the y_i are all $poly(\tau)$ bits long, where $poly(\cdot)$ is some fixed polynomial. Let $T = \big\{ (\{0,1\}^\tau)^n \mid \tau, n \in \mathbb{N}_{\geq 1} \big\}$ denote set of n-tuples of fixed-length strings.

Example. For propositions $p(x, y)$ asserting knowledge and equality of discrete logarithms, as in the actual protocols we consider in this paper, $R = \big\{ (x_i, y_i) = \big((g_i, h_i), y_i\big) \in \mathbb{G}^2 \times \mathbb{Z}_p \mid \log_g g_i = \log_h h_i = y_i \big\}$. If $p(x, y)$ is the "AND" proposition, then L is the language of strings comprised entirely of 1s; if $p(x, y)$ is the "OR" proposition, then L is the language of strings with nonzero Hamming weight. For our own k-out-of-n proofs, L is the language of strings with Hamming weight at least k. Note that in general P is proving *partial knowledge* of witnesses for R, with the strings in L reflecting which subsets of witnesses P might actually know.

We now recall the standard notions of a *simulator* for verifier V, which we use to formalize what it means for $\big(P_x(y), V_x(z)\big)$ to be "zero-knowledge", and of a *knowledge extractor* for P, which we use to formalize what it means for $\big(P_x(y), V_x(z)\big)$ to be a "proof of knowledge".

Definition 1. A probabilistic function S_{V^*} is a *simulator* for verifier-language pair (V^*, L_R) if the probability ensembles $\big\{ \mathrm{tr}_{P,V^*}(x, z) \big\}_{x \in L_R}$ and $\big\{ S_{V^*}(x, z) \big\}_{x \in L_R}$ are (computationally, statistically, or perfectly [17, Definitions 3,4]) indistinguishable, where $S_{V^*}(x, z)$ is the string-valued random variable describing the output of S_{V^*} on input (x, z).

An *oracle machine* for P^* is a function E^{P^*} that is endowed with *rewinding black box oracle access* to P^*. In other words, E^{P^*} is able to 1) submit arbitrary challenges to P^* and get truthful responses in a single time step, and 2) "rewind" P^* to a previous state to get several responses for the same input and random coin flips but different challenges. (Note that E^{P^*} is generally *not* privy to P^*'s inputs or internal state.)

Definition 2. Let $\kappa\colon T \to [0,1]$ and let $q(x)$ denote the probability that V outputs "true" in $\bigl(P_x^*(y), V_x(z)\bigr)$. An oracle machine E^{P^*} is a *knowledge extractor* (with knowledge error $\kappa(\cdot)$) for the prover-language pair (P^*, L_R) if there exists a positive polynomial $g(\cdot)$ such that, for all n-tuples $x \in L_R$, if $q(x) \geq \kappa(x)$ then, with probability at least $\frac{q(x) - \kappa(x)}{g(|x|)}$, $E^{P^*}(x)$ outputs an n-tuple y' for which $\varphi_R(x, y') \in L$.

Given the above definitions, we formally define what it means for a pair of interactive functions to implement a system of *batch zero-knowledge proofs* or a system of *batch zero-knowledge proofs of knowledge* for the language-relation pair (L, R). What sets our Definition 3 apart from the standard zero-knowledge definitions is that we include an explicit *conciseness* condition, which characterizes the cost of proving $\varphi_R((x_1, \ldots, x_n), (y_1, \ldots, y_n)) \in L$ in terms of the cost of proving $(x_1, y_1) \in R$.

For example, consider an interactive protocol A between P and V in which, on common input $x_0 \in \{0,1\}^\tau$, P convinces V that there exists (or, perhaps, that it "knows") some y_0 such that $(x_0, y_0) \in R$. Let $a_0(\tau)$ and $a_1(\tau)$ respectively denote the computation cost (for both P and V) and the bidirectional communication cost of A. Now, consider a second interactive protocol B between P and V in which, on common input $x \in (\{0,1\}^\tau)^n$, P convinces V that there exists (or it "knows") some y such that $\varphi_R(x, y) \in L$. Let $b_0(\tau, n)$ and $b_1(\tau, n)$ respectively denote the computation cost (for both P and V) and the bidirectional communication cost of B. For a fixed pair of constants $\alpha, \beta \in [0,1]$, we say that B is (α, β)-*concise* if there exists a constant $\delta > 0$ such that, for all $\epsilon > 0$, we have

$$b_0(\tau, n) \in O\bigl(n^\alpha a_0(\tau) + n^{\beta+\epsilon}\tilde{a}_0(\tau)\bigr) \text{ for some } \tilde{a}_0(\tau) \in o\bigl(a_0(\tau)^{1-\delta}\bigr),$$

and

$$b_1(\tau, n) \in O\bigl(n^\alpha a_1(\tau) + n^{\beta+\epsilon}\tilde{a}_1(\tau)\bigr) \text{ for some } \tilde{a}_1(\tau) \in o\bigl(a_1(\tau)^{1-\delta}\bigr).$$

(That is, the computation cost and communication cost of B grow no faster than n^α times the corresponding cost of A plus at most about n^β times some function that grows at least polynomially slower than the corresponding cost of A as τ grows large. The ϵ and δ factors are present so that we may ignore the contribution of polylogarithmic terms.) Recalling that $\alpha, \beta \in [0,1]$, we call B a *batch proof (of knowledge)* for (L, R) if it is (α, β)-concise for any $\alpha < 1$, or, very roughly, if the cost of the protocol grows slower than n times the cost of A as we let both n and τ tend to infinity.

Example.

1. Consider Peng et al.'s protocol for proofs of complete knowledge [30, §4.1], our repaired version of Peng and Bao's protocol in §3 for proofs of partial knowledge, and the forthcoming protocol in §5 for proofs of partial knowledge. In each, we find that $a_0(\tau) \in \Omega\bigl(\tau^2 \lg^2 \tau\bigr)$ and $a_1(\tau) \in \Omega(\tau)$ while, for all $\epsilon > 0$ and for any soundness parameter $\lambda \in \mathbb{N}$, we find that $b_0(\tau, n) \in O\bigl(a_0(\tau) + n^{1+\epsilon}\lambda\tau \lg^2 \tau\bigr)$ and $b_1(\tau, n) \in O\bigl(a_1(\tau) + n\lambda\bigr).$[2] For any fixed $\delta < 1/2$, we have that $\tilde{a}_0(\tau) =$

---

[2] We assume here that multiplication in $\mathbb{G}$ requires $O(\tau \lg \tau \lg \lg \tau) \in O(\tau \lg^2 \tau)$ bit operations using the Fast Fourier Transform (FFT) [14].

$\lambda \tau \lg^2 \tau \in o(a_0(\tau)^{1-\delta})$ and $\tilde{a}_1(\tau) = \lambda \in o(a_1(\tau)^{1-\delta})$, and therefore each of these protocols is $(0, 1)$-concise; moreover, since $\alpha = 0 < 1$, each protocol satisfies our conciseness criterion for a batch proof of knowledge.

2. Brands, Demuynck, and De Decker describe a protocol [8, §3.4] to prove that a given commitment commits to a different value than every other commitment on a list. As in the previous example, we find that $a_0(\tau) \in \Omega(\tau^2 \lg^2 \tau)$ and $a_1(\tau) \in \Omega(\tau)$ but, in this case, we have $b_0(\tau, n) \in O(n^{1/2}\tau^2 \lg^2 \tau)$ and $b_1(\tau, n) \in O(n^{1/2}\tau)$. Thus, letting $\delta = 1/2$ and letting $\tilde{a}_0(\tau)$ and $\tilde{a}_1(\tau)$ be arbitrary constant functions, we see that Brands et al.'s protocol is $(\frac{1}{2}, 0)$-concise; moreover, since $\alpha = \frac{1}{2} < 1$, it satisfies our conciseness criterion for a batch proof.

Definition 3. (System of batch zero-knowledge proofs (of knowledge)). Let $\Lambda \colon \mathbb{N} \to \mathbb{N}$ be a nondecreasing *soundness function* and let $\alpha, \beta \in [0, 1]$ be constants such that $\alpha < 1$. An interactive protocol $(P_x(y), V_x(z))$ is a *system of (α, β, Λ)-batch zero-knowledge proofs* for the language-relation pair (L, R) if there exists a negligible function $\varepsilon_0 \colon \mathbb{N} \to \mathbb{R}$ for which $(P_x(y), V_x(z))$ satisfies each of the following four conditions.

1. **Complete:** For any $n \in \mathbb{N}$ and pair (x, y) such that $\varphi_R(x, y) \in L$, if y is input to honest P and x is input to P and honest V, then V outputs "true".
2. **(Unconditionally) sound:** For every (possibly malicious) prover P^*, $\tau \in \mathbb{N}$, $n \in \mathbb{N}$, and $x \in (\{0,1\}^\tau)^n \setminus L_R$, if P^* and honest V receive x as common input then, with probability at least $1 - \varepsilon_0(\Lambda(\tau))$, V outputs "false".
3. **(General) zero-knowledge:** For every (possibly malicious) PPT verifier V^*, there exists a PPT simulator S_{V^*} for (V^*, L_R).
4. **(α, β)-concise:** If $a_0(\tau)$ and $a_1(\tau)$ respectively denote the computation and communication cost of $(P_x(y), V_x(z))$ when n is fixed as 1, then there exists some constant $\delta > 0$ and functions $\tilde{a}_0(\tau) \in o(a_0(\tau)^{1-\delta})$ and $\tilde{a}_1(\tau) \in o(a_1(\tau)^{1-\delta})$ such that, for every $\epsilon > 0$, we have that
   a. for every (possibly malicious) PPT verifier V^*, $\tau \in \mathbb{N}$, and pair (x, y) such that $\varphi_R(x, y) \in L$, if y is input to honest P and x is input to P and V^*, then P runs in $O(n^\alpha a_0(\tau) + n^{\beta+\epsilon}\tilde{a}_0(\tau))$ time and sends $O(n^\alpha a_1(\tau) + n^{\beta+\epsilon}\tilde{a}_1(\tau))$ bits to V; and
   b. for every (possibly malicious) prover P^*, $\tau \in \mathbb{N}$, and n-tuple x, if x is input to P^* and honest V, then V runs in $O(n^\alpha a_0(\tau) + n^{\beta+\epsilon}\tilde{a}_0(\tau))$ time and sends $O(n^\alpha a_1(\tau) + n^{\beta+\epsilon}\tilde{a}_1(\tau))$ bits to P^*.

If $(P_x(y), V_x(z))$ additionally satisfies the following condition, then it is a system of (α, β, Λ)-batch zero-knowledge proofs *of knowledge* for (L, R).

5. **(Unconditionally) knowledge extractable:** There exists an oracle machine E and function $\kappa \colon T \to [0, 1]$ such that, for every (possibly malicious) prover P^*, E^{P^*} is an expected PPT knowledge extractor for (P^*, L_R) with knowledge error $\kappa(\cdot) \leq \varepsilon_0(\Lambda(\tau))$.

We also consider the following two (standard) relaxations of the above definition. First, if $(P_x(y), V_x(z))$ satisfies Conditions 1, 2, 4 (and 5) as stated above, but it only satisfies the weaker Condition 3b as stated below (instead of Condition 3), then it is a system of *honest-verifier* (α, β, Λ)-batch zero-knowledge proofs (of knowledge) for (L, R).

3b. **(Honest-verifier) zero-knowledge:** There exists a PPT simulator S_V for (V, L_R), where V is the *honest verifier*.

If there exists a negligible function $\varepsilon_1 : \mathbb{N} \to \mathbb{R}$ for which $\big(P_x(y), V_x(z)\big)$ satisfies Conditions 1, 3[b], and 4 as stated above, but only satisfies the weaker Conditions 2b (and 5b) as stated below, then it is a computationally convincing system of [honest-verifier] (α, β, Λ)-batch zero-knowledge *arguments* (of knowledge) for (L, R).

2b. **(Computationally) sound:** For every (possibly malicious) PPT prover P^*, there exists a constant τ_0 such that, for every $\tau > \tau_0$ and $n \in \mathbb{N}$, if P^* and honest V receive $x \in (\{0,1\}^\tau)^n \setminus L_R$ as common input then, with probability at least $1 - \varepsilon_0\big(\Lambda(\tau)\big) - \varepsilon_1\big(\tau\big)$, V outputs "false".

5b. **(Computationally) knowledge extractable:** There exists an oracle machine E^{P^*} and function $\kappa : T \to [0,1]$ such that, for every (possibly malicious) PPT prover P^*, there exists a constant τ_0 such that, for every $\tau > \tau_0$ and $n \in \mathbb{N}$, E^{P^*} is an expected PPT knowledge extractor for (P^*, L_R) with knowledge error $\kappa(\cdot) \leq \varepsilon_0\big(\Lambda(\tau)\big) + \varepsilon_1\big(\tau\big)$.

5 Batch Proof of Knowledge and Equality of k-out-of-n Pairs of Discrete Logarithms

Our new protocol draws inspiration from the repaired version of Peng and Bao's protocol outlined in §3, but it improves on that protocol by letting k vary in the all-but-k mercurial commitments, which allows us to prove a more general class of propositions. More precisely, the new protocol generalizes from a system for proofs of knowledge and equality of one-out-of-n pairs of discrete logarithms to a system for arguments of knowledge and equality of k-out-of-n pairs of discrete logarithms for any $k \in [1, n]$. We defer a formal security analysis of the new protocol to the extended version of this paper [23, Appendix B] wherein we prove that, for any fixed k and soundness parameter $\lambda \in \mathbb{N}$, it is a system for honest-verifier $(0, 1, \min\{\tau, \lambda\})$-batch zero-knowledge proofs of knowledge (in the sense of Definition 3). The latter analysis uses efficiency characteristics of the underlying construction for all-but-k mercurial commitments [22]. Using Henry and Goldberg's all-but-k mercurial commitment scheme [22], which is computationally binding under the n-Strong Diffie-Hellman assumption [7, §3], yields a system of honest-verifier batch zero-knowledge arguments. We note that in this particular instantiation, the prover is assumed to be computationally bounded not in the bit-length τ but in the security parameter for the all-but-k mercurial commitments. Standard tricks from the literature [19] can relax the honest-verifier assumption at only a small cost to efficiency. Swapping in unconditionally binding all-but-k mercurial commitments would yield a system of proofs rather than arguments.

Table 1. This table compares the communication cost (in bits) and the computation cost (in τ-bit multiplications) for four different protocols that each implement honest-verifier zero-knowledge proofs of knowledge and equality of k-out-of-n pairs of discrete logarithms for some k in a group with τ-bit order. The "**Concise**" column indicates the conciseness of the protocol (in the sense of Definition 3); the "**Batch?**" column indicates if the protocol satisfies our definition of a batch proof; the "**k-out-of-n**" column lists values of k that the protocol supports; the "**Sound?**" column indicates if the protocol achieves overwhelming soundness in the soundness parameter λ. Note that $\lambda = \tau$ in the protocol by Cramer et al.; for the other protocols, typically $\lambda \ll \tau$ and λ is fixed as the smallest value yielding a palatable soundness error.

Protocol	Communi-cation	Computation	Concise	Batch?	k-out-of-n	Sound?
Cramer et al. [12]	$\Theta(\tau n)$	$\Theta(\tau n)$	$(1,0)$	✗	$k \in [1,n]$	✓
Peng-Bao [28]	$\Theta(\tau + \lambda n)$	$\Theta(\tau + \lambda n)$	$(0,1)$	✓	$k = 1$	✗
Peng et al. [30]	$\Theta(\tau + \lambda n)$	$\Theta(\tau + \lambda n)$	$(0,1)$	✓	$k = n$	✓
This work	$\Theta(\tau + \lambda n)$	$\Theta(\tau + \lambda n \lg n)$	$(0,1)$	✓	$k \in [1,n]$	✓

Table 1 compares the cost of our protocol and those arising from a naive application of Cramer et al.'s framework [12], Peng and Bao's protocol [28], and Peng et al.'s protocol [30]. The latter three protocols are all systems for *proofs* of knowledge; ours is a system for *arguments* of knowledge. Observe that Peng et al.'s protocol is both sound and a batch protocol, *but it only handles the simple $k = n$ case*, and that Peng and Bao's protocol is a batch protocol and handles the interesting $k = 1$ case, *but it is not sound*. Cramer et al.'s framework is sound and handles every $k \in [1,n]$, *but it is not a batch protocol*.

5.1   The Protocol

Suppose that **ABK** = (ABK-Init, ABK-Commit, ABK-Open, ABK-Verify) is a secure all-but-k mercurial commitment scheme. Fix a soundness parameter $\lambda \in \mathbb{N}$ and use ABK-   to generate a common reference string PK. Protocol 2 implements a system for batch zero-knowledge proofs or arguments of knowledge and equality of k-out-of-n pairs of discrete logarithms for any pair of nonnegative integers (k,n) with $k \leq n$ and $n \leq n_0$. In the protocol, we use $\mathbf{V}_q^{n \times k}$ to denote the column-wise $n \times k$ *rectangular Vandermonde matrix* with entries reduced modulo q:

$$\mathbf{V}_q^{n \times k} = \begin{bmatrix} 1 & 1 & 1 & \cdots & 1 \\ 1 & 2 & 2^2 & \cdots & 2^k \\ 1 & 3 & 3^2 & \cdots & 3^k \\ \vdots & \vdots & \vdots & \ddots & \vdots \\ 1 & n & n^2 & \cdots & n^k \end{bmatrix} \bmod q.$$

Note that because q is prime with $n < q$ and $k \leq n$, every subset of k rows of $\mathbf{V}_q^{n \times k}$ has full rank and thus forms a non-singular (i.e., invertible) square matrix modulo q. If desired, one could replace $\mathbf{V}_q^{n \times k}$ with any other matrix that has this property when all arithmetic is modulo q.

The setting for the new protocol is similar to before. Both P and V know the same two generators g, h of an order-p group $\mathbb{G}$, the above-generated all-but-k reference string PK, and a set of $n \in [1, n_0]$ pairs of group elements $\{(g_i, h_i) \mid i \in [1, n]\}$, but only P knows a size-k subset $S \subseteq [1, n]$ of indices and corresponding set $x_S = \{x_j \in \mathbb{Z}_p \mid j \in S\}$ of exponents such that $\log_g g_j = \log_h h_j = x_j$ for all $j \in S$. The goal of the protocol is for P to convince V that she knows such a (S, x_S) pair without revealing any additional information. For ease of notation below, we let $H = [1, n] \setminus S$ for the (S, x_S) pair that honest P is proving knowledge of.

Intuitively, our k-out-of-n proof replaces the all-but-one mercurial commitment from the repaired Peng-Bao proof with an all-but-k mercurial commitment. P commits to $\{c_i \mid i \in H\}$ in Step P2, thus assuring V that she can choose at most $k = |S|$ of the c_i after V sends the challenge in Step V3. Rather than challenge P to produce c_i that sum to c modulo q, V challenges P to produce c_i that obey a system of k non-degenerate linear constraints induced by $\mathbf{V}_q^{n \times k}$ and the k free components in $\langle c_1, \ldots, c_n \rangle$. V verifies the constraints in Step V5 by checking if $\langle c_1, \ldots, c_n \rangle \cdot \mathbf{V}_q^{n \times k} \stackrel{?}{\equiv} \langle c, 0, \ldots, 0 \rangle \pmod{q}$; the all-but-$k$ commitment ensures that P chose all but k of the c_i before she received c. This assures V that c uniquely determined a size-k subset of the c_i, although he learns no information about which subset. From here, P essentially uses Peng et al.'s batch "AND" proof for the size-k subset she is proving knowledge of, and "simulates" the proof for the remaining $n - k$ predicates, as in a standard proof of partial knowledge.

Protocol 2. (Generalized batch proof of partial knowledge).

V1: Choose $t_i \in_R [0, 2^\lambda - 1]$ for each $i \in [1, n]$. Send $(t_1, \ldots, t_n)$ to P.

P2: Receive $(t_1, \ldots, t_n)$ from V. Choose $r \in_R \mathbb{Z}_p^*$ and $c_i \in_R [0, q-1]$ for $i \in H$. Compute $a = g^r \prod_{i \in H} g_i^{c_i t_i}$, $b = h^r \prod_{i \in H} h_i^{c_i t_i}$, and $\mathcal{C} \leftarrow$ ABK-$_{\text{PK}}\langle c_1, \ldots, c_n \rangle$). Send $(a, b, \mathcal{C})$ to V.

V3: Receive $(a, b, \mathcal{C})$ from P. Choose $c \in_R [0, q-1]$ and send it to P.

P4: Receive c from V. Solve for $\mathbf{c} = \langle c_1, \ldots, c_n \rangle \in \mathbb{Z}_q^n$ such that $\mathbf{c} \cdot \mathbf{V}_q^{n \times k} \equiv \langle c, 0, \ldots, 0 \rangle \pmod{q}$, then compute $v = r - \sum_{j \in S} c_j t_j x_j \bmod p$ and $\omega \leftarrow$ ABK-$_{\text{PK}}(\mathcal{C}, k, \mathbf{c})$. Send $(\mathbf{c}, v, \omega)$ to V.

V5: Receive $(\mathbf{c}, v, \omega)$ from P. Output "true" if and only if $a \stackrel{?}{=} g^v \prod_{i=1}^n g_i^{c_i t_i}$, $b \stackrel{?}{=} h^v \prod_{i=1}^n h_i^{c_i t_i}$, $\mathbf{c} \cdot \mathbf{V}_q^{n \times k} \stackrel{?}{\equiv} \langle c, 0, \ldots, 0 \rangle \pmod{q}$, and ABK-$_{\text{PK}}(\mathcal{C}, \mathbf{c}, k, \omega) \stackrel{?}{=}$ "true"; otherwise, output "false".

As before, some remarks about this protocol are in order. Protocol 2 follows the same basic recipe as Protocol 1, with V starting the conversation in Step V1 by sending to P a list of short exponents for small-exponent batching. In fact, one easily sees by inspection that the repaired version of Protocol 1 is just the special case of Protocol 2 with k fixed to one. (The only difference being that the former protocol uses $q = 2^\lambda - 1$ since it does not require a prime q to guarantee linearly independent constraints.) Completeness holds trivially by inspection and constructing a simulator for honest V is equally straightforward. In the extended version of this paper [23, Appendix B], we prove that using Henry and

Goldberg's all-but-k mercurial commitment construction [22] in our protocol yields a system for honest-verifier $(0, 1, \min\{\lg p, \lambda\})$-batch zero-knowledge arguments of knowledge of a size-k subset $S \subseteq [1, n]$ of indices and corresponding set $x_S = \{x_j \in \mathbb{Z}_p \mid j \in S\}$ of exponents such that $\log_g g_j = \log_h h_j = x_j$ for all $j \in S$.

6   Applications

In the introduction, we listed the following example applications in which the need to prove propositions about large batches of predicates naturally arise: cryptographic voting [11, 25], anonymous blacklisting and reputation systems [2, 3], priced symmetric private information retrieval [24], threshold ring signatures [34], verifiable mix networks [21, 31], and cryptographic auctions [9]. We now briefly discuss how our new protocol can directly speed up and extend two such constructions from the literature.

Symmetric private information retrieval. Henry, Olumofin, and Goldberg [24] describe a symmetric variant of Goldberg's information-theoretic private information retrieval protocol [16] that achieves data privacy by having each client commit to her query using polynomial commitments [26] and then exhibit a zero-knowledge proof that the committed query is "well formed". The final step in their proof—which dominates the computation cost of their enhancements and contributes considerable communication overhead to the protocol—is a proof of equality of one-out-of-r pairs of discrete logarithms, where r is the number of records in the database. The authors suggest small-exponent batch testing to speed up the verification at the database servers; however, playing the role of prover in that interaction still accounts for a significant fraction of a client's per-query computational expenditure. Simply swapping in our protocol leads to significant reductions in both the computation overhead and the communication overhead of their protocol.

Cryptographic voting systems. The *JCJ protocol* of Juels, Catalano, and Jakobsson [25] underlies a number of protocols for coercion-resistant, receipt-free verifiable Internet voting [1, 11, 35]; indeed, Spycher et al. [32] opine that "[JCJ is] the only known protocol for remote e-voting that offers individual verifiability and receipt-freeness simultaneously under somewhat acceptable trust assumptions". The bottleneck operation in JCJ is its *vote authorization* phase, which eliminates fake votes and duplicate votes prior to tallying. The computational cost of both steps grows quadratically in the number of votes cast: JCJ detects fake votes by having voters attach zero-knowledge proofs (made non-interactive via the *Fiat-Shamir heuristic* [13]) that they are on the registered voters roster, and it detects duplicate votes by employing a pairwise *plaintext equivalence test* on each vote. Several papers suggest strategies that can detect duplicate votes in linear time [1, 32, 35]; however, eliminating fake votes in linear time appears to necessitate a weakening the protocol's security guarantees. In particular, some existing schemes have voters prove membership within some smaller *anonymity set* rather than the entire roster [11, 32]. Our batch proof of partial knowledge may help to reduce the cost of this step and thereby allow for significantly larger anonymity sets; for smaller elections, it might even make the quadratic algorithm practical.

A second cryptographic operation that frequently arises in end-to-end verifiable voting systems is "proofs of re-encryption" of El Gamal ciphertexts: that is, given two sets of pairs $\left\{(g^{y_i}, m_i\, h^{y_i}) \mid i \in [1, n]\right\}$ and $\left\{(g^{y_i'}, m_i'\, h^{y_i'}) \mid i \in [1, n]\right\}$ of El Gamal ciphertexts encrypted under public key $h = g^x$, prove that $m_i = m_i'$ for all $i \in S$ (where S is a subset of indices suitably defined by the application). Such proofs work by considering the quotients $(m_i\, h^{y_i})/(m_i'\, h^{y_i'}) = (m_i/m_i')\, h^{y_i - y_i'}$ and $g^{y_i}/g^{y_i'} = g^{y_i - y_i'}$ and noting that $\log_h (m_i/m_i')\, h^{y_i - y_i'} = \log_g g^{y_i - y_i'}$ if and only if $m_i = m_i'$. Thus, batch proofs of knowledge and equality for k-out-of-n pairs of discrete logarithms imply batch proofs of re-encryption of k-out-of-n El Gamal ciphertexts.

7   Conclusion

We have examined "batch zero-knowledge" protocols for communication- and computation-efficient proofs of propositions composed of many simple predicates. Our primary contribution is a novel system for batch zero- knowledge arguments of knowledge and equality of k-out-of-n discrete logarithms for fixed $k \in [1, n]$. We also suggested the first general definitions for *batch zero-knowledge proofs and arguments (of knowledge)*. Our new definitions introduce a *conciseness* property that describes the asymptotic performance of a protocol relative to one formed by sequential composition of single-instance protocols. Our new argument system came about when we analyzed and uncovered a critical flaw in the security proof for Peng and Bao's [28] batch proofs of knowledge and equality of one-out-of-n discrete logarithms. A malicious prover can exploit the flaw to cause unsuspecting verifiers to accept proofs when the claimed equality of logarithms is false. Fortunately, we showed that the flaw is not fatal: we sketched a fix based on *all-but-k* mercurial commitments with $k = 1$ and then generalized to our main result by varying k in the repaired protocol. In addition, we illustrated the usefulness of our new protocol by sketching some example applications where its adoption could result in noteworthy speedups.

Acknowledgements. We thank Jalaj Uphadyay and Colleen Swanson for helpful discussions and the anonymous reviewers for their comments. The first author is supported by a GO-Bell Graduate Scholarship and by the Natural Sciences and Engineering Research Council of Canada (NSERC) through a Vanier Canada Graduate Scholarship. The second author thanks NSERC for further funding this research through a Discovery Grant and a Discovery Accelerator Supplement.

References

1. Araujo, R., Foulle, S., Traoré, J.: A practical and secure coercion-resistant scheme for remote elections. In: Frontiers of Electronic Voting, Schloss Dagstuhl, Germany. Dagstuhl Seminar Proceedings, vol. 7311 (July 2007)
2. Au, M.H., Tsang, P.P., Kapadia, A.: PEREA: Practical TTP-free revocation of repeatedly misbehaving anonymous users. ACM Transactions on Information and System Security 14(4), Article No. 29 (2011)
3. Au, M.H., Kapadia, A., Susilo, W.: BLACR: TTP-free blacklistable anonymous credentials with reputation. In: Proceedings of NDSS 2012, San Diego, CA, USA (February 2012)
4. Bellare, M., Garay, J.A., Rabin, T.: Batch verification with applications to cryptography and checking. In: Lucchesi, C.L., Moura, A.V. (eds.) LATIN 1998. LNCS, vol. 1380, pp. 170–191. Springer, Heidelberg (1998)
5. Bellare, M., Garay, J.A., Rabin, T.: Fast batch verification for modular exponentiation and digital signatures. In: Nyberg, K. (ed.) EUROCRYPT 1998. LNCS, vol. 1403, pp. 236–250. Springer, Heidelberg (1998)
6. Bellare, M., Goldreich, O.: On defining proofs of knowledge. In: Brickell, E.F. (ed.) CRYPTO 1992. LNCS, vol. 740, pp. 390–420. Springer, Heidelberg (1993)
7. Boneh, D., Boyen, X.: Short signatures without random oracles and the SDH assumption in bilinear groups. Journal of Cryptology 21(2), 149–177 (2008)
8. Brands, S., Demuynck, L., De Decker, B.: A practical system for globally revoking the unlinkable pseudonyms of unknown users. In: Pieprzyk, J., Ghodosi, H., Dawson, E. (eds.) ACISP 2007. LNCS, vol. 4586, pp. 400–415. Springer, Heidelberg (2007)
9. Cachin, C.: Efficient private bidding and auctions with an oblivious third party. In: Proceedings of CCS 1999, Singapore, pp. 120–127 (November 1999)
10. Catalano, D., Fiore, D., Messina, M.: Zero-knowledge sets with short proofs. In: Smart, N.P. (ed.) EUROCRYPT 2008. LNCS, vol. 4965, pp. 433–450. Springer, Heidelberg (2008)
11. Clark, J., Hengartner, U.: Selections: Internet voting with over-the-shoulder coercion-resistance. In: Danezis, G. (ed.) FC 2011. LNCS, vol. 7035, pp. 47–61. Springer, Heidelberg (2012)
12. Cramer, R., Damgård, I., Schoenmakers, B.: Proof of partial knowledge and simplified design of witness hiding protocols. In: Desmedt, Y.G. (ed.) CRYPTO 1994. LNCS, vol. 839, pp. 174–187. Springer, Heidelberg (1994)
13. Fiat, A., Shamir, A.: How to prove yourself: Practical solutions to identification and signature problems. In: Odlyzko, A.M. (ed.) CRYPTO 1986. LNCS, vol. 263, pp. 186–194. Springer, Heidelberg (1987)
14. Fürer, M.: Faster integer multiplication. SIAM Journal on Computing 39(3), 979–1005 (2009)
15. Gennaro, R., Leigh, D., Sundaram, R., Yerazunis, W.S.: Batching schnorr identification scheme with applications to privacy-preserving authorization and low-bandwidth communication devices. In: Lee, P.J. (ed.) ASIACRYPT 2004. LNCS, vol. 3329, pp. 276–292. Springer, Heidelberg (2004)
16. Goldberg, I.: Improving the robustness of private information retrieval. In: Proceedings of IEEE S&P 2007, Oakland, CA, USA, pp. 131–148 (May 2007)
17. Goldreich, O.: A note on computational indistinguishability. Information Processing Letters 34(6), 277–281 (1990)

18. Goldreich, O., Micali, S., Wigderson, A.: Proofs that yield nothing but their validity or languages in NP have zero-knowledge proof systems. Journal of the ACM 38(3), 691–729 (1991)
19. Goldreich, O., Sahai, A., Vadhan, S.P.: Honest-verifier statistical zero-knowledge equals general statistical zero-knowledge. In: Proceedings of STOC 1998, Dallas, TX, USA, pp. 399–408 (1998)
20. Goldwasser, S., Micali, S., Rackoff, C.: The knowledge complexity of interactive proof systems (extended abstract). In: Proceedings of STOC 1985, Providence, RI, USA, pp. 291–304 (May 1985)
21. Groth, J.: A verifiable secret shuffle of homomorphic encryptions. Journal of Cryptology 23(4), 546–579 (2010)
22. Henry, R., Goldberg, I.: All-but-k mercurial commitments and their applications. Technical Report CACR 2012-26, University of Waterloo, Waterloo, ON, Canada (November 2012)
23. Henry, R., Goldberg, I.: Batch proofs of partial knowledge. Technical Report CACR 2013-08, University of Waterloo, Waterloo, ON, Canada (February 2013)
24. Henry, R., Olumofin, F.G., Goldberg, I.: Practical PIR for electronic commerce. In: Proceedings of CCS 2011, Chicago, IL, USA, pp. 677–690 (October 2011)
25. Juels, A., Catalano, D., Jakobsson, M.: Coercion-resistant electronic elections. In: Proceedings of WPES 2005, Alexandria, VA, USA, pp. 61–70 (November 2005)
26. Kate, A., Zaverucha, G.M., Goldberg, I.: Constant-size commitments to polynomials and their applications. In: Abe, M. (ed.) ASIACRYPT 2010. LNCS, vol. 6477, pp. 177–194. Springer, Heidelberg (2010)
27. Lenstra, A.K., Lenstra, H.W., Lovász, L.: Factoring polynomials with rational coefficients. Mathematische Annalen 261(4), 515–534 (1982)
28. Peng, K., Bao, F.: Batch ZK proof and verification of OR logic. In: Yung, M., Liu, P., Lin, D. (eds.) Inscrypt 2008. LNCS, vol. 5487, pp. 141–156. Springer, Heidelberg (2009)
29. Peng, K., Bao, F.: Batch range proof for practical small ranges. In: Bernstein, D.J., Lange, T. (eds.) AFRICACRYPT 2010. LNCS, vol. 6055, pp. 114–130. Springer, Heidelberg (2010)
30. Peng, K., Boyd, C., Dawson, E.: Batch zero-knowledge proof and verification and its applications. ACM Transactions on Information and System Security 10(2), Article No. 6 (2007)
31. Sako, K., Kilian, J.: Receipt-free mix-type voting scheme. In: Guillou, L.C., Quisquater, J.-J. (eds.) EUROCRYPT 1995. LNCS, vol. 921, pp. 393–403. Springer, Heidelberg (1995)
32. Spycher, O., Koenig, R.E., Haenni, R., Schläpfer, M.: A new approach towards coercion-resistant remote e-voting in linear time. In: Danezis, G. (ed.) FC 2011. LNCS, vol. 7035, pp. 182–189. Springer, Heidelberg (2012)
33. Tsang, P.P., Au, M.H., Kapadia, A., Smith, S.W.: BLAC: Revoking repeatedly misbehaving anonymous users without relying on TTPs. ACM Transactions on Information and Systems Security 13(4), Article No. 39 (2010)
34. Tsang, P.P., Wei, V.K., Chan, T.K., Au, M.H., Liu, J.K., Wong, D.S.: Separable linkable threshold ring signatures. In: Canteaut, A., Viswanathan, K. (eds.) INDOCRYPT 2004. LNCS, vol. 3348, pp. 384–398. Springer, Heidelberg (2004)
35. Weber, S.G., Araujo, R., Buchmann, J.: On coercion-resistant electronic elections with linear work. In: Proceedings of ARES 2007, Vienna, Austria, pp. 908–916 (April 2007)

Efficient Signatures of Knowledge
and DAA in the Standard Model

David Bernhard[1], Georg Fuchsbauer[2,*], and Essam Ghadafi[1]

[1] University of Bristol, UK
[2] Institute of Science and Technology, Austria

Abstract. Direct Anonymous Attestation (DAA) is one of the most complex cryptographic protocols deployed in practice. It allows an embedded secure processor known as a Trusted Platform Module (TPM) to attest to the configuration of its host computer without violating the owner's privacy. DAA has been standardized by the Trusted Computing Group and ISO/IEC.

The security of the DAA standard and all existing schemes is analyzed in the random-oracle model. We provide the first constructions of DAA in the standard model, that is, without relying on random oracles. Our constructions use new building blocks, including the first efficient signatures of knowledge in the standard model, which have many applications beyond DAA.

Keywords. DAA, group signatures, signatures of knowledge, standard model.

1 Introduction

Direct Anonymous Attestation (DAA) is a protocol for a secure embedded processor known as a Trusted Platform Module (TPM) to authenticate itself and sign messages attesting to the state of its host while preserving the privacy of its owner. The first DAA protocol by Brickell, Camenisch and Chen [10] was standardized in 2004 by the Trusted Computing Group (TCG) [32] as the TPM 1.2 standard and has since been adopted as an ISO/IEC standard [28]; millions of TPMs have been shipped with personal computers.

In DAA a party owning a TPM can join a group and then sign messages as a member of this group. DAA signatures sign pairs of data, a message and a *basename*, which can be thought of as the identity of the intended verifier. Two signatures on the same basename can be *linked*, that is, they reveal whether they were produced by the same signer. Apart from this, signatures are anonymous; in particular, signatures on different basenames (or empty basenames) hide whether they come from the same user.

Many DAA schemes have been proposed, including [11,16,17,18,19,20], improving both the efficiency of DAA and refining the security model. While the first schemes were analyzed in a simulation-based model, recent papers have switched to game-based models. We prove our results in the most recent model of Bernhard et al. [6] who pointed out shortcomings in the models of some previous papers [10,11,16,17,18,19].

---

* Work done while at University of Bristol.

M. Jacobson et al. (Eds.): ACNS 2013, LNCS 7954, pp. 518–533, 2013.

The novelty of our schemes is that they are in the *standard model*, where one does not need to rely on the so-called *random-oracle* heuristic [3], which was required in all previous DAA schemes but is problematic in cryptographic theory [13]. It is common practice nowadays to investigate which schemes can be implemented without random oracles. Standard-model schemes are generally less efficient than their random-oracle-based ancestors; we do not intend to improve on the efficiency of earlier DAA schemes but construct efficient schemes in the standard model.

A Blueprint for DAA. As argued in [6], all existing DAA schemes follow the same "blueprint" and are constructed from the same building blocks: a Randomizable weakly Blind Signature (RwBS), a Linkable Indistinguishable Tag (LIT) and a Signature of Knowledge (SoK). We discuss these concepts in more detail in Sect. 3 and 4. DAA users hold secret keys, on which they receive a (blind) signature as a certificate from the issuer when joining a group. A DAA signature consists of this certificate, a LIT on the basename under the user's key and a SoK on the message, proving knowledge of a key corresponding to the certificate and the LIT. Our first standard-model DAA scheme largely follows this blueprint; for our second scheme we propose an alternative method of constructing DAA yielding a more efficient scheme.

The security model from [6] operates in two steps: first, the authors discuss *pre-DAA* schemes, which are fully functional DAA schemes but without the option for the TPM to delegate non-security critical operations to its more powerful host computer. Secondly, they give generic methods to perform such delegation securely given a pre-DAA scheme. Since their second step is independent of the random-oracle model (ROM), it is also applicable to our schemes. We therefore restrict ourselves to constructing standard-model pre-DAA schemes in this paper.

LIT in the Standard Model. A DAA signature contains a deterministic tag on the basename. This LIT should look random, so tags under different keys are indistinguishable, which is trivially achievable by using a random oracle. Like Verifiable Random Functions (VRF) [30], LITs are much harder to construct in the standard model, in particular, for large input spaces. LITs are somewhat stronger than VRFs, and we do not know of any large-domain VRF which yields a LIT. (See the discussion in Sect. 4.2.)

For DAA, we believe it is reasonable to postulate that the number of possible basenames is polynomial in the security parameter. While the set of *messages* which users can sign must be large, the number of possible verifiers (corresponding to basenames) will be efficiently enumerable.

Overview of our Paper and Contributions. In Sect. 2 we introduce some notation as well as the (pre-)DAA definition and security notions from [6].

In Sect. 3 we introduce and construct the first efficient signatures of knowledge [14] without random oracles, which may be of independent interest. SoKs are a generalization of digital signatures and use a witness to an NP statement as the signing key. We build them from Proofs of Knowledge (PoK), of which Groth-Sahai proofs [26] are the only known efficient standard-model instantiation. While the transformation from PoK to SoK is almost trivial in the random-oracle model, Groth-Sahai proofs cannot be used directly since SoKs require strong security properties akin to simulation-sound extractability [25]. Instead, we revert to a known technique, used by Groth [25], to overcome this limitation.

In Sect. 4 we discuss and construct randomizable weakly blind signatures and linkable indistinguishable tags. In order to construct DAA, these building blocks must be compatible with each other and the Groth-Sahai-based SoK. The challenges here are that Groth-Sahai proofs apply only to a limited class of statements and are even more restrictive in security proofs: the language on which we make proofs is that of pairing-product equations [25], in which we can only prove knowledge of elements of a bilinear group. It follows that we have to choose our RwBS and LIT with some care: the RwBS implicitly used in previous DAA schemes, even those that do not require a random oracle directly, are not Groth-Sahai compatible for example. We build on the signature schemes of Abe et al. [1] and Ghadafi [22] to construct different RwBS schemes. As the LIT used in previous schemes is only secure in the ROM, we construct a new LIT based on the VRF by Dodis and Yampolskiy [21].

Using these building blocks, we construct two DAA schemes in Sect. 5 and 6. These are the first DAA schemes in the standard model. Our first construction relies solely on existing, non-interactive assumptions. To improve efficiency, our second construction uses some components from the literature which rely on interactive assumptions.

To evaluate efficiency, we consider the most closely related cryptographic primitive: dynamic group signatures [4], which do not require linkability and handle tracing differently. Our DAA signatures are shorter than Groth's group signatures [24], which is currently the most efficient scheme in the standard model. Moreover, our join protocol involves fewer rounds. See the full version [5] for details.

2   Preliminaries

Notation. A bilinear group is a tuple $\mathcal{P} = (p, \mathbb{G}_1, \mathbb{G}_2, \mathbb{G}_T, e, P_1, P_2)$ where $\mathbb{G}_1, \mathbb{G}_2$ and $\mathbb{G}_T$ are groups of prime order p; P_1 and P_2 are generators of $\mathbb{G}_1$ and $\mathbb{G}_2$ respectively and $e \colon \mathbb{G}_1 \times \mathbb{G}_2 \to \mathbb{G}_T$ is bilinear (i.e. $e([x]Q_1, [y]Q_2) = e(Q_1, Q_2)^{xy}$ for all Q_1, Q_2, x and y) and $e(P_1, P_2)$ generates $\mathbb{G}_T$. All group operations are efficiently computable and $[x]P$ denotes the x-fold composition of an element P with itself. We use *asymmetric* bilinear groups (which are more efficient), for which there are no known efficiently computable homomorphisms from $\mathbb{G}_1$ to $\mathbb{G}_2$ or vice versa. We let $\mathbb{G}^\times := \mathbb{G} \setminus \{0_{\mathbb{G}}\}$.

Assumptions. Our constructions rely on the following assumptions from the literature:

SXDH. The DDH assumption holds in both groups $\mathbb{G}_1$ and $\mathbb{G}_2$.

CDH$^+$ [7]**.** Given $(P_1, P_2, [a]P_1, [b]P_1, [a]P_2)$, it is hard to compute $[ab]P_1$. This is identical to CDH in symmetric bilinear groups.

q-SDH [8]**.** Given $(P_1, [x]P_1 \ldots, [x^q]P_1, P_2, [x]P_2)$ for $x \leftarrow \mathbb{Z}_p^\times$, it is hard to output a pair $(c, [\frac{1}{x+c}]P_1) \in \mathbb{Z}_p \times \mathbb{G}_1$ for an arbitrary $c \in \mathbb{Z}_p \setminus \{-x\}$.

q-DDHI [2]**.** Given $(P_i, [x]P_i, [x^2]P_i, \ldots, [x^q]P_i)$ where $x \leftarrow \mathbb{Z}_p^\times$ it is hard to distinguish $[\frac{1}{x}]P_i$ from a random element of $\mathbb{G}_i$. Here i can be either 1 or 2.

q-SFP [1]**.** Given $A, B \in \mathbb{G}_1$, $\tilde{A}, \tilde{B}, G_Z, F_Z, G_R, F_U \in \mathbb{G}_2$, and q random tuples $(Z_i, R_i, S_i, T_i, U_i, V_i, W_i)$ each satisfying $e(A, \tilde{A}) = e(Z_i, G_Z)e(R_i, G_R)e(T_i, S_i)$ and $e(B, \tilde{B}) = e(Z_i, F_Z)e(U_i, F_U)e(W_i, V_i)$, it is hard to output a new such tuple $(Z^*, R^*, S^*, T^*, U^*, V^*, W^*)$ with $Z^* \notin \{Z_i\}_{i=1}^q \cup \{0_{\mathbb{G}_1}\}$.

DH-LRSW [22]. Given $([x]P_2, [y]P_2)$ for random $(x, y) \leftarrow \mathbb{Z}_p^2$ and an oracle that, on input a *Diffie-Hellman* pair (M_1, M_2) of the form $([m]P_1, [m]P_2)$ for some $m \in \mathbb{Z}_p$, picks a random $a \leftarrow \mathbb{Z}_p$ and outputs a DH-LRSW tuple of the form $([a]P_1, [ay]P_1, [ay]M_1, [ax]P_1 + [axy]M_1)$, it is hard to compute a DH-LRSW tuple for $([m']P_1, [m']P_2)$ that was never queried to the oracle.

Groth-Sahai Proofs. Groth-Sahai (GS) proofs [26] are non-interactive proofs in the Common Reference String (CRS) model. We will use GS proofs that are secure under the SXDH assumption (which, as noted by [23], yields their most efficient instantiation) and that prove knowledge of a satisfying assignment for a pairing-product equation

$$\prod e(A_j, \underline{Y_j}) \prod e(\underline{X_i}, B_i) \prod \prod e(\underline{X_i}, \underline{Y_j})^{\gamma_{i,j}} = \prod e(G_\ell, H_\ell) \qquad (1)$$

(the variables are underlined, all other values are constants). The language for these proofs is of the form $\mathcal{L} := \{ \text{statement} \mid \exists \text{witness} : E(\text{statement}, \text{witness}) \text{ holds} \}$ where $E(\text{statement}, \cdot)$ is a set of pairing-product equations. The GS proof system is formally defined by a tuple of algorithms

(GSSetup, GSProve, GSVerify, GSExtract, GSSimSetup, GSSimProve) .

GSSetup takes as input the description of a bilinear group $\mathcal{P}$ and outputs a *binding* reference string crs and an extraction key xk. GSProve takes as input crs, a set of equations statement and a witness, and outputs a proof Ω for the satisfiability of the equations. We write GSProve$_{\text{SEC}}$(crs, {witness} : statement $\in \mathcal{L}$), where SEC = ZK means the proofs are zero-knowledge and WI means they are witness-indistinguishable. Given crs, a set of equations and a proof, GSVerify and outputs 1 if the proof is valid, and else 0.

GSExtract takes as input a binding crs, the extraction key xk and a valid proof Ω, and outputs the witness used for the proof. GSSimSetup, on input a bilinear group $\mathcal{P}$, outputs a *hiding* reference string crs$_{\text{Sim}}$ and a trapdoor key tr that allows to simulate proofs. GSSimProve takes crs$_{\text{Sim}}$, a statement and the trapdoor tr and produces a simulated proof Ω_{Sim} without a witness. The distributions of strings crs and crs$_{\text{Sim}}$ are computationally indistinguishable and simulated proofs are indistinguishable from proofs output by GSProve. The proof system has prefect completeness, perfect soundness, composable witness-indistinguishability or composable zero-knowledge. We refer to [26] for the formal definitions.

Direct Anonymous Attestation: The pre-DAA Model. The syntax and security model for pre-DAA were defined in [6]. A pre-DAA scheme consists of a tuple of algorithms

(Setup, GKg, UKg, ⟨Join, Iss⟩, GSig, GVf, Identify$_T$, Identify$_S$, Link) .

Setup, on input the security parameter 1^λ, outputs public parameters param, which is an implicit input to all other algorithms. GKg outputs (gmpk, gmsk), a public/secret key pair for the group manager (issuer), and UKg generates a secret key sk for a user.

⟨Join(sk$_i$, gmpk), Iss(gmsk, gmpk)⟩ are the user- and issuer-side procedures for an interactive protocol by means of which a user joins a group. The user takes a secret key sk$_i$ and the issuer's public key gmpk as input, whereas the issuer has as input a key pair $(\mathsf{gmpk}, \mathsf{gmsk})$. If completed successfully, the user obtains a *group signing key* gsk. We assume w.l.o.g. that gsk contains the issuer's public key gmpk.

$\mathsf{GSig}(\mathsf{gsk}_i, \mathsf{sk}_i, m, \mathsf{bsn})$ is the signing algorithm. It takes as input a group signing key gsk_i, a user secret key sk_i, a message m and a basename bsn and outputs a DAA signature σ on the message m under the basename bsn.

$\mathsf{GVf}(\mathsf{gmpk}, \sigma, m, \mathsf{bsn})$ is the verification algorithm. It returns 1 if the signature σ is valid on the message m and the basename bsn w.r.t. gmpk. Otherwise, it returns 0.

$\mathsf{Identify}_\mathsf{T}(\mathsf{gmpk}, \mathcal{T}, \mathsf{sk}_i)$ is a transcript-tracing algorithm. It is mainly used in the security model although it could be used to trace dishonest users who reveal their secret key. This algorithm takes as input gmpk, a transcript $\mathcal{T}$ of a join/issue protocol execution and a secret key sk_i. It returns 1 if this transcript could have been produced by an honest user with secret key sk_i, and 0 otherwise.

$\mathsf{Identify}_\mathsf{S}(\mathsf{gmpk}, \sigma, m, \mathsf{bsn}, \mathsf{sk}_i)$ is a signature-tracing algorithm. Like $\mathsf{Identify}_\mathsf{T}$, its use is in the security model and possibly to trace dishonest users. On inputs gmpk, a signature σ, a message m, a basename bsn and a secret key sk_i, it returns 1 iff σ could have been produced by an honest user with the secret key sk_i.

$\mathsf{Link}(\mathsf{gmpk}, m_0, \sigma_0, m_1, \sigma_1, \mathsf{bsn})$ is the linking algorithm. Its inputs are gmpk, two messages and signatures $m_0, m_1, \sigma_0, \sigma_1$ and a basename bsn. It returns 1 iff both signatures were produced by the same user on their respective messages and under the non-empty basename bsn.

Security Definitions of pre-DAA. Here we provide an informal description of the different security requirements. The formal definitions can be found in [6].

Correctness: This demands that signatures produced by honest users are accepted by the verifier, and that the user who produced a valid signature can be traced. Moreover, two signatures by the same user on the same non-empty basename link.

Anonymity: An adversary, who may control the group issuer, cannot distinguish which of two users of his choice signed a message as long as he cannot trivially decide this using the linking property.

Traceability: No group of users can create an untraceable signature as long as the issuer is honest. (A dishonest issuer could always join untraceable users to his group.) There are two notions of traceability which deal with untraceable signatures and signatures that do not link although they should. Since unlike in group signatures, users do not have public keys corresponding to their secret keys, the group-join transcript is used to identify the user.

Non-frameability: No adversary, who may even control the group issuer, can frame an honest user by claiming that this user signed a message he did not sign. There are again two notions: framing a user by creating a signature that traces to his key, or one that links to a previous signature created by that user.

3   Efficient Signatures of Knowledge without Random Oracles

Let $\mathcal{L}$ be an *NP language*, defined by a polynomial-time computable relation R as $\mathcal{L} = \{x \mid \exists w : (x, w) \in R\}$. We call x a *statement* in $\mathcal{L}$ and w a *witness* for x

if $(x, w) \in R$. A *signature of knowledge* (SoK) for $\mathcal{L}$ consists of the following three algorithms: SoKSetup takes a security parameter 1^λ and outputs parameters par. If $(x, w) \in R$ then SoKSign(par, R, x, w, m) outputs a signature σ on the message m w.r.t. statement x. The signature is verified by SoKVerify(par, R, x, m, σ) outputting 0 or 1. Signatures produced by SoKSign on inputs par output by SoKSetup, and any (R, x, w, m) such that $(x, w) \in R$ should be accepted by SoKVerify. The (game-based) security definition for SoK, called *SimExt security* [14] requires the following:

Simulatability: There exists a *simulator* which can simulate signatures without having a witness for the statement. It consists of SoKSimSetup and SoKSimSign: the former outputs parameters together with a *trapdoor* tr and the latter outputs signatures on input (par, tr, R, x, m). It is required that no adversary can distinguish the following two situations: (1) It is given par output by SoKSetup and access to a SoKSign oracle. (2) It is given par output by SoKSimSetup and an oracle SoKSim that on input (R, x, w, m) outputs SoKSimSign(par, tr, R, x, m) if $(x, w) \in R$.

Extraction: There exists an algorithm SoKExtract such that if an adversary, given par $\leftarrow$ SoKSimSetup and an oracle SoKSim as above, outputs a tuple (R, x, m, σ), we have: if SoKVerify(par, R, x, m, σ) $= 1$ and (R, x, w', m), for any w', was never queried to the SoKSim oracle then SoKExtract extracts a witness for x from σ with overwhelming probability.

Chase and Lysyanskaya [14] offer a generic construction satisfying SimExt security, but it is inefficient due to the use of general Non-Interactive Zero-Knowledge (NIZK) proofs. Our construction is based on Groth-Sahai proofs [26] which are efficient NIZK proofs that do not rely on random oracles but only apply to a restricted language. Our SoKs are thus for the same language, namely *satisfiability of sets of Pairing-Product Equations (PPE)*.

If we generate a binding CRS using GSSetup, we can use GSExtract to extract a witness from a valid proof. However, in order to simulate GS proofs, we need to set up the CRS via GSSimSetup. In this case proofs become information-theoretically independent of their witnesses, thus we cannot extract anymore. In order to realize simulatability and extractability simultaneously, we revert to a well-known trick that was employed by Groth in the context of PPEs [25]. Our SoK parameters are a binding CRS and a signature-verification key and a SoK is a proof of the following statement: one either knows a witness for the original statement *or* knows a signature on the original statement and the message to be signed, under the key contained in the parameters.

To simulate SoKs, we can now use the corresponding key to sign the statement and the message, and use this signature as a witness for the modified statement. Witness indistinguishability of GS proofs guarantees that simulated SoKs are indistinguishable from SoKs that use the witness of the original statement. Extractability follows since from any SoK we can extract a witness for the *modified* statement. This witness must be for the original statement, as a signature on a statement/message pair which was never signed by the SoKSim oracle would be a forgery.

Choosing the Signature Scheme. As we need to prove knowledge of a signature, we require a scheme whose signatures consist of group elements and whose validity is verified by evaluating PPEs. An ideal candidate would be the signatures by Waters

[33], which are secure under the Computational Diffie-Hellman (CDH) assumption, which is implied by the assumptions required for GS proofs. (Their main drawback is a long public key, which will result in long parameters for our SoK.) Waters signatures are defined over *symmetric* bilinear groups (where $\mathbb{G}_1 = \mathbb{G}_2$). Using the Groth-Sahai instantiation over these groups, our construction yields SoKs for the same statements and under the same assumption as GS proofs. To allow for a more general class of statements, we use the following generalization of Waters signatures to asymmetric groups from [7]:

Parameter Generation. Given a bilinear group $\mathcal{P}$, to sign messages of the form $m = (m_1, \ldots, m_N) \in \{0,1\}^N$, choose $(Q, U_0, \ldots, U_N) \leftarrow \mathbb{G}_1^{N+2}$.

Key Generation. Choose a secret key $\mathsf{sk} \leftarrow \mathbb{Z}_p$ and set $\mathsf{vk} := [\mathsf{sk}]P_2$.

Signing. To sign $(m_1, \ldots, m_N)$ using key sk, choose a random $r \leftarrow \mathbb{Z}_p$ and output

$$\left(W_1 := [\mathsf{sk}]Q + [r](U_0 + \textstyle\sum_{i=1}^{N}[m_i]U_i),\ W_2 := [-r]P_1,\ W_3 := [-r]P_2\right)\ .$$

Verification. Check whether $e(W_1, P_2)\,e(U_0 + \sum_{i=1}^{N}[m_i]U_i, W_3) = e(Q, \mathsf{vk})$ and $e(W_2, P_2) = e(P_1, W_3)$.

This scheme is unforgeable under chosen-message attack under the CDH$^+$ assumption. In order to sign arbitrary messages, we assume a collision-resistant hash function $\mathcal{H} \colon \{0,1\}^* \to \{0,1\}^N$ (for a suitable N).

Disjunctions of Pairing-Product Equations. Groth [25] shows how to express disjunctions of two sets of PPEs as a new set of PPEs. The idea is the following: introduce a "selector equation" of the form $e(P_1, \underline{S} + \underline{T} - P_2) = 1$, which can only be satisfied if either S or T are different from 0. Setting one of them to 0 will enable us to simulate one clause of the disjunction. To do so, for every variable Groth introduces an auxiliary variable and adds an equation.

We choose a more efficient approach inspired by that from [26]. In order to simulate equations of the form (1), it suffices to replace the constants G_ℓ by auxiliary variables G'_ℓ, as then, setting all variables to 0 is a satisfying assignment for (1). Now it only remains to ensure that a signer without the trapdoor is forced to set G'_ℓ to G_ℓ, which is done by adding equations $e(G_\ell - \underline{G'}_\ell, \underline{S}) = 1$, where S can only be set to 0 when the prover knows a signature under the public key from the CRS.

With this intuition in mind we now define our signature of knowledge of a satisfying assignment for a set of pairing-product equations. Regarding the Chase-Lysyanskaya definition, we have fixed the relation R to be the set of all pairs $\left((E_k)_{k=1}^K, ((X_i)_{i=1}^m, (Y_j)_{j=1}^n)\right)$ such that $((X_i), (Y_j)) \in \mathbb{G}_1^m \times \mathbb{G}_2^n$ satisfy E_k for all $1 \leq k \leq K$.

3.1 A Construction of Signatures of Knowledge without Random Oracles

Setup. On input $\mathcal{P}$, run $(\mathsf{crs}, \mathsf{xk}) \leftarrow \mathsf{GSSetup}(\mathcal{P})$ and choose parameters $(Q, U_0, \ldots, U_N) \leftarrow \mathbb{G}_1^{N+2}$ and a key pair for Waters signatures: choose $t \leftarrow \mathbb{Z}_p$ and set $T := [t]P_2$. SoKSetup outputs $\mathsf{par} := (\mathsf{crs}, (Q, U_0, \ldots, U_N, T))$, whereas SoKSimSetup additionally outputs (xk, t) as an extraction/simulation trapdoor.

Signing. Let $E := (E_k)_{k=1}^K$ be the set of equations representing the statement w.r.t. which we sign, where E_k is

$$\prod_{j=1}^n e(A_{k,j}, \underline{Y_j}) \prod_{i=1}^m e(\underline{X_i}, B_{k,i}) \prod_{i=1}^m \prod_{j=1}^n e(\underline{X_i}, \underline{Y_j})^{\gamma_{k,i,j}} = \prod_{\ell=1}^{M_k} e(G_{k,\ell}, H_{k,\ell}) , \quad (E_k)$$

and let $((X_i)_{i=1}^m, (Y_j)_{j=1}^n)$ be a witness for E. We define a new set of equations E':

(i) Modified equations. For all $1 \le k \le K$:

$$\prod e(A_{k,j}, \underline{Y_j}) \prod e(\underline{X_i}, B_{k,i}) \prod e(G'_{k,\ell}, -H_{k,\ell}) \prod \prod e(\underline{X_i}, \underline{Y_j})^{\gamma_{k,i,j}} = 1 .$$

(ii) Selector equations. For all $1 \le k \le K, 1 \le \ell \le M_k$: $e(G_{k,\ell} - G'_{k,\ell}, T - \underline{T'}) = 1$.

(iii) Signature-verification equations.

$$e(\underline{W_1}, P_2) e(U_0 + \textstyle\sum_{i=1}^N [h_i] U_i, \underline{W_3}) = e(Q, \underline{T'}) \qquad e(\underline{W_2}, P_2) = e(P_1, \underline{W_3})$$

To sign a message $m \in \{0,1\}^*$ under par $:= (\mathsf{crs}, (Q, U_0, \ldots, U_N, T))$ for the statement E using witness $((X_i), (Y_j))$ proceed as follows:

- Set $T' = W_1 = W_2 = W_3 := 0$ and $G'_{k,\ell} := G_{k,\ell}$, for all k and ℓ.
- Compute $h = (h_1, \ldots, h_N) := \mathcal{H}(E\|m) \in \{0,1\}^N$, where E is an encoding of the original equations.
- The SoK is a GS proof Σ of satisfiability of the set of equations E', using as witness

$$(T', W_1, W_2, W_3, X_1, \ldots, X_m, Y_1, \ldots, Y_n, G'_{1,1}, \ldots, G'_{K,M_K}) . \quad (2)$$

Verification. Under par $:= (\mathsf{crs}, (Q, U_0, \ldots, U_N, T))$, to verify a SoK Σ on m for the statement E, verify that under crs the GS proof Σ is valid on the statement E' for the values $A_{k,j}, B_{k,i}, G_{k,\ell}, H_{k,\ell}$ and $\gamma_{k,i,j}$ from the description of E, values T and $(Q, U_0, \ldots, U_N)$ from par and h defined as $\mathcal{H}(E\|m)$.

Theorem 1. *The above is a signature-of-knowledge scheme satisfying SimExt security for the language of sets of pairing-product equations.*

Proof sketch. To simulate a signature without knowing a witness, one uses the trapdoor t to make a signature (W_1, W_2, W_3) on $(h_1, \ldots, h_N) := \mathcal{H}(E\|m)$, and sets $T' := T$ and all remaining witnesses components $X_i = Y_j = G'_{k,\ell} := 0$, which satisfies E'. Simulatability then follows from witness indistinguishability of GS proofs.

For "Extraction", consider an adversary that has never queried a signature for a pair (E, m), but outputs a SoK Σ for it. By soundness of GS proofs, we can extract from Σ a witness for E' of the form (2). We must have $T' \ne T$, as otherwise (W_1, W_2, W_3) would be a forgery on $(E\|m)$ (which was never queried to the simulator) by equations (iii) of E'. Together with equations (ii) of E', $T' \ne T$ implies that $G'_{k,\ell} = G_{k,\ell}$ for all k, ℓ, and therefore, by (i), $((X_i), (Y_j))$ is a witness for the original equation E. We have thus extracted a witness for E. $\square$

To reduce the parameter length, but relying on stronger ("*q*-type") assumptions, we could replace Waters signatures with any of the structure-preserving schemes from [1].

4   New Building Blocks

4.1   Randomizable Weakly Blind Signatures

Bernhard et al. [6] introduce Randomizable Weakly Blind Signatures (RwBS) as one of the building blocks for DAA. These are similar to blind signatures [15,31] except that blindness must hold only against adversaries that never get to see the message they signed, that is, a signature should not be linkable to its issuing session.

Randomizability means that given a signature, anyone can produce a fresh signature on the same message. We construct two RwBS that do not rely on random oracles. The syntax and security definitions for RwBS can be found in [6,5].

Partially Randomizable Weakly Blind Signatures. To work with our SoKs, we require our scheme to be *structure-preserving*: the signatures and the messages it signs must be group elements and the verification equations must be pairing-product equations. For our first construction we use a standard-model signature scheme based on non-interactive assumptions by Abe et al. [1], which we call AHO after its authors. Its security relies on the q-SFP assumption (see Sect. 2). Abe et al. show that six of the seven group elements which constitute an AHO signature can be randomized. (We are not aware of a fully randomizable structure-preserving scheme based on non-interactive assumptions.)

This randomizability is useful, since we show that if the signer is given parts of a (partial) randomization of a signature he issued earlier, they are independent of the original signature. When used as a certificate for DAA, we thus only need to hide part of the certificate in a DAA signature to guarantee anonymity. We therefore further relax the notion of weak blindness from [6] to *partial weak blindness* defined w.r.t. a projection function π. In the security game a signer blindly signs a message chosen by the game. He is then either given the projection of a (partial) randomization of his signature or of a signature on another message and should not be able to distinguish the two cases. The details of this notion and our construction can be found in the full version [5].

Fully Randomizable Weakly Blind Signatures. In order to provide a more efficient DAA scheme, we construct a RwBS satisfying the original definition of [6]. Our construction uses a fully randomizable signature scheme by Ghadafi [22] called NCL, which is a structure-preserving variant of CL-signatures [12] based on a variant of the LRSW assumption [29] (see Sect. 2).

Messages of NCL are of the form $([m]P_1, [m]P_2) \in \mathbb{G}_1 \times \mathbb{G}_2$ for some $m \in \mathbb{Z}_p$. The secret and verification keys are of the form $(x, y) \in \mathbb{Z}_p^2$ and $([x]P_2, [y]P_2)$, respectively. A message (M_1, M_2) is signed by choosing a random $a \leftarrow \mathbb{Z}_p^\times$ and outputting

$$\left(A := [a]P_1, \ B := [y]A, C := [ay]M_1, \ D := [x](A + C)\right) \ .$$

The verification equations are $A \neq 0$, $e(B, P_2) = e(A, Y)$, $e(C, P_2) = e(B, M_2)$, $e(D, P_2) = e(A, X) e(C, X)$ and $e(M_1, P_2) = e(P_1, M_2)$. A signature is randomized by choosing $a' \leftarrow \mathbb{Z}_p^\times$ and setting $A' := [a']A, B' := [a']B, C' := [a']C, D' := [a']D$.

We observe that to compute a signature on a message (M_1, M_2), only M_1 is required, whereas verification of the signature could be done using M_2 only. A first idea to construct a weakly blind signature from NCL is to define BSRequest as only sending

Experiment: $\mathsf{Exp}^{\text{w-}f\text{-IND}}_{\mathsf{LIT},\mathcal{A}}(\lambda)$	Experiment: $\mathsf{Exp}^{\text{w-LINK}}_{\mathsf{LIT},\mathcal{A}}(\lambda)$
• $b \leftarrow \{0,1\}$; par $\leftarrow$ GlobalSetup(1^λ).	• $(\mathsf{sk}_0, m_0, \mathsf{sk}_1, m_1, \tau) \leftarrow \mathcal{A}(\mathsf{par})$.
• $\mathsf{sk}_0, \mathsf{sk}_1 \leftarrow$ LITKeyGen(par).	• Return 1 if and only if :
• $(m_1, \ldots, m_q, m^*, \mathsf{St}) \leftarrow \mathcal{A}_1(1^\lambda)$.	$\circ$ LITTag(sk_0, m_0) $= \tau$.
• For $i = 1$ to q do	$\circ$ LITTag(sk_1, m_1) $= \tau$.
$\circ$ If $m_i = m^*$ then $\tau_i := \perp$	$\circ$ Either ($\mathsf{sk}_0 = \mathsf{sk}_1$ and $m_0 \neq m_1$)
$\circ$ Else $\tau_i \leftarrow$ LITTag(sk_0, m_i).	or ($\mathsf{sk}_0 \neq \mathsf{sk}_1$ and $m_0 = m_1$).
• $\tau^* := $ LITTag(sk_b, m^*).	
• $b^* \leftarrow \mathcal{A}_2(\mathsf{St}, \mathsf{par}, f(\mathsf{sk}_0), \tau_1, \ldots, \tau_q, \tau^*)$.	
• Return 1 if $b^* = b$, else 0.	

Fig. 1. Security games for indistinguishability (left) and linkability (right) of LIT.

M_1. However, in the security proof of weak blindness, the simulator (playing the user) will not have M_2 (otherwise it could break the notion itself) and can therefore not verify the correctness of the adversary's signature. We therefore require the signer to provide a NIZK proof of correctness of the signature.

Moreover, in the reduction of blind-signature unforgeability to unforgeability of NCL, the simulator (playing the signer) needs the full message (M_1, M_2) to query its signing oracle. Therefore, when requesting a signature, the user must provide a NIZK proof of knowledge of M_2. These NIZK proofs use different CRSs (as the reductions exploit different properties) and are efficiently implemented using Groth-Sahai proofs. We refer to the full version [5] for the details of our scheme and a security proof.

4.2 Linkable Indistinguishable Tags

The second building block introduced to construct DAA schemes generically in [6] is a *Linkable Indistinguishable Tag* (LIT). These tags are similar to MACs, but have stronger security requirements. LIT schemes are defined w.r.t. a one-way function $\mathsf{PK}()$ such that a tag created with a secret key sk can be verified given $\mathsf{PK}(\mathsf{sk})$ rather than sk. Thus, $\mathsf{PK}(\mathsf{sk})$ can be viewed as a public key for the tag. A LIT scheme is defined by the following algorithms. W.l.o.g. we assume that there is an algorithm GlobalSetup which generates global parameters par (such as a bilinear group), which all algorithms take as an (implicit) input.

LITKeyGen(par) takes global parameters par and outputs a secret key sk.

LITTag(sk, m) is deterministic, takes as input a secret key sk and a message m, and outputs a tag τ.

LITVerify($\mathsf{PK}(\mathsf{sk}), m, \tau$) is given the image of sk under PK, a message m and a tag τ and checks whether τ is a valid tag on the message m w.r.t. sk, outputting 1 or 0.

Security. Besides correctness, [6] defines the notions linkability and indistinguishability, of which we only require relaxations. A LIT is *weakly linkable* if the following holds: if two tags are identical then they are either w.r.t. the same key and the same message, or both keys *and* both messages are different. In particular, two tags

LITKeyGen($\mathcal{P}$)	LITTag(sk, m)	LITVerify(PK(sk), m, τ)
Return sk $\leftarrow \mathbb{Z}_p$.	If $m = -$sk then return $\perp$.	If $e(\tau, \text{PK(sk)} + [m]P_2) = e(P_1, P_2)$
	Return $\tau := [\frac{1}{\text{sk}+m}]P_1$.	then return 1, else return 0.

Fig. 2. The WBB-based Linkable Indistinguishable Tag (WBB-LIT).

under different keys on the same message (or under the same key on different messages) must be different. Weak linkability was used implicitly in [6]. We formalize it by experiment $\text{Exp}_{\text{LIT},\mathcal{A}}^{\text{w-LINK}}(\lambda)$ in Fig. 1 and say a LIT scheme is *weakly linkable* if $\text{Adv}_{\text{LIT},\mathcal{A}}^{\text{w-LINK}}(\lambda) := \Pr[\text{Exp}_{\text{LIT},\mathcal{A}}^{\text{w-LINK}}(\lambda) = 1]$ is negligible in λ for any PPT adversary $\mathcal{A}$.

The LIT f-*indistinguishability* is defined w.r.t. a one-way function f and states that no adversary, having access to a LITTag(sk, $\cdot$) oracle, can distinguish a tag on a message of his choice (for which he did not query the oracle) from a tag produced under a different random key. This should hold even if the adversary is given the image $f(\text{sk})$ of the secret key in question. We weaken this property by requiring that the adversary submit all the oracle queries and announce the message to be challenged on *before* seeing the parameters and the image of the secret key. This is formalized by $\text{Exp}_{\text{LIT},\mathcal{A}}^{\text{w-}f\text{-IND}}(\lambda)$ in Fig. 1 and we say a LIT scheme is *weakly f-indistinguishable* if $\text{Adv}_{\text{LIT},\mathcal{A}}^{\text{w-}f\text{-IND}}(\lambda) := |2 \cdot \Pr[\text{Exp}_{\text{LIT},\mathcal{A}}^{\text{w-}f\text{-IND}}(\lambda) = 1] - 1|$ is negligible in λ for any PPT adversary $\mathcal{A}$.

Small Message Spaces. If the size of the message space is polynomial in the security parameter then f-indistinguishability from [6] is implied by its weak version: assuming an adversary $\mathcal{A}$ breaking the standard notion, we can construct an adversary $\mathcal{B}$ breaking the weak notion as follows: Let $\{m_1, \ldots, m_\ell\}$ be the message space, with $\ell = poly(\lambda)$. Then $\mathcal{B}$ randomly picks $i \leftarrow \{1, \ldots, \ell\}$ and outputs its queries and the challenge as $(m_1, \ldots, m_{i-1}, m_{i+1}, \ldots, m_\ell, m^* := m_i)$. With non-negligible probability $\mathcal{A}$ will ask to be challenged on m_i, in which case $\mathcal{B}$ can simulate all Tag queries and use $\mathcal{A}$ to break weak f-indistinguishability.

A Weak LIT in the Standard Model. The weak Boneh-Boyen signature scheme [8] was used in [21,2] to construct verifiable random functions [30] for small message spaces under two variants of the DDHI assumption. The proof of pseudorandomness uses a technique similar to that for the unforgeability of weak Boneh-Boyen signatures in [8]: if the queried messages $m_1, \ldots, m_n$ and the challenge m^* (whose VRF value is to be distinguished from random) are known in advance then given a DDHI instance, we can set up the VRF parameters and the public key so that we can (1) construct the VRF values on $m_1, \ldots, m_n$ and (2) use the DDHI challenge to construct a challenge for m^*. Using the proof strategy for small message spaces discussed above, this suffices to prove pseudorandomness. We define our LIT as the VRF from [2] and use the first part of their proof of pseudorandomness of VRFs to prove weak f-indistinguishability w.r.t. $f(\text{sk}) := [\text{sk}]P_1$.

Theorem 2. *The* WBB-LIT *in Fig. 2 is a LIT for* $\text{PK(sk)} := [\text{sk}]P_2$. *It is weakly linkable and satisfies weak f-indistinguishability for* $f(\text{sk}) := [\text{sk}]P_1$ *if the DDHI assumption holds in group* $\mathbb{G}_1$.

Since it is impossible to have $\tau = \mathsf{LITTag}(\mathsf{sk}_0, m_0) = \mathsf{LITTag}(\mathsf{sk}_1, m_1)$ with ($\mathsf{sk}_0 = \mathsf{sk}_1$ and $m_0 \neq m_1$) or ($\mathsf{sk}_0 \neq \mathsf{sk}_1$ and $m_0 = m_1$), weak linkability holds unconditionally. Weak f-indistinguishability is proved analogously to the pseudorandomness property of the VRF under the q-DDHI assumption (see [21, Theorem 2]).

LIT vs. VRF. To construct a LIT which is fully indistinguishable *and* supports large domains, a natural approach would be to consider large-domain VRFs. There have been several such schemes in the recent literature, e.g. [9,2,27]. Unfortunately, all of the aforementioned schemes violate the weak linkability requirement for LITs, as it is easy to find $\mathsf{sk}_0 \neq \mathsf{sk}_1$ and m such that $\mathsf{LITTag}(\mathsf{sk}_0, m) = \mathsf{LITTag}(\mathsf{sk}_1, m)$. While in the random-oracle model LITs are easy to construct, it is not clear how to construct fully indistinguishable LITs for large basename spaces without resorting to interactive assumptions. VRFs are already hard to construct, but due to the subtle linkability requirement, LITs seem even harder.

5 A Generic Construction of pre-DAA in the Standard Model

Our first construction of pre-DAA uses AHO signatures as partially weakly blind signatures, the VRF from [2] given in Fig. 2 as a LIT and Waters signatures [33] implicitly for the signatures of knowledge, which are themselves Groth-Sahai proofs [26].

The setup algorithm outputs a bilinear group and parameters for the SoK. The issuer generates an AHO signature key pair as $(\mathsf{gmsk}, \mathsf{gmpk})$. To join a group, a user creates a LIT key sk and sends $F_1 := [\mathsf{sk}]P_1$ to the issuer, who replies with an AHO signature cred on F_1. To make a DAA signature on a message m under a basename bsn, a user first (partially) randomizes his AHO signature cred and then splits it into a public part cred_P and a part cred_H which he will include in the witness for the SoK. Next, he creates a LIT tag $\tau := \mathsf{LITTag}(\mathsf{sk}, \mathsf{bsn})$ on the basename using his key. He then computes a signature of knowledge Σ on the message $\mathsf{bsn}\|m$ proving knowledge of a LIT key sk and the hidden part of an AHO signature cred_H such that the tag and the AHO signature both verify w.r.t. this key. The DAA signature is $\sigma := (\mathsf{cred}_P, \tau, \Sigma)$.

We formalize the above. The language of the SoK needs to be a pairing-product equation as in (1) with witnesses in $\mathbb{G}_1$ and $\mathbb{G}_2$. Rather than proving knowledge of sk, the witness will be $F_1 := [\mathsf{sk}]P_1$ and $F_2 := [\mathsf{sk}]P_2$. The AHO signature is on F_1 rather than sk so F_1 is also sufficient to verify it. The signature is split into a public part $\mathsf{cred}_P := (S, T, V, W)$ and a hidden part $\mathsf{cred}_H = (Z, R, U)$ (see the full version [5] for the details). We let $\mathsf{BSVerify}'(\mathsf{gmpk}, F_1, (\mathsf{cred}_H, \mathsf{cred}_P))$ denote the AHO verification algorithm of a split signature on F_1.

The value F_2 is the public key for the LIT from Sect. 4.2, so τ can be verified using $\mathsf{LITVerify}(F_2, \mathsf{bsn}, \tau)$. It remains to prove that (F_1, F_2) is a Diffie-Hellman pair, that is, of the form $([\mathsf{sk}]P_1, [\mathsf{sk}]P_2)$. The language of the SoK is thus

$$\mathcal{L} : \big\{ \big((\mathsf{gmpk}, \mathsf{cred}_P, \mathsf{bsn}, \tau), (F_1, F_2, \mathsf{cred}_H)\big) : e(-P_1, F_2)\, e(F_1, P_2) = 1$$
$$\wedge\ \mathsf{BSVerify}'(\mathsf{gmpk}, F_1, (\mathsf{cred}_H, \mathsf{cred}_P)) = 1 \wedge \mathsf{LITVerify}(F_2, \mathsf{bsn}, \tau) = 1 \big\} .$$

If $\mathsf{bsn} = \bot$ then the DAA signature is $(\mathsf{cred}_P, \Sigma)$, where Σ is a SoK for the language $\mathcal{L}' : \big\{ \big((\mathsf{gmpk}, \mathsf{cred}_P), (F_1, \mathsf{cred}_H)\big) : \mathsf{BSVerify}'(\mathsf{gmpk}, F_1, (\mathsf{cred}_H, \mathsf{cred}_P)) = 1 \big\}$.

To verify a DAA signature, one verifies the SoK. To link two signatures under the same basename, one compares the contained tags τ and returns 1 if they are equal; to identify a transcript given sk, one checks if the first message by the user is the value $[\mathsf{sk}]P_1$; and to identify a signature, one checks the LIT tag τ using sk and bsn. Our construction follows closely the blueprint from [6] (except for proving knowledge of a function of sk and hiding parts of the certificate) and is proven analogously.

6   A More Efficient pre-DAA Scheme in the Standard Model

To construct a truly efficient pre-DAA scheme, we replace the *partially* randomizable AHO-based *partially* weak blind signatures by the fully randomizable NCL-based RwBS; this avoids having to include parts of the certificate in the SoK. In addition, we replace the SoKs by more efficient Proofs of Knowledge (PoK).

The main obstacle in doing so is that the user secret key sk is used both for the tag on bsn and (implicitly in the SoK) for the signature on the message m. Suppose we replaced the SoK of sk by a regular Groth-Sahai proof of knowledge of sk and of a signature on m. Non-frameability corresponds to a forgery of a signature on m, to which the notion must be reduced. In the reduction we thus have to extract a signature from the PoK, and therefore cannot simulate proofs, as GS proofs only allow extraction *or* simulation (while SimExt security of SoKs allows both at the same time.) However, if we do not simulate the PoK then when answering DAA-signing queries, we need to provide actual tags—for which we do not have the user's secret key.

We overcome this by using a novel approach: we use a signature scheme which in the reduction allows us to simulate tags under the same secret key and a tag scheme which allows us to simulate signatures. We do so by choosing the schemes in a way that tags of one scheme and signatures of the other scheme have the same form—although the security requirements are different, and they are based on different assumptions. In particular, note that the values of the VRF from [2] are essentially "weak" Boneh-Boyen signatures [8]. (These signatures are only secure against adversaries which make all signing queries before seeing the public key.) Weak signatures can easily be turned into standard signatures using a hybrid construction, where one signs a verification key of a one-time signature and uses the corresponding secret key to sign the actual message. Unlike for the message space of the LIT (i.e. the basename space), there is no restriction on the message spaces of the signature schemes (and thus the message space of our DAA is big enough to sign messages of arbitrary length by hashing them first).

We separate the domains for the messages of the weak signatures and the messages of the tags by prepending a bit to the messages. In the reduction of non-frameability to weak signature unforgeability we can then use our (weak) signing oracle to obtain signatures *and* simulate the tags: The basename space is polynomial in size and the verification keys of the one-time signatures can be produced beforehand; we can therefore make our signature queries on all basenames and on the one-time keys beforehand.

Then, in the proof of anonymity we use the trick the other way round and simulate signatures using the tag oracle. In the reduction to weak f-indistinguishability of the tags, we can again make all tag queries (on basenames and one-time verification keys) upfront. Another advantage of this approach is that, since weak signatures have the form of LITs, they are unlinkable to the key that produced them, which means that we can

Setup(1^λ)

- $(\mathcal{P}, \mathsf{crs}_1, \mathsf{crs}_2) \leftarrow \mathsf{BSSetup}(1^\lambda)$.
- Return param := $(\mathcal{P}, \mathsf{crs}_1, \mathsf{crs}_2)$.

GKg(param)

- $(\mathsf{gmpk}, \mathsf{gmsk}) \leftarrow \mathsf{BSKeyGen}(\mathsf{param})$.
- Return $(\mathsf{gmpk}, \mathsf{gmsk})$.

UKg(param)

- $\mathsf{sk}_i \leftarrow \mathsf{LITKeyGen}(\mathcal{P})$.
- Return sk_i.

⟨Join, Iss⟩

- Run (BSRequest, BSIssue) for message
  $(f_1(\mathsf{sk}_i), f_2(\mathsf{sk}_i)) \in \mathcal{M}_{\mathsf{BS}}$.
- User has input $((f_1(\mathsf{sk}_i), f_2(\mathsf{sk}_i)), \mathsf{gmpk})$.
- Issuer has input gmsk.
- User's output is $\mathsf{gsk}_i = \mathsf{cred}$.

GSig($\mathsf{gsk}_i, \mathsf{sk}_i, m, \mathsf{bsn}$)

- $\mathsf{cred} \leftarrow \mathsf{BSRandomize}(\mathsf{gsk}_i)$.
- $(\mathsf{vk}_{\mathsf{ots}}, \mathsf{sk}_{\mathsf{ots}}) \leftarrow \mathsf{OTSKeyGen}(1^\lambda)$.
- $\sigma_w \leftarrow \mathsf{BBSign}(\mathsf{sk}_i, 1||\mathsf{vk}_{\mathsf{ots}})$.
- If $\mathsf{bsn} \neq \perp$
  - $\tau \leftarrow \mathsf{LITTag}(\mathsf{sk}_i, 0||\mathsf{bsn})$.
  - $\varphi := (\mathsf{gmpk}, \mathsf{cred}, \mathsf{bsn}, \tau, \mathsf{vk}_{\mathsf{ots}}, \sigma_w)$.
  - $\Sigma \leftarrow \mathsf{GSProve}(\mathsf{crs}_1, \{(f_1(\mathsf{sk}_i),$
    $f_2(\mathsf{sk}_i))\} : \varphi \in \mathcal{L})$.
- Else
  - $\tau := \emptyset; \ \varphi := (\mathsf{gmpk}, \mathsf{cred}, \mathsf{vk}_{\mathsf{ots}}, \sigma_w)$.
  - $\Sigma \leftarrow \mathsf{GSProve}(\mathsf{crs}_1, \{(f_1(\mathsf{sk}_i),$
    $f_2(\mathsf{sk}_i))\} : \varphi \in \mathcal{L}')$.
- $\sigma_{\mathsf{ots}} \leftarrow \mathsf{OTSSign}(\mathsf{sk}_{\mathsf{ots}}, (m, \tau, \mathsf{bsn}))$.
- $\sigma := (\mathsf{cred}, \tau, \sigma_w, \mathsf{vk}_{\mathsf{ots}}, \Sigma, \sigma_{\mathsf{ots}})$.

GVf($\mathsf{gmpk}, m, \mathsf{bsn}, \sigma$)

- Parse σ as $(\mathsf{cred}, \tau, \sigma_w, \mathsf{vk}_{\mathsf{ots}}, \Sigma, \sigma_{\mathsf{ots}})$.
- If $\mathsf{OTSVerify}(\mathsf{vk}_{\mathsf{ots}}, (m, \tau, \mathsf{bsn}), \sigma_{\mathsf{ots}}) = 0$, return 0.
- If $\mathsf{bsn} \neq \perp$ then
  - $\varphi := (\mathsf{gmpk}, \mathsf{cred}, \mathsf{bsn}, \tau, \mathsf{vk}_{\mathsf{ots}}, \sigma_w)$.
  - Return $\mathsf{GSVerify}(\mathsf{crs}_1, \varphi \in \mathcal{L}, \Sigma)$.
- If $\tau = \emptyset$ then
  - $\varphi := (\mathsf{gmpk}, \mathsf{cred}, \mathsf{vk}_{\mathsf{ots}}, \sigma_w)$.
  - Return $\mathsf{GSVerify}(\mathsf{crs}_1, \varphi \in \mathcal{L}', \Sigma)$.
- Return 0.

Identify$_T$($\mathsf{gmpk}, \mathsf{sk}_i, \mathcal{T}$)

- If $\mathcal{T}$ is a valid transcript then check if the user message
  in $\mathsf{Join}^0 = \mathsf{BSRequest}^0$ is $(f_1(\mathsf{sk}_i), \Omega)$, for some Ω.
- If so return 1, otherwise return 0.

Identify$_S$($\mathsf{gmpk}, \mathsf{sk}_i, m, \mathsf{bsn}, \sigma$)

- Parse σ as $(\mathsf{cred}, \tau, \sigma_w, \mathsf{vk}_{\mathsf{ots}}, \Sigma, \sigma_{\mathsf{ots}})$.
- If $\mathsf{BSVerify}(\mathsf{gmpk}, (f_1(\mathsf{sk}_i), f_2(\mathsf{sk}_i)), \mathsf{cred}) = 0$
  then return 0.
- If $\mathsf{OTSVerify}(\mathsf{vk}_{\mathsf{ots}}, (m, \tau, \mathsf{bsn}), \sigma_{\mathsf{ots}}) = 0$
  then return 0.
- Return 1 iff one of the following hold
  - $\mathsf{bsn} = \perp, \tau = \emptyset$ and
    $\mathsf{BBVerify}(f_2(\mathsf{sk}_i), 1||\mathsf{vk}_{\mathsf{ots}}, \sigma_w) = 1$.
  - $\mathsf{bsn} \neq \perp, \mathsf{LITVerify}(f_2(\mathsf{sk}_i), 0||\mathsf{bsn}, \tau) = 1$
    and $\mathsf{BBVerify}(f_2(\mathsf{sk}_i), 1||\mathsf{vk}_{\mathsf{ots}}, \sigma_w) = 1$.

Link($\mathsf{gmpk}, \sigma_0, m_0, \sigma_1, m_1, \mathsf{bsn}$)

- If $\mathsf{bsn} = \perp$ return 0.
- For $b = 0, 1$:
  If $\mathsf{GVf}(\mathsf{gmpk}, m_b, \mathsf{bsn}, \sigma_b) = 0$, return $\perp$.
  Parse σ_b as $(\mathsf{cred}_b, \tau_b, \sigma_{w_b}, \mathsf{vk}_{\mathsf{ots}_b}, \Sigma_b, \sigma_{\mathsf{ots}_b})$.
- Return 1 if and only if $\tau_0 = \tau_1$.

Fig. 3. An efficient pre-DAA scheme construction in the standard model

even include the weak signatures in the clear in the DAA; we thus only need to prove knowledge of the secret key.

Our construction is shown in Fig. 3 and uses the LIT scheme from Fig. 2 and the NCL-based RwBS described in Sect. 4.1. As in the generic scheme, the user group signing key gsk is a credential (i.e. a blind signature) obtained from the issuer when joining the group. To make a DAA signature, the user randomizes gsk to cred, chooses a one-time signature key pair ($\mathsf{sk}_{\mathsf{ots}}, \mathsf{vk}_{\mathsf{ots}}$) and uses his secret key sk to generate a LIT tag τ on $0||\mathsf{bsn}$ (if $\mathsf{bsn} = \perp$ then $\tau := \emptyset$), and a weak signature σ_w on $1||\mathsf{vk}_{\mathsf{ots}}$. The user then produces a GS PoK Σ of $(f_1(\mathsf{sk}) := [\mathsf{sk}]P_1, f_2(\mathsf{sk}) := [\mathsf{sk}]P_2)$ showing well-formedness, that cred is valid on it and that τ and σ_w both verify under $f_2(\mathsf{sk})$.

The DAA signature is defined as $\sigma := (\mathsf{cred}, \tau, \sigma_w, \mathsf{vk}_{\mathsf{ots}}, \Sigma, \sigma_{\mathsf{ots}})$, where σ_{ots} is a one-time signature produced with $\mathsf{sk}_{\mathsf{ots}}$ on the tuple (m, τ, bsn). Note that the one-time signature also only needs to be weakly unforgeable, as the message (m, τ, bsn) is known before $\mathsf{vk}_{\mathsf{ots}}$ is chosen. The languages for the GS proofs are defined as follows, where $\mathcal{L}'$ is used when $\mathsf{bsn} = \perp$ and $\mathcal{L}$ otherwise.

$$\mathcal{L} : \big\{ ((\mathsf{gmpk}, \mathsf{cred}, \mathsf{bsn}, \tau, \mathsf{vk}_{\mathsf{ots}}, \sigma_w), (F_1, F_2)) : e(-P_1, \underline{F_2}) e(\underline{F_1}, P_2) = 1$$
$$\wedge\ \mathsf{BSVerify}(\mathsf{gmpk}, (\underline{F_1}, \underline{F_2}), \mathsf{cred}) = 1 \wedge \mathsf{LITVerify}(\underline{F_2}, 0 || \mathsf{bsn}, \tau) = 1$$
$$\wedge\ \mathsf{BBVerify}(\underline{F_2}, 1 || \mathsf{vk}_{\mathsf{ots}}, \sigma_w) = 1 \big\}$$

$$\mathcal{L}' : \big\{ ((\mathsf{gmpk}, \mathsf{cred}, \mathsf{vk}_{\mathsf{ots}}, \sigma_w), (F_1, F_2)) : e(-P_1, \underline{F_2}) e(\underline{F_1}, P_2) = 1$$
$$\wedge\ \mathsf{BSVerify}(\mathsf{gmpk}, (\underline{F_1}, \underline{F_2}), \mathsf{cred}) = 1 \wedge \mathsf{BBVerify}(\underline{F_2}, 1 || \mathsf{vk}_{\mathsf{ots}}, \sigma_w) = 1 \big\}$$

A detailed analysis of the efficiency of the construction can be found in the full version [5], where we also give a proof of the following.

Theorem 3. *If the NCL-based RwBS scheme is unforgeable and weakly blind, the LIT scheme is weakly linkable and weakly f-indistinguishable, the Groth-Sahai proof system is sound and zero-knowledge, and the one-time signature scheme is weakly unforgeable then the construction in Fig. 3 is a secure pre-DAA scheme.*

Acknowledgements. This work was supported by ERC Advanced Grant ERC-2010-AdG-267188-CRIPTO, EPSRC via grant EP/H043454/1 and the European Commission through the ICT Programme under Contract ICT2007216676 ECRYPT II.

References

1. Abe, M., Fuchsbauer, G., Groth, J., Haralambiev, K., Ohkubo, M.: Structure-preserving signatures and commitments to group elements. In: Rabin, T. (ed.) CRYPTO 2010. LNCS, vol. 6223, pp. 209–236. Springer, Heidelberg (2010)
2. Belenkiy, M., Chase, M., Kohlweiss, M., Lysyanskaya, A.: Compact e-cash and simulatable VRFs revisited. In: Shacham, H., Waters, B. (eds.) Pairing 2009. LNCS, vol. 5671, pp. 114–131. Springer, Heidelberg (2009)
3. Bellare, M., Rogaway, P.: Random oracles are practical: A paradigm for designing efficient protocols. In: CCS 1993, pp. 62–73. ACM (1993)
4. Bellare, M., Shi, H., Zhang, C.: Foundations of group signatures: The case of dynamic groups. In: Menezes, A. (ed.) CT-RSA 2005. LNCS, vol. 3376, pp. 136–153. Springer, Heidelberg (2005)
5. Bernhard, D., Fuchsbauer, G., Ghadafi, E.: Efficient signatures of knowledge and DAA in the standard model. Cryptology ePrint Archive. Report 2012/475, http://eprint.iacr.org/2012/475
6. Bernhard, D., Fuchsbauer, G., Ghadafi, E., Smart, N.P., Warinschi, B.: Anonymous attestation with user-controlled linkability. Cryptology ePrint Archive. Report 2011/658, http://eprint.iacr.org/2011/658
7. Blazy, O., Fuchsbauer, G., Pointcheval, D., Vergnaud, D.: Signatures on randomizable ciphertexts. In: Catalano, D., Fazio, N., Gennaro, R., Nicolosi, A. (eds.) PKC 2011. LNCS, vol. 6571, pp. 403–422. Springer, Heidelberg (2011)
8. Boneh, D., Boyen, X.: Short Signatures without random oracles and the SDH assumption in bilinear groups. Journal of Cryptology 21(2), 149–177 (2008)
9. Boneh, D., Montgomery, H.W., Raghunathan, A.: Algebraic pseudorandom functions with improved efficiency from the augmented cascade. In: CCS 2010, pp. 131–140. ACM (2010)
10. Brickell, E., Camenisch, J., Chen, L.: Direct anonymous attestation. In: CCS 2004, pp. 132–145. ACM (2004)
11. Brickell, E., Chen, L., Li, J.: Simplified security notions for direct anonymous attestation and a concrete scheme from pairings. Int. Journal of Information Security 8, 315–330 (2009)

12. Camenisch, J., Lysyanskaya, A.: Signature schemes and anonymous credentials from bilinear maps. In: Franklin, M. (ed.) CRYPTO 2004. LNCS, vol. 3152, pp. 56–72. Springer, Heidelberg (2004)
13. Canetti, R., Goldreich, O., Halevi, S.: The random oracle methodology, revisited (preliminary version). In: STOC 1998, pp. 209–218. ACM (1998)
14. Chase, M., Lysyanskaya, A.: On signatures of knowledge. In: Dwork, C. (ed.) CRYPTO 2006. LNCS, vol. 4117, pp. 78–96. Springer, Heidelberg (2006)
15. Chaum, D.: Blind signatures for untraceable payments. In: CRYPTO 1982, pp. 199–203. Plenum Press (1983)
16. Chen, L.: A DAA scheme requiring less TPM resources. In: Bao, F., Yung, M., Lin, D., Jing, J. (eds.) Inscrypt 2009. LNCS, vol. 6151, pp. 350–365. Springer, Heidelberg (2010)
17. Chen, L., Morrissey, P., Smart, N.P.: Pairings in trusted computing. In: Galbraith, S.D., Paterson, K.G. (eds.) Pairing 2008. LNCS, vol. 5209, pp. 1–17. Springer, Heidelberg (2008)
18. Chen, L., Morrissey, P., Smart, N.P.: On proofs of security for DAA schemes. In: Baek, J., Bao, F., Chen, K., Lai, X. (eds.) ProvSec 2008. LNCS, vol. 5324, pp. 156–175. Springer, Heidelberg (2008)
19. Chen, L., Morrissey, P., Smart, N.P.: DAA: Fixing the pairing based protocols. Cryptology ePrint Archive. Report 2009/198, http://eprint.iacr.org/2009/198
20. Chen, X., Feng, D.: Direct anonymous attestation for next generation TPM. Journal of Computers 3, 43–50 (2008)
21. Dodis, Y., Yampolskiy, A.: A verifiable random function with short proofs and keys. In: Vaudenay, S. (ed.) PKC 2005. LNCS, vol. 3386, pp. 416–431. Springer, Heidelberg (2005)
22. Ghadafi, E.: Formalizing group blind signatures and practical constructions without random oracles. In: Cryptology ePrint Archive, Report 2011/402, http://eprint.iacr.org/2011/402.pdf
23. Ghadafi, E., Smart, N.P., Warinschi, B.: Groth–Sahai proofs revisited. In: Nguyen, P.Q., Pointcheval, D. (eds.) PKC 2010. LNCS, vol. 6056, pp. 177–192. Springer, Heidelberg (2010)
24. Groth, J.: Fully anonymous group signatures without random oracles. In: Kurosawa, K. (ed.) ASIACRYPT 2007. LNCS, vol. 4833, pp. 164–180. Springer, Heidelberg (2007)
25. Groth, J.: Simulation-sound NIZK proofs for a practical language and constant size group signatures. In: Lai, X., Chen, K. (eds.) ASIACRYPT 2006. LNCS, vol. 4284, pp. 444–459. Springer, Heidelberg (2006)
26. Groth, J., Sahai, A.: Efficient non-interactive proof systems for bilinear groups. In: Smart, N.P. (ed.) EUROCRYPT 2008. LNCS, vol. 4965, pp. 415–432. Springer, Heidelberg (2008)
27. Hohenberger, S., Waters, B.: Constructing verifiable random functions with large input spaces. In: Gilbert, H. (ed.) EUROCRYPT 2010. LNCS, vol. 6110, pp. 656–672. Springer, Heidelberg (2010)
28. International Organisation for Standardisation (ISO). ISO/IEC 11889: Information technology – Trusted Platform Module (2009)
29. Lysyanskaya, A., Rivest, R.L., Sahai, A., Wolf, S.: Pseudonym systems (Extended abstract). In: Heys, H.M., Adams, C.M. (eds.) SAC 1999. LNCS, vol. 1758, pp. 184–199. Springer, Heidelberg (2000)
30. Micali, S., Rabin, M.O., Vadhan, S.P.: Verifiable random functions. In: FOCS 1999, pp. 120–130. IEEE Computer Society (1999)
31. Pointcheval, D., Stern, J.: Security arguments for digital signatures and blind signatures. Journal of Cryptology 13(3), 361–396 (2000)
32. Trusted Computing Group. TCG TPM specification 1.2 (2003), http://www.trustedcomputinggroup.org
33. Waters, B.: Efficient identity-based encryption without random oracles. In: Cramer, R. (ed.) EUROCRYPT 2005. LNCS, vol. 3494, pp. 114–127. Springer, Heidelberg (2005)

Analysis and Improvement of Lindell's UC-Secure Commitment Schemes

Olivier Blazy[1], Céline Chevalier[2], David Pointcheval[3], and Damien Vergnaud[3]

[1] Ruhr-Universität Bochum, Germany
[2] Université Panthéon-Assas, Paris, France
[3] ENS, Paris, France[*]

Abstract. In 2011, Lindell proposed an efficient commitment scheme, with a non-interactive opening algorithm, in the Universal Composability (UC) framework. He recently acknowledged a bug in its security analysis for the adaptive case. We analyze the proof of the original paper and propose a simple patch of the scheme. More interestingly, we then modify it and present a more efficient commitment scheme secure in the UC framework, with the same level of security as Lindell's protocol: adaptive corruptions, with erasures. The security is proven in the standard model (with a Common Reference String) under the classical Decisional Diffie-Hellman assumption. Our proposal is the most efficient UC-secure commitment proposed to date (in terms of computational workload and communication complexity).

1 Introduction

Related Work. The Universal Composability (UC) framework introduced by Canetti [5] is a popular security paradigm. It guarantees that a protocol proven secure in this framework remains secure even if it is run concurrently with arbitrary —even insecure— protocols (whereas classical definitions only guarantee its security in the stand-alone setting). The UC framework enables one to split the design of a complex protocol into that of simpler sub-protocols.

Commitment schemes are one of the most important tools in cryptographic protocols. This is a two-phase protocol between two parties, a committer and a receiver. In the first *commit* phase, the committer gives the receiver an *in silico* analogue of a sealed envelope containing a value m. In the second *opening* phase, the committer reveals m in such a way that the receiver can verify it. As in the sealed envelope analogy, it is required that a committer cannot change the committed value (*i.e.*, he should not be able to open to a value different from the one he committed to), this is called the *binding* property. It is also required that the receiver cannot learn anything about m before the opening phase, this is simply called the *hiding* property.

The security definition for commitment schemes in the UC framework was presented by Canetti and Fischlin [7]. A UC-secure commitment scheme achieves

---

[*] ENS, CNRS & INRIA – UMR 8548.

M. Jacobson et al. (Eds.): ACNS 2013, LNCS 7954, pp. 534–551, 2013.
© Springer-Verlag Berlin Heidelberg 2013

the binding and hiding properties under any concurrent composition with arbitrary protocols and it was shown, in [7], that it cannot be securely realized without additional assumptions. The common reference string (CRS) setting is the most widely used assumption when considering commitment schemes. In this setting, all parties have access to public information ideally drawn from some predefined distribution.

From a theoretical viewpoint, UC-secure commitments are an essential building block to construct more complex UC-secure protocols such as zero-knowledge protocols [11] and two-party or multi-party computations [9]. Moreover, a UC-secure commitment scheme provides *equivocability* (*i.e.*, an algorithm that knows a secret related to the CRS can generate commitments that can be opened correctly to any value) and *extractability* (*i.e.*, another algorithm that knows a secret related to the CRS can correctly extract the content of any valid commitment generated by anybody). Therefore, since their introduction, UC-secure commitments have found numerous practical applications in the area of Authenticated Key Exchange, either in Password Authenticated Key Exchange like [1,8,13], or the recent generalization to Language Authenticated Key Exchange [2].

Several UC-secure commitment schemes in the CRS model have been proposed. Canetti and Fischlin [7] and Canetti, Lindell, Ostrovsky, and Sahai [9] proposed inefficient non-interactive schemes from general primitives. On the other hand, Damgård and Nielsen [11], and Camenish and Shoup [4] (among others) presented interactive constructions from several number-theoretic assumptions.

Lindell [15] has recently presented the first very efficient commitment schemes proven in the UC framework. They can be viewed as combinations of Cramer-Shoup encryption schemes and Σ-protocols. He presented two versions, one proven against static adversaries (static corruptions), while the other can also handle adaptive corruptions. These two schemes have commitment lengths of only 4 and 6 group elements respectively, while their total communication complexity amount to 14 and 19 group elements respectively. Their security relies on the classical Decisional Diffie-Hellman assumption in standard cryptographic groups. Fischlin, Libert and Manulis [12] shortly after adapted the scheme secure against static corruptions by removing the interaction in the Σ-protocol using non-interactive Groth-Sahai proofs [14]. This transformation also makes the scheme secure against adaptive corruptions but at the cost of relying on the Decisional Linear assumption in symmetric bilinear groups. It thus requires the use of computationally expensive pairing computations for the receiver and can only be implemented over groups twice[1] as large (rather than the ones that do not admit pairing computations).

Contributions of the Paper. Recently, Lindell edited the ePrint version of his paper [16], to signal a bug in the original proof of the protocol design for adaptive corruptions. While there is no known detail on this bug, we detail on this paper a possible inconsistency on the *binding* property of the scheme. In

---

[1] It may be possible to adapt the scheme from [12] to asymmetric bilinear groups using the instantiation of Groth-Sahai proofs based on the Strong eXternal Diffie-Hellman assumption but our scheme will nevertheless remain more efficient.

order to avoid the above concern, we propose a simple patch to Lindell's scheme making it secure against adaptive corruptions.

However, our main contribution is on improving both Lindell's commitment schemes [15]. As mentioned above, the committer encrypts the value m (encoded as a group element) using the Cramer-Shoup encryption scheme [10]. In the opening phase, he simply reveals the value m and uses a Σ protocol to give an interactive proof that the message is indeed the one encrypted in the ciphertext. In Lindell's schemes, the challenge in the Σ protocol is sent to the committer using a "dual encryption scheme". Our improvement consists in noting that the receiver can in fact send this challenge directly without having to send it encrypted before. With additional modifications of the schemes, we can present two new protocols secure under the DDH assumption in the UC framework, against static and adaptive corruptions. Both schemes require a smaller bandwidth and less interactions than the original schemes:

- Static corruptions: the scheme requires the communication of 9 group elements and 3 scalars, where Lindell's original proposal requires 10 group elements and 4 scalars. The commit phase is non-interactive and the opening phase needs 3 rounds (instead of 5 in Lindell's scheme).
- Active corruptions: the scheme requires the communication of 10 group elements and 4 scalars, where Lindell's original proposal requires 12 group elements and 6 scalars. The commitment phase needs 3 rounds (instead of 5 in Lindell's scheme) and the opening phase is non-interactive.

Implemented on suitable elliptic curves over 256-bit finite fields, our schemes provide a 128-bit security level with a communication complexity reduced to only 3072 and 3584 bits respectively (see Table 1 for a detailed comparison). The computational workload of the new schemes has also slightly decreased compared to Lindell's original proposal and is significantly better than Fischlin *et al.*'s scheme from [12] since the new schemes do not require any expensive pairing computation and can be implemented in much smaller groups.

Table 1. Efficiency comparison of UC-secure commitment schemes (128-bit security)

Scheme	Communication Complexity (in bits)			Round Complexity		Computation Complexity		Adaptivity
	Commit	Decommit	Total	Commit	Decommit	exp.	pair.	
[15, § 3]	1024	2560	3584	1	5	27	-	✗
[15, § 4]	3072	1536	4608	5	1	36	-	✓
[12, § 3]	2560	8192	10752	1	1	41	69^2	✓
[12, § 4]	18944	1536	20480	1	1	88	129^2	✓
Fig. 5	1024	2048	3072	1	3	22	-	✗
Fig. 6	2048	1536	3584	3	1	26	-	✓

---

[2] These numbers can be reduced using batching techniques [3] but at the cost of additional exponentiations.

Outline of the Paper. We start by reviewing the standard definitions, in Section 2. We then present the original Lindell's commitment schemes in Section 3, followed by an explanation of a possible inconsistency and a simple correction.

Section 4 focuses on improving the original protocols. We will show how to reduce both the number of rounds and the number of elements exchanged, in both schemes. We then provide complete security proofs under the same computational assumption as for the original schemes, namely the DDH assumption.

2 Definitions

2.1 Commitments

A commitment scheme $\mathcal{C}$ is defined by 3 algorithms:

- Setup(1^k), where k is the security parameter, generates the global parameters param of the scheme, implicitly given as input to the other algorithms;
- Commit($m; r$) produces a commitment c on the input message $m \in \mathcal{M}$, using the random coins $r \xleftarrow{\$} \mathcal{R}$, and also outputs the opening information w;
- Decommit($c, m; w$) decommits the commitment c using the opening information w; it outputs the message m, or $\perp$ if the opening check fails.

Such a scheme should be both *binding*, which means that the decommit phase can successfully open to one value only, and *hiding*, which means that the commit phase does not reveal any information about m.

These two properties can be obtained in a perfect, statistical or computational way, according to the power an adversary would need to break them. But essentially, a *perfectly binding* commitment scheme guarantees the uniqueness of the opening phase. This is achieved by an encryption scheme, which on the other hand provides the *computational hiding* property only, under the IND-CPA security. A *perfectly hiding* commitment scheme guarantees the perfect secrecy of m.

Some additional properties are sometimes required. The first is *extractability*, for a *perfectly binding* commitment scheme. The latter admits an indistinguishable Setup phase that also generates a trapdoor allowing message extraction from the commitment. Again, an encryption scheme is an extractable commitment, where the decryption key is the trapdoor that allows extraction. The second one is *equivocability*, for a *perfectly hiding* commitment scheme. The latter admits an indistinguishable Setup phase that generates a trapdoor allowing to open a commitment in any way.

2.2 Universal Composability Framework

The Universal Composability framework was introduced in [5]. The aim of the following is just to give a brief overview to have some common conventions.

In the context of multi-party computation, one wants several users P_i with inputs x_i to be able to compute a specific function $f(x_1, \ldots, x_n) = (y_1, \ldots, y_n)$

without leaking anything except y_i to P_i. One can think about Yao's Millionaires' problem [18]. Instead of following the classical approach which aims at listing exhaustively all the expected properties, Canetti did something else and tried to define how a protocol should ideally work: what are the inputs, and what are the available outputs. For that, he specified two worlds: the real world, where the protocol is run with some possible attacks, and the ideal world where everything would go smoothly, and namely no damage can be done with the protocol. For a good protocol instantiation, it should be impossible to distinguish, for an external player, the real world from the ideal one.

In the *ideal world* there is indeed an incorruptible entity named the *ideal functionality*, to which players can send their inputs privately, and then receive the corresponding outputs without any kind of communication between the players. This way the functionality can be set to be correct, without revealing anything except what is expected. It is thus perfectly secure. A protocol, in the *real world* with real players and thus possibly malicious players, should create executions that look similar to the ones in the previous world. This is to show that the communications between the players should not give more information than the description of the functionality and its outputs.

As a consequence, the formal security proof is performed by showing that for any external entity, that gives inputs to the honest players and gets the outputs but that also controls the adversary, the executions in the two above worlds are indistinguishable. More concretely, in order to prove that a protocol $\mathcal{P}$ realizes an ideal functionality $\mathcal{F}$, we consider an environment $\mathcal{Z}$ which can choose inputs given to all the honest players and receives back the outputs they get, but which also controls an adversary $\mathcal{A}$. Its goal is to distinguish in which case it is: either the real world with concrete interactions between the players and the adversary, or the ideal world in which players simply forward everything to and from the ideal functionality and the adversary interacts with a simulator $\mathcal{S}$ to attack the ideal functionality. We have to build a simulator $\mathcal{S}$ that makes the two views indistinguishable to the environment: since the combination of the adversary and the simulator cannot cause any damage against the ideal functionality, this shows that the adversary cannot cause any damage either against the real protocol.

The main constraint is that the simulator cannot rewind the execution as often done in classical proofs, since it interacts with an adversary under the control of the environment: there is no possible rewind in the real word, it is thus impossible too in the ideal world.

The adversary $\mathcal{A}$ has access to the communication but nothing else, and namely not to the inputs/outputs for the honest players. In case of corruption, it gets complete access to inputs and the internal memory of the honest player, and then gets control of it.

2.3   Ideal Functionality of Commitment

The ideal functionality of commitment is presented on Figure 1. It is borrowed from [6, 15], where a *public delayed output* is an output first sent to the adversary $\mathcal{S}$ that eventually decides if and when the message is actually delivered to

---

$\mathcal{F}_{\mathsf{mcom}}$ with session identifier sid proceeds as follows, running with parties $P_1, \ldots, P_n$, a parameter 1^k, and an adversary $\mathcal{S}$:

- Commit phase: Upon receiving a message $(\mathsf{Commit}, \mathsf{sid}, \mathsf{ssid}, P_i, P_j, x)$ from P_i where $x \in \{0, 1\}^{\mathsf{polylog}\,k}$, record the tuple $(\mathsf{ssid}, P_i, P_j, x)$ and generate a *public delayed output* $(\mathsf{receipt}, \mathsf{sid}, \mathsf{ssid}, P_i, P_j)$ to P_j. Ignore further Commit-message with the same $(\mathsf{sid}, \mathsf{ssid})$.
- Reveal/decommit phase: Upon receiving a message of the form $(\mathsf{reveal}, \mathsf{sid}, \mathsf{ssid})$ from party P_i, if a tuple $(\mathsf{ssid}, P_i, P_j, x)$ was previously recorded, then generate a *public delayed output* $(\mathsf{reveal}, \mathsf{sid}, \mathsf{ssid}, P_i, P_j, x)$ to P_j. Ignore further reveal-message with the same $(\mathsf{sid}, \mathsf{ssid})$ from P_i.

Fig. 1. Ideal Functionality $\mathcal{F}_{\mathsf{mcom}}$ of Commitment

the recipient. In case of corruption of the committer, if this is before the receipt-message for the receiver, the adversary chooses the committed value, otherwise it is provided by the ideal functionality, according to the Commit-message.

2.4 Useful Primitives

Hash Function Family. A hash function family $\mathcal{H}$ is a family of functions H_K from $\{0, 1\}^*$ onto a fix-length output, either a bitstring or $\mathbb{Z}_p$. Such a family is said to be *collision-resistant* if for any adversary $\mathcal{A}$ on a random function $H_K \xleftarrow{\$} \mathcal{H}$, it is hard to find a collision. More precisely, this means that $\Pr[H_K \xleftarrow{\$} \mathcal{H}, (m_0, m_1) \leftarrow \mathcal{A}(H_K) : H_K(m_0) = H_K(m_1)]$ should be small.

Pedersen Commitment. The Pedersen commitment [17] is an *equivocable* commitment:

- $\mathsf{Setup}(1^k)$ generates a group $\mathbb{G}$ of order p, with two independent generators g and ζ;
- $\mathsf{Commit}(m; r)$, for a message $m \xleftarrow{\$} \mathbb{Z}_p$ and random coins $r \xleftarrow{\$} \mathbb{Z}_p$, produces a commitment $c = \mathsf{Ped}(m, r) = g^m \zeta^r$, while r is the opening information;
- $\mathsf{Decommit}(c, m; r)$ outputs m and r, which opens c into m, and allows the validity test $c \overset{?}{=} g^m \zeta^r$.

This commitment is computationally binding under the discrete logarithm assumption: two different openings (m, r) and (m', r') for a commitment c, lead to the discrete logarithm of ζ in basis g. On the other hand, with this discrete logarithm value as additional information from the setup, one can equivocate any dummy commitment, when the input and opening values are known.

Cramer-Shoup Encryption. The Cramer-Shoup encryption scheme [10] is an IND-CCA version of the ElGamal encryption. By merging the Setup and KeyGen algorithm into a unique Setup algorithm, we make it into an extractable commitment scheme CS, where dk is the extraction key, and r is the witness for the opening.

- Setup(1^k) generates a group $\mathbb{G}$ of order p.
- KeyGen(param) generates $(g_1, g_2) \xleftarrow{\$} \mathbb{G}^2$, dk $= (x_1, x_2, y_1, y_2, z) \xleftarrow{\$} \mathbb{Z}_p^5$, and sets $c = g_1^{x_1} g_2^{x_2}$, $d = g_1^{y_1} g_2^{y_2}$, and $h = g_1^z$. It also chooses a Collision-Resistant hash function H_K in a hash family $\mathcal{H}$ (or simply second-preimage resistant). The encryption key is ek $= (g_1, g_2, c, d, h, H_K)$.
- Encrypt(ek, $M; r$), for a message $M \in \mathbb{G}$ and a random scalar $r \in \mathbb{Z}_p$, the ciphertext is $C = \mathsf{CS}(M; r) = (\mathbf{u} = (g_1^r, g_2^r), e = M \cdot h^r, v = (cd^\omega)^r)$, where v is computed afterwards with $\omega = H_K(\mathbf{u}, e)$.
- Decrypt(dk, C): one first computes $\omega = H_K(\mathbf{u}, e)$ and checks whether the equality $u_1^{x_1 + \omega y_1} \cdot u_2^{x_2 + \omega y_2} = v$ holds or not. If the equality holds, one computes $M = e/(u_1^z)$ and outputs M. Otherwise, one outputs $\bot$.

The IND-CCA security can be proven under the DDH assumption and the fact the hash function used is collision-resistant or simple second-preimage resistant. This also leads to a non-malleable commitment scheme, that is additionally extractable when the Setup outputs the decryption key dk.

3   Lindell's Commitment Protocols

We now have all the tools to review the two original Lindell's commitment schemes [15]. The first variant can be found on Figure 2. It only prevents static corruptions: the adversary can decide to run the protocol on behalf of a player, with its inputs, from the beginning, but cannot corrupt anybody when the execution has started. The second variant prevents adaptive corruptions with erasures.

3.1   Description of the Scheme for Adaptive Corruptions

It is presented on Figure 3. The main difference from the static case is to move some proof from the decommit phase to the commit phase.

3.2   Discussion

Adaptive Corruptions. Lindell has proven both schemes secure under the DDH assumption, the former in details but a sketch of proof only for the latter. And actually, as noted by Lindell in the last version of [16], the security against adaptive corruptions might eventually not be guaranteed.

He indeed proves that no adversary can choose a message x' beforehand, and do a valid commit/decommit sequence to x' where the simulator extraction, at the end of the commit phase, would output an x different from x'. However this is not enough as an adversary could still do a valid commit/decommit sequence to x' where the simulator extraction at the end of the commit phase would output an x different from x'. The difference between the two experiments is how much the adversary controls the value x': in the former x' has to be chosen beforehand, while in the latter x' is any value different from x.

We describe, on top of Figure 4, such a situation in which the adversary $\mathcal{A}$ plays as P_i, and makes the simulator extract the value x, while in fact committing

---

We have a CRS, consisting of $(p, \mathbb{G}, g_1, g_2, c, d, h, h_1, h_2)$, where $\mathbb{G}$ is a group of order p with generators g_1, g_2; $c, d, h \in \mathbb{G}$ are random elements in $\mathbb{G}$ and $h_1 = g_1{}^\rho$ and $h_2 = g_2{}^\rho$ for a random $\rho \in \mathbb{Z}_p$.

Intuitively, $(p, \mathbb{G}, g_1, g_2, c, d, h)$ is a Cramer-Shoup encryption key and $(p, \mathbb{G}, g_1, g_2, h_1, h_2)$ is the CRS of a dual-mode encryption scheme.

Let $G : \{0,1\}^n \to \mathbb{G}$ be an efficiently computable and invertible mapping of a binary string to the group.

The commit phase. Upon receiving a message $(\mathsf{Commit}, \mathsf{sid}, \mathsf{ssid}, P_i, P_j, x)$, where $x \in \{0,1\}^{n-\log^2(n)}$ and $\mathsf{sid}, \mathsf{ssid} \in \{0,1\}^{\log^2(n)/4}$, party P_i works as follows:

1. P_i computes $m = G(x, \mathsf{sid}, \mathsf{ssid}, P_i, P_j)$.
2. P_i picks $r \overset{\$}{\leftarrow} \mathbb{Z}_p$ and computes $C = \mathsf{CS}(m; r)$, we will note ω the hash of the first three terms.
3. P_i sends $(\mathsf{sid}, \mathsf{ssid}, C)$ to P_j.
4. P_j stores $(\mathsf{sid}, \mathsf{ssid}, P_i, P_j, C)$ and outputs $(\mathsf{receipt}, \mathsf{sid}, \mathsf{ssid}, P_i, P_j)$.
   P_j ignores any later commitment messages with the same $(\mathsf{sid}, \mathsf{ssid})$ from P_i.

The decommit phase. Upon receiving a message $(\mathsf{reveal}, \mathsf{sid}, \mathsf{ssid}, P_i, P_j)$, P_i works as follows:

1. P_i sends $(\mathsf{sid}, \mathsf{ssid}, x)$ to P_j.
2. P_j computes $m = G(x, \mathsf{sid}, \mathsf{ssid}, P_i, P_j)$
3. (a) P_j picks $R, S \overset{\$}{\leftarrow} \mathbb{Z}_p$, a random challenge $\varepsilon \overset{\$}{\leftarrow} \{0,1\}^n$.
      He then sends $c' = (g_1{}^R g_2{}^S, h_1{}^r h_2{}^S G(\varepsilon))$ to P_i.
   (b) P_i picks $s \overset{\$}{\leftarrow} \mathbb{Z}_p$ and computes $(\alpha, \beta, \gamma, \delta) = (g_1{}^s, g_2{}^s, h^s, (cd^\omega)^s)$.
      He then sends $(\mathsf{sid}, \mathsf{ssid}, \alpha, \beta, \gamma, \delta)$ to P_j.
   (c) P_j now opens c' by sending $(\mathsf{sid}, \mathsf{ssid}, R, S, \varepsilon)$ to P_i.
   (d) P_i checks if this is consistent with c' otherwise he aborts.
      P_i now computes $z = s + \varepsilon r$ and sends $(\mathsf{sid}, \mathsf{ssid}, z)$ to P_j.
   (e) P_j outputs $(\mathsf{reveal}, \mathsf{sid}, \mathsf{ssid}, P_i, P_j, x)$ if and only if
      $$g_1{}^z = \alpha u_1{}^\varepsilon, g_2{}^z = \beta u_2{}^\varepsilon, h^z = \gamma(e/m)^\varepsilon, (cd^\omega)^z = \delta v^\varepsilon$$

Fig. 2. Lindell's Commitment Protocol, UC-Secure against Static Adversaries

(or actually opening) to another value x', but that is too late when the simulator discover the mistake. For the sake of clarity, we only mention the differences between this situation and the real protocol presented on Figure 3.

Any extraction done on C at the end of the commit phase would lead the simulator to believe to a commit to x, however the valid decommit outputs x'. Note however that this attack does not succeed very often since one needs, for a random ε, that $G^{-1}(mD^{1/\varepsilon})$ exists and can be parsed as $(x', \mathsf{sid}, \mathsf{ssid}, P_i, P_j)$.

Static Corruptions. We stress that this possible inconsistency comes from the move forward of the proof in the commit phase, even before the message x is strongly committed. The first protocol does not suffer from this issue.

We have a CRS, consisting of $(p, \mathbb{G}, g_1, g_2, c, d, h, h_1, h_2, \zeta, H_K)$, where $\mathbb{G}$ is a group of order p with generators g_1, g_2; $c, d, h \in \mathbb{G}$ are random elements in $\mathbb{G}$ and $h_1 = g_1{}^\rho$ and $h_2 = g_2{}^\rho$ for a random $\rho \in \mathbb{Z}_p$; H_K is randomly drawn from a collision-resistant hash function family $\mathcal{H}$.

Intuitively, the tuple $(p, \mathbb{G}, g_1, g_2, c, d, h, H_K)$ is a Cramer-Shoup encryption key, the tuple $(p, \mathbb{G}, g_1, g_2, h_1, h_2)$ is the CRS of a dual-mode encryption scheme, and the tuple $(p, \mathbb{G}, g, \zeta) =$ is the CRS of a Pedersen commitment scheme.

Let $G : \{0, 1\}^n \to \mathbb{G}$ be an efficiently computable and invertible mapping of a binary string to the group.

The commit phase. Upon receiving a message $(\mathsf{Commit}, \mathsf{sid}, \mathsf{ssid}, P_i, P_j, x)$, where $x \in \{0, 1\}^{n - \log^2(n)}$ and $\mathsf{sid}, \mathsf{ssid} \in \{0, 1\}^{\log^2(n)/4}$, party P_i works as follows:

1. P_i computes $m = G(x, \mathsf{sid}, \mathsf{ssid}, P_i, P_j)$.
2. P_i picks $r \xleftarrow{\$} \mathbb{Z}_p$ and computes $C = \mathsf{CS}(m; r)$, we will note ω the hash of the first three terms.
3. P_i picks $k_1 \xleftarrow{\$} \mathbb{Z}_p$, computes $c_p^1 = \mathsf{Ped}(H_K(C); k_1)$ and sends it to P_j.
4. P_j picks $R, S \xleftarrow{\$} \mathbb{Z}_p$, $\varepsilon \xleftarrow{\$} \{0, 1\}^n$ and sends $c' = (g_1{}^R g_2{}^S, h_1{}^R h_2{}^S G(\varepsilon))$ to P_i.
5. P_i picks $s, k_2 \xleftarrow{\$} \mathbb{Z}_p$ and computes $(\alpha, \beta, \gamma, \delta) = (g_1{}^s, g_2{}^s, h^s, (cd^\omega)^s)$. He then computes and sends $c_p^2 = \mathsf{Ped}(H_K(\alpha, \beta, \gamma, \delta); k_2)$ to P_j.
6. P_j now opens c' by sending (R, S, ε) to P_i.
7. P_i checks if this is consistent with c' otherwise he aborts.
8. P_i now computes $z = s + \varepsilon r$, and erases r, s. He also opens c_p^1 by sending C, k_1 to P_j.
9. P_j verifies the consistency of c_p^1. If yes, he stores $(\mathsf{sid}, \mathsf{ssid}, P_i, P_j, c, \varepsilon, c_p^2)$ and outputs $(\mathsf{receipt}, \mathsf{sid}, \mathsf{ssid}, P_i, P_j)$. He ignores any later commitment messages with the same $(\mathsf{sid}, \mathsf{ssid})$ from P_i.

The decommit phase. Upon receiving a message $(\mathsf{reveal}, \mathsf{sid}, \mathsf{ssid}, P_i, P_j)$, P_i works as follows:

1. P_i sends $(x, \alpha, \beta, \gamma, \delta, k_2, z)$ to P_j.
2. P_j computes $m = G(x, \mathsf{sid}, \mathsf{ssid}, P_i, P_j)$, and outputs $(\mathsf{reveal}, \mathsf{sid}, \mathsf{ssid}, P_i, P_j, x)$ if and only if c_p^2 is consistent and:
$$g_1^z = \alpha u_1{}^\varepsilon, g_2{}^z = \beta u_2{}^\varepsilon, h^z = \gamma(e/m)^\varepsilon, (cd^\omega)^z = \delta v^\varepsilon$$

Fig. 3. Lindell's Commitment Protocol, UC-Secure against Adaptive Adversaries

3.3 A Simple Patch

In order to avoid the above concern, a simple patch consists in committing $m = G(x, \mathsf{sid}, \mathsf{ssid}, P_i, P_j)$ in the second Pedersen commitment c_p^2. This leads to the simple change in the protocol presented on the bottom part of Figure 4, where x is now strongly committed before the proof, and then the previous issue does not occur anymore.

4 Our Optimization of the Commitments Protocols

We now focus on much more efficient protocols, with the above modification, and additional ones. We kept the original notations, but as done in [2], we can note

---

The commit phase. Upon receiving a message $(\mathsf{Commit}, \mathsf{sid}, \mathsf{ssid}, P_i, P_j, x)$ where $x \in \{0,1\}^{n-\log^2(n)}$ and $\mathsf{sid}, \mathsf{ssid} \in \{0,1\}^{\log^2(n)/4}$, $\mathcal{A}$ works as follows:

5. $\mathcal{A}$ picks $s, k_2 \xleftarrow{\$} \mathbb{Z}_p$, $\underline{D \xleftarrow{\$} \mathbb{G}}$ and computes $(\alpha, \beta, \gamma, \delta) = (g_1{}^s, g_2{}^s, h^s \underline{D}, (cd^\omega)^s)$. $\mathcal{A}$ then computes and sends $c_p^2 = \mathsf{Ped}(H_K(\alpha, \beta, \gamma, \delta); k_2)$ to P_j.

8. $\mathcal{A}$ <u>checks</u> if $G^{-1}(mD^{1/\varepsilon})$ exists and can be parsed as $(x', \mathsf{sid}, \mathsf{ssid}, P_i, P_j)$ for a random x'. If so, $\mathcal{A}$ now computes $z = s + \varepsilon r$, and erases r, s. It also opens c_p^1 by sending C, k_1 to P_j.

The decommit phase. Upon receiving a message $(\mathsf{reveal}, \mathsf{sid}, \mathsf{ssid}, P_i, P_j)$, $\mathcal{A}$ works as follows:

1. $\mathcal{A}$ sends $(\underline{x'}, \alpha, \beta, \gamma, \delta, k_2, z)$ to P_j.
2. P_j computes $\underline{m'} = G(\mathsf{sid}, \mathsf{ssid}, P_i, P_j, \underline{x})$, and outputs $(\mathsf{reveal}, \mathsf{sid}, \mathsf{ssid}, P_i, P_j, \underline{x'})$ if and only if c_p^2 is consistent and:
$$g_1^z = \alpha u_1{}^\varepsilon, g_2{}^z = \beta u_2{}^\varepsilon, h^z = \underline{h^s(e'D^{1/\varepsilon})^\varepsilon} = \gamma(e/\underline{m'})^\varepsilon, (cd^\omega)^z = \delta v^\varepsilon$$

The commit phase.

5. P_i picks $s, k_2 \xleftarrow{\$} \mathbb{Z}_p$ and computes $(\alpha, \beta, \gamma, \delta) = (g_1{}^s, g_2{}^s, h^s, (cd^\omega)^s)$. He then computes and sends $c_p^2 = \mathsf{Ped}(\underline{m}, H_K(\alpha, \beta, \gamma, \delta); k_2)$ to P_j.

Fig. 4. Inconsistent Extraction/Opening and Simple Patch w.r.t. Figure 3

that C is actually a Cramer-Shoup encryption of m, and $(\alpha, \beta, \gamma, \delta)$ is a partial Cramer-Shoup encryption of 1 with the same ω as in the first ciphertext: the double Cramer-Shoup encryption of (m, m') was denoted by $\mathsf{DCS}(m, m'; r, s) = (C_1, C_2)$, where

- C_1 is a real Cramer-Shoup encryption $C_1 = \mathsf{CS}(m; r)$ of m for a random $r \xleftarrow{\$} \mathbb{Z}_p$: $C_1 = (\mathbf{u}_1 = (g_1{}^r, g_2{}^r), e_1 = m \cdot h^r, v_1 = (cd^\omega)^r)$, where v_1 is computed afterwards with $\omega = H_K(\mathbf{u}_1, e_1)$;
- C_2 is a partial Cramer-Shoup encryption $C_2 = \mathsf{PCS}(m'; \omega, s)$ of m' for a random $s \xleftarrow{\$} \mathbb{Z}_p$ with the above ω value: $C_2 = (\mathbf{u}_2 = (g_1{}^s, g_2{}^s), e_2 = m' \cdot h^s, v_2 = (cd^\omega)^s)$, where v_2 is computed directly with the above $\omega = H_K(\mathbf{u}_1, e_1)$.

In addition, when ω is fixed, we have an homomorphic property: if $(C_1, C_2) = \mathsf{DCS}(m, m'; r, s)$, with a common ω, the component-wise product $C_1 \times C_2 = \mathsf{PCS}(m \times m'; \omega, r+s)$. In particular, we can see the last tuple $(\alpha u_1^\varepsilon, \beta u_2^\varepsilon, \gamma e^\varepsilon, \delta v^\varepsilon)$ as $C_2 \times C_1^\varepsilon$. It should thus be $\mathsf{PCS}(m^\varepsilon; \omega, \varepsilon r + s) = \mathsf{PCS}(m^\varepsilon; \omega, z)$, which is the final check. We now use these new notations in the following.

4.1   Improvement of the Static Protocol

The improvement presented below consists in noting that the receiver can directly send the value ε in the decommit phase, without having to send a commitment first. To allow this, we simply ask the sender to send a Pedersen commitment of $C_2 = (\alpha, \beta, \gamma, \delta)$ prior to receiving ε. This reduces the number

We have a CRS, consisting of $(p, \mathbb{G}, g, g_1, g_2, c, d, h, \zeta, H_K)$, where $\mathbb{G}$ is a group of order p with generators g, ζ, g_1, g_2; $c, d, h \in \mathbb{G}$ are random elements in $\mathbb{G}$; H_K is randomly drawn from a collision-resistant hash function family $\mathcal{H}$.

Intuitively $(p, \mathbb{G}, g_1, g_2, c, d, h, H_K)$ is a Cramer-Shoup public key and $(p, \mathbb{G}, g, \zeta)$ is a CRS for a Pedersen commitment.

Let $G : \{0,1\}^n \to \mathbb{G}$ be an efficiently computable and invertible mapping of a binary string to the group, as before.

The commit phase. Upon receiving a message $(\mathsf{Commit}, \mathsf{sid}, \mathsf{ssid}, P_i, P_j, x)$ where $x \in \{0,1\}^{n - \log^2(n)}$ and $\mathsf{sid}, \mathsf{ssid} \in \{0,1\}^{\log^2(n)/4}$, party P_i works as follows:

1. P_i computes $m = G(x, \mathsf{sid}, \mathsf{ssid}, P_i, P_j)$.
2. P_i picks $r, s \xleftarrow{\$} \mathbb{Z}_p$ and computes $(C_1, C_2) = \mathsf{DCS}(m, 1; r, s)$. We note $C_2 = (\alpha, \beta, \gamma, \delta)$.
3. P_i sends $(\mathsf{sid}, \mathsf{ssid}, C_1)$ to P_j.
4. P_j stores $(\mathsf{sid}, \mathsf{ssid}, P_i, P_j, C_1)$ and outputs $(\mathsf{receipt}, \mathsf{sid}, \mathsf{ssid}, P_i, P_j)$. He ignores any later commitment messages with the same $(\mathsf{sid}, \mathsf{ssid})$ from P_i.

The decommit phase. Upon receiving a message $(\mathsf{reveal}, \mathsf{sid}, \mathsf{ssid}, P_i, P_j)$, P_i works as follows:

1. P_i picks $k_2 \xleftarrow{\$} \mathbb{Z}_p$, computes $c_p^2 = \mathsf{Ped}(H_K(m, C_2, \mathsf{sid}, \mathsf{ssid}, P_i, P_j); k_2)$. He then sends $(\mathsf{sid}, \mathsf{ssid}, x, c_p^2)$ to P_j.
2. P_j computes $m = G(x, \mathsf{sid}, \mathsf{ssid}, P_i, P_j)$, picks $\varepsilon \xleftarrow{\$} \mathbb{Z}_p$ and sends it to P_i.
3. P_i now computes $z = s + \varepsilon r$ and sends $(\mathsf{sid}, \mathsf{ssid}, C_2, k_2, z)$ to P_j.
4. P_j outputs $(\mathsf{reveal}, \mathsf{sid}, \mathsf{ssid}, P_i, P_j, x)$ if and only if c_p^2 is consistent and

$$g_1^z = \alpha u_1^\varepsilon, g_2^z = \beta u_2^\varepsilon, h^z = \gamma (e/m)^\varepsilon, (cd^\omega)^z = \delta v^\varepsilon$$

Fig. 5. Our New Commitment Protocol UC-Secure against Static Adversaries

of flows of the decommit phase (from 5 downto 3) and the number of elements sent by the receiver, (from 2 group elements and 3 scalars down to only 1 scalar, the challenge), simply increasing the number of elements sent by the sender by 1 group element and 1 scalar (the Pedersen commitment).

4.2   Sketch of Proof of the Static Protocol

For lack of space, we do not give here the full proof of the protocol. One may note that it is very similar to the one given in [15]. The only change lies in the decommit phase, where we make the receiver directly send his challenge value ε rather than encrypting it first. But this change is made possible by the sender sending a Pedersen commitment c_p^2 of C_2 before having seen ε, as in the commit phase of the adaptive version of our protocol.

The proof can thus be easily adapted from the one given for our adaptive protocol (see Section 4.4). The only difference is that in the static version, the sender does not commit to his value C_1, so that the simulator cannot change its mind on the value it gave inside this ciphertext later on. But one can note that in the proof of the adaptive protocol, this commitment c_p^1 has to be equivocated only in case of adaptive corruptions (if the latter occur before the adversary has sent ε). This yields to the same simulator as in the adaptive case (see Section 4.5) with the following modifications, when P_i is honest only:

COMMIT STAGE: Exactly as in the adaptive case except there is no corruption to deal with.

DECOMMIT STAGE: Upon receiving the information that the decommitment has been performed on x, with $(\mathsf{reveal}, \mathsf{sid}, \mathsf{ssid}, P_i, P_j, x)$ from $\mathcal{F}_{\mathsf{mcom}}$, $\mathcal{S}$ first chooses a random z and computes the ciphertext $C_3 = \mathsf{PCS}(m; \omega, z)$. It then chooses a random k_2, a random C_2, computes the associated Pedersen commitment c_p^2 and simulates the first flow of the decommit phase to P_j. Upon receiving ε from P_j, it then adapts $C_2 = C_3/C_1^{\varepsilon}$ and uses the trapdoor for the Pedersen commitment to produce a new value k_2 corresponding to the new value C_2. It then simulates the third flow of the decommit phase to P_j.

4.3   Improvement of the Adaptive Protocol

As for the static version of the protocol, the main improvement presented on Figure 6 below consists in noting that the receiver can directly send the value ε, without having to send an encryption before. To allow this, we simply ask the sender to send his two Pedersen commitments prior to receiving ε.

This reduces, in the commit phase, the number of rounds (from 5 downto 3) and the number of elements sent by the receiver (from 2 group elements and 3 scalars down to only 1 scalar, the challenge). Contrary to the static version, there is no additional cost. This is illustrated in Section 5, which sums up the differences between Lindell's protocol and ours, in the same setting: UC-security against adaptive corruption with erasures.

In addition, in order to slightly increase the message space from $n - \log_2(n)$ to n, we move the sensitive prefix $(\mathsf{sid}, \mathsf{ssid}, P_i, P_j)$ into the second Pedersen.

Eventually, in order to definitely exclude the security concerns presented in Section 3.2, we include the value m to the second Pedersen to prevent the adversary from trying to open his commitment to another value.

4.4   Security Proof

We now provide a full proof, with a sequence of games, that the above protocol emulates the ideal functionality against adaptive corruptions with erasures. This sequence starts from the real game, where the adversary interacts with real players, and ends with the ideal game, where we have built a simulator that makes the interface between the ideal functionality and the adversary.

As already explained, we denote by $C_3 = C_2 C_1^{\varepsilon}$, the tuple involved in the last check. It should be a partial encryption of m under randomness $z = s + \varepsilon r$: $C_3 = \mathsf{PCS}(m; \omega, z)$ where ω is the hash value of the first three terms of C_1.

Game G_0:   This is the real game, in which every flow from the honest players is generated correctly by the simulator which knows the input x sent by the

We have a CRS, consisting of $(p, \mathbb{G}, g, g_1, g_2, c, d, h, \zeta, H_K)$, where $\mathbb{G}$ is a group of order p with generators g, ζ, g_1, g_2; $c, d, h \in \mathbb{G}$ are random elements in $\mathbb{G}$; H_K is randomly drawn from a collision-resistant hash function family $\mathcal{H}$.
Intuitively $(p, \mathbb{G}, g_1, g_2, c, d, h, H_K)$ is a Cramer-Shoup public key and $(p, \mathbb{G}, g, \zeta)$ is a CRS for a Pedersen commitment.
Let $G : \{0,1\}^n \to \mathbb{G}$ be an efficiently computable and invertible mapping of a binary string to the group, as before.
The commit phase. Upon receiving a message $(\mathsf{Commit}, \mathsf{sid}, \mathsf{ssid}, P_i, P_j, x)$, party P_i works as follows, where $x \in \{0,1\}^n$ and $\mathsf{sid}, \mathsf{ssid} \in \{0,1\}^{\log^2(n)/4}$:

1. P_i computes $m = G(x)$.
2. P_i picks $r, s \xleftarrow{\$} \mathbb{Z}_p$ and computes $(C_1, C_2) = \mathsf{DCS}(m, 1; r, s)$.
   We note $C_2 = (\alpha, \beta, \gamma, \delta)$.
3. P_i picks $k_1, k_2 \xleftarrow{\$} \mathbb{Z}_p$.
   He computes $c_p^1 = \mathsf{Ped}(H_K(C_1); k_1)$, $c_p^2 = \mathsf{Ped}(H_K(m, C_2, \mathsf{sid}, \mathsf{ssid}, P_i, P_j); k_2)$.
   He sends (c_p^1, c_p^2) to P_j.
4. P_j picks $\varepsilon \xleftarrow{\$} \mathbb{Z}_p$ and sends it to P_i.
5. P_i now computes $z = s + \varepsilon r$, and erases r, s.
   He also opens c_p^1 by sending (C_1, k_1) to P_j.
6. P_j verifies the consistency of c_p^1.
   If yes, he stores $(\mathsf{sid}, \mathsf{ssid}, P_i, P_j, C_1, \varepsilon, c_p^2)$ and outputs $(\mathsf{receipt}, \mathsf{sid}, \mathsf{ssid}, P_i, P_j)$.
   He ignores any later commitment messages with the same $(\mathsf{sid}, \mathsf{ssid})$ from P_i.

The decommit phase. Upon receiving a message $(\mathsf{reveal}, \mathsf{sid}, \mathsf{ssid}, P_i, P_j)$, P_i works as follows:

1. P_i sends (x, C_2, k_2, z) to P_j.
2. P_j computes $m = G(x)$, and outputs $(\mathsf{reveal}, \mathsf{sid}, \mathsf{ssid}, P_i, P_j, x)$ if and only if c_p^2 is consistent and:
$$g_1^z = \alpha u_1^\varepsilon, g_2^z = \beta u_2^\varepsilon, h^z = \gamma(e/m)^\varepsilon, (cd^\omega)^z = \delta v^\varepsilon$$

Fig. 6. Our New Commitment Protocol UC-Secure against Adaptive Adversaries

environment to the sender. There is no use of the ideal functionality for the moment.

Game G_1: In this game, we focus on the simulation of an honest receiver interacting with a corrupted sender. Executions with an honest sender are still simulated as before, using the input x. The simulator will generate the CRS in such a way it knows the Cramer-Shoup decryption key, but ζ is a discrete logarithm challenge.

Upon receiving the values (c_p^1, c_p^2) from the adversary, the simulator simply chooses a challenge ε at random and sends it to the adversary, as P_j would do with P_i. After receiving the values (C_1, k_1), the simulator checks the consistency of the Pedersen commitment c_p^1 and aborts in case of failure. It then uses the Cramer-Shoup decryption key to recover the value m' sent by the adversary, and computes $x' = G^{-1}(m')$. In case of invalid ciphertext, one sets $x' = \bot$ (an element not in the domain of G). It stores $(\mathsf{sid}, \mathsf{ssid}, P_i, P_j, C_1, \varepsilon, c_p^2)$ and $(x', \mathsf{sid}, P_i, P_j)$ (this will correspond later to the Commit query to the ideal functionality, in the ideal game). Upon receiving the values (x, C_2, k_2, z), the simulator does as P_j would do in checking the commitment c_p^2 and that $C_3 = \mathsf{PCS}(m^\varepsilon; \omega, z)$, but accepts x' as the opening for the commitment.

The only difference with the previous game is that P_i will accept x', as decrypted from $C_1 = \mathsf{CS}(m' = G(x'); r)$, for the decommitment instead of the value x output at the decommitment time, which leads to $m = G(x)$ that matches with $C_3 = \mathsf{PCS}(m^\varepsilon; \omega, z)$, but that is also contained in c_p^2 together with C_2. We will show that under the binding property of the Pedersen commitment, one necessarily has $x' = x$, and thus there is no difference.

Let us assume that $x' \neq x$ in at least one of such executions: for the first one, we rewind the adversary up to the step 4., and send a new random challenge ε'. Then the adversary should send the same C_1, otherwise one extracts the discrete logarithm of ζ in basis g or a collision for H_K, and the same pair (m, C_2) in the decommit phase for the same reason, but possibly a different z'. Then, the final checks guarantee that $C_3 = \mathsf{PCS}(m^\varepsilon; \omega, z)$ in the first execution and $C_3' = \mathsf{PCS}(m^{\varepsilon'}; \omega, z')$ in the second execution. From the homomorphic property: C_2 encrypts $(m/m')^\varepsilon$ in the first execution, but $(m/m')^{\varepsilon'}$ in the second execution, which are thus equal. Since $\varepsilon' \neq \varepsilon$, this implies that $m' = m$. For the same reason, one can note that if C_1 is not a valid ciphertext, C_3 cannot be valid either (for the fixed ω). We stress that the rewind here is just for the proof of indistinguishability of the two games, but not in the simulation.

In case of corruption of the receiver, one can note that he has no secret.

Game G_2: In this game, we start modifying the simulation of an honest sender, still knowing his input x. For the honest verifier against a corrupted sender, we still have to know the Cramer-Shoup decryption key to run the same simulation as in the previous game. But we now need to know the discrete logarithm for equivocating the Pedersen commitment.

This game is almost the same as the previous one excepted the way the double Cramer-Shoup ciphertext is generated: $(C_1, C_2) = \mathsf{DCS}(m, n; r, s)$, for a random n instead of 1. The rest of the commit phase is unchanged.

At the decommit phase, $\mathcal{S}$ chooses random coins z and computes $C_3 = \mathsf{PCS}(m; \omega, z)$, and then "repairs" $C_2 = C_3/C_1^\varepsilon$, and k_2 for being able to open c_p^2 to this new value.

Thanks to the homomorphic property, the repaired C_2 is a correct ciphertext of 1, and the equivocation of the Pedersen commitment guarantees a correct opening. This game is thus perfectly indistinguishable from the previous one.

In case a corruption of P_i occurs before the decommit phase, the simulator anticipates the equivocation of c_p^2.

Game G_3: One can note that in the previous game, r is not used anymore to compute z. One could thus ignore it, unless P_i gets corrupted before ε has been sent, since we should be able to give it. But in such a case, one can compute again C_1 knowing r and equivocate c_p^1. We then alter again the way the double Cramer-Shoup ciphertext is generated: $(C_1, C_2) = \mathsf{DCS}(m', n; r, s)$, for random m' and n. Everything remains unchanged.

The unique change is thus the ciphertext C_1 that encrypts a random m' instead of m. One can run the IND-CCA security game, in an hybrid way, to show this game is indistinguishable from the previous one. To this aim, one has to show that the random coins r are not needed to be known, and that the challenge ciphertexts are never asked for decryption (where the decryption key here is replaced by an access to the decryption oracle, hence the IND-CCA security game). The former point has been discussed above. For the latter, we have shown that the value actually encrypted in C_1 by the corrupted sender is the value sent at the decommit phase, which would even break the one-wayness of the encryption. Hence, if such a replay happens, one knows that the decommit phase will fail.

In case of corruption of P_i before receiving ε, Pedersen commitments only have been sent, and they can thus be equivocated with correct values (given by either the ideal functionality or the adversary). In case of corruption of P_i after having received ε, one does has before, anticipating the equivocation of c_p^2.

Game G_4: This is the ideal game, in which the simulator works as described below: when P_i is corrupted, one uses the decryption of C_1 to send the Commit query to the ideal functionality, when P_i is honest one can wait for the receipt and reveal confirmations from the adversary to conclude the simulation of the real flows.

4.5   Description of the Simulator

Setup. The simulator generates the parameters, knowing the Cramer-Shoup decryption key and the Pedersen equivocation trapdoor.

When P_i is Honest.

COMMIT STAGE: Upon receiving the information that a commitment has been performed, with $(\mathsf{receipt}, \mathsf{sid}, \mathsf{ssid}, P_i, P_j)$ from $\mathcal{F}_{\mathsf{mcom}}$, $\mathcal{S}$ computes $(C_1, C_2) = \mathsf{DCS}(m', n; r, s)$, for random m' and n but then follows as P_i would do. If P_j is honest too, one just has to send a random ε.

In case of corruption of P_i before receiving ε, one can equivocate c_p^1, otherwise one equivocates c_p^2, as explained below, in both cases using the value given either by the ideal functionality or the adversary, according to the time of the corruption.

DECOMMIT STAGE: Upon receiving the information that the decommitment has been performed on x, with $(\mathsf{reveal}, \mathsf{sid}, \mathsf{ssid}, P_i, P_j, x)$ from $\mathcal{F}_{\mathsf{mcom}}$, $\mathcal{S}$ exploits the equivocability of the Pedersen commitment: it first chooses a random z and computes the ciphertext $C_3 = \mathsf{PCS}(m = G(x); \omega, z)$. It then adapts $C_2 = C_3/C_1{}^\varepsilon$ and uses the trapdoor for the Pedersen commitment to produce a new value k_2 corresponding to the new value C_2. It then simulates the decommit phase to P_j.

When P_i is Corrupted and P_j is Honest.

COMMIT STAGE: Upon receiving (C_1, k_1) from the adversary, $\mathcal{S}$ decrypts the Cramer-Shoup ciphertext C_1 and extracts x from G. If the decryption is invalid, $\mathcal{S}$ sends (Commit, sid, ssid, $P_i, P_j, \perp$) to $\mathcal{F}_{\mathsf{mcom}}$. Otherwise, $\mathcal{S}$ sends (Commit, sid, ssid, P_i, P_j, x).

DECOMMIT STAGE: $\mathcal{S}$ acts as a regular honest user P_j from the incoming message of $\mathcal{A}$ on behalf of P_i. In case of validity, send the query (reveal, sid, ssid).

5   Conclusion

As a conclusion, let us graphically present a comparison of the two protocols.

5.1   The Original Lindell's Protocol for Adaptive Adversaries

The commit phase

$$m = G(x, \text{sid}, \text{ssid}, P_i, P_j)$$
$$r \overset{\$}{\leftarrow} \mathbb{Z}_p, k_1 \overset{\$}{\leftarrow} \mathbb{Z}_p, C = \mathsf{CS}(m; r)$$
$$c_p^1 = \mathsf{Ped}(H_K(C); k_1) \xrightarrow{\quad c_p^1 \quad} R, S \overset{\$}{\leftarrow} \mathbb{Z}_p, \varepsilon \overset{\$}{\leftarrow} \{0,1\}^n$$
$$s \overset{\$}{\leftarrow} \mathbb{Z}_p, k_2 \overset{\$}{\leftarrow} \mathbb{Z}_p \xleftarrow{\quad c' \quad} c' = (g_1{}^R g_2{}^S, h_1{}^R h_2{}^S G(\varepsilon))$$
$$(\alpha, \beta, \gamma, \delta) = (g_1{}^s, g_2{}^s, h^s, (cd^\omega)^s)$$
$$c_p^2 = \mathsf{Ped}(H_K(\alpha, \beta, \gamma, \delta)); k_2) \xrightarrow{\quad c_p^2 \quad}$$
$$\text{Aborts if } c' \text{ inconsistent} \xleftarrow{\quad R, S, \varepsilon \quad}$$
$$z = s + \varepsilon r, \text{ erases } r, s \xrightarrow{\quad k_1, C \quad} \text{Aborts if } c_p^1 \text{ inconsistent}$$

The decommit phase

$$\xrightarrow{(x, \alpha, \beta, \gamma, \delta, k_2, z)} m = G(x, \text{sid}, \text{ssid}, P_i, P_j) \text{ checks } c_p^2 \text{ and whether}$$
$$g_1^z = \alpha u_1{}^\varepsilon, g_2{}^z = \beta u_2{}^\varepsilon, h^z = \gamma(e/m)^\varepsilon, (cd^\omega)^z = \delta v^\varepsilon$$

5.2   Our Protocol

The commit phase

$$m = G(x), r \overset{\$}{\leftarrow} \mathbb{Z}_p, s \overset{\$}{\leftarrow} \mathbb{Z}_p$$
$$(C_1, C_2) = \mathsf{DCS}(m; 1; r, s), k_1, k_2 \overset{\$}{\leftarrow} \mathbb{Z}_p$$
$$c_p^1 = \mathsf{Ped}(H_K(C_1); k_1)$$
$$c_p^2 = \mathsf{Ped}(H_K(C_2, m, \text{sid}, \text{ssid}, P_i, P_j); k_2) \xrightarrow{\quad c_p^1, c_p^2 \quad}$$
$$\xleftarrow{\quad \varepsilon \quad} \varepsilon \overset{\$}{\leftarrow} \mathbb{Z}_p$$
$$z = s + \varepsilon r, \text{ erases } r, s \xrightarrow{\quad k_1, C_1 \quad} \text{Aborts if } c_p^1 \text{ inconsistent}$$

The decommit phase

$$\xrightarrow{(x, C_2, k_2, z)} m = G(x), \text{ checks } c_p^2 \text{ and whether}$$
$$g_1^z = \alpha u_1{}^\varepsilon, g_2{}^z = \beta u_2{}^\varepsilon, h^z = \gamma(e/m)^\varepsilon, (cd^\omega)^z = \delta v^\varepsilon$$

Acknowledgments. We thank Yehuda Lindell for his fruitful comments. The first author was funded by a Sofja Kovalevskaja Award of the Alexander von Humboldt Foundation and the German Federal Ministry for Education and Research. This work was supported in part by the French ANR-12-INSE-0014 SIM-PATIC Project and in part by the European Commission through the FP7-ICT-2011-EU-Brazil Program under Contract 288349 SecFuNet.

References

1. Abdalla, M., Chevalier, C., Pointcheval, D.: Smooth projective hashing for conditionally extractable commitments. In: Halevi, S. (ed.) CRYPTO 2009. LNCS, vol. 5677, pp. 671–689. Springer, Heidelberg (2009)
2. Ben Hamouda, F., Blazy, O., Chevalier, C., Pointcheval, D., Vergnaud, D.: Efficient UC-secure authenticated key-exchange for algebraic languages. In: Kurosawa, K., Hanaoka, G. (eds.) PKC 2013. LNCS, vol. 7778, pp. 272–291. Springer, Heidelberg (2013)
3. Blazy, O., Fuchsbauer, G., Izabachène, M., Jambert, A., Sibert, H., Vergnaud, D.: Batch Groth–Sahai. In: Zhou, J., Yung, M. (eds.) ACNS 2010. LNCS, vol. 6123, pp. 218–235. Springer, Heidelberg (2010)
4. Camenisch, J., Shoup, V.: Practical verifiable encryption and decryption of discrete logarithms. In: Boneh, D. (ed.) CRYPTO 2003. LNCS, vol. 2729, pp. 126–144. Springer, Heidelberg (2003)
5. Canetti, R.: Universally composable security: A new paradigm for cryptographic protocols. In: 42nd FOCS, pp. 136–145. IEEE Computer Society Press (October 2001)
6. Canetti, R.: Universally Composable Security: A New Paradigm for Cryptographic Protocols. On the Cryptology ePrint Archive, Report 2000/067 (December 2005)
7. Canetti, R., Fischlin, M.: Universally composable commitments. In: Kilian, J. (ed.) CRYPTO 2001. LNCS, vol. 2139, pp. 19–40. Springer, Heidelberg (2001)
8. Canetti, R., Halevi, S., Katz, J., Lindell, Y., MacKenzie, P.: Universally composable password-based key exchange. In: Cramer, R. (ed.) EUROCRYPT 2005. LNCS, vol. 3494, pp. 404–421. Springer, Heidelberg (2005)
9. Canetti, R., Lindell, Y., Ostrovsky, R., Sahai, A.: Universally composable two-party and multi-party secure computation. In: 34th ACM STOC, pp. 494–503. ACM Press (May 2002)
10. Cramer, R., Shoup, V.: A practical public key cryptosystem provably secure against adaptive chosen ciphertext attack. In: Krawczyk, H. (ed.) CRYPTO 1998. LNCS, vol. 1462, pp. 13–25. Springer, Heidelberg (1998)
11. Damgård, I., Nielsen, J.B.: Perfect hiding and perfect binding universally composable commitment schemes with constant expansion factor. In: Yung, M. (ed.) CRYPTO 2002. LNCS, vol. 2442, pp. 581–596. Springer, Heidelberg (2002)
12. Fischlin, M., Libert, B., Manulis, M.: Non-interactive and re-usable universally composable string commitments with adaptive security. In: Lee, D.H., Wang, X. (eds.) ASIACRYPT 2011. LNCS, vol. 7073, pp. 468–485. Springer, Heidelberg (2011)
13. Gennaro, R., Lindell, Y.: A framework for password-based authenticated key exchange. In: Biham, E. (ed.) EUROCRYPT 2003. LNCS, vol. 2656, pp. 524–543. Springer, Heidelberg (2003)

14. Groth, J., Sahai, A.: Efficient non-interactive proof systems for bilinear groups. In: Smart, N.P. (ed.) EUROCRYPT 2008. LNCS, vol. 4965, pp. 415–432. Springer, Heidelberg (2008)
15. Lindell, Y.: Highly-efficient universally-composable commitments based on the DDH assumption. In: Paterson, K.G. (ed.) EUROCRYPT 2011. LNCS, vol. 6632, pp. 446–466. Springer, Heidelberg (2011)
16. Lindell, Y.: Highly-efficient universally-composable commitments based on the DDH assumption. Cryptology ePrint Archive, Report 2011/180 (2011)
17. Pedersen, T.P.: Non-interactive and information-theoretic secure verifiable secret sharing. In: Feigenbaum, J. (ed.) CRYPTO 1991. LNCS, vol. 576, pp. 129–140. Springer, Heidelberg (1992)
18. Yao, A.C.: Theory and applications of trapdoor functions. In: 23rd FOCS, pp. 80–91. IEEE Computer Society Press (November 1982)

Primeless Factoring-Based Cryptography
–Solving the Complexity Bottleneck of Public-Key Generation–

Sonia Bogos*, Ioana Boureanu, and Serge Vaudenay

École Polytechnique Fédérale de Lausanne, CH-1015 Lausanne, Switzerland

Abstract. Factoring-based public-key cryptosystems have an overall complexity which is dominated by the key-production algorithm, which requires the generation of prime numbers. This is most inconvenient in settings where the key-generation is not an one-off process, e.g., for forwards secrecy. To this end, we extend the Goldwasser-Micali (GM) cryptosystem to a provably secure system, denoted SIS, where the generation of primes is bypassed. By developing on the correct choice of the parameters of SIS, we align SIS's security guarantees (i.e., resistance to factoring of moduli, etc.) to those of other well-known factoring-based cryptosystems. Taking into consideration different possibilities to implement the fundamental operations, we explicitly compare and contrast the asymptotic complexity of well-known public-key cryptosystems (e.g., GM and/or RSA) with that of SIS's. The latter shows that once we are ready to accept an increase in the size of the moduli, SIS offers a generally lower asymptotic complexity than, e.g., GM or even RSA.

1 Introduction

Setting. Several, widely used public-key cryptosystems have a setup phase where prime numbers are generated and/or primality tests are run. The computational complexity yielded by the generation of a prime number of length L is generally in $O(L^4)$ and –if optimised– $O^{\sim}(L^3)$, as we will detail next in this section. Such generations occur, for instance, in the case of RSA [21] and/or in the Goldwasser-Micali (GM) probabilistic cryptosystem [7], as each of them defines its operation over $\mathbf{Z}_n^*$, for n being a product of two, distinct large prime numbers generated therein.

Moreover, there exist settings in which the key-generation in asymmetric cryptosystems is not an one-off process, e.g., key agreement with forward secrecy [1], secure delegation protocols [18], EKE password-based key exchange [3], zero-knowledge proofs of knowledge without any setups, where a new commitment key is used at each session. *Secure* delegation protocols [18] are based on homomorphic public-key encryption schemes and in each of the runs of such a protocol, the keys need to be re-issued freshly. Hence, the asymptotic complexity of prime-generation for the homomorphic encryptions used therein [18] (e.g., GM, RSA, Paillier's encryption, etc.) becomes an alarming bottleneck of the delegated computation. The scheme that we propose in this paper is homomorphic and it is aimed at overcoming precisely the shortcoming of such bottlenecks. In this context, in our comparisons, we focus mostly on (homomorphic)

* Supported by a grant of the Swiss National Science Foundation, 200021_143899/1.

M. Jacobson et al. (Eds.): ACNS 2013, LNCS 7954, pp. 552–569, 2013.

schemes that are commonly used in these settings i.e., factoring-based ones, and do not compare with public-key cryptosystems different in nature. I.e., we do not refer to the McEliece cryptosystem [17] based on algebraic codes, which may indeed have faster key-generation procedures; neither do we relate to Diffie-Hellman cryptosystems (e.g., EC-based) for which primes are not key-specific. We are interested in systems where the security gravitates around problems related to primality, e.g., factoring of moduli. More precisely, we extend and compare with the Goldwasser-Micali (GM) cryptosystem [7].

Comparisons at a Glance. The security of the RSA cryptosystem is based on the integer prime-factorisation problem (i.e., the RSA modulus n should be hard-to-factor). Thus, a fair security guarantee is to take the length L of the modulus n large enough to be considered practically hard-to-factor using, e.g., the general number field sieve (GNFS) factorisation algorithm [14]. Given the complexity of the latter factorisation for a number of the order 2^L and measuring its hardness in the order of 2^s (s is a security parameter), we conclude that a secure length L for the RSA-generated modulus is $O^\sim(s^3)$.

The commonplace implementation of the RSA cryptosystem has a complexity of $O(L^4)$ for the setup phase, due to prime-generation numbers. The "schoolbook" multiplication method of $O(L^2)$ can be replaced by "fast multiplication" techniques in the key-generation process, i.e., by the Karatsuba algorithm [12] in $O(L^{\log_2 3})$ or by methods [23] based on the Fast Fourier Transform (FFT) in $O(L \times \log L)$. In the FFT-based optimisation cases, the complexity of RSA is lowered[1] to $O^\sim(L^3)$. Thus, in the best case of FFT-optimisation, primality-testing based cryptosystems would run in $O^\sim(s^9)$.

The GM cryptosystem is semantically secure under the assumption that the quadratic residuosity (QR) problem modulo a composite integer n is hard. The QR problem stipulates that, given this modulus n and a number $x \in \mathbf{Z}_n^*$, when the Jacobi symbol [10] for $x \in \mathbf{Z}_n^*$ with respect to n is 1, it is difficult to determine whether x is a quadratic residue modulo n. If the prime-factorisation of n is known, then the QR problem is easy. In this context of complexity-analysis, it is to be mentioned that the Jacobi symbol [10] itself generally has quadratic complexity, as schoolbook multiplication is most often used within. We briefly recall the GM scheme somewhat more detailedly. In the key-generation algorithm, firstly two different (large) prime numbers p and q are independently generated and $n = pq$. Then, a non-residue x is found such that its Legendre symbol [10] with respect to p and q are equal to -1, i.e., $\left(\frac{x}{p}\right) = \left(\frac{x}{q}\right) = -1$, whereas the Jacobi symbol with respect to n is 1. The public key is defined by the pair (x, n), whereas the prime factors p and q are kept secret. To encrypt a bit b, an integer y is randomly picked from $\mathbf{Z}_n^*$, i.e., $y \leftarrow_U \mathbf{Z}_n^*$, and its encryption is calculated as $c = y^2 x^b \pmod{N}$. To decrypt, the secret key (p, q) is used and it is to check whether the encrypted value c is a quadratic residue, i.e., to solve $\left(\frac{c}{p}\right) = (-1)^b$, in the unknown b.

Contribution. In this paper, we endeavour in extending the GM scheme into a public-key scheme that bypasses prime-generation procedures. The GM scheme has the same aforementioned complexity bottlenecks. We show reduction in complexity, from the

---

[1] $O^\sim(t(n))$ is equal to $O(t(n) \times (\log t(n))^c)$, for some constant $c \geq 0$.

best $O^\sim(s^9)$ to $O^\sim(s^4)$, at the cost of generating larger, composite numbers (where s is the security parameter). This comes to the special benefit of applications like the aforementioned, where the overwhelming key-generations repeat at each run.

Structure of the Paper. In Section 2, we present the computational problems relevant to our cryptosystem and discuss their hardnesses. In Section 3, we describe our cryptosystem denoted SIS. In Section 4, we discuss the necessary conditions for the selection of parameters and their asymptotic behaviours. In Section 5, we discuss the complexity of our scheme and compare it to RSA and GM. We provide experimental results that show that our asymptotic analysis is valid.

2   Preliminaries

We present here some essential background; the computational problems that found the basis of our security analyses, and results with respect to their hardness.

2.1   Foundations

Let G be an Abelian group. A *character* χ is a group homomorphism from $(G, +)$ to $\mathbb{C}^*$. The set of characters over G has a group structure with component-wise multiplication over $\mathbb{C}^*$. This group is called the *dual group* $\widehat{G}$ of G and it is isomorphic with G [10]. Each character will have an order in this group. For all $a \in G$, $\chi(a)$ is a $\lambda(G)$-th root of the unity, where $\lambda(G)$ is the exponent of the group G. A character χ of order 2 is such that $\chi(a) \in \{-1, 1\}$, for all $a \in G$. Let ε be the trivial character, i.e., $\varepsilon(a) = 1$. The set of characters χ for which $\chi^2 = \varepsilon$ consists of ε and characters of order 2.

Let $p \in \mathbf{Z}$ be an odd prime. The only character in $\mathbf{Z}_p^*$ of order 2 is the Legendre symbol $\chi(a) = (\frac{a}{p})$, for any $a \in \mathbf{Z}_p^*$. For the standard properties of the Legendre symbol, as well as its generalisation to the Jacobi symbol w.r.t. composed numbers, see [10]. For $n = pq$ with p and q being two different odd primes, there are 3 characters of order 2: the Legendre symbol $(\frac{\cdot}{p})$, the Legendre symbol $(\frac{\cdot}{q})$, and the Jacobi symbol $(\frac{\cdot}{n})$. The latter is easy to compute, but the former are allegedly hard to compute when the primes p and q are unknown. We call these former characters *hard characters* of order 2.

We recall that QR_n is a usual notation for the subgroup of Z_n^* of all quadratic residues. We refer to the problem of deciding whether an element of Z_n^* is quadratic residue or not as the QR problem.

The main scope of this paper is to use characters of order 2, in order to design public-key encryption schemes that elude the generation of prime numbers, thus reducing the general asymptotic complexity of the usual schemes of the kind.

2.2   Computational Problems

In this paper, we first consider the following combinatorial problem:

CHI Problem (Character Interpolation Problem):
Parameters: a modulus n, $x_1, \ldots, x_t$ in $\mathbf{Z}_n^*$, t elements $y_1, \ldots, y_t \in \{-1, +1\}$, all defining a unique character χ on $\mathbf{Z}_n^*$ such that $\chi(x_i) = y_i$ for $i = 1, \ldots, t$ and $t \geq 1$.

Input: $x \in \mathbf{Z}_n^*$.
Problem: Find $y = \chi(x)$.

An instance of this problem is defined by fixing some parameters and providing a corresponding input x. Then, it requires the computation of a character of order 2 for a number $x \in \mathbf{Z}_n^*$, given t elements in $\mathbf{Z}_n^*$ and their respective characters. Note that the above problem can be generalised to the case of characters of order d, i.e., by replacing the set $\{-1, +1\}$ with a group of order d. Also, observe the **CHI** problem can be immediately rewritten as the **MOVA**^{2} problem presented in [19].

We now give a combinatorial problem presented in [20]:

GHI Problem (Group Homomorphism Interpolation Problem):
Parameters: G and H two Abelian groups, S be a subset of $G \times H$, $r \geq 1$ such that S interpolates in a homomorphism between G and H.
Input: r elements $x_1, \ldots, x_r$ in G.
Problem: Find $y_1, \ldots, y_r \in H$ such that there exists a group homomorphism φ such that $\varphi(x_i) = y_i$ for $i = 1, \ldots, r$ and $\varphi(x) = y$ for all $(x, y) \in S$.

An instance of the above problem demands that once given r numbers lying in G, one provides r points in H that together with S interpolate in the group homomorphism φ.

Obviously, the **CHI** problem is a specialisation of the **GHI** problem in which $G = \mathbf{Z}_n^*$, $H = \{-1, +1\}$, $r = 1$, and the homomorphism is unique.

We recall the following theorem:

Lemma 1. *(Lemma 4.3 in [20]) Let G and H be two finite Abelian groups, where the group operation is denoted additively. We denote by d the order of H. Let $x_1, x_2, \ldots, x_r \in G$ which span G'. The following properties are equivalent. In this case, we say that $x_1, x_2, \ldots, x_r$ H-generate G.*

- *For all $y_1, y_2, \ldots, y_r \in H$, there exists at most one group homomorphism $Hom: G \to H$ such that $Hom(x_i) = y_i$ for all $1 \leq i \leq r$.*
- $G' + dG = G$.
- $x_1 + dG, \ldots, x_r + dG$ *span G/dG.*

We denote $span_d(x_1, \ldots, x_t) = \langle x_1, \ldots, x_t \rangle + dG$. Then, saying that $\{x_1, \ldots, x_t\}$ H-generates G for $H = \{-1, +1\}$ is equivalent to $span_2(x_1, \ldots, x_t) = G$.

When one can compute discrete logarithms in $G = \mathbf{Z}_n^*$, one can easily solve the **CHI** problem by solving a linear system. The discrete logarithm is easy when n has only small prime factors. Therefore, for the **CHI** problem to be hard, we need that n has large prime factors. This is the case if n is hard-to-factor. Similarly, when n is easy to factor, we can easily evaluate the characters in certain subgroups of $\mathbf{Z}_n^*$, and therefore solve the **CHI** problem. For details, an efficient Karp reduction of the **CHI** problem to the factorisation problem is present in [19].

Definition 1 (CHI and QR Hardness Assumptions). *Given a probabilistic algorithm* $\mathsf{Gen}(1^s) \to (n, \chi, t)$ *such that χ is a character of order 2 in $\mathbf{Z}_n^*$, say that the **CHI** problem* *is* hard *relative to* Gen *if for every probabilistic algorithm* $\mathcal{A}$ *which is polynomial in s, we have*

$$\left| \Pr \left[\mathcal{A}(x,n,x_1,\ldots,x_t,\chi(x_1),\ldots,\chi(x_t)) = \chi(x) \middle| \begin{array}{l} \mathsf{Gen}(1^s) \to (n,\chi,t), \\ x,x_1,\ldots,x_t \in_U \mathbf{Z}_n^*, \\ \mathsf{span}_2(x_1,\ldots,x_t) = \mathbf{Z}_n^* \end{array} \right] - \frac{1}{2} \right| < \mathsf{negl}(s) \ .$$

We say that the QR problem is hard *relative to* Gen *if for every probabilistic algorithm* $\mathcal{A}$ *which is polynomial in s, we have*

$$\left| \Pr \left[\mathcal{A}(x,n) = 1_{x \in QR_n} \middle| \begin{array}{l} \mathsf{Gen}(1^s) \to (n), \\ x \in_U \mathbf{Z}_n^*, \\ \left(\frac{x}{n}\right) = 1 \end{array} \right] - \frac{1}{2} \right| < \mathsf{negl}(s) \ .$$

Then, we have the following amplification result.

Lemma 2. *Given the parameters* $n, x_1, \ldots, x_t, y_1, \ldots, y_t$ *for an instance of the* **CHI** *problem, i.e., defining a unique* χ *on* $\mathbf{Z}_n^*$, *if* $\mathcal{A}$ *is a probabilistic algorithm which is polynomial in s such that*

$$\left| \Pr[\mathcal{A}(x) = \chi(x) | x \in_U \mathbf{Z}_n^*] - \frac{1}{2} \right| > \theta \ ,$$

then one can define an algorithm $\mathcal{A}'$ *calling* $\mathcal{A}$ *a number of* $\frac{1}{2}\theta^{-2} \ln \frac{2}{\varepsilon}$ *times such that*

$$\Pr\left[\mathcal{A}'(x) = \chi(x) | x \in_U \mathbf{Z}_n^* \right] \geq 1 - \varepsilon \ ,$$

with $\theta > 0$ *and* $\varepsilon > 0$.

Proof. Let $\mathcal{A}$ be a probabilistic algorithm which is polynomial in s. Let

$$p = \Pr\left[\mathcal{A}(x) = \chi(x) | x \in_U \mathbf{Z}_n^* \right] \ .$$

We define the following algorithm $\mathcal{A}'(x)$:

1: initialize $c_1 \leftarrow 0$ and $c_2 \leftarrow 0$
2: **for** $i = 1$ to k **do**
3:     pick some random bits $b_1, \ldots, b_t$ and $r \in_U \mathbf{Z}_n^*$
4:     set $x' \leftarrow x x_1^{b_1} \cdots x_t^{b_t} r^2 \bmod n$
5:     $c_1 \leftarrow c_1 + \mathcal{A}(x') y_1^{b_1} \cdots y_t^{b_t}$
6:     pick some random bits $b_1, \ldots, b_t$ and $r \in_U \mathbf{Z}_n^*$
7:     set $x' \leftarrow x_1^{b_1} \cdots x_t^{b_t} r^2 \bmod n$
8:     $c_2 \leftarrow c_2 + \mathcal{A}(x') y_1^{b_1} \cdots y_t^{b_t}$
9: **end for**
10: output the sign of $c_1 c_2$

Since $p \neq \frac{1}{2}$, we observe that x' at step 7 is uniformly distributed in $\mathbf{Z}_n^*$ and such that $\chi(x') = y_1^{b_1} \cdots y_t^{b_t}$. For this, see Lemma 3 given below.

So, c_2 is incremented with probability p and decremented with probability $1 - p$. Due to the Chernoff bound [4], the final value of c_2 has the sign of $p - \frac{1}{2}$ with probability at least $1 - e^{-2k(p-\frac{1}{2})^2}$. Similarly, c_1 multiplied by the sign of $p - \frac{1}{2}$ will have the sign of $\chi(x)$ with probability at least $1 - e^{-2k(p-\frac{1}{2})^2}$. So, the algorithm produces the correct value of $\chi(x)$ with probability at least $1 - 2e^{-2k(p-\frac{1}{2})^2}$.

By taking $k = \frac{1}{2}\theta^{-2}\ln\frac{2}{\varepsilon}$ and since $|p - \frac{1}{2}| > \theta$, we attain the required probability of "success" for the algorithm $\mathcal{A}'$ thus-wise constructed, where ε is the "error" in the text of the theorem. $\qquad\square$

Lemma 3 (Lemma 4.16 in [20]). *Let G and H be two finite Abelian groups. We denote by d the order of H, where the group operation is denoted additively. Let $x_1, x_2, \ldots, x_r \in G$. If $x_1, \ldots, x_t$ H-generate G then by picking $r \in_U dG$ and $b_1, \ldots, b_t \in_U \{0, \ldots, d-1\}$ then $dr + b_1x_1 + \cdots + b_tx_t$ is uniformly distributed.*

Now assume a ppt. algorithm Gen_{GM} which generates a modulus $n = pq$ as in the Goldwasser-Micali cryptosystem [7] and $t > 1$, i.e., $\mathsf{Gen}_{GM}(1^s) \to (n)$. We define $\mathsf{Gen}_{CHI}(1^s) \to (n, (\frac{\cdot}{p}), t)$, given that we have $\mathsf{Gen}_{GM}(1^s) \to (n)$, p being one of the two prime factors of n selected at random, and $t = 2$. We can then see that the hardness of quadratic residuosity implies the hardness of the **CHI** problem relative to Gen_{GM}. Formally, this is proven below.

Theorem 1. *If the QR problem is hard relative to Gen_{GM}, then* **CHI** *problem is hard relative to Gen_{CHI}.*

Proof. Let $\mathcal{A}$ be an adversary against CHI. Let $\mathsf{Gen}_{QR}(1^s) \to (n)$. We pick one of the two hard characters χ at random. Let

$$p_n = \Pr[\mathcal{A}(x, n, x_1, x_2, \chi(x_1), \chi(x_2)) = \chi(x)|n, \mathrm{span}_2(x_1, x_2) = \mathbf{Z}_n^*].$$

over $x, x_1, x_2 \in_U \mathbf{Z}_n^*$ and χ. Due to the definition of Gen_{CHI}, what we have to prove is that $E(p_n)$ is negligible when the QR problem is hard relative to Gen_{QR}.

We construct an adversary $\mathcal{B}(u, n)$ against QR as follows. By definition, we have $(u/n) = +1$. Then, we pick $v \in_U \mathbf{Z}_n^*$ until $(v/n) = -1$ and $\sigma \in_U \{-1, +1\}$. Let χ be the only hard character of $\mathbf{Z}_n^*$ of order 2 such that $\chi(v) = \sigma$. Clearly, χ is a uniformly distributed hard character. Then, we select bits a, b, c, d until $\begin{vmatrix} a & b \\ c & d \end{vmatrix}$ is odd. Finally, $r, r' \in_U \mathbf{Z}_n^*$. We define $x_1 = u^a v^b r^2 \bmod n$ and $x_2 = u^c v^d (r')^2 \bmod n$.

The residue u is quadratic if and only if $\chi(u) = +1$. When it is not, then $\mathrm{span}_2(u, v) = \mathbf{Z}_n^*$. In that case, (x_1, x_2) is randomly distributed over the pairs such that $\mathrm{span}_2(x_1, x_2) = \mathbf{Z}_n^*$. Still in the case that $\chi(u) = -1$, we note that $\chi(x_1) = (-1)^a \sigma^b$, $\chi(x_2) = (-1)^c \sigma^d$. Let $x = u^\alpha v^\beta (r'')^2 \bmod n$ with $\alpha, \beta \in_U \{0, 1\}$ and $r'' \in_U \mathbf{Z}_n^*$. Clearly, x is uniformly distributed in $\mathbf{Z}_n^*$ and $\chi(x) = (-1)^\alpha \sigma^\beta$. Thanks to the good distributions, we have

$$\Pr[\mathcal{A}(x, n, x_1, x_2, (-1)^a \sigma^b, (-1)^c \sigma^d) = (-1)^\alpha \sigma^\beta|n, \chi(u) = -1] = p_n.$$

In the case $\chi(u) = +1$, the inputs to $\mathcal{A}$ are independent from α. So, the above probability becomes $\frac{1}{2}$.

We define

$$\mathcal{B}(u,n) = 1_{\mathcal{A}(x,n,x_1,x_2,(-1)^a\sigma^b,(-1)^c\sigma^d) \neq (-1)^\alpha\sigma^\beta}.$$

Clearly, for $(u/n) = -1$, we have $\Pr[\mathcal{B}(u,n) = 0|n] = p_n$. For $(u/n) = -1$, we have $\Pr[\mathcal{B}(u,n) = 1|n] = \frac{1}{2}$. So,

$$\Pr[\mathcal{B}(u,n) = 1_{u \in QR_n}] = \frac{1}{4} + \frac{E(p_n)}{2}.$$

Assuming that the QR problem is hard relative to Gen_{QR}, we obtain that $\left| \frac{E(p_n)}{2} - \frac{1}{4} \right|$ is negligible. Therefore, $|E(p_n) - \frac{1}{2}|$ is negligible as well. Since this holds for all $\mathcal{A}$, we deduce that the CHI problem is hard relative to Gen_{CHI}.   □

In this paper, we use the CHI problem with $\chi(\cdot) = \left(\frac{\cdot}{\alpha} \right)$ over $\mathbf{Z}_n^*$, for a factor α of n. For the CHI problem to be hard, α must be a hard factor of n. So, we tune our parameters to ensure this. So far, we know no algorithm better than finding α to solve the CHI problem. So, we believe that our selection method is enough to guaranty security.

3   SIS: A Primeless Public-Key Cryptosystem

Our proposed scheme, denoted SIS, is described below. We assume a security parameter s. Based on s, other parameters of SIS will be defined, namely t, k, and ℓ. The exact way to choose these parameters is discussed in Section 4.

3.1   The Core of the Cryptosystem

In Algorithm 1, we describe the *key generation procedure* of our SIS cryptosystem. As usual, the procedure runs in the security parameter s. Algorithm 1 generates and uses within a parameter denoted t, which will have its expression in this security parameter s made clear in the next section.

This key generation procedure produces a pair (α, n) of integers such that α is an odd factor of n. We note that the value n is part of the public key, whereas the integer α is kept secret. Therefore, the Jacobi symbol $\left(\frac{\cdot}{\alpha} \right)$ is a character of order 2 in $\mathbf{Z}_n^*$. Then, in the generation procedure, t values, $x_1, x_2, \ldots, x_t$, are randomly picked from $\mathbf{Z}_n^*$. Using the Jacobi symbol $\left(\frac{\cdot}{\alpha} \right)$, the values y_i are computed as $\left(\frac{x_i}{\alpha} \right)$, for all $1 \leq i \leq t$. If all y_i's are equal to 1, then all the x_i values are dropped and the procedure restarts by choosing again all these values, in the same fashion. (In any case, this occurrence of re-starting is rare: it happens with a probability close to 2^{-t}; there are rare cases where all y_i's are always 1, i.e., when α is a square.)

1: **Input:** Security parameter s.
   Output: Public key: $(n, x_1, x_2, \ldots x_t, y_1, y_2, \ldots y_t)$; Private key: α.

2:   compute t, k, and ℓ depending on s, as per (1) in p. 562 and (2)-(4) in p. 563
3:   pick random odd integers α_i and β_i of size ℓ, $i = 1, \ldots, k$;
4:   compute $\alpha = \alpha_1 \times \cdots \times \alpha_k$
5:   compute $\beta = \beta_1 \times \cdots \times \beta_k$
6:   compute $n = \alpha \cdot \beta$
7:   pick $x_1, x_2, \ldots, x_t \in_U \mathbf{Z}_n^*$
8:   compute $y_i = \left(\frac{x_i}{\alpha}\right)$ for all $1 \le i \le t$
9:   **if** $y_i = 1$ for all $1 \le i \le t$, **then** go-to step 3

Algorithm 1. SIS: Key generation

Intuitively, we could expect that taking $k = 1$ would be the optimal option. We will see in the analysis in the next section that there is an advantage in taking k larger.

In Algorithm 2 below, we show how to encrypt a bit b using our SIS cryptosystem.

1: **Input:** a bit b.
   Public key: $(n, x_1, x_2, \ldots x_t, y_1, y_2, \ldots y_t)$.
   Output: the encryption z, $z \in \mathbf{Z}_n^*$.

2:   find $y_i = -1, i \in \{1, \ldots, t\}$
3:   pick $b_1, b_2, \ldots, b_{i-1}, b_{i+1}, \ldots, b_t \in_U \{0, 1\}$

4:   compute $P = \prod_{j \neq i} y_j^{b_j}$
5:   **if** $P = (-1)^b$ **then** $b_i \leftarrow 0$ **else** $b_i \leftarrow 1$.
6:   compute $z' = x_1^{b_1} \cdots x_t^{b_t} \pmod{n}$
7:   pick $r \in_U \mathbf{Z}_n^*$
8:   compute $z = r^2 \cdot z' \pmod{n}$

Algorithm 2. SIS: Encryption

From the public values y_i, the encryption procedure firstly selects t bits such that $\prod_i y_i^{b_i} = (-1)^b$. The value $z = r^2 \times x_1^{b_1} \cdots x_t^{b_t} \pmod{n}$ is computed, where the number r is randomly picked. The result denotes the ciphertext of the bit b. Having got the ciphertext z and knowing value α, one decrypts z by solving $(-1)^b = \left(\frac{z}{\alpha}\right)$, where $\left(\frac{z}{\alpha}\right)$ is the Jacobi symbol of z with respect to α. This is presented in Algorithm 3.

1: **Input:** the encryption z, $z \in \mathbf{Z}_n^*$.
   Secret key: α.
   Output: a bit b.

2:   compute $\left(\frac{z}{\alpha}\right)$.
3:   **if** $\left(\frac{z}{\alpha}\right) = 1$ **then** $b = 0$ **else** $b = 1$.

Algorithm 3. SIS: Decryption

Correctness. The SIS encryption scheme is correct, i.e., if z is the encryption of a bit b as above, then one can decrypt z to b, provided that it knows the secret value α. To see this, we give the following lemma.

Lemma 4. $\left(\frac{z}{\alpha}\right) = (-1)^b$, *where the values z, α, the bit b are honestly computed/selected as in the SIS cryptosystem.*

Proof. From $z = r^2 x_1^{b_1} \cdots x_t^{b_t}$ (mod n) as in the scheme and α a divisor of n, it follows that $z = r^2 x_1^{b_1} \cdots x_t^{b_t}$ (mod α). Using the standard properties for the Legendre symbol, we obtain that the value $\left(\frac{z}{\alpha}\right)$ is as follows:

$$\left(\frac{z}{\alpha}\right) = \left(\frac{r^2 x_1^{b_1} \cdots x_t^{b_t}}{\alpha}\right) = \left(\frac{r}{\alpha}\right)^2 \left(\frac{x_1}{\alpha}\right)^{b_1} \cdots \left(\frac{x_t}{\alpha}\right)^{b_t} = 1 \cdot y_1^{b_1} y_2^{b_2} \cdots y_t^{b_t} = (-1)^b. \qquad \square$$

3.2 Security Analysis

It is clear that to perform a secret key recovery attack, an attacker needs to find the factor α of n. So, SIS strongly relies on the factoring problem.

Take now the goal of the adversary to be guessing whether b is 0 or 1. We follow the standard lines in saying that our cryptosystem is IND-CPA secure if for every polynomial adversary A outputting a bit b', its advantage $Adv_A(s) = \Pr_{\alpha,n,X,B}[b = b'] - \frac{1}{2}$ is negligible in terms of s, where n and α are the modulus used and its secret factor generated in the scheme, b is the encrypted bit, X and B respectively denote the values x_i and b_i that are picked during a run of the scheme.

Let a ppt. algorithm Gen such that $\mathsf{Gen}(1^s) \to (n,\chi,t)$ with $\chi(\cdot) = \left(\frac{\cdot}{\alpha}\right)$ as per our system. Then, the following corollary follows.

Corollary 1. *Assuming that the **CHI** problem is hard relative to Gen, the SIS scheme is IND-CPA secure.*

Proof. It follows from the definition of hardness of the **CHI** problem in Section 2.2, Lemma 2 and the construction of the SIS scheme, i.e., the bit that an $\mathcal{A}$ is supposed to output correctly to break IND-CPA security is the character $\left(\frac{z}{\alpha}\right)$, where z is generated in Algorithm 2 and α is the secret generated at the setup phase. $\qquad \square$

Thus, we reduced the IND-CPA security of the SIS scheme to the hardness of the **CHI** problem (which is assumed to be hard). Since the SIS-scheme is homomorphic, it is clearly not IND-CCA secure.

4 Selection of the Parameters

4.1 The Local Parameter t

Let us assume that the parameters k and ℓ are chosen and we attempt to gauge the right choice for t. Let $s \in \mathbb{Z}$ be the security parameter and $L = 2k\ell$ be the bitlength of n. We pick the value t such that we obtain the uniqueness of the homomorphism in the **GHI** corresponding problem. Namely, we pick t to be greater than the value r specified by Lemma 1, specialised here for $d = 2$.

Theorem 2. *(Theorem 4.29 in [20]) Let G, H be some Abelian groups, and d the order of H. The probability P_{gen} that some elements $g_1, \ldots, g_s \in_U G$ picked uniformly at random H-generate G satisfies*

$$P_{gen} \geq \prod_{q \in \mathcal{P}_d} \left(1 - \frac{q^{k_q} - 1}{(q-1) \cdot q^s}\right),$$

where $\mathcal{P}_d$ is the set of all prime factors of $\gcd(\#G, d)$ and k_q is the rank of the maximal q-subgroup of G. (Given a prime q, the q-subgroup of G is the subgroup A_q of elements whose order are powers of q. The rank k_q is the integer such that there exists a unique sequence of integers $a_{q,1} \leq \cdots \leq a_{q,k_q}$ such that A_q is isomorphic to $\mathbf{Z}_{q^{a_{q,1}}} \oplus \cdots \oplus \mathbf{Z}_{q^{a_{q,k_q}}}$).

To apply the above theorem to our case, we give the following corollary.

Corollary 2. *The probability that $\{x_1, \ldots, x_t\}$ in the $\mathtt{SIS}$ scheme $\mathbf{Z}_2$-generates $\mathbf{Z}_n^*$ is*

$$P_{gen} \geq 1 - 2^{k_2 - t},$$

where k_2 is the rank of the group A_2 and A_2 is the maximal 2-subgroup of $\mathbf{Z}_n^*$.

In order to enforce $1 - P_{gen} \leq 2^{-s}$, we get a sufficient bound for t: i.e., $t \geq k_2 + s$. Further, the rank k_2 of the 2-subgroup of $\mathbf{Z}_n^*$ is closely related to $\omega(n)$, i.e., the number of distinct prime factors of n [8]. More precisely the relation is as follows.

Lemma 5. *The rank k_2 of the 2-subgroup of $\mathbf{Z}_n^*$ is: $\omega(n)$, if n is odd or 4 divides n and 8 does not divide n; $\omega(n) - 1$, if 2 divides n and 4 does not divide n and $\omega(n) + 1$, if 8 divides n.*

Proof. We write n as $\prod_{i=1}^{r} p_i^{\alpha_i} \times 2^{\alpha_0}$, where p_i are different, odd primes. Then, by properties of Abelian groups, $\mathbf{Z}_n^*$ is isomorphic with the group $\prod_{i=1}^{r} \mathbf{Z}_{p_i^{\alpha_i}}^* \times \mathbf{Z}_{2^{\alpha_0}}^*$. The group $\mathbf{Z}_{p_i^{\alpha_i}}^*$ is cyclic of 2-rank equal to 1, for each p_i as above. The group $\mathbf{Z}_{2^{\alpha_0}}^*$ is: either the trivial group, hence of 2-rank equal to 0 (if $\alpha_0 = 0$ or $\alpha_0 = 1$); or $\mathbf{Z}_2$, hence of 2-rank equal to 1 (if $\alpha_0 = 2$); or of 2-rank equal to 2 (if $\alpha_0 > 2$). Since the 2-rank of a product is the sum of the 2-ranks, we compute the 2-rank of $\mathbf{Z}_n^*$ in terms of r. We conclude with the fact that $\omega(n) = r$ if n is odd and $\omega(n) = r + 1$, otherwise. $\square$

So, since n to be generated in the $\mathtt{SIS}$ scheme is odd, we conclude as follows:

Corollary 3. *For $t \geq \omega(n) + s$, $x_1, \ldots, x_t$ $\mathbf{Z}_2$-generate $\mathbf{Z}_n^*$ with a probability greater than or equal to $1 - 2^{-s}$.*

By the Ramanujan-Hardy theorem [8], the average number $\omega(m)$ of distinct prime factors of a random number m is $\ln(\ln m)$. Further, by the Erdös-Kac theorem [5] says that $\frac{\omega(m) - \ln \ln m}{\sqrt{\ln \ln m}}$ follows the standard normal distribution, for such a random number m. So, $\Pr\left[\omega(m) > \ln \ln m + \sqrt{2s.\ln 2.\ln \ln m}\right]$ is $F(-\sqrt{2s.\ln 2})$, where F is the standard normal cumulative distribution function.

We can apply the arguments above using the numbers α_i and β_i that the Key generation algorithm produces. Namely, first see that $\omega(n) \leq \Sigma_{i=1}^{2k}(\omega(\alpha_i) + \omega(\beta_i))$. So, we can bound the mean of the variable $\omega(n)$ with that expected value $2k \times \ln \ln \ell$. So,

$$\Pr\left[\omega(n) \geq 2k \times \ln\ln 2^\ell + \sqrt{2s} \times \ln 2 \times 2k \times \ln\ln 2^\ell\right] \leq F(-\sqrt{2s.\ln 2}) .$$

Since $F(-x)$ can be approximated with $\frac{1}{\sqrt{2\pi}}e^{\frac{-x^2}{2}}/x$, then the probability is smaller than $\frac{1}{\sqrt{4\pi s \ln 2}}2^{-s}$. Thus, all things considered, we can take:

$$t = \left\lceil 2k\ln\ln 2^\ell + \sqrt{2s.\ln 2.2k.\ln\ln 2^\ell} + s \right\rceil . \tag{1}$$

Hence, t can be taken of the order of $\sqrt{s \cdot k \cdot \log \ell} + s$. The final estimation of t asymptotically in s will be clear at the end of this section, after we see exactly how k and ℓ vary in s.

Note: As one can see, one dominant component in the asymptotic expression (1) of t is the standard deviation of the random variable characterising $\omega(n)$, i.e., in the term $\sqrt{2s.\ln 2.2k.\ln\ln 2^\ell}$. We ran several experiments with smaller α's and β's and we observed that in practice this standard deviation is in fact smaller than $\sqrt{2k \times \ln(\ln(2^\ell))}$ and even smaller than the value of $\sqrt{\ln(2k\ell\ln 2)^2}$. So, in practice, t could potentially be taken smaller than the asymptotic approximation proven here.

4.2   The Local Parameters k and ℓ

It can be seen (as developed in Section 3.2) that in order for the **CHI** problem to be hard and, separately for key recovery attacks to be impossible, α and β need to be hard to find.

Let n be a positive integer and let its unique prime decomposition be as follows: $n = n_1 n_2 \cdots n_\nu$, with $n_1 \geq n_2 \geq \ldots \geq n_\nu$. In [13], Knuth *et al.* look at the probability that, for a random number n, the rth largest of its prime factors, n_r, is smaller than n^x where $0 < x < 1$. We recall some commonplace notations describing this:

- $F_r(x) = \lim_{N \to +\infty} \frac{P_r(x,N)}{N}$, where $P_r(x,N) = \#\{1 \leq n \leq N | n_r \leq N^x\}$;
- $\psi(x,y) = P_1\left(\frac{\log y}{\log x}, x\right)$ is the de Brujin function [9] and the ratio $\psi(x,y)/x$ can be interpreted as the probability that an integer chosen at random in the interval $[1,x]$ has all its prime factors smaller than or equal to y. This function has several approximations [9,13].
- Thus, $F_1(x) = \lim_{N \to +\infty} \frac{\psi(N,N^x)}{N} = \rho(1/x)$ where ρ is Dickman's function. Since $\rho(u) \leq \frac{1}{u!}$, we use a convenient upper bound $(F_1(x))^{-1} \geq \frac{1}{x}!$. In [16], van de Lune and Wattel provide a numerical table for $\rho(u)$ when u is large.

---

[2] This would be the standard deviation predicted by the Erdös-Kac theorem, if the latter were applicable directly to an n generated like ours.

We express our security desiderata (the hardness on n's factorisation); to do so, we will use some value $x \in (0,1)$. To ease our explanations, we start by recalling the complexities of factoring with elliptic curves, ECM and with the generalised number sieves, GNFS.

- Given the constants $c, \varepsilon \in \mathbb{R}$ we define a function
  $C_{GNFS}(L,c,\varepsilon) = c \times (e^{\left(\sqrt[3]{\frac{64}{9}}+\varepsilon\right)(\ln 2^L)^{\frac{1}{3}}(\ln\ln 2^L)^{\frac{2}{3}}}$. The complexity of factoring n with GNFS [14] is in $C_{GNFS}(\log_2 n, O(1), o(1))$. We deduce that we can reasonably take $\varepsilon \approx 0$ and $c \approx 2^{-14}$. In what follows, $C_{GNFS}(L) = C_{GNFS}(L, 2^{-14}, 0)$. We take for granted that $C_{GNFS}(1\,248) \approx 2^{80}$ [2].

- We define a function $C_{ECM}(L, c', \varepsilon') = c' \times e^{\sqrt{2+\varepsilon'}\sqrt{\ln 2^L \ln\ln 2^L}}$. The complexity of factoring a number n with ECM [15] is in $C_{ECM}(\log_2 p, O(1), o(1))$, where p is the smallest factor of n. In what follows, $C_{ECM}(L) = C_{ECM}(L, 2^{-14}, 0)$ as in C_{GNFS}. So, even though one would find all factors of n of length smaller than $x\ell$, one would not isolate α.

Now, we impose our conditions to align the security of SIS to the security levels of factoring moduli in general, in public-key cryptography. First, we impose equation (2). This equation stipulates that factors of n with no divisors of size less than $x\ell$ are hard to find with ECM. There is one such factor in α_i, respectively in β_i, with probability $1 - F_1(x)$. Equation (4) ensures that we have at least k' of such factors in n and at least one in α or in β, respectively. Equation (3) means that the product of hard-to-find factors is also hard to factor with GNFS.

$$C_{ECM}(x\ell) \geq 2^s \qquad (2)$$

$$C_{GNFS}(k'x\ell) \geq 2^s \qquad (3)$$

$$\sum_{i=0}^{k'-1} \binom{2k}{i} F_1(x)^{2k-i}(1 - F_1(x))^i + 2 \sum_{i=k'}^{k} \binom{k}{i} F_1(x)^{2k-i}(1 - F_1(x))^i \leq 2^{-s} \qquad (4)$$

The latter condition would approximate to $\binom{2k}{k'} F_1(x)^{2k-k'+1} + 2F_1(x)^k \leq 2^{-s}$, where the second term could be neglected for $k' > k$. Practically, using SAGE [22], we derive the following parameters.

s	80	128	192	256	320	384	448	512
x	0.0561	0.0654	0.0653	0.0652	0.0651	0.0574	0.0585	0.0593
k	1	2	3	4	5	5	6	7
k'	2	3	4	5	6	6	7	8
ℓ	10978	16553	31080	50143	73204	117776	145499	181116
$k'x\ell$	1232	3248	8118	16347	28593	40562	59581	85921
$2k\ell$	21956	66212	186480	401144	732040	1177760	1745988	2535624
t	143	247	379	512	648	743	880	1018

We recall that $2k\ell$ is the modulus size and that $k'x\ell$ would be the modulus size for GM or RSA with equivalent security.

Interpreting the Optimised Parameters. For instance, with $s = 128$, the probability that α_i resp. β_i is $2^{x\ell}$-smooth is $F_1(x) \approx 2^{-65.3}$ and the probability that we do not have at least 3 non-smooth factors out of $2k = 4$ is $2^{-128.0}$. So, we could count on at least 3 factors with no prime divisor of length lower than $x\ell$, i.e., on a hard-to-factor integer of $3x\ell$ bits.

On Choosing k. Asymptotically, we can take $x \sim \frac{\log\log s}{\log s}$, $k \sim \frac{s}{\log s}$, $k' = uk$ given a constant u, and $\ell \sim s^2$. Clearly, (2)-(3) are satisfied. We have $\binom{2k}{k'} \leq 2^{2k}$. By using $F_1(x)^{-1} \geq \frac{1}{x}!$, we can show that $F_1(x)^{-1} \geq s^{O(1)}$, so $\binom{2k}{k'} F_1(x)^{2k-k'+1} \leq 2^{-s}$ by tuning u appropriately. This makes sure that (4) is satisfied. So, we have $2k\ell \in O\left(s^3(\log s)^{-1}\right)$. Since we already showed that $t \in O(\sqrt{s.k.\log\ell} + s)$, obtain $t \in O(s)$. We recall that (according to the note on page 562) experiments indicate that this could be a pessimistic approximation of t and suggest that, in practice, t could be taken smaller.

In contrast, $k = 1$ and $k' = 2$ leads us to $x \in O\left(\frac{\log s}{s}\right)$ then to $2k\ell = O\left(s^4(\log s)^{-3}\right)$ which is asymptotically larger than before. So, there is an advantage in taking k larger than 1 (which was maybe not intuitive to begin with).

5   Complexity of the Scheme

5.1   Asymptotic Complexity

In the modulus-generation phase, $2k$ integers of size ℓ are randomly picked and $2k - 1$ multiplications are performed, in order to obtain the value n. These operations are performed in $O(2k\ell + \Sigma_i 2^i C_{mul}(alg, \frac{k\ell}{2^i}))$, $i = 0, 1, \ldots, \log_2 2k - 1$, where $C_{mul}(alg, \ell)$ denotes the complexity of multiplying numbers of ℓ bits using a particular algorithm, i.e., $C_{mul}(\text{schoolbook}, \ell) = O(\ell^2)$, $C_{mul}(\text{Karatsuba}, \ell) = O(\ell^{\log_2 3})$, $C_{mul}(\text{FFT-optimised}, \ell) = O(\ell \log \ell)$. In the next, "*sch.*" denotes the schoolbook multiplication and "*FFT*" denotes the FFT-based multiplication algorithm [23].

Thus, the complexity of modulus generation in SIS, $O(\text{SIS-Gen})$, is

$$O(2k\ell + \Sigma_i 2^i C_{mul}(alg, \frac{k\ell}{2^i})) = \begin{cases} O((k\ell)^2), & \text{if alg is sch.} \\ O(k\ell \log k\ell), & \text{if alg is FFT.} \end{cases}$$

The choices for the values x_i from $\mathbf{Z}_n^*$ and the computation of the values y_i are done in $O(2tk\ell + tC_{Jac}(alg, 2k\ell))$, where $C_{Jac}(alg, x)$ denotes the complexity to calculate the Jacobi symbol on an input of two x-bit integers, using the algorithm alg for the multiplication needed inside the calculation of the symbol. We know that $C_{Jac}(alg, L) = C_{mul}(alg, L) \log L$, for L being a size of the inner modulus. Thus,

$$O(2tk\ell + tC_{Jac}(alg, 2k\ell)) = \begin{cases} O(t \times (k\ell)^2 \log k\ell), & \text{if alg is sch.} \\ O(t \times (k\ell)(\log k\ell)^2), & \text{if alg is FFT.} \end{cases}$$

For encryption, one performs at most $t + 1$ multiplications to compute z, which takes $O(tC_{mul}(alg, 2k\ell))$. The value P is then computed within a complexity of order $O(t)$. This gives a total complexity of the order of $\begin{cases} O(t \times (k\ell)^2), & \text{if alg is sch.} \\ O(t \times (k\ell) \log k\ell), & \text{if alg is FFT.} \end{cases}$

For decryption, we need to compute one Jacobi symbol. This implies a complexity
of $\begin{cases} O((k\ell)^2 \log k\ell), & \text{if alg is sch.} \\ O((k\ell)(\log k\ell)^2), & \text{if alg is FFT.} \end{cases}$

By SIS-s, we denote the SIS cryptosystem over the domain $\{0,1\}^s$, in which –of course– the encryption and decryption have an overhead factor of s. We do consider s-bit messages since, while having a security 2^s, one would be interested in encrypting a symmetric key of s bits to use a consistent security level in hybrid encryption.

We would now like to compare our complexity with the complexity of the GM and RSA schemes. Given the existent optimised implementations of RSA, we will consider the most expensive multiplication algorithm, e.g., schoolbook multiplication, as well as the cheapest multiplication one, e.g., FFT-based.

An additional fact to consider in this comparison is that –in general– the key-generation in public-key cryptosystem is a one-time process, i.e., one generates the keys once and encrypts/decrypts several times. An exception to this case is, as we mentioned in the introduction, the context of forwards secrecy and secure delegation of linear algebra computation. In these cases, the secure delegation protocols require re-generation of each run of the secret/public keys. Outside this setting, it is compelling to consider separately the case of the complexity of RSA without the key generation and draw a corresponding comparison with the complexity of the system herein.

Another thing to bare in mind in this comparative study is that the SIS cryptosystem in its presented form encrypts a single bit. The GM system has also a "bit-by-bit" fashion. So, if we were to compare SIS asymptotically with the RSA that encrypts s bits at once, then we ought to consider s encryptions of the SIS cryptosystem.

For this comparison, we take the asymptotic values $k\ell \in O\left(s^3(\log s)^{-1}\right)$ and $t \in O\left(s^{\frac{3}{2}}(\log s)^{-\frac{1}{2}}\right)$ that we obtained. We consider the GM cryptosystem first. By looking carefully at the complexity of the GM cryptosystem, one can conclude with Table 1.

Table 1. Asymptotic Complexities in Security Parameter s for GM vs. SIS

		key-generation	encryption	decryption
schoolbook multiplication	GM	$O(s^{12}(\log s)^{-8})$	$O(s^6(\log s)^{-4})$	$O(s^6(\log s)^{-5})$
	SIS	$O(s^7(\log s)^{-1})$	$O(s^7(\log s)^{-2})$	$O(s^6)$
FFT-based multiplication	GM	$O(s^9(\log s)^{-5})$	$O(s^3(\log s)^{-1})$	$O(s^3)$
	SIS	$O(s^4(\log s))$	$O(s^4)$	$O(s^3 \log s)$

We consider now the RSA cryptosystem. Let us denote by RSA the instance of RSA when we have a random full-size e. When we take the public exponent of RSA as a constant, e.g., $e = 2^{16} + 1$, we will refer to using RSA$_{e\,\text{cte.}}$.

We wrap the complexity comparison between RSA and SIS-s in Table 2.

Table 2. Asymptotic Complexities in Security Parameter s for $\text{RSA}_{e \text{ cte.}}$ vs. SIS

		key-generation	encryption	decryption
schoolbook multiplication	$\text{RSA}_{e \text{ cte.}}$	$O(s^{12}(\log s)^{-8})$	$O(s^6(\log s)^{-4})$	$O(s^9(\log s)^{-6})$
	RSA	$O(s^{12}(\log s)^{-8})$	$O(s^9(\log s)^{-6})$	$O(s^9(\log s)^{-6})$
	SIS-s	$O(s^7(\log s)^{-1})$	$O(s^8(\log s)^{-2})$	$O(s^7)$
FFT-based multiplication	$\text{RSA}_{e \text{ cte.}}$	$O(s^9(\log s)^{-5})$	$O(s^3(\log s)^{-1})$	$O(s^6(\log s)^{-3})$
	RSA	$O(s^9(\log s)^{-5})$	$O(s^6(\log s)^{-3})$	$O(s^6(\log s)^{-3})$
	SIS-s	$O(s^4(\log s))$	$O(s^5)$	$O(s^4\log s)$

5.2 Experimental Results

To assess the correctness of our analysis, we implemented and compared the running time of RSA and SIS-s. The experimental environment consists of a Linux kernel 3.2.0-31 that runs on a Intel Xeon 3.33Ghz CPU. The implementation was done in C and for our large numbers we used the GMP library [6]. The implementations of both SIS-s and RSA were tested for the same security parameters illustrated in the table from page 563, namely s varies from 80 to 512.

SIS-s Implementation. Our implementation verifies the asymptotic complexities we provide in Table 2. In practice, if we compute the slope of the regression line for the logarithmic running time of key generation, encryption and decryption against $\log s$, we get 5.7 for the key generation, 6.2 for the encryption and 6.0 for the decryption algorithm. Indeed these values are slightly smaller than the ones in Table 2 as GMP has efficient implementations of its operations, e.g., multiplication or computation of the Jacobi symbol.

Comparing RSA and SIS-s. Besides verifying that the asymptotic complexity of SIS-s is valid, we are also interested in comparing the running time of RSA and SIS-s for the generation of the key.

Figure 1 illustrates both the running time (Figure 1a) and the logarithmic running time (Figure 1b) of the key generation for RSA and SIS-s, where the security parameter s takes values between 80 and 512. The running time is measured in seconds. For small values of s, the generation of primes for RSA is faster than our primeless method. But one may notice that once we increase the value of the security parameter the two plots intersect at around $s = 300$ and clearly the key generation of our SIS-s becomes faster than the one of RSA. This behaviour reinforces our asymptotic study.

We conclude that, by comparison with GM and RSA, SIS exhibits improved asymptotic complexities for all procedures, apart from encryption. The result is sustained also by our experimental results. This would solve the bottlenecks of the execution of secure delegation of computation and/or key agreement with forward secrecy [1], i.e., of all settings where the key-generation is not an one-off process.

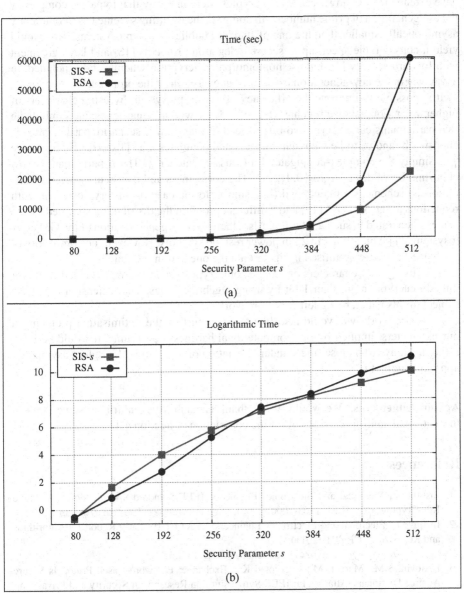

Fig. 1. Key generation SIS-s vs. RSA

6   Conclusions

In this paper, using the same, main idea of relying on hard characters of order 2, we have extended the Goldwasser-Micali cryptosystem in a way that bypasses completely the use/generation of prime numbers. In doing so, the resulting scheme has a complexity asymptotically smaller than the one of standard public-key cryptosystems. This would yield a considerable speed-up to secure delegation protocols [18] and key agreement with forward secrecy [1] that use homomorphic encryption schemes, GM included, in a way where the key-generation is repeated at every run of the protocol.

It is possible to improve the efficiency of our cryptosystem by using characters of higher order. For instance for characters of order 4, with the quartic residue symbol, the two participants can encrypt two bits instead of one. In this scenario, participant A is choosing β_i and α_i to be Gaussian integers and computes n as $\prod_i \alpha_i \cdot \bar{\alpha}_i \cdot \beta_i \cdot \bar{\beta}_i$, where $\bar{\gamma}_i$ is simply the complex-conjugate of a Gaussian integer γ_i. The B participant is now choosing the values b_i from $\{0,1,2,3\}$. The correctness and the security proof of this optimised scheme are maintained (i.e., similar to the case of our cryptosystem, with reductions to the **MOVA**⁴ [19] and a different proof on the distribution spawned by the values z generated in such a scheme). Also, there exists a generalization of the GM cryptosystem [11] which is using 2^k-th power residue symbols. However, the complexity of a scheme thus-wise optimised is higher than the one herein presented.

Still, using only characters of order 2, our cryptosystem can be extended so that it directly encrypts more than 1 bit by using algebraic codes. This extension is not the subject of this paper, being left for future work.

As future work, we would also like to study further the optimisation problem on our parameters, implied by our computational hardness constraints. It would be interesting to study from closer the standard deviation of $\omega(n)$, to find a tighter asymptotic approximation of t.

Acknowledgements. We would like to thank Hannah Muckenhirn for some input in the statistical analysis carried out for the completion of Section 4.1.

References

1. Institute of Electrical and Electronics Engineers: IEEE Standard Specifications for Public Key Cryptography. IEEE 1363-2000 (2000), http://grouper.ieee.org/groups/1363/
2. Institute of Electrical and Electronics Engineers: ECRYPT II Yearly Report on Algorithms and Key Sizes. ECRYPT (2011),
   http://www.ecrypt.eu.org/documents/D.SPA.17.pdf
3. Bellovin, S.M., Merritt, M.: Encrypted Key Exchange: Password-Based Protocols Secure Against Dictionary Attacks. In: IEEE Symposium on Research in Security and Privacy, pp. 72–84 (1992)
4. Chernoff, H.: A Measure of Asymptotic Efficiency for Tests of a Hypothesis Based on the sum of Observations. The Annals of Mathematical Statistics 23(4), 493–507 (1952)
5. Erdös, P., Kac, M.: The Gaussian Law of Errors in the Theory of Additive Number Theoretic Functions. American Journal of Mathematics 62(1), 738–742 (1940)
6. The GNU Multiple Precision Arithmetic Library, http://gmplib.org

7. Goldwasser, S., Micali, S.: Probabilistic Encryption. J. Comput. Syst. Sci. 28(2), 270–299 (1984)
8. Hardy, G., Ramanujan, S.: The Normal Number of Prime Factors of a Number n. Quart. J. Math. 48, 76–92 (1917)
9. Hildebrand, A., Tenenbaum, G.: Integers without Large Prime Factors. Prépublications de l'Institut Elie Cartan. Dép. de Math., Univ. de Nancy I (1991)
10. Ireland, K., Rosen, M.: A Classical Introduction to Modern Number Theory. Springer (1990)
11. Joye, M., Libert, B.: Efficient Cryptosystems From 2^k-th Power Residue Symbols. In: EUROCRYPT (2013)
12. Karatsuba, A., Ofman, Y.: Multiplication of Multidigit Numbers on Automata. Soviet Physics Doklady 7, 595–596 (1978)
13. Knuth, D.E., Pardo, L.T.: Analysis of a Simple Factorization Algorithm. Theoretical Computer Science 3(3), 321–348 (1976)
14. Lenstra, A.K., Lenstra Jr., H.W. (eds.): The Development of the Number Field Sieve. Lecture Notes in Mathematics, vol. 1554. Springer, Berlin (1993)
15. Lenstra Jr., H.W.: Factoring Integers with Elliptic Curves. Ann. of Math. (2) 126(3), 649–673 (1987)
16. van de Lune, J., Wattel, E.: On the Numerical Solution of a Differential-Difference Equation Arising in Analytic Number Theory. Mathematics of Computation 23, 417–421 (1969)
17. Mceliece, R.J.: A Public-Key Cryptosystem Based on Algebraic Coding Theory. Tech. rep., Jet Propulsion Lab Deep Space Network Progress Report (1978)
18. Mohassel, P.: Efficient and Secure Delegation of Linear Algebra. Cryptology ePrint Archive, Report 2011/605 (2011), http://eprint.iacr.org/
19. Monnerat, J.: Short Undeniable Signatures: Design, Analysis, and Applications. Ph.D. thesis, École Polytechnique Fédérale de Lausanne (2006)
20. Monnerat, J., Vaudenay, S.: Short Undeniable Signatures Based on Group Homomorphisms. Journal of Cryptology 24(3), 545–587 (2011)
21. Rivest, R.L., Shamir, A., Adleman, L.: A method for Obtaining Digital Signatures and Public-Key Cryptosystems. Commun. ACM 21, 120–126 (1978)
22. Sage Mathematics Software, http://www.sagemath.org
23. Schönhage, A., Strassen, V.: Schnelle Multiplikation grosser Zahlen. Computing 7, 281–292 (1971)

Author Index